etc.—Train
...way services

Continued on back endpapers

SCIENCE MUSEUM/NATIONAL RAILWAY MUSEUM

A BIBLIOGRAPHY OF BRITISH RAILWAY HISTORY

COMPILED BY

GEORGE OTTLEY

of the British Museum Library

*with the co-operation of William J. Skillern, Charles R. Clinker,
John E. C. Palmer, and Charles E. Lee, fellow members of the
Railway & Canal Historical Society*

FOREWORD BY PROFESSOR JACK SIMMONS

LONDON: HER MAJESTY'S STATIONERY OFFICE

First published 1983
ISBN 0 11 290334 7*

Printed in the UK for HMSO
Dd 717054 C31 4/83

To my wife,
fireman on this journey

CONTENTS

Although railways have been in use in this country, in some form, for more than 350 years, it is only quite lately that their history has become the subject of serious and detailed inquiry. In the nineteenth century, when the railway's power was at its height, some well-written studies appeared, which retain a permanent value—those of Francis, for example, in the fifties and of Acworth in the eighties and nineties. But they were sketches, not works of research: they did not aim at historical completeness.

The first major historical enterprise to be devoted to British railways was the second volume of Jackman's *Transportation in Modern England*, which was published in 1916: a work of massive learning, intelligently used. It has been a quarry for all its successors, partly because the author—a trained economic historian—marshalled his materials well and shaped them into a coherent narrative and analysis; but not less because of the indefatigable pains he took to document all his statements and to provide an account of the literature of his subject in the invaluable bibliography of sixty pages appended to the work.

Ten years later, when the centenary of the Stockton & Darlington Railway came to be celebrated, two books appeared that at once became standard works: Lewin's *Early British Railways, 1801–44*, a series of annals, recording the development of the railway system, illustrated with an invaluable set of maps; and Ahrons's study *The British Steam Railway Locomotive, 1825–1925*, a work that no one has attempted to supersede. It is worth noting that the first and third of the books that have been mentioned, having been unobtainable for a long time, have now reappeared in editions photographically reprinted: a clear tribute to the steadily-continuing demand for them.

Nearly forty years have passed since then; and they have brought a stream of contributions to railway history in this country—a stream that since 1945 has swollen into a sizeable river. Much of this work is ephemeral, some of it poor in quality. The student cannot neglect it, however; and up to now his difficulty has been to locate it. For this is an ill-disciplined literature; useful pieces of it have been published not in London but in out-of-the-way places—Lingfield, Dawlish, Ashbourne, Sevenoaks. How is it to be found?

The problem is not a new one. For throughout the past century and a half the railways have called forth a great volume of pamphlets: on Sunday travelling, on methods of traction and break of gauge, on relations with rival forms of transport, on government policy, on the grievances of shareholders—above all, and at all times, on the complaints of traders and passengers about rates and fares. Many of these pamphlets are eccentric, some lie well within the borders of lunacy; few of them are anything but partisan. Yet again they must not be neglected. The mere fact that such views were being advanced may have a significance independent of the folly or the merit of the ideas themselves. Once again, how is this large literature to be explored?

Jackman made a valiant start on the labour of mapping this jungle. But, though his title speaks of 'modern England', his survey stops at 1850. What we have wanted ever since 1916 has been a successor to Jackman, bold enough to carry on his bibliography from the point at which he left off.

[9]

Now at last we have found him, and found him in the right place. No one could be in a better position to assemble and describe this great mass of material than a member of the library staff at the British Museum, which under the terms of the Copyright Acts is entitled to receive one copy of every book and pamphlet published in this country. Mr. Ottley has brought to his task all the patience and diligence it needs, guided and informed by the bibliographical skill of the trained librarian, accustomed to the protracted hunt for his quarry and relentless in the pursuit of it—often into unlikely places. He has taken great pains with the organization of his book: no easy matter, as any one who has attempted the simplest exercise of the kind will know. Above all he has kept in mind the convenience of the user, making a strenuous and persistent effort to set out his material in the shape that makes reference easiest.

The large growth in the literature of railway history during recent years reflects the growth in the number of serious students of the subject: a growth stimulated, in its turn, by other things that lie on the fringes of this book or beyond it. The most notable of these was the great step taken by the British Transport Commission in 1951, in establishing its Departments of Historical Records and Historical Relics, which offer the opportunity of adding a whole new dimension to our knowledge of the economic history of the nineteenth and twentieth centuries. But the history of British railways is not of interest to railway historians alone. At countless points it touches and leads into the modern history of our whole society and of the innumerable societies and communities within it. Historians of all towns and most villages in Britain, of industry and agriculture and trade, all need to know what has been written about railways. To them, as well as to the dedicated students of the subject for its own sake, Mr Ottley's book may be commended as an indispensable work of reference. They will join with me in thanking him for undertaking it.

JACK SIMMONS

COMPILER'S INTRODUCTION
TO THE FIRST EDITION
SCOPE AND NATURE OF SUBJECT COVERAGE AND OF MATERIAL REPRESENTED, AND SOURCES USED

This bibliography is a classified arrangement of entries relating to books, parts of books, pamphlets, etc., on the history and description of rail transport in the British Isles from the earliest times down to the present.

The work is based primarily upon the resources of the British Museum Library in this subject, but in order to include items not represented there[1] and classes of material not normally deposited there, such as reprints of articles from serial publications, typescript reproductions of papers read to meetings of societies, privately printed works, and unpublished university theses, a series of visits was made to other London libraries known to specialize in transport. In addition, a number of relatively unknown items have been brought to light through the co-operation of provincial librarians and railway historians in response to appeals for details of locally-produced pamphlets[2].

With few exceptions the entries were made from examination of the actual works at one or other of the libraries visited. A location symbol indicates where each was seen, but it is necessary to point out that the frequency at which any one symbol occurs must not be taken as an indication of the relative value of these libraries as sources for railway history, for as the tour progressed so the proportion of items 'not yet seen' decreased; also, throughout the course of compiling, constant reference has been made to the Catalogue of the Department of Printed Books of the British Museum. As custodians of the nation's books, the Trustees of the British Museum are under an obligation to accept for preservation material deposited under the Copyright Act. This unique responsibility adds a quality of permanence and dependability to any bibliographical reference to its holdings and whenever possible preference has been given to a BM location.

The following is a list of the contributing libraries, other than the British Museum Library, in the order visited:

† Institution of Civil Engineers   ICE
† London School of Economics (British Library of Political and Economic Science, University of London)   LSE
† Institute of Transport   IT
† Trades Union Congress   TUC
‡ Railway Club   RC
‡ Institution of Mechanical Engineers   IME
† University of London (Goldsmiths' Library of Economic Literature) UL (GL)
* British Railways Board Historical Records (London)   BR
‡ Stephenson Locomotive Society   SLS
* Science Museum (Science Library)   SL
* Patent Office   PO
* Guildhall Library, London   GL
† National Liberal Club (Gladstone Library)   NLC

* With certain reservations, admission may be given to any applicant.
† For members only, but single-visit admission may be granted to non-members within the terms of the regulations.
‡ Not accessible to non-members.

Charles E. Lee (private collection)   pc
Charles R. Clinker (private collection)   pc
Charles E. R. Sherrington (private collection)   pc

Single visits were also made to the National Union of Railwaymen; Labour Research Department; Railway Research Service (British Railways); British Railways (Western Region) General Manager's Office and Publicity and Public Relations Office; British Railways (London Midland Region) Publicity and Public Relations Office; Holborn Public Library[3]; Eltham Public Library[3]; Ian Allan Ltd., and The Oakwood Press.

Items from the Haliday Collection in the Royal Irish Academy, Dublin, were borrowed through the agency of the National Central Library, London.

It is neither possible nor desirable to muster into a railway bibliography the countless prospectuses, minute books, rules and regulations, reports to shareholders, etc., which are the official documentary records of the thousand or more companies that have shaped the course of our railway history. A comprehensive collection of such material already exists and is freely available for reference and study. In 1951, three years after the nationalization of the public railways of England, Scotland, and Wales, the British Transport Commission set up its 'Historical Records' Department, with repositories in London, York, and Edinburgh[4]. At these centres, documents of all railway and canal undertakings affected by the Transport Act (1947) may be consulted. The London collection is supplemented by a large reference library, and similar facilities are now available at York and Edinburgh. Together this amounts to what is virtually a National Transport Archives and Library.

From 1840, with the introduction of the Railway Department of the Board of Trade, railway affairs were subjected to increasing control by Government. Departmental records of the Board of Trade Railway Department and its successor the Ministry of Transport, and records of other government bodies which exercised measures of control and influence over railway development, are preserved for use at the Public Record Office, London[5].

For *printed* sources of primary material for the study of British railway history—Parliamentary Papers, Acts (General and Private), Bills, Light Railway Orders, *Hansard*, the *London Gazette*, and all publications of government departments—the State Paper Room of the British Museum provides a comprehensive collection. A file of *The Times* is also available, and in the same building an extension of one's research is made possible by the resources of the Map Room. Furthermore, at Colindale Newspaper Library (British Museum) all newspapers (national and local) and all weekly publications are to be found.

The House of Lords Record Office provides a valuable specialized service by making available classes of official material, both manuscript and printed, of a more restricted nature such as Private Bills, Deposited Plans and Sections, Books of Reference, Minutes of Evidence on Private Bills, and Light Railway Orders[6].

From this brief survey three observations may be made:
1. The locating of railway company records is facilitated by their having followed the pattern of ever-widening amalgamation which characterizes British railway history, so that with the eventual unification of the railway companies under nationalization in 1948 came the ultimate assembling, arranging and indexing by the British Transport Commission Archivist of all relevant material.
2. The locating of printed sources of Parliamentary and Departmental

published material presents no difficulty. It is all available in the British Museum Library (State Paper Room).

3. For groundwork and detail and for the convenience of having all related matter to hand, London offers advantages not available at provincial centres of study. This is a circumstance which is not likely to remain unchallenged, since the time is not far distant when it will be possible to consult large series like the Sessional Papers of the House of Commons on microfilm without coming to London. For the present, however, the main sources of British railway history rest upon the shelves of the British Museum Library, British Railways Board Historical Records, the Public Record Office, and the House of Lords Record Office. All of these centres are, with some reservations, freely accessible for study.

The object of this present work has been to harvest that class of material which must be regarded as secondary to the authoritative outpourings of officialdom. In railway history research this bibliography, therefore, has a complementary function. Its aim is to show what has appeared in the form of printed and published information *about* railway development.

It follows that most of the items recorded are from unofficial (i.e. non-railway and non-government) sources and are in fact books or pamphlets. I have, however, included publications which have been issued by railway authorities for the information of the general public, and exception has sometimes been made with regard to 'private and confidential' items intended for limited distribution among railway officials or shareholders. Some of these have nevertheless found their way on to the shelves of one or other of the above-mentioned libraries and the fact that they are there has persuaded me to include them whenever the information contained was thought to be too valuable to disregard. Also included are university theses[7], papers read to meetings of various societies, itineraries of rail tours organized by groups of railway enthusiasts, and volume collections of documentary and miscellaneous material forming part of the resources of libraries visited.

It will be some time before a supplementary volume for serials and periodical articles is produced, and for this reason I have included in this present work essays from the *Journal of Transport History*, published twice yearly by the University of Leicester since 1953. About forty of these come within subject range of this bibliography and although this represents a numerical proportion to the whole work of only 1 in 150 (0·67 per cent), their proportionate value is without any doubt far higher.

In general, the criterion has been to bring together into an ordered sequence all monographs which contribute to knowledge of our railways and tramways in their historical, geographical, social, and economic aspects.

EXCLUSIONS

The following classes of publication are, with some exceptions, excluded:

Children's books which are so ephemeral as to be of little or no value to the railway historian, ranging from picture books for the very young to simple readers for school use. Among books for older children, however, are some informative introductory works with good illustrations, and these are included. Also included are 'spotters' books'. These have a distinct value as reliable contributions to pure fact.

Highly technical works on specialized subjects. These are usually beyond the scope and needs of railway history research, but exceptions are allowed in respect of works of this kind written before 1851, during the formative, experimental period when railway technology was still a matter of opinion rather than experience; also, technical works have been included when there is a secondary theme or aspect which qualifies for inclusion, especially if the subject has not appeared elsewhere.

Topographical works containing railway information. Generally this is found to be scant and somewhat unreliable. There are, however, some notable exceptions such as Michael Robbins' *Middlesex* (1953) which has 166 passages in its text concerning railway and tramway development within that county. Likewise, certain volumes in the *Victoria History of the Counties of England* contain authentic descriptions of railway development.

The great number and variety of railway guides presents a problem. Although their railway information may be sometimes relatively slight, and their dating of events often incorrect, railway guides are so closely linked to the ventures they describe that it is hardly permissible to ignore them. But to try to describe all editions of every guide and companion from the 1830's onwards is impracticable, and would add very little to what is already known, so I have confined their admission to a selection of those issued upon the opening of particular lines, or soon after[8].

Rule books call for similar treatment. Every company had its rules and regulations for employees, and tramways their instructions to motormen, and I have thought it sufficient for our purpose to include a selection from those which have come to hand in the course of compiling.

Discretion was needed in selecting works of fiction for the section 'Railways in Literature'. The isolation of the passenger coach compartment on a train journey has provided many an opening chapter of a mystery novel with circumstances upon which the story can develop, but this bibliography cannot allow itself to be padded out with examples of fiction in which the author, in search of a convenient setting for crime, decides to have it happen on a railway journey. As a principle for selection I have required novels to show that railway working is an essential element of the story, or, where incidents or settings are taken from the past, I have judged their usefulness for our purposes upon their value as accounts of actual railway happenings or places.

Railways are well represented in all forms of English literature, from Wordsworth to Paul Jennings, and the discovery of items for inclusion in the 'Railways in Literature' section has been perhaps one of the most pleasurable features of the compiling; but I have not extended the survey to include examples of railway metaphor—that is a subject for literary, not railway, research.

Generally, I have tried to present examples of writing into which some aspect of the life and character of railways has been integrated, as opposed to merely being used.

Exception has also been required in a few cases where books have appeared with titles which seem to belie their content. Such is *Twenty-five years at King's Cross* by G. H. Cator (1936), a collection of miscellaneous essays produced for a charitable cause, only two of which have some slight relationship to the title. Misleading titles of this kind are nevertheless recorded in the Index, followed by the abbreviation (ex), for 'excluded'.

ARRANGEMENT AND USE

The entries are grouped by subject and arranged chronologically within each section—with the exception of 'Railways in Literature' which is presented alphabetically under authors. By this process the subject-content of books may be set into a pattern—the Classification Scheme.

But books and their subjects often overlap. There is sometimes more than one subject to account for; authors vary in their approach to a theme and in the treatment of it; and also, hidden within the book itself there may be information not revealed by the wording on the title-page which needs to be brought to light. To correlate these differences and to give due place to fringe elements within the text, and to ensure that relationships between subjects are preserved, Class headings are provided with contents notes, followed by references to related subjects and aspects.

Some sections of the Bibliography are necessarily large and contain sub-ordinate divisions. Even so, it has sometimes been found useful to carry sub-division a stage further by introducing a system of marginal symbols to pick out features common to some entries within the section, thus bringing them into *visual* relief when scanning. Throughout the Bibliography marginal symbols **b** and **c** are so used to single out bibliographies and chronologies.

The Index is the key to the full resources of the Bibliography. Basically for authors, titles and subjects, it is extended to include also, persons, places, and anything significant or noteworthy in the wording of titles of individual works or in my own footnotes to entries. I have also extended the subject analysis of the works represented by including in the Index, so far as this is practicable, subjects in books which are not embraced by the wording of their title-pages.

It is important to remember that although some works have duplicate and occasionally multiple entries within the Scheme (the same work appearing in more than one place) it may sometimes still be necessary to refer to a heading in the Index other than the most obvious. In following up information on the Talyllyn Railway, for example, besides the main group of entries arranged under that heading in **L**, 'Individual Railways', there will be in **C 3**, 'Railways in Wales', and in **D 2**, 'Narrow Gauge Railways', some works which will have contributions to make. It is hardly possible to index a bibliography so minutely as to include the complete range of subject matter contained within works of a very general nature. As a general rule, whenever a detailed study of a subject is required, it is wise to examine the genus as well as the species, not forgetting that the first 156 items of the 'Generalia' section **A** provide 156 possible sources of information on any and every topic covered by the Bibliography.

The First Schedule of the Railways Act (1921) and the alphabetical lists of railways amalgamated under this Act and under the Transport Act (1947), and the genealogical tables of some of our large railway systems are included as an aid to research into company histories. I should mention that the reproduction of these tables within this present work involved the making of new blocks from the printed pages of the *Railway Gazette* and reducing the size.

At the end of compiling I was left with a number of unauthenticated references collected from a variety of sources, including booksellers' catalogues. Items in this *Phantasmagoria* probably relate to extracts, or manuscripts, or are abbreviated and manufactured descriptions of works already in; other items are perhaps announcements of projects which miscarried. Most will no doubt be found to have no substance whatever and none has been included in this present work.

Supplementary entries will be incorporated into a later volume planned to cover periodical literature, which J. E. C. Palmer and I hope to produce (see item no. 7895) and we shall be grateful for information on any items which have escaped our notice.

Although this work was conceived in the Reading Room of the British Museum Library, and nurtured in its surrounding book-stacks, it is a private venture, and the compilation has been undertaken without any undue interruption of official duties over a period of ten years. Undoubtedly an extension of visits to provincial libraries would bring to light some omissions, particularly of small locally-produced pamphlets, and variant editions of early guides and companions, but such a tour is impracticable. It is also impracticable—and this must be so in any work of this kind—to go on adding and improving. 'Even a journey on the Eastern Counties,' remarked W. M. Thackeray, 'must have an end at last!' So it is with the present work. There comes a time when one must say 'It is not complete, it is not perfect, but it is adequate—it will serve'. I hope that the work as it now stands will be found useful.

POSTSCRIPT FOR LIBRARIANS
(Some additional notes on modifications and style)

The work is essentially a practical guide for historians and students, and a free-flowing style in collation and note has been preferred to the use of the bibliotechnical algebraics which one would expect to find in a work of more scholarly intention.

In the employment of capitals, a middle course is found between the old use of too many and the modern use of too few. Capitals are used for titles of works in imaginative literature, for figurative and satirical expressions, and for titles which are 'reflexive'—describing the actual book as distinct from its subject. They are also used for Parliamentary publications (Bills, Acts, Standing Orders, Minutes of Evidence, etc.). Apart from these instances, I think it is sometimes permissible to capitalise by intuition, in order to convey some special meaning or subtlety which is implied in the title of a work[9].

A small proportion of the entries have been made from existing bibliographies and catalogues. These are for works which undoubtedly exist but which do not appear to be in the libraries I have visited. The selection of such items has been restricted to those whose descriptions carry enough detail to allow them to be accepted as representations of actual works, for I have found that no firm reliance can be placed upon check lists indirectly compiled from information sent in by contributing libraries.

Duplicate entries have been made for works which demand them, and multiple entries are given for books like Roger Lloyd's *Railwaymen's Gallery*, a volume of miscellaneous essays which cannot be adequately embraced by any one Class. But where a book contains *minor* topics which fall outside the scope of the Class in which it is placed, these are represented by subject entries in the Index.

The publisher is omitted in describing works issued before 1936 except in cases where to know the publisher is to know the approach to the subject. From 1936 the name of the publisher is given. In that year The Oakwood Press began to produce railway books with a distinctive style and content. Since then a tendency towards specialized forms for railway books has been adopted by The Locomotive Publishing Company, and Ian Allan, Ltd. Also, several new 'railway publishers' have appeared in response to the apparently ever-growing demand for more and more knowledge of railway history, particularly railway company history, and tramways, and it has become possible to visualize more accurately the nature of modern railway books if the publisher is known.

A few entries with BM locations have no collation. These are for older works not represented fully in the British Museum catalogue which were destroyed during the War (1939–45) and for which no alternative location or description has been found.

Headings for corporate bodies associated with localities, but whose names commence with a word other than the name of the locality, appear thus: [BURY.] COUNTY BOROUGH OF BURY.

For economy rather than for preference, shortened descriptions are sometimes used for successive editions, and for works in which it is necessary for our purpose to describe only a small part of the text. Authors' names appear fully only in the Index.

Editions of works which have become part of English Literature (Class O) are not defined. A systematic enumeration was beyond the bounds of practicability in this present work.

The ampersand (&) is used as a conjunction in composite names of railways—London & North Western Railway. Thus used it makes a closer bond than 'and', and '&' and 'and' can be used distinctively in such phrases as 'The London, Brighton & South Coast and South Eastern & Chatham'.

The marginal symbols may be something of an innovation. They are introduced to facilitate identification of bibliographies, chronologies, minor subjects or special aspects or emphases within a Class, and to avoid the inconvenience caused by conventional multiple references from an index entry. They are used sparingly, for noteworthy cases.

In collations, inserted square-bracketed pagination, e.g. pp. 13[15], means 'actually 15', but of course, pp. 13,[15,] would mean 13 numbered pages followed by 15 un-numbered pages.

The larger Classes are divided into two sections: 'Historical', for general and retrospective coverage of a subject, and 'Contemporaneous'. By 'contemporaneous' I mean books about contemporary events. A *contemporary* work is not necessarily contemporaneous in its treatment of a subject. It is rather a fine distinction but, I am sure, a valid one.

I have not ventured to evaluate the works described; a reliable guide to the best reading is to be found in Professor Jack Simmons's *The Railways of Britain* (1961) in the chapter 'Literature and Maps', and in Michael Robbins's *The Railway Age* (1962) in his 'Notes on Sources'. The best current reviews of railway books are in the *Journal of Transport History* and in *British Transport Review*. The *Railway Magazine* and the *Railway World* also feature short reviews of new books.

NOTES

(1) The Copyright Act of 1911 obliges publishers to deposit in the British Museum a copy of every book published in the United Kingdom. Previous legislation embodied in the series of Acts passed during the nineteenth century made similar provision; but in fact this obligation was only gradually accepted by publishers and there are in consequence gaps in the collections of the B.M. Library, especially in respect of material published during the first half of the nineteenth century.

(2) Appeals for information on locally-produced pamphlets appeared in the *Railway Magazine*, February 1956, and in the *Library Association Record*, January 1959.

(3) A scheme for subject specialization among libraries of the London boroughs, known as the Metropolitan Non-Fiction Special Collections, was initiated by the Association of Metropolitan Chief Librarians in 1950. Under this scheme, Holborn and Eltham are responsible for Transport. (Dewey classification, Holborn, 380–389; 650–659; Woolwich, 620–628, of which Eltham Branch is responsible for 621.7–628.)

In recent years other regions have established subject specialization schemes, and since 1959 there has been a national scheme for the purchase of British books, under which Glasgow Public Library is responsible for 380–382 and 384–387.4; Widnes Public Library for 621.13 and 625–625.6; and Middleton Public Library for 621.33.

(4) British Railways Board Historical Records, 66 Porchester Road, London, W.2. Also at the General Railway Office, North Eastern Region, York, and at 23 Waterloo Place, Edinburgh, Scotland. See 'Historical Records of the British Transport Commission' by L. C. Johnson (B.T.C. Archivist) in *Journal of Transport History*, vol. 1, no. 2, November 1953, pp. 82–96. Also, 'The Scottish Records of the British Transport Commission' by Jack Simmons, in *Journal of Transport History*, vol. 3, no. 3, May 1958, pp. 158–67.

(5) See 'Sources for the history of railways at the Public Record Office' by D. B. Wardle, in *Journal of Transport History*, vol. 2, no. 4, November 1956, pp. 214–34.

(6) See 'Materials for transport history amongst the records of Parliament' by Maurice Bond, in *Journal of Transport History*, vol. 4, no. 1, May 1959, pp. 37–52.

(7) The availability of theses is governed by the regulations of the university responsible for their custody.

(8) During the years 1837 to 1840, when our first trunk routes were opened, a large number of guides and companions appeared. They were sometimes issued in combined editions, varying according to the travel patterns then emerging from various end-on connections of separate companies soon to resolve into main-line railway systems. Not only were there variations in the sectional make-up of these publications—the rapid expansion of lines at this time made necessary the frequent issue of new editions, perhaps with only slight differences in pagination and imprint.

Apart from the inclusion of current time-tables, and sometimes a map, these early guides and companions rarely provide more than a brief reference to actual railway matters. There is sometimes an account of a trip down the line, but generally their value as contributions to knowledge is so slight that I do not feel that a prolonged search for variants is required of me.

(9) *Great Western Steam*, the title of a book by W. A. Tuplin, for example. *Great Western steam* would mean, surely, a book about the vapour exhausted by GWR locomotives, which is absurd. In cataloguing, we should not ignore the nuances which authors have introduced into the titles of their works.

COMPILER'S INTRODUCTION
TO THE SECOND EDITION

The original printing of this work ran to 2000 copies and when in the early 1970s all had been sold, the question arose of the possibility of compiling a new edition. The now out-of-print work was still in demand but a factor of more pressing concern was the ever-increasing number of railway books that had been published since the cut-off date, 1963. By 1975 this was running into thousands. The Railway Book Mania, which had its beginnings in the 1950s, was now, twenty-five years later, just showing signs of being on the wane, indicating that the time was about right to begin work on a new edition. By the time the work was ready for publication—if indeed this was found to be practicable—the phenomenon would surely have run itself out of steam.

Professor Jack Simmons of the University of Leicester—who may fairly be regarded as the Edward Pease of railway bibliography—discussed the feasibility of a new edition with interested publishers but it soon became clear that a re-setting of the work as a revised and enlarged edition would be impracticable. Thousands of new entries would have to be inserted into as many places within the existing text. This, and the consequent re-numbering and re-indexing, would add hundreds of pages to an already bulky volume, and to attempt to print and publish such a work would be folly. No one would be able to afford to buy it. It was therefore decided to compile a Supplement and to seek to publish also a photo-litho reprint of the original work into which corrections would be incorporated.

The present work, then, is a reprint with minor corrections. Additions and amendments to entries which needed space, for the describing, for example, of a subsequent (i.e. a post-1963) edition of a work, or an explanatory note, are listed numerically in the Supplement volume and are linked by an asterisk placed against the relevant entry in this Reprint. This always means 'See the Supplement'.

The main body of the Supplement consists of descriptions of works published in 1963–1980 and works of earlier date which have subsequently come to light. The style and presentation conforms to that of the earlier volume, with some slight alterations to the Classification Scheme made necessary by changes in subject area representation in railway literature over the past twenty-five years.

ACKNOWLEDGEMENTS
TO THE FIRST EDITION

In his *English express trains* (1884) Professor E. Foxwell says: 'Railways are incessantly persuading men into a disposition of more kindliness.' There are times—on the 5.30 from Charing Cross, for example—when this comes as a severe challenge to one's powers of imagination, but what the professor has in mind is that mystical quality in railways which enables them to be seen as avenues of pure delight, releasing in some inexplicable way little springs of pleasantness whenever we watch a train go by. This is not 'railway enthusiasm': a railway enthusiast is one who is burdened with an unbridled obsession for the aesthetics of railways and for the collecting of their ephemera—tickets, numberings, re-numberings, bits of old locomotives—especially nameplates—and any and every imaginable item of discarded bric-à-brac, including buttons from guards' old tunics. Professor Foxwell means that everyone *likes* railways. A few love them, but everyone likes them. I am sure that this is more or less true, except that they are not liked in towns, where they tend to have wrong emphases, but everyone likes them otherwise and I think he is right in believing that in a most curious and interesting way, reserves of goodwill are somehow enlivened by the sight and sound and being of railways. Perhaps deep down in the soul-centred source of all attitudes, where likes and dislikes kindle, form and pair off, it might be found, if that were possible, that railways and friendliness have a natural affinity, being really two expressions of what is in essence that most fundamental of human urges, the desire to communicate.

That having an interest in railways goes with a natural disposition towards friendliness is a theory borne out in fact by the co-operation that railway historians and enthusiasts have displayed in gathering material for this bibliography. They are a fraternity, characterized by a universal willingness to share knowledge. Librarians also have this quality and it is true to say that it is a mark of their calling. Some have supplied lists from their local collections; others have sent details of particular items. From railway historians and librarians I have received no less than five hundred letters; they have welcomed me into their homes and their libraries, and the whole career has been one of cheerful and ready co-operation.

The work, almost from its outset, has progressed under the blessing of the Railway & Canal Historical Society, unique among amateur transport societies in having the bibliography of railway history as one of its stated aims. Its past president has played a prominent part in its furtherance, and two librarian members have given much time and energy to biblio-technical aspects of the work.

For practical reasons I have to set some limit in acknowledging individuals, and the following list does not include the innumerable instances of help received in respect of single items.

To all who have helped me I give my thanks. I wish to thank particularly: William J. Skillern, F.L.A., of Stockport, and John E. C. Palmer, B.A., of the National Central Library, London, librarians and fellow members of the Railway & Canal Historical Society who have shared the problems encountered and have brought their opinions, criticisms and suggestions to bear upon the decisions made.

Charles R. Clinker and Charles E. Lee, authors, the former a past president of the Railway & Canal Historical Society, and the latter, President of the Railway Club and a past president of the Newcomen Society, for much valuable advice on points of railway history, and for access to their private collections.

Professor Jack Simmons, M.A., Department of History, University of Leicester, and joint editor of the *Journal of Transport History*, for his encouragement throughout the course of the work, and for writing the Foreword.

Sir Frank Francis, K.C.B., M.A., F.S.A., F.M.A., Director and Principal Librarian, British Museum, for advice at an early stage on broad principles of approach and for his interest in the progress of the work.

Robert A. Wilson, C.B., M.A., Principal Keeper of the Department of Printed Books, British Museum, for allowing me to arrange my duties so as to facilitate the visiting of other libraries.

E. J. Coates, F.L.A., of the British Technology Index, Library Association, for ideas on formulating a classification scheme for this subject.

For the privilege of free access to material and for personal assistance, the following librarians:

H. C. Richardson, A.L.A., Librarian, Institution of Civil Engineers.

G. Woledge, B.A., Librarian, Miss M. E. Dawson, M.A., and James and Betty Downey, of the British Library of Political and Economic Science, London School of Economics.

Doris Crowther, Librarian, Trades Union Congress.

J. H. P. Pafford, B.Litt., M.A., F.S.A., Goldsmiths' Librarian, University of London.

Miss M. F. Webb, B.Sc., Head of Library, and D. R. Jamieson, F.L.A., Patent Office.

Miss H. J. Parker, B.Sc., and L. R. Day, M.Sc., of the Science Library, Science Museum.

G. E. V. Awdry, M.A., F.L.A., Librarian, Gladstone Library, National Liberal Club.

L. C. Johnson, former Archivist, and Edward Atkinson, present Archivist, and Philip J. Kelley, British Railways Board Historical Records.

For sending lists of railway items from their local collections and for supplying subsequent information, the following librarians:

A. J. I. Parrott, F.L.A., City Librarian, Gloucester.

V. H. Woods, M.A., F.L.A., City Librarian, Birmingham.

P. Hepworth, M.A., F.L.A., F.R.S.A., City Librarian, Norwich.

H. Nichols, F.L.A., Reference Librarian, Central Library, Leeds.

Miss M. Y. Williams, B.A., A.L.A., Archivist, Lambeth.

Victor A. Hatley, B.A., A.L.A., Librarian, Central College of Further Education, Northampton.

Edward Robertson, M.A., D.D., D.Lttt., former Librarian, John Rylands Library, Manchester.

Percy Clare, M.B.E., A.L.A., Chief Librarian, Bermondsey.

Denis A. G. Wilson, M.A., A.L.A., Librarian, Portsmouth College of Art.

D. I. Colley, M.A., F.L.A., City Librarian, Manchester.

K. W. Humphreys, B.Litt., M.A., Librarian, University of Birmingham.

P. D. Hancock, M.A., University of Edinburgh Library.

R. J. Lee, F.L.A., Deputy Borough Librarian, Reading.

Norman Crawford, Burgh Librarian, Arbroath.

F. S. Green, M.A., F.L.A., County Librarian, Isle of Wight.

Mrs M. Lowther, F.L.A., Borough Librarian, Darlington.

ACKNOWLEDGEMENTS

E. Austin Hinton, B.A., F.L.A., City Librarian, Newcastle upon Tyne.
Ernest Bletcher, F.L.A., Borough Librarian, Derby.
B. G. Owens, M.A., Keeper of MSS. and Records, National Library of Wales.
Miss Máire Ní Dhomhnilláin, M.A., Assistant Librarian, Royal Irish
Academy, Dublin, for finding and sending to me volumes of rare pamphlets
from the Haliday Collection relating to Irish railways.
Professor A. C. O'Dell, M.Sc., F.R.S.(Edin.), Department of Geography,
University of Aberdeen, for descriptions of railway items in Aberdeen
University Library.
Alan Small, M.A., of the same Department, for subsequent information.

I am also grateful to:

Charles E. R. Sherrington, founder and for the whole period of its existence
from 1924 to 1962, head of the Railway Research Service, British Railways,
for access to his private collection.
B. D. J. Walsh, Hon. Secretary, The Railway Club, for access to the Railway
Club Library over a long period.
T. P. Hally-Brown and R. F. Roberts, M.A., of the Stephenson Locomotive
Society, for access to the S.L.S. Library and for the loan of material.
Ian Allan, for access to file copies of publications of Ian Allan, Ltd., Hampton
Court.
Roger W. Kidner, for access to file copies of publications of The Oakwood
Press, Lingfield, Surrey.
Frank T. Sabin, of Rutland Gate, London, for sending me a complete set
of his catalogues of railway prints and books.
B. W. C. Cooke, of the Tothill Press, for his kind permission to reproduce
genealogical tables (Appendix III) from the *Railway Gazette*.
Leslie Blackmur, of the British Museum Library, for help in alphabetizing
the Index; also to Trevor Payne for compiling the lists in the Appendix and
to E. G. Winskell and Alan Throp for practical help in the book-stacks.
Hildegard Schill, Ph.D., for revising the German entries. Philip Handsaker,
B.A., Research Assistant, Department of Printed Books, British Museum,
for revising the French entries.
Geoffrey T. Martin, B.A., who amalgamated the author, title and subject
entries into one sequence for the Index.

For expressed interest in the progress of the work over ten years of
compiling, friendly encouragement, and the sense of shared faith which
good-will raises up, I am more grateful than is perhaps realised. Apart from
those already mentioned, and colleagues in my own library, I would like to
acknowledge the help so given by the following:

Philip S. Bagwell, B.Sc.(Econ.), Ph.D., School of Commerce, The Polytechnic,
Regent Street, London.
Edwin A. Course, B.Sc.(Econ.), Ph.D., Department of Adult Education,
University of Southampton.
Henry W. Parris, M.A., Ph.D., Department of Extramural Studies, University
of Sheffield.
Professor Geoffrey Tillotson, M.A., B.Litt., of Birkbeck College, University
of London.
Professor Kathleen M. Tillotson, M.A., B.Litt., of Bedford College, Uni-
versity of London.
Philip Unwin, of George Allen & Unwin, Ltd. The actual appearance of
this work is due to his confidence in the project, his understanding of the
nature of the difficulties encountered, and his immeasurable patience.

ACKNOWLEDGEMENTS

For typing I am chiefly indebted to Eileen Dyer, Maureen Kennedy, Sally Wimbush, and to my wife's sisters, Catherine Brooker and Irene Hammond.

For alphabetizing at various times it is a pleasure to have to thank my own teenage daughters, Marian Elizabeth and Meredith Ann.

For careful and devoted work on the Index I am grateful to my wife's father, Fred Hammond of Caversham, Berkshire.

Lastly, praise is due, and here most warmly recorded, to my dear wife, Kay, not only for much typing and arranging, but for her loyalty and companionship over the long course which this work has led us. Much of our time together has been sacrificed, and the littering-up of the home which this kind of work involves made it hard to believe that normal home life would one day return. Having proposed to her between a cluster of milk churns and the waiting engine on the departure platform at Kings Cross, I think she feels that she should try to have some interest in railways, and she may even agree with Professor Foxwell that railways have indeed persuaded at least one man into a disposition of more kindliness! For her sake I hope so.

CHISLEHURST   G.O.
July 1964

ACKNOWLEDGEMENTS
TO THE SECOND EDITION

In a large complex bibliography set in double column in crown octavo and running into several hundred pages, an incidence of one mistake to a page might be regarded as an indication that an acceptable degree of accuracy had been achieved. The present work, in its original edition has been found to have a considerably lower proportion.

Modern printing technology and skill has made it possible to rectify all discovered blemishes. Most of these were minor ones (a wrong letter or figure), but in a few instances some movement of type was necessary. In all about 200 corrections have been incorporated into this Reprint—one to about every four pages. No doubt others will come to light as time goes by, but it would seem that we have good reason to believe that most delinquencies have now been put right.

Almost all of these errors were spotted by historians and scholars who took the trouble to note their discoveries, list them and send them in, and users of this revised work are invited to join with the compiler in acknowledging their co-operation. The difference between the original volume and this revision is largely the sum of their efforts.

Occasional single corrections were received from friends, and colleagues and others previously unknown to me, but the main contributors are, in alphabetical order: C. R. Clinker of Harlyn Bay, Cornwall; David Garnett of Little Somerford, Wiltshire; Norman Kerr of Cartmel, Cumbria; Michael J. T. Lewis of Hull; Harry Paar of Chigwell, Essex; John E. C. Palmer of Harpenden, Hertfordshire; Michael Robbins of Wimbledon; Jack Simmons of Leicester and William J. Skillern of Stockport.

Finally, the work owes its actual appearance to the enterprise of Professor Jack Simmons, and the spirited co-operation of Terry Walls of HMSO, Norwich and Philippa Richardson of the Science Museum, London. Without their goodwill and active interest the work would still be in manuscript.

LEICESTER   G.O.
July 1982

ABBREVIATIONS

(*locations and sources*)

AU	Aberdeen University
BM	British Museum Library
BM(MAPS)	British Museum, Map Room
BM(MSS)	British Museum, Department of Manuscripts
BM(P&D)	British Museum, Department of Prints & Drawings
BR	British Transport Commission Historical Records, now British Railways Board Historical Records, and for a few items seen at the former Railway Research Service, and at the Regional Publicity and Public Relations Offices of British Railways
BRE	* Bureau of Railway Economics, Washington, D.C.
CIE	Córas Iompair Eireann, Information Office, Kingsbridge, Dublin
G	Guildhall Library, London
H	* Daniel C. Haskell, *A Tentative Check-List of Early European Railway Literature* (1955)
HRL	* Hopkins Railway Library, Stanford Junior University
HZ	Max Hoeltzel, *Aus der Frühzeit der Eisenbahnen, mit einer Bibliographie* (1935)
ICE	Institution of Civil Engineers
IME	Institution of Mechanical Engineers
IT	Institute of Transport
LC	* Library of Congress, Washington, D.C.
LCC	London County Council
LSE	London School of Economics
NCL	National Central Library
NLC	National Liberal Club (Gladstone Library)
NLW	National Library of of Wales
P	* William Barclay Parsons Collection, New York Public Library (catalogue)
pc	private collection
PL	Public Library (e.g. Norwich PL)
PO	Patent Office
RC	Railway Club
RIA(H)	* Royal Irish Academy, Dublin (Haliday Collection)
SL	Science Library, Science Museum
SLS	Stephenson Locomotive Society
TUC	Trades Union Congress
UL	University of London
UL(GL)	University of London (Goldsmiths' Library)

* Microfilm copies of items with locations other than BM, especially those marked *, may have been subsequently acquired by the British Museum Library.

CLASSIFICATION SCHEME
Summary Table

A GENERAL HISTORY AND DESCRIPTION OF RAIL TRANSPORT IN THE BRITISH ISLES

B RAIL TRANSPORT AT PARTICULAR PERIODS——

  B 1 ORIGIN, ANTIQUITY, AND EARLY USE OF RAIL TRANSPORT
  Prepared stone trackways of ancient times—Wagonways in mines and quarries in mediaeval Europe—Their evolution in England during the 16th, 17th, and 18th centuries as feeders from mines and quarries to canals, rivers, and the coast

  B 2 THE TRANSITIONAL PERIOD, FROM MINERAL WAGONWAY TO PUBLIC PASSENGER RAILWAY, 1800–1830 ... 1850

  B 3 1830–1914 THE RAILWAY AGE

  B 4 1914–1918 RAILWAYS IN THE BRITISH ISLES DURING THE FIRST WORLD WAR

  B 5 1918–1923 POST-WAR RECOVERY AND THE PERIOD ENDING WITH THE 'BIG FOUR' AMALGAMATIONS OF 1923 (Railways Act, 1921)

  B 6 1921–1939 THE 'BIG FOUR' AMALGAMATIONS OF 1923 (Railways Act, 1921) AND RAILWAYS DURING THE 1920'S AND 1930'S

  B 7 1939–1945 RAILWAYS IN THE BRITISH ISLES DURING THE SECOND WORLD WAR

  B 8 1945–1947 POST-WAR RECOVERY, AND RAILWAYS DURING THEIR FINAL YEARS OF PRIVATE OWNERSHIP

  B 9 NATIONALIZATION, 1948. THE ESTABLISHMENT OF THE BRITISH TRANSPORT COMMISSION AND 'BRITISH RAILWAYS' (Transport Act, 1947)

  B 10 1948–   RAILWAYS OF THE BRITISH ISLES IN GENERAL AND 'BRITISH RAILWAYS'

  B 10 (ER)   Eastern Region
  B 10 (LMR) London Midland Region
  B 10 (NER) North Eastern Region
  B 10 (Sc.R) Scottish Region
  B 10 (SR)   Southern Region
  B 10 (WR) Western Region

C RAIL TRANSPORT IN PARTICULAR AREAS Historical and descriptive accounts of railways and tramways in various parts of the British Isles——

  C 1 ENGLISH LOCALITIES London—Geographical regions of England—Counties —The East and West Coast routes to Scotland and the 'Railway Races' to Scotland

  C 2 SCOTLAND

  C 3 WALES

  C 4 IRELAND

  C 5 ISLE OF WIGHT—Solent Tunnel scheme

  C 6 ISLE OF MAN

  C 7 CHANNEL ISLANDS

  C 8 ENGLISH CHANNEL TUNNEL and other Channel crossing schemes

  C 9 SCOTLAND TO IRELAND TUNNEL SCHEME

  C 10 BRITISH RAIL TRANSPORT COMPARED WITH THAT OF OTHER COUNTRIES

  C 11 INTERNATIONAL CO-OPERATION

D SPECIAL TYPES OF RAILWAY AND LOCOMOTION——

D 1 LIGHT RAILWAYS AND TRAMWAYS, including electric tramways (general works)

D 2 NARROW GAUGE RAILWAYS (with gauges less than 4 ft. 8½ in. down to 1 ft. 3 in.)

D 3 INDUSTRIAL, MINERAL, DOCK, HARBOUR, AND PUBLIC UTILITIES' SYSTEMS

D 4 ELECTRIC AND UNDERGROUND RAILWAYS (General works)

D 5 UNUSUAL FORMS OF RAILWAY AND LOCOMOTION—General—Monorail—Suspension—Elevated—Cable—Cliff—Wireways, etc.

D 6 MINIATURE RAILWAYS Passenger-carrying railways of 2 ft. gauge and less

E RAILWAY ENGINEERING (General)

E 1 BIOGRAPHIES OF RAILWAY ENGINEERS (Civil and Mechanical)

E 2 CIVIL ENGINEERING (General)—Construction and maintenance—Problems of terrain (gradients, cuttings, tunnelling, and embanking)

E 3 PERMANENT WAY

E 4 ELECTRIC RAILWAY ENGINEERING—Electrification—Underground electric railways (tube and subway)

E 5 ARCHITECTURE AND DESIGN—Bridges, viaducts, stations, tunnel entrances, etc.

E 6 MECHANICAL ENGINEERING (General) Locomotives, carriages, wagons—Trains

E 7 LOCOMOTIVES General works on steam, electric, diesel, etc., locomotives

E 8 STEAM LOCOMOTIVES

E 9 ELECTRIC LOCOMOTIVES AND TRAINS

E 10 DIESEL, DIESEL-ELECTRIC, AND OTHER SELF-GENERATING TYPES OF LOCOMOTIVE AND TRAIN

E 11 ROLLING STOCK (Carriages and wagons)

E 12 CARRIAGES—Pullman cars—Lighting and heating

E 13 WAGONS and other vehicles for special classes of work

E 14 BRAKES and passenger communication apparatus

E 15 SAFETY ENGINEERING—Signals and signalling methods—Interlocking

E 16 OTHER RAILWAY EQUIPMENT

F RAILWAY ADMINISTRATION—Constitution, promotion, and ownership of railways—Cost of construction—Internal finance (income and expenditure)—Accounts and auditing—Dissolution

F 1 RATES, CHARGES, FARES, AND TOLLS

F 2 INTER-RAILWAY RELATIONS—Competition—Co-operation and amalgamation—Running powers and working arrangements—Gauge controversy

F 3 CLEARING HOUSE SYSTEM

G RAILWAY MANAGEMENT AND OPERATION

G 1 OPERATION OF RAILWAY SERVICES—Train control

G 2 FREIGHT TRAFFIC—Marshalling—Cartage

G 3 PASSENGER TRAIN SERVICES—Pullman trains—Speed

G 4 RAILWAY ROAD SERVICES (Omnibus and freight)

G 5 RAILWAY WATER SERVICES—Docks, harbours, steamships, etc.—Train ferries and boat trains—Canal and inland waterway services

G 6 PUBLIC RELATIONS AND PUBLICITY

G 7 ANCILLARY SERVICES—Hotels, catering, camping coaches, and other special facilities—Station kiosks and bookstalls

G 8 RESEARCH

H RAILWAY LABOUR Work and working conditions of railway servants and railway navvies and labourers—Pay, welfare, pensions, and superannuation—Labour/management relations, labour questions and disputes, trade unions, strikes—Staff training—Safety of employees—Medical services—Memoirs of railway life

K RAILWAYS AND THE NATION Railways and their problems within the framework of national life—Fear of monopoly *vis-à-vis* the wastage of unbridled competition—The call for reform—Arguments for and against private ownership, and for and against government supervision, control, purchase, and state ownership—Railways and politics—Railways in relation to other forms of transport (road, canal, air, and coastwise shipping) as competitors and in co-operation—Integration of all forms of transport—Railway rating (taxation)—Railways and the future

K 1 RAILWAYS AND SOCIETY—The effect of railways upon the life of the people—Opposition to railways from owners of property—Spoliation of land and of scenery—Displacement of the poor caused by railway development—Relief of poverty by means of employment in railway construction and by railway taxation—Objections to Sunday trains—Suburban development and the creation of new centres of population—The effects of increased facilities for travel and recreation made possible by railways—The effects upon railways of social change—Railways and public health—Workmen's trains

K 2 RAILWAYS AND THE PASSENGER—Travelling conditions—Discomforts of early rail travel—Classes of accommodation—Passenger duty (Travelling tax)

K 3 SAFETY IN TRANSIT—Accidents and their prevention—Problems, theories, and reforms relating to safety of the travelling public as a social aim

K 4 RAILWAYS AND INDUSTRY, TRADE, AND AGRICULTURE—Railway facilities from the viewpoint of the distributor—Rates and charges reform—Private sidings and private wagon ownership

K 5 RAILWAYS AND THE MONEY MARKET—Investment—The effects of over-speculation—The 'Railway Manias'

K 6 GOVERNMENT CONTROL AND INSPECTION—Parliament and the railways—Legislation—Select Committees—Procedure—Standing Orders—Railway Department of the Board of Trade—Railway Commission—Railway Inspectorate—Ministry of Transport

K 7 RAILWAY LAW—Manuals and treatises on statute and case law relating to railways—Collections of Acts—Legal obligations of railways and of passengers and consignors of goods

K 8 RAILWAYS AND CRIME—Offences against railways or committed upon railway property

K 9 RAILWAYS AND THE POST OFFICE—Travelling Post Offices—Post Office Underground Railway—Railway letter stamps

K 10 RAILWAYS AND NATIONAL DEFENCE The use of public railways for movements of troops and equipment

K 11 MILITARY RAILWAYS Systems owned, operated, and maintained by military authorities

L INDIVIDUAL RAILWAYS The history and description of individual lines, including accounts of their locomotives, etc.

(Collected works, followed by an alphabetical arrangement of railway 'families')

M HERALDRY AND LIVERY

N THE RAILWAY IN ART—Fine Art—Posters—Ceramics—Medals and tokens

O THE RAILWAY IN LITERATURE

P HUMOUR, HUMOROUS DRAWING, AND SATIRE—Anecdotes—Allegory—Curiosa and Miscellanea

Q APPRECIATION OF RAILWAYS The appeal of railways and locomotives—Railway aesthetics

    Q 1 EXHIBITIONS, DISPLAYS, AND PAGEANTS of a general and historical nature —Museums

    Q 2 MODEL RAILWAY ENGINEERING

    Q 3 RAILWAY PHOTOGRAPHY

    Q 4 ILLUSTRATIONS

R RESEARCH AND STUDY OF RAILWAYS AND RAILWAY HISTORY—Sources and methods—Bibliography

S STATISTICAL METHOD The science of compiling railway statistics

T GENERAL DIRECTORIES, GAZETTEERS, ATLASES, GUIDE BOOKS, LISTS OF STATIONS, DISTANCE TABLES, TIME-TABLES

USE THE INDEX for detailed and extensive research and for special aspects and minor subjects. Basically for authors, titles and subjects, the Index is extended to include persons, places, and anything significant or noteworthy in the wording of titles of individual works or in the compiler's footnotes to entries. The subject content of works represented in the Bibliography is accommodated generally by the Classification Scheme, but an extended analysis of subjects not embraced by the wording of title-pages is incorporated, so far as this is practicable, into the Index.

It is important to remember that although some works have duplicate and occasionally multiple placings within the Scheme it may sometimes still be necessary to refer to a heading in the Index other than the most obvious. In following up information on the Festiniog Railway, for example, it will be found that besides the main group of entries arranged under that heading in **L** 'Individual Railways' there will be in **C 3** 'Railways in Wales' and in **D 2** 'Narrow Gauge Railways' some works which have contributions to make.

It is hardly possible to index a bibliography so minutely as to include the complete range of subject matter contained within works of a very general nature. As a general rule, whenever a detailed study of a subject is required, it will be found profitable to examine the genus as well as the species (for Steam Locomotives, **E 7** as well as **E 8**) not forgetting that the 156 items which make up the 'Generalia' section **A** provide 156 possible sources of information on any and every topic covered by the Bibliography. In cases like the Festiniog, which is an offspring of the marriage of two subject areas, 'Railways in Wales' and 'Narrow Gauge Railways', it will be found advisable to examine the genera from which the subject under survey proceeds.

Research will be facilitated by using the Bibliography in conjunction with a good general history. Among modern books *British Railway History* by C. Hamilton Ellis is unrivalled for subject coverage; *The Railways of Britain* by Jack Simmons, and for social aspects *The Railway Age* by Michael Robbins, both include authoritative annotated guides to the best reading on general and specific subjects.

A full account of the subject coverage of this Bibliography, material represented, and sources used, is given in the Compiler's Introduction (pages 13–20).

For collective histories of individual railways see L *(Collective Works)*
For railways in general at particular periods see B
For railways in particular localities see C

Marginal symbols: **b** bibliographies
c chronologies

1 COMPANION to the Almanack; or, Year-Book of General Information, for 1828 (–1888). *London*, [1827–1887].   BM
——An Analytical Index to the Companion to the Almanack . . . 1828 to 1834 [with] an index . . . for 1834 and 1835. *London*, 1835. pp. 89.   BM
—— A Complete Index to the Companion to the Almanac, from 1828 to 1843, inclusive. *London*, 1843. pp. 561.   BM
Issued as a running supplement to the *British Almanac*. The editions for the years 1837 to 1852 (1850 excepted) provide a most reliable contemporary source of information on current railway development generally, and for particular lines.
In the 1841 edition is a ten-column table of 135 railways.
After 1852 there is a sharp falling off in railway information, undoubtedly due to the appearance in 1850 of the first edition of a serial publication which at once surpassed the *Companion to the Almanack* as a source for railway information. This was *Bradshaw's General Railway Directory, Shareholders' Guide, Manual and Almanack* (1850 to 1923). (*See* 7949.)
In the 1868 edition, however, is a 24-page account by Arthur Locker of the findings of the Royal Commission on Railways (1865–7), and in the 1871 edition a special article appears with the title 'Metropolitan locomotion' by Robert Smiles (pp. 110–31).

2 HERAPATH, J. On railways. [*London*, 1836.] pp. 32, with illus.   LSE
Reprints from the *Mechanics Magazine*, vol. 22, 1835; vol. 23, 1836.

*3 PRIESTLEY, J. Historical account of the navigable rivers, canals and railways throughout Great Britain, as a reference to Nichols, Priestley & Walker's 'New Map of Inland Navigation', derived from original and parliamentary documents in the possession of Joseph Priestley. *London*, 1831. pp. xiv, 702, viii.   BM
—— another edn. *London*, 1831. pp. xii, 776, x.   MANCHESTER PL
—— another edn. *London*, 1838. pp. xii, 776, x.   H

*4 GILBERT, J. The Railways of England, containing an account of their origin, progress and present state, a description of the several parts of a railway and a history of their invention; together with a map with all the lines carefully laid down. *London* [1838.] pp. 126.   BM

In his *History of British railways down to the year 1830* (1938), C. F. Dendy Marshall wrongly ascribes this work to Frederic Moore, who was born in 1830.

5 LECOUNT, P. Railways. *In* 'Encyclopaedia Britannica', 7th edn., 1841. pp. [13]–58, with plates 420–9.   BM

6 PENNY Cyclopaedia. *London*, 1833–43. BM
vol. 6, 1836. pp. 219–25, 'Canal'. Includes tables of canals in the British Isles; those with railway feeder lines being noted in the 'Remarks' column.
vol. 19, 1841. pp. 245–67, 'Railway'. Includes tables listing 124 lines in the British Isles opened between 1801 and 1840, with details.
—— The Supplement to the Penny Cyclopaedia. *London*, 1845, 1846. 2 vols.   BM
vol. 2, 1846. pp. 659–84, 'Transit, railway'. This is a supplementary article to that in vol. 19, with a supplementary list.

7 STANESBY, J. T. Railways. [*London*, 1841.] pp. [65]–80. [*Knight's Store of Knowledge*, no. 5.]   LSE

8 KLETKE, G. M. Literarische Übersicht von Schriften welche über das Eisenbahnwesen
b ... bis jetzt erschienen sind. *Berlin*, 1844. pp. 31.   BM
Includes items on British railways.

9 LEGOYT, M. A. Le Livre des chemins de fer: construits, en construction et projetés; ou, Statistique générale de ces voies de communication en France et a l'étranger. *Paris*, 1845. pp. 298.   BM
pp. 29–47, 'Angleterre', and a bibliography on pp. 268–9, 271.

10 MOGG, E. Mogg's Handbook for Railway Travellers; or, Real Iron Road Book; being an entirely original and accurate description of all the travellable railways hitherto completed between the Thames and the Tweed, with notices of those in progress and projected ... *London*, 1839. pp. viii, 235, 13, with 2 maps.   BR
—— 2nd edn. *London*, 1840. pp. vi, 235, 13.
—— Appendix to Mogg's Handbook for Railway Travellers. *London*, 1840. pp. 101, 34.   BM
—— 3rd edn., with an Appendix. *London*, 1846. pp. irreg.   BM
Maps published separately with a general title-page, *List of the Maps that accompany Mogg's Handbook*.   BM

11 RITCHIE, R. Railways: their rise, progress and construction; with remarks on railway accidents and proposals for their prevention . . . illustrated by numerous woodcuts. *London*, 1846. pp. viii, 444.   BM

12 PROGRESS, Peter, *pseud.* [R. Y. Clarke.] The rail, and the electric telegraph; comprising a brief history of former modes of travelling and telegraphic communication; with an account of the electric clock, etc., with illustrative anecdotes and engravings. *London*, 1847. pp. 60, 84.   UL(GL)

13 CLARKE, R. Y. Railway appliances in the nineteenth century; or, The rail, steam, and electricity; with illustrative anecdotes, engravings and diagrams. *London*, 1848. pp. 60, 84, 77.   BM
In three sections: *A short history of the origin and progress of tramroads and railways*; *The electric telegraph*; *The steam engine*. Also published separately under the pseudonym 'Peter Progress'.
—— 3rd edn. *London*, 1850. pp. 60, 77, 84.   LSE

14 STEPHENSON, R. M. Railways: an introductory sketch . . . part I . . . *London*, 1850. pp. 119, with illus.   BM
Cover title, *Rudimentary treatise on railways*.

15 CHAMBERS, W. Railway communications. [*London*, 1851?] pp. 31[32]. [*Chambers' Papers for the People*, no. 89, vol. 12.]   LSE

*16 FRANCIS, J. A history of the English railway: its social relations and revelations, 1820–1845. *London*, 1851. 2 vols.   BM
A detailed work, including accounts of G. Stephenson, I. K. Brunel, S. M. Peto, G. C. Glyn, and G. Hudson.

17 LARDNER, D. The steam engine, steam navigation, roads, and railways, explained and illustrated. Eighth edition, revised & improved; with numerous illustrations. *London*, 1851. pp. xi, 422.   BM
pp. 339–418, Railways.

18 PORTER, G. R. The progress of the nation in its various social and economic relations, from the beginning of the nineteenth century to the present time. *London*, 1838. pp. 367.   BM
pp. 62–77, Railways; with table of lines completed.
—— another edn. *London*, 1847. pp. xxiii, 846.   BM
—— another edn. *London*, 1851. pp. xxvii, 843.   BM

19 HEBERT, L. The Engineer's and Mechanic's Encyclopaedia . . . *London*, 1836. 2 vols.   BM
vol. 2, pp. 373–584, 'Railway', with illus.
—— new edn., *London*, 1852.   BM
(vol. 2, pp. 373–550.)
Includes a complete list of railway patents down to 1846.

20 DICKSON, W. E. Railways and locomotion . . . *London*; *Society for Promoting Christian Knowledge*, 1854. pp. vi, 122.   BM

21 SCOTT, B. The progress of locomotion; being two lectures on the advances made in artificial locomotion in Great Britain. *London: Working Men's Educational Union*, 1854. pp. 80   BM
pp. 60–72, Railways.

22 TOMLINSON, C. Cyclopaedia of Useful Arts, mechanical and chemical, manufactures, mining and engineering; edited by C. Tomlinson, *London & New York*, 1854.   BM
vol. 11, pp. 536–63, Roads and railroads.

23 BAKER, T. The Steam Engine; or, The powers of flame; an original poem in ten cantos. *London*, 1857. pp. iv, 260   BM
Cantos 8, 9, and 10 relate to locomotives and various aspects of railways, including the Liverpool & Manchester, and to navvies. The 'additional notes' (pp. 239–60) are very informative, but their references to places in the text are sometimes incorrectly given.

24 STEPHENSON, R. Résumé of the railway system and its results. *In* 'The life of George Stephenson' by S. Smiles. 1857. pp. 477–512.   BM
Robert Stephenson's presidential address to the Institution of Civil Engineers, January 1856.

25 PERDONNET, A. Notions générales sur
b les chemins de fer . . . suivées . . . d'une bibliographie raisonnée. *Paris*, [1859.] pp. vii, 452.   BM
Contains very little about British railways but the bibliography has six pages of 'ouvrages anglais'.

26 MACNAY, T. A lecture on our roads & railways, delivered at the Mechanics' Hall, Darlington, on Friday February 1st, 1861. *Darlington*, 1861. pp. 24.   LSE
Stockton & Darlington Rly., and railway development generally.

27 AUDIGANNE, A. Les Chemins de fer aujourd'hui et dans cent ans chez tous les peuples; économie financière et industrielle, politique et morale des voies ferrées. *Paris*, 1852–62. 2 vols.   BM
vol. 1, pp. 65–99, 'Les pays étrangers durant la période originelle des chemins de fer, l'Angleterre'.
vol. 2, pp. 28–67, 'Grandes exploitations britanniques'.

28 CHAMBERS, W. About railways. *London & Edinburgh*, [1865.] pp. 103.   BM

29 DODD, G. Railways, steamers and telegraphs: a glance at their recent progress
c and present state. *London & Edinburgh*, 1867. pp. vi, 326, with 7 plates.   BM
pp. 1–186, 'Railways'; with chronology.
c —— another edn. *London*, 1868. pp. vi, 326.   BR

30 STUERMER, G. Geschichte der Eisenbahnen:
Entwickelung und jetzige Gestaltung sämmt-
c licher Eisenbahnnetze der Erde. *Bromberg*, 1872. pp. 247.   BM
pp. 89–126, 'Grossbritannien'; with lists of
companies, including (pp. 109–26) a chronology
of openings, 1825–1871.

31 COHN, G. Untersuchungen über die
englische Eisenbahnpolitik. *Leipzig*, 1874–
75. 2 vols. pp. xiii, 370; xii, 646.   BM
Bd. 1, Die Entwickelung der Eisenbahngesetzgebung in England.
Bd. 2, Zur Beurteilung der englischen Eisenbahnpolitik.
A very detailed survey of the development of
British railways in general, with special emphasis
on government control and legislation,
finance, and amalgamation.
Part of this work is incorporated into this
author's *Die englische Eisenbahnpolitik der
letzten zehn Jahre, 1873–1883* (1883). This
later work has an index for all three volumes.

32 CROAL, T. A. A Book about Travelling,
past and present . . . with numerous illustrations. *London & Edinburgh*, 1877. pp. 608. BM
Reprinted 1880.
pp. [453]–606, 'The railway'.

33 PARSLOE, J. Our railways: sketches historical and descriptive, with practical information as to fares and rates, etc. and a
chapter on railway reform. *London*, 1878.
pp. xii, 294.   BM

34 SAX, E. Die Eisenbahnen. *Wien*, 1879.
pp. viii, 552.   BM
pp. 470–82, 'Die Entwicklung in den wich-
tigsten Ländern: England', with bibliographical notes.

35 STEINER, F. Bilder aus der Geschichte des
Verkehrs: die historische Entwicklung der
Spurbahn. Eine Festschrift zum fünfzigsten
Gedenktage des Sieges Stephensons bei
Rainhill, 1829 . . . mit 33 Abbildungen im
Texte und einem Kärtchen. *Prag*, 1880.
pp. iv, 153[155].   LSE
pp. 113–28, Von Liverpool nach Manchester.
pp. 139–53, Die Wettfahrt von Rainhill.

36 BACLÉ, L. Les Voies ferrées . . . 143 figures
dans le texte et 4 planches hors texte. *Paris*,
1882. pp. vii, 322.   BM
Includes British railways.

37 TIMBS, J. Wonderful inventions, from the
mariner's compass to the electric telegraph
cable; with numerous engravings. *London*,
1870. pp. xiv, 400.   pc
pp. [280]–314, The railway and the locomotive.
—— another edn. *London*, 1882. pp. xix, 423.
                                         pc

38 MACLIVER, P. S. The growth of the railway system: a lecture. *London*, [1883?]
pp. 12.   NLC
Reprinted from the *Railway Review*.

39 WOODS, E. Address of Mr. Edward Woods,
President of the Institution of Civil Engineers, 9th November 1886. *London*, 1886.
pp. 63.   UL(GL)
On railway development.

40 MONTEFIORE, A. All about our railways.
London, 1887. pp. 140.   BM
Introductory.

41 WARD, T. H. The reign of Queen Victoria:
a survey of fifty years of progress. *London*,
1887. 2 vols.   BM
vol. 2, pp. 83–111, Locomotion and transport: part 1, railways.

*42 WILLIAMS, F. S. Our Iron Roads: their
history, construction and social influences;
with numerous illustrations. *London*, 1852.
pp. x, 390.   BM
Includes a table of accidents.
—— 2nd edn. [1883.] pp. viii, 514.   BM
—— 3rd, 1883. pp. xvi, 514.   IME
—— 4th, 1883. pp. xvi, 514.   BM
—— 5th, 1884. pp. xvi, 514.   UL(GL)
—— 6th, 1885. pp. xvi, 514.   pc
—— 7th, 1888. pp. xvi, 514.   BM

43 MACDERMOTT, E. R. Railways. *Philadelphia*, 1891. pp. 31.
Reprinted from *Chambers' Encyclopaedia*.

44 MULHALL, M. G. The Dictionary of
Statistics. *London*, 1892.   BM
pp. 495–512, 'Railways'.

45 BAKER, E., *publisher*. A Bibliography and
Priced Catalogue of Early Railway Books;
b the collection forming a complete history of
railways, 1824–1860 . . . Compiled by S.
Cotterell. *Birmingham*, 1893. pp. 23.   pc
Items are annotated with remarks and
opinions.

46 FRITH, H. The Flying Horse: the story of
the locomotive and the railway; with numerous illustrations. *London*, 1893. pp. xii,
290.   BM
A popular history with some unique illustrations.

47 BORGHT, R. van der. Das Verkehrswesen.
Leipzig, 1894. pp. x, 468. [*K. Frankenstein,
Hand\und\Lehrbuch\der\Staatswissenschaften*.
Iste. Abt., Bd. 7.]   BM
pp. 273–350, 'Der Eisenbahnverkehr'. Includes British railway development; with
bibliographical notes and a bibliography.

*48 BAKER, E. *publisher*. A Handbook to
various publications, documents and charts
b connected with the rise and development of
the railway system chiefly in Great Britain
and Ireland . . . (Compiled by S. Cotterell.)
Birmingham, 1893. pp. 128.   pc
—— Supplement to the Railway Handbook,
being a new price list . . . a list of additional
books and pamphlets . . . index to the Railway Handbook . . . (Compiled by S. Cotterell.) *Birmingham*, 1895. pp. 92.   pc

49 TEGGART, F. J. Catalogue of the Hopkins Railway Library. *Palo Alto: Leland Stanford Junior University*, 1895. pp. ix, 231. [*Publications of the Library, Leland Stanford Junior University*, no. 1.]   BM
Includes British railways (pp. 99–130).

50 GORDON, W. J. The story of our railways. *London*, [1896.] pp. 159, with illus.   BM

51 PENDLETON, J. Our railways: their origin, development, incident and romance. *London*, 1894. 2 vols, with 294 illus.   BM
—— another edn. *London*, 1896.   BM
Issued serially in 18 parts.

*52 ACWORTH, W. M. The railways of England . . . *London*, 1889. pp. xvi, 427, with 56 illus.   BR
—— 2nd edn. *London*, 1889. pp. xvi, 427.   UL
—— 3rd, *London*, 1889. pp. xvi, 427.   BM
—— 4th, *London*, 1890. pp. xvi, 427.   IT
—— 5th, *London*, 1900. pp. xxiv, 480, with 67 illus. (Reprint, *London: Ian Allan*, 1964.)   BM
Collected historical accounts of the main line companies.

53 FISHER, J. A. The railways of the United Kingdom: fifty years of progress. *London*, May 1900. pp. 19.   BR
Reprinted from the *Anglo-Saxon Guide to the Paris Exhibition, 1900.*

54 LAURENT DE VILLEDEUIL, P. C. Bibliographie des chemins de fer, 1771–1846. *Paris*, 1907. pp. 826.   BM
In tome 1, fascs. 1, 2 & 3, pp. 1–240, 638 items are described of which about 60 (excluding brief entries for patent specifications) are concerned in varying degrees with railways in Gt. Britain.

55 HOWDEN, J. R. The Boys' Book of Railways; with over one hundred illustrations from photographs. *London*, 1909. pp. xviii, 242.   BM

56 GORDON, W. J. Our home railways: how they began and how they are worked; with 36 coloured plates . . . and 300 illustrations . . . *London*, 1910. 2 vols. pp. xvi, 268: x, 248.   BM
Also issued separately in 12 parts.
—— reprinted, *London: Ian Allan*, 1962, 63. [*Classics of Railway Literature.*]   BM
Plates in monochrome.

57 HARTNELL, F. S. All about railways: a book for boys . . . with a colour frontispiece and a large number of illustrations from photographs. *London*, [1910.] pp. viii, 374.   BM

58 IVATTS, E. B. Railway information: a collection of MS. notes and press cuttings, *c.* 1860–1910. 8 vols, with an index.   LSE

59 WILLIAMS, A. The romance of modern locomotion; containing interesting descriptions in non-technical language of the rise and development of the railroad systems in all parts of the world. *London*, 1904. pp. 367, with 25 illus.   BM
Includes short accounts of the Midland, the G.W. Rly., locomotive development, and the 'Railway Mania'. Introductory.
—— another edn. *London*, 1910. pp. 368.   BM

60 DEFRANCE, P. Les Chemins de fer de la Grande Bretagne et de l'Irlande: étude au point de vue commercial et financier. *Bruxelles & Paris*, 1911. pp. 292.   BM

*61 PRATT, E. A. History of inland transport and communication in England. *London*, 1912. pp. xii, 532.   BM
p. 195 to end, mostly on railways.

62 LAWSON, W. R. British railways: a financial and commercial survey. *London*, 1913. pp. xxxii, 320.   BM
A survey of all aspects of railway development except technical engineering. pp. 1–60, Finance; pp. 161–217, Rates; pp. 218–53, Administration; pp. 268–320, Railways and the State.

63 BRITISH railway progress shown by the Board of Trade Returns [1870–1912]. *In* 'Jubilee of the Railway News, 1864–1914.' *London*, [1914.] pp. 32–3.   BM
A table (28 columns).

64 RAILWAY NEWS. The Jubilee of the Railway News, 1864–1914. *London*, [1914.]
c pp. 348, 120, with many illus., incl. 12 colour reproductions of railway posters.   BM
A collective reprint of a selection of informative articles covering a wide range of railway activities and developments, historical and descriptive. There are many tables and much statistical data. The second section (120 pages) is concerned with railway engineering. There are 120 pages of illustrated advertisements relating to railway services and railway equipment.

65 TALBOT, F. A. Railway wonders of the world; illustrated, with colour plates and photographs. *London*, [1913–14.] 2 vols. pp. 760, with 24 col. plates & over 300 photographs.   BM
Issued serially in 24 fortnightly parts, April 1913–March 1914.

66 PROTHEROE, E. The railways of the world; with 16 coloured plates and 419 illustrations from photographs in the text. *London*, [1914.] pp. xx, 752.   BM
pp. 1–528, British railways.

67 PARSONS, W. B. Railways. (Paper to be read at a meeting of the International Engineering Congress, San Francisco, 1915.) [*San Francisco*, 1915.] pp. 46, with many tables.   IT
'Advance copy; printed, not published.'
A general comparative account of railway development in many countries.

*68 JACKMAN, W. T. The development of transportation in modern England. *Cam-*
b *bridge*, 1916. 2 vols. (pp. xv, 459; vi, 461–820), with many bibliographical notes and an extensive bibliography.   BM

A very detailed work.

vol. 2. pp. 461–603, Development of railways, up to 1850.

pp. 604–23, Effects of steam upon road transportation.

pp. 624–749, Competition of railways and canals.

pp. 750–811, Bibliography.

—— reprinted in 1 vol. with a new introduc-
b tion by W. H. Chaloner. *London: Frank Cass & Co.*, 1962. pp. xxxiii, 820, with maps.   BM

*69 WILLIAMS, J. B. A guide to some aspects of English social history, 1750 to 1850. *New*
b *York*, 1916. pp. 149.   BM

pp. 134–49, 'Railways'. An annotated bibliography of 106 items.

70 BOASE, F. Modern English biography; containing many thousand concise memoirs of persons who have died since the year 1850, with an index of the most interesting matter. *Truro*, 1892–1921. 6 vols.   BM

Under 'Railways' in the indexes to each volume is a large number of subject entries relating to the activities of persons engaged in various branches of railway development.

71 TIMES *newspaper*. Railway Number, August 15, 1921. (no. 42,799. Supplement.) *London*, 1921. pp. xxiv.   LSE

72 JACKSON, G. G. All about our British railways. *London*, 1923. pp. xi, 288, with 62 plates.   BM

73 TALBOT, F. A. Railways of the world; with numerous illustrations. *London*, [1924.] 2 vols. (pp. 728.)   BM

Issued in 18 fortnightly parts, 26 March–19 Nov., 1924.

74 HALLOWS, R. W. Modern railways … *London*, 1924. pp. 124.   BM

Introductory.

75 ASPINALL, J. A. F. Some railway notes, old and new. *London: Institution of Mechanical Engineers*, [1925.] pp. 1107–51, with illus. & diagrams.   BR

Excerpt *Min. Proc. I.M.E.*, 6 Nov. 1925.

Miscellaneous remarks on some by-ways of railway development. (Thomas Hawksley Lecture.)

76 DARLINGTON CORPORATION. Railway Centenary Souvenir. [*Darlington*, 1925.] pp. 47, with illus. (some col.).   IT

77 DAVIES, R. The Railway Centenary: a retrospect. *London*, [1925.] pp. 49, with 18 plates.   BM

Mostly about the Stockton & Darlington Rly.

78 LOCOMOTIVE, RAILWAY CARRIAGE & WAGON REVIEW. Railway Centenary Supplement. *London*, June 30, 1925. pp. 124, with 28 plates (7 col.).   PO

Historical essays by various writers on each of the components of the main line companies and the underground railways of London, including their locomotive history.

79 LONDON & NORTH EASTERN RLY. Catalogue of the collection of railway relics and modern stock at Faverdale, Darlington, in connection with the Railway Centenary Celebrations, July 1925. 4th edition. *York*, [1925.] pp. 95.   BM

Pictures, prints, models, documents, locomotives, rolling stock, permanent way and signalling apparatus lent by the main line companies.

80 LONDON & NORTH EASTERN RLY. Commemoration of the centenary of railways, Wednesday 1st July to Friday 3rd July, 1925. [*Leeds*, 1925.] pp. 30.   BM

Summary of proceedings, programme, list of exhibits, etc.

81 RAILWAY GAZETTE. Special British Railway Centenary Number, June 22, 1925. *London*, 1925. pp. 128, with many illus., maps & diagrams.   IT

In English and French.

82 SCIENCE MUSEUM [London]. Land transport: Railway Centenary Exhibition Supplement; compiled by E. A. Forward. *London*, 1925. pp. 29. [*Catalogue of the Collections in the Science Museum.*]   BM

Description of the 189 items which made up this special exhibition.

83 TIMES *newspaper*. Imperial and Foreign Trade and Engineering Supplement: Railway Centenary section. July 4, 1925. pp. ix–xxiv.   RC

84 HIND, J. R. The Book of the Railway; with over 250 illustrations, including 26 plates in full colour. *London & Glasgow*, 1927. pp. 384.   BM

British and foreign railways described to young readers.

85 JACKSON, G. G. The world's railways; illustrated by Barnard Way. *London*, [1927.] pp. 165, with 13 plates (6 col.) & illus. in text.   BM

For older children.

86 WILLIAMS, A. The Book of Trains. [*London*,] 1927. pp. 112, with illus.   BM

For young readers, with questions and answers. An earlier edition, 1926, had no illustrations.

87 HIND, J. R. Train, station and track; with 100 illustrations including 6 blocks in full colour. *London & Glasgow*, [1928.] pp. 128.   BM

88 WOOD, W. V. *and* STAMP, J. C. Railways. *London*, 1928. pp. 252. [*Home University Library*, no. 137.]   BM

89 GRAFTON & Co. Railways. (Catalogue 87.)
 London, 1930. pp. 48.   PC
b Books, maps, and pamphlets, from 1791 to
c 1930, in chronological order. Graftons
   specialised in railway books and almost all their
   catalogues contained a railway section.

90 HAWKS, E. The Railway Book for Boys.
 London, [1930.] pp. 256, with 16 col. plates
 & many illus.   BM

91 HIND, J. R. Railwayland; with over 250
 illustrations, including 16 plates in full
 colour. *London*, [1930.] pp. 192.   BM

92 JACKSON, G. G. British railways: the
 romance of their achievement. *London*,
 [1930.] pp. xii, 244, with 105 illus. on 32
 plates.   BM

93 'MERCURY'. The fascination of our railways: a series of instructive railway talks for
 boys. *London*, [1930.] pp. 115, with 56
 illus. on 37 plates.   BM

94 THOMAS, C. E. Collection of railway
 books, railroadiana . . . *Burgess Hill*, 1931.
b pp. 57[58].   PC
   A catalogue, with descriptive annotations to
   each entry. Some titles are much abbreviated.

95 GAIRNS, J. F. Railways for all; with a
 hundred illustrations. *London*, 1923. pp.
 384, with illus. on plates.   BM
   Introductory.
   —— 4th edn., rev. & enl. by J. K. Taylor.
 London, [1934.] pp. 320.   BM
   The 2nd and 3rd editions were reprints, with
   minor alterations (not in BM).

*96 SHERRINGTON, C. E. R. A hundred years
 of inland transport, 1830–1933. [*London:*]
 Duckworth, 1934. pp. 376.   BM
   Mostly relating to the development of railways and to the effect upon them of the introduction of later modes of transport. Also,
   railways and the Post Office.

97 DOLLFUS, C. *and* GEOFFROY, E. de. Histoire de la locomotion terrestre; les chemins
 de fer. *Paris*, 1935. pp. xiii, 376, with 49
 plates (16 col.) & many illus. in text.   BM
   Includes British railways.

98 JACKSON, G. G. The railways of Great
 Britain: the story of their rise and progress
 to the date of their new grouping; illustrated
 with photographs. *London*, [1923.] pp. 278,
 with 38 illus. on plates.   BM
   —— rev. edn. *London*, [1935.] pp. 271. BM

99 SOMMERFIELD, V. Speed, space and time.
 London, [1935.] pp. xv, 299.   BM
   pp. 115–200, 'The Railway'; with plates &
 illus.

100 WINCHESTER, C. Railway wonders of the
 world. *London*, [1935.] 2 vols. (pp. 1604),
 with many illus. & detailed index.   BM
   Issued in weekly parts, 1 Feb. 1935 to 10 Jan.
 1936.

*101 LEWIN, H. G. The Railway Mania and its
 aftermath, 1845–1852: being a sequel to
 'Early British railways'. *London: Railway
 Gazette*, 1936. pp. xx, 500, with 13 maps (5
 fold.) & 15 tables.   BM
   Some apparent mis-statements are noted by
 M. D. Greville in *Jnl. Railway & Canal Hist.
 Soc.*, vol. 2, no. 1, Jan. 1956, and in vol. 3,
 no. 3, May 1957.

102 ANDREWS, C. B. The Railway Age. *London: Country Life*, 1937. pp. xi, 145, with 82
 plates, many illus. & some verse.   BM
   Railways in the 19th century.

103 SOMMERFIELD, V. English railways: their
 beginnings, development and personalities.
 London: Nelson, 1937. pp. xx, 362, with 11
 plates & 6 maps.   BM
   Historical sketches, with a chapter on post-
 grouping developments and possibilities.

104 BELL, W. J. The Modern Book of Railways.
 London, 1935. pp. 142, with 16 plates. BM
   For young readers.
   —— 2nd edn. *London*, 1938. pp. 146.   BM

105 GARBUTT, P. E. A survey of railway de-
 velopment and practice. *London: A. H.
 Stockwell*, [1938.] pp. 112.   BM
   Introductory.

106 NATIONAL LIBERAL CLUB—GLADSTONE
 LIBRARY. Early railway pamphlets, 1825–
b 1900. *London*, 1938. pp. 60. [*Gladstone
 Library Pamphlet Collection. Subject List
 no. 1.*]   BM
   Compiled by R. Pennington.

107 SOMMERFIELD, V. The Wheel. *London:
 Nicholson & Watson*, 1938. pp. x, 248, with
b 24 illus. on 16 plates; chronology (10 pp.);
   bibliography (9 pp.).   BM
c General history of transport, including
   railways.

*108 CLAPHAM, J. H. An economic history of
 modern Britain: the Early Railway Age,
 1820–1850. *Cambridge: Cambridge University Press*, 1926. pp. xviii, 623.   BM
   A very detailed work.
   —— 2nd edn. *Cambridge*, 1930. pp. xvi,
 623.   BM
   —— 2nd edn., repr. with corr.; *Cambridge*,
 1939, 1950.   BM

109 EMDEN, P. H. Quakers in commerce: a
 record of business achievement. *London:
 Low*, 1939. pp. xiii, 273.   BM
   pp. 61–8, 'Rail magnates and Bradshaw.'
 Brief notes on Edward Pease; Joseph Sturge;
 John Ellis; James Cropper; Charles May;
 James Ransome; Thomas Edmondson; George
 Bradshaw and others. With a portrait of J.
 Ellis.

110 ALLEN, C. J. The romantic story of the
 Iron Road; with 193 illustrations. *London
 & Melbourne: Hutchinson*, 1940. pp. 328.
                                                 BM

111 JONES, G. P. *and* POOL, A. G. A hundred years of economic development in Great Britain. *London: Duckworth*, 1940. pp. 420. BM
Includes railways.

112 SHERRINGTON, C. E. R. Inland transport, 1900–1940. *In* 'English economic history, mainly since 1700.' By C. R. Fay. *Cambridge*, 1940. pp. 227–33. BM
Reprinted 1948.

113 EWALD, K. 20000 Schriftquellen zur
b Eisenbahnkunde. *Kassel*, 1941. pp. 928. BM
A bibliography of references, mainly to periodical articles, a small number relating to British railways and locomotives.

114 NEW YORK PUBLIC LIBRARY. Catalogue of the William Barclay Parsons Collection.
b *New York*, 1941. pp. 108. BM
Reprinted from Bull. N.Y.P.L., Jan. & July 1941.
pp. 18–79, 'Transportation & communication'. Includes railways in the British Isles.

115 ELTON, A. British railways . . . *London: Collins*, 1945. pp. 46, with 8 col. plates & 30 illus. BM

116 TATFORD, B. The story of British railways. *London: Low*, 1945. pp. xvi, 343, with 24 col. plates & many illus. in text. BM

117 COLLIER, R. A. H. [Lord Monkswell.] Railways: their history and organization. *London*, 1928. pp. 78. [*Benn's Sixpenny Library*, no. 22.] BM
British and foreign railways.
—— Railways and their future. *London: Benn*, 1946. pp. 96. BM
Their past (especially their past mistakes) also reviewed. Based on his *Railways: their history and organization* (1928).

118 KIDNER, R. W. A short history of mechanical traction and travel: vol. 2, Rail. [*South Godstone:*] *Oakwood Press*, 1947. pp. 150, with 96 illus. on 40 plates, & many illus. BM
Originally issued separately.

119 GREENLEAF, H. Britain's Big Four: the story of the London Midland & Scottish, London & North Eastern, Great Western, and Southern Railways. *London: Winchester Publications*, 1948. pp. 228, with many illus., some col. BM

*120 REDMAYNE, P. Transport by land; designed and edited by Paul Redmayne. Text, Thomas Insull; drawings, Francis McNally; maps, Frank T. Lockwood. *London: John Murray*, 1948. pp. 47. BM
pp. 24–39, a graphic presentation of the history of railways, tramways, locomotives, coaches and wagons.
—— 2nd edn. *London*, 1960. pp. 47. BM

121 LIBRARY ASSOCIATION. Train and track: a booklist. (Compiled by William J. Skillern.)

b [*London*, 1949.] pp. [8.] Folder. [*Library Association Booklist*, no. 13.] BM
A select list of twenty-seven current railway books, with an introduction and descriptive notes.

122 NOCK, O. S. The railways of Britain, past and present. *London: Batsford*, 1948. pp. viii, 120, with 117 illus. on 68 plates. BM
—— 2nd edn. *London*, 1949. pp. viii, 120. BM
—— 2nd edn. reprinted, with paper covers. *London*, 1962. pp. 224, with illus. BM

123 TOWNEND, P. The Modern World Book of Railways. *London: Sampson Low, Marston & Co.*, [1949.] pp. 159, with many illus. BM
Introductory.

124 BOULTON, W. H. The railways of Britain: their history, construction, and working. *London: Sampson Low*, 1950. pp. 384, with many illus. BM
Introductory.

125 LIBRARY ASSOCIATION—COUNTY LIBRARIES SECTION. Readers' Guide to Books
b on Transport. *London*, 1950. pp. 23. BM
pp. 9–14, Rail transport. Seventy-six items for 'general readers'.

126 WEBSTER, H. C. Railways for all. Edited by H. C. Webster; with over fifty illustrations. (New edition.) *London: Ward, Lock*, 1950. pp. 254, with plates. BM

127 ELLIS, C. H. The beauty of old trains. *London: Allen & Unwin*, 1952. pp. 147, with 60 illus. on 32 plates (8 col.). BM

128 BRITISH TRANSPORT COMMISSION. A hundred years of railway statistics in Great
c Britain, 1853–1952. [*London*,] July 1953. pp. 16. *Reproduced typescript.* BR
Chronological tables—'Locomotives'; 'train miles'; 'Mileage of track', etc.

129 GREENWOOD, M. Railway revolution, 1825 to 1845. *London: Longmans*, 1955. pp. iv, 92, with illus. BM

130 HOUGH, R. A. Six great railwaymen: Stephenson, Hudson, Denison, Huish, Stephen, Gresley. *London: Hamish Hamilton*, 1955. pp. 200, with portraits. BM
Note: George Stephen was a pioneer and first president of the Canadian Pacific Railway.

131 BEIRMAN, B. The Dumpy Book of Railways of the World. *London: Sampson Low*, [1956.] pp. 285. BM
A pocket book introduction to the history and description of railways, with many line illustrations, including locomotives, company insignia, maps, and gradient profiles.

132 ELLIS, C. H. A Picture History of Railways. *London: Hulton Press*, 1956. pp. 18 (text) & 408 illus. BM
The text 'Railway Saga' is a summary of British railway history. Each illustration is described.

133 SUNDAY DISPATCH *newspaper*. A Pictorial History of Railways, with an anthology of 19th century railway chronicles. [*London*, Feb. 1956.] pp. 47.   BR

134 ALLEN, C. J. Railways of Britain. *London: Nelson*, July [1958.] pp. viii, 136, with 45 illus. on plates, & tables.   BM
History and description.

135 FRY, L. Railways. *London: Educational Supply Association*, 1951. pp. 89, with illus., diagrams & maps.   BM
History and description. Introductory.
—— 2nd edn. *London*, 1953.   BM
—— 3rd, *London*, 1954.   BM
—— 4th, *London*, 1956.   BM
—— 5th, *London*, 1958.   BM

136 MAXWELL, H. Railway Magazine Miscellany, 1897–1919. Edited by Henry Maxwell. *London: Allen & Unwin*, 1958. pp. 213.   BM
A selection of articles and illustrations representing railway progress during this period.

137 ROLT, L. T. C. Railways. [*London:*] *Newman Neame*, [1958.] pp. 15, with illus. [*Take Home Book*.]   BM

138 ELLIS, C. H. British railway history: an outline from the accession of William IV to the nationalisation of railways. *London: Allen & Unwin*, 1954, 1959. 2 vols.   BM
vol. 1, 1830–1876. pp. 443, with 45 illus. on 25 plates.
vol. 2, 1877–1947. pp. 416, with 25 illus. on 14 plates, & a map.

139 THOMAS, D. St. J. Great moments with trains; with 20 drawings by E. W. Fenton. *London: Phoenix House*, 1959. pp. 128. BM
Introductory essays on some highlights of railway history, including: Geo. Stephenson and the Liverpool & Manchester Rly; Thos. Cook; Queen Victoria's rail journeys; the railway races of 1888 and 1895; London's railways; broad gauge conversion, 1892; Talyllyn Railway Preservation Society.

140 THORNHILL, P. Railways for Britain; illustrated by R. Barnard Way. *London: Methuen & Co.*, 1954. pp. 84.   BM
A concise but comprehensive introduction to British railway history, with regional sketch maps to illustrate certain crucial developments.
—— reprint, with minor corrections. *London*, 1959.   BM

141 CAMPBELL, J. M. Index to the Railway Magazine, 1897–1957. [1958.] *c.* 500 pp.
b *Typescript*.   BR
Compiled for the use of staff of B.T.C. Historical Records. Three copies only, at London, York, and Edinburgh.
A very detailed and accurate analysis of articles and significant smaller items arranged alphabetically by subject. A continuation has been maintained on cards. Mr. Campbell retired from the B.T.C. in 1960.
The Railway Magazine issues an index at the completion of each volume, but no general index has been published.

142 ADAMS, J. *and* WHITEHOUSE, P. B. Railway Roundabout: the book of the T.V. programme. *London: Ian Allan*, 1960. pp. 72, with 8 col. plates & many illus. BM
Ten essays by various authors on subjects of popular and topical interest.

143 ALLEN, G. C. Railways. British railways from their beginning until 1960. *Oxford: Basil Blackwell*, 1960. pp. viii, 112, with 28 illus. on 19 plates & line drawings in text; pp. [90]–104, notes on the plates & drawings.   BM

144 CARTER, E. F. The Boys' Book of World Railways. *London: Burke*, 1960. pp. 144, with many illus.   BM

*145 CENTRAL OFFICE OF INFORMATION— REFERENCE DIVISION. Inland transport in the United Kingdom. *London*, Oct. 1960. pp. 13. [R.4689, superseding R.3900 of 1958 & earlier issues.]   BM
A concise account of the history and present state of British railways.

146 RANSOME-WALLIS, P. On railways, at home and abroad. *London: Batchworth Press*, 1951. pp. 299, with plates. BM
pp. 19–65, general survey, 1923–50.
—— 2nd edn. *London: Spring Books*, [1960.] pp. 300, with plates.   BM

147 ALLEN, G. F. Ian Allan Book of Railways: re-issue of favourite stories by G. Freeman Allen from the Ian Allan Loco-spotters' Annual, nos. 1 to 3. *London: Ian Allan*, [1961.] pp. 71, with 7 col. plates & many illus.   BM

148 NOCK, O. S. British steam railways . . . with eight plates in colour and 94 photographs. *London: A. & C. Black*, 1961. pp. xii, 326.   BM
A treasury of British railway history as it was seen and experienced.

149 ROGERS, H. C. B. Turnpike to Iron Road. *London: Seeley, Service & Co.*, 1961. pp. 271, with 63 illus. on 32 plates, & 53 illus. in text.   BM
The transition from road to rail, and railways in Great Britain until 1914.

*150 SIMMONS, J. The railways of Britain: an historical introduction. *London: Routledge*
b & *Kegan Paul*, 1961. pp. xii, 264, with 25 illus. on 17 plates, & 14 figures & 6 maps in text.   BM
Special features: pp. 233–50, Literature & maps; a classified and annotated select bibliography; pp. 253–5, List of historic locomotives preserved in Britain; pp. 186–232, Railways on the ground; three lineal surveys—Fenchurch St. (London) to Rochester, Derby to Man-

chester, Glasgow to Edinburgh, and a fourth, an area survey of the railway development of Suffolk.

151 THE HORIZON Book of Railways, with contributions from T. M. Simmons, P. Ransome-Wallis, A. J. F. Wrottesley, Walken Fisher, Derek Waldren, Cecil J. Allen, J. R. Day. *London: Paul Hamlyn*, 1961. pp. 159, with 180 illus. & diagrs., incl. 43 in col.   BM
   Twenty-eight essays on British and foreign railways, for young readers.

152 STOECKL, F. Die Eisenbahnen der Erde: Band 1, Grossbritannien. *Wien*, 1961. pp. 108, with 3 col. plates & many illus.   NCL

153 WALLER, C. E. Marshall's Book of Railways. *London: Percival Marshall*, [1961.] pp. 111, with col. plates, illus. & maps.   BM

154 APPLETON, J. H. The geography of communications in Great Britain. *London: pub-*

b *lished for the University of Hull by the O.U.P.,* 1962. pp. xix, 251, with 42 plates, 43 maps, & a bibliography.   BM
   Includes the relationship between land contours, waterways, etc., upon the course of railway routes and the pattern of their resultant network.

155 SIMMONS, J. Transport. *London: Vista Books*, 1962. pp. x, 69, 199–206, with 239 illus. on 128 plates, & 82 notes [*Visual History of Modern Britain* Series.]   BM
   A pictorial survey, introduced by a concise account of main features in the development of all forms of transport from the 13th century to the present day, with 56 illustrations relating to railways and tramways.

156 VEALE, E. W. P. Railway Scrapbook. *London: Railway Publications*, 1962. pp. 160, with 8 plates.   BM
   Miscellaneous essays on subjects in railway history.

B RAIL TRANSPORT AT PARTICULAR PERIODS

For this subject related to localities see **C**

B1 ORIGIN, ANTIQUITY AND EARLY USE OF RAIL TRANSPORT

Prepared stone trackways of ancient times—Wagonways in mines
and quarries in mediæval Europe—their evolution in England
during the 16th, 17th, and 18th centuries as feeders from mines
and quarries to canals, rivers, and the coast

Marginal symbols: **b** bibliographies

c chronologies

157 HASELBERGER, J. Der Ursprung gemeynner Berckrecht wie die lange zeit von den alten erhalten worde darauss die Künigklichen vn Fürstlichen bergks ordnungen uber alle Bergrecht geflossen welcher sich eyn jetzlicher in zufelligen Berckhandlungen vor dem öbristen Berckmeister und anderen Berckrichtern zurecht wol gebrauchen mag. Auch ein anzeygung der clüfft und geng des Metallischen ärtz wie die in berg unnd thal streichent und jhr geschickt haben. Mit artlichen Figuren verzeichnet. Sampt eyner anzeygung vil höflicher und fündiger Berckwerck der löblichen Cron zu Beham. Holzschnitt CUM GRATIA ET PRIVILEGIO C.M. [At end:] Durch Iohan Haselberger auss der Reichenaw in druck verordnet. [c. 1535–1538.] pp. 44. 4to.   BM
The BM copy is a photo reproduction supplied by New York Public Library.
The work contains the earliest known illustration of the use of rail transport.

158 AGRICOLA, G. De Re Metallica. Translated from the first Latin edition of 1556, with biographical introduction, annotations and appendixes . . . By Herbert Clark Hoover and Lou Henry Hoover. *London,* 1912. pp. xxxi, 640.   BM
pp. 156, description and illustration of the type of wagon used in Europe in the 16th century.
—— new edn. (reprint) *New York,* 1950. PC
Earlier editions—
Basle, 1556. pp. 538. (Latin.)   BM
Basle, 1557. 'Vom Bergkwerck.' pp. ccccxci. (German.)   BM
Basle, 1561. pp. 502. (Latin.)   BM
Basle, 1563. pp. 542. (Italian.)   BM
Frankfurt-am-Mayn, 1580. 'Bergwerck Buch.' (German.)   BM
Basle, 1621. 'Bergwerck Buch.' pp. ccccxci. (German.)   BM
Basle, 1621. pp. 502. (Latin.)   BM
Basle, 1657. pp. 708. (Latin.)   BM
Other works by Agricola are bound in with this edition.
For information on these editions and on the possible existence of others, see pp. xxv–xxvii of Hoover's introduction and his 'Appendix A' for bibliographical notes.

159 RAMELLIS, A. de. Le diverse et artificiose machine; composte in lingua Italiana et Francese. *Paris,* 1588. pp. 338.   BM
Figure 138, wagons being hauled up a sloping runway by means of horse-powered gins. The runway is double and the course of the wagons is guided by vertical side-flanges, similar in principle to the 18th century plateway.
—— Schatzkammer mechanische Künste. *Leipzig,* 1620. pp. 462. (Figure 138.)   BM

160 LORINI, B. Delle fortificationi . . . *Venetia,* 1596. pp. [x,] 219.   BM
pp. 194–6, 'Strumento et ordine facilissimo per portar dentro la terra da terrapienar le fortezze.' With 4 illus. of equipment for hauling earth, etc., in wagons up the ramparts of forts in trackways.
—— another edn. *Venetia,* 1609. pp. [x,] 303. (pp. 219–21.)   BM

161 VERANCSICS, F. Machinæ novæ. *Venetiis,* [1620?]   BM
Engravings, with short descriptions.
pl. 36, an aerial ropeway over a river.

162 MUENSTER, S. Cosmographia Universalis. [Various editions, 1544–1628. Title varies.]   BM
Among the many woodcuts which are repeated throughout the 47(?) editions are three (one large and two small) showing 16th century wagonways in the silver mines of Alsace. The large one (a) is reproduced in C. E. Lee's *Evolution of Railways,* 1937 (enl. edn. 1943). The two smaller ones show a wagon emerging from a tunnel (b) to the left of the picture, and (c) towards the right.
The quality of printing varies considerably between editions. Among those in the BM the following were found to be good examples:
(a) *Basle,* 1550. p. 9.
(b) *Basle,* 1556. p. dclxxxviii.
(c) *Basle,* 1550. p. 716.
A brief description of the wagons is given in the text. A translation is included in Mr. Lee's book.
For commentaries on *Cosmographia* see 'Sebastian Münster: Leben, Werk, wissenschaftliche Bedeutung' by Viktor Hantzsch, in *Abhandlungen der Philologisch-Historischen Classe der Königl. Sächsischen Gesellschaft der Wissenschaften,* Band 18, nr. 3 (1898), pp. 50–69; 153–7. Also 'A. Ortelii Catalogus Carto-

graphorum', by Leo Bagrow, in 2te Teil, Ergänzungsheft nr. 210 of *Petermann's Mitteilungen* (1930), pp. 19–29.

163 MACKWORTH, H. The case of Sir Humphry Mackworth and of the Mine Adventurers with respect to the irregular proceedings of several justices of the peace for the county of Glamorgan and of their agents and dependents. *London*, 1705. pp. 16.   BM
With reference to his 'waggon-way on wooden rails'.

164 BARROW, J. A Supplement to the New and Universal Dictionary of Arts and Sciences. *London*, 1754.   BM
Under the heading 'Carriage'—a description of the carriages made use of by Ralph Allen to carry stone from his quarry, etc. (4 columns).

165 DE LABELYE, C. A description of the carriages made use of by Ralph Allen, Esq., to carry stone from his quarries situated on the top of a hill, to the waterside of the River Avon near the City of Bath. *In* Desaguliers, J.T., 'A course of experimental philosophy.' 1734.   BM
vol. 1, pp. 274–9 & plates 21, 22 & 23.
—— another edn. *London*, 1745.   BM
vol. 1, pp. 283–8 & plates 21, 22 & 23.
—— another edn. *London*, 1763.   BM
vol. 1, pp. 283–8 & plates 21, 22 & 23.

166 YOUNG, A. A six months' tour through the north of England. *London*, 1770. 4 vols.
   BM
vol. 3, pp. 12–13, description of wagonways in coal mines at Newcastle and (pp. 274–5) at Worsley.
—— 2nd edn. *London*, 1770, 1771. 4 vols. BM
(vol. 3, pp. 12–13, & pp. 226–7.)
—— Extracts from Mr. Young's 'Six months' tour through the north of England'. [*London*,] 1774. pp. 29.   BM
pp. 17 et seq., wagonways in mines.

167 STUKELEY, W. Itinerarium Curiosum; or, An account of the antiquities and remarkable curiosities in nature and art observed in travels through Great Britain; illustrated . . . 2nd edn., centuria II. *London*, 1776. pp. 177.   BM
pp. 68–9 refers to cart-ways in wooden frames for the transport of coal in wagons at Newcastle, and to Col. Lyddal's coal works at Tanfield, where cuttings, bridges and embankments were found.

168 JARS, G. Voyages métallurgiques; ou, Recherches et observations sur les mines . . . en Allemagne, Suède, Norwège, Angleterre, et Écosse . . . avec figures . . . *Lyon & Paris*, 1774–81. 3 vols, with fold. plates, & fold maps.   BM
vol. 1, pp. 200–5, and plate V, mineral railways.

168a YOUNG, A. A tour to Shropshire. *In* 'Annals of Agriculture', vol. 4, 1785. pp. 138–90.   BM
On p. 166 is a passing reference to the Coalbrookdale wagonway being laid with cast iron rails instead of wood (13 June, 1776).
—— reprinted. *London*, 1932. [*London School of Economics and Political Science. Reprints of Scarce Tracts in Economic and Political Science*, no. 14.] (p. 150.)   BM

169 BRAND, J. The history and antiquities of the town and county of . . . Newcastle upon Tyne. *Newcastle*, 1789. 2 vols.   BM
vol. 2, pp. 687–8, 'Waggons and waggonways'.

170 SMEATON, J. Narrative of the building and description of the construction of the Eddystone Lighthouse with stone . . . *London*, 1791. pp. xiv, 198, with 23 plates.   BM
p. 94 (note to para. 151), description of the plateway and turntables (diagrams, pl. 17).
—— another edn. *London*, 1793. pp. xiv, 198.   BM

171 FOX, J. General view of the agriculture of the county of Monmouth. *Brentford: Board of Agriculture*, 1794. pp. 43.   BM
p. 25, reference to extensive 'rail roads' at Blaen Avon iron works.

*172 CURR, J. The Coal Viewer and the Engine Builder's Practical Companion. *Sheffield*, 1797. pp. 96.   BM
Includes a detailed description, with folding diagrams, of the method of constructing wagons ('corves') and plate-ways.

173 ERSKINE, J. F. On iron roads, or waggonways. *In* 'Communications to the Board of Agriculture.' vol. 1, *London*, 1797. pp. 203–4.   BM

174 FULTON, R. A treatise on the improvement of canal navigation . . . illustrated. *London*, 1796. pp. xvi, 144.   BM
pp. 101–4, Cast iron railroads (for the conveyance of small boats between canals of different levels).
—— another edn. *Lisbon*, 1800.

175 WILKES, J. On iron railways. *In* 'Communications to the Board of Agriculture.' vol. 2, 1800. pp. 474–8. (Communication no. 29.)   BM
Two letters on experiments with coal haulage by horse-drawn wagons on rails at Measham Colliery, Derbyshire. (Text headed 'Iron railways'.)

176 BAILEY, J. *and* CULLEY, G. General view of the agriculture of the county of Northumberland, with observations on the means of its improvement, drawn up for the consideration of the Board of Agriculture and Internal Improvement. 2nd edn. *Newcastle*, 1797. pp. viii, 317.   BM
pp. 10–11, description of the 'Newcastle coal

waggon' and the wagonway, including a sketch, dimensions and footnotes.

—— 3rd edn. *London*, 1805. pp. xx, 361.
BM

—— reprint, 1813.   BM
The first edition (1794) was a much smaller work, of 70 pages, and does not mention wagonways.

177 NORTH, R. The life of . . . Francis North, Baron of Guilford . . . *London*, 1742. pp. 333.   BM
pp. 136–7, description of colliery wagonways at Newcastle.
—— 2nd edn. *London*, 1808. 2 vols.   BM
(vol. 1, p. 265.)
—— abridged edn. *London*, [1939.] pp. 247. (pp. 119–20.)   BM

178 ALLNUTT, Z. Useful and correct accounts of the navigation of the rivers and canals west of London . . . 2nd edn., much improved. *Henley*, [c. 1810.] pp. 20.   BM
pp. 17–18, account of the canals and railroads in South Wales.

179 BAILEY, J. General view of the agriculture of the county of Durham. *London: Board of Agriculture*, 1810. pp. xiv, 412.   BM
Also issued with a similar title page but dated 1813.
pp. 33–5, description of method of conveying coal, illustrated by diagram of 'iron railways'.
Author forsees 'public rail-ways' for the supply of coal to London.

180 SMEATON, J. Reports of the late John Smeaton. *London*, 1812.   BM
vol. 3, pp. 396–403, Earl of Egremont's coals: the report . . . respecting the practicability of exporting coals, etc.
Considers proposed wagonways.

181 DUPIN, F. P. C. Narratives of two excursions to the ports of England, Scotland and Ireland in 1816, 1817 and 1818, together with a description of the breakwater at Plymouth . . . translated from the French. *London*, [1819.] pp. viii, 96.   BM
pp. 63–4, a description of the railway from the quarries to the breakwater at Plymouth.

182 DUTENS, J. M. Mémoires sur les travaux publics de l'Angleterre. *Paris*, 1819. pp. xx, 374.   BM
pp. 61–2, railways as feeders to canals. Plates 4 & 7 show plateways at Coalport and Hay-on-Wye and on the Surrey Iron Rly. (points and crossovers).

183 AYTON, R. A voyage round Great Britain undertaken in the summer of 1813 . . . *London*, 1814–25. 8 vols.   BM
vol. 2, pp. 150–2, a description of a colliery railway at Whitehaven, with an eye-witness account of its working.
vol. 6, between pp. 58 & 59, an engraving of Sunderland Pier, showing the wagonway.

184 DUNN, M. A historical, geological and descriptive view of the coal trade of the North of England, comprehending its rise, progress,

present state and future prospects . . . *Newcastle-upon-Tyne*, 1844. pp. ix, 248. BM
pp. 11–38, a chronology of the rise and progress of the coal trade.
Includes many references to railways and wagonways.

185 YOUNG, T. A course of lectures on natural philosophy and the mechanical arts. *London*, 1807. 2 vols.   BM
vol. 1, pp. 218–19, description of wagonways for surface transport at collieries as substitutes for canals, and for drawing loaded boats over inclined planes.
—— new edn. *London*, 1845.   BM
pp. 167–8.

186 SCOTT, W. The extracts from the Letter Book of William Scott . . . (Compiled by M. A. Richardson.) *Newcastle-upon-Tyne*, 1848. pp. 52, with notes & references. BM
W. Scott was in business in Newcastle, supplying rails and wheels for local wagonways. The entries selected are from the period Sept. 1745 to May 1748 and contain frequent references to materials used, and to problems of supply and demand.

187 RATHBONE, H. M. Letters of Richard Reynolds, with a memoir of his life . . . *London*, 1852. pp. 310.   BM
pp. 27, alleged first use of iron rails, at Coalbrookdale, some time between 1763 and 1768.

188 WALKER, W. Memoirs of distinguished men of science of Great Britain living in the years 1807–8. *London*, 1862. pp. xii, 228.
BM
pp. 111–15, William Jessop, from *Memoir of Wm. Jessop* by S. Hughes.
—— 2nd edn. *London*, 1862. pp. viii, 160.
BM

189 SMILES, S. Industrial biography: iron workers and tool makers. *London*, 1863. pp. xiv, 342.   BM
pp. 77–98, Coalbrookdale Iron Works, the Darbys, and the Reynolds. (p. 89, the first use of iron for rails.)

190 GALLOWAY, R. L. A history of coal mining in Great Britain. *London*, 1882. pp. xi, 273.   BM
Includes the origin and use of early mineral railways.

191 GRAY, W. Chorographia; or, A survey of Newcastle-upon-Tyne . . . *Newcastle*, 1649. pp. 48.   BM
pp. 24–5, the coal trade and wagonways.
—— *In* 'Harleian Miscellany', vol. III. *London*, 1745. pp. 256–72.   BM
—— *Newcastle*, 1813. pp. ix, 43.   BM
—— *Newcastle*, 1818. pp. 48.   BM
—— *In* Richardson, T. M., 'Antiquities of the Border Counties', 1881. pp. 1–36 at end.
BM
—— *Newcastle*, 1884. pp. 121[124]. BM

192 MARGGRAFF, H. Die Vorfahren unserer Eisenbahnen und Dampfwagen; mit 20 in den Text gedruckten Abbildungen. *Berlin*,

1884. pp. 64. [*Sammlung Gemeinverständlicher, Wissenschaftlicher Vorträge*, herausgegeben von Rud. Virchow und Fr. von Holtzendorff. Serie 19, Hefte 435, 436. Seite 93–156.]   PO

193 STRETTON, C. E. A few notes on early railway history, from 1630 to 1830 . . . *London*, [1884.] pp. 7.   BM

194 STRETTON, C. E. The history of the Loughborough and Nanpantan edge-rail-way. [1889.] pp. [3.]   BM
—— another edn. pp. [8.]   BM

195 HAARMANN, A. Das Eisenbahngeleise. *Leipzig*, 1891 (1892). 2 Theile.   BM
   Bd. 1, Geschichtlicher Teil. pp. xl, 852, with 1837 illus.
   Bd. 2, Das Eisenbahngeleis: kritischer Teil. 1892. pp. ix, 277, with 503 illus.
   A very detailed history and description of railway track, including British; with bibliographical notes.

196 STRETTON, C. E. The history of the Belvoir Castle edge-railway: a paper read at the 'Peacock Hotel', Belvoir, upon the occasion of the centenary of the opening of the line, 1893. [1893.] pp. [7,] with 1 illus.   BM

197 PEACH, R. E. M. The life and times of Ralph Allen. *London*, 1895. pp. xvi, 247, with illus.   BM
   pp. 76–82, R. Allen's wagonways from his quarries at Hampton Down and Combe Down through Priory Park to the Avon, *c.* 1731.

198 BECK, T. Beiträge zur Geschichte des Maschinenbaues. *Berlin*, 1899. pp. vii, 559.   BM
   pp. 128–30, mediaeval mine railways (from G. Agricola's *De Re Metallica*).
   pp. 246–7, wagonways on inclines in mediaeval forts (from Lorini's *Della Fortificationi*).
—— 2. Aufl. *Berlin*, 1900. pp. 582.

199 STRETTON, C. E. Early tramroads and railways in Leicestershire. *Burton-on-Trent*, 1900. pp. 14.   BM

200 KOEHLER, G. Lehrbuch der Bergbaukunde; mit 823 Holzschnitten und 6 lithographische Tafeln. *Leipzig*, 1884. pp. xxii, 708.   BM
   pp. 295–305, Early English wagonways and wagons described.
—— 2nd edn. *Leipzig*, 1887.
—— 3rd, *Leipzig*, 1892.
—— 4th, *Leipzig*, 1897.
—— 5th, *Leipzig*, 1900.   BM
—— 6th *Leipzig*, 1903.

201 STRETTON, C. E. The history of the Bagworth Colliery (private) Railway: a paper read at Bagworth at the meeting of the Permanent Way Institution. *Bagworth*, 1904. pp. [5.]   BM

202 GALLOWAY, R. L. Annals of coal mining and the coal trade: the invention of the

steam engine and the origin of the railway. *London*, 1898. pp. x, 533, illus.   BM
   The text contains many references to other works.
—— 2nd series. *London*, 1904. pp. xiii, 409.   BM

203 GALLOWAY, R. L. Papers relating to the history of the coal trade and the invention of the steam engine . . . *London*, 1906. pp. 34.   BM
   pp. 9–12, a brief survey of the use of wagonways in mines.

204 FORRER, R. Reallexikon der prähistorischen, klassischen und frühchristlichen Altertümer . . . *Stuttgart*, 1908. pp. viii, 943.   BM
   p. 59, prehistoric trackways at Pompeii and elsewhere.

205 FELDHAUS, F. M. Ruhmesblätter der Technik von den Urerfindungen bis zur
b Gegenwart. *Leipzig*, 1910. pp. viii, 631. BM
   pp. [503]–524, 'Bahnen'. There are thirty-four references to works containing information on mediaeval railways and wire-ways in Europe, including the following manuscripts which have illustrations of 15th-century wire-ways: 'Feuerwerksbuch von Hartlieb', 1411. (Abb. 202. Hof und Staatsbibliothek, Vienna.) A manuscript by an Italian engineer, Jacopo Mariano, 1449. (Bibliotheque Nationale, Paris, Cod. lat. 7239, folio 23 recto.)

206 HISTORICAL MANUSCRIPTS COMMISSION. Report on the manuscripts of Lord Middleton preserved at Wollaton Hall, Nottinghamshire. *London: H.M.S.O.*, 1911. pp. xv, 746, viii. [Cd. 5567.]   BM
   On p. 169 and elsewhere are entries indicating the existence of a wagonway for coal transport at Wollaton Hall interpreted as 1597–8, but since established by Richard S. Smith (*See* 228) as 1604.

207 HALL, C. The early history of the railway. *In* Modern railway working', ed. by J. Macaulay, 1912–14. Section 1, part 1., pp. 3–68.   BM

*208 JACKMAN, W. T. The development of transportation in modern England. *Cam-*
b *bridge*, 1916. 2 vols, with many bibliogr. notes and an extensive bibliography.   BM
   vol. 2, pp. 461–603, 'The development of railways', up to 1850.
—— Reprint, with a new introduction by
b W. H. Chaloner. *London: Frank Cass & Co.*, 1962. pp. xxxiii, 820, with maps.   BM

209 CODRINGTON, T. Roman roads in Britain. *London*, 1903. pp. 392.   BM
—— 2nd edn. *London*, 1905. pp. iv, 404.   BM
—— 3rd, *London*, 1918. pp. 317.   BM
   Includes an account of the excavation of Watling Street at Abbey Dore, revealing Roman wheel tracks of 4' 8" gauge.

210 FUERST, A. Die Welt auf Schienen: Eine Darstellung der Einrichtungen und des

Betriebs auf den Eisenbahnen des Fernverkehrs nebst einer Geschichte der Eisenbahn. *München*, 1918. pp. 539, with many illus. BM
>pp. 3–86 are concerned with the history and antiquity of railways and track.

211 ASHTON, T. S. *and* SYKES, J. The coal industry in the eighteenth century. *Manchester*, 1919. pp. ix, 268. BM
>pp. 63–9, colliery railways.

212 PEDDIE, R. A. Railway literature, 1556–1830: a handlist. *London*, 1931. pp. 73. BM
b Brief descriptions, in chronological order, of 750 contemporary books, Acts, plans, documents and articles, on British and foreign rail-
c ways.

213 NEF, J. U. Rise of the British coal industry.
b *London*, 1932. 2 vols. BM
>Includes mineral wagonways, with many bibliographical notes.

214 NEWLANDS, A. The railway highway. [*London*, 1934.] pp. 35. BR
>Jubilee Lecture, Permanent Way Institution, 1934. Reprinted from the *Journal of the P.W.I.*, vol. 52, pt. 2, August 1934.
>History of 'railed ways' from the 15th century.

215 JENKINS, R. Railways in the sixteenth century. *In his* 'Collected Papers'. *Cambridge*, 1936. pp. 36–7. BM
>Printed for the Newcomen Society at the University Press.

216 LEE, C. E. The evolution of permanent way. *London*, 1937. pp. 64, with illus. & bibliogr. notes. BM
>Paper, Permanent Way Inst., 8 March 1937: Supplement, *Jnl. P.W. Inst.*, vol. 55, August 1937.
>—— another edn. of the same work. 'The evolution of railways.' *London: Railway Gazette*, 1937. pp. viii, 64. BM
>—— 2nd edn. rev & enl. *London*, 1943. pp. viii, 108. BM

217 LEE, C. E. The world's oldest railway: three hundred years of coal conveyance to the Tyne staiths. [*London*, 1946.] pp. 141–62, with illus., on plates & in text, maps, & bibliogr. notes. BM
>Excerpt, *Trans. Newcomen Society*, vol. 25.
>The Ravensworth wagonway (Tanfield Branch, LNER).

218 DOTT, G. Early Scottish colliery wagonways. *Westminster*, 1947. pp. 32, with bibliogr. notes. BM
>Reprint from *Colliery Engineering*.
>Contains lists with details, illustrations, and maps.

219 LEE, C. E. The highways of antiquity: a study of the relationships between the development of roads and the rise of the ancient empires. *London: Railway Gazette*, 1947. pp. 33, with bibliogr notes. *Reproduced typescript.* BM

Includes evidence of the use of artificial wheel ruts in ancient times.

220 NORDMANN, H. Die Frühgeschichte der Eisenbahnen. *Berlin*, 1948. pp. 27. [*Abhandlungen der Deutschen Akademie der Wissenschaften zu Berlin. Jahrg.* 1947. *Math.-Wiss. Klasse, nr.* 4.] LSE
>Includes early British railway history.

221 LEE, C. E. Tyneside tramroads of Northumberland: some notes on the engineering background of George Stephenson. [*London*, 1949.] pp.28[32], with 3 maps, & a plan. BM
>Paper, Newcomen Society, 9 March, 1949.

222 BIRKS, J. A. *and* COXON, P. An account of railway development in the Nottinghamshire coalfield. *Mansfield*, 1950. pp. 77, with plates, time-tables, map, & bibliography. BM
>Published by the authors in reproduced typescript.

223 COOTE, C. *and* MOTTRAM, R. H. Through five generations: the history of the Butterley Company. *London: Faber & Faber*, 1950. pp. 181. BM
>Contains details on Benjamin Outram and his wagonways.

224 LEE, C. E. The wagonways of Tyneside. *Gateshead-on-Tyne: Society of Antiquaries of Newcastle-upon-Tyne*, 1951. pp. 135–202, with 3 plates, illus., & 7 maps. BM

225 HUGHES, E. North Country life in the eighteenth century: the North East, 1700–50. *Oxford: O.U.P.*, 1952. pp. xxi, 435. BM
>pp. 153–8, and elsewhere, wagonways.

226 SIMMONS, J. Parish and Empire: studies and sketches. *London: Collins*, 1952. pp. 256. BM
>pp. 146–54, 'William Jessop, civil engineer'; with portrait, & bibliogr. notes.

227 RAISTRICK, A. Dynasty of iron founders: the Darbys and Coalbrookdale. *London: Longmans Green & Co.*, 1957. pp. xvi, 308, with plates, illus., & maps. BM
>pp. 171–92, 'Railways and canals, 1745–1800'. Wagonways at Coalbrookdale and the introduction of iron rails there, *c.* 1767.

228 SMITH, R. S. Huntingdon Beaumont: adventurer in coal mines. *In* 'Renaissance and
b Modern Studies', vol. 1, 1957. pp. [115]–153, with 79 bibliogr. & other notes. BM
>Includes (pp. 129–51) fifteen letters reprinted from the Middleton Collection, University of Nottingham, dated 1601(?) to 1624. (*See* 206.)

229 NATIONAL REGISTER OF ARCHIVES. North MSS., reproduced from originals prepared by the Bodleian Library, Oxford. *London*, 1958. pp. 68. *Reproduced typescript.* BM
>A catalogue of documents relating to Francis North, 1st Earl of Guilford. (*See*

230 NATIONAL REGISTER OF ARCHIVES. North of England Institute of Mining & Mechanical Engineers, Newcastle on Tyne. Handlist of manuscripts. [*London*,] 1960. pp. 73. *Reproduced typescript.* BM

Period, end of 17th century to end of 19th century. Some of the items listed may have information on early mineral lines.

—— Supplement and Index of Places. Compiled by H. A. Taylor. 1961. pp. 75–135.

Some of the items in the original Handlist have been listed in greater detail. Index covers both Handlist and Supplement.

231 BOROUGH, C. M. Calendar of the papers of the North family, from Wroxton Abbey, now in the Bodleian Library, Oxford. *London: National Register of Archives,* 1960. pp. 459. *Reproduced typescript.* BM

232 NATIONAL REGISTER OF ARCHIVES. University of Nottingham, Department of Manuscripts. Middleton manuscripts, 12C–20C: part 1. [1960.] BM

Deposited in 1947. Records of the Wil-loughby family, mostly title deeds, but including manorial records, estate, household, and coal-mining accounts. This collection was inspected and reported upon by W. H. Stevenson for the Historical Manuscripts Commission in 1911. (*See* 206.) It may contain earlier references to the use of rail transport than those discovered in the 1911 survey and mentioned in C. E. Lee's *Evolution of Railways* (2nd edn., 1943).

Part 2, which will also contain coal mining records, is yet to be published.

233 SMITH, R. S. England's first rails: a recon-
b sideration. *Nottingham: Sisson & Parker*, [1960.] pp. [119]–134, with 50 bibliogr. notes. BM

Reprinted from *Renaissance and Modern Studies*, vol. 4, 1960.

233a LEE, C. E. Some railway facts and fallacies
b . . . [*London*, 1961.] pp. 16, with 4 plates, 5 illus. in text, & 50 bibliogr. notes. BM

Excerpt, *Transactions of the Newcomen Society*, vol. 33, 1960–61. (Presidential Address.)

Events and dates in the history of rail transport, 2000 B.C. to A.D. 1860.

B 2 THE TRANSITIONAL PERIOD, FROM MINERAL WAGONWAY TO PUBLIC PASSENGER RAILWAY, 1800–1830 . . . 1850

The experimental and formative period which saw the developments in locomotives and track following the success of Richard Trevithick's Pen-y-darran engine of 1804, and which resulted in the establishment of the first public passenger railway, between Liverpool and Manchester, in 1830.

Included here are works on the comparative merits of railways, canals, and roads during this period, and works presenting analyses of current theories and practices associated with the development of the idea of rail transport as a new means of communication between towns. For works on the later relationship between railways as an established feature of national life and other forms of transport (canals, road, air, and coastwise shipping), and for this subject in general, see **K**.

For unusual forms of railway and locomotion which appeared later, and for this subject in general, see **D 5**.

This period of transition is not easy to define by dates. The general superiority of the steam locomotive over other forms of traction was made clear by the success of George Stephenson's 'Rocket' during the trials at Rainhill on the Liverpool & Manchester Railway in October 1829, and the general form which public passenger railways were to take was settled when this line was opened in September 1830. The Liverpool & Manchester was the first railway to provide safe travelling at fixed rates by a regular service of steam-hauled passenger trains owned by the railway. While 1830 may be regarded for convenience as marking the end of the experimental period and the beginning of the era of the modern railway, it must be borne in mind that there was no sudden end to experimentation at this point, and that the urge to try out new methods and to improve the old is with us still. This section, however, is concerned with the efforts made to solve the *primary* problems presented by the idea of an extended use of wagonways.

It was not until 1845 that uncertainty regarding choice of gauge of new railways was finally settled by the recommendations of the Gauge Commission, and experiments with atmospheric propulsion as an alternative to steam locomotion continued until 1848. Contemporary writings on these matters were, however, part of the general process of ideas which in the main preceded the advent of the Liverpool & Manchester in 1830, and are included here.

Safety problems received no serious attention until the 1850's, by which time the increasing speed, weight, and frequency of trains, and growing public concern, forced the railway owners to devise better protection for the travelling public. Consequent developments in signalling, brakes, interlocking of points, and passenger communication are subjects *created by* the process of transition from mineral wagonway to public passenger railway and are not included here.

For problems of safety in transit see **K 3**
For safety engineering and operation see **E 15**

Marginal symbols: **a** atmospheric and other unconventional systems
b bibliographies
c chronologies

234 WILKES, J. On the utility of iron rail-ways: from the second volume of 'Communications to the Board of Agriculture'. *In* 'The Repertory of Arts and Manufactures' vol. 3. *London*, 1800. pp. 167–71.   BM

235 ANDERSON, J. Recreations in agriculture ... *London*, 1799–1802. 6 vols.   BM
  vol. 4, pp. 198–217, 'On cast-iron railways': pp. 473–7, 'Minutes to be observed on the construction of rail-ways'.
  vol. 5, pp. 290–3, 'On iron rail-ways': a letter by Bulstrode on the Surrey Iron Railway.

236 TELFORD, T. Some account of the inland navigation of the county of Salop. *In* 'General view of the agriculture of Shropshire' by J. Plymley (1803). pp. 284–316, & 2 fold. plates.   BM
  Includes description of railways on inclined planes for conveying boats on wagons between the locks of the Shropshire & Shrewsbury Canal.

237 CHAPMAN, W. Mr. Chapman's report on the means of obtaining a safe and commodious communication from Carlisle to the sea. *Carlisle*, 1807. pp. 18.   BM
  p. 10, possibility of a railway considered.

238 MEDHURST, G. A new method of conveying letters and goods with great certainty and
a rapidity by air. *London*, 1810. pp. 11.   BM
  Pneumatic system.

239 MEDHURST, G. On the properties, power and application of the Æolian engine, with a
a plan and particulars for carrying it into execution upon a scale that will embrace all the principal objects to which it can be applied with full effect. *London*, [1810?] pp. 23.   BM
  Compressed air generated by a mechanism worked by wind pressure bearing upon sails.

240 MEDHURST, G. Calculations and remarks tending to prove the practicability, effects and
a advantages of a plan for the rapid conveyance of goods and passengers upon an iron road through a tube of 30 feet in area, by the power and velocity of air. *London*, 1812. pp. 18.   BM
  Pneumatic system.

241 CHAPMAN, W. Report of William Chapman, civil engineer, on various projected lines of navigation from Sheffield. *Sheffield*, 1813. pp. 35, with map.   NLC
  Strongly advocates, as an alternative, a railway.

242 CHAPMAN, W. *and* CHAPMAN, E. W. Copy of the specification of a patent granted to William Chapman . . . and Edward Walton Chapman . . . dated the 30th day of December 1812, for their invention of a method, or methods, of facilitating the means and reducing the expence, of carriage on railways and other roads. *Newcastle-upon-Tyne*, 1813. pp. 14, with 2 fold. diagrams.
                    PO
  A geared drive on to a chain laid between the rails.

243 ACCOUNT of an invention for reducing the expense of carriage on railways and other similar roads: being a copy of a letter transmitted to the Secretary of the Society of Arts in London, June fourth, 1814. *Newborough*, [1814.] pp. 7.   BM
  Power transmitted to a train by means of an endless chain and toothed wheels.
  Note: On the first page of the text is a footnote—'An engraving, to face the following page, is in preparation, and will speedily be published.' This engraving has not been inserted into the BM copy, and may not have appeared in fact.

244 EDGEWORTH, R. L. An essay on the construction of roads and carriages. *London*, 1813. pp. ix, 202, 194.　BM
pp. 36–9, a plan for constructing railways on existing roads.
—— 2nd edn. *London*, 1817. pp. iv, 171.　BM

245 REES, A. Cyclopaedia; or, Universal dictionary of arts, sciences and literature. *London*, 1819. 39 vols.　BM
vol. 6, 'Canal'. Written in 1805. Includes descriptions of wagonways.
vol. 29, 'Railways'. pp. [5.]

246 THOMPSON, B. Copy of the specification of a patent granted to Benjamin Thompson . . . for his invention of 'a method of facilitating the conveyance of carriages along iron and wood rail-ways, tram-ways, and other roads'. Dated the 24th day of October, 1821 . . . with remarks thereon by the patentee, and the result of a trial of the invention . . . *Newcastle*, [1821.] pp. 19, with illus.　P

247 A HISTORY of useful arts & manufactures. *Dublin*, 1822. pp. 175.　BM
pp. 156–7, a description of mineral railways at Whitehaven using trains of wagons hauled by Blenkinsop's rack locomotive.

248 WOOD, N. On the conveyance of goods along railroads. 1822.
A pamphlet written at Killingworth Colliery, March 16, 1822, and published in the *Newcastle Magazine*, April 1822.

249 CUMMING, T. G. Illustrations of the origin and progress of rail and tram roads and steam carriages or locomotive engines: also, interesting descriptive particulars of the formation, construction, extent and mode of working some of the principal railways now in use within the United Kingdom, particularly those great and unequalled communications projected between Liverpool and Birmingham, and Liverpool and Manchester, with a view to the more general employment of steam carriages, or locomotive engines for the conveyance of passengers as well as merchandise with remarks on the public advantages likely to accrue therefrom . . . with an explanatory plate. *Denbigh*, 1824. pp. 64.　BM

250 PALMER, H. R. Description of a railway on a new principle, with observations on those hitherto constructed, and a table shewing the comparative amount of resistance on several now in use . . . and a description of an improved dynamometer for ascertaining the resistance of floating vessels and carriages moving on roads and railways. *London*, 1823. pp. viii, 60, with 2 fold. plates.　SL
An overhead suspension railway from the Royal Victualling Yard at Deptford to the Thames.

—— 2nd edn. *London*, 1824. pp. viii, 60.　BM

251 STEVENSON, R. Essays on rail-roads, presented to the Highland Society; edited by Robert Stevenson. *In* 'Prize Essays and Transactions of the Highland Society of Scotland', vol. 6, 1824. pp. 1–146, with plates.　BM
Essays by Alexander Scott, George Robertson, George Douglas, John Ruthven, James Dickson, James Walker of Lauriston, James Walker of Carron, James Allan, John Fraser, John Wotherspoon, John Moore; also an account of 'Mr. John Baird's model of road-tracks' at Port Dundas, 1816. The collection ends with 'Notes by Mr. Stevenson in reference to the preceding essays on railways' (pp. 130–46).

252 [VALLANCE, J.] On facility of intercourse.
a *London*, 1824. pp. 13[15].　ICE
Pneumatic system.

253 DUPIN, F. P. C. The commercial power of Great Britain; exhibiting a complete view of the public works of this country . . . translated from the French. In two volumes with a quarto atlas of plans, elevations . . . *London*, 1825. pp. xlvi, 393.　BM
vol. 1, pp. 206–20, wooden and iron railways.

254 The FINGER POST; or, Direct road from John-o'-Groats to the Land's End; being a discussion of the railway question. By ??? *London*, [c. 1825.] pp. xvi, 48, with bibliogr. notes.　BM
On the future planned development of railways.
—— 3rd edn. *London*, [1825.] pp. xvi, 60.　BM

255 GEORGE, C. M. The National Waggon-Post, to travel at the rate of twenty miles per hour carrying one thousand ton weight, all over the Kingdom of England, with passengers, goods and stock; also a letter from the Chancellor of the Exchequer, and the author's reply. *Paris*, 1825. pp. vii, 47. BM
An iron roadway as an alternative to railways.

256 GRAY, T. Observations on a general iron rail-way, or land steam-conveyance, to supersede the necessity of horses in all public vehicles: shewing its vast superiority in every respect over all the present pitiful methods of conveyance by. turnpike roads, canals and coasting traders. Containing every species of information relative to railroads and loco-motive engines. 5th edition, with maps and plates illustrative of the plan. *London*, 1825. pp. xxiv, 233.　BM
The four earlier editions were published anonymously:
—— Observations on a general iron rail-way, shewing its great superiority over all the present methods of conveyance, and claiming

the particular attention of all merchants, manufacturers, farmers, and indeed, every class of society. *London*, 1820. pp. 22. ICE
—— 2nd edn. *London*, 1821. pp. 60. BM
Includes two extracts; one from a 'Plymouth paper' relating to T. Tyrwhitt's proposal for a 'Plymouth & Dartmoor Railway', and the other from *Martin's Circle of the Mechanical Arts* relating generally to the history and development of railways, and ending with an extract from the *Philosophical Magazine*, July 1811, concerning wagons and railroad dimensions and costs.
—— 3rd edn. Observations on a general iron rail-way; with a geographical map of the plan, showing its great superiority by the general introduction of mechanic power, over all the present methods of conveyance by turnpike roads and canals . . . 3rd edn., revised and considerably enlarged. *London*, 1822. pp. xii, 131. RC
—— 4th edn. Observations on a general iron rail-way, with plates and map illustrative of the plan . . . 4th edn., considerably improved. *London*, 1823. pp. xii, 131. BM

257 LETTER to James Caldwell, Esq., on canals and railroads. 2nd edn. *London*, 1825. pp. 10. ICE
Arguments in favour of canals rather than railways. Caldwell was chairman of the Grand Trunk Canal.

258 M[ACLAREN], C[harles]. Railways compared with canals and common roads and their uses and advantages explained; being the substance of a series of papers published in 'The Scotsman' [December 1824] and now re-published with additions and corrections. *Edinburgh*, 1825. pp. 66, with bibliogr. notes. (Signed 'C.M.') BM
—— another edition in 'The Pamphleteer', vol. 26, 1826. pp. 57–92[96]. BM
—— reprinted in his 'Select Writings'. *Edinburgh*, 1869. vol. 2, pp. 3–62. BM

259 OBSERVATIONS on the general comparative merits of inland communication by navigation or railroads, with particular reference to those projected or existing between Bath, Bristol and London. In a letter to Charles Dundas. (By a Proprietor of Shares in the Kennet and Avon Canal.) *Bath*, 1825. pp. 62, with fold. plate. BM

260 OVERTON, G. A description of the faults or dykes of the mineral basin of South Wales: part 1, introductory observations on the mineral basin tramroads, railways, etc., etc. *London*, 1825. pp. 79. BM
Regards as absurd the idea of a national system of railways.

261 [PARKES, J.] A statement of the claim of the subscribers to the Birmingham & Liverpool Rail Road to an Act of Parliament in reply to the opposition of the canal companies. *London*, 1825. pp. 67 BM
Although he claims to be impartial, the author supports the proposed railway.

—— 2nd edn. *London*, 1825. pp. viii, 93. BM

*262 SYLVESTER, C. Report on rail-roads and locomotive engines, addressed to the Chairman of the Committee of the Liverpool & Manchester projected Rail-Road. *Liverpool*, 1825. pp. 39. LSE
Findings of 'an examination of the locomotive engines at the Killingworth and Hetton collieries'.
—— 2nd edn. *Liverpool*, 1825. pp. 39. BM

263 VALLANCE, J. Considerations on the expediency of sinking capital in railways.
a *London*, 1825. pp. 39. BM
J. Vallance, eager to dissuade would-be investors from speculating in conventional railway ventures, assures them 'the novelty will soon wear off'. He follows with a supplement entitled *On facility of intercourse* (pp. [41]–112), in which he explains a system of atmospheric propulsion of his own invention.

264 ADAMSON, J. Sketches of our information as to rail-roads. Also, an account of the Stockton & Darlington Rail-Way; with observations on rail-ways, etc., etc. Extracted from the Caledonian Mercury. *Newcastle*, 1826. pp. 60, with fold. plate. BM
pp. 30–60, Stockton & Darlington.
—— another edn. *Newcastle*, 1826. pp. 26. LSE

265 BAADER, J. R. von. Über die Vortheile einer verbesserten Bau-art von Eisenbahnen und Wagen . . . *München*, [1826.] pp. 72. ICE
Railway experiments in England discussed, including Palmer's Suspension Railway.

265a STRICKLAND, W. Reports on canals, railways, roads, and other subjects, made to the Pennsylvania Society for the Promotion of Internal Improvement. *Philadelphia*, 1826. BM
pp. 23–31, 'Railways, locomotive engines, etc.' followed by 'Extract from a report of Mr. Jessop, civil engineer, upon a proposed railway from Cromford to the Peak Forest Canal, at Whaley, in the county of Derby.'
plates 42–55: detailed drawings of rails, fastenings, points, locomotive, wagons and wheels; also a folding diagram of Brandling's Railway.

266 GERSTNER, F. von. Mémoire sur les grandes routes, les chemins de fer et les canaux de navigation. *Paris*, 1827. pp. clxiv, 164. BM
pp. v–clxiv (by P. S. Giraud) has many references to British railways.

267 HILL, T. A treatise upon the utility of a rail-way from Leeds to Selby and Hull, with observations and estimates upon rail-ways generally as being pre-eminent to all other modes of conveyance for dispatch and economy. *Leeds*, 1827. pp. 32, with 3 plates. (*See* 274.) ICE

*268 OEYNHAUSEN, C. von *and* DECHEN, H. von. Über Schienenwege in England: Bemera kungen gesammelt auf einer Reise in den Jahren 1826 und 1827 . . . *Berlin*, 1829. [*Archiv für Bergbau und Hüttenwesen.* Band 19, Heft 1, pp. 3–253.]

ROYAL SOCIETY: BM

A very detailed record of an extensive tour of railways and wagonways in England, Wales & Ireland. The accounts of each line occupy from one to ten pages, but in the case of the Hetton wagonway a much longer report is given (pp. 74–96).

The survey includes observations on locomotives, track, wagons, the Atmospheric, Palmer's Monorail, etc., and ends with a general comparative summary, with tables.

—— Mémoire sur les chemins à ornières d'Angleterre (Extrait des *Archives de Karsten*, Ire livraison du 19me volume, traduit de l'allemand par Auguste Perdonnet). 1830. pp. 106.

—— Report on railways in England in 1826–27: translated and reviewed by E. A. Forward. *In* Transactions of the Newcomen Society, vol. 29, 1958. pp. 1–12.   BM

Paper, Newcomen Society, 14 October, 1953.

A translation of the descriptive section of the report—70 per cent of the whole work.

269 MEDHURST, G. A new system of inland conveyance for goods and passengers cap-
a able of being applied and extended throughout the country; and of conveying all kinds of goods, cattle, and passengers, with the velocity of sixty miles in an hour at an expense that will not exceed the one-fourth part of the present mode of travelling, without the aid of horses or any animal power. *London*, 1827. pp. 38.   BM

Carriages propelled through a tube by air.

270 VALLANCE, J. A letter to M. Ricardo, Esq., in reply to his letter to Dr. Yates on the
a proposed method of pneumatic transmission or conveyance by atmospheric pressure. *Brighton*, 1827. pp. 118.   ICE

271 RANKINE, D. A popular exposition of the effect of forces applied to draught; with illustrations of the principles of action, & tables of the performance of horses & locomotive engines on railways ... *Glasgow*, 1828. pp. 76.   BM

272 DRYDEN, J. Observations on the construction of railways, and upon mechanics. *London*, 1829. pp. viii, 158.   PO

*273 EXPERIMENTS on rail roads in England, illustrative of the safety, economy, and speed of transportation which this system, as now improved, is capable of affording. *Baltimore*, 1829. pp. 16.   P

274 HILL, T. A Supplement to the short treatise on rail-roads generally, explaining particularly the Liverpool and Manchester, also the Leeds, Selby and Hull rail-roads; the consequent great change that will be effected by them ... & which will shew that

horse-power is cheaper, preferable & more expeditious than locomotive engines ... also, a description of an inclined plane, when it cannot be avoided, with machinery to assist the horses . . . *Leeds*, 1829. pp. 16, with 2 diagrs., & a map. (*See* 267.)   ICE

275 JACKSON, W. Lecture on rail roads, delivered . . . before the Massachusetts Charitable Mechanics Association. *Boston*, 1829. pp. 32.   BM

British practice and experience explained in relation to American transport problems.

276 BREWSTER, D. Railway. *In* 'Edinburgh Encyclopædia . . . in eighteen volumes.' vol. 17, *Edinburgh*, 1830. pp. 303–10, & plate 477.   BM

277 COSTE, L. *and* PERDONNET, A. Mémoire sur les chemins à ornières. *Paris*, 1830. pp. 200, with 3 fold. plates & tables in text.   BM

Reprinted with additions from *Annales des Mines*, 2me ser., tome VI, 1829.

Railways in general; the Rainhill Trials and the Liverpool & Manchester.

278 DICK, M. Description of the suspension railway invented by Maxwell Dick, with engravings. *Irvine*, 1830. pp. 26, with diagrs. on 2 fold. plates.   BM

—— another edn. *Irvine*, 1830. pp. 27.   BM

279 EARLE, T. A treatise on rail-roads and internal communication: compiled from the best and latest authorities, with original suggestions and remarks. *Philadelphia*, 1830. pp. 120.   BM

Mostly American but includes British railway practice, with diagrams and descriptions of early locomotives.

280 ESSAY on railroads. *Philadelphia*, [1830.] pp. 26.   UL(GL)

Extracts from newspapers and magazines.

281 'INVESTIGATOR.' On tunnels and inclined planes as forming part of railways. [*Manchester*, 1830?] s.sh.   ICE

Reprinted from the *Manchester Guardian*.

282 MANN, W. A description of a new method of propelling locomotive machines ...
a *London*, 1830. pp. 56, with frontis., la. fold. plate showing Mann's patent Locomotive Air Carriage.   BM

Compressed air carried by the locomotive.

283 MILNE, J. A practical view of the steam engine . . . with an account of the mercurial statical dynamometer, and results of the draught of horses, quantum of friction on railways, etc., as proved by this instrument. *Edinburgh & London*, 1830. pp. xix, 175, with 4 plates.   ICE

English and French.

284 RENWICK, J. Treatise on the steam engine. *New York*, 1830. pp. 328.   BM
  pp. 29–69, steam locomotion applied to railroads.

285 STEPHENSON, R. *and* LOCKE, J. Observations on the comparative merits of locomotive and fixed engines as applied to railways: being a reply to the report of Mr. James Walker to the directors of the Liverpool & Manchester Railway, compiled from the reports of Mr. George Stephenson, with an account of the competition of locomotive engines at Rainhill in October 1829, and of the subsequent experiments. *Liverpool*, [1830.] pp. viii, 83, with frontis.   LSE

286 'DETECTOR.' Conveyance upon canals and railroads compared. *London*, 1831. pp. 17.   ICE

287 GRAHAME, T. A letter addressed to Nicholas Wood, Esq. on that portion of chapter IX of his Treatise on Railroads entitled 'Comparative performances of motive power on canals and railroads.' *Glasgow*, 1831. pp. 40.   BM

288 P[AGE], F. A letter to a friend containing observations on the comparative merits of canals and railways occasioned by the reports of the committee of the Liverpool & Manchester Railway. *London*, 1832. pp. 32, 5. Signed 'F. P.'   BM
  pp. 14–18 includes a report and estimate of the Cromford & High Peak Rly.
  —— 2nd edn. '. . . with additions arising from the Evidence of the London & Birmingham Rly.' *London*, 1832. pp. 42.   BM

289 BADNALL, R. A treatise on railway improvements, explanatory of the chief difficulties and inconveniences which at present attend the general adoption of railways, and the means by which these objections may be overcome, as proved by a series of interesting experiments to which are added various remarks on the operation and effect of locomotive power. *London*, 1833. pp. 142, with illus.   BM

290 CUNDY, N. W. Inland transit; the practicability, utility and benefit of railroads: the comparative attraction and speed of steam engines on a railroad, navigation, and turnpike road. Report of a Select Committee of the House of Commons on Steam Carriages, with an abstract of the Evidence taken before Parliament on the Birmingham Railroad Bill, with the preamble; also, the plans, sections and estimates of the projected Grand Southern and Northern railroads. *London*, 1833. pp. iv, 161, with charts, & a plate. BM
  —— 2nd edn. *London*, 1834. pp. iv, 161.   BM

291 POPPE, J. H. M. Die Telegraphen und Eisenbahnen im ganzen Umfange . . . mit Abbildungen auf sechs Steintafeln. *Stuttgart*, 1834. pp. 162.   BM
  pp. 53 to end, 'Die Eisenbahnen'.
  pp. 158–62, a bibliography.

292 MACERONI, F. Expositions and illustrations interesting to all those concerned in steam power, whether as applied to railroads, common roads, or to sea and inland navigation. *London*, 1835. pp. 126, with plates & illus.   NLC

*293 TREDGOLD, T. A practical treatise on railroads and carriages, shewing the principles of estimating their strength, proportions, expense, and annual produce, and the conditions which render them effective, economical and durable . . . illustrated by four engravings and numberous useful tables. *London*, 1825. pp. xi, 184.   UL(GL)
  —— 2nd edn. *London*, 1835. pp. xi, 184. BM
  —— 'Caminos de hierro: tratado practico del ingeniero ingles, Mr. Tredgold.' *Madrid*, 1831. pp. xv, 126[132], 2 pl.   UL(GL)

294 WOOD, N. A practical treatise on railroads and interior communication in general, with original experiments and tables of the comparative value of canals and railroads; illustrated by engravings. *London*, 1825. pp. 314, with 6 fold. plates.   BM
  —— [2nd] edn. '. . . containing an account of the performances of the different engines at and subsequent to the Liverpool contest; upwards of two hundred and sixty experiments with tables of the comparative value of canals and railroads and the power of the present locomotive engines, illustrated by numerous engravings.' *London*, 1831. pp. xxiii, 530, 11 plates, 1 fold. table.   BM
  —— 2nd edn. [with another printer's title-page, of different format to, but with the same wording as, the 1831 edition.] *London*, 1832. pp. xxiii, 530, 11 plates, 1 fold. table. BM
  —— 3rd edn. '. . . containing numerous experiments on the powers of the improved locomotive engines; and tables of the comparative cost of conveyance on canals, railways and turnpike roads . . . illustrated by several new engravings.' *London*, 1838. pp. xxvii, 760, 13 plates, 4 tables.   BM

295 LENGTHS and levels to Bradshaw's maps of canals, navigable rivers and railways from actual survey. *London: T. G. White*, 1832. pp. 15.   BM
  —— another edn. *London: E. Ruff*, 1833. pp. 20.   BM

296 VALLANCE, J. A letter to the Kensington
 a Canal Company on the substitution of the pneumatic railway for the common railway, by which they contemplate extending their line of conveyance. Printed by order of the Company. *London*, 1833. pp. 74[75].   PO
  Advocating his pneumatic railway for conveying passengers between Kensington and the

London & Birmingham Rly. Inserted in the Patent Office copy is a MS. letter from J. Vallance to the editor of *The Times*.

297 GRAHAME, T. A letter to the traders and carriers on the navigations connecting Liverpool and Manchester, showing the easy means they possess of establishing, on the navigations between those towns, an elegant and comfortable conveyance for passengers at the rate of ten miles an hour, at fares only one-fourth of those on the railway, and the means they possess of conveying goods between Liverpool and Manchester with despatch equal to that of the railway, at a charge lower than the bare railway outlays. *Glasgow*, 1833. pp. 29.
—— 2nd edn. *Glasgow*, 1834. pp. 36. BM

298 GRAHAME, T. A treatise on internal intercourse and communication in civilized states, and particularly in Great Britain. *London*, 1834. pp. xiii, 160. BM
pt. 1 on railways (pt. 2 not published?).
Existing railways examined; arguments in favour of horse traction.

299 HEDLEY, O. D. A descriptive account of the means used on the Tyne and Wear for effecting the safe transit of railway carriages in ascending and descending steep planes; together with a historical sketch of the brake, as applied to railway carriages; being the subject of a paper read to the Literary & Philosophical Society of Newcastle at the November monthly meeting, 1834. *Newcastle-on-Tyne*, 1834. pp. 32, with 13 figures on 3 plates. SL

300 WARD, J. Manual labour superior to steam used upon railways: a new discovery whereby manual labour can be most advantageously substituted for steam power upon railways, as being greatly preferable, and much cheaper ... being an exposition of the merits and national importance of Mr. Snowden's Patent Improvements in Railways and Carriages ... *London*, 1834. pp. 19. UL(GL)

301 GORDON, A. The fitness of turnpike roads and highways for the most expeditious, safe, convenient and economical internal communication. *London*, 1835. pp. 32. BM
Roads preferred to railways.

302 GRAHAME, T. Essays and letters on subjects conducive to the improvement and extension of inland communication and transport. *Westminster*, 1835. pp. 61. BM
pp. 59–60 refer to boats used to convey loaded coal wagons from the Monkland & Kirkintilloch Rly.

303 LOUDON, J. C. An Encyclopaedia of Agriculture ... *London*, 1825. PC
Book 2, pt. 3, pp. 539–42, 'Rail-roads'.
A general account; also, granite carriageways, sometimes referred to at this period as 'tramways', designed to provide a smooth surface for road vehicles.
—— 2nd edn. *London*, 1831. pp. 613–16. BM
—— 3rd edn. *London*, 1835. pp. 613–16. BM

304 FAIRBAIRN, H. A plan for converting turnpike roads into railroads, and for superseding the whole of the joint stock railway schemes. *London*, 1836. pp. 34. ICE

305 GORDON, A. An historical and practical treatise upon elemental locomotion by means of steam carriages on common roads ... *London*, 1832. pp. v, 192, with plates. BM
Road locomotives preferable to railways or canals.
—— 2nd edn. A treatise upon elemental locomotion and interior communication wherein are explained and illustrated the history, practice and prospects of steam carriages, and the comparative value of turnpike roads, railways and canals. *London*, 1834. pp. xiv, 326. BM
—— 3rd edn. *London*, 1836. pp. xiv, 344. BM
—— German edns. 'Historische und praktische Abhandlung über Fortbewegung ohne Tierkraft ...' *Wien*, 1832; *Weimar*, 1833.

306 NAVIER, C. L. M. H. On the means of comparing the respective advantages of different lines of railway and on the use of locomotive engines. Translated from the French ... by John MacNeill. *London*, 1836. pp. xv, 97. BM
Various principles examined in the light of mathematical theory. (*See* 317.)

307 ADAMS, W. B. English pleasure carriages ... with an analysis of the construction of common roads and railroads, and the public vehicles used on them. *London*, 1837. pp. xviii, 315. BM

308 'CAUTUS.' A second letter to Sir Robert Peel on railway legislation. By Cautus. *London*, 1837. pp. 23. BM
Urging support for proposal by E. Pease for a parliamentary enquiry into varying gauges, and other reforms.

309 An EXPOSURE of the costly fallacies of railroad engineering, involving a wasteful outlay of original capital, a ruinous annual expenditure in repairs, and considerable risk to human lives. By 'Common Sense'. *London*, 1837. pp. 31. BM
A layman's advice to railway engineers and railway management.

310 GORDON, A. Observations addressed to those interested in either rail-ways or turnpike-roads, showing the comparative expedition, safety, convenience and public economy of these two kinds of road for internal communication. *London*, 1837. pp. 31. BM
Roads preferred to railways.

311 HEBERT, L. A practical treatise on railroads and locomotive engines for the use of
c engineers, mechanics and others, in which
the mechanical construction of edge, tram,
suspension and all other railways and the
various locomotive carriages designed for
rail and common roads are described in
chronological order, accompanied by an
analysis of the whole, including an explanation of every patent that has hitherto been
granted in England for improvements in the
mechanics of locomotion. Illustrated by
nearly 250 engravings. *London*, 1837. pp.
216. LSE

312 A FEW general observations on the principal
railways executed, in progress, and projected,
in the midland counties & north of England,
with the author's opinion upon them as investments; illustrated with maps. *London*,
1838. pp. xvi, 64, with 4 fold. maps. BM

313 LONGRIDGE, M. [*and* BIRKINSHAW, J.]
Remarks on the comparative merits of cast
metal and malleable iron railways, and an
account of the Stockton & Darlington Railway . . . *Newcastle*, 1827. pp. iv, 22, 39. PO
—— another edn. '. . . and the Liverpool &
Manchester Railway,' by Henry Booth.
Newcastle, 1832. pp. 26, 39, 38. PO
—— another edn. *Newcastle*, 1838. pp. 32,
38, 38, with two lithograph letters to M.
Longridge from the London & Birmingham
Railway and from Peter Barlow. SL
A collection of correspondence, newspaper
extracts, reports from railway companies, etc.,
brought together by Michael Longridge and
John Birkinshaw of Bedlington Iron Works.
Also issued with an additional work bound
in: *Sketches of our information as to railroads*
by James Adamson. [*Newcastle*, 1826.] p. 26.
PO

314 PARNELL, H. A treatise on roads . . .
London, 1833. pp. 438, with 7 fold. plates.
BM
pp. 101–19, 'Iron railroads'. Horses preferred to locomotives.
—— 2nd edn. *London*, 1838. pp. xii, 465.
BM
pp. 101–4, 'Iron railways'.
pp. 363–6, 'Horse railways', by J. MacNeill.

315 ADCOCK, H. Rules and data for the steam
engine, both stationary and locomotive, and
for railways, canals, and turnpike roads . . .
London, 1839. pp. 88. ICE
pp. 51–64, 'Roads & railways', and 'Railways
& canals'.

316 CLEGG, S. Clegg's patent atmospheric
a railway. *London*, 1839. pp. 20. UL(GL)

317 NAVIER, C. L. M. H. Die Grundsätze und
Bedingungen der Bewegung der Locomoti-
ven auf Eisenbahnen, für den Zweck, die
absoluten Transport kosten von Waaren und
Passagieren berechnen und miteinander
vergleichen zu können; nach dem Englischen
des MacNeill . . . von Chr. Heinr. Schmidt.
Leipzig, 1839. (*See* 306.) H

318 BIOGRAPHICAL notice of William James,
projector of the railway system in England.
London, [1840.] pp. 16. BM

319 CLEGG, S. *and* SAMUDA, J. d'A. Clegg and
Samuda's atmospheric railway. *London*,
a 1840. pp. 23, with fold. plate. BM
Locomotive power and atmospheric system
compared; tables of trials on the Birmingham,
Bristol & Thames Junction Rly., and a summary of advantages of the atmospheric.

320 CURTIS, W. J. Curtis's inventions for railways, steam-vessels . . . *London*, 1840. pp.
v, 78, with frontis. & illus. ICE
pp. 7–17, Animal locomotive (horse working
treadles).

321 PINKUS, H. Prospectus of a new agrarian
system invented by H. Pinkus. (The New
a agrarian system and the pneumatic-atmos-
pheric and gaso-pneumatic railway, common
road and canal transit.) *London*, 1840.
pp. 50. BM

322 CHEMINS de fer atmosphériques en Angle-
a terre et en Irlande. [*Paris*, 1841.] pp. 2. BM

323 GORDON, A. Observations on railway
monopolies and remedial measures. *London*, 1841. pp. 57. BM
Recommends government control, and a
more extensive use of steam-carriages on roads.

*324 PIM, J. The atmospheric railway: a letter
to the Earl of Ripon, President of the
a Board of Trade . . . *London*, 1841. pp. 26,
with 4 la. fold. plates. ICE

325 PIM, J. Irish railways. The atmospheric
railway: a letter to . . . Viscount Morpeth.
a *London*, 1841. pp. 15. BM
Proposing a trial of the atmospheric system
on the Dublin & Kingstown Rly.

326 ROGERS, J. W. Plan proposed by Sir
James C. Anderson . . . and J. W. Rogers . . .
for establishing steam carriages for the conveyance of goods and passengers on the mail
coach roads of Ireland . . . *Dublin*, 1841.
pp. 15, with fold. letter at end by Wm. Bald,
civil engineer. BM
Roads preferred to railways.

327 RANKINE, W. J. M. An experimental inquiry into the advantages attending the use
of cylindrical wheels on railways; with an
explanation of the theory of adapting curves
for those wheels . . . *Edinburgh*, 1842. pp.
16. ICE

328 SHUTTLEWORTH, J. G. The hydraulic
railway, being a carefully digested but plain
statement of the advantages to be derived,
and impediments removed, in establishing
hydraulic propulsion on railways. *London*,
1842. pp. xi, [9]–106, with 2 fold. plates. BM

329 SMITH, F. *and* BARLOW, P. Report of Lt.
Col. Sir Frederic Smith and Prof. Barlow to
a the . . . Earl of Ripon, President of the

Board of Trade, on the atmospheric railway.
London, 1842. pp. 19.   BM
   Parliamentary Papers, 1842. XLI. pp. 381–
99. Various railways, including, pp. 15–19, 'A
letter from Mr. Pim of the Dalkey & Kingstown Rly. to the Earl of Ripon'.

330 BERGIN, T. F. The atmospheric railway:
    observations on the report of Lt. Col. Sir
 a Frederic Smith, R.E. and Prof. Barlow on
    the atmospheric railway: addressed to
    Francis Low, Esq., chairman of the Dublin
    and Kingstown Rly. Co. *Dublin*, 1843.
    pp. 86.   BM
       In support of atmospheric system for the
    D. & K. Rly.

331 ARAGO, D. F. J. Mons. Arago's report on
    the atmospheric railway system . . . *London*,
 a 1844. pp. 12.   BM
       General description of the system, and of the
    Kingstown & Dalkey Rly.

332 BECKER, F. Atmosphärische Eisenbah-
    nen: nach den Berichten von Smith, Mallet,
 a Samuda, Pim, usw., und englischen Quellen
    bearbeitet. *Frankfurt-am-Main*, 1844.   HZ

333 CANALS and railways. [*London*, 1844.]
    pp. 4.   RIA(H)
       Examples of decreasing revenue and falling
    off of share values in canal undertakings where
    a railway has been built to run parallel.

334 HORSE-POWER applied to railways at
    higher rates of speed than by ordinary
    draught: its economy and practicability
    considered in reference to subsidiary lines,
    with some general observations on railroads,
    other roads and locomotive power . . .
    London, 1844. pp. 52.   BM

335 PILBROW, J. Atmospheric railway and
    canal propulsion, and pneumatic telegraph.
 a *London*, 1844. pp. 39, with 3 la. fold.
    diagrams.   PO
    —— 2nd edn. *London*, 1844. pp. 42.   LSE

336 SAMUDA, J. d'A. The atmospheric rail-
 a way. *London*, 1844. pp. 29, with illus. ICE
    Excerpt, *Min. Proc. I.C.E.*, vol. 3, 1844.

337 SAMUDA, J. d'A. A treatise on the adapta-
    tion of atmospheric pressure to the purposes
 a of locomotion on railways. *London*, 1841.
    pp. 50, with 2 plates.   BM
    —— *London*, 1844. pp. 50.   BM
    —— 'Railways atmosphériques; ou, Appli-
    cation de la pression atmosphérique a la
    traction sur les railways.' *Paris*, 1842.
    pp. 48.   PO

338 STEPHENSON, R. Report on the atmos-
    pheric railway system. *London*, 1844. pp.
 a 44, 73, & a vol. of plates. (1 fold. table,
    86 diagrs. on 26 plates & 10 tables at end.)
                                    BM
       Addressed to the directors of the Chester &
    Holyhead Rly. Stephenson's reports on the

Dublin & Kingstown Rly. and the London &
Blackwall Rly. The second part of this volume
is Robert Mallet's *Three reports upon improved
methods of constructing and working atmospheric railways.*

339 BARLOW, P. W. Comparative advantages
    of the atmospheric railway system; with an
 a appendix containing experiments on the
    Tyler Hill inclined plane of the Canterbury
    & Whitstable Railway . . . *London*, 1845.
    pp. 40.   ICE

340 BERKELEY, G. The peculiar features of the
    atmospheric railway system. *London*, 1845.
 a pp. 42.   ICE
       Excerpt, *Min. Proc. I.C.E.*, vol. 4, 1845.

341 HEWLETT, J. G. On atmospheric traction in
    general with explanations and illustrations of
 a Pilbrow's atmospheric railway and canal
    propulsion; being the substance of a paper
    read before the Society of Arts, March 19,
    1845. *London*, 1845. pp. 19, with fold.
    diagram.   ICE

342 JONES, W. A popular sketch of the various
    proposed schemes of atmospheric railway,
 a demonstrating the applicability of the
    mechanical properties of the atmosphere as
    a motive power; illustrated by numerous
    wood-cuts; being the substance of lectures
    delivered on the subject at the Royal
    Adelaide Gallery in the month of February
    1845, with additions and corrections by
    the late proprietor, William Jones. *London*,
    1845. pp. xviii, 108.   BM
       Appendix, pp. 101–8, Report of the Select
    Committee (House of Commons) appointed to
    inquire into the merits of the Atmospheric
    System of Railway; dated April 22, 1845.

343 MALLET, R. Report of the Institute of
    France upon M. Arnollet's system of atmos-
 a pheric railways. *Dublin*. 1845. pp. 16. BM
    French and British systems compared.

344 MALLET, R. Three reports upon improved
    methods of constructing and working
 a atmospheric railways. *London*, 1845. pp.
    73, with 10 fold. plates.   BM
       From *Weale's Quarterly Papers on Engineer-
    ing.*
       pp. 58–73, seventeen letters concerning
    patent rights and priorities of invention, and
    substantiating the date at which his inventions
    were made and communicated.

345 PARSEY, A. Parsey's patent locomotive and
    stationary air engines. [*London*, 1845.]
 a pp. 11.   ICE
       Compressed air carried in container on
    locomotive and replenished at intervals along
    the line.

346 DUBERN, H. A. De l'application de l'air
    atmosphérique aux chemins de fer: resumé
 a des opinions des ingénieurs français et
    anglais sur les chemins de fer atmosphér-
    iques. *Paris*, 1846. pp. 81.   BM

347 GALLOWAY, E. Description of an improved system of railway traction and remarks on some of its advantages as compared with the locomotive and atmospheric systems. *London*, 1846. pp. 41, with 2 plates.
BM
Motion by wire ropes from stationary engines.

348 NAIRNE, W. Description of William Nairne's new mode of propelling carriages along railways; with estimates of first cost, working expenses . . . [*Milnhaugh*, 1846.] pp. 11, with fold. diagram.   H

349 OBSERVATIONS on the means of providing against the dangers and fatal accidents so
a much complained of in railway travelling, and of obtaining much greater power and economy by such improvements in the atmospheric system as will render iron rails and cylinders unnecessary. *London*, [1846.] pp. 49.   PO
Inherent dangers of conventional railways.

350 VIGNOLES, C. B. Vignoles' steam railway . . . Explanatory circular. [*Bradford*,] 1846.
a pp. 7, with la. fold. diagram.   ICE
Steam atmospheric system.

351 BESSEMER, H. On the resistance of the atmosphere to railway trains, and a means of lessening the same; together with an account of some improvements in railway carriage axles. *London*, 1847. pp. 15, with illus. BM

352 STATISTICS of locomotion compared with the velocity of the wind; the latter calculated by Professor Ferguson. *London*, April 1847. s.sh.   BM
Tables of comparative speeds of various forms of travel, including railways.

353 TURNBULL, W. An essay on the air-pump and atmospheric railway containing formu-
a lae and rules for calculating the various quantities contained in Robert Stephenson's report on atmospheric propulsion, for the directors of the Chester & Holyhead Railway. *London*, 1847. pp. 96, with 6 illus.   BM

354 BARLOW, P. W. Investigation of the power consumed in overcoming the inertia of railway trains and of the resistance of the air to the motion of railway trains at high velocities. *London*, 1848. pp. 34, with 10 tables.
BM

355 BEADON, G. Ten minutes' reading of plain observations upon canals and navigable rivers . . . *London*, 1848. pp. 38.   BM
Advantages of canals over railways.

356 SOWERBY, W. Description of Harlow and Young's patent atmospheric railway, with
a observations on the atmospheric system. *London*, 1848. pp. 12, with la. fold. diagram.   BM

357 GORDON, L. D. B. Railway economy: an exposition of the advantages of locomotion by locomotive carriages instead of the present expensive system of steam tugs. *Edinburgh*, 1849. pp. 67.   BM
Steam rail-cars instead of locomotives.

358 PARSEY, A. Compressed air power and the patented compressed air engine, popu-
a larly described; with an engraving. *London*, 1851. pp. 24.   PO

359 GRAHAME, T. Correspondence between the Board of Trade and T. Grahame on railway and canal combination. *London*, 1852. pp. 43.   BM
'. . . calling attention to a system of legislation equally hostile to the agricultural, manufacturing & mercantile interests of the country.'

360 BRADFIELD, J. E. The public carriages of Great Britain: a glance at the rise, progress, struggles and burthens of railways, stage coaches . . . with an appendix containing Report of the Committee of the House of Commons against the taxation of internal conveyances; statistics and other useful information. *London*, 1855. pp. vi, 117.
BM
pp. 23–5, comparison of coach and railway fares.

*361 PERDONNET, A. Traité élémentaire des
a chemins de fer. *Paris*, 1855–6. 2 vols. BM
Brief accounts only of British railways, but some engravings of early British locomotives and many illustrations.
pp. 459–89, a detailed account of English atmospheric system, with illustrations.

362 KINGSLEY, J. Invention: water instead of coal the impelling power: the steam engine
a superseded: applicable to . . . short atmospheric railways. *London*, 1857. pp. 8. BM

363 GURNEY, G. Mr. Goldsworthy Gurney's account of the invention of the steam-jet or blast and its application to steamboats and locomotive engines in reference to the mistaken claim put forth by Mr. Smiles in his 'Life of the late George Stephenson'. *London*, 1859. pp. 24.   BM

364 WILSON, T. The railway system and its author, Thomas Gray . . . *London*, 1845. pp. 39.   BM
—— new edn. *London*, 1860. pp. vii, 63.
ICE
pp. 31–63, Press opinions.

365 P[AINE], E. M. S. The two James's and the two Stephensons; or, The earliest history of passenger transit on railways. *London*, 1861. pp. viii, 121, with fold. plan.
BM: UL(GL)
Based on family records; asserting the claim of Wm. James to the title of 'Father of railways'. Inserted in a pocket at the end of the UL(GL) copy are three holograph letters from

E. M. S. Paine to Lord Bagot, dated April and May, 1866.
—— Centenary reprint, with an introduction by L. T. C. Rolt. *Dawlish : David & Charles*, 1961. BM

*366 JEAFFRESON, J. C. The life of Robert
a Stephenson ... *London*, 1864. 2 vols. BM
vol. 1, pp. 292–363, The atmospheric system.

367 PASSY, F. Le Petit poucet du XIXe siècle: Georges Stephenson et la naissance des chemins de fer. *Paris*, 1881. pp. 192, with illus. BM

368 ARCHER, M. William Hedley, the inventor of railway locomotion on the present principle. *Newcastle-upon-Tyne*, 1882. pp. 66, with 4 plates (1 fold.), & map. BM
—— 3rd edn. *London*, [1885.] pp. xvi, 80. BM

369 ARCHER, M. Letters on the subject of William Hedley's invention of railway locomotion on the present principle. *Newcastle-upon-Tyne*, 1883. pp. 17. BM
A sequel to his *Wm. Hedley, the inventor of railway locomotion* (1882).

370 [BURROWS, E.] The triumphs of steam; or, Stories from the lives of Watt, Arkwright and Stephenson. *London*, 1859. pp. viii, 263. BM
pp. 83–263 relate to G. Stephenson, and to the Liverpool & Manchester Rly.
—— another edn. by H. Frith, *London*, 1892. pp. xii, 263. BM

371 PEASE, M. H. Henry Pease: a short story of his life. By M. H. P. *London*, 1897. pp. 112, with 5 plates. BM

372 KIRKWOOD, S. Thomas Gray and the origin of the British railway system. pp. 24. *Typescript*. RC
Paper, Railway Club, June 1906.

373 PEASE, A. E. The Diaries of Edward Pease, the Father of English Railways. Edited by Sir Alfred E. Pease. *London*, 1907. pp. 10, 407, with 13 plates, & fold. genealogical chart. BM
As a background to the biography the author provides as a preface (pp. 1–40) a 'general idea of the principles upon which the Quakers based their religion and worship and regulated their conduct'. [His exposition is perhaps unrivalled for its clarity and appeal.—G. O.]

374 HALL, C. The early history of the railway. *In* 'Modern railway working', edited by John Macaulay. 1912–14. vol. 1, pp. 3–68. BM

375 LEWIN, H. G. The British railway system: outlines of its early development to the year
c 1844. *London*, 1914. pp. vii, 67, with 9 fold. maps, & table. BM
Arranged chronologically.

376 SOME pictorial records of the early days of railways. *In* 'Jubilee of the Railway News, 1864–1914.' *London: Railway News*, [1914.] pp. 4–20. BM
Includes the 'Atmospheric', the Railway Mania, and the Battle of the Gauges.

*377 JACKMAN, W. T. The development of transportation in modern England. *Cam-
b bridge*, 1916. 2 vols. (pp. xv, 459; vi, 461–820), with many bibliogr. notes & an extensive bibliography (pp. 750–811). BM
vol. 2, pp. 461–603, 'The development of railways'. A very detailed account of British railway history up to 1850.
pp. 604–23, Effects of steam upon road transportation.
pp. 624–749, Competition of railways and canals.
pp. 750–811, Bibliography.
—— reprinted with a new introduction
b by W. H. Chaloner. *London: Frank Cass & Co.*, 1962. pp. xxxiii, 820, with maps. BM

*378 YOUNG, R. Timothy Hackworth and the locomotive. *London*, 1923. pp. xxxii, 406, with illus. BM
Very detailed work containing much information on early railways and locomotives.

379 D[IXON], W. Intimate story of the origin of railways. By 'W. D.' *Darlington*, 1925. pp. 22, with illus., & maps. BM
Boyhood reminiscences of his acquaintanceship with early railway pioneers, augmented with extracts from diaries, records and drawings in his possession, mostly concerning John Dixon and Edward Pease.

380 FUERST, A. Die Hundertjährige Eisenbahn; wie Meisterhände sie schufen; mit vielen Abbildungen. *Berlin*, 1925. pp. 308. BM

381 LEWIN, H. G. Early British railways: a short history of their origin and development, 1801–1844. *London & New York*, 1925. pp. xii, 202. with 8 illus., 8 maps. BM
Among maps are four showing all railways in operation in 1836, 1839, 1842 and 1844; also a table of 7 pp. showing railways up to 1844 with subsequent amalgamations.

382 STOCKTON-ON-TEES RAILWAY CENTENARY COMMITTEE. The Centenary of Public Railways, at their birthplace, Stockton-on-Tees, with a brief history of the town prior to and since 1825. *Stockton-on-Tees*, 1925. pp. 105[107], with illus. RC
pp. 22–83, Early railway and locomotive history, and the Stockton & Darlington Rly.

383 WILLIAMS, H. D. The Steel Highway: a romance of the railway. *London*, [1925.] pp. 253. BM
The story of the pioneer days of railways centred around George Stephenson and others; the Stockton & Darlington, and the Rainhill Trials.

*384 CLAPHAM, J. H. An economic history of modern Britain: The Early Railway Age, 1820–1850. *Cambridge: Cambridge University Press*, 1926. pp. xviii, 623.   BM
A very detailed work.
—— 2nd edn. *Cambridge*, 1930. pp. xvi, 623.   BM
—— 2nd edn., repr. with corr. *Cambridge*, 1939; 1950.   BM

385 PEDDIE, R. A. Railway literature, 1556–1830: a handlist. *London*, 1931. pp. 73.
b   BM
Brief descriptions, in chronological order, of 750 contemporary books, Acts, plans, documents and articles, on British and foreign railways.

386 OUTRAM, M. F. Margaret Outram, 1778–1863 . . . *London*, 1932. pp. xiv, 358.   BM
Contains references to Benjamin and Joseph Outram; extracts from a Newcomen Society paper by Fred Bland on John Curr's rails; 'Minutes to be observed in the construction of railways' by B. Outram (1803 or 4); the derivation of the word 'tram' by Edwin A. Pratt; and a record by John Curr of what is almost certainly the first use of an iron plateway in Sheffield.

387 HOELTZEL, M. Aus der Frühzeit der Eisenbahnen; mit einer Bibliographie . . .
b *Berlin*, 1935. pp. 111.   BM
pp. 29–111, 'Bibliographie der Eisenbahnen in ihrer Frühzeit'. (1801–1850.)

*388 DENDY MARSHALL, C. F. A history of British railways down to the year 1830.
b *London: O.U.P.*, 1938. pp. xi, 246, with 101 illus. on plates & in text, bibliography of 12 pages, a glossary of 22 pages, & many bibliographical notes.   BM

389 BROWN, K. With men, horses or otherwise. pp. 10, 9. *Typescript*, with added pages in MS.   RC
Paper, Railway Club, 9 July, 1941.
Early methods of haulage on railways.

390 LEE, C. E. The evolution of permanent way. *London*, 1937. pp. 64, with illus. & bibliogr. notes.   BM
Paper, Permanent Way Institution, 8 March, 1937: Suppl., *Jnl. P. W. Instn.*, vol. 55, Aug. 1937.
—— another edn. 'The evolution of railways.' *London: Railway Gazette*, 1937. pp. viii, 64. (The same work.)   BM
—— 2nd edn., rev. & enl. *London*, 1943. pp. viii, 108.   BM

391 HARVARD GRADUATE SCHOOL OF BUSINESS ADMINISTRATION–BAKER LIBRARY.
b The pioneer period of European railroads: a tribute to Mr. Thomas W. Streeter. *Boston, Mass.*, 1946. p. 71. [*Kress Library of Business and Economics*, no. 3.]   BM
A list of items relating to European railroad development, published between 1734 and 1848, which are available in the Baker and other Harvard libraries.
pp. [3]–13, an introductory essay: 'The pioneer period of railroads in England, France, and the United States', by Arthur L. Dunham. (*See* 397.)

392 BARMAN, C. Early British railways; with sixteen reproductions of old prints and drawings. *Harmondsworth*, 1950. pp. 39. [*King Penguin Books*, no. 56.]   BM

393 GUEST, C. E. Lady Charlotte Guest: extracts from her journal, 1833–1852. Edited by the Earl of Bessborough. *London: J. Murray*, 1950. pp. ix, 309.   BM
Includes several short accounts of journeys by rail and impressions of newly opened railways. Some entries refer to the supply of rails from Dowlais Iron Works.

394 GARNETT, E. The railway builders; illustrated by Wardill. [*London:*] *Hodder & Stoughton*, 1952. pp. 231.   BM
For young readers. A general account of the early days of railways, and of the men who built them.

395 LLOYD, R. Railwaymen's Gallery. *London: Allen & Unwin*, 1953. pp. 166.   BM
pp. 11–31, Pioneers! O Pioneers!

396 GREENWOOD, M. Railway revolution, 1825 to 1845. *London: Longmans*, 1955. pp. iv, 92, with illus.   BM

397 HASKELL, D. C. A Tentative Check-List of early European Railway Literature, 1831–
b 1848; prepared by Daniel C. Haskell, with a prefatory note by Arthur H. Cole, Librarian. *Boston, Mass.: Baker Library, Harvard Graduate School of Business Administration*, 1955. pp. 192.   BM
This work is an extension of *The Pioneer Period of European Railroads*, issued in 1946. The arrangement is similar (chronological by date of publication) but the period covered is limited to 1831–1848. The earlier work was for Harvard, but this one records items from six American libraries. To this are added transcriptions from other printed library catalogues and booksellers' catalogues.

398 SIMMONS, J. For and against the locomotive. *In* 'Journal of Transport History', vol. 2, no. 3, May 1956. pp. 144–51, with 24 bibliogr. notes.   BM
The locomotive and alternative means of propulsion before 1830.

399 DAY, J. R. *and* WILSON, B. G. Unusual railways. *London: F. Muller*, 1957. pp.
a 212, with 44 illus. on 20 plates.   BM
Historical and descriptive survey. (*See also* 402.)

400 ROLT, L. T. C. Thomas Telford. *London: Longmans*, 1958. pp. xv, 211.   BM
pp. 153–72, 'The coming of railways'. The effects on canals.

*401 HADFIELD, C. British canals: an illustrated history. *London: Phoenix House,*

1950. pp. 259, with 8 plates, 44 illus., 17 maps, & a bibliography.   BM
The index has 84 entries relating to various railways.
pp. 177–92, 'War with the railways'.
—— 2nd edn., completely revised, *London*, 1959. pp. 291, with 8 plates, 44 illus., maps, bibliogr. notes, & a bibliography.   BM
pp. 196–227, 'Canals and railways'.

402 DAY, J. R. More unusual railways. *London: F. Muller*, 1960. pp. 214, with

a 45 illus. on 20 plates, & 10 diagrams.   BM
Historical and descriptive. A sequel to *Unusual railways*, by J. R. Day and B. G. Wilson (1957). (*See also* 399.)

403 BANKES, J. H. M. *and* HARRIS, J. R. The first Lancashire locomotive. *In* 'Journal of Transport History', vol. 5, no. 3, May 1962. pp. 146–8, with plate & 5 notes.   BM
Robert Daglish's locomotives (the first, 1813) on the Orrell Mount Colliery wagonway to the Leeds & Liverpool Canal.

B 3   1830–1914   THE RAILWAY AGE

For historical accounts see **A**

Marginal symbols: **a** atmospheric system
c chronologies

404 ALBERT, L. P. Verzeichnis von 119 Eisenbahnen welche in England, Frankreich, Belgien, Holland, Deutschland, und Nordamerika teils erbaut, teils im Bau begriffen oder zur Ausführung bestimmt sind. *Ulm*, 1835.   HZ
—— 2 Ausgabe, für 141 Eisenbahnen. *Ulm*, 1836.   HZ

405 DESCRIPTION des locomotives Stephenson, circulant sur les chemins de fer en Angleterre et en France, et sur celui de Bruxelles à Malines; précédée d'un aperçu historique sur les chemins, les rails, le vapeur, et les machines à vapeur. *Bruxelles*, 1835. pp. 72, with 6 fold. plates.   H

406 FAIRBAIRN, H. A treatise on the political economy of railroads, in which the new mode of locomotion is considered in its influence upon the affairs of nations. *London*, 1836. pp. xvi, 248.   BM

407 KLEINSCHROD, C. T. von. Grossbritanniens Gesetzgebung über Gewerbe, Handel und Innere Communicationsmittel statistisch und staatswirthschaftlich erläutert; mit mehreren Tabellen. *Stuttgart & Tübingen*, 1836. pp. x, 479.   BM
pp. 472–6, Brief financial tables of British railways to date.

408 MUDGE, R. Z. Observations on railways, with a reference to utility and profit and the obvious necessity for a national system. *London*, 1837. pp. 73, with fold. map showing all existing and proposed railways, 3 tables showing receipts and profits, and a list of 101 Railway Bills for the ensuing Session.   BM

409 FRAENZL, M. J. Statistische Übersicht der Eisenbahnen, Canäle und Dampfschiffahrten Europas und Amerikas. *Wien*, 1838 pp. 73, with fold. map.   BM
pp. 16–19, Eisenbahnen, Gross Britannien.

410 WHISHAW, F. Analysis of railways, consisting of a series of reports on the twelve hundred miles of projected railways in England and Wales now before Parliament, together with those which have been abandoned for the present Session, to which are added a table of distances from the proposed London termini to eight well-known places in the Metropolis . . . and other useful information. *London*, 1837. pp. xv, 296.   BM
—— 2nd edn. with additions & corrections. *London*, 1838. pp. xv, 298.   ICE

411 LECOUNT, P. A practical treatise on railways, explaining their construction and management, with numerous woodcuts and ten plates; being the article 'Railways' in the 7th edition of the Encyclopaedia Britannica, with additional details. *Edinburgh*, 1839. pp. v, 422, with 10 fold. plates, & 49 illus. in text.   BM
A very detailed work on all aspects of railways.

412 The ROADS and railroads, vehicles and modes of travelling of ancient and modern countries, with accounts of bridges, tunnels and canals in various parts of the world. *London*, 1839. pp. viii, 340.   BM
pp. 262–340, Railways and locomotives.

413 HEAD, G. A home tour through the manufacturing districts of England in the Summer of 1835. *London*, 1836. pp. xi, 434. HRL
Impressions of railways visited, principally the Leeds & Manchester and the Leeds & Selby.
—— new edn. *London*, 1836. pp. xi, 440.   BM
—— A home tour through the manufacturing districts and other parts of England, Scotland, and Ireland . . . *London*, 1840. pp. xi, 440. (2 vols.)   BM

414 BINEAU, J. M. Chemins de fer d'Angleterre; leur état actuel; législation qui les

régit; conditions d'art de leur tracé . . .; application à la France des résultats de l'expérience de l'Angleterre et de la Belgique. *Paris*, 1840. pp. 456, with la. col. map & tables.   LSE

415 DUNOYER, C. Esprit et méthodes comparées de l'Angleterre et de la France dans les entreprises de travaux publics, et en particulier des chemins de fer . . . *Paris*, 1840. pp. ii, 110.   H

416 PERDONNET, A. Notes sur les chemins de fer anglais et belges à la fin de l'année 1839. *Paris*, 1840. pp. 47, with fold. diagram.   H

417 POUSSIN, G. T. Notice sur les chemins de fer anglais; ou, Résumé analytique des principaux renseignements contenus dans les publications officielles du Parlement en 1839. *Paris*, 1840. pp. vii, 280.   H

418 RAILWAY TIMES. Railway Calendar for 1840. *London*, 1840. la. fold. s.sh.   LSE
   Diagrams of thirty-two railways, showing comparative lengths of line, surrounded by tables of miscellaneous general information.
   —— Railway Calendar for 1841. *London*, 1841.   LSE
   Only fifteen railways depicted, but with more details in the tables, and including the text of Lord Seymour's Act for Regulating Railways, 1840.

419 DAMMERT, A. H. Auszug aus einem . . . Berichte über einen Aufenthalt in England zur Besichtigung der dortigen Eisenbahnen. *Hannover*, 1841. pp. 45.   ICE

*420 WHISHAW, F. The railways of Great Britain and Ireland, practically described and illustrated. *London*, 1840, 1841. pp. xxvi, 500, lxiv, with 15 fold. plates.   BM
   Detailed accounts of fifty-eight railways, with tables compiled from results of experimental runs extending to 7000 miles, and tables relating to the performances of 630 locomotives. Also Standing Orders of the House of Commons relating to Railway Bills.
   —— 2nd edn. *London*, 1842. pp. xxvi, 500, lxiv, with 19 plates.   LSE

421 ARMENGAUD, J. E. Das Eisenbahnwesen; oder, Abbildungen und Beschreibungen von den vorzüglichsten Dampf-, Munitions-, Transport-, und Personenwagen, von Schienen, Stühlen, Drehscheiben, usw., die auf den Eisenbahnen Englands, Deutschlands, Frankreichs, Belgiens, usw. in Anwendung stehen . . . Aus dem Französischen übersetzt. *Weimar*, 1841. (Text & atlas.)   H

422 COWDIN, J. Description and testimonials of the patent locomotive steam double pile driving and railway grading machine, together with statistics giving the square miles of territory and the population of each state in Europe and America; also, Remarks on railways in Europe and America; with illustrations. *London*, 1842. pp. 26.   BM

423 TEISSERENC, E. De la politique des chemins de fer et de ses applications diverses. *Paris*, 1842. pp. vi, 584.   BM
   pp. 169–82, 'Les chemins de fer d'Angleterre'.

424 BEIL, J. A. Stand und Ergebnisse der deutschen, amerikanischen, englischen, französischen, belgischen, hollandischen, italienischen und russischen Eisenbahnen am Schlusse des Jahres 1843; mit einem Anhang enthaltend Beschreibung und detaillierte Übersichten der ausgeführten und im Bau begriffenen englischen und amerikanischen Eisenbahnen. *Frankfurt-am-Main*, 1844. pp. 250, xxviii, 9.   BM
   pp. 20–49, 'Englische Eisenbahnen'.
   —— another edn. 'Stand und Ergebnisse der europäischen Eisenbahnen bis zu dem Jahr 1845.' *Wien*, 1845. pp. 138.   BM
   —— another edn. '. . . bis zu dem Jahr 1847.' *Wien*, 1847. pp. 296.   BM

425 [GALT, W.] Railway reform: its expediency and practicability considered; with a copius appendix containing a description of all the railways in Great Britain and Ireland . . . *London*, 1843. pp. 108.   BM
   —— 2nd edn. *London*, 1843. pp. 116.   BM
   —— 3rd edn. *London*, 1844. pp. 116.
   —— People's edn. *London*, 1844. pp. 76   BM

426 BIGG, J., *publisher*. Reports of the Railway Department of the Board of Trade on schemes for extending railway communication, Session 1845. With a copious index. *Westminster*, [1845.] pp. 252.   BM

427 BIGG, J., *publisher*. Reports of the Railway Department of the Board of Trade on schemes for extending railway communication and on amalgamations of railways, Session 1845. With a copious index. *Westminster*, Sept. 1845. pp. 269.   UL(GL)
   Twenty-two reports. Plans to accompany this work were issued separately.

428 BROWN, K. British railways in 1845. pp. 48, with 2 maps & 31 illus. mounted in text. *Typescript*.   RC
   Paper, Railway Club, 20 February, 1936.

429 JULLIEN, A. Notes diverses sur les chemins de fer en Angleterre, en Belgique et en France. *Paris*, 1845. pp. 80.   H
   Extract, *Annales des Ponts et Chaussées*, mars et avril 1845.

430 MICHELOT, P. *and* BOUSSON, A. Observations sur les chemins de fer d'Angleterre. *Paris*, 1845. pp. 36.   ICE

431 SALT, S. Statistics and calculations essentially necessary to persons connected with railways or canals, containing a variety of information not to be found elsewhere. (New & cheap edition.) *Manchester*, 1845. pp. 116.   BM

432 SPACKMAN, W. F. An analysis of the railway interest of the United Kingdom, embracing all companies registered to the 31st day of October, 1845, shewing the defects of the present system of railway management and the necessity for amendments in the law of provisional registration. [*London*,] 1845. pp. 54.   BM

433 CLARKE, H. Contributions to railway statistics in 1845. *London*, 1846. pp. 35.
                                                                    LSE
Financial, traffic, and commodities.

434 COLLINS, C. J. The projected new railways: an epitome of the new lines of railway in England which Parliament will probably sanction, with reasons for their doing so. *London*, 1846. pp. 32.   BM

435 CLARKE, H. Contributions to railway statistics in 1846, 1847 and 1848 . . . *London*, 1849. pp. 55.   BM
Passengers and fares, commodities, parcels and mail and rolling stock.

436 CHEVALLIER, J. G. A. Mémoire sur l'exploitation des chemins de fer anglais. *Paris*, 1847. pp. 146, with tables, & 6 fold. plates.   H

437 GLYNN, H. Reference Book to the incorporated railway companies of England
c and Wales, alphabetically arranged, including a list of their directors, offices and officers, constitution and capital, shewing also the lines suspended in Session 1847, and applications for Bills in 1848 . . . *London*, 1847. pp. xii, 227.   BM
pp. [215]–227, chronological table of special railway Acts (Local & Personal) sessionally arranged, with year, chapter, and date of royal assent; names of companies, alphabetically arranged from 1801 to 1847 inclusive, showing also length of each line, amount of share capital and borrowing powers.

438 HARDING, W. Facts bearing on the progress of the railway system; from the 'Journal of the Statistical Society of London', November 1848. [*London*, 1848.] pp. 24.
                                                                    BM
General review of the development of railways, and their benefits and problems.

439 SALT, S. Facts and figures, principally relating to railways and commerce. *London*, & *Manchester*, 1848. pp. 152.   BM
A supplement to his *Statistics and Calculations*. Statistical extracts.

* 440 LARDNER, D. Railway economy: a treatise on the new art of transport, its management, prospects and relations, commercial, financial and social . . . *London*, 1850. pp. xxiii, 528.   BM
Very detailed work on railways in general and on specific aspects and problems.
—— another edn. *New York*, 1850. pp. xxiii, 442.

441 SALT, S. Railway and commercial information. *London*, 1850. pp. xi, 240.   LSE
Miscellaneous information under 290 headings, with index. Includes some unusual aspects and quaint comments.

442 HEBERT, L. The Engineer's and Mechanic's Encyclopaedia . . . *London*, 1836. 2
a vols.   BM
vol. 1, pp. 35–40, Pneumatic railways.
   pp. 40–6, Air-motive engines.
vol. 2, pp. 373–584, 'Railway'; with illus.
—— new edn. *London*, 1852.   BM

443 POOLE, B. Statistics of British commerce . . . *London*, 1852. pp. vii, 332.   BM
pp. 251–62, 'Railways'. Seventeen tables and other statistical information.

444 ADAMS, W. B. Practical remarks on railways and permanent way as adapted to the various requirements of transit; with diagrams. *London*, 1854. pp. 16, with fold. plate of W. B. Adams' 'improved rails and fastenings'.   BM
A discourse on the salient features of street railways, light, elevated and underground railways, and 'moveable lines'.

445 CHATTAWAY, E. D. Railways: their capital and dividends, with statistics of their working in Great Britain and Ireland, etc., etc.; being a second volume to Mr. [R. M.] Stephenson's work on railways in this series. *London*, 1855–56. pp. vii, 133. BM
Cover title, 'Rudimentary treatise on railways'.

446 STEPHENSON, R. Address of Robert Stephenson . . . on his election as president of the Institution of Civil Engineers, Session 1855–56. *London*, 1856. pp. 34.   BM
Excerpt, *Min. Proc. I.C.E.*, vol. 15.
General review of British railway development.

447 GALTON, D. Statistics of railways in the United Kingdom. [An analysis of a report by Capt. Douglas Galton presented to the Lords of the Privy Council for Trade on Railways, for the year 1858.] *In* 'A Treatise on the steam engine.' By J. Bourne. 5th edn. *London*, 1861. pp. 482.   BM

448 WILLIAMS, E. L. Reasons why the Oxford, Worcester & Wolverhampton Railway Company should neither be allowed to abandon their Diglis branch nor obtain the control of the Worcester and Birmingham Canal. *Worcester*, [1858.] pp. 4.   ICE

449 ADAMS, W. B. Roads and rails and their sequences, physical and moral. *London*, 1862. pp. xii, 372.   BM
General and rather discursive observations.

450 ADAMS, W. B. Railways: their permanent way and rolling stock. *London*, 1864. pp. 12.   BM

451 LLOYD, J. T. Lloyd's Numerical and Alphabetical Index to the railways in actual operation in the British Isles up to January 1867, with the number and official name of each railway, and its total length, the names of the extreme terminal stations on each railway line, alphabetically and numerically arranged, to accompany Lloyd's County & Railway Map of the British Isles. *London*, 1867. pp. 25.   pc

452 NORTH EASTERN RLY. Summary of railway statistics for the years 1859 . . . 1865, including all the railways in the United Kingdom. Compiled from the Returns of the Board of Trade. *York*, 1867 (a fold. table).   NCL

453 HAUCHECORNE, G. Tableaux statistiques des chemins de fer de l'Europe en exploitation pendant l'exercice 1866. *Cologne*, 1868. pp. 45.   ICE
'From official sources.'
IV partie, section G, 'Grande-Bretagne et Irlande'.

454 RONEY, C. P. Rambles on railways . . . *London*, 1868. pp. xii, 519, with diagrs., maps & appendices.   BM
A very detailed general survey of contemporary railways.

455 FRANCE—MINISTERE DE L'AGRICULTURE, DU COMMERCE ET DES TRAVAUX PUBLICS—DIRECTION GÉNÉRALE DES PONTS ET CHAUSSÉES ET DES CHEMINS DE FER. Chemins de fer de l'Europe: résultats généraux de l'exploitation. *Paris*, 1869. pp. 115.   BM
pp. 32–47, tables showing financial position of all railways of British Isles, 1862 and 1863 (in francs).
pp. 96–103, the same, for 1863 and 1864.

456 FIGUIER, L. Les Merveilles de la science; ou, Description populaire des inventions modernes. *Paris*, 1867–70. 4 vols.   BM
vol. 1, pp. 262–398, 'La locomotive et les chemins de fer'. Includes British railways.

457 GILLESPIE, W. M. A Manual of the Principles and Practice of Road-making,
a   comprising the location, construction and improvement of roads . . . and railroads. 2nd edn. *New York*, 1848. pp. 344.   BM
pp. 241–312, 'Railways'. Current theories and experiments described, including an account of the atmospheric system.
—— 3rd edn. *N.Y.*, 1849. pp.3 72. UL(GL)
—— 8th. *N.Y.*, 1855. pp. 372.   BM

—— 9th. *N.Y.*, 1868. pp. 372.   BM
—— 10th. *N.Y. & Chicago*, [1871.] pp. 464.   BM

458 SCHWABE, H. Étude sur les chemins de fer anglais d'après des notes recueillies dans un voyage en Angleterre . . . traduit de l'allemand par A. Huberti et A. Habets; avec une carte des chemins de fer de Londres et des environs. *Paris*, 1872. pp. xx, 259, with statistical tables.   BM
pp. 47–102, railways in London.

459 BAYNES, J. A. Railways in the U.K. and in India. *Hampstead*, 1873. pp. 4.   ICE
Reprinted from *The Times* of 1st Sept. 1873. A statistical summary.

460 FRANQUET DE FRANQUEVILLE, A. C. Les Chemins de fer en France et en Angleterre. *Paris*, 1873. pp. 24.   BM

461 BAYNES, J. A. Memorandum on the cost, traffic and working of the railways in the United Kingdom and in India for the year 1873 compared with 1872. *London*, 1874. pp. 4.   ICE
Signed 'J. A. Baynes, Bombay, Baroda & Central India Rly. . . . London.'

462 BAYNES, J. A. Memorandum on the cost, traffic and working of the railways in the United Kingdom and in India for the year 1874 compared with 1873. *London*, 1875. pp. 8.   ICE

463 FRANQUET DE FRANQUEVILLE, A. C. Du régime des travaux publics en Angleterre. *Paris*, 1874. 4 vols.
Largely concerned with British railways and their legislation.
—— 2e edn. *Paris*, 1875. 4 vols.   BM

464 CLARK, D. K. Railways. *In* 'British manufacturing industries', by G. P. Bevan. *London*, 1876. vol. 9, pp. 168–214.   BM

465 STUERMER, G. Geschichte der Eisenbahnen: 2. Theil, Statistische Darstellung der Entwickelung sowie der Verkehrs und finanziellen Verhältnisse sämmtlicher Eisenbahn-Netze der Erde während der Jahre 1871 bis 1875. *Bromberg*, 1876. pp. 79. PO
pp. [31]–35, Grossbritannien.

466 MALEZIEUX, E. Les Chemins de fer anglais en 1873: rapport de mission par M. Malezieux. *Paris*, 1874. pp. 155, with 2 la. fold. maps.   BM
Issued by the Min. des Travaux Publics. Also in *Annales des Ponts et Chaussées*.
—— 2e edn. *Paris*, 1874. pp. 179.

467 FLEMING, W. The Index to our Railway System and Leading Lines: a clear and comprehensive analysis of the capital, nature, extent and weight of traffic, working expenditure, profits, mileage, etc. for the year 1875 and the years 1874 and 1871 for com-

parison, whereby the condition and prospects of railway property in each division of the United Kingdom, and of each line in itself and relatively to other lines can be viewed in detail and sound opinions derived therefrom: a guide to investors, capitalists and stockbrokers, an aid to railway directors, and managers . . . a reliable record to statisticians and others interested in railway enterprise. *London*, [1876.] pp. 15, with 2 la. fold. tables.　　　　　　　　　　　　BM
　Includes Irish railways, 'deduced from Board of Trade returns'.

—— 2nd number. *London*, [1878.] pp. 93.
　　　　　　　　　　　　　　　　　BM
　Results for 1876 with a fuller comparative analysis than 1st edn.

—— 3rd number. *London*, [1879.] pp. 125.
　　　　　　　　　　　　　　　　　BM
　For 1877, 1878 and 1879.

—— 4th number. *London*, [1880.] pp. 135.
　　　　　　　　　　　　　　　　　BM
　For 1879, 1880 and the first six months of 1880.

468 SCHWABE, H.　Über das englische Eisenbahnwesen: Reisestudien von H. Schwabe; nebst eirner Karte. *Berlin*, 1871. pp. 133, with bibliogr. notes & a fold. map.　　BM
　pp. 25–47, stations; pp. 48–54, London underground railways.
—— Neue Folge. *Wien*, 1877. pp. 208,
c 'mit einem Atlas enthaltend 16 Blatt Zeichungen'.　　　　　　　　　　　　BM
　This much enlarged edition has a chronology of the growth of lengths of line from 1825 to 1875; pp. 9–96, English stations; pp. 97–130, London underground railways. The atlas contains large folding maps and plans of stations, mostly in London.

469 FERRARIS, M. Note sulle ferrovie Inglese *Rome*, 1881. pp. 110.　　　　　　ICE
　Description of the economy and working of railways in the British Isles.

470 COHN, G.　Die englische Eisenbahnpolitik der letzten zehn Jahre, 1873–1883. *Leipzig*, 1883. pp. viii, 196.　　　　　　　BM
　A revised edition of part of his *Untersuchungen über die englische Eisenbahnpolitik* (1874–5) with index for both works. *See* 31.

471 RUSSELL, H. V.　The financial position of British railways for the second half-year of 1883. [1883.] s.sh.　　　　　　NLC

472 EASON, C.　Manual of Financial, Railway, Agricultural and other Statistics, for politicians, economists and investors. *London*, [1884.] pp. 91.　　　　　　　BM
　pp. 19–34, railway statistics for 1882–3.

473 RUSSELL, H. V.　The financial position of British railways on 4th May 1884. 1884. s.sh.　　　　　　　　　　　　NLC

474 SEARGEANT, L. J.　The English railway system. *Chicago*, 1885. pp. 9.　　LC
　Reprinted from the *Railway Review*.

475 FRANK, E.　Der Betrieb auf den englischen Bahnen; mit sechs Tafeln. *Wien*, 1886. pp. 91, with illus. & fold. maps.　　BM
　A record of observations on English railway working made on a visit in 1885.

* 476 ALL about our railways. *London*, [1887.] pp. viii, 184.　　　　　　　　BM
　A miscellany on railways and their working.

477 DORSEY, E. B.　English and American railroads compared . . . *New York*, 1887. pp. 142.　　　　　　　　　　　BM
　Excerpt, American Society of Civil Engineers *Transactions*, vol. 15, 1886.
　Statistical analyses of all aspects of railways; sixty tables and four folding plates. (An edition of 78 pages with a 58-page supplement was published in New York in 1886.)

478 ROUS-MARTEN, C.　Notes on the railways of Great Britain. *Wellington, N.Z.*, 1887. pp. 20.　　　　　　　　　　　　LSE
　Addressed to the Minister for Public Works, New Zealand. Notes from records of an inspection recently made. Describes engineering, locomotives, practical working and maintenance, including some unusual observations such as painting of equipment, etc.

479 Les CHEMINS de fer de l'Europe en exploitation: nomenclature des compagnies; lignes composant leurs réseaux respectifs, etc. *Paris*, 1888. pp. vi, 131.　　BM
　pp. 73–96, 'Grande Bretagne et Irlande'. An alphabetical list of railways in operation in 1884.

480 MARSHALL, W. P.　Modern railways and railway travelling. *Birmingham*, 1888. pp. [183]–204.　　　　　　　　　　ICE
　Reprint, *Proceedings of the Birmingham Philosophical Society*, vol. 6, pt. 2.

481 ACWORTH, W. M.　English and American railways: a comparison and a contrast. *In* 'Compendium of Transportation Theories', Kensington Series, First Book; edited by C. C. McCain. *Washington*, 1893. pp. 139–47.　　　　　　　　　　BM

482 PATTINSON, J. P.　British railways; their passenger services, rolling stock, locomotives, gradients, and express speeds . . . *London*, 1893. pp. xiv, 249, with 35 plates.　　BM

483 SCHWEIGER-LERCHENFELD, A. von. Vom rollenden Flügelrad. *Wien*, 1894. 2 vols. (pp. 783), with many illus.　　　　BM
　General description of railways in various countries, including Gt. Britain.

484 HEAD, J.　American rail- and tram-ways. *Middlesbrough*, 1895. pp. 64, with illus.
　　　　　　　　　　　　　　　　　ICE
　Comparison between British and American railways.

485 MACDERMOTT, E. R.　Railways. *London* 1904. pp. vii, 197.　　MANCHESTER PL

486 UNITED STATES OF AMERICA—DEPART-MENT OF COMMERCE AND LABOR—BUREAU OF STATISTICS. Transportation routes and systems of the world. Development of steam-carrying power on land and sea, 1800 to 1905. *Washington: Government Printing Office*, 1905. pp. 1549–59, with la. fold. map.   IT
    Reprint, *Monthly Summary of Commerce and Finance* for November 1905.
    pp. 1550–1, comparative statistics for railways in various countries for 1903.

487 DIACOMIDIS, J. D. Statistical tables of the working of railways in various countries up to the year 1904 . . . 2nd edn. *Cairo*, 1906. pp. 84.   BM
    pp. 17–23, 'Details for 24 railways in Gt. Britain & Ireland obtained from . . . the Board of Trade for the year 1904'.

488 BUREAU OF RAILWAY ECONOMICS [Washington]. Comparative railway statistics of the United States, the United Kingdom, France and Germany, for 1900 and 1909. *Washington*, 1911. pp. 47. [*Bulletin*, no. 24.]   BRE

489 FAY, S. Presidential address. (London School of Economics, Railway Students' Union, October 24, 1911.) *London*, 1911. pp. 8.   LSE
    The future of railways: a forecast.

490 GRINLING, C. H. The ways of our railways . . . *London*, 1905. pp. xvi, 338, with 191 illus., tables & diagrams.   BM
    —— new edn. *London*, 1911. pp. 350.   RC

491 FRAHM, J. Das englische Eisenbahn-wesen; mit 353 Text Figuren und 1 Eisenbahn-Karte. *Berlin*, 1911. pp. 323.   BM
    General description of contemporary English railways. Illustrations include drawings of railway equipment and buildings.

492 LONDON MUNICIPAL SOCIETY—DEPARTMENT OF SOCIAL ECONOMICS. Railway statistics for the United Kingdom, 1910. *London*, 1912. pp. 16. [*Statistical & Other Memoranda*. Second series, no. 4.]   LSE
    A summary of Board of Trade Returns for 1910.

493 COLLIER, R. A. H. The railways of Great Britain. *London*, 1913. pp. viii, 303, with 18 plates.   BM
    —— another edn. *London*, [1926.] pp. 254, with 27 plates & 3 la. fold. gradient profiles.   BM

494 MITTON, G. E. The Book of the Railway; with 12 illustrations in colour by Allan Stewart. *London*, 1909. pp. ix, 356.   BM
    An introductory work on railway working of this period.
    —— [2nd edn.] *London*, 1914.   RC
    A re-issue with 9 illustrations.

B 4   1914–1918   RAILWAYS IN THE BRITISH ISLES DURING THE FIRST WORLD WAR

495 FELL, A. The Channel Tunnel and food supplies in time of war. *London*, 1913. pp. 11.   BM

496 FELL, A. The position of the Channel Tunnel question in May 1914: statement on behalf of the House of Commons Channel Tunnel Committee. *London*, 1914. pp. 19.   BM

497 GOBEY, F. E. British and Continental ambulance trains supplied to the War Office by the Lancashire & Yorkshire Railway. *Horwich; Horwich Railway Mechanics' Institute Engineering & Scientific Club* (*L. & Y. Rly.*), [1916.] pp. 45, with 23 plates.   BR
    Lecture, 11 January 1916.

498 JOINT COMMITTEE OF THE BRITISH RED CROSS SOCIETY AND THE ORDER OF ST. JOHN. Hospital trains: how they are saving soldiers' lives. [1916.]   LSE

499 RECORDS of railway interests in the War. *London: Railway News*, 1915–17. 4 pts., with many illus., diagrams & statistical tables.   BM

    Contains a great variety of news items, among which are many concerning hospital trains.

500 BRITISH railways under war conditions. (Confidential. Dec. 12, 1917.) pp. 73. *Typescript.*   LSE

501 BUREAU OF RAILWAY ECONOMICS [Washington]. Experience of British railways under war control. *Washington*, 1917. pp. 3. [*Leaflet* no. 34, April 26, 1917.]   LC

502 MACKENZIE, F. A. British railways and the War. *London*, 1917. pp. 31.   BM
    Includes post-war problems.

503 WEBB, S. J. How to pay for the War: being ideas offered to the Chancellor of the Exchequer by the Fabian Research Department; edited by Sidney Webb. *Westminster: Fabian Society*, [1916.] pp. xv, 278, with bibliogr. notes.   BM
    pp. 51–111, A public service of railway and canal transport.
    —— 2nd edn. *London*, 1917. pp. xv, 278. xii.   BM

504 DIXON, F. H. *and* PARMELEE, J. H. War administration of the railways in the United States and Great Britain. *New York*, 1918. pp. x, 155. [*Carnegie Endowment for International Peace. Preliminary Economic Studies of the War.*]   BM
pp. 71–127 and supplementary chapters, Great Britain.
—— another edn. *N.Y.*, 1919. pp. vi, 203.   LSE

505 RAILWAY EXECUTIVE COMMITTEE. British ambulance trains on the Continent. [*London*, 1918.] pp. 8[9], with 10 illus. & fold. diagram of complete train of 16 coaches.   BR

506 FRIENDS AMBULANCE UNIT—NO. 17 AMBULANCE TRAIN. Lines of communication: a souvenir volume: being pages from the Train Magazines which were published whilst on active service together with descriptions of ambulance train life. *London*, 1919. pp. 124, with 27 illus.   LSE
Voluntary medical service by British Quakers and others in France during the Great War, 1914–1918.

507 GATTIE, A. W. How to solve the food problem. *London*, 1918. pp. 10,[2.]
Reprinted from *The Nineteenth Century and After*, April 1918.

508 HORNIMAN, R. How to make the railways pay for the War; or, The transport problem solved . . . *London*, 1916. pp. xx, 348, with 22 illus., & bibliogr. notes.   BM
Urgency of economic reforms and the need for a central clearing house in London.
—— 2nd edn. *London*, 1917. pp. xx, 340.   BM
—— 3rd. *London*, 1919. pp. xvi, 375. BM

509 ST. PAUL'S CATHEDRAL. Divine service in memory of those railwaymen who laid down their lives for their country in the Great War, 1914–1918. Wednesday, May 14, 1919. [*London*:] *Railway Companies Association*, [1919.] pp. 152.   BM
pp. 13–152, 'Names of railwaymen . . . who have died . . .' alphabetically arranged under companies.

510 DARROCH, G. R. S. Deeds of a great railway: a record of the enterprise and achievements of the London & North Western Rly. Co. during the Great War . . . *London*, 1920. pp. xvi, 217, with 18 plates & 22 illus. BM

511 RAILWAY GAZETTE. Special War Transportation Number. *London*, 21 Sept., 1920. pp. 80, 160. (pp. 49–96, illus.)   IT

512 AZCARATE FLOREZ, P. de. La Guerra y los servicios publicos de caracter industrial. I, el regimen ferroviario inglés y la guerra. *Madrid*, 1921. pp. 140, with bibliogr. notes.   BM

513 PRATT, E. A. British railways and the Great War: organisation, efforts, difficulties and achievements. *London*, 1921. 2 vols. (pp. xx, 1194), with 73 illus., and 27 maps & diagrams.   BM

514 MOORE, G. A. The birth and early days of our hospital trains in France, August 1914 to April 1915. (By 'Wagon Lit'.) *London*, 1921. pp. 19, with illus. on front cover.   BM
—— *London*, 1922. pp. 24, with 5 illus. (by G. A. Moore).   RC

515 GREAT WESTERN RLY. A few observations on railways. (By Felix J. C. Pole.) *London*, [1927.] pp. 21.   LSE
Railways and their difficulties during the Great War and since the amalgamations of 1923.

516 FAY, S. The War Office at war. *London*: *Hutchinson*, 1937. pp. 288.   BM
Includes accounts of the work of the Railway Executive Committee.

B 5   1918–1923   POST-WAR RECOVERY AND THE PERIOD ENDING WITH THE 'BIG FOUR' AMALGAMATIONS OF 1923

517 The FUTURE of English railways. [*London*, 1917.] pp. 84–103.   BM
Reprinted from the *Edinburgh Review*, January 1917.

518 ASPINALL, J. A. F. Address . . . as president of the Institution of Civil Engineers, 5 November, 1918. *London*, 1918. pp. 25.   ICE
Railways and the immediate future.

519 GATTIE, A. W. A statement made by Mr. A. W. Gattie to the Select Committee of the House of Commons appointed to examine into the conditions of transport in the United Kingdom (to which is appended a list of defects and inaccuracies of the Board of Trade Railway Returns for . . . 1913, with notes). *London*: *Transport Reform Society*, 1918. pp. 17.   BM

520 RAILWAY NATIONALISATION SOCIETY. Nationalisation of Railways Bill. *London*, 1918. pp. 16. [*R.N.S. Pamphlet*, no. 14.]   LSE
Introductory notes, with the text of the Bill.
—— another edn. *London*, 1919. pp. 15.   TUC

521 ACWORTH, W. M. Historical sketch of state railway ownership. *London*, 1920. pp. xv, 104.   BM
Review of nationalization of foreign railways and opinion as to its application to British railways in the post-war period.

522 BUREAU OF RAILWAY ECONOMICS [Washington]. Comparative railway statistics, United States and foreign countries, 1912. *Washington*, 1915. pp. 78. [*Consecutive Series*, no. 83.]   LSE
pp. 63–4, Basic tables for U.K. railways in 1912, compiled from official Board of Trade Returns.
pp. 65–78, Comparative tables.
—— another edn. for 1913. *Washington*, 1916. pp. 78. [*Consecutive Series*, no. 100; *Miscellaneous Series*, no. 25.]   IT
—— another edn. for 1916. *Washington*, 1920. pp. 66. [*Consecutive Series*, no. 170; *Miscellaneous Series*, no. 35.]   IT

523 ASSOCIATED SOCIETY OF LOCOMOTIVE ENGINEERS & FIREMEN *and* RAILWAY CLERKS ASSOCIATION. Railway reorganisation: memorandum on the proposals of the Minister of Transport as to the future organisation of transport undertakings in Great Britain and their relation to the State, as outlined in . . . Cmd. 787. *London*, 1921. pp. 7.   TUC

524 BANBURY, F. G. Railways Bill. Memorandum by the chairman of the Great Northern Railway Co. *London*, 12 May 1921. pp. 4.   LSE
Addressed to all proprietors of the G.N. 'Railways should be handed back.' Amalgamations to be carried out, but by private arrangement between companies.

525 RAILWAY NATIONALISATION SOCIETY. Memorandum on the Railways Bill, 1921. *London*, [1921.] pp. 8. [*R.N.S. Pamphlet*, no. 17.]   LSE
Summary of the Bill's proposals, with observations and criticisms. Resolution, complete unification of railways.

526 THOMAS, J. H. The Red Light on the railways. *London*, 1921. pp. 143[144].   BM
The case for nationalization. Includes (pp. 138–44) Ministry of Transport's outline of proposals as to the future organisation of transport.

527 AGGS, W. H. *and* KNOWLES, G. W. Handbook on Railways: being the Railways Act, 1921; with full notes and an introduction and index. *London*, 1922. pp. 108.   BM

528 AZCARATE FLOREZ, P. de. La Guerra y los servicios publicos de caracter industrial. IV, la nueva ley inglesa de ferrocarriles. *Madrid*, 1922. pp. 34, with bibliogr. notes.
                                              BM

529 KENYON, T. A. Railway statistics in Great Britain. *Manchester: Manchester Statistical Society*, 1922. pp. 63–89, 15, with 15 statistical diagrams for 1921.   BM
An outline of the broad features of the statistical returns made by railway companies to the Board of Trade.

530 MANCHESTER GUARDIAN *newspaper*. Railway Supplement. *Manchester*, 13 March 1922. pp. XII.   LSE
The Grouping of British railways. By A. Watson.

531 RAILWAY CLERKS ASSOCIATION. The Railways Act, 1921: notes and observations mainly for the information of the staff employed in the railway service of Great Britain. *London*, 1922. pp. 97. [By A. G. Walkden.]   BM
—— 3rd edn. *London*, [1922.] pp. 97. LSE

532 ROYLE, R. W. The Railways Act, 1921. *Manchester*, 1924. pp. 20.   BM
A companion to the Act with simplified interpretation of parts and sections.

533 SAMS, J. G. B. How to reform our railways: a discussion on cheapening transport. *London*, 1923. pp. 62.   BM
Criticisms of the Grouping scheme, 1921 (1923).

534 SOMMERFIELD, V. The Railway Grouping scheme: a handbook for stockholders and investors. *London: Financial News*, [1923.] pp. 36.   BM
Tables showing constituent and subsidiary companies with their joint undertakings and principal officers.

535 CAMPBELL, C. D. British railways in boom and depression: an essay in trade fluctuations and their effects, 1878–1930. *London*, 1932. pp. 125, with bibliogr. notes.
                                              LSE
Includes the amalgamations of 1921 (1923).

536 LEAGUE OF NATIONS—ORGANISATION FOR COMMUNICATIONS AND TRANSIT. Transport problems which arose from the War of 1914–1918 and the work of restoration undertaken in this field by the League of Nations. *Geneva*, July 1945. pp. 52. [*Publications Series VIII. Transit.* 1945. VIII. 2.]
                                              BM
A guide to anticipated post-war transport problems.

537 ALDCROFT, D. H. The decontrol of British shipping and railways after the First World
b   War. *In* 'Journal of Transport History', vol. 5, no. 2, November 1961. pp. 89–104, with 115 bibliogr. notes.   BM

B 6 1921 – 1939 THE 'BIG FOUR' AMALGAMATIONS OF 1923 (Railways Act, 1921) AND RAILWAYS DURING THE 1920's AND 1930's

For schedule and list of amalgamations see Appendix I

538 TIMES *newspaper*. Railway Number, August 15, 1921. (no. 42,799.) *London*, 1921. pp. xxiv.   LSE
The Grouping and the future of the railways.

539 MANCHESTER GUARDIAN *newspaper*. Railway Supplement. *Manchester*, 13 March, 1922.   LSE
Progress and possibilities of electrification. By W. E. Simnett.

540 MATHIESON, F. C. & SONS, *publishers*. Railway stocks officially quoted on the Stock Exchange on the last day of 1922; with prices, yields, highest and lowest for two years, dividends, etc. *London*, 2 January, 1923. pp. [4.]   BM

541 SHERRINGTON, C. E. R. A comparison of the probable consequences of the United States 'Transportation Act', 1920, and the British 'Railways Act', 1921. A paper read at the Economic Section of the British Association, Liverpool, September 13, 1923. [*Oxford*, 1923.] pp. 16.   LSE

542 SMITH, H. B. A. The re-organization of railways in Great Britain: its progress and prospects. *Washington: Government Printing Office*, 1923. pp. 28, with 12 tables of official statistics. [*Department of Commerce, Trade Information Bulletin*, no. 79.]   BM
Supplement to *Commerce Reports*, issued by the Bureau of Foreign and Domestic Commerce.

543 SHERRINGTON, C. E. R. Some economic results of the British Railways Act of 1921. pp. [227]–239.   PC
Reprint, *American Economic Review*, vol. 14, no. 2, June 1924.

544 STEPHENSON, W. T. Communications. *London*, 1924. pp. 180. [*Resources of the Empire Series*.]   BM
pp. 73–88, Railways of the U.K. A general account of the present position.

545 GOOD, E. T. Fair play for railways: some unacknowledged facts. *London: Great Western Railway*, 1925. pp. 12. [*Great Western Pamphlets*, no. 14.]   LSE
Reprinted from *The Financial Review of Reviews*, April–June 1925.
A defence against unfair and irresponsible criticism.

546 COLLIER, R. A. H. [Lord Monkswell.] The railways of Great Britain. *London*, 1913. pp. viii, 303, with 18 plates.   BM
—— another edn. *London*, [1926.] pp. 254, with 27 plates & 3 la. gradient profiles.   BM

547 GREAT WESTERN RLY. General Strike, May 1926. *London*, [1926.] pp. 123.   BR
A detailed record of the strike with reproductions of documents, correspondence, statements of various bodies, notices displayed by the G.W.R. and numerous statistical tables showing the effects of the strike on various aspects of G.W.R. traffic and working.

548 GREAT WESTERN RLY. A few observations on railways. (By Felix J. C. Pole.) *London*, [1927.] pp. 21.   LSE
Railways and their difficulties during the Great War and since the amalgamations of 1923.

549 'MERCURY.' The fascination of our railways: a series of instructive railway talks for boys. *London*, 1927. pp. 115, with 37 plates.   BM
General description of contemporary railways.

550 ALLEN, C. J. The Steel Highway . . . *London*, 1928. 2 parts in 1 vol. (pp. xii, 132: 144, with plates.)   BM
An introductory description of the modern railway. Part 1, 'Railway planning and making'. Part 2, 'Trains and their control'. Also published separately:
—— Railway planning and making. *London*, 1928. pp. vii, 132, with plates.   BM
—— Trains and their control. *London*, 1928. pp. xv, 144, with plates.   BM

551 BELL, R. The railways in 1927. *London*, 1928. pp. 19.   IT
Paper, L.N.E.R. (Lond.) Lecture & Debating Society, 13 March 1928.

552 KIDD, H. C. A new era for British railways: a study of the Railways Act, 1921, from an American standpoint, with special reference to amalgamation. *London*, 1929. pp. 158, with 4 maps in text.   BM

553 WOOD, W. V. *and* SHERRINGTON, C. E. R. The railway industry of Great Britain, 1927. *London: Royal Economic Society*, January 1929. pp. 26[27], with 34 tables. [*Memorandum* no. 11.]   BM
General situation since 1923; financial results and miscellaneous statistics, with 34 tables.
Also issued by The London & Cambridge Economic Service, London School of Economics, as *Special Memorandum* no. 27. January 1929. pp. 26[27].   BM

554 ALLEN, C. J. Railways of today: their evolution, equipment and operation . . . with exhaustive index and illustrated with 36 coloured plates . . . 200 photographic illustrations . . . *London*, 1929. pp. xvi, 400.   BM
Plates include company heraldry.
—— [2nd] edn. 'with Supplement'. *London*, 1930. pp. xvi, 400, 8.   PC

555 INTERNATIONAL UNION OF RAILWAYS. The main line railways of Great Britain, 1923–30: a study by the Railway Research Service based on official figures. *Westminster*, 1931. pp. 46, with 57 tables. French and German translations appeared in *Bulletin*, no. 4 of the I.U. of R., April 1931. BM

A detailed statistical survey of railway finance, mileage, operation, staff and accidents.

556 DAILY EXPRESS *newspaper*—FINANCIAL INFORMATION BUREAU. British railway stocks and the investor. *London*, [1932.] pp. 33. [*Daily Express Aids to Investors.*] BM

An outline of the financial state of British railways with a review of economic factors which have caused a decline, the present position and future prospects. With financial tables of the main line companies for 1929, 1930 and 1931.

557 TIMES *newspaper*. The railways: six special articles together with two leading articles, reprinted from 'The Times', May 12, 13, 14, 16, 17, & 18, 1932. *London*, [1932.] pp. 21. BR

Current problems, especially road rivalry.

558 FENELON, K. G. British railways since the War. 1933. pp. 57, with 42 tables. IT

Paper, Royal Statistical Society, 21 March, and in *Journal of the R.S.S.*, vol. 96, pt. 3, 1933.

559 HALLSWORTH, H. M. The rail transport industry. *In* 'Britain in depression: a record of British industries since 1929.' British Association for the Advancement of Science. *London*, 1935. pp. [189]–210, with 10 tables. BM

560 NEWLANDS, A. The British railways . . . *London: Longmans*, 1936. pp. 134. BM

'An attempt to dissect and analyse the cost of working the British railways for one year (1933) by the use of a common denominator, and to co-relate such cost with the volume of work done and the revenue earned.'

561 BRITISH RAILWAYS PRESS OFFICE. British railways plans for 1937. *London*, 1937. pp. 2. [*Press Release.*] BM

562 LONDON PASSENGER TRANSPORT BOARD. The Coronation, 1937: a record of services on the Underground. *London*, 1937. pp. 19, with illus., charts & diagrams. BM

A souvenir brochure issued to staff.

563 WAY, R. B. *and* GREEN, N. D. Railways. *London: Wells, Gardner & Co.*, 1937. pp. 155, with many illus. BM

All aspects of modern railway locomotive and train working described.

564 GREENLEAF, H. *and* HAYDEN, H. Britain's railways. *London: Frederick Muller*, 1938, pp. xii, 232, with plates & diagrams. BM

565 RAILWAY RESEARCH SERVICE. The main-line railways of Great Britain, 1923–1937. *Westminster*, June 1938. pp. 60. 'Private. For official use only.' Detailed statistical review in fifty-three tables.

566 STEVENS, W. J. The future of British railways: a plea for co-operation . . . *London: P. S. King & Son*, 1938. pp. xiii, 101. BM

Co-operation between all railway interests essential to ensure successful future of railways. pp. 62–end, financial position of the four main line companies, with tables, 1929–1936.

567 WATERS, W. L. Rationalization of British railways; presented before the American Society of Mechanical Engineers, Railroad Division, Metropolitan Section, New York, May 11, 1938. *New York*, 1938. pp. 9. TUC

A study of the results of the 1921 amalgamations upon railway economy, management and operation.

568 FENELON, K. G. British railways today. *London: Nelson*, 1939. pp. 187, with plates. [*Discussion Books*, no. 39.] BM

Includes chapters on state control, railways and the public, railway operation, finance, and railway *versus* roads.

569 COMING of Age of Railway Grouping: G.W.R., L.M.S.R., L.N.E.R., S.R. *London Railway Gazette*, 1944. pp. iii, 64, with portraits of senior railway officials. BM

A review of British railways since 1923.

B 7 1939–1945 RAILWAYS IN THE BRITISH ISLES DURING THE SECOND WORLD WAR

570 BEVIN, E. Transport in war-time: address . . . to the Members of the Institute of Transport . . . January 8, 1940. pp. 9. *Reproduced typescript.* TUC

571 LONDON, MIDLAND & SCOTTISH RLY. Air raid precautions: special instructions for the working of railways. November 1940. pp. 35. BR

572 ALLEN, C. J. Our railways in war-time. [*London*, 1942.] pp 31, with illus. BM

573 MINISTRY OF WAR TRANSPORT. Transport goes to war. *London*, 1942. pp. 79 [81], with illus. BM

574 YOUNG, P. C. Transportation and total war. *London: Faber & Faber*, 1942. pp. 144, with 7 diagrams & a map.

The need for maximum efficiency and co-ordination.

*575 BRITISH RAILWAYS PRESS OFFICE. Facts about British railways in wartime. *London,* 1940. pp. 32, with illus.   BM
—— *London,* 1941. pp. 43.   BM
—— *London,* 1942. pp. 39[40].   BM
—— *London,* 1943. pp. 64.   BM

576 CURNOCK, G. C. Heroes of road and rail: a book of the Great War in Britain, fully illustrated with 47 contemporary photographs. *London: Simpkin,* 1943. pp. 98, with 38 plates.   BM

577 EMETT, R. Engines, Aunties and Others: a book of curious happenings. *London: Faber & Faber,* 1943. pp. [60.]   BM
Humorous drawings, mostly concerning railways under war-time conditions.

578 HIND, J. R. The British railways can 'take it'. *Dundee & London: Valentine,* 1943. pp. [24.]   BM
Plates with brief descriptions showing war-time conditions and damage on the railways.

579 RAILWAY posters and the War. *London: Railway Gazette,* 1939–1943. 6 parts.   BR
Reproductions of notices relating to alterations in services displayed to passengers, including, for comparison, some from the Great War, 1914–18.

580 SHERRINGTON, C. E. R. Transportation problems in Great Britain. *In* 'The Annals of the American Academy of Political & Social Science', vol. 230, Nov. 1943. pp. 134–40.   PC

581 TAMBIMUTTU, J. M. The Man in the Street. *In* 'Talking to India . . . a selection of English language broadcasts, edited . . . by George Orwell.' *London: Allen & Unwin,* [1943.] pp. 35–9.   LSE
Air-raid sheltering in tube stations as a social feature of war-time London.

582 BRITISH RAILWAYS PRESS OFFICE. British railways in peace and war. *London,* 1944. pp. 72, with illus.   LSE

583 COMING of Age of Railway Grouping: G.W.R., L.M.S.R., L.N.E.R., S.R. *London: Railway Gazette,* 1944. pp. iii, 64, with plates.   BM
Railways since 1923.

584 KNOX, C. The Un-beaten Track. *London: Cassell,* 1944. pp. 199, with plates.   BM
The Great Western Rly. during the War. Appendix contains lists of officials and of awards to staff.

585 MCGIVERN, C. Junction 'X': a dramatisation of events that occurred at a vital cross-roads on the path to victory on a certain day in 1944 between the hours of 10 a.m. and 10 p.m. A broadcast, showing how British railways are successfully carrying out their vital and gigantic war task in conditions of unparalleled difficulty. Written and produced by Cecil McGivern, with the full co-operation of the L.M.S., L.N.E., G.W. and Southern Railways. *London,* June 1944. pp. 55, with illus.   BM
—— 2nd edn. *London,* Nov. 1944. pp. 55.   BM

586 [LEE, C. E.] The Railway Executive Committee and its headquarters: a description of government control of railways in wartime, and of the preparation of adequately protected deep-level headquarters in a disused London tube station for the staff to work, eat and sleep. *London: Railway Gazette,* 1944. pp. 19, with fold. plan & illus. & plans in text.   IT
Reprint, *Railway Gazette,* 17 & 24 Nov., 1944.

587 BROWN, A. Dunkirk and the Great Western: a plain and authentic account of the experiences of some Great Western steamships during the evacuation of the Expeditionary Force from Dunkirk and Western France. *London: G.W. Rly.,* [1945.] pp. 39, with illus., map & a list of ships.   BM

588 [DOW, G.] It can now be revealed: more about British railways in peace and war. *London: British Railways Press Office,* 1945. pp. 64, with illus.   BM

589 BISHOP, F. C. Queen Mary of the Iron Road: the autobiography of an engine-driver. *London: Jarrolds,* 1946. pp. 150.   BM
Includes an account of the L.M.S. Rly. during the war.

590 DARWIN, B. R. M. War on the line: the story of the Southern Railway in war-time. *London: Southern Rly.,* 1946. pp. iv, 215, with illus. (4 col.) on plates, tables & a map.   BM

591 BELL, R. History of the British railways during the War, 1939–1945. *London: Railway Gazette,* 1946. pp. 291.   BM
A detailed record with many reference tables, data and lists of personnel, etc., in appendices, pp. 253–85.

592 NASH, G. C. The LMS at war. *London: L.M.S. Rly.,* 1946. pp. 87, with plates (some col.).   BM

593 NEWTON, C. H. British railways during the War. Paper presented to the Fifth Pan-American Railway Congress, Buenos Aires, 1946. *London,* [1946.] pp. 29.   LSE

594 WILDISH, G. N. Engines of War: an illustrated booklet of the locomotives and

freight cars of the British Ministry of Supply and of the U.S. Army Transportation Corps. *London: Ian Allan*, 1946. pp. 24, with 23 illus.   BM
Descriptions, notes and lists.

595 CRUMP, N. By rail to victory: the story of the L.N.E.R. in wartime. [*London:*] *L.N.E. Rly.*, 1947. pp. xii, 196, with plates & a map.   BM

*596 GRAVES, C. London Transport carried on: an account of London at war, 1939–1945. *London: L.P.T.B.*, 1947. pp. 95[97], with many illus.   IT

597 JOHN, Evan, *pseud.* [E. J. Simpson.] Time table for victory: a brief and popular account of the railways and railway-owned dockyards of Great Britain and Northern Ireland during the Six Years War, 1939–45. *London,* 1947. pp. 268, with maps, diagrams and illus.   BM
'Published by the British railways.'

598 RAILWAY CLEARING HOUSE. Tables of statistical returns relating to the railways of Great Britain, years 1938 to 1946. *London,* [1947.] pp. 34.   IME

599 BRITISH RAILWAYS. British railways in war time. [*London,* 1948?] pp. 32.   BM
Illustrations with captions.

600 RAILWAY CLEARING HOUSE. Tables of statistical returns relating to the railways of Great Britain, years 1938 to 1947. *London,* [1948.] pp. 34.   TUC
Summary tables 'similar to those on pp. 20–25 of the Railway Returns issued by the Ministry of Transport in July 1939'.

601 HANCOCK, W. K. *and* GOWING, M. M. British war economy. *London: H.M.S.O.,* 1949. pp. xvii, 583, with bibliogr. notes. BM
Includes railways.

602 LLOYD, R. The fascination of railways. *London: Allen & Unwin,* 1951. pp. 160.   BM
pp. 137–49, The war record of the railway service, 1939–1945.

603 LLOYD, R. Railwaymen's Gallery. *London: Allen & Unwin,* 1953. pp. 166, with plates.   BM
pp. 119–35, The Highland Rly. at war, 1939–45.

604 SAVAGE, C. I. Inland transport. *London: H.M.S.O.,* 1957. pp. xvii, 678, with tables & bibliogr. notes. [*History of the Second World War. United Kingdom Civil Series.*]   BM
A detailed record, including railways.

B 8   1945–1947   POST-WAR RECOVERY, AND RAILWAYS DURING THEIR FINAL YEARS OF PRIVATE OWNERSHIP

605 JOHNSTON, K. H. Railway electrification and post-war reconstruction. *In* 'Creative Demobilisation', vol. 2, 'Case Studies in National Planning', by E. A. Gutkind. *London,* 1943. pp. 145–65.   BM

606 LABOUR PARTY. Post-war organisation of British transport. *London,* [1943.] pp. 23.   BM

607 A NATIONAL transport programme: the approach to a long-term plan . . . *London: Railway Gazette,* 1943. pp. 27.   IT

608 [RAILWAY COMPANIES ASSOCIATION.] Memorandum: post-war policy. Private and confidential. *Waterloo Station* [*London*], June 1943. pp. 5. *Reproduced typescript.*   BR
Report of the general managers of the four main line companies.

609 MODERN TRANSPORT. A plan for post-war transport . . . with a foreword by . . . Sir Arthur Griffith-Boscawen. *London,* [1944.] pp. 51.   IT
Reprinted from *Modern Transport*, 12 Feb.–25 March, 1944.
Co-ordination under private ownership.

610 PARKINSON, H. Who owns the railways? A series of articles . . . reprinted from the 'Financial News' of October 31, November 1, 2 & 3, 1944. [*London,* 1944.] pp. 14, with 2 fold. financial tables.   LSE
Public ownership of railways. Railways already publicly owned—by a large body of stockholders.

611 DAVIES, E. British transport: a study in industrial organisation and control. *London: Fabian Society,* 1945, pp. 25.   BM
War-time control measures related to post-war problems.

612 LEAGUE OF NATIONS—ORGANISATION FOR COMMUNICATIONS & TRANSIT. Transport problems which arose from the War of 1914–1918 and the work of restoration undertaken in this field by the League of Nations. *Geneva,* July 1945. pp. 52. [*Publications Series VIII. Transit.* 1945. VIII, 2.]   BM
A guide to anticipated post-war transport problems.

613 LIBERAL PARTY. The future of British transport: report of a Liberal committee under the chairmanship of B. Seebohm

Rowntree. *London*, [1945.] pp. 39[40]. BM
Proposes that railways should be transferred to a public utility corporation.

614 WOOD, W. V. Railway and allied transport. *In* 'Post-war Britain' by J. Marchant. *London*, 1945. pp. 178–203. BM
Past experience and future needs.

615 DUNNAGE, J. A. Transport plans and Britain's future: some long-term aspects . . . *London: Industrial Transport Publications*, 1946. pp. 35. LSE
Against nationalisation. Suggested plan for general reforms.

616 LONDON & NORTH EASTERN RLY. Statistics; railways, roads, canals. [*London*,] 1946. pp. 32. BR
A handbook. Comparative figures for main line railways and all railways.

617 LONDON, MIDLAND & SCOTTISH RLY. The LMS answers your questions. *London*, 1946. pp. 20, with illus. BM
Post-war conditions and difficulties.

618 LONDON, MIDLAND & SCOTTISH RLY. State ownership and control of transport. [*Watford*, 1946.] pp. [4.] BR
A letter to stockholders asking their views, and an extract from the Chairman's speech at the Annual General Meeting, 1st March, 1946.

619 [RAILWAY COMPANIES ASSOCIATION.] British railways and the future . . . Issued by the G.W.R., L.M.S., L.N.E.R., S.R. *London*, 1946. pp. 20. LSE

620 STANLEY, A. H. [Lord Ashfield.] Speeches by . . . Lord Ashfield, Chairman of the Board, at the staff reunion victory dinners, 5 and 10 July, 1946. *London: L.P.T.B.*, August 1946. pp. 17. BR

621 LABOUR PARTY. Transport for the Nation. Prepared for the Labour Party by the Fabian Society. *London*, January 1947. pp. [4.]
An illustrated folder giving outline rail and road statistics and facts about the Transport Bill, 1946.

622 RAILWAY CLEARING HOUSE. Tables of statistical returns relating to the railways of Great Britain, years 1938 to 1947. *London*, [1948.] pp. 34. TUC
Summary tables 'similar to those on pp. 20–25 of the Railway Returns issued by the Ministry of Transport in July 1939'.

623 WILLIAMSON, J. W. Railways today. *London: O.U.P.*, 1938. pp. 160, with 23 plates. (2nd impr., 1942; 3rd impr., 1946.) BM
—— 2nd edn. *London*, 1951. pp. xviii, 154. BM

B9 NATIONALIZATION, 1948 THE ESTABLISHMENT OF THE BRITISH TRANSPORT COMMISSION AND 'BRITISH RAILWAYS'

For a list of undertakings affected by the Transport Act (1947) see Appendix II

624 COLLIER, R. A. H. [Lord Monkswell.] Railways and their future. *London: Benn*, 1946. pp. 96. BM
Their past (especially their past mistakes) also reviewed. Based on his *Railways: their history and organization* (1928).

625 NATIONAL UNION OF MANUFACTURERS. Nationalisation of transport. Feb. 1946. pp. 3. *Reproduced typescript.* IT
Preferring the recommendations of the Transport Advisory Council in April 1939 to the proposed nationalisation.

626 PARLIAMENT—HOUSE OF COMMONS—LIBRARY. Inland transport. Bibliography no. 13. *London*, December 1946. pp. 26. *Reproduced typescript.* BM
'A guide to official publications and other printed material relevant to the subject matter of the Transport Bill (1946).' Includes books, pamphlets, periodical and newspaper articles.
—— 13a, Addenda. Nov. 1949. pp. 17. BM
—— 13b, Second Addendum. May 1952. pp. 7. BM
—— 13c, Third Supplement. Nov. 1952. pp. 4. BM
—— 21, 'Inland transport: a guide to com-

ment on the Transport Bill in newspapers and periodicals.' Feb. 1947. pp. 8. BM
Contains a short list of addenda to Bibliography no. 13, dated Feb. 1947.

627 BRITISH TRANSPORT COMMISSION. The Transport Act, 1947. Scheme of delegation of functions by the British Transport Commission to the Railway Executive. *London: B.T.C.*, 1947. pp. 6. IT

628 COMMERCIAL MOTOR. The Operator's Guide to the Transport Act, 1947. By the legal adviser to 'Commercial Motor'. *London*, April 1947. pp. iv. 36. IT
Reprinted from *Commercial Motor*.

629 LONDON & NORTH EASTERN RLY. An outline of the Transport Act. [*London*,] 1947. pp. 25. BR
A simplified guide issued to staff.

630 BRITISH RAILWAYS. Memorandum for the information and guidance of all officers and staff of the main line railways as to procedure during the period beginning January 1st, 1948. [*London*,] Nov. 1947. pp. [4.] BR

631 MOTOR TRANSPORT. The Transport
Act, 1947: a simplified version. *London*,
[1947.] pp. 6.   IT
Reprint, *Motor Transport*, 13 Sept., 1947.

632 CAMERON, M. A. The Transport Act in
action. pp. 31. *Typescript, with alterations in MS.*   IT
Paper, Institute of Transport, Western Section, 2 December, 1948.

633 KARMEL, D. *and* BEDDINGTON, R. The
Transport Act, 1947. *London: Butterworth*,
1948. pp. viii, 296.   BM

634 ASSOCIATION OF AMERICAN RAILROADS
—BUREAU OF RAILWAY ECONOMICS LIB-
RARY. Nationalization of railways, 1939–
1949: a list of references. *Washington*,
November 1949. pp. 30.   LSE
pp. 16–24, articles in periodicals on nationalisation in Gt. Britain.

635 WILSON, G. L. An appraisal of nationalised transport in Great Britain; parts 1 & 2.
pp. 20, 23, with bibliogr. notes. *Reproduced typescript.*   IT
Paper, American Economic Association, 28
Dec., 1949, New York.

*636 WILSON, G. L. Nationalization of trans-
port in Great Britain. *Washington: Traffic
Service Corporation*, 1949. pp. 24.   IT

637 ZIEGLER, O. Die Nationalisierung des
Verkehrswesens in Grossbritannien. *Hamburg*, 1949. pp. [160]–174. [*Sonderdruck
WeltwirtschaftlichesArchiv*, Band 62, Heft 1,
1949.]   IT

638 WILSON, H. The financial problem of
British transport. [*London*, 1951.] pp. 43,
xiii. *Reproduced typescript.*   TUC

Compensation to stockholders upon Nationalization, and general financial results of
transport since 1948, followed by conclusions
and recommendations. Appendix contains a
schedule of valuations on stock of pre-1948
companies; summary of the debate on the
financial provisions of the Transport Bill,
March–May 1947; principal provisions in the
Transport Act (1947) relating to compensation;
main increases in transport costs, 1948–1951.

639 LABOURRESEARCHDEPARTMENT. Transport robbery: exposure of Tory plan; with
Appendices on (1) Railway profits before
nationalisation, (2) Transport Commission
1951 Accounts, (3) Plans of railway companies and hauliers before nationalisation.
London, 1952. pp. 11.   TUC
Based on legislation proposed to be introduced by the Conservative Party (*Cmd.* 8538).

640 BRITISH Transport Directory of Officials.
Westminster: Railway Gazette, [1948.] pp.
39.   BM
Reprinted from the *Railway Gazette*.
—— *Westminster*, [1949.] pp. 39.   BM
Supplement, *Railway Gazette*, Jan. 14, 1949.

641 HURCOMB, C. The organisation of British
transport. *London: British Transport Com-
mission*, 1948. pp. 24[25].   TUC
An outline of the powers and functions of the
B.T.C. and its components under the Transport
Act (1947).

642 ALLEN, C. J. British Railways for boys.
London: English Universities Press, 1949.
pp. 96, with 57 illus. & 8 diagrams. [*Junior
Teach Yourself Books.*]   BM

643 BRITISH RAILWAYS. British Railways
today and tomorrow. *London*, 1949. pp.
48, with 48 illus.   BM

B 10 1948–   RAILWAYS OF THE BRITISH ISLES IN GENERAL
AND 'BRITISH RAILWAYS'

For London Transport see C 1 (London)

644 JOHNSTON, K. H. British Railways and
economic recovery: a sociological study of
the transport problem. *London: Clerke &
Cockeran*, 1949. pp. 352, with plates &
bibliogr. notes.   BM
A plan for more efficient railways. Electrification.

645 BRITISH RAILWAYS. A step forward:
revision of regional boundaries. [*London*,
1940.] pp. 8.   BR
Changes to be made on 2 April, 1950, with a
list of lines and stations involved. A guide to
B.R. staff.

646 HURCOMB, C. The development of the
organisation of the British Transport
Commission: address . . . to the Institute of

Public Administration, 21 April, 1950
pp. 33. *Reproduced typescript.*   IT

647 REED, B. Modern railways. *London:
Temple Press*, 1950. pp. 104, with plates &
illus. [*Boys' Power & Speed Library.*]   BM

648 BRITISH RAILWAYS. Your British Rail-
ways. [*London*,] 1951. pp. 48.   BM
A well-illustrated 'picture story of British
Railways'.

649 BRITISH TRANSPORT COMMISSION. Electrification of railways. *London*, 1951. pp.
xi, 94, with 10 tables & 7 maps.   BM
Survey of existing electrification systems, and
recommendations for future development.

650 CASSERLEY, H. C. Service suspended: a pictorial souvenir of British passenger services that are no longer in operation. *London: Ian Allan,* [1951.] pp. 40. BM
Sixty illustrations with descriptions, followed by (pp. 33–40) a detailed list of passenger services withdrawn.

651 INTERNATIONAL UNION OF RAILWAYS. The position of the European railways: difficulties, causes, and possible remedies. *Paris,* 1951. pp. 36[37]. LSE

652 LLOYD, R. The fascination of railways. *London: Allen & Unwin,* 1951. pp. 160. BM
pp. 150–60, British Railways in 1960: a forecast.

653 NOCK, O. S. Boys' Book of British Railways. *London: Ian Allan,* 1951. pp. 128, with many illus. (6 col.). BM
Essays on contemporary equipment and working.

654 SAMPSON, H. World railways . . . edited and compiled by Henry Sampson. *London: Sampson Low's World Railways,* [1951– .] In progress. Bi-annual. BM
A comprehensive work of reference for the technical and mechanical features of the railways of all countries, with special emphasis on locomotives and rolling stock, and many illustrations. Includes underground railways. The Foreword gives a summary account of current developments, problems and trends.
The sixth edition (1961) was a complete revision covering a wider range of information than hitherto, with 412 pages, 653 illustrations, 141 maps, 80 loading and clearance-gauge diagrams, a table of data in 32 columns for 1500 railways in 108 countries (pp. 1–125), followed by a further table giving 'amplified details of major railways and manufacturers' (pp. 127–381).
The current edition (7th, 1962) has 435 pages.

655 WILLIAMSON, J. W. Railways today. 2nd edn. *London: O.U.P.,* 1951. pp. xviii, 154, with plates. (1st edn. 1938.) BM

656 WILSON, H. The financial problem of British transport. [*London,* 1951.] pp. 43. *Reproduced typescript.* TUC
Compensation to stockholders upon nationalisation; financial results of transport in general since 1948; conclusions and recommendations. Appendix contains a schedule of valuations on stock of pre-1948 railway companies; a summary of the debate on the financial provisions of the Transport Bill, March–May 1947; the principal provisions in the Transport Act (1947) relating to compensation; and a summary of the main increases in transport costs, 1948–1951.

657 ALLEN, G. F. Railways the world over. *London: Ian Allan,* [1952.] pp. 128, with many illus., some col. BM
Introductory.

658 CONSERVATIVE PARTY. Transport Bill. [*Westminster,*] 15 Sept. 1952. pp. [4.] IT
Reply to the Labour Party and T.U.C. campaign against the Bill.

659 WEBSTER, H. C. Railway motive power . . . *London: Hutchinson,* 1952. pp. 310, with 50 plates, & 57 drawings in text. BM
Modern locomotives of all kinds, related to current problems of running costs, maintenance, etc.

660 KARMEL, D. *and* POTTER, K. The Transport Act, 1953, with general introduction and annotations. *London: Butterworth,* 1953. pp. 7, 333. BM

661 INTERNATIONAL Railway Congress. *London: Railway Gazette,* May 1954. pp. 250. IT
pp. 23–88, reports on the progress of each Region of British Railways.

662 ST. JOHN, J. Britain's railways today. *London: Naldrett Press,* 1954. pp. 192, with 92 illus. on plates. BM

663 BRITISH TRANSPORT COMMISSION. Modernisation and re-equipment of British Railways. *London,* 1955. pp. 36. BM

664 FINANCIAL TIMES. The railway modernisation plan [and other articles]. *London,* August 17, 1955. pp. IV. LSE
A supplement.

665 MANCHESTER GUARDIAN *newspaper.* Supplement. Planning for a new railway age [and other articles]. *Manchester,* 14 July, 1955. pp. 7–14. LSE

666 BRITISH TRANSPORT COMMISSION. Modernisation of British Railways: the system of electrification of British Railways. *London,* [1956.] pp. 24, with a map. BM

*667 MINISTRY OF TRANSPORT AND CIVIL AVIATION. Proposals for the railways, presented by the Minister of Transport and Civil Aviation to Parliament. *London: H.M. Stationery Office,* [1956.] pp. 43, with tables. *Cmd.* 9880. BM
Present policy and future plans, with estimates.
pp. [9]–30, 'Review of policy and prospects, with special reference to the railways'.
pp. 31–9, 'The programme for railway modernisation'.

668 ROBERTSON, B. B.T.C. future prospects: report to Minister of Transport. *London: British Transport Commission,* Oct. 1956. pp. 4. *Reproduced typescript.* IT

669 ROBERTSON, B. The British transport system. *London: British Transport Commission,* 1956. pp. 19, with 6 diagrams. TUC
Paper, Royal United Services Institution, 1st Feb., 1956.
The progress and achievements of the B.T.C. since its inception.

670 SCOTSMAN *newspaper.* Survey of the modernisation of British Railways. *Edinburgh*, 19 March, 1956. pp. 12.
A supplement.

671 BURLEIGH, L. G. 'Are the railways finished?' asks a user. 1957. pp. 11. *Reproduced typescript.*   IT
Paper, Institute of Transport, Irish Section, 2 April, 1957.
Current trends in the development of transport and a re-assessment of the part to be played by railways.

672 BRITISH TRANSPORT COMMISSION. British Railways facts for teachers. *London*, 1958.   BM
A wallet containing five items—
1. All along the line (general booklet).
2. Know your trains (picture strip in colour).
3. Facts and figures about British Railways, 1958 edn.
4. Diesel-electric main-line locomotive (wall chart).
5. Yours for the asking (list of publications and film strips).

673 FINANCIAL TIMES. Rail modernisation. *London*, 18th August, 1958. pp. VII.   LSE
A supplement.

674 MINISTRY OF TRANSPORT AND CIVIL AVIATION. The British Transport Commission: re-appraisal of the plan for the modernisation and re-equipment of British Railways. *London: H.M. Stationery Office*, [1959.] pp. 52. *Cmnd.* 813.   BM

675 ALLEN, G. F. British Railways today and tomorrow. *London: Ian Allan*, 1959. pp. 194, with many illus. on plates.   BM
—— 2nd edn. *London*, 1960. pp. 196. BM
—— 3rd edn., rev. & enl., *London*, 1962. pp. 240, with col. frontis., and 162 illus. on 48 plates.   BM

*676 CENTRAL OFFICE OF INFORMATION— REFERENCE DIVISION. Inland transport in the United Kingdom. *London*, October 1960. pp. 13. [*Publication* no. R 4689, superseding R 3900 of 1958 & earlier issues.]   BM
A summary for reference use, including an account of the railway system since 1947.

677 BRITISH TRANSPORT COMMISSION. Modernisation progress report. *London*, May 1961. pp. 47, with 30 illus.   BM

678 BRITISH RAILWAYS BOARD. The reshaping of British Railways. *London: H.M. Stationery Office*, 1963. pp. ii, 148, with 12 [13] col. fold. maps in sep. folder.   BM
The 'Beeching Report'. Proposals for rationalization of the railways. Recommended reductions in services and closure of lines. Railways to be employed for classes of traffic for which they are most suited within the framework of transport as a whole. Produced under the chairmanship of Dr. Richard Beeching.

679 HAMMOND, R. Railways tomorrow: a study of railway transport problems, with special emphasis on the modernisation plan for British Railways. *London: Alvin Redman*, 1963. pp. xv, 187, with frontis., 29 illus. on 24 plates, & 44 diagrams in text.   BM

B 10 (ER) Eastern Region

680 DOW, G. By electric train from Liverpool Street to Shenfield. *London: British Railways*, 1949. pp. 15, with illus.   BM
The electrification to Shenfield.

681 ANDERSON, A. The Flying Scotsman; illustrated by the author. *Leicester: Brockhampton Press*, 1949. pp. 63[65], with a time schedule, gradient profile, & maps on end papers. [*Famous Train Journeys*, no. 1.]   BM
—— *Leicester*, [1952.] pp. 63, with photographs added. [*Famous Trains and their Routes.*]   BM

682 BRITISH RAILWAYS—EASTERN REGION. Ilford Electric Train Depot. [1954.] pp. [6.] Folder, with 5 illus. & a plan.   BR

683 ENGLISH ELECTRIC COMPANY. Liverpool St.—Shenfield service, British Railways, Eastern Region. *London*, [1954.] pp. 12, with illus.   BR

684 BRITISH RAILWAYS—EASTERN REGION. Potters Bar, new main line station. *London*, Nov. 1955. pp. 6 (folder), with 11 illus.   BR

685 BRITISH RAILWAYS—EASTERN REGION. Electric Control Station, Chadwell Heath. 1957. pp. [6.] Folder, with an illus. & a plan.   BR

686 CASSERLEY, H. C. *and* ASHER, L. L. Locomotives of British Railways, London & North Eastern Group: a pictorial record. *London: Dakers*, [1958.] pp. 148, with 216 illus. on plates.   BM
—— Combined edn. (all regions). *London*, 1961. pp. 488, with 732 illus. on 366 plates.   BM
A complete record of all steam locomotives of British Railways, acquired upon nationalization, and built since.

687 ALLEN, C. J. ABC, British express trains: no. 4, Eastern and North Eastern Regions. *Hampton Court: Ian Allan*, [1959.] pp. 64, with illus. & train schedules.   BM

688 ALLEN, C. J. Great Eastern. *London: Ian Allan*, [1959.] pp. 64, with illus.   BM
History, description, and recent progress with electrification and improved services.

689 BRITISH RAILWAYS—EASTERN REGION. Electrification. Opening, Wednesday 16th November, 1960. *London*, 1960. pp. [20,] with illus.   BR
Brochure.

B 10 (LMR) London Midland Region

690 BRITISH RAILWAYS—LONDON MIDLAND REGION. Souvenir of the inaugural cruise of the motor vessel 'Cambria', Wednesday 25 May, 1949. [*London*,] 1949. pp. [6.]
BR

691 MODERNISED 'up' marshalling yard at Toton, British Railways Midland Region. *London: Railway Gazette*, 1951. pp. 31, with many illus. & diagrams.   IT
Reprinted from the *Railway Gazette*, Nov. and Dec., 1951.

692 ANDERSON, A. The Royal Scot; illustrated by the author. *Leicester: Brockhampton Press*, [1952.] pp. 63, with photographs, route map & gradient profile. [*Famous Train Journeys and their Routes.*]   BM

693 WESTINGHOUSE BRAKE AND SIGNAL COMPANY. Euston re-signalling. *London*, [1952.] pp. 10, with illus. & la. fold. diagram.   IT
Reprinted from the *Railway Gazette*, 19 Dec., 1952.

694 BRITISH INSULATED CALLENDER'S CONSTRUCTION COMPANY. High volttage A.C. traction equipment installed on the Lancaster–Morecambe–Heysham section of British Railways, London Midland Region. *London*, August 1953. pp. 15, with illus. & a map. [*Publication* no. 12.]   IT

695 ANDERSON, A. The Irish Mail. *Leicester: Brockhampton Press*, [1954.] pp. 63, with illus. by the author, photographs, a route map & gradient profile. [*Famous Trains and their Routes.*]   BM

696 DOW. G. The third Woodhead Tunnel. Issued by British Railways, Midland Region, to commemorate the formal opening of the new Woodhead Tunnel . . . 1954. *London*, 1954. pp. 27, with illus., map & diagrams.
BM

697 ENGLISH ELECTRIC CO. Liverpool–Southport service, British Railways, London Midland Region. *London*, [1954.] pp. 11, with illus.   BR

698 ANDERSON, A. The Thames–Clyde Express. *Leicester: Brockhampton Press*, [1955.] pp. 55[63], with route map & gradient profile. [*Famous Journey Series.*]
BM

699 CASSERLEY, H. C. *and* ASHER, L. L. Locomotives of British railways, London, Midland & Scottish Group: a pictorial record. *London: Dakers*, 1955. pp. 114. BM
172 illustrations on plates, with descriptions, preceded by an introduction of 27 pages.
—— Combined edn. (all Regions). *London*,

1961. pp. 488, with 732 illus. on 366 plates.   BM
A complete record of all steam locomotives of British Railways, acquired upon nationalization and built since.

700 BRITISH RAILWAYS. Euston Station: a brief historical sketch. [*London*,] September 1957. pp. [4.]   BR

701 BRITISH RAILWAYS—LONDON MIDLAND REGION. St. Pancras re-signalling. [*London*, 1959.] pp. 8, with 6 illus. & diagram.
BM
Reprinted from the *Railway Gazette*.

702 ALLEN, C. J. ABC, British express trains: no. 3, London Midland Region. *Hampton Court: Ian Allan*, [1960.] pp. 72, with illus. & train schedules.   BM

703 BRITISH RAILWAYS—LONDON MIDLAND REGION. Change at Crewe: commemorating the completion of stage one, Manchester to Crewe, of the Manchester–Liverpool–Euston electrification scheme. *Euston (London)*, Sept. 1960. pp. 42, with illus. (some col.).   BM

704 BRITISH RAILWAYS—LONDON MIDLAND REGION. The Midland Pullman. *London*, March 1960. pp. [12,] with plate, illus. & diagrams.   BM
Includes historical notes.

705 BRITISH RAILWAYS—LONDON MIDLAND REGION. Todays' London Midland express freight. *London*, [1960.] pp. [16,] with many illus.   BM

B 10 (NER) North Eastern Region

706 WESTINGHOUSE BRAKE & SIGNAL COMPANY. York resignalling, British Railways, North Eastern Region. *London*, 1951. pp. 23, with illus. & fold. diagram of layout.
BR

707 ANDERSON, A. The Flying Scotsman; illustrated by the author. *Leicester: Brockhampton Press*, 1949. pp. 63[65], with a time schedule, gradient profile, & maps on end papers. [*Famous Train Journeys*, no. 1.]   BM
—— *Leicester*, [1952.] pp. 63, with photographs added. [*Famous Trains and their Routes.*]   BM

708 ALLEN, C. J. ABC, British express trains: no. 4, Eastern and North Eastern Regions. *Hampton Court: Ian Allan*, [1959.] pp. 64, with illus. & train schedules.   BM

B 10 (Sc.R) Scottish Region

709 ANDERSON, A. The Flying Scotsman; illustrated by the author. *Leicester: Brockhampton Press*, 1949. pp. 63[65], with a

time schedule, gradient profile, & maps on end papers. [*Famous Train Journeys*, no. 1.]
BM

—— *Leicester*, [1952.] pp. 63, with photographs added. [*Famous Trains and their Routes*.]
BM

710 ANDERSON, A. The Royal Scot; illustrated by the author. *Leicester: Brockhampton Press*, [1952.] pp. 63, with photographs, route map, & gradient profile. [*Famous Train Journeys and their Routes*.]
BM

711 ANDERSON, A. The Thames–Clyde Express. *Leicester: Brockhampton Press*, [1955.] pp. 55[63], with route map & gradient profile. [*Famous Journey Series*.]
BM

712 MARGETTS, F. C. Modernisation of marshalling yards in the Scottish Region. *Aberdeen: Railway Students Association Convention*, 1957. pp. 8. *Reproduced typescript*.
IT

713 ALLEN, C. J. ABC, British express trains: no. 5, Scottish Region, including Anglo-Scottish services. *Hampton Court: Ian Allan*, [1960.] pp. 72, with illus. & train schedules.
BM

714 BLAKE, G. Glasgow Electric: the story of Scotland's new electric railway. *Glasgow: British Railways Scottish Region*, 1960. pp. [36,] with many illus., incl. 13 in full colour, & a map.
BM

B 10 (SR) Southern Region

715 TILLING, W. G. The locomotives of the Southern Region of British Railways. *London*, 1948. pp. 84.
BM
Published by the author.
Detailed lists, notes, and illustrations.

716 SAVILL, R. A. The changing face of the Southern. *London: British Railways (S.R.) Lecture & Debating Society*, 1949. pp. 13.
IT

717 ANDERSON, A. The Devon Belle; illustrated by the author. *Leicester: Brockhampton Press*, 1950. pp. 63[65], with time schedule, gradient profile, & maps on end papers. [*Famous Train Journeys*, no. 2.] BM

*718 ALLEN, C. J. *and* TOWNROE, S. C. The Bulleid pacifics of the Southern Region. *London: Ian Allan*, 1951. pp. 80, with lists, & illus. on plates.
BM
Design and performance.

719 RAILWAY CORRESPONDENCE & TRAVEL SOCIETY. The Kemp Town Branch, Southern Region. *Leamington Spa*, Oct. 1952. pp. 3[4].
BR
Reprint, *Railway Observer*.
An itinerary of the Kemp Town Branch

Special, 5 Oct., 1952, with an historical account by Derek W. Winkworth.

720 RAILWAY CORRESPONDENCE & TRAVEL SOCIETY. Report of an unofficial traffic survey: Southern Region, Western Section, Saturday, August 23rd, 1952. [By B. Knowlman.] pp. 11. *Reproduced typescript*. IT
A practical enquiry by 23 observers over a period of 8–10 hours.

721 ARMSTRONG, P. Southern Region allocations: all steam and diesel locomotives allocated to the Southern Region. *High Wycombe: Locomotive Club of Great Britain*, [1953.] pp. 31, with 24 illus. on 8 plates. BM
Lists, with details of number, class, name, date and place of construction, designer, shed, of all locomotives in service on 3 March, 1953.

722 ANDERSON, A. The Golden Arrow. *Leicester: Brockhampton Press*, [1954.] pp. 63, with illus. by the author, photographs, route map, & gradient profile. [*Famous Trains and their Routes*.]
BM

723 CASSERLEY, H. C. *and* ASHER, L. L. Locomotives of British Railways, Southern Group: a pictorial record. *London: Dakers*, [1956.] pp. 106.
148 illustrations on plates, with descriptions, preceded by an introduction of 31 pages.
—— Combined edn. (all Regions). *London*, 1961. pp. 488, with 732 illus. on 366 plates.
BM
All steam locomotives acquired by British Railways upon nationalization and built since.

724 BUCKNALL, R. Boat trains and Channel packets: the English short sea routes. *London: Vincent Stuart*, 1957. pp. xi, 218, with col. frontis. & 108 illus. on 46 plates, maps & diagrams in text, & a bibliography (29 items).
BM
The history of the boat and boat train services of the South Eastern, the London, Chatham & Dover, the South Eastern & Chatham, the Southern Railway, and British Railways (Southern Region).

725 ALLEN, C. J. ABC, British express trains: no. 2, Southern Region. *Hampton Court: Ian Allan*, [1959.] pp. 64, with illus., & train schedules.
BM

*726 MOODY, G. T. Southern Electric: the history of the world's largest suburban electrified system. *London: Ian Allan*, 1957. pp. vii, 172, with 86 illus. on 72 plates, maps, diagrams & tables.
BM
—— 2nd edn. *London*, 1958. (Reprint).
BM
—— 3rd edn. *London*, 1960. pp. vii, 189.
BM

B 10 (WR) Western Region

727 ANDERSON, A. The Cornish Riviera Express, Paddington to Penzance; illustrated by the author. *Leicester: Brockhampton*,

Press, [1952.] pp. 63, with photographs, route map & gradient profile. [*Famous Trains and their Routes*.] BM

728 INSTITUTION OF MECHANICAL ENGINEERS—BRISTOL MEETING. Visit to the Swindon Works of the Western Region, British Railways, June 19th, 1952. pp. 12, with 4 plates & fold. plan. *Reproduced typescript.* IME

729 ARMSTRONG, P. Western Region allocations: all steam and diesel locomotives allocated to Western Region. *High Wycombe: Locomotive Club of Great Britain*, [1953.] pp. 40, with 32 illus. on 8 plates, & a supplementary list (1 page). BM
Lists with details of number, class, name, date and place of construction, designer, shed, of all locomotives in service on 27 May, 1953.

730 ANDERSON, A. The Red Dragon. *Leicester: Brockhampton Press*, [1954.] pp. 63, with illus. by author, photographs, route map & gradient profile. [*Famous Trains and their Routes*.] BM
Paddington–Severn Tunnel–Carmarthen.

731 [BRITISH RAILWAYS.] Two anniversaries: centenary of Paddington Station; jubilee of Cornish Riviera Express. [*London*, 1954.] pp. 15, with illus. BM

732 BRITISH RAILWAYS—WESTERN REGION. Swindon Locomotive and Carriage Works. *London*, 1954. pp. 48, with many illus. & a plan of the works. BM
Cover title—'Swindon Works'.

733 BRITISH RAILWAYS—WESTERN REGION. Swindon Locomotive Works. *London*, 1956. pp. 36, with many illus. & a plan of the works. BM

734 BRITISH RAILWAYS—WESTERN REGION. Swindon Carriage & Wagon Works. *London*, 1957. pp. 35, with many illus. & a plan of the works. BR

735 BRITISH RAILWAYS. Introduction of diesel-hydraulic main line locomotives in the Western Region: a new chapter in railway modernisation. [*London*,] 1958. pp. 8, with fold. diagram. BM
Description of type '4' locomotive.

736 CASSERLEY, H. C. *and* ASHER, L. L. Locomotives of British Railways, Great Western Group: a pictorial record. *London: Dakers*, [1958.] pp. 114. BM
Text (31 pages) followed by 164 illustrations on plates, with descriptions.
—— Combined edn. (all Regions). *London*, 1961. pp. 488, with 723 illus. on 366 plates. BM
All steam locomotives acquired by British Railways upon nationalization, and built since.

737 BRITISH RAILWAYS—WESTERN REGION. British Railways at your service in Bristol (Cardiff, Gloucester, Newport, Plymouth, Reading, Swansea, Worcester). [*London*,] 1958. BM
A series of booklets giving information about W.R. facilities (passenger and goods) at these places.

738 ALLEN, C. J. ABC, British express trains: no. 1, Western Region. *Hampton Court: Ian Allan*, [1960.] pp. 64, with illus. & train schedules. BM

C RAIL TRANSPORT IN PARTICULAR AREAS OF THE BRITISH ISLES

For England as a whole see A for general works and B for contemporaneous works
For the Regions of British Railways see B 10 (ER), etc.

Marginal symbols: **b** bibliographies, **c** chronologies

C1 English localities (London—Geographical regions of England—The East and West Coast routes to Scotland and the 'Railway Races to Scotland')
C 2 Scotland
C 3 Wales
C 4 Ireland
C 5 Isle of Wight

C 6 Isle of Man
C 7 Channel Islands
C 8 English Channel Tunnel scheme
C 9 Scotland to Ireland Tunnel scheme
C 10 Comparisons between British and foreign railways
C 11 International co-operation

C 1 ENGLISH LOCALITIES London—Geographical regions of England—Counties—The East and West Coast routes to Scotland and the 'Railway Races to Scotland'

London and the London Suburban Area

This section is subdivided by a modified version of the main scheme, as follows:

A General history and description
B Contemporaneous works
C Particular areas of London
D 1 Tramways

D 4 Underground railways
E Engineering
H Labour
K Social aspects

C 1 (London) A General history and description of all forms of rail transport of London

739 METROPOLITAN BOARD OF WORKS [London]. Report upon Metropolitan railway and other schemes of Session 1855/6, *etc.* By J. W. Bazalgette, Engineer. *London,* 1856–1889. G
Annual reports on railway and tramway projects.

740 COMMISSIONERS OF SEWERS [City of London]. Report to the Hon. the Committee upon Improvements of the Commissioners of Sewers of the City of London, upon the railways and other companies applying for powers to construct works within the City of London. (By W. Haywood, Engineer and Surveyor to the Commissioners.) *London,* 1860–1898. G
Annual reports on railway and tramway projects.

741 DAY & SON. Iron Road Book and Railway Traveller, 1866: a pocket companion comprising all railways and branches in Great Britain and Ireland . . . Part 1, Metropolitan and suburban railways and branches. *London,* [1866.] pp. 37[44], with map. BM
No more issued.

742 FIGUIER, L. Les Chemins de fer métropolitains, Londres, New York . . . *Paris,* [1886.] pp. xii, 272. BM
pp. 15–58, 'Londres'; with 5 illus., diagram and map.

743 MACDERMOTT, F. The railway system of London. *London,* [1891.] pp. 20. G

744 KEMMANN, G. Der Verkehr Londons, mit besonderer Berücksichtigung der Eisenbahnen; mit 8 Plänen und zahlreichen in der Text gedruckten Abbildungen. *Berlin,* 1892. pp. 197. RC
A very detailed work.

745 LONDON COUNTY COUNCIL—SURVEY COMMITTEE. The Survey of London . . . Edited by C. R. Ashbee. *London,* 1900– . *In progress.* BM
This very detailed and well illustrated work is published in separate volumes for each parish. It includes railways and stations.

746 BENNETT, A. R. London and Londoners in the eighteen-fifties and sixties. *London,* 1924. pp. 371. BM
Includes railways.

747 SOMMERFIELD, V. London Transport: a record and a survey. *Westminster: L.P.T.B.,* c 1934. pp. viii, 68, with 37 illus. on plates & a chronology. BM
Includes, pp. 43–68, 'Historical and statistical particulars of the concerns vested in the L.P.T.B.'
—— another edn. 1935. pp. 71. BM

748 MONOD, N. Transports publics à Londres: gestion unique et socialisation. *Paris,* [1936.] b pp. 302. BM
Detailed history and description of London transport, including railways and tramways. The L.P.T.B., with genealogical chart and a bibliography.

749 CENTRAL OFFICE OF INFORMATION— REFERENCE DIVISION. London transport and traffic. *London,* April 1958. pp. 4. [*Fact Sheets on Britain,* no. R2541/39.] BM

A concise general description, including a brief historical outline and an explanation of current problems.

750 SEKON, G. A. Locomotion in Victorian London. *London*, 1938. pp. xi, 211, with plates & illus. in text. BM
Includes railways and tramways.

751 DAVIES, E. National enterprise: the development of the public corporation. *London*, 1946. pp. 173. BM
Includes the L.P.T.B.

752 LONDON TRANSPORT EXECUTIVE. London Transport basic facts: general facts &
c figures. *London*, October 1958. pp. 22. *Reproduced typescript.* BR
A concise history and description of London Transport.
pp. 13–16, Chronology of underground railways in London, 1843–1954.
pp. 17–22, Statistics.

753 COURSE, E. London railways. *London. Batsford*, 1962. pp. 280, with 61 illus. on 24 plates, 8 maps & diagrams in text, & a table (5 pp.) of closed stations. BM
A detailed historical and geographical survey of the development of lines in and around London, and of stations and termini.

*754 BARKER, T. C. *and* ROBBINS, M. A history
b of London transport: passenger travel and the development of the metropolis; volume 1, the nineteenth century. [By T. C. Barker.] *London: Allen & Unwin* for the *London Transport Board*, 1963. pp. xxxii, 412, with frontis., & 118 illus. on 58 plates, 11 maps, 1055 bibliogr. notes, and detailed lists of early omnibuses, routes, and owners. BM
London Transport Board's official history. A detailed and authentic record of the development of all forms of passenger transport in London, related throughout to the social, economic, and historical factors which by cause and effect shaped the course of London's transport during the nineteenth century.
An index will be included in vol. 2.

755 BENNETT, A. E. *and* BORLEY, H. V. London Transport Railways: a list of opening, closing, and renaming dates of lines and stations. *Dawlish: David & Charles; London: Macdonald*, 1963. pp. 32, with 2 maps (1 fold.). BM
A comprehensive and highly accurate record.

*756 LONDON TRANSPORT BOARD. London Transport posters; with an introduction and notes by Harold F. Hutchinson. *London*, 1963. pp. 23, 124,[4.] BM
Fifty years of pictorial poster art represented in 124 colour plates.

*757 WHITE, H. P. Greater London . . . *London: Phoenix House*, 1963. pp. xii, 227, with frontis., 43 illus. on 16 plates, 30 sm. maps, diagrams & tables, a bibliography, & a fold. col. map. [*Regional History of the Railways of Great Britain*, vol. 3.] BM

C1 (London) B

Contemporaneous Works

758 TATHAM, W. London Canal and Rail-Road! Explanatory remarks on the projected London Canal and Railroad addressed to the public interests of the Metropolis and to the consideration of the nobility, gentry and others, convened at the Crown and Anchor on the invitation of the New River Company by William Tatham, one of the sufferers. *London*, 1803. pp. 21. ICE

759 COCK, S. Case of the London Dock Company. *London*, 1825. pp. iv, 92. BM
p. 21, mention of a Bill proposing railways from the docks to Aldgate.

760 CUNDY, N. W. Inland transit: the practicability, utility and benefit of railroads: the comparative attraction and speed of steam engines on a railroad, navigation and turnpike road. Report of a Select Committee of the House of Commons on Steam Carriages . . . *London*, 1833. pp. iv, 161. BM
'The advantages that would emanate from the establishment of five railroads from the Metropolis.'

—— 2nd edn. *London*, 1834. pp. iv, 161. BM

761 COMMERCIAL ROAD [London] —TRUSTEES. Report of the Trustees of the Commercial Road to the proprietors, affording a comparative view of the capabilities of the Commercial and East India Dock Roads with reference to the projected railways to the East and West India Docks and Blackwall. [By W. Baker, Clerk.] *London*, 1835. pp. 13. BM
Describes the 'tramway' (i.e. granite carriageway) along the Commerical Road.

762 STATEMENTS illustrative of the necessity for additional means of communication between London and Blackwall; with an examination of the comparative suitableness of the railways projected by the London & Blackwall Railway Co . . . and the Blackwall Commercial Railway Co. to supply those additional means. *London*, 1836. pp. 26. BM

763 CITY RAILWAY TERMINUS COMPANY. [A collection of leaflets, memorials, etc. 1853.] G

764 PARSONS, P. M. Proposed London railway to afford direct railway communication between the City and Westminster and all the western suburbs . . . and to unite the existing metropolitan railways both north and south of the Thames and provide them with a general central station . . . *London*, [1853.] pp. 29, with 2 la. fold. maps. BR
A ground-level railway, elevated in parts.

765 TAYLOR, G. L. On metropolitan communications and improvements. *London*, 1856.
pp. 27, with 2 fold. maps. (one of London
termini).   BM
Includes the Report of the Select Committee
of the House of Commons on Metropolitan
Communications to and in the Metropolis,
dated 23 July, 1855. Intercommunication between railways in London. Thirty-four schemes
commented upon.

766 YEATMAN, H. J. The junction of the
Metropolitan railways: a letter addressed
to Sir Benjamin Hall . . . First Commissioner of Works. *London*, 1857. pp. 7. BM
A scheme for connecting all London railways.

767 LANE, C. B. Railway communication in
London and the Thames Embankment.
London, 1860. pp. 23.   BM
Through stations to relieve congestion, and
J. Fowler's scheme for a railway along the
Embankment.

—— 2nd edn. *London*, 1861. pp. 24. BM

768 SAMUEL, J. *and* HEPPEL, J. M. The
Thames Viaduct Railway described and
commented on. *Westminster*, 1863. pp. 8.
     BM
A proposed elevated railway along the centre
of the Thames between the City of London and
Westminster.

769 REMARKS upon some of the London rail-
way projects of 1864, comprising Mr.
Fowler's Outer Circle and Inner Circle, Mr.
Hawkshaw's lines, the Metropolitan Grand
Union, etc.; with a map. *London*, [1864.]
pp. 4.   BM

770 SERAFON, F. Étude sur les chemins de fer,
les tramways, et les moyens de transport en
commun à Paris et à Londres, suivie d'une
notice sur la construction et l'exploitation
des tramways avec carte et planches. *Paris*,
1872. pp. viii, 110, with 3 fold. plates in
pocket.   BM

771 HOVENDEN, T. H. New railways and new
streets: a few hints to those affected by proposed public improvements. *London*, 1872.
pp. 36.   BM
Proposed London railways.

—— another edn. *London*, 1873. pp. 36.
     BM

772 HARTWICH, E. H. Aphoristische Bemer-
kungen über das Eisenbahnwesen und
Mitteilungen über die Eisenbahnen in London,
nebst Vorstädten. *Berlin*, 1874. pp. 46. BRE

773 SCHWABE, H. Über das englische Eisenbahnwesen: Reisestudien von H. Schwabe;
nebst einer Karte. *Berlin*, 1871. pp. 133,
with bibliogr. notes & a fold. map.   BM
pp. 25–47, stations; pp. 48–54, London
underground railways.

—— Neue Folge. *Wien*, 1877. pp. 208,
c 'mit einem Atlas enthaltend 16 Blatt Zeich-
nungen'.   BM
This much enlarged edition has a chronological table of the growth of lengths of line
from 1825 to 1875; pp. 9–96, English stations;
pp. 97–130, London underground railways.
The atlas contains large folding maps and plans
of stations, mostly in London.

—— Étude sur les chemins de fer anglais
d'après des notes receuillies dans un voyage
en Angleterre . . . traduit de l'allemand par
A. Huberti et A Habets; avec une carte des
chemins de fer de Londres et des environs.
Paris, 1872. pp. xx, 259.   BM

774 [ALLEN, E. E.] Proposed City Union Railway and Outer and Inner Circle completion.
[*London*,] 1878. pp. 10.   ICE
Inter-connection of Cannon St. station and
Fenchurch St. station via Inner Circle Line, and
an outer circle surburban railway. (ICE copy
signed 'Edward E. Allen'.)

775 SERAFON, F. Les Chemins de fer métropolitains et les moyens de transport en commun à Londres, New York, Berlin, Vienne
et Paris. *Paris*, 1885. pp. 126, with 8
illus.   ICE
pp. 9–57, Londres.

776 FRANK, E. Der Betrieb auf den englischen
Bahnen; mit sechs Tafeln. *Wien*, 1886.
pp. 91, with illus. & fold. map.   BM
A record of observations on English railway
working, mostly in London, made on a visit in
1885.

777 REA, S. Railways terminating in London;
with a description of the terminal stations
and the underground railways. *New York*,
1888. pp. 56, with la. col. fold. map in
pocket & 3 fold. tables.
Contains statistical details of each railway.

778 'W.' Der Eisenbahnverkehr in London.
[By] 'W.' *Berlin*, [1899.] pp. [401]–404.
     LSE
Sonderabdruck aus *Zeitschrift für Klein-
bahnen*, Heft 8, 1899.
Traffic and financial statistics.

779 ROBINSON, J. C. Electric traction: London's tubes, trams, and trains, 1902. *London*, 1902. pp. 19, with map.   PC
Paper, Society of Arts, 19 March, 1902, and
reprinted from the *Journal of the Society of
Arts*, 21 March, 1902.

780 BEAVAN, A. H. Tube, train, tram and car;
or, Up-to-date locomotion . . . *London*, 1903.
pp. xviii, 291, with many illus.   BM

781 HARPER, E. J. Statistics of London
traffic. *London: Royal Statistical Society*,
1904. pp. 51.   IT
Reprint, *Journal of the R.S.S.*, vol. 67, pt. 1,
30 June, 1904.
Includes railways.

782 MEIK, C. S. *and* BEER, W. The improvement of London traffic. *London*, 1905. pp. 15, with 3 fold. plates.   LSE
Paper, Society of Engineers, 5 June, 1905.
Tramways; elevated railways; underground railways.

783 ROYAL COMMISSION ON LONDON TRAFFIC. Report of the Royal Commission appointed to inquire into and report upon the means of locomotion and transport in London. *London*, 1905. 8 vols. [*Parliamentary Papers, Cd.* 2597; 2751; 2752; 2987; 2798; 2799; 2743; 2744.]   BM
Report, Minutes of Evidence and Appendices, maps, diagrams, illustrations and reports by the Advisory Board of Engineers. The whole work is minutely indexed.

*784 KEARNEY, E. W. C. Rapid transit in the future: the Kearney High-Speed Railway. 2nd edn. *Westminster*, [1911.] pp. 55, with illus.   PC
A proposed mono-rail underground railway for London.

785 BOARD OF TRADE. Report of the London Traffic Branch of the Board of Trade, 1914. *London*, 1915. pp. 94, with 9 maps & diagrams. [*Cd.* 7757.]   BM

786 KEEGAN, G. *and* WOOD, F. T. Transportation facilities of London and Paris as of October 1913. Report prepared by George Keenan, assistant to Vice-President and General Manager, Inter-borough Rapid Transit Company; F. T. Wood, assistant to Vice-President and General Manager, New York Railways Company. [*New York*, 1915.] pp. v, 126, with fold. tables & fold. diagrams.   LC
pp. 1–86, London railways and tramways.

787 STONE, H. W. D. The principles of urban traffic. *London*, 1917. pp. viii, 130.   BM
pp. 77–96, Railways. (London suburban traffic problems.)

788 GORDON, H. H. Some aspects of metropolitan road and rail transit . . . with a report of the discussion. *London*, 1919. pp. 83, with 10 diagrams & 18 tables.   BM
Lecture, Institution of Civil Engineers, 25 Nov., 1919.
Problems of traffic conditions. Includes railways, tube railways, tramways, and motor buses. (Discussion, pp. 54–83.)

789 WEBB, A. London of the future. By the London Society, under the editorship of Sir Aston Webb. *London*, 1921.   BM
pp. 49–66, Roads, streets and traffic of London. By R. C. Hellard.
pp. 67–90, London railway reconstruction. By A. J. Leaning. With maps.
pp. 115–24, London and the Channel Tunnel. By Sir Arthur Fell.

790 LONDON COUNTY COUNCIL. London traffic: report presented to the Council on 9th May, 1922, dealing with the passenger transport systems of Greater London, with special reference to the Council's tramways. [*London*, 1922.] pp. 28.   LSE

791 TURNER, D. L. New York, London, Paris, & Berlin transit conditions compared. *New York*, Dec. 1922. pp. 73. *Reproduced typescript.*   IT

792 SWINTON, G. S. C. London: her traffic, her improvement, and Charing Cross Bridge. *London*, 1924. pp. vii, 90.   BM
Potential increased usefulness of the Bridge and Station by widening and by having two levels.

793 LONDON UNDERGROUND GOODS RAILWAYS. Descriptive note of the London Underground Goods Railways. *Westminster*, January 1926. pp. 8.   PC

794 MINISTRY OF TRANSPORT. Report of Messrs. Mott, Hay & Anderson and . . . G. W. Humphreys as to proposed bridge at Charing Cross. *London*, 1928. pp. 7, with 3 fold. maps.   LSE

795 DEELEY, R. M. Road and bridge improvements at Charing Cross. [*London*? 1929?] with diagram.   TUC

796 LONDON GOODS RAILWAY. The London Goods Railway via underground tunnels: what the proposal is and the public advantages accruing. *London*, August 1929. pp. 8, with a map of proposed system. LSE
Seventy-five miles of standard gauge.

797 MURRAY, J. The 'Empire Bridge' at Charing Cross. *London*, [1929.] pp. 12, with fold. diagram.   TUC

798 ARE the Lambeth slums to last for ever? The Charing Cross Bridge problem. [By] 'Pro Bono Publico.' [*London*? 1930?] pp. [3,] with 2 diagrams.   TUC

799 KEEN, A. Charing Cross Bridge. *London*, 1930. pp. 78, with plates & plans.   LSE
A review of schemes, official and otherwise.

800 WALLER, A. G. The proposed bridge at Charing Cross. *London*, Feb. 1930. pp. 20, with 4 fold. maps & diagrams.   TUC
pp. 7–10, History of Charing Cross (Hungerford) Bridge.

801 WORLD POWER CONFERENCE, 1933. The handling of urban and suburban passenger traffic by railway, electric traction, tramways, and motor omnibuses. *Stockholm*, [1933.] pp. 48, with illus., diagrams & map.   BR
Submitted by the Underground Group of Companies, Great Britain, for the information

of Group 42, Section 8, of the World Power Conference.

802 BAILEY, E. D. The economics of London suburban electrification. September 1936. pp. 49. *Typescript.*   LSE

803 DAUTRY, R. La Formule anglaise des 'public trusts' appliquée à la gestion des grands services publics. Les transports de Londres. *Paris*, 1936. pp. 72, with maps (1 fold.) & tables.   LSE
Extrait, *Revue Générale des Chemins de Fer*, nos. des Ier août, sept., oct., et nov., 1936.
Development and present position of rail and road transport in London, and its co-ordination.

804 LONDON PASSENGER TRANSPORT BOARD. The Coronation, 1937: a record of services on the Underground. *London*, 1937. pp. 19, with illus., charts & diagrams.   BM
A souvenir brochure issued to staff.

805 LONDON PASSENGER TRANSPORT BOARD. London Transport today. *London*, 1937. pp. [22.]   LSE
Reproductions of two series of newspaper advertisement-announcements (17 in all) explaining the work, problems and plans of the LPTB.

806 STRAUSS, F. Angaben über den Londoner Verkehr und das Londoner Verkehrsamt. *Wien*, April 1937. pp. 22. *Typescript.*   IT

807 COCHRANE, W. Charing Cross Road and Rail Bridge. [*London*, 1938?] pp. 7, with 2 diagrams.   TUC
Paper, Southern Railway Debating Society, March 24.

808 GORDON, L. The public corporation in Great Britain. *London*, 1938. pp. viii, 351.   BM
pp. 245–315, 'The London Passenger Transport Board'. With many references to parliamentary publications.

809 IMPROVING London's transport . . . describing the new works scheme of the L.P.T.B., the L.N.E.R. and the G.W.R. *London: Railway Gazette*, May 1946. pp. 108, with many illus., diagrams & maps.   IT
Post-war improvements.

*810 GRAVES, C. London Transport carried on: an account of London at war, 1939–1945. *London: London Passenger Transport Board*, 1947. pp. 95[97], with many illus.   IT

811 LONDON PASSENGER TRANSPORT BOARD. London Transport ABC: an index to London on the move. *London*, July 1947. pp. 27.   BR
Facts and figures.

812 LONDON CHAMBER OF COMMERCE. London's transport. *London*, 1948. pp. 3. *Typescript.*

813 DAVIES, E. Transport in Greater London. *London: London School of Economics*, 1962. pp. 15. [*Greater London Papers*, no. 6.] BM

C 1 (London) C Rail transport in specific areas of London

North London

814 FINCHLEY RESIDENTS OPPOSITION. Finchley residents' opposition to the Northern Junction Railway Bill. *Finchley*, [1914.] pp. [3.]   FINCHLEY PL
Reprints of three letters and a leading article from *The Times* of January 1914.

815 FINCHLEY RESIDENTS OPPOSITION. The Northern Junction Railway menace. *Finchley*, [1914.] s.sh.   FINCHLEY PL
A broadside consisting of two coloured pictures 'Finchley as it is: keep it so!' and 'Finchley as it may be', and the words: 'Support the opposition; stop the Railway!'

816 LAKE, G. H. The railways of Tottenham: a detailed description and historical survey of their development. *London*, 1945. pp. 91, with illus., maps & tables, incl. timetables.   BM
The Great Eastern Rly. and the Tottenham & Hampstead Rly.

*817 WILMOT, G. F. A. The railway in Finchley: a study in suburban development. *Finchley: Finchley Public Libraries Committee*, 1962. pp. 62, with 5 illus. & 2 maps. [*Old Finchley Series*, no. 4.]   BM

North East London

818 HACKNEY BOARD OF WORKS [London]. Report of the Surveyor (J. Lovegrove) on the several railways proposed to be constructed through the Hackney district, Session 1863–4. Printed by order of the Board. *London*, 1863. pp. 14.   BM
Local objections.

819 REES, H. The north-eastern expansion of London since 1770. Thesis, M.Sc. (Econ.), University of London, 1946. pp. vi, 209, with 4 appendices, 31 maps & diagrams; also a MS. map (6 colours for 6 periods). *Typescript.*   UL
pp. 103–28, Expansion during the Railway Age.

820 GIBBINS, P. G. A historical survey of Walthamstow Tramways. *London: Omnibus Society*, 1959. pp. 11, with illus. & a map.   SL

East London

821 ALDGATE WARD RATEPAYERS ASSOCI-ATION [London]. Report on the projected railway schemes affecting the Ward of Aldgate, of Session 1864, and remarks on the unjust state of the law of compensation. (Prepared by E. D. Rogers.) *London*, [1864.] pp. 14, with map.

822 MACCALL, A. W. Bus and tram services from Aldgate to Barking. *London: Omnibus Society*, Dec. 1956. pp. 7. pc
Paper, 29 October, 1956.

823 POLLINS, H. Public passenger transport in East London . . . a lecture given to the East London History Group, 18 October, 1956. pp. 20. *Typescript*. BR

South London

824 DYOS, H. J. Victorian suburb: a study of the growth of Camberwell. *Leicester: University Press*, 1961. pp. 240, with 20 maps & diagrams, & 6 tables. BM
pp. 69–80, and elsewhere, Railways, tramways, and the 'workmen's'.

825 CHADWICK, G. F. The works of Sir Joseph Paxton, 1803–1865. *London: Architectural Press*, 1961. pp. 275, with plates, illus. & diagrams. BM
Includes railways promoted by Paxton, and railways and the Crystal Palace, Sydenham (L.B. & S.C., also the L. & S.W. and the L.C. & D.).

826 'SOUTHEASTERN.' The tramways of Woolwich and South East London; edited by
b G. E. Baddeley. *London: Light Railway Transport League*, in collaboration with *The*
c *Tramway and Light Railway Society*, 1963. pp. 248, with frontis., 109 illus., 4 maps, tables, diagrams, lists, chronology & bibliography. BM
Compiled by F. Merton Atkins, Geoffrey E. Baddeley, Reginald J. Durrant, Richard Elliott, and Alan A. Jackson.

C 1 (London) D 1 Tramways

Historical

827 NEWMAN, S. A. Overground: a review of London's transport, 1900–1947 . . . *London: Ian Allan*, 1947. pp. 40, with illus. LSE
pp. 15–18, Trams.
—— 2nd ed. rev. *London*, [1954.] pp. 32. BM

828 POOLE, S. L. The ABC of London's transport. No. 2, Trams and trolleybuses. *London: Ian Allan*, 1948. pp. 58. BM
pp. 1–16, The history of London's tramways. Lists and illustrations.
—— 2nd edn. *London*, [1949.] pp. 72. BM

829 BETT, W. H. Some notes on the 'Effra Road' tickets of the L.C.C. Tramways and their successors. *London: Light Railway Transport League*, [1951.] pp. 19. BM

*830 KIDNER, R. W. The London tramcar, 1861 to 1951. *South Godstone: Oakwood Press*, 1951. pp. 46, with illus. & lists. [*Locomotion Papers*, no. 7.] BM

831 GILLHAM J. C. London horse omnibus routes at the beginning of 1895. *London*, April 1953. pp. 5. *Reproduced typescript*. IT
Compiled from a list published by the London County Council Statistical Dept. in 1895; re-arranged and tabulated by J. C. Gillham. 176 routes, with a map.

832 GILLHAM, J. C. London horse tramway routes at the beginning of 1895. *London*, April 1953. pp. 4, with la. fold. map. *Reproduced typescript*. IT
Compiled from a list published by the London County Council Statistical Dept. in 1895, re-arranged and tabulated by J. C. Gillham.

833 MORRIS, O. J. Fares, please: the story of London's road transport. A symposium edition. *London: Ian Allan*, 1953. pp. 176, with plates. BM
Includes tramway history.

834 DRYHURST, M. Trams of bygone London. [*London:*] *Dryhurst Publications*, [1958.] pp. 40. BM
Sixty-six illustrations, with descriptions and historical notes.

835 PRICE, J. H. London's first electric railway. *In* 'Journal of Transport History', vol. 3, no. 4, November 1958. pp. 205–11, with map, & 34 bibliogr. notes. BM
Alexandra Park Electric Rly., 1898–9.

836 FLEETWOOD, R. The London tramway network, 1861–1952: a bibliography sub-
b mitted in part requirement for the University of London Diploma in Librarianship, May 1961. pp. 131, with la. fold. map. *Typescript*. UL
pp. 3–6, historical introduction; pp. 12–38, Acts; pp. 39–43, Light Railway Orders; pp. 44–8, Maps; pp. 49–71, General (incl. official papers); pp. 72–80, Horse and early mechanical; pp. 81–93, Electric.

*837 GIBBS, T. A. The Metropolitan Electric Tramways: a short history. *London: The Tramway & Light Railway Society*, 1961. pp. 22, with 6 illus., map, tables of rolling stock and routes. BM

*838 DUNBAR, C. S. London's tramway subway. *London: Light Railway Transport League*, [1964.] pp. 23, with 27 illus., diagram & 2 maps. BM
The Kingsway Tramway Subway.

Contemporaneous

839 GREENE, C. *and* RIPPON, G. P. Street railways in London: special reports of the debates in the Representative Council of Saint Marylebone upon the application of

George Francis Train, Esq., of Boston, U.S., to establish street railways in London; with introduction, incidents, opinion of the Press, and Appendix. *London*, 1860. pp. 128. BM

840 CARTER, J. A letter addressed to ... Lord Palmerston on the proposed embankment of the Thames. *London*, 1861. pp. 11. NLC
Proposes a carriage way, a double line of rails and footways. Suggests that trams should be drawn by horses, not propelled by steam.

841 [TRAIN, G. F.] Report of the banquet given by George Francis Train . . . at St. James's Hall, Piccadilly, to inaugurate the opening of the first street railway in London, The Marble Arch line, March 23rd, 1861; with opinions of the press and extracts on the subject of street railways. *London*, 1861. pp. 110. LSE
pp. 51–110, Press opinions.

842 [NOBLE, J. & Co.] Tramways as a means of facilitating the street traffic of the Metropolis; providing first class public carriages at reduced fares; a more easy and pleasant means of transit, and relieving the rate-payers of the expense of maintaining a large portion of the public streets and roads. *London*, 1865. pp. 16, with diagrams. LSE

843 NOBLE, J. & Co. Observations upon Mr. Bradfield's pamphlet on tramways or railways on Metropolitan streets, in which the assertion of the writer that they 'will be mischievous and dangerous obstructions and nuisances' is completely disproved. *London*, 1866. pp. 18. BM

844 BRADFIELD, J. E. Tramways or railways on Metropolitan streets will be mischievous and dangerous obstructions and nuisances. *London*, 1865–6. pp. 23. LSE
—— another edn. *London*, 1867. pp. 24 BM

845 NOBLE, J. & Co. Metropolitan tramways and omnibus misrepresentations: a reply to Mr. Bradfield's pamphlet on tramways or railways on Metropolitan streets. *London*, 1867. pp. 20. BM
Bradfield's statements 'completely disproved'.

846 [NOBLE, J. & Co.] Metropolitan tramways: explanatory statement and map, proving the advantages of tramways as applied to the traffic of the Metropolis, with tables showing the width of American streets compared with those of London, and traffic returns of London and New York. *London*, 1867. pp. 22, with fold. map showing proposed routes, & tables. BM
pp. 7–15, objections to tramways, and replies.

847 BRADFIELD, J. E. Street railways or street tramways will be mischievous and danger-ous obstructions and nuisances in the crowded streets of London ... *London*, 1868. pp. 27. BM

848 BRIGHT, H. Remarks on street tramways applied to London and its suburbs. *London*, 1868. pp. 15, with 3 plates & a map. BM
Cover title, *The tramway question as applied to London and its suburbs.*

849 MACKAY, C. Street tramways for London: their utility, convenience, and necessity ... *London*, 1868. pp. 19. BM

850 METROPOLITAN BOARD OF WORKS [London]. Analysis of the Bill to Facilitate the Construction and Regulate the Working of Tramways. *London*, 1870. pp. [2.] [no. 417.] G
Signed 'W. Wyke Smith'.

851 SCOTT, W. B. Report on tramways in the Metropolis. *London*, 1870. pp. 70. BM
Addressed to the Parish of St. Pancras General Purposes Committee, December 9, 1869.

852 CARR, H. Metropolitan street traffic: suggested improvements. *London*, 1871. pp. 7. BM
Tramways in *centre* of streets.

853 METROPOLITAN BOARD OF WORKS [London]. Form of Consent to tramway schemes. [*London*, 1871.] pp. 4. G
Meeting of 20 Jan., 1871.

854 METROPOLITAN tramways: statement of obstructions to business and accidents to vehicles, horses and persons caused by existing tramways. *London*, 1873. pp. 23. BM

855 LONDON REFORM UNION. The London County Council and the tramways of London. By J. Allen Baker. *London*, [1887.] pp. 8. [*Progressive Pamphlet* no. 26.] LSE
Public, not private, interests should be first concern of the L.C.C. Comparison with tramways administration in other towns.

856 HOPKINS, A. B. Tramway legislation in London, and tramways belonging to local authorities. By Mr. A. Bassett Hopkins, chairman of the Highways Committee. Second issue, revised and amended. *London: London County Council*, 1891. pp. 90, with 8 statistical tables. BM
An annotated list of Private Acts and Orders, clauses of the Tramways Act (1870), L.C.C. Byelaws, and a list of provincial tramways owned by local authorities.

857 LONDON COUNTY COUNCIL. London County Council *v.* the London Street Tramways Company. Minutes of Evidence and proceedings, Nov. 29–Dec. 2, 1892. LSE

858 LONDON STREET TRAMWAYS. Rules and regulations for the officers & servants. [*London*, 1892.] pp. 39. LSE

859 LONDON COUNTY COUNCIL. Light railways. Conference held at the County Hall

. . . on 12th July 1898, between a Joint Sub-Committee of the Parliamentary and Highways Committees of the Council, and representatives of local authorities affected by the applications to the Light Railway Commissioners for Orders authorising the construction of the London, Barnet, Edgware, and Enfield Light Railways, and the London Southern Light (Electric) Railways. [*London*, 1898.] pp. 9. BM

860 LONDON COUNTY COUNCIL. Light railway schemes, 1899. Reports by the Solicitor. [*London*, 1899.] pp. 2. BM

861 LONDON COUNTY COUNCIL. The Light Railways Act, 1896. Proceedings at the inquiry held at the County Hall, Spring Gardens, on 25th and 26th April 1900, by the Light Railway Commissioners, with regard to the application of the London County Council for orders, under the Light Railways Act, 1896, to authorise the construction of light railways within the County . . . Evidence. [*London*, 1900.] pp. 56. BM

862 LONDON COUNTY COUNCIL—HIGHWAYS COMMITTEE. Tramways. The Council and electrical traction for tramways. Statement of the action taken by the Council with regard to the adoption of electrical traction on its tramways, and description of the system provisionally adopted by the Council subject to approval by the Board of Trade. *London*, 1901. pp. 8, with 6 illus. LCC

863 LONDON COUNTY COUNCIL. Inauguration by . . . the Prince of Wales of the first sections of the Council's electrical tramways, from Westminster and Blackfriars to Tooting, on Friday 15th May, 1903. *London*, [1903.] pp. 32, with 9 plates & map. LCC

864 LONDON COUNTY COUNCIL. Conference on the reconstruction of the Council's northern tramways for electrical traction. Notes of the proceedings at meetings . . . 14 July and 27 October 1904, to consider the systems of electrical traction to be adopted . . . *London*, 1904. pp. 18. LCC

865 LONDON COUNTY COUNCIL. Special inspection of the New Cross and Greenwich tramways on 12 January, 1904. Electrification of the Council's southern tramways. *London*, 1904. pp. 4. LCC

866 LONDON COUNTY COUNCIL. London County Council tramways statistics, 1904. Return prepared by the Statistical Officer . . . showing, for each week and quarter of 1904, the number of passengers carried on the Council's tramways at each fare, on each route, receipts from passengers carried on each route, and number of passengers for the whole year carried on each route . . . *London*, May 1905. pp. 21. LCC
Tables.

867 LONDON COUNTY COUNCIL. Opening of Kingsway and Aldwych by . . . the King, accompanied by . . . the Queen, on Wednesday, 18th October, 1905. *London*, 1905. pp. 40, with 45 plates, including some illustrating the Subway under construction. LCC

868 LONDON COUNTY COUNCIL. [A collection of reports, financial returns and other papers, with illustrations and maps, relating to tramways and steamboat services in London, and to subways in the U.S.A. Twenty-five items, 1899–1906.] LCC

869 LONDON COUNTY COUNCIL. Opening of the tramway over Westminster Bridge and along the Victoria Embankment. Inspection of the line on Friday, 14th December, 1906. [*London*, 1906.] pp. 8. BM

870 LONDON COUNTY COUNCIL. Opening of the tramway subway in connection with the new tramway route between the Strand and Islington. Inspection of the line on Saturday, 24th February, 1906. [*London*, 1906.] pp. 6. LCC

871 LONDON MUNICIPAL SOCIETY. The Tramway Scandal. How the Progressives reckon 'profits'. Report of the debate in the London County Council. *London*, [1906.] pp. 42. LSE

872 BINGHAM, W. G. London electricity and London traffic. *London*, 1908. pp. 22. LSE
Bulk supply of electricity for lighting and tramway extension, and the desirability of having this under control of a public trust.

873 LONDON COUNTY COUNCIL. London County Council Tramways. Financial results. Report of the Finance Committee . . . 22 January, 1907, showing the financial results of the Council's tramways up to that date, with tables summarising the results. *London*, [1908.] pp. 8, 19, with 16 tables. [*Publication* no. 1025.] LCC

874 LONDON COUNTY COUNCIL. Official Tramways Guide. [1st edn.] *London*, 1908. pp. xx, 132, with illus. [*Publication* no. 1169.] BM
Details of routes, with times and route diagrams.

875 LONDON COUNTY COUNCIL. Report on the Council's tramways. Report prepared by Mr. W. B. Peat, President of the Institute of Chartered Accountants, and Mr. F. W. Pixley, F.C.A. . . . upon the accounts of the Council's tramways. *London*, 1908. pp. 19, & 16 schedules. [*Publication* no. 1144.] BM

876 LONDON COUNTY COUNCIL. Special inspection of the tramway subway, Aldwych to the Victoria Embankment, on Friday, 10th April, 1908, at 3 o'clock p.m. [*London*, 1908.] pp. 8, with plate. LCC

877 WOOD, T. M. The so-called 'commercial audit' of the L.C.C. Tramways: a speech ... delivered in the London County Council, 24 March, 1908. [*London*, 1908.] pp. 16. [*L.C.C. Progressive Pamphlets*, no. 29.] LSE

878 HUME, G. H. L.C.C. Tramways, and London electricity supply. *London: London Municipal Society for the Promotion of Municipal Reform*, 1919. pp. 11. BM
London tramways during the war; management/labour relations; development and future plans.

879 LONDON MUNICIPAL SOCIETY. Tramways. [*London*, 1919.] pp. 66[65]–71. [*London Series*, no. 8.] BM
London tramways during the war.

880 LONDON COUNTY COUNCIL—STAFF ASSOCIATION. [Series of lectures given by officers in the Tramways Department at New County Hall, 1921–22.] 7 lectures. *Reproduced typescript.* LCC
[1,] The scope and objects of tramways and other forms of locomotion. By R. G. Thomas. pp. 11.
[2,] Cars: their design, control and repair. By H. S. May. pp. 11.
[3,] Fares, time-tables, through running, etc. By T. E. Thomas. pp. 10, with 9 tables.
[4,] Electric power and distribution. By T. L. Horn. pp. 15.
[5,] Discipline, delays, licences, etc. By S. R. Geary. pp. 9[11].
[6,] Ordering, checking and distribution of stores. By G. T. Dickins. pp. 17, with col. diagram.
[7,] Construction, re-construction and maintenance of track. By J. R. Wignall. pp. 10, with 16 mounted photographs.

881 LONDON COUNTY COUNCIL. London County Council Tramways. [*London*, 1922.] pp. 32[33], with 4 illus. LCC
Produced for the Institute of Transport Congress, May 17–19, 1922. Finance, maintenance, power supply and equipment of L.C.C. Tramways.

882 ROMER, C. The Metropolitan Traffic Manual, containing the law relating to road, river, and air traffic in London and elsewhere. *London: H.M.S.O.*, 1922. pp. xv, 474, 96, xxxv, with 2 fold. maps & tables of statutes and cases. BM
Includes bye-laws and regulations of various tramways.

883 ANTI-SOCIALIST UNION. A costly experiment in municipal socialism: the L.C.C. Tramways. *London*, [1926.] pp. 3[4]. BM

884 MATTHEWS, C. W. The L.C.C. Tramways. *London: London Municipal Society* and *National Union of Ratepayers' Associations*, 1928. pp. 24, with tables. BM
History of the economics of London's tramways. Issued in connection with L.C.C. election, 1928.

885 LONDON COUNTY COUNCIL. A record of selected papers read at depot meetings during Winter Session, 1928–29. *London*, [1929.] pp. 31, with illus. LCC
Three prize-winning essays, relating to improvements in tramway economy and efficiency.

886 LABOUR PARTY—RESEARCH AND INFORMATION DEPARTMENT. The electricity interests and the L.C.C. Tramways. ('Private & confidential.' By J. T. Walton Newbold.) *London*, January 1929. pp. 11. [*Research*, no. 180.] LSE
—— Addendum, Feb. 1929. pp. 2. [*Research*, no. 180x.] LSE

887 UNION CONSTRUCTION COMPANY. Notes concerning tramcar no. 320, built by the Union Construction Co. Ltd., Feltham, Middlesex, for the Metropolitan Electric Tramways, January 1929. *Feltham*, 1929. pp. [7,] with fold. diagrams. PO
Privately printed and distributed.

888 UNION CONSTRUCTION COMPANY. Specimen cars for the Metropolitan Electric Tramways built by the Union Construction and Finance Co. Ltd. *Feltham*, August 1929, with 22 plates, drawings & illustrations. PO
Descriptions of cars 1 and 2 (fleet nos. 320 and 330).

889 LONDON COUNTY COUNCIL. A Guide to Kingsway Tramway. [*London*, 1931.] pp. 32, with illus. & time tables. IT
Issued on the occasion of the re-opening after enlargement.

*890 UNDERGROUND ELECTRIC RAILWAYS. The 'Feltham' car of the Metropolitan Electric and London United Tramways. [*London*,] 1931. pp. 17, with 14 illus. PC

891 LONDON COUNTY COUNCIL. London County Council Tramways: a description of the system of L.C.C. Tramways prepared on the occasion of the Annual Conference of the Tramways, Light Railways & Transport Association, May 1932. *London*, May 1932, with illus. & diagrams. IT

*892 LONDON COUNTY COUNCIL. London County Council Tramways. The Pullman Review; issued in connection with efficiency meetings and essay competition, 1932–33. [*London*,] May 1932. pp. 44, with 37 illus. & 4 diagrams. LCC
General and statistical information.

C 1 (London) D 4 Underground railways

For a genealogical table of the London Passenger Transport Board see Appendix IIId

Historical

893 The HISTORY of the Metropolitan Inner Circle Railway and the efforts to complete it by means of the link line sanctioned by Parliament in 1874, and the attempts made

to delay and prevent its construction. *London*, [1879.]   pp. 63.   pc

894 FRITH, H. The triumphs of modern engineering. *London*, [1891.]   BM
pp. 59–68, 'The Metropolitan railways of London'.

895 MACKAY, T. Life of Sir John Fowler. *London*, 1900. pp. ix, 403, with 18 illus. BM
pp. 145–78, his work on the Metropolitan Rly.

896 EDMONDS, A. History of the Metropolitan District Railway Company to 1908. pp.
c   233, [11.] *Typescript.*   BM

897 METROPOLITAN RLY. The Jubilee of the Metropolitan Railway. *Westminster*, 1913.
c   pp. 7, with illus. & chronology.   PO
Reprinted from the *Railway Gazette*, 10 January, 1913.

898 The UNDERGROUND Electric Railways of London. *In* 'Jubilee of the Railway News, 1864–1914.' *London: Railway News*, [1914.] pp. 149–58, with illus.   BM
History and description.

*899 METROPOLITAN RLY. Diamond Jubilee of the 'Metro': a souvenir of the occasion with a brief review of the Metro's history during its sixty years of public service. *London*, January 1923. pp. 24, with illus. & col. frontis.   RC

900 METROPOLITAN RLY. Metropolitan Railway: a brief review of the Metro's history during its sixty years of public service. [*London, c.* 1923.] pp. 15. [*Lantern Lecture Series.*]   BR

901 METROPOLITAN DISTRICT RLY. Diamond Jubilee, 1868–1928. Exhibition of
c   rolling stock, past and present: some particulars of the exhibits, with notes on the history and operation of the District Railway. South Kensington Station, November 5–10, 1928. [*London*, 1928.] pp. 12[14], with illus., statistics & a chronology of the District Rly.   LSE

902 HIDER, R.C. Report on early history of the Metropolitan Railway, with special reference to the extension to Aylesbury. Dec. 1931. pp. 33, with 2 maps. *Typescript.*   BR

903 PASSINGHAM, W. J. Romance of London's Underground. *London*, [1932.] pp. x, 243, with 87 illus.   BM
Historical and descriptive.

904 LUZZETTI, C. A. The construction of the London Underground Railways: a study of

b the creation of an important public utility by private enterprise. (Thesis, B.Litt., Univ. Oxford, 1939.) pp. 153, with tables, bibliogr. notes & a bibliography largely consisting of official reports and publications. No map. *Typescript.* UNIV. OXFORD
The effects of original financing, constructing and routing, and of subsequent extentions, upon the fortunes of the companies and upon suburban development.

905 BUILDING the Inner Circle Railway: a remarkable series of early constructional photographs reprinted from 'The Railway Gazette', November . . . 1945. *Westminster: Railway Gazette*, 1946. pp. 32.   BM
Thirty-three illustrations with accompanying texts, and a section on the architecture of Metropolitan Railway stations.

906 LONDON   PASSENGER   TRANSPORT BOARD. The story of the Underground: a London Transport lantern lecture. *Westminster*, [1947.] pp. 19.   pc
Notes for lecturers, to accompany a sequence of ninety-four pictures.

907 LONDON TRANSPORT EXECUTIVE. The first electric tube railway in the world opened sixty years ago: Diamond Jubilee of the 'City Tube'. *London*, 1950. pp. 5[6], with a map showing the development of the Northern Line. [*T.P.N.* 816.] *Reproduced typescript.*   IT

908 LONDON   TRANSPORT   EXECUTIVE— PRESS & PUBLICATIONS OFFICE. The Two-penny Tube reaches its half century. Central Line Jubilee, July 30, 1950. [*London*, 1950.] pp. 5. *Typescript.*
A short history of the Central Line.

909 WILSON, B. G. *and* HARAM, V. S. The Central London Railway. *London: Fairseat Press*, 1950. pp. 49, with 12 illus.   BM
Published by the authors.

910 BAKER, J. C. Y. The Metropolitan Railway. *South Godstone: Oakwood Press*, 1951, pp. 76, with 15 plates, illus., & a bibliography. [*Oakwood Library of Railway History*, no. 7.]   BM
—— Reprinted, *Lingfield*, 1960. pp. 76, with additional illus. and a revised map. BM

911 MORRIS, O. J. London's Underground: a pictorial survey. (London's Underground in pictures.) *London: Ian Allan*, 1951. pp. 32.   BM
137 illustrations, being the pictorial section of H. F. Howson's *London's Underground* (1951).

912 KEEN, P. A. Metropolitan Railway road services. *In* 'Journal of Transport History',
b   vol. 1, no. 4, November 1954. pp. 216–37, with map, 2 tables of services, & 100 bibliogr. notes.   BM

913 LASCELLES, T. S. The City & South London Railway. *Lingfield: Oakwood Press*, 1955. pp. 36, with 13 illus. on 8 plates, map, & tables of locomotives & rolling stock in text. [*Oakwood Library of Railway History*, no. 11.]   BM

914 BALL, A. W. London underground railways (1863–1956). Bibliography submitted
b in part requirement for University of London Diploma in Librarianship, May 1956. pp. 122. *Typescript.*   UL(GL)
A detailed bibliography of general, historical, economic and technical works, Acts of Parliament, and maps. Annotated. An historical introduction (pp. 1–7).

915 BETT, W. H. The evolution of the Tube ticket office. *Sidcup: Electric Railway Society*, July 1956. pp. 41–8. *Reproduced typescript* from *El. Rly. Soc. Jnl.* [*Booklet* no. 1.]   BM

916 BETT, W. H. Early tube tickets: and The evolution of the Tube ticket office, 2nd end. *Sidcup: Electric Railway Society*, July 1956. pp. iv, 41–8. *Reproduced typescript.* [*Booklet* no. 1., rev.]   BM

917 LEE, C. E. The Metropolitan District Railway. *Lingfield: Oakwood Press*, 1956.
c pp. 51, with 21 illus. & maps on 13 plates, chronologies, & lists of stations & officials. [*Oakwood Library of Railway History*, no. 12.]   BM

*918 LEE, C. E. Fifty years of the Hampstead Tube. *London: London Transport*, 1957. pp. 28, with 15 illus. on 8 plates & a map.   BM

The Northern Line.

919 PRIGMORE, B. J. London Transport tube stock, 1923–34: an analysis. *Sidcup: Electric Railway Society*, Jan. 1957. pp. [4,] with a list. [*Booklet* no. 2.]   BM

920 PRIGMORE, B. J. *and* ATKINSON, F. G. London Underground tube stock, 1900–20: an analysis. *Sidcup: Electric Railway Society*, March 1958. pp. [4,] with a list. *Reproduced typescript.* [*Booklet* no. 4.]   BM

921 ROBBINS, R. M. Lord Kelvin on electric railways. *In* 'Journal of Transport History', vol. 3, no 4, November 1958. pp. 235–8, with 5 bibliogr. notes.   BM
William Thompson (1824–1907). Includes a long letter from him to Francis A. Lucas, Chairman, Central London Rly., 6 January, 1893.

922 BETT, W. H. Scheme tickets on the London Underground. *Sidcup: Electric Railway Society*, in association with the *Ticket & Fare Collection Society*, 1959. pp. xv [*Booklet* no. 6.]   IT
Reprint, *Journal of the Electric Railway Society.*

923 PRIGMORE, B. J. London Transport tube stock till 1939. *Sidcup: Electric Railway Society*, [1960.] pp. 12[20]. [*Booklet* no. 8.]   BM

*924 HOWSON, F. H. London's Underground. *London: Ian Allan*, 1951. pp. 144, with
c many illus. on plates & a chronology.   BM
—— rev. edn. *London*, 1960. pp. 119.   BM
—— 3rd edn. *London*, 1962. pp. 125.   BM

925 JACKSON, A. A. *and* CROOME, D. F. Rails through the clay: a history of London's
c tube railways. *London: Allen & Unwin*, 1962. pp. 406, with 34 illus. on 16 plates, 3 maps, diagrams, chronology, and lists of accidents, power failures, fires and strikes.   BM
A detailed survey with social, political and financial background, including the important place of Charles Tyson Yerkes.
pp. [373]–384, 'some notes on tube tickets and ticket issuing machines'.

926 BENEST, K. Metropolitan electric locomotives. *Sutton: Lens of Sutton*, 1963. pp. 44, with 16 illus. on 4 plates, scale drawing of a locomotive, map, & 2 tables.   BM

*927 DAY, J. R. The story of London's Underground. *London: London Transport*, 1963. pp. v, 153, with 30 illus. on 16 plates, & a col. map inserted.   BM

928 DOUGLAS, H. The Underground story. *London: Robert Hale*, 1963. pp. 208, with 23 illus. on 12 plates, & 3 maps.   BM
An account of the birth and development of the London underground railways (subway and tube), with particular emphasis on social aspects and biographical elements (Charles Pearson, Charles Tyson Yerkes, John Fowler, and Lord Ashfield).

929 THE EARLY history of the Metropolitan District and Metropolitan railways in Wembley. *Wembley: Wembley Transport Society*, 1963. pp. 43, with 6 illus. on 2 plates, 4 illus., drawings, diagrams, & 2 maps. *Reproduced typescript.* [*Publication* no. 3.]   BM

930 GADSDEN, E. J. S. Metropolitan Steam. *Northwood: Roundhouse Books*, 1963. pp. 43, with frontis., 56 illus. on 30 plztes, tables, & bibliography.   BM

931 TIMES *newspaper.* The Times Supplement on the Centenary of the London Underground. *London*, 24 May, 1963. pp. xxvi, with 50 illus. & a map.   BM

Contemporaneous

932 NEW Metropolitan railways: a view of the comparative merits of the various Metropolitan railway projects, and the projects for effecting through lines between the railways of the north and the railways of the west of England via London, and the railways or ports and watering places of the south and south-east of England. *London*, 1845. pp. 37, with fold. map. HRL

933 PEARSON, C. Central City Terminus: letters from Charles Pearson to W. H. Ashurst, Member of the Corporation of London, and Chairman of the Committee of City Lands, and from Mr. Ashurst to the Members of the Corporation of London, and others connected with trade in the City of London, on the importance of a central City terminus to the citizens and to the retail trade of the City. [*London*, 1845.] pp. 20
PO

934 PEARSON, C. [A letter to W. H. Ashurst of the City of London Court of Common Council on a proposed Central City Terminus for the proposed London & Manchester Railroad, at Farringdon Street; a reply from Ashurst, and a letter from him on the subject to the Members of the Corporation of London.] *London*, Oct. 1845. pp. 20. G

935 PEARSON, C. Upon the importance of a Central City Terminus . . . Petitions presented to the Court of Common Council upon the subject. *London*, 1845. G

936 WILLIAMS, J. Sub-railways in London: letters to Her Majesty's ministers, the Commissioners for Metropolitan Improvements and the Commissioners for the Health of Towns in 1844 and 1845, respecting a great improvement in the streets of London, which is equally necessary in all the cities and towns in the Kingdom; to which is added a proposal for sub-railways in the Metropolis. *London*, [1845.] pp. 35. BM
Fifteen letters followed by a description of the author's conception of sub-railways.

937 OGIER, J. C. H. Proposal for a general Metropolitan railway: a letter to the Commissioners appointed to investigate projects for Metropolitan railway termini. *London*, 1846. pp. 14, with fold. map. PO
A railway encircling London and bisecting it, with no terminus, but with numerous stations.

938 PEARSON, C. The substance of several speeches . . . developing a project . . . for the purpose of effecting great street improvements in the City and suburbs of London, in combination with the erection of spacious railway stations in Farringdon Street . . . *London*, [1851.] pp. 48, with fold. plan of proposed stations & a fold. sketch (frontis.). BM
Cover title—*City improvements & railroad termini.*

939 PEARSON, C. An address to the electors of London. *London*, 1852. pp. 12, with fold. plan. UL(GL)
A railway through the heart of London with a central station in Farringdon Road area, to relieve traffic congestion.

940 PEARSON, C. An imaginary speech, supposed to have been delivered by the City Solicitor at a meeting of Common Councilmen proposed to have been held on the 7th February, 1853, preparatory to the election of City Officers. *London*, 1853, with maps and plans. G
On his proposed Central City Terminus.

941 PEARSON, C. [Speech at a meeting of the shareholders of the City Railroad Terminus Company on his retiring as honorary director.] *London*, [1853.] G

942 WILLIAMS, J. Metropolitan sub-arch railways, and the streets of London made perfect, without disturbing the paving for pipes, sewers, or any other purpose. The line of railway is shown and this entirely new system clearly described. *London*, 1854. pp. 19.
BM
Prefaced by reprints of letters to *The Times* and to Lord John Russell.

943 TAYLOR, G. L. Programme and plan of the Metropolitan General Junction Railways and Roads. *London*, 1855. pp. 26, with la. fold. map & plan. BM
'A connection of the various railways with one another.'

944 FOOTMAN, W. A practical means of providing an efficient accommodation for the traffic of the Metropolis. *London*, 1856. pp. 16. BM
Railway inter-communication with through routes. Other schemes reviewed and compared.

945 MITCHELL, J. Practical suggestions for relieving the over-crowded thoroughfares of London, securing improved means of locomotion . . . in a letter addressed to Sir Benjamin Hall . . . Chief Commissioner to the Board of Works. *London*, 1857. pp. 26, with 3 plates, fold. map & fold. diagram.
BM
A proposal for a submerged railway, partly covered, partly in open cuttings, from Kensington Gardens to the City.

946 PEARSON, C. Correspondence between the Great Northern Railway Company and Charles Pearson, City Solicitor . . . relative to the Fleet Valley Railway and City Terminus. *London*, 1858. G

947 WILKINSON, W. A. Metropolitan railway terminal accommodation and its effect on traffic results. [*London*, 1858.] pp. 15.
                                                             BM
From the *Journal of the Statistical Society of London*, June 1858.
Remoteness of Paddington a detriment to G.W.R. prosperity.

948 PEARSON, C. Letter to the citizens of London in favour of the Metropolitan Railway and City station. *London*, 1859.   G

949 PEARSON, C. Proceedings at a public meeting held at the London Tavern on the 1st December 1858. *London*, 1859. pp. 55.   NLC
Concerning the proposed Metropolitan Rly.

950 PEARSON, C. A twenty-minutes letter to the citizens of London in favour of the Metropolitan Railway & City Station. *London*, 1859. pp. 22, with prospectus. BM

951 METROPOLITAN RLY. London Metropolitan Railway, from Paddington to Finsbury Circus. Photographic views to illustrate the work in progress. [*London*,] July 1862.   G
An album of mounted photographs; 28 views, 15 plans and a map.

952 HOLLINGSHEAD, J. Underground London. *London*, 1862. pp. 244.   BM
pp. 203–12, Underground railways (the Metropolitan Rly.).

953 GILES, F. The Great City & West End Railway. Report upon the route and general character of the Great City & West End Railway, and estimated cost; with a map and section. *London*, June 1863. pp. 3, with la. fold. map & section.   G
A proposed underground railway from Oxford Circus via Trafalgar Square to the Mansion House, with stations at Trafalgar Square, Chancery Lane and Farringdon Street. Tunnel to be from 12 ft. to 20 ft. below the surface.

954 MAYHEW, H. The shops and companies of London, and the trades and manufactories of Great Britain. *London*, 1865.   BM
vol. 1, pp. 142–53, 'The Metropolitan Railway'; with 3 illus. & 4 tables.

955 METROPOLITAN Railway: a peep into the future of the Metropolitan Underground Railway and a forecast of the next dividend: with extracts from official documents, etc. By One Who Knows. *London*, 1865. pp. 18.   BM

956 BARLOW, P. W. On the relief of London street traffic, with a description of the Tower Subway, now shortly to be executed. *London*, 1867. pp. 29.   BM
Proposes manually propelled carriages on rails in a tunnel: pp. 17–23, 'Observations on the system . . .' by John C. Adagh.

957 LYTHGOE, J. P. The Metropolitan Railway: its position and prospects examined. By J. P. Lythgoe, Public Accountant. *London*, 1868. pp. 21[23], with financial tables.   BR
'Conclusions very widely at variance with those indicated in the reports of the directors, etc.'

958 METROPOLITAN BOARD OF WORKS [London]. Report of the Works and General Purposes Committee as to the course taken by the Board with regard to the construction of the Metropolitan District Railway works along the line of the Thames Embankment, North, and the new street to the Mansion House. *London*, [1868.] pp. 20.   G

959 The METROPOLITAN Railway: what dividend will it really pay? An unexaggerated statement. *London*, 1868. pp. 23.   PC
The financial history, present position and future prospects of the Met. Rly.

960 'VERITAS'. The Metropolitan Railway; its public convenience, its capital, its traffic, its dividends. By Veritas. *London*, 1868. pp. 16.   BM

961 LYTHGOE, J. P. The Metropolitan Railway: its position and prospects again examined. *London*, 1870. pp. 21[25]. NLC

962 P., E. C. The Metropolitan District Railway: its approaching completion and consequent prospects. *London*, [1870?] pp. 16.   NLC

963 BARLOW, P. W. The relief of street traffic; advantages of the City & Southwark Subway, with reasons why the proposed connection of street tramways from the Elephant and Castle through the City is unnecessary and undesirable. Second pamphlet. *London*, 1871. pp. 6.   BM
Plan to transfer tramway passengers to an underground railway to relieve congestion in the City.

964 [SMILES, R.] Metropolitan District Railway. Opening of the line from Blackfriars Bridge to the Mansion House Station, Queen Victoria Street, and of the enlarged station at South Kensington, and of the North Junction between Kensington High Street Station and the West London Railway: with a report of the proceedings at the banquet . . . July 1st, 1871. [*London*, 1871.] pp. 31.   BM

965 BARLOW, P. W. A description of the Southwark & City double line of subway, or tunnel, shewing the important effect it will have in relieving the traffic of London Bridge. *London*, 1873. pp. 8, with map.
                                                             NLC

966 METROPOLITAN, METROPOLITAN DISTRICT *and* ST. JOHN'S WOOD RAILWAYS. Report of interview with the Chancellor

of the Exchequer on the subject of passenger duty. (Passenger duty on the underground railways.) *London*, 1873. pp. 8.   LSE

967 WALFORD, E. [Thornbury's] Old and new London ... *London*, 1873. 5 vols.   BM
vol. 5, pp. 224–42, 'Underground London, its railways, subways & sewers'; with 3 illus. The Metropolitan Rly.

968 The METROPOLITAN Railway and its prospects. By a Proprietor. [*London*,] 1875. pp. 4.   ICE
'Hold fast to your stock!'

969 HUET, M. Les Chemins de fer métropolitains de Londres. (Étude d'un réseau de chemins de fer métropolitains pour la ville de Paris.) *Paris*, 1878. pp. 132, with tables, 3 plates, & a fold. map.   ICE
pp. 10–76, Metropolitan and Metropolitan District Rlys.

970 METROPOLITAN *and* METROPOLITAN DISTRICT RAILWAYS. Memorandum of interview, with deputation from the public bodies, at the Board of Works ... October 27th, 1879. *London*, 1879. pp. 15.   PC
—— Memorandum of further interview ... November, 3rd 1879. *London*, 1879. pp. 12.   PC

971 WATKIN, E. W. In arbitration. The Metropolitan and Metropolitan District Railways (City Lines & Extensions) Act, 1879. Proceedings in this reference before G. S. Venables. [*London*, 1879.] pp. 56.   NLC
E. W. Watkin's evidence.

972 PINKS, W. J. The history of Clerkenwell ... *London*, 1865.   BM
pp. 357–68, 'The Metropolitan Railway', with 2 illus.
—— 2nd edn. *London*, 1881.   BM

973 MACALPINE, W. J. The New York Arcade Railway as projected, compared with the underground railways of London. Report to the Broadway Underground Railway Co. [*New York*,] 1884. pp. 24.   P

974 ILLUSTRATIONS. The District Railway and the London 'Circle' train service. [*London*, c. 1886.] pp. 7.   BR
Reprinted from Francis George Heath's pictorial magazine, *Illustrations*.

975 SCOTT, W. B. Critical condition of the Underground Railway: reports of W. B. Scott on the extraordinary sinking and lateral movement of the railway tunnel in Euston Road in November and December, 1885 ... never before published. *London*, 1886. pp. 16.   BM

976 MATHER AND PLATT. City of London & Southwark Subway: description of proposed scheme for working by electricity, and esti-

mate of cost. *Manchester*, [Sept. 1888.] pp. 11.   LSE

977 MATHER AND PLATT. City of London & Southwark Subway: proposed scheme for working by electricity. Private and confidential. *Manchester*, [May 1888.] pp. 11.   LSE

978 [METROPOLITAN RLY.] The Metropolitan Railway: a fifteen per cent. paying line. 10th edn. *London*, 1888. pp. 52.   LSE
Assurance to shareholders of the good prospects ahead for the Metropolitan Rly.

979 CENTRAL LONDON RLY. Statement as to the proposed railway (In Parliament, Session 1890). [*London*, 1889.] pp. 11.   LSE
Criticisms answered.

980 HAZARD, R. R. Underground railway communication in great cities. (Automatic ventilating superficial subway system) (London Central Subway Railway). 3rd edn. *London*, 1889. pp. 26, 2, with 3 illus.   ICE
Proposed to be built under the main streets of London. Pages 15–26, Press opinions.

981 CALLARD, E. The ventilation of the Metropolitan Railway tunnels: the case for mechanical ventilation. Memorandum submitted to the Committee appointed by the Board of Trade (Departmental Committee on the Ventilation of the London underground railways). *London*, 1898. pp. 36.   ICE

982 CITY & SOUTH LONDON RLY. City & South London Railway. Description of the works. Inaugurated by ... the Prince of Wales on Tuesday, 4th November 1890. [*London*, 1890.] pp. 16, with 12 illus. & map.   PC

983 FRITH, H. The triumphs of modern engineering. *London*, [1891.]   BM
pp. 104–11, 'The South London Subway'.

984 LUIGGI, L. La nuova ferrovia elettrica sotteranea di Londra: note di viaggio. *Roma*, 1891. pp. 20, with fold. plate.   BM
The City & South London Rly.

985 CENTRAL LONDON RLY. The Central London Railway. [*London*, 1892.] pp. 29 [33], with illus & map.   LSE
History and description; financial and traffic statistics.

986 TROSKE, L. Die Londoner Untergrundbahnen. *Berlin*, 1892. pp. 102, mit 2 lithographierten Tafeln und 156 in den Text gedruckten Abbildungen.   LSE
Reprinted from *Zeitschrift des Vereines deutscher Ingenieur*, 1891 and 1892.

987 HOPKINSON, E. Electrical railways. *London*, 1893. pp. 24, with fold. plate.   LSE
Excerpt, *Min. Proc. I.C.E.*, vol. 112. Session 1892–93. part ii.
The City & South London Rly.

988 EXPLORATION COMPANY. Notes on the Central London Railway. (Private: not for circulation.) *London*, 1895. pp. 31, with illus. & 2 maps.   LSE
History and description. The appendix contains letters between F. A. Lucas and Lord Kelvin, and statistical tables for London traffic, 1867–1893.

989 GREATHEAD, J. H. The City & South London Railway; with some remarks upon subaqueous tunnelling by shield and compressed air . . . *London*, 1895. pp. 37, with 3 fold. sheets at end with diagrams, maps and sections of the line and its stations.   LSE

990 BRITISH THOMSON-HOUSTON COMPANY. The Central London Railway. *London*, 1898. pp. 30, with 51 diagrams & map. PO

991 LEIGHTON, J. Tubular transit for London. (The need and the remedy.) *London*, 1902. pp. 16, with diagrams.   BM
Plan for a symmetrical network of underground railways.

992 BRITISH WESTINGHOUSE ELECTRIC AND MANUFACTURING COMPANY. Electric traction on the Metropolitan Railway. *London*, [1904.] pp. 28, with illus., diagrams & map.   PO
Reprinted from the *Tramway & Railway World*, July 1904.

993 STATIST. The Underground Electric Railways Company of London, Ltd. *London: U.E. Rlys.*, Sept. 1904.   RC
A large folded map, issued with the *Statist*, 15 Oct., 1904, to accompany an article (pp. 656–60), 'London's new underground railways'.

994 BRITISH THOMSON-HOUSTON COMPANY. Electrification of the Metropolitan District Railway. [*London*, 1905.] pp. 39, with illus., diagrams & map.   BR
From the *Tramway & Railway World*, Feb. 1905.

995 BRITISH THOMSON-HOUSTON COMPANY. Metropolitan District Railway electrification. *London*, 1905. pp. 39. la. 4°, with 38 illus., diagrams & a map.   BR
Reprinted from the *Tramway & Railway World*, Feb. 1905.

996 CENTRAL LONDON RLY. Report and record of four years working. By Granville C. Cunningham, General Manager. [*London*,] 1905. pp. 29, with 6 statistical tables.   LSE
Addressed to chairman and directors, period, 1901–1904.

997 FORTENBAUGH, S. B. The electrification of the London Underground Electric Railways Company's system. pp. 34, with 71 illus. & diagrams.   BR

Reprinted from the *Street Railways Journal*, 4 March, 1905.
S. B. Fortenbaugh was Electrical Engineer to the U.E. Rlys. Co.

998 TEBB, W. S. The chemical and bacteriological conditions of the air on the City & South London Railway. *London*, 1905. pp. 14.   BM
A report to Southwark Borough Council.

999 BAKER STREET & WATERLOO RLY. Baker Street & Waterloo Railway, March 1906. Description. *London*, 1906. pp. 25, with illus., maps & diagrams.   LSE
Reprinted from *Tramway & Railway World*, 8 March, 1906.

1000 BRITISH WESTINGHOUSE ELECTRIC & MANUFACTURING CO. The Metropolitan Railway, 1863–1906. *London & Manchester*, 1906. pp. 41, with 28 illus., including several of Neasden Power Station, & a map.   LSE
Largely concerned with generation of current.

1001 GREAT Northern, Piccadilly & Brompton Railway. *London: Tramway & Railway World*, 1906. pp. 16, with illus., diagrams & maps.
Reprinted from *Tramway & Railway World*, 6 December, 1906.

1002 GREAT NORTHERN, PICCADILLY & BROMPTON RLY. Illustrated description of the Great Northern, Piccadilly & Brompton Railway. [*London*, 1906.] pp. 48, with 12 illus., timetable & a fold. map.

1003 GREAT NORTHERN, PICCADILLY & BROMPTON RLY. Souvenir of the opening of the Great Northern, Piccadilly & Brompton Railway, December 15th, 1906 . . . [*London*, 1906.] pp. 28, with illus., tables & a fold. map.   LSE
A description of the railway.

1004 WESTINGHOUSE BRAKE COMPANY. Automatic signalling on the underground railways of London. *London*, 1906. pp. 68, with 36 illus. & diagrams. [*Signalling Pamphlet, no. 9.*]   BR
The Metropolitan District; Baker St. & Waterloo; Great Northern, Piccadilly & Brompton.

1005 CHARING CROSS, EUSTON & HAMPSTEAD RLY. Charing Cross, Euston & Hampstead Railway . . . Formal opening, Saturday June 22, 1907. *London*, 1907. LSE
Reprinted from the *Railway Times*.

1006 CHARING CROSS, EUSTON & HAMPSTEAD RLY. Illustrated description of the Hampstead Tube. (Souvenir of the Opening, June 22, 1907.) *London*, 1907. pp. 31, with illus., tables & a map.   LSE

1007 CHARING CROSS, EUSTON & HAMPSTEAD RLY. Report of proceedings at the luncheon at the Car Depot, Golders Green, on the occasion of the opening . . . of the Charing Cross, Euston & Hampstead Railway on Saturday, 22nd June, 1907 . . . [*London*, 1907.] pp. 27.　LSE

1008 CITY & SOUTH LONDON RLY. Extension to King's Cross, St. Pancras, and Euston. Souvenir of the Opening Ceremony (11th May 1907). *London*, 1907. pp. 30[31], with 11 illus., map & financial tables, 1890–1906.　PC

1009 HALDEN, G. M. Setting out of tube railways. *London*, 1907. pp. 68, with 4 plates, illus., & 4 fold. route plans.　BM
　Great Northern & City Railway.

1010 HAY, H. H. D. The tube railways of London: their design and construction. *In* 'Engineering wonders of the world', edited by Archibald Williams. *London*, [1909, 1910.] vol. 1, pp. 227–40; 300–11, with illus.　BM

1011 CENTRAL LONDON RLY. Report of Manager on proposed extension into the Thames Valley. *London*, 1912. pp. 20[21], with 5 tables.　LSE
　Shepherds Bush via L. & S.W. Rly. to Richmond.

1012 METROPOLITAN RLY. Baker Street Station alterations. *London*, 1912. pp. 8, with illus.　PO
　Reprinted from the *Railway Gazette*, 1st December, 1911.

1013 PEARSON, C. An Alphabet of T.O.T.: train, omnibus, tram; illustrated by Charles Pearson. [*London*]: *Underground Electric Railways*, [*c*. 1914.] pp. [28.]　PC
　Twenty-seven coloured drawings of contemporary scenes.

1014 SMITH, J. S. The progress and future of the Metropolitan Railway. *In* 'Jubilee of the Railway News, 1864–1914.' pp. 141–8, with illus.　BM

1015 METROPOLITAN RLY. London Traffic Enquiry, 1919. Statement submitted to the Select Committee by the General Manager of the Metropolitan Railway Company. *London*, [1919.] pp. 11, with tables.　LSE
　Basic facts concerning the administration and operation of the Metropolitan Rly. since 1913.

1016 LONDON COUNTY COUNCIL. Report of meeting of November 1st, 1921, to discuss E. Davies' motion for the construction of a municipal tube. 1921. pp. 46. *Typescript.*　LCC

1017 UNDERGROUND ELECTRIC RAILWAYS. Some particulars about London's Underground. [*London*, 1921.] pp. [8,] with illus.　IT

1018 UNDERGROUND ELECTRIC RAILWAYS. Acton Rolling Stock Overhaul Works. *London*, 1924. pp. 11, with illus. [*Facts concerning London's Underground, no. 3.*] LSE

1019 UNDERGROUND ELECTRIC RAILWAYS. Engineering developments. *London*, 1924. pp. 14, with illus. [*Facts concerning London's Underground, no. 4.*]　LSE

1020 UNDERGROUND ELECTRIC RAILWAYS. The Power House. *London*, 1924. pp. 19, with illus. [*Facts concerning London's Underground, no. 1.*]　LSE

1021 [UNDERGROUND ELECTRIC RAILWAYS.] Re-opening of the City & South London Railway, Monday, 1st December, 1924 . . . Some account of the origin and history of the railway and a description of the new works. [*London*, 1924.] pp. 31, with illus.　LSE

1022 UNDERGROUND ELECTRIC RAILWAYS. Signalling, safety and speed on the Underground. *London*, 1924. pp. 8, with illus. [*Facts concerning London's Underground, no. 5.*]　LSE

1023 UNDERGROUND ELECTRIC RAILWAYS. How a tube railway is constructed. *London*, 1926. pp. 16, with illus. [*Facts concerning London's Underground, no. 7.*] LSE

1024 UNDERGROUND ELECTRIC RAILWAYS. Opening of the Morden Extension and the Kennington Loop, Monday, 13 September, 1926, with some account of other extensions and improvements carried out on the Underground system. [*London*, 1926.] pp. 39, with 27 illus. & 6 maps & diagrams. LSE

1025 PALMER, A. The 'District' Signalman. *In his* 'Straphangers.' *London*, 1927. pp. 38–46; with plate.　BM
　Description of his work.

1026 THOMAS, J. P. Handling London's Underground traffic. *London*, 1928. pp. vii, 237.　BM
　Includes illustrations of early equipment and scenes.

1027 [UNDERGROUND ELECTRIC RAILWAYS.] Acton Rolling Stock Overhaul Works. [*London*,] 1928. pp. 31, with 37 illus. & plans.　LSE

1028 [UNDERGROUND ELECTRIC RAILWAYS.] The new Piccadilly Circus Station, opened . . . December 10th 1928: a description of the new station and its supplementary works, with some account of the engineering difficulties . . . *Westminster*, [1928.] pp. 24, with illus.　IT

1029 HALL, H. The new Piccadilly Circus Station, *London*, 1929. pp. 25, with 2 la. fold. plates.   BR
    Excerpt, *Min. Proc. I.C.E.*, vol. 22, Session 1928–29.

1030 UNDERGROUND ELECTRIC RAILWAYS. A description of the new administrative offices of the Underground Group of Companies. [*Westminster*, 1929.] pp. 15, with 6 illus. & a diagram.   PC
    Cover title, *55 Broadway*.

1031 METROPOLITAN VICKERS ELECTRICAL COMPANY. Metropolitan Railway electrification. [*Manchester*, 1923.] pp. 50, with illus.   PO

1032 EATON, I. C. London Underground Railway construction: a description of the Southgate extension of the Piccadilly Line, with special reference to the setting out. [1932.] pp. 75, with tables & diagrams. *Reproduced typescript.*   IME
    Paper, Glasgow Association of Students of the I.C.E., 18 November, 1932.

1033 [UNDERGROUND ELECTRIC RAILWAYS.] The Overhaul Works of London's Underground, Acton. [*London*,] August 1932. pp. 47, with illus. & la. fold. plan.   IT

1034 UNDERGROUND extensions and improvements. *London: Railway Gazette*, 1932. pp. 68, with illus. Supplement to *Railway Gazette*, 18 Nov. 1932.   IT
    London Underground.

1035 BRITISH ELECTRICAL & ALLIED MANUFACTURERS ASSOCIATION. Electrical equipment for London's Underground Railways. *London*, Nov. 1933. pp. 83, with many illus.   BR

1036 LONDON PASSENGER TRANSPORT BOARD. How a tube railway is constructed. *Westminster*, 1934. pp. 20, with illus.   BM

1037 LONDON PASSENGER TRANSPORT BOARD. The overhaul of Underground rolling stock. *Westminster*, 1934. pp. 52, with illus. & a fold. diagram.   BM

1038 LONDON PASSENGER TRANSPORT BOARD. Safety on the Underground. *Westminster*, 1934. pp. 12, with illus. BM

1039 SOMMERFIELD, V. Underground railways; their construction and working. *London*, 1934. pp. xi, 105, with illus.   BM
    Mainly London Underground railways.

1040 LONDON PASSENGER TRANSPORT BOARD. Underground: a series of press advertisements reprinted from The Times, Daily Telegraph, Financial News, Financial Times, Evening News, Evening Standard, Star, September–October, 1938. [*London* 1938.] pp. [8.]   BR
    Brief facts and statistics.

1041 LONDON PASSENGER TRANSPORT BOARD. The Central Line extension, Liverpool Street to Stratford. *Westminster*, [1946.] pp. 30[31], with 23 illus. & a route diagram.   PC

1042 LONDON PASSENGER TRANSPORT BOARD. How London's tube railways are built: a London Transport lantern lecture. *Westminster*, [1947.] pp. 21.   PC
    Notes for lecturer, to accompany a sequence of sixty-four pictures.

1043 LONDON PASSENGER TRANSPORT BOARD. Seven more stations on the Central Line. *Westminster*, [1947.] pp. 31, with illus.   IT
    Leytonstone to Woodford and to Newbury Park.

1044 LONDON TRANSPORT EXECUTIVE. Central Line extensions, November 1948. *Westminster*, [1948.] pp. 31, with 28 illus. & map.   BM

1045 NEURATH, M. Railways under London. *London: Adprint*, 1948. pp. 32.   BM
    Instructive coloured diagrams of tube railways, with descriptions.

1046 LONDON TRANSPORT EXECUTIVE. The Circle Line and its rolling stock. [*London*,] Oct. 1950. pp. 6. [*T.P.N.* 773.] *Reproduced typescript.*   IT

1047 MINISTRY OF TRANSPORT AND CIVIL AVIATION. The Victoria Line: Report by the London Travel Committee to the Minister of Transport and Civil Aviation. (Chairman, Alex Samuels.) *London*, 1959. pp. 40, with 2 maps & an errata slip.   BM
    Walthamstow to Victoria. The report begins with a general survey of the present transport situation in London (pp. 1–9).

1048 TURNER, F. S. P. Preliminary planning for a new tube railway across London. *London: I.C.E.*, 1959. pp. 19–38, with 2 fold. diagrams. [*Paper* 6343.]   IT
    Excerpt, *Procs. I.C.E.*, vol. 12, Jan. 1959. Victoria to Walthamstow.

*1048a GARBUTT, P. E. How the Underground works. *London: London Transport*, 1963. pp. viii, 116, with frontis., 28 illus. on 16 plates, & 23 diagrams & maps.   BM
    Construction, power supply, signalling, operation, and organization; with statistics for 1962.

C 1 (London) E Engineering (civil and mechanical)

Electrification

1049 MOODY, G. T. London's electrifications, 1890–1923. *Sidcup: Electric Railway Soci-*

ety, 1961. pp. 14. *Reproduced typescript.*
BM
Origins of electric traction on all London railways, main line and underground.

Station Architecture

1050 BETJEMAN, J. First and Last Loves. *London: Murray*, 1952. pp. xi, 244. BM
pp. 75–89, London railway stations.
Previously published in *Flower of Cities: a book of London. Studies and sketches by twenty-two authors* (1949). pp. 13–30.

1051 KNIGHT, C. London. Edited by C. Knight. *London*, 1841–4. 6 vols. BM
vol. 6, pp. 305–20, Railway termini; with 4 illus.

1052 KNIGHT, C. Knight's Cyclopædia of London. *London*, 1851. BM
pp. 839–60, Metropolitan (i.e. London) railway stations.

1053 GLEIM, C. O. Neuere Stadt und Vorortbahnen in London, Liverpool und Glasgow . . . *Berlin*, 1896. pp. 14, with maps & diagrams. ICE
From the *Deutsche Bauzeitung*.

Locomotives, Rolling Stock and Signalling

1054 TATFORD, B. The ABC of London Transport services. *London: Ian Allan*, 1945. pp. 48. BM
Historical notes, lists, and illustrations of railway locomotives and tramcars.

1055 The ABC of London Transport Railways: part 1, by S. L. Poole. *London: Ian Allan*, [1950.] pp. 73, with lists & illus. BM
—— part 2, by S. L. Poole. *London: Ian Allan*, [1951.] pp. 64. BM
Descriptions, with detailed lists of rolling stock.
—— rev. edn., by S. A. Newman. *London*, [1954.] pp. 56. BM
—— another edn. [anon.] *London*, [1957.] pp. 63. BM
—— another edn. [anon.] *London*, [1959.] pp. 64. BM

1056 LONDON PASSENGER TRANSPORT BOARD. Rolling stock overhaul. *London*, [1934.] pp. [14.] IT
Fourteen plates showing various repair operations.

1057 DENSHAM, P. Locomotives of the Metropolitan Railway, excluding G. N. & C. Railway locos, 1863 to 1943. *North Harrow: Denton Equipment.*, 1944. pp. 18. BM
Lists with notes and outline drawings.
—— 2nd edn. 'London Transport: its locomotives' . . . *North Harrow: Denton Equipment*, 1947. pp. 34.

1058 WESTINGHOUSE BRAKE AND SIGNAL COMPANY. The jubilee of automatic and power signalling on London Transport lines. *London*, [1955.] pp. 19, with 30 illus. & 2 maps. IT

1059 BRITISH TRANSPORT COMMISSION. London on Wheels: an exhibition of London travel in the nineteenth century. *London*, 1953. pp. 30, with illus. BM
—— 2nd edn. *London*, 1962. pp. 24.

C 1 (London) H Railway Labour

1060 [RAILWAY CLERKS ASSOCIATION.] The London Passenger Transport Act, 1933: a summary of its main provisions with special articles on the Negotiation Machinery established to deal with salaries, wages and conditions of service . . . also, particulars of the personnel of the new Board with terms and conditions of appointment and a two-page map of the Transport Board Area. *London*, [1933.] pp. 12[13]. TUC
Reprinted from the *Railway Service Journal*, June and July 1933.

*1061 LONDON TRANSPORT EXECUTIVE. Welcome to London Transport: a booklet of information for the staff of the London Transport Executive. *Westminster*, [1948.] pp. 31, with illus., diagrams & 3 insets in pocket at end relating to staff & social activities. BR
—— another edn. *London*, Jan. 1953. pp. 26, also with insets. BR

1062 CLEGG, H. A. Labour relations in London Transport. *Oxford: Blackwell*, 1950. pp. viii, 188, with bibliogr. notes. BM

1063 LONDON PASSENGER TRANSPORT BOARD. Scheme for establishment of staff councils, as provided for in accordance with Clauses 69–71 of the London Passenger Transport Act, 1933. [*London*,] Feb. 1934. pp. 20. PC

C 1 (London) K Social aspects

Historical

1064 DYOS, H. J. Victorian suburb: a study of the growth of Camberwell. *Leicester: University Press*, 1961. pp. 240, with 20 maps & diagrams, & 6 tables. BM
pp. 69–80 and elsewhere, railways, tramways, and the 'workmen's'.

1065 REES, H. The north-eastern expansion of London since 1770. Thesis, M.Sc.(Econ.) London, 1946. pp. vi. 209, with 4 appendices, 31 maps & diagrams; also a MS. map (6 colours for 6 periods). *Typescript.* UL
pp. 103–28, Expansion during the Railway Age.

1066 MOORE, M. L. A century's extension of passenger transport facilities, 1830–1930,
b within the present London Transport Board's area, and its relation to population spread.
c pp. v, 380, xxxv, with a bibliography (61 items), & la. portfolio of maps. Thesis, Ph.D., Univ. Lond. 1948. *Typescript.* UL
Appendix, pp. i–xxxiv, Dates of opening. Changes over ten-year periods.

1067 DYOS, H. J.   The suburban development of Greater London south of the Thames, 1836–1914. pp. cxxvi, 449, with many tables, 37 maps & diagrams, 11 plates.   216 notes. *Typescript.* (Thesis, Ph.D., Univ. Lond., 1952.)   UL

1067a ROBBINS, M. Middlesex. *London: Collins,* 1953. pp. xxii, 456, with frontis., 74 illus. on 48 plates, & 12 maps (2 on end-papers). [*A New Survey of England,* vol. 1.]   BM
pp. 77–83 and elsewhere, railways (including underground) and tramways. Rail transport is closely interwoven into the text throughout and is represented in the index by no less than 166 references.

1068 REES, M.   The economic and social development of extra-Metropolitan Middlesex during the nineteenth century (1880–1914). pp. vi, 617, with tables & notes.   *Typescript.* (Thesis, M.Sc.Econ., Univ. Lond., 1954.) UL
The nature and course of the transformation from a largely agricultural area into a suburban dormitory.
pp. 49–97, Rail transport.

1069 MORRIS, O. J.   Grandfather's London; with an introduction by John Pudney. *London: Putman,* 1956.   pp. 127.   BM
Fifty full-page photographs of street scenes, mostly in Greenwich, London, in the 1880's, with descriptive commentaries on the facing pages. Four are of tramways and four of railways.

1070 DYOS, H. J.   Some social costs of railway
b   building in London.   *In* 'Journal of Transport History', vol. 3, no. 1, May 1957. pp. 23–30, with plate, a table (pp. 25–9) of 'displacements of labouring classes by railways in London, 1853–1900' (61 instances) & 13 bibliogr. notes.   BM

Contemporaneous

1071 STEVENSON, J.   New railways in London: how and where they should be constructed so as to avoid the destruction of house property, and be of the most service to the public and their undertakers, with information respecting the passenger and goods traffic in the streets, amount of railway communication wanted, and the number of houses required to be built annually in the Metropolis. *Hounslow,* 1866.   pp. 16.   NLC

1072 LONDON railways: a contribution to the Parliamentary Papers of the Session. By a Middle-aged Citizen. *London,* 1867.   pp. 36.   BM
'The requirements of Londoners have been sacrificed to the interests of great provincial railways.' Lack of facilities for efficient interurban transport. Plan to replace termini with through stations.

1073 [LONDON.] CORPORATION OF THE CITY OF LONDON.   Ten years' growth of the City of London. Report, Local Government & Taxation Committee of the Corpora-

tion, etc. . . . By J. Salmon, chairman of the Committee. *London,* 1891.   IT
pp. 33–47, Census of passenger and vehicular traffic. Tables.

1074 LONDON COUNTY COUNCIL—PUBLIC HEALTH & HOUSING COMMITTEE. Reports of the Public Health and Housing Committee giving results of inquiries instituted by the Council with reference to the service of the workmen's trains provided by the thirteen railway companies having termini in the Metropolis. February and April, 1892. [*London,* 1892.]   pp. 49, with tables.   BM

1075 LONDON COUNTY COUNCIL. Locomotive service . . . Return of services and routes by tramways, omnibuses, steamboats, railway and canals, in the County of London and in extra-London, together with an examination in detail of the present system of locomotive service and of the requirements to meet the needs of London. By G. L. Gomme, Statistical Officer.   Part 1, Tramways, omnibuses and steamboats. [*London,*] May 1895.   pp. iv, 199, with a map supplement.   LCC
pp. 2–47 and elsewhere, Tramways.

1076 LONDON COUNTY COUNCIL. Workmen's trains.   Reports by the Statistical Officer on workmen's trains on the London, Brighton & South Coast and the City & South London railways. [*London,* 1896.]   pp. 8, with tables.   BM

1077 LONDON COUNTY COUNCIL Workmen's trains.   Report of the Statistical Officer on the inadequacy of the workmen's train services of the South London railways. *London,* 1897.   pp. 17, with tables. [*Publication* no. 365.]   BM

1078 LONDON COUNTY COUNCIL. Workmen's trains.   Report of the Statistical Officer on the need for a general extension of the service of workmen's trains on metropolitan railways to 8 a.m. *London,* 1897.   pp. 17, with tables. [*Publication* no. 366.]   BM

1079 LONDON COUNTY COUNCIL. Workmen's trains.   Extract from the reports of the Housing of the Working Classes Committee, adopted by the Council on 22 February 1898. [*London,* 1898.]   pp. 4.   BM

1080 BARRY, J. W.   Address on the streets & traffic of London, delivered at the . . . Society of Arts on Wednesday, November 16, 1898. *London,* 1899.   pp. 44, with tables.   IT
Problems of transport arising from the growth of London and its population.

1081 LONDON COUNTY COUNCIL. Workmen's Trains Inquiry.   Evidence prepared by the Statistical Department of the L.C.C. in regard to the application to the Board of Trade of the National Association for the Extension of Workmen's Trains, for a reduction in the workmen's fares from certain stations on the London & South Western Railway. [*London*, 1900.] pp. 13, with tables.   BM

1082 BOOTH, C.   Improved means of locomotion as a first step towards the cure of the housing difficulties of London. *London*, 1901. pp. 24.   LSE
   'Browning Hall Conference' lectures. Includes recommendations for the extension of tramways and underground railways.

1083 LONDON COUNTY COUNCIL.   Third class season tickets. Report of Statistical Officer as to the metropolitan railway companies which issue third-class season tickets. *London*, 1901. pp. 9, with a table (6 pp.) of season ticket rates in the London area. BM

1084 LONDON COUNTY COUNCIL.   Workmen's Trains Inquiry. Evidence prepared by the Local Government and Statistical Department in regard to the need for a service of workmen's trains on the Great Eastern Railway (Palace Gates Branch). [*London*, 1901.] pp. 5[6], with tables.   BM

1085 LONDON COUNTY COUNCIL.   Workmen's Trains Inquiry. Evidence prepared by the Statistical Officer of the London County Council as to the services of workmen's trains on the railways between Willesden Junction and Broad Street owned and jointly worked by the London & North Western Railway and North London Railway Companies. [*London*, 1901.] pp. 13, with tables.   BM

1086 LONDON COUNTY COUNCIL.   Workmen's Trains Inquiry. Report prepared by the Local Government and Statistical Department of the London County Council as to the need for earlier workmen's trains on the North London Railway. [*London*, 1901.] pp. 7, with tables.   BM

1087 LONDON COUNTY COUNCIL.   Workmen's Trains Inquiry. Supplementary report prepared by the Local Government & Statistical Department of the London County Council as to the need for earlier workmen's trains on the North London Railway. [*London*, 1901.] pp. 9, with letters between the N.L. Rly., Board of Trade, & L.C.C. on the L.C.C.'s replies to points in the N.L. Rly's statements.   LCC

1088 BROWNING HALL CONFERENCES ON HOUSING AND LOCOMOTION. Report of Sub-Committee on Locomotion. [*London*, 1902.] .pp. 14.   LSE
   Proposed railway, tramway and underground railway extensions around London.

1089 LONDON COUNTY COUNCIL—LOCAL GOVERNMENT & STATISTICAL DEPARTMENT. Third class season tickets: report by the Statistical Officers as to the issue of third class season tickets on railways having termini in London; and return showing the comparative cost of season and ordinary return tickets of all classes issued between London railway termini and stations within 20 miles thereof . . . By Edgar Harper, Statistical Officer. *London*, May 1902. pp. xxvi, 81. BM
   Tables showing the comparative cost of season and ordinary return tickets of all classes issued between London termini and stations within twenty miles.

1090 WRIGHT, A.   The truth about the trams. *London*, 1905. pp. 16.   BM
   Reasons for rejection by the House of Lords of the London County Council's Bill concerning tramways across the Thames; the problem of congestion; and the advent of the motor bus.

1091 BROWNING HALL CONFERENCES ON HOUSING AND LOCOMOTION. Report of Sub-Committee on Housing and Locomotion in London, 1902–1907 . . . [*London*,] 1907. pp. 35.   LSE

1092 DAVIES, A. E. *and* GOWER, E. E.   Tramway trips and rambles: cheap delightful trips by tram and foot in the London countryside. *London*, [1907.] pp. 136, with 23 illus.   BM

1093 GATTIE, A. W.   How to improve London's transport. *London*, [1910.] pp. 19, with 3 plates & illus. [*Lecture* no. 2.]   BM
   A central clearing house for goods.

1094 GATTIE, A. W.   Improvements in the transport and distribution of goods in London. *London*, [1911.] pp. 27.   BM
   A goods clearing house for all London railways.

1095 GATTIE, A. W.   How to cheapen transport. *London*, [1912.] pp. 15. [*Lecture* no. 4.]   BM
   A clearing house for goods from all London railways.

1096 GATTIE, A. W.   A plea for more light on railway administration. *London*, [1913.] pp. 31. [*Lecture* no. 7.]   BM
   pp. 10–31, Detailed table of estimated traffic from all London railways to and from the proposed goods clearing house.

1097 STANLEY, A. H. [Lord Ashfield.] London traffic in 1913: a paper to be presented at a meeting of the International Engineering Congress, 1915, in San Francisco, Cal., September 20–25, 1915. [*London*, 1915.] pp. 40.   BM
   Problems of congestion.

1098 PRATT, E. A.   A London Transport Trust: criticism of an impracticable scheme. *London*, 1916. pp. 70.   BM
   Objections to A. W. Gattie's scheme for a central goods clearing house.

1099 [CONFERENCE OF LONDON MEMBERS OF PARLIAMENT] 1919. London traffic, 1919. Conference of London Members of Parliament on Monday, May 5, 1919: statement prepared on behalf of the Metropolitan District Rly., the London Electric Rly., the City & South London Rly., the Central London Rly., and the London General Omnibus Co., for submission to the Conference. *London*, 1919. pp. 25.   LSE
London traffic problems.

1100 PICK, F. London traffic: a programme. A report upon the London traffic situation, with special reference to a programme of works and improvements for meeting the situation to arise in the ensuing twelve years. In five parts. 1919.
Not published.
pt. 2, pp. 16–34, Railways.

1101 ASPINALL, J. A. F. Some post-war problems of transport. *London*, 1922. pp. 39. ICE
Excerpt, *Min. Proc. I.C.E.*, vol. 214, pt. ii.
Expanding London.

1102 LONDON COUNTY COUNCIL. Tramways, trolley vehicles, and motor vehicles compared: report presented to the Council on 15th July 1924, dealing with the operation of tramways, trolley omnibuses (rail-less tramcars) and petrol (motor) omnibuses. [*London*, 1924.] pp. 8, with tables.   LCC

1103 STANLEY, A. H. [Lord Ashfield.] London's traffic problem reconsidered. *London*, 1924. pp. 14.   PC
Reprinted from *The Nineteenth Century and After*, August 1924.

1104 LONDON LABOUR PARTY. London's traffic problem. How to secure low fares, better services and greater comfort; being the Report of the Special Joint Committee representing the London Labour Party, London Members of Parliament, and the London County Council Labour Party. *London*, 1927. pp. 13, with tables. [*London Municipal Pamphlets*, no. 7.]   LSE

1105 MORRISON, H. The London Traffic Fraud: being the true story of the London Traffic Monopoly Bills. *London: London Labour Party Publications*, 1929. pp. 23. [*London Municipal Pamphlets*, no. 8.]   LSE
'The purpose of the Bills is to wrest the L.C.C. tramways from public ownership and to run them for private profit by the "London Traffic Combine".'

1106 LONDON MUNICIPAL SOCIETY. Memorandum on the London Traffic Scheme of the Labour–Socialist Government. *London*, 1929. pp. 11. [*London Municipal Pamphlet*, no. 36.]   LSE
A reply to H. Morrison's pamphlet, *The London traffic fraud*. Argument against state ownership.

1107 HARRIS, P. A. London and its government . . . *London*, 1931. pp. x, 261, with illus. BM
pp. 145–64, Traffic. Contemporary problems and the future.

1108 BENNETT, E. P. L. A Londoner looks on. [*London*, 1932.] pp. 14, with 4 plates.   IT
An essay on new facilities for increased enjoyment of rural London made available by the northerly and westerly extensions of the Piccadilly Line.

1109 LABOUR RESEARCH DEPARTMENT. The London Traffic Combine: a study of the finances and ramifications of the London Traffic Combine. *London*, [1932.] pp. 16.   TUC

1110 PONSONBY, G. J. London's passenger transport problem. *London*, 1932. pp. ix, 106.   BM
Unification of various transport bodies necessary for future efficient administration and service.

1111 MORRISON, H. Socialisation and transport: the organisation of socialized industries with particular references to the London Passenger Transport Bill. *London*, 1933. pp. xi, 312[313].   BM

1112 STANLEY, A. H. [Lord Ashfield.] London Passenger Transport. *London: Royal Institution of Gt. Britain*, 1933. pp. 43, with illus., maps, diagrams & tables.   IT
Lecture, 24 March, reprinted from *Proc. Royal Inst.*, vol. 27, pt. 5.
The LPTB and the development of London, and problems of congestion.

1113 STANLEY, A. H. [Lord Ashfield.] Practical aspects of the London Passenger Transport problem. By . . . Lord Ashfield of Southwell. Lecture delivered at the London School of Economics on March 5th, 1934. pp. 27 [28]. *Typescript*.   IT

1114 LONDON SCHOOL OF ECONOMICS. The New Survey of London Life and Labour. *London*, 1930–35. 9 vols.   BM
vol. 1, pp. 171–99, Travel and mobility. Suburban system, underground railways, tramways. Changes between 1890 and 1930. With four maps and tables.
vol. 4, maps 1–7, showing railways.
vol. 7, maps 8–13, showing railways.

1115 BUCKINGHAM, D. Fast trains to town. *London: British Council*, 1944. pp. 31, with illus. [*Britain Advances*.]   BM
Electrification and resultant outer-suburban development. The transport of London workers to and from their homes.

1116 ROYAL ACADEMY PLANNING COMMITTEE. Road, rail, and river in London: the Royal Academy Planning Committee's Second Report. (Chairman, G. G. Scott.) *London: Country Life*, July 1944. pp. 38, with many illus. of plans & drawings for the replanning of London.   IT

1117 COWDEROY, J. E. Public co-operation in transport. [*London:*] *Institute of Transport, Metropolitan Section*, 1948. pp. 25, with 12 charts & tables, & 2 maps.   IT
The travelling public in London. Present trends and future plans.

1118 POWNALL, J. F. The rank bad planning of London Transport. *London: Oliver Moxon*, 1949. pp. 15.   IT
Concerning the Bakerloo extension to Stanmore, the Central Line extension to Epping and Newbury Park, and the 1944 London Railways Plan. This is followed by the author's plan for a 'railway hour' network for London.

1119 LONDON TRANSPORT EXECUTIVE. London Travel Survey, 1949. *London*, 1950. pp. 46, with 19 tables.   BM
Survey of suburban travel patterns and of traffic density, including railways.

1120 LONDON TRANSPORT EXECUTIVE. London's travelling public: an advertising survey. *London*, 1950. (9 fold. tables.)   IT
An analysis of the 1949 Travel Survey presented graphically, with a summary.

1121 MINISTRY OF TRANSPORT—LONDON AND HOME COUNTIES TRAFFIC ADVISORY COMMITTEE. London traffic congestion. *London*, 1951. pp. 57.   BM

1122 LONDON TRANSPORT EXECUTIVE. London Travel Survey, 1954. *London*, 1956. pp. 63, with 19 tables.   BM
Suburban travel patterns and traffic density, including railways.

1123 MINISTRY OF TRANSPORT AND CIVIL AVIATION. 'Crush hour' travel in Central London: report of the first year's work of the Committee for Staggering of Working Hours in Central London. *London*, 1958. pp. 45, with tables & map.   BM

1124 LONDON COUNTY COUNCIL. County Planning Report: first review, 1960. *London*, 1960, pp. xii, 2481. [*Publication* no. 4065.]   BM
pp. 77–81, London and the Railway Modernisation Plan.

East Anglia

1125 [BARRETT, H.] Observations on railways, addressed to the nobility, gentry, clergy, agriculturists, . . . particularly to those situate on the line and connected with the Grand Northern & Eastern Railroad projected by N. W. Cundy. *Yarmouth*, 1834. pp. 55.   BM
—— 2nd edn. *Yarmouth*, 1835. pp. 59. BM
The BM copy of the 2nd edn. is inscribed: 'With the Compiler's compliments. Henry Barrett.'

1126 [B., H.] An address to the inhabitants of the Eastern Counties of England: being a slight historical sketch of ancient roads; with some observations on the adaptation of the modern railway to the development of the resources of a country. *London*, 1839. pp. xvi, 44.   H
In verse. By Henry Barrett(?) See also 1128.

1127 [B., H.] Pooh! Pooh!: a poem; by one of Job's Comforters. [*London,*] 1839. pp. 23.   BM
Verses on the coming of railways to East Anglia. Reprinted in *Reminiscences of Railway Making* (1845). By Henry Barrett(?)

1128 [B., H.] Reminiscences of railway making: rhymes, etc. *London*, 1845. pp. iv, 122.   BM
Verses, mostly on the coming of railway to East Anglia, 1839–1841. The BM copy is inscribed 'R. Patterson, Esq., Ch. of the Northern & Eastern Railway Co., with H.B.'s best comps. Not published.' [By Henry Barrett?]
pp. [71]–122[123], 'An address to the inhabitants of the eastern counties of England . . . ' (1839).

1129 REDDIE, J. The Railway Quadrille; composed and respectfully dedicated to the chairman and directors of the East Anglian railways, by Josiah Reddie. *King's Lynn*, [*c.* 1850.]

1130 CASTLE, H. J. A few words to the shareholders of the Eastern Counties Rly. Co. *London*, [1851.] pp. 24.   BM
Urging amalgamation of the E.C. Rly., Eastern Union Rly. and Norfolk Rly., to gain control of East Anglia before the Great Northern Rly.

1131 SAUNDERS, J. F. Railways in the Eastern Counties district: the mode by which a fair fusion of railway interests eastward of the Great Northern Railway may be effected, the lines not yet under agreement with the Eastern Counties company be placed under their control, and the injury to all that has ensued from competition be arrested. Recommended to the consideration of all shareholders in the above district. *London*, [1852.] pp. 11.   BM

1132 ALLEN, G. F. Regional rounds: no. 1, Eastern and North Eastern Regions. *London: Ian Allan*, [1949.] pp. 48.   BM
No more published.
Historical and descriptive essays, including:
pp. 16–22, 'The Back Line'. By A. G. Cramp. (Nottingham.)
pp. 23–32, 'Cambridge'. By G. F. Allen.
pp. 33–9, 'The Midland & Great Northern Rly.' By H. C. Casserley.

1133 TAYLOR, G. H. The tramways of East Anglia: being some account of the systems once operating at Colchester, Great Yarmouth, Ipswich, Lowestoft, and Norwich. February 1950. pp. 18, with map & a supplement (1 p.). *Reproduced typescript.* PC
Paper, Light Railway Transport League, 15 Feb., 1950.

Midlands

1134 ALDERSON, R. Report on the Manchester, Cheshire [&] Staffordshire, and the South Union lines of railway, by order of the Master-General and Board of Ordnance. *In* 'Papers on Subjects connected with the Corps of Royal Engineers.' vol. 2. *London*, 1838. pp. 91–113, with 2 fold. maps.   BM

1135 SIMMONS, J. Some railway schemes in the West Midlands, 1833–1865. pp. 33, with 4 maps. *Typescript.*   BM
Paper, Railway Club, 9 Sept., 1937.

1136 POWNALL, J. F. The Liverpool and Stoke-on-Trent railway hour section and also Birmingham and Nottingham hour sections to speed up railways in the Midlands. *Birmingham: Cotterell*, 1943. pp. 12.   BM
'Hour section' schedules.

1137 [CLINKER, C. R.] Railways of the West Midlands: a chronology, 1808–1954. *Lon-*
c   *don: Stephenson Locomotive Society*, [1954.] pp. 64, with 32 illus. on 16 plates; fold. map (loose).   BM

1138 WEBB, J. S. Tramways of the Black Country: company-operated lines of South Staffordshire and North Worcestershire. *Bloxwich: the author*, [1954.] pp. 65, with illus.   IT

1139 LEICESTER COURT OF QUARTER SESSIONS. Deposited railway plans: reproduced
c   by the Historical Manuscripts Commission from originals prepared by the Leicestershire Record Office ... [*London: National Register of Archives*,] 1958.   BM
Description of 385 items relating to railways in the Midlands, 1829–1952, arranged in chronological order.

1140 POTTERIES MOTOR TRACTION COMPANY. The story of the Potteries Motor Traction Company Limited. By J. Wentworth Day. *Stoke-on-Trent*, [1958.] pp. 22, with 37 illus. & a map.   PC
Includes tramways.

1141 TONKS, E. S. The ironstone railways and tramways of the Midlands. *London: Loco-*
b   *motive Publishing Co.*, 1959. pp. 316, with col. frontis., col. plate, 62 maps (8 fold.), 124
c   illus. on 32 plates, many bibliogr. notes, chron. list of ironstone tramways (pp. 284–92), and a list of locomotives (pp. 293–303).   BM
History and details of 144 systems and their locomotives.
—— 2nd impr. (revised). *London*, 1961. pp. 316.

*1142 HADFIELD, C. *and* NORRIS, J. Waterways to Stratford. *Dawlish: David & Charles; London: Phœnix House*, 1962. pp. 176, with 35 illus. on 20 plates, 4 illus. in text, 11 maps, & 181 bibliogr. notes.   BM
pp. 15–70, 'The Avon Navigation' by Charles Hadfield; pp. 73–123, 'The Stratford-upon-Avon Canal' by Charles Hadfield; pp. 127–59, 'The Stratford & Moreton Tramway' by John Norris.

William James' interest and activity in canal and railway promotion in this area, and his scheme (*c.* 1820) for a 'Central Junction Railway' from Stratford to London are important elements in this detailed survey. Also featured (pp. 104–13) is the relationship between the Stratford Canal Company, the Oxford, Worcester & Wolverhampton Rly. and the Birmingham & Oxford Junction Rly.

North East England

1143 OBSERVATIONS on the practicability and advantages of the continuation of the Stockton & Darlington Railway from Croft Bridge to the City of York and by means of collateral branches to effect a speedy, cheap and direct communication between the counties of Northumberland and Durham, the ports of Newcastle and Stockton, and the agricultural districts of the North Riding of Yorkshire, and the manufacturing and commercial districts of Yorkshire and Lancashire. *Ripon*, 1827. pp. 18.   BM
Signed 'A Practical Farmer'.

1144 HILL, T. A short treatise, showing the only practicable method (upon a scale to remunerate the subscribers) of connecting the important towns of Manchester, Leeds, Halifax, Huddersfield, Bradford, Wakefield and Dewsbury, consequently the ports of Liverpool, Hull, Selby and Goole, by rail roads; with observations on others in operation, etc. *Wakefield*, 1833. pp. 16.   LEEDS PL

1145 RICHARDSON, M.A. The Local Historian's Table Book of remarkable occurrences, historical facts . . . connected with the counties of Newcastle-upon-Tyne, Northumberland, and Durham. Historical Division. *London*, 1841–6. 5 vols.   BM
Includes items of news concerning railways, such as openings of new lines, and accidents.

1146 TONE, J. F. On the railways and locomotives of the districts adjoining the rivers Tyne, Wear and Tees. *In* 'Industrial resources of the . . . Tyne, Wear and Tees', by William George Armstrong. *London*, 1864. pp. 277–84, with la. fold. map.   BM
—— 2nd edn. *London*, 1864. pp. 321–28.   BM

1147 FORDYCE, T. Local records, or historical register, of remarkable events which have occurred in Northumberland and Durham, Newcastle-upon-Tyne and Berwick-upon-Tweed. *Newcastle*, 1866–1876. 4 vols. BM
Many references to railways, in vols. 3 & 4, by T. Fordyce, and some in vols. 1 & 2 by J. Sykes.

1148 FLETCHER, J. R. The development of the railway system in Northumberland and Durham. *Newcastle upon Tyne*, 1902. pp. 47, with 2 fold. maps & fold. diagram. BR
Address, I.C.E. Newcastle on Tyne Association of Students, 7 Nov., 1901.

1149 KINDON, K. A. Contribution of railways to the industrial development of Tees-side. 1957. pp. 12. *Typescript.*   IT
Paper, Institute of Transport, 18 Oct., 1957

North West England

1150 NICHOLSON, C. The London & Glasgow Railway through Westmoreland and Cumberland: the interests of Kendal considered. *Kendal*, 1837. pp. 19. LSE
The necessity, probable advantages, and objections.

1151 RASTRICK, J. U. *and* HAGUE, J. West Cumberland, Furness & Morecambe Bay Railway. Reports. *London*, [1838.] pp. 23, with fold. map. BM

1152 RASTRICK, J. U. West Cumberland, Furness & Morecambe Bay Railway. Report . . . on the intended line of railway from Lancaster to Maryport, via Furness and Whitehaven. *Whitehaven*, 1839. pp. 11. BM
On the title-page the author's name appears as J. M. Rastrick.

1153 STOCKDALE, J. Facts proving the fertility of the soil in Morecambe Bay, extracted from the published letters of James Stockdale, Esq., by the Committee of the West Cumberland Railway. *Whitehaven*, 1839. pp. 8. H

1154 LARMER, G. Report of the railway communication with Scotland between Lancaster, Kendal, Penrith and Carlisle. *Carlisle*, 1840. pp. 12. LSE

1155 POLLARD, S. North-west coast railway politics in the eighteen-sixties. *Kendal*,
b 1953. pp. 160–77, with map & 39 bibliogr. notes. BR
Reprinted from the Cumberland & Westmoreland Antiquarian & Archaeological Society's *Transactions*, new series, vol. 52. Read at Bangor, 4 September, 1952.
Concerning attempts to form a Furness–Cumberland coast route to Scotland.

South East England

1156 COURSE, E. A. The evolution of the railway network of South East England. 1958. 2 vols. (pp. 926), with many photographs & maps inserted. *Typescript*. (Thesis, Ph.D, Univ. Lond.) UL

Southern England

1157 TRITTON, G. At a meeting of gentlemen held at the Spread Eagle in Wandsworth on Thursday the 3rd of June, 1802, George Tritton, Esq., in the chair, it was represented, that from the view of the Iron Railway . . . from Wandsworth to Croydon, and the proofs which had been made of its utility . . . it had been thought advisable to enquire whether the work might not be extended through the counties of Surrey, Sussex and Hants, so as to open a communication with the sea-ports in the Channel, and particularly with Portsmouth . . . *London*, 1802. pp. 10. BM
Includes W. Jessop's survey.

1158 MARSHALL, R. An examination into the respective merits of the proposed canal and iron railway from London to Portsmouth. *London*, 1803. pp. 20. UL(GL)

1159 [JAMES, W.] Report or essay, to illustrate the advantages of direct inland communication through Kent, Surrey, Sussex and Hants, to connect the Metropolis with the ports of Shoreham (Brighton), Rochester (Chatham) and Portsmouth, by a line of engine railroad, and to render the Grand Surrey Canal, Wandsworth and Merstham Rail-Road, Shoreham Harbour and Waterloo Bridge shares productive property, with suggestions for diminishing poor-rates, and relieving agriculture. *London*, 1823. pp. 31, with fold. map (frontis.). BM

1160 COMMERCIAL docks on the southern coast of England. *London*, [1836.] pp. 35, with fold. map & fold. plan of proposed railways from Southampton. BM

1161 FOWLER, J. South Wales and Southampton Railway, for connecting the Bristol Channel with the South Coast. *London*, 1854. pp. 8. NLC

1162 NORRIS, W. An address to the Southampton Chamber of Commerce upon a direct communication by railway and steam ferry between Southampton and South Wales. *London*, July 1854. pp. 8, with a map. NLC
Proposes a railway from Salisbury via Wells to Weston.

1163 SOUTHAMPTON CHAMBER OF COMMERCE. Southampton and Bristol united by direct railway communication. *Southampton*, [1854.] pp. 16. NLC

1164 COOPER, C. F. G. Railways of Britain; no. 1, Southern England. *London: Daily Mail School-Aid Dept.*, [1947.] pp. 31, with maps & illus. in text. [*Young Britain: Educational Series.*] BM
History and description.

*1165 HADFIELD, C. The canals of Southern England. *London: Phœnix House*, 1955. pp. 383, with plates & maps. BM
pp. 264–336, 'The railways and after', and many other references to railways and tramroads elsewhere in the text.

*1166 WHITE, H. P. Southern England . . . *London: Phœnix House*, 1961. pp. lx, 214, with frontis., 36 illus. on 16 plates, 18 sm. maps & diagrams, bibliography, & fold. col. map. [*Regional History of the Railways of Great Britain*, vol. 2.] BM
Covering England south of the Thames (Kent, Surrey, Sussex, Hampshire, Dorset, and the Isle of Wight).

West of England and the West Country

1167 [RESOLUTIONS passed] at a numerous and respectable meeting of manufacture[r]s and

others interested in the reduction of charges for the carriage of coals and goods from the River Severn to the town of Stroud . . . 24 September, 1824. [1824.] pp. 4.
GLOUCESTER PL
With a report, estimates, etc., on the proposed Stroud & Severn Railroad.

1168 [TOWNSEND, R. E. A.] Visions of the Western Railways . . . London, 1838. pp. 90, 36. BM
Printed for private circulation.
Miscellaneous poems, some about railways in Cornwall and the West Country.

—— an. edn. London, 1838. pp. 49, 36. BM
Some poems, not railway ones, omitted.

1169 DEVON & CORNWALL RLY. Devon and Cornwall Railway. Report of the committee appointed at a meeting of the County of Cornwall on the 21st of October, 1840, to inquire into the practicability of constructing a railway through the County of Cornwall; together with the tables of traffic, and the engineer's reports. Truro, [1840.] pp. 39, with la. fold. map. BM

1170 BRISTOL, BATH & POOLE RLY. Observations touching the capabilities and character of the Port of Poole. [Sherborne, 1844.] s.sh. BM
Reprint, Sherborne Journal.
On the advantages of Poole as a terminus for the proposed 'Bristol & English Channel Junction Rly.'

1171 COLOMBINE, D. E. Letter addressed to . . . Lord Carteret . . . Lord Vivian, Sir William L. S. Trelawney . . . Francis Rodd . . . and the chief magistrates, landowners and merchants of the County of Cornwall. London, 1845. pp. 10, with fold. map. BM
The claims of the proposed London & Exeter Rly. in preference to the Exeter, Yeovil & Dorchester Rly., the Salisbury & Yeovil Rly. and the L. & S.W. Rly.

1172 WORTH, R. H. Early western railroads. [Plymouth,] 1888. pp. 15. BM
Reprinted from Transactions of the Plymouth Institution and Devon & Cornwall Historical Society, 1887–8.
Origins and history of rail transport in Devon and Cornwall. Tavistock Canal & Incline; Portreath Rly.; Heytor Rly.; Bude Canal; Plymouth & Dartmoor Rly.; Redruth & Chasewater Rly.; Bodmin & Wadebridge Rly.; West Cornwall Rly.; Treffry Rly.

1173 COOPER, C. F. G. Railways of Britain; no. 2, West of England. London: Daily Mail School-Aid Dept., [1949.] pp. 30, with illus. & maps in text. [Young Britain: Educational Series.] BM
Historical and descriptive.

1174 GENTRY, P. W. The tramways of the West of England. London: Light Railway Trans-

port League, 1952. pp. 139, with maps & many illus. BM
Includes cliff railways.

—— 2nd edn. London, 1960. pp. 173. BM

*1175 THOMAS, D. St. J. The West Country . . . London: Phœnix House, 1960. pp. ix, 212, with frontis., 55 illus. on 20 plates, 4 maps, 5 diagrams, 4 tables, diagrams, bibliography, & a fold. col. map. [Regional History of the Railways of Great Britain, vol. 1.] BM

1176 BARTON, D. B. A historical survey of the mines and mineral railways of East Cornwall and West Devon. Truro: D. B. Barton, Truro Bookshop, 1964. pp. 102, with 10 maps, and 13 line drawings by the author. BM

Bedfordshire

1177 BLYTH, T. A. The History of Bedford and Visitors' Guide. London & Bedford, [1868.] pp. 318. with illus. BM
pp. 209–16, Accounts from the Bedford Times of the Parliamentary battle preceding the incorporation of the Bedford & Cambridge, 1862, and of the dinner at the opening of the Leicester & Hitchin branch of the Midland, 1857.

1178 HAMSON, J. Bedford town and townsmen: a record of the local history of Bedford during the last half century. Bedford, 1896. pp. xx, 168. BM
Includes several references to railways.

Berkshire

1179 JORDON, H. E. The tramways of Reading. London: Light Railway Transport League, 1957. pp. 93, with 30 illus., tables & a map. BM

Buckinghamshire

1180 FOWLER, J. K. Echoes of old country life. London & New York, 1892. pp. x, 264. BM
pp. 186–95, Railways in Buckinghamshire.

1181 FOWLER, J. K. Recollections of old country life . . . London, 1894. pp. xx, 235. BM
pp. 124–5, Robert Stephenson at Aylesbury, prospecting for a branch line from his London & Birmingham Rly.

1182 ELAND, G. The Chilterns and the Vale; with six illustrations in colour by E. Saunders. London, 1911. pp. xiv, 170. BM
pp. 146–55, The railway systems of mid-Bucks (chiefly the Aylesbury & Buckingham line).

1183 MARKHAM, S. F. The Nineteen Hundreds: being the story of the Buckinghamshire towns of Wolverton and Stony Stratford during the years 1900–1911. Buckingham: E. N. Hillier & Sons, [1951.] pp. xii, 152 [154]. BM
pp. 21–3, 'The Stony Stratford District Light Railway Co.'; with 3 illus.
pp. 14–19 & elsewhere, Wolverton Carriage & Wagon Works, L. & N.W.R.; with 3 illus.

1184 GADSDEN, E. J. S. Duke of Buckingham's railways. [London:] Bledlow Press, 1962. pp. 54, with 7 illus. & a map. Reproduced typescript.   BM
Railways in the Vale of Aylesbury promoted by the Duke of Buckingham and Sir Harry Verney and later controlled by the Metropolitan & Great Central Joint Committee. Includes the Brill branch, and the Wotton Tramway.

Cambridgeshire

1185 FELLOWS, R. B. Railway communication between London and Cambridge, and how the Great Northern Railway got to Cambridge. pp. 27. Typescript.   RC
Paper, Railway Club, 1936.

*1186 FELLOWS, R. B. London to Cambridge by train, 1845 to 1938. Cambridge: Walter Lewis, 1939. pp. 31, with 23 illus. & timetable on 15 plates, & illus. in text.   BM
140 copies printed.

*1187 FELLOWS, R. B. Railways to Cambridge, actual and proposed. South Godstone: Oakwood Press, 1948. pp. 28, with 4 plates.   BM

1188 TURTON, T. F. Cambridge transport. 1949. pp. [30.] Typescript.   IT
Paper, Institute of Transport, Beds., Cambs. & Hunts. Section, 9 Nov. 1949.
Includes railways and the Cambridge Tramways Co.

Cheshire

1189 LIVERPOOL STANDARD newspaper. Descriptive account of the railway accommodation of Lancashire and Cheshire, together with a map of the district illustrating the same. Presented gratuitously to the purchasers of the Liverpool Standard. Liverpool, 1846. pp. 16.   LSE
Supplement to the issue of Tuesday, 28 April, 1846.

1190 TRAIN, G. F. Report of the banquet given by George Francis Train of Boston, U.S., to inaugurate the opening of the first street railway in Europe at Birkenhead, August 30, 1860; with opinions of the press on the subject of street railways. Liverpool, 1860. pp. 117, with fold. plate.   BM

1191 CREWE GUARDIAN newspaper. The Jubilee of Crewe; containing a brief history of the rise and progress of the Borough from 1837 to 1887, together with an account of the Jubilee Rejoicings on June 21st and July 4th, 1887 on which occasions were celebrated the fiftieth anniversary of the opening of the Grand Junction Railway through Crewe, the completion of the 3,000th engine made in Crewe Works, and the dedication of the New Queen's Park, given by the London &

North Western Railway Company to the Town. Crewe, [1887.] pp. 108, with illus.   BR

1192 CHALONER, W. H. The social and economic development of Crewe, 1780–1923. Manchester: Manchester University Press, 1950. pp. xx, 326.   BM
pp. 1–38, the transformation and development of Crewe by the railway.

1193 LLOYD, R. Railwaymen's Gallery. London: Allen & Unwin, 1953. pp. 166, with plates.   BM
pp. 94–118, 'Railway towns' (Crewe and Swindon).

1194 WYATT, W. L. The development of corporation public transport in Stockport up to August 31st 1951. 1953. pp. [125,] with illus., tables, & a bibliography. Typescript.   STOCKPORT PL
Includes tramways.

*1195 GREVILLE, M. D. Chronological List of the Railways of Cheshire, 1837–1939. c [Liverpool, 1955.] pp. 135–44.   BM
Reprinted from the Transactions of the Historic Society of Lancashire and Cheshire, vol. 106, 1954.

1196 MAUND, T. B. Local transport in Birkenhead and district. Blackpool: Omnibus Society, January 1959. pp. 39, with 16 illus. & 2 maps.   IT
Includes local tramway history.

1197 RAILWAY CORRESPONDENCE & TRAVEL SOCIETY—LANCASHIRE & NORTH WESTERN BRANCH. The Cheshire rail-tour, Saturday, 26th March 1960. Itinerary. pp. [7,] with double-page map. Reproduced typescript.   STOCKPORT PL

1198 WILMOT, G. F. A. The evolution of railways in the Wirral Peninsula. 1961. pp. 4. Reproduced typescript   PC
A concise survey issued on the occasion of a tour of the area by members of the Railway and Canal Historical Society, 7 May, 1961.

Cornwall

1199 WHISHAW, F. Report on the proposed railway for connecting the town of Truro with the mining district of Perran, in the County of Cornwall. London, 1831. pp. 15, with map.   ICE

1200 WHISHAW, F. and THOMAS, R. Report on the proposed line of railway from Perran-Porth to Truro by Perran Alms-House. Truro, 1831. pp. 12, with fold. map.   BM

1201 WHISHAW, F. and THOMAS, R. Report on two proposed lines of railway between Perran Porth and Truro, in the County of Cornwall. London, 1831. pp. 14, with fold. map (frontis.).   BM

1202 TREMENHEERE, S. Observations on the proposed breakwater in Mount's Bay, and on its connection with a railway into Cornwall, in a letter to Richard Moyle, Esq., Mayor of Penzance . . . *Penzance*, 1839. pp. 20, with map.   BM
'A harbour would be an inducement to the G.W.R. to bring its railway to Penzance.'

1203 SIMMONS, G. N. The Corporation of Truro and the West Cornwall Railway, and Baron Vivian's Estate Acts. *Truro*, 1853. pp. 15.   BM
Resistance by the Town Council to the adoption of the quay by the proposed railway.

1204 ROBBINS, A. F. Launceston past and present: a historical and descriptive sketch. *Launceston*, 1888. pp. x, 450, with bibliogr. notes.   BM
pp. 349–56, railways and railway projects in and around Launceston and in Cornwall.

1205 ROWE, W. J. Cornwall in the age of the Industrial Revolution. *Liverpool: University Press*, 1953. pp. x, 367, with bibliogr. notes & a bibliography.   BM
Includes railways.

1206 CLINKER, C. R. The railways of Cornwall, 1809–1963: a list of authorising Acts of
c Parliament: opening and closing dates; with other historical information, compiled from original and contemporary sources by C. R. Clinker. *Dawlish: David & Charles*, 1963. pp. 32, with map.   BM

Cumberland

1207 CHAPMAN, W. Mr. Chapman's report on the means of obtaining a safe and commodious communication from Carlisle to the sea. *Carlisle*, 1807. pp. 18.   BM
p. 10, possibility of a railway considered.

1208 STEPHENSON LOCOMOTIVE SOCIETY— North West Area *and the* MANCHESTER LOCOMOTIVE SOCIETY. The West Cumberland Railtour, Sunday, 5th September, 1954. Descriptive notes on the route, by W. McGowan Gradon. [*Manchester*, 1954.] pp. 8. *Reproduced typescript.*   SLS

*1209 HEARSE, G. S. Tramways of the City of Carlisle. *Corbridge: the author*, 1962. pp. viii, 50, with 20 illus. & a plan.   BM

Derbyshire

1210 STRETTON, C. E. The Little Eaton outram-way: a paper read at Little Eaton, 29th July, [1903.]   BM
One newspaper column, with two illustrations.

1211 BAXTER, B. Early railways in Derbyshire. Paper, [Newcomen Society] Science Museum, London, 9 February 1949. pp. 185–97, with plates 32–35 (8 illus.) & map   SLS

1212 [HOLLICK, J. R.] The railway history of Ashbourne. pp. 11. *Reproduced typescript*   PC
'From a paper read to the Adelphi Club of Ashbourne, 12 December, 1955.'

1213 COCHRAN, A. D. Railway operating problems in the Derby district. pp. 23. *Reproduced typescript*, with 5 maps & diagrams at end.   IT
Paper, Convention of Railway Students' Association, Derby, 23 July, 1956.

1214 NIXON, F. Notes on the engineering history of Derbyshire. *Derby: Derbyshire Archaeological & Natural History Society*, February 1956. pp. 19, with illus.   BM
pp. 13–17, early railways (Outram, Jessop, Brunton): Little Eaton to Derby Rly.: Cromford & High Peak Rly.: Stephenson's Clay Cross Co.)

1215 STANDEN, J. D. The social, economic and political development of Derby, 1835–88.
b (Thesis, M.A., Leeds University, 1958.) pp. v, 261, with 2 plates & a bibliography (pp. 251–61). *Typescript.*   LEEDS UL

Devon

1216 DUPIN, F. P. C. Narratives of two excursions to the ports of England, Scotland and Ireland in 1816, 1817 and 1818, together with a description of the breakwater at Plymouth . . . translated from the French . . . *London*, [1819.] pp. viii, 96.   BM
pp. 63–4, a description of the railway from the quarries to the breakwater at Plymouth.

1217 HOPKINS, R. Report of a committee appointed by the subscribers to ascertain the capability and probable cost of constructing a railway between the port of Bideford and Okehampton, containing the different lines with their respective estimates, suggested and surveyed by Roger Hopkins. [*Okehampton*, 1831.] pp. 25, with tables & map.   H
Three proposed schemes.

1218 BESLEY, H., *publisher*. The Route Book of Devon, for rail and road. *Exeter*, [1871.] pp. 438, with maps.
This, and other guide books produced by this compiler entitled *Hand Book of North Devon*; *Hand Book of South Devon*; *The South of Devon*, etc., all contain descriptions of rail journeys within the county.

1219 WHITE, J. T. The history of Torquay: illustrated. *Torquay*, 1878.   BM
pp. 226–37; 289–90, railways.

1220 PLYMOUTH Passenger Transport: seventy years of progress. *London: Modern Transport*, [1943.] pp. 16, with illus. & maps. IT
Includes tramways.

1221 ADAMS, E. A. The old Heytor granite railway. pp. 5[6]. *Typescript.* pc
Extracted from the *Report & Transactions of the Devonshire Association*, vol. 68, 1946. pp. 153–60.

1222 BRITISH RAILWAYS—SOUTHERN REGION. Railway Centenary Exhibition, 1849–1949, to be held at the Museum & Art Gallery, Plymouth, 31st March–10th April, 1949. [*London*, 1949.] pp. 8. BR
Description of 125 exhibits and (pp. 1–4) 'How the railways came to Plymouth'. (G.W.R. and L. & S.W.R.)

1223 HOSKINS, W. G. Devon. *London: Collins*, 1954. pp. xx, 600. [*New Survey of England.*] BM
pp. 158–65, 'Railways'; with map.

1224 THOMAS, D. St. J. Rural transport: a report . . . sponsored by Dartington Trustees, Dartington Hall, Devon. *Dawlish: David Charles*, 1960. pp. 28. BM
pp. 15–18, train services and road/rail competition in South Devon and in Northumberland.

Dorset

1225 WARREN, F. C. Early railway days in Dorset. *Dorchester: Dorset Natural History & Archaeological Society*, 1933. pp. [77]–85, with map. BR
Reprinted from the *Proceedings of the D.N.H. & A.S.*, vol. 55. Read 21 Nov., 1933.

Durham

1226 BAILEY, J. General view of the agriculture of the County of Durham . . . *London: Board of Agriculture*, 1810. pp. xiv, 412. BM
pp. 33–5 describes wagonways in use in this area.

1227 'ALEXIS.' On the intended communication between Stockton and the collieries in the Auckland district. *Durham*, 1818.

1228 [RICHARDSON, T.] History of the Darlington & Barnard Castle Railway; with notices of the Stockton and Darlington, Clarence, West Hartlepool, and other railways and companies in the district. By 'An Inhabitant of Barnard Castle'. *London*, 1877. pp. iv, 93. BM

1229 GATESHEAD & DISTRICT OMNIBUS COMPANY. From trams to buses. Issued . . . to celebrate the running of the last tram on the completion of the change-over to motor omnibuses, 4th August, 1951. *Gateshead*, [1951.] pp. 12, with 8 illus. pc

1230 MOSES, F. K. *and* MACLEOD, C. R. Sunderland Corporation Transport: a history and survey. *London: Omnibus Society*, [1960.] pp. 28, with 21 illus., fleet lists, & a map. BM

Essex

1231 ILFORD & DISTRICT RAILWAY USERS' ASSOCIATION. The case for a tube rail-

way and electrification of the L. & N.E.R. *Ilford*, [1934.] pp. 48, with 2 maps & 2 statistical tables. IT
Reports of meetings reprinted from the *Ilford Recorder*. Urging an extension from Liverpool St. Station via Ilford to Romford.

1232 CHELMSFORD—BOROUGH—PUBLIC LIB-
c RARY & MUSEUM COMMITTEE. Essex railways, 1836–1956: an exhibition to mark the extension of British Railways electrification to Chelmsford. Central Library, Duke Street . . . 8–23 June, 1956. *Chelmsford*, 1956. pp. 7, with 5 illus. BM
pp. 2–5, 'A chronology of Essex railway history'.

1233 POWELL, W. R. A history of the County of
b Essex. Edited by W. R. Powell. *London: Institute of Historical Research*, 1959. [*Victoria History of the Counties of England.*] BM
Bibliography, pp. 48–51, 'Railways.' Primary and secondary sources.

1234 SMITH, A. *and* WILLIAMS, J. The railways of Essex. *Ilford: Narrow Gauge & Light Railway Society*, [April 1959.] pp. [12.] [*N.G. & L.R.S. Handbook*, no. 1.] BM
A revised form of a booklet issued in 1958.
A brief summary of the railways, and some tramways.

Gloucestershire and the Forest of Dean

1235 OUTRAM, B. Report and estimate of the proposed rail-ways from the collieries in the Forest of Dean to the rivers Severn and Wye. *Hereford*, 1801.

1236 'PUBLICUS.' The Stroud & Severn Rail Road: a fallacy as it regards public benefit and private speculation. *Stroudwater*, 1825. pp. 25. P

1237 COMPARATIVE view of the projected lines of railway between North and South Wales, Gloucester, Hereford, Worcester, Cheltenham, Oxford and London, founded on Mr. Brunel's examination before the Committee of the House of Lords, as contrasted with his original statements in Cheltenham. *Cheltenham*, [1836.] pp. 63. BR
In favour of the Cheltenham & Oxford line and opposed to the Great Western.

1238 CHELTENHAM DISTRICT OF TURNPIKE ROADS—TRUSTEES. Road works on railways: a statement made by the Trustees of the Cheltenham District of Turnpike Roads to the Trustees and persons interested in turnpike roads. *Gloucester*, 1842. pp. 15. BM
Railway bridges and existing roadways: the need for protective legislation.

1239 The NEW lines of railway between Cheltenham and London promoted by the London & North Western and Great Western Companies respectively considered in reference to the interests of Gloucester and the neigh-

bourhood. By 'A Gloucester Man'. *Gloucester*, 1846. pp. 16.   BR
  In support of the London, Oxford & Cheltenham lines (L.&N.W.) via Tring and in opposition to the G.W.R. line via Oxford.

1240 WALKER, A. C. Narrow gauge grooveless and noiseless tramways for Cheltenham . . . *London*, 1879. pp. 24.   BM

1241 MORRIS, T. E. R. The Forest of Dean tramroads. pp. 11. *Typescript.*   pc
  From *The Locomotive*, January–April 1931.

*1242 SHIREHAMPTON, W. J. P. Tramroads and railways in the Forest of Dean: a historical outline. [*Coleford*, 1961.] pp. 10, with 2 maps. *Reproduced typescript.* [*Forest of Dean Local History Society Occasional Papers*, no. 2.]   BM

1243 PAAR, H. W. The Severn & Wye Railway:
  b a history of the railways of the Forest of Dean; part one, by H. W. Paar, based on the work of 'Dean Forester'. *Dawlish: David & Charles; London: Macdonald*, 1963. pp. 173, with col. frontis., 39 illus. on 16 plates, 9 maps (1 fold.), list of locomotives, and 97 bibliogr. notes   BM
  Includes the Severn Bridge Rly.

Hampshire

1244 EDINGTON, R. A descriptive plan for erecting a penitentiary house for the employment of convicts . . . to which are added . . . a plan of a rail-way from London to Portsmouth, on a construction superior to any thing seen in this country. *London*, [1803.] pp. ii, 85, with fold. plan & plates. BM
  pp. 73–85, plan of a railway from London to Portsmouth. A visit to the Surrey Iron Rly. is also described.

1245 PORTSMOUTH TRADES COUNCIL. The report of the campaign against trams and bus fares. [*Portsmouth*,] Sept., 1936. pp. [8.]   LSE
  Concerning Portsmouth Corporation Transport Undertaking and its withdrawal of cheap tickets and short stages.

1246 HARRISON, S. E. The tramways of Portsmouth. *London: Light Railway Transport League* 1955. pp. 138, with 57 illus., & 7 maps.   BM
  —— 2nd edn., rev. *London: L.R.T.L.*, 1963. pp. 175, with 68 illus. & 7 maps.   BM

1247 ANDERSON, R. C. The tramways of Bournemouth and Poole. *London: Light Railway Transport League*, 1964. pp. 119, with frontis., 44 illus., 2 maps, 9 diagrams (1 fold.), & 4 fold. tables.   BM

Hertfordshire

1248 OBSERVATIONS on the proposed rail-way. from the Grand Junction Canal at BelSwaine's to the town of St. Albans. By an Inhabitant. *St. Albans*, 1817. pp. 16. NLC
  Addressed to those attending a public meeting to be held on February 4th.

1249 WHISHAW, F. Hertfordshire Grand Union Railway. Report to the promoters of a proposed line of railway between the Northern Railway and the London and Birmingham Railway yb [*sic*] which a direct communication would be effected between the towns of Watford, St. Albans, Hatfield, Hertford, Ware and the Metropolis, and nearly all the counties of England. *Hertford*, 1836. pp. 15.   BM

1250 LUCAS, W. A Quaker Journal: being the diary and reminiscences of William Lucas of Hitchin, 1804–1861, a Member of the Society of Friends. Edited by G. E. Bryant and G. P. Baker . . . *London*, 1934. 2 vols. pp. 580. with illus.   BM
  There are seventy-four references to railways. These concern W. Lucas's railway journeys, accounts of accidents, his views on various railway enterprises, in some of which he had small investments, the Railway Mania, etc. Many railways are mentioned, but most frequently those in Hertfordshire.

1251 HUTTON, K. Hatfield and its people: book 5, Roads and railways and population changes. *Hatfield: Workers' Educational Association, Hatfield Branch*, Nov. 1960. pp. 32, with 6 illus., 4 maps, diagrams & tables.   BM

Kent

1252 [KENTISH RAILWAYS.] [A collection of company prospectuses, share certificates, reports, announcements of train services, plans and sections, posters, illustrations, pamphlets and extracts from newspapers and periodicals. 177 items mounted on 36 folios, with an index.]   BM

1253 LONDON & DOVER RAIL ROAD. Prospectus of a proposed rail road between London and Dover, with a steam ferry across the River Thames, forming a communication between the counties of Kent and Essex, and a steam boat dock, connected by the rail road with the Metropolis. *London*, 1832. pp. 8, with fold. map.   BM
  Limehouse (London), Woolwich Ferry, Erith, Greenhithe, Gravesend, Chatham, Sittingbourne, Faversham, Canterbury, Dover.

1254 KENT RLY. Comparison of the Kent Railway with the South Eastern, and the South Eastern, Canterbury, Ramsgate & Sandwich railways. *London*, [1836.] la. s.sh.   BM
  A proposed line through north Kent.

1255 'CALCULUS.' Remarks on some of the proposed railway projects for connecting Rochester, Chatham and Strood with Gravesend or Rosherville, with a map of the country, showing the two competing lines. By Calculus. *Chatham*, 1844. pp. 21.   BM
  Argument to show how the Chatham, Rochester & Gravesend Rly. would be far better than the Rosherville & Chatham Rly.

1256 The BOARD of Trade and the Kentish railway schemes. *London*, 1845. pp. 41. BM
Criticism. 'Their duty to advise and assist Parliament; not to decide.'

1257 DOULL, A. Random hints on railways and railway legislation. *London*, 1848. pp. 43. BM
Suggested reforms. Kentish railways cited as examples.

1258 MORGAN, W. T. W. The development of settlement on the Isle of Thanet in its geographical setting, with special reference to the growth of the holiday industry. (Thesis, M.Sc.(Econ.) Univ. Lond., 1950.) pp. 2, viii, 192, with 55 illus., 7 tables & bibliography. UL
pp. 56–70, Railways.

1259 HORN, J. V. The story of Dover Corporation Tramways, 1897–1936. *London: Light Railway Transport League*, 1955. pp. 88, with illus. IT

1260 JESSUP, F. W. A history of Kent; with maps and pictures. *London: Finlayson*, 1958. pp. 191. BM
pp. 162–71, 'Urban and railway development in the nineteenth century'; with map.

1261 KENT COUNTY COUNCIL—KENT ARCHIVES OFFICE. Transport in Kent: catalogue of documents from the Kent Archives Office displayed . . . at the Museum, St. Faith Street, Maidstone . . . 24th June–25th July, 1959. [*Maidstone*, 1959.] pp. 30. *Reproduced typescript.* PC
Includes eighteen items relating to railways in Kent.

Lancashire, including Manchester and Liverpool

1262 'OBSERVER.' Thoughts on railways and projected railways. *Liverpool*, 1833. pp. 15. ICE
Reasons against the proposed extension of the Manchester, Bolton & Bury Rly. to the north end of Liverpool and against a rival line to the Liverpool & Manchester Rly.

1263 WALKER, J. *and* BURGES, A. North Liverpool Railway: report on the proposed line of railway from the Manchester & Bolton Railway to the north end of Liverpool. *Westminster*, 1835. pp. 8, with 2 fold. maps. ICE

1264 WHEELER, J. Manchester: its political, social and commercial history, ancient and modern. *London*, 1836. pp. xi, 538. BM
pp. 275–304, mostly on local railways.

1265 MANCHESTER as it is; or, Notices of the institutions, manufactures, commerce, railways, etc. of the metropolis of manufactures . . . with numerous steel engravings and a map. *Manchester*, 1839. pp. 244. BM
pp. 168–78, railways.

1266 LOCH, J. *and* LAWS, J. M. Correspondence . . . on the subject of a railway connexion between the Liverpool & Manchester Railway and the other railways diverging from the latter place . . . *Manchester*, 1842. pp. 20. LSE

1267 ASHURST, W. H. Direct London & Manchester Railway: letters to the Manchester Times, Journal of Commerce, and Morning Herald by W. H. Ashurst and George Remington, August 1845. pp. 17. UL(GL)
No title-page in UL(GL) copy.

1268 REPORT of the Board of Trade on the projected railways in the Manchester and Leeds district; including the Leeds & West Riding Junction, West Yorkshire, Leeds, Dewsbury & Manchester, Leeds & Bradford Extension to Skipton & Colne, Bury & Burnley branches, and Barnsley Junction; also, Report of the Select Committee of the House of Commons on Railway Bills. *Leeds: Baines & Newsome*, [1845.] pp. 24. LEEDS PL
The last page is dated 28 February, 1845.

1269 LIVERPOOL STANDARD, *newspaper*. Descriptive account of the railway accommodation of Lancashire and Cheshire, together with a map of the district illustrating the same. Presented gratuitously to the purchasers of the Liverpool Standard. *Liverpool*, 1846. pp. 16. LSE
Supplement to the issue of 28 April, 1846.

1270 REASONS in favour of a direct line of railroad from London to Manchester. *London*, 1846. pp. 35. BM

1271 BAINES, T. History of the commerce and town of Liverpool . . . *London*, 1852. pp. xvi, 844, 13. BM
pp. 591–622, formation of the Liverpool & Manchester Railway. Also, in ch. 20, opening of the Grand Junction Rly., and the London & Birmingham Rly.; and in ch. 23, internal communications of Liverpool by means of railways, with tables of goods traffic.

1272 BAINES, T. Lancashire and Cheshire past and present . . . with an account of the rise and progress of manufactures and commerce, and of civil and mechanical engineering in these districts by William Fairbairn . . . *London*, 1852. 2 vols. BM
vol. 2, pp. xlix–lvi, Railways.

1273 GRANTHAM, J. Improvements in working the Liverpool Docks. High level railway for goods and passengers. *Liverpool*, 1853. pp. 26, with fold. map & 2 fold. diagrams. ICE
Recommending an elevated railway.

1274 GRANTHAM, J. Railways within the Borough of Liverpool. *Liverpool*, 1856. pp. 15, with fold. map & fold. gradient profile. ICE

1275 LIVERPOOL TOWN COUNCIL. Report on horse railways. (By James Newlands, Borough Engineer, to a Special Joint Sub-Committee on Tramways.) *Liverpool*, 1860. pp. 18.   ICE

1276 RATES of carriage to and from Liverpool: report of the proceedings of a public meeting of the inhabitants of the Borough of Liverpool held in the Corn Exchange . . . March 2nd . . . *Liverpool*, 1865. pp. 40.   BM
Resolved: 'That the rates now charged are excessive.'

1277 NOBLE, J. & Co. Liverpool tramways: explanatory statement and map. *Liverpool*, 1866. pp. 15.
The introduction of tramways into Liverpool.

1278 LIVERPOOL—SPECIAL COMMITTEE ON RAILWAY AMALGAMATIONS. Amalgamations of railway companies. London & North Western and Lancashire & Yorkshire Railway Companies' Amalgamation Bill. Report of Special Committee. *Liverpool*, 1872. pp. 39.   LSE
Need for protection of commercial interests against railway monopoly in Liverpool.

1279 LIVERPOOL CHAMBER OF COMMERCE. Railway companies' amalgamation: report of the Railways, Transit & Parliamentary Committee on the Report from the Joint Select Committee of the House of Lords and the House of Commons appointed to inquire into the subject of the amalgamation of railway companies . . . *Liverpool*, 1873. pp. 19.   LSE
Fear of a rates monopoly which could result from a L. & N.W.R. and L. & Y.R. union.

1280 SALFORD BOROUGH COUNCIL. Tramways: report. (Report of the Parliamentary Sub-Committee to the Council of the Borough of Salford.) [Chairman, T. Barlow.] *Salford*, 1873. pp. 15.   IT
Report of an inspection of tramway systems in London, Glasgow and Edinburgh.

1281 LIVERPOOL BOROUGH COUNCIL. Tramways: report of Special Committee appointed by the Council on the 7th day of May, 1873. [Chairman, S. G. Rathbone.] *Liverpool*, 1874. pp. 27.   ICE
Report on existing and prospective tramways within the borough, and upon tramways generally.

1282 LIVERPOOL BOROUGH COUNCIL. Tramways: reconstruction of the Inner Circle: report of the Borough Engineer [George F. Deacon]. Copy agreement & specification. *Liverpool*, 1876. pp. 22.   ICE

1283 LIVERPOOL—JOINT COMMITTEE OF THE CITY COUNCIL, DOCK BOARD & MERCANTILE ASSOCIATIONS. Railway rates and railway administration as affecting the trade of Liverpool: report of the meeting of the deputation from the Joint Committee of the City Council, Dock Board, mercantile associations, with the directors of the railway companies who have termini in Liverpool, held at Euston Station on Tuesday, 8 March, 1881; together with tables of inequalities of rates . . . *Liverpool*, 1881. pp. 57.   LSE

1284 CLARKE, H. Morecambe Bay railway reclamation in 1836 and 1883. *London*, 1884. pp. 16.   BM
Various railway schemes.

1285 FOSTER, T. B. Suggested Manchester Circular Railway plan and short particulars. *Manchester*, 1885. pp. 2, with fold. map.   MANCHESTER PL

1286 MANCHESTER CORPORATION *and* LANCASHIRE AND CHESHIRE CORPORATIONS. Railway rates and charges. Proposed alteration of rates and charges and imposition of terminal charges by nine of the leading railway companies of England. Report on the Bills by Sub-Committee on Proposed Alterations in the Law. *Manchester*, 1885. pp. 61.   BM

1287 AXON, W. E. A. The Annals of Manchester: a chronological record from the earliest
c times to the end of 1885. *Manchester & London*, 1886. pp. xvii, 456.   BM
Contains forty-three references to railways in Manchester.

1288 [LIVERPOOL.] CITY OF LIVERPOOL. Corporation Tramways. Report of City Engineer as to works executed in tramway streets within the City from 1880 to 1885. *Liverpool*, 1886. pp. 17, with fold. map, fold. table, & 5 fold. diagrams.   PO

1289 PICTON, J. A. City of Liverpool municipal archives and records, 1700–1835. *Liverpool*, 1886.   BM
pp. 301, 302, 358–62, Minutes of the City Council regarding the Liverpool & Manchester Railway, 1824–1835.

1290 HAVESTADT, C. Die Eisenbahn Anlagen in Liverpool und Birkenhead. *Berlin*, 1887. pp. 16, with 5 fold. plates.
Reprinted from *Zeitschrift für Bauwesen*.

1291 'PROGRESS.' Deep water railway docks in the Mersey, versus Manchester Ship Canal. *Edinburgh*, 1887. pp. 12, with 3 diagrams.   BM
Advantages of a railway dock.

1292 SMITH, M. H. The Blackpool Electric Tramway: a paper read before the British Association at Birmingham, with the discussion thereon. *London*, 1887. pp. 33, with diagrams.   IME
Reprinted from *The Electrician* 10 Sept., 1886.

1293 LIVERPOOL CORPORATION TRAMWAYS. Official Handbook and Illustrated Map of the electric tramway routes. *Liverpool*, 1904. pp. 68.

1294 DEVELOPMENT of the railway system of Southport and the Fylde district: proposal to link up the Cheshire Lines Extension Railway with the Fylde Railway system . . . *Southport*, [1905.] pp. 10.   LSE
Reprinted from the *Southport Visitor*, 7 and 10 October, 1905.

1295 LIVERPOOL CORPORATION TRAMWAYS. Stages and fares: report of the General Manager (C. R. Bellamy). *Liverpool*, 1905. pp. 12.   IT
On the consequences to be expected from the proposed introduction of ½d. fare stages and of lower fares for workmen.

1296 HARDMAN, S. Linking the railways. The proposed Wigan & Blackpool Railway and the suggested new port on the Ribble Estuary. *Southport*, [1906.] pp. 16, with fold. map.   BR

1297 STEVENS, M. Railway reform and traffic distribution as they affect the Mersey: an address . . . delivered under the auspices of the Liverpool Chamber of Commerce . . . 20 December 1917. *Liverpool*, [1917.] pp 47.   BM
Rates, station accommodation, competition between railways, etc.

1298 WILLIAMS, W. H. Early railways in South-West Lancashire. [1923.] pp. 13, with 14 illus.   BR
Reprinted from the *Transactions of the Historic Society of Lancashire & Cheshire*, 1923.

1299 MALLINS, C. W. The story of the Tramway: fifty years of progress in Liverpool, with amusing reminiscences. *Birkenhead*, [1926.] pp. 74.   PC
Tramways in Liverpool.

1300 LYTHAM ST. ANNES EXPRESS, *newspaper*. Proposed Ribble Bridge: road and rail-plane structure from Lytham to Southport. *Lytham St. Annes*, 3 February, 1928. s.sh.   TUC
A reprint, with 2 illus.
Bennie railplane scheme.

1301 JOINT MUNICIPAL PASSENGER TRANSPORT BOARD FOR SOUTH-EAST LANCASHIRE AND EAST CHESHIRE [PROPOSED]. Summary and reports of the general managers, town clerks and treasurers of authorities concerned in the proposal. *Manchester*, [August, 1933,] with detailed schedules covering all aspects of tramway and omnibus operation in the areas proposing to amalgamate, & 3 fold. maps.   LSE

1302 JONES, D. C. The Social Survey of Merseyside. *Liverpool: University Press of Liverpool*, 1934. 3 vols.   BM
vol. 2, pp. 145–89, Inland transport; rail,

road and canal: employment conditions of transport workers; with 15 tables and a map.

1303 MANCHESTER CORPORATION TRANSPORT DEPARTMENT. A hundred years of road passenger transport in Manchester, 1835–1935. *Manchester*, [1935.] pp. 32, with illus.   LSE

1304 SIMEY, T. S. *and* CAMPBELL, C. D. Merseyside: co-ordination of passenger transport services. *Liverpool: University Press of Liverpool*, 1935. pp. 39, with 6 tables & a fold. map. [*University of Liverpool, Social Science Department, Statistics Division. Publications*, new series, no. 2.]   BM
Includes descriptions of various transport undertakings and their services.

1305 DAVIES, A. Railways and the Lancashire of tomorrow. *In* 'Transport in Lancashire' issued by the Manchester Chamber of Commerce. *Manchester*, 1938. pp. 9–28, with 2 maps (1, Railways of Lancashire; 2, Suggested Manchester underground railway).   IT

1306 HALLIWELL, D. Passenger transport facilities in South-East Lancashire. *Manchester: Manchester Statistical Society*, 1945. pp. 21.   BM
The need for improvements and for underground railways and electrification of suburban lines around Manchester.

1307 [DARWEN.] BOROUGH OF DARWEN TRANSPORT DEPARTMENT. Souvenir of the abandonment of tramways, 5th October 1946. (A brief survey of the tramways of the Borough.) [*Darwen*, 1946.] pp. [8.]   IT

1308 [BOLTON.] COUNTY BOROUGH OF
c BOLTON TRANSPORT DEPARTMENT. Abandonment of tramways, 29th March 1947. Commemoration dinner. pp. [4.]   PC
On p. 4 is a chronological list headed 'Brief history of tramways' [of Bolton].

1309 ENGLISH ELECTRIC Co. New tramcars for Blackpool. *London*, [1948.] pp. 7, with illus.   IT

1310 FORBES, N. N. The Great Crosby tramways. *Cricklewood: Light Railway Transport League*, [c. 1948.] pp. 15, with 7 illus. & map.   RC
Reprinted from *The Modern Tramway*.

1311 MANCHESTER CORPORATION TRANSPORT DEPARTMENT. Souvenir Brochure
c on the occasion of the abandonment of the last tram service . . . [*Manchester*, 1949.] pp. 31, with 18 illus., chart & 2 fold. plans.   BM
Historical. Contains a chronological list of services, and statistics of growth and decline of tramways in relation to buses.

1312 GILLHAM, J. C. A history of Bolton Corporation Transport. *London*, 1950. pp. 20, with map. *Reproduced typescript.* PC
Paper, Omnibus Society, 19 March, 1948.

1313 MANCHESTER CORPORATION TRANSPORT DEPARTMENT. Golden Jubilee of
c the Passenger Transport undertaking, 1901-1951. *Manchester*, 1951. pp. 32, with illus. & chronology. BM

1314 MELVILLE, J. *and* HOBBS, J. L. Early railway history in Furness. *Kendal*, 1951. pp. 75, with bibliogr. notes & 4 maps. [*Cumberland & Westmoreland Antiquarian & Archaeological Society. Tract Series,* no. 13.] BM

1315 SALFORD CITY TRANSPORT. 50 years of municipal passenger transport operation, 1901-1951. Commemoration brochure. *Salford*, [1951.] pp. 28. PC

1316 SHERRINGTON, C. E. R. Manchester's contribution to transport. pp. 13. *Typescript.* PC
Paper, Manchester & District Traffic Association, 16 November, 1951.
Canals, railways, locomotive building, electrification, etc.

1317 ASHTON-UNDER-LYNE CORPORATION PASSENGER TRANSPORT. 50 years of municipal passenger transport, 1902-1952. *Ashton-under Lyne*, [1952.] pp. 14, with illus. IT

1318 ROCHDALE CORPORATION. 50 years of municipal transport operation, 1902-1952. Commemoration brochure. *Rochdale*, [1952.] pp. 23, with illus. & statistics. IT

*1319 [BURY.] COUNTY BOROUGH OF BURY TRANSPORT DEPARTMENT. 50 years of municipal transport operation, 1903-1953. Commemoration brochure. *Bury*, [1953.] pp. 23, with illus. & statistics IT

1320 ATKINSON, R. *and* BETT, W. H. The tickets of Salford and Bury Corporation Transport Departments. *London: Ticket & Fare Collection Society*, 1954. pp. 19. BM

1321 BARKER, T. C. *and* HARRIS, J. R. A Merseyside town in the Industrial Revolution: St. Helens, 1750-1900. *Liverpool: Liverpool University Press*, 1954. pp. xviii, 508, with bibliogr. notes. BM
pp. 181-92, The coming of the railway.
pp. 327-37, The transport monopoly, 1845-72.

1322 GREVILLE, M. D. Chronological List of the Railways of Lancashire, 1828-1939.
c [*Liverpool*, 1954.] pp. 187-201. BM
Reprinted from the *Transactions of the Historic Society of Lancashire and Cheshire*, vol. 105, 1953. Some corrections by M. D. Greville appear in the *Journal of the Railway & Canal Historical Society*, vol. 1, no. 4, p. 37.

1323 BAILEY, F. A. A history of Southport. *Southport: Angus Downie*, 1955. pp. 237. BM
pp. 144-59, Communications: canal, road, and rail.

1324 HARRIS, J. R. Railways of the St. Helens coalfield down to 1830: a note. *In* 'Journal
b of Transport History', vol. 2, no. 3, May 1956. pp. 175-6, with 16 bibliogr. notes. BM

1325 MANCHESTER LOCOMOTIVE SOCIETY *and* STEPHENSON LOCOMOTIVE SOCIETY—NORTH WEST AREA. The 'Old' Manchester Rail-Tour, Saturday 12th May 1956: descriptive notes on the tour by G. Harrop. *Manchester*, May 1956. pp. 12, with la. fold. map. *Reproduced typescript.* PC

1326 PLATT, E. N. T. South Lancashire coalfield Rail Tour, Railway Correspondence & Travel Society, 29 September 1956. Descriptive and historical notes. pp. 9. *Reproduced typescript.* PC

1327 LIVERPOOL CORPORATION PASSENGER TRANSPORT UNDERTAKING. The first sixty years: a pictorial record of the Liverpool Corporation Passenger Transport Undertaking issued on the occasion of the last tramcar running in Liverpool on the 14th September 1957. [*Liverpool*, 1957.] pp. 40, with 62 illus. & 2 charts. PC

1328 TAYLOR, C. Manchester Corporation Tramways. Rolling stock summary: passenger cars. *Rochdale: the author*, 1957. pp. [9.] BR

1329 RAWTENSTALL BOROUGH COUNCIL. The Golden Jubilee of the Rawtenstall Corpora-
c tion Transport Department, 1908-1958. Souvenir brochure; including some notes on the general history of passenger transport in the Rossendale area. *Rawtenstall*, 1958. pp. 16, with 12 illus. & a chronology. BM
Includes tramways.

1330 SMITH, L. J. The South Lancashire development area: a selective study of changes
b within an emerging problem area, 1830-1945. Thesis, M.A., London University, 1958. pp. xii, 297, with 24 mounted photographs, bibliogr. notes, & a bibliography; also a volume of 53 maps. *Typescript.* UL
Growth and relationship of industry, transport and population, with (pp. 228-66) a detailed examination of Newton-le-Willows.

1331 BARDSLEY, J. R. The railways of Bolton, 1824-1959. [*Bolton: the author*, 1960.] pp. 34[35], with 8 illus. on 4 plates, & a map. BM
The L. & Y. Rly. and the L. & N.W. Rly.

1332 [BLACKPOOL.] COUNTY BOROUGH OF BLACKPOOL. 75 years of electric street tramway operation. [*Blackpool*, 1960.] pp. 13, with 19 illus. BM

1333 CORMACK, I. L. Seventy-five years on wheels: the history of public transport in Barrow-in-Furness, 1885–1960. *Glasgow: Scottish Tramway Museum Society*, [1960.] pp. 55, with 32 illus., fleet lists & a map. BM

1334 MAUND, T. B. Transport in Rochdale and district. *London: Omnibus Society*, [1960.] pp. 22, with 10 illus., lists & a map. BM
An historical account, including tramways.

1335 KIDD, C. *and* BETT, W. H. Manchester Corporation, 1901–1961: sixty years of tickets. *Petts Wood (Orpington): Ticket & Fare Collection Society*, 1961. pp. 34, with 2 plates, & tables. BM

1336 RUSH, R. W. The tramways of Accrington, 1886–1932; with brief notes on the adjoining systems of Blackburn, Darwen, Haslingden and Rawtenstall. *London: Light Railway Transport League*, 1961. pp. 88, with plates (incl. maps), tables, diagrams, & a bibliography. BM

1337 YEARSLEY, I. A. The Manchester tram. *Huddersfield: Advertiser Press*, 1962. pp. 255, with 78 illus., 3 plans & 2 maps on endpapers. BM
A detailed historical account.

1337a YEARSLEY, I. A., PRICE, J. H. *and*
c TAYLOR, C. Manchester Tramway Diary: a record of tramway events in East Lancashire and North Cheshire from 1940 to 1951. *Castleton*, August 1961. pp. 20, with maps & diagrams. BM
Issued on behalf of the Manchester Transport Historical Collection as a chronological appendix to I. A. Yearsley's *The Manchester Tram* (1962).

Leicestershire

1338 STRETTON, C. E. Early tramroads and railways in Leicestershire. *Burton-on-Trent*, 1900. pp. 14. BM

*1339 LEICESTER CORPORATION TRAMWAYS. Rules and instructions to motormen. *Leicester*, [1907.] pp. 25[27]. BM

1340 STRETTON, C. E. The stone roads, canals, edge rail-ways, outram-ways and electric rail-ways in the county of Leicester . . . *Leicester*, [1907.] pp. 231–47. BM
Reprint from *Guide to Leicester & district* (1907).

1341 THOMAS, G. O. On a certain town. *In* his 'Things big and little.' *London*, 1922. pp. 58–64 (61–4). BM
Reminiscences of boyhood in Leicester. The fascination of watching trains.

1342 [LEICESTER.] CITY OF LEICESTER— TRAMWAYS AND MOTOR OMNIBUS DEPARTMENT. Report to the Chairman and members of the Motor Omnibus Committee on the financial position of the Department and the replacement of tramways by other forms of traction. [By] H. Pool, General Manager. *Leicester*, [September 1934.] pp. 26, with tables. IT
'Private and confidential.'
Trams to be replaced by buses.

1343 LEICESTER CITY TRANSPORT. Report by the General Manager and Engineer to the Chairman and members of the Transport Committee on the future of the electric tramways. *Leicester*, 11 October 1937. pp. 70, with illus. IT
'Private and confidential.'
The scrapping of tramways recommended.
—— Supplementary Report, 5 January 1938. IT

1344 THOMAS, G. O. Autobiography, 1891–1941. *London: Chapman & Hall*, 1946. pp. 267. BM
Including boyhood reminiscences of railways in Leicester.

1345 LEICESTER CITY TRANSPORT. Official Brochure of the Leicester City Transport. *Leicester*, [1949.] pp. 64, with illus. & a map. PC
pp. 5–21 (18–21), 'The evolution of road passenger transport [in Leicester].'

1346 SMITH, K. W. The story of Leicester's trams, told by a passenger. *Cricklewood: Light Railway Transport League*, October 1950. pp. 15, with illus. *Reproduced typescript.* PC

1347 ABBOTT, R. The railways of the Leicester Navigation Company . . . *Leicester*, 1955. pp. 51–61, with map. BM
Reprinted from the *Transactions of the Leicestershire Archaeological & Historical Society*, vol. 31, 1955.

1348 SIMMONS, J. Railways. *In* 'A history of
b the County of Leicester': vol. 3. *London: Institute of Historical Research*, 1955. pp. 108–27, with 2 illus., map, & 93 bibliogr. notes. [*Victoria History of the Counties of England.*] BM

*1349 CLINKER, C. R. *and* HADFIELD, C. The
b Ashby-de-la-Zouch Canal and its railways. *Leicester: Leicester Archaeological & Historical Society*, 1958. pp. 53–76, with 2 maps, tonnage & revenue tables, 1806–1906, & 107 bibliogr. notes, mostly referring to original documents. BM

1350 LEICESTER COURT OF QUARTER SES-
c SIONS. Deposited railway plans: reproduced by the Historical Manuscripts Commission from originals prepared by the Leicestershire Record Office . . . [*London: National Register of Archives*,] 1958. BM
Summary descriptions of 385 plans deposited between 1829 and 1952.

1351 LEICESTER MUSEUMS *and* LEICESTER
c CITY TRANSPORT. Public transport in Leicester, 1874–1961. (A pictorial calendar published to mark the Diamond Jubilee of Leicester City Transport, 1901–1961.) *Leicester*, [1961.] pp. 28, with 40 illus., a tramway route map (1927), & 5 chronological tables. BM
Thirty tramway scenes are depicted.

Lincolnshire

1352 LINCOLN. Report of the committee appointed at Lincoln to examine the proposals for a Northern Railway. (March 1835.) [*Lincoln*, 1835.] pp. 16.
  Signed, 'Thos. Norton, Mayor, Chairman'.
  The comparative merits of a Yorkshire–London main line to pass through Lincolnshire, and a 36-mile branch from Lincoln to the proposed Midland Counties Rly. at Nottingham.

1353 BRACE, H. W. A Chronology of Gainsborough's railways. *Gainsborough*, 1952.
  c s.sh.   PC
  Produced by the 'Friends of the Old Hall' Association for an exhibition about railways. Period, 1845–1882.

Monmouthshire

1354 COXE, W. Historical tour in Monmouthshire. *London*, 1801.   BM
  pp. 230–1, 'Blaenafon Iron Works', with illus.
  —— another edn. *Brecon*, 1904.   BM
  pp. 201–2, with illus.

1355 JONES, T. E. The history of the Industrial Revolution in Monmouthshire. (Thesis, M.A., University of Wales, 1929.) 4 parts. pp. 428,[76.] *Typescript.*   NLW
  pt. 4, Communications. Includes railways and early tramroads.

1356 SWALLOW, M. A. History of the means of communication in the County of Monmouth. (Thesis, Ph.D., Univ. Lond., 1932.) pp. 205. *Reproduced typescript.*   UL
  Includes early mineral wagonways and later public railways.
  Appendix, List of Acts relating to railways in Monmouthshire, followed by a large collection of miscellaneous detailed information (*c.* 130 pp.)

1356a DAVIES, E. M. E. Port developments and commerce of Newport, 1835–1935. (Thesis, M.A., University of Wales, 1938.) pp. 154, xxvii, with maps. *Typescript.*   NLW
  Contains sections on transport.

1357 BARRIE, D. S. *and* LEE, C. E. The Sirhowy Valley and its railways. *London: Railway Publishing Co.*, 1940. pp. 36, with illus., maps & diagrams.   BM

1358 STEPHENSON LOCOMOTIVE SOCIETY—MIDLAND AREA. Monmouthshire Valleys Rail Tour, July 11th, 1953: historical and other notes on the route, by D. S. Barrie. pp. 9. *Reproduced typescript.*   SLS

1358a RAILWAY AND CANAL HISTORICAL SOCIETY. Monmouthshire Rail Tour, Saturday, 7 May, 1960. Itinerary (by William J. Skillern). pp. 8, with a map. *Reproduced typescript.*   NEWPORT PL
  Historical and descriptive notes.

1359 SHIREHAMPTON, W. J. P. Monmouth's railways: a historical survey. 2nd edn. *Monmouth: Monmouth & District Field Club & Antiquarian Society*, [1958.] pp. 7, with a map. [*Memorials of Monmouth*, no. 6.] *Reproduced typescript.*   BM

—— 3rd edn. *Monmouth*, [1961.] pp. 8, with a map.   BM

1360 STEPHENSON LOCOMOTIVE SOCIETY—MIDLAND AREA. Monmouth and its railways. Photographic souvenir and historical notes in connection with the last passenger train on the Monmouth–Ross and Monmouth–Chepstow branches of the Western Region of British Railways (formerly G.W.R.), Sunday 4th January 1959. *Birmingham*, 1949. pp. [8,] with 10 illus. & a map.   SL

1361 RAILWAY AND CANAL HISTORICAL SOCIETY. Coach tour of Monmouthshire and Brecknock & Abergavenny canals, Sunday, 8 May 1960. Itinerary. *With* Monmouthshire Canal: historical notes, by Charles Hadfield, *and* The Caerleon Tramroad [historical notes], by William J. Skillern. pp. [3.] *Reproduced typescript.* NEWPORT PL

1362 PRITCHARD, A. J. Historical notes on the railways of South East Monmouthshire. *Lingfield: Oakwood Press*, 1962. pp. 48, with 4 plates & 3 maps. [*Locomotion Papers*, no. 17.]   BM
  'The Newport, Abergavenny & Hereford Railway': 'Chepstow; a vital link for the South Wales railways.'

Norfolk

1363 The NORWICH tramways, 1900–1935. *Norwich: Tramway & Omnibus Historical Society*, [1960.] pp. 24, with 5 illus, & a list of dividends, 1901–1933.   BM
  Four essays: The coming of the trams to Norwich, by Geoffrey Goreham; The development, by A. B. Dennis; Memories of the Norwich trams, by C. J. W. Messent; Some facts and figures, by R. W. Gamble.

Northamptonshire

1364 WAKE, J. Northampton vindicated; or, Why the main line missed the town. *Northampton: the author*, 1935. pp. 31, with bibliogr. notes, portrait & map.   BM
  The story of Northampton's objection to the London & Birmingham Rly.'s proposed route.

1365 NORTHAMPTONSHIRE ARCHIVES COMMITTEE. Guide to an Exhibition on Transport and Communications at the Northampton Art Gallery & Museum. *Northampton*, 1958.   BR
  pp. 20–8, Railways. Documents, maps, prints, photographs, paintings, books, models and objects.

1366 HATLEY, V. A. Northampton re-vindicated: more light on why the main line missed the town. *In* 'Northamptonshire Past and Present', vol. 2, no. 6. 1959. pp. 305–9, with a map & bibliogr. notes.   BM
  The relationship between Northampton and the course of the London & Birmingham Rly. An extension of the enquiry by Joan Wake in her *Northampton vindicated* (1935).

1367 PERRIN, R. The history of New England [*Peterborough*, 1958.] pp. 44, with 6 illus-
pc
Privately issued to commemorate the New England Old Boys' Reunion and the centenary of the Great Northern Railway's New England School, 1857–1957.

1368 CLINKER, C. R. The railways of North-amptonshire, including the Soke of Peter-
c borough, 1800–1960: a list of authorising Acts of Parliament, opening and closing dates, with other historical information, compiled from original and contemporary sources. *Rugby: the author*, February 1960. pp. 14. *Reproduced typescript.* SL

1369 PERRIN, R. G.N.R. schools: the history of the old railway church schools, 1856–1911. [*Peterborough*, 1961.] pp. 51, with 16 illus., incl. portraits of groups. pc
Privately issued to members of the New England Old Boys' Association.

Northumberland, including Newcastle

1370 GRAY, W. Chorographia; or, A survey of Newcastle upon Tyne. *Newcastle*, 1649. pp. 48. BM
pp. 24–5, the coal trade and wagonways.
—— *In* 'Harleian Miscellany', vol. III, 1745. pp. 256–72. BM
—— *Newcastle*, 1813. pp. ix, 43. BM
—— *Newcastle*, 1818. pp. 48. BM
—— *In* Richardson, T. M., 'Antiquities of the Border Counties', 1881. pp. 1–36 at end. BM
—— *Newcastle*, 1884. pp. 121[124]. BM

1371 NORTH, R. The life of . . . Francis North, Baron of Guilford . . . *London*, 1742. pp. 333. BM
pp. 136–7, description of colliery wagonways at Newcastle.
—— 2nd edn. *London*, 1808. 2 vols. BM
(vol. 1, p. 265.)
—— abridged edn. *London*, [1939.] pp. 247. BM
(pp. 119–20.)

1372 STUKELEY, W. Itinerarium Curiosum; or, An account of the antiquities and remark-able curiosities in nature and art observed in travels through Great Britain; illustrated . . . 2nd edn., Centuria II. *London*, 1776. pp. 177. BM
pp. 68–9 refer to cart-ways in wooden frames for the transport of coals at Newcastle, and to Col. Lyddal's coal works at Tanfield where cuttings, bridges and embankments were found.

1373 BRAND, J. The history and antiquities of the town and county of . . . Newcastle upon Tyne. *Newcastle*, 1789. 2 vols. BM
vol. 2, pp. 687–8, 'Waggons and waggon way'.

1374 GRAINGER, R. A proposal for concen-trating the termini of the Newcastle &

Carlisle, the Great North of England, and proposed Edinburgh railways, and for providing spacious and eligible depots with convenient access from these several rail-ways to the town of Newcastle . . . *Newcastle*, 1836. pp. 8, with fold. map. BM

1375 BOARD OF TRADE—RAILWAY DEPART-MENT. Report of the Railway Department of the Board of Trade, on the schemes for ex-tending railway communication from New-castle to Berwick. *London*, 24 February, 1845. pp. 7, with la. fold. map. LSE

1376 NEWCASTLE & CARLISLE RLY. In Chan-cery. Her Majesty's Attorney-General at the relation of Alexander George Gray & John Humber versus the Mayor, Aldermen & burgesses of the Borough of Newcastle-upon-Tyne. The affidavits, valuations and other proceedings in the above cause to-gether with the judgement . . . and the in-junction . . . served upon the Corporation of Newcastle-upon-Tyne. With a litho-graphed plan. *Newcastle*, 1845. pp. 51.
LSE
Concerning ground in Neville St. to be given up to the Newcastle & Carlisle Rly.

1377 NEWCASTLE UPON TYNE TOWN COUN-CIL. Report of a discussion in Newcastle Town Council at a special meeting held Jan. 8, 1845, on the question of assenting to a railway passing through Newcastle-upon-Tyne, and involving the construction of a high-level bridge. *Newcastle-upon-Tyne*, 1845. pp. 24. BM

1378 NEWCASTLE UPON TYNE TOWN COUN-CIL. Report of the discussion in the Town Council of Newcastle-on-Tyne, Wednesday, February 3, 1847, on the railways projected through the Team Valley by the Leeds & Thirsk, and York & Newcastle railway companies. *Newcastle-upon-Tyne*, 1847. pp. 47. BM

1379 NEWCASTLE UPON TYNE TOWN COUN-CIL. Third discussion in Newcastle Town Council on the Team Valley Railways. *Newcastle*, [1847.] pp. 12. LSE

1380 EVIDENCE concerning the High Level Bridge over the Tyne at Newcastle, taken at the Guildhall in that town on the 2nd of August, 1848, before Captain Washington, R.N., of the Harbour Department of the Admiralty. *Newcastle*, 1848. pp. 24. BM
Obstruction to river traffic. Complaints by keelmen and watermen against the York, New-castle & Berwick Rly. Co.'s erections in the river.

1381 LANGLEY, J. B. The dangers of the North British Railway policy; or, A question for the consideration of the inhabitants of New-castle and the surrounding towns, candidly stated and impartially discussed. 2nd edn. *Newcastle*, [1861.] pp. 16. BM

1382 LEE, C. E. Tyneside tramroads of Northumberland: some notes on the engineering background of George Stephenson. [*London*, 1949.] pp. 28[32], with 3 maps & a plan.   BM
> Paper, Newcomen Society, 9 March, 1949.

1383 THOMAS, D. St. J. Rural transport: a report . . . sponsored by Dartington Trustees, Dartington Hall, Devon. *Dawlish: David Charles*, 1960. pp. 28.   PC
> pp. 15–18, Train services and road/rail competition in South Devon and Northumberland.

1384 HEARSE, G. S. The tramways of Northumberland. *Blanchland: the author*, 1961. pp. viii, 104, with frontis., 64 illus., 4 maps, (1 la. fold), & tables.   BM

Nottinghamshire

1385 NOTTINGHAM CITY TRANSPORT. Golden Jubilee, 16th October 1947. *Nottingham*,
c 1947. pp. 18, with 37 illus.   PC
> pp. 11 & 13, Chronological table of events; and, p. 18, Comparative statistics, 1899 and 1947.

1386 CRAMP, A. G. The 'Back Line'. *In* Allen, G. F., 'Regional Rounds no. 1, Eastern and North Eastern Regions'. 1949. pp. 16–22.   BM
> Nottingham and district.

1387 BIRKS, J. A. *and* COXON, P. An account of railway development in the Nottinghamshire coalfield. *Mansfield: the authors*, 1950. pp. 77, [4,] with 7 illus. & diagrams on 3 plates, & 2 maps (1 fold). *Reproduced typescript*.   BM

1388 [NOTTINGHAM.] CORPORATION OF NOTTINGHAM. Records of the Borough
c of Nottingham: being a series of extracts from the archives of the Corporation of· Nottingham. vol. 9, 1836–1900. *Nottingham: Thos. Forman & Sons*, 1956. pp. xix, 462, with fold. map.   BM
> A chronological arrangement, with over 100 extracts from entries relating to railways and tramways.

1389 MARSHALL, R. A history of Nottingham City Transport, 1897–1959. *Nottingham:*
c *Nottingham Corporation Transport Department*, July 1960. pp. 136 with 6 illus. & a table.   PC
> A chronological record.

Oxfordshire

1390 BRUNTON, J. The Oxford & District Tramways. *London: Institution of Civil Engineers*, 1882. pp. 6, with 4 diagrams.   ICE
> Excerpt, *Min. Proc. I.C.E.*, vol. 67, Session 1881–82, pt. 1.

Shropshire

1391 DENTON, J. H. A tour of the railways and canals between Oakengates and Coalbrookdale. *Codsall: Cottage Press*, [1962.] pp. 8, with map.   BM

Somerset

1392 TAUNTON GRAND WESTERN RAIL-ROAD. At a meeting of landowners and others resident in Taunton and its neighbourhood, held this 3rd day of January 1825 . . . for the purpose of taking into consideration the expediency of forming a rail-road from the town of Taunton to Bristol, and from Taunton to Exeter, with a branch to Tiverton. Malachi Blake in the Chair. *Taunton*, 1825. pp. [3.]   BM
> Resolutions.

1393 BRITTON, J. Lecture on the road-ways of England, pointing out the peculiarly advantageous situation of Bristol for the commerce of the West; with remarks on the benefits likely to arise from a rail-road between that port and London. *Bristol*, [1833.] pp. 14.   BM
> Read before the Literary & Philosophical Society of Bristol, October 19, 1833.

1394 BIDE, W. Deception unmasked. *Yeovil*, 1847. pp. 16, 56.   YEOVIL PL
> Two pamphlets comprising four letters addressed 'to the inhabitants of Yeovil on the railway question', in defence of Great Western proposals and of the broad gauge.

1395 BRISTOL TRAMWAYS & CARRIAGE CO. Electric tramways. *Bristol*, [1895.] pp. 48, with illus. & diagrams.   ICE
> Issued to celebrate the inauguration of the Bristol, St. George & Kingswood Electric Tramways, 14 Oct., 1895.

1396 BRISTOL TRAMWAYS & CARRIAGE CO. Pictorial Bristol, and Handbook of the Bristol Tramways & Carriage Company, Limited. *Bristol*, [June, 1897.] pp. 72, with 10 route plans, timetables, & other information.   PC

1397 LATIMER, J. The Annals of Bristol in the nineteenth century. *Bristol*, 1887, 1902. 2 vols.   BM
> vol. 1, 1801–1886. pp. 552.
> vol. 2, 1887–1900. pp. 108.
> Includes railways and tramways.

1398 ARROWSMITH, J. W., *publisher*. Half a century of railway progress in the Bristol district. *Bristol*, July 1904. pp. 12.   RC

1399 The 'IRON LORD' of the Brendon Hills. *In* 'Echoes of Exmoor: a record of the discussions and doings of the Men-of-Exmoor Club, under the eye of A Spectator. Second series.' *London*, 1924. pp. [1]–27 (5–10).   BM
> The aerial rope-way, and the Brendon Hill incline for cable haulage of iron-stone. Includes a dramatic account of a runaway truck, 1867, and (p. 24) 'Jack Crascombe's Strike Song' (4 verses in dialect), 1880.

1400 GAILEY, T. W. H. Passenger transport in Bristol in the Victorian Era . . . *London: Omnibus Society*, [1956.] pp. 7, with 6 illus. & a map. LSE

1401 LITTLE, B. D. G. The City and County of Bristol: a study in Atlantic civilisation. *London: Werner Laurie*, 1954. pp. xix, 399. BM
Includes railways.

1402 WINSTONE, R. Bristol as it was, 1914–1900. *Bristol: R. Winstone*, 1957. pp. 78 [80]. BM
A photographic record, with many pictures of Bristol tramways.

1403 WINSTONE, R. Bristol as it was, 1939–1914. *Bristol: R. Winstone*, 1957. pp. 79. BM
A photographic record, including pictures of Bristol tramways.

1404 WINSTONE, R. Bristol in the 1890's . . . the photographs collected by, and the book designed and published by, Reece Winstone. *Bristol*, 1960. pp. 79. BM
Includes tramway and railway scenes, with brief descriptions.

1405 ELTON, A. The pre-history of railways, with special reference to the early quarry railways of North Somerset. *[Taunton:]*
b *Somerset Archaeological and Natural History Society*, [1963.] pp. 31–59, with 6 illus., 2 maps, & 52 bibliogr. notes. BM
Presidential address, reprinted from the *Proceedings of the S.A. & N.H.S.*, vol. 107 (1963).
A concise but well circumscribed general survey of present knowledge of railway antiquity is followed (pp. 36 to end) by a more detailed account of Ralph Allen's wagonway and other shorter lines in the vicinity of 18th-century Bath.

Staffordshire

1406 TAYLOR, G. H. Some account of the tramways of Wolverhampton. *[Cricklewood,]* July 1951. pp. 15, with lists & map. *Reproduced typescript.* pc
Paper, Light Railway Transport League, 28 July, 1951.

1407 HOLLICK, J. R. The Caldon Low tramways. pp. 10, with fold map. *Reproduced typescript.* pc
Paper, Cheadle Historical Society, 24 March, 1954.

1408 WALSALL CORPORATION TRANSPORT. Golden Jubilee Celebration and official opening of Birchill's Trolley Vehicle Depot . . . on Thursday 7th October 1954. *[Walsall*, 1954.] pp. [20,] with 25 illus. & map. pc

1409 HUFFER, D. B. M. The economic development of Wolverhampton, 1750–1850. (The-
b sis, M.A., Univ. Lond., 1957.) pp. 363, vi, & bibliography. UL
pp. 100–31, Railways.

1410 WARRILLOW, E. J. D. A sociological history of the City of Stoke-on-Trent . . . *Hanley: Etruscan Publications*, June 1960. pp. [ix,] 418, with 233 illus. BM
pp. 10–127, Communications. Includes railways and tramways.

Suffolk

*1411 SIMMONS, J. The railways of Britain: an historical introduction. *London*, 1961. BM
pp. 197–209, 'The railways of Suffolk'; with illus. and map.

Surrey

1412 PRICE, H. H. Report . . . respecting the completion of the Grand Surrey Canal to the Thames at Vauxhall and laying a railway on the bank thereof, to connect the Southampton, Croydon, Greenwich, and proposed Brighton, Tunbridge Wells, Gravesend, and Dover railways together, with branches . . . *London*, 1835. pp. 13, with fold. map. BM
The Grand Surrey Canal & Railway.

1413 O'DELL, A. C. Transport and population changes in the Croydon district. *Croydon*, [1941.] pp. 83–90, with a population table, 1541–1931, a local railway chronology, & a series of clock diagrams showing density of passenger train service for various years. pc
Reprinted from *Procs. Croydon Natural History & Scientific Society*, vol. 40, 1935–1941.

1414 LEE, C. E. Early railways in Surrey: the Surrey Iron Railway and its continuation, the Croydon, Merstham & Godstone Iron Railway: a paper presented to the Newcomen Society, Dec. 11, 1940. *London*, 1944. pp. 40, with 10 illus. on 4 plates, map & illus. in text, & bibliogr. notes. BM

1415 TOWNSEND, C. E. C. Further notes on early railways in Surrey. pp. 12,[8,] with 12 maps and an inserted page headed 'Appendix no. 3'. *Reproduced typescript.* pc
Paper, Newcomen Society, 11 January, 1950. Supplementing *Early railways in Surrey*, by Chas. E. Lee (1944). Some notes by C. E. Lee are included.

1416 CARTER, E. F. The story of Redhill as a railway centre. *Redhill: Holmesdale Press*, [1954.] pp. 12, with 5 illus. (2 on cover). BM

1417 'SOUTHMET.' The tramways of Croydon. By 'Southmet'. *London: Light Railway*
c *Transport League*, 1960. pp. 212, with frontis., 78 illus., tables, fold. map, & chronology (4 pp.). BM
Compiled by Geoffrey E. Baddeley, Reginald J. Durrant, Richard Elliott, George L. Gundry, and Ronald M. Harmer.

Sussex

1418 'TOWNSMAN.' A series of four letters addressed to the inhabitants of Brighton

on the subject of a railway communication between that town and London. *Brighton*, 1837. pp. 36.   SL
Dated 26 December, 1836, to 27 February, 1837.
Comparing the various proposed schemes, and favouring the Direct (Cundy's) Line.

1419 BROOKFIELD, H. C. A regional study of urban development in coastal Sussex since the eighteenth century. Thesis, Ph.D., University of London, March 1950. pp. ix, 378, with maps & tables. *Typescript.*   UL
pp. 314–22, The railway, 1840–1880.

*1420 JACKSON, A. A. Volk's Electric Railway, Brighton, 1883–1964. *London: Light Railway Transport League*, [1964.] pp. 20, with 20 illus. & map.   BM
Cover title, *Volk's Railway, Brighton, 1883–1964.*

Warwickshire, including Birmingham

1421 OBSERVATIONS on the projected improvements of the town, in reference to railways . . . By 'Common Sense'. *Birmingham*, [1838.] pp. 12.   H
Birmingham.

1422 BIRMINGHAM CENTRAL TRAMWAYS. The cable system. Reprinted from Birmingham and Glasgow newspapers. *Birmingham*, 1886. pp. 25, with illus. & map.   ICE
Considerations on the proposed use of cable traction on the Hockley route.

1423 BIRMINGHAM CORPORATION. Report of the Sub-committee on Tramway Traction, April 1897. [Chairman, J. Hopkinson.] *Birmingham*, 1897. pp. 50.   ICE
Recommendations following visits to tramways in Great Britain and in Europe.

1424 COVENTRY CORPORATION TRANSPORT COMMITTEE. Diamond Jubilee of mechanical passenger transport in Coventry, 1884–1944. Compiled by James Taylor, City Development Officer. *Coventry*, [1944.] pp. 19, with 21 illus.   IT
Includes tramways.

1425 BAYNES, R. H. A Bibliography of Railways in the Birmingham area, to 1844.
b Submitted for the Diploma in Librarianship, University of London, May 1949. pp. 46. *Typescript.*   UL
Ninety-two items.

1426 CAMWELL, W. A. The ABC of Birmingham City Transport: part one, trams and trolleybuses. [*London:*] *Ian Allan*, 1950. pp. 55, with illus. & map.   BM
History and description.

1427 BIRMINGHAM JUNIOR CHAMBER OF COMMERCE. Survey and report on Birmingham suburban passenger transport facilities. *Birmingham*, April 1952. pp. 32, with tables.   IT

1428 CLARK, P. L. Studies in the railway geography of the Birmingham region. Thesis, M.A. (Geography), University of Birmingham, 1952. pp. ix, 291. *Typescript.*   BU
The forty maps and plans which form part of this thesis are with the top copy in the Geography Department.

1429 BIRMINGHAM TRANSPORT DEPARTMENT, City of Birmingham Transport Department
c Jubilee, 1904–1954. Brochure to commemorate the undertaking's Jubilee. *Birmingham*, 1954. pp. [30.]   BM
Includes tramways and contains a chronology.

1430 HARVEY, P. D. A. *and* THORPE, H. The printed maps of Warwickshire, 1576–1900
c . . . Published by the Records and Museum Committee of the Warwickshire County Council in collaboration with the University of Birmingham. *Warwick*, 1959. pp. x, 279.   BM
pp. 53–9, Dates of completion or projection of the principal railways appearing on Warwickshire maps.

Wiltshire

1431 WELLS, H. B. Swindon in the nineteenth and twentieth centuries. *In* 'Studies in the
b history of Swindon' by L. B. Grinsell and others. 1950. pp. 91–157, with 4 plates, maps, illus., & 275 bibliographical and other notes.   BM
Swindon and the G.W.R.

1432 LLOYD, J. B. The development of education in Swindon, with particular reference to
b the influence and requirements of the Railway Works and the local industries. (Thesis, M.A., Bristol University, 1957.) pp. 333, with maps, diagram & a bibliography (5 pp.). *Typescript.*   BRISTOL UNIV

1433 CLINKER, C. R. Railways. *In* 'A history of Wiltshire', edited by Elizabeth Crittall: v. 4.
b *London: Institute of Historical Research*, 1959. pp. 280–93, with map and 91 bibliogr. notes. [*Victoria History of the Counties of England.*]   BM

Worcestershire

1434 TURBERVILLE, T. C. Worcestershire in the nineteenth century. *London*, 1852. pp. 335.   BM
pp. 150–64, 'Railways'. The Birmingham & Gloucester; the Grand Connection project; the Oxford, Worcester & Wolverhampton.

1435 NORRIS, J. E. The railways of Worcester. pp. 21. *Typescript.*   RC
Paper, Railway Club, September 1953.

Yorkshire

1436 KNARESBOROUGH RAILWAY COMMITTEE. Report of the Knaresborough Railway Committee. *Leeds*, [1819.] pp. 36, with a map.   UL(GL)
Proposed railway along the Nidd Valley.

1437 PEMBERTON, J. An address to the County of York, respecting the formation of a railway company and the making a railway from York to the Darlington Railway, with a branch to Ripon; and the rules of such Company. *York*, [1827.] pp. 16. UL(GL)
A proposed 'Yorkshire Railway Company'.

1438 RENNIE, G. B. The preliminary report on the Bridlington & York Railway . . . published by the Committee, 1834. *York*, 1834. pp. 12, iv.

1439 REPORT of the Board of Trade on the projected railways in the Manchester and Leeds district; including the Leeds & West Riding Junction, West Yorkshire, Leeds, Dewsbury & Manchester, Leeds & Bradford Extension to Skipton & Colne, Bury and Burnley branches, and Barnsley Junction; also, Report of the Select Committee of the House of Commons on Railway Bills. *Leeds: Baines & Newsome*, [1845.] pp. 24. LEEDS PL
The last page is dated 28 February, 1845.

1440 REPORT of the Board of Trade on the Yorkshire Railways, detailing their reasons for reporting to Parliament in favour of the Leeds & West Riding Junction Railways; also, Report of the Select Committee of the House of Commons on Railway Bills. *Leeds*, [1845.] pp. 24. LEEDS PL
The last page is dated 28 February, 1845.

1441 [BAXTER, R.] Letter to Richard Monckton Milnes, Esq., M.P., on his erroneous statements in the debate in the House of Commons leading to the rejection of the South Yorkshire Isle of Axholme Bill, 23 February, 1852. *Doncaster*, 1852. pp. 8. LEEDS PL
The letter is dated from Doncaster, 5 March, 1852, and is signed by Robert Baxter.

1442 PHILLIPS, J. Railway excursions from York, Leeds, and Hull. *Hull*, 1853. pp. 106. LEEDS PL

1443 [PHILLIPS, J.] Phillips' excursions in Yorkshire by the North Eastern Railway. 3rd edition, illustrated. *York*, [1855.] pp. 88. LEEDS PL
Added in pencil, 'By John Phillips'.

1444 FAWKES, F. H. North Eastern Railway: an address to the landowners of Wharfedale. *Otley*, 1861. pp. 15. BM
The proposed line of the Leeds & Thirsk Rly. considered in relation to the plan of the North Eastern and the Midland Rly. for a line between Otley and Ilkley. Appendix, five letters between F. H. Fawkes and the N.E. Rly.

1445 GARNETT, J. North Eastern Railway: a reply to Mr. Fawkes's remarks on the Wharfedale Railway. *Otley*, 1861. pp. 7. BM
Criticising Fawkes' opposition to a railway between Otley and Arthington.

1446 FILLITER, E. Report upon the railway schemes affecting the Borough of Leeds, in Parliament in 1864. *Leeds*, 1864. pp. 12, with la. fold. map. ICE

1447 LEATHER, J. W. Letter to Mr. Alderman Kitson, on the proposed new Central Railway Station, and the lines projected by the North Eastern Company for connecting the railways on the Western and Eastern sides of Leeds. Second edition, corrected and improved, and to which is added an Appendix showing how a grand central low level passenger station may be formed on the south side of Wellington Street, to which all the railways now using the Midland Station and the existing central station can conveniently be brought; showing also a line by which the Leeds & Selby Railway may be connected with such a grand central low level station, etc. without objectionably interfering with any of the principal streets of the town; with suggested new approaches to such station and certain desirable improvements of the adjacent streets and roads. Illustrated by new and additional maps and sections. *Leeds*, 1864. pp. 50. LEEDS PL
A corrigenda note explains that the five maps and plans referred to may be seen at various libraries.

1448 WHEATER, W. How to approach Roundhay Park: Mr. Wheater's scheme. [*Leeds*, c. 1875.] pp. 8. LEEDS PL
A plan and description of a proposed 'circular railway', a loop line passing near Roundhay Park and connecting with the North Eastern Rly. Not built.

*1449 MACTURK, G. G. A history of the Hull railways. *Hull*, 1879. pp. 164. BM

1450 BRADFORD BOROUGH COUNCIL. Queries and replies re tramways. By J. H. Cox, Borough Surveyor. [*Bradford*,] 1882. la. fold. s.sh. IT
A table of eight questions with answers from thirty-six towns which already have tramways.

1451 INDUSTRY illustrated: a memoir of the life of Thomas Jackson of Eltham Park, Kent, showing what he did, how he did it and what he became. *London*, 1884. pp. vii, 109, with illus. & a portrait. WOOLWICH PL
Includes his work as a contractor on railway construction in Yorkshire in the 1840's.

1452 JEFFERSON, J. C. and PULLON, J. T. A description of the proposed elevated single rail railway to Roundhay Park . . . *Leeds*, 1887. pp. 23, with 3 fold. plates. BM
Elevated mono-rail.

1453 LEEDS CITY CORPORATION. Report on the various systems of tramway haulage. By the City Engineer, Thomas Hewson. *Leeds*, 1895. pp. 43. LSE
Includes detailed recommendations for improvement of Leeds tramways, and tables of returns.

1454 [SHEFFIELD.] CITY OF SHEFFIELD. Tramway traction. (Report of the Deputation as to Tramway Traction, January 1897.) *Sheffield*, 1897. pp. 120, with illus.   pc

1455 IMPERIAL TRAMWAYS CO. The Middlesbrough, Stockton, and Thornaby electric tramways: history, construction, equipment. [1898?] pp. 29, with maps & diagrams in text.   BM

1456 BRADFORD CITY TRAMWAYS. The Bradford Picturesque Tram Guide containing timetables, lengths of the various lines and description of the routes, and other information, etc., etc. [*Bradford*, 1903?] pp. 63.   BM

1457 SHEPPARD, T. Early means of transport in the East Riding . . . *Hull*, 1928. pp. 36. [*Hull Museum Publications*, no. 154.]   BM
Reprinted from the *Transactions of the East Riding Antiquarian Society*, 1928.
Mostly pre-railway transport, but a few pages and illustrations are given to railways and to railway pottery.

1458 DICKINSON, H. D. Transport economics in the West Riding of Yorkshire. pp. 11.   IT
Paper, L.S.E. Rly. Student's Assoc., Leeds Convention, 5 July, 1930.
Includes railways and tramways.

1459 MIDDLESBROUGH COUNTY BOROUGH. The transport services within the County Borough of Middlesbrough. Memorandum, data and statistics prepared in connection with the negotiations with Mr. T. Hornsby, Divisional General Manager of the London & North Eastern Railway Company on behalf of the United Services Automobile Services, Ltd. *Middlesbrough*, 1930. pp. 15.   TUC
'Strictly private and confidential.'

1460 SHEFFIELD TRANSPORT DEPARTMENT. A brief history of the progress of municipal
c   transport in Sheffield since 1896 . . . *Sheffield*, July 1946. pp. 32, with 62 illus., incl. ports.   IT
pp. 9–22, a chronology, 1852–1946. Includes tramways.

1461 GILLHAM, J. C. A history of Halifax Corporation Tramways: summary of a paper read before a London meeting of the Light Railway Transport League . . . 23 February 1946. *London: L.R.T.L.*, January 1948. pp. 22, with map. *Reproduced typescript.*

1462 HALIFAX CORPORATION. 50 years of transport in Halifax: Jubilee, June 29th, 1948. *Halifax*, 1948. pp. 12, with illus.   IT
Includes tramways.

1463 HANSON, J. L. Transport development in West Yorkshire from the Industrial Revo-
b   lution to the present day. (Thesis, Ph.D., Univ. Lond., 1948.) pp. v, 367, with 36 maps & diagrams, bibliogr. notes & a detailed bibliography. *Typescript.*   UL
Primarily road transport, including tramways, but there is a substantial section on railways.

1464 HULL CORPORATION TRANSPORT. A brief history of municipal passenger transport in Kingston-upon-Hull, Jubilee Day, 5th July 1949. *Kingston-upon-Hull*, 1949. pp. 27 [30], with illus.   pc

1465 LINES to Leeds, and Leeds Loco Stock Book; illustrated. *Pool-in-Wharfedale: the author*, 1950. pp. 48.   BM
Handbook of local railway information, much of it historical.

1466 DUNN, J. M. The Nowells: a remarkable Dewsbury family: contractors, railway builders and tunnel makers. November 1951. pp. 21. *Reproduced typescript.*   pc
Extracted from *The Reporter* of 30th July, 1932.
Railway construction in Yorkshire.

1467 DONCASTER CORPORATION. The story of Doncaster Corporation Transport, 1902–
c   1952. *Doncaster*, [1952.] pp. 51, with illus. & a chronology.   BM
pp. 13–23, Tramways.

1468 [HUDDERSFIELD.] COUNTY BOROUGH OF HUDDERSFIELD—PASSENGER TRANSPORT DEPARTMENT. History of Undertaking, 1882–1952: 70 years of operation. [*Huddersfield*, 1952.] pp. 24[25], with illus., statistics, & map.   IT

1469 YORKSHIRE TRACTION COMPANY. 50-years of public service and progress. (Jubilee, 7th November 1952.) [*Barnsley*,] 1952 pp. 29, with illus.   pc
Includes tramways, with statistics.

*1470 MACMAHON, K. A. The beginnings of the East Yorkshire railways. *York*, 1953. pp. 31. [*East Yorkshire Local History Society. Local History Series*, no. 3.]   BM
Twenty-three railways and branches. Includes G. Hudson's activities in this area.

1471 GILLHAM, J. C. A history of Huddersfield Corporation Tramways. 3rd edn. n.p., 1955. pp. 26, with map. *Reproduced typescript.*   IT

1472 PARRIS, H. W. Railway building and the effect on the economic and social life of
b   some Yorkshire dales. (Thesis, M.A., Leeds University, 1955.) pp. xxiv, 284, with 5 plates & (pp. viii–xiv) a bibliography. *Typescript.*   LEEDS UNIV

1473 APPLETON, J. H. The railway network of Southern Yorkshire. pp. 159–69, with maps in text.

Reprint, *Transactions and Papers of the Institute of British Geographers*, Publication no. 22, 1956.

*1474 SHEFFIELD CITY LIBRARIES—DEPARTMENT OF LOCAL HISTORY AND ARCHIVES.
c A Railway Chronology of the Sheffield area. [*Sheffield*,] 1956. pp. 8, with map. *Reproduced typescript. [Local History Leaflets*, no. 5.]   BM

—— new enl. edn. *Sheffield*, 1961. pp. 12, with illus. & 2 maps.

1475 APPLETON, J. H. Communications. *In* 'A survey of Whitby', edited by G. H. J. Daysh. 1958. pp. 207–43, with illus., maps & diagrams.   BM
Includes railways.

1476 BRADFORD CITY TRANSPORT. Diamond Jubilee, 1898–1958. [*Bradford*, 1958.] pp. 11, with 10 illus.   pc
Includes tramways.

1477 BROCK, J. R. The railways of Harrogate. 1958.] pp. 9. *Typescript.*   LEEDS PL
b Gives separate chronologies for each of the nine railways involved, including Harrogate
c Gasworks Railway, and a bibliography of twenty-three books and periodical articles.

1478 PRICE, J. H. Leeds City Tramways, 1956. *London: Light Railway Transport League*, [1958.] pp. 12, with 8 illus., map, & list. BM

1479 STOCKS, W. B. Pennine journey: being the history of the railways, tramways and
c canals in Huddersfield and district . . . Illustrations by John P. Hanson. *Huddersfield: Advertiser Press*, [1958.] pp. 94, with 3 plates, & illus. & maps in text.   BM
London & North Western and Lancashire & Yorkshire railways and other minor railways and industrial lines. The Appendix (pp. 79 to end) contains much varied supplementary information, including a chronology and a list of Acts.

1480 BONSER, K. J. *and* NICHOLS, H. Printed maps and plans of Leeds, 1711–1900. *Leeds: The Thoresby Society*, 1960. pp. xxiv, 147, with 12 fold. plates. [*Publications of the Thoresby Society*, vol. 47, no. 106.]   BM
374 descriptions, including 48 of railways and tramways.

1481 BREARLEY, H. Tramways in West Yorkshire. *South Godstone: Oakwood Press*, 1960. pp. 43, with 23 illus., lists, & a map. [*Locomotion Papers*, no. 13.]   BM

1482 BROOK, R. The tramways of Huddersfield: a history of Huddersfield Corporation
c Tramways, 1883–1940. *Huddersfield: Ad-*

vertiser Press, [1960.] pp. 120, with 37 illus., fold. map, lists, & chronology.   BM

1483 DICKINSON, G. C. The development of suburban road passenger transport in Leeds,
b 1840–95. *In* 'Journal of Transport History', vol. 4, no. 4, November 1960. pp. 214–23, with map, 2 tables, & 36 bibliogr. notes.   BM

1484 LEE, C. E. Early industry and transport in East Yorkshire. [*London*, 1960.] pp. 129–33.   BM
Excerpt, *Transactions of the Newcomen Society*, vol. 32, 1959–60.

1485 SHEFFIELD TRANSPORT DEPARTMENT. The tramway era in Sheffield: souvenir
c brochure on the closure of the tramways, 8th October 1960. *Sheffield*, [1960.] pp. 32, with 46 illus., chronology, & tables. BM

1486 TATE, W. E. *and* SINGLETON, F. B. A history of Yorkshire, with maps and pictures. Cartography by G. Bryant. *London: Darwen Finlayson*, 1960. pp. 72.   BM
pp. 57–9, Yorkshire transport: railways; with map and 4 illus. on plates.

1487 WARD, J. T. West Riding landowners and the railways. *In* 'Journal of Transport
b History', vol. 4, no. 4, November 1960. pp. 242–51, with 50 bibliogr. notes.   BM

1488 PARRIS, H. W. Transport [in the City of York]. *In* 'A history of Yorkshire', edited
b by P. M. Tillott. The City of York. *London: Institute of Historical Research*, 1961. pp. 472–81, with 3 illus., map, & 187 bibliogr. notes. [*Victoria History of the Counties of England.*]   BM

England to Scotland
The East Coast and West Coast routes to Scotland—The 'Railway Races'

1489 WHISHAW, F. Railway communication with Scotland: Mr. Whishaw's report on the proposed Lancaster & Penrith Railway. *London*, [1840.] pp. 8, with a sectional diagram of Gate Scarth and the Summit Tunnel.   LSE

1490 The RIVAL rails; or, Reply to the 'Remarks on the proposed railway between England and Scotland'. *Carlisle*, 1841. pp. 40, with tables.   LSE
Clydesdale route (Lancaster via Carlisle to Edinburgh) preferred to another via the East Coast. Reports of meetings (pp. 35–40).

1491 BLACK, A. M. P. & Co., *publishers*. Black's Iron Highway from London to Edinburgh: being a descriptive guide to the railway lines

between these cities via Rugby, Birmingham, Derby, York, Newcastle and Berwick, with charts exhibiting the continuous lines and their branches . . . *Edinburgh*, 1850. pp. 59.
                                BM
    L. & N.W.; Midland; York, Newcastle & Berwick; & North British.

1492 REID, A. Reid's 'Railway Ride' from London to Edinburgh . . . shewing the towns, villages, roads, and distance of each station from London. *Newcastle*, [c. 1850.] pc
    A folded route chart.

1493 MITCHELL, J. O. Glasgow to London. [*Glasgow*, 1888.] pp. 8. LSE
    Privately printed from the *Glasgow Herald* of 14th July, 1888.
    Brief history of rail communications between Glasgow and London.

1494 SCOTT, W. J. Kinnaber; or, The great railway race of 1895, with notes on Scottish

train speeds . . . *London*, [1895.] pp. 46, with illus. BM
    Record of the five-weeks' struggle between the L. & N.W.R. and Caledonian (West Coast route), and the G.N.R., N.E., and N.B. (East Coast route) for the quickest journey from London to Aberdeen via Kinnaber Junction, 15 July to 22 August, 1895.

*1495 NOCK, O. S. The Railway Race to the North. *London: Ian Allan*, [1959.] pp. 168, with col. frontis. & 61 illus. on plates, incl. ports., map & tables. BM
    —— new edn. *London*, [1962.] pp. 176, with plates, etc. BM

1496 NOCK, O. S. *and* TREACY, E. Main lines across the Border. *London: Nelson*, 1960. pp. xvi, 155, with 62 plates of photographs taken by Eric Treacy, & tables of train timings. BM
    Lines north of Lancaster, Settle and Newcastle, to Carstairs, Kilmarnock and Edinburgh.

C2 SCOTLAND

For the East and West Coast routes from London to Scotland and for the 'Railway Races' see the end of the previous section, C1

Historical

1497 BRITISH MUSEUM—DEPARTMENT OF PRINTED BOOKS. [Documents relating to railways in Scotland. A collection of prospectuses, reports, maps, pamphlets, etc. concerning 17 railway companies under formation between 1835 & 1865; with an index.]
                           BM(MAPS)

1498 GLASGOW TRAMWAY & OMNIBUS CO. History of the Glasgow Tramway & Omnibus Company, Limited, from its formation in 1871 till 1894. Issued to the shareholders under the authority of the Company's Board of Directors. *Glasgow*, 1894. pp. 26. pc

1499 NEWLANDS, A. The Scottish railways: a sketch of their growth and recent developments. *In* 'Jubilee of the Railway News, 1864–1914.' [*London*, 1914.] pp. 65–73. BM

1500 MACKINNON, J. The social and industrial history of Scotland from the Union to the present time. *London*, 1921. pp. viii, 298.
                                  BM
    pp. 131–45, 'Railways'.

1501 NEWLANDS, A. The Scottish railways: a sketch of their growth and recent developments. *London*, 1921. pp. 28. RC
    Reprinted from the *Railway Gazette*.

1502 GLASGOW CORPORATION TRAMWAYS. Jubilee of the Glasgow Tramways, 1872–1922. *Glasgow*, [1922.] pp. 107, with 20 plates, incl. portraits. IT

1503 GARDNER, J. W. F. London, Midland & Scottish Railway: origin and subsequent development of the railways in Scotland. *Glasgow*, 1934. pp. 75, with plates. LSE
    Cover title: *Railway enterprise*. Published by the author.

1504 GLASGOW CORPORATION TRANSPORT DEPARTMENT. Glasgow municipal transport: an historical account of the inauguration and development of the Corporation Transport Services. Compiled from information supplied by Lachlan Mackinnon, General Manager. *Glasgow*, 1934. pp. 143, with illus. & maps. IT
    Tramways, bus, and Glasgow District Subway.

1505 O'DELL, A. C. A geographical examina-
b tion of the development of Scottish railways.
c 1939. pp. [129]–148, with maps & diagrams in text, 6 tables, incl. a chronology, notes, & a bibliography. pc
    Newbiggin Memorial Essay, 1938. Reprinted from the *Scottish Geographical Magazine*, vol. 55, May 1939.

1506 DOTT, G. Early Scottish colliery wagon-ways. *Westminster*, 1947. pp. 32, with bibliogr. notes. BM
    Reprint from *Colliery Entineering*.
    Contains lists with details, illustrations and maps.

1507 CHAMBERLAIN, L. G. Transport and the North-West Highlands. pp. 19. *Reproduced typescript.* IT
    Paper, Institute of Transport Metropolitan Graduate & Student Society, 11 Nov., 1952.
    Historical and descriptive. Includes railways.

1508 STEPHENSON LOCOMOTIVE SOCIETY. Edinburgh excursion, 6th September 1952. pp. 5, with map. *Reproduced typescript.* BR
Historical notes on railways in the Edinburgh district.

1509 STEPHENSON LOCOMOTIVE SOCIETY. Special Rail Tour, May 3rd, from Glasgow St. Enoch to Glasgow Central. *Clarkston,* [1952.] pp. 4, with map of route. *Reproduced typescript.* SLS
Itinerary.

1510 COONIE, I. M. *and* CLARK, R. R. The tramways of Paisley and district, 1885–1954. *Glasgow: Scottish Tramway Museum Society,* [1954.] pp. 24, with 17 illus. on 8 plates, & tables. BM
Issued in celebration of the Golden Jubilee of electric tramways in Paisley.

1511 HUNTER, D. L. G. The Edinburgh cable tramways. *In* 'Journal of Transport History', vol. 1, no. 3, May 1954. pp. 170–184, with map, table of services, & bibliogr. notes. BM

1512 HOGG, R. M. The historical development of the railways of Scotland. pp. 11, & map. *Typescript.* BR
Paper, Edinburgh University, Oct. 1957. Company histories.

1513 O'DELL, A. C. Railways and geography in N.E. Scotland. 1957. pp. 15. *Reproduced typescript,* with tables. IT
Paper, Railway Students' Association, Aberdeen Convention, 30 Sept., 1957.
A detailed historical and descriptive review of the geographical and economic factors relating to railway development in this area.

1514 ABERDEEN CORPORATION TRANSPORT DEPARTMENT. Sixty years of progress. *Aberdeen,* [1958.] pp. 21, with 38 illus. pc

1515 BRITISH TRANSPORT COMMISSION—HISTORICAL RECORDS DEPARTMENT, EDINBURGH. List of railway companies in Scotland prior to 1923. pp. 17. *Reproduced typescript,* dated July 1958. BR

1516 EMSLIE, J. A. N. Glasgow tramway and railway rolling stock: an illustrated guide to the vehicles operated by the Tramway and Underground Sections of the Glasgow Corporation Transport Department, past and present. *Glasgow: Scottish Tramway Museum Society,* [1958.] pp. [29.] BM
Lists, notes and illustrations.

1517 SCOTTISH TRAMWAY MUSEUM SOCIETY. The rise and fall of the Glasgow tram. *Glasgow,* [1958.] pp. 7, with 10 illus. BM
Reprinted from *Colville's Magazine,* Winter 1958.

1518 NOCK, O. S. Scottish railways. *London: Nelson,* 1950. pp. ix, 214, with 38 plates (14 col.) & illus. (No map.) BM
—— rev. edn. *London,* 1961. pp. x, 230, with 38 plates (14 col.), tables & diagrams. BM

1519 STEPHENSON LOCOMOTIVE SOCIETY—SCOTTISH AREA. Wigtownshire Rail Tour, Saturday, 2nd September, 1961. *Glasgow,* [1961.] pp. 12. *Reproduced typescript.* SLS
Notes and itinerary.

1520 CORMACK, I. L. Glasgow tramways, 1872–1962: ninety glorious years. *Cricklewood (London): Light Railway Transport League,* [1962.] pp. 16, with illus. & a bibliography. BM

1521 HUNTER, D. L. G. Edinburgh's transport. *Huddersfield: Advertiser Press,* 1964. pp. 398, with frontis., 75 illus., 2 sets of diagrams, & 2 fold. maps. BM
Includes tramways and suburban railways.

*1522 THOMAS, J. The Springburn Story: the history of the Scottish railway metropolis. *Dawlish: David & Charles. London: Macdonald,* 1964. pp. 260, with frontis. & 44 illus. on 10 plates. BM
The locomotive works of the Caledonian Rly. and the North British Rly.

Contemporaneous

1523 SINCLAIR, J. The Statistical Account of Scotland, drawn up from the communications of the ministers of the different parishes. *Edinburgh,* 1791–9. 21 vols. BM
vol. 8, pp. 617–18, a description of the wagonway at Alloa coal mine, constructed 1768.

1524 BUCHANAN, R. Report relative to the proposed rail-way from Dumfries to Sanquhar. *Dumfries,* 1811. pp. 46. UL(GL)

1525 STEVENSON, R. Report relative to the Strathmore Canal . . . *Edinburgh,* 1817. pp. 17, 2, with map showing the course which a railway might take.

1526 EDINBURGH. Minute of the . . . Lord Provost, magistrates and Council, respecting the projected railway in the vicinity of Edinburgh. *Edinburgh,* 18 March, 1818. pp. [6.] LSE
Giving it their 'countenance and approbation'.

1527 MEMORIAL humbly submitted to . . . the Lord Provost and magistrates of Edinburgh respecting the projected railways. [*Edinburgh,*] March 1818. pp. 8. LSE
By Messrs. Gibson & Oliphant, agents for the Railway Committee. An eloquent appeal for support for a line from Edinburgh to Leith.

1528 STEVENSON, R. Report relative to an iron railway between the port of Montrose and the town of Brechin. *Edinburgh,* 1819. pp. 23, with fold. map at end, followed by a four-page abstract of the report and a fold. map. ICE

1529 STEVENSON, R.   Report relative to various lines of railway from the coal-field of Midlothian to the city of Edinburgh and port of Leith, with plans and sections, showing the practicability of extending these lines of railway to Dalkeith, Musselburgh, Haddington and Dunbar . . . *Edinburgh*, 1819. pp. 47, with 4 fold. plans.   ICE

1530 STEVENSON, R.   Memorial relative to opening the great valleys of Strathmore and Strathearn by means of a railway or canal with branches to the sea from Perth, Arbroath, Montrose, Stonehaven and Aberdeen, together with observations on interior communication in general. *Edinburgh*, 1821. pp. 13, with fold. map.   BM

1531 BAIRD, H.   Report on the proposed railway from the Union Canal at Ryal to Whitburn, Polkemmet and Benhar; or, The West Lothian Railway. *Edinburgh*, 1824. pp. 14, 4, with fold. map.   BM

1532 GRIEVE, J.   Report on the utility of a bar-iron railway from Edinburgh to Dalkeith and to the harbour of Fisherrow, and of a relative survey. *Edinburgh*, 1824. pp. 18.   ICE

1533 DUNN, M.   Observations upon the line of railroad projected by Mr. Landale from Dundee to the Valley of Strathmore. *Dundee*, [1825.] pp. 5.   ICE

1534 LANDALE, C.   Report of . . . a survey to ascertain whether it is practicable and expedient to construct a railway between the Valley of Strathmore and Dundee. *Dundee*, 1825. pp. 10, with plan & section on fold. plate (col.).   ICE

1535 STEEDMAN, J.   Report to the subscribers to the survey of the proposed railway from the Forth & Clyde Canal to Stirling and Callander of Monteith, and to Alloa Ferry, near Kersie Nook. *Edinburgh*, 25 August 1827. pp. 18, with la. fold. col. map. UL(GL)

1536 STEVENSON, R.   Report relative to lines of railway surveyed from the ports of Perth, Arbroath and Montrose into the Valley of Strathmore; with an appendix containing estimates of expense and revenue . . . and a book of reference shewing the adjacent property with the names of the owners and occupiers in the year 1826. *Edinburgh*, 1827. pp. ii, 79, with tables & 2 charts.   ICE

1537 GRAINGER, T. *and* MILLER, J.   Report relative to the proposed railway to connect the Clydesdale or upper coal field of Lanarkshire with the city of Glasgow, and the east and west country markets. *Edinburgh*, 1828. pp. 17, with 3 plans.   ICE

1538 REMARKS on the report, by Messrs. Grainger and Miller, on the subject of the proposed railway and tunnel from Saint Rollox, in the north quarter of the city of Glasgow to the Broomielaw . . . *Glasgow*, 1829. pp. 19.   P

1539 LETTER to the author of 'Remarks on the report by Messrs. Grainger and Miller on the proposed railway and tunnel from the north quarter of Glasgow to the Broomielaw'. *Glasgow*, 1829. pp. 16.   P
Signed, 'A Friend to the Tunnel'.

1540 GRAINGER, T. *and* MILLER, J.   Report and estimate of the probable expense of the proposed extension of the Garnkirk & Glasgow Railway to Port Dundas. *Edinburgh*, 1829. pp. 8, with fold. map.   ICE

1541 OBSERVATIONS on the proposed railway and tunnel for connecting the River Clyde with the canals, etc. at Glasgow, and on the opposition to that measure; addressed to the magistrates and other municipal authorities and citizens of Glasgow, the trustees and others interested in the River Clyde, the feuars of Blythswood, the proprietors of the Union Canal, and others. *Glasgow*, 1829. pp. 22.   P

1542 SCOULLER, J. *and* HARVIE, R.   Report of a particular survey of a level line of railway from the Garnkirk & Glasgow Railway, by Cumbernauld, to the Edinburgh & Glasgow Union Canal, and to Falkirk . . . *Glasgow*, 1830. pp. 28, with col. chart.   P

1543 STRACHAN, J.   Prospectus of a railway between Edinburgh and the Port of Leith, as projected by Mr. John Strachan. *Edinburgh*, [1830?] pp. 12.   UL(GL)

1544 GRAINGER, T. *and* MILLER, J.   Report relative to a proposed railway communication between the City of Glasgow and the towns of Paisley and Johnstone. *Edinburgh*, 1831. pp. 19[20], with fold. map.   LSE

1545 GRAINGER, T. and MILLER, J.   Report relative to the proposed railway from the River Clyde at Renfrew Ferry, to Paisley. *Edinburgh*, 1834. pp. 12, with tables.   H

1546 STATEMENT shewing the advantages a great Scotch northern railway company would possess by forming a railway through the counties of Fife and Forfar, in connection with the new Great Northern Turnpike in course of formation from Forfar to Elgin and the Murray Firth. *Edinburgh*, 1835. pp. 11, with plan.   H

1547 [DUMFRIES.] PROVISIONAL COMMITTEE FOR PROMOTING THE RAILWAY FROM CARLISLE THROUGH THE VALE OF EVAN TO EDINBURGH & GLASGOW.   Reports

on the proposed line of railway from Carlisle to Glasgow and Edinburgh by Annandale. [*Dumfries*,] 1838. pp. 11[12.] BM
pp. 9–11, A report from J. Locke reprinted for the subscribers, with an additional report from the Committee.

1548 STEPHENSON, R. To the committee appointed for the promotion of a railway from Newcastle to Edinburgh. *Newcastle*, [1838.] pp. 22. LSE
Text dated 13 Sept., 1838. The LSE copy is incomplete.

1549 GRAINGER, T. *and* MILLER, J. Report relative to a railway communication from Montrose to Brechin, and the railways lately formed in the County of Forfar. *Montrose*, 1839. pp. 8, with map. FORFAR PL

1550 MILNE, J. Fife Railway question: being an article from the 'Fife Herald', April 22nd, 1841, on a recently published pamphlet of Mr. J. Milne, engineer. *Cupar*, 1841. pp. 36. AU
The advantages and disadvantages of a railway through Glenfarg from Burntisland to Perth, as opposed to a line from Burntisland to Dundee via Cupar and a bridge over the Tay.

1551 REPLY to the observations addressed by Mr. Thomas Grainger to the Committee of the Chamber of Commerce of the City of Edinburgh, on the proposed railways through Fife. *Edinburgh*, 1841. pp. 63. H

1552 LIZARS, W. H. Lizars' Guide to the Edinburgh, Glasgow, Paisley, Greenock, and Ayr Railways; including tables of distances, fares, arrivals and departures of the different railway trains . . . *Edinburgh*, [1842.] pp. 42, with a map. BR
Edinburgh & Glasgow; Glasgow, Paisley & Greenock; Glasgow, Paisley & Ayr railways.

1553 MURRAY, A. The September Time Tables, with Road Book & Companion for the Traveller in Scotland. *Glasgow*, 1844. pp. 48. LSE
Includes, pp. 12–17, railway timetables.

1554 [WALKER, J.] Scottish Central Railway: correspondence as to the appointment of a consulting or principal engineer. *London*, 1844. pp. 28. ICE
James Walker was not appointed.

1555 BOARD OF TRADE—RAILWAY DEPARTMENT. Report of the Railway Department of the Board of Trade on the schemes for extending railway communication in Scotland. *Edinburgh: Thomas Allan & Co.*, [1845.] pp. 23. UL(GL)

1556 GLASGOW. Report and resolutions of a public meeting held at Glasgow on Friday, March 20, in support of Sir Robert Peel's suggestions in reference to railways. *Glasgow*, 1846. pp. 14. H

1557 STATEMENT in relation to proposed Highland lines of railway and to the proposed Scottish Grand Junction Railway. January 1846. pp. 15. AU
A proposed line between Oban and the head of Loch Lomond.

1558 GLYNN, H. Reference Book to the incorporated railway companies of Scotland, c alphabetically arranged, including a list of their directors, offices and officers, constitution and capital. Gauge of way, 4 feet 8½ inches. *London*, 1847. pp. xl, 60, with fold. map (front) & a chronological table (4 pages). BM

1559 LIZARS, W. H. Lizars' Guide to the Edinburgh & Glasgow, Glasgow, Paisley, Kilmarnock, Ayr, and Greenock Railways. [*Edinburgh*, 1847.] la. fold sh. (text & map). UL(GL)

1560 DUNDEE. Statement by the magistrates and Town Council of the Rural Burgh of Dundee in reference to the proposed plans of the Dundee & Arbroath Railway (Dundee Junction) shewing a connecting line of railway through the said burgh. *Dundee*, 1848. pp. 9.

1561 BAIRD, R. *and* BYERS, W. Two letters addressed to the editor of the 'Aberdeen Journal' on the mail route between Perth and Aberdeen. *Aberdeen*, 1849. pp. 16. AU
The first letter, by Richard Baird, manager of the Dundee & Perth & Aberdeen Junction Rly., defends criticisms of the company's mail train service, and the second letter, from W. Byers, manager of the Scottish Midland Junction Rly., answers with his company's views.

1562 MOFFAT, A. Scottish railways: their present and future value considered as an investment for capital. *Edinburgh*, 1849. pp. 39. AU

1563 SCOTTISH Railway Shareholder's Manual, containing introductory view of railways, statistical account of railway companies, law regulating companies, revenue, expenditure, and traffic, the invester's guide and reckoner, names of directors and officers; with an appendix of financial statements. Illustrated with maps. *Edinburgh*, 1849. pp. xii, 182, lxxvi. LSE

1564 NOTMAN, R. R. Railway amalgamation: addressed to the shareholders of the Aberdeen, Scottish Midland, Dundee & Arbroath, Scottish Central and Caledonian railway companies. *London*, 1852. pp. 30. BM
In favour.

1565 MARSHALL, W. Railway legislation and railway reform considered with special reference to Scottish lines. *Edinburgh & London*, 1852. pp. iv, 111. BM
—— 2nd edn. *Edinburgh.*, 1853. pp. 114. BM

1566 REPORT of Evidence taken before the Committee of the House of Commons on the subject of the proposed interference with the public links belonging to the community of Aberdeen, by the Harbour Branch of the Aberdeen, Peterhead & Fraserburgh Railway Company, May and June, 1856. *Aberdeen*, 1856. pp. 64, with fold. map.   AU

1567 ABERDEEN ROYAL INFIRMARY. Proceedings relative to a proposed railway tunnel along Woolmanhill and under a portion of the grounds of Aberdeen Royal Infirmary. [*Aberdeen*, 1863.] pp. 32.   AU
Extracts from the minute books.

1568 RAILWAY amalgamation: a letter to Sir J. Campbell . . . by a Glasgow merchant. *Glasgow*, 1864. pp. 10.   NLC
Dated 27 Jan., 1864.
A protest against the proposed amalgamation of the Caledonian, Edinburgh & Glasgow, and Scottish Central railways.

1569 RAILWAY amalgamation: a second letter to Sir J. Campbell . . . by a Glasgow merchant. *Glasgow*, 1864. pp. 10.   NLC
Dated 6 Feb., 1864.

1570 CAMPBELL, D. Railway amalgamations: their bearing on the interests of Scotland; with special reference to the proposed amalgamation between Midland, and Glasgow & South-Western railways. Treated in a letter to . . . C. Fortescue, M.P. *Greenock*, 1873. pp. 23.   BM
Prejudicial effects of proposed amalgamations with English railways.

1571 GREIG, A. Extension of the Dundee street tramways. *London: Institution of Civil Engineers*, 1881. pp. 9, with 4 diagrams & 3 tables.   ICE
Excerpt, *Min. Proc. I.C.E.*, vol. 67, Session 1881–82, pt. 1.

1572 ROBINSON, J. C. Tramways; with a description of the wire cable system. *Edinburgh*, 1883. pp. 29.   ICE
Practical, not engineering aspects. Robinson was General Manager and Secretary, Edinburgh Street Tramways.

1573 WILSON, A. Memorandum as to suggested railway connections in the east end of Glasgow from Bridgeton Cross. *Glasgow*, 1887. pp. 8.   BM

1574 N., J. Tramway car sketches. *Glasgow*, 1889. pp. 48.   BM
Cover title, *Glasgow tramway car sketches.*
Seventy-two humorous drawings depicting travelling conditions and episodes in the working life of tramway men on the Glasgow horse trams.

1575 ACWORTH, W. M. Edinburgh railway schemes: reports by W. M. Acworth to the Corporation of Edinburgh. *Edinburgh*, October 1890. pp. 7.   LSE

His views on proposals for railway improvements in the city by the North British and the Caledonian.

1576 ACWORTH, W. M. The railways of Scotland: their present position, with a glance at their past and a forecast of their future; with a map of the Scottish railway system. *London*, 1890. pp. viii, 199.   BM

1577 GLASGOW CHAMBER OF COMMERCE. North British and Glasgow & South Western amalgamation. *Glasgow*, 1890. pp. 3.   LSE

1578 STRATHAAR, E. Scheme for new Scottish main line railway system. By 'Eon Strathaar'. 2nd ed., with enlarged map. *London & Glasgow*, [1890.] pp. 20.   BM
Amalgamation of the North British, Caledonian, and G. & S.W. railways.

1579 GLASGOW HERALD. Tramway motors: lessons from America, reported after independent enquiry by the Commissioner from the 'Glasgow Herald' staff. *Glasgow*, [1897.] pp. 56.   PO
Reprinted from the *Glasgow Herald.*
Glasgow advised to adopt electric traction for its tramways.

1580 MORTON, A. H. The Glasgow District Subway: its construction, plant and working. *Glasgow*, [1897.] obl. 4°. pp. 43, 24, with frontis. & 24 plates, incl. map & fold. section. (24 pp. adverts. at end.)   IME

1581 SULLIVAN, P. F. Comparison of street railway conditions and methods in Europe and the United States. *Chicago*, 1897. pp. 30.   LSE
Glasgow tramways taken as a British example.

1582 MACLEAN, A. Local industries of Glasgow and the West of Scotland. Edited by Angus McLean. *Glasgow: Local Committee for the Meeting of the British Association*, 1901. pp. 288.   BM
pp. [119]–131, Transport. By David T. Sandeman. (Also pp. 66–77, locomotive and other railway mechanical engineering manufacture, and pp. 263–7, tramways.)

1583 GALLOWAY, T. L. The Campbeltown Colliery & Light Railway . . . *Glasgow*, 1902. pp. 16, with 3 illus.   SLS
Paper, Glasgow Association of Students of the Institution of Civil Engineers, Session 1901–2.

*1584 GIBSON, R. Glasgow District Subway: its construction and equipment. *Glasgow*, 1905. pp. 48.   PC

1585 WATSON, T. The Glasgow District Subway. *Glasgow*, 1906.
A descriptive pamphlet. Construction and equipment.

1586 GLASGOW CORPORATION TRAMWAYS. Illustrated description of Glasgow Corporation tramway system. *Glasgow*, 1911. pp. 60, with illus. & diagrams (no map). IT

1587 PRATT, E. A. Scottish canals and waterways, comprising state canals, railway-owned canals, and present-day ship canal schemes. *London*, 1922. pp. xi, 299, with 19 maps & diagrams, bibliogr. notes & a bibliography. BM

1588 GARDINER, R. Railway transportation progress in Scotland. pp. 41, with map. *Reproduced typescript.* BR
Paper, Annual Convention, London School of Economics Railway Students' Association, 1937.
R. Gardiner was Superintendent, Southern Scottish Area, London & North Eastern Rly.

1589 LAMONT, A. How Scotland lost her railways . . . and the case for nationalisation on a Scottish basis. [*Glasgow: Scottish Secretariat*, 1945.] pp. 24. BM
Detrimental effects of amalgamation with English railway companies brought about by pressure from the Scottish Railway Stockholders' Association in the interests of shareholders.

1590 POWNALL, J. F. The Scottish railway network: a project for reconstructing the Scottish railways according to certain new railway network principles. *Birmingham: Cotterell*, 1946. pp. 72. BM
'Railway hour sections.'

1591 GLASGOW CORPORATION TRANSPORT. A report on the future development of passenger transport in Glasgow . . . By E. R. L. Fitzpayne, General Manager, Glasgow Corporation Transport. *Glasgow*, May 1948. pp. 38, with 6 fold. maps, & 6 fold. plates. IT
On the extension of the Underground, and the proposed replacement of tramways by electric railways.

1592 BRITISH TRANSPORT COMMISSION—GLASGOW & DISTRICT TRANSPORT COMMITTEE. Passenger transport in Glasgow and district. *Edinburgh*, 1951. pp. ix, 81, with 8 fold. maps & tables. BM
Present problems, including relocation of railway stations, electrification, road-rail co-ordination, etc. Chairman, Robert Inglis.

1593 WHITE, H. P. South-Eastern Scotland: transport. pp. 152–61, with 5 maps. PC
Reprinted from *Scientific survey of South-Eastern Scotland*, British Association for the Advancement of Science, 1951.
Includes railways.

1594 GLASGOW CORPORATION TRANSPORT. Inglis Report: observations by General Manager [E. R. L. Fitzpayne]. January, 1952. pp. 12. *Reproduced typescript.* IT
Addressed to Transport Committee. Criticisms of Inglis Committee Report.

1595 DUNDEE CORPORATION TRANSPORT DEPARTMENT. Report by Engineer and Manager on acquisition of tramcars . . . *Dundee*, August 1954. pp. 13[15], with statistics & estimates. IT
Trams to be replaced by buses.

1596 LIGHT RAILWAY TRANSPORT LEAGUE—SCOTTISH SECTION. The future of Glasgow's tramways: a fresh approach to an old problem. *Glasgow*, July 1958. pp. 31, with 19 illus. & a diagram. (Second printing, Feb. 1959.) BM

*1597 CORMACK, I. L. Green Goddesses go East. *Cambuslang: Scottish Tramway Museum Society*, 1961. pp. 24, with 16 illus. BM
Ex-Liverpool tramcars in Glasgow, 1953–60.

1598 9 DALMUIR West. *London: North London Artists*, [1963.] pp. [36.] BM
Forty-two photographs commemorating the last days of Glasgow's tramways; with commentary.

C3 WALES

Historical

1599 LLOYD, J. The early history of the South Wales iron works, 1760–1840. From original documents. *London*, 1906. pp. viii, 218, with fold. map. BM
p. 163, an extract from the account of the Blaenafon Iron Works by Archdeacon Coxe, in his *Historical tour in Monmouthshire* (1801).
p. 101, 'Proposed railway from Dowlais to the Valley of the Usk, 1836.

1600 HOWELLS, C. S. Transport facilities in the mining and industrial districts of South Wales and Monmouthshire: their history and future development. *London & Cardiff*, 1911. pp. 56. BM
pp. 12–19, 'Railways'.

1601 BEASLEY, A. Railway developments in South Wales. *In* 'Jubilee of the Railway News, 1864–1914.' *London: Railway News*, [1914.] pp. 62–5. BM

1602 JONES, W. H. History of the Port of Swansea. *Carmarthen*, 1922. pp. xv, 383, with maps & illus. BM
pp. 102–27, Development of canals and railroads.
pp. 261–72, Development by railways.

1603 JOHN, D. G. An economic and historical survey of the development of the anthracite

industry, with special reference to the Swansea Valley. Thesis, M.A., University of Wales, 1923. *Typescript.*　　　NLW
Contains a section on 'the industrialisation of South Wales by the development of mechanical transport and its effect on the anthracite industry'.

1604 PHILLIPS, D. R. History of the Vale of Neath. *Swansea*, 1925. pp. 816.　　　BM
pp. 338–46, Quarry tramroads, South Wales Rly., Vale of Neath Rly., South Wales Mineral Rly., and other smaller lines in the locality.

1605 DAVIES, J. The industrial history of the Rhymney Valley, with special reference to the iron, steel, and tinplate industries, coal mining, lead mining and smelting and quarrying. (Thesis, M.Sc., University of Wales, 1926.) pp. 141. *Typescript.*　NLW
ch. 19, Communications: roads and railways.

1606 BEVAN, T. The industrial development of the Llynfi, Ogmore and Garw valleys, with special reference to transport facilities in the area. (Thesis, M.A., University of Wales, 1928.) pp. 214,[13,] with 4 maps & plans. *Typescript.*　　　NLW

1607 JOHN, D. G. Contributions to the economic history of South Wales. (Thesis, D.Sc., University of Wales, 1930.) 2 vols, with 3 rolls of maps. (Sectional pagination.) *Typescript.*　　　NLW
part 1, The organisation and activity of the chartered companies in South Wales, with special reference to the development of ferrous and non-ferrous industries.
part 2, Geographical and economic factors associated with the variations in the distribution and density of the population of South Wales, from Tudor to modern times.
part 2 contains a section on 'the transport of minerals, 1700–1850'. This includes tramroads and railways. There are maps in the text.

1608 DODD, A. H. The Industrial Revolution in North Wales. *Cardiff*, 1933. pp. xxxi, 439.　　　BM
pp. 112–19, 'Railways': with bibliogr. notes.

1609 DAVIES, L. N. A. The history of the Barry Dock & Railways Company in relation to the development of the South Wales coalfield. (Thesis, M.A., University of Wales, 1938.) pp. 193, 10, with maps (some printed), mounted photographs (cuttings), and diagrams, including a graph. *Typescript.* NLW

1610 THOMAS, I. Top Sawyer: a biography of David Davies of Llandinam. . . . *London:*
b *Longmans*, 1938. pp. xvi, 355, with frontis., 19 plates, 2 maps, diagrams, & a reproduced holograph letter.　　　BM
Many bibliographical sources are given in the author's Preface, and in notes to the text.
David Davies' work as contractor/financier to various Welsh railway projects.

1611 CHAPPELL, E. L. History of the Port of Cardiff. *Cardiff: Priory Press*, 1939. pp.
c xxxviii, 135.　　　BM
Contains many references to railways, and a chronology.
pp. 82–106, Taff Vale Rly., Rhymney Rly., & South Wales Rly. (G.W.R.), Barry Docks & Rly.

1612 ALLCHIN, M. C. V. Locomotives of the smaller Welsh railways and of the Midland & South Western Junction Railway: types, building dates, etc. *Fareham: the author,* [1943.] pp. 12.　　　BM

1613 LEE, C. E. Narrow-gauge railways in North Wales. *London: Railway Publishing Co.,* 1945. pp. 136, with 63 illus. on 44 plates, diagrams, maps, tables & bibliogr. notes.　　　BM

1614 HODGES, T. M. History of the Port of Cardiff in relation to its hinterland, with special reference to the years 1830–1914. (Thesis, M.Sc.(Econ.), Univ. Lond., 1946.) pp. 416[417], with maps & bibliogr. notes.　　　UL

1615 WALKER, E. The development of communications in Glamorgan, with special reference to the growth of industry between 1760 and 1840. (Thesis, M.A., University of Wales, 1947.) pp. xxv, 316, xviii, with maps & plans. *Typescript.*　　　NLW
ch. 4, Canals and railroads.
ch. 6, The dawn of the Railway Age.

1616 BOYD, J. I. C. Narrow-gauge rails to Portmadoc: a historical survey of the Festiniog–Welsh Highland Railway and its ancillaries. [*South Godstone:*] *Oakwood Press*, 1949. pp. iii, 158, with plates, illus. in text, & map.　　　BM

1617 LERRY, G. G. Henry Robertson, pioneer of railways into Wales. *Oswestry: Woodalls*, 1949. pp. 52, with 3 illus., & a portrait.　　　BM

1618 WILLIAMS, C. R. The industrialisation of Flintshire in the nineteenth century: being an examination of the changes and developments in the principal industries from 1815 to 1914. (Thesis, M.A., University of Wales, 1950.) pp. 201, with maps. *Typescript.*　　　NLW
ch. 4, Communications in the nineteenth century; river and railway.

1619 BARRIE, D. S. M. Historical notes on the railways of the Western Region in South Wales and Monmouthshire. [1951.] pp. 12.　　　BR
Reprinted from the *Proceedings of the South Wales & Monmouthshire Railways & Docks Lecture & Debating Society*, Session 1950–51, no. 2. Read 2 January, 1951.

*1620 BOYD, J. I. C. Narrow-gauge rails in Mid-Wales: a historical survey of the narrow gauge railways in Mid-Wales. *South Godstone: Oakwood Press*, 1952. pp. vi, 146, with illus. BM

1621 FRASER, M. Wales: vol. 2, The Country. *London: Hale*, 1952. pp. ix, 233–492. BM
pp. 256–64, 'Railway recollections'. Brief historical sketch with personal observations. Includes narrow gauge lines.

1622 HARRIS, M. I. The railway network of Wales. (Thesis, M.A., University of Wales, 1953.) 2 vols. pp. v, 160: atlas, figs. 1–35 (maps). *Typescript.* NLW

1623 POLLINS, H. The Swansea Canal. *In*
b 'Journal of Transport History', vol. 1, no. 3, May 1954. pp. 135–54, with map, 2 tables, & 125 bibliogr. notes. BM
Includes railways and wagonways and their relationship to the Canal.

1624 KIDNER, R. W. The narrow gauge railways of North Wales. *Sidcup: Oakwood Press*, 1936. pp. 15, with 5 plates, maps, & illus. [*Light Railway Handbooks*, no. 2.] BM
—— 2nd edn. *Sidcup*, 1937. pp. 29–44. BM
—— 3rd, 'The narrow gauge railways of Wales.' *Chislehurst*, 1947. pp. [29]–44. BM
—— 4th, *Lingfield*, 1956. pp. 23. BM

1625 RICHARDS, G. The role of transport and communication and distribution in the Welsh economy. (Thesis, M.A., University of Wales, 1957.) pp. viii, 207, with tables. *Typescript.* NLW
Includes some statistics relating to railways.

1626 STEPHENSON LOCOMOTIVE SOCIETY *and* MANCHESTER LOCOMOTIVE SOCIETY. The Caernarvonshire Rail Tour, 5th May, 1957. Notes on the route by J. M. Dunn. pp. 10. *Reproduced typescript.* SLS

1627 MORRIS, J. R. *and* WILLIAMS, L. J. The South Wales coal industry, 1841–1875. *Cardiff*, 1958. pp. xii, 289, with 2 maps. BM
Includes railway development in South Wales.

1628 DAVIES, D. The Llwchr and Amman valleys to 1939: a study in industrial development. (Thesis, M.A., University of Wales, 1959.) pp. 180, 6. *Typescript.* NLW
ch. 4, The Railway Age, 1841–1866. A general survey, including railways; with maps.

1629 LEWIS, E. D. The Rhondda Valleys: a study in industrial development, 1800 to the present day. *London: Phœnix House*, 1959. pp. xiii, 312, with plates & maps. (Thesis, D.Sc., University of Wales, 1960.) NLW
pp. 105–29, Transport.

*1630 HADFIELD, C. The canals of South Wales and the Border; with plates and map. *Cardiff: University of Wales Press*; *London: Phoenix House*, 1960. pp. 272, with 9 illus. on 8 plates, & 9 maps in text. BM
Includes many references to horse tramroads and railways.

1631 ROBERTS, E. The development of public passenger transport services in Wales. (Thesis, M.Sc., University of Wales, 1960.) 2 vols. pp. iii, 186, [19.]: figs. 1–42 (maps & mounted photographs). *Typescript.* NLW
Includes railways and tramways.

Contemporaneous

1632 ALLNUTT, Z. Useful and correct accounts of the navigation of the rivers and canals west of London . . . 2nd edn., much improved. *Henley*, [1810.] pp. 20. BM
pp. 17–18, Account of the canals and railroads in South Wales.

1633 PRICE, H. H. Report of Henry Habberly Price, civil engineer, relative to a Grand Western railway communication from London into South Wales, with a comparative view of the merits of the London & Reading and London & Windsor railway scheme[s]. *London*, 1834. pp. 14. LSE
Addressed to Charles Tennant, on behalf of the Earl of Jersey, and dated 7 March, 1834.

1634 SAINT GEORGE'S HARBOUR & RAILWAY. Report and Evidence before the Select Committees of the House of Commons on Harbours of Refuge and Shipwrecks . . . *London*, 1836. pp. 53, with fold. plate. BM
Proposes (pp. 7–8) a line from St. George's Bay, Caernarvonshire, to Chester (60 miles).

1635 STEPHENS, E. L. A review of the national advantages to be derived by the improvement of Fishguard Harbour . . . *Haverfordwest*, 1837. pp. 17. BR
Includes a report of a proposed railway from Gloucester to Fishguard.

1636 WALKER, J. Communication with Ireland [*London*,] 1843. pp. 14, with 5 drawings (maps) appended. ICE
Addressed to the Secretary to the Admiralty. Concerned partly with the crossing of the Menai Straits by railway.

1637 REMARKS on the pre-eminent natural advantages of Milford as the western terminal point to the railways of Great Britain. *London*, 1847. pp. 10, with 3 plates & 3 maps. BM

1638 ROBERTS, S. Letters on improvements, addressed to landlords and Road Commissioners, with a petition to Parliament . . . By a Llanbrynmair Farmer. *Llanbrynmair*, 1852. pp. 59. BM
pp. [33]–36, 'A rail to Newtown'.

1639 ROBERTS, S. Letters on railways. *Dolgelly* 1856. pp. 61.   BR
The need for a railway through Central Wales.

1640 PROCEEDINGS to promote the introduction of tramways and to improve the town of Swansea. [*Swansea?*] 1874. s.sh. (fold.)   ICE
Two plans, with explanatory text.

1641 WILLIAMS, R. Montgomeryshire worthies. 2nd ed. *Newtown*, 1894. pp. 340.   BM
pp. 30–6, David Davies of Llandinam.

1642 GREAT WESTERN RLY. Welsh mountain railways. *London*, May 1924. pp. 26, with 16 plates & a fold. map.   pc

1643 MAYNARD, A. The Great Western Railway as a factor in the prosperity of Cardiff. [*London: Great Western Rly.*, 1932.] [*Great Western Pamphlets*, no. 7, 1932.]   BR
Addressed to Cardiff Publicity Club. A. Maynard was speaking as Chief Goods Manager, G.W.R.

1644 DICKSON, S. B. A report of an unofficial traffic survey held on the North Wales Coast on the 15th August, 1953. [*Llanfairfechan*, 1953.] pp. 9. *Reproduced typescript.*   pc
The collected findings of ten observers stationed at various points between 9.0 a.m. and 7.0 p.m.

1645 MORGAN, L. A. Operating railway branch lines in South Wales. 1953. *Typescript.*   IT
Paper, Institute of Transport, South Wales & Monmouthshire Section, 19 Nov., 1953.
Passenger services: problems arising from closures.

1646 MANCHESTER LOCOMOTIVE SOCIETY. North Wales Traffic Survey, Saturday, 31st July, 1954. Report of the Survey by Stirling B. Dickson. [*Manchester,*] November 1954. pp. 31. *Reproduced typescript.*   pc
From 8.30 a.m. to 7.0 p.m.; twenty-five observers at various places; Saturday preceding Bank Holiday.

1647 COUNCIL FOR WALES AND MONMOUTHSHIRE. Report on the rural transport problem in Wales. *London: H.M.S.O.*, 1962. pp. 46, with map of Radnorshire communications. *Cmnd.* 1821.   BM
Includes railways.

C 4 IRELAND

This section is subdivided by a modified version of the main Scheme

C 4 A General history and description of railways in Ireland

1648 MURLAND, J. W. Observations on Irish railway statistics: a paper read before the Dublin Statistical Society. *Dublin*, 1849. pp. 13.   RIA(H): LSE
A statistical survey of past railway development in Ireland.

1649 EASON, C. Manual of financial, railway, agricultural and other statistics for politi-
c cians, economists, and investors. *London*, [1884.] pp. 91.   BM
Includes (pp. 62–9) an historical and general account of Irish railways and a chronology.

1650 TATLOW, J. Irish railways: their progress during the last decade of the last century. *Dublin*, 1901. pp. 18.   BR
'Printed for the Institution of Civil Engineers of Ireland.'

1651 INGRAM, J. Irish railways. *In* 'Jubilee of the Railway News, 1864–1914'. *London: Railway News*, [1914.] pp. 74–7.   BM

1652 CONROY, J. C. A history of railways in Ireland. *London*, 1928. pp. viii, 386, with bibliogr. notes.   BM

1653 TATLOW, J. Fifty years of railway life in England, Scotland and Ireland. *London*, 1920. pp. vi, 223.   BM
J. Tatlow was with the Belfast & County Down; Midland; Glasgow & South Western; Midland Great Western of Ireland; Dublin & Kingstown. Several well-known railwaymen are mentioned.
—— 2nd edn. *London*, 1948. pp. 223, with a biographical introduction by Charles E. Lee.   BM

C 4 B Contemporaneous

1654 GRIFFITH, R. J. Second report on the proposed rail-road from Cork to Limerick. *Cork*, 1826. pp. 32, with tables.

1655 NIMMO, A. Report of Alexander Nimmo on the proposed railway between Limerick and Waterford. *Dublin*, 1825. pp. 24.   ICE
Addressed to the Secretary of the Hibernian Rly. Co. This project failed but the two towns were eventually linked by the Waterford & Limerick Rly. (8 & 9 Vict., c.cxxxi.)
—— another edn. *Dublin*, 1826. pp. 39   UL(GL)

1656 MOSS, S. Some considerations of the benefits and evils of steam power. *Dublin*, 1831. pp. 23.   BM
The application of steam to manufactures. Locomotives also considered.

1657 STEPHENSON, G. A report on the practicability and utility of the Limerick & Waterford Railway, or of such parts thereof as ought to be completed immediately. *London*, 1831. pp. 16, with tables.   H

1658 BERMINGHAM, T. Additional statements on the subject of the River Shannon to the reports published in 1831. *London*, 1834. pp. 15[40].   BM
   Appendix, Proposals of the American Steam Carriage Co. for the construction of locomotive engines, etc. This is missing from the BM copy.

1659 BOOTH, H. A letter to His Majesty's Commissioners on Railways in Ireland, in reply to a communication from H. D. Jones, Esq., Secretary to the Commissioners. *Liverpool*, 1836. pp. 12.   UL(GL)
   Advice based upon experience of six years' working of the Liverpool & Manchester Rly., and an invitation to the Commissioners to come and see the line for themselves.

1660 A BRIEF sketch of a proposed new line of communication between Dublin and London, via Portdynllaen (Carnarvonshire), Worcester and Oxford, capable of being travelled in twelve hours by means of steam packets and railways; to which are added the Report of T. Rogers, engineer, lighthouse builder, etc., etc. to . . . the Commissioners of . . . Revenue in Ireland and other documents published in 1807, shewing its advantages at that time over the Holyhead Line, and demonstrating the utility of Portdynllaen as an asylum harbour; together with the resolutions of two public meetings, one held in the County of Carnarvon and the other in the City of Dublin. 2nd edn. *Dublin*, 1836. pp. xii, 40.   UL(GL)

1661 The ESTABLISHMENT of a general packet station on the south-west coast of Ireland connected by railways with Dublin and London considered with reference to the advantages which it would afford in facilitating the intercourse between Europe and America . . . and in promoting the improvement of Ireland. *London*, 1836. pp. 32, with fold. map.   LSE

1662 KNIGHT, P. Erris in the 'Irish Highlands', and the 'Atlantic Railway'. *Dublin*, 1836. pp. vii, 178, with fold. map & illus.   BM
   pp. 147–63, preference for Erris, rather than Valencia or Galway, for the terminus of a proposed railway from Dublin.

1663 WALKER, J. Two letters to Matthew Barrington, on proposed southern rail-roads in Ireland, with an introductory letter to . . . Thomas Spring Rice, Chancellor of the Exchequer . . . and an explanatory map. *Limerick*, 1837. pp. 16.   BM
   1, Concerning Kilkenny's exclusion from proposed route; 2, on the advantages of completing a railway to Limerick and the Shannon.

1664 IRISH RAILWAY COMMISSION, Second report of the Commissioners appointed to inquire into the manner in which railway communications can be most advantageously promoted in Ireland. Abridged edition. *Dublin*, 1838. pp. iv, 213, with la. fold. map.
                                                        UL(GL)
   Final report, with index.

1665 BERMINGHAM, T. A letter to . . . Lord Viscount Morpeth . . . upon the advantages certain to accrue to Ireland by the introduction of railway communication to the River Shannon . . . *London*, 1839. pp. 13.   BM

1666 GALE, P. A letter to the Commissioners of Railway Inquiry in Ireland, on the advantages to the Empire from increased facilities of international communication; also, observations on the proper position for a main trunk to the South and West of Ireland. *Dublin*, 1837. pp. 34 [35].   PO
—— 2nd edn., corr., *Dublin*, 1837. pp. 35[36].
                                                        LSE

1667 BERMINGHAM, T. First report and proceedings of the General Railway Committee. *Dublin*, 1838. pp. 23, with fold. map.   ICE
   Object—to influence railway development so as to serve Ireland with maximum benefit.

1668 BERMINGHAM, T. Irish railways: a full and interesting report of the public proceedings on this important question, with extracts from the statistical journals of the day, on foreign—especially those in Belgium—and English railways, shewing the advantage of their construction both as a private or public undertaking; also, Observations on the advantageous prospects on forming railways in Ireland, with a map of Ireland, showing the lines projected by private parties, as also the three trunk lines proposed to be made by Government. *London*, 1839. pp. 24, 50, 8.   UL(GL)
   (1) A statistical account of foreign and English railways . . . *London*, 1839. pp. 24, with fold. map.
   (2) A report of the proceedings at two public meetings held at the Thatched House Tavern, 13th & 20th April, 1839, for the purpose of taking into consideration the necessity of forming railways throughout Ireland. *London*, 1839. pp. 50.
   (3) Irish railways: proceedings of the Deputation. *London*, 1839. pp. 8.

1669 FLYNN, H. E. An appeal to the wisdom, justice, and mercy of the Imperial Parliament, in behalf of the Irish peasantry on the subject of a national system of railways in Ireland. *Dublin*, 1839. pp. 8.   H

1670 PIM, J. Irish railways: a letter to . . . Frederick Shaw. *London*, 1839. pp. 16. BM
   Proposes government control.

1671 QUIN, M. J. A letter to the House of Commons on railways in Ireland. *London*, 1839. pp. 40.   NLC

1672 SMYTH, G. L. Railways and public works in Ireland: observations upon the Report of the Irish Railway Commissioners, with a review of the failures which have already occurred under the different Government Boards and Commissions connected with public works in Ireland. Addressed to . . . Viscount Duncannon. *London*, 1839. pp. 86, with 3 fold. maps & bibliogr. notes. BM

1673 BERMINGHAM, T. Statistical evidence in favor of state railways in Ireland, with the speech of T. Bermingham . . . also an appendix containing above twenty statistical tables . . . with a map of Ireland shewing . . . the lines of the Irish Railway Commissioners, with additions recommended by the author. *Dublin*, 1841. pp. 22, xciv.   BM

1674 PEMBERTON, B. An address to the nobility, gentry, and mercantile classes, on the extension of railway communication to the west of Ireland by the formation of a line from the steam packet station of the North Wall to the town of Trim . . . with casual observations on the extraordinary conduct of the Railway Commissioners in reference thereto . . . *Dublin*, 1841. pp. iv, 18.   NLC

1675 RAILWAYS for Ireland . . . *London*, 1841. pp. 15.   RIA(H)
From the *Railroad Monthly Journal*, June 1841.

1676 ROGERS, J. W. Plan proposed by Sir J. C. Anderson and J. W. Rogers . . . for establishing steam carriages for the conveyance of goods and passengers on the mail coach roads of Ireland. *Dublin*, 1841. pp. 15. BM
Steam road vehicles preferable to railways. At the end is a report by William Bald, civil engineer.

1677 [VIGNOLES, C. B.] Railways in Ireland . . . [*Dublin*, 1842.] pp. 15.   ICE
From the *Dublin Magazine*, January 1842.

1678 DORAN, L. Irish railways: five letters on the Irish railways projected in 1844 and to be produced to Parliament in 1845. Addressed to . . . the Earl of Dalhousie, Vice-President of the Board of Trade. *London*, 1845. pp. 26, with map.   BM

1679 IRISH railways and the Board of Trade, considered in a letter to . . . Lord Brougham; accompanied by a railways map of Ireland. *Dublin*, 1845. pp. 66.   RIA(H)
Signed 'Locomotive'.

1680 KANE, R. The industrial resources of Ireland. *Dublin*, 1844. pp. xii, 417.   BM
pp. 328–71, Importance of internal communication to industry and progress in Ireland, including (pp. 346–71) railways.
—— 2nd edn. *Dublin*, 1845. pp. xvi, 438. (Railways, pp. 363–90.)   BM

1681 [LINDSAY, H. L.] Railway communication from Dublin to the North of Ireland. *Armagh*, 1845. pp. iv, 24, with fold. gradient profile.

1682 LOYAL NATIONAL REPEAL ASSOCIATION. Report of the Parliamentary Committee of the Loyal National Repeal Association on the subject of having the enquiries connected with Irish railway legislation transacted in Dublin. [*Dublin*, 1845.] pp. [95]–103.   BM
Read at a meeting of the Association on Monday 22 December, 1845.

1683 MULOCK, T. Railway revelations: being letters on the proposed Direct London & Manchester Railways. *London*, 1845. pp. 46.   ICE
pp. 38–46. 'Supplement. Irish railways.' A 'system' of railways wanted, not a 'series of schemes'.

1684 TOWNSEND, R. W. Report on the proposed Cork, Passage & Kinsale Railway and its expected advantages as a main trunk line leading from Cork to the west of the county. *Cork*, 1845. pp. 8, with fold. map & gradient profile.   ICE

1685 IRISH GREAT WESTERN RLY. Digest of Evidence received by the Select Committee of the House of Commons appointed to inquire into the merits of the Bill for the formation of a railway from Dublin to Galway. [1846.] pp. 75.   NLC
Not enacted.

1686 BENTINCK, W. G. F. C. Railways in Ireland: the speech of . . . George Bentinck on moving for leave to bring in a Bill 'to stimulate the prompt and profitable employment of the people by the encouragement of railways in Ireland', in the House of Commons on Thursday, February 4th, 1847. Extracted from Hansard's Parliamentary Debates. [*London*,] 1847. pp. 34   UL(GL)
—— another edn. *London*, 1847. pp. 47. BM

1687 BROWN, H. Irish wants and practical remedies: an investigation on practical and economical grounds as to the application of a government system of railways in Ireland. *London*, 1848. pp. iv, 67[71], with bibliogr. notes & 5 tables.   BM

1688 WHITE, G. P. Letter to . . . Lord John Russell, on the expediency of promoting railways in Ireland. *London*, 1849. pp. 40.   BM

1689 LOW, W. Letter to . . . Lord John Russell . . . explanatory of a financial system for extending railways in Ireland and for restoring confidence in railway property generally. *London*, 1850. pp. 16.   BM
'. . . the relief of distress among labouring classes in Ireland by promoting railways [with the help of a loan fund]'.

1690 WEBB, C. L. Suggestions on the present condition of Ireland, and on government aid for carrying out an efficient railway system. *London*, 1852. pp. 46.   BM

1691 WHITE, G. P. Transatlantic packet station. Preliminary report on the south western harbours of Ireland and the practicability of

connecting them by railway. *London*, [1852.] pp. 16.   UL(GL)
Addressed to the Bandon & Crookhaven Rly. & Transatlantic Packet Station.

692 FEW remarks on the railways of the north of Ireland, with special reference to the proposed railway from Armagh to Cavan, via Clones. *Dublin*, 1853. pp. 19.   NLC
Belfast & West of Ireland Juction Rly. Not incorporated.

693 SPROULE, J. The Irish Industrial Exhibition of 1853: a detailed catalogue of its contents ... also, a portrait of Mr. Dargan engraved on steel, accompanied by a memoir ... *Dublin*, 1854. pp. xvii, 502.   BM
pp. ix–xiv, Memoir of William Dargan, the Irish railway contractor and financier.

694 'TIRESIAS.' Rail and waterway competition: pleasing dividends. 2nd edn., rev. & corr. *Dublin*, 1858. pp. 15.   RIA(H)

695 HEMANS, G. W. On the railway system in Ireland, the government aid afforded, and the nature and results of county guarantees. *London*, 1859. pp. 28.   BM
Excerpt, *Min. Proc. I.C.E.*, vol. 18.

696 'PAX.' The projected railways in connection with Lough Derg, considered in reference to their amalgamation. *Dublin*, 1861. pp. 10.   RIA(H)

697 IRISH railways: government loans. Memorial of certain of the companies to the Lords Commissioners of Her Majesty's Treasury, praying for legislation to enable Government to lend money to pay off their debts, and finish the construction of their railways ... also financial and statistical statement in relation thereto. *Limerick*, 1866. pp. 23, with tables.   NLC

698 JACKSON, R. Hand Book of Irish Railway Reform; containing copy of memorial addressed to the Lords Commissioners of Her Majesty's Treasury by the people of Ireland together with the resolutions passed at public meetings ... and other data. Compiled by Robert Jackson. *Dublin*, 1866. pp. 63.   BM
R. Jackson was Secretary of the Irish Railway Reform Committee.

699 STATEMENT as to the acceleration of the mail service from London to Belfast and the North of Ireland via Portpatrick and Donaghadee. *Belfast*, 1866. pp. 28.   NLC

1700 CONSOLIDATION of Irish railways: letter to the ... Earl of Derby ... *Dublin*, 1867. pp. 14.   ICE
Suggests the formation of one company under government supervision, for the whole of Ireland.

1701 FISHER, J. Railway reform ... *Dublin*, 1867. pp. 4[9], with map.   BM

1702 HANCOCK, W. N. Report on a plan for the state purchase of railways for Ireland. *Dublin*, 1867. pp. 26.   ICE
'Confidential'.
Lord Naas's plan. 'Government purchase the only complete solution.'

1703 IRISH railways: should Government purchase the Irish railways? A question for the shareholders and the public. *Dublin*, 1867. pp. 16.   BM
In favour of government purchase.

1704 PIM, J. T. The condition of our railways considered with reference to their purchase by the State. *Dublin*, 1867. pp. 22[27]. BM

1705 DODDS, J. Railway reform a public necessity; with practical suggestions. *Belfast*, 1868. pp. 23, with early railway map of Ireland.   BM
Government to undertake management of railways.

1706 OGILBY, W. Irish railways: their present depression and future prospects of amelioration. *Dublin*, 1868. pp. 25.   NLC

1707 WHITE, G. P. [Letter advocating further construction of railways in Ireland.] [*London*, 1868.] pp. 48.   LSE
pp. 21–48, extracts from various sources, in support.

1708 B., J. The Irish church property devoted to the purchase of Irish railways: a letter to ... W. E. Gladstone. *London*, 1869. pp. 8.   BM

1709 WATSON, J. H. Irish railway reform: a scheme for amalgamating the different railway companies in Ireland; proving that uniform fares ... would be profitable to the State. *London*, 1870. pp. 16.   BM
Against monopoly and abuse of power by directors, and advocating government control. Previous schemes by Galt and Brandon considered.

1710 FEARNLEY, B. L. Irish railways and the Irish Board of Public Works: being a review of some of the unused powers of the Loan Commissioners, with suggestions for their practical employment. *Dublin*, 1871. pp. 43, with tables.   NLC

1711 BLENNERHASSETT, R. Irish railways: speech ... in the House of Commons on 17th July, 1872, on proposing the second reading of his Bill for the purchase of Irish railways by the State. *London*, [1872.] pp. 19. BM

1712 CROWE, G. R. The Queen's Highway: being an argument for the amalgamation of the Irish railways under the Queen's Government in trust for the use and benefit of the Queen's subjects, showing the good it would do, the evil it would remove, and how it can be done without any expenditure of public money. *Belfast*, 1873. pp. 22.   NLC

1713 JEPHSON, H. L. Irish railway reform: a paper read before the Statistical & Social Inquiry Society of Ireland ... 15 April, 1873. *Dublin*, 1873. pp. 23.   BM
Control of railways by public boards representing the interests of each district.

1714 DILLON, J. On the railways of Ireland and the causes which have led to the stoppage of railway enterprise, and the best way of providing for the improvement and extension of the railway system. Read before the Dublin Society. *Dublin*, 1871. pp. 32, with fold. map.   BM
Cheap light railways preferable for Ireland.
——3rd edn. 'On the railways of Ireland and the most economical method of providing for the construction of cheap branch railways.' *Dublin*, 1879. pp. 32.   BM

1715 WATHERSTON, E. J. Our railways: should they be private or national property?
c *London*, 1879. pp. 60.   BM
Historical survey of railways, with tables from 1854 to 1878, followed by descriptions of individual Irish lines, with financial tables. State ownership desirable.

1716 DOYLE, J. P. Old Ireland improved and made New Ireland ... *London*, 1881. pp. xvi, 275.   BM
Among reforms suggested is a plan for a nationally owned system of narrow gauge as well as standard gauge railways.

1717 ARMSTRONG, R. O. Improved postal and passenger communication between England and Ireland. *Dublin*, 1882. pp. 14, with map showing proposed spurs to link up railways terminating in Dublin.   NLC
'Issued 31st May, 1882: re-issued with additions, 16th June, 1882.'

1718 K., J. W. Remarks on the necessity and practicability of railway extensions in Ireland. By J. W. K. *Dublin*, 1883. pp. 13, with fold. map.   NLC

1719 PIM, J. T. The Irish mail contract. *Dublin*, [1883.] pp. 15, with tables.   NLC
'Written in the public interest.'

1720 GALT, W. Acceleration of the Irish mail trains: a general review of the present state of the mail service throughout Ireland and in connection with England; with suggestions for its improvement. [*Dublin?*] 1884. pp. 20.   ICE

1721 FINDLAY, G. Irish railways and state purchase. *London*, 1886. pp. 48.   BM
Letters from *The Times* followed (pp. 14–42) by extracts from Evidence, H. of C. Committee of Inquiry 1885, and ending with further suggestions.

1722 B., W. Remarks on the Report of the Royal Commission on Irish Public Works: Railways. 2nd edn. *London: Railway News*, [1889.] pp. 27.   LSE
A reprint of a series of articles in the *Railway News*.

1723 DALY, J. B. Glimpses of Irish industries. *London*, 1889. pp. xvi, 219.   BM
pp. 25–56, Railway autocracy; with tables.
Mismanagement of railway administration an obstacle to national progress. Railways 'under the control of a handful of commercial speculators'.

1724 The WAR of the gauges in Ireland, 1889: the evils of a mixed gauge. *London: Railway News*, [1889.] pp. 14.   LSE
Reprinted from the *Railway News & Joint-Stock Journal*.

1725 IRISH railways and the 'Fortnightly Review' ... *London: Railway News*, [1893.] pp. 24.   LSE
Reprinted from the *Railway News*, 18 November, 1893.
Reply to an article 'The Ireland of today' by 'X' in the *Fortnightly Review*, November 1893.

1726 LOUGH, T. England's wealth, Ireland's poverty ... *London*, [1896.] pp. xiv, 221, with 9 diagrams.   BM
pp. 88–94, effects of English profit-motivated railway promotion upon Irish economy; with two tables.
—— 3rd edn., rev. & corr. *London*, 1897. pp. xv, 223.   BM

1727 FIELD, W. Irish railways compared with state-owned and managed lines. *Dublin*, 1898. pp. 22.   LSE
In favour of nationalization.

1728 DAILY EXPRESS [Dublin], *newspaper*. Irish railway amalgamation. By an English railway expert ... *Dublin*, [1899.] pp. 45, with map.   IT
Reprint, *Daily Express*, 24 & 25 January, 1899.
—— 2nd edn. [with subsequent letters to the 'Daily Express' added] *Dublin*, [1899.] pp. 63.   IT

1729 EDWARDS, C. State railways for Ireland. *London: Fabian Society*, October 1899. pp. 15. [*Fabian Tract*, no. 98.]   BM

1730 FIELD, W. High rates and railway monopoly in Ireland: amendment to Queen's speech ... *Dublin*, 1899. pp. 50.   LSE
Present rates and charges an intolerable grievance to the Irish people. State control wanted. Text consists of two of W. Field's speeches in the H. of C. and, pp. 22–47, press opinions, English and Irish newspapers.

1731 IRISH RAILWAY COMPANIES. Irish railways and their critics: issued under the authority of the Irish Railway Companies. *Belfast*, 1899. pp. 38.   LSE
A reply to charges by Wm. Field, M.P. and Prof. James Long, with Long's series of articles reprinted with the railway companies' replies alongside.

1732 FIELD, W. Trade and transit travel together. Irish railways, and letter to the Lord

Lieutenant. Ireland's case summarized. *Dublin*, 1901. pp. 23.   LSE
Reprinted from the *New Ireland Review*.
'Public utilities should be owned and controlled by the people.'

733 TAYLOR, J. S. Transit, trade and traffic in Ireland. *Dublin*, [1905.] pp. 16.   LSE
A collection of views of manufacturers and traders, expressing dismay at high railway rates.

734 IRISH REFORM ASSOCIATION. Irish railways: their retarded development and influence on industry: a plea for consolidation and state control. *Dublin*, [1906.] pp. 29.   LSE
The need for a special Railway Department for Ireland which will make returns available to the public.
Enclosed with the LSE copy is a separate publication entitled *Dublin, Wicklow & Wexford Rly. Co. mismanagement! What it means to the shareholders!* pp. [4.] This has comparative tables ·for 1896 and 1906.

735 IVATTS, E. B. The Irish railways: what can be done with them. [*Birmingham*, 1908.] pp. [6.]   LSE
Substantial reduction in local rates and in cross-Channel rates from Ireland. State purchase no solution.

736 [O'CONNOR, J.] Statement sent to the Vice-Regal Commission on Irish railways on 7th March, 1908. *Dublin*, 1908. pp. 24. LSE
Signed 'J.O'C.'
Adverse effects which proposed nationalization would have on rates and on railway traffic.

737 'SENTRY.' The commercial conquest of Ireland by the John Bull Syndicate, aided by our selected national economists. *Dublin*, 1909. pp. 8.   BR
Signed 'Sentry'.
Alleged plan by British financial interest to gain complete monopoly of Irish railways, cross-Channel routes and the industrial resources of Ireland.

738 MURPHY, W. M. The reports of the Vice-Regal Commissioners on Irish railways, reviewed by William M. Murphy. *Dublin*, September 1910. pp. 34.   BR

739 PRATT, E. A. Irish railways and their nationalisation: a criticism of the report of the Vice-Regal Commission. 2nd impression. *London*, 1910. pp. 44.   BM

740 PIM, F. W. The railways and the State. *London*, 1912. pp. 302.   BM
State purchase or control of Irish railways. Considerations and advantages.

741 GOOD, T. M. Irish transport chaos: how railways may survive: possibilities of road-rail clearance centres. *Dublin*, 1931. pp. 13.
                                               BM
Road–rail co-ordination.

1742 CÓRAS IOMPAIR ÉIREANN. Around the Bend: passenger services. *Dublin*, 1946. pp. 32, with sketches, photographs & diagrams.   CIE
An account of passenger services in Southern Ireland during the war, and their future prospects.

1743 CÓRAS IOMPAIR ÉIREANN. Seven lean years: freight services. *Dublin*, May 1946. pp. 32, with sketches, photographs & diagrams.   CIE
An account of the effect of the war years upon freight services in Southern Ireland.

1744 MINISTRY FOR INDUSTRY AND COMMERCE [Republic of Ireland]. Report on transport in Ireland. (By J. Milne.) *Dublin: Stationery Office*, 1948. pp. 85. [P. no. 9201.]   BM

1745 LEMASS, F. Public transport in Ireland. pp. 22. *Reproduced typescript.*   IT
Paper, Institute of Transport, Irish Branch, 6 April, 1954.
Land transport problems and future plans.

1746 COMMITTEE OF INQUIRY INTO INTERNAL TRANSPORT [Republic of Ireland]. Report, *Dublin*, [1957.] pp. 259, with 66 tables, 3 charts, fold. map. & diagram.   BM

1747 SITES, J. N. Quest for Crisis: a world-ranging search for clues to the transport future. *New York: Simmons-Boardman; London: Technical Press*, 1963. pp. xvi [xxiii], 223, with illus. & tables.   BM
pp. 22–35, 'Opposite trends in the two Irelands'.

C 4c Railways in particular areas of Ireland

Cork

1748 MACNEILL, J. B. Cork & Cove Railway: report on a proposed railway between the city of Cork and the town of Cove in the South of Ireland. *London*, 1837. pp. 10, with fold. map.   ICE

Donegal

1749 M'FADDEN, J. The present and the past of the agrarian struggle in Gweedore; with letters on railway extension in Donegal. *Londonderry*, 1889. pp. ii, 148.   NLC
pp. 137–40, Developing Donegal.

1750 TUKE, J. H. The condition of Donegal: letters reprinted from 'The Times' of May 20, 28, and June 29, 1889; with further suggestions for the . . . promotion of light railways, fisheries . . . *London*, 1889. pp. 50, with a map.   BM

Dublin

1751 BALLAST CORPORATION [Dublin]. A concise statement of the proceedings of the Ballast Corporation, and the consequent state of the harbour: an inquiry into the

promised and probable consequences to the trade and commerce of Dublin from the proposed railway between Kingstown and Dublin ... *Dublin*, [1833.] pp. 60, with fold. map.   BM
Opposing the railway.

1752 MEMORANDA deduced from official and public documents and intended to show the comparative advantages desirable to the trade and commerce of Dublin from the project of a railway for commercial purposes. *Dublin*, [1833 ?] pp. 43.   HRL

1753 'SCRIBBLE, William.' Dublin destroyed; or, The witches' cauldron of railway horrors!: a mysterious Shakespeareana, in one act. By William Scribble [pseud., William Smith.] 3rd edn. *Dublin*, [1862.] pp. 30.   BM
'To shew how Dublin might be soon destroyed By railway bridges and by line for train, Till of her boasted beauties none remain ...'

1754 [NOBLE, J. & Co.] City of Dublin Tramway: approval of the Municipal Corporation at a special meeting held on the 1st November, 1866 ... *London*, 1866. pp. 10.   BM

1755 LALOR, W. Remarks in connection with a proposal for extending the railway accommodation of Dublin ... *Dublin*, 1872. pp. 12, with la. fold. map & section.   LSE

1756 BARRINGTON, W. L. North Dublin tramways: a letter to those interested in the prosperity of Dublin. *Dublin*, 1875. pp. 12, with a map of the proposed tramway and a detachable share application form.   NLC

1757 DUBLIN SOUTHERN DISTRICT TRAMWAYS Co. Dublin electric tramways. [*Dublin*, 1896.] pp. 59, with illus., diagrams & a map.   ICE
Issued to celebrate the electrification.

Galway

1758 STRYPE, W. G. Galway as a packet station. [1888.] pp. 14,   NLC

Mayo

1759 RAILWAY extension to Mayo: exposition of the fallacy of the proposed scheme, called 'The Grand Junction Railway of Ireland', with a county guarantee. *Dublin*, 1854. pp. 12.   RIA(H)

Meath

1760 FORD, W. A letter addressed to the resident proprietors, merchants, farmers, mill owners, shopkeepers, mechanics, and labourers, of the County of Meath, on the important subject of railway communication between the County [of] Meath and the City of Dublin, containing suggestions as to the mode whereby such communication should be effected, and which it would be well for the people of that county and the several counties north of it, to adopt. *Dublin*, 1845. pp. 24.   RIA(H)

Northern Ireland

1761 NORTHERN IRELAND. Transport conditions in Northern Ireland. Report by Sir Felix J. C. Pole. *Belfast*, [August 1934.] pp. 54, with 20 statistical tables. *Cmd.* 160. IT
'Co-ordination now a matter of urgency.'

1762 CLARKE, D. L. Statement on the Road and Rail Transport Act (Northern Ireland), 1935. By D. L. Clarke, Chairman, Northern Ireland Road Transport Board. *Belfast*, 1935. pp. 16.   IT
Responsibilities of the N.I.R.T.B. under the Act.

1763 WHAT the railways mean to Northern Ireland. [*Belfast*,] 1939. pp. 23.   PC
Issued jointly by the Belfast & County Down Rly., the Great Northern Rly. (I.), and the L.M.S. Rly. (N.C.C.).
Rail facts and figures to meet the threat of closure.

1764 BRITISH ROAD FEDERATION. The Northern Ireland transport mess: £11,600 deficit. *London*, March 1946. pp. 6.   IT
'An outstanding example of complete failure.'

1765 MACCORMICK, W. P. The railways of Northern Ireland and their locomotives. 2nd edn. [*Belfast*,] 1946. pp. 30, with illus. Privately printed.   BR

1766 MINISTRY OF COMMERCE [NORTHERN IRELAND]. Public transport in Northern Ireland. *Belfast*, 1946. pp. 8. *Cmd.* 232. BM
Proposal to merge road and rail undertakings.

1767 JOHN, E. Time table for victory: a brief and popular account of the railways and railway-owned dockyards of Great Britain and Northern Ireland during the Six Years War, 1939–45. *London: British Railways*, 1947. pp. 268, with maps, diagrams & illus.   BM

1768 MACCORMICK, W. P. Main line railways of Northern Ireland. [*Belfast*, 1948.] pp. 47, with illus., lists & map.
Great Northern Rly. (Ireland); London, Midland & Scottish Northern Counties Committee; Belfast & County Down Rly.

1769 [BELFAST.] CITY AND COUNTY BOROUGH c OF BELFAST—TRANSPORT DEPARTMENT. Tramcar Souvenir Brochure. Closing ceremony of last tramcar, Saturday 27th February, 1954. *Belfast*, [1954.] pp. 23, with 16 illus. & table of annual statistics, 1906–1953.   PC

1770 MACNEILL, D. B. Ulster tramways and light railways. *Belfast: Belfast Museum & Art Gallery*, [1956.] pp. 34, with 20 illus., map, & bibliogr. notes. [*Transport Handbook* no. 1.]   BM
Histories of individual lines.

1771 MORTON, R. G. Standard gauge railways in the North of Ireland. *Belfast: Belfast Museum & Art Gallery*, 1962. [*Transport Handbooks*, no. 5.]   BM

C 4D Light and narrow-gauge railways and tramways

1772 LEWIS, W. Narrow gauge railways, Ireland. pp. 64, with tables & 2 fold. diagrams. [With] Green, C. F. Light railways, or remunerative railways for thinly-populated districts. pp. 31–77, with tables & 2 fold. diagrams. *Dublin*, 1882.   BM

1773 SLOANE, J. S. A few words on tramways and light railways applicable to the requirements of Ireland at the present time. *Dublin*, 1883. pp. 23.   ICE

1774 The TRAMWAYS Map of Ireland: showing all the proposed new lines of tramways and light railways. *Dublin*, 1884.   ICE
A la. fold. map with explanatory table of 4 pages.

1775 DAILY EXPRESS [Dublin], *newspaper*. Mr. Balfour's Light Railway Act: the scheduled lines with text of the Act by a special contributor. [*Dublin*, 1889.] pp. 44. [*Daily Express Extras*, no. 1.]   LSE
Explanatory.

1776 FAYLE, H. The narrow gauge railways of Ireland. *London: Greenlake Publications*, 1946. pp. 204, with 129 illus. on plates; maps & diagrams.   BM

1777 KIDNER, R. W. Narrow gauge railways of Ireland. 3rd edn. *Lingfield: Oakwood Press*, [*c*. 1954.] pp. 28, with plates. [*Light Railway Handbooks*, no. 4.]   BM
A combined edition of *The three-foot gauge railways of Northern Ireland* (1950) and *The light railways of Eire* (1949).

1778 KIDNER, R. W. Three-foot gauge railways of Northern Ireland. *Sidcup: Oakwood Press*, 1937. pp. 62–76, with 6 plates, diagrams & maps. [*Light Railway Handbooks*, no. 5.]   BM
—— 2nd edn. *South Godstone*, 1950. pp. [11]–[27.]   BM
—— 3rd, forming part of 'The narrow gauge railways of Ireland'. *Lingfield*, 1954.   BM

1779 KIDNER, R. W. The light railways of Eire, Isle of Man, and Channel Islands. *Sidcup: Oakwood Press*, 1938. pp. [77]–92, with 6 plates, diagrams & map. [*Light Railway Handbooks*, no. 6.]   BM
—— 2nd edn. *South Godstone*, 1949. pp. [17]–32.   BM
—— 3rd, forming part of 'The narrow gauge railways of Ireland'. *Lingfield*, 1957.   BM

1780 WHITEHOUSE, P. B. Narrow Gauge Album. *London: Ian Allan*, 1957. pp. 141, with 129 illus., (2 col.), & 10 maps.   BM
Includes Irish lines.
pp. 136–[142,] 'Tabulated information covering railways mentioned in detail in text.' (10 columns.)

1781 MACGRATH, W. Some industrial railways of Ireland, and other minor lines . . . *Cork*, 1959. pp. 96, with 42 illus.   BM
Published by the author.

1782 COLE, D. Irish industrial and contractors' locomotives. *London: Union Publications*, 1962. pp. 48. Lists, with 16 illus.   BM

C 4E Engineering

1783 COTTON, C. P. Manual of Railway Engineering in Ireland, with appendices including the Irish Tramway Acts. *Dublin*, 1861. pp. iv, 111, with 2 fold. plates (specimen deposited plans).   BM
—— 2nd edn. 'Manual of Railway Engineering for the field and the office.' *Dublin*, 1874. pp. 181.   BM

1784 MILLS, W. H. Remarks made by W. H. Mills . . . at the close of the discussion on the papers on narrow gauge railways and light railways at the meeting on the 4th May, 1881. [*Dublin*,] 1881. pp. 10.   LSE
'For private circulation only.'
Arguments (engineering) against narrow gauge at a meeting of the Institution of Civil Engineers of Ireland.

1785 MAHON, G. R. Railways and bogs in Ireland. *In* 'Journal of Transport History', vol. 5, no. 2, November 1961. pp. 116–26, with a map.   BM

C 4G Operation

1786 IRISH RAILWAY CLEARING HOUSE. Coaching Arrangements Book, embracing the general regulations relating to traffic by passenger train, 1st May, 1900. *London*, 1900. pp. xxviii, 217.   BM
'Private and not for publication.'

C 4H Railway labour

1787 CROKER, E. J. Retrospective lessons on railway strikes, United Kingdom. *London & Cork*, 1898. pp. vi, 205.   BM
Irish railway labour disputes, especially that of the Cork, Bandon & South Coast Rly., 1897–8. Criticism of trade unions.

1788 IRISH TRANSPORT & GENERAL WORKERS' UNION. Three men and three days: a fight for Irish trade unionism. The story of the unsuccessful attempt of an English trade union operating in Ireland to deprive a number of Irish workers of their livelihood because they joined an Irish trade union. *Dublin*, [1934.] pp. 23.   LSE

Press articles, letters, and trade union circulars relating to a T. & G.W.U. demand for dismissal of three Dublin tramwaymen who joined the Irish T. & G.W.U.

C 4 L Individual railways

Collective works

1789 [CURRY.] W. CURRY JNR. & CO. The Irish Railway Guide, containing a correct account of the hours of departure of the railway trains, with a list of coaches, cars, etc. starting from the various railway stations, and a map of Ireland, showing the working lines of railway. *Dublin*, 1846. pp. 44, with fold. map.   LSE

Issued as a Supplement to their *Handbook for Travellers in Ireland.*

—— another edn. *Dublin*, 1847. pp. 50.   UL(GL)

1790 GLYNN, H. A Reference Book to the incorporated railway companies of Ireland, alphabetically arranged, including a list of their directors, offices and officers, constitution and capital. Gauge of way, 5 feet 3 inches. *London*, 1847. pp. xvi, 84, with fold. map.   BM

1791 IRISH Railway Charts: Dublin to Belfast. *Dublin*, [c. 1850?]   BM

A fold. chart depicting stations, line features, and places of interest, Dublin & Drogheda, Dublin & Belfast Junction, and Ulster railways.

1792 The DUBLIN & Kingstown, the Waterford, Wexford, Wicklow & Dublin, and the Dublin, Dundrum & Rathfarnham railway companies. *London*, 1851. pp. 12.   RIA(H)

1793 MEASOM, G. S. The Official Illustrated Guide to the Midland Great Western . . . Great Southern & Western and Dublin & Drogheda railways . . . with 400 engravings . . . and maps. *London*, [1866.] pp. xxxii, 384.   UL(GL)

1794 BRITISH   MUSEUM—DEPARTMENT   OF PRINTED BOOKS. [Documents relating to railways in Ireland. A collection of prospectuses, reports, maps and pamphlets relating to forty-three railway companies under formation between 1844 and 1875. With an index.]   BM (maps)

1795 IRISH   RAILWAY   CLEARING   HOUSE. Handbook of Distances, 1875. *Dublin*, [1875.] pp. xiii, 157.   BM

Arranged under companies.

1796 BROWNING, W. W. Handbook of Railway Distances (Ireland): compiled . . . from the official returns etc. of the various railway companies . . . revised by the Railway Clearing House, Dublin. *London*, 1869. pp. 126, with la. fold. map in end pocket. BM

—— 2nd edn., *London*, 1874. pp. x, 131. BM

—— 3rd, *London*, 1884. pp. xi, 118.   BM

1797 SEALY, BRYERS AND WALKER, *publishers.* Irish Travelling Guide, and Railway Stations Handbook. [*Dublin*,] 1890. pp. 96, with illus.   LSE

Individual railways

Belfast & County Down Railway

1798 BELFAST & COUNTY DOWN RLY. Extension from Comber to Downpatrick, with branch from Saintfield to Ballynahinch. Declaration in favour of the above extension from landed proprietors in the County of Down, and merchants, bankers, manufacturers, and traders of Belfast, Downpatrick, Newry . . . *London*, [1853.] pp. 20, with map.   BM

A short statement followed by seventeen pages of signatories.

1799 LLOYD, T. I. Roadway or railway? between Belfast and Bangor. *Belfast*, 1933. pp. 46, with map.   BM

The Belfast & County Down Rly. should convert their railway into a roadway, with motor-buses.

1800 PATTERSON, E. M. The Belfast & County Down Railway. *Lingfield: Oakwood Press*, 1958. pp. 51, with illus. on plates, lists, gradient profiles & a map. [*Oakwood Library of Railway History*, no. 15.] BM

Cavan & Leitrim Railway

1801 DIGGES, J. G. How the Cavan & Leitrim Railway Extension Bill was killed. *Dublin: Irish Homestead*, 1906. pp. 38.   LSE

Reprint of a series of articles in the *Irish Homestead*, 24 March–9 June, 1906. Cover title, *Fighting industries and financing emigration in Ireland, 1906.*

A detailed account of the circumstances surrounding the Leitrim County Council's opposition to the Bill.

Cork & Macroom Railway

1802 CREEDON, C. The Cork & Macroom Direct Railway: a short history. [*Cork*, 1960.] pp. 35[40], with illus., map & diagrams. BM

Cork & Youghall Railway

1803 CROKER, J. D. Letter of J. Dillon Croker, Esq., auditor of the Cork & Youghal Railway Company, to the shareholders of the said company. *London*, 1857. pp. 8. RIA(H)

County Donegal Railways Joint Committee

1804 PATTERSON, E. M. The County Donegal Railways . . . *Dawlish: David & Charles; London: Phœnix House*, 1962. pp. 157, with col. frontis., 37 illus. on 16 plates, maps, plans, gradient profiles, lists, & a fold. table. [*A History of the Narrow Gauge Railways of North-West Ireland*, part one.]
BM

Dublin & Blessington Railway

1805 FAYLE, H. *and* NEWHAM, A. T. The Dublin & Blessington Steam Tramway. *Lingfield: Oakwood Press*, 1963. pp. 32, with 16 illus. on 8 plates & a map. [*Locomotion Papers*, no. 20.]   BM

Dublin & Drogheda Railway

1806 BALD, W. *and* HENRY, D. J. Report upon the proposed railways between Dublin, Navan, and Drogheda. *Dublin*, 1836. pp. 16, with fold. section & fold. map. PO:RIA(H)
Addressed to the Committee of Management of the Dublin & Drogheda Inland Line of Railway.

1807 CUBITT, W. The report of William Cubitt, civil engineer, to the provisional committee of the Dublin & Drogheda, or Grand Northern Trunk Railway. *Dublin*, 1836. pp. 15.
RIA(H)

1808 DUBLIN & DROGHEDA RLY. In the House of Commons. Minutes of Evidence taken before the Committee on the Dublin & Drogheda Railway (5 May—9 June, 1836). *London*, 1836. pp. 447.   RIA(H)

1809 JONES, J. E. *and* RADCLYFFE, E. Six views on the Dublin & Drogheda Railway: part one. [*Dublin*, 1836.] 6 plates (engravings).   BM(PD)
No more published.

1810 D'ALTON, J. The history of Drogheda, with its environs, and an introductory memoir of the Dublin & Drogheda Railway; in two volumes. *Dublin*, 1844. pp. cxxxiv, 260. BM
Published by the author.
The 'introductory memoir' of 134 pages is mostly concerned with the topography of the towns and estates through which the line passes, and the genealogy of various landowners. An account of the formation of the D. & K. is given, and the course is described. Six of the engravings are views of the railway.

1811 WALSH, N., *publisher*. The Hand Book to the Dublin & Drogheda Railway . . . with a map and a view of the Dublin terminus. *Dublin*, [1844.] pp. 70[80].   BM
pp. [1]–11, A brief historical sketch of the

Dublin & Drogheda Railway; the Dublin terminus (with an engraving).

1812 BRODIGAN, T. Statement of special services rendered to the Dublin & Drogheda Railway Company by Thomas Brodigan, Esq., addressed to the directors. *Dublin*, 1845. pp. 42.   RIA(H)

1813 HEMANS, G. W. Description of the rails, sleepers and fastenings on the Dublin & Drogheda Railway. *London*, 1846. pp. 16.
ICE
Excerpt, *Min. Proc. I.C.E.* 1845. vol. 4.

1814 BRODIGAN, T. A letter written by Thomas Brodigan, Esq., to George A. Hamilton, Esq., M.P., respecting his claims against the Dublin & Drogheda Railway Company, including in an appendix, a report of the trial of the cause of Brodigan against the Company, August 1847. *Dublin*, 1847. pp. 32.   RIA(H)

1815 DUBLIN & DROGHEDA RLY. Statement of the directors of the Dublin & Drogheda Railway respecting the claims of Mr. Thomas Brodigan for special services . . . *Dublin*, 1847. pp. 36.   RIA(H)

1816 MACNEILL, J. Report on the extension northwards of the Dublin & Drogheda Railway, and on its junction with lines in the north-east of Ireland. *London*, 1893. pp. 10, with map.

Dublin & Enniskillen Railway

1817 'ENNISKILLENER.' Dublin & Enniskillen Railway: public notice, to the editor of 'The Railway Times'. [1845.] s.sh.   RIA(H)

1818 O'BEIRNE, J. L. *and* MALLEY, J. Dublin & Enniskillen Railway. *Dublin*, 1845. pp. 2, with la. fold. map.   RIA(H)
Dated 9th September, 1845.
Refutations of statements by 'R. D. Kane' regarding the proposed railway, and reasons for supporting the line. O'Beirne and Malley were solicitors to the railway. The prospectus is appended.

1819 STEPHENSON, R. *and* ROSS, A. M. To the provisional committee of the Dublin & Enniskillen Railway. *London*, 1845. s.sh.
RIA(H)
Report, dated August 25th, of an inspection of the proposed line.

Dublin & Kingstown Railway
and the Kingstown & Dalkey (atmospheric) Railway

1820 BALLAST CORPORATION [Dublin). A concise statement of the proceedings of the

Ballast Corporation, and the consequent state of the harbour: an inquiry into the promised and probable consequences to the trade and commerce of Dublin from the proposed railway between Kingstown and Dublin . . . *Dublin*, [1833.] pp. 60, with fold. map.   BM

Opposing the railway.

1821 NICHOL, A. Five views of the Dublin & Kingstown Railway, from drawings taken on the spot by A. Nichol; with a description of this important work. *Dublin*, 1834. pp. 8, with 5 plates.   BM

*1822 CLAYTON, R. Thirteen views on the Dublin & Kingstown Railway. *Dublin*, 1834. pp. 16.   BM

Woodcuts by R. Clayton. The text describes the line and the locomotive 'Hibernia'.

—— another edn. *Dublin*, 1835. pp. 15. SL

1823 BRIDE, A. S. A few remarks on the eligibility of extending the railway from Bray to the town of Wicklow, addressed to the directors and proprietors of the Kingstown Railroad. *Dublin*, 1836. pp. 16, with tables of exports & imports, Wicklow, 1833–1836.
RIA(H)

1824 STEVENSON, D. Observations on the Liverpool & Manchester Railway, with remarks on the Dublin & Kingstown Railway. [*Edinburgh*, 1836.] pp. 16.   ICE

From the *Transactions of the Society of Arts for Scotland*, as published in the *Edinburgh New Philosophical Journal*, March 1835.
pp. 11–16, D. & K. Rly.

1825 PIM, J. Irish railways. The atmospheric railway: a letter to . . . Viscount Morpeth. *London*, 1841. pp. 15.   BM

Proposing a trial of the atmospheric system on the D. & K. Rly.

1826 BERGIN, T. F. The atmospheric railway: observations on the report of Lt. Col. Sir Frederick Smith, R. E. and Prof. Barlow on the atmospheric railway: addressed to Francis Low, Esq., Chairman of the Dublin and Kingstown Rly. Co. *Dublin*, 1843. pp. 86.   BM

In support of atmospheric system for the D. & K. Rly.

1827 ARAGO, D. F. J. Mons. Arago's report on the atmospheric railway system . . . *London*, 1844. pp. 12.   BM

Includes an account of the D. & K. Rly.

1828 BEYSE, A. W. Neueste Erfahrungen im Eisenbahnwesen. *Karlsruhe*, 1844. 3 Hefte.
BM

vols. 2 & 3 contain descriptions of the Kingsown & Dalkey Atmospheric Rly.

1829 HALLETTE, A. Tube propulseur-Hallette: système d'exécution et d'exploitation des chemins de fer par la pression atmosphérique. *Batignolles*, [1844.] pp. 45, with 2 fold. plates.   BM

French and British systems compared: pp. 17 to end describe the K. & D. Rly.

1830 IRWIN, G. O'M. The Illustrated Hand-Book to the County of Wicklow: being a guide to the stranger and a companion to the resident; with an account of the Atmospheric Railway . . . *London*, 1844. pp. x, 84.   BM

pp. 75–84, an account of the Atmospheric Railway (Kingstown & Dalkey) 'now in operation'; with 3 diagrams.

1831 MALLET, R. Report on the railroad constructed from Kingstown to Dalkey in Ireland, upon the atmospheric system, and upon the application of this system to railroads in general. [*Paris*, 1844.] pp. 55, with 4 fold. plates.   UL(GL)

—— Rapport sur le chemin de fer établi suivant le système atmosphérique de Kingstown à Dalkey en Irlande . . . *Paris*, 1844. pp. 71, with fold. map.   PO

1832 MALLET, R. Mallets Bericht über die atmosphärische Eisenbahn von Dublin nach Dalkey in Irland, ausgeführt und in Betrieb gesetzt von den Herrn Clegg und Samuda; mit einem Stahlstich-'Aufsicht der atmosphärische Eisenbahn von Dublin nach Dalkey'. *Darmstadt*, 1844. pp. 14.   ICE

1833 An APPEAL to . . . the Lord Lieutenant on behalf of the labouring classes. *Dublin*, [1846.] pp. 54.   LSE

Concerning the demolition of 'the bathing places of the poor' at Salt Hill, Kingstown, by the K. & D. Rly. for the purpose of constructing their line along the coast.

1834 STEPHENSON, R. Report on the Atmospheric Railway . . . to the directors of the Chester & Holyhead Railway. [*London*,] 1844, with la. fold. table & 86 graphs on 26 plates. ICE

R. Stephenson's report on the D. & K. Rly.

—— 'Die Atmosphärische Eisenbahn', translated by M. M. von Weber. *Berlin*, 1845.

Dublin & Limerick Railway

1835 DUBLIN & LIMERICK Rly. Prospectus of the Dublin & Limerick Railway, being the second extension of the Great Leinster & Munster Railway, with the report of the Government Commissioners on the importance of the Shannon, and observations as to the Western Packet Station; also a letter from the president of the Chamber of Commerce at Limerick to Mr. Barrington, and his reply. *London*, 1836. pp. 15, 10. BM

pp. 1–10, 'On a Western Packet Station at Limerick, and a railroad between that city and Dublin', by Matthew Barrington.

1836 MEMORANDUM relating to the Dublin & Limerick Railway Bill, 1842. [*Limerick, 1842.*] s.sh.   BM(MSS)
Printed.
The BM copy is prefaced by a MS. letter from Archdeacon Keating, Limerick, 17 May, 1842, addressed to Sir Robert Peel, on the unfair liabilities imposed upon landowners for capital.

Dublin, Wicklow & Wexford Railway

1837 FLOOD, E. S. Observations upon the present position of the Waterford & Wexford Railway Co. and the best means of developing its traffic. *Dublin*, 1873. pp. 23.   ICE

1838 DUBLIN, WICKLOW & WEXFORD RLY. Servants' Time Bill for October, 1889. *Dublin*, 1889. pp. 28.   LSE
Instructions to staff, and time-tables.

1839 GRIERSON, T. B. The enlargement of Westland Row terminus, part 2 . . . read before the Institution of Civil Engineers of Ireland, April 5, 1893. *Dublin*, 1893. pp. 15.   ICE
(Part 1 of this lecture appeared in vol. 18 of the Institution's *Minutes*.)

1840 IRISH REFORM ASSOCIATION. Dublin, Wicklow & Wexford Railway Company mismanagement: what it means to the shareholders. [1906.] pp. [4.]   LSE
Containing comparative tables for 1896 and 1906. This pamphlet is enclosed with the LSE's copy of *Irish railways: their retarded development and influence on industry* (1906), also issued by the Irish Reform Association.

Dundalk & Enniskillen Railway

1841 DUNLOP, D. Dundalk & Enniskillen Railway Company: a statement in reply to the comments appended by the directors to the report of the Committee of Investigation. *Dublin*, 1848. pp. 64.   H

1842 PORTER, J. G. V. Lord Erne's mistakes as chairman of the Dundalk Railway Company. *Dublin*, 1858. pp. 22.   RIA(H)
—— 2nd edn. Mistakes of the Dundalk & Enniskillen Railway Company's directors. *Dublin*, 1858.   RIA(H)

1843 COURT OF QUEEN'S BENCH. Earl of Erne, plaintiff: John Grey Vesey Porter, defendant. Report of a trial of an action for libel. *Dublin*, 1859. pp. 115.   RIA(H)

1844 PORTER, J. G. V. Reply to statements since trial, February 14, 1859. *Dublin*, 1859. pp. 21.   RIA(H)

Dundalk, Newry & Greenore Railway

1845 DUNDALK & GREENORE RLY. Opening of the railway and harbour, Greenore, on Wednesday the 30th April, 1873.   BR
A collection of newspaper reports.

*1846 BARRIE, D. S. M. The Dundalk, Newry & Greenore Railway, and the Holyhead-Greenore steamship service. [*Lingfield:*] *Oakwood Press*, 1957. pp. 68, with col. frontis., 37 illus., 2 maps & 3 plans.   BM

Giant's Causeway Tramway

1847 MACGUIGAN, J. H. The Giant's Causeway Tramway. *Lingfield: Oakwood Press*, 1964. pp. vi, 107, with 24 illus. on 12 plates, map, diagrams, & table of tickets & fares.   BM

Great Leinster & Munster Railway

1848 GREAT LEINSTER & MUNSTER RLY. Prospectus of the Great Leinster & Munster Railway; first extension, from the City of Dublin to the City of Kilkenny, with estimated annual revenue, engineer's report, etc., etc. *London*, 1836. pp. 26.   PO

Great Northern Railway (Ireland)

1849 MILLS, W. H. List of some of the principal new works carried out on the Great Northern Railway (Ireland) between January 1st, 1877 and January 1st, 1890. [1890.] pp. 8.   LSE
'For private circulation only.'

1850 STUART, C. R. G. Some notes on main line train services and locomotive performance on the Great Southern and Great Northern railways of Ireland. pp. 31, with tables. *MS.*   RC
Paper, Railway Club, 5 May, 1933.

1851 MURRAY, K. The Great Northern Railway Ireland: past, present and future . . . *Dublin: G.N.R. (I)*, 1944. pp. xii, 148, with 82 illus., fold. diagram, & fold. map.   BM
Issued to mark the centenary of the Dublin & Drogheda Rly. Compiled from official sources. The constituent railways historically described are, Ulster; Dublin & Drogheda; Dublin & Belfast Junction; Irish North Western.

1852 GREAT NORTHERN RLY. (IRELAND). Dundalk Works: visit of Institute of Transport, Northern Ireland Section, October 26th, 1945. [*Dundalk*, 1945.] pp. [24,] with 12 plates.   IT

1853 SHIELDS, B. F. An analysis of the financial and operating statistics of the Great Southern Railway Co. and Great Northern Railway Co., 1938–44. *Dublin: Statistical Social Inquiry Society of Ireland*, [1946.] pp. 19 with tables.   IT
Paper, 31 January, 1946.

1854 PATTERSON, E. M. The Great Northern
b Railway of Ireland. *Lingfield: Oakwood
Press*, 1962. pp. 188, with 45 illus. on 21
plates, map, gradient profile, tables, many
lists, incl. ten 10-column lists of locomotives
of the GN(I) and its nine constituent companies, and a bibliography of 94 items.   BM

Great Southern & Western Railway

1855 GRAND CANAL COMPANY. Dublin &
Cashel Railway, and Grand Canal Company,
Ireland. Statement on behalf of the Grand
Canal Company. *London*, 1844. pp. 14,
with fold. map.   RIA(H)
Opposition to a proposed line of railway to
run parallel to the canal from Dublin to Sallins.
(In this same volume of pamphlets (vol. 1897 of
the Haliday Collection) is a prospectus of the
Grand Canal Atmospheric Company, formed
in 1844 in opposition to the proposed Dublin
& Cashel Rly.).

1856 MACNEILL, J. B. Atmospheric railway.
Report of Sir John MacNeill to the provisional committee of the Great Southern &
Western Railway, Ireland, and letter from
the chairman to Mr. Pim. [*Dublin*, 1844.]
pp. 20.   LSE
Proposed Dublin to Cashel line, which James
Pim opposed. The letter to him is reprinted
from the *Railway Record* and is dated 6 June,
1844.

1857 MACNEILL, J. B. Report on a proposed
line of railway from Dublin to Cashel,
being the first division of a main trunk to
the south and south-west of Ireland, including a branch therefrom to Athy and
Carlow. *Dublin*, 1844. pp. 16.   RIA(H)
Report of a survey, with tables of estimated
cost, traffic, and of gradients.

1858 MACNEILL, J. B. Reports . . . to the pro-
visional committee of the Dublin & Cashel
Railway. *Dublin*, 1844. pp. 24.   NLC
One report considers the atmospheric system.

1859 HALIDAY, C. Remarks on the Dublin
terminus of the Cashel, or Great Southern
& Western Railway. [*Dublin*,] 1845. pp.
16.   RIA(H)
The advantages of having a terminus at
King's Bridge, Dublin, and not at Portobello.

1860 D'ALTON, J. A Memoir of the Great
Southern & Western Railway of Ireland,
and its branches: part the first, comprising a
memoir of the main line to Cherryville and
of the thence diverging branch to Carlow.
Dublin, 1846. pp. 136.   RC
No more published.

1861 GREAT SOUTHERN & WESTERN RLY.
Rules and regulations for engine-drivers
and firemen in the employ of the G.S. & W.
Rly. Co. *Dublin*, 1847. pp. 32.   LSE

1862 IRISH Railway Charts. Dublin to Tipper-
ary and Limerick (Great Southern & Western Railway.) *Dublin*, [*c.* 1850?]   BM
A fold. chart.

1863 MINUTES of correspondence between the
directors of the Grand Canal Company and
the directors of the Great Southern &
Western and of the Midland Great Western
railway companies. *Dublin*, 1853. pp. 27.
                                    RIA(H)
—— CORRESPONDENCE and minutes between the directors of the Midland Great Western and Great Southern & Western railway
companies and Grand Canal Company.
Dublin, 1854. pp. 44.   RIA(H)

1864 MEASOM, G. S. The Official Illustrated
Guide to the Great Southern & Western
Railway . . . with numerous engravings.
London, 1866. pp. xxiv, 410, with map. UL(GL)

1865 ROY, K. Tales of an engineer; being facts
and fancies of railway life. *London*, 1896.
pp. 94.   BM
Seven short stories, mostly centred upon the
G.S. & W. Rly., Ireland.

Great Southern Railways

1866 STUART, C. R. G. Great Southern Railways (Ireland). [pp. 32 and 8 pp. tables.] RC
Paper, Railway Club, 8 May, 1931.
An account of the railways which amalgamated in 1924.

1867 W., S. J. Locomotives of the Great Southern
Railways of Ireland. *London: A. H. Stock-
well*, 1937. pp. viii, 77.   BM
Notes, lists and illustrations.

1868 SHIELDS, B. F. An analysis of the financial
and operating statistics of the Great Southern Railway Co. and Great Northern Railway Co., 1938–44. *Dublin: Statistical
Social Inquiry Society of Ireland*, [1946.]
pp. 19, with tables.   IT
Paper, 31 January, 1946.

Irish Great Western Railway

1869 IRISH Great Western Railway, from Dublin
to Galway. [*Dublin*, 1844.] pp. [4.] RIA(H)
Title on reverse, *Traffic Statement of the Irish
Great Western Railway*.
Four detailed tables, revealing the nature and
extent of traffic (passenger and merchandise) by
mail coaches, stage coaches, gigs, carts, and by
horse, observed and recorded by a team of
enumerators stationed at various points over a
period of fourteen consecutive days.

1870 ROWE, W. C. Irish Great Western Railway.
Speech of W. C. Rowe on the petition of the
Grand Canal Company. 1845. pp. 53. RIA(H)

Londonderry & Lough Swilly Railway

1871 PATTERSON, E. M. The Londonderry &
Lough Swilly Railway. *Dawlish: David &
Charles; London: Macdonald*, [1964.] pp.
189, with col. frontis., 24 plates, illus., maps,
plans, tables, diagrams & a bibliography.
[*History of the Narrow Gauge Railways of
North-West Ireland*, pt. 2.]   BM.

Midland Great Western Railway

872 MULLINGAR, ATHLONE & LONGFORD RLY. Observations of the provisional directors of the Mullingar, Athlone & Longford Railway on the report of the Board of Trade on railways proposed to be made in Ireland, westward from Dublin. *Dublin*, 1845. pp. 54.   ICE
Includes the text of the Board of Trade Report.

873 MIDLAND Great Western Railway: Dublin to Galway. [*Dublin*,] 1853.   BM
A fold. travelling chart.

874 MINUTES of correspondence between the directors of the Grand Canal Company and the directors of the Great Southern & Western and of the Midland Great Western railway companies. *Dublin*, 1853. pp. 27.
RIA(H)

—— CORRESPONDENCE and minutes between the directors of the Midland Great Western and Great Southern & Western railway companies, and Grand Canal Company. *Dublin*, 1854. pp. 44.   RIA(H)

875 MIDLAND GREAT WESTERN RLY. Western Highlands, Connemara: opinions of the press . . . 2nd edn. *Dublin*, [1860.] pp. 51.   PC

876 CLEMENTS, R. N. M.G.W.R., 1847–1947. *Dublin: Coras Iompair Eireann*, [1947.] pp. 12[14], with 5 illus. of locomotives. SLS
Reprinted from the June 1947 issue of *Cuislei na Tire*.

Northern Counties Committee

877 BRITISH RAILWAYS—NORTHERN COUNTIES COMMITTEE. Centenary of the opening c of the Belfast & Ballymena Railway. *Belfast*, 1948. pp. 71, with illus. (incl. seals) & map.
IT
pp. 3–35, 'Chronology of the N.C.C.'
pp. 38–72, 'Journey on the main line'.

Schull & Skibbereen Tramway and Light Railway

878 NEWHAM, A. T. The Schull & Skibbereen Tramway and Light Railway. [*Lingfield:*] *Oakwood Press*, 1964. pp. 32, with 15 illus., timetable & gradient profile on 8 plates, map & diagrams. [*Locomotion Papers*, no. 24.] BM

Sligo, Leitrim & Northern Counties Railway

879 BRIEF summary of the history of the Sligo, Leitrim & Northern Counties Railway, and negotiations for reconstruction. *Dublin*, 1895. pp. 20.   LSE
Legal and financial history.

880 MORRISSEY, DANIEL & SONS. Sligo, Leitrim & Northern Counties Railway (Republic

of Ireland Section). Auction of approximately 32 miles of railway track, bridges, sleepers, etc., locomotives, etc. *Dublin*, [1959.] pp. 54, with diagrams of sections of the line.   PC
A sale catalogue. A complete (?) inventory of the components of the S.L. & N.C. Rly.

Suir & Shannon Junction Railway

881 SMYTH, G. L. The Suir & Shannon Junction Railroad: an exposition of the expenditure, revenue, and general advantages of the proposed railroad from Limerick to Waterford, with a distinct terminus at Carrick-on-Suir . . . *London*, 1836. pp. 35.   NLC

Tralee & Dingle Light Railway

882 WHITEHOUSE, P. B. The story of the Tralee & Dingle Light Railway; by P. B. Whitehouse in collaboration with A. J. Powell. *London: Locomotive Publishing Co.*, [1958.] pp. iv, 69[76], with many illus., maps, diagrams & gradient profiles.   BM

Waterford & Limerick Railway

883 FURTHER reasons for granting a loan to the Waterford & Limerick Railway. (By a Citizen of Waterford, not a shareholder.) *Waterford*, 1849. pp. 8.   ULC

884 LEVY, J. History of the mismanagement of the Waterford & Limerick Railway Board: the legal consequences to directors of paying a dividend not warranted by profits! With an appendix . . . *Dublin*, 1856. pp. 34.   BM
A speech and six letters addressed to shareholders and to the *Waterford Chronicle*. Tables of receipts and expenditure for 1855.

Waterford & Tramore Railway

885 NEWHAM, A. T. Waterford and Tramore Railway. rev. edn., 1957. pp. 23. *Typescript*.   SLS

West Cork Railways

886 WEST CORK RAILWAYS. Land plans and contract sections. *Westminster: H. Conybeare*, [1864.] pp. 90.   PO
Privately printed for use by surveyors.

Wexford & Valencia Railway

887 WALKER, J. Wexford & Valencia Railway, Killarney to Valencia . . . Report of James Walker . . . to the . . . Admiralty, on the Harbour of Valencia, Ireland. *London*, 1846. pp. 20.   NLC

888 WEXFORD and Valencia Railway: a letter to the scripholders, by a Scripholder. 2nd edn. *London*, [1847.] pp. 30.   BM
Advantages of the proposed railway and of a harbour at Valencia.

1889 WEXFORD & VALENCIA RLY. Evidence and opinions on the Harbour of Valencia, Ireland, as to its fitness for a Western packet station; submitted to . . . Lord John Russell, First Lord of the Treasury. Compiled by the solicitors of the Wexford & Valencia Railway Company; with map. *London*, 1847. pp. 34.   RIA(H)
—— 2nd edn. *London*, 1847. pp. vii, 61.   BM

Wexford, Carlow & Dublin Junction Railway

1890 WEXFORD, CARLOW & DUBLIN JUNCTION RLY. The Evidence given before the Committee on the Bill in the House of Commons; printed from the short hand writer's notes. *London*, 1845. pp. 236.   RIA(H)

C 4Q Appreciation and aesthetics

1891 MORTON, J. B. The Old Trams. *In* 'Essays of the Year (1930–31)', compiled by Frederick J. H. Darton. *London*, 1931. pp. 187–92. BM
Sentiments aroused by the replacement of trams by buses in Ireland.

1892 ALLEN, P. On the old lines: locomotives round the world. *London: Cleaver-Hume Press*, 1957. pp. 184[186].   BM
pp. 110–17, 'Ireland'; with 8 illus. on 4 plates.
—— 2nd edn. *London*, 1958. pp. 190[192].   BM

1893 RANSOME-WALLIS, P. On railways, at home and abroad. *London: Batchworth Press*, 1951. pp. 299, with plates.   BM
—— 2nd edn. *London, Spring Books*, [1960.] pp. 300.   BM
pp. 204–14, Railways in Ireland.

C 5   ISLE OF WIGHT – Solent Tunnel Scheme

1894 MITCHELL, W. The Isle of Wight and its railways: its risk and its remedy . . . *Edinburgh*, 1912. pp. 36 with map.   BM
The strategic position of the Isle of Wight for a military base and for a tunnel to the mainland.
—— 2nd edn. *Edinburgh*, 1912. pp. 34. BM

1895 WALKER, P. C. The locomotives of the railways of the Isle of Wight. *London*, [1919.] pp. 8.   BM

1896 ALLEN, P. C. The railways of the Isle of Wight. *London*, 1928. pp. 83, with 32 illus. & 2 maps.   RC

1897 GREENIDGE, T. L. A Branch-line Holiday. *In* 'Holidays and Happy Days', by Oswell Blakeston. *London*, 1949. pp. 69–84. BM
The appeal of railways, especially those of the Isle of Wight.

1898 ROBBINS, R. M. The Isle of Wight railways. *South Godstone: Oakwood Press*, 1953. pp.
c   37, with 34 illus. on 17 plates, maps, tables, chronology & bibliogr. notes. [*Oakwood Library of Railway History*, no. 54.] BM

1899 TURTON, F. The history of the Solent Tunnel Scheme and railways associated with it . . . *Ilfracombe: Stockwell*, 1945. pp. 64, with illus.   BM
—— 2nd edn. *Cowes: S. Wroath*, 1946. pp. vi, 59.
—— 3rd, *Cowes: S. Wroath*, 1946. (reprint.)
—— 4th, *Cowes: S. Wroath*, 1948. pp. vi, 60.
—— rev. edn. 'A Solent Tunnel?' *Southampton: G. F. Wilson*, 1953. pp. 63.   BM
Editions 2, 3 & 4 are in the County Seely Library, Isle of Wight.

1900 RAILWAY DEVELOPMENT ASSOCIATION. Isle of Wight Railways. Report of inquiry held in London, June 1953. *Kennington (London)*, [1953.] pp. [8.]   PC
Reprinted from the *Isle of Wight County Press*, June 20, 1953.

1901 FAULKNER, D. The Isle of Wight Railway. *Morden: Falcon Publishing Co.; Teddington: Branch Line Handbooks*, 1963. pp. 34[36], with 14 illus., 9 diagrams, 2 tables, brief chronology & fold. map. *Reproduced typescript.* [*Regional Railway Histories.*] BM

C 6   ISLE OF MAN

1902 F., R. Beyond the Silver Streak in Manxland: the great electric railway; written and illustrated by R. F. *London*, [1894.] pp. 72, with illus.   BM
pp. 9–72, a descriptive tour by tram.

*1903 MACNAB, I. A history and description of the Isle of Man Railway. *London: Greenlake Publications*, 1945. pp. 100, with many illus. on plates.   BM

1904 ISLE OF MAN—TYNWALD. Interim report of the committee appointed by Tynwald to report on insular transport. (Chairman, T. G. Moore.) *Douglas*, July 1947. pp. 7.   IT

—— Final report. *Douglas*, April 1949. pp. 14, with fold. map.   IT
Recommending that railways should be abandoned and road services substituted.

1905 DOUGLAS, M. Manx Electric Railway: descriptive booklet on coast and mountain electric railways. *Douglas: Manx Electric Rly. Co.*, 1938. pp. 52, with illus. & maps.   BM
Cover title, *See the Isle of Man by the Manx Electric Railway.*
—— another edn. *Douglas*, 1950. pp. 39.   BM
—— another edn. *Douglas*, 1951. pp. 35.   BM

*1906 PEARSON, F. K. Snaefell Mountain Railway 1895–1955. *London: Light Railway Transport League*, 1955. pp. 11, with illus. & map.   PC

1907 [DOUGLAS.] BOROUGH OF DOUGLAS TRANSPORT DEPARTMENT. The Douglas Bay Tramway, 1876–1956; by F. K. Pearson. (Souvenir Brochure, 7th August, 1956. 80th anniversary, horse trams.) *Douglas*, 1956. pp. 21, with 9 illus.   IT

1908 KIDNER, R. W. The light railways of Eire, Isle of Man and Channel Islands. *Sidcup: Oakwood Press*, 1938. pp. [77]–92, with 6 plates, maps & diagrams. [*Light Railway Handbooks*, no. 6.]   BM
—— 2nd edn. *South Godstone*, 1949. pp. [17]–32.   BM
—— 3rd, forming part of 'The narrow-gauge railways of Ireland'. *Lingfield*, 1957.   BM

1909 PEARSON, F. K. The Manx Electric Railway. *London: Light Rly. Transport League*, [1957.] pp. 20, with illus., lists & a map. IT

*1910 BOYD, J. I. C. The Isle of Man Railway: a history of the Isle of Man Railway and the former Manx Northern Railway, together with notes on other steam railways in the Island . . . with drawings by J. M. Lloyd. *Lingfield: Oakwood Press*, 1962. pp. 215, with 80 illus. on 44 plates, many diagrams, specimen timetables, drawings of locomotives and rolling stock, and gradient profiles.   BM
  Includes details of Corrin's Hill tramroad, Port Erin Harbour of Refuge tramway, Great Laxey Mining Co. tramway, West Baldwin River Reservoir contract tramways, and the Groundle Glen (miniature) Railway.

C 7 CHANNEL ISLANDS

1911 GUERNSEY RLY. Guide to Glorious Guernsey: bus time table and Island tours. *St. Peter Port*, [1955.] pp. 68, with illus. BM
  Includes a short account of the Guernsey Railway Company, 1878–1934.

1912 KIDNER, R. W. The light railways of Eire, Isle of Man and the Channel Islands. *Sidcup: Oakwood Press*, 1938. pp. [77]–92, with illus. on 6 plates. [*Light Railway Handbooks*, no. 6.]   BM
  Notes, diagrams and maps.
—— 2nd edn. *South Godstone*, 1949. pp. 18–32.   BM
—— 3rd, forming part of 'The narrow-gauge railways of Ireland'. *Lingfield*, 1957.   BM

1913 BURT, R. G. The old Jersey railways, *Jersey: The Museum*, 1961. pp. 91–100,

with 4 illus. on 2 plates, diagram, map & gradient profile.   BM
  The Jersey Western Rly. and the Jersey Eastern Rly.

1914 GINNS, M. Transport in Jersey; by Michael Ginns, in collaboration with Eric N. Osborne: an historical survey of public transport facilities by rail and road in the Island of Jersey, 1788–1961. *London: Transport World*, 1961. pp. 64.   BM
  With ten illustrations and two maps.

1915 BONSOR, N. R. P. The Jersey Railway (J.R. & T.) *Lingfield: Oakwood Press*, 1962. pp. 87, with 17 illus. on 16 plates, 5 tables & a map. [*Oakwood Library of Railway History*, no. 58.]   BM

C 8 ENGLISH CHANNEL TUNNEL and other Channel-crossing Schemes

For Channel train ferry services see G 5

Historical

1916 PILLET, J. E. Histoire d'un tunnel sous-marin. *Rouen*, 1888. pp. 363, with illus. [*Bibliothèque Morale de la Jeunesse*.]

1917 HANNING, W. The Channel Tunnel: a paper read before the British Chamber of Commerce in Paris on December 15th, 1906. *London*, 1907. pp. 35, with fold. plate. ICE
  History of schemes and problems, geological, military, etc.

1918 WEBB, D. M. Channel Tunnel. *In* 'Bulletin of the British Library of Political Science',
  b no. 4, January 1913. pp. 11–14.   LSE
  A bibliography.

1919 COLOMBOS, C. J. Le Tunnel sous la Manche et le droit international: thèse pour le doctorat (Université de Paris). *Paris*, 1915. pp. 116[117].   BM
  History, problems and present position.

1920 D'ALTOFF, A. C. T. Le Tunnel sous la Manche. *Paris*, 1919. pp. 45.   BM
Historical survey from various aspects.

1921 LONDON SCHOOL OF ECONOMICS—
b BRITISH LIBRARY OF POLITICAL AND ECONOMIC SCIENCE. Channel Tunnel. (Select Bibliography no. 45.) *In* 'Bulletin of the British Library of Political Science', March 1929. pp. 29–35.   LSE

1922 GAIN, P. H. La Question du Tunnel sous la Manche. *Paris*, [1932.] pp. viii, 300, with
b a bibliography of 102 items.   BM
History of the project; technical, military, economic, political and legal aspects.

1923 The CHANNEL Tunnel project. *London*, [1948.] pp. 15.   BM
History and prospects.

1924 HARRINGTON, J. L. The Channel Tunnel and Ferry. *South Godstone: Oakwood Press*, 1949. pp. 18, with illus. & map. [*Locomotion Papers*, no. 4.]   BM

1925 SLATER, H. *and* BARNETT, C. The Channel Tunnel; by H. Slater and C. Barnett, with the collaboration of R. H. Géneau. *London: Allan Wingate*, 1958. pp. 213, with 27 illus. on 14 plates & in text, & map on end papers.   BM
The history of Channel Tunnel schemes, and present and future prospects.

1926 SMITH, H. The Channel Tunnel. *London: Library Association*, 1958. pp. 11. [*Special
b Subject List*, no. 24.] *Reproduced typescript.*   BM
244 references to printed material on the Channel Tunnel in the English language, 1858–1958.

1927 WHITESIDE, T. The Tunnel under the Channel. *London: Rupert Hart-Davis*, 1962. pp. 133, with 21 illus. on plates, & map on end papers.   BM

Contemporaneous

1928 TURNER, R. *and* TURNER, T. Proposed submarine railway from Dover to Cape Grisnez. *Dublin*, [c. 1840.] s. sh.   ICE
Three diagrams with explanatory text.
A tube railway laid on the sea bed and covered 'with a mound of ballast'.

1929 THOMÉ DE GAMOND, A. Étude pour l'avant-projet d'un tunnel sous-marin entre l'Angleterre et la France reliant sans rompre charge les chemins de fer de ces deux pays par la ligne de Grinez à Eastware; avec la carte du tracé . . . *Paris*, 1857. pp. 180, with 3 fold. plates.   BM

1930 NICKLÈS, M. J. Le Moteur des convois des grands tunnels et en particulier du tunnel sous-marin. *Nancy*, 1858. pp. 32, with bibliogr. notes.   BM
T. de Gamond's plan for impelling trains through tunnels by force of air.

1931 PLANS for a submarine communication between England and France, 1858. *Dublin*, 1858. pp. 13.   ICE
Atmospheric system with passengers conveyed in a piston-car of 6 ft. diameter.

1932 ROBERT, G. Chemin de fer de Paris à Londres: construction d'une jetée de Douvres à Calais. *Paris*, 1860. pp. 16.   BM

1933 CHALMERS, J. The Channel Railway, connecting England and France. *London*, 1861. pp. 47, with fold. map and la. fold. diagrams.   BM
—— 2nd edn. *London*, 1867. pp. iv, 50.   BM

1934 BATEMAN, J. F. *and* RÉVY, J. J. Channel railway: description of a proposed cast-iron tube for carrying a railway across the Channel between the coasts of England and France. *Westminster*, 1869. pp. 59.   BM
The tunnel 'to rest on sea bed'.

1935 NURSEY, P. F. A paper on English and continental intercommunication. Read before the Society of Engineers . . . on 18 October, 1869. [*London*, 1869.] pp. 40.   ICE

1936 YOUNG, E. W. International Floating Tunnel. *London*, 1869. pp. 14, with chart & 2 diagrams.   BM
From Dover to Gris Nez in a tunnel floating under the surface and secured by mooring cables.

1937 THOMÉ DE GAMOND, A. Atlas containing the plans and sections of the submarine tunnel between England and France reduced from those shown at the Universal Exhibition of 1867, to accompany the account of the new project of . . . A. Thomé de Gamond. *London*, 1870. 3 fold. plates.   BM

1938 WALKER, W. T. Construction of a railway across the Channel beneath the sea, between the coasts of England and France. *London*, 1870. pp. 37, with fold. plan.   IME
Lecture, Highgate Literary & Scientific Institute, 15 November, 1870. 'For presentation only.'

1939 OBACH, T. *and* LEBRET, B. The Channel Railroad Ferry for a safe and regular steam service between England and the Continent . . . *London*, 1874. pp. 18, with a fold. plate at end showing view, section & plan proposed.   BM
A submerged bridge with rails and a movable platform upon which to transport trains.

1940 PRESTWICH, J. On the geological conditions affecting the construction of a tunnel between England and France; with an abstract of the discussion upon the paper. Edited by James Forrest. *London*, 1874. pp. 64, with fold. map & section at end. BM
Excerpt *Min. Proc. I.C.E.*, vol. 27.

1941 HESSE, E. A. VON. Der Unterseeische Tunnel zwischen England und Frankreich, vom geologischen, technischen und finanziellen Standpunkte beleuchtet; mit zwei Karten und einer Tafel . . . *Leipzig*, 1875. pp. 32.   BM

1942 LAHORE, G. P. Projet de construction d'une chaussée avec ou sans tunnel de Calais à Douvres, pour l'établissement d'un chemin de fer entre la France et l'Angleterre. *Foix*, 1875. pp. 23, with fold. plate.   BM
Previous schemes outlined.

1943 BISHOP, P. J. The Channel Railway, tube or tunnel: the advantages considered of constructing and laying a submarine tube as a means of communication across the Channel. *London*, 1876. pp. 23.   BM
Includes a survey of previous schemes.

1944 MARCHEGAY, A. Le Chemin de fer sous-marin entre la France et l'Angleterre. *Lyon*, 1876. pp. 46, with plan.

1945 NURSEY, P. F. A paper on the Channel Railway; read before the Society of Engineers . . . on 6 March 1876. [*London*, 1876.] pp. 17–64, with 2 fold. diagrams.
ICE
Anchored tubes. Previous schemes analysed.

1946 ASSOCIATION DU CHEMIN DE FER SOUS-MARIN ENTRE LA FRANCE ET L'ANGLE-TERRE. Assemblée Générale du 6 juin, 1877. Rapports présentés aux membres de l'Association. *Paris*, 1877. pp. 81.   LC

1947 WEBER, C. P. M. M. VON. Der Eisenbahn Betrieb durch lange Tunnels . . . mit 7 Tafeln mit einem Anhang: die Wechselwirkungen zwischen den continentalen und den englischen Bahnsystemen nach der Vollendung des Unterseeischen Tunnels. *Wien*, 1877. pp. 76[77]. [*Populäre Erörterungen von Eisenbahn Zeitfragen*, no. 5.]

1948 TOPLEY, W. Report on the recent French explorations connected with the Channel Tunnel, to the chairman and committee of the Channel Tunnel Co. Ltd. *London*, 1878. pp. 14, with fold. plate.   BM
Geology of the sea bed.

1949 LESLIE, B. Channel Railway, 1880. *Calcutta*, [1880.] pp. 16 with 2 fold. diagrams.
BM
A submerged, buoyant, cylindrical steel tunnel, moored to the sea bed.

1950 The BATTLE of Boulogne; or, How Calais became English again: another version of the Channel Tunnel affair. By 'The Demure One.' *London*, 1882. pp. 51.   BM
Signed 'Hector Chauvin' ex-Prime Minister of France.
An imaginary forecast of an attempted invasion of England by the French via the Tunnel in 1890, and of a successful counter-attack by British forces.

1951 BERNEY, T. The Battle of the Channel Tunnel and Dover Castle and forts: a letter to W. E. Gladstone, First Lord of the Treasury. [*Norwich*, 1882.] pp. 12.   ICE
Privately printed and sent to all M.P.'s. Fears of invasion dramatically presented.

1952 The CHANNEL Tunnel: a true view of it . . . *London*, 1882. pp. 8.   BM
Verses against the Tunnel.

1953 CRAMPTON, T. R. Crampton's system of excavating the Channel Tunnel by hydraulic machinery. [*Southampton*, 1882.] pp. 8.
BM

1954 DAWKINS, W. B. The Channel Tunnel: read before the Manchester Geological Society, May 2, 1882. *Salford*, [1882.] pp. 20.
LSE
Geological problems.

1955 'GERMAN OFFICER.' A German opinion on the projected Channel Tunnel; by a German Officer. 1882. pp. 20.   LSE
Translated from *Militär Wochenblatt*, no. 30, 1882, by T. J. Denne.
Military dangers to Great Britain of the proposed tunnel.

1956 'GRIP.' How John Bull lost London; or, The capture of the Channel Tunnel. 4th edn. *London*, 1882. pp. 127.   BM
A forecast of a French invasion via the proposed Tunnel.

1957 HAWKSHAW, J. C. The Channel Tunnel. *Westminster*, 1882. pp. 19, with 2 la. fold. plates.   BM
Geological aspects.

1958 LAVALLEY, A. The Channel Tunnel railway between England and France: report on the geological explorations made in 1875 and 1876. *London*, 1882. pp. 31.   ICE
—— Chemin de fer sous-marin entre la France et l'Angleterre: rapports . . . 1875 et 1876. *Paris*, 1877. pp. 55, with plate, maps & plans.

1959 PARLIAMENT. Correspondence between the governments of France and England respecting the proposed Channel Tunnel and Railway: presented to both Houses of Parliament by command of Her Majesty, 1875. London, [1882?] pp. 199.   BM
Reprinted for the Channel Tunnel Co.

1960 POTTER, G. The Channel Tunnel and international progress. [1882.] pp. 24.   LSE
The Tunnel as a communication for international understanding and co-operation.

1961 SUBMARINA; or, Green eyes and blue glasses: an amusing spectacle of short sight, as exhibited by the glorious year of light A.D. 1882, recalled and recorded one hundred years after. (Channel Tunnel: danger to England or no danger?) *London*, 1882. pp. 48.   LSE

1962 SUBMARINE CONTINENTAL RLY. CO. Channel Tunnel: report of a meeting of the members . . . held at the Charing Cross Hotel on Friday the 20th January, 1882; Sir Edward Watkin in the chair. *London*, 1882. pp. 47.
BM

1963 VINDEX. England crushed: the secret of the Channel Tunnel revealed: being the literal translation of a secret despatch recently revised and adopted by an Austrian Federal Cabinet. (Warning—It will be dangerous to be found with this in possession on the Continent.) *London*, 1882. pp. 16. BM
An imaginary German plan to regain its 'old Saxon province of Kent' by capturing the Tunnel and using it for re-inforcements and supplies for the conquest of Gt. Britain.

1964 BRAMWELL, F. The Channel Tunnel. *London*, 1883. pp. 34. BM

1965 BRIGHT, J. The Channel Tunnel: Mr. Bright's remarkable forecast. *London*: *Channel Tunnel Co.*, [1883.] s.sh. BM
John Bright's speech to the Institution of Civil Engineers, 7th April, 1883.

1966 FORBES, H. C. G. Shall we have a Channel Tunnel? *Aberdeen*, 1883. pp. 39. BM
Reasons against.

1967 FORTH, C. Surprise of the Channel Tunnel. (A sensational story of the future.) *Liverpool*, 1883. pp. 22. BM
Invasion!

1968 KNOWLES, J. T. The Channel Tunnel and public opinion, compiled by James Knowles, editor of 'The Nineteenth Century'. *London*, 1883. pp. viii, 136. LSE
Reprints of fifty-one articles from *The Nineteenth Century* and other magazines, and from the correspondence columns of newspapers, all voicing opposition to the Tunnel project. The main contributors are: James Knowles; Prof. Goldwin Smith; Gen. Lintorn Simmons; Lord Bury; Sir E. Hamley; Lord Dunsany; John Fowler; Prince George, and Gen. Garnet J. Wolseley.

1969 WHITE, S. Shall we have the Channel Tunnel? Yes! *Andover*, [1883.] pp. 20. BM
A paper read before the Andover Debating Society on 21 November, 1882.

1970 WORKMEN'S COMMITTEE. The Channel Tunnel and industrial opinion: deputation of English workmen to Paris . . . *London*, 1883. pp. 47. BM
Speeches, including that of John Bright, and a report of the visit to Paris. The aim was to unite working class opinion in favour of the Tunnel and to make this known to the people of France. This was in opposition to the campaign against the Tunnel then running in *The Nineteenth Century* magazine.
See 1968, *The Channel Tunnel and public opinion* (1883), edited by J. T. Knowles of *The Nineteenth Century*.

1971 BERLIER, J. B. The pneumatic transmission of messages and parcels between Paris and London via Calais and Dover. Preliminary study and surveys. *London*, 1885. pp. 17, with map. BM
Two pneumatic tubes, diam. 11.8″, for telegrams, letters, and parcels up to 11 lb.

1972 BRADLAUGH, C. The Channel Tunnel: ought the democracy to oppose or support it? *London*, 1887. pp. 20. BM
Objections analysed: 'I am in favour.'

1973 CHANNEL Tunnel mysteries. *London*, 1887. pp. 43. LSE
Fears and doubts examined.

1974 GRIFFITHS, R. J. Under the deep, deep sea: the story of the Channel Tunnel; illustrated by Melton Prior. *London*, [1887.] pp. 95, with 7 illus., incl. diagrams of machinery and one of the railway tunnel entrance. BM

1975 The CHANNEL Tunnel: report of a meeting held at St. James's Hall, Piccadilly, 25th May, 1888. *London*, 1888. pp. 15. BM

1976 GLADSTONE, W. E. The Channel Tunnel: great speech in the House of Commons on June 27th, 1888, as revised by Mr. Gladstone. *London*, 1888. pp. 39. BM
pp. 5–24, a preface by Francis Lawley.

1977 HOZIER, H. M. The Channel Tunnel: a paper. *London*, 1888. pp. 12. BM
Advantages and military questions. 'No French general would dream of invading through a tunnel.'

1978 WATKIN, E. W. *and* SMITH, W. H. [Reprint of correspondence between E. W. Watkin and W. H. Smith, M.P. concerning the Channel Tunnel, June–July 1888.] pp. 14. BR
Privately printed.

1979 WHAT the press said on the Channel Tunnel, 1868–1875. *London*, 1888. pp. 51. LSE
Extracts from *The Times*, *Daily Telegraph*, and *Daily News*.

1980 CHANNEL BRIDGE & RAILWAY COMPANY. Le Pont sur la Manche: exposé complet de la question avec documents, cartes et planches. *Paris & London*, 1892. pp. 185. BM

1981 CHANNEL BRIDGE & RAILWAY COMPANY. Channel Bridge: detailed description of the project for the construction of a bridge across the English Channel . . . *London*, 1893. pp. 166, with 10 fold. plans. BR

1982 COLLARD, W. Draft Prospectus of the London & Paris Railway. [*London*, 1893.] pp. 24, with map, dated 28/12/1893. LSE
'Strictly private and confidential.'
A proposed railway from London via Chisle-

hurst, Maidstone, Wye, Dover, with ferry across to Calais and thence by rail to Paris.
—— Supplemental Note to the Draft Prospectus of the London & Paris Railway, by William Collard. December 1894. pp. 12.
LSE

1983 DAWKINS, B. On the history of the discovery of the South-Eastern coalfield. *In* 'Transactions of the Manchester Geological Society,' vol. 25, pt. 1, Session 1896–97. pp. 155–63. BM
Coal discovered in Channel Tunnel borings, 1886–1891, by B. Dawkins working under orders of E. W. Watkin, Chairman, South Eastern Rly. and Channel Tunnel Co.

1984 RODAKOWSKI, E. DE. The Channel Ferry: advantages and feasibility of a train-ferry between England and France . . . *London*, 1905. pp. xv, 236, with 19 tables & 49 plates. BM
pp. 16–34, previous attempts, including tunnel schemes.

1985 SARTIAUX, A. The Channel Tunnel from a military point of view. [1906.] pp. 6. BTCHR
Invasion of England via the Tunnel not possible. A. Sartiaux was General Administrator to the 'Association du Chemin de Fer Sousmarin entre la France et l'Angleterre'.

1986 BARCLAY, T. The Channel Tunnel. (Reprinted from 'The Westminster Review' of February 1907.) pp. 4. IME

1987 BUTLER, W. F. The Channel Tunnel. *London: Channel Tunnel Co.*, [1907.] s.sh. BM
No fear of invasion via Tunnel.

1988 The CHANNEL Tunnel, by a military railway expert. *London*, 1907. pp. 6. BM
Considerations in favour.

1989 CHANNEL TUNNEL CO. The Channel Tunnel. Relief model. [*London*, 1907?] 3 col. charts with an explanatory 2 page folder. BM

1990 The CHANNEL Tunnel. Royal United Service Institution. Important discussion, February 13th, 1907. [*London*, 1907.] pp. 10. BM
Discussion between Sir Charles Campbell, Francis Fox, Col. Maude, Arthur Diosy, Adml. F. A. Close, Lord Kingsburgh, and Sir J R. Colomb (chairman).

1991 NATIONAL DEFENCE ASSOCIATION. Proceedings of the National Defence Association: no. 1, The Channel Tunnel. [*London*, 1907.] pp. 24. LSE
Views of various prominent people.

1992 PERKINS, W. T. Channel Tunnel: reports by British and foreign engineers; [and] Papers on national defence by Gen. Sir William Butler, Maj.-Gen. Sir Alfred Turner, and Vice-Adml. Sir Charles Campbell. Edited by W. T. Perkins, Literary Secretary, Channel Tunnel Company. *Westminster*, 1907. pp. 56, with diagrams, maps, a fold. section of Tunnel, & bibliogr. notes.
BM
pp. 5–14, Report by Sir Douglas Fox & Partners.
pp. 15–39, Report by [A.] Sartiaux, from *Revue politique et parlementaire*, July 1906. This contains accounts of previous schemes.

1993 SARTIAUX, A. Le Tunnel sous-marin entre la France et l'Angleterre: conférence faite à la Société Industrielle du Nord de la France dans sa séance solennelle du 20 janvier, 1907. Extrait du Bulletin de la Société . . . 1907. *Lille*, 1907. pp. 59, with illus. & maps in text. BM

1994 TURNER, A. E. The Channel Tunnel: its chimerical dangers. [1907.] s.sh. BM
Fears of invasion via the Tunnel discounted.

1995 OPPENHEIM, L. Der Tunnel unter dem Ärmelkanal und das Völkerrecht. [1908.] pp. 16, with bibliogr. notes. BM
Sonderausdruck aus *Zeitschrift für Völkerrecht und Bundesstaatsrecht*, Band 2.

1996 VIERNOT, G. Le Tunnel sous la Manche. (Un grande problème international et militaire.) Ses rapports avec la securité de la France et de la Grande-Bretagne. *Paris*, [1908?] pp. 166, with bibliogr. notes. BM
Military considerations.

1997 FELL, A. The Channel Tunnel and food supplies in time of war. *London*, 1913. pp. 11. BM

1998 PERKINS, W. T. Channel Tunnel: deputation to the Prime Minister: full details of the present scheme; military, engineering, financial. Special articles by Lord Sydenham, Albert Sartiaux, Sir William Butler, Sir Alfred E. Turner, Lt.-Col. Alsager Pollock, Cmmdr. E. Hamilton Currey. Food supplies in time of war. Benefit of the Channel Tunnel to British trade. The late Sir Robert Giffen's Evidence. Opinions of the Press. [*London*:] *Channel Tunnel Co.*, December, 1913. pp. 136, with illus., diagrams, portraits, maps, & a fold. section. BM
Reprints of articles, pamphlets, speeches and reports 'issued while the Channel Tunnel Scheme is under the consideration of the Committee of Imperial Defence'.

1999 By TUBE to France: England's chance to aid great scheme for a Channel Tunnel. *London*, 1914. pp. 75. LSE
A collection of extracts, letters, speeches and illustrations from many sources.

2000 CLARKE, G. S. The Channel Tunnel: military aspect of the question. [*London*,] 1914. pp. 36. BM
An address to the House of Commons Channel Tunnel Committee: pp. 22–35, other Members' comments.

2001 DE HORSEY, A. F. R. National defence versus the Channel Tunnel. *London*, 1914. pp. 15.   BM
'Stupendous folly of connecting Great Britain with the Continent of Europe.'

2002 D'ERLANGER, E. The Channel Tunnel. *In* 'Jubilee of the Railway News, 1864–1914.' *London: Railway News*, [1914.] pp. 208–10.   BM

2003 FELL, A. The position of the Channel Tunnel question in May 1914: statement on behalf of the House of Commons Channel Tunnel Committee. *London*, 1914. pp. 19.   BM

2004 CHANNEL TUNNEL CO. The Channel Tunnel and the World War: deputation to Mr. Asquith: House of Commons Committee. *London*, January 1917. pp. 242. BM
A collection of essays and, pp. 74–195, press opinions, from many sources.

2005 DAILY CHRONICLE, *newspaper*. Charing Cross to Bagdad: an account by various experts of the great after-war combined reconstruction scheme including . . . the construction of the Channel Tunnel on a larger scale than hitherto contemplated. *London*, 1917. pp. 28.   LSE
Contains eleven essays on the Channel Tunnel, by P. C. Tempest, F. Fox, Lord Sydenham, and others.

2006 FELL, A. The British Government and the Channel Tunnel. *London*, 1917. pp. 15. BM
Urging Government support to build the Tunnel after the War.

2007 FELL, A. The Channel Tunnel: demands for German control. *Westminster: House of Commons Channel Tunnel Committee*, [1917.] s.sh.   BM
A reprint from *The Times* of 19 Dec., 1917, revealing German intentions for control of the Tunnel.

2008 FOX, F. Geographical aspects of the Channel Tunnel: paper read . . . at the meeting of the Royal Geographical Society, 23 April 1917. *London*, 1917. pp. 11, with diagram, map, & plate.   BM
From the *Geographical Journal*, August 1917.

2009 FELL, A. *and others*. The Channel Tunnel. 1, London and the Channel Tunnel: paper read by Sir Arthur Fell; 2, International Parliamentary Conference—the Tunnel in its commercial aspects: address by Sir A. Fell; 3, History, benefits and prospects of the Tunnel: lecture to British soldiers in Paris, by Baron Emile d'Erlanger; 4, From London to the Cape by rail: French and Spanish scheme of M. H. Bressler. [*London*, 1918.] pp. 89, with illus., maps & plans. BM

2010 CHANNEL TUNNEL CO. The Channel Tunnel: recent Parliamentary history. [*London*, 1920.] pp. 4.   BM

2011 PARLIAMENT—HOUSE OF COMMONS—CHANNEL TUNNEL COMMITTEE. Report of meeting in Standing Committee Room no. 14, Monday, 5th July 1920. Protest against delay of work. Support of Labour Party. Deputation to Prime Minister, Wednesday, 12 November, 1919. Reply of Mr. Lloyd George. [*London*, 1920.] pp. 30.   BM

2012 BALFOUR, A. Le Tunnel sous la Manche et les transports par ferry-boats. *Paris: Chambre du Commerce Internationale*, 1921. pp. 5–7.   LSE
Paper no. 1 of the First Congress, held in London, 1st July, 1921.

2013 FELL, A. The Channel Tunnel: its position in October 1921; strategic value of the Channel Tunnel: remarkable testimony by Marshal Foch. Unemployment at home: how the Tunnel would afford immediate relief. *London*, 1921. pp. 15.   BM

2014 PARLIAMENT—HOUSE OF COMMONS—CHANNEL TUNNEL COMMITTEE. Verbatim report of meeting held on July 18, 1923. Addresses by Baron Emile d'Erlanger and Sir Percy Tempest. *London*, [1923.] pp. 18.   LSE
Reprinted from the *Railway Gazette*, 27 July, 1923.

2015 PARLIAMENT—HOUSE OF COMMONS—CHANNEL TUNNEL COMMITTEE. Verbatim report of deputation to the Prime Minister . . . J. Ramsay MacDonald, Thursday, 26th June 1924, and Memorandum to the Cabinet and to the Committee of Imperial Defence. *London*, [1924.] pp. 30.   LSE
Reprinted from the *Railway Gazette*, 27 June & 4 July, 1924.

2016 METROPOLITAN-VICKERS ELECTRICAL CO. London & Paris Railway: estimated working expenses. [c. 1927.] pp. 33. *Typescript*.   LSE

2017 The CHANNEL Tunnel. [1928.] pp. 12. BM
A collection of articles on the imaginary danger of invasion via the Tunnel, published as a pamphlet.
pp. 1–3, 'The Channel Tunnel and national defence', by Gen. Sir Wm. Butler.
pp. 4–9, 'Military fears dispelled', by Maj.-Gen. Sir A. E. Turner.
pp. 10–12, 'A naval view', by Vice-Adml. Sir Chas. Campbell.

2018 COLLARD, W. Proposed London & Paris Railway: London and Paris in four and a half hours. *London*, 1895. pp. 26, with fold. map.   BM
London–Dover–Paris with steamer connection between Dover and Calais.
—— another edn. *Westminster*, 1928. pp. vi, 292.   BM
Includes Channel Tunnel schemes.

019 BURTT, P. London and Paris: proposed high speed electric railway. *Harpenden*, July 1929. pp. 17. *Reproduced typescript.* IT
A report addressed to 'Mr. Collard' concerning estimated receipts and expenses for a Channel Tunnel railway.

020 'CALLISTHENES.' Channel Tunnel articles reprinted from 'The Times' at the request of some Members of Parliament. *London: Selfridge & Co.*, Feb. 12, 1929. 8 la. fold. sheets. LSE
Fifty-one articles by 'Callisthenes.'

021 JAEGER, J. New avenues for British trade: proposed double jetty across the Channel, carrying railways and motor-roads on parallel dams and enclosing a canal of still water for barges. *Gryon S. Bex, Switzerland*, 1929. pp. 4, with an illus. of the proposed bridge. LSE

022 KENDALL, P. F. The proposed tunnel under 'la Manche' ... *London*, 1929. pp. 327–32. LSE
Reprinted from *The Naturalist* for October 1929.
Views of a geologist.

023 MARCHAL, J. Union douanière et organisation européenne. *Paris*, 1929. pp. 231. LSE
Includes Channel Tunnel.

024 RYVES, R. A. The Channel Tunnel project. *London*, 1929. pp. 56, with 3 illus. & a fold. diagram. BM
Largely concerned with William Low's scheme, but chap. 1 is an historical summary.

At the end of one of the BM copies (8236.e.18) is a typewritten inset of 8 pp. entitled 'The Author's addenda, May 1944,' and a further page in MS. is signed by him and dated 'June 1945'.

2025 BULL, W. The Channel Tunnel: a reply to the Government's decision. [*London*,] June 24, 1930. pp. 11. BM
Comments on the Report of the Channel Tunnel Committee, Economic Advisory Council (Cmd. 3513).

2026 CARVALHO, H. N. The Channel Tunnel. [*London*, 1930.] pp. 143–65. BM
An extract. Lecture delivered to the Institution of Sanitary Engineers, 18 December, 1929.

2027 SZLUMPER, G. S. Cross Channel transport. *London: Société des Ingénieurs Civils de France, British Section*, 1930. pp. 27. BM
Lecture, 5 March, 1930. A review of various methods of crossing; ship, train ferry, tunnel, bridge, aircraft. pp. 16–27, discussion.

2028 SHERRINGTON, C. E. R. The economic and traffic aspects of a Channel Tunnel. pp. 20. *Typescript.* IT
Paper, Institute of Transport, Guildford Group, 29 March, 1949.

2029 KEEN, P. A. The Channel Tunnel project. *In* 'Journal of Transport History,' vol. 3, no. 3, May 1958. pp. 132–44, with map, & 31 bibliogr. notes. BM

2030 ABEL, D. Channel underground: a new survey of the Channel Tunnel question. b *London: Pall Mall Press*, 1961. pp. xvi, 127, with frontis., 4 plates, diagrs. & a bibliography. BM

C9 SCOTLAND TO IRELAND TUNNEL SCHEME

031 MACASSEY, L. L. *and* SCOTT, W. Report on proposed railway tunnel between Scotland and Ireland. *London*, [1868.] pp. 16, with fold. plan & section. BM

032 NEALE, J. O'N. The real remedy for Ireland: an engineering solution; humbly submitted to an august and gracious lady. *London*, 1868. pp. 17. BM
A proposal to connect Ireland with Scotland by means of a causeway from Mould to Tor Point, 11 miles long and carrying six lines of railway.

033 ASHBURY, T. Proposed sub-marine tunnel between Scotland and Ireland. [1902.] pp. 73–8. *In his* 'Miscellaneous Papers.' *Manchester*, 1904. pc

034 ASHBURY, T. Submarine railways: is one from Great Britain to Ireland practicable?

pp. 37–41. *In his* 'Miscellaneous Papers'. *Manchester*, 1904. pc

2035 A PROPOSED tunnel under the Irish Channel. *In* 'Jubilee of the Railway News, 1864–1914.' *London: Railway News*, [1914.] p. 212, with 2 diagrams. BM

2036 TYRRELL, H. G. A tube to Ireland: a remedy for Ireland's unrest and a plea for its commercial betterment by means of a constructive enterprise rather than by fruitless legislation. An important link in the British Imperial Highway: in connection with the Labrador Railroad will shorten the time by several days from the Canadian West to London. [*Chicago*, 1914.] pp. 8, with map in text. BM

C 10 BRITISH RAIL TRANSPORT COMPARED WITH THAT OF OTHER COUNTRIES

2037 JACKSON, W. Lecture on rail roads, delivered . . . before the Massachusetts Charitable Mechanics Association. *Boston*, 1829. pp. 32. BM
British practice and experience explained in relation to American transport problems.

2038 FRAENZL, M. J. Statistische Übersicht der Eisenbahnen, Canäle und Dampfschiffahrten Europas und Amerikas. *Wien*, 1838. pp. 73, with fold. map. BM
pp. 16–19, Eisenbahnen, Gross-Britannien.

2039 DUNOYER, C. Esprit et méthodes comparés de l'Angleterre et de la France dans les entreprises de travaux publics, et en particulier des chemins de fer . . . *Paris*, 1840. pp. ii, 110. H

2040 COWDIN, J. Description and testimonials of the patent locomotive steam double pile driving and railway grading machine . . . also, remarks on railways in Europe and America . . . *London*, 1842. pp. 26, with illus. BM

2041 LANG, G. H. Letter to . . . W. E. Gladstone, M.P. . . . on the importance in a national point of view of railway extension . . . *London*, 1844. pp. 28. ICE
British railways handicapped by existing laws. The adaptation of law to railways in France and other countries.

2042 BEIL, J. A. Stand und Ergebnisse der deutschen, amerikanischen, englischen, französischen, belgischen, hollandischen, italienischen und russischen Eisenbahnen am Schlusse des Jahres 1843; mit einem Anhang enthaltend Beschreibung und detaillierte Übersichten der ausgeführten und im Bau begriffenen englischen und amerikanischen Eisenbahnen. *Frankfurt-am Main*, 1844. pp. 250, xxviii, 9. BM
pp. 20–49, 'Englische Eisenbahnen.'
—— another edn. 'Stand u. Ergebnisse der europäischen Eisenbahnen bis zu dem Jahr 1845.' *Wien*, 1845. pp. 138. BM
—— another edn. '. . . bis zu dem Jahr 1847.' *Wien*, 1847. pp. 296. BM

2043 ADAMS, W. B. The construction and duration of the permanent way of railways in Europe . . . *London*, 1854. pp. 57, with illus. ICE
Excerpt, *Min. Proc. I.C.E.*, vol. 11, 1851/2.

2044 COLBURN, Z. and HOLLEY, A. L. The permanent way and coal-burning locomotive boilers of European railways: with a comparison of the working economy of European and American lines and the principles upon which improvement must proceed . . . with

fifty-one engraved plates by J. Bien. *New York*, 1858. pp. 168. BM

2045 HAUCHECORNE, G. Tableaux statistiques des chemins de fer de l'Europe en exploitation pendant l'exercice 1866. *Cologne*, 1868. pp. 45. ICE
IV partie, Section G, 'Grande Bretagne et Irlande.' 'from official sources.'

2046 BAYNES, J. A. Railways in the U.K. and in India. *Hampstead*, 1873. pp. 4. ICE
Reprinted from *The Times* of 1st Sept., 1873. A statistical summary.

2047 FRANQUET DE FRANQUEVILLE, A. C. Les Chemins de fer en France et en Angleterre. *Paris*, 1873. p. 24. BM

2048 BAYNES, J. A. Memorandum on the cost, traffic and working of the railways in the United Kingdom and in India for the year 1873 compared with 1872. *London*, 1874. pp. 4. ICE
Signed 'J. A. Baynes, Bombay, Baroda & Central India Rly. . . . London.'

2049 BAYNES, J. A. Memorandum on the cost, traffic and working of the railways in the United Kingdom and in India for the year 1874 compared with 1873. *London*, 1875. pp. 8. ICE

2050 [EVANS, W. W.] American v. English locomotives: correspondence, criticism and commentary respecting their relative merits. *Leeds*, 1880. pp. 79. ICE
—— another edn. *New York*, 1880. pp. 78. BM

2051 MINOT, R. S. Railway travel in Europe and America; with 25 tables of recent and novel statistics of journeys, speeds, fares, etc., for travellers and others. *Boston*, 1882. pp. 28. BM

2052 EDDY, W. L'Employé de chemins de fer: sa condition en France et en Angleterre. *Paris*, 1883. pp. 56. BM
A comparison of various aspects of railway employment in France and in Britain.

2053 MACALPINE, W. J. The New York Arcade Railway as projected, compared with the underground railways of London. Report to the Broadway Underground Railway Co. [*New York*,] 1884. pp. 24. P

2054 DORSEY, E. B. English and American railroads compared . . . *New York*, 1887. pp. 142. BM
Excerpt, *Trans. Amer. Soc. Civil Engineers*, vol. 15, 1886.
Statistical analyses of all aspects of railways; 60 tables & 4 fold. plates. (An edition of 78 pp. + 58 pp. suppl. was published in New York in 1886.)

2055 JEANS, J. S. Railway problems: an inquiry into the economic conditions of railway working in different countries. *London*, 1887. pp. xxviii, 560.　　　　　BM

2056 PICARD, A. Traité des chemins de fer: économie politique, commerce, finances, administration, droit. Études comparées sur les chemins de fer étrangers. *Paris*, 1887. 4 vols.　　　　　LSE

2057 ADAMS, C. F. Railroads: their origin and problems. *New York*, 1878. pp. 216.　　BM
　　pp. 1–36, railways in the U.K. up to the Liverpool & Manchester, and at various points after; comparisons with American practice.
　　pp. 80–216, The difficulties of adapting existing legislation to railways in various countries, incl., pp. 80–94, Gt. Britain.
　　—— rev. edn. *New York & London*, 1886. pp. 230.　　　　　RC
　　—— rev. edn. *New York & London*, 1888.　　　　　PO

2058 GOMEL, C. Les Droits de l'état sur les tarifs de chemins de fer en Angleterre et aux États-Unis. *Paris*, 1891. pp. 28.　　BM

2059 JEFFERDS, M. R. Chart showing the railway mileage area, density of population increase of railways since 1881, and the adequate railway service required for the principal countries of the world, as compared with Belgium. *London*, 1892. s.sh.　　BM

2060 ACWORTH, W. M. English and American railways: a comparison and a contrast. *In* MacCain, C. C., 'Compendium of Transportation Theories.' Kensington Series. First Book. *Washington*, 1893. pp. 139–47.　　　　　BM

2061 HEAD, J. American rail- and tram-ways. *Middlesbrough*, 1895. pp. 64, with illus.　　　　　ICE
　　Comparisons between British and American railways.

2062 LEIGHTON, G. B. Observations of English railway practice with some account of the Fifth Session of the International Railway Congress. [*St. Louis*,] 1896. pp. 15.　　BM
　　Reprinted from *Journal of the Association of Engineering Societies*, vol. 16, no. 1, January 1896.

2063 SULLIVAN, P. F. Comparison of street railway conditions and methods in Europe and the United States. *Chicago*, 1897. pp. 30.　　　　　LSE
　　Glasgow tramways taken as a British example.

2064 HINES, W. D. Railway regulation: the English system contrasted with the demands of the Interstate Commerce Commission. *Louisville*, 1898. pp. 8.　　　　　LSE

2065 PANGBORN, J. G. Side lights on management: world systems railways. *Baltimore*, 1901. pp. 245.　　　　　BM
　　pp. [167]–200, British railways (management, government control, etc.), compared with U.S. practice.

2066 CHAPMAN, S. J. Work and wages, in continuation of Lord Brassey's 'Work and wages' and 'Foreign work and wages.' Part 1, Foreign competition . . . *London*, 1904. pp. xxxv, 301.　　　　　BM
　　pp. 257–96, 'Railways'.

2067 DIGBY, W. P. Statistics of British and American rolling-stock. *London: Society of Engineers*, 1905. pp. 16.　　　　　LSE
　　Relationship between the number of locomotives and rolling stock and volume of traffic, 1894–1904.

2068 ACWORTH, W. M. Railroad accounting in America vs. England. *New York*, 1910. pp. 12.　　　　　LSE
　　Reprinted from the *North American Review*, March 1910.

2069 BUREAU OF RAILWAY ECONOMICS [Washington]. Comparative railway statistics of the United States, the United Kingdom, France and Germany, for 1900 and 1909. *Washington*, 1911, pp. 47. [*Bulletin*, no. 24.]　　　　　BRE

2070 PARSONS, W. B. Railways. [*San Francisco*, 1915.] pp. 46, with many tables.　　IT
　　'Advance copy; printed, not published.' Paper to be read at a meeting of the International Engineering Congress, San Francisco, 1915.
　　A general comparative account of railway development in many countries.

2071 ACWORTH, W. M. Historical sketch of government ownership of railroads in foreign countries; presented to the Joint Committee of Congress on Interstate Commerce, May 1917. *Washington*, 1917. pp. 63.　　LSE
　　Includes government control over railways in the British Isles.

2072 JACKSON, D. C. *and* MACGRATH, D. J. Street railway fares. *New York*, 1917.　BM
　　pp. 112–25, Some comparisons of American and British fare systems.

2073 WIENER, L. Train speeds. *Westminster*, [1919.] pp. 57, with 56 tables, & 51 maps & diagrams.　　　　　BM
　　Reprinted from the *Railway Gazette*.
　　A very detailed survey of contemporary scheduled runs on railways in various European countries, including Britain.

2074 BUREAU OF RAILWAY ECONOMICS [Washington]. Comparative railway statistics: United States and foreign countries, 1912. *Washington*, 1915. pp. 78. [*Consecutive Series*, no. 83.]　　　　　LSE

pp. 63–4, Basic tables for U.K. railways in 1912, compiled from official Board of Trade Returns.
pp. 65–78, Comparative tables.
—— another edn., for 1913. *Washington,* 1916. pp. 78. [*Consecutive Series*, no. 100; *Miscellaneous Series*, no. 25.]   IT
—— another edn., for 1916. *Washington,* 1920. pp. 66. [*Consecutive Series*, no. 170; *Miscellaneous Series*, no. 35.]   IT

2075 TURNER, D. L. New York, London, Paris, & Berlin transit conditions compared. *New York*, 1922. *Reproduced typescript.*   IT

2076 INTERNATONAL TRANSPORT WORKERS' FEDERATION, AMSTERDAM—RAILWAY-MEN'S SECTION Working conditions of railwaymen in different countries. *Amsterdam,* 1924. pp. 139.   TUC
pp. 65–98, Gt. Britain.

2077 BROWN, J. D., *and others.* Railway Labor Survey, prepared by J. Douglas Brown and associates. *New York: Social Science Research Council, Division of Industry & Trade,* 1933. pp. 153. *Reproduced typescript.*   LC
A comparison, U.S.A., Canada, and Gt. Britain.

2078 JOHNSTON, K. H. British Railways and economic recovery: a sociological study of the transport problem. *London: Clerke & Cockeran*, 1949. pp. 352, with bibliogr. notes.   BM
pp. 217–344, British and foreign railways compared.

2079 GIRARD, J. M. La Productivité du travail dans les chemins de fer: Allemagne, États-Unis, France, Grande-Bretagne. *Paris: Centre d'Études et de Mesures de Productivité,* [1956.] pp. 139, with tables & charts.   IT

C11 INTERNATIONAL CO-OPERATION

2080 REES, A. W. The international organisation of railway communications. Thesis, M.A., University of Wales 1938. pp. vi, 357. *Typescript.*   NLW

2081 INTERNATIONAL railway associations. *London: Railway Gazette*, 1943. pp. 22.   IT
Reprint, *Railway Gazette*, Dec. 1942.
Objects, scope and work of twenty associations, mostly European.

2082 MANCE, H. O. Frontiers, peace treaties and international organization. *London: Royal Institute of International Affairs*, 1946. pp. x, 196. [*International Transport & Communications.*]   BM

2083 WEDGWOOD, R. L. International rail
b   transport. *London: Oxford University Press,* [1946.] pp. xii, 162, with a bibliography. [*International Transport & Communications.*]   BM
Railways within the framework of growing international co-operation. Contains much

information on national and international organisations concerned wholly or partly with railway administration.

2084 ZWALF, M. European transport: the way to unity: a report prepared for a Committee of the Fabian International Bureau by M. Zwalf. *London: Fabian Society*, March 1946. pp. 39.   BM
'No real solution so long as the worship of the national state and its sovereignty prevents the internationalization of European transport.' (Leonard Woolf's Foreword.)

2085 HAUSTEIN, W. Das internationale öffentliche Eisenbahnrecht. *Frankfurt-am-Main,* 1953. pp. xxxi, 304.   IT

2086 GEAR, J. H. S. *and* DEUTSCHMAN, Z. Disease control and international travel: a review of the international sanitary regulations. *Geneva: World Health Organization,* 1956. pp. 73.   BM

D SPECIAL TYPES OF RAILWAY AND LOCOMOTION

Marginal symbols: **b** bibliographies
c chronologies

D1 LIGHT RAILWAYS AND TRAMWAYS

including electric tramways (general works)

Historical

2087 THOMPSON, C. L. A Catalogue of Books, reports, papers and articles relating to light
b railways. *London*, 1895. pp. 39.   BM

2088 TRAIN, G. F. My life in many states and in foreign lands, dictated in my seventy-fourth year . . . *New York*, 1902. pp. xxi, 348, with 8 plates, incl. portraits.   pc
pp. 259 et seq., Building the first street railways in England.

2089 ALLEN, E. & CO. Tramway evolution: part one; tramway track, 1883 to 1923; or, 40 years of tramway practice. By Fred Bland. Part two, Points and crossings. 4th edn. [*Sheffield*, 1928.] pp. 58, with many illus.   IME
Manufacturer's catalogue.

2090 SHEPPARD, T. Early fare collecting boxes. *In* 'Early tramcars, and record of additions.' *Hull: Hull Railway Museum*, 1940. pp. 6, with illus. [*Publication* no. 210.]   pc
Reprinted from *Transport World*, April 11, 1940.
Horse trams and buses.

2091 SHEPPARD, T. England's oldest tramcar. *In* 'Early tramcars, and record of additions.' *Hull: Hull Railway Museum*, 1940. pp. 16, with 4 illus. [*Publication* no. 210.]   BM
Reprinted from *Passenger Transport Journal*, 11 October, 1940.
An account of the earliest horse tram, Ryde Pier Co., 1863. Included is a second essay, pp. 11–16, 'No. 1 steam tram' describing a Kitson car of 1882, Portstewart Tramway Co., Northern Ireland; with 2 illus.

2092 GRUNDY, A. G. My fifty years in transport . . . *London: Transport World*, 1944. pp. 39, with illus.   BM
A. G. Grundy was with North Staffordshire Steam Tramways; Blackburn Tramways; Stalybridge, Hyde, Mossley, & Dukinfield Transport & Electricity Board.

2093 KIDNER, R. W. The light railways of Britain: a survey of the development of narrow gauge and light standard gauge passenger railways, with notes on present-day locomotive stocks. *Chislehurst: Oakwood Press*, 1947. pp. 40, with illus., tables & maps.
                BM

2094 KIDNER, R. W. Multiple unit trains, railmotors and tramcars, 1829–1947: cable, atmospheric, steam, electric, petrol, petrol-electric, battery-electric, compressed air, heavy oil. *South Godstone: Oakwood Press*, 1947. pp. 107–50, with 40 plates. [*A Short History of Mechanical Traction & Travel*, part 6.]   BM
Also issued as part of a collected edition, vol. 2, Rail. 1947.

2095 KIDNER, R. W. A short history of mechanical traction and travel. vol. 2, Rail. *Chislehurst: Oakwood Press*, 1947. pp. 150, with 40 plates.   BM
pp. 107–50, Multiple-unit trains, rail-motors and tramcars, 1825–1947. Part of a collected edition. Previously published separately, 1947.

2096 KIDNER, R. W. The Colonel Stephens railways. *Sidcup: Oakwood Press*, 1936. pp. 12, with 5 plates, maps & illus. [*Light Railway Handbook*, no. 1.]   BM
Kent & East Sussex; East Kent; Shropshire & Montgomeryshire; Weston, Clevedon & Portishead; West Sussex.
—— 2nd edn., *Chislehurst*, 1937. pp. 12. BM
—— 3rd, *South Godstone*, 1948. pp. 16. BM

2097 THORNTON, W. The nine lives of Citizen Train. *New York*, 1948. pp. xii, 327, with 11 plates, incl. portraits, a bibliography.   BM
pp. 49–107, Pioneer of British street railways. [George F. Train.]

2098 KIDNER, R. W. British light railways: narrow gauge and independent standard gauge passenger-carrying lines. [*Sidcup:*] *Oakwood Press*, 1938. pp. 100, with many illus. on plates and in text.   BM
A composite edition of the *Light Railway Handbooks*, nos. 1–6, revised.
The Colonel Stephens railways (Kent & East Sussex; East Kent; Shropshire & Montgomeryshire; Weston, Clevedon & Portishead; West Sussex); Standard gauge light railways; Narrow gauge railways of North Wales; English narrow gauge railways; Three-foot gauge railways of Northern Ireland; Light railways of Eire, Isle of Man and Channel Islands; Addenda and errata.
——2nd edn. 'The Light Railway Handbook: a collected edition including Handbooks 1–6 and 8. A summary of the history and equipment of light railways constructed under the Acts of 1864 and 1896, and other public narrow-gauge and lightly-laid standard gauge lines.' (Second revised edition [of 'British light railways', 1938]).

South Godstone, 1950. pp. [119,] with, pp. 65–80, 'Light and narrow gauge locomotives' [with detailed lists]; and 'Appendices to Light Railway Handbook' [with plates & maps].   BM
Similar revised editions are issued from time to time.

2099 TONKS, E. S. Light and miniature railway locomotives of Great Britain. [*Birmingham:*] *Birmingham Locomotive Club*, 1950. pp. 44, with 20 illus. on 10 plates, & detailed lists.   BM

*2100 ROLT, L. T. C. *and* WHITEHOUSE, P. B. Lines of Character. *London: Constable*, 1952. pp. 188, with 66 illus. on plates.   BM
Essays on railway 'byways' in Great Britain and Ireland.

2101 LEE, C. E. The English street tramways of
b George Francis Train. *In* 'Journal of Transport History,' vol. 1, no. 1, May 1953. pp. 20–7, *and* vol. 1, no. 2, November 1953, pp. 97–108, with 31 bibliogr. notes.   BM

*2102 ELLIS, C. H. Popular carriage: two centuries of carriage design for road and rail. *London: British Transport Commission*, 1954. pp. 32, with illus.   BM
Includes tram-cars.

2103 WHITCOMBE, H. A. The history of the steam tram. *Lewes*, 1937. pp. 55, with 2 fold. plates, & illus. in text.   BM
Reprinted from the *Journal of the Institution of Locomotive Engineers, Paper* no. 367.
—— another edn. *South Godstone: Oakwood Press*, 1954. pp. 48. [*Locomotion Papers*, no. 9.]   BM

2104 BRITISH ELECTRIC TRACTION COMPANY. Five decades of B.E.T.: the story of the British Electric Traction Company, Ltd. [By] Roger Fulford. *London*, Oct. 1946. pp. 84, with illus. & fold. map.   BR
Includes tramways.
—— Supplementary volume: 'The sixth decade, 1946–1956.' *London*, Oct. 1956. pp. xxi, 86[87].   BR

2105 MACNEILL, D. B. Ulster tramways and light railways. *Belfast: Belfast Museum & Art Gallery*, [1956.] pp. 34, with 20 illus., map & bibliogr. notes. [*Transport Handbook* no. 1.]   IT
Histories of individual lines.

2106 NOCK, O. S. Branch lines. *London: Batsford*, 1957. pp. 184, with plates & illus.   BM

2107 KIDNER, R. W. The railcar, 1847–1939. *Sidcup: Oakwood Press*, 1939. pp. 65, with illus. on plates, & diagrams.   BM
—— The development of the railcar. *South Godstone: Oakwood Press*, 1958. pp. 56, with 25 illus. on 8 plates, & diagrams. [*Locomotion Papers*, no. 12.] (2nd edn. of 'The railcar'.)   BM

2108 KIDNER, R. W. Standard gauge light railways. *Sidcup: Oakwood Press*, 1937. pp. 13–28, with 6 plates, maps & diagrams. [*Light Railway Handbooks*, no. 4.]   BM
—— 2nd edn. *Chislehurst*, 1947. pp. [13]–28.   BM

—— 4th, *Lingfield*, [1958.] pp. 40, with 16 plates. [*Light Railway Handbooks*, no. 1.]   BM

2109 KIDNER, R. W. Light and narrow gauge locomotives. 2nd edn. *South Godstone: Oakwood Press*, 1949. pp. 65–80, with 11 plates. [*Light Railway Handbooks*, no. 8.]   BM
—— 3rd edn, *Lingfield*, [1959.] pp. 32.

*2110 LEWTHWAITE, G. C. Branch Line Index:
b a list of articles on branch lines in Great Britain which have appeared in the following magazines, from their inception to the end of 1957: Railway Magazine; Trains Illustrated; Railway World. Compiled by G. C. Lewthwaite for the Branch Line Society. *Leeds: Branch Line Society*, 1960. pp. 15. [*Occasional Publications*, no. 1.]   BM
—— Supplement, 1958–62. *Leeds*, 1962. pp. [7.] *Reproduced typescript.* [*Occasional Publications*, no. 1a.]   BM
Articles appearing in 1963 and onwards are to be published annually in the Society's magazine, *Branch Line News*.

2111 CARTER, E. F. Trams and tramways. *London: W. & G. Foyle*, 1961. pp. 95, with 15 illus.   BM

2112 JOYCE, J. The British tramway scene. *Cricklewood: Light Railway Transport League*, 1961. pp. 31, with 93 illus.   BM
A selection of illustrations from the *Modern Tramways* since 1938.

*2113 KLAPPER, C. The golden age of tramways.
b *London: Routledge & Kegan Paul*, 1961.
c pp. xiii, 327, with 47 plates & 14 illus. in text.   BM
The appendix includes a bibliography, a list of tramway abandonments, 1914–1952, and a list of tramway vehicles preserved.

2114 WILSON, F. E. The British tram. *London: Percival Marshall*, 1961. pp. vii, 87, with frontis., illus., & diagrams.   BM

*2115 BETT, W. H. *and* GILLHAM, J. C. Great British tramway networks. *London: Light Railway Transport League*, 1940. pp. 85, with 6 maps, & illus.   BM
—— 2nd edn. *London*, 1944. pp. 96.   BM
—— 3rd edn. *London*, 1957. pp. 223, with 113 illus. & 19 maps (9 fold. in pocket).   BM
The third edition, completely revised and much enlarged, and with a detailed index, provides a record of every tramway and light railway planned, constructed or operated in the British Isles, including pier railways, miniature railways and cliff lifts.

—— 4th edn. *London*, 1962. pp. 200, with 122 illus. on 56 plates & 20 maps (9 fold. in pocket). BM

A further revision with added subject coverage and historical detail. Every known tramway or electric light railway in the British Isles is described or referred to, and depicted on maps.

2116 PRICE, J. H. Tramcars. *London: Ian Allan*, [1963]. pp. 64, with 54 illus., & a list of 114 preserved cars. [*Veteran & Vintage Series.*] BM

Descriptions of vehicles representing a century of tramway development.

2117 DAVIES, W. J. K. Light railways: their rise and decline. *London: Ian Allan*, 1964. pp. 312, with frontis., 64 illus. on 32 plates, 26 maps, plans & diagrams, 48 tables, a glossary & a bibliography. BM

A detailed survey related throughout to economic and geographic factors of cause and effect, generally and locally. pp. 49–82, British Isles.

Included in the Appendices; a letter giving Sir Arthur Heywood's views on light railways, Sir Robert Walker's views on agricultural light railways, notes on the theories and work of E. R. Calthrop, and a transcript of the Light Railways Act (1896).

Contemporaneous

2118 ADAMS, W. B. Road progress; or, Amalgamation of railways and highways for agricultural improvement. *London*, 1850. pp. 76, with 3 fold. diagrams. BM

Railways on roads; light railways.

2119 SHARPE, E. A letter on branch railways addressed to . . . Lord Stanley of Alderley . . . containing suggestions for the creation of a system of secondary railways for the agricultural districts; with an appendix and a map. *London*, 1857. pp. 36. BM

Narrow-gauge railways.

2120 BRUCE, G. B. Street railways. [*Westminster*, 1860.] pp. 10. ICE

Returning from a visit to the U.S.A., G. B. Bruce writes in favour of their adoption in Britain.

2121 LIVERPOOL TOWN COUNCIL. Report on horse railways. (By J. Newlands, Borough Engineer.) *Liverpool*, 1860. pp. 18. ICE

2122 TRAIN, G. F. Observations on horse railways . . . addressed to Milner Gibson, M. P., President of the Board of Trade. *London & Liverpool*, 1860. pp. 56, with plate. ICE

'The age of omnibuses in crowded cities is passed. The age of horse railways has commenced.' Examples drawn from American tramways but British also referred to.

2123 TRAIN, G. F. Observations on street railways by George Francis Train, addressed to . . . Milner Gibson, M.P., President of the Board of Trade, London. Second edition, with Appendix. *London & Liverpool*, 1860. pp. viii, 114. BM

A collection of reports, letters, extracts from journals and Press opinions on street railways generally, in America, and on the eve of the introduction of the first tramway in Europe, between Woodside Ferry and Birkenhead Park.

2124 TRAIN, G. F. Report of the banquet given by George Francis Train of Boston, U.S. to inaugurate the opening of the first street railway in Europe at Birkenhead, August 30, 1860; with opinions of the press on the subject of street railways. *Liverpool*, 1860. pp. 117, with fold. plate. BM

2125 TRAIN, G. F. Street railways: a lecture delivered before the members of the Greenwich Literary Institution, December 18, 1860. *London*, 1860. pp. 21. NLC

2126 HAWORTH, J. Paper on street railways . . . *Manchester*, 1861. pp. 7. BM

Advocating his patent rail for street railways.

2127 [TRAIN, G. F.] Report of the banquet given by George Francis Train . . . at St. James's Hall, Piccadilly, to inaugurate the opening of the first street railway in London, The Marble Arch line, March 23rd, 1861; with opinions of the press and extracts on the subject of street railways. *London*, 1861. pp. 110. LSE

pp. 51–110, Press opinions.

2128 [GILES, J.] The railway system: how to make it pay the shareholders and accom[m]odate the public. *London*, 1865. pp. 8. [*Exchange Essays*, no. 1.] LSE

Branch lines the cause of financial difficulties of railways. Solution—road locomotives instead. Ends with an advert. of Giles' light road passenger engines.

2129 NOBLE, J. & Co. Drawing and description of the Crescent rail; also, an article on street railways . . . *London*, 1866. pp. 8. BM

2130 NOBLE, J. & Co. Facts respecting street railways: the substance of a series of official reports from the cities of New York, Brooklyn, Boston . . . *London*, 1866. pp. 55. BM

2131 FOX, C. D. On the construction of future branch railways in the United Kingdom. *London*, 1867. pp. 16. BM

2132 BRIGHT, H. Remarks on street tramways applied to London and its suburbs. *London*, 1868, pp. 15, with 3 plates & map. BM

Cover title *The tramway question as applied to London and its suburbs.*

2133 MACKAY, C. Street tramways for London: their utility, convenience, and necessity . . . *London*, 1868. pp. 19. BM

On p. [20,] 'Description of the Crescent rail' [of John Noble & Co.].

2134 NOBLE, J. & Co. Street tramways as they will affect the ordinary users of the roads and householders: a reprint of a pamphlet

issued by the London General Omnibus Company, with observations thereon . . . *London*, [1868.] pp. 11.   LSE
A point for point reply.

2135 MUIR, W. J. C. Light railways . . . *Edinburgh*, 1869. pp. 20.   ICE
Advantages and disadvantages.

2136 ADAMS, W. B. Tramways for streets and roads, and their sequences . . . *London*, 1870. pp. 32.   LSE
Reprinted from the *Journal of the Society of Arts*, 11 March, 1870.

2137 GROVER, J. W. The facilities of 'flexible' rolling stock for economically constructing, maintaining and working railways or tramways. *London*, 1870. pp. 23.   ICE

2138 ELLIS, H. S. Light railways. *Exeter*, [1872.] pp. 20.   BM
Advocating standard-gauge light railways.

2139 SERAFON, F. Étude sur les chemins de fer, les tramways, et les moyens de transport en commun à Paris et à Londres, suivie d'une notice sur la construction et l'exploitation des tramways, avec carte et planches. *Paris*, 1872. pp. viii, 110, with 3 fold. plates in pocket.   BM

2140 STREET tramways, the cars drawn by horses. *Melbourne*, 1872. pp. 12.   BM
Contains accounts of tramways in London and Glasgow.

2141 PAIN, A. C. Light railways and tramroads: their advantages to landowners, cost, mode of construction and working; with remarks on the raising of the necessary capital. *London*, 1873. pp. 24.   BM
Reprinted from *The Field*.
pp. 18–24, extracts from relevant Acts.

2142 SALFORD BOROUGH COUNCIL. Tramways: report. (Report of the Parliamentary Sub-Committee to the Council of the Borough of Salford.) [Chairman, T. Barlow.] *Salford*, 1873. pp. 15.   IT
Report of an inspection of tramway systems in London, Glasgow and Edinburgh.

2143 COTTON, C. P. Manual of Railway Engineering in Ireland, with appendices including the Irish Tramway Acts. *Dublin*, 1861. pp. iv, 111, with 2 fold. plates (specimen deposited plans).   BM
—— 2nd edn. 'Manual of Railway Engineering for the field and the office'. *Dublin*, 1874. pp. 181.   BM

2144 GRANTHAM, J. Grantham's steam car for tramways. *London & Aylesbury*, 1874. pp. 15, with plate.   ICE

2145 TODD, L. J. Some remarks on working street tramway lines by steam power, with description of various engines. *Leith*, 1874. pp. 15, with 9 sheets (some fold.) of detailed coloured drawings of locomotives (steam, ammonia and accumulator).   ICE
With the ICE copy is a letter from the author.

2146 DOWSON, J. E. *and* DOWSON, A. Tramways: their construction and working. *London*, 1875. pp. 65.   BM

2147 CLARK, D. K. Tramways. *In* Bevan, G. P. 'British manufacturing industries.' *London*, 1876. pp. 215–8.   BM

2148 LONGRIDGE, J. A. Railway extension. *London*, 1877. pp. 48.   ICE
Light railways for rural and for hilly districts using specially constructed locomotives; with estimates of quantities and costs.

2149 MATHESON, E. Tramways in town and country. Reprinted from 'Aid book to engineering enterprise abroad' [by Matheson.] *London*, 1878. pp. 41.   BM
Historical and contemporary review of tramways.

2150 [WEBB, W.] A few observations on mechanical power on tramways; together with the reports of the three Select Committees of the House of Commons upon the subject. [*London*,] 1878. pp. 55.   ICE
Steam power for tramways.

2151 GUNSON, W. T. Paper on an improved system of tramway construction. *Manchester*, 1879. pp. 14.   ICE
Problem of the subsiding of sets adjacent to rails. Suggests embedding rails in longitudinal granite curbs.

2152 JONES, A. W. A paper on modern tramway construction; read before the Society of Engineers on 3 Nov., 1879. [1879.] pp. 179–96, with fold. plate.   ICE

2153 RANSOMES & RAPIER. The tramway nuisance and its true remedy; with coloured illustrations. An address to local authorities. *London*, [1879.] pp. 11.   BM
Advocating wider grooves to accommodate road vehicles also.

2154 VIGNOLES, C. B. Permanent way for tramways. *Westminster*, [1879.] pp. 5, with la. fold. plate.   ICE
—— another edn. [1879.] pp. 5, with 2 fold. plates.   ICE

2155 MILLS, W. H. Remarks made by W. H. Mills, Vice President of the Institution of Civil Engineers of Ireland, at the close of the discussion on the papers on narrow gauge railways and light railways, at the meeting on the 4th May, 1881. [*Dublin*, 1881.] pp. 10.   LSE
'For private circulation only.'
Comments on the papers by C. F. Green and by W. Lewis. Some commonly held ideas on the advantages of narrow gauge disputed. The Ballymena & Larne Rly. referred to.

2156 SCHOOL OF MILITARY ENGINEERING [Chatham]. Lectures. Light and temporary railways (by Charles Douglas Fox), *and*

Temporary expedients in engineering construction (by Charles Lean). *Chatham*, 1881. pp. 52, with 23 diagrams.　　ICE
'Printed for private circulation only.'

2157 PAIN, C. S. Hints on tramways. *Liverpool*, [1882.] pp. 4, with 4 la. diagrams.　　ICE
Introducing his patent 'lift out' rail.

2158 SLOANE, J. S. A few words on tramways and light railways applicable to the requirements of Ireland at the present time. *Dublin*, 1883. pp. 23.　　ICE

2159 BALLARD, S. Cheap railways for rural districts. *Malvern*, [1884.] pp. 11.　　BM

2160 COLE, T. Steam tramways: a paper read before the Civil & Mechanical Engineers' Society on the 26 March, 1884. *London*, 1884. pp. 13.　　ICE

2161 LONGRIDGE, J. A. Longridge's patent locomotive. *London*, 1885. pp. 11, with 4 fold. diagrams.　　ICE
For light railways with heavy gradients and sharp curves.

2162 DUDLEY & STOURBRIDGE TRAMWAYS COMPANY. Tramway and omnibus companies: drivers' and conductors' wages: scheme [of] Dudley & Stourbridge Tramways Company for payment by result. *Birmingham*, [1886.] 3 parts (s.sh. & 2 ruled ledger pages).　　BM
A plan to dispense with way bills. Instead, penny tickets only, to be collected and destroyed at the end of every stage and when the passenger leaves the car. Wages based upon the number of tickets issued.

2163 LAWFORD, W. Paper on light railways; read before the Society of Engineers, 1 Oct., 1888. [*London*, 1888.] pp. 161–90.　　ICE
Lecture and discussion on the merits of light railways.

2164 SELLON, S. P. W. d'A. A few arguments in favour of light or road railways: a paper read before the British Association at Bath. *London*, [1888.] pp. 15.　　ICE
Light railways for rural areas.

2165 WALTON, J. B. Railways for rural and under-developed districts: a paper read before the Civil & Mechanical Engineers' Society . . . 26 April, 1888. *London*, 1888. pp. 23.　　ICE
Light railways, narrow gauge, and road railways, and steam tramways.

2166 DAILY EXPRESS [Dublin], *newspaper*. Mr. Balfour's Light Railway Act: the scheduled lines with text of the Act by a special contributor. [*Dublin*, 1889.] pp. 44. [*Daily Express Extras*, no. 1.]　　LSE
Explanatory.

2167 MORE, J. Tramway permanent way. *London: Institution of Civil Engineers*, 1891. pp. 32, with diagrams.　　PO
Excerpt, *Min. Proc. I.C.E.*, vol. 103, Session 1890–91. pt. 1.

2168 The WALLER-MANVILLE system of electric traction. *London*, 1891. pp. 11, with la. fold. diagram.　　ICE
Underground (conduit) conductors for tramways.

2169 WYNNE, F. Direct electric tramway traction with surface construction. (Wynne's Patents.) *London*, [1892.] pp. 9, with illus. & 2 fold. diagrams.　　PO
Surface rail contact energised by passing car.

2170 ACWORTH, W. M. Light railways. *London*, 1894. pp. 21.　　LSE
'Author's reprint' from the *Journal of the Royal Agricultural Society of England*, vol. 5, 3rd series, part 4.
Light railways and their advantages.

2171 CLARK, D. K. Tramways: their construction and working; embracing a comprehensive history of the system with an exhaustive analysis of the various modes of traction, including horse power, steam, heated water and compressed air; a description of the varieties of rolling stock and ample details of cost and working expenses, with special reference to the tramways of the United Kingdom . . . *London*, 1878. pp. xxii, 434, with fold. plates, & illus.　　BM
—— 2nd edn., rewritten and greatly enlarged, *London*, 1894. pp. xxxv, 758.　　BM
—— Tramways: construction et exploitation . . . par D. K. Clark. Ouvrage traduit de l'anglais . . . par M. O. Chemin. *Paris*, 1880. 2 vols. (text & plates.)
—— Die Strassenbahnen: deren Anlage und Betrieb . . . *Leipzig*, 1879, 80.
—— another edn., *Leipzig*, 1886.

2172 HAMMOND, R. Electric street tramways. pp. 30, with illus.　　UL(GL)
Paper, Annual Meeting, Incorporated Association of Municipal & County Engineers, London, 21, 22 & 23 June, 1894.

2173 TECHNICAL CORRESPONDENCE AGENCY. Report on light railways for agricultural districts: presented to the Railway Department of the Board of Trade, December 1894. pp. 17. *Typescript*.　　LSE

2174 HEWSON, T. Tramways . . . *Leeds*, 1895. pp. 20, with 11 diagrams on 6 fold. plates.　　ICE
Paper, I.C.E. Yorkshire Students' Assoc.
On tramway track; based on twenty years experience with Leeds tramways.

2175 LEEDS CITY CORPORATION. Report of the Sub-Highways (Tramways) Committee to the Highways Committee . . . of their investigations as to tramway traction, and recommendations thereon. *Leeds*, 1895. pp. 35.   LSE

2176 OWEN, L. *and* RUSSELL, J. Engineering notes as to light railways. [*London*, 1895.] pp. 8.   LSE
Non-technical.

2177 PAIN, A. C. Paper on light railways. *London: Surveyors' Institution*, [1895.] pp. [199]–346 (including pp. 233–346, discussion). [*Transactions of the Surveyors' Institution*, Session 1894–95, vol. 27, pts. 7 & 8. Paper 208.]   BM

2178 WHITE, J. W. Light railways: papers read before the Liverpool Chamber of Commerce and the Society of Chemical Industry . . . partly printed from 'Engineering.' *Widnes*, 1895. pp. 128, with illus.   BM

2179 CALTHROP, E. R. The economics of light railway construction. *Leeds*, 1896. pp. 26, with 12 illus.   LSE

2180 DODD, C. *and* ALLAN, C. E. The law relating to light railways, comprising the Light Railways Act, 1896, together with the enactments relating thereto, with notes and index; also the rules made by the Board of Trade and the Standing Orders applicable, annotated. *London*, 1896. pp. xix, 334.   BM

2181 JOHNSON, F. R. Practical hints for light railways at home and abroad. *London*, 1896. pp. 31, [5,] with 6 plates.   PO

2182 MACKAY, J. C. Light railways for the United Kingdom, India and the colonies: a practical handbook . . . *London*, 1896. pp. xii, 322.   BM
Mostly colonial and foreign, but contains much information about lines in Great Britain and a list (pp. 96–9) of British light railways.

2183 PENARTH TRAMWAY SYNDICATE. Electric tramways as a means of rapid transit in and near towns. *Cardiff*, [1896.] pp. 16.   BM

2184 SCHOLEY, H. Electric tramways and railways, popularly explained. *London*, 1896. pp. 62, with illus.   BM

2185 BRITISH ELECTRIC TRACTION CO. On various methods of tramway working, with special reference to electric traction. *London*, [1897.] pp. 7, with 2 illus.   LSE

2186 DAWSON, P. Electric railways and tramways: their construction and operation: a practical handbook . . . entirely revised, enlarged . . . *London*, 1897. pp. xxvi, 677.   BM
pp. 371–439, British electric railways.

2187 [DOUGLAS.] BOROUGH OF DOUGLAS. Report and proceedings in relation to electric traction, presented to the Mayor, aldermen and councillors of the Borough of Douglas, by Thomas H. Nesbitt. *Douglas*, 1897. pp. 8, v-ccl, with plates.   PO
Reports on tramways in Bristol and in Prescot.

2188 FABIAN SOCIETY. The municipalization of tramways. *London*, 1897. pp. 15. [*Fabian Tract*, no. 77.]   BM

2189 HALDANE, J. W. C. Railway engineering, mechanical and electrical; with many plates and other illustrations. *London*, 1897. pp. xx, 562.   BM
Includes light railways and tramways.

2190 LIVERPOOL CHAMBER OF COMMERCE—SPECIAL COMMITTEE ON LIGHT RAILWAYS. Reports of papers and discussion . . . *Liverpool*, 1897. pp. 82.   LSE

2191 PAIN, A. C. What is true and false economy in light railway construction? [*London*, 1897.] pp. 3.   LSE
I.C.E. Engineering Conference, Section 1, Railways, 26 May, 1897. Paper no. 2.

2192 ROBINSON, L. S. Light railways . . . *London & Newcastle-on-Tyne*, 1897. pp. 21.   LSE
Paper, Federated Institution of Mining Engineers, 3 June, 1897. Reprinted from the *Transactions of the F.I.M.E.*

2193 STEWARD, H. A. The Light Railways Act, 1896, annotated; with an introduction and note upon the light railway systems of the Continent and of Ireland, together with the Board of Trade Rules . . . *London*, 1897. pp. x, 138.   RC

2194 BLACKPOOL CORPORATION. Electric tramways: report of a deputation on continental systems of electric traction. [*Blackpool*,] March 1898. pp. 25.   LSE

2195 LIVERPOOL CHAMBER OF COMMERCE. Report of a Special Committee on Light Railways upon schemes having for their object reduction in the cost of transit of merchandise between Liverpool and Manchester and the adjacent districts. (Chairman, G. H. Cox.) *Liverpool*, 1898. pp. 132, with diagrams & maps.   UL(GL)
A plateway, a tramway, and a system of conveying road vehicles on railway wagons are among the various schemes explained.

2196 LONDON COUNTY COUNCIL. Tramway traction: report on some forms of mechanical tramway traction that have been tried and more or less successfully worked in various towns and cities in England, on the Continent of Europe, and in America. By J. Allen Baker. *London*, [1898.] pp. 29, with 26 illus. on plates & 17 in text; tables. LCC

2197 LONDON UNITED TRAMWAYS. Electric tramways: verbatim reports of the leading municipal corporations of the United

Kingdom with lists of cities in which electric traction has been adopted. *London*, [1898.] pp. 24. LSE

2198 RICHMOND [SURREY] TOWN COUNCIL —TRAMWAYS SUB-COMMITTEE. Memorandum on municipal tramways, drafted at the request of the Tramways Sub-Committee, May 1898. (By W. Thompson.) *London*, [1898.] pp. 20. TUC
'Reprinted for the Fabian Society.'
A review of tramway undertakings of various types in operation, with financial and other details.

2199 BOUGHEY G. F. O. Light railways and the effect of recent legislation thereon. *Chatham*, 1899. pp. 19. [*Professional Papers of the Corps of Royal Engineers. Occasional Paper Series*, vol. 25. Paper IX. 1899.] BM
On the benefits to be expected for light railways from the Light Railways Act, 1896.

2200 CASSIER'S MAGAZINE. Electric Railway Number. (Vol. 16, no. 4.) *London*, August 1899. pp. [253]–540, with many illus. & pp. 229 (adverts.). BM
Electric railways and tramways.
—— Reprinted by Light Railway Transport League, 1960. BM

2201 COLE, W. H. Light railways at home and abroad . . . *London*, 1899. pp. x, 339, with plates & illus. BM

2202 LONDON COUNTY COUNCIL. Mechanical traction on tramways. Report by Alex. B. W. Kennedy. *London*, 1899. pp. 5. [*Publication* no. 438.] LCC
On the best system other than steam or cable; where an experimental line could be set up; general comments.

2203 ROBINSON, J. C. Electric traction on tramways: history, position and prospects. *London: British Thompson Houston Co.*, [1899.] pp. 40. PO
Paper, Cleveland Institute of Engineers, Stockton-on-Tees, 29 May, 1899.

2204 GREATOREX, A. D. Electric tramway
b traction. *London*, 1900. pp. 74[76], with 46 illus., bibliogr. notes & a bibliography. IT
A general reference work for the guidance of municipal engineers and town councils. Includes short accounts of individual tramways.

2205 INTERNATIONAL TRAMWAYS AND LIGHT RAILWAYS EXHIBITION. Official Catalogue of the International Tramways and Light Railways Exhibition held at the Horticultural Hall, Islington, London N., June 23rd to July 4th, 1900. *London*, [1900.] pp. 174. BM
Descriptions of exhibits at ninety-eight stalls. Not illustrated.

2206 A MEMORANDUM on co-operative railroads . . . by an expert . . . *London*, [1900.] pp. 30, x, with maps & tables. BM
A plan for financing light railways by groups of local public authorities.

2207 OCEAN ACCIDENT & GUARANTEE CORPORATION. Tramway statistics. *London*, [1900.] pp. 16. LSE
A directory with tabulated details of tramways and light railways (electric, steam and cable). Issued for general information. Contains a section on insurance at end.

2208 ASKHAM BROTHERS & WILSON, LTD. Special track work: tramway passing places, junctions, crossings, depot sidings, lay-outs, terminus junctions, etc. *Sheffield*, [1902.] pp. [46,] with illus. of layouts at Farnworth, Sheffield, Leeds, & Nottingham. PO

2209 BRICE, S. The law relating to tramways and light railways . . . *London*, 1898. pp. xxiv, 487. BM
—— 2nd edn. 'The law specially relating to tramways and light railways.' *London*, 1902. pp. xlii, 551. BM

2210 HOPKINSON, C. *and others*. Electric tramways. *London: Institution of Civil Engineers*, 1902. pp. 44, with la. fold. chart. LSE
Excerpt, *Min. Proc. I.C.E.*, vol. 151; Session 1902–3, pt. 1.
Mechanical and electrical principles.

2211 KEEN, F. N. Tramway companies and local authorities . . . *London*, 1902. pp. 295. BM
A collection of enactments.

2212 BOWKER, W. R. Practical construction of electric tramways. *London*, 1903. pp. viii, 119. BM
A technical work with illustrations of equipment in text. Chapter VII describes various tramways.

2213 OXLEY, J. S. Light railways procedure: reports and precedents. *London*, 1901, 1903. 2 vols. BM
A large number of reports of Light Railway Commissioners on applications relating to proposed or existing light railways and tramways.

2214 RIDER, J. H. Electric traction: a practical handbook on the application of electricity as a locomotive power . . . *London*, 1903. pp. xvi, 453, with 194 illustrations. IT
Mostly on tramways.

2215 SUTHERS, R. B. The truth about the trams. *London: Clarion Press*, 1903. pp. 16. [*Clarion Pamphlet* no. 39.] LSE
The case for retaining tramways under municipal ownership. Examples of comparative wages, receipts and fares, under private and under municipal ownership, of sixteen tramways.

2216 SUTTON, H. The Tramways Acts of the United Kingdom; with notes on the law and practice, an Introduction . . . and an Appendix . . . *London*, 1874. pp. lxviii, 224. BM

—— 2nd· edn. *London*, 1883. pp. lxxxviii, 292.   BM

—— 3rd edn. 'The law of tramways and light railways in Great Britain', by G. S. Robertson. *London*, 1903. pp. lxxvi, 708.   BM

2217 BOWKER, W. R. Management of electric tramways and light railways. *London*, 1904. pp. ix, 298.   BM

2218 ARNALL, T. Permanent way for tramways and street railways. *London*, 1905. pp. 246 [248], with diagrams. [*Railway Series of Textbooks & Manuals*, no. 6.]   BM
pp. 197 to end, Acts, Orders and Regulations relating to tramways.

2219 MACLEAN, M. Modern electric practice. Editor, Magnus Maclean. *London*, 1904–5. 6 vols., with many illus. & diagrams.   BM
vol. 3, pp. 249–65, 'Electric tramways: the rails'. By John R. Wignall; pp. 267–85, 'Electric tramways: rail bonding'. By Victor Watlington.
vol. 4, pp. 1–64, 'Electric tramways: overhead construction', by I. Everson Winslow; pp. 65–92, 'Tramway feeders', by I Everson Winslow; pp. 93–154, 'Electric tramways: surface contact systems', by I. Everson Winslow; pp. 155–202, 'Conduit systems of electric traction', by A. G. Seaman; pp. 203–61, 'Rolling stock and equipment' (tramways), by H. C. Buckmaster.

2220 SMITH, R. H. Electric traction . . . *London & New York*, 1905. pp. xxii, 442, with 333 illus. & 14 tables.   BM
pp. 24–206, Tramways.

2221 HELLER, A. Der Automobilmotor im Eisenbahnbetriebe . . . mit 82 Abbildungen im Text. *Leipzig*, 1906. pp. 116.   PO
Includes British rail-motors.

2222 GARCKE, E. The progress of electrical enterprise: reprints of articles from the Engineering Supplement of 'The Times' on the British electrical industries. *London*, [1907.] pp. 87.   BM
pp. 49–70, Tramways. Legislation and various economic aspects and problems.

2223 SAYERS, H. M. Brakes for tramway cars. *London*, [1907.] pp. iv, 76.   BR
pp. 56–68, Report on the Highgate accident of 1906, by Col. Yorke.

2224 BRITISH WESTINGHOUSE ELECTRIC & MANUFACTURING COMPANY. Some British electric tramways. *London*, June 1908. pp. 40, with 18 illus., incl. 9 of tramcars. PC

2225 EVERARD, E. E. W. Light railways in Great Britain under the Light Railways Acts, 1896 and 1912, and the Light Railway Commission. *In* 'Jubilee of the Railway News, 1864–1914.' *London: Railway News*, [1914.] pp. 59–61.   BM

2226 BAGNALL, W. G., LTD. Locomotives and light railway stock and materials. (Cata-

logue no. 18.) *Stafford*, [1912.] pp. 68, with illus.   PO

—— Catalogue no. 19. *Stafford*, [1917.] pp. 82.   PO

2227 BAIN, W. & Co. Light railways: a catalogue of material and equipment for light railway construction. *Coatbridge*, [1918.] pp. 47, with illus.   PO
Wagons, locomotives and permanent way.

* 2228 AGNEW, W. A. The Electric Tramcar Handbook for motormen, inspectors, and depot workers. *London*, 1904. pp. vii, 106, with illus.   BM
Maintenance and operation of tramcars, simply described.

—— 6th edn. *London*, 1911. pp. vii, 124. BM
—— 8th edn. *London*, 1920. pp. vii, 132. BM

2229 IBBETSON, W. S. Tramway Motorman's Handbook . . . *London*, 1920. pp. vi, 208, with fold. diagram of L.C.C. tramcar, & illus. in text.   BM
Theory and practice for tram-drivers.

2230 ALLEY, S. E. Some notes on railway matters. *London: Sentinel Waggon Works*, [1926.] pp. 64, with many illus. & a fold. diagram.   LSE
Saving of running costs by using Sentinel rail coaches and locomotives.

2231 MACKINNON, L. Paper on tramways burdens. [*Glasgow*, 1927.] pp. 10.   LSE
Submitted by L. Mackinnon, General Manager, Glasgow Corporation Tramways, at 5th Annual Conference of the Scottish Tramways & Transport Association, 20 May, 1927.
Permanent way maintenance and taxation.

2232 SENTINEL WAGGON WORKS. Some railway problems of today and their solution. *London*, 1927. pp. 64, with illus. & diagrams.   BR
The branch line problem; light traffic on main lines; shunting economies; the carriage of small quantities at a profit.

2233 BAGULEY, LTD. Steam and internal combustion locomotives . . . rail and tram cars, light railway carriages and wagons . . . *Burton-on-Trent*, [c. 1930.] pp. 56.   SLS
Illustrations and descriptions.

2234 PILCHER, R. S. Road transport operation: passenger. *London*, 1930. pp. x, 209, with 34 illus.   IT
An outline for students: includes tramways.

2235 SPENCE, A. H. Tramway Motormen's Guide. *Dundee*, Sept. 1930. pp. 60, with illus.   IT

2236 GLEDHILL, A. H. Standard costs and their influence on transport policy. *London: Municipal Tramways & Transport Association*, 1931. pp. 24.   IME
Paper, Annual Meeting, Manchester, 11 Sept., 1931.

High tramway maintenance costs compared with estimated savings which would result from the adoption of rail-less vehicles.

2237 WATSON, H. Street traffic flow. *London*, 1933. pp. xii, 395, with illus. & diagrams. BM
Includes tramway problems such as narrow streets and obstructions.

2238 LONDON PASSENGER TRANSPORT BOARD. The overhaul of tramcars. *London*, 1935. pp. 25, with illus. & la. fold. chart of Charlton Works. LSE

2239 CHESTER, D. N. Public control of road passenger transport: a study in administration and economics. *Manchester: Manchester University Press*, 1936. pp. xi, 226. IT
Includes tramways.

2240 METROPOLITAN-VICKERS ELECTRICAL CO. The Metro-Vick-Cammell railcar. *Manchester*, [1937.] pp. 20, with illus. & diagrams. IT
Diesel.

2241 LIGHT RAILWAY TRANSPORT LEAGUE. 50 questions & answers about trams. [*London*, 1943.] pp. 8. BM

2242 BETT, W. H. The theory of fare collection on railway and tramways. *Cricklewood: Light Railway Transport League*, 1945. pp. 64, with 11 plates showing tickets, with notes. BM

2243 DUNCAN, I. G. T. The ABC of the locomotives of the minor British railways. *Staines: Ian Allan*, 1945. pp. 32, with tables & illus. BM

2244 BIZERAY, C. R. Towards ideal transport in town planning and reconstruction. *London: Light Railway Transport League*, 1944. pp. 44, with 15 plates. BM
Detailed arguments in favour of tramways.

—— 2nd edn. *London: L.R.T.L.*, 1947. pp. 52[54]. BM

2245 KLAPPER, C. F. Buses and trams; edited by Charles F. Klapper. *London: Ian Allan*, [1949.] pp. 96, with illus. BM
Essays include 'Trams of bygone London'; 'Some memories of Southampton trams'; 'Cable days in Edinburgh'.

2246 MUNICIPAL PASSENGER TRANSPORT ASSOCIATION. Cost guide . . . recommended for use by all Municipal passenger transport undertakings. *London*, Sept. 1950. pp. 18, with 11 schedules showing the data required for estimating costs of power and maintenance. IT

2247 MUNICIPAL PASSENGER TRANSPORT ASSOCIATION. Standard form of accounts for municipal passenger transport undertakings. *London*, Jan. 1950. pp. 17. IT
Recommended schedules. Produced in co-operation with the Institute of Municipal Treasurers & Accountants.

2248 PHILLIPS, D. F. *and* PEARSON, F. V. The tram that went to America. *London: Light Railway Transport League*, [1958.] pp. 16, with illus. BM
Reprinted 1960.
Blackpool Corporation's car no. 144 and its acquisition by the New England Electric Railway Historical Society, Kennebunkport, Maine.

2249 PRIGMORE, B. J. The future and rapid transit. *London: Light Railway Transport League*, 1959. pp. 23, with illus. PO

2250 LIGHT RAILWAY TRANSPORT LEAGUE. The truth about tramways and light railways: some questions and answers. *Cricklewood (London)*, June 1960. pp. 15. BM
Forty-four questions and answers.

D 2 NARROW GAUGE RAILWAYS

(with gauges less than 4 ft. 8½ in. down to 1 ft. 3 in.)

For mineral railways see **D 3**
For miniature railways see **D 6**

2251 FAIRLIE, R. F. Locomotive engines: what they are and what they ought to be. *London*, 1864. pp. 36, with 13 fold. diagrams. ICE
The advantages of his patent locomotives: questions and answers.

2252 FAIRLIE, R. F. Opinions of the press on the Fairlie engine: being a series of articles reprinted from the leading scientific and

other journals. *London*, 1868. pp. v, 142, with illus. (some fold.). BR

2253 FAIRLIE, R. F. Paper on the gauge for 'the railways of the future'; read before the British Association at Liverpool, 1870. *Liverpool*, 1870. pp. 16. LSE
The advantages of narrow gauge.

2254 [FAIRLIE, F. R.] Second series of experiments with the Fairlie engines on the Festiniog, Brecon & Merthyr, and Burry Port & Gwendreath Valley railways, on June 16, 17, 18 & 20, 1870. [*London,*] 1870. pp. 23, with plates.   NLC

2255 FAIRLIE, R. F. A comparison between the Fairlie and the ordinary engines, and the refutation of the oft-repeated assertion that a Fairlie engine is only two engines coupled together. [*London,* 1878.] pp. 8, with diagrams.   BR
  The BR copy is accompanied by a number of printed letters of testimony, reports of trials, etc.

2256 SPOONER, C. E. Narrow gauge railways. *London,* 1871. pp. 128, with 11 illus. & 25 fold. charts.   BM
  pp. 10–57, Festiniog Rly.
  —— 2nd edn. *London,* 1879. pp. 128.   BM

2257 LEWIS, W. Narrow gauge railways, Ireland. pp. 64, with tables & 2 fold. diagrams. [with] Green, C. F. Light railways, or unremunerative railways for thinly-populated districts. pp. 31–77, with tables & 2 fold. diagrams. *Dublin,* 1882.   BM

*2258 NORTH BRITISH LOCOMOTIVE COMPANY. Locomotives for narrow gauge railways. (Catalogue of narrow gauge locomotives.) *Glasgow,* Feb. 1912. pp. 79, with illus. & constructional details.   BR

2259 DUNCAN, I. G. T. The ABC of the locomotives of the minor British railways. *Staines: Ian Allan,* 1945. pp. 32, with tables & illus.   BM

2260 LEE, C. E. Narrow-gauge railways in North Wales. *London: Railway Publishing Co.,* 1945. pp. 136, with plates & maps.   BM

*2261 FAYLE, H. The narrow gauge railways of Ireland. *London: Greenlake Publications,* 1946. pp. 204, with 129 illus. on plates, maps and diagrams.   BM

2262 KIDNER, R. W. The light railways of Britain: a survey of the development of narrow-gauge and light standard-gauge passenger railways, with notes on present-day locomotive stocks. *Chislehurst: Oakwood Press,* 1947. pp. 40, with illus., tables & maps. BM

2263 HOWSON, F. H. Narrow gauge railways of Britain. *London: Ian Allan,* 1948. pp. 79, with illus.   BM

2264 BOYD, J. I. C. Narrow-gauge rails to Portmadoc: a historical survey of the Festiniog–Welsh Highland Railway and its ancillaries. [*South Godstone:*] *Oakwood Press,* 1949. pp. iii, 158, with plates, map & illus.   BM

2265 TONKS, E. S. Light and miniature railway locomotives of Great Britain. [*Birmingham:*] *Birmingham Locomotive Club,* 1950. pp. 44, with 20 illus. on 10 plates, & detailed lists. BM

*2266 BOYD, J. I. C. Narrow gauge rails in Mid-Wales: a historical survey of the narrow gauge railways in Mid-Wales. *South Godstone: Oakwood Press,* 1952. pp. vi, 146, with plates, & maps in text.   BM
  Corris; Talyllyn; Glyn Valley; Fairbourne; Vale of Rheidol; Welshpool & Llanfair, and other smaller lines.

2267 KIDNER, R. W. English narrow gauge railways. *Sidcup: Oakwood Press,* 1937. pp. 16, with 6 plates, diagrams & maps. [*Light Railway Handbooks,* no. 3.]   BM
  —— 2nd edn. *Chislehurst,* 1946. pp. 45–60.
                                         BM
  —— 3rd. *South Godstone,* 1947. pp. [45]–60.
                                         BM
  —— 4th. *Lingfield,* [1957.]   BM

2268 WHITEHOUSE, P. B. Narrow Gauge Album. *London: Ian Allan,* 1957. pp. 141, with 129 illus. (2 col.) & 10 maps.   BM
  Includes Irish lines.
  pp. 136–[142,] 'Tabulated information covering railways mentioned in detail in text'. (10 columns.)

2269 JONES, R. B. British narrow gauge railways . . . *London: Black,* 1958. pp. 110, with 35 illus. on 23 plates.   BM

2270 SHAW, F. Little railways of the world. *Berkeley, California,* 1958. pp. ix, 261, with illus., maps & diagrams.
  Includes: R.H.' & D.; Festiniog; Talyllyn; Ravenglass & Eskdale; Lynton & Barnstaple; Vale of Rheidol. Also short biographies of W. J. Bassett-Lowke; Henry Greenly.

2271 KIDNER, R. W. Light and narrow-gauge locomotives. 2nd edn., *South Godstone: Oakwood Press,* 1949. pp. 65–80, with 11 plates. [*Light Railway Handbooks,* no. 8.]   BM
  —— 3rd edn. *Lingfield,* [1959.] pp. 32. BM

2272 JUX, F. British narrow gauge steam: a current survey. *Richmond: the author,* May 1960. pp. 19, with an addenda slip.   BM
  Lists and illustrations of locomotives.

2273 DAVIES, W. J. K. ABC, narrow gauge railways. *London: Ian Allan,* [1961.] pp. 80, with 42 illus., sketch maps & select bibliographies.   BM
  Detailed historical and descriptive notes, stock lists and routes of forty-four railways, past and present, in Great Britain and Ireland. Includes industrial railways and a list of preserved items.

2274 LIGHT Railway Guide and Timetables; edited by G. Body and R. L. Eastleigh. *Dawlish: David & Charles*, 1963. pp. 40.   BM
   A handbook to existing light railway services, with historical and descriptive details, illustrations, maps and time-tables.

—— another edn. *Dawlish*, 1964. pp. 48.
                                          BM
—— A previous edn., 'Light Railway

Guide and Timetable, Summer, 1962.' *Enfield: Trans-Rail Publications*, 1962. pp. 25. *Reproduced typescript.*   BM

2275 WHITEHOUSE, P. B. On the narrow gauge. *London: Nelson*, 1964. pp. xii, 148, with col. frontis. & 116 illus. on 66 plates.   BM
   pp. 1–90, historical and descriptive accounts of narrow gauge railways in the British Isles.

D 3 INDUSTRIAL, MINERAL, DOCK, HARBOUR, AND PUBLIC UTILITIES SYSTEMS

For dock and harbour railways owned and operated by railway companies see G 5 *for general works and* L *for individual companies. For docks and harbour railways owned and operated by British Railways see* B 10

2276 COOPER, W. R. Electric traction on roads and mineral railways: a paper read before the Institution of Mining Engineers General Meeting at London, May 30th 1902. *London*, 1902. pp. 24.   IME

2277 BARCLAY, A., SONS & CO. Instructions for drivers of small locomotives. *Kilmarnock*, 1921. pp. 30[32], with 1 illus. & 6 diagrams.
                                          BM

2278 CADBURY BROTHERS. Bournville transport, 1925. *Bournville*, [1925]. pp. 48.   LSE
   Includes the Bournville Works railway system, with illus. and map.

2279 BASS & CO. A notable brewery railway system: being the copy of an article which' recently appeared in the 'Railway Gazette' and the 'Railway Magazine' . . . *Burton-on-Trent*, 1926. pp. 19, with map.   BM
   Cover title, *Our model railway and all about it.*

2280 KITSON & CO. Manning Wardle type locomotives. *Leeds*, [c. 1930.] pp. 23.   SLS
   In English, French, Italian and Spanish. (pp. 19–23 are perforated for detachment.)
   Specifications and illustrations of eight industrial locomotives.

2281 PARKER, J. W. Factory transport: a guide to internal movement and works' handling appliances. *London*, 1931. pp. 102.   LSE
   Includes advice on construction and operation of industrial railways.

2282 HOBSON, J. W. The care and maintenance of the industrial steam locomotive. *Newcastle-upon-Tyne: North East Coast Institution of Engineers & Shipbuilders*, 1932. pp. 42.   IT
   A paper with (pp. 21 to end) discussion.

2283 HEDLEY, R. Modern traction for industrial and agricultural railways. *London*, 1935. pp. 182, with many illus. & tables.   BM
   Steam, petrol, diesel, electric and compressed air locomotives.

2284 DUNCAN, I. G. T. The ABC of the locomotives of the minor British railways. *Staines: Ian Allan*, 1945. pp. 32, with tables & illus.   BM

2285 MACDONALD, D. G. I. The function and organisation of an industrial transport department. 1946. pp: 16. *Reproduced typescript.*   IT
   Paper, Institute of Transport, Birmingham, 15 January, 1948.
   Includes works railways.

*2286 TONKS, E. S. Pocket Books (Industrial Locomotive Pocket Books). *Birmingham: Birmingham Locomotive Club*, 1947–1958.
                                          BM
   Lists and illustrations.
   Industrial locomotives of:
   no. 1, West Midlands. 1947. pp. 42.
   no. 2, East Midlands. 1947. pp. 58.
   no. 3, Southern England. 1949. pp. 44.
   no. 4, Eastern England. 1950. pp. 56.
   no. 5, North Wales & English Border Counties. 1950. pp. 48.
   no. 6, South Wales & Monmouthshire. 1951. pp. 60.
   no. 7, Lancashire. 1952. pp. 329–428.
   no. 8, Yorkshire (E. & W. Ridings). 1954. pp. 429–530.
   A, West Midlands (2nd edn. of no. 1). 1957. pp. 90.
   B, Southern England (2nd edn. of no. 3). 1958. pp. 75.
   C, South-Eastern England. 1958. pp. 123.

2287 MARDON, H. H., CHAPMAN, H. A. *and* BRISBY, M. D. J. The traffic of iron and steel works: the application of very high frequency radio communication. *London: British Iron & Steel Research Assoc.*, April 1950. pp. 425–38, with illus. of equipment. IT
   Reprint, *Jnl. BI. .& S.R.A.*, April 1950.

2288 ROYAL SOCIETY FOR THE PREVENTION OF ACCIDENTS. I.C.I. Engineering Codes and Regulations, Group A, vol. 1 (4). Railways and haulages: design: safety precautions. Published for Imperial Chemical Industries Ltd. by the Royal Society for the Prevention of Accidents. *London*, [1950.] pp. 19. SL

Design and installation of works railways, sidings and haulages.

2289 TONKS, E. S. Light and miniature railway locomotives of Great Britain. [*Birmingham:*] *Birmingham Locomotive Club*, 1950. pp. 44, with 20 illus. on 10 plates, & detailed lists. BM

2290 ROYAL SOCIETY FOR THE PREVENTION OF ACCIDENTS. I.C.I. Engineering Codes and Regulations, Group A, vol. 1 (5). Railways and haulages: operation and maintenance: safety precautions. Published for Imperial Chemical Industries Ltd. by the Royal Society for the Prevention of Accidents. *London*, 1951. pp. 24. SL

2291 PEACOCK, T. B. P.L.A. Railways. *London: Locomotive Publishing Co.*, 1952. pp. xiii, 117, with 61 illus., 3 maps, 3 diagrams & bibliography. BM

The railway system of the Port of London Authority.

2292 [IMPERIAL CHEMICAL INDUSTRIES.] Memento of the opening of the light railway, Gorstage to Wallerscote. [1953.] BR

A collection of thirty-three photographs, mounted, with captions, of the line constructed from the London Midland Region to the I.C.I. salt plant at Wallerscote. Privately compiled.

2293 KIDNER, R. W. Mineral railways. *Sidcup: Oakwood Press*, 1938. pp. 16, with notes, diagrams & maps, 4 plates, & a bibliography. [*Light Railway Handbooks*, no. 7.]
—— 2nd edn. *Chislehurst*, 1946. pp. 16. BM
—— 3rd. *South Godstone*, 1954. pp. 24. BM

2294 BRISBY, M. D. J. The traffic of iron and steelworks locomotive operating. [*London*, 1956.] pp. 30–7, with tables. IT

Reprinted from *Journal of the Iron & Steel Institute*, vol. 182, Jan. 1956.

Comparative economic values of steam and diesel, with tables.

2295 DAVIES, W. J. K. Pike Bros., Fayle & Co. Ltd., Furzebrook. *Leeds & London: Narrow Gauge Railway Society*, [1958.] pp. 33, with 9 illus. on covers, & maps in text. *Reproduced typescript.* (A page of errata inserted.) [*N.G.R.S. Handbook* no. 1.] BM

2296 DAVIES, W. J. K. Parish's Loam Quarries, Erith . . . *Leeds & London: Narrow Gauge Railway Society*, 1959. pp. 32, with 8 illus. on 4 plates, & maps. [*N.G.R.S. Handbook* no. 2.] BM

History and description.

2297 MACGRATH, W. Some industrial railways of Ireland, and other minor lines . . . *Cork: the author*, 1959. pp. 96, with 42 illus. BM

2298 TONKS, E. S. The ironstone railways and tramways of the Midlands. *London: Loco-*
c *motive Publishing Co.*, [1959.] pp. 316, with maps & illus. on plates; chronological table & locomotive list. BM

History and details of 144 systems and their locomotives.

2299 PEARSON, H. M. Railway works construction. *London: Odhams*, 1960. pp. 303, with illus. & diagrams. BM

A textbook for railway and contractors works staff.

*2300 TOWNSEND, J. L. The Dorking Greystone Lime Co. Ltd. and 'Townsend Hook'. *London: Narrow Gauge Railway Society*, [1961.] pp. 43, with 8 illus. & map. BM

Cover title, *The history of the Dorking Greystone Lime Co., Ltd. and the locomotive 'Townsend Hook'*.

2301 PRICE, J. H. London's last horse tramway. *In* 'Journal of Transport History', vol. 5, no. 3, May 1962. pp. 149–58, with plan, 3 diagrams & 37 notes. BM

A tramway system from the Thames to the River Hospitals, Dartford, for the conveyance of small-pox patients, 1897–1925.

2302 WELLS, A. G. Bowaters' Sittingbourne railway. *Leeds & London: Narrow Gauge Railway Society*, 1962. pp. 46, with 22 illus., 6 diagrams of wagons, & 4 maps. BM

D 4 ELECTRIC AND UNDERGROUND RAILWAYS (General Works)

For electric tramways see **D 1**
For the Post Office (London) Underground Railway see **K 9**
For electric railway engineering and electrification of steam railways see **E 4**

2303 BARLOW, P. W. On the relief of London street traffic, with a description of the Tower Subway, now shortly to be executed. *London*, 1867. pp. 29. BM

Proposes manually propelled carriages on rails in a tunnel. 'Observations on the system . . .' by John C. Adagh (pp. 17–23).

2304 BARLOW, P. W. The relief of street traffic: advantages of the City & Southwark Subway, with reasons why the proposed connection of street tramways from the Elephant & Castle through the City is unnecessary and undesirable. Second pamphlet. *London*, 1871. pp. 6. BM

Plan to transfer tramway passengers to an

underground railway to relieve congestion in the City.

2305 GRIST, W. Locomotion, non-electric and electric: an illustrated and descriptive account of the Electric Railway (Binko's System) as working at the Crystal Palace, preceded by an historical sketch of early roads, tramways, railways & means of locomotion. *Crystal Palace (London): International Electric Rly. Co.*, 1882. pp. 16, with illus.   RC

2306 EWING, J. A. Electric railways. *In* 'Chambers' Encyclopædia', 1889. vol. 4, pp. 284–6.
          BM
Quoted as an authoritative article in *Nature.* October 24, 1889.

2307 SCHOLEY, H. Electric tramways and railways popularly explained. *London*, 1896. pp. 62, with illus.   BM
Historical and descriptive.

2308 DAWSON, P. Electric railways and tramways, their construction and operation: a practical handbook . . . entirely revised, enlarged . . . *London*, 1897. pp. xxvi, 677.
          BM
pp. 371–439, British electric railways.

2309 CASSIER'S MAGAZINE. Electric Railway Number. (vol. 16, no. 4.) *London*, August 1899. pp. [253]–540 + pp. 229, adverts., with many illus.   BM
Electric railways and tramways.
—— Reprinted by the Light Railway Transport League, 1960.   BM

2310 BLONDEL, A. *and* PAUL-DUBOIS, P. F.
b   La Traction électrique sur voies ferrées . . . avec 1014 figures dans le texte. *Paris*, 1898. 2 vols. (pp. xxxviii, 841; 863.)   BM
vol. 2, pp. 791–811, Bibliography.
—— another edn. *Paris*, 1901.   BM

2311 SMITH, R. H. Electric traction . . . *London & New York*, 1905. pp. xxii, 442, with 133 illus. & 14 tables.   BM
pp. 207–99, Underground railways of London (tube and subway).

2312 HOBART, H. M. Electric trains. *London & New York*, 1910. pp. xviii, 210, with illus. on plates.   BM
For electrical engineers, but contains detailed statistical tables of rolling stock, etc., of British underground and electric railways.

2313 WHYTE, A. G. Electricity in locomotion: an account of its mechanism, its achievements and its prospects. *Cambridge*, 1911. pp. vi, 143, with 18 illus.   BM
Introductory.

2314 ENGLISH ELECTRIC Co. Industrial locomotives: small sizes for factories, mines, quarries . . . battery, trolley-wire or third rail. *London*, 1930. pp. 11, with illus.   PC

2315 SALMOND, H. G. Notes on tube railway construction. *Calcutta: Railway Board*, 1931. pp. 42, with diagrams. [*Technical Paper*, no. 278.]   LSE
Report of a six-weeks' inspection of the City & South London Railway and the Hampstead Railway. A general and technical description.

2316 LONDON PASSENGER TRANSPORT BOARD. The overhaul of Underground rolling stock. *Westminster*, 1934. pp. 52, with illus. & fold. diagram.   BM

2317 EVERYDAY knowledge in pictures. *London: Odhams Press*, [1943.] pp. 320.   BM
pp. 158–80, 'How a tube railway works'; with 27 illus. and diagram.

2318 CANSDALE, J. H. Electric Traction Jubilee, 1896–1946: a brief survey of electric traction with some account of the part played by the British Thomson-Houston Co. Ltd. [*Rugby:*] *B.T.H.Co.*, 1946. pp. 66.   BM

2319 ALLEN, G. F. ABC of British electric trains. *London: Ian Allan*, 1948. pp. 68, with lists & illus.   BM
Includes historical data.

2320 LINECAR, H. W. A. British electric trains. *London: Ian Allan*, 1947. pp. 133, with plates.   BM
History and description of electric railways and their trains.
—— 2nd edn. *London*, [1949.] pp. 132.   BM

2321 BERGER, R. Untergrundbahnen und ihre Einsatzgrenzen . . . *Berlin*, 1951. pp. viii, 99, with 39 illus., 35 tables & 21 plans.   IT
Comparison of economic aspects of underground railways in various cities, including London, Liverpool, and Glasgow.

2322 BRITISH TRANSPORT COMMISSION. Electrification of railways. *London*, 1951. pp. xi, 94, with 10 tables & 7 maps.   BM
Survey of existing electrification methods and recommendations for future development.

2323 WROTTESLEY, A. J. F. Famous underground railways of the world. *London: F. Muller*, 1956. pp. 144, with plates & illus. BM
pp. 9–105, in London, Glasgow, and Liverpool.
—— 2nd edn. *London*, 1960. pp. 144.   BM

2324 MOODY, G. T. The development of electric railway rolling stock. *Sidcup: Electric Railway Society*, July 1957. pp. 12. *Reproduced typescript.* [*Booklet* no. 3.]   BM
Includes underground railways.

D5 UNUSUAL FORMS OF RAILWAY AND LOCOMOTION

General—Monorail—Suspension—Elevated—Cable—Cliff—
Wireways, etc.

*For early experimental forms (atmospheric, stationary engine and
cable, horse traction, etc.) see* **B 2**

2325 JONES, W. A popular sketch of the various systems of atmospheric railway, demonstrating the applicability of the mechanical properties of the atmosphere as a motive power; illustrated by numerous wood cuts; being the substance of lectures delivered on the subject at the Royal Adelaide Gallery . . . February 1845, with additions and corrections. By the late proprietor, William Jones. *London*, 1845. pp. xviii, 10, 8, with diagrams.

           BM

     Appendix, pp. 101–8, Report of the Select Committee, House of Commons, appointed to inquire into the merits of the atmospheric system of railway; dated April 22, 1845.

2326 [PROSSER, W.] Some remarks on the advantages of Prosser's patent railway guide wheels on either iron or wooden rails. *London*, 1845. pp. 8, with diagram.   SL
— another edn. *London*, May 1845. pp. 8.   SL

2327 WESTLY, W. K. An account of the portable farm railway. [1854.] pp. 3, with plate.   ICE
     Monorail.

2328 WESTLY, W. K. On the uses and applications of the portable farm railway. [1854.] pp. 8.   ICE

2329 BOYDELL, J. Explanatory remarks upon Boydell's patent for propelling locomotive engines. *London*, [1857.] pp. 16. (Patent no. 3127, 1857.)   NLC
     Propulsion by 'a direct forward push to the carriage'. (?)

2330 RAMMELL, T. W. A new plan for street railways. *London*, 1857. pp. 11, with 2 la. fold. diagrams.   LSE
     Elevated atmospheric.
—— another edn. London, 1857. pp. 14.   BM

2331 NICKLÈS, M. J. Le moteur des convois des grandes tunnels et en particulier du tunnel sous-marin, *Nancy*, 1858. pp. 32, with bibliogr. notes.   BM
     T. de Gamond's plan for impelling trains through tunnels by force of air.

2332 BURN, C. On the construction of horse railways for branch lines in England and the colonies. *London*, 1860. pp. 59, with 18 diagrams on plates, illustrating types of track.   BM
—— 2nd edn. *London*, 1860. pp. 81.   PO

2333 NEWLANDS, J. Report on horse railways. *Liverpool*, 1860. pp. 18.   ICE
     Addressed to the Liverpool Town Council. J. Newlands was Borough Engineer.

2334 TRAIN, G. F. Observations on horse railways . . . addressed to Milner Gibson, M.P., President of the Board of Trade. *London & Liverpool*, 1860. pp. 56, with plate.   ICE
     'The age of omnibuses in crowded cities is passed; the age of horse railways has commenced.'

2335 LILLIE, J. S. Suggestions for improvements in railway travelling by atmospheric pressure as the only means of providing against the dangers which have been recently increasing to such an alarming degree by the increase of traffic on existing railways as to induce Her Majesty to direct the attention of various railway companies to the subject. [*London, c.* 1866.] pp. 11.   BM
     No title-page in BM copy.
     Atmospheric tunnel alongside running rails serving also as a continuous platform.

2336 BARLOW, P. W. On the relief of London street traffic, with a description of the Tower Subway, now shortly to be executed. *London*, 1867. pp. 29.   BM
     Proposes manually propelled carriages on rails in a tunnel. 'Observations on the system . . .' by John C. Adagh (pp. 17–23).

2337 ADAMS, W. B. Railway practice and railway possibilities as affecting dividends and safety; with diagrams of engines, trains, and brakes. *London*, 1868. pp. 26, with 9 fold. plates.   BM
     Radial system of locomotive and rolling-stock construction.

2338 FIGUIER, L. Les Mervielles de la science; ou, Description populaire des inventions modernes. *Paris*, 1867–70. 4 vols.   BM
     vol. 1, pp. 391–3, a description, with illustrations, of Rammell's experimental pneumatic railway at the Crystal Palace, Sydenham, 1864.

2339 BEALE, M. Wire tramways: Hodgson's patents: description of Hodgson's system of wire-rope transport . . . *London: Wire Tramway Co.*, [1870.] pp. 23, with illus.   BM
     Includes a list of wire tramways constructed, five of which are in the British Isles; press opinions.

2340 BLACKBURN, B. Description of the proposed Wheelway from London to Manchester, to perform the distance in two hours at the rate of 94 miles an hour: departures every five minutes, fares one halfpenny per mile, total expenses 19% of receipts. *London,* 1870. pp. 7. BR

Wheels mounted in stationary bearings placed at 25 ft. intervals along the line are made to rotate continuously. The rails are fixed under the floors of the carriages.

2341 HUMPHREYS, H. T. Description of Humphrey's Patent Post and Rail-way. [*Limerick,*] 1870. pp. 8, with fold. diagram. BM

Monorail (James Samuel's patent).

2342 FELL, J. B. Description of the patent narrow gauge railway at the Parkhouse Mines near Furness Abbey. *Westminster,* [1871.] pp. 4. ICE

A railway on a series of raised beams.

2343 FELL, J. B. Patent narrow-gauge railways adapted for inexpensive branches to main lines of railway ... *London,* 1871. pp. 3, with 3 fold. plates. ICE

Rails laid on a series of raised beams; the carriages designed to overhang on either side.

2344 HADDAN, J. L. Economical one-rail railways for India, the colonies, and sparsely populated countries. *London,* 1871. pp. 13, with 6 diagrams on 3 plates. BM

Includes a description of the monorail system.

2345 FELL, J. B. Lecture delivered at a meeting of the United Services Institution at Plymouth ... on the use of improved narrow gauge railways in the operations of war, and for other special objects. *Aldershot,* 1873. pp. 30. ICE

2346 PATENT OFFICE. Patents for inventions. Abridgments of specifications relating to air, gas, and other motive power engines, A.D. 1635–1866. (Compiled by B. Woodcroft.) *London,* 1873. pp. xxiv, 474. BM:PO

Includes atmospheric and pneumatic systems of propulsion.

2347 HANDYSIDE, H. A treatise on an improved method of overcoming steep gradients on railways, whereby an ordinary locomotive capable of hauling a given load up a gradient of 1 in 80 can take the same up 1 in 8. *London,* 1874. pp. 31, with 4 plates. BM

Winches fitted to locos.

—— 'A treatise on a safe and improved method for overcoming steep gradients on railways.' *Bristol,* 1875. pp. 24, with fold. frontis. ICE

2348 FELL, J. B. Military field railways . . . *Ulverston,* 1876. pp. 10. ICE

Fell's 'two-rail' monorail.

2349 [FELL, J. B.] Reports of the Royal Engineers Committee and correspondence with the Secretary of State for War, on the experiments made at Aldershot with Mr. J. B.

Fell's system for the rapid construction of military field railways. *Ulverston,* 1876. pp. 19. ICE

2350 CARRINGTON, T. H. Wire tramways: description of the various systems of wire rope transport in operation in different parts of the world, constructed under the patents and from designs furnished by the Wire Tramway Co. [*London,* 1878.] pp. 27, with illus. ICE

2351 HADDAN, J. L. Military railways, including also, description and estimates of the 'Pioneer' steam caravan, or test line, for the proposed Euphrates Valley Railway . . . *London,* [1878.] pp. 34. BM

2352 PATENT OFFICE. Patents for inventions. Abridgments of specifications relating to air, gas, and other motive power engines: part 2, A.D. 1867–1876. (Compiled by H. Reader Lack.) *London,* 1881. pp. xvii, 923. BM: PO

Includes methods of working locomotives from portable reservoirs of compressed air.

2353 DEVOOGHT, F. Cable railroad and cable tramways without locomotives nor horses, the carriage rolling alone on the road . . . *Antwerp,* 1882. pp. 16, with la. fold. diagram. ICE

2354 ROBINSON, J. C. Tramways; with a description of the wire cable system. *Edinburgh,* 1883. pp. 29. ICE

Cable tramways; practical, not engineering, aspects. Robinson was General Manager and Secretary, Edinburgh Street Tramways.

2355 TIPTON, T. C. Digest of English patents relating to propelling cars by traveling ropes or cables, from no. 3126 of 1808 to no. 4433 of 1881. *Washington,* 1883. pp. 31. PO

2356 BEHR, F. B. A paper on the Lartigue single-rail railway, read before the Society of Engineers . . . on the 4th October 1886. [*London,* 1886.] pp. 31, with map & section. PO

2357 BIRMINGHAM CENTRAL TRAMWAYS. The cable system; reprinted from Birmingham and Glasgow newspapers. *Birmingham,* 1886. pp. 25, with illus. & map. ICE

2358 EVANS, W. W. The Abt system of railway for steep inclines. *New York,* 1886. pp. [147]–180, with diagrams. [*Transactions of the American Society of Civil Engineers,* vol. 15, March 1886. Paper no. 323.] LSE

A foreign system often referred to in proposals for mountain railways in the U.K. and actually used for the Snowdon Mountain Railway.

2359 INTERNATIONAL EXHIBITION, Liverpool, 1886. Lifts and pneumatic railways exhibited . . . vertical or inclined lifts worked by the pressure of fluids, etc. Translated from the French. *Lausanne,* 1886. pp. 26[31], with diagrams. ICE

2360 PERRY, J. Telpherage. *London*, 1886. pp. 50, with illus. & fold. diagram.   ICE
pp. 16–22, The Glynde telpher line.

2361 JEFFERSON, J. C. *and* PULLON, J. T. A description of the proposed elevated single rail railway to Roundhay Park . . . *Leeds*, 1887. pp. 23, with 3 fold. plates.   BM
Elevated mono-rail.

2362 SMITH, J. B. A treatise upon cable or rope traction as applied to the working of street and other railways. Revised and enlarged from 'Engineering'. *London*, 1887. pp. xii, 195, with fold. plates & illus.   BM
Mostly describing cable tramways in U.S.A., but includes, pp. 94–105, a review (partly chronological) of examples of this system in the U.K., especially the Highgate Hill Cable Tramway.

2363 SMITH, W. On the conveyance of ships over land: the ship railway. *Paris*, 1889. pp. 18.   LSE
Suggested ship railways between Humber and Mersey, Forth and Clyde, Bristol and Southampton, and other places, with a map indicating possible lines.

2364 BARRE, A. A short description of the Gliding Railway patented by A. Barre, on exhibition at the Crystal Palace, Sydenham. *London*, 1891. pp. 13, with 3 illus.   ICE
Wheel-less, sliding trains, propelled by squirts of water.

2365 BENNETT, A. R. On an electrical parcel exchange system. *Manchester*, 1891. pp. 13, with 9 fold. diagrams.   PO
Paper, Section G, British Association, Cardiff, 25 August, 1891.
A miniature electric railway system laid in rectangular tubes.

2366 BEHR, F. B. Lightning Express Railway service; 120 to 150 miles per hour. *London*, 1893. pp. 32, with 7 fold. plates.   BM
Lartigue monorail system.

2367 ROPEWAYS SYNDICATE LTD. Improved aerial ropeways for economical transportation. [*London*.] 1893. pp. 10, with illus. on 12 plates.   ICE

2368 ROWAN, F. J. A one-rail, or trestle system of light railway. *London & Newcastle-on-Tyne*, 1898. pp. 10, with diagrams on fold. plates.   ICE
Excerpt, *Transactions of the Federated Institution of Mining Engineers*.

2369 BEHR, F. B. Lecture on the proposed Lightning Express Railway between Liverpool and Manchester in eighteen minutes . . . *Liverpool*, [1899.] pp. 14, with illus.   BM
Proposed electric monorail system.

2370 The MANCHESTER & Liverpool Electric Express Railway Company. [*London*, 1901.] pp. 24, with illus., fold. plate, & diagrams.
A proposed monorail.   LC

2371 BLONDEL, A. *and* PAUL-DUBOIS, P. F. La Traction électrique sur voies ferrées . . . *Paris*, 1898. 2 vols.   BM
vol. 2, pp. 12–22, monorail system.
—— another edn. *Paris*, 1901.

2372 MANCHESTER & LIVERPOOL ELECTRIC EXPRESS RLY. Extracts from Evidence before Parliament. [*London*, 1902.] pp. 24, with diagrams & map.   RC
A proposed monorail.

2373 ASHBURY, T. Mono-rail systems. *In his* 'Miscellaneous Papers.' *Manchester*, 1904. pp. 101–8.   PC

2374 PARTICULARS of the Brennan mono-rail system of locomotion as exhibited at Gillingham, Kent, 1909–10. pp. 5. *Reproduced typescript.*   IME

2375 KEARNEY HIGH-SPEED TUBE RLY. CO. The Kearney High-Speed Railway. Brochure no. 1, Inter-urban railways; street railways. (American edition.) *London*, [*c.* 1910?] pp. 16, with 3 illus. & 4 diagrams.   PC

*2376 KEARNEY, E. W. C. Rapid transit in the future: the Kearney High-Speed Railway. 2nd edn. *Westminster*, [1911.] pp. 55, with illus.   PC
An underground monorail railway.

*2377 KEARNEY, E. W. C. The Kearney High-Speed Railway. *Westminster*, 1917. pp. [307]–356, with illus., tables, & diagrams.   PC
Reprinted from *Transactions of the Society of Engineers*, 1917.
Includes a comparison with underground railways.

2378 TAYLER, A. J. W. Aerial or wire-rope tramways: their construction and management . . . *London*, 1898. pp. viii, 216, with 81 illus.   BM
General descriptions of components and of particular installations.
—— another edn. *London*, 1911. pp. viii, 246.   BM
—— 2nd edn. *London*, 1920. pp. viii, 252.   BM

2379 BENNIE railplane system on elevated tracks. *London: Tramway & Railway World*, 16 September, 1926. pp. 4, with 6 illus.   TUC
A reprint.

2380 ENOCK, C. R. The new type of railway: a revolution in land transport. *Froxfield*, 1927. pp. 12.   LSE
Flangeless wheels and lateral guide wheels; light single-unit vehicles instead of trains.

2381 KEARNEY HIGH-SPEED TUBE RLY. CO. The Kearney High-Speed Tube Railway. *London*, [1927.] pp. 25, with 7 illus. & plan.   SLS

2382 BENNIE, G. The George Bennie Railplane system of transport. *Edinburgh*, [*c.* 1928.] pp. 24, with 13 illus. & diagrams.　　IT

2383 LYTHAM ST. ANNES EXPRESS, *newspaper*. Proposed Ribble Bridge: road and railplane structure from Lytham to Southport. *Lytham St. Annes*, 3 February, 1928. s.sh, with 2 illus.　　TUC
A reprint.
Bennie railplane scheme.

2384 MANCHESTER GUARDIAN, *newspaper*. Plan to bridge the Ribble Estuary: railplane invention explained. [*Manchester*, 2 February, 1928.] pp. 4, with 1 illus.　TUC
A reprint.
The Bennie railplane scheme.

2385 BENNIE, G. The George Bennie Railplane system of transport. (Rail transport, past, present & future, commemorating the opening of the test line of the George Bennie Railplane System of transport erected on the LNER line, Milngavie, near Glasgow, 8 July 1930.) *Glasgow & London*, [1930.] pp. 20, with 12 illus. & a portrait.　LSE

2386 KEARNEY HIGH-SPEED TUBE RLY. CO. The Kearney High-Speed Railway: souvenir of first exhibition in Australia of the working model . . . [*Sydney*, 1930.] pp. 15, with illus.　　PC

2387 INTER-COUNTIES, LTD. The Railplane system of transport. *London*, 1935. pp. 28, with 6 illus. & 2 maps (1 fold. showing proposed railplane route connecting N.E. suburbs of London.)　　LSE

2388 KIDNER, R. W. Multiple unit trains, railmotors and tramcars, 1829–1947: cable, atmospheric, steam, electric, petrol, petrol-electric, battery-electric, compressed air, heavy oil. *South Godstone: Oakwood Press*, 1947. pp. 107–50, with 40 plates. [*A Short History of Mechanical Traction and Travel*, part 6.]　　BM
Also issued as part of a collected edition, vol. 2, 'Rail', 1947.

2389 DAY, J. R. *and* WILSON, B. G. Unusual railways. *London: F. Muller*, 1957. pp. 212, with 44 illus. on 20 plates.　　BM
Historical and descriptive survey.

2390 DEAN, F. E. Famous cableways of the world. *London: F. Muller*, 1958. pp. 144, with plates.　　BM
Introductory: the telphers at Baldock and at Glynde (pp. 14–16).

2391 BOTZOW, H. S. D. Monorails. *New York: Simmons-Boardman*, 1960. pp. vii, 104, with
b　plates, & a bibliography (pp. 75–102).　BM
Includes British experiments.

2392 CARTER, E. F. Unusual locomotives. *London: Frederick Muller*, 1960. pp. 221, with 20 plates & 18 drawings in text.　BM
Historical; British and foreign.

2393 DAY, J. R. More unusual railways. *London: F. Muller*, 1960. pp. 214, with 45 illus. on 20 plates, & 10 diagrams.　　BM
Historical and descriptive. A sequel to *Unusual railways*, by J. R. Day and B. G. Wilson (1957).

2394 TRAVIS, A. S. A short survey of Road-Rails and Neverstop railway systems at the British Empire Exhibition, Wembley, 1924–25. *Wembley: Wembley Transport Society*, 1961. pp. [9,] with map & diagrams. *Reproduced typescript*.　　BM

D 6　MINIATURE RAILWAYS

(Short passenger-carrying railways of 2 ft. gauge and less)

For garden railways and model railway engineering see Q2

*2395 HEYWOOD, A. P. Minimum gauge railways: their application, construction and working; being an account of the origin and evolution of the 15 in. gauge line at Duffield Bank, near Derby; also of the installation of a similar line at Eaton Hall, near Chester; together with various notes on the uses of such railways, and on the results of some experimental investigations relating thereto. 3rd edn. *Derby*, 1898. pp. 59, with 23 illus. & maps on plates.　　IME
Printed for private circulation.
Contains the General Regulations (sixty-three in number) for the working of the Eaton Railway.
—— A typescript reproduction with plates issued separately, 1950. pp. 48[49].　BR

2396 ROBERTSON, L. S. Narrow-gauge railways of two-feet gauge and under. *Westminster*, 1898. pp. 376–403.　　LSE
Excerpt, *Min. Proc. I.M.E.* Meeting, 26 July, 1898.
With descriptions of various lines and illustrations of Duffield Bank Rly., Eaton Hall Rly., and Woolwich Arsenal Rly.

2397 PARVER MODELS, LTD. Catalogue of parts, castings and equipment for passenger-hauling railways, 1 inch scale to 15 inch gauge. *Southport*, January 1935. pp. 56, with illus. & diagrams.　　BM

2398 BASSETT-LOWKE, LTD. Fifty years of model making. (The story of Bassett-Lowke

Ltd. from the turn of the century.) Recorded by George Holland. [*Northampton*, 1949.] pp. 64, with many illus.   BM

2399 BASSETT-LOWKE, LTD. Model railways: a handbook on the choice of model locomotives and railway equipment, including designs for rail formations, and model railway signalling. *Northampton: W. J. Bassett-Lowke & Co.*, [1905]. pp. 72, with frontis., & 76 illus. & diagrams.   pc
Includes garden railways and locomotives.

—— 2nd edn., rev. & enl. *Northampton*, [1907.] pp. 82.   pc
—— [3rd.] 'Model Railway Handbook.' *Northampton*, [1910.] pp. 91.   pc
—— 4th, rev. & enl. *London & Northampton*, [1912.] pp. 96.   pc
——5th, rev. & enl. *London*, [1914.] pp. 142.   PO
—— 6th, rev. & enl. *Northampton*, [1920.] pp. 120.   pc
—— 7th, *London, Edinburgh & Northampton*, [1922.] pp. 132.   pc
—— 8th, by W. J. Bassett-Lowke and C. J. Allen. *London*, [1928.] pp. 135.   pc
—— 9th, completely revised & rewritten, by W. J. Bassett-Lowke. *Northampton*, 1940. pp. 148.   BM
—— 10th, *Northampton*, 1943. pp. 149.   pc
—— 11th, *Northampton*, [1944.] pp. 149.   BM
—— 12th, *Northampton*, [1946.] pp. 149 pc
—— 13th, *Northampton*, 1947. pp. 149.   pc
—— 14th, *Northampton*, 1948. pp. 157.   pc
—— 15th, *Northampton*, 1950. pp. 157. BM

2400 TONKS, E. S. Light and miniature railway locomotives of Great Britain. [*Birmingham:*] *Birmingham Locomotive Club*, 1950. pp. 40, with 20 illus. on 10 plates, & detailed lists.   BM

2401 EMETT, R. *and* KEELING, V. The Emett Festival Railway. *Harmondsworth*, 1951. pp. 30. [*Puffin Cut-Out Book*, no. 7.]   BM
Model, designed by V. Keeling, of the train which ran during the Festival of Britain, 1951 (The Far Twittering & Oyster Creek Rly.).

2402 MALDEN AND DISTRICT SOCIETY OF MODEL ENGINEERS. Souvenir of the Malden & District Model Railway. *Thames Ditton*, [1960.] pp. [12,] with 17 illus. & a map.   pc
A passenger-carrying railway of 7-inch gauge.

2403 STAPLEFORD MINIATURE RAILWAY The Stapleford Miniature Railway. *Hampton Court: Ian Allan*, [1960.] pp. 21[24], with 17 illus., map, & gradient profile.   BM
A 10½-inch gauge railway, 1133 yards long, in the grounds of Stapleford Park, Leicestershire.

2404 WILSON, B. G. ABC, miniature railways. *London: Ian Allan*, [1961.] pp. 64, with 58 illus.   BM
Descriptions, with details of locomotives and rolling stock of forty lines in England, Wales, and the Isle of Man.

*2405 HILTON VALLEY Rly. The Hilton Valley Railway: souvenir booklet. [*Worfield*, 1963.] pp. 4, with 8 illus. & plan.   BM
A passenger-carrying line of ¾ mile on 7¼" gauge.

*2406 JAMES, N. D. G. The Bicton Woodland Railway. *East Budleigh (Devon): [Clinton Devon Estates,]* 1963. pp. 28, with 13 illus., 2 maps & 2 diagrams.   BM
A passenger-carrying railway in Bicton Gardens; ¾ mile, 18-inch gauge.

2407 BOYLET, L. J. Eastbourne Tramways. *London: Ian Allan*, [1964.] pp. 27, with 17 illus. & a map.   BM
A 2-ft. gauge electric tramway with overhead current supply, owned and operated by Modern Electric Tramways, Ltd. with a fleet of replica tramcars.

2408 WOODCOCK, G. Miniature steam locomotives. *Dawlish: David & Charles*, 1964. pp. 80, with frontis., & 32 illus. on 14 plates, & 6 diagrams.   BM
The history of small-scale passenger-hauling steam locomotive construction and operation, with accounts of past and present lines, locomotives and builders, and details of notable features and developments.

Marginal symbols: **b** bibliographies
c chronologies

2409 SIMMS, F. W. Public works of Great Britain; consisting of railways, rails, chairs, blocks, cuttings, embankments, tunnels, oblique arches, viaducts, bridges, stations, locomotive engines, etc. *London*, 1838. pp. xii, 72, 32, 24, 70, with 153 plates & tables. BM
 Division 1, pp. 1–72, Railways, locomotive engines and carriages. (London & Birmingham; Great Western; London & Southampton; London & Greenwich; London & Croydon; Birmingham, Bristol & Thames Junction; Glasgow & Garnkirk.)
—— 2nd edn. *London*, 1846. pp. 72, 32, 24, 70. ICE

2410 BARLOW, P. A treatise on the strength of timber, cast iron, malleable iron, and other materials, with rules for application in architecture, construction of suspension bridges, railways, etc., with an appendix on the power of locomotive engines and the effect of inclined planes and gradients. *London*, 1837. pp. xii, 492, with 7 fold. plates & diagrams. BM
—— another edn. *London*, 1851. pp. xii, 492. BM

2411 DEMPSEY, G. D. The practical railway engineer: examples of the mechanical and engineering operations and structures combined in the making of a railway . . . with fifty engravings. *London*, 1847. pp. 157, with 50 plates. BM
—— 4th edn. *London*, 1855. pp. vi, 428, 44, with 71 plates. BM

2412 COLBURN, Z. *and* HOLLEY, A. L. The permanent way and coal-burning locomotive boilers of European railways; with a comparison of the working economy of European and American lines and the principles upon which improvement must proceed . . . with fifty-one engraved plates by J. Bien. *New York*, 1858. pp. 168. BM

2413 JACQUIN, A. Nouvel album des chemins de fer. *Paris*, [1860.] pp. 42, with 51 plates. BM
 Hundreds of line drawings of railway equipment and architecture, including British.

2414 MORANDIÈRE, J. Mémoire sur l'exploitation et le matériel des chemins anglaises en 1865. *Paris*, 1866. pp. iv, 90, with 5 fold. plates & tables. LSE

2415 BARRY, J. W. Railway appliances: a description of details of railway construction subsequent to the completion of the earthworks and structures, including a short

notice of railway rolling stock. *London*, 1876. pp. xiii, 299, with many illus. BM
—— 2nd ed. *London*, 1878. pp. xiii, 301. BR
—— 6th ed. *London*, 1890. pp. xiii, 331. BM

2416 SERAILLIER, L. Vocabulaire technique des chemins de fer: Railway technical vocabulary: French, English and American terms. *London*, 1897. pp. xx, 222. BM

2417 SEKON, G. A. Dictionary of Railway Terms and Phrases . . . *London*, 1901. pp. 61. BM

2418 BODMER, G. R. The inspection of railway materials . . . *London*, 1902. pp. ix, 149, with 3 plates & 19 diagrams. IT

2419 BOSHART, A. Railway construction and operation. Compiled by August Boshart; with about 1900 illustrations and numerous formulæ. *London*, 1909. pp. xiii, 870. [*The Deinhardt-Schlomann Series of Technical Dictionaries in Six Languages*, vol. 5.] BM
 German, English, French, Russian, Italian, and Spanish.

2420 KEMPTHORNE, W. O. Kempthorne's Railway Stores Price Book: being a handbook of prices of stores and material used in the construction and maintenance of railways . . . *London*, 1909. pp. 487. BM

2421 GARCIA, A. J. R. V. Dictionary of Railway Terms in Spanish–English and English–Spanish. *London*, 1912. pp. 350. BM

2422 ALLEN, C. J. The production of iron and steel for railway purposes. *London*: 'Railway Engineer', [1924.] pp. 39, with illus. IT
 Reprinted articles.
 Manufacture of permanent way, structures, and rolling stock.

2423 ALLEN, C, J. The Iron Road. Railway building [and] Locomotives and their work . . . *London*, [1926.] pp. viii, 192, with illus. BM

2424 GRIBBLE, C. Railway engineering in Great Britain in the first half of the twentieth century. *London*, [1946.] pp. 22. BM
 Presidential address, Société des Ingénieurs Civils de France, British Section.

2425 MORRIS, O. J. The Ian Allan Spotters'

Logbook. *London: Ian Allan*, 1948. pp. 112.
BM
A pocket reference for gradients, bridges, viaducts, tunnels, etc., and for various records.

2426 BARMAN, C. Public transport. *Harmondsworth: Penguin Books*, [1949.] pp. 64, with many illus. [*The Things We See*, no. 5.] BM
Historic and modern design, comparatively portrayed. (pp. 1–15, text; 16–62, illustrations, with notes.)

2427 JOINT ENGINEERING CONFERENCE. Proceedings of the Joint Engineering Conference, 1951 . . . part 2, Railways. *London*, [1951.] IT
pp. 39–91, Recent developments in all branches of railway engineering.

2428 BRITISH RAILWAYS. Careers in the railway service. [*London*, 1952.] pp. 32. BM

2429 INGLIS, R. A. An introduction to railway engineering: a short textbook of the theory and practice of railway surveying, construction and signalling, for the use of students and engineers. *London: Chapman & Hall*, 1953. pp. xiv, 200. BM

2430 FRY, L. Get to know—British Railways. Illustrated by C. W. Huxtable. *London: Methuen*, 1950. pp. 47. [*Get to Know Series*.]
BM
Track, signals, engineering works and stations. Concise descriptions illustrated by drawings of the physical features of contemporary railways.
—— 2nd edn. *London*, 1955. pp. 47. BM

2431 BRITISH RAILWAYS. Careers with a future, through graduateships and engineering apprenticeships in mechanical and electrical engineering on British Railways. *London*, 1956. pp. 20, with illus. & diagrams.
IT

2432 SIMON, H. *and* FENTON, W. About railways. *London: Penguin Books*, 1957. pp. 30, with illus. & diagrams (some col.). [*Puffin Picture Books*, no. 113.] BM
Modern railway equipment, mostly locomotives. Introductory.

2433 INTERNATIONAL UNION OF RAILWAYS. Lexique Général des Termes Ferroviaires. (General Dictionary of Railway Terms.) *Berne*, 1957. pp. 829. SL
50,000 terms and expressions in French, English, German, Italian and Spanish.

2434 ELLIS, C. H. The development of railway engineering. *In* 'A history of technology', edited by Charles Singer & others, 1958. vol. 5, 'The late nineteenth century, *c*. 1850 to 1900'. pp. 322–49, with diagrams. BM

2435 FRY, L. On a railway journey. *London: Educational Supply Association*, 1959. pp. 27, with illus. & diagrams. BM
A simple introduction to the physical features of railways.

2436 HERBERT, J. Glossary of Railway Terms; English, French, German, Italian, Spanish, Swedish. *London*, 1960. pp. 413. BM
Published under the authority of the International Union of Railways.

E 1   BIOGRAPHIES OF RAILWAY CIVIL ENGINEERS
(including the civil/mechanical engineers)

For locomotive engineers see **E 8**
For civil and mechanical engineers whose work is strongly associated with a particular railway (such as I. K. Brunel) see **L**

Collected Biographies

2437 LAYSON, J. F. George Stephenson, the locomotive and the railway. *London*, [1881.] pp. 128, with illus. BM
A biography.

2438 LAYSON, J. F. The Stephensons and other railway pioneers. *London*, [1881.] pp. 304. [*Memorable Men of the Nineteenth Century*, no. 6.] LSE
Geo. and Robt. Stephenson. Also, pp. 233 to end, R. Trevithick, Wm. Hedley, T. Hackworth, and I. K. Brunel.

2439 SMITH, G. B. Leaders of modern industry: biographical sketches. *London*, 1884. pp. vi, 477. BM
pp. 1–72, The Stephensons.
pp. 301–33, Thomas Brassey.

pp. 335–78, The Fairbairns.
pp. 421–69, The Rennies.

2440 PIKE, W. T. British engineers and allied professions in the twentieth century: contemporary biographies. *Brighton*, 1908. pp. 436. [*Pike's New Century Series*, no. 24.] BM
Includes a few railwaymen, with portraits.

2441 NOCK, O. S. The railway engineers. *London: Batsford*, 1955. pp. 256, with 65 illus. on plates & in text. BM

Francis Fox

2442 FOX, F. River, road and rail: some engineering reminiscences . . . *London*, 1904. pp. xii, 218, with 67 illus. on plates & in text. BM
Includes accounts of Charles Fox.

2443 Fox, F. Sixty years of engineering, scientific and social work. *London*, 1924. pp. xii, 338.   BM

    pp. 23–122, Railways and tunnels. An auto-biography.

William James

2444 P[AINE,] E. M. S. The two James's and the two Stephensons; or, The earliest history of passenger transit on railways. *London*, 1861. pp. viii, 121, with fold. plan.   BM: UL(GL)

    Based on family records, asserting the claim of William James rather than George Stephenson to the title of 'the Father of Railways'. Inserted in the pocket at the end of the UL(GL) copy are three holograph letters from E. M. S. Paine to Lord Bagot, dated April and May 1866.

    —— A centenary reprint, with an introduction by L. T. C. Rolt. *Dawlish: David & Charles; London: Phœnix House*, 1961. pp. xiv, 121, with portrait & map.   BM

Joseph Locke

2445 DEVEY, J. Life of Joseph Locke, civil engineer. *London*, 1862. pp. iv, 366.   BM

George *and* Robert Stephenson

2446 CORDEROY, E. Progress: life of George Stephenson: a lecture. [1858.] pp. 68.   PC

    Privately printed.

2447 OLIVER, T. The Stephenson Monument: what should it be?: a question and answer addressed to the subscribers. 2nd edn. *Newcastle upon Tyne*, 1858. pp. 17.   BM

2448 The LIFE of George Stephenson, the little mechanic and great engineer. *London*, 1861. pp. 24.   BM

2449 JEAFFRESON, J. C. The life of Robert Stephenson . . . *London*, 1864. 2 vols. (pp. xv, 363; ix, 335.)   BM

2450 LUCCHESINI, A. Vita di Giorgio Stephenson. *Firenze*, 1869. pp. 108.   ICE

2451 ANDRESON, A. George Stephenson: grundlæggeren af Jaernbanerne . . . efter Samuel Smiles 'Lives of the engineers'. *København*, 1877. pp. 144.   BM

2452 SUMMERSIDE, T. Anecdotes, reminiscences and conversations of and with the late George Stephenson, father of railways, characteristically illustrative of his adroitness, sarcasm, benevolence, and intrepidity. By T. Summerside, who knew him when he was poor, served him when he was rich, and assisted to carry him to his final resting place. *London*, [1878.] pp. xi, 116, with 2 portraits.   BM

2453 WILLIAMS, E. L. George Stephenson. *Manchester*, 1880. pp. 24.   LSE

    Paper, Manchester Association of Employers, Foremen & Draughtsmen.

*2454 DUNCAN, W. The Stephenson Centenary, containing the proceedings of the day, the processions and decorations, with the speeches delivered upon the occasion; illustrated with views. Edited by Wm. Duncan, Newcastle. *London*, [1881.] pp. xii, 118. BM

    Chiefly compiled from the *Newcastle Chronicle*, 10 June, 1881.

2455 GEORGE STEPHENSON CENTENARY FESTIVAL COMMITTEE. Centenary Festival, 1881. George Stephenson . . . his life and work as founder of the railway locomotive system. . . *London & Derby*, [1881.] pp. 109, with illus.   RC

2456 MACNAY, C. George Stephenson and the progress of railway enterprise . . . *Newcastle upon Tyne*, 1881. pp. 32, with illus.   PC

    Issued in connection with the George Stephenson Centenary Exhibition, 9 June, 1881.

2457 NEWCASTLE ON TYNE—GEORGE STEPHENSON CENTENARY, 1881. Official Programme of the grand procession and demonstration on Thursday, 9 June, 1881. *Newcastle on Tyne*, [1881.] pp. 8.   IME

2458 NEWCASTLE WEEKLY CHRONICLE. Stephenson Centenary Supplement, Saturday, June 11, 1881. pp. 4.   IME

2459 RAILWAY SERVANTS ORPHANAGE, DERBY. Life of George Stephenson. [*Derby*, 1881.] pp. 109.   IT

    Issued to raise funds to build a 'George Stephenson Wing'.

2460 BOWES, I. George Stephenson, the locomotive, and the first public railway: a lecture delivered at the Salford Royal Museum and Library. *Manchester & London*, 1883. pp. 24.   MANCHESTER PL

2461 SMITH, J. F. Frederick Swanwick: a sketch. [*Edinburgh*,] 1888. pp. xii, 105.   BM

    'Printed for private circulation.'

    His work as a railway engineer, mostly in association with George Stephenson. Includes letters from G. S. and Smith's speech at the Centenary of Stephenson's birth, held at Chesterfield, 9 June, 1881, reprinted from the *Derbyshire Courier*.

2462 HATTON, J. George Stephenson. *In his* 'Old lamps and new: an after-dinner chat.' [1890.] pp. 265–314.

2463 MATEAUX, C. L. George and Robert Stephenson. *London*, 1891. pp. 128.   RC

2464 [BURROWS, E.] The triumphs of steam; or, Stories from the lives of Watt, Arkwright, and Stephenson. *London*, 1859. pp. viii, 263. BM
    pp. 83–263 relate to G. Stephenson and the Liverpool & Manchester Rly.
—— another edn., by H. Frith, *London*, 1892. pp. xii, 263. BM

2465 CHAMBERS, W. & R., *publishers*. The story of Watt and Stephenson . . . *London*, [1892.] pp. 136, with plates. BM
    Bound with *Eminent engineers: Watt, Stephenson, Telford, and Brindley*.

2466 BOWES, I. Rails and waterways. George Stephenson and M. Ferdinand de Lesseps: the men and their work: the first public railway in the world, and the Suez and Panama Canals. *London*, [1893.] pp. 62. BM
    pp. [7]–28, G. Stephenson: The Locomotive: The Stockton & Darlington Rly.

2467 DEANE, D. J. George Stephenson, father and founder of the railway system. *London*, [1899.] pp. 176, with illus. BM

2468 WERTHER, G. Erinnerungen an die Zeit der ersten Eisenbahnen und ihren Urheber, George Stephenson. *Hannover*, [1901.] pp. 30. ICE
    Reprint from *Zeitschrift für Lokomotivführer*.

2469 ALEXANDER, J. The two Stephensons, pioneers of the railway system . . . *London*, [1903.] pp. 160, with illus. BM

2470 P[AINE,] E. M. S. The two James's and the two Stephensons; or, The earliest history of passenger transit on railways. *London*, 1861. pp. viii, 121, with fold. plan. BM: UL(GL)
    Based on family records, asserting the claim of William James rather than George Stephenson to the title of 'the Father of Railways'. Inserted in the pocket at the end of the UL(GL) copy are three holograph letters from E. M. S. Paine to Lord Bagot, dated April and May 1866.
—— A centenary reprint, with an introduction by L. T. C. Rolt. *Dawlish: David & Charles; London: Phœnix House*, 1961. pp. xiv, 121, with portrait & map. BM

*2471 SMILES, S. The life of George Stephenson, railway engineer. *London*, 1857. pp. xvi, 516. BM
    pp. 477–512, 'Resumé of the railway system and its results' by Robert Stephenson.
—— 2nd edn. *London*, 1857. pp. xvi, 528. IME
—— 3rd, *London*, 1857. pp. xvi, 546. BM
—— 4th (reprint), *London*, 1857. BM
—— 5th, *London*, 1858. pp. xvi, 557. BM
—— German edn. 'Georg Stephenson geschildert in seinem Leben und Wirken.' *Stuttgart*, 1859. pp. viii, 504. BM
—— abridged edn. 'The story of the life of George Stephenson.' *London*, 1859. pp. xii, 356. (Reprinted 1860, 1862 & 1863.) BM
—— new edn. 'The story of the life of George Stephenson.' *London*, 1864. pp. xiv, 388. BM

—— Centenary edn. *London*, 1881. pp. x, 229. BM
—— —— New impr. *London*, 1903. BM

*2472 SMILES, S. Lives of the engineers; with an account of their principal works, comprising also a history of inland communication in Britain. *London*, 1861–2. 3 vols. BM
    vol. 3, George and Robert Stephenson. pp. xx, 512, with illus.
—— another edn. *London*, 1868. vol. 3, pp. lii, 542. BM
—— New & rev. edn. *London*, 1874. pp. xl, 388. BM
—— Popular edn. *London*, 1904. pp. xliv, 466. BM

2473 GEORGE Stephenson . . . the founder of railways. 2nd edn. *London*, 1907. pp. 39. [*Anna Library*.] BM

2474 MAXWELL, R. George Stephenson . . . *London*, 1920. pp. 191, with 9 illus. BM
    Introductory.

2475 FUERST, A. Die Hundertjährige Eisenbahn, wie Meisterhände sie schufen . . . *Berlin*, 1925. pp. 308, with many illus. BM
    pp. 96–123, 'Der Meister'. G. Stephenson.

2476 CHESTERFIELD CORPORATION—EDUCATION COMMITTEE. Chesterfield education: the record of four years of experiment and reconstruction . . . *Chesterfield*, 1932. BM
    pp. 212–32, Tapton House. This includes an account of the house during George Stephenson's occupation.

2477 PARSONAGE, W. R. A short biography of George Stephenson. [*London*,] 1937. pp. 373–91, with 6 illus. on 4 plates. IME
    Excerpt, *Min. Proc. I.M.E.*, vol. 136, 1937.

2478 INSTITUTION OF MECHANICAL ENGINEERS. Centenary celebrations, 9th–13th June, 1947: brief guide to exhibition of Stephenson relics at the Institution. [*London*, 1947.] pp. 13. BM
    Includes reproductions of holograph letters.

2479 CHESTERFIELD—GEORGE STEPHENSON CENTENARY COMMEMORATION. British Railways Exhibition, Chesterfield . . . August 12–15, 1948. Programme. [*Chesterfield*, 1948.] pp. [8.] PC
    A descriptive list of exhibits.

2480 CHESTERFIELD—GEORGE STEPHENSON CENTENARY COMMEMORATION. Guide to Visitors. *Chesterfield*, 1948. pp. 48, with illus. & portrait. PC
    pp. 5–12, a short biography, by W. R. Parsonage.

2481 INSTITUTION OF MECHANICAL ENGINEERS. George Stephenson: list of relics at the Science Museum and other places. 1948. *Typescript*. pp. 18. IME

2482 LAING ART GALLERY [Newcastle upon Tyne]. George Stephenson Centenary Exhibition, 12th–21st August 1948. Compiled

by C. Bernard Stevenson, Curator. [*Newcastle-upon-Tyne*, 1948.] pp. 35, with 12 plates. PC
Description of 128 exhibits and a short biography of G. Stephenson.

2483 MICKLEWRIGHT, G. R. Stephenson Centenary Commemoration. Bibliography, com-
b piled by G. R. Micklewright. *Chesterfield: Chesterfield Library & Museum Committee*, [1948.] pp. 12. SL

2484 MCCARTNEY, D. George Stephenson. *London: Harrap*, 1951. pp. 64, with illus. [*Harrap's Great Engineers Library*.] BM

2485 THOMAS, J. The story of George Stephenson; illustrated by Serena Chance. *London: O.U.P.*, 1952. pp. 171. BM
Introductory.

2486 HALWARD, L. Famous British engineers. *London: Phoenix House*, 1953. pp. 192. BM
pp. 124–59, George Stephenson.

2487 ROWLAND, J. H. S. George Stephenson, creator of Britain's railways. *London: Odhams Press*, 1954. pp. 239, with plates & a bibliography. BM

2488 WYMER, N. G. George Stephenson. [*London:*] *O.U.P.*, [1957.] pp. 31, with illus. [*Lives of Great Men & Women*.] BM

2489 NOCK, O. S. Father of Railways: the story of George Stephenson; illustrated by Robert Hodgson. *Edinburgh: Nelson*, 1958. pp. 84. BM

2490 WILLIAMSON, J. A. George and Robert Stephenson; illustrated by Peter Dunbar. *London: Black*, 1958. pp. 94. [*Lives to Remember* Series.] IT

2491 ELLIS, C. H. The young George Stephenson; illustrated by William Randell. *London: Max Parrish*, 1959. pp. 120. BM
For young readers.

*2492 ROLT, L. T. C. George and Robert Stephenson: the railway revolution; with drawings and maps by Kenneth Lindley. *London: Longmans*, 1960. pp. xviii, 356, with 23 plates, drawings & maps. BM

Robert Stevenson

2493 STEVENSON, A. Biographical sketch of the late Robert Stevenson . . . civil engineer. *Edinburgh*, 1861. pp. 32. BM
pp. 25–7, his railway survey work and his examination of the essays submitted to the Highland Society in 1818 on the subject of railroads, published in the Society's *Transactions*. Also a letter from George Stephenson inviting him to Killingworth.

2494 STEVENSON, D. Life of Robert Stevenson. *London & New York*, 1878. pp. x, 283. BM
pp. 111–29, Railways, 1812–26.

Thomas Telford

2495 GIBB, A. The story of Telford . . . *London*, 1935. pp. xx, 357. BM
pp. 320–1, details of his work in the construction of seven railways.

E 2   CIVIL ENGINEERING (General)

Construction and maintenance—Problems of terrain (gradients, cuttings, tunnelling, and embanking)

Historical

2496 VIGNOLES, C. B. Address . . . on his election as President of the Institution of Civil Engineers, Session 1869–70. *London*, 1870. pp. 59. BM
Engineering progress, and some reminiscences.

2497 PATENT OFFICE. Patents for inventions. Abridgments of specifications relating to railways, A.D. 1803–1866. 2nd edn. (Compiled by B. Woodcroft.) *London*, 1873. pp. xxxiii, 673. BM: PO
Construction and arrangement of railways and tramways.

2498 RENNIE, J. Autobiography of Sir John Rennie . . . *London*, 1875. pp. viii, 464. BM
pp. 415–21, his work on railway construction.

2499 COLE, H. Fifty years of public work of Sir Henry Cole, accounted for in his deeds,

speeches, and writings. *London*, 1884. 2 vols. BM
vol. 1, pp. 70–97, 'Work with railways and docks.'

2500 GALE, T. A brief account of the making and the working of the great Box Tunnel; with illustrations. By Thomas Gale, native of Box, late office porter at the G.W.R. Station, Bath. Introduced and revised by R. E. Peach. *Bath*, 1884. pp. 16, with illus. NLC
Produced and sold to help Gale during a period of impoverishment and in retirement.

2501 PATENT OFFICE. Patents for inventions. Abridgments of specifications relating to railways: part 2, A.D. 1867–76. (Compiled by H. Reader Lack.) *London*, 1884. pp. xix, 1308. BM: PO

2502 MACDERMOTT, F. The life and work of Joseph Firbank . . . railway contractor. *London*, 1887. pp. v, 144, with illus. on plates & in text, & a list of contracts. BM

*2503 HELPS, A. Life and labours of Mr. Brassey, 1805–1870. *London*, 1872. pp. xiv, 386, with 7 plates.
pp. 161–6, table of railway and other contracts.
—— 2nd edn. (reprint). *London*, 1872.   BM
—— 3rd (reprint). *London*, 1872.   BM
—— 7th, *London*, 1888. pp. x, 212.   BM

2504 SPENCER, H. An Autobiography. *London*, 1904. 2 vols.   BM
In vol. 1, Surveying for the London & Birmingham under Charles Fox, 1838 (with a narrative of his ride in a brakeless, uncoupled wagon from Harrow to Willesden); surveying for the Birmingham & Gloucester at Worcester, Powick and Bromsgrove, under W. S. Moorsom; his work under William B. Prichard on several schemes in 1845, including the Northampton, Daventry, Leamington & Warwick; the South Wales Rly.; impressions of I. K. Brunel; memoirs on the life and work of a railway surveyor in the 1840's; his views on the mania for speculation, 1844–6, and on corruption in the conduct of railway affairs generally.
—— reprinted, *London*, 1926. 2 vols.

2505 HOBSON, G. A. The life of Sir James Falshaw . . . by his nephew . . . *Chiswick (London): Caradoc Press*, 1905.   BM
Limited edition, 100 on paper, two on vellum.
pp. 45–76, James Falshaw's work as a railway civil engineer and contractor, Leeds & Selby; Whitby & Pickering; Stockton & Hartlepool; Scottish Central; South Midland; North British.

2506 GAIRNS, J. F. Fifty years of railway engineering, 1864–1914. *In* 'Jubilee of the Railway News, 1864–1914.' [*London*, 1914.] (pp. 1–24 of Engineering section), with illus.   BM

2507 SCIENCE MUSEUM [London]. Land transport; IV, railway construction and working. Compiled by E. A. Forward. *London*, 1927. pp. 84, with 20 illus. on 10 plates. [*Catalogue of the Collections in the Science Museum*]   BM
Description of 227 exhibits.

2508 ALLEN, C. J. Railway planning and making; with four colour plates and illustrations from photographs. *London*, 1928. pp. vii. 132.   BM
Also published as part one of his *The Steel Highway* (1928).
Introductory.

2509 INSTITUTION OF CIVIL ENGINEERS. A brief history of the Institution of Civil Engineers, with an account of the Charter Centenary Celebration, June 1928. [*London*, 1928.] pp. 95, with plates & illus.   IT

2510 KIRBY, R. S. *and* LAURSON, P. G. The early years of modern civil engineering. *New Haven*, 1932. pp. xvi, 324, with illus. on plates & bibliogr. notes.   BM
pp. 87–131, Railroads. Includes early history and development of the railways in Gt. Britain up to the London & Birmingham (1838);

atmospheric system, etc., and chapters on bridges and tunnels.

2511 JUBILEE Souvenir of the Permanent Way Institution: a supplement to the July 1934 issue of 'The Railway Engineer'. *London: Railway Engineer*, 1934. pp. 24, with illus.   BM
History of the Institution followed by essays on early permanent way, the development of signalling, and 'Brunel, our inspiration'.

2512 BLACK, A. The story of tunnels. *New York*, 1937. pp. xv, 245, with plates.   BM
Includes some British tunnels and the Channel Tunnel schemes.

2513 BRUNTON, J. John Brunton's Book, 1812–1899: being the memories of J. Brunton, engineer; from a manuscript in his own hand written for his grandchildren and now first printed. *Cambridge*, 1939. pp. viii, 163. BM

2514 BRODIE, R. The reminiscences of a civil engineering contractor. *Bristol: Wright*, 1942. pp. 106, with 3 plates.   PC
Includes accounts of his work in constructing the Montrose & Arbroath, Whitby & Loftus, Scarborough & Whitby, Mersey, and Burntisland & Inverkeithing railways.

*2515 GRADIENTS of the British main line railways. *London: Railway Magazine*, 1936. pp. 90.   BM
211 gradient profiles, with index.
—— *London*, 1947. pp. viii, 104.   BM
245 gradient profiles, with index.

2516 BRITISH RAILWAYS. A short survey of railway civil engineering. [*London*, May 1950.] pp. 29.   BR
Issued in connection with Exhibition of Railway Civil Engineering jointly presented by the I.C.E. and the Railway Executive, May 1950.

2517 FEDERATION OF CIVIL ENGINEERING CONTRACTORS. The British civil engineering contracting industry: illustrated history. *London*, 1956. pp. 188[191]. la. 4°.   BR
pp. [12]–19, 'Railways'; with 15 illus.

2518 NORRIE, C. M. Bridging the years: a short history of British civil engineering. *London: Edward Arnold*, 1956. pp. 212, with illus., incl. portraits.   BM
Includes railway construction and contracting.

Contemporaneous

2519 LENGTHS and levels to Bradshaw's maps of canals, navigable rivers, and railways, from actual survey. *London*, 1832. pp. 15.   UL(GL)
—— another edn. 'Lengths and levels to Bradshaw's Maps of the Canals, navigable rivers and railways in the principal parts of England.' *London*, 1833. pp. 20   UL(GL)

2520 BRUNTON, W. Description of a practical and economical method of excavating ground and forming embankments for railways . . . *London*, 1836. pp. 30. BM

2521 REYNOLDS, J. An explanation of a mode of constructing railways on the 'continuous bearing' principle. *London*, 1837. pp. 21. BM
Rails embedded in ballast. pp. 15–21, two reports by H. R. Palmer and by Messrs. Grainger & Miller on Reynolds' system.

2522 SIMMS, F. W. Secto-planography: a description of Mr. MacNeill's method of laying down railway sections and plans in juxtaposition, as adapted by the Standing Order Committee of the House of Commons, 1837. *London*, 1837. pp. 11, with 3 fold. plates. LC

2523 BRADSHAW, G. Tables of the gradients to Bradshaw's map of the railways of Great Britain, containing particulars of the lengths, levels and gradients of all the principal railways in the Kingdom. Dedicated to James Walker. *Manchester: George Bradshaw*, 1839. pp. 26[28]. BR

2524 KOLLMANN, G. A. Some observations on the imperfections of the present system of constructing railways; with an account of the new method of construction invented by Mr. Kollmann. *London*, 1839. pp. 16. [*Railway Papers*, no. 1.] BM

2525 A PRACTICAL inquiry into the laws of excavation and embankment upon railways . . . with Appendix and plates . . . By a resident assistant engineer. *London*, 1840. pp. 173, with 3 plates. UL(GL)

2526 COWDIN, J. Description and testimonials of the patent locomotive steam double pile driving and railway grading machine . . . also; remarks on railways in Europe and America; with illustrations. *London*, 1842. pp. 26. BM

2527 GALBRAITH, W. Trigonometrical surveying, levelling and railway engineering. *Edinburgh & London*, 1842. pp. viii, 161, 20, with geodetical tables. BM

2528 BEYSE, A. W. Neueste Erfahrungen im Eisenbahnwesen. *Karlsruhe*, 1844. 3 Hefte. BM
vol. 1 contains a description of Joseph Cowdin's pile driver in use in England, with letters and extracts from British periodicals (in German) and a picture of the machine.

2529 BREES, S. C. A Glossary of Civil Engineering . . . *London*, 1844. pp. 310[311], with illus. ICE
Includes railway terms.

2530 CASTLE, H. J. Railway curves . . . *London*, [1845?] pp. 29, with plates and diagrams. BM

2531 DARBYSHIRE, G. C. Tables for setting out railway curves. *Derby*, 1846. pp. [14.] BM

2532 GREENHOW, C. H. Exposition of the danger and deficiencies of the present mode of railway construction; with suggestions for its improvement. *London*, 1846. pp. 29, with 5 plates. ICE
Suggests concave tyres and convex rails, etc.

2533 HASKOLL, W. D. The Assistant Engineer's Railway Guide in Boring . . . *London*, 1846. pp. 136, with 60 illus., tables, & 3. la. fold. plates. BM

2534 LOWE, J. Earthwork table for parliamentary and working sections of railways. *London*, 1846. pp. vi, [30.] BM

2535 MACNEILL, J. B. Tables for calculating the cubic quantity of earth work in the cuttings and embankments of canals, railways, and turnpike roads. *London*, 1833. pp. xxxviii, 254, with diagrams on 4 plates. BM
—— 2nd edn. 'Tables for facilitating the calculation of earth work in the cuttings and embankments of railways, canals, and other public works. 2nd edn., corrected & considerably enlarged.' *Dublin*, 1846. pp. xxxvi, 368, with diagrams on 4 plates. BM

2536 QUESTED, J. A treatise on railway surveying and levelling in which the author has endeavoured to simplify the most approved methods now adopted by surveyors. *London*, 1846. pp. viii, 73. BM

2537 BRODIE, R. Rules for ranging railway curves with the theodolite and without tables. *London*, 1847. pp. 16. BM

2538 CASTLE, H. J. Engineering field notes on parish and railway surveying and levelling, with plans and sections; being a sequel to his Elementary Text Book, with practical formulae . . . 2nd edn. *London*, 1847. pp. xv, 303, 13, 13, 16, with frontis., illus. & 9 plates (some fold., incl. diagrams). LC

2539 GARDNER, E. V. An easy introduction to railway mensuration, illustrated by drawings from original works that have been carried out upon various English railway lines . . . *London*, 1847. pp. xi, 63. BM

2540 HILL, W. An essay on the theory and practice of setting out railway curves. *London*, 1847. pp. 24. ICE

2541 HUNTINGDON, J. B. Tables and rules for facilitating the calculation of earthwork, land, curves, distances, and gradients, required in the formation of railways, roads, and canals. *London*, 1846. H
—— 2nd edn. *London*, 1847. pp. xvii, clxxii, [173]–300. BM

2542 IBBETSON, D. J. H. Practical rules for ascertaining the relation between alterations in gradients and the corresponding changes in contents. *London*, 1847. pp. 24. BM

2543 KELLY, W. Tables for determining the cubical content of earthwork in the construction of railways and common roads, whether on level ground or side cutting. *Dublin*, 1847. pp. 69, with 4 diagrams on 2 plates.　BM

2544 LAW, H. Examples of the modes of setting out railway curves. [1847.] pp. 39.　ICE
pp. 23 to end, 'On setting out the widths of ground required for the works of a railway or canal'. By F. W. Simms.

2545 MAY, R. C. A new method of setting out railway curves, by reflecting the angle in a segment. 2nd edn. *London*, 1847. pp. 31. BM

2546 SIBLEY, C. K. *and* RUTHERFORD, W. Tables for estimating the contents in cubic yards of the earthwork of railways and other public works. *London*, 1847.　BM
Ten detailed tables.

2547 BAKER, T. Railway engineering; or, Field work preparatory to the construction of railways . . . *London*, 1848. pp. 64, with fold. table.　ICE

2548 DAY, J. A practical treatise on the construction and formation of railways, showing the practical application and expense of excavating, haulage, embanking and permanent-way laying . . . *London*, 1839, pp. xii, 210, with illus.　PC
A non-technical work.
—— 2nd edn. *London*, 1839. pp. xii, 210. BM
—— 3rd. *London*, 1848. pp. xii, 216.　BM

2549 HASKOLL, W. D. Assistant Engineer's Railway Guide, containing instructions for setting out the lines and levels of railway works . . . illustrated by upwards of 120 woodcuts, etc., part 2. *London*, 1848. pp. iv, 192[223].　BM
A supplementary volume to his *Assistant Engineer's Railway Guide in Boring* (1846).

2550 KENNEDY, A. *and* HACKWOOD, R. W. Tables for setting out curves for railways, canals, roads, etc. *London*, 1849. pp. 66. BM

2551 WILLIAMS, R. P. The cyclograph: a new instrument for setting out railway curves . . . illustrated with engravings and woodcuts. *London*, 1849. pp. 13, with 3 plates.　ICE

2552 ADAMS, W. B. Practical remarks on railways and permanent way as adapted to the various requirements of transit; with diagrams. *London*, 1854. pp. 16, with fold. plate of W. B. Adams' 'Improved rails and fastenings'.　BM
A discourse on the salient features of street railways, light, elevated and underground railways, and 'moveable lines'.

2553 HASKOLL, W. D. Railway construction, from the setting out of the centre line to the completion of the works . . . *London*, 1857. 2 vols. (pp. x, 368), with 28[43] plates (some fold.).　UL(GL)

2554 BREES, S. C. Railway practice: a collection of working plans and practical details of construction in the public works of the most celebrated engineers . . . on the several railways . . . throughout the Kingdom: a series of original designs for every description of railway works, in various styles of architecture . . . *London*, 1837. pp. xxxii, 108, with 77 plates.　BM
—— 2nd edn. *London*, 1838. pp. xxxvi, 106. (81 pl.)　ICE
—— Appendix, 1839. pp. vii, 373. (6 pl.) BM
—— 2nd series, 1840. pp. 124. (61 pl.)　BM
—— 3rd series, 1847. pp. xv, 247. (69 pl.)　BM
—— 4th series, 1847. pp. 46, clii. (69 pl.) BM
—— 3rd edn. *London*, 1847. pp. 164. (70 pl.)　UL(GL)
—— [4th edn.] *London*, 1859. pp. 247. SL
—— 'Science pratique des chemins de fer.' *Liège*, 1840, *Bruxelles*, 1841, and *Paris*, 1841.

2555 NESBIT, A. A complete treatise on practical land surveying . . . 9th edition, to which are now added, Plane trigonometry . . . Railway engineering. *London*, 1847. pp. xxiii, 426[428], with fold. plate & tables at end. BM
—— 10th edn. *London*, 1855. pp. xxii, 426. BM
—— 11th, *London*, 1864. pp. xxi, 486. BM
—— 12th, *London*, 1870. pp. xxiii, 499. BM

2556 RICHARDSON, C. The Severn Tunnel: a paper read at the forty-fifth meeting of the British Association, held at Bristol, August 25, 1875. *Bristol*, 1875. pp. 23.　BM
Description of its construction.

2557 MORRISON, G. J. The ventilation and working of railway tunnels . . . *London*, 1876. pp. 79, with fold. diagram.　UL(GL)
Excerpt, *Min. Proc. I.C.E.*, vol. 44, 1875/6.

2558 JONES, A. W. A paper on modern tramway construction, read before the Society of Engineers on 3 Nov., 1879. [1879.] pp. 179–96, with fold. plate.　ICE

2559 BARRY, J. W. *and* BRAMWELL, F. J. Railways and locomotives: lectures delivered at the School of Military Engineering at Chatham in 1877. *London*, 1882. pp. ix, 427, with illus.　BM
Principles of railway construction and of signalling.

2560 LAW, H. The rudiments of civil engineering for the use of beginners. *London*, 1848–9. 2 pts. in 1 vol.　BM
pt. 2, pp. 16–69, railway construction, including two plates and twenty-two illustrations.
—— 6th edn. *London*., 1881. pp. xxii, 638.　BM
pp. 100–60, railway and tramway construction.
—— 7th, *London*, 1884.　BM

2561 RICHARDSON, C. The Severn Tunnel: a paper read before the Clifton Scientific Club,

12 March, 1887. [*Bristol*,] 1887. pp. 28. ICE
History of the scheme up to its opening.

2562 WALKER, T. A. The Severn Tunnel. *London*, 1887. pp. 26. ELTHAM PL

2563 RICHARDSON, C. The Severn Tunnel: its origin and construction. [*Bristol*,] 1888. pp. 8. ICE

2564 WALKER, T. A. The Severn Tunnel, its construction and difficulties, 1872–1887; with five portraits and upwards of forty sketches and plans. *London*, 1888. pp. xv, 188. BM
—— 2nd edn. *London*, 1890. pp. xxi, 188. BM
—— 3rd. *London*, 1891. pp. xxi, 195. BM

2565 NEWMAN, J. Scamping tricks and odd knowledge occasionally practised upon public works; chronicled from the confessions of some old practitioners. *London*, 1893. pp. viii, 129. LSE
pp. 103–14 and elsewhere, permanent way, railway tunnel and bridge construction.

2566 SIMMS, F. W. Practical tunnelling; explaining in detail the setting out of the works . . . and the construction of the brickwork of tunnels . . . as exemplified by . . . Bletchingley and Saltwood Tunnels. *London*, 1844. pp. xi, 174, with 13 plates (8 fold.) & 47 illus. BM
—— 2nd edn. with additional plates. *London*, 1859. pp. 189. BM
—— 3rd, *London*, 1877. pp. xviii, 354. BM
—— 4th, greatly extended. *London*, 1896. pp. xxxii, 548. BM

2567 FULLER, H. J. The preparation of parliamentary plans for railways. *London*, 1897. pp. 39. ICE

2568 CALLARD, E. The ventilation of the Metropolitan Railway tunnels: the case for mechanical ventilation. Memorandum submitted to the Committee appointed by the Board of Trade (Departmental Committee on the Ventilation of London Underground Railways.) *London*, 1898. pp. 36. ICE

2569 MILLS, W. H. Railway construction . . . *London*, 1898. pp. vi, 365, with illus. BM
Outline descriptions of construction and maintenance of works and equipment.

2570 WOOD, O. T. The design and construction of earthworks. *In* 'Modern railway working', edited by John Macaulay. vol. 2, 1912. pp. 117–41, with diagrams. BM

2571 COPPERTHWAITE, W. C. Tunnel construction with shields and compressed air. *In* 'Modern railway working', edited by John Macaulay. vol. 3, 1913. pp. 55–109, with illus. & diagrams. BM

2572 PLANNING and setting out. *In* 'Modern railway working', edited by John Macaulay. vol. 2, 1913. pp. 97–116, with diagrams. BM

2573 TRAVERS, W., MILEHAM, G. S. *and* JOSCELYNE, A. B. Re-inforced concrete in railway construction. *In* 'Modern railway working', edited by John Macaulay. vol. 3, 1913. pp. 111–56, with illus. & diagrams. BM

2574 The INSTITUTION of Civil Engineers. *In* 'Jubilee of the Railway News, 1864–1914.' *London: Railway News*, [1914.] pp. 176–9. BM

2575 OLDFIELD, F. W. F. Sidings and warehouses: notes and suggestions on construction and equipment. *Hull*, [*c.* 1906–14.] pp. 13.

2576 WINN, R. G. A. The goods clearing house system and machinery explained. *Westminster*, 1917. pp. [194]–232, with illus. & diagrams.
Paper, Society of Engineers, 7 May, 1917.
Gattie's system.

2577 HULL, H. A. Railway maintenance problems. *London: Railway Gazette*, 1936. pp. vii, 82, with diagrams. BM
Practical advice for maintenance of permanent way, earthworks, drainage, buildings, etc.

2578 BEAVER, S. H. Geography from a railway train. [*London*, 1937.] pp. 19. LSE
Reprinted from *Geography*, Dec. 1936.
Notes made on journeys on main line railways from London. Geographical and geological features, and gradients.

2579 CEMENT AND CONCRETE ASSOATCIION. Concrete in railway construction. *London*, 1941. pp. 51, with 85 illus., tables & diagrams. SL

2580 [CLARK, R. H.] Rail and platform plans of British stations: part one. *South Merstham: Railway & Technical Press*, 1947. pp. 96. [*British Railways Illustrated*: series 2, part 1.] BM
Eighty-nine diagrams.
No more published.

2581 BRITISH RAILWAYS. Railway civil engineering as a career. *London*, [1953.] pp. 36, with many illus. IT

*2582 O'DELL, A. C. Railways and geography. *London: Hutchinson*, 1956. pp. 198. BM
The influence of geographical factors on the construction and operation of railways; including urban problems.

2583 PEARSON, H. M. Railway works construction. *London: Odhams*, 1960. pp. 303, with illus. & diagrams. BM
A textbook for railway and contractors works staff.

E 3   PERMANENT WAY

For special forms of track see **D 1 – 5**
For the 'War of the Gauges' see **F 2**

Historical

2584 PATENT OFFICE. Patents for inventions. Abridgment of specifications relating to railways, A.D. 1770–1863. (Compiled by B. Woodcroft.) *London*, 1868. pp. xiv, 538.
BM: PO
Permanent way and other equipment. Generally excluding locomotives, rolling stock, and signalling.

2585 POLE, W. Some notes on the early history of railway gauge. *Birmingham*, [1875.] pp. 66–90.   BM
Excerpt, *Min. Proc. I.M.E.*

2586 VIGNOLES, O. J. Life of Charles Blacker Vignoles, soldier and civil engineer . . . a reminiscence of early railway history. *London & New York*, 1889. pp. xx, 407, with illus.   BM

2587 HAARMANN, A. Das Eisenbahngeleise. *Leipzig*, 1891(1892). 2 vols.   BM
Bd. 1, Geschichtlicher Teil. pp. xl, 852, with 1837 illus.
Bd. 2, Das Eisenbahngeleis. Kritischer Teil. 1892. pp. ix, 227, with 503 illus.
A very detailed history and description of permanent way, including British; with bibliographical notes.

2588 ALLEN, C. J. Modern British permanent way . . . *London*, 1915. pp. xv, 147, with diagrams.   BM
pp. 3–8, 'The history and development of the modern bull-headed steel rail'.

2589 RAIDABURGH, G. P. Origin and development of the railway rail, English and American, wood, iron and steel. *Philadelphia*, 1915. pp. 54, with 49 illus. in text.   BM
Cover title—'The railway rail'.

2590 BLAND, F. A century of permanent way . . . Section 1. *Sheffield*, 1925. pp. 72, with many illus.   LSE
'A paper prepared for the Annual Convention of the Permanent Way Institution, 8 July, 1925.' Reprinted articles from *Edgar Allen News*.

2591 FUERST, A. Die Hundertjährige Eisenbahn; wie Meisterhände sie schufen; mit vielen Abbildungen. *Berlin*, 1925. pp. 308.   BM
pp. 168–212, 'Geschichte des Gleises'.

2592 NEWLANDS, A. The railway highway. [*London*, 1934.] pp. 35.   BR
Jubilee Lecture, Permanent Way Institution, 1934. Reprinted from *P.W.I. Journal*, vol. 52, pt. 2, August 1934.
History of railed ways from 15th century, and the present road-rail problem.

2593 LEE, C. E. The evolution of permanent way. *London*, 1937. pp. 64, with illus & bibliogr. notes.   BM
Paper, P.W. Inst., 8 March, 1937: Suppl., *Jnl. P.W. Inst.*, vol. 55, August 1937.
—— another edn. 'The evolution of railways.' *London: Railway Gazette*, 1937. pp. viii, 64.   BM
—— 2nd edn., rev. & enl. *London*, 1943. pp. viii, 108.   BM

2594 PERMANENT WAY INSTITUTION. Diamond Jubilee Souvenir, July 1944. *London*, 1944. pp. 76, with illus., incl. ports., on plates; illus. & diagrams in text.   IT

2595 GREENLEAF, H. *and* TYERS, G. The permanent way (Britain's railroads in the making); with 78 illustrations in photogravure and 4 colour plates. *London: Winchester Publications*, 1948. pp. xi, 196.
BM
Includes descriptions of some tunnels, bridges and viaducts, with a 9-page list.

2596 DEARDEN, J. The centenary of the steel rail. pp. 11–24.   BR
Reprinted from *Railway Steel Topics*, vol. 4, no. 1, 1957.

2597 SMITH, R. S. England's first rails: a reconsideration. *Nottingham: Sisson & Parker*, [1960.] pp. [119]–34, with 50 bibliogr. notes.   BM
Reprinted from *Renaissance and Modern Studies*, vol. 4, 1960.

Contemporaneous

*2598 CURR, J. The Coal Viewer and the Engine Builder's Practical Companion. *Sheffield*, 1797. pp. 96.   BM
Includes a detailed description of the method of constructing wagons ('corves') and plateways.

2599 LONGRIDGE, M. [*and* BIRKINSHAW, J.] Specification of John Birkinshaw's patent for an improvement in the construction of malleable iron rails to be used in rail roads; with remarks on the comparative merits of cast metal and malleable iron rail-ways, with a plate. *Newcastle*, 1821. pp. 10.   BM
—— another edn. *Newcastle*, 1822. pp. 10.   UL(GL)
—— another edn. *Newcastle*, 1824. pp. 14, 8.   SL

2600 BARLOW, P. Experiments on the transverse strength and other properties of malleable iron, with reference to its uses for railway bars . . . *London*, 1835. pp. 97.   ICE

—— Expériences sur la force transversale et les autres propriétés du fer malléable dans son application aux chemins de fer . . . *Paris*, 1838. pp. 151. BM

2601 LECOUNT, P. An examination of Professor Barlow's reports on iron rails. *London*, [1836. pp. 192,] with 2 plates (1 fold.) & diagrams. BM

2602 LECOUNT, P. A letter from 'Jonah' to Professor Barlow, on iron rails. *London*, 1836. pp. 41. BM

2603 LECOUNT, P. Remarks on the cheapest distance for railway blocks. *London*, [1836.] pp. 93. (i–xxxi, [32]–93.) ICE
In his introduction (pp. i–xxxi) P. Lecount explains his differences with P. Barlow's opinions and includes a reprint of articles by Barlow and himself from the *Philosophical Magazine*.

2604 PARKIN, T. A letter on important matters addressed to the proprietors of the London & Birmingham Railway, together with Dr. Birkbeck's and Professor Barlow's opinions on Mr. Parkin's patent railway invention, and which will interest the proprietors of all railways yet to be made. *London*, 1836. pp. 24, with fold. diagram. LSE
Deploring Stephenson's 'fishbelly rail' and offering his own, on continuous sleepers; with letters testifying to its success.

2605 REYNOLDS, J. Mr. Reynolds' plan for railways. [1836.] pp. [125]–130. LSE
From the *Railway Magazine* for June 1836. Continuous bearing principle for rails.

2606 BARLOW, P. Second report addressed to the directors and proprietors of the London & Birmingham Railway Co., founded on an inspection of, and experiments made on, the Liverpool & Manchester Railway. *London*, 1835. pp. 116, with illus., tables & diagrams. ICE
—— 2nd edn. 'Report on the weight of rails, the description of chairs and fastenings, the distance of the support and the size of blocks, of the Liverpool & Manchester Railway.' *London*, 1837. pp. 116. ICE

2607 WHITE, J. Description of certain improvements on railways, consisting of a newly invented railway chair and of a slate block constructed by machinery . . . *London*, 1837. pp. 16, with diagram. BM

2608 LONGRIDGE, M. [*and* BIRKINSHAW, J.] Remarks on the comparative merits of cast metal and malleable iron rail-ways, and an account of the Stockton & Darlington Railway . . . *Newcastle*, 1827. pp. iv, 22, 39. PO
—— another edn. '. . . and the Liverpool & Manchester Railway, by Henry Booth.' *Newcastle*, 1832. pp. 26, 39, 38. PO
—— another edn. *Newcastle*, 1838. pp. 32, 38, 38, with two lithograph letters to M.

Longridge from the London & Birmingham Rly. and from Peter Barlow. SL
A collection of correspondence, newspaper extracts, reports from railway companies, etc., brought together by Michael Longridge and John Birkinshaw of Bedlington Iron Works.
Also issued as an additional work bound in *Sketches of our information as to railroads*, by James Adamson. [*Newcastle*, 1826.] pp. 26.

2609 'GEOMETRICUS.' Round rail versus T rail; or, The principles of the geometrical railway system explained. By 'Geometricus'. *London*, 1846. pp. 29. BM
Advocating round rails.

2610 HOPKINS, J. A drawing and explanation of a new safety rail for railways invented by John Hopkins . . . *London*, [1846.] pp. 14, with la. fold. plate. ICE

2611 STEPHENSON, R. The double gauge: observations by Mr. R. Stephenson on Mr. Brunel's report on the double gauge. *London*, 1847. pp. 27, with 10 fold. diagrams. ICE
The difficulties of mixed gauge.

2612 BARLOW, W. H. On the construction of permanent way of railways; with an account of the wrought-iron permanent way laid down on the main line of the Midland Railway. *London*, 1850. pp. 25, with fold. diagram. ICE
Excerpt, *Min. Proc. I.C.E.*, vol. 9, 1849/50.

2613 SMITH, B. An improved system of working railways, whereby the assimilation of the broad and narrow gauges may be effected. *Carnarvon*, 1851. pp. 16, with diagrams. LSE
Narrow gauge track laid within broad gauge.

2614 WILLSON, H. B. Reports and correspondence on the 'patent compound rail'. *London*, 1851. pp. 20. BM
A split rail for smoother running.
—— another edn. *London*, 1852. pp. 16. UL(GL)

2615 LOCARD, E. Recherches sur les rails et leurs supports, extrait des ouvrages anglais de P. Barlow et N. Wood . . . *Paris*, 1853. pp. viii, 616. BM
—— Atlas. *Paris*, 1853. pp. XV. BM

2616 ADAMS, W. B. The construction and duration of the permanent way of railways in Europe . . . *London*, 1854. pp. 57, with illus. ICE
Excerpt, *Min. Proc. I.C.E.*, vol. 11, 1851/2.

2617 PERMANENT WAY CO. The Permanent Way Company's Circular, October 1855. *London*, [1855.] pp. 38[40], with 11 fold. diagrams. PC

2618 ADAMS, W. B. The varieties of permanent way, practically used, or tried, on railways up to the present period . . . and some recent improvements in the permanent way of railways by P. M. Parsons; with an abstract of the discussion upon both papers. Edited by Charles Manby. *London*, 1857. pp. 73, with fold. plate & 2 fold. tables. UL(GL)

Excerpt, *Min. Proc. I.C.E.*, vol. 16, Session 1856–57.

2619 PERMANENT WAY Co. Observations and experiments on cast-iron sleepers . . . *London*, 1857. pp. 24, with diagrams & tables. BM

*2620 PERMANENT WAY Co. Observations of the Permanent Way Company upon opinions expressed at the meeting of the Institution of Civil Engineers on Tuesday, Feb. 10 [7], 1857. *London*, 1857. pp. 14. BM

Engineers and the taking out of patents.
In the BM copy the date of the meeting on the title page is altered in ink from '10th' to '7th'.

2621 HAWORTH, J. Paper on street railways . . . *Manchester*, 1861. pp. 7. BM

Advocating his patent rail for street railways.

2622 FOX, F. On the results of trials of varieties of iron permanent way . . . *London*, 1862. pp. 35, with fold. tables. ICE

Excerpt, *Min. Proc. I.C.E.*, vol. 20, 1860/1.

2623 HOLLEY, A. L. American and European railway practice in the economical generation of steam . . . and in permanent way . . . *New York & London*, 1867. pp. 192, with 69 plates. 4°. BM

2624 MALLET, R. Mallet's patent iron buckled plate elastic permanent way. *London*, 1868. pp. 6, with la. fold. diagram. LSE

2625 GRIFFIN, G. F. Griffin's new railway systems, 1870: extracts of reports by the Royal Commission on Railways, and from the Board of Trade Returns, etc. *Westminster*, 1870. pp. 16, with 3 fold. diagrams. BM

Griffin's patent permanent way.

2626 SANDBERG, C. P. Safety of permanent way, with drawings and tables concerning punching and notching of rails. *London*, 1873. pp. 12[16], with 4 tables & 3 la. fold. diagrams. BM

'For private circulation only.'

2627 WILLIAMS, R. P. On the permanent way of railways . . . *London*, 1876. pp. 65, with 20 tables (some fold.). UL(GL)

Excerpt, *Min. Proc. I.C.E.*, vol. 46, Session 1875–76, pt. 4.
The greater durability of steel rails over iron.

2628 SIMON, H. Hilf's system of wrought-iron permanent way for railways . . . *Manchester*, 1877. pp. 8, with la. fold. diagram. ICE

2629 VIGNOLES, C. B. Permanent way for tramways. *Westminster*, [1879.] pp. 5, with la. fold. plate. ICE

—— another edn. [1879.] pp. 5, with 2 fold. plates. ICE

2630 DE BERGUE, C. Patent permanent way. *London*, [c. 1880?] pp. 8, with plates. ICE

Cast iron sleeper-chairs.

2631 BONNYN, W. W. Seaton's patent safety rail, and improvements in the permanent way of railways . . . *London*, [1881?] pp. 12. ICE

Rails laid down along 10-inch timber baulks.

2632 STRETTON, C. E. A few remarks on railway permanent way. *London*, 1884. pp. 11, with 3 illus. (2 fold.). BM

The necessity for good permanent way to prevent accidents.

2633 STRETTON, C. E. A paper on railway permanent way . . . *Leicester*, [1884.] pp. 11. (cf. his *Few Remarks on Railway Permanent Way*.) BM

2634 COLE, W. H. Notes on plate-laying, maintenance, curves and points . . . *London*, 1885. pp. vi, 36. BM

2635 TRATMAN, E. E. R. English railroad track. *New York*, 1888. pp. 217–52, with diagrams on 6 plates. [*Trans. Amer. Soc. Civil Engineers*, vol. 18, no 388.] ICE

2636 MEMORANDUM on three-feet gauge railways in Ireland, approved by the chairmen of the Cavan, Leitrim & Roscommon, the Clogher Valley, the West Donegal, and the Finn Railway & Tramway companies. *Dublin*, August 1889. pp. 7. LSE

The advantages of narrow gauge over the Irish standard 5 feet 3 inches, and some objections to break of gauge.

2637 SANDBERG, C. P. On the use of heavier rails for safety and economy in railway traffic. *London*, 1889. pp. 21, with diagrams on fold. plate. LSE

Sandberg's patent rail.

2638 WILLIAMS, R. P. Steel permanent way. *London*, 1898. pp. 41. ICE

Reprinted from *Journal of the Iron & Steel Institute*, no. 1, 1898.
The demands made upon rails by the increase of traffic.

2639 HOLT, A. Plateways: a description of the proposed plateway system; its necessity, convenience and economy . . . and an account of the proposed Lancashire Plateway Co. . . . *Liverpool*, 1883. pp. 43, with illus. ICE

—— 2nd edn. *Liverpool*, 1899. pp. 53. ICE

2640 PERMANENT WAY INSTITUTION. The Permanent Way Institution, established 1884. *Nottingham*, [1906.] pp. 20 [21]. BM

A descriptive booklet.

2641 MODERN British permanent way: no. 1, Rails. *London: Railway News*, Dec. 1911. pp. 10, with diagrams.   IT
Reprinted from *Railway News*.

2642 PERMANENT way. By 'a permanent way engineer'. *In* 'Modern railway working', edited by John Macaulay. vol. 3, 1913. pp. 157–93, with illus. & diagrams.   BM

2643 LESLIE, B. A new chapter in the history of permanent way. 1924. pp. 22, with 17 diagrams on plates.   ICE
Privately printed.
B. Leslie's improved track to meet the demands of increasing traffic density and axle loads.

2644 COLE, W. H. Notes on permanent-way material, platelaying, and points and crossings. *London*, 1890. pp. vii, 90, with 18 plates.   BM
—— 2nd edn. *London*, 1896. pp. xii, 164. BM
—— 3rd. *London*, 1900. pp. x, 170.   BM
—— 4th, rev. *London*, 1903. pp. x, 176. BM
—— 5th, rev. *London*, 1905. pp. xii, 176. BM
—— 6th, rev. *London*, 1912. pp. xiii, 202. BM
—— 7th, rev. 'Permanent-way material, platelaying, and points & crossings. *London*, 1915. pp. xvi, 236.   BM
—— 8th, rev. by G. R. Hearn. *London*, 1920. pp. viii, 276.   BM
—— 9th, rev. by G. R. Hearn. *London*, 1928. pp. vii, 245.   BM
—— 10th, completely rewritten. 'Cole's permanent way material, maintenance, points and crossings.' By Colonel Sir Gordon Hearn. *London*, 1940. pp. vi, 196.   BM

2645 PERMANENT WAY INSTITUTION. Memorandum and articles of association of the Permanent Way Institution. *Faversham*, [1931.] pp. 17.   BM

2646 WALLIS, E. Junction layouts. pp. 23. *Typescript*.   RC
Paper, Railway Club, 2 Oct., 1931.

2647 WALLACE, W. K. Permanent way maintenance and the effect of speed. 1936. pp. 16. *Typescript*.   IME
Paper, L.S.E. Railway Students' Association.

2648 DOW-MAC (Products) LTD. Dow-Mac prestressed concrete sleepers. *Stamford*, [1950.] pp. 19, with illus.   IT

2649 TRAIN, J. C. L. Permanent way mechanised equipment. *London: British Railways*, Oct. 1951. pp. 30, with illus.   PC

2650 SUMMERSON, T. & SONS. The Summerson Book of Railway Sidings. *Darlington*, [1952.] pp. 72[73], with illus. & diagrams. PO
A trade catalogue with details of various rail formations and maintenance equipment.

2651 SUMMERSON, T. & SONS. Tables and diagrams of switches and crossings: a handy platelayer's guide. 3rd edn. *Darlington*, 1895. pp. 90, with many tables & diagrams.   PO
—— 5th edn. 'Platelayers' Guide.' *Darlington*, 1904. pp. 106.   PO
—— 6th, *Darlington*, 1924. pp. 195. PO
—— 7th, *Darlington*, 1954. pp. 94.   PO

* 2652 PERMANENT WAY INSTITUTION. British railway track: design, construction and maintenance. Compiled by a committee of the P.W.I. Edited by R. A. Hamnett. *Nottingham*, 1943. pp. 338[341]. (Reprinted 1947.)   IT
Textbook (mostly technical) on practical permanent way work.
—— 2nd edn. *Nottingham*, 1956. pp. 446 [453].   IT

2653 PEARSON, H. M. Track for heavy freight trains. *London: United Kingdom Railway Advisory Service*, 1962. pp. 12, with 16 illus.   BM

E 4 ELECTRIC RAILWAY ENGINEERING

Electrification—Underground electric railways (tube and subway)

For electric locomotives and trains see **E 9**
For electrical safety engineering see **E 15**
For train lighting see **E 12**

2654 HOOD, J. W. J. Electric traction in its relation to existing railways: a paper read before the London & South Western Rly. Debating Society, May 1902. *London*, 1902. pp. 18.   ICE
'Private.'

2655 ASHBURY, T. Electrical development. *In his* 'Miscellaneous Papers'. *Manchester*, 1904. pp. 69–72.   PC
Railways.

2656 LANGDON, W. E. Modern electrical appliances employed in the operation of railways. *In* 'Modern electric practice', edited by M. Maclean. vol. 6, 1905. pp. 247–73, with illus.   BM

2657 KAPP, G. The electrification of railways. [*London*, 1908.] pp. 45 (in double-column 4to.), with many illus.   SLS
Two lectures to the Royal Institution, 18 & 25 January, 1908. Reprinted from the *Electrical Engineer*.

2658 WESTINGHOUSE, G. The electrification of railways. *London*, 1910. [*Times Engineering Supplement*, 3 August, 1910.]　ICE
A unified system desirable.

2659 DAWSON, P. Electric traction on railways. *In* 'Modern railway working', edited by John Macaulay. vol. 6, 1913. pp. 29–158; with diagrams, illus. & tables.　BM

2660 PROGRESS of railway electrification. *In* 'Jubilee of the Railway News, 1864–1914'. *London: Railway News*, [1914.] pp. 25–37 of the Engineering section.　BM

2661 TREWMAN, H. F. Electrification of railways. *London*, 1920. pp. 78.　BM
Economic aspects.

2662 MANCHESTER GUARDIAN, *newspaper*. Railway Supplement. *Manchester*, 13 March, 1922.　LSE
Progress and possibilities of electrification. By W. E. Simnett.

2663 HIGHFIELD, W. E. Main line electrification in England. pp. 15. *Reproduced typescript*.　RC
Paper, Railway Club, 9 May, 1924.
Advantages and problems.
—— Answer to the discussion on the paper. pp. 15.　RC

2664 RAVEN, V. Railway electrification & electric locomotives; being papers read by Sir Vincent Raven . . . and reprinted by permission. *Manchester: Metropolitan Vickers Electrical Company*, [1924.] pp. 36, with illus.　PO
pt. 1, Railway electrification.

2665 O'BRIEN, H. F. The future of main-line electrification on British railways. *London*, [1924.] pp. 729–81, with illus.　LSE
Reprint, *Journal of the Institution of Electrical Engineers*, vol. 62, no. 333. Sept. 1924.

2666 TREWMAN, H. F. Railway electrification: a complete survey of the economics of the different systems of railway electrification from the engineering and financial points of view. *London*, 1924. pp. xii, 244.　IT

2667 METROPOLITAN VICKERS ELECTRICAL COMPANY. Electrification work for British railways. *Manchester*, [1930.] pp. 48, with illus.　PO

2668 LONDON PASSENGER TRANSPORT BOARD. How a tube railway is constructed. *Westminster*, 1934. pp. 20, with illus.　BM
London underground railways.

2669 BRITISH ELECTRICAL DEVELOPMENT ASSOCIATION. The case for electrification of the railways. *London*, 1935. pp. 23.　LSE

2670 JOHNSTON, K. H. Railway electrification and post-war reconstruction. *In* 'Creative demobilisation', vol. 2, 'Case Studies in National Planning' by E. A. Gutkind. 1943. pp. 145–65.　BM

2671 LONDON PASSENGER TRANSPORT BOARD—PERMANENT WAY DIVISION. Safety on the track. (By R. J. Macleod.) *Westminster*, [1948.] pp. 65, with diagrams.　IT
A safety hand-book for permanent-way men.

2672 METROPOLITAN VICKERS ELECTRICAL COMPANY. 1899–1949. [By] John Dummelow. *Manchester*, [1949.] pp. x, 249, with illus.　BR
Produced to commemorate the Golden Jubilee of the Company. Includes railway electrification, and the manufacture of locomotives (turbine, electric, diesel-electric, gasturbine and petrol-electric).

2673 BRITISH TRANSPORT COMMISSION. Electrification of railways: report of a committee appointed by the Railway Executive and the London Transport Executive. London, 1951. pp. xi, 94, with 7 fold. maps.　BM
Review of past methods and suggestions for future development.

2674 BRITISH RAILWAYS. Lancaster–Morecambe–Heysham Line conversion to 50-cycle, single-phase a.c. system of electric traction. *London*, Sept. 1953. pp. 10, with illus. & diagrams.　IT

2675 BRITISH RAILWAYS (EASTERN and LONDON MIDLAND REGIONS). Electrification of the Manchester, Sheffield & Wath lines. Issued to commemorate the inauguration . . . of electrically hauled passenger services between Manchester and Sheffield, 14 September, 1954. *London*, [1954.] pp. 31, with illus. & fold. map.　BR

2676 BRITISH TRANSPORT COMMISSION. Modernisation of British Railways: the system of electrification for British railways. *London*, [1956.] pp. 24, with a map.　BM

2677 GENERAL ELECTRIC COMPANY. G.E.C. and the railways. *London*, Dec. 1956. pp. 31, with illus.　IT
Description of equipment.

2678 BRITISH RAILWAYS ELECTRIFICATION CONFERENCE, 1960. British Railways Electrification Conference, 1960. Exhibition at Battersea. *London: British Electrical & Allied Manufacturers Association*, [1960.] pp. [60,] with illus. & a plan of the exhibition.　BM

2679 BRITISH RAILWAYS ELECTRIFICATION CONFERENCE, 1960. Railway electrification at industrial frequency. Proceedings. *London*, [1961.] pp. 496, with many illus. & diagrams.　BM

2680 MOODY, G. T. London's electrifications, 1890–1923. *Sidcup: Electric Railway Society*, 1961. pp. 14. *Reproduced typescript.*　BM
Origins of electric traction on all London railways, main line and underground.

E 5 ARCHITECTURE AND DESIGN

Bridges, viaducts, stations, tunnel entrances, etc.

Historical

2681 ROBBINS, R. M. Railway stations and architecture. pp. 20[21]. *Reproduced type-script.*　　　　　　　　　　　RC
Paper, Railway Club, April 1935.

2682 ANDREWS, C. B. The Railway Age. *London: Country Life*, 1937. pp. xi, 145, with 82 plates, & illus.　　　　BM
Includes architecture.

2683 [CLARK, R. H.] British railway stations; illustrated. *South Merstham: Railway & Technical Press*, 1947–[48.]　BM
Book One, Cornwall, Devon & Somerset. 1947. pp. 60.
Book Two, North Wales. [1948.] pp. 60.
Book Three, Kent, Surrey & Sussex. [1948.] pp. 60.
Photographs (fifty-five to each book) with descriptions.

2684 ARSCHAVIR, A. The development of the British railway station. M.A. thesis, University of Manchester, 1948. pp. 4, 176, [13,] with 90 mounted photographs & 22 plans. *Typescript.*　　MANCHESTER UL
The photographs are of old prints and contemporary scenes.

2685 CASSON, H. An introduction to Victorian architecture. *London: Art & Technics*, 1948. pp. 96, with plates & illus.　　BM
Includes railway architecture.

2686 GLOAG, J. *and* BRIDGWATER, D. A history of cast iron in architecture. *London: Allen & Unwin*, 1948. pp. xx, 395.　　BM
pp. 163–78, Cast iron in railway architecture. With 26 illustrations.

2687 BARMAN, C. An introduction to railway architecture. *London: Art & Technics*, 1950. pp. 104. (pp. 41–104, plates, with notes.) BM

2688 BUCKLE, C. H. *and* STEEL, K. Railway architecture: a series of fifteen views drawn by Claude H. Buckle and Kenneth Steel. [*London*,] *British Railways, London Midland Region*, [1951.] 23 in. by 7½ in. In colour.　　　　　　　　　　　BR

2689 KU, C. H. Railway station planning in Great Britain. M.A. thesis, University of Manchester, 1952. pp. 59.[4,] with 14 mounted photographs & 17 plans.
　　　　　　　　　　MANCHESTER UL

2690 PEVSNER, N. The buildings of England: London, except the cities of London & Westminster. *Harmondsworth: Penguin Books*, 1952. pp. 496. [*The Buildings of England*, no. BE6.]　　BM
Includes descriptions of railway stations.

*2691 HITCHCOCK, H. R. Early Victorian architecture in Britain. *London*, 1954. 2 vols. [*Yale Historical Publications: History of Art*. no. 9.]　　　　　　　　BM
vol. 1, pp. 492–529, Early railway stations.
(vol. 2 contains 55 illus. on 17 plates relating to this section.)

2692 MEEKS, C. L. V. The railway station: an architectural history. *London: Architectural*
b *Press; New Haven: Yale University Press*, 1957. pp. xxvi, 203, with 231 illus. [*Yale Historical Publications: History of Art*, no. 2.]　　　　　　　　　　BM
A detailed study of architectural and artistic aspects of railway stations in Great Britain and the U.S.A., with a bibliographical essay.

2693 CARTER, E. F. Famous railway stations of the world and their traffic; illustrated by Kenneth E. Carter. *London: F. Muller*, [1959]. pp. 143, with plates.　　BM
pp. 9–61, British stations (history & description).

2694 WALTERS, D. British railway bridges. *London: Ian Allan*, 1963. pp. 72, with 44 illus. & 3 tables.　　　　　　BM
An historical survey, followed by descriptions, with constructional details, of a selection of twenty-seven bridges.

Contemporaneous

2695 NICHOLSON, P. The Guide to Railway Masonry, containing a complete treatise on the oblique arch . . . *London*, 1839. pp. 10, lvi, 50, with 39 plates.　　　UL(GL)
—— 2nd edn. *London*, 1840. pp. 10, lii, 50. (40 plates.)　　　　　　BM
—— 3rd. *London*, 1846. pp. 10, lxviii, 57. (42 plates.)　　　　　　　UL(GL)

2696 STEPHENSON, R. Reports of Mr. Robert Stephenson, Mr. Wm. Fairbairn and Mr. E. Hodgkinson, upon the experiments made to ascertain the practicability of erecting a Tubular Bridge across the Menai Straits, for the passage of railway trains. *London*, 1846. pp. 20.　　　　　　　BM

2697 FAIRBAIRN, W. An account of the construction of the Britannia and Conway Tubular Bridges, with a complete history of their progress . . . *London*, 1849. pp. xii, 291, with 21 fold. plates & 78 illus.　BM

2698 [HEAD, F. B.] Highways and Dry-ways; or, The Britannia and Conway Tubular Bridges; by the author of 'Stokers and Pokers'. *London*, 1849. pp. 83.　　　BM
Criticisms of Thomas Fairbairn.

2699 CLARK, E. The Britannia and Conway Tubular Bridges . . . in two volumes. *London*, 1850. pp. xii, 821, iv, with a third vol. of 45 plates.　　　　　　BM

2700 [CLARK, L.] General description of the Britannia and Conway Tubular Bridges on the Chester & Holyhead Railway. Published with the permission of Robert Stephenson, civil engineer. By a Resident Assistant. *London*, 1849. pp. 34.   LSE
—— 3rd edn. *London*, 1849. pp. 34.
—— 5th, *London*, 1850. pp. 40.
—— 7th, *London*, 1850. pp. 40   UL(GL)

2701 DEMPSEY, G. D. Iron applied to railway structures, comprising an abstract of re-results of experiments conducted under the authority of the Commissioners appointed . . . to inquire into the application of iron to railway structures; with practical notes . . . *London*, 1850. pp. 42, with 10 plates. BM

2702 FAIRBAIRN, T. Britannia and Conway Tubular Bridges: truths and tubes on self-supporting principles. A few words in reply to the author of 'Highways and Dry-ways'. [F. B. Head.] *London*, 1849. pp. 62.   BM
A refutation of charges made against him by F. B. Head in relation to the contract for building of the bridges.
—— 2nd edn. *London*, 1850. pp. 63.   IT

2703 JACKSON, T. Tourist's Guide to Britannia Bridge . . . 4th edn. *London*, 1850. pp. 42 [43].   BM
—— 6th edn. *London*, 1851. pp. 44[45]. RC
—— 12th edn. *London*, 1854. pp. 44. BM
—— 13th edn. *London*, 1856.

2704 HOOD, R. J. On the arrangement and construction of railway stations. *London*, 1858. pp. 36, with 13 illus.   LSE
Excerpt, *Min. Proc. I.C.E.*, vol. 17, 1857–58. The layout of stations.

2705 HISTORY of the Royal Albert Bridge for the Cornwall Railway, across the River Tamar at Saltash . . . *Devonport*, [1859.] pp. [5,] with illus.   BM

2706 MAYNARD, H. N. Handbook to the Crumlin Viaduct, Monmouthshire . . . *Crumlin*, 1862. pp. 32, with 15 plates.   BM

* 2707 DEMPSEY, G. D. Rudimentary treatise: tubular and other girder bridges, particularly the Britannia and Conway Tubular Bridges . . . *London*, 1850. pp. viii, 132, with plate & 41 illus.   BM
A technical work containing also some general information on various railways.
—— 3rd edn. *London*, 1865. pp. viii, 136. BM

2708 DICKSON, W. E. Tubular and other iron girder bridges . . . 3rd edn. *London*, 1865. pp. viii, 136.   BM
This entry is a mistake. *See* 2707.

2709 GROVER, J. W. Examples of station buildings and their cost, as executed on several railways: being an Appendix to 'Estimates and diagrams of railway bridges', by J. W. Grover. *London*, 1871. 47 plates.   BM

2710 MAW, W. H. *and* DREDGE, J. Modern examples of road and railway bridges, illustrating the most recent practice of leading engineers in Europe and America. *London*, 1872. pp. iv, 180, with 94 plates.   BM
Includes bridges in Gt. Britain.

2711 COENE, J. DE. Les Chemins de fer en Angleterre: construction et exploitation des gares à marchandises dans les grandes villes . . . *Paris*, 1877. pp. 38, 34.   BRE
Includes a description of the interior of St. Pancras Station, Midland Rly., London.

2712 The TAY Bridge: its history and construction; the introductory note and lithograph drawings by Albert Grothe. *Dundee: John Leng & Co.*, 1878. pp. 111, with 4 fold. diagrams.   RC
pp. 90–111, an account of the opening, 31 May, 1878.

2713 MIDDLETON, R. E. The Forth Bridge: a paper read before the Civil & Mechanical Engineers' Society, 13 April, 1887. *London*, 1887. pp. 9.   ICE
The foundations.

2714 TAY Bridge Guide. *Dundee*, [1887.] pp. 16; with illus.   ICE
An account, for visitors, of the new Tay Bridge.

2715 The FORTH Bridge and all about it. *Edinburgh*, [1888.] pp. 16.   BM
A description for tourists.

2716 WALMISLEY, A. T. Iron roofs: examples of design: description, illustrated with working drawings. *London*, 1884. pp. 37, with 64 plates. la. 4°.   BM
Includes many examples of railway station roofs.
—— 2nd edn. *London*, 1888. pp. 91, with 70 plates. la. 4°.   BM

2717 BARLOW, C. The New Tay Bridge . . . *London*, 1889. pp. 46, with 23 plates.   BM

2718 MORISON, A. A popular description of the Forth Bridge; illustrated. 1890. pp. 47. BM

2719 PHILLIPS, P. The Forth Bridge in its various stages of construction and compared with the most notable bridges of the world. 2nd edn. *Edinburgh*, [1890.] pp. 203, with 55 plates. la. obl. 4°.   BR

2720 PHILLIPS, P. Sketches of the Forth Bridge; or, The Giant's Anatomy, from various points of view. *Edinburgh*, 1888. pp. 47. BM
Construction described. Has also the text to accompany a series of forty photographs, separately published.
—— The Forth Railway Bridge: being the expanded edition of 'The Giant's Anatomy', by the author of 'The Forth Bridge in its various stages of construction' . . . *Edinburgh*, 1890. pp. 40, with 20 plates.   BM

—— 3rd ('Popular') edn. Sketches of the Forth Bridge; or, The Giant's Anatomy . . . *Edinburgh*, 1890. pp. 36[37], with 7 illus. BM

2721 WESTHOFEN, W. The Forth Bridge. *London*, [1890.] pp. 31, with 19 plates & 156 illus. in text.   BM
Reprinted from *Engineering*, 28 Feb., 1890.

2722 PARKER, H. A. Report of a visit to the Forth Bridge . . . *London: London Association of Foremen Engineers & Draughtsmen*, 1891. pp. 16, with 16 fold. plates.   PC

2723 RAILWAY HERALD. The Railway Herald Station Album. *London*, [1899.] pp. [20.]
SLS
Twenty illustrations, with brief details of London and provincial termini.

2724 STRETTON, C. E. The history of the Britannia Tubular Bridge. *Leeds*, 1900. pp. 12.
BM

2725 ASHBURY, T. The Forth Bridge: a paper read . . . 10th November, 1888. *Manchester: Manchester Association of Engineers*, 1888. pp. [149]–177, with 2 fold. plates. *In his* 'Miscellaneous Papers'. *Manchester*, 1904.
PC

2726 The NEW High Level Railway Bridge over the River Tyne. *London: Railway Gazette*, [1906.] pp. [10.] with illus., & diagrams. BR
Reprinted from the *Railway Gazette*, 25 May, 1906.

2727 HISTORY of the Forth Bridge. *Edinburgh: Banks & Co.*, 1911. pp. 46, with 10 illus. & la. fold. map.   RC

2728 CONNAL, E. Railway masonry works. *In* 'Modern railway working', edited by John Macaulay. vol. 2, 1912. pp. 143–86, with diagrams.   BM

2729 FIDLER, T. C. The bridges upon a line of railway: their design and execution. *In* 'Modern railway working', edited by John Macaulay. vol. 3, 1913. pp. 1–15, with diagrams.   BM

2730 NICHOLAS, J. S. The design and construction of railway steelwork. *In* 'Modern railway working', edited by John Macaulay. vol. 3, 1913. pp. 17–53, with illus. & diagrams.   BM

2731 PURVIS, R. Sir William Arrol: a memoir . . . *Edinburgh*, 1913. pp. x, 150, with 16 plates.
BM
Includes his building of the second Tay Bridge and the Forth Bridge.

2732 WEBSTER, T. H. The new High Level Bridge and its origin. *Newcastle upon Tyne*, 1928. pp. 40, with illus. & diagrams.   PC

2733 BICKERTON, J. F. *and* PROTOPAPADAKIS, P. Notes on the design and layout of large passenger stations. *London: Institution of Civil Engineers*, 1946. pp. 40, with 5 diagrams.   BR
Paper, 26 Feb., 1946.

2734 MARTIN, J. L. Unit-built stations. [*London*, 1946.] pp. 8, with illus. & diagrams.
BR
Reprint, the *Architectural Review*, March 1946.
Historical development and present practice.

2735 NEWTON, C. H. The design of railway stations. pp. 17. *Reproduced typescript.*   IT
Presidential Address, L.S.E. Railway Students' Association, 13 November, 1946.

2736 COUNCIL OF INDUSTRIAL DESIGN. The 1951 Design Congress. Main paper, 'Design in London Transport', by Lord Latham. 1951. pp. 8. *Reproduced typescript.*   IT

2737 ROYAL INSTITUTE OF BRITISH ARCHI-
b   TECTS—LIBRARY. Railway stations, 1949–1956: a select list of references to material in the R.I.B.A. Library. November 1956. pp. 4. *Reproduced typescript.*   RIBA
Books and periodicals, British and foreign stations.

*2738 PREBBLE, J. The High Girders. *London. Secker & Warburg*, 1956. pp. ix, 219, with plates, incl. portrait of Thomas Bouch.   BM
A graphic account of the rise and fall of the first Tay Bridge.
—— *London: Pan Books*, 1959. pp. 184[185], with plates.   BM

2739 BRITISH RAILWAYS (WESTERN REGION). Centenary of Royal Albert Bridge, Saltash, and opening of Cornwall Railway from Plymouth to Truro. (1859–1959.) *Paddington (London)*, [1959.] pp. 8, with illus.   BR

E 6 MECHANICAL ENGINEERING (General)

Locomotives, carriages, and wagons—Trains
For the operation of trains and train services see G1, G2 *and* G3

Historical

2740 The INSTITUTION of Mechanical Engineers. *In* 'Jubilee of the Railway News, 1864–1914'. *London: Railway News*, [1914.] pp. 179–80 (of Engineering section).   BM

*2741 SCIENCE MUSEUM [London]. Land transport: III, Railway locomotives and rolling stock. Compiled by E. A. Forward. *London*, 1923. pp. 96, with 10 plates. [*Catalogue of the Collections in the Science Museum.*]   BM

198 exhibits in the permanent exhibition described.
—— another edn. *London,* 1931, 2 parts.
BM
Part One: Historical review. pp. 99, with 52 illus. on plates.
Part Two: Descriptive Catalogue. pp. 118 [119], with 24 illus. on plates.

2742 SANDERS, T. H. The evolution of railway vehicle suspension. *London: Institution of Locomotive Engineers,* [1934.] pp. 31, with 21 drawings. [*Paper* 334.]　　　PC

*2743 ELLIS, C. H. The trains we loved. *London: Allen & Unwin,* 1947. pp. 196, with 69 illus. on 40 plates (8 col.).　　　BM

2744 KIDNER, R. W. A short history of mechanical traction and travel. vol. 2, Rail. *Chislehurst: Oakwood Press,* 1947. pp. 150, with 40 plates & many illus.　　　BM
A collected edition. Originally issued in separate parts, 1946–47.
pp. [1]–38, The early history of the railway locomotive, 1804–1879.
pp. [39]–81, The development of the railway locomotive, 1880–1946.
pp. 81–104, The railway carriage, 1825–1946.
pp. 107–50, Multiple unit trains, rail-motors and tramcars, 1829–1947.

2745 PARSONS, R. H. A history of the Institution of Mechanical Engineers, 1847–1947: Centenary memorial volume. *London: I.M.E.,* 1947. pp. xi, 299, with plates & illus.　　BM

2746 NOCK, O. S. British trains, past and present. *London: Batsford,* 1951. pp. x, 117, with 105 illus., incl. plates (some col.).　　　BM

2747 ALLEN, C. J. Royal trains. *London: Ian Allan,* [1953.] pp. 40, with 48 illus.　　BM

2748 TIDEY, H. G. Those were the trains! *London: Ian Allan,* 1954. pp. 64.　　　BM
117 illustrations with captions, photographed between *c.* 1900 and 1923.

2749 ELLIS, C. H. Royal journey: a retrospect of royal trains in the British Isles. *London: British Transport Commission,* 1953. pp. 32, with illus.　　　BM
—— revised edn. *London,* 1960. pp. 31. BM

2750 PAYNE, P. L. Rubber and railways in the nineteenth century: a study of the Spencer Papers. *Liverpool: Liverpool University Press,* 1961. pp. xiv, 246, with 12 diagrams, 12 tables, lists (incl. list of patents), & many footnotes.　　　BM
Bearing springs, buffers, and other equipment, from 1826 onwards.

2751 STEPHENSON LOCOMOTIVE SOCIETY. Railway progress, 1909–1959. Jubilee year publication, volume two. *London,* [1963.] pp. 141–224, with 69 illus. on 28 plates. BM
Signalling, mechanical engineering and railway operation.

Contemporaneous

2752 ARMENGAUD, J. E. *and* C. L'Industrie des chemins de fer; ou, Dessins et descriptions des principales machines locomotives . . . wagons de transport . . . en usage sur les routes en fer de la France, d'Angleterre . . . *Paris,* 1839. pp. 174.　　　BM

2753 DIRCKS, H. Account of a patent improved metallic railway wheel with wood-faced tyre. *Liverpool,* 1840. pp. 8, with 5 illus.　　H

2754 LARDNER, D. *and* WOODS, E. Reports on the determination of the mean value of railway constants; from the Report of the British Association for the Advancement of Science for 1841. *London,* 1842. pp. 205–306.　　　BM
Reports of experiments with the speed of trains on various lines in 1839.

2755 GREENHOW, C. H. Exposition of the danger and deficiencies of the present mode of railway construction, with suggestions for its improvement. *London,* 1846. pp. 29, with 5 plates.　　　ICE
Suggests concave tyres and convex rails, etc.

2756 HARDING, W. On the resistance to railway trains at different velocities . . . *London,* 1846. pp. 66, with 5 fold. tables.　　　BM

2757 THORNEYCROFT, G. B. On the manufacture of malleable iron, with the results of experiments on the strength of railway axles. *London,* 1850. pp. 11, with fold. plate.　BR
Excerpt, *Min. Proc. I.C.E.,* vol. 9.

2758 BARLOW, H. B. A comparative account and delineation of railway engine and carriage wheels, compiled and arranged by H. B. Barlow, consulting engineer. *London,* 1848. pp. 51, with la. fold. plate showing 80 diagrams of various wheels.　　　SL

2759 BARLOW, H. B. Railway engine and carriage wheels, vol. 2. *Manchester,* 1856. pp. 78, with la. fold. plate depicting various wheel patterns.　　　SL
An account of patents obtained from May 1847 to November 1855.

2760 CLARK, D. K. Railway machinery: a treatise on the mechanical engineering of railways . . . illustrated . . . *London,* 1855. 2 vols. (text & plates). pp. 328; pl. 60, 10.　BM
—— another edn. *Glasgow, Edinburgh & London,* 1861. 2 vols. (pp. xxiv, 335, with 353 diagrams; pl. 70.)　　　SL

2761 CLARK, D. K. The exhibited machinery of 1862: a cyclopaedia of the machinery represented at the International Exhibition. *London,* [1862.] pp. xxiv, 447.　　　SL
part 1, pp. 1–43, Railway plant, with 6 plates & 35 illus. Also, a railway ticket printing machine described and illustrated, pp. 243–5.

2762 COLBURN, Z. Locomotive engineering and the mechanism of railways: a treatise on the principles and construction of the locomotive engine, railway carriages and railway plant, with examples; illustrated by 64 large engravings and 240 woodcuts. *London & Glasgow*, [1871.] pp. xiv, 320 (text) & a vol. of 64 plates & diagrams. la. 4°. LSE

2763 DIGBY, W. P. Statistics of British and American rolling-stock. *London: Society of Engineers*, 1905. pp. 16. LSE
Relationship between numbers of locomotives and rolling-stock, and the volume of traffic carried, 1894–1904.

2764 MACKAY, F. E. Britain's famous expresses. *London*, 1911. pp. [12.] RC
Twelve mounted photographs with descriptions.
—— another edn. *London*, 1912. RC

2765 RAILWAY views. *London*, [1916.] BM
A series of eight booklets each containing eleven photographs, with captions. A selection of fifty of these, with no title page, was also issued.

2766 RAILWAY mechanical engineering: a practical treatise of engineering experts. *London*, 1923. 2 vols. BM
Technical matters, but has many illustrations on plates and in text.

2767 MILLER, B. E. Painting of railway equipment. *New York*, 1924. pp. 39, with illus. in text. IT

2768 DENDY MARSHALL, C. F. The resistance of express trains. *London*, 1925. pp. ix, 76. BM
pp. 65–70, description of a G.W.Rly. dynamometer car, with illustrations and diagrams.

2769 ALLEN, C. J. Famous trains. *Liverpool: Meccano Ltd.*, 1928. pp. viii, 191, with 58 illus. [*Meccano Library*, no. 1.] BM
Contemporary trains.

2770 MACBETH, C. Rubber and railways. *London: Rubber Growers' Association*, 1931. pp. 62, with illus. BM
pp. 1–14, 'Rubber on British railways'. The use of rubber on locomotives and rolling stock.
—— 2nd edn. *London: Rubber Publicity Assoc.*, 1939. pp. 216. BM

2771 WAY, R. B. Famous British trains: a chronicle of the daily work of the named expresses. *London: Nicholson & Watson*, 1936. pp. xv, 232, with plates. BM

2772 WEBSTER, H. C. British railway rolling stock. *London: O.U.P.*, [1942.] pp. 159, with illus. & descriptions of locomotives, coaches & wagons. BM

2773 LOCOLLECTION. *London: Ian Allan*, July 1946. pp. [32.] BM
Photographs of trains, with descriptions.

2774 WILDISH, G. N. Engines of War: an illustrated booklet of the locomotives and freight cars of the British Ministry of Supply and of the U.S. Army Transportation Corps. *London: Ian Allan*, 1946. pp. 24, with 23 illus. BM
Descriptions, notes and lists.

2775 FAMOUS British trains: photographs from 'The Times Weekly Review'. *London: The Times*, 1949. pp. 16. SL
Nine illustrations of present-day named expresses.

2776 SAMPSON, H. World railways . . . edited and compiled by Henry Sampson. *London: Sampson Low's World Railways*, [1951– .] BM
In progress. Bi-annual.
A comprehensive work of reference for the technical and mechanical features of the railways of all countries, with special emphasis on locomotives and rolling stock, with many illustrations. Includes underground railways. The Foreword gives a summary of current developments, problems, and trends.
The 6th edition (1961) was a complete revision covering a wider range of information than hitherto, with 412 pages, 653 illustrations, 141 maps, 80 loading and clearance gauge diagrams, a table of data in 32 columns for 1500 railways in 108 countries (pp. 1–125), followed by a further table giving 'amplified details of major railways and manufacturers' (pp. 127–381).
The current edition (7th, 1962) has 435 pages.

2777 SELECTED railway photographs. *London: Railway World*, [1952.] pp. [24.] BM
Twenty-seven illustrations from the periodical *Railways (Railway World)*.

*2778 ALLEN, C. J. Titled trains of Great Britain. *London: Ian Allan*, 1946. pp. 128, with plates. BM
—— 2nd edn. *London*, 1947. pp. 204. BM
—— 3rd, *London*, 1953. pp. 224. BM
—— 3rd [with a supplement], *London*, [1954.] pp. 240. BM

2779 ALLEN, C. J. Titled trains in pictures: reprint of the photographs from 'Titled trains of Great Britain'. *Hampton Court: Ian Allan*, [1953.] pp. [32.] BM
Seventy photographs, with descriptions.

2780 BRITISH RAILWAYS. Exhibition of locomotives, carriages, wagons and engineering plant at Willesden. [*London*, 1954.] pp. [82,] with many illus. & a plan. IT

2781 ALLEN, G. F. Famous trains. [*Hampton Court:*] *Ian Allan*, [1955, 56,] with illus. & route diagrams. BM
1, The Elizabethan. [1955.] pp. 28.
2, The Royal Scot. [1955.] pp. 28.
3, The Cornish Riviera Express. [1955.] pp. 28.
4, The Atlantic Coast Express. [1955.] pp. 29.
5, The South Wales Pullman. [1955.] pp. 29.
6, The Queen of Scots. [1956.] pp. 29.
7, The Royal Wessex, and the Bournemouth Belle. [1956.] pp. 28.

2782 BRITISH TRANSPORT COMMISSION. Modern railway travel. [*London*,] June 1957. pp. 24.   BR
    Brochure describing thirty-three exhibits at Battersea.

2783 FAMOUS Trains Colour Book. *London: Ian Allan*, [1958.] pp. [12.]   BM
    Twelve pictures in full colour, with short descriptions.

2784 STOECKL, F. Europäische Eisenbahnzüge mit klangvollen Namen. *Darmstadt*, 1958. pp. 266.

2785 ALLEN, C. J. Modern railways: their engineering, equipment, and operation. *London: Faber & Faber*, 1959. pp. 307, with 247 illus. on 64 plates, 22 diagrams, & 11 tables.   BM

*2786 TRAINS Album. *London: Ian Allan*, 1953–59.   BM
    Photographs, with captions.
    1, London Midland Region. [1953.]. pp. 32.
    2, Eastern, and North Eastern Regions. 1954.] pp. 32.
    3, Western Region. [1954.] pp. 32.
    4, Southern Region. [1954.] pp. 32.
    5, Scottish, and London Midland Regions. [1954.] pp. 32.
    6, Scottish, Eastern, and North Eastern Regions. [1954.] pp. 32.
    7, Western Region. [1954]. pp. 32.
    8, Southern Region. [1955.] pp. 32.
    9, London Midland Region. [1957.] pp. 32.
    10, Scottish, Eastern, and North Eastern Regions. [1957.] pp. 32.
    11, Western Region. [1958.] pp. 32.
    12, London Midland Region. [1958.] pp. 32.
    13, Eastern, and North Eastern Regions. [1959.] pp. 32.
    14, Southern Region. [1959.] pp. 32.
    15, London Midland Region. [1959.] pp. 32.

E7 LOCOMOTIVES

(General works on steam, electric, diesel, etc. locomotives)

2787 The ABC of British Railways locomotives. *London: Ian Allan*, [1948/49–]   BM
    Various editions; since 1950, twice yearly. In progress.
    A series of booklets containing lists, illustrations, and historical and descriptive notes. Until 1961 issued in four parts, and since 1958 also as a combined edition. In 1961 parts 5, 6, & 7 were introduced.
    1, Western Region.
    2, Southern Region.
    3, London Midland Region and Scottish Region.
    4, Eastern, North Eastern, and Scottish Regions.
    5, Diesel and electric locomotives.
    6, Diesel multiple units.
    7, Electric multiple units.

2788 ROSLING, G. *and* BRAY, J. Western and Southern Regions Locomotive Reference Book. Classified locomotive stock; named locomotives; complete allocation. Motive power depots and sub-sheds. Electric multiple-units. *Bristol: British Locomotive Society*, December 1948. pp. 104.   BM
    Locomotive re-numberings.

2789 The 20,000 British locomotives. *Huddersfield: Quadrant Publications*, 1948. pp. iv, 52.   BM
    Number, class, and name of every locomotive in service at the end of 1947.

2790 BELL, A. M. Locomotives: their construction, maintenance and operation; with notes on electric, internal combustion and other forms of motive power. *London: Virtue & Co.* [1935.] 2 vols. (pp. viii, 431), with 7 col. plates & fold. diagrams, & many illus. in text.   BM

—— 2nd edn. *London*, 1935.   BM
—— 4th, *London*, 1937.   BM
—— 5th, *London*, 1946.   BM
—— 6th, *London*, 1948.   BM
—— 7th, *London*, 1949.   BM

2791 LOCOMOTIVE MANUFACTURERS' ASSOCIATION OF GREAT BRITAIN. LMA Handbook. *London*, 1949. pp. 464.   BM
    A general reference work containing a history of the locomotive manufacturing industry; B.S. Specifications, and (pp. 100–373) dictionary of locomotive terms in English, French, Spanish, Portuguese & German, with diagrams.

2792 REED, B. Modern railway motive power. *London: Temple Press*, 1950. pp. vi, 170, with 11 plates, illus., & a bibliography.   BM

2793 ROSLING, G. *and* BRAY, J. British Railways locomotive reference, 1–39999, including all multiple-unit electric stock. Classified locomotive stock, named locomotives; complete allocation. Motive power depots and codes, etc. Second edition. *Bristol: British Locomotive Society*, January 1951. pp. 105.   BM

2794 BRITISH standard locomotives: names, numbers, photographs, diagrams and dimensions. *London: Locomotive Publishing Co.*, [*c*. 1952.] pp. 19.   IT
    Locomotives of British Railways.

2795 COCK, C. M. Motive power for railways. 1952. pp. 24.   IT
    Presidential address, Institution of Locomotive Engineers, 24 Sept., 1952.
    Alternatives to steam.

2796 COOK, K. J. Statistical approach to locomotive maintenance. pp. 21. *Reproduced typescript, with mounted photographs.* IT
Paper, York Locomotive Society, 13 Nov., 1952.

2797 SIMPSON, C. R. H. *and* ROBERTS, F. B. Locomotives and their working; with a section on gas turbine, diesel and electric locomotives. *London: Virtue,* 1952. 2 vols. (pp. 562), with many plates, illus., & diagrams (some col., and some in detailed perspective by V. C. Stockton.) BM
A textbook for enginemen and mechanics on the construction and maintenance of locomotives.

2798 WEBSTER, H. C. Railway motive power . . . *London: Hutchinson,* 1952. pp. 310, with 50 plates, & 57 drawings in text. BM
Modern locomotives of all kinds, related to current problems of railway economics.

2799 BRITISH RAILWAYS (LONDON MIDLAND REGION). Derby Locomotive Works Training School. *Derby,* June 1953. pp. 32, with illus. IT

2800 LUND, G. H. K. Future developments in motive power. 1956. pp. 15. *Typescript.* IT
Paper, Institute of Transport, Merseyside Section, 5 April, 1956.

2801 NELSON, R. I. Modern motive power in service. Paper read before the Stephenson Locomotive Society, January 1956. pp. 67, with 2 illus. inserted. *Typescript.* SLS
Successors to steam.

2802 COOPER, B. K. Modern railway working. *London: L. Hill,* 1957. pp. xii, 114, with 105 illus. on plates and 6 figures in text. BM
Includes comparative merits of steam, diesel and electric locomotives.

2803 MACKILLOP, N. Top link locomotives. *London: Nelson,* 1957. pp. xiii, 187, with 24 illus. on 11 plates. BM
Driving modern locomotives; steam, diesel, electric and gas-turbine.

*2804 THE OBSERVER's Book of Railway Locomotives of Great Britain. (By E. F. Carter.) *London: Warne,* 1955. pp. 281, with over 200 illus. & 8 col. plates. BM
Details of all classes of locomotives in use.
—— Subsequent revised editions by H. C. Casserley:
—— *London,* 1957. pp. 284. BM
—— *London,* 1958. pp. 286. BM
—— *London,* 1960. pp. 282. BM
—— *London,* 1962. pp. 285. BM
—— *London,* 1964. pp. 256. BM

2805 REED, B. Locomotives. *London: Temple Press,* 1958. pp. 138, with plates and diagrams. IT

2806 The ABC Locoshed Book. *London: Ian Allan,* 1959– BM
A series, in progress.
Shed allocations for all British locomotives. A companion to 'ABC of British Railways Locomotives'.

2807 RANSOME-WALLIS, P. The Concise Encyclopaedia of World Railway Locomotives; edited by P. Ransome-Wallis . . . *London: Hutchinson,* 1959. pp. 512, with 144 plates (16 col.), & many illus. & diagrams in text. BM
A comprehensive and authoritative work.
pp. 25–106, Diesel railway traction, by J. M. Doherty.
pp. 107–42, Diesel traction in North America, by David P. Morgan.
pp. 143–238, Electric motive power, by F. J. G. Haut.
pp. 239–318, The reciprocating steam locomotive, by C. R. H. Simpson.
pp. 319–85, Illustrated survey of modern steam locomotives, by H. M. Le Fleming.
pp. 386–410, The testing of locomotives, by S. O. Ell.
pp. 411–38, The steam locomotive in traffic, by O. S. Nock.
pp. 439–56, The organisation of a steam motive power depot, by G. Freeman Allen and P. Ransome-Wallis.
pp. 457–77, Unconventional forms of motive power, by P. Ransome-Wallis.
pp. 478–93, The gas turbine in railway service, by P. Ransome-Wallis.
pp. 494–503, Concise biographies of famous locomotive designers and engineers, by H. M. Le Fleming.

2808 DAY, J. R. *and* COOPER, B. K. Railway locomotives . . . illustrated by Michael G. Young. *London: F. Muller,* 1960. pp. 144. with 26 illus. on 12 plates, & diagrams. BM
Steam, diesel, diesel-electric, and electric.

2809 LOCOMOTIVE AND ALLIED MANUFACTURERS' ASSOCIATION OF GREAT BRITAIN. British locomotives. *London,* [1961.] pp. 88, with many illus., incl. 31 in colour. BM
pp. 30–53, The evolution of the British locomotive industry.

2810 LORD, S. E. Factors affecting choice of motive power. *London: United Kingdom Railway Advisory Service,* 1962. pp. 16, with 'Transart' six-section diagram of an electric locomotive. BM

E 8   STEAM LOCOMOTIVES

For locomotives of particular railways see **L** *and* **B 10**
For narrow gauge and other special forms of locomotive see **D 1 – 6**

Historical

2811 STUART, R. Anecdotes of steam engines. *London*, 1829. 2 vols. (pp. xlii, 650.)   BM
c   Stationary engines, but includes early experiments in locomotion with details of inventors and a chronological list of their patents.

2812 HEDLEY, O. D. Who invented the locomotive engine?; with a review of Smiles' 'Life of Stephenson'. *London*, 1858. pp. 92, with 4 plates.   BM
     Supporting the claims of Wm. Hedley.

2813 BOUCHOT, J. C. Invention de la locomotive par Cugnot, Nic.-Jos. né le 26 févr. 1725 à Void (Meuse). *Bar-le-Duc*, [1861.] pp. 7.

2814 EDMONDS, R. The Lands' End district . . . also a brief memoir of Richard Trevithick. *London*, 1862. pp. 269.   BM
     pp. 254–66, 'Contributions to the biography of Richard Trevithick'.

2815 WALKER, W. Memoirs of distinguished men of science of Great Britain living in the years 1807–8. *London*, 1862. pp. xiii, 228. BM
     pp. 193–200, R. Trevithick.
     —— 2nd edn. *London*, 1862. pp. viii, 160.   BM

2816 PATENT OFFICE. Patents for inventions. Abridgments of specifications relating to the steam engine: part 1, A.D. 1618–1859, in two volumes. (Compiled by B. Woodcroft.) *London*, 1871. pp. xxxvi, 2030.   BM:PO
     Includes locomotives.

2817 PATENT OFFICE. Patents for inventions. Abridgments of specifications relating to the steam engine: part 2, A.D. 1860–1866; in two volumes. (Compiled by B. Woodcroft.) *London*, 1871. pp. xxviii, 1364. BM:PO
     Includes locomotives.

2818 TREVITHICK, F. The life of Richard Trevithick, with an account of his inventions; illustrated . . . *London & New York*, 1872. 2 vols. in one (pp. xii, 388; vii, 403), with 18 plates.   BM

2819 EVERS, H. Steam and the steam engine: land, marine and locomotive. *London & Glasgow*, 1873. pp. 373, with diagrams. BM
     pp. [225]–243, History and description of locomotives.

2820 WEBER, C. P. M. M. von. Zur Erinnerung an die fünfzigjährige Gedenkfeier der ersten Lokomotiv-Wettfahrten bei Rainhill . . . *Berlin*, 1879. pp. 23.   ICE

2821 GALLOWAY, R. L. The steam engine and its inventors: a historical sketch. *London*, 1881. pp. xix, 260.   BM
     pp. 201–32, locomotive engines on railways.

2822 [DAVIS, J.] Memorial Edition of the life of Richard Trevithick. *London*, 1883. pp. 24, with 5 plates, & illus.   BM

2823 ARCHER, M. William Hedley, the inventor of railway locomotion on the present principle. *Newcastle-on-Tyne*, 1882. pp. 66, with 4 plates (1 fold.); map.   BM
     —— 3rd edn. *London*, [1885.] pp. xvi, 80.   BM

2824 ARCHER, M. Letters on the subject of William Hedley's invention of railway locomotion on the present principle. *Newcastle-upon-Tyne*, 1883. pp. 17.   BM
     A sequel to his 'William Hedley, the inventor of railway locomotion on the present principle', 1882.

2825 WEST, T. An outline of the growth of the locomotive engine, and a few early railway
c   carriages. July 1885. la. fold. sh.   BR
     Seventy-seven line drawings with captions, showing chronological development.

2826 DEGHILAGE, A. L. Origine de la locomotive. *Paris*, 1886. pp. 44, with 12 plates.   BM
     Includes early British locomotives.

2827 STRETTON, C. E. Locomotive development. *Leeds: Associated Society of Locomotive Engineers & Firemen*, [1889.] pp. 40.
                                                ICE
     Special number of the Society's monthly journal.
     Arranged under railways.

2828 CHURCH, W. C. Life of John Ericsson. *London*, 1890. 2 vols, with illus.   BM
     vol. 1, pp. 53–66 & elsewhere, Rainhill Trial.

2829 TOMLINSON, J. Address of the President, Joseph Tomlinson. *Westminster: Institution of Mechanical Engineers*, 1890. pp. 181–202, with 46 plates (locomotives).   IME
     Excerpt, *Min. Proc. I.M.E.*, 1st May, 1890.
     Recollections of early locomotives, from 1837.

*2830 JUBILEE of the world's first public railway, the Stockton & Darlington, 1875; a chapter in the history of railway locomotion, and a memoir of Timothy Hackworth, the father of locomotives; with a portrait and a list of some of his principal inventions. *Leamington Spa*, [1893.] pp. 36.   BM
     pp. 3–13, 'A chapter in the history of railway

locomotion', reprinted from the *Practical Mechanics Journal*, 1851.
pp. 14–20, 'Memoir of Timothy Hackworth', reprinted from the *Practical Mechanics Journal*, 1851.
pp. 22–33, Appendix, 'Timothy Hackworth's inventions'. By John Wesley Hackworth.

2831 MARTIN, J. Chats on invention . . . *London*, 1894. pp. 142, with diagrams. RC
Reprinted from *Invention*.
Includes the steam locomotive.

2832 PANGBORN, J. G. The world's railway: historical, descriptive, illustrative. Edition de luxe. *New York: Winchell Printing Co.*, 1894. pp. 164. la. 4°. BM
A locomotive history, including development in Gt. Britain.

2833 MARSHALL, W. P. Evolution of the locomotive engine. *London: I.C.E.*, 1898. pp.
c 77, with 5 fold. plates. ICE
Excerpt, *Min. Proc. I.C.E.*, vol. 133, pt. 3.
A chronological record of the development of locomotives and their components.

2834 SEKON, G. A. The evolution of the steam locomotive, 1803 to 1898. *London*, 1899. pp. iv, 327, with many illus. BM
—— 2nd edn. *London*, 1899. pp. vii, 327. BM

2835 COOKE, C. J. B. British locomotives: their history, construction and modern development; with numerous illustrations . . . and reproductions of official drawings and photographs. *London*, 1893. pp. xvi, 381, with 145 illus. BM
—— 2nd edn. *London*, 1894. pp. xvi, 381. RC
—— 3rd, with additional illus. *London*, 1900. pp. xix, 422. BM

2836 WEST, T. The evolution of the locomotive engine. *Darlington* [c. 1900]. 14 plates. RC
c Hundreds of small drawings presented in fourteen series. The introduction includes a biographical account of Theodore West. One of the series, 'Types of railway locomotive engines on the Stockton & Darlington and the North Eastern lines, 1825–1848' is reproduced in *Jubilee of the Railway News* (1914).

2837 STRETTON, C. E. The locomotive engine and its development: a popular treatise . . . with numerous illustrations. *London*, 1892. pp. x, 154. BM
—— 2nd edn. *London*, 1893. pp. x, 204. BM
—— 3rd, *London*. 1895. pp. x, 208. BM
—— 4th, *London*. 1896. pp. xii, 228. BM
—— 5th, *London*. 1896. pp. xii, 252. BM
—— 6th, *London*. 1903. pp. xii, 270. BM

2838 PATENT OFFICE. Patents for inventions. Abridgments of specifications. Class 79, Locomotives and motor vehicles for road and rail, period 1867–76. *London*, 1904. pp. xxii, 247, with diagrams. BM: PO

2839 BENNETT, A. R. Historic locomotives and 'moving accidents' by steam and rail . . . *London*, 1906. pp. 15, with 10 col. plates. BM.

2840 MATSCHOSS, C. Die Entwicklung der Dampfmaschine. *Berlin*, 1908. 2 vols. SL
vol. 1, pp. 773–834, Die Entwicklung der Locomotive. With illus. & bibliogr. notes.
Includes British locomotive development.

2841 HAWTHORN, R. & W., LESLIE & CO. Short history of R. & W. Hawthorn, Leslie & Co. Ltd., locomotive manufacturers. *Newcastle-on-Tyne*, [c. 1910.] pp. 18, with illus. & diagrams. pc

2842 The STORY of the locomotive; compiled from authoritative sources. (Illustrated to show progress from 1769 to 1910; including a coloured dissected model of a passenger express locomotive.) *London & New York*, 1910. pp. 18, with fold. diagram. BM

2843 HARPER, E. K. A Cornish Giant: Richard Trevithick, the father of the locomotive-engine . . . *London*, 1913. pp. 61, with 12 illus. BM

2844 AHRONS, E. L. The development of British locomotive design. *London*, 1914. pp. 223, with illus. & many diagrams on fold. plates & in text. IME

2845 GAIRNS, J. F. Fifty years of locomotive engineering, 1864–1914. *In* 'Jubilee of the Railway News, 1864–1914.' [*London*, 1914.] pp. 38–66, with 55 illus., & tables. BM

2846 SNELL, S. A story of railway pioneers: being an account of the inventions and works of Isaac Dodds and his son, Thomas Weatherburn Dodds. *London*, [1921.] pp. xvi, 159, with 44 illus. on plates & in text. BM

*2847 WARREN, J. G. H. A century of locomotive building by Robert Stephenson & Co., 1823–1923. *Newcastle upon Tyne*, 1923. pp. vii, 461, with many illus. & bibliogr. notes. BM

*2848 YOUNG, R. Timothy Hackworth and the locomotive. *London*, 1923. pp. xxxii, 406, with illus. BM
Very detailed work containing much information on early railways and locomotives.

*2849 AHRONS, E. L. The British steam railway locomotive, 1825 to 1925. *London*, 1927. pp. 391, with 473 illus. BM
A very detailed work. Contains a short biography of E. L. Ahrons.
—— Reprint. *London: Locomotive Publishing Co. (Ian Allan)*, [1961.] pp. 391. BM

*2850 BENNETT, A. R. The chronicles of Boulton's Siding . . . *London*, 1927. pp. 272, with 93 illus. BM
Locomotives rebuilt by Isaac Watt Boulton.

2851 BEYER PEACOCK & CO. The British locomotive industry. [*Gorton*, 1927.] pp. [17.]
                                        SLS
Reprint of editorial articles from the *Daily
Telegraph*, 27 Feb. to 6 March, 1927, embodying
the history of Beyer Peacock & Co., and an
account of the Gorton Foundry.

2852 BEYER PEACOCK & CO. Hermann Ludwig
Lange. *Manchester*, 1928. pp. 28, with
illus., incl. portraits.   BR
Reprint, *B.P. Quarterly Review*, April 1928.
His work with Beyer Peacock.

2853 HIND, J. R. The locomotive, at work and at
rest; with 100 illustrations including 6 blocks
in full colour. *London & Glasgow*, [1928.]
pp. 136.   BM
History and description.

2854 DENDY MARSHALL, C. F. Two essays in
early locomotive history . . . *London*, 1928.
c pp. 119, with illus.   BM
pp. 9–86, 'The first hundred railway engines.'
Includes a chronological table and bibliographical notes.

2855 SCOTT, E. K. Matthew Murray, pioneer
engineer: records from 1765 to 1826 *Leeds*,
b 1928. pp. 132.   BM
Includes details of other contemporary steam
c engineers and their locomotives; notes on the
Middleton Colliery Rly; chronology of M.
Murray and also of engineering and other
events from 1758–1875; bibliography of 5 pages
and a pedigree of the Murrays.

2856 JACKSON, G. G. British locomotives: their
evolution and development. *London*, [1929.]
pp. x, 246, with many illus. on plates. BM
Arranged under companies.

2857 [STEPHENSON.] ROBERT STEPHENSON &
CO. The 'Rocket'. *Darlington*, May 1929.
pp. 2.   SLS
The replica built for Henry Ford's Mechanical Museum, Detroit, U.S.A.

2858 The VULCAN Locomotive Works, 1830–
1930. *London*, 1930. pp. 122, with plates
& illus.   BM

*2859 WIENER, L. Articulated locomotives. *Lon-
don*, 1930. pp. xv, 628, with 213 illus. & 112
c tables.   BM
pp. 588–96, Chronological sequence of the
invention and progress of articulated locomotives.

2860 INGLIS, C. E. Trevithick Memorial Lecture
delivered at the Institution of Civil Engineers . . . April 24th, 1933. [*London*, 1933.]
pp. 15. with illus.   IT
Trevithick Centenary Commemoration.

2861 PENDRED, L. St. L. Richard Trevithick: a
eulogy delivered by L. St. L. Pendred at
Dartford Parish Church on Sunday, April
23, 1933. *London*, [1933.] pp. [2.]   IT
Trevithick Centenary Commemoration.

2862 DICKINSON, H. W. *and* TITLEY, A. Richard
Trevithick, the engineer and the man: Tre-
b vithick Centenary Commemoration memor-
c ial volume. *Cambridge*, 1934. pp. xvii, 290,
with 18 plates, 41 illus. in text, bibliography,
chronology & fold. pedigree.   BM

2863 HAMBLETON, F. C. John Ramsbottom, the
father of the modern locomotive. [1937.]
pp. 30, with drawings & lists.   RC
pp. 1–6 reprinted from the February 1937
issue of the *Journal of the Stephenson Locomotive Society*.

2864 MUSGRAVE, G. A. The history, evolution
and construction of the steam locomotive.
London: L.N.E.Rly., 1937. pp. 37, with
illus.   PC
A reprint of a series of articles in the L. &
N.E. Rly. Magazine, written for the instruction
of young enginemen.

2865 CLARK, E. K. Kitsons of Leeds, 1837 to
1937: a firm and its folk, by one of them.
London: Locomotive Publishing Co., [1938.]
pp. 185, with plates & fold. diagrams. BM

2866 DENDY MARSHALL, C. F. Early British
locomotives: a supplement to the first of the
author's 'Two essays in early locomotive
history.' *London: Locomotive Publishing Co.*,
1939. pp. 107, with plates, illus. & bibliogr.
notes.   BM

2867 MATSCHOSS, C. Great engineers. *London:
Bell*, 1939. pp. xi, 381.   BM
pp. 154–89, R. Trevithick; G. & R. Stephenson.

2868 STEPHENSON LOCOMOTIVE SOCIETY.
Locomotive drawings, comprising a selec-
tion of work by F. C. Hambleton, L. Ward,
J. N. Maskelyne, J. C. Cosgrave, G. F. Bird,
R. C. Menzies . . . *New Malden*, [1939.] pp.
61.   BM
Over 200 drawings reprinted from the *Journal
of the S.L.S.*.

2869 THURSTON, R. H. A history of the growth
of the steam engine. *London*, 1878. pp. xviii,
490, with illus.   BM
pp. 144–220, 'Steam locomotion on railroads,
1800–1840'; with illus.
—— Centennial edn. *Ithaca*, 1939. pp. xii,
555.   BM

2870 FAY, C. R. Trevithick and Cornwall. *In*
'English economic history, mainly since
1700.' *Cambridge: W. Heffer & Sons*, 1940.
pp. 164–70, with bibliogr. notes.   BM
Reprinted 1948.

2871 TATFORD, B. The ABC of Irish locomotives. *Staines: Ian Allan*, 1945. pp. 32. BM
Lists, historical data, and illustrations.

2872 CASSERLEY, H. C. Veterans of the track.
London: Ian Allan, 1946. pp. 36.   BM

Photographs of old locomotives still in use, with short descriptions, prefaced by an introductory essay.

2873 KIDNER, R. W. The development of the railway locomotive, 1880–1946. *Chislehurst: Oakwood Press*, 1946. pp. [39]–81 & pl. IX–XX. [*Short History of Mechanical Traction & Travel*, pt. 4.]   BM
Also issued as part of a collected edition, vol. 2, 'Rail,' 1947.

2874 ALLEN, C. J. Locomotive practice and performance in the twentieth century. *Cambridge: W. Heffer & Sons*, 1949. pp. xv, 302, with 149 illus. on plates, 82 tables & 24 gradient profiles.   BM
From the series 'British locomotive practice and performance' which first appeared in the *Railway Magazine* in the September issue, 1901, and which is still in progress. C. J. Allen produced the articles from August 1909 until December 1958.

2875 BISHOP, P. M. K. Tandem compound locomotives: a historical review; drawings by the author. *London*, 1949. pp. 70.   BM
Mostly American, some European, a few British.

2876 CLEMENTS, R. N. *and* ROBBINS, J. M. The ABC of Irish locomotives. *London: Ian Allan*, 1949. pp. 56, with 45 illus. & a map.   BM
Historical notes and lists.

2877 DEWHURST, P. C. Norris locomotives in England, 1838–1842. *London: Newcomen Society*, [1949]. pp. 13–45 & pl. IV–XII, with bibliogr. notes.   BR
Excerpt, *Transactions, Newcomen Society*, vol. 26, 1947/48–1948/49.

2878 ELLIS, C. H. Some classic locomotives. *London: Allen & Unwin*, 1949. pp. x, 173, with 80 illus. (8 col.) on plates.   BM

2879 ALLEN, C. J. The locomotive exchanges, 1870–1948. *London: Ian Allan*, 1949. pp. 176, with 63 illus. on 32 plates, & tables. BM
—— New light on the locomotive exchanges: a detailed analysis of the official report of the Railway Executive. *London: Ian Allan*, 1950. pp. 59, with illus. on 8 plates.   BM
The 1948 exchanges; a supplement to *The locomotive exchanges* (1949).
—— The locomotive exchanges. [2nd edn.] *London*, [1950.] pp. 176, lix.   pc
A combined edition.

2880 DOW, G. British Steam Horses. *London: Phoenix House*, 1950. pp. 128, with 57 illus. on 32 plates, & 7 diagrams.   BM
An explanatory and descriptive appreciation of the locomotive, with details of its construction and working, and a biographical chapter on some locomotive designers.

2881 SHILDON—TIMOTHY HACKWORTH CENTENARY COMMEMORATION COMMITTEE. Timothy Hackworth, 1786–1850, father of the locomotive: souvenir on commemoration of the centenary of his death, July 7th, 1950. (Compiled by Frederick Dewell and Charles V. Browne.) *Shildon*, 1950. pp. 43, with illus.   BR

2882 FORWARD, E. A. Chapman's locomotives, 1812–1815: some facts and some speculations. pp. 22. *Reproduced typescript.*   SLS
Paper, Newcomen Society, 10 October, 1951. William Chapman, 1749–1832.

2883 HOLLOWOOD, B. Cornish engineers; illustrated by Terence Cuneo, with reproductions of contemporary photographs and documents. *Camborne: Holman Bros.*, [1951.] pp. 95.   pc
'Published for private circulation.'
Includes Trevithick.

2884 LEE, C. E. Adrian Stephens, inventor of the steam whistle. [*London*, 1951.] pp. 163–73, & pl. XXXVI & XXXVII.   BM
Excerpt, *Transactions of the Newcomen Society*, vol. 27, 1949/50 and 1950/51.

2885 CASSERLEY, H. C. Locomotive Cavalcade; a comprehensive review, year by year, of the changes in steam locomotive development and design which have taken place on the railways of the British Isles between the years 1920 and 1951. *Berkhamsted: the author*, 1952. pp. 216, with over 300 illus.   BM

2886 POULTNEY, E. C. British express locomotive development, 1896–1948 . . . *London: Allen & Unwin*, 1952. pp. 175, with 82 illus.   BM
pp. 19–28, The railway races to Aberdeen of 1895.

2887 DENDY MARSHALL, C. F. A history of railway locomotives down to the end of the year 1831. *London: Locomotive Publishing Co.*, 1953. pp. xii, 271, with 105 illus., bibliogr. notes & an index of locomotives.   BM

2888 NORTH BRITISH LOCOMOTIVE CO. A history of the North British Locomotive Co. Ltd. *Glasgow*, 1953. pp. 115, with illus. (some col.).   BR
Histories of Sharp, Stewart & Co., Neilson, Reid & Co. and Dübs & Co., which amalgamated in 1903, and accounts of present locomotive production.

2889 CHALONER, W. H. John Galloway, 1804–1894, engineer of Manchester, and his 'Reminiscences'. *Manchester*, 1955. pp. 93–116, with illus., portrait & 80 bibliogr. notes.   BM
Reprinted from the *Transactions of the Lancashire & Cheshire Antiquarian Society*, vol. 64, 1954.
Personal accounts of experiments with the

locomotive 'Manchester' on the Liverpool & Manchester Rly. in 1831, and of his firm's subsequent work in the manufacture of boilers.

*2890 NOCK, O. S. Steam locomotive: a retrospect of the work of eight great locomotive engineers. *London: British Transport Commission*, 1955. pp. 40, with illus., incl. portraits.　BM
　　Robert Stephenson, John Ramsbottom, Edward Fletcher, Patrick Stirling, Samuel Waite Johnson, Dugald Drummond, G. J. Churchward, and H. N. Gresley.

2891 DEWHURST, P. C. The Crampton locomotive in England. pp. 16. *Reproduced typescript.*　BR
　　Paper, Newcomen Society, 11 April, 1956.

2892 ODGERS, J. F. Richard Trevithick, 'the Cornish Giant', 1771–1833: memorials and commemorations in Camborne and district. *Camborne*, September, 1956. pp. 40, with 13 illus.　BM
　　A record of various commemorations held in Cornwall in honour of R. Trevithick.

2893 SIMMONS, J. For and against the locomotive. *In* 'Journal of Transport History,' vol.
b　2, no. 3, May 1956. pp. 144–51, with 24 bibliogr. notes.　BM
　　The locomotive and alternative means of propulsion before 1830.

2894 ELLIS, C. H. Famous locomotives of the world: sketches by the author. *London: F. Muller*, 1957. pp. 143, with 37 illus. on 12 plates & illus. in text.　BM
　　Mostly of railways in the British Isles.

*2895 NOCK, O. S. Steam locomotive: the unfinished story of steam locomotives and steam locomotive men on the railways of Great Britain. *London: Allen & Unwin*, 1957. pp. 233, with 106 illus. on 32 plates.　BM

2896 ELLIS, C. H. Twenty locomotive men. *London: Ian Allan*, 1958. pp. viii, 214, with 42 illus. on plates & a bibliography.　BM

W. B. Adams	S. W. Johnson
J. H. Beattie	W. Stroudley
J. C. Craven	D. Jones
R. Sinclair	F. W. Webb
D. Gooch	T. W. Worsdell
T. R. Crampton	D. Drummond
A. Sturrock	W. Dean
P. Stirling	J. Mason
W. Adams	J. Aspinall
C. R. Sacré	G. J. Churchward

*2897 FENTON, E. W. Locomotives in retirement. (Illustrated and described by E. W. Fenton.) *London: Hugh Evelyn*, 1958. 10 la. col. plates with descriptive text.　BM

2898 VULCAN FOUNDRY *and* ROBERT STEPHENSON & HAWTHORNS. Built by Stephenson: the early history of two locomotive builders. *London*, [1958.] pp. 24, with 22 illus.　IT

2899 WAY, R. B. The story of British locomotives. *London: Methuen*, 1953. pp. 75, with illus.　BM
　　—— 2nd edn. *London*, 1958. pp. 76.　BM

2900 WESTCOTT, G. F. The British railway locomotive: a brief pictorial history of the first fifty years of the British steam railway locomotive, 1803–1853. *London: Science Museum*, 1958. pp. 14, with 32 plates & col. frontis.　BM

2901 MASKELYNE, J. N. Locomotives I have known. *London: Percival Marshall*, 1959. pp. 133. obl. 4°.　BM
　　Two-page descriptions of sixty-six locomotives, each accompanied by scale drawings, table of dimensions and the company's seal.

2902 NOCK, O. S. Historical steam locomotives; with a plate in colour and 68 photographs. *London: Black*, 1959. pp. xii, 162, with 32 plates.　BM
　　Thirty-one locomotives which have been preserved.

2903 BRITISH locomotives, 1825–1960. *London: Percival Marshall*, [1960.] pp. [32,] with illus.　BM

2904 CASSERLEY, H. C. The Historic Locomotive Pocketbook, from the 'Rocket' to the end of steam. *London: Batsford*, 1960. pp. 255, with many illus.　BM
　　Descriptions of classes, with dimensions.

2905 ROLT, L. T. C. The Cornish Giant: the story of Richard Trevithick, father of the steam locomotive. *London: Lutterworth Press*, 1960. pp. 160, with 12 plates, and 13 drawings by Francis, Richard Trevithick's son.　BM

2906 STEPHENSON LOCOMOTIVE SOCIETY. Railway progress, 1909–1959. Jubilee Year publication; volume one. *London*, [1960.] pp. 139, with 65 illus. on 24 plates.　PC
　　Locomotive development on various railways.

2907 BROWN, F. A. S. Nigel Gresley, locomotive engineer. *London: Ian Allan*, 1961. pp. 256, with illus. on 32 plates.　BM

*2908 CASSERLEY, H. C. *and* ASHER, L. L. Locomotives of British Railways: a pictorial record. *London: Spring Books*, 1961. pp. 488, with 732 illus. on 350 pp.　BM
　　All steam locomotives acquired by British Railways upon nationalization, and built since, up to March 1960. A combined and revised edition of the work of the same name previously published in four parts.

2909 EVANS, M. Atlantic Era: the British atlantic locomotive. *London: Percival Marshall*, 1961. pp. 94, with frontis., illus. & tables. BM

2910 EVANS, M. Pacific Steam: the British pacific locomotive. *London: Percival Marshall*, 1961. pp. vii, 80, with illus. & tables.　BM

2911 ALLEN, C. J. British pacific locomotives. *London: Ian Allan*, 1962. pp. 240, with 116 illus. on 49 plates, diagrams, & many tables.   BM

2912 CARTER, E. F. British steam locomotives. *London: W. & G. Foyle*, 1962. pp. 92, with
c   26 illus. on 8 plates, diagrams, & a chron. table of locomotive classes since 1900. [*Foyles Handbooks.*]   BM

2913 MASKELYNE, J. N. A further selection of locomotives I have known. *London: Percival Marshall*, 1962. pp. 71. obl. 4°.   BM
Thirty-three essay descriptions with line drawings.

2914 CASSERLEY, H. C. British locomotive names of the twentieth century. *London: Ian Allan*, 1963. pp. 177, with many lists & 115 illus. on 32 plates.   BM

2915 BULLEID, H. A. V. Master builders of Steam. *London: Ian Allan*, 1963. pp. 190, with 107 illus. on 32 plates, & 44 diagrams, tables & line illus. in text.   BM
The main achievements in locomotive design of H. A. Ivatt, H. N. Gresley, O. V. S. Bulleid, G. J. Churchward, W. A. Stanier, and H. G. Ivatt, with a detailed biographical background of their railway and workshop life.

Contemporaneous

2916 CUMMING, T. G. Illustrations of the origin and progress of rail and tram roads, and steam carriages or locomotive engines; also, interesting descriptive particulars of the formation, construction, extent and mode of working some of the principal railways now in use within the United Kingdom, particularly those great and unequalled communications projected between Liverpool and Manchester, with a view to the more general employment of steam carriages or locomotive engines for the conveyance of passengers as well as merchandise, with remarks on the public advantages likely to accrue therefrom . . . with an explanatory plate. *Denbigh*, 1824. pp. 64.   BM

2917 SYLVESTER, C. Report on rail-roads and locomotive engines, addressed to the Chairman of the Committee of the Liverpool & Manchester projected Rail-road. *Liverpool*, 1825. pp. 39.   LSE
Findings of 'an examination of the locomotives of the Killingworth and Hetton collieries.'
—— 2nd edn. *Liverpool*, 1825. pp. 39.   BM

2918 PARTINGTON, C. F. A course of lectures on the steam engine, delivered before the members of the London Mechanics Institution . . . *London*, 1826. pp. 92.   UL(GL)
pp. 48–9, locomotives.

2919 Essay on railroads. *Philadelphia*, [1830.] pp. 26.   UL(GL)
pp. 5–26, Extracts from newspapers and magazines, mostly on the Rainhill Trial.

2920 MOSS, S. Some considerations of the benefits and evils of steam power. *Dublin*, 1831. pp. 23.   BM
The application of steam to manufactures. Locomotives also considered.

2921 ALDERSON, M. A. An essay on the nature and application of steam, with an historical notice of the rise and progressive improvement of the steam engine. *London*, 1834. pp. xvi, 124, with plates.   UL
Includes locomotives.

2922 DESCRIPTION des locomotives Stephenson, circulant sur les chemins de fer en Angleterre et en France, et sur celui de Bruxelles à Malines; précédée d'un aperçu historique sur les chemins, les rails, la vapeur, et les machines à vapeur. *Bruxelles*, 1835. pp. 72, with 6 fold. plates.   H

2923 GALLOWAY, E. History and progress of the steam engine; with practical investiga-
c   tion of its structure and application . . . to which is added an extensive Appendix . . . by Luke Hebert . . . *London*, 1830. pp. 863, with illus. & a chron. list of patents.   UL(GL)
pp. 568–640, Railways, including the Liverpool & Manchester, the Rainhill Trials, and Palmer's suspension railway.
—— *London*, 1831. pp. 863.   BM
—— *London*, 1832. pp. 863.   H
—— *London*, 1836. pp. 863.   H

2924 PARTINGTON, C. F. An historical and descriptive account of the steam engine . . . *London*, 1822. pp. xvi, 187, 90.   UL(GL)
p. 50, Blenkinsop's locomotive.
—— 2nd edn. corr. & enl. *London*, 1826. pp. xiv, 300.   BM
—— 3rd edn. 'A popular and descriptive account of the steam engine' . . . *London*, 1836. pp. xvi, 330.   UL(GL)

2925 MARSHALL, W. P. Description of the patent locomotive steam engine of Messrs. Robert Stephenson & Co., with four elaborate engravings and numerous woodcuts of details. *London*, 1838. pp. 67.   PO
From *The Steam Engine* by T. Tredgold (1838–39).
Stephenson's 2-2-2 used in the construction of the London & Birmingham Rly.
—— Description de la machine locomotive de MM. Robert Stephenson et Cie . . . *Bruxelles*, 1839. pp. 100.   H

2926 REID, H. The steam engine; being a popular description of the construction and action of that engine, with a sketch of its history . . . *Edinburgh*, 1838. pp. xi, 203.   BM
pp. 85–9, 'Locomotive engines on rail-roads'.

2927 STUART, R. A descriptive history of the steam engine. *London*, 1824. pp. vi, 228. BM
pp. 162–4, Trevithick and Vivian's locomotive.
—— 2nd edn. *London*, 1824. pp. vi, 228.   UL(GL)

—— 3rd, *London*, 1825. pp. vi, 228. UL(GL)
—— another edn. *London*, 1838. pp. vi, 249.
BM

2928 TEMPLETON, W. The Engineer's Common-
place Book of Practical Reference, consisting
of practical rules and tables adapted to land,
marine and locomotive steam engines . . .
with lithograph illustrations. *London*, 1839.
pp. 138, 37–48, 153–66.   BM
Later editions exclude locomotives.

*2929 TREDGOLD, T. The steam engine: its in-
vention and progressive improvement: an
investigation of its principles and its application to navigation, manufactures and railways. A new edition . . . revised and edited
by W. S. B. Woodhouse. *London*, 1838, 1839.
2 vols. (text, pp. xix, 500; plates, pp. 250.)
BM

2930 GUYONNEAU DE PAMBOUR, F. M.
Practical treatise on locomotive engines
upon railways . . . founded upon a great
many new experiments . . . on the Liverpool
& Manchester Railway. *London*, 1836. pp.
xxxi, 365, incl. tables & 4 fold. plates. BM
A translation from the French, *Traité
théorique et pratique des machines locomotives.*
—— 2nd edn. *London*, 1840. pp. xlviii, 583.
BM
—— French edn. *Paris*, 1840. pp. xlv, 660.
H

2931 HAWTHORN, R. & W. Experiments by R.
and W. Hawthorn of two locomotive engines
the 'Sun' and 'Star' upon the Newcastle-
upon-Tyne & Carlisle Railway, as to the
consumption of coke and water. *Newcastle-
upon-Tyne*, 1840. pp. 71, with tables.   ICE

2932 GRAY, J. Improvements in steam engines,
etc. *Hull*, 1841. pp. 8.   LSE
Advantages of his improved engine on the
Liverpool & Manchester and Hull & Selby
railways.

*2933 GREGORY, C. H. Practical rules for the
management of a locomotive engine; in the
station, on the road, and in cases of accident.
London, 1841. pp. 48.   H

2934 RUSSELL, J. S. On the nature, properties,
and application of steam, and on steam
navigation; from the seventh edition of
Encyclopaedia Britannica. *Edinburgh*, 1841.
pp. xii, 378.   BM
Includes an account of the locomotive steam
engine from the treatise on railways by P.
Lecount.

2935 HOBLYN, R. D. A Manual of the Steam
Engine; illustrated with numerous engravings
on steel and wood. *London*, 1842. pp. xviii,
293[297].   RC
pp. 138–93, 'Of locomotive engines on railways . . .'

*2936 WHISHAW, F. The railways of Great
Britain and Ireland, practically described

and illustrated. *London*, 1840, 41. pp. xxvi,
500, lxiv, with 15 fold. plates.   BM
Detailed accounts of fifty-eight railways, with
tables of experimental runs extending to 7000
miles, and tables relating to the performances of
630 locomotives.
—— 2nd edn. *London*, 1852. pp. xxvi, 500,
lxiv, with 19 plates.   LSE

2937 BASIRE, J. The locomotive engine illustrated
on stone. 2nd edn. *London*, 1844. 4 la.
double-page diagrams, with 2 pp. text. BM

2938 CURR, J. Railway locomotion and steam
navigation: their principles and practice.
London, 1847. pp. 181.   BM

2939 CURR, J. The Learned Donkeys of eighteen
hundred and forty seven . . . being a review
of the reviewers of 'Railway locomotion and
steam navigation; their principles and practice.' *London: John Williams & Co.*, 1847.
pp. 185–98.   LSE
Letters by J. Curr to the editors of the
Mechanics Magazine, the *Artizan*, and the *Civil
Engineer & Architects' Journal*, etc. 'Ten thous-
and copies of this satire will be printed, to
exhibit the mal-practices of mechanical critics.'

2940 'VERITAS VINCIT.' Railway locomotive
management, in a series of letters reprinted
from the 'Railway Record.' *Birmingham &
London*, 1847. pp. iv, 232.   BM
On the mismanagement of various locomotive
superintendents and other officials of the period.

2941 PORTWINE, E. The Handbook to the Steam
Engine, including atmospheric railways . . .
a new edition, illustrated by wood engravings. *London*, 1848. pp. 116.   H

2942 PROGRESS, Peter, *pseud.* [R. Y. Clarke].
The locomotive; or, The steam engine
applied to railways, common roads, and
water; and an account of the atmospheric
railway. *London*, 1848. pp. 77, with illus.
BM

*2943 TEMPLETON, W. The locomotive engine
popularly explained and illustrated by lithographic designs . . . also, interesting statistical particulars connected with railways.
London, 1841. pp. 100, with fold. frontis.,
fold. plate, & tables.   BM
—— 2nd edn. 'Locomotive engines popularly explained'. *London*, 1848. pp. 106. BM

2944 FLACHAT, E. *and* PETIET, J. The Student's
Guide to the Locomotive Engine; being a
description of the different modes of constructing locomotives, details of their component parts, and the nature of their employment; with observations on the management
of locomotives. Illustrated by seventy-two
copperplate engravings. *London*, 1849. pp.
142.   BM

2945 STEWART, W. Causes of the explosion of
steam engine boilers explained, and means

suggested for its prevention. 2nd edn. *London*, 1849. pp. 16, 11.   BM
Appendix 'Invention of the locomotive steam engine.' Claims to be the inventor of the steam locomotive. 'These statements are here published simply because the inventions are my right and because I see others disposed unjustly to claim them.'

2946 ARMSTRONG, R. On the dimensions of the locomotive engine boiler in relation to evaporative power. *In* 'The principles and practice and explanation of the machinery of locomotive engines' by Thomas Tredgold. (Division A, Locomotive engines, 3rd paper.) *London*, 1850. pp. 12, with 13 plates.   BM

2947 BARLOW, H. B. Description of the outside-cylinder tank engine constructed by Messrs. Sharp Brothers & Co. of Manchester with five elaborate engravings and numerous woodcuts of details. [*London*,] 1848. pp. 40, with 5 plates. (Division A, Locomotive engines, 4th paper.) *In* 'The principles and practice and explanation of the machinery of locomotive engines' by Thomas Tredgold. *London*, 1850.   BM

2948 DESCRIPTION and specification of Crampton's patent locomotive engine 'Liverpool'. (Division A, Locomotive engines, 10th paper.) *In* 'The principles and practice and explanation of the machinery of locomotive engines . . .' by Thomas Tredgold. *London*, 1850. pp. 4, with 4 plates.   BM

2949 DESCRIPTION and specification of the passenger locomotive engine 'Wrekin,' constructed by Messrs. Bury, Curtis, & Kennedy of Liverpool, for the Shrewsbury & Birmingham Railway Company; with three elaborate engravings. (Division A, Locomotive engines, 8th paper.) *In* 'The principles and practice and explanation of the machinery of locomotive engines' by Thomas Tredgold. *London*, 1850. pp. 8, with 4 plates.   BM

2950 DESCRIPTION of the first-class express engine made by R. & W. Hawthorn, of Newcastle-upon-Tyne, November 1849. (Division A, Locomotive engines, 9th paper.) *In* 'The principles and practice and explanation of the machinery of locomotive engines' by Thomas Tredgold. *London*, 1850. pp. 16, with 4 plates.   BM

2951 STEPHENSON, R. Description of the patent locomotive steam engine made by Messrs. Robert Stephenson & Co., of Newcastle-upon-Tyne, for conveying the earth excavated in the construction of a line of railway. (Division A, Locomotive engines, 6th paper.) *In* 'The principles and practice and explanation of the machinery of locomotive engines' by Thomas Tredgold. *London*, 1850. pp. 68, with 4 plates.   BM

2952 TREDGOLD, T. The principles and practice and explanation of the machinery of loco-

motive engines in operation on the several lines of railway . . . forming the first volume of the new edition of Tredgold on the steam engine. *London*, 1850.   BM
A collection of ten papers by various authors, with 55 illus., & 41 la. fold. plates.

2953 WOODS, E. Observations on the consumption of fuel and the evaporation of water in locomotive and other steam engines. (Division A, Locomotive engines, 5th paper.) *In* 'The principles and practice and explanation of the machinery of locomotive engines' by Thomas Tredgold. *London*, 1850. pp. 44, with 2 plates.   BM

2954 HAWTHORN, R. & W. R. & W. Hawthorn's first-class passenger locomotive engine 'The Hawthorn,' sent to the Great Exhibition of 1851. *London*, 1851. pp. 12.   UL(GL)

2955 BURN, R. S. The steam engine, its history and mechanism; being descriptions and illustrations of the stationary, locomotive and marine engine . . . *London*, 1854. pp. viii, 189.   BM
pp. 140–66, 'Railway locomotion and locomotive engines.'

—— 2nd edn. *London*, 1857. pp. 142.   pc
—— 5th, *London* [n.d.], pp. 142.   pc
—— 8th, *London*, 1894. pp. vi, 184.   BM

2956 LARDNER, D. The steam engine familiarly explained and illustrated, with an historical sketch of its invention and progressive improvement, its application to navigation and railways, with plain maxims for railway speculators. 5th edn., considerably enlarged. *London*, 1836. pp. xii, 379, with plates, diagrams & tables.   BM
The earlier editions contain only passing references to railway locomotives.

—— Die Dampfmaschine, fasslich beschrieben und erklärt . . . nach der 5. Ausgabe. *Leipzig*, 1836.
—— 3rd American, from the 5th London edn. *Philadelphia*, 1836.   P
—— 6th, *London*, 1836. pp. xii, 391.   IT
—— 7th, *London*, 1840. pp. xix, 535.   BM
—— 8th, 'The steam engine, steam navigation, roads, and railways'. *London*, 1851. pp. xi, 422.   BM
—— 6th American, from the 5th London edn. *New York & Cincinnati*, 1856. pp. 324.   P

2957 [FLACHAT, E. *and* PETIET, J.] The Railway Engine-driver's Guide: being an explanation of the action and the mechanism of the several parts of locomotives and observations on their management; illustrated with numerous copper-plate engravings. *London*, 1856. pp. 142, with 72 plates.   SLS
Consists principally of a translation from *Guide du mécanicien conducteur de machines locomotives, terminé par des calculs et tableaux. Paris*, 1840 (in BM), but most of the plates are of British locomotives. At the end is a French and English vocabulary of engineering terms.

2958 LARDNER, D. Steam and its uses; including the steam engine, the locomotive and steam navigation . . . *London*, 1856. pp. 193–208, with 89 illus.   BM
Reprinted from this author's *The Museum of Science & Art*, 1854–6.
Contains details on running and maintenance practices.

2959 CLARK, D. K. Railway locomotives: their progress, mechanical construction and performance . . . illustrated by an extensive series of plates, and numerous engravings on wood. *Glasgow*, 1860. 2 vols. (text & plates.)   BM
Published in twenty-five parts.

2960 CLARK, D. K. *and* COLBURN, Z. Recent practice in the locomotive engine; being a supplement to 'Railway Machinery'; comprising the latest English improvements . . . illustrated by a series of plates and numerous engravings on wood. *Glasgow*, 1860. pp. vi. 82, with 51 plates & detailed drawings. BM

2961 CHAMBERS, W. & R. Locomotive steam engine. [*London*,] 1861. la. fold. sh.   BM
Description and four diagrams of a 2–4–0 tank engine.

2962 HOLLEY, A. L. American and European railway practice in the economical generation of steam . . . and in permanent way . . . with 77 plates. *New York & London*, 1867. pp. 192, with 69 plates.   BM

2963 FLETCHER, JENNINGS & CO. An illustrated description of some of the tank locomotive engines etc. constructed by Fletcher, Jennings & Co., Engineers . . . *London*, [*c.* 1870.] pp. 17.   ICE
Illustrations with descriptions.

2964 BOURNE, J. A Treatise on the Steam Engine. *London*, 1846–72.   BM: SL
Ten editions, each containing a brief section on locomotives.

*2965 DEMPSEY, G. D. A rudimentary treatise on the locomotive engine in all its phases, popularly described, with illustrations for students and non-professional men. Fifty-four illustrative explanatory diagrams. *London*, 1856. pp. iv, 150, with an atlas of 14 plates, separately bound.   BM
—— 2nd edn. *London*, 1857. pp. iv, 150.   UL(GL)
—— 2nd edn. *London*, 1862. pp. iv, 150. BM
—— 3rd, *London*, 1866. pp. 152.   BM
—— [3rd edn.] with additions by D. K. Clark. *London*, 1879. pp. xii, 240.   BM

2966 REYNOLDS, M. The model locomotive engineer, fireman and engine-boy; comprising a historical notice of the pioneer locomotive engines and their inventors, with a project for the establishment of certificates of qualification in the running service of railways. *London*, 1879. pp. xii, 256.   BM
—— new edn., with revised Appendix. *London*, 1896. pp. xiv, 258.   BM
A reprint, with revised Appendix.

2967 DANIELS, T. The locomotive of 1879. *Manchester*, 1880. pp. 19.   RC
Paper, Manchester Association of Employers, Foremen & Draughtsmen, 24 Jan., 1880.
Description of the contemporary locomotive.

2968 [EVANS, W. W.] American v. English locomotives: correspondence, criticism and commentary respecting their relative merits. *Leeds*, 1880. pp. 79.   ICE
—— another edn. *New York*, 1880. pp. 78.   BM

*2969 BOURNE, J. A Catechism of the Steam Engine . . . *London*, 1847. pp. vi, 276.   BM
—— 4th edn., greatly enl., improved & illustrated. *London*, 1856. pp. xvi, 558.   BM
—— 5th, *London*, 1857. pp. xii, 558.   BM
—— 11th, *London*, 1865. pp. xxiii, 564.   BM
—— new edn., much enl. & mostly rewritten. *London*, 1885. pp. xii, 610.   BM
Includes advice on the duties of locomotive engine drivers. The earlier (1st to 3rd) editions deal only briefly with locomotive engines.

2970 DEMOULIN, M. Étude sur les locomotives anglaises. *Paris*, 1885. pp. 110, with 6 fold. diagrams.   ICE
Description of locomotives in current use.

2971 STRETTON, C. E. A lecture on the breaking of locomotive driving axles. *Leicester*, [1885.] pp. 12.   ICE
Introducing his patent for strengthening the webs or throws of cranks.

2972 STROUDLEY, W. The construction of locomotive engines, with some results of the working of those on the London, Brighton & South Coast Railway; with an abstract of the discussion on the paper. *London: I.C.E.*, 1885. pp. 93, with 8 tables & fold. plate.   ICE
Excerpt. *Min. Proc. I.C.E.*, vol. 81, pt. 3, 1885.

2973 CRAMPTON, T. R. Crampton's new design for locomotive engines. *London*, [1886.] pp. 5.   ICE
Translation, *Mémoires . . . de la Société des Ingénieurs-Civils*, Paris; Meeting of 5 March, 1886.

2974 CLARK, D. K. The steam engine . . . *London*, 1890. 2 vols.   BM
vol. 2, pp. 487–643, 'Railway locomotives.' Constructional details with many diagrams. Includes (pp. 638–43) tramway locomotives.
—— another edn. *London*, 1891.   ICE

2975 ROUND the works of our great railways; by various authors . . . *London*, [1893.] pp. 232, with illus.   BM
The London & North Western Railway Works at Crewe. C. J. B. Cooke.
The Midland Railway Works at Derby. C. H. Jones.
The Great Northern Railway Works at Doncaster. A. J. Brickwell.

The North Eastern Railway and its engines. W. Worsdell.

The Great Eastern Railway Works at Stratford. A. P. Parker.

The Great Western Railway Works at Swindon. A. H. Malan.

Old broad gauge engines and their successors. A. H. Malan.

The North British Railway Works at Cowlairs. A. E. Lockyer.

2976 LOCOMOTIVE engines of the railways of the United Kingdom: illustrations and dimensions. *London: Railway Herald*, [1896.] pp. 43.   BM
    Twenty passenger engines.

2977 PEARCE, T. The locomotive: its failures and remedies. *Wolverhampton*, 1896. pp. 88,[16,] with diagrams of 8 positions of motion in the course of one revolution of driving wheels.   BM
    Published by the author.
    A textbook for enginemen.
    —— 3rd edn. rev. & enl. *Wolverhampton*, 1896. pp. 96,[32,] with 16 positions (left & right sides).   BM

2978 ASPINALL, J. A. F. Petroleum as steam-engine fuel. [*London*, 1897.] pp. 8. [*Institution of Civil Engineers Engineering Conference. Section III, Machinery & Transmission of Power. 26 May, 1897. Paper no. 3.*]   LSE
    James Holden's experiments on the G.E. Rly., with diagrams.

2979 MALLET, A. Les locomotives étrangères a l'Exposition Universelle de 1900. *Paris*, 1900. pp. 36.   ICE
    Extract, *Mémories de la Société des Ingénieurs Civils de France*.
    pp. 12–15, 'Locomotives anglaises'.

2980 ROUS-MARTEN, C. Notes on English and French compound locomotives. *London: Society of Engineers*, 1900. pp. 27. LSE
    Read at the Royal United Service Institution, 7 Nov., 1900.

2981 COOKE, C. J. B. Some recent developments in locomotive practice . . . *London*, 1902. pp. viii, 75.   BM

2982 MALLET, A. Twenty-fifth anniversary of the compound locomotive, 1877–1902. *Paris*, [1902.] pp. 4, with 2 illus.   ICE

2983 ASHBURY, T. Short communication . . . on locomotive engines. *Manchester: Manchester Association of Engineers*, 1887. Reprinted *in his* 'Miscellaneous Papers'. *Manchester*, 1904. pp. [168]–177.   PC

2984 LAKE, C. S. The world's locomotives: a digest of the latest locomotive practice in the railway countries of the world; with eight folding plates and over 300 photographs and detailed drawings. *London*, [1905.] pp. 380.   BM

2985 HARDY, T. The locomotive: its defects and remedies. [*Leeds*, 1906.] pp. 51.   BM
    —— 2nd edn. *Leeds*, 1906. pp. 62.   BM
    pp. 3–13, fatherly advice to young enginemen.

*2986 LOCOMOTIVE Handbook of Useful Memoranda and Data. *London*, 1906. pp. 99. with diagrams.   BM
    A revised presentation of the series of articles entitled 'Locomotive running' which appeared in the *Locomotive Magazine*.

2987 BEYER PEACOCK & CO. The locomotive works of Beyer Peacock & Co., Ltd., Gorton Foundry, Manchester. *London*, 1907. pp. 43, with many illus.   PC
    Reprinted from *Engineering*, 4 & 18 January, 1907.

2988 HOWDEN, J. R. The Boy's Book of Locomotives; with over one hundred illustrations from photographs. *London*, 1907. pp. xviii, 264.   BM

2989 LAKE, C. S. Locomotives of 1906. *London* [1907.] pp. 39.   BM
    Illustrations with descriptions.

2990 MONTAGU, G. Ten years of locomotive progress. *London*, 1907. pp. viii, 159, with 48 illus. on 16 plates, & tables. '   BM
    Semi-technical account of development from 1896 to 1906.

2991 FRENCH, J. W. Modern power generation: steam, electric and internal combustion, and their application to present-day requirements; with many diagrams and pictorial illustrations and a series of composite sectional models. Prepared under the direction of J. W. French. *London*, 1908. 2 vols.
                                        BM
    vol. 1, pp. 123–64 [166], The steam locomotive.

2992 LAKE, C. S. Locomotives of 1907. *London*, [1908.] pp. 44.   BM
    Illustrations with descriptions.

2993 PENDRED, V. The railway locomotive: what it is and why it is what it is. *London*, 1908. pp. xi, 310, with 94 illus.   BM
    A 'physiological' presentation of the locomotive; addressed to 'non-locomotive' engineers.

2994 PETTIGREW, W. F. Manual of Locomotive Engineering; with an historical introduction . . . *London*, 1899. pp. xvi, 430, with 9 plates and 280 illus.   BM
    A technical work, but includes useful general and historical data.
    —— 2nd edn. *London*, 1901. pp. xvi, 430.
                                        BM
    —— 3rd, *London*, 1909. pp. xv, 356.   BM

2995 RAILWAY scenes. *London*, [1909.]   SLS
    Thirty-three full-page illus. (6 col.) of locomotives, British and foreign.

2996 [BEYER PEACOCK & CO.] The further development of the steam locomotive: notes on the 'Garratt' type. *Altrincham*, 1911. pp. 26[27].   SLS
Cover title, 'The Garratt patent locomotive', End of text signed 'H.W.G.'

2997 FRY, L. H. Locomotive proportions. [*London*, 1911.] pp. 18, with 17 tables.   BM
Reprinted from the *Engineer*.
Showing how average trends in design are related to general progress towards more efficient performance.

2998 ALLEN, C. E. The modern locomotive. *Cambridge*, 1912. pp. viii, 174, with illus. & diagrams. [*Cambridge Manuals of Science & Literature.*]   BM

2999 CLAYTON, J. The organisation of the locomotive department. *In* 'Modern railway working', edited by John Macaulay. vol. 2, 1912. pp. 47–69.   BM

3000 BELL, A. R. Modern locomotive design. *In* 'Modern railway working', edited by John Macaulay. vol. 4, 1913. pp. 37–90, with 45 illus. & tables (some fold.).   BM

3001 CHALMERS, W. Locomotive maintenance and repair. *In* 'Modern railway working' edited by John Macaulay. vol. 5, 1913. pp. 17–51, with diagrams.   BM

3002 LOCOMOTIVE engine. *London*, [1913.] pp. 2.   BM
A folding diagram showing details of a contemporary locomotive.

3003 NASH, T. Tests of materials used in British locomotive construction. *In* 'Modern railway working', edited by John Macaulay. vol. 5, 1913. pp. 1–15, with diagrams.   BM

3004 SHAWCROSS, G. N. Locomotive workshop practice and equipment. *In* 'Modern railway working', edited by John Macaulay. vol. 4, 1913. pp. 105–87, with illus.   BM

3005 GAIRNS, J. F. Superheating on locomotives: the why and the wherefore . . . *London*, [1911.] pp. 99, with la. fold. diagram in pocket.   RC
—— 2nd edn. *London*, 1914. pp. 120.   RC

3006 TAYLOR, A. T. Modern British locomotives: 100 diagrams and principal dimensions. *London*, 1907. pp. viii, 110.   BM
—— 2nd edn. *London*, 1914. pp. vi, 123. (112 diagrams.)   BM

3007 LOCOMOTIVE running shed notes. *London*, [1915.] pp. 98, with diagrams.   BM
A selection of articles from the *Locomotive Magazine*.

3008 DEARBERG, H. W. The 'Garratt' locomotive . . . *Lewes: Institution of Locomotive*

Engineers, 1916. pp. 67, with 18 illus. on plates & fold. diagrams.   IME
Reprinted from the *Journal of the I.L.E.*, July–August 1916.

3009 WRIGHT, R. V. *and* SAUTER, F. H. Locomotive Dictionary and Encyclopedia. 5th edn. *New York*, 1919.   BM
pp. 915–27, 'War service locomotives. Photographs of the various types of locomotive built for war service in the U.S. and abroad.' Forty-two photographs, with dimensions. Some of these engines were employed in Britain.

3010 AHRONS, E. L. The steam railway locomotive, explaining the component parts and method of working of modern steam railway locomotives. *London*, [1920.] pp. ix, 114, with diagrams.   RC

3011 NORTH BRITISH LOCOMOTIVE COMPANY. North British Locomotive Company. An account of the manufacture of locomotives and war material, 1914–1919. [*Glasgow*, 1920.] pp. 123, with many illus.   BR

3012 YORKSHIRE ENGINE COMPANY. [Catalogue of haulage (stationary) engines and locomotives.] *Sheffield*, [*c.* 1920.]   SLS

3013 DRUMMOND, D. Lectures delivered to the enginemen and firemen of the London & South Western Railway Company, on the management of their engines. *London*, 1908. pp. 189, with diagrams.   RC
Cover title: 'Lectures on the working of locomotive engines.'
—— another edn. *London*, 1908. pp. 202.   BR
—— 4th edn. *London*, 1910. pp. 202.   SLS
—— 6th, *London*, 1921. pp. 243.   LSE

3014 HOWDEN, J. R. Locomotives of the world; illustrated in colour. *London*, 1910. pp. 80.   BM
Sixteen mounted colour plates, with descriptions of locomotives and their railways in text.
—— rev. edn. *London*, [1923.] pp. 79.   BM

3015 [FOWLER.] JOHN FOWLER & CO. Locomotives. *Leeds*, [1924.] pp. 36, with illus.   SLS
Trade catalogue.

3016 JACKSON, G. G. The Book of the Locomotive; fully illustrated with coloured plates and photographs. *London*, 1924. pp. xii, 244, with 40 plates.   BM

3017 OLIVER, A. Locomotive engine driving. *London: Co-operative Printing Society*, [*c.* 1925.] pp. xi, 226, with illus. & diagrams (some fold.).   BM

3018 PATERSON, W. *and* WEBSTER, H. [C.] A Manual of Locomotive Running Shed Management. *London*, 1925. pp. xiii, 200, with tables.   LSE

3019 SAUNDERS, H. H. The central control systems for the scheduling of operations in locomotive repair workshops in England. January 1924. *Calcutta: Railway Board,* 1925. pp. i, 38. [*Technical Paper* no. 339.]   LSE
Various works visited and described, with specimen forms.

3020 SENTINEL WAGGON WORKS. Sentinel-Cammell steam rail coaches. *Westminster,* 1925. pp. 60, with many illus., diagrams & tables.   LSE

3021 ALLEN, C. J. Locomotives and their work; with 119 illustrations. *London,* [1926.] pp. iv, 192, with col. plates.   RC

3022 The LOCOMOTIVE in service. *London,* [1926.] pp. 187, with illus., la. fold. plate & diagrams.
A manual for engine-men.

*3023 The LOCOMOTIVE of today; reprinted with revisions and additions from the 'Locomotive Magazine'. *London,* 1899. pp. 178, with 16 plates & 38 illus. in text.   SLS
—— 3rd edn. *London,* 1904. pp. 180.   SLS
—— 6th, *London,* 1915. pp. 184, 4.   SLS
—— 8th, *London,* 1927. pp. 316.   SLS

3024 SENTINEL WAGGON WORKS. Sentinel-Cammell steam rail coaches: comparative running costs. *Westminster,* [1927?] pp. [4.]   LSE
A comparison with internal-combustion rail coaches and light trains.

3025 HATHAWAY, A. The locomotive: its peculiarities, failures, and remedies, in question and answer form. *Newport, Monmouthshire,* 1928. pp. 72.   BM
Produced for G.W. Rly. engine-men.

3026 SENTINEL WAGGON WORKS. Gear driven 'Sentinel-Cammell' rail cars. *London,* [1928.] pp. 24, with illus.   SLS

3027 SENTINEL WAGGON WORKS. A geared steam rail car. *London,* [1928.] pp. 8, with 6 illus. & 3 diagrams.   SLS
Reprinted from the *Engineer,* 18 May, 1928.

3028 JACKSON, G. G. British locomotives: their evolution and development. *London,* [1929.] pp. x, 246, with many illus. on plates.   BM

3029 SENTINEL WAGGON WORKS. Sentinel-Cammell gear driven rail cars. *Westminster,* 1929. pp. 83, with many illus. & 3 fold. charts.   SLS

3030 PHILLIPSON, E. A. Essays of a locomotive man. *London,* [1930.] pp. 143, with illus. BM
On locomotive running and maintenance, and locomotive shed management.

*3031 SENTINEL WAGGON WORKS. 'Sentinel' patent locomotives. *London,* July 1927. pp. 72, with many illus.   LSE
A detailed catalogue.

—— another edn. *Shrewsbury,* December 1931, pp. 84, with many illus.   SLS

3032 BELL, W. J. British locomotives illustrated. *London,* 1933. pp. 95.   BM
Forty-three full-page illustrations with origin, description and constructional details on facing pages.

3033 REED, B. Railway engines of the world. *London,* 1934. pp. 159, with plates.   BM
pp. 20–41, British locomotives.

3034 LAKE, C. S. The locomotive simply explained . . . fully illustrated with drawings and photographs. 3rd edn. *London,* [1935.] pp. 56.   BM

*3035 RAILWAY CORRESPONDENCE AND TRAVEL SOCIETY. The locomotive stock as at 31 December, 1934, of the main line companies of Great Britain, including alterations to stock during 1934. [*Leamington Spa,* 1935.] pp. xx.   BR
Supplement to the *Railway Observer.* A forerunner of the serial publication *Locomotive Stock Book.*

3036 WAY, R. B. How, why and when: railway engines, their history, growth and development shown in pictures for young people and their elders. *London,* 1935. pp. 128, with many line illus. & diagrams.   BM

3037 OLIVER, J. Railways round the world. Compiled by J. Oliver. *Oxford: O.U.P.,* 1936. pp. [80.]   ELTHAM PL
Illustrations, with descriptions, including British locomotives.

3038 PHILLIPSON, E. A. Steam locomotive design: data and formulae. *London: Locomotive Publishing Co.,* 1936. pp. 444, with 27 plates.   BM
Technology and design.

3039 SELLS, M. P. How the locomotive works, and why. *London: Locomotive Publishing Co.,* 1936. pp. 93, with illus. & fold. diagrams.
A much enlarged edition appeared in 1951 as *The steam locomotive of today.*

3040 LOEWY, R. The locomotive: its esthetics. *London: The Studio,* 1937. pp. [104.]   ICE
125 photographs with short descriptions, showing the development of locomotive design in the U.S.A. and elsewhere, including Gt. Britain.

3041 ALFLOC, LTD. Locomotive feed water. *London,* [1938.] pp. 101, with illus.   IT
Softening and conditioning of water. Installations for railways.

3042 DOWNEY, R. The cleaner's locomotive. *Lancaster: Locomotive College,* [1938.] pp. 47, with 13 diagrams. [*Locoman Series no. 1.*]   BM
A manual for engine-men.

3043 LOCOMOTIVE COLLEGE [Lancaster]. The Walschaert valve gear simplified. *Lancaster,* [1938.] pp. 24, with 6 diagrams. [*Locoman Series, no. 2.*]   BM
A manual for engine-men.

3044 KIDNER, R. W. Narrow gauge locomotives. *Sidcup: Oakwood Press,* 1939. pp. viii, 28. [*Light Railway Handbook, no. 8.*]   BM
Notes, lists, illustrations and maps.

3045 DALZIEL, J. The Outdoor Machinery Department. *London: Railway Gazette,* 1940. pp. viii, 31.   BM
Maintenance and repair.

3046 The BRITISH austerity locomotive. *Westminster: Railway Gazette,* [1943.] pp. 8, with illus. & diagrams (1 la. fold.).   IT
Reprint, *Railway Gazette,* 10 Sept., 1943.

3047 BRITISH-built austerity 2-10-0 locomotive. *Westminster: Railway Gazette,* [1944.] pp. 8, with illus. & fold. diagram.   IT
Reprint, *Railway Gazette,* 15 Dec., 1944.

3048 RUDGARD, H. L.M.S.R. locomotive casualty report system: methods used for reporting, and dealing with, engine failures. *London: Railway Gazette,* 1944. pp. 8.   BM
Notes for guidance in the inspection of locomotives. H. Rudgard writes as Superintendent of Motive Power, LMS.

3049 CLAYTON, J. The 'Paget' locomotive: hitherto unpublished details of Sir Cecil Paget's heroic experiment . . . *London,* 1945. pp. 12.   BM
Reprinted from the *Railway Gazette,* 2 Nov., 1945.
Includes biographical details of C. Paget.

3050 STOCKTON, V. C. Sectioned perspective view of locomotive front end: a notable drawing of L.M.S.R. class '7P' 4-6-2 locomotive of the latest type. *Westminster: Railway Gazette,* 1945. pp. 3.   BM
A la. fold. diagram drawn by V. C. Stockton, with descriptive text.

3051 BEYER PEACOCK & CO. Locomotives by Beyer Peacock & Co. *Manchester,* 1946. pp. 63.   BM
Illustrations and dimensions of a selection of locomotives built in recent years at Gorton Works.

3052 BRITISH locomotive types; compiled by the Railway Gazette from official drawings supplied by the Chief Mechanical Engineers of the four main-line railways. *London: Railway Gazette,* Sept. 1937. pp. vii, 113. BM

—— 2nd edn. *London,* 1937.   RC
—— 3rd, *London,* 1938.   RC
—— 4th, *London,* 1939.   RC
—— 5th, *London,* 1943. pp. viii, 127.   BM
—— 6th, *London,* 1946. pp. viii, 140.   BM

3053 CONVERSION of locomotives from coal to oil burning. Ministry of Transport plan for converting 1,217 locomotives. Equipment of oil burning locomotives on the G.W.R. fully described and illustrated. *London: Railway Gazette,* 1946. pp. 8, with illus. & diagrs.   IT
Reprint, *Railway Gazette,* 18 Jan., 16 & 30 August, 1946.

3054 CRESWELL, A. J. LMS numbers, names and classes; LNER second re-numberings; stock changes, LNER, GWR, SR, July 1946. *Huddersfield: Quadrant Publications,* 1946. pp. viii, 16.   BM

3055 CRESWELL, A. J. What to see in engines: an illustrated locomotive guide. *Huddersfield: Quadrant Publications,* 1946. pp. 40.   BM

3056 POLLOCK, D. R. *and* WHITE, D. E. The 2-8-0 and 2-10-0 locomotives of the War Department, 1939–1945. *London: Railway Correspondence & Travel Society,* 1946. pp. 40, with 8 illus. on plates, & 4 diagrams.   RC
Very detailed and extensive record of Stanier, Robinson & 'Austerity' locomotives on war service.

3057 WEBSTER, H. C. What engine is that? *London: Sampson Low,* [1946.] pp. vi, 201.   BM
Drawings, with details of history, construction, and use.

3058 CRESWELL, A. J. On the footplate. *Huddersfield: Quadrant Publications,* [1947.] pp. 40.   BM
Short essays.

3059 EATON, R. J. Oil-burning locomotive . . . illustrated by R. Barnard Way. *London: Transportation Press,* [1947.] pp. 31.   BM

3060 BASSETT-LOWKE, W. J. *and* MANN, P. Locomotives. *Harmondsworth,* 1947. pp. 30, with illus., some col. [*Puffin Picture Books, no. 74.*]   BM
Introductory.

3061 NOCK, O. S. British locomotives at work. *London: Greenlake Publications,* 1947. pp. 260, with illus., diagrams, maps, & gradient profiles.   BM
Descriptions of footplate journeys between 1934 and 1939.

3062 WAY, R. B. Meet the locomotive; written and illustrated by R. B. Way. *London: Transportation Press,* [1947.] pp. 49.   BM
The function of various parts of the steam locomotive simply explained.

3063 WEBSTER, H. C. Introduction to the locomotive. *London: Sampson Low*, [1947.]
pp. vi, 56.　　　　　　　　　　　　　BM
Constructional details of the modern locomotive simply described; with detailed diagrams.

3064 WEBSTER, H. C. Locomotive running shed
practice: the maintenance and servicing of
locomotives; by Harry Webster. *London:
O.U.P.*, 1947. pp. vii, 222.　　　　　　IT

3065 BRITISH RAILWAYS. Locomotive Testing Station, Rugby, 1948. *London*, 1948.
pp. 15, with illus.　　　　　　　　　　BM

3066 The 'LIBERATION' locomotive: 2-8-0 type
with double-bogie tender for European use:
a detailed account of the Vulcan Foundry's
design for international service on the Continent. *London: Railway Gazette*, [1948.]
pp. 8, with illus. & la. fold. diagram.　IT
Reprint, *Railway Gazette*, 28 June, 1946.

3067 The 20,000 British locomotives. *Huddersfield: Quadrant Publications*, 1948. pp. iv,
52.　　　　　　　　　　　　　　　　BM
Class, name and number of every locomotive
in service at the end of 1947.

3068 RANSOME - WALLIS, P. Locomotives
through the lens. *London: Ian Allan*, 1948.
pp. 95.　　　　　　　　　　　　　　BM
200 photographs taken between 1923 and
1947, with descriptions.

3069 WARD, [L.]. Modern locomotives;
compiled & illustrated in full colour by
WARD. *Birmingham: Ryle, Ltd.*, 1948. pp.
32.　　　　　　　　　　　　　　　　BM
Fourteen locomotives, with constructional
details and descriptions.

3070 WAY, R. B. *and* WARDALE, R. W. British
passenger locomotives. *Redhill: Wells Gardner, Darton & Co.*, 1948. pp. 128. [*Quick
Spotter Book*.]　　　　　　　　　　　BM
Notes and illustrations on contemporary
locomotives.

3071 ALLEN, G. F. *and* BALDWIN, A. W.
Studies in Steam: [no. 1.] *London: Ian Allan*,
1947. pp. 32.　　　　　　　　　　　　BM
Photographs of trains, with captions.
—— no. 2. *London*, 1949. pp. 32.　　BM

3072 BRITISH RAILWAYS. Report of the Locomotive Testing Committee on the Locomotion Interchange Trials, 1948. [1949.] pp.
131. *Reproduced typescript.*　　　　　IT
Object, to establish principles for future
locomotive design. Detailed tables.

3073 PHILLIPSON, E. A. The steam locomotive
in traffic . . . *London: Locomotive Publishing
Co.*, 1949. pp. 252, with diagrams, specimen
forms, etc.　　　　　　　　　　　　　BM
A textbook of locomotive operation and
maintenance.

3074 WAY, R. B. *and* WARDALE, R. W. Freight
and mixed traffic locomotives. *Redhill:
Wells Gardner, Darton & Co.*, 1949. pp.
128. [*Quick Spotter Book*, no. 2.]　　BM
A companion work to *British Passenger
Locomotives* (1948), by the same authors.

3075 BARTON, D. F. British Railways locomotive reference, 60001–90774. Classified locomotive stock, named locomotives. Complete allocation. Motive power depots and
codes. *Bristol: British Locomotive Society*,
[1950.] pp. 94[95].　　　　　　　　　BM
Ex-L.N.E.R. locomotive re-numberings.
Code numbers of depots of *all* Regions.

3076 NOCK, O. S. British locomotives from the
footplate. *London: Ian Allan*, 1950. pp. 224,
with 56 illus. on 32 plates.　　　　　　BM
Footplate journeys described.

3077 REED, B. Modern locomotive classes. *London: Locomotive Publishing Co.*, 1945. pp.
62.　　　　　　　　　　　　　　　　BM
Photographs, descriptions and diagrams of
sixty-one classes.
—— another edn. *London*, 1950. pp. 64. IT

3078 FAWCETT, B. Let me drive. *London &
Glasgow: Blackie*, [1951.] pp. 64, with 13
col. plates, & illus.　　　　　　　　　BM
A description of the parts, motion and working of a locomotive, addressed to boys.

3079 POLITICAL AND ECONOMIC PLANNING.
Locomotives: a report on the organisation
and structure of the industry, its products
and its market prospects at home and abroad.
London, November 1951. pp. 75, with 10
tables, 4 diagrams & 9 plates. [*Engineering
Reports*, no. 3.]　　　　　　　　　　BM

3080 POULTNEY, E. C. Steam locomotion:
the construction, working principles and
practical operation of steam locomotives.
London: Caxton Publishing Co., 1951. 2
vols. (pp. viii, 329: vi, 333), with plates and
many diagrams & illus. in text.　　　　BM
A practical handbook for enginemen.

3081 SELLS, M. P. The steam locomotive of today: its construction, operation and upkeep.
London: Locomotive Publishing Co., 1951.
pp. 250, with many illus. & diagrams.　BM
A much enlarged edition of *How the locomotive works, and why* (1936).

3082 LOCOMOTIVE shed code, British Railways.
London: Locomotive Publishing Co., 1952.
pp. 8.　　　　　　　　　　　　　　　PC

3083 NOCK, O. S. Four thousand miles on the
footplate. *London: Ian Allan*, 1952. pp. vii,
223, with illus. on plates, and performance
tables.　　　　　　　　　　　　　　BM
Accounts of journeys on locomotives in 1951.

3084 REED, B. Modern locomotives. *London: Temple Press*, 1949. pp. 85, with plates. [*Boys' Power & Speed Library*.] BM
Introductory.
—— 2nd edn. *London*, 1952. pp. 87, with 14 plates. BM

3085 BRITISH RAILWAYS (LONDON MIDLAND REGION). Rugby Locomotive Testing Station. [*London*, 1954.] pp. 20, with illus. & diagrams (1 fold.). BR

3086 HODGSON, J. T. *and* WILLIAMS, J. Locomotive management from cleaning to driving. *London*, [1909.] pp. xvi, 383. [*Railway Series of Text Books & Manuals*, no. 8.] BM
—— 2nd edn., [1912.] pp. xvi, 409. BM
—— 3rd, [1914.] pp. xv, 529. BM
—— 4th, [1920.] pp. xvi, 437. BM
—— 5th, [1924.] pp. xxvi, 421. BM
—— 6th, [1928.] pp. xiv, 449 BM
—— 7th, 'Locomotive management: cleaning, driving, maintenance,' by J. T. Hodgson, rev. by Chas. S. Lake. [1939.] pp. xi, 492. BM
—— 8th, by J. T. Hodgson & C. S. Lake, pp. xi, 492. BM
—— 9th, 1948. pp. xi, 512. BM
—— 10th, rev. by W. R. Oaten, 1954. pp. xi, 512. BM

3087 BRITISH TRANSPORT COMMISSION—RAILWAYS DIVISION. Good firemanship. *London*, 1956. pp. 31, with 10 col. diagrams. IT
A handbook for locomotive firemen.

3088 BRITISH RAILWAYS (LONDON MIDLAND REGION). Horwich Locomotive Works Training School: foundation stone laying ceremony, 25 October 1957. *Derby*, 1957. pp. 22[24], with illus. BR
The work of the school and a description of the locomotive works.

*3089 BRITISH TRANSPORT COMMISSION. Handbook for railway steam locomotive enginemen. *London*, 1957. pp. 196, with diagrams (some col.). IT
The anatomy of locomotives, and their operation.

3090 MANN, R. H. Steam locomotive design. *Richmond (Surrey): Association of Engineering & Shipbuilding Draftsmen*, 1957. 2 parts, with illus. & diagrams. SL

3091 RANSOME-WALLIS, P. On engines in Britain and France. *London: Ian Allan*, 1957. pp. ix, 244, with 64 illus. on 32 plates, & logs of journeys. BM
Locomotive and train working.

3092 TALYLLYN RLY. The first 'Giesl ejector' front end in Great Britain. [*Towyn*, Oct. 1958.] pp. 8, with 3 illus. PC

3093 BRITISH RAILWAYS (WESTERN REGION). Naming ceremony of the last steam locomotive to be built by British Railways, Swindon Works, Western Region, 18th March, 1960. *London*, 1960. pp. [8,] with 8 illus. BR
Class 9F 2–10–0 no. 92220, 'Evening Star.'

*3094 FULLER, A. L. F. The British Locomotive Shed Directory. *Birmingham*, 1947. pp. 108[110]. BM
Published by the author.
The location and accessibility of numerous locomotive sheds.
——7th edn. *Birmingham*, 1956. pp. iii [113]. BM
Five supplements were issued successively to the first edition, and when a new complete edition appeared in 1956 this was called the 7th.
—— 8th, *Birmingham*, 1958. pp. 122[125]. BM
—— 9th, *Birmingham*, [1960.] pp. 123. BM
—— 10th, *London: Railway Publications*, 1961. pp. 112. BM
—— 11th, *London*, 1962. pp. 112. BM
—— 12th, *London*, 1963. pp. 112. BM

3095 McKILLOP, N. Ace enginemen. *London: Nelson*, 1963. pp. x, 117, with 56 illus., incl. ports., on 20 plates, & 16 logs of actual runs. BM
A record of present day and recent steam locomotive performance from the aspect of individual achievement of drivers and firemen. A narrative of twenty-eight runs.

E9   ELECTRIC LOCOMOTIVES AND TRAINS

For those of particular railways see L and B 10

3096 STEAM superseded: an account of a newly-invented electro-magnetic engine, for propulsion of locomotives, ships, mills, etc: translated from the original German by Dr. Taylor. *London*, 1841. pp. viii, 36, with fold. plan. AU

3097 BENNETT, A. R. Electric traction. *Edinburgh*, [1889.] pp. 13. BM
General principles explained.

3098 BRUSH ELECTRICAL ENGINEERING COMPANY. The works of the Brush Electrical Engineering Company Ltd. *London*, 1902. pp. 14, with illus. PC
Reprinted from *Engineering*, 7 & 14 February, 1902.

3099 DAWSON, P. Electric traction on railways. *In* 'Modern electric practice', edited by M. Maclean. vol. 4, 1905. pp. 287–304, with illus. BM

3100 BRUSH ELECTRICAL ENGINEERING COMPANY. Rolling stock, 1905: a review of progress in railway, tramway and road vehicles for public service. *Loughborough*, 1905. pp. 84, with many illus. pc

3101 METROPOLITAN VICKERS ELECTRICAL COMPANY. Railway electrification & electric locomotives; being papers read by Sir Vincent L. Raven . . . and reprinted by permission. *Manchester*, [1924.] pp. 36, with illus. PO
pt. 2, Electric locomotives.

3102 ENGLISH ELECTRIC COMPANY. English Electric locomotives for industrial purposes. *London*, January 1927. pp. 23, with illus. LSE

3103 METROPOLITAN VICKERS ELECTRICAL COMPANY. Electric locomotives. *Manchester*, [1928.] pp. 40, with illus. PO

3104 CHLORIDE ELECTRICAL STORAGE CO. A solution of the shunting problem; describing various types and sizes of shunting locomotives equipped with Exide-Ironclad batteries. *Manchester*, 1932, with illus. & graphs. [*Publication* no. 113.] pc

3105 ENGLISH ELECTRIC COMPANY. The English Electric Company and its activities in rail and road transport, with special reference to the Rolling Stock Works, Preston. *London*, [1937.] pp. 42, with illus. pc

3106 AGNEW, W. A. Electric trains: their equipment and operation; including notes on electric locomotives . . . *London: Virtue*, 1937. 2 vols. (pp. x, 506), with fold. plates, illus. & diagrams. BM
A manual for maintenance and operational staff.
—— Supplement. 'Main and control circuits of London Passenger Transport 1938 tube rolling stock.' *London*, [1938.] pp. 31. IT

3107 HILLS, S. M. Battery-electric vehicles . . . *London: Newnes*, 1943. pp. viii, 206. BM
pp. 109–28, Locomotives; with illus.

3108 ANDREWS, H. H. Electricity in transport: over sixty years' experience, 1883–1950. *London: English Electric Co.*, 1951. pp. 183, with 103 illus. BM

Detailed survey of railway electrification, diesel-electric, tramways, industrial and mining locomotives. The history of the E.E. Co.'s electric traction.

3109 ENGLISH ELECTRIC COMPANY 'English Electric' electric rolling stock . . . a summary of the electric traction achievements of the English Electric Co. . . . [*London*, 1952.] BM
Prepared for private circulation.

3110 ENGLISH ELECTRIC COMPANY. 'English Electric' traction. *London*, 1952– . BM
Various editions. In progress.
Descriptions and illustrations of locomotives and trains supplied to British and foreign railways.

3111 HAUT, F. J. G. The early history of the electric locomotive. *Purley: the author*, 1952. pp. 16, with 14 illus. on 4 plates. BM

3112 COOPER, B. K. Electric trains and locomotives. *London: L. Hill*, 1953. pp. xvii, 111, with 72 illus. on plates & in text. BM
Contemporary British and foreign trains.

3113 BINNEY, E. A. Electric traction engineering. *London: Cleaver-Hulme*, 1955. pp. 224, with plates & diagrams. [*Cleaver-Hulme Electrical Series*, no. 10.] BM

3114 COOK, K. J. Electric and diesel traction. [*London*, 1957.] pp. 13[14], with illus. & diagrams. BR
Reprint, *British Railways (ER) Magazine.*

3115 ALLEN, G. F. British trains of tomorrow. *London: Ian Allan*, [1960.] pp. 40, with 69 illus. BM
The present and future in diesel and electric traction.

3116 COX, E. S. British Railways' experience with diesel and electric traction: record of a paper read at the Witwatersrand University, Johannesburg, on 22nd March 1961. *London: H.M. Stationery Office*, 1961. pp. 32, with 4 plates, 2 diagrams, & 7 tables, and a verbatim record of the discussion following the reading of the paper. BM

3117 ILLINGWORTH, T. Battery traction on tramways and railways. *Lingfield: Oakwood*
b *Press*, July 1961. pp. 23, with 4 plates, illus., & a bibliography. [*Locomotion Papers*, no. 14.] BM

E 10   DIESEL, DIESEL-ELECTRIC, AND OTHER SELF-GENERATING TYPES OF LOCOMOTIVE AND TRAIN

For narrow gauge and other special forms see D 1 – 5

3118 LONDON, MIDLAND & SCOTTISH RLY. Diesel oil electric train. Joint report [of trials on the Blackpool–Lytham Section of the L.M.S., July 1928 to April 1929]. *Derby*, July 1929. pp. 9,[15,] with tables & diagrams. BR

3119 ARMSTRONG-WHITWORTH & CO. Diesel-electric traction: an alternative to the proposals of the Weir Committee. *London*, 1931. pp. 11. LSE
Reprinted from *Modern Transport*, 4, 11 & 18 July, 1931.

3120 FRANCO, I. *and* LABRYN, P. Internal combustion locomotives and motor coaches.
b *The Hague*, 1931. pp. 249, with illus. & a detailed bibliography. BR
Includes British examples.

3121 HARDY MOTORS, LTD. The 'Hardy' rail car. *Southall*, 1933. pp. 13, with illus. & la. fold. diagrams. IT
Petrol and diesel types.

3122 HARDY MOTORS, LTD. A new streamlined oil-engined railcar. *Southall*, 1933. pp. 7, with illus. & fold. diagrams. IT
Reprint, the *Engineer*, 27 Oct., 1933.

3123 REED, B. Diesel locomotives and railcars. *London: Locomotive Publishing Co.*, [1935.] pp. 190[193], with illus. & diagrams. BM
—— 2nd edn. *London*, [1939.] pp. 210. BM

3124 L.M.S.R. diesel-electric shunting locomotives: a review of developments . . . from the operative standpoint. *London: Railway Gazette*, [1943.] pp. 24, with illus. BM

3125 DIESEL locomotives for industrial shunting. *London: Railway Gazette*, 1944. pp. 7. BM
Reprinted from the *Railway Gazette* Diesel Railway Traction Supplement.

3126 ENGLISH ELECTRIC COMPANY. Diesel-electric shunting locomotives. *London*, [1945.] pp. 13, with illus. pc
—— another edn. *London*, [1948.] pp. 9 [11]. pc

3127 BRITISH RAILWAYS (WESTERN REGION). The first British built gas turbine locomotive, no. 18100: a description of the 3000 h.p. gas turbine electric locomotive built for British Railways by Metropolitan-Vickers Electrical Co. Ltd. *London*., April 1952. pp. 24, with 11 illus. & fold. diagrams. BR

3128 ENGLISH ELECTRIC COMPANY. 'English Electric' diesel-electric traction equipment . . . a summary of the achievement of the English Electric Company . . . [*London*, 1952.] BM
Tables, diagrams, and illustrations.

3129 LOCOMOTIVE MANUFACTURERS' AS-SOCIATION INTERNAL COMBUSTION GROUP. British diesel locomotives and railcars. *London*, 1953. pp. 48, with illus. IT
Examples of the products of seventeen manufacturers.

3130 TIMES *newspaper*. Diesel locomotives: photographs from the 'Times Weekly Review'. *London*, [1953.] pp. [16.] BM
Ten illustrations, with descriptive text, of British diesel and gas-turbine locomotives and diesel rail-cars.

3131 BONAVIA, M. R. Lightweight diesel trains. *London: B.T.C.*, 1954. pp. 9, with illus. & diagrams. BR
Reprint, *British Transport Review*, vol. 3, no. 1, April 1954.

3132 BRITISH PRODUCTIVITY COUNCIL. A review of productivity in the diesel locomotive industry. *London*, August 1954. pp. 21, with illus. BM

3133 [UTAH.] UNIVERSITY OF UTAH—DE-PARTMENT OF PHYSICS. An atomic locomotive: a feasibility study. *Salt Lake City*, January 1954. pp. 54, with 11 diagrams. *Reproduced typescript*. IT

3134 ENGLISH ELECTRIC COMPANY. Britain's first main-line diesel-electric locomotives. *London*, [1955.] pp. 12[13], with illus. [*Diesel-Electric Traction Series*, no. 103.] pc

3135 BOND, R. C. Some aspects of diesel traction. 1956. pp. 22, with tables. *Reproduced typescript*. IT
Paper, L.S.E. Railway Students Association, 25 Jan., 1956.

3136 BRITISH RAILWAYS. Multiple-unit diesel trains built at the Swindon Works of Western Region. [*London*,] 1956. pp. 7, with fold. diagram. BR
Long-distance diesel trains.

3137 ASTON, R. L. The diesel locomotive. *London: Thames & Hudson*, 1957. pp. x, 116, with 53 illus. BM
Principles, working and maintenance.

3138 COOK, K. J. Electric and diesel traction. [*London*, 1957.] pp. 13[14], with illus. & diagrams. BR
Reprint, *British Railways (ER) Magazine*.

*3139 BOLTON, W. F. Railwayman's Diesel Manual: a practical introduction . . . *London: G. H. Lake & Co.*, 1956. pp. 96, with illus. & diagrams. IT
—— 2nd edn. *London*, 1958. pp. 120. IT

3140 BRITISH RAILWAYS. Introduction of diesel-hydraulic main line locomotives in the Western Region: a new chapter in railway modernisation. [*London*,] 1958. pp. 8, with fold. diagram. BR
Description of type '4' locomotive.

3141 POWER PETROLEUM COMPANY. Diesel centenary. *London*, 1958. pp. 43, with plates, incl. portrait. IT

3142 SELF-CHANGING GEARS, LTD. Railcar progress around the British Isles: a short survey of railcar progress. *Coventry*, [1958.] pp. 24, with 14 illus., 4 gradient profiles, & 2 maps of railcar routes in Gt. Britain and Ireland. BM

3143 TERRY, T. H. The diesel electric shunting locomotive simply explained; with illus-

trations by the author. *Shrewsbury*, 1958.
pp. 79, with diagrams.   BM
    A guide for ex-steam locomotive drivers.

—— 2nd edn. *London*, 1961. pp. 88.

3144 DIESEL locomotives. *London: Ian Allan*,
1956– . In progress.   BM
    An annual review of current developments,
with many illustrations (some coloured) and
diagrams.

3145 ALLEN, G. F. British trains of tomorrow.

London: Ian Allan, [1960.] pp. 40, with
69 illus.   BM
    The present and future in diesel and electric
traction.

3146 COX, E. S. British Railways' experience with
diesel and electric traction: record of a
paper read at the Witwatersrand University,
Johannesburg, on 22nd March 1961. *London: H.M. Stationery Office*, 1961. pp. 32,
with 4 plates, 2 diagrams, 7 tables, and a
verbatim record of the discussion following
the reading of the paper.   BM

E 11   ROLLING STOCK (Carriages and Wagons)

For Travelling Post Offices see K 9

3147 ADAMS, W. B. Road progress; or, Amalgamation of railways and highways for agricultural improvement and steam farming, in
Great Britain and the colonies; also, Practical economy in fixed plant and rolling stock
for passenger and goods trains. *London*,
1850. pp. 76, with 3 fold. plates.   BM

3148 SMITH, G. Patent wheels. *Belfast*. 1867.
pp. [3.] (1 p. text & 2 pp. diagrams.)   ICE

3149 GROVER, J. W. The facilities of 'flexible'
rolling stock for economically constructing,
maintaining and working railways or tramways. *London*, 1870. pp. 23.   ICE

3150 PATENT OFFICE. Patents for inventions.
Abridgments of specifications relating to
carriages and other vehicles for railways,
A.D. 1807–1866. (Compiled by B. Woodcroft.) *London*, 1871. pp. xxxiv, 1496.
                                    BM: PO

3151 MIDLAND RAILWAY-CARRIAGE AND
WAGON COMPANY. [A brochure of ninety-nine illustrations of all types of railway and
tramway vehicles, with notes.] *London*,
[1896.] pp. 99.   BM

3152 MACDONALD, N. D. Railway rolling stock,
present and future: a paper read before
Section G of the British Association at
Glasgow. *Glasgow*, 1907. pp. 24.

3153 BOSHART, A. Railway rolling stock. Compiled by August Boshart; with about 2100
illustrations and numerous formulæ. *London*, 1909. pp. xiii, 796. [*The Deinhardt-Schlomann Series of Technical Dictionaries
in Six Languages*, vol. 6.]   BM
    German, English, French, Russian, Italian,
and Spanish.

3154 STONE, S. Railway carriages and wagons:
their design and construction . . . *London*,
[1911.] pp. viii, 176[178], with illus. [*Railway Series of Text Books & Manuals*, no. 4.]
                                    BM

3155 WARNER, S. The design and construction
of carriages and wagons. *In* 'Modern railway working', edited by John Macaulay.
vol. 5, 1913. pp. 53–215, with illus. & many
diagrams.   BM

3156 INSPECTION cars. *In* 'Jubilee of the Railway
News, 1864–1914.' *London: Railway News*,
[1914.] pp. 95–8, with 7 illus.   BM

3157 L., J. F. Train lighting by electricity. *London*, 1914. pp. 22, with illus. & diagrams. RC
    General descriptions of systems in operation.

3158 RAILWAY rolling stock. *In* 'Jubilee of the
Railway News, 1864–1914.' *London: Railway News*, [1914.] pp. 118–25, with 19 illus.
                                    BM

3159 SANDERS, L. I. The Railway Carriage and
Wagon Handbook. *London: Locomotive
Publishing Co.*, [1937.] pp. 366, with illus.
& diagram.   BM
    Constructional detail and maintenance.

3160 BRITISH RAILWAYS (LONDON MIDLAND
REGION). The London Midland Region
Carriage & Wagon Works at Derby. [*London*,] 1949. pp. 15, with 17 illus. & a plan.
                                    BR

3161 BRITISH RAILWAYS (LONDON MIDLAND
REGION). Earlestown Works, Carriage and
Wagon Engineer's Department, 1853–1953.
London, [1953.] pp. 16, with illus. & fold.
plan.   IT
—— New training school at Earlestown
Carriage and Wagon Works: officially
opened on 1st April 1955. *London*, 1955.
pp. 16, with illus. & plan of the school.
                                    BR

3162 LYNES, L. Railway carriages and wagons:
theories and practices. *London: Locomotive
Publishing Co.*, 1959. pp. 272, with 110 illus.,
diagrams & tables.   BM
    A guide to design, construction and maintenance.

3163 ALUMINIUM DEVELOPMENT ASSOCIATION. An International Exhibition of
Aluminium in railway rolling stock; orga-

nised by the Centre International de Développement de l'Aluminium, and held at Strasbourg, June 21 to 26, 1960. *London*, December 1960. pp. 87, with many illus. (some col.) & diagrams.   BM
Includes British developments.

3164 GLOUCESTER RAILWAY CARRIAGE & WAGON COMPANY, A history of the Gloucester Railway Carriage & Wagon Company. *London: Weidenfeld & Nicholson*, 1960. pp. 64, with illus.   G
A centenary publication.

E 12 CARRIAGES

Pullman Cars—Lighting and heating

For Pullman Car services see G 3

3165 HILL, T. A treatise upon the utility of a rail-way from Leeds to Selby and Hull, with observations on railways generally as being pre-eminent to all other modes of conveyance for dispatch and economy. *Leeds*, 1827. pp. 32, with 3 plates.   ICE
Includes description of Hill's patent railway carriages.

3166 KOLLMANN, G. A. Some observations on the imperfections of the present system of constructing railways, with an account of the new method of construction invented by Mr. Kollmann. *London*, 1839. pp. 16. [*Railway Papers*, no. 1.]   BM
Low gravity carriages with flangeless, free-running wheels, and a centre guide rail.

3167 FOTHERGILL, B. Railway Carriage and Steam Boat Gas Lighting Company Ltd . . . Report on James Newall's invention for supplying gas to railway carriages, steam boats, etc. *Bury*, [1862.] pp. 17, with fold. plate.   NLC

3168 FAIRLIE, R. F. Observations on the construction of railway carriages, together with a paper [pp. 11 to end] on railways and their management. *London*, 1868. pp. 35.   ICE
An improved coupling arrangement.

3169 MASSEY, W. H. Notes on a train lighting experiment. *London*, 1884. pp. 40.   ICE
Excerpt, *Min. Proc., Soc. Telegraph Engineers & Electricians*, 13 & 17 Mar., 1884.
Carried out on District Rly.

3170 CARSWELL, T. P. Automatic electrical lighting of trains. [*Glasgow*, 1887.] pp. 6, with fold. diagram.   ICE
Extract, *Proc. Philos. Soc. of Glasgow*, vol. 18.
Lighting in tunnels by means of a conductor rail.

3171 DRUMMOND, D. On the heating of carriages by exhaust steam on the Caledonian Railway. *London: Institution of Civil Engineers*, 1888. pp. 7, with diagrams.   ICE
Excerpt, *Min. Proc. I.C.E.*, vol. 92, Session 1887-8, pt. 2.

3172 LANGDON, W. E. On railway-train lighting. *London*, 1891. pp. 57, with tables & a fold. plate of 11 diagrams. Discussion, pp. 27-end.   LSE

Excerpt, *Min. Proc. I.C.E.*, vol. 106, Session 1890-91. pt. 4.
Comparing oil, gas and electricity, but mostly on electrical methods.

3173 STONE, J. & Co. Stone's electric light system for railway carriages. *Deptford (London)*, *c.* 1905. pp. 80, with many illus.   SL

3174 TURNER, J. M. The Coaching Department; being a complete and detailed account of the work done in the Passenger Department, composed of two parts: first, the Parcels Office; second, the Booking Office. Written for the benefit and instruction of the junior clerk, particularly the G.N.R. junior. *Stamford*, 1905. pp. 55.   BM

3175 WESTINGHOUSE BRAKE CO. Heating of railway carriages; steam at atmospheric pressure; automatic regulation of temperature. *London*, 1908. pp. 30, with illus. & fold. diagram.   BM

3176 LEITNER, H. Train lighting. *London*, [1909.] pp. 93, with plates.   BM

3177 BAZLEY, B. M. Passenger carriages of British railways. pp. 36. *Typescript.*   RC
Paper, Railway Club, Oct. 1912.

3178 FOWLER, H. Railway carriage lighting. *In* 'Modern railway working', edited by John Macaulay. vol. 6, 1913. pp. 1-28, with illus. & diagrams.   BM

3179 RAILWAY carriage. *London: Gresham Publishing Co.*, [1913.] pp. 2.   BM
A folding diagram showing details of a carriage, with key.

3180 CARRIAGE furniture and fittings. *In* 'Jubilee of the Railway News, 1864-1914.' *London: Railway News*, [1914.] pp. 126-35 of the Engineering section, with illus. BM

3181 HUSBAND, J. The story of the Pullman car . . . *Chicago*, 1917. pp. 161, with plates. BM
pp. 61-9, 113-18, in Gt. Britain.

3182 STONE, J. & Co. Stone's electrical installations for the lighting of railway carriages: general instructions. 5th edn. *London*, 1924. with diagrams.   RC

3183 LONDON PASSENGER TRANSPORT BOARD. The overhaul of Underground rolling stock. *Westminster*, 1934. pp. 52, with illus. & a fold. diagram.   BM

3184 LEE, C. E. Passenger class distinctions. *London: Railway Gazette*, 1946. pp. 76, with 24 illus. & 9 tables.   BM

The development and subsequent modification of classes of passenger accommodation on British railways in relation to changes in social and economic conditions. Based upon a paper presented to the Institute of Transport which received a Railway Companies Association Award in the 1944/45 Session.

3185 KIDNER, R. W. A short history of the railway carriage. *Chislehurst: Oakwood Press*, 1946. pp. 81–104, with 19 illus. on 8 plates, & 68 illus. in text. [*A Short History of Mechanical Traction and Travel*, part 5.]   BM

Also issued as part of a collected edition, vol. 2, 'Rail,' 1947.

3186 ELLIS, C. H. Nineteenth century railway carriages in the British Isles, from the eighteen-thirties to the nineteen-hundreds. *London: Modern Transport Publishing Co.*, 1949. pp. 176, with many illus.   BM

3187 BRITISH RAILWAYS (LONDON MIDLAND REGION). New carriage cleaning and servicing depot at Willesden, officially opened on 9th March 1953 . . . *London*, 1954. pp. 20, with illus. & la. fold. plan.   BR

Willesden Carriage Cleaning & Servicing Depot.

3188 BRITISH RAILWAYS (LONDON MIDLAND REGION). New training school at Wolverton Carriage and Wagon Works, officially opened on 2nd April 1954 . . . [*London*, 1954.] pp. 14[16], with illus. & a plan of the school.   BR

*3189 ELLIS, C. H. Popular carriage: two centuries of carriage design for road and rail. *London: British Transport Commission*, 1954. pp. 32, with illus.   BM

3190 INTERNATIONAL Railway Congress. *London: Railway Gazette*, May 1954. pp. 250. IT
pp. 89–96, The Pullman Car Co., Ltd. An historical review; with illus.

*3191 KICHENSIDE, G. M. ABC of British Railways coaches: standard steam & electric. *London: Ian Allan*, [1958.] pp. 64.   BM
Lists and illustrations.

E13   WAGONS and other vehicles for special classes of work

3192 ASPINALL J. A. F. Experiments on the tractive resistance of loaded railway wagons. *London*, 1904. pp. 7, with diagrams.   LSE
Excerpt, *Min. Proc. I.C.E.*, vol. 158, Session 1903–4, pt. 4.

3193 WOODS, A. R. T. Inland transport of perishable produce . . . [*London*, 1917.] pp. 56. LSE
Includes railway refrigerator wagons.

3194 DEPARTMENT OF SCIENTIFIC & INDUSTRIAL RESEARCH—FOOD INVESTIGATION BOARD. On the design of railway wagons for the carriage of perishable foods. (Interim report of the Refrigerator Cars & Barges Sub-Committee.) *London*, 1919. pp. 8. [*Special Report*, no. 1.]   BM
Recommendations.

3195 TUCKER, S. The relationship between tonnage and cubic capacity and its effect upon the design of freight wagon stock. [*c.* 1927.] pp. 82, with 13 fold. tables. *Typescript.*   LSE

3196 SAUNDERS, P. H. Wagon details and construction, describing the latest methods and machines applied to the building of steel railway wagons. *London*, 1932. pp. xv, 143.   BM

A hand-book with sixty-nine illustrations.

3197 BRITISH STEELWORK ASSOCIATION. Modern mineral transport. *London*, [*c.* 1934.] pp. 16, with 11 illus. of wagons.   LSE
The advantages of the new all-steel wagons for improved efficiency.

3198 GLOSSOP, W. H. Refrigeration problems on the L.M.S. Railway. [1934.] pp. 16.   IT
Paper, British Assoc. of Refrigeration, 7 Feb, 1934.

3199 OGDEN, F. Railway wagon and tank construction and repair. *London: Isaac Pitman*, 1948. pp. xiv, 174, with illus. & diagrams. BM
pp. 10–19 'Progress of wagon design from 1800.'

3200 BRITISH RAILWAYS. Freight Rolling Stock Exhibition. *London*, 1952. pp. 29.   BR
Forty-four new types illustrated and described.

3201 BRITISH TRANSPORT COMMISSION. Freight transport: equipment used by British Railways and British Road Services. *London*, 1958. pp. 37, with 52 illus.   IT

E 14   BRAKES and passenger communication apparatus

3202 HEDLEY, O. D. A descriptive account of the means used on the Tyne and Wear for effecting the safe transit of railway carriages in ascending and descending steep planes; together with a historical sketch of the brake, as applied to railway carriages; being the subject of a paper read to the Literary and Philosophical Society of Newcastle at the November monthly meeting, 1834. *Newcastle-on-Tyne*, 1834. pp. 32, with 13 figures on 3 plates.   SL

3203 POWER, J. Mode of preventing the disastrous effects of collision, preceded by an enquiry into the causes of the Brighton Railway accident. *Cambridge*, 1842. pp. [301]–317.   ICE
From the *Trans. Cambridge Phil. Soc.*, vol. 7, pt. 3.
'The accident in Copyhold Cutting, Oct. 2 1841, and the problem of simultaneous braking of two engines coupled, with a train behind.'

3204 PREVENTION of railway accidents. By a Practical Engineer. *Kingston*, 1853. pp. 12, with diagram.   BM
A communication cord on trains.

3205 FITZPATRICK, M. The Fitzpatrick invention for the prevention of accidents on railways. *London*, 1854. pp. 20.   BM
Pneumatic woollen cushions between each vehicle.

3206 NEWALL, J. Newall's patent railway break illustrated by reports of experiments made on the London & North Western, and East Lancashire railways; extracted from the leading journals . . . *Manchester*, 1854. pp. 20.   ICE

3207 FAY, C. A letter to Captain Galton . . . in reply to Lieut. Col. Yolland's report on comparative experiments with Messrs. Newall and Fay's breaks. *Manchester*, 1858. pp. 8.   ICE
Fay explaining to the Board of Trade why his brakes are better than Newall's.

3208 HALL, W. Hall's patent railway brake apparatus. *Erith*, 1859. pp. 4.   ICE

3209 NEWALL, J. Newall's patent railway break: copy of letter from the Railway Department of the Board of Trade addressed to the railway companies . . . *Bury*, 1859. pp. 16.   ICE

3210 HIGGIN, J. An enquiry into the theory and application of railway breaks, with suggestions of improvement on the present plan. . . . *Manchester: British Association for the Advancement of Science*, 1861. pp. 12.   LSE

3211 FAIRBAIRN, W. On the efficiency of various kinds of railway breaks, with experimental researches on their retarding powers. *London*, 1862. pp. 38.   BR
Excerpt, *Min. Proc. I.C.E.*, vol. 19, Session 1859–60.

3212 CREAMER, W. G. Railway safety; By a practical engineer. *London*, 1863. pp. 10.   ICE
Describing a patent communication cord and brakes manufactured by Creamer & Mannion.

3213 PREECE, W. H. On the best means of communicating between the passengers, guards, and drivers of trains in motion. *London*, 1867. pp. 40, with fold. plate.   LSE
Excerpt, *Min. Proc. I.C.E.*, vol. 26, Session 1866–67.

3214 CLERK, H. On the application of hydraulic buffers to prevent the destructive effects of railway collisions. *Woolwich*, 1868. pp. 8.   ICE

3215 NAYLOR, W. Motive power and break power on railways. *London*, 1868. pp. 22.   ICE

3216 SPAGNOLETTI, C. E. A letter on the subject of intercommunication between passengers, guards and drivers of trains whilst in motion, to J. Grierson . . . General Manager of the Great Western Railway. *London*, 1868. pp. 7.   BR
Spagnoletti writing from the Telegraph Dept., Paddington Station, G.W.R., 1st December, 1868. Recommends electric, rather than mechanical, appliances.

3217 CHAMBERS, A. *and* CHAMPION, W. H. Chambers and Champion's railway breaks. *London*, [*c.* 1870?] pp. 6, with diagrams on 2 plates.   ICE
Brakes applied throughout the train by one brake screw.

3218 FOX, W. H. Two papers on continuous railway brakes, read before the Society of Engineers. *London*, [1874.] pp. 33–137, with 4 fold. plates.   SL

3219 BROWNE, W. R. On Robert's patent communicator for railway trains. *Bridgwater*, 1875. pp. 8.   ICE
Electrical.

3220 DAY, ST. J. V. Paper on recent arrangements of continuous brakes, read before the Society of Engineers . . . on the 7th June 1875. [*London*, 1875.] pp. [87]–128, with 8 fold. diagrams.   PO

3221 STEEL, J. The 'Steel-McInnes' patent pneumatic reaction brake . . . *London*, 1875. pp. 15, with diagrs. on 4 la. fold. sheets.   BM
Compressed-air brakes.

222 TYLER [H. W.] Brakes: how the brake question is being manipulated in England. [By] Captain Tyler. *Glasgow*, 1877. pp. 66. BM

Lecture and discussion on continuous brakes for railways. Also published in the May 1877 issues of *Society of Arts Journal*, and *Iron*.

223 GALTON, D. Memorandum . . . on brake experiments made by the North Eastern Railway Company at York on 14 & 15 July 1879 upon a train fitted with the Westinghouse Automatic Brake. *London*, [1879.] pp. 10, with fold. table. ICE

224 HAGGARD, F. T. Remarks upon railway continuous brakes . . . *London*, [1879.] pp. 24. BM

225 GALTON, D. Report by Douglas Galton on brake experiments made at Gisburn on the Lancashire & Yorkshire Railway on the 14th, 15th & 16th July, 1880. *London*, July 1880. pp. 14, with la. fold. table. BR

226 HAGGARD, F. T. Arguments against the use of continuous self-acting railway brakes. 1880. pp. 10. ICE

227 SMITH, W. P. The automatic screw brake. [*London*, 1880.] pp. 5, with 2 fold. diagrams. ICE

The Parker-Smith railway brake.

228 WILSON, J. Description of the continuous brake invented in 1848 . . . read before the Royal Scottish Society of Arts on 10th May 1880. [1880.] pp. 6, with plate. BM

Title-page missing in BM copy.
Invention accredited to John Wilson.

229 WESTINGHOUSE CONTINUOUS BRAKE COMPANY. Driver's Book. *London*, 1881. pp. 19,[2,] with 3 fold. diagrams. PO

230 HAGGARD, F. T. Railways. Simplicity v[ersus] complexity; or, Simple and self-acting continuous brakes. *London*, 1882. pp. 22. BM

231 PILBROW, J. The eccentric railway brake; its automatic and continuous method of actuation and the shaft attachment or coupling of the carriages of a train, *Tunbridge Wells*, [1882.] pp. 8, with 4 fold. diagrams. ICE

232 REYNOLDS, M. Continuous railway brakes: a practical treatise of the several systems in use in the United Kingdom . . . with copious illustrations and numerous tables. *London*, 1882. pp. x, 228, with 9 fold. plates & 83 illus. BM

pp. 3–20, Historical survey.

233 WESTINGHOUSE BRAKE COMPANY. The Brake Returns and the relative value and progress of automatic and non-automatic brakes considered. *London*, 1882. pp. 52. LSE

Reply to the Vacuum Brake Co.'s 'unwarrantable statements' reflecting on the Westinghouse Brake and the Board of Trade Returns.

3234 WESTINGHOUSE BRAKE COMPANY. Experiments showing the amount of efficiency to be obtained by Automatic Vacuum Brakes. [*London*,] 1882. pp. 29, with fold. tables & graphs. LSE

Cover title: 'Railway brakes: the vacuum principle: startling facts.'

3235 NASMITH, J. On the necessity for an automatic railway coupling: a paper read before the Manchester Association of Employers, Foremen & Draughtsmen . . . on January 27, 1883. *Manchester*, 1883. pp. 24, with fold. diagrams. LSE

The prevention of accident through faulty coupling.

3236 GRAVELL, D. Continuous brakes: a paper read before the Civil & Mechanical Engineers' Society on 18 January 1886. *London*, 1886. pp. 14, with tables. ICE

Various types of brake described.

3237 KIERNAN, G. Continuous pneumatic railway brakes: reprint of a paper read by Mr. G. Kiernan before the members of the Manchester Association of Engineers, 26th February 1887. *Manchester*, 1887. pp. 24, with la. fold. diagram. SL

3238 MARSHALL, W. P. Railway brakes. *London*, 1887. pp. 17, with illus. ICE

Various types of brake described.

3239 ORTON, R. H. Description of Orton's steam continuous automatic railway brake. *London*, 1888. pp. 8, with fold. diagram. PO

3240 BLAKENEY, W. H. Continuous railway brakes, and appendix with copious illustrations of the Westinghouse automatic and Vacuum automatic. *London*, 1889. pp. 30, with 23 fold. diagrams. BM

3241 GALTON, D. Memorandum on experiments made by the Vacuum Brake Company . . . on the Manchester, Sheffield & Lincolnshire Railway on the 21st July, 1889. pp. 2. BR

Trials between Doncaster and Thorpe. Enclosed with the BR copy are two letters; 1, from Alfred Louis Sacré of the North British, and 2, from J. Tomlinson to J. L. Sacré.

3242 HARRIS, H. G. Continuous brakes. *Chatham*, 1889. pp. 41, with diagrams on 8 fold. plates. [*Corps of Royal Engineers. Professional Papers*, vol. 14, paper no. 4, 1888.] BM

Westinghouse and Vacuum brakes described.

3243 WESTINGHOUSE BRAKE COMPANY. The Westinghouse Automatic Brake described and illustrated. 4th edn. *London*, 1886. pp. 27, with 3 fold. plates. SL

—— 6th edn. *London*, 1889. pp. 27. BR

3244 The FROZEN vacuum brake; in a series of
eight articles reprinted from the Saturday
Review; with especial reference to the accident to the London & North Western train
at Carlisle Station on the 4th March, 1890.
[London,] 1890. pp. 59.   BR

3245 KIERNAN, G. New methods of signalling
by railway passengers, and slip coach arrangement of the vacuum automatic brake.
Manchester, 1890. pp. [227]–236.   SL
Paper, Manchester Association of Engineers,
22 November, 1890.
Pneumatic communication.

3246 VACUUM BRAKE COMPANY. The Vacuum
Automatic Brake. London, [c. 1890?] pp.
16[19], with 3 fold. diagrams.   BR

3247 POLLITT, H. Intercommunication in railway trains: a paper read before the International Congress of Railways at St. Peters-
burg, 1892. Manchester, 1892. pp. 43.   pc
Printed for private circulation.

3248 WESTINGHOUSE BRAKE COMPANY. The
Westinghouse Quick-Acting Brake: illustrated description. London, 1893. pp. 45,
with diagrams (2 fold.).   PO

3249 GALTON, D. The effect of brakes upon
railway trains; reprinted, with a preface,
by the Westinghouse Air Brake Company.
Pittsburgh, 1894. pp. 217, with diagrams.
                                          LSE
Three excerpts from Min. Proc. I.M.E. of
1878 & 1879.

3250 WESTINGHOUSE BRAKE COMPANY. The
Westinghouse Ordinary Automatic Brake:
illustrated description. London, 1895. pp.
29, with diagrams (2 fold.).   PO

3251 [CLOUD, E. W.] Continuous brakes: Board
of Trade Returns. London, 1900. pp. 26. LSE
A critical analysis of Returns from 1894–
1898; the alleged superiority of Westinghouse.

3252 [CLOUD, E. W.] Continuous brakes on passenger trains. London, 1900. pp. 7.   LSE
Advantages over 'automatic' brakes.

3253 VACUUM BRAKE COMPANY. Passenger
communication in connection with the

Vacuum Automatic Brake. London, [c. 1900.
pp. 2.   BM

3254 VACUUM BRAKE COMPANY. The Rapid
Acting Vacuum Brake and its successes.
London, [1901.] pp. 20, with 4 fold. tables. BM
Comparisons with the Westinghouse brake.

3255 WESTINGHOUSE BRAKE COMPANY.
Railway brakes. London, 1901. pp. 13.   pc
Comparison between Vacuum and Westing-
house. Includes an analysis of Board of Trade
Returns on Brakes between 1893 and 1900.

3256 PHILIPSON, W. Brakes for retarding the
motion of carriages in descending inclines . . .
Apsley Guise, 1902. pp. 197–216 of 'Papers
read before the Institute of British Carriage
Manufacturers,' 1883–1901, with illus.   BM
History of Newcastle coal wagon brakes.

3257 KNIGHT, S. Y. Railway brakes. London,
1904. pp. 51, with 3 fold. diagrams.   PO
Historical and modern. The use of various
types of brake by different railways.

3258 WESTINGHOUSE CONTINUOUS BRAKE
Co. Reference Book. Liverpool, [1874,]
with illus. & 18 fold. diagrams.   IT
—— London, 1880. pp. ix, 22, 16, with 17
la. diagrams (some fold.).   SL
—— London, 1904. pp. 100, with many
diagrams (some fold.).   BR

3259 KNIGHT, S. Y. Notes on the Vacuum
Automatic Brake; with a note on 'slipping
carriages.' London, 1909. pp. viii, 93, with
diagrams.   BR

3260 The WESTINGHOUSE Air Brake: a description of the system and its working.
London, [1921.] pp. 80, with illus., incl. fold.
diagrams.   PO

3261 BRINKWORTH, R. E. The Vacuum Brake
and related appliances: their operation and
maintenance. London, [c. 1931.] pp, iv,
140.   BM
Detailed descriptions with many illustrations
and diagrams.

3262 MOORE, I. G. Vacuum brakes. London:
United Kingdom Railway Advisory Service,
1962. pp. 15, with 10 diagrams.   BM
Modern developments.

E 15 SAFETY ENGINEERING

Signals and signalling methods—interlocking

For general (non-technical) and social aspects of safety see **K 3**

Historical

3263 PATENT OFFICE. Patents for inventions.
Abridgments of specifications relating to rail-
way signals and communicating apparatus,
A.D. 1840–1866. (Compiled by B. Woodcroft.)
London, 1869. pp. xii, 480.   BM: PO

3264 IVATTS, E. B. Origin of the train staff . . .
[Dublin, 1888.] pp. 10.   ICE

Reprinted from the *Railway Herald*, 15 & 22
Dec., 1887.
History of its use in the British Isles.

3265 COOKE, W. F. Extracts from the private
letters of the late Sir William Fothergill
Cooke, 1836–39, relating to the invention
and development of the electric telegraph;
also a memoir by Latimer Clark. Edited by

F. H. Webb. *London & New York*, 1895. pp. 95, with diagrams & lithograph letters. SL
  Includes his experiment on the London & Birmingham between Euston Square and Camden Town, and his work for the Great Western.

3266 PIGG, J. Railway block signalling: the principles of train signalling and apparatus for ensuring safety . . . *London*, 1899. pp. 387, with illus.   BM
  pp. 1–26, Early methods.

3267 WARREN, A. George Westinghouse, 1846–
c 1914. pp. 32, with 2 portraits & a chrono-biographical table.   PC
  Privately issued.

3268 BYLES, C. B. The first principles of railway signalling; including an account of the legislation in the United Kingdom affecting the working of railways and the provision of signalling and safety appliances. *London*, 1910. pp. viii, 146, 18, with illus.   BM
  Historical and descriptive.
  — 2nd edn. *London*, 1918. pp. viii, 146.   IT

3269 LEUPP, F. E. George Westinghouse: his life and achievements; illustrated from photographs. *Boston*, 1918. pp. ix, 304, with 11 plates.   BM
  —— reprinted, *London*, 1919.   BM

3270 PARSONS, J. *and* COOKE, B. W. Notes on railway signalling: an elementary handbook on the practical side of the subject. *London*, [1922.] pp. 74.   BM
  pp. 1–13, 'Evolution of railway signalling.'

3271 PROUT, H. G. A life of George Westinghouse. *London*, 1922. pp. xii, 375, with 8 plates.   BM

3272 WILLIAMS, A. Marvels of railways: interesting accounts of the rise and development of railroad systems in many parts of the world . . . *London*, 1924. pp. 249, with illus.
                    ELTHAM PL
  pp. 18–34, Midland Rly.
  pp. 35–52, G.W. Rly.
  pp. 174–214, Safety.

3273 WESTINGHOUSE BRAKE AND SAXBY SIGNAL COMPANY. Thirty years of power
c signalling, 1897–1927. *London*, 1928. pp. 22, with illus. & a chron. list of installations.
                    BR

3274 LEWIS, L. P. Railway signal engineering: mechanical. *London*, 1912. pp. xviii, 358, with 250 illus.   BM
  An engineering text-book, but contains also much information on early practice and describes current methods of working.
  —— 2nd edn. *London*, 1920. pp. xviii, 358.
                    BM
  —— 3rd, rev. & enl. by J. H. Fraser. *London*, 1932. pp. xx, 391.   BM

3275 WESTINGHOUSE BRAKE AND SIGNAL COMPANY. A centenary of signalling, 1856–1956. John Saxby, 1821–1913, and his part in the development of interlocking and of the

signalling industry which began with his patent of 1856 for protecting junctions. *London*, [1956.] pp. 24[25], with illus., incl. portraits of Saxby and Farmer.   ICE

3276 NOCK, O. S. Fifty years of railway signalling; in celebration of the Golden Jubilee of
b the Institution of Railway Signal Engineers, 1912–1962. *London: I.R.S.E. through Ian Allan*, 1962. pp. 222, with col. frontis. & 61 illus. (incl. ports.) on 32 plates.   BM
  pp. [189]–[216], Author and subject indexes to papers read, 1910 to 1962.

Contemporaneous

3277 CURTIS, W. J. Curtis's inventions for railways, steam-vessels . . . *London*, 1840. pp. v, 78, with illus.   ICE
  Includes brakes and signals, and (pp. 73–4) patent low-gravity coaches as supplied to the London & Greenwich.

3278 CURTIS, C. B. Particulars of a method or methods, by self-acting apparatus to be used on railways, for obviating collisions between successive trains . . . *London*, [1841.] pp. 12, with 3 diagrams on fold. plate.   BM
  Signals.

3279 COOKE, W. F. Telegraphic railways; or, The single way recommended by safety, economy and efficiency, under the safeguard and control of the electric telegraph; with particular reference to railway communication with Scotland and to Irish railways. *London*, 1842. pp. 39, with 4 plates.   BM

3280 GREENHOW, C. H. Exposition of the danger and deficiencies of the present mode of railway construction, with suggestions for its improvement. *London*, 1846. pp. 29, with 5 plates.   ICE
  Suggests concave tyres and convex rails.

3281 PROGRESS, Peter, *pseud.* [R. Y. Clarke]. The electric telegraph . . . *London*, 1847. pp. 84.   UL(GL)
  Includes, pp. 42–7, early telegraph methods on railways.

3282 WALKER, C. V. Electric telegraph manipulation . . . *London*, 1850. pp. 107.   BM
  pp. 83–90, railway telegraphs.

3283 HUISH, M. Railway accidents, their cause and means of prevention (detailing particularly the various contrivances which are in use and have been proposed). *London*, 1852. pp. 19.   BM
  Excerpt, *Min. Proc. I.C.E.*, vol. 11.

3284 WACHTER, J. P. Plan for preventing railway trains from running off the rails, and for stopping them instantaneously. *Rotterdam*, 1852. pp. 14.   ICE
  A centre guide-rail.

3285 OGAN, A. Railway collisions prevented. *London*, 1855. pp. xx, 34.   BM
  Tyer's electro-magnetic signals. Includes a general survey of the problems of safety.

3286 WILSON, G. Researches on colour-blindness; with a supplement on the danger attending the present system of railway and marine coloured signals. *Edinburgh*, 1855. pp. xx, 180.　　　　　　　　　BM

3287 WALKER, C. V. System of train signalling by which also disabled trains may telegraph for assistance without the aid of portable apparatus. *London*, [1857.] pp. 3.　　ICE
Abstract from *Proc. Roy. Soc.*, 19 Mar., 1857.

3288 BARANOWSKI, J. J. J. Baranowski's patent automaton railway signals for exhibiting the danger signal after the passage of each train during a given time—say, for five minutes, or until the train has arrived at a given distance beyond—say, one mile. *London*, 1858. pp. 8, with diagrams on 2 plates.　ICE

3289 BARANOWSKI, J. J. J. Baranowski's patent automaton distant signal as now in use on the North London Railway between Hackney and Kingsland stations ... *London*, 1859. p. 1, with la. fold. plate.　　　ICE

3290 HIPP, M. Electric safety distance signal for railways. [*London*, 1862.] pp. 2.　　ICE
In operation at Battersea Goods Station, London, Chatham & Dover Rly.

3291 PREECE, W. H. On railway telegraphs and the application of electricity to the signalling and working of trains. *London*, 1863. pp. 75, with diagrams.　　　　　　LSE
Excerpt, *Min. Proc. I.C.E.*, vol. 22, Session 1862-3. Paper and discussion.

3292 BRAE, A. E. Electrical communication in railway trains: the causes considered which have hitherto prevented its successful application; with a list of the several patents for the attainment of that object to the present time. *London*, 1865. pp. 36, with 4 plates showing diagrams of safety appliances.　　　　　　　　　　　　　BM

3293 PREECE, W. H. On railway electric signalling. *London*, 1865. pp. 39, with diagrams & fold. plate.　　　　　　　　LSE
Explanation of the block system.

3294 DAPPLES, E. Le Matériel roulant des chemins de fer au point de vue du confort et de la sécurité des voyageurs: moyens d'intercommunication proposés pour permettre aux voyageurs de tous les compartiments et aux conducteurs des trains de communiquer entr'eux pendant la marche. *Lausanne*, 1866. pp. 31.　　　　　　　　　ICE
pp. 12-21. Inter-communication on British trains.

3295 WEBER, C. P. M. Das Telegraphen-und Signalwesen der Eisenbahnen: Geschichte und Technik ... *Weimar*, 1867. pp. xx, 319.　　　　　　　　　　　　　BM
A good proportion of the work is devoted to British practice.

3296 TARDIEU, A. Étude sur les signaux de chemins de fer employés en Angleterre dans les bifurcations et les grandes gares. *Paris*, 1869. pp. 12, with fold. diagrams.　ICE

3297 PREECE, W. H. *and* MALLOCK, Captain. On the block system of working on railways. [*London*, 1873.] pp. 23.　　　BM
Two papers read at a meeting of the Society of Telegraph Engineers.

3298 BARR, H. J. General Barr's automatic danger signals for railways. [*Aberdeen*, 1874.] pp. 16.　　　　　　　ICE
Title-page missing from ICE copy.
Detonator operated by, and with movement of, semaphor signal. pp. 7-11 are extracts from *Simplicity as the essential element of safety and efficiency in the working of railways* by Henry Whatley Tyler. pp. [13]-16, 'Provisional Specification'.

3299 [BURN.] R. BURN & SON. Robert Burn's optional audible signal; simple, reliable and inexpensive. *Epsom*, 1874. pp. 8.　　ICE
Whistle in cab operated by ramp on track.

3300 HUCKVALE, H. W. Huckvale's improved railway switch and locking apparatus. *London*, 1874. pp. 7, with la. fold. plate. ICE

3301 RAPIER, R. C. On the fixed signals of railways. *London*, 1874. pp. 110, with 150 diagrams on 6 fold. plates.　　　　　IT
Excerpt, *Min. Proc. I.C.E.*, vol. 38, 1873-4.

3302 TYER & CO. Tyer's patent train signalling telegraphs. (Tyer's block telegraph and electric locking signals.) *London*, [1862?] pp. 23, with illus.　　　　　　ICE
—— 2nd edn. *London*, [c. 1870.] pp. 58. BR
—— 5th, *London*, 1874. pp. 96, with 5 fold. plates.　　　　　　　　　　　　　BM

3303 BRAMWELL, F. J. Railway safety appliances. [*Bristol*, 1875.] pp. 24, with 19 diagrams & tables on fold. plates.　　ICE

3304 A PATENT law scandal. Patents for improvements in apparatus for locking and controlling railway points and signals; or, The history of the locking catch-rods instead of levers. [*c.* 1875.] pp. 16.　　NLC

3305 SALOMONS, D. New method of signalling on railways. [*Southborough*,] 1874. pp. 32.　　　　　　　　　　　　　BM
Electrical indicators in engine cab worked from a centre rail.
—— 2nd edn. *Southborough*, 1874. pp. 32.　　　　　　　　　　　　　NLC
—— another edn. *Tunbridge Wells*, 1875. pp. 59.　　　　　　　　　　ICE

3306 WHITEHURST, F. F. Great undertakings interspersed with anecdotes of distinguished persons. *London*, 1875. pp. 48.　BM
The electric telegraph; the G.W. Rly., etc. The author who was with the G.W.R. claims

that the electric telegraph is the greatest invention of mankind and that he invented it.

3307 BURN, R. The missing link: signalling trains in fogs and snow-storms, with . . . opinions of some eminent railway officers & engineers. *London*, 1877. pp. 20.　　ICE
Burn's apparatus.

3308 HOLMGREN, F. Holmgren's method of testing for colour. [*London:*] *London & North Western Rly.*, [*c.* 1880.] pp. 17, with a colour chart.　　BR

3309 HARFORD, E. Suggestions for safe railway working, made in reply to numerous inquiries. *London: Amalgamated Society of Railway Servants*, [1885.] pp. 7.　　BM
Twenty-three necessary requirements.

3310 BARANOWSKI, J. J. Automatic railway signals invented by J. J. Baranowski. *London*, 1887. pp. 4.　　ICE
A single sheet diagram with explanatory notes, intended to be used with the above work, was published later. In the ICE copy the two are together. The text has no p. 3.

3311 [SYKES.] W. R. SYKES INTERLOCKING SIGNAL COMPANY. The 'Sykes' system of interlocking railway signals and points with block instruments. *London*, 1887. pp. 13. PO

3312 MALAN, E. de M. Apparatus for protecting trains standing at a signal cabin on either the right or wrong line. *Howden*, 1890. pp. 2.　　ICE

As employed on the Hull & Barnsley.

3313 POLLITT, H. Means of communication between intermediate places and stations; also, use of the telephone, especially on lines of small traffic: a paper read before the Fourth Session of the International Congress on Railways at St. Petersburgh, June, 1892. Question XVIII. Section B. *Manchester*, [1892.] pp. 88, with 36 fold. plates illustrating signalling equipment.　　PO

3314 POLLITT, H. Means of communication between trains while on the journey and the stations along the line, or vice versa: a paper read before the Fourth Session of the International Congress on Railways at St. Petersburgh, August 1892. Question XVIII, Section C. *Manchester*, [1892.] pp. 9, with 2 fold. plates.　　IT

3315 SAUVAGE, E. Le Système anglais des signaux de chemins de fer. *Paris*, 1893. pp. 96, with 5 fold. plates.　　ICE

3316 WESTINGHOUSE, G. Electro-pneumatic automatic block signalling. *London*, 1895. pp. 14, with la. fold. plate.　　ICE

3317 WESTINGHOUSE BRAKE COMPANY. The electro-pneumatic signalling and interlocking system. *London*, 1895. pp. 18, with 2 la. fold. plates.　　ICE

3318 BOULT, W. S. Boult's system of railway signalling. *Manchester*, 1896. pp. 16, with illus.　　LSE
Reprinted from the *Practical Engineer*.
Armature on engine passes through magnetic field on track, giving signals direct to train.

3319 LANGDON, W. E. Application of electricity to railway working. *London*, 1877. pp. xv, 315, with many illus.　　BM
Mainly about signalling apparatus and methods; includes specimen forms for entering train movements.
—— another edn. *London*, 1897. pp. xvi, 331.　　BM

3320 BOULT, W. S. Signalling without contact: a system of railway signalling. *London*, [1899.] pp. 11, with illus.　　LSE
Armature on locomotive passing through magnetic field on track.

3321 MALAN, E. de M. Electro-pneumatic signalling. *Chatham*, 1901. pp. 24, with 8 fold. diagrams. [*Corps of Royal Engineers. Professional Papers*, vol. 27, no. 2.]　　BM

3322 ELECTRIC RAILWAY SIGNALLING SYNDICATE. Electric automatic signals. The International Tramways and Light Railways Exhibition, Agricultural Hall, Islington, July 1–12, 1902. *London*, 1902. pp. 4, with diagrams.　　PO

3323 REDMAYNE, R. N. Electric signalling on railways: particulars of the Brown-Mackenzie system. *Newcastle*, [1902.] pp. 15, with illus.　　BR
In English and French.
Direct signalling from track to driver's cab

3324 WESTINGHOUSE BRAKE COMPANY. The Westinghouse electro-pneumatic system for the operation of railway points and signals. *London*, April 1902. pp. 62, with illus. & diagrams of layouts.　　BR

3325 FRENCH, J. W. Modern power generation: steam, electric and internal combustion, and their application to present-day requirements; with many diagrams and pictorial illustrations and a series of composite sectional models. Prepared under the direction of J. W. French. *London*, 1908. 2 vols. BM
vol. 1, pp. 167–201, Continuous railway brakes.

3326 HADLEY, E. S. Railway working and appliances . . . *London*, 1909. pp. viii, 120.　BM
Cover title—'The appliances and operations on railways in Great Britain.'
Describes safety appliances.

3327 WILSON, H. R. Railway signalling. *In* 'Engineering wonders of the world', by Archibald Williams. vol. 2, 1909. pp. 225–40, with illus.   BM

3328 WILSON, H. R. Railway signalling. *London*, [1900.] pp. xviii, 161. [*Railway Series of Text Books & Manuals*, no. 1.]   BM
Mechanical (not electrical) signalling; with detailed drawings and illustrations of installations and of apparatus of all kinds, including signal cabins, crossing gates, etc.

—— 2nd edn. 'Mechanical railway signalling.' *London*, [1910.] pp. xx, 193.   BM
Same series.

3329 [SYKES.] W. R. SYKES INTERLOCKING SIGNAL COMPANY. The four-position block instrument. *Clapham* [*London*], [191–.] pp. 5, with fold. diagram.   PO

3330 [SYKES.] W. R. SYKES INTERLOCKING SIGNAL COMPANY. The improved electric lock and block system, style 'L.' *London*, [191–.] pp. 18, with illus. & diagrams. PO

3331 WILSON, H. R. Power railway signalling. *London*, 1910. pp. xix, 342, with many drawings & illus. [*Railway Series of Text Books*, no. 5.]   BM

3332 GAIRNS, J. F. The possibilities of flash signalling in British railway practice. *Stockholm*, 1913. pp. 17[20], with diagrams. RC
Reprinted from *Bulletin of the International Railway Congress Assoc.*, vol. 27, no. 1, Jan. 1913.

3333 GREAT WESTERN RLY. Synopsis of course of instruction on the subject of safe working of railways and the appliances used in connection therewith, for the use of signalling class students. *London*, 1913. pp. 79, with illus. & diagrams.   LSE
'Private & not for publication.'

3334 MORGAN, H. E. Signalling and train control. *In* 'Modern railway working', edited by John Macaulay. vol. 6, 1913. pp. 159–222; vol. 7, 1913. pp. 1–60, with many illus. & diagrams.   BM

3335 RAILWAY signalling. *In* 'Jubilee of the Railway News, 1864–1914.' *London: Railway News*, [1914.] pp. 136–48, with illus. BM

3336 BOUND, A. F. A review of the art of signalling, and some suggestions. *In* 'Proceedings of the Institution of Railway Signal Engineers,' 1915. pp. 14–139, with 2 fold. diagrams.

3337 [SYKES.] W. R. SYKES INTERLOCKING SIGNAL COMPANY. The 'rotary' system of lock and block. *London*, [1916.] pp. 12, with illus.   PO

3338 TATTERSALL, A. E. Modern Developments in railway signalling . . . track circuit-

ing, power signalling and automatic train control. *London*, 1921. pp. 299.   BM

3339 INSTITUTION OF RAILWAY SIGNAL ENGINEERS. Report of the Committee on Three-position Signalling appointed by Council Minute 751 of March 29, 1922. *Reading*, 1922. pp. 22.   LSE

3340 The RAILWAY Signal and Permanent Way Engineer's Pocket Book. *London*, [1920.] pp. 259, with illus., diagrams & tables. BM
—— another edn. *London*, [1922.] pp. 326.   BM

3341 The RE-SIGNALLING of the Liverpool Overhead Railway with daylight colour-light signals. *London*, [1922.] pp. 12, with 9 illus. & a diagram.   BM
Reprinted from the *Engineer*, 4 Nov., 1921.

3342 WILSON, F. R. Railway signalling: automatic: an introductory treatment of the purposes, equipment & methods of automatic signalling & track circuits for steam and electric railways . . . *London*, 1922. pp. xiii, 116, with illus.   BM

3343 [SYKES.] W. R. SYKES INTERLOCKING SIGNAL COMPANY. Harper's block telegraph instruments. [*London*, 1923.] pp. 8.   PO

3344 WILSON, F. R. Railway signalling: mechanical: an introductory treatment of the principles, methods & equipment . . . and the principles of interlocking . . . *London*, 1923. pp. xiii, 109, with illus. & diagrams. BM

3345 GREAT WESTERN RLY. A Great Western Railway signal box: souvenir of the exhibit at the British Empire Exhibition, Wembley, [1925.] *London*, 1925. pp. 30, with 12 illus. & fold. map.   BR

3346 LONDON, MIDLAND & SCOTTISH RLY. Signalling model, British Empire Exhibition, Wembley, 1925. [*London*, 1925.] pp. 20, with 3 plates, 5 mounted photographs & 2 fold. charts (col.).   BM
A guide to the principles and method of signalling as demonstrated by the model railway used at one of the LMS signalling schools.

3347 TWEEDIE, M. G. *and* LASCELLES, T. S. Modern railway signalling. *London*, 1925.
b   pp. 259, with bibliography.   BM
Includes description of methods of working.

3348 WAGENRIEDER, B. Railway signalling from a traffic point of view. pp. 11. *Typescript*.   RC
Paper, Railway Club, 15 Jan., 1926.

3349 DE BRAY, M. R. G. Outdoor interlocking apparatus: paper read before the Railway Club, October 17, 1927. pp. 28, with diagrams.   RC
Printed pamphlet.

3350 DUTTON, S. T. Railway signalling: theory and practice: a practical manual for engineers . . . *London*, 1928. pp. viii, 148. BM

3351 WESTINGHOUSE BRAKE AND SAXBY SIGNAL COMPANY. The re-signalling of Victoria and Exchange Stations, Manchester, L.M. & S. Rly.: some details regarding the largest re-signalling undertaking let out to contract in recent years. *London*, April 1930. pp. 28, with illus., diagram & a la. fold. plan (col.). IT

3352 WESTINGHOUSE BRAKE AND SAXBY SIGNAL COMPANY. Power signalling at Cardiff, G.W.R. *London*, June 1934. pp. 15, with la. fold. diagram. BR

3353 SIEMENS AND GENERAL ELECTRIC RAILWAY SIGNAL COMPANY. Resignalling, Fenchurch Street Station, L.N.E.R. *Westminster*, [1935.] pp. 6, with illus. & plans. IT
Reprinted from the *Railway Gazette*, 17 May, 1935.

3354 GILBERT, F. Wrong line orders and their uses. *Sheffield: F. Gilbert*, [1938.] s.sh. obl. fol. BM

3355 WESTINGHOUSE BRAKE AND SIGNAL COMPANY. Resignalling of Portsmouth, Mid-Sussex, and coastal lines, Southern Railway. *London*, 1939. pp. 16, with illus., maps & fold diagram. LSE
Reprinted from the *Railway Gazette*, 24 Feb., 1939.

3356 AITKEN, J. Modern railway signalling on British railways; illustrated. 2nd edn. *Lennoxtown*, [c. 1944.] pp. 175. BR
Privately distributed.

*3357 AITKEN, J. The railway signalman; incorporating the 'Signalman's Pocket Book'. War edition. *Lennoxtown*, [c. 1944.] pp. 116, with diagrams. BR
Privately distributed.

3358 AITKEN, J. Single line working during repairs or obstruction, by means of pilotman. 2nd edn. *Lennoxtown*, [c. 1944.] pp. 40, with diagrams. BR
Privately distributed.

3359 LONDON & NORTH EASTERN RLY.—SIGNAL & TELEGRAPH ENGINEER'S DEPARTMENT. Lectures on signalling and telegraph work, Southern Area. [1946.] pp. [275], with over 230 diagrams. *Reproduced typescript*. BR
'Private. For use of the Company's staff only.'
Thirteen lectures.

3360 [TATTERSALL, A. E.] Railway signalling and communications: installation and maintenance. *London: St. Margaret's Technical Press*, [Dec. 1940.] pp. xv, 416, with 25 plates, 16 illus. & 339 diagrams. IT
—— 2nd edn. *London*, May 1946. pp. xv, 416, etc. IT

3361 WESTINGHOUSE BRAKE AND SIGNAL COMPANY. Coded continuous cab signalling. *London*, November 1946. pp. 12, with illus. & diagrams. SL

3362 NOCK, O. S. British railway construction and operation: no. 1, semaphore signals. *London: Greenlake Publications*, [1947.] pp. 31, with illus. BM

3363 TAYLOR, M. Railway signalling . . . *London: Sampson Low*, 1949. pp. 84, with plates. BM
Historical and descriptive.

3364 HYATT, A. P. *and* SHEPHERD, G. J. Automatic train control: its application to British railways from the operating and economic points of view. September 1955. pp. 39, with 3 diagrams. *Typescript*. ICE

3365 BRITISH TRANSPORT COMMISSION. Railway signal engineering as a career. *London*, 1956. pp. [16,] with illus. IME

3366 NOCK, O. S. Signalling from the driver's point of view. *London: Institution of Railway Signalling Engineers*, 1956. pp. 15. IT
A paper, 28 March, 1956.

3367 DAY, J. R. *and* COOPER, B. K. Railway signalling systems. *London: F. Muller*, 1958. pp. 144, with plates & illus. BM

3368 WESTINGHOUSE BRAKE AND SIGNAL COMPANY, Signalling for railway modernisation. *London*, [1959]. pp. 36, with illus. SL
Various installations described.

3369 LANGLEY, P. A. Level crossing protection. *London: Institution of Railway Signal Engineers*, [1961.] pp. 98, with illus. & diagrams. BM

3370 COLEY, J. P. Remote control in railway signalling. *London: United Kingdom Railway Advisory Service*, 1962. pp. 16, with 4 illus. & 5 diagrams. BM

3371 DENNISON, H. F. Double wire signalling. *London: United Kingdom Railway Advisory Service*, 1962. pp. 22, with 2 illus. & 13 diagrams. BM
General introduction to the double wire system of signal and point operation.

3372 LOOSEMORE, J. P. Relay interlocking. *London: United Kingdom Railway Advisory Service*, 1962. pp. 20, with 10 illus. & 12 circuit diagrams. BM

*3373 KICHENSIDE, G. M. *and* WILLIAMS, A. British railway signalling. *London: Ian Allan*, 1963. pp. 104, with many illus. & diagrams, incl. 8 pp. of signal diagrams in colour. BM
A concise but comprehensive account (pp. 5–13, historical) of safety engineering and operation.

E16   OTHER RAILWAY EQUIPMENT

3374 VULLIAMY, B. L. On the construction and regulation of clocks for railway stations; with an abstract of the discussion. *London*, 1845. pp. 16.   BM
Excerpt, *Min. Proc. I.C.E.*

3375 YOUNG, C. D. A short treatise on the system of wire fencing, gates, etc. as manufactured by C. D. Young & Co. . . . with explanatory copper-plate engravings, to which is appended an illustrated and descriptive catalogue . . . *Edinburgh*, 1861. pp. xvi, 100, xi, pl. 38. (Catalogue, pp. 155.)   BM
Includes fencing, gates and railings for railways.

3376 SMILES, R. Brief memoir of the late William Muir, mechanical engineer of London and Manchester. [*London*, 1888.] pp. 26.   BM
pp. 15–17, his work with Thomas Edmondson in the making of ticket printing machines.
—— another edn. *Manchester*, [1888.] pp. 45. (pp. 25–7.)   BM

3377 LANGDON, W. On the employment of the electric light for railway purposes. Paper, read 28 March, 1895. *London*, 1895. pp. 278–372, with illus. & fold. diagram.   BM
Excerpt, *Journal & Proceedings* of the Institute of Electrical Engineers.
Based on Midland Rly. practice.

3378 FOWLER, H. The lighting of railway premises. *In* 'Modern railway working', edited by John Macaulay. vol. 4, 1913. pp. 1–34, with illus. & diagrams.   BM

3379 NETTELBLADT, N. T. C. C. F. F. R. The introduction of platform tickets in Great Britain, 1913 . . . with an Appendix containing instructions for attending B.E.A.M. platform ticket machines. *London: British Electric Automatic Machines*, [1913.] pp. 23, with 7 plates & a map.   pc

3380 TYPES of British railway companies' horses. *In* 'Jubilee of the Railway News, 1864–1914.' *London: Railway News*, [1914.] pp. 24–5.   BM
Six illustrations; no text.

3381 JACOB, A. Weighing machines on railways. *In* 'Jubilee of the Railway News, 1864–1914.' *London: Railway News*, [1914.] pp. 159–63, with 9 illus.   BM

3382 BULKELEY, G. Mechanical appliances for handling railway traffic. *London*, 1921. pp. 132, with illus.   BM

3383 RAILWAY CLEARING HOUSE. Use of mechanical appliances and labour saving devices in connection with goods train traffic. Report of Sub-Committee, 3 December 1918. pp. 15, with illus.   IT
'Private & not for publication.'
—— Second Report, Oct. 1920. pp. 58.   IT
—— Final Report, April 1922. pp. 22, with illus.   IT

3384 MITCHELL CONVEYOR & TRANSPORTER COMPANY. Material handling: a reference book of mechanical appliances. *London*, [1925.] pp. xv, 127, with illus.   IT
Includes locomotive coaling plants, wagon tippers, aerial ropeways and telphers.

3385 LEAD INDUSTRIES DEVELOPMENT COUNCIL. Railway painting. *London*, [1940.] pp. 78. [*Technical Publication* no. 12.]   IT
Advice on technique.

3386 WILLIAMS, T. L. *and* BROWN, D. W. Plastics in railway engineering. *London: Railway Gazette*, 1944. pp. 4, with illus. pc
Reprinted from *Railway Gazette*, 31 May, 1944.

F RAILWAY ADMINISTRATION

Constitution, promotion and ownership of railways—Cost of construction—Internal finance (income and expenditure)—Accounts and auditing—Dissolution

For general statistical accounts of railways at any period see **B 3 – 10**
For investment in railways from the viewpoint of the investor, and for social and national economic aspects of speculation, see **K 5**

Marginal symbols: **b** bibliographies
c chronologies

Historical

3387 BUREAU OF RAILWAY ECONOMICS [Washington]. Railway economics: a collec-
b tive catalogue of books in fourteen American libraries. *Illinois*, 1912. pp. x, 446. BM
pp. 373–87, 'British railways'.

3388 LAWSON, W. R. British railways: a financial and commercial survey. *London*, 1913. pp. xxxii, 320. BM
pp. 1–60, Finance.

3389 BAILEY, W. Railway accounts, old and new. *In* 'Jubilee of the Railway News, 1864–1914.' *London: Railway News*, [1914.] pp. 78–86. BM

3390 [BRITISH railway finance, 1850–1914.] *In* 'Jubilee of the Railway News, 1864–1914.'
c *London: Railway News*, [1914.] pp. 29–39. BM

Articles and detailed tables.

3391 BRITISH railway progress shown by the Board of Trade Returns. *In* 'Jubilee of the Railway News, 1864–1914.' *London: Railway News*, [1914.] p. 32–3. BM
A detailed record, in 28 columns, of railway finance from 1870 to 1912. Other tables precede and follow (pp. 29–35).

3392 LABOUR RESEARCH DEPARTMENT. Labour and capital on the railways. *London*, 1923. pp. 64. [*Studies in Labour & Capital*, no. 4.] LSE
Wastage of capital in early railway enterprises (1830–1859); the process of amalgamation and legislative control; pp. 42 to end, history of railway trade unions and present labour position.

3393 CAMPBELL, C. D. Cyclical fluctuation in the railway industry. *Manchester: Manchester Statistical Society*, 1929. pp. 47, with 19 tables in text & 12 graphs on 3 folded sheets at end. LSE
An historical and statistical review.

3394 FENELON, K. G. Railway economics. *London*, 1932. pp. xii, 288, with a biblio-
b graphy (107 items). BM
General and historical.

3395 SHERRINGTON, C. E. R. The economics of rail transport in Great Britain. *London*, 1928. 2 vols. BM

vol. 1, 'History and development'. pp. xii, 283.
vol. 2, 'Rates and service'. pp. xii, 332.
—— 2nd edn. of vol. 2. *London*, 1937. pp. xv, 336, with 3 fold. tables. BM

3396 LABOUR RESEARCH DEPARTMENT. Railways for the nation. *London*, 1945. pp. 31, with bibliogr. notes. LSE
History of railway ownership and finance. Labour's case for nationalization.

3397 KIRKALDY, A. W. *and* EVANS, A. D. The history and economics of transport. *London*, [1915.] pp. ix, 338. BM
pp. 26–196, Railways. With tables.
—— 2nd edn. *London*, 1920, pp. xi, 358. BM
—— 3rd, *London*, 1924. pp. xi, 410. BM
—— 4th, *London*, 1927. pp. xi, 426. BM
—— 5th, *London*, 1931. pp. xi, 455. BM
—— 6th, 'Transport: its history and economics', by A. D. Evans. *London*, 1946. pp. vi, 122. BM

3398 POLLINS, H. A note on railway constructional costs, 1825–1850. [1952.] pp. 395–407. BR
Reprinted from *Economica*, November 1952.

3399 FULFORD, R. Glyn's, 1753 to 1953 . . . *London: Macmillan & Co.*, 1953. pp. xvi, 266, with plates (some col.). BM
Appendix IV, Railways which had accounts with Glyn's.

*3400 POLLINS, H. Aspects of railway accounting before 1868. *In* 'Studies in the history of
b accounting', by A. C. Littleton and B. S. Yamey. *London: Sweet & Maxwell*, 1956. pp. 332–55, with many bibliogr. notes. BM

3401 POLLINS, H. Railway auditing: a report of 1867. pp. 22. BR
Reprinted from *Accounting Research*, vol. 8, no. 1, Jan. 1957.
L. & N.W. Rly.

*3402 POLLINS, H. Railway contractors and the finance of railway development in Britain.
b *In* 'Journal of Transport History', vol. 3, no. 1, May 1957. pp. 103–10, with 94 bibliogr. notes. BM

3403 ROBBINS, M. The Railway Age. *London: Routledge & Kegan Paul*, 1962. pp. x, 227,
b   with 12 plates.   BM
    pp. 104–25, 'Capital, earnings, and public control'.
    pp. 107–8, Notes on sources.

Contemporaneous

3404 FITZPATRICK, R. W. Railway rights and liabilities arising before an Act of Incorporation is obtained. *London*, 1845. pp. 27. BM
    The law relating to the formation of railway companies.

3405 INSTRUCTIONS for the preparation of the Book of Reference. [*c.* 1845.] pp. 4.   LSE

3406 LEWIS, G. H. The liabilities incurred by the projectors, managers and shareholders of railway and other joint-stock companies considered and also the rights and liabilities arising from transfers of shares. Written expressly for non-professional use. *London*, 1845. pp. 79.   BM

3407 CLARK, G. D. Provisional railway code, with instruction to scripholders: being a summary of the legislative measures of this Session to protect scripholders and facilitate the dissolution of railway companies. Compiled and arranged from Parliamentary Reports and official documents. *London*, 1846. pp. 24.   BM

3408 CLARK, G. D. Railway Companies Dissolution Act, 9 & 10 Victoria, c. 28; with an analysis by George D. Clark. *London*, [1846.] pp. 16.   BM

3409 HODGES, W. The law relating to railways and railway companies, with all the cases . . . decided in the Courts of Law and Equity. *London*, 1847. pp. xxviii, 721, 278.   BM

3410 SIMMS, F. W. Report upon the project of the Calcutta & Diamond Harbour Railway & Dock Co. [*Calcutta*, 1847.]   BM
    pp. 86–8, 95–6, The average cost per mile of the principal railways in the United Kingdom (and cost of permanent way). Tables.

3411 DOULL, A. Random hints on railways and railway legislation. *London*, 1848. pp. 43.
                                            BM
    Suggested reforms, especially with regard to law relating to railway construction.

3412 KING, G. Uniformity of railway accounts: a few remarks on the subject of railway economy; also, proposal of a method of keeping railway accounts on one uniform plan, and of closing capital accounts in a way that shall not encroach unduly upon present dividends. *London*, 1849. pp. 84, with tables.   BM

3413 NOTLEY, S. Suggestions for the management of railway accounts; and a word or two on audit. *London*, 1849. pp. 27.   BM

3414 HARDCASTLE, D. Railway audit . . . *London*, 1850. pp. 32.   BM
    The prevention of irregularities.

3415 MACPHERSON, P. I. The law expenditure of railway companies considered with a view to its speedy and effectual reduction. *London*, [1850.] pp. 24.   BM

3416 PENNINGTON, W. Suggestions as to the best mode of auditing railway accounts. [*Manchester*,] 1850. pp. [3.]   BM
    'As long as the Executive has the control of the internal audit of any railway it will be almost impossible to prevent fraud.'

3417 LAING, S. Audit of railway accounts: letter to the proprietors of the London, Brighton & South Coast Railway Company. [*London*, 1851.] pp. 16.   LSE
    Objection to government interference with railway companies' accounts (the subject of two Bills presented in that Session).

3418 THORBURN, T. Diagrams: railway economics. *Edinburgh*, 1853. [pp. irreg.] LSE
    Eight diagrams showing comparative figures for railway companies in respect of mileage, cost of construction, traffic and finance, in 1852.

3419 COMPARATIVE statement of railway accounts for the years 1853 & 1854, compiled from the published returns of the railway companies. *London*, 1855. pp. [40.] BM
    —— Comparative statement . . . for the first half of 1854 and 1855 . . . *London*, 1855. pp. [249.]   LSE
    Arranged under sixty companies, with a comparative summary table at end.

3420 CHATTAWAY, E. D. Railways: their capital and dividends, with statistics of their working in Great Britain and Ireland, etc., etc.; being a second volume to Mr. R. M. Stephenson's work on railways in this series. *London*, 1855–56. pp. vii, 133.   BM
    Cover title, *Rudimentary treatise on railways*. For part one see 14.

3421 YEATS, J. S. Comparative statement of English, Scotch and Irish railway capital and revenue accounts for the years 1855 and 1856, compiled from the published accounts of the railway companies . . . *London*, 1857. pp. 103.   UL(GL)
    Tables for all railways.

3422 GRINSTED, J. The finance of the railways in the United Kingdom, compiled from official statistics; reprinted from 'The Times'. *London*, 1859. pp. 20.   BM
    From *The Times* of 25–30 August.
    pp. 7–10, tables for 1858, for all railways.

3423 WARMINGTON, E. Railroad mismanagement: its evils and remedy, showing how the

dividends of shareholders can be greatly augmented, and railroad property put on a sound and solid basis. *London*, 1859. pp. 24.
BM

3424 MOORE, A. A Hand-book of Railway Law: containing the Public General Railway Acts from 1838 to 1858 inclusive, and statutes connected therewith, with an introduction containing statistical and financial information . . . *London*, 1859. pp. cxvi, 404. BM
—— 2nd edn. *London*, 1860. pp. cxvi, 488.
LSE

3425 HAND-BOOK Guide to Railway Situations, including the complete system of railway accounts and returns, to which are added, valuable hints on commercial employments generally. *London & New York: Cassell, Petter & Galpin*, 1861. pp. 60. BR

3426 KINGDOM, W. Suggestions for improving the value of railway property and for the eventual liquidation of the national debt. *London*, [1850.] pp. 15. BM
Government to assist in railway finance.
—— 2nd edn. 'Suggestions for the liquidation of the national debt by means of railway property . . .' *London*, 1855. pp. 15. BM
—— 3rd, *London*, 1855. pp. 14. BM
—— 4th, 'Suggestions for the increase of railway dividend . . .' *London*, 1859. pp. 12.
BM
—— 7th, *London*, 1863. pp. 12. BM

3427 COATES, T. Railway deposits discussed in a letter to the chairman of the Committee. *London*, 1864. pp. 23. BM
Addressed to J. H. Scourfield, chairman of the Select Committee on Standing Orders (Parliamentary Deposits). 'The passage of an act should not be impeded by financial difficulties arising from construction expenses. Money should be deposited until act is passed.'

3428 LEES, H. The North British Railway: its past and future policy; with remarks on the duties and responsibilities of directors in reference to accounts. *Edinburgh*, 1866. pp. 18. BM

3429 LIVESEY, W. A financial scheme for the relief of railway companies, submitted to directors, shareholders, and the public. *London*, 1866. pp. 40. BM
Proposes mutual control, under government supervision, of railway company finance, to end irregularities concerning borrowed capital.

3430 PATTERSON, R. H. Railway finance. *Edinburgh & London*, 1867. pp. vi, 76. BM

3431 TARRANT, H. J. Lloyd's bonds: their nature and uses. *London*, 1867. pp. 18. BM
Their usefulness to railway company promoters.

3432 WHITEHEAD, J. Railway finance. *London*, [1867]. pp. 21. LSE
Criticism of the continued expenditure of

capital on railways; with tables for main line companies from 1862–1866.

3433 AYRES, H. The financial position of railways, and observations on the railway systems of accounts in the United Kingdom; showing the necessity for a more systematic and uniform plan of publishing railway accounts periodically under the authority of Parliament, the advantages to be derived from a complete system of registration for railway securities and the establishment of a special department of Government for the purpose of controlling the railway affairs of the country; with a variety of information respecting the railway property in the United Kingdom. *London*, 1868. pp. lxiii, 41. BM

3434 BARLOW, W. H. An analytical investigation of the Board of Trade Returns of the capital and revenue of railways in the United Kingdom. *London*, 1868. pp. 48. BM
Period 1846–1866.

3435 BIRD, H. E. Railway accounts: a comprehensive analysis of the capital and revenue of the railways of the United Kingdom, with a few observations thereon. *London*, [1868.] pp. [20,] 9. BM
Figures for 1865 to 1867 tabled and analysed.

3436 HULSE, W. W. Model form of railway accounts submitted . . . to the National Conference of Railway Shareholders, Manchester, April 15, 1868. [*Manchester*, 1868.] pp. [5.] ICE
Twelve specimen forms.

3437 LEES, H. Railway affairs: suggestions with a view to investing shareholders with more direct control, ensuring more reliable accounts and maintaining distinction between capital and revenue charges. *Edinburgh*, 1868. pp. 32. BM

3438 SKELLORN, S. B. Railway business and accounts: the details of railway management in general, with the accounts in all branches practically explained. New & improved edn. *Liverpool*, 1868. pp. viii, 144, with specimen forms. RC
A manual for railway clerks.

3439 [FRANCE]—MINISTÈRE DE L'AGRICULTURE, DU COMMERCE ET DES TRAVAUX PUBLICS.—DIRECTION GÉNÉRALE DES PONTS ET CHAUSSÉES ET DES CHEMINS DE FER. Chemins de fer de l'Europe: résultats généraux de l'exploitation. *Paris*, 1869. pp. 115. BM
pp. 32–47, tables showing financial position of all railways of British Isles in 1862 and 1863 (in francs).
pp. 96–103, the same, for 1863 and 1864.

3440 GODEFROI, H. *and* SHORTT, J. Law of railway companies. *London*, 1869. pp. xxxvii, 552, ccclxiv. BM

3441 HAGGARD, F. T. A mile of railway in the United Kingdom. *London*, 1869. pp. 40, with tables.   BM
Urging financial reform.

3442 MORGAN, H. L. Accounts and audits: remarks on the new 'Regulation of Railways Act'. 2nd edn. *London*, 1868. pp. 24.   BM
—— 3rd, *London*, 1868. pp. 26.   BM
—— 5th, *London*, 1869. pp. 40.   BM

3443 WOOD, W. An analysis of the half-yearly reports of the principal railway companies, second half-year, 1872, compared with the corresponding period, 1871, expressed in decimals. *London*, 1873. pp. 46.   BM
Tables arranged under railways.

3444 GASKELL, T. P. Railways: their financial position and prospects. *London*, 1874. pp. 31.   BM

3445 DOWDEN, T. F. Railway dividends. *London*, 1876. pp. 16.   ICE
Reforms and economies to avoid wastage of capital.

3446 COHN, G. Die englische Eisenbahnpolitik der letzten zehn Jahre, 1873–1883. *Leipzig*, 1883. pp. viii, 196.   BM
A revised edition of part of his *Untersuchungen über die englische Eisenbahnpolitik* (1874–75), with an index serving both works.

3447 PERKS, R. W. Is it desirable to alter the law which prohibits railway companies from paying interest out of capital?—being notes upon the Report of the Select Committee of 1882 on Standing Order 167. *London*, 1883. pp. 46.   BM

3448 HAGGARD, F. T. The profit of railway travelling in the United Kingdom versus the train mile run considered. *London*, 1884. pp. 8.   LSE
An increase of train mileage but a decrease in profits.

3449 PEASE, J. W. Payment of interest out of capital during construction of works. *London*, 1885. pp. 28.   UL(GL)
Harmful effects which the proposed alteration of statute law and of Parliamentary Standing Orders would have on the economic stability of the State. 'It can be no part of the duty of the State to allow inducements to be held out to investors which all financial authorities and every man's common sense must declare to be both delusive and dangerous.'

3450 BIRD, H. E. Railway accounts: a concise view for the last four years, 1881 to 1884, and an estimate for 1885, with remarks on the relation of capital to revenue and on vital statistics of the working of railways. *London*, 1886, pp. 20, with tables.   BM

3451 GUTHRIE, E. Payment of interest on capital during construction of works: a paper read by Mr. Edwin Guthrie at a meeting of the Society . . . January 29, 1886. [*Manchester:*] *Manchester Society of Chartered Accountants*, 1886. pp. 19.   BM

3452 TENNANT, R. Railway administration. *Geneva*, 1886. pp. 36.   ICE
The economics of British railway administration.

3453 JEANS, J. S. Railway problems: an inquiry into the economic conditions of railway working in different countries. *London*, 1887. pp. xxviii, 560.   BM
Mostly financial problems.

3454 PICARD, A. Traité des chemins de fer: économie politique, commerce, finances, administration, droit. Études comparées sur les chemins de fer étrangers. *Paris*, 1887. 4 vols.   LSE

3455 FINANCIAL TIMES. Railway capital expenditure. Reprinted from the 'Financial Times' [of July & August 1893]. *London*, [1893.] pp. iv, 38.   LSE
Increase of capital investment, but decrease of yield.

3456 BROWNE, G. A. R. Report on the system of accounts in force on English railways and in the English Railway Clearing House. *Calcutta: Government of India Printing Office*, 1896. pp. vii, 107, with specimen forms.   BR
The railways visited were the G.W.R., L. & N.W.R. and L.B. & S.C.R.

3457 WOOLSTON AND BEETON. Statistical Chart of British railways, 1899. *London*, [1900.] la. fold. sh.   UL(GL)
Four graphs showing the cost of railways per mile and amount of ordinary capital per mile on each of the railways of Great Britain.

3458 HAGGARD, F. T. Our railways in the United Kingdom: a disastrous policy made clear. *Tunbridge Wells*. 1901. pp. 11.   BTCHR
Suggested financial reforms based on examination of returns between 1870 and 1900. Increase in 3rd class travel and decrease in 1st and 2nd, ruinous to shareholders.

3459 MACCOLL, D. Tramway book-keeping and accounts . . . *London*, 1902. pp. xi, 226. [*The Accountants' Library*, vol. 15.]   BM

3460 FRASER, J. English railways statistically considered. *London*, 1903. pp. xii, 279, 12. BM
Criticisms of railway accounting methods and of management; pp. 175–235, suggestions for increased safety, with illus. Includes tables of accounts of L.B. & S.C. and of Midland railways for 1900.

3461 SHEFFIELD, G. H. Problems in transportation by rail. (Presidential address, Institu-

tion of Civil Engineers, 12 November, 1903.) *London*, 1903. pp. 24, with 18 illus. & tables. ICE
Economic aspects of rolling stock capacity, etc.

3462 WALL, W. W. British railway finance: a guide to investors. *London*, 1902. pp. xii, 410. BM
An analysis of the financial state of each of the main-line companies,
—— 2nd edn. 'How to invest in railways.' *London*, 1903. pp. xii, 410. BM

3463 RAILWAY expenditure under Abstract 'A'; being a course of lectures delivered to the railway students of the London School of Economics. By a Railway Officer. [*London*, 1905.] pp. 92, with 4 financial charts. LSE

3464 GRINLING, C. H. British railways as business enterprises. *In* 'British industries: a series of general reviews for business men and students', edited by W. J. Ashley. *London*, 1903, pp. 150–72. BM
Railways as commercial undertakings.
—— 2nd edn. *London*, 1907. pp. 150–72. BM

3465 MACCOLL, D. Tramway book-keeping and accounts simplified. *London*, 1907. pp. vii, 44. BM

3466 SOWRAY, J. R. British railway finance; with special reference to capital charges. *London*, 1907. pp. 25. BM
Criticism of railway finance and accounting methods based on a study of Board of Trade Returns from 1890–1906. Addressed to shareholders.

3467 STEVENS, W. J. British railway extravagance. *London*, [1907.] pp. 24. [*Popular Financial Booklets*, no. 36.] LSE
Reprint, *Financial Review of Reviews*, December 1907.

3468 ANDERSON, A. C. Digest on railway accounts . . . based upon notes made during a study of Mr. J. A. Fisher's well-known work, 'Railway accounts and finance from an accountant's standpoint'. *London*, 1908. pp. 93. BM

3469 WILLIAMS, S. C. S. The economics of railway transport. *London*, 1909. pp. x, 308. BM

3470 ACWORTH, W. M. Railroad accounting in America vs. England. *New York*, 1910. pp. 12. LSE
Reprint, *North American Review*, March 1910.

3471 BROWNE, J. H. B. *and* THEOBALD, H. S. The law of railway companies. *London*, 1881. pp. lv, 859. BM
—— 2nd edn. *London*, 1888. pp. lv, 916. BM
—— 3rd, *London*, 1899. pp. lxi, 1036. BM
—— 4th, *London*, 1911. pp. lxxxvii, 1285. BM

3472 LOMAS, A. D. Railway economics: the Finance Act, compulsory acquisition of land, and taxation of railways. *London*, [1911]. pp. 14. LSE
Six lectures delivered October–November 1911 at Manchester University, and reprinted from the *Railway News*.

3473 FISHER, J. A. Railway accounts and finance: an exposition of the principles and practice of railway accounting in all its branches. *London*, 1891. pp. xvi, 514. BM
—— 2nd edn. *London*, 1893. pp. xvi, 542. BM
—— 3rd, *London*, 1911. pp. xl, 588. RC
—— 4th, *London*, 1912. pp. xl, 588. IT

3474 M'DERMOTT, F. The constitution of railway companies: their financial and legal status. *In* 'Modern railway working' edited by John Macaulay. vol. 1, 1912. pp. 69–126, with illus. & tables. BM

3475 POLE, F. J. C. *and* MILNE, J. The economics of passenger traffic. *In* 'Modern railway working', edited by John Macaulay. vol. 7, 1913. pp. 161–236, with illus. & tables. BM

3476 NEWHOOK, A. E. Railway accounts and finance: Railway Companies (Accounts & Returns) Act, 1911. *London*, [1914.] pp. xix, 128. BM
The Act is reproduced in full.

3477 RAILWAY companies and profit sharing. *In* 'Jubilee of the Railway News, 1864–1914.' *London: Railway News*, [1914.] pp. 195–9. BM

3478 JARVIS, W. H. Railway stores methods and problems. *London*, 1918. pp. ii, 116. BM
Includes accounting.

3479 REED, L. C. W. Accounting in respect of railway goods, mineral, cattle traffic, and miscellaneous parcels traffic, carriage paid. *Carmarthen*, [*c*. 1918.] pp. 7. BM
Suggested reform for simpler accounting.

3480 WANG, CHING-CH'UN. Legislative regulation of railway finance in England. *Urbana*,
b 1918. pp. 196, with a bibliography. [*University of Illinois Studies in the Social Sciences*, vol. 7, nos. 1 & 2.] BM

3481 LEA, J. W. Britain's decline: her economic disorder and its only remedy. *Birmingham*, 1922. pp. xiv, 79, with tables & a graph. BM
pp. 1–33, Depreciation of British home investments. Includes facts and figures relating to British railway investments. The problem of low output per man.

3482 FINANCIAL TIMES. Special Railway Supplement, 1st January, 1923. pp. 36. RC
Articles on current railway financial situation.

3483 MARSH, S. B. N. Organisation and administration of the Tramways Department. *London*, 1923. pp. 163.   BM
Accounts.

3484 KNOOP, D. Outlines of railway economics. *London*, 1913. pp. xvi, 274.   BM
—— 2nd edn. *London*, 1923. pp. xxviii, 274.   BM

3485 HOMBERGER, L. Wirtschaftsführung und Finanzwesen bei den englischen Eisenbahnen. *Berlin*, 1928. pp. viii, 64, with tables & forms.   LSE

3486 WAGSTAFF, H. W. An enquiry into the method of preparation of periodical returns on the railways of Great Britain, Egypt and Palestine. *Calcutta*, 1929. pp. 50. [*Government of India Central Publications Branch. Technical Paper* no. 275.]   LSE

3487 WOOD, W. V. *and* SHERRINGTON, C. E. R. The railway industry of Great Britain, 1927. *London: Royal Economic Society*, January 1929. pp. 26[27]. [*Memorandum* no. 11.]   BM
General situation since 1923; financial results and miscellaneous statistics, including thirty-four tables.

3488 NEWTON, C. H. Railway accounts: their statutory form and the practice of railway companies to give effect thereto. *London*, 1930. pp. ix, 245.   BM

3489 FENELON, K. G. Transport and communications. *London*, 1931. pp. ix, 101.   BM
pp. 26–48, Economics of rail transport.

3490 HARRINGTON, J. L. Economic aspects of railway electrification. [*London*, 1931.] pp. 11.   IT
Paper, London Association of Foremen Engineers, 7 Feb., 1931. Previously read to Institute of Transport Metropolitan Graduate & Student Society, 4 Nov., 1930.
Initial expenditure; running costs; traffic receipts.

3491 ACWORTH, W. M. Elements of railway economics. *Oxford*, 1905. pp. 159.   BM
—— new edn. by W. M. Acworth and W. T. Stephenson. *Oxford*, 1924. pp. 216.   BM
—— another edn. *Oxford*, 1932. pp. 216. LSE
—— German edns., 'Grundzüge der Eisenbahnwirtschaftslehre.' 1907. 1926.

3492 DAWSON, P. The economics of railway electrification. pp. 16. *Typescript.*   IT
Paper, City of Birmingham Commercial College, 24 Feb., 1932.
Economic advantages.

3493 FOX, W. *and others.* Ten years of railway finance: a study of the railways of Great Britain; their 'watered' capital, their directors, earnings, reserves and dividends, road transport interests, and the position of the railway workers. *London: Labour Research Department*, 1932. pp. 23.   BM
Proposed reduction in railwaymen's wages shown against an analysis of railway finances.

3494 FINANCIAL and operating results of the British group railways in 1932. *London: Railway Gazette*, 1933. pp. 32.   IT
Supplement *Railway Gazette*, 12 May, 1933.
Analysis of published reports.

3495 FOX, W. Seven years of railway finance, 1928–1934; with three charts. *London: Labour Research Department*, 1935. pp. 31.   BM
Railway finance in relation to railwaymen's wages. A revision of this author's *Ten years of railway finance* (1932).

3496 PEARSON, A. J. Economic aspects of railway signalling. pp. 14. *Printed. Advance copy.*   IT
Paper, Institution of Railway Signal Engineers, 10 April, 1935.
Relationship between cost of signalling and traffic receipts.

3497 GLEDHILL, A. H. Application of the theory of relativity to transport. *Halifax: Municipal Tramways & Transport Association*, February 1936. pp. 19, with 6 charts. [*Pamphlet* no. 5.]   IT
The inadequacy of a mere 'cost per mile' basis for estimating the cost of alternative forms of road transport. Varying conditions require all relevant factors to be brought into account.

3498 NEWLANDS, A. The British railways . . . *London: Longmans*, 1936. pp. 134.   BM
'An attempt to dissect and analyse the cost of working the British railways for one year (1933) by the use of a common denominator, and to co-relate such cost with the volume of work done and the revenue earned.'

3499 RAILWAY RESEARCH SERVICE. The main-line railways of Great Britain, 1923–1937. *Westminster*, June 1938. pp. 60.   IT
'Private. For official use only.'
Detailed statistical review in fifty-three tables.

3500 STEVENS, W. J. The future of British railways: a plea for co-operation . . . *London. P. S. King & Son*, 1938. pp. xiii, 101.   BM
Co-operation between all railway interests essential to ensure successful future of the railways.
pp. 62 to end, financial position of the four main line companies; with tables, 1929–1936.

3501 WATERS, W. L. Rationalization of British railways; presented before the American Society of Mechanical Engineers, Railroad Division, Metropolitan Section, New York, May 11, 1938. *New York*, 1938. pp. 9. TUC
A study of the results of the 1921 amalgamations upon railway economy, management, and operation.

3502 FENELON, K. G. British railways today. London: Nelson, 1939. pp. 187 with plates. [*Discussion Books*, no. 39.] BM
Includes chapters on state control, railways and the public, railway operation, finance, and railways *versus* roads.

3503 INTERNATIONAL CHAMBER OF COMMERCE. Commission on Rail Transport, Paris, 1939. Meeting of February 13. Documents 6823, 6742, 6743, 6745, 6746, & 6750. *Paris*, 1939. *Reproduced typescript.* IT
Finance and organisation. Methods in various countries compared.

3504 BONAVIA, M. R. Some aspects of railway capital. pp. 21. *Typescript.* IT
Paper, Institute of Transport, Yorkshire Section, Leeds, 15 Nov., 1944.
Finance simply explained; including a survey of its development.

3505 BRADLEY, W. The present aspect of finance in municipal passenger transport. *London: Municipal Passenger Transport Association*, [1946.] pp. 18, with tables. IT

3506 WEBSTER, H. C. Railway motive power . . . London: Hutchinson, 1952. pp. 310, with 50 plates & 57 drawings. BM
Modern locomotives of all kinds related to problems of railway economics.

3507 BONAVIA, M. R. The economics of transport. *London: Nisbet*, 1936. pp. x, 202. BM
Includes railways.
—— New edn. *London*, 1947. pp. xiii, 202. LSE
—— another edn. *London*, 1949. pp. xvi, 202. LSE
—— another edn. *London*, 1954. pp. xii, 219. BM

3508 WILSON, R. Finance in public administration, with particular reference to passenger transport. *London: British Transport Commission*, 1954. pp. 21. IT

3509 MILNE, A. M. The economics of inland transport. *London, Pitman*, 1955. pp. vii, 292, with a bibliography. BM
Includes sections on railway working costs.
—— rev. ed. *London*, 1960. pp. vii, 292. BM
—— 2nd edn. By J. C. Laight. *London*, 1963. pp. vii, 288. BM

*3510 SCHUMER, L. A. The elements of transport. *London: Butterworth*, 1955. pp. xii, 196. BM
An introduction to transport economics and operation, including railways.

3511 TAIT, A. W. Costs and charges. pp. 15. *Reproduced typescript.* IT
Paper, L.S.E. Railway Students' Assoc., 26 Jan., 1955.
The relationship between costs and charges in railway economics.

3512 BRITISH TRANSPORT COMMISSION. Reassessment of B.T.C. finances: report to Minister of Transport: subsidy not required: big financial benefits expected from railway modernisation. *London*, Oct. 1956. pp. 7. *Reproduced typescript.* IT

3513 WILSON, R. Economics of transport, with special reference to road–rail questions in the United Kingdom; presented to the British Association for the Advancement of Science, Sections F & G, York, 8th September 1959. *York*, 1959. pp. 41[42]. BR

F 1 RATES, CHARGES, FARES, AND TOLLS

For social aspects see **K 2**
For this subject from the viewpoint of the user (consignor) see **K 4**

Historical

3514 EDMONDSON, J. B. To whom are we indebted for the railway ticket system? *Manchester*, [1878.] pp. 19. RC
Reprinted from the *English Mechanic and World of Science* of 2 August, 1878.
Thomas Edmondson.

3515 LAWSON, W. R. British railways: a financial and commercial survey. *London*, 1913. pp. xxxii, 320. BM
pp. 161–217, Rates.

3516 DAVIS, W. J. *and* WATERS, A. W. Tickets and passes of Great Britain and Ireland . . . described with occasional notes. *Leamington Spa*, 1922. pp. viii, 347, [6.] BM
pp. 325–30, Railway tickets and passes.

3517 SHEPPARD, T. Yorkshire tramway tokens and counters . . . Hull: *Hull Museum*, 1922. pp. 139–44. [*Hull Museum Publications*, no. 127.] BM
Reprinted from *Transactions of the Yorkshire Numismatic Society*, vol. 2, pt. 4, 1922.

3518 PINDER, R. W. Transport by railway: some practical elements of rate making and the evolution of railway rates in Great Britain. *London*, [1924.] pp. 20, with tables. RC

3519 HADLEY, A. T. Principles and methods of rate regulation . . . *New Haven*, 1927. pp. [417]–432. LSE
Reprinted from the *Yale Review* for April 1927.
In Gt. Britain and the U.S.A.; an historical review.

3520 LEEMANN, E. Die Personenfahrpreise der englischen Eisenbahnen; Dissertation der rechts- und staatswissenschaftlichen Fakultät der Universität Zürich . . . vorgelegt von E. Leemann. *Berlin*, [1931.] pp. xii, 144. LSE
Reprinted from *Archiv für Eisenbahnwesen*, 1931. Hefte 1–3.
A detailed historical and descriptive analysis.

3521 HERDMAN, E. F. Transport tokens, tickets, passes and badges of Great Britain & Ireland. *Bishop Auckland*, 1932. pp. 33. BM

3522 GARDINER, R. S. History of the, railroad ticket. *Boston: Rand Avery Supply Co.*, 1938. pp. 21. IT
Printed for private circulation: offset from plates of the original edition, 1898.
pp. 4–10, Edmondson and early British railway tickets and issuing methods.

3523 BEZZANT, R. Newspaper carriage and parcels traffic on British railways. *London: Dawson*, [1951.] pp. xi, 140. BM
The development of newspaper railway carriage charges and parcel rates.

3524 PIKE, J. R. Charges as a factor in inland transport. pp. 16. *Typescript.* IT
Paper, Institute of Transport, Irish Section, 3 Nov., 1953.
Historical background to the pattern of transport charges; the present position and the Transport Act, 1953; changes in the basis and control of railway rates.

Contemporaneous

3525 DEGRAND, P. P. F. An address by P. P. F. Degrand on the advantages of low fares and low rates of freight, practically illustrated by the deep researches of the British, French and Belgian governments. *Boston*, 1840. pp. 39. BM

3526 WILKINSON, W. A. The toll question on railways exemplified in the case of the Croydon and Greenwich companies. *London*, 1841. pp. 16. BM
This pamphlet is discussed in *Railway travelling and the toll question* (anon.), 1843.

3527 SIDNEY, S. Speed on railways considered in a commercial point of view. *London*, 1847. pp. 22. BM
A plea for more cheap, frequent, slower, stopping trains and fewer fast ones. The G.W. Rly. criticised.

3528 RATES of carriage to and from Liverpool: report of the proceedings of a public meeting of the inhabitants of the Borough of Liverpool held in the Corn Exchange . . . March 2nd . . . *Liverpool*, 1865. pp. 40[41]. BM
Resolved 'that the rates now charged . . . are excessive'.

3529 HAGGARD, F. T. Railway facts and lower fares. *London*, 1869. pp. 31. BM
Reasons against lowering of fares.

3530 HAUGHTON, B. The paying and the non-paying weights pulled by the locomotive engine in 1867, as shown from the statistical railway tables published by the Board of Trade . . . considered in connection with the existing charges for the carriage of passengers and goods. [*London*, 1869.] pp. 14. BM

3531 IMRAY, J. British railways as they are and as they might be: suggestions as to cheap and uniform fares with increased and guaranteed dividends. *London*, 1869. pp. 32. BM

3532 JONES, G. W. G. W. Jones's plan for universal penny railways, by the application of turnpikes to railways: a practical plan, suitable to the genius of the people, and calculated to satisfy the locomotive requirements of the country. *London*, 1869. pp. viii, 55. BM
Nationalization, and a toll system with turnstiles at entrances to stations.

3533 BRANDON, R. Railways and the public: how to make railways remunerative to the shareholders, beneficial to the public and profitable to the state. *London*, 1868. pp. 22. BM
Any distance for the same fare.
—— 2nd edn. *London*, 1869. pp. 31. BM
—— 7th, *London*, 1870. pp. 15. LSE
—— 8th, *London*, 1871. pp. 8. BM

3534 CARTER, S. Railway legislation: the railway companies and the Railway Commissioners: proposed transfer to the Commissioners of the power of fixing rates on railways, and repeal of existing parliamentary rates. Letters and correspondence. *Westminster*, 1874. pp. 34. BM
Nine letters, mostly by S. Carter, on W. H. Wait's motion for increasing the powers of the Railway Commissioners.

3535 JONES, G. W. The million on the rail: a few statistics showing the expediency of encouraging the third-class passenger to travel: dedicated to the shareholders of the Midland, London & North Western, and Great Northern railway companies. *London*, 1874. pp. 19. BM
On Allport's fares reform on the Midland, with tables revealing receipts of these three companies for each class, 1866–73.

3536 REITZENSTEIN, E. Über einige Verwaltungseinrichtungen und das Tarifwesen auf den Eisenbahnen Englands. *Berlin*, 1876. pp. v, 212. LSE

3537 LIVERPOOL—JOINT COMMITTEE OF THE CITY COUNCIL, DOCK BOARD, & MERCANTILE ASSOCIATIONS. Railway rates and railway administration as affecting the trade of Liverpool: report of the meeting of the deputation from the Joint Committee . . . with the directors of the railway companies

who have termini in Liverpool, held at Euston Station . . . 8 March 1881, together with tables of inequalities of rates . . . *Liverpool*, 1881. pp. 57.   BM
'The excessive rates of railway carriage to and from Liverpool.'

3538 CONDER, F. R. The actual and the possible cost of conveyance between Manchester and Liverpool. *London*, 1882. pp. 29–44.
                                             ICE
A Manchester Statistical Society reprint.
'Fifty years after the opening of the Liverpool & Manchester Railway it costs more to convey a bale of cotton . . . than it did in 1829.'

3539 An ENQUIRY into the terminal charges of railway companies. *London*, 1882. pp. 40. BM

3540 MINOT, R. S. Railway travel in Europe and America; with 25 tables of recent and novel statistics of journeys, speeds, fares, etc., for travellers and others. *Boston*, 1882. pp. 28.   BM

3541 HORROCKS, J. Railway rates. *London*, 1883. pp. 83, with tables.   BM

3542 RAILWAY & CANAL TRADERS' ASSOCIATION—PARLIAMENTARY DEPARTMENT. Report . . . on Railway Bills introduced in Session 1883. *London*, 1883. pp. 16.   LSE
Signed 'W. A. Hunter'.
Rates of new railway companies.

3543 POPE, J. B. Railway rates and Radical rule: being a series of practical questions vitally affecting the interests of traders and agriculturists throughout the country, and suggested to them for consideration as electors. *London*, 1884. pp. 364.   BM

3544 HAGGARD, F. T. Railway fares; or, Penny wise, pound foolish . . . *London*, 1885. pp. 7.   LSE
The relation between fares of 1st, 2nd and 3rd classes and of the respective receipts. Includes two tables of the Midland Rly. for the years 1865 to 1884.

3545 HUNTER, W. A. The new railway rates Bills: report and analysis; published by the secretary to the Railway and Canal Traders' Association. *London*, 1885. pp. 37.   BM
—— rev. edn. *London*, [1885.] pp. 40.   LSE

3546 MANCHESTER CORPORATION *and* LANCASHIRE & CHESHIRE CORPORATIONS. Railway rates and charges. Proposed alteration of rates and charges, and imposition of terminal charges, by nine of the leading railway companies of England: report on the Bills by Sub-Committee on Proposed Alterations in the Law. *Manchester*, 1885. pp. 61.   BM

3547 RAILWAY rates and charges Bills: three articles on the proposed railway legislation:

revised and reprinted from the 'Northern Echo'. *Darlington*, 1885. pp. 22.   BM
Analysis of Bills proposed for the 1885 Session.

3548 SAMUELSON, B. A report to C. M. Norwood, president of the Association of the Chambers of Commerce of the United Kingdom, on the railway goods tariffs of Germany Belgium and Holland compared with those of this country. *Birmingham*, [1885.] pp. 41.
                                             ICE
pp. 24 to end, tables of commodities.

3549 BOON, W. The ABC Railway Parcels Rate Guide versus rates by parcels post, showing at a glance a saving of about 50 per cent in the charges by railway companies compared with parcels post . . . *London*, [1886.] pp. 28.   BM
Various editions in 1886 and 1887.

3550 GRIERSON, J. Railway rates, English and foreign. *London*, 1886. pp. viii, 208, lxxii. BM

3551 RAILWAY RATES COMMITTEE. Railway rates. Joint deputation of the Railway Rates Committee and the Conference of Municipal Corporations of Lancashire and Cheshire to . . . A. J. Mundella, M.P., President of the Board of Trade . . . *London*, 1886. pp. 29.   LSE

3552 VENABLES, G. S. Railway and Canal Traffic Bill. Speech delivered . . . at a special meeting of Great Western Railway proprietors held at the Paddington Station, April 5, 1886. *London*, 1886. pp. 15.   NLC
Protest against the Bill, which proposes Board of Trade control over the fixing of rates.

3553 GILES, R. W. Railway passenger traffic: a few words to railway passengers and railway proprietors. By one of themselves. *London*, 1887. pp. 22.   BM
Suggests a broader basis for passenger classes.

3554 BUTTERWORTH, A. K. A treatise on the law relating to rates and traffic on railways and canals, with special reference to the Railway and Canal Traffic Act, 1888, and an appendix of statutes, rules, etc. *London*, 1889. pp. xxxii, 235, 108.   BM

3555 BUTTERWORTH, A. K. The practice of the Railway and Canal Commission: being the Railway and Canal Commission Rules, 1889, and the Railway and Canal Traffic Acts, 1854, 1873, and 1888; with notes and index and a compendium of the practice. *London*, 1889. pp. v, 86, 79.   BM
Issued as a supplement to this author's *Treatise on the law relating to rates and traffic* (1889).

3556 COTSWORTH, M. B. Railway and Canal Traffic Act, 1888. Proposed parliamentary classifications of goods and minerals . . . *London*, 1889.   BM

3557 GYE, P. New law of rates and charges . . . under the Railway Traffic Act, 1888. *London*, 1889. pp. vi, 101.　　　　　BM

3558 HUNTER, W. A. The Railway and Canal Traffic Act, 1888: part 1, an exposition of Section 24 of the Act. *London*, 1889. pp. xv, 212.　　　　　BM
　　Cover title, *Railway rates*.

3559 RICHARDS, H. C. *and* MACGEAGH, B. S. F. A Popular Manual of the law of railway rates . . . *London*, [1889.] pp. 134[142].　　BM

3560 BROWNE, J. H. B. The Railway and Canal Traffic Act, 1888. Hearing of objections to revised classifications of merchandise traffic and schedules of maximum rates and charges proposed by various railway companies . . . Speech . . . reprinted from the official minutes for the Lancashire and Cheshire Conference on Railway Rates and Charges. *Manchester*, [1890.] pp. 191.　　LSE

3561 GOMEL, C. Les Droits de l'État sur les tarifs de chemins de fer en Angleterre et aux États Unis. *Paris*, 1891. pp. 28.　　BM

3562 A ZONE system of passenger fares: its advantages to the railway companies, shareholders, and general public; with tables of fares and distances. *London*, 1891. pp. 55.　　　　　BM
　　The preface signed 'H'.
　　Each station the centre of a series of concentric zones.

3563 MANSION HOUSE ASSOCIATION ON RAILWAY TRAFFIC. Report on the nine Railway (Rates & Charges) Order Confirmation Acts, 1891. *London*, 1892. pp. 39. BM
　　Advantages and disadvantages to traders.

3564 DARLINGTON, H. R. The railway rates and the carriage of merchandise by railway. *London*, 1893. pp. xxxvi, 581.　　BM

3565 DAVIES, J. Railway rates, charges and regulations of the United Kingdom: being a summary of the Railway Rates and Charges (Order Confirmation) Acts, 1891 and 1892. *London*, [1893.] pp. 234.　　BM

3566 MACEWEN, R. How should railway fares be charged? The telescope system. *London*, 1893. pp. 8.　　BM
　　Maximum fare for shortest distance.

3567 TABLES for ascertaining the charges on merchandise by railway. *London*, 1893. pp. 121.　　BM
　　Rate book.

3568 DODSHON, E. Memorandum on maximum railway rates for coal. *London*, 1896. pp. x, 57.
　　　　　BM

3569 WILLIAMS, R. P. Railway rates and terminal charges. *London*, 1896. pp. 44.　　ICE
　　Reprinted from the *Journal of the Royal Statistical Society*, vol. 59, pt. 3, Sept. 1896.
　　Contains many tables and charts relating to income, expenditure and traffic on the L. & N.W. Rly.

3570 HODGSON, W. A new method of booking parcels, fish, horses, carriages, dogs, excess luggage, etc. *Newcastle-upon-Tyne*, 1897. pp. 20.　　　　　BM
　　Hodgson's type-numbered debit label system; with specimen forms.

3571 BUTTERWORTH, A. K. The law relating to maximum rates and charges on railways; being a treatise on the Railway Rates and Charges Order Confirmation Acts, 1891 to 1896 and the Railway and Canal Traffic Act, 1894. *London*, 1897. pp. xi, 113, 232,[14.] BM
　　The latter portion is an analysis of the Acts of 1891 and 1892, with lists of all railway companies affected, and other tables, etc.

—— another edn. *London*, 1898. pp. 177.
　　　　　BM

3572 MARTIN, W. B. Parcels and cloak room tickets: case and accounts. *Nottingham*, 1904. pp. 15.　　　　　BM

3573 BEMROSE, W. & SON. Bemrose's Railway Rate Book of the stations, sidings and collieries on the English railways (with principal Scotch and Irish stations) alphabetically arranged. 4th edn. *London*, [1893?] 2 vols.
　　　　　HRL
—— 6th edn. *London*, 1905. pp. xvii, 513. BM

3574 RATES charged by British railway companies in respect of the carriage of foreign and colonial farm dairy and market garden produce: the railway companies' case; reprinted with additions and alterations from the 'Railway News'. *London: Railway News*, [1905?] pp. 40.　　　　　LSE

3575 ACWORTH, W. M. The railways and the traders: a sketch of the railway rates question in theory and practice. *London*, 1891. pp. 14, 378.　　　　　BM
—— Popular edn. *London*, 1906. pp. xvi, 378.　　　　　BM

3576 PRATT, E. A. Railways and their rates, with an appendix on the British canal problem. *London*, 1905. pp. ix, 361, with plates.　　BM
—— 2nd edn. *London*, 1906. pp. vii, 361. BM

3577 WAGHORN, T. Agriculture and railway rates. *London: Central Associated Chambers of Agriculture*, 1906. pp. 46.　　LSE
　　Comparative rates for railway transport of home and foreign meat and fruit.

3578 FITTON, J. H. Railway rates and how to check them. *Huddersfield*, 1907. pp. 61. BM
　　A handbook for traders.

3579 RUSSELL, H. H. Railway rates and charges orders: the law under the Railway Rates and Charges Orders Confirmation Acts, 1891 and 1892, and the Railway and Canal Traffic Act, 1894. *London*, 1907. pp. xvi, 160.   BM

3580 HARBERT, C. L. Railway rates from Dundee. *Edinburgh*, 1909. pp. 384.   BM

3581 HORROCKS, J. Railway rates: the method of calculating equitable rates and charges for merchandise carried on railways . . . *London*, 1909. pp. viii, 485.   BM

3582 RAILWAY CLEARING HOUSE. List of Ticket Nippers in use by the railway and steamship companies. [*London*,] March 1909. pp. 54.   RC
'Private and not for publication.'
Code signs and letters for stations.

3583 COTSWORTH, M. B. Railway maximum rates and charges. *London*, 1892. pp. 130. BM
A pocket reference work, with tables.
—— 2nd edn. *London*, 1898. pp. 177, xvi. BM
—— 3rd, *London*, 1904. pp. 191, xvi.   BM
—— 4th, *London*, 1910. pp. iv, 208.   BM

3584 COUTTS, W. B. Railway reform. Railway Companies (Accounts & Returns) Bill, 1910: first reading, Wednesday June 8 . . . second reading Wednesday, June 15. *London*, 1910. pp. 35.   LSE
'A great opportunity for reform is lost by the Bill, which does not go far enough with reforms.'
Memorandum of Evidence given by W. B. Coutts, M.P., before the Board of Trade Departmental Committee on Railway Accounts & Statistical Returns. An eleventh-hour plea, dated June 13.

3585 LISSENDEN, G. B. The Railway Trader's Guide to forwarding, receiving, railway charges, and all other matters incidental to transactions with the railway companies. *London*, 1910. pp. viii, 236.

3586 MARRIOTT, H. The fixing of rates and fares. *London*, 1908. pp. 85, with tables.   BM
—— 2nd edn. *London*, 1910. pp. 85.   IT

3587 LISTER, H. L. The principles of railway goods rates. *In* 'Modern railway working' edited by John Macaulay. vol. 7, 1913. pp. 131–60, with tables.   BM

3588 ARNOLD, W. C. Royal railways with uniform rates: a proposal for amalgamation of railways with the General Post Office and adoption of uniform fares and rates for any distance. *London*, 1914. pp. 61.   BM

3589 JEPSON, W. A. Railway companies' rates. *In* 'Jubilee of the Railway News, 1864–1914.' *London: Railway News*, [1914.] pp. 89–98.   BM

3590 TRAVIS, C. Railway rates and traffic: translated from the third (1907) edition of C. Colson's 'Transports et tarifs.' . . . *London*, 1914. pp. viii, 195.   BM
Principles of rate determination.

3591 BUREAU OF RAILWAY ECONOMICS [Washington]. Comparison of railway freight rates in the United States [with] the principal countries of Europe . . . *Washington*, 1915. pp. 131.   LSE
Tables.

3592 RAILWAY charges and prices of provisions. *London: Railway News*, Sept. 1916. pp. 8.   LSE
'Percentage of cost attributable to transport by rail is negligible.'

3593 JACKSON, D. C. *and* MACGRATH, D. J. Street railway fares. *New York*, 1917.   BM
pp. 112–25, Some comparisons of American and British fare systems.

3594 The COASTING trade: what must be done at once to keep the coasting services and the smaller ports going? [*London*,] 1920. pp. 6   LSE
Asking for the raising of railway rates to allow coastal traffic to compete on an equal footing.

3595 PICK, F. The fixing of a fare. [*London*, 1920.] pp. 14.   LSE
Lecture, London School of Economics, 18 Nov., 1920.
General principles related to social, economic and geographic aspects of London.

3596 GREAT NORTHERN RLY. Workmen's tickets: a résumé of the practices governing the issue of workmen's tickets on the Great Northern Railway from the commencement of their issue on March 1st, 1871 to September 1920. [1920.] pp. 9[11]. 11 la. sheets. *Typescript*.   LSE

3597 GENERAL increase of goods rates, 1915–1920. *London: Great Western Rly.*, Jan. 1921. pp. 30. [*Great Western Pamphlets*, no. 6.]   BR
The case for increased rates to meet higher running costs.

3598 STANLEY, A. H. The problem of the fare. *London*, 1921. pp. 19, with tables.
Reprint, *Nineteenth Century & After*, June 1921.

3599 JONES, G. G. Railway Rates Tribunal: jurisdiction and practice. *London*, [1922.] pp. 120.   BM
Powers of the Tribunal under the Railways Act (1921) explained. Includes text of part III, 'Railway Charges' and the Tribunal's Rules of Procedure.

3600 THE BRISTOL Railway Rate Book, comprising all class and special rates between Bristol and about 6,000 stations in Great Britain, Ireland and Continental ports. *Birmingham*, 1922. pp. 190.   BM

3601 ROCHESTER, A. E. Railway rates and the cost of living: a defence of the enemy: the real railway charges. *London: Great Wes-*

tern Rly., 1922. pp. 14. [*Great Western Pamphlets*, no. 10.] BR
Reprinted from the *Railway Review*, 8 December, 1922.

3602 RAILWAY rates and charges: effect of reduction on companies' financial position. *London: Great Western Rly.*, June 1923. pp. 20[23]. [*Great Western Pamphlets*, no. 12.] BR

3603 GRIFFITHS, R. P. The Railways Act, 1921: a survey of the work of the Railway Rates Tribunal. *London*, 1925. pp. 72. BM

3604 BURTT, P. Railway rates: principles and problems. *London*, 1926. pp. vii, 167. BM

3605 ORIGIN of the flat rate addition on rates for the conveyance of coal class traffic. *London: Great Western Rly.*, Feb. 1926. pp. 9. [*Great Western Information*, no. 1, 1926.] BR

3606 FORD, E. South Wales shipment coal rates. *London: Great Western Rly.*, Dec. 1927. pp. 23, with tables. [*Great Western Pamphlets*, [no. 2?] 1927.] BR

3607 GORST, E. M. A Guide to the Railway Rates Tribunal. *London*, 1927. pp. xv, 316, with a bibliography. BM

3608 RAILWAY & SHIPPING JOURNAL. Tables for calculating revised railway rates applicable between places in Great Britain, from 1*d*. to £5, officially compiled on February 1st, 1927 . . . *Birmingham*, [1927.] pp. 16. LSE

*3609 RAILWAY CLEARING HOUSE. The new railway rates: how they affect the cost of living. *London*, March 1920. pp. 14. LSE
Tables showing the negligible effect of increased rates on retail prices.
—— 'Railway rates: how they affect the cost of food.' *London*, 1923. pp. 19. TUC
—— 'Railway rates: how they affect the cost of living.' *London*, Jan. 1925. pp. 21. LSE
—— 'Railway rates: how little they affect the cost of food.' *London*, Feb. 1927. pp. 20. LSE

3610 GOOD, E. T. From pit to port. *London: Great Western Rly.*, 1928. pp. 18. [*Great Western Pamphlets*, no. 6, 1928.] BR
Some misconceptions regarding the apparent high cost of rail charges when compared with foreign railways. An explanation to users.

3611 METROPOLITAN CONFERENCE. General instructions and charges in respect of warehouse rent, wharfage and fixed spaces. January 1928. *London*, 1928. pp. 29. LSE

3612 METROPOLITAN CONFERENCE. Scales of charges and arrangements in London for the collection and delivery of traffic and other services, 1st January, 1928. *London*, 1928. pp. 78. LSE
Instructions to railway staff.

3613 METROPOLITAN CONFERENCE. Scales of weights for various traffic forwarded from London . . . *London*, 1929. pp. 30. LSE
'Private and for use of companies' servants only.'

3614 GREENWOOD, C. Reduced railway fares as a means of increasing railway travel and revenue. pp. 20. 1931. *Typescript.* LSE

3615 PIGOU, A. C. Economics of welfare. *London*, 1920. pp. xxxvi, 976, with bibliogr. notes. BM
pp. 256–82, Railway rates.
—— 2nd edn. *London*, 1924. pp. xxviii, 783. BM
—— 3rd, *London*, 1929. pp. xxxi, 835. BM
—— 4th, *London*, 1932. pp. xxxi, 837. BM

3616 SIMS, E. A. Note on the methods by which the provisions regarding rates and fares embodied in the English Railways Act of 1921 were framed . . . *Calcutta*, 1933. pp. 23. [*Government of India Central Publications Branch. Technical Paper* no. 285.] LSE

3617 BIRD, C. K. Recent developments in railway rates. *Stratford (London): L. & N.E. Rly.*, [1935.] pp. 11. IT
Paper, Manchester & District Traffic Association, 17 Oct., 1935.

3618 WILLIAMSON, A. Tickets in rolls, books or pads. *Ashton-under-Lyne*, [*c.* 1937.] pp. 56. IT
A ticket and ticket-punch manufacturer's catalogue including railway and tramway tickets, with illustrations in colour.

3619 SCHROIFF, F. Die Eisenbahntariftheorien
b in Deutschland, England und Amerika: eine kritische Betrachtung. *Münster*, 1938. pp. 58[59], with bibliogr. notes & bibliography of 9 pages. [*Verkehrswissenschaftliche Forshungen aus dem Verkehrs-Seminar an den Westf. Wilhelms-Universität zu Münster, I.W.* Heft 13.] LSE

3620 WIENER, L. Passenger tickets; abstracted from the Bulletin of the International Railway Congress Association. *London: Railway Gazette*, [1939.] pp. xxix, 357, with many illus. BM

3621 SCOTT, W. G. An aspect of the British 'Railways Act', 1921. *In* 'Essays in transportation in honour of W. T. Jackman', edited by H. A. Innis. *Toronto*, 1941. pp. 119–44, with bibliogr. notes. BM
The maintenance of the standard revenue by the Railway Rates Tribunal.

3622 BETT, W. H. The theory of fare collection on railways and tramways. *Cricklewood: Light Railway Transport League*, 1945. pp. 64, with 11 plates showing tickets, with notes. BM

3623 BRITISH TRANSPORT COMMISSION. Draft outlines of principles proposed to be embodied in a charges scheme for merchandise traffic. *London*, 1949. pp. 26. TUC

3624 HURCOMB, C. Speech ... Tees-side Chamber of Commerce, Darlington, 28 March, 1950. pp. 11. *Reproduced typescript.* IT
Economic problems of the railways.

3625 LABOUR RESEARCH DEPARTMENT. London fares. *London*, [March 1950.] pp. 15. LSE
Opposition to the B.T.C.'s proposal to raise fares.

3626 WOOD, W. V. Railway charges: efficiency and integration policy. pp. 15[19]. *Reproduced typescript.* IT
Paper, Liverpool Economic & Statistical Society, 1st Dec., 1950.
The relationship and interdependence of these factors.

3627 HAYMAN, A. The foundations of tolls, rates and charges in the development of transport: a paper submitted to the Institute of Transport ... *Manchester*, [1952.] pp. 42. *Typescript.* LSE

3628 EATON, R. J. Mechanization of ticket printing and issue. pp. 13, with 5 la. fold. charts, & tables in text. *Reproduced typescript.* IT
Paper, Operational Research Society, 15 Feb., 1955.

3629 JENSON, A. G. Black Country tram tickets. *London: Ticket & Fare Collection Society*, 1955. pp. 13. *Reproduced typescript.* BM
Mostly concerned with early examples.

3630 BERRY, J. Relating cost, competition and revenue to railway rates. 1956. pp. 25. *Typescript.* IT
Paper, Institute of Transport, April 1956.

3631 BRITISH TRANSPORT COMMISSION. Goods by railway. *London*, 1957. pp. 7. LSE
An outline memorandum on the terms of the Merchandise Charges Scheme, 1957.

3632 BROADBENT, E. G. *and* BETT, W. H. Liverpool Corporation: some notes on tickets and fares ... *London: Ticket & Fare Collection Society*, 1960. pp. 15. *Reproduced typescript.* BM

F2 INTER-RAILWAY RELATIONS

Competition—Co-operation and amalgamation—Running powers and working arrangements—Gauge controversy

For national aspects of gauge controversy see **K**
For the amalgamations of 1923 *see* **B 6**

Historical

3633 SCOTT, W. R. Competition and combination in railway transportation in Great Britain. *Glasgow: Royal Philosophical Society of Glasgow*, 1910. pp. 18. LSE
From the *Proceedings of the R.P.S. of Glasgow*. Read 5 January, 1910.

3634 ROBERTSON, W. A. Combination among railway companies. *London*, 1912. pp. 105. [*Studies in Economics & Political Science*, no. 26.] BM

3635 STEVENS, E. C. English railways: their development and their relation to the state.
b *London*, 1915. pp. xvi, 332, with 2 fold. maps of railways in 1848 and 1872, & many detailed bibliogr. notes. BM
The course of amalgamations in British railway history.

3636 SIMNETT, W. E. Railway amalgamation in Great Britain. *London*, 1923. pp. 276, with
b a bibliography. BM

3637 LEWIN, H. G. Early British railways: a short history of their origin and develop-

c ment, 1801–1844; with 8 illustrations and 8 maps. *London & New York*, 1925. pp. xii, 202, with table of 7 pp. showing railways up to 1844 with their subsequent amalgamations. BM

3638 STAMP, J. C. Industrial and railway amalgamations. *London*, 1928. pp. 31. BM

3639 BROWN, K. Railway amalgamation before 1921: read before the Railway Club on 4th April 1940. pp. 40. *Typescript.* RC

3640 BROWN, K. The Battle of the Gauges: an address given to the Railway Club on 18th March 1944. pp. 36. *Typescript.* RC

3641 BROWN, K. Some sidelights on the War of the Gauges: a paper read before the Railway Club on 4th March 1955. pp. 29. *Typescript.* RC

Contemporaneous

3642 RAILWAYS; their uses and management. *London*, 1842. pp. 65. BM
Combinations and competition. Government control and supervision needed.

3643 The NARROW & wide gauges considered: also, effects of competition and government supervision. *London*, 1845. pp. 36.   BM

3644 The BROAD gauge proved the one best adapted to the commercial wants of the nation, most suited to the increasing traffic of the country, as well as being the safest and speediest means of transit and most eligible investment for capital; in a letter to the . . . Earl of Dalhousie, President of the Board of Trade, etc., etc. By 'An Engineer'. *London*, 1846. pp. 32.   BM

3645 CLARKE, H. Two articles on the ga[u]ge question, and on the performance of the Great Western leviathan locomotive. *London*, 1846. pp. 28.

3646 [COLE, H.] Dialogues of the gauges: reprinted from the 'Railway Record'. *London*, 1846. pp. 23.   BM
Imaginary conversations arranged to conclude in favour of narrow gauge. Broad and narrow gauge 'territories' shown on a map; also points where break of gauge is encountered. (The florid introduction is noteworthy.)

3647 [COLE, H.] Fallacies of the broken gauge. Mr. Lushington's arguments in favour of broad gauge and breaks of gauge refuted; being a reply to the remarks of a late Fellow of Trinity College, Cambridge, on the Report of the Gauge Commissioners. By a Fellow of two Royal Societies. *London*, 1846. pp. 40.   BM
General objections to break of gauge and comments on locomotive experiments on both gauges, with a list of thirty prominent railwaymen in favour of uniform gauge, and four against.
—— 2nd edn. *London*, 1846. pp. 40.   BM

3648 EXPERIMENTAL trip of the 'Great Western' new locomotive passenger engine, made on the 13th June, 1846. Extracted from the 'Morning Herald' of the 15th June. *London: W. Snell*, [1846.] pp. 16.
Written on behalf of broad gauge (i.e. G.W. Rly.) interests.

3649 [COLE. H.] A few of the miseries of the break of gauge at Gloucester, which occasions the shifting of passengers, luggage and goods from one carriage to another. [1846?] s.sh.

3650 A FEW plain reasons why the Gauge Commissioners' Report should receive legislative sanction, illustrated with drawings of ordinary and monster engines for both gauges shewing the capability of the narrow gauge both in power and speed and why the public cannot be called on to pay compensation to the Great Western Railway, etc. By One of the Public. *London*, 1846. pp. 45, 24, with tables & appendix.   BM

3651 [GREAT WESTERN RLY.] Observations on the Report of the Gauge Commissioners presented to Parliament. *Westminster*, 1846. pp. 49   BM
Appendix—G.W. Rly. reports to the Commissioners.

3652 [GREAT WESTERN RLY.] Supplemental observations on the published Evidence and Appendix of the Gauge Commission. *Westminster*, 1846. pp. 33.   BM
Appendix—letters from and to the G.W. Rly., tables and folded plate.

3653 REPLY to 'Observations' of the Great Western Railway Company on the Report of the Gauge Commissioners. *London*, 1846. pp. 75.   BM
Survey of the gauge controversy; the inquiry; attitude of G.W.R. to its findings; the races, etc.; pp. 61–75, Reports to the London & Birmingham Rly.

3654 HARDING, W. The question of the ga[u]ges commercially considered. By A Practical Man. *London*, 1846. pp. 52.   BM
Condemns broad gauge and the Great Western's attitude to the Gauge Commission and its Report.
—— 2nd edn. *London*, 1846. pp. 58.   UL(GL)

3655 HUNT, T. Unity of the iron network, showing how the last argument for the break of gauge competition is at variance with the true interests of the public. *London*, 1846. pp. 31.
'The fallacy of Great Western competition.'
—— 3rd edn. *London*, 1846. pp. 31.

3656 LUSHINGTON, H. The broad and the narrow gauge; or, Remarks on the Report of the Gauge Commissioners. *Westminster*, 1846. pp. 64.   BM
Criticising the decision of the Commissioners. In favour of retaining broad gauge.

3657 LUSHINGTON, H. Postscript on the Gauge Evidence; witnesses and judges. *Westminster*, 1846. pp. 50.   BM
Reaction of broad gauge interests.

3658 MELVILLE, H. S. Narrow gauge speedier than broad gauge railways, as well as cheaper. *London*, 1846. pp. 15, with map.   PC
—— 2nd edn. *London*, 1846. pp. 15.   UL(GL)
—— 3rd, *London*, 1846. pp. 15.   BM

3659 NATIONAL uniformity of gauge: a letter to Lord Dalhousie submitting reasons for preferring the original recommendations of the Gauge Commissioners to the recent proposals of the Board of Trade. *London*, 1846. pp. 16.   BM

3660 POWELL, *Capt.* [H. B. Powell.] A description and explanation of an invention for obviating the difficulties experienced by the break of gauge, and at the same time doing away with the necessity for a central ter-

minus . . . *London*, 1846. pp. 27, with 12 illus.   BM
Upper parts of wagons transferable by means of 'wheels and slides'. See 3799.

*3661 SIDNEY, S. Gauge Evidence. The history and prospects of the railway system illustrated by the Evidence given before the Gauge Commission; with a map. *London*, 1846. pp. xxxix, 400.   BM
A very detailed work.

—— 2nd edn. *London*, 1846. pp. lxxi, 400.   LSE

—— 3rd, *London*, 1846. pp. lxxi, 400.   BR

*3662 SIDNEY, S. A brief history of the gauge system illustrated: being the introductory chapter, revised and corrected, of 'The railway system illustrated' [i.e. 'Gauge Evidence: the history and prospects of the railway system illustrated']. *London*, 1846. pp. 59.   BM

3663 SIDNEY, S. The double gauge railway system: danger to travellers and injury to shareholders threatened by a combination of the broad gauge and narrow gauges. *London*, 1847. pp. viii, 88, with plates.   BM

3664 SIDNEY, S. The commercial consequences of a mixed gauge on our railway system examined. *London*, 1848. pp. 47.   BM
Against broad gauge and mixed gauge.

3665 RAILWAY competition: a letter to George Carr Glyn, Chairman of the London & North Western Railway. *London*, 1849. pp. 31.   BM
The evils of competition; harmony between railway companies essential to successful railway progress.

3666 MALINS, W. Two letters to Lord Barrington, Chairman of the Great Western Railway; first, on continuing the 'narrow gauge' from Reading to Paddington, and secondly, on Great Western affairs generally. *London*, 1857. pp. 23.   BM

3667 THOMAS, J. L. A letter on the present position of railways, addressed to railway shareholders. *London*, 1867. pp. 21.   BM
The evils of competing lines and the remedy in government assistance in finance.

3668 FAIRLIE, R. F. Railways or no railways. Narrow gauge, economy with efficiency; or broad gauge, costliness with extravagance. *London*, 1872. pp. 147, with 7 plates (1 fold.) & 3 fold. diagrams.   BM
Cover title, *The Battle of the Gauges renewed*.
A reply to S. Seymour's *Review of the theory of narrow gauges* (1871).

—— German edn. 'Die Richtige Praxis der Schmalspurbahnen.' *Zürich*, 1873.
—— French edn. 'Chemins de fer ou absence de chemins de fer.' *Paris*, 1872.

—— Spanish edn. 'Ferro-carriles o no ferro-carriles.' *Londres y Paris*, 1872.

3669 LATROBE, B. H. A letter on the railway gauge question . . . also, Extracts from English engineers' reports to the British government on railway gauges and economy in construction, maintenance and working, published by W. W. Evans. *New York*, 1872. pp. 35.   ICE

3670 BAZAINE, M. A. Étude sur le monopole et la concurrence dans les chemins de fer d'Angleterre, 1872–1873. *Paris*, 1874. pp. 44.
Extract from *Annales Industrielles*, livraisons des 5, 12, 19 et 26 avril, et du 3 mai, 1874.

3671 BOGLE, W. R. Our railways and the zone system fully explained and practically illustrated, as applied to the Caledonian Railway Company. *London*, 1891. pp. 8.   LSE
Reprinted from *Tinsley's Magazine*, July 1891.
Centralisation of railway management,

3672 WAGHORN, T. The effect of railway competition on railway dividends. *London*, 1904. pp. 38.   BR
Competition between companies the main cause of diminishing dividends, 1883–1903.

3673 RAILWAY amalgamations and agreements. *In* 'Jubilee of the Railway News, 1864–1914.' *London: Railway News*, [1914.] pp. 42–5.   BM

3674 MARSHALL, A. Industry and trade: a study of industrial technique and business organisation and of their influences on the conditions of various classes and nations. *London*, 1919. pp. xxiv, 875.   BM
pp. 445–506, Competition and monopoly among railways.

—— 2nd edn. *London*, 1919. pp. xxiv, 874.   BM

3675 RAILWAY CLERKS' ASSOCIATION. Railway pooling proposals and joint working arrangement . . . Employees' case for safeguards, as submitted to the Railway Pool Committee, October 31–November 2, 1932. *London*, November 1932. pp. 63.   LSE

3676 GRUMBRIDGE, J. L. Railway pooling: the potentialities of the pooling agreements recently made between certain of the main line railway companies, both from the point of view of the public, and the companies themselves. 1934. pp. 53. *Typescript*.   LSE
Rosebery Prize Essay, London School of Economics.

3677 WESTCOTT, L. F. The potentialities of the pooling agreements recently made between certain of the main line railway companies,

both from the point of view of the public and of the companies themselves. 1934. pp. 65. *Typescript.*   LSE
Rosebery Prize Essay, London School of Economics.

3678 SHERRINGTON, C. E. R. The economics of railway pooling. pp. 12.   PC
Reprinted from *Railway accounts and finance*, published by the Railway Board of India, July 1935.

F3 CLEARING HOUSE SYSTEM

For Gattie's London Goods Clearing House proposal see **K 4**

3679 MORISON, K. The origin and results of the clearing system which is in operation on the narrow gauge railways, with tables of the through traffic in the year 1845. *London*, 1846. pp. 26.   BM
'Narrow gauge' in the sense used here refers to what later came to be known as 'standard gauge' (4 ft. 8½ in.).

—— [The origin and results of the clearing system.] Reprint of a pamphlet on the origin and results of the clearing system published in 1846, and of articles and correspondence from 'The Times' of January 1869 and January 1893; also of an article in 'The Railway Official Gazette' of January 1892. [*London*,] April 1892. pp. 26, 11, 37.   LSE
Issued to celebrate the fiftieth year of the Railway Clearing House.

3680 PENNINGTON, W. Proposals for increasing the efficiency of the Railway Clearing House. *Manchester*, 1850. pp. 4.   LSE
Proposes that the R.C.H. should be taken away from London and be made the centre of a community for the training of railway clerks.

3681 PENNINGTON, W. Railway Clearing House. *Manchester*, 1850. s.sh.   LSE
A letter dated 4 March to G. C. Glyn, Chairman of the Railway Clearing House Committee on Reform of the R.C.H., suggesting reforms.

3682 BABBAGE, C. An analysis of the statistics of the Clearing House during the year 1839; with an appendix on the London and New York Clearing Houses, and on the London Railway Clearing House. *London*, 1856. pp. 33.   BM
pp. 29–33, The Railway Clearing House.

3683 DOWDEN, T. F. The railway clearing system as practised in the English Clearing House in 1876. *London*, 1877. pp. iv, 164.
Printed for H.M.S.O.   ICE
A very detailed account, with reproductions of specimen forms in current use.

3684 RAILWAY CLEARING HOUSE. Regulations, 1st January, 1856. *London*, 1856. pp 61.   AU

—— another edn. *London*, 1874. pp. viii, 196, xxviii, 64.   PC
—— another edn. *London*, 1878. pp. viii, 225, xxxiv, 112.   UL(GL)

3685 CARLILE, H. Allgemeine Darstellung des Centralen Eisenbahn-Abrechnungs-Systems in England und Betrachtungen über die Vortheile der Einführung dieses Systems in Russland. *Riga*, 1880. pp. 56, with tables.
The Clearing House system.   ICE
—— another edn. in Russian. *Riga*, 1880. pp. 60, with tables.

3686 [SEKON, G. A.] Railway Clearing House: illustrated interview with Mr. Harry Smart . . . [*London*, 1898.] pp. 15, with illus.   BM
Reprinted from the *Railway Magazine*, November 1898.

*3687 The RAILWAY Clearing House: its object, work and results . . . *London*, 1876. pp. 32.
                                              BM
Reprinted from the *Railway Fly Sheet & Official Gazette*.
—— rev. edn. *London*, 1901. pp. 51.   BM

3688 SMART, H. C. The R.C.H. (Railway Clearing House): what it is and what it does . . . [*London*, 1912.] pp. 15, with illus.
Reprinted from the *Railway and Travel Monthly*, May 1912.

3689 SMART, H. C. The Railway Clearing House. *In* 'Jubilee of the Railway News, 1864–1914.' *London: Railway News*, [1914.] pp. 53–9. BM

3690 The WORK of the Railway Clearing House, 1842–1942. *Westminster: Railway Gazette*, 1943. pp. 24, with illus. incl. portraits.   BM
Reprint, *Railway Gazette*, 2 Jan., 19 and 26 June, 1942.

3691 BRITISH TRANSPORT COMMISSION. The Railway Clearing House. [*London*,] 1957. pp. 12, with 3 illus.   IT
Historical and descriptive.
—— another edn. [*London*,] 1960. pp. 12, with 3 illus.   BM

G RAILWAY MANAGEMENT AND OPERATION

Marginal symbols: **b** bibliographies
c chronologies

3692 RAILWAYS: their uses and management. *London*, 1842. pp. 65. BM

3693 ECKERSLEY, P. Railway management: observations on two letters to George Carr Glyn . . . by John Whitehead of the Stock Exchange, London, and Mark Huish, General Manager of the London & North Western Railway. *London*, 1848. pp. 22. BM
Mainly criticising Whitehead's pamphlet and supporting that of Huish. P. Eckersley was connected with the Lancashire & Yorkshire Rly. See 6522–5.

3694 BROWN, H. Railway accidents, railway amalgamation and railway management, in a series of letters to 'The Morning Chronicle' by 'A Gloucestershire M.P.' *London*, 1853. pp. 45. BM
Seven letters, generally concerned with cricitisms of railway administration.

3695 CHAPLIN, F. A plan for the better management of railroads. *London*, 1856. pp. 15. BM
'. . . to divide each railway company into two, one to hold the line, and the other to conduct the carrying trade upon it . . .'

3696 COHN, G. Untersuchungen über die englische Eisenbahnpolitik. *Leipzig*, 1874–5. 2 vols. (pp. xiii, 370; xii, 646.) BM
Bd. 1, Die Entwickelung der Eisenbahngesetzgebung in England.
Bd. 2, Zur Beurtheilung der englischen Eisenbahnpolitik.
A very detailed work. This author's 'Die englische Eisenbahnpolitik der letzten zehn Jahre, 1873–1883' (1883) incorporates a revision of part of this work and has an index for all three volumes.

3697 PANGBORN, J. G. Side lights on management, world systems railways. *Baltimore*, 1901. pp. 245. BM
pp. [167]–200, British railways, railway management, governmental control, etc., compared with railways in the U.S.A.

3698 ROSS, H. M. British railways: their organisation and management. *London*, 1904. pp. vii, 245, with illus. BM

3699 BURTT, P. Scientific method in the railway world . . . a paper read at the York Railway Lecture & Debating Society on October 13, 1908. *London*, 1908. pp. 16, with fold. diagram. LSE
The wisdom of basing railway management on accurate data. (P. Burtt was Deputy General Manager, North Eastern Rly.)

3700 LAWSON, W. R. British railways: a financial and commercial survey. *London*, 1913. pp. xxxii, 320. BM
pp. 218–53, Administration and management.

3701 GATTIE, A. W. The coming trouble in the railway world. *London*, 1914. pp. 16, with illus. LSE
Paper, Birmingham Chamber of Commerce, 14 July, 1914.
Waste in railway organisation and operation, and the solution.

3702 DIXON, F. H. *and* PARMELEE, J. H. War administration of the railways in the United States and Great Britain. *New York*, 1918. pp. x, 155. [*Carnegie Endowment for International Peace. Preliminary Economic Studies of the War.*] BM
pp. 71–127, and later chapters, 'Gt. Britain'.
—— another edn. *N.Y.*, 1919. pp. vi, 203. LSE

3703 RAILWAY re-organisation: a study of possibilities of staff re-organisation and economical working, with a tabular analysis of all British railway costs based on Board of Trade Returns for the year 1913. By a Railway Officer. *London*, 1919. pp. xii, 108. BM

*3704 MODERN railway administration: a practical treatise by leading railway experts. *London*, 1925. 2 vols., with plates, illus. diagrams & fold. tables. BM
vol. 1, pp. 1–78, The early history of the railway; by Cyril Hall, rev. by F. H. Graveson: pp. 81–128, The constitution of railway companies: their financial and legal status; by F. M'Dermott and J. F. Gairns: pp. 131–155, Railway rating and valuation; by Walter Ingleby: pp. 159–195, The elements of railway goods rates; by H. L. Lister: pp. 199–266, The working of the goods department; by Henry W. Ede and G. E. Sellers.
vol. 2, pp. 3–33, The organization of the docks and marine department; by James R. Bailey: pp. 37–82, The economics of dock administration; by John Macaulay, revised by James R. Bailey: pp. 85–161, The economics of passenger traffic; by Felix J. C. Pole and James Milne: pp. 163–211, The manipulation of passenger traffic; by D. W. Barrie: pp. 213–248, Labour organization on British railways; by J. H. Thomas: pp. 251–279, The administrative reorganisation of the railways following the War; by Felix J. C. Pole: pp. 283–309, The law relating to railways; by Arthur Gaunt.

3705 NNOKES, G. A. [*pseud.* G. A. Sekon.] Railway control by railway stockholders, not by railway directors. *Burgess Hill*, [1929.] pp. 32. BM

3706 [RAILWAY COMPANIES ASSOCIATION.] Memorandum, post-war policy. Private and confidential. *Waterloo Station* [*London*], June 1943. pp. 5. *Reproduced typescript.* BR
Report of the general managers of the four main line companies.

3707 The RAILWAY Executive Committee and its headquarters: a description of Government control of railways in wartime, and of the preparation of adequately protected deep-level headquarters in a disused London tube station for the staff to work, eat and sleep. *London: Railway Gazette*, 1944. pp. 19, with fold. plan & illus., & plans in text.   IT
   Reprint, *Railway Gazette*, 17 & 24 Nov., 1944.

3708 DAVIES, E. British transport: a study in industrial organisation and control. *London: Fabian Society*, 1945. pp. 25.   LSE
   War-time control measures related to post-war problems.

3709 ELLIOT, J. The functions of management in an age of change. 1950. pp. 11. *Reproduced typescript.*   IT
   Presidential address, L.S.E. Railway Students' Association, 18 Oct., 1950.
   The principal functions of transport and railway management.

3710 UNIFICATION of British railways: administrative principles and practice; by members of the Railway Executive. *London: Modern Transport*, 1951. pp. 64, with illus.   TUC

3711 LATHAM, C. London Transport. *In* 'Efficiency in the nationalised industries' [issued by] the Institute of Public Administration. *London*, 1952. pp. 29–42.   IT
   Management, and co-ordination of work and services.

3712 EATON, R. J. Elements of transport. *London: Pitman*, 1936. pp. ix, 83.   BM
   Organisation and administration of railways.
   —— another edn. 'for the use of H.M. Forces: not for resale.' *London*, 1945. pp. ix, 82.   UL
   —— 2nd edn. *London*, 1953. pp. ix, 93.   BM

3713 SLEEMAN, J. F. British public utilities. *London: Pitman*, 1953. pp. 290.   BM
   pp. 53–90, Railways.

3714 ROBBINS, M. The Railway Age. *London: Routledge & Kegan Paul*, 1962. pp. x, 227,
b with 12 plates.   BM
   pp. 87–103, 'Railway directors, managers and shareholders.'
   pp. 206–7, Notes on sources.

G1 OPERATION OF RAILWAY SERVICES

Train control

3715 NASH, C. Railway carrying and carriers' law: the liabilities . . . of railways, carriers, and others, as to goods, luggage, passengers, etc., etc. *London*, 1846. pp. 92.   BM

3716 The RAILWAY Station Master's and Booking Clerk's Manual: or, Practical guide to the duties of persons intrusted with the management of railways. By a Railway Superintendent. *London*, [1849.] pp. 71.   RC

3717 MACDONNELL, G. Railway management with or without railway statistics. *London*, [1854.] pp. 37.   BM
   Occasions when reports from personnel to the Executive are called for.

3718 IVATTS, E. B. The Handbook of Railway Station Management. *Liverpool*, 1861. pp. 142, with illus.   BM

3719 LAWFORD, W. Railway management . . . *London*, 1874. pp. 14.   ICE
   Railway traffic management. Suggestions for increasing working capacity.

3720 WEIR, F. C. Suggestions for railway management to simplify working and for the prevention of accidents . . . *Bristol*, [1874.] pp. [5,] with fold. diagram.   ICE

3721 FORREST, J. Railway management; comprising the following papers: 1, The working of railways, by George Findlay; 2, On sorting railway trains by gravitation, by William Cudworth; 3, On railway statistics, by John Thornhill Harrison; with an abstract of the discussion upon the papers. Edited by J. Forrest. *London: Institution of Civil Engineers*, 1875. pp. 84.   BR
   Excerpt, *Min. Proc. I.C.E.*, vol. 41, 1874/5.

3722 WILLIAMS, R. P. On the economy of railway working. [*London*, 1879.] pp. 96–153, pl. 10–17, with 20 tables.   BM
   Excerpt, *Min. Proc. I.M.E.*, 1879.

3723 MACLEAN, J. L. The British railway system: a description of the work performed in the principal departments. *London*, 1883. pp. 103.   BM
   Based on Caledonian Rly. practice.

3724 FINDLAY, G. Report of a lecture delivered . . . at the School of Military Engineering, Chatham, 8 March, 1888. Subject, 'The working of an English railway'. *London*, 1888. pp. 37.   ICE
   Exemplified by the L. & N.W. Rly.

3725 FERGUSON, J. Railway rights and duties: a summary of the law relating to a railway in operation. *Edinburgh*, 1889. pp. xx, 402. BM

3726 COLE, W. H. Report on signalling and interlocking, station arrangements, train working and permanent way on British and French railways. [*Calcutta*,] 1893. 2 vols. ICE

*3727 FINDLAY, G. The working and management of an English railway . . . *London*, 1889. pp. vi, 270, with illus.   BM
   The London & North Western Rly.
   —— 2nd edn. *London*, 1889. pp. vi, 300. BM

—— 3rd, *London*, 1890. pp. vi, 300.   BM
—— 4th, *London*, 1891. pp. vi, 354.   BM
—— 5th, with a biographical sketch of George Findlay. *London*, 1894. pp. 412. BM

3728 LEIGHTON, G. B. Observations of English railway practice, with some account of the Fifth Session of the International Railway Congress. [*St. Louis*,] 1896. pp. 15.   BM
Reprinted from *Journal of the Association of Engineering Societies*, vol. 16, no. 1, January 1896.

3729 WEDGWOOD, R. L. A question of railway organisation: a paper read . . . before the York Railway Lecture and Debating Society, November 7th, 1905. [*Newcastle upon Tyne*, 1905.] pp. 20.   LSE
Improvements in railway economy and efficiency by amalgamation of Locomotive and Engineering Departments with Operating Departments. American practice considered.

3730 GREAT WESTERN RLY. Information for the guidance of railway officials with regard to police regulations. [*London*,] 1906. pp. 46.   PC
'Private & not for publication.'
Extracts from various Acts and GWR by-laws, with notes and details of powers of arrest.

3731 KEMPTHORNE, W. O. The principles of railway stores management. *London*, 1907. pp. viii, 268.   BM
A textbook.

3732 MITTON, G. E. The Book of the Railway; with 12 illustrations in colour by Allan Stewart. *London*. 1909. pp. ix, 256.   BM
An introductory work on railway working.
—— [2nd] edn. *London*, 1914.   RC
A re-issue with 9 illustrations.

3733 IVATTS, E. B. Railway management at stations. *London*, 1885. pp. vi, 598.   BM
Goods and passenger work. Includes a 27-page glossary of railway terms.
—— 2nd edn. *London*, 1887. pp. vi, 608. ICE
—— 3rd, *London*, 1898. pp. viii, 608. ICE
—— 4th, *London*, 1904. pp. 605.   LSE
—— 5th, *London*, 1910. pp. 605.   LSE

3734 HALL, C. The organization of the departments of the General Manager and the Superintendent of the Line. *In* 'Modern railway working', edited by John Macaulay. vol. 2, 1912. pp. 1–11.   BM

3735 HALL, C. The organization of the Engineering Department. *In* 'Modern railway working', edited by John Macaulay. vol. 2, 1912. pp. 33–45.   BM

3736 TRAVIS, C., LAMB, D. R. *and* JENKINSON, J. A. The elements of railway operating economics . . . *London*. 1913. pp. x, 228. BM
Reprinted from the *Railway News*. A companion work to *Practical railway working* (1915).

3737 HALLSWORTH, H. M. The elements of railway operating. [*York*, 1914.] pp. 350.
Printed and issued for private circulation only, by the North Eastern Rly. Co.

3738 MACAULAY, J. Modern railway working: a practical treatise by engineering and administrative experts under the editorship of John Macaulay, assisted by Cyril Hall. *London*, 1912–14. 8 vols., with plates, illus. & diagrams.   BM

3739 JENKINSON, J. A., LAMB, D. R. and TRAVIS, C. Railway operation: passenger and goods station management and working . . . *London*, 1915. pp. 173, 149.   BM
Reprinted from the *Great Central Journal*, April 1913 to April 1914.

3740 TRAVIS, C., LAMB, D. R., *and* JENKINSON, J. A. Practical railway working; with numerous illustrations; reprinted, with numerous additions, from the 'Railway News'. *London*, 1915. pp. 326.   BM
A companion work to *Elements of railway operating economics* (1913).

3741 GATTIE, A. W. Problems of transport: the latest crisis; reprinted from 'The Field' newspaper of July 28 and August 4, 1917. *London*, 1917. pp. 18.   LSE
Economic reforms in use of locomotives and rolling stock to avoid long periods of idleness between journeys. Proposes a central clearing depot.

3742 STONE, H. W. D. The principles of urban traffic. *London*, 1917. pp. viii, 130.   BM
pp. 77–96, 'Railways'. London suburban traffic problems.

3743 COLES, W. G. Monograph on control systems of train working. 30 September, 1918. pp. 48. *Typescript.*   LSE

3744 GREAT EASTERN RLY. A lecture on tickets and ticket holders and the method of dealing with them: delivered in the Essex Room of the Great Eastern Hotel, Liverpool Street, on June 12, 1917 . . . By A. W. Brenes, Chief Traffic Manager's Department. *Stratford*. [1918.] pp. 19.   LSE
'For official use only.'

3745 JARVIS, W. H. Railway stores methods and problems. *London*, 1918. pp. ii, 116.   BM

3746 DAVIES, A. Lancashire & Yorkshire Railway: a paper on statistics as applied to railway operation read by Mr. Ashton Davies at a meeting of the Zetetic Society, Department of the Superintendent of the Line, held at Victoria Station, Manchester, Thursday, January 16th, 1919. [*Manchester*, 1919.] pp. 16, with 6 diagrams and 34 examples of forms in use on the L. & Y.   BR

3747 TURNER, R. J. Railway Police Manual; with railway by-laws and precedents; revised. *Derby*, 1920. pp. 152.   BM

3748 WATSON, A. Some advantages of control as applied to traffic on railways. [*London*, 1921.] pp. 22, 51.   LSE
Paper, Institute of Transport, April 18, 1921.
Train control. The address is followed by a fifty-one page booklet entitled *A survey of the comprehensive control system operating on the Lancashire & Yorkshire Railway*, by A. Watson, General Manager. This contains many illustrations and diagrams, some coloured.

3749 RAILWAYS: their history: constructional requirements from an operating point of view: systems of control. [1922.] pp. 30.   IT
Privately printed. A lecture, Institute of Transport.
Signalling and train control.

3750 MAIN line control: North Eastern area, London & North Eastern Railway. *London: Railway Gazette*, [1923.] pp. 12, with la. fold. train diagram & 15 illus., diagrams & tables in text.   IT
Reprinted from the *Railway Gazette*, 2 March, 1923.

3751 MOSSOP, C. P. Railway operating statistics. *London*, 1911. pp. 131, with specimen diagrams of tables used on the N.E. Rly.   BM
Objects, principles and methods.

—— 2nd edn., revised by F. H. Graveson. *London*, 1923. pp. 150.   IT

3752 PICK, F. The objects and effects of traffic control. *London*, 1923. pp. 32.   LSE
Printed for private circulation among students of the London School of Economics, 15 November, 1923.

3753 WAGENRIEDER, B. Railway rules and regulations. pp. 16. *Typescript.*   RC
Paper, Railway Club, 12 Oct., 1923.
The relationship between safe and efficient service, and staff discipline and method.

3754 BURTT, P. Control on the railways: a study in methods. *London*, 1926. pp. 255, with plates & illus.   BM
Centralised and co-ordinated system of communicating, controlling, and supervising the movements of trains.

3755 ALLEN, C. J. Trains and their control; with four coloured plates and illustrations from photographs. *London*, 1928. pp. xv, 144.   BM
Also published as part of this author's *The steel highway* (1928).

3756 WARD, V. M. B. Modern train operating requirements and organisation. [1928.] pp. 10. *Typescript.*   IT
Paper, L.N.E. Rly. (London) Lecture & Debating Society, 14 Nov., 1928.

3757 BURTT, P. Railway electrification and traffic problems. *London*, 1929. pp. xvi, 197, with illus. & maps.   BM
Problems in applying electrification to traffic working.

3758 TRAFFIC control on the L.M.S.R. .... *Westminster: Railway Gazette*, [1929.] pp. 20, with maps, diagrams & illus.   BM

3759 HARE, T. B. British railway operation. *London*, 1927. pp. 156.   BM

—— 2nd edn. By T. B. Hare and R. L. Wedgwood. *London*, 1927. pp. 156, xvi. BM
—— 3rd, *London*, 1930. pp. 156.   IT

3760 HARDT, K. Die Verkehrsprobleme im
b   Eisenbahnwesen von Grossbritannien. (Doctoral thesis, Technischen Hochschule, Stuttgart, 1931.) pp. 91, with maps, tables, diagrams & a bibliography. *Printed.*   pc

3761 HARE, T. B. Practical railway operating. *London*, [1931.] pp. viii, 168, with tables. BM

3762 WESTINGHOUSE BRAKE & SAXBY SIGNAL COMPANY. Centralised traffic control. *London*, 1931. pp. 22, with illus. & diagrams.   PO

3763 WILLIAMSON, J. W. A British railway behind the scenes. *London*, 1933. pp. ix, 213, with 32 illus. on plates.   BM
The L.M.S. Rly.

3764 VALLANCE, H. A. How railways fight the snow. pp. 16. *Reproduced typescript.*   RC
Paper, Railway Club, 31 May, 1935.

3765 CODD, E. C. Life in a booking office. pp. 32. *MS.*   RC
Paper, Railway Club, 11 June, 1936.

3766 EARLEY, A. H. High speed on railways. pp. 40, with 3 diagrams. *Typescript.*   IT
Paper, Institute of Transport, Newcastle-on-Tyne, 13 Nov., 1936.
An examination of the prospect of greatly increased speed from the viewpoint of operation.

*3767 AITKEN, J. The Railway trainman; incorporating the trainman's manual. 11th edn. *Lennoxtown, c.* 1937. pp. 128, with illus. & diagrams.   BR
Privately distributed.

3768 GRESLEY, H. N. Development of high-speed running on railways; being the Watt Anniversary Lecture for 1937. *Greenock: Greenock Philosophical Society*, 1937. pp. 24.   BM

3769 WATERS, W. L. Rationalization of British railways; presented before the American Society of Mechanical Engineers, Railroad Division, Metropolitan Section, New York, May 11, 1938. *New York*, 1938. pp. 9. TUC
A study of the results of the 1921 amalgamations upon railway economy, management and operation.

3770 LONDON, MIDLAND & SCOTTISH RLY. Air Raid Precautions. Special instructions for the working of railways. November 1940. pp. 35.   BR

3771 POWNALL, J. F. New railway network principles: a project for applying them to

British railways. *Birmingham: Cotterell*, 1940. pp. 23.   BM
'Hour section' schedules.

3772 POWNALL, J. F. Transport reform in Great Britain; illustrated by a map: the bits and pieces character of British railways crystallised out . . . *London*, [*c.* 1940.] pp. [4.] BM
Published by the author.
A large folding map illustrating a proposed re-alignment of the railways to enable the working of his 'railway hour' system.

3773 LAMB, D. R. Modern railway operation. *London*, 1926. pp. xiii, 169, with illus. BM
—— 2nd edn. *London*, 1927. pp. xiv, 169. IT
—— 3rd, *London*, 1941. pp. xix, 243. (reissued 1946.) BM

3774 POWNALL, J. F. The Liverpool and Stoke-on-Trent railway hour section and also Birmingham and Nottingham hour sections to speed up railways in the Midlands. *Birmingham: Cotterell*, 1943. pp. 12. BM
'Hour section' schedules.

3775 ALLEN, C. J. Railways and their working. *In* 'Inside Information: how the nation's services work: an illustrated guide . . .' *London*, 1945. pp. 205–27. BM

3776 RAILWAY CLEARING HOUSE. Rules for observance by employees. (Rule Book.) January 1933, Reprint 1945, including Supplements 1 to 13 and alterations comprising Supplement no. 14. [*London*, 1945.] pp. 248, xlvii. IT

3777 CAMERON, T. F. An outline of railway traffic operation . . . *London: Railway Publishing Co.*, 1946. pp. 205, with illus. BM

3778 BRITISH RAILWAYS. Memorandum for the information and guidance of all officers and staff of the main line railways as to procedure during the period beginning January 1st, 1948. [*London*,] Nov. 1947. pp. [4.] BR

3779 EATON, R. J. Transport services research . . . : a talk given to the London Centre of the Institute of Traffic Administration . . . 12 May, 1948. *London: Transportation Press*, [1948.] pp. 20. BM
Improvement of services.

3780 JAMES, P. G. How can operational efficiency in transport be measured? [*Felixstowe*, 1950.] pp. 41. BR
Paper, British Transport Commission Second Officers' Conference, Felixstowe, First Session, 25 & 26 October, 1950. Printed but not published.

3781 DICKEN, E. R. H. The history of truncheons. *Ilfracombe: Stockwell*, 1952. pp. 136. BM
pp. 44–54, Railway police truncheons: with 3 plates.

3782 LATHAM, C. London Transport. *In* 'Efficiency in the nationalised industries'. *London: Institute of Public Administration*. 1952. pp. 29–42. IT
Management, and co-ordination of work and services.

3783 SANDERSON, H. F. Railway commercial practice. *London: Chapman & Hall*, 1952. 2 vols. with 60 illus. on plates, and illus. & plans in text. BM
vol 1, General and passenger.
vol. 2, Freight.
A comprehensive work based on practical knowledge covering all subjects relating to the running of services as they affect the travelling public and the consigner of goods.
—— Supplement to vols. 1 & 2: 'The Transport Act 1953, Railway re-organisation, Charges schemes, Modernisation Plan and other developments'. *London*, 1955. pp. 48. BM

3784 WEBSTER, H. C. Railway motive power . . . *London: Hutchinson*, 1952. pp. 310, with 50 plates, & 57 drawings in text. BM
Modern locomotives of all kinds, related to current problems of running costs, maintenance, etc.

3785 AHRONS, E. L. Locomotive and train working in the latter part of the nineteenth century. Edited by L. L. Asher . . . *Cambridge: Heffer*, 1951–4. 6 vols., each with 48 illus., on 24 plates. BM
Deals separately with all main railways.
A very detailed and informative record.

3786 INTERNATIONAL Railway Congress. *London: Railway Gazette*, 1954. pp. 250. IT
pp. 5–22, The railways of Britain, 1924–54. Technical and operational progress.

3787 BRITISH RAILWAYS. Ideas pay. *London*, 1955. pp. [12.] LSE
Issued to staff to encourage ideas for improved efficiency and use of railways. Awards for accepted suggestions.

*3788 SCHUMER, L. A. The elements of transport. *London: Butterworth*, 1955. pp. xii, 196. BM
An introduction to transport economics and operation, including railways.

3789 COCHRAN, A. D. Railway operating problems in the Derby district. 1956. pp. 23. *Reproduced typescript*, with 5 maps & diagrams at end. IT
Paper, Convention of the L.S.E. Railway Students' Association, Derby, 23 July, 1956.

*3790 O'DELL, A. C. Railways and geography. *London: Hutchinson*, 1956. pp. 198. BM
The influence of geographical factors on the construction and operation of railways; including urban problems.

3791 COOPER, B. K. Modern railway working. *London: L. Hill*, 1957. pp. xii, 114, with 105 illus. on plates. BM

3792 Cox, L. W. Modernisation on the railways as particularly affecting the Operating Department. 1957. pp. 9. *Reproduced typescript.*　IT
　Paper, L.S.E. Railway Students Association, 13 Feb., 1957.

3793 ALLEN, C. J. Modern railways: their engineering, equipment, and operation. *London: Faber & Faber*, 1959. pp. 307, with 247 illus. on 64 plates, 22 diagrams, & 11 tables.　BM

3794 PARKES, G. R. Railway snowfighting equipment and methods. *Hadfield: the author*, 1961. pp. 95, with 95 illus., & diagrams.　BM

3795 WHITBREAD, J. R. The railway policeman: the story of the constable on the track . . .

London: Harrap, 1961. pp. 269, with 36 illus. on 15 plates.　BM

3796 DENNISON, H. F. Economics of railway signalling and track capacity as applied to single line railways. (Abridged version by E. Procter of original paper prepared by H. F. Dennison.) *London: United Kingdom Railway Advisory Service*, 1962. pp. 34, with 21 diagrams.　BM

3797 SAMUEL, H. Railway operating practice. *London: Odhams Press*, 1962. pp. 256, with 29 plates.　BM

*3798 BAILEY, M. R. The ABC of British Railways head-codes: a complete list of all British Railways headlamp, disc and two-and four-character codes. [1962.] pp. 96, with illus., tables & diagrams.　BM

G2 FREIGHT TRAFFIC

Marshalling—Cartage (*see also* **G 4**)

3799 POWELL, H. B. Description of the great advantages to be derived by Government, the mercantile community, and railway companies, from the universal use of patent sectional transferable railway carriages invented by Captain Powell of the Grenadier Guards, whereby the difficulty of the difference of the gauge is obviated, and great facility afforded for the transmission of goods or stores by railways to places at distances from the railway station. *Lymington*, 1846. pp. 8.　BM(MSS)
See 3660.

3800 POOLE, B. A Report to the Road and Traffic Committee of the Northern Division of Directors of the London & North Western Railway Company on coal traffic, ordered 15th June, 1849. [*Liverpool*,] 1849. pp. 21.　BM
　The possibilities of increasing coal traffic from Lancashire coalfields.

—— Extracts from a report to the Road & Traffic Committee. [*Liverpool*,] 1849. pp. 11.　BM

3801 CUDWORTH, W. On sorting railway trains by gravitation. *In* 'Railway management', edited by J. Forrest. 1875. pp. 21–35.　BM

3802 CHAPMAN, S. The marshalling, shunting and working of goods traffic on railways on an improved system, combining greater safety and economy; with an address to the directors of the Great Eastern Company. By S. Chapman, 34 years in the service of the said company. *London*, 1881. pp. iv, 107.　LSE

3803 LUIGGI, L. Il servizio merci sulle ferrovie Inglesi. *Roma*, 1888. pp. 15, with fold. diagrams.　ICE

3804 JEFFERDS, M. R. On tube-frame goods wagons of light weight and large capacity, and their effect upon the working expenses of railways. *Westminster*, [1890.] pp.475–527 with 10 diagrams.　LSE
　Excerpt, *Min. Proc. I.M.E.*, Meeting of 29 October, 1890.

3805 TWELVETREES, M. M. Organisation for the collection and delivery of goods and parcels consigned by railway. *London*, 1895. pp. 3–24. [*International Railway Congress. Fifth Session, 1895. Question XII, Cartage & Delivery.*]　LSE
　Author was Chief Goods Manager, Great Northern Rly.

3806 PAISH, G. The British railway position . . . *London*, 1902. pp. xiv, 322.　BM
　Reprinted from the *Statist.*
　Urging the adoption of the American practice of heavily loaded goods trains for increase of traffic with greater economy.

3807 The ORGANIZATION of a goods train service. [*London*, April 1905.] pp. 10. *Typescript.*　LSE

3808 WAGHORN, T. Carriers and railway companies. *London: Carriers Publishing Co.*, 1907. pp. 24.　LSE
　Reprinted from the *World's Carriers & Contractors' Review.*
　Traces the growth of the idea and practice of monopoly of cartage by railway companies.

809 LISSENDEN, G. B. The Railway Trader's Guide to forwarding, receiving, railway charges, and all other matters incidental to transactions with the railway companies. *London*, 1910. pp. viii, 236.

810 GOTT, W. The organization and duties of the Goods Department. *In* 'Modern railway working', edited by John Macaulay. vol. 2, 1912. pp. 13–32, with illus.   BM

811 WEST, F. W. The railway goods station: a guide to its control and operation. *London*, 1912. pp. xv, 192, with illus.   BM

812 BIRCHAM, B. O. Railway consignment notes and their conditions. *London*, 1913. pp. xviii, 194, 10.   BM
The carriage of goods and animals.

813 EDE, H. W. The working of the Goods Department. *In* 'Modern railway working', edited by John Macaulay. vol. 7, 1913. pp. 63–129.   BM

814 JENKINSON, J. A., LAMB, D. R. *and* TRAVIS, C. Railway operation: the goods depot. *London*, 1915. pp. 149.   IT
A handbook.

815 REED, L. C. W. The shortage of railway wagons: a pooling scheme. [*London*,] 1918. pp. 3.   BM
Reprint, *Railway Gazette*, 4 Oct., 1918.
Pooling of all railway wagons, private and railway owned.

816 LISSENDEN, G. B. How to send goods by road, rail and sea. *London*, 1922. pp. v, 85.
A handbook.

817 HORNER, F. C. English cartage practice: a standard for our railway terminal trucking. [*New York*,] 1923. pp. 30, with 6 illus. LSE
Reprinted from the May 1923 issue of the *Journal of the Society of Automotive Engineers*.
Delivery and collection to and from railway goods depots.

818 BURTT, P. The principal factors in freight train operating. *London*, 1923. pp. 208, with plates; illus. & tables in text.   BM
—— *London*, 1924. pp. 208.   BM

819 HINTS on the management of a goods station. *London: Great Western Rly.*, 1929. pp. 44. [*Great Western Information*, no. 4.]   BR
'The more traffic carried, the less it costs to carry.'

820 LONDON & NORTH EASTERN RLY.— SOUTHERN AREA. Goods station work and accounts. [*London*, 1929.] pp. 80.
'Private—for Company's staff only.'
Synopses of lectures to clerks.

821 DAVIES, E. H. The lay-out, organisation and operation of a large goods station.

pp. 14, with 5 diagrams & tables. *Reproduced typescript.*   IT
Paper, Institute of Transport, 1931.

3822 BARR, J. W. H. A new and improved system of freight transport by rail and road devised by J. W. Barr, combining a more economic and a more rapid distribution of goods by both passenger and freight train services and a more intensive use of existing railway facilities. *Bournemouth*, 1931. pp. 16, with 31 diagrams on 13 fold. sheets.   BM
Transfer of freight containers from train to platform and vice versa. Direct service from consigner to consignee. Elimination of shunting.

3823 BULKELEY, G. Railway and seaport freight movement . . . *London*, 1930. pp. xiv, 221, with illus., diagrams & tables.   BM
Describes contemporary methods in handling goods traffic.
—— Students' edn. *London*, 1932. pp. xiv, 221.   IT

3824 BACHSCHMIDT, F. W. Die englische Eisen-bahn-Kraftwagen Politik von 1918 bis 1933.
b *Heidelberg*, 1934. pp. v, 96, with bibliogr. notes & a bibliography.   BM
Legislation bearing upon road transport by railways.

3825 HARTLEY, H. The transport of food by rail. *London*, 1935. pp. 9.   BR
Reprinted from the *Journal of the Society of Chemical Industry*, 26 July, 1935.

3826 JAMES, S. H. The history of Pickfords. pp. 14. *Reproduced typescript.*   IT
Paper, Institute of Transport, 23 March, 1935.
Includes brief mention of their link with railways, especially with the L. & N.W. and the L.B. & S.C.

3827 LONDON, MIDLAND & SCOTTISH RLY.— SCHOOL OF TRANSPORT. Cartage. *London*, 1938. pp. v, 124, with tables, specimen forms, etc.   BR

3828 LONDON, MIDLAND & SCOTTISH RLY.— SCHOOL OF TRANSPORT. Goods station working. *London*, August 1938. pp. viii, 213, with fold. diagrams.   BR
'For use of Company's servants only. Not for publication.'

3829 RAILWAY COMPANIES ASSOCIATION. Ride with me on the Early Bird! *London*, [1939.] pp. [20,] with illus.   BM
Night goods train working exemplified by the 7.25 from Acton to Cardiff.

3830 HADLEY, E. S. The Shunter's Manual: a practical guide to ways of saving time, work and engine power in shunting and marshalling; with more than seventy diagrams. *London: the author*, 1944. pp. 48.   BM

3831 BLEE, D. Railway collection and delivery services for freight traffic; their organisation and scope. pp. 25. *Reproduced typescript.*   IT
Paper, Institute of Transport, Birmingham, 18 December, 1945.

3832 HAY'S WHARF CARTAGE CO. Transport saga, 1646–1947. *London*, 1947. pp. 63, with illus.   IT
pp. 22–4, Pickfords and the railways.

3833 RAILWAY CLEARING HOUSE. The Livestock Handbook: instructions relating to the transport of livestock by rail . . . and road . . . [*London*,] December 1947. pp. 56.
'Private and not for publication.'
For the use of station masters, goods agents, yard masters, and others.

3834 DYSON, R. A. & Co. Road/rail trailers. *London*, [1948.] pp. 17, with illus.   LSE

3835 KRUGER, J. A. Design and operation of marshalling yards. pp. 19. *Reproduced typescript.*   IT
Paper, Institute of Transport, Johannesburg Section, 11 May, 1948.
Includes British examples.

3836 BEZZANT, R. Newspaper carriage and parcels traffic on British railways. *London: Dawson*, [1951.] pp. xi, 140.   BM

3837 BRITISH RAILWAYS (LONDON MIDLAND REGION). Toton Marshalling Yards. [*London*, 1952.] s.sh. (fold.).   BM
An illustrated folder for visitors.

3838 HAWKES, J. R. Report on the container problem. *York*, March 1952. pp. 44, with diagrams. *Typescript.*   IT
Robert Bell Travelling Scholarship, 1951/52 Award.
A survey covering N.W. Europe and the U.K.

3839 HALL, J. A. Compilation and use of railway cartage statistics. 1954. pp. 8, with specimen forms. *Typescript.*   IT
Paper, Institute of Transport, York, 11 January, 1954.

3840 MITCHELL ENGINEERING LTD. Mechanical wagon-marshalling system. *London*, [1954.] pp. 17[20], with illus. & diagrams.
                                                      IME

3841 STARR, H. H. Railway transport terminal facilities. 1954. pp. 12. *Reproduced typescript.*   IT
Paper, Institute of Transport, Gloucester–Cheltenham Group, 2 March, 1954.
Developments over the past thirty-five years, generally, and on the G.W.R.

3842 STEELE, E. Livestock by rail from the Port of Birkenhead. 1955. pp. 6. *Typescript.* IT
Paper, Institute of Transport, Merseyside Section, 6 January, 1955.
The handling and entraining of cattle, pigs and sheep landed from Ireland.

3843 WARDELL, B. M. Marshalling yards. 1957. pp. 8. *Typescript.*   IT
Paper, Institute of Transport, York, 19 November, 1957.
Descriptions of various types of yards, and of their work.

3844 DODDS, J. K. Gravity marshalling yards. *London: United Kingdom Railway Advisory Service*, 1962. pp. 28, with 9 illus., 14 diagrams & a table of rolling resistance.   BM

3845 WHITTINGHAM, E. K. Mechanical handling and alternative means of loading and unloading heavy freight bogie wagons. *London: United Kingdom Railway Advisory Service*, 1962. pp. 11, with 12 illus.   BM

G3 PASSENGER TRAIN SERVICES

Special trains, excursions, Pullman trains, royal trains—Speed—Closed lines
For engineering aspects, and for descriptions of named trains, royal trains, etc., see E6

Historical

3846 RAE, W. F. The business of travel: a fifty years' record of progress . . . *London*, 1891. pp. 318.   BM
Origin and progress of Thomas Cook & Son.

3847 FORTUNES made in business: life struggles of successful people; illustrated. *London: Harmsworth*, 1910.   BM
Issued serially.
pp. 182–90, Thomas Cook; with portrait.

3848 CHARLEWOOD, R. E. Dining cars on British railways: their history and importance. pp. 31. *MS.*   RC
Paper, Railway Club, 12 Feb., 1907.

3849 'COACHING.' Passenger services past and present. *In* 'Jubilee of the Railway News'. *London: Railway News*, [1914.] pp. 122–3. BM

3850 COOK, T. & SON. The origin and development of excursion traffic. *In* 'Jubilee of the Railway News, 1864–1914'. *London: Railway News*, [1914.] pp. 200–1.   BM

3851 PULLMAN CAR COMPANY. The story of the Pullman organisation; being in the main a reprint of extracts from articles which appeared in 'The Daily Telegraph' on August, 14th, 16th, 19th, 21st, & 23rd, 1929.

[*London*, 1929.] pp. 56, with 14 illus.　BM
Cover title, *The history of the Pullman car in Great Britain*.
Includes a description of services, construction, fittings, decor, and cuisine.

852 DANIELS, G. W. T. Slip coach services. pp. 60, with tables. *MS*.　RC
Paper, Railway Club, 9 November, 1934.
From 1858 to the present.

853 FELLOWS, R. B. British non-stop expresses historically considered. pp. 26, with tables. *Typescript*.　RC
Paper, Railway Club, 11 May, 1934.

854 FELLOWS, R. B. The history of slip-coach working. pp. 28. *Typescript*.　RC
Paper, Railway Club, 11 October, 1941.

855 BURTT, F. *and* BECKERLEGGE, W. Pullman and perfection. *London: Ian Allan*, 1948. pp. 40.　BM
History of the Pullman Car service. Contents inside front cover. Includes 9 pp. list of cars in service, and 5 pp. list of cars withdrawn.

856 SANDERS, E. M. British railway restaurant car services. pp. 28. *Typescript*.　RC
Paper, Railway Club, 3 November, 1950.
A survey of progress over the past thirty years.

857 CASSERLEY, H. C. Service suspended: a pictorial souvenir of British passenger services that are no longer in operation. *London: Ian Allan*, [1951.] pp. 40.　BM
Sixty illustrations with descriptions: pp. 33–40, 'Passenger services no longer in operation': a detailed list including dates of closure.

858 PUDNEY, J. The Thomas Cook story. *London: M. Joseph*, 1953. pp. 264, with plates & illus.　BM
pp. 72–81, Railway excursions.

859 FELLOWS, R. B. Non-stop runs by trains
b in Great Britain, 1845–1928. *In* 'Journal of Transport History', vol. 2, no. 1, May 1955. pp. 1–10, with 10 bibliogr. notes.　BM

860 GREVILLE, M. D. *and* SPENCE, J. Hand-
c book to Closed Passenger Lines of England and Wales, 1827 to 1939. *Caterham*, 1955. pp. [41,] with 5 maps. *Reproduced typescript*.
Published by the authors.　BM
411 closures listed, with details and remarks.

861 HARDING, F. D. M. The Pullman Car Company. pp. 11. *Typescript*.　BR
Paper, Institute of Transport, Southern Section, 12 Jan., 1955.
The history of Pullman by its General Manager.

862 BEHREND, G. The history of 'Wagon-Lits', 1875–1955. *London: Modern Transport*, 1959. pp. 32, with illus.　BM

863 BEHREND, G. Pullman in Europe. *London: Ian Allan*, 1962. pp. 360, with 81 illus. on 32 plates, & 12 very detailed multicolumn tables (pp. 242–356).　BM
The history of Pullman cars and services in Europe, including Great Britain. The tables, compiled by Howard Turner, provide a complete and accurate record of every Pullman car which has run in Gt. Britain, and of other cars owned by the Pullman Car Company.

***3864** DANIELS, G. *and* DENCH, L. Passengers no more: closures of stations and branch lines (1952–1962). *Brighton*, December 1962. pp. 33. *Reproduced typescript*, with 2 pp. addenda & errata. 'A GLO Publication.'　BM
Alphabetical list, giving company or Region, date of closure and map reference. Also supplementary lists of stations changed to halts, new stations, halts, and lines, and re-openings. Great Britain and Ireland.

—— 2nd edn. *Brighton*, Feb. 1963. pp. 34.　BM

***3865** CLINKER, C. R. Register of Closed Passenger Stations and Goods Depots in England, Scotland and Wales, 1923–1962. *Harlyn Bay, Cornwall: the author*, 1963. pp. viii, 91[1.] *Reproduced typescript*.　BM
Issued to subscribers only. 4287 closures.

—— Supplement no. 1. July 1963. pp. ii, 11.　BM

—— Supplement no. 2. Jan. 1964. pp. i, 16.　BM

***3866** GREVILLE, M. D. *and* SPENCE, J. A Handbook to Closed Passenger Lines of Scotland up to 1939. *Caterham: Railway & Canal Historical Society*, 1963. pp. 12, with 3 maps.　BM

Contemporaneous

3867 MINOT, R. S. Railway travel in Europe and America; with 25 tables of recent and novel statistics of journeys, speeds, fares, etc. for travellers and others. *Boston*, 1882. pp. 28.　BM

3868 FOXWELL, E. English express trains: two papers. *London*, 1884. pp. 128.　BM
The second paper, pp. 59–128, contains tables and notes on long runs, gradients, etc.

3869 [FOXWELL, E.] The best trains; with particulars of the summer services of 1888 and the railway race to Edinburgh. *London*, [1888.] pp. 47. [*Pall Mall Gazette Extra* no. 42.]　LSE
A collection of articles, mostly concerning the speeds of various express trains, and E. Foxwell's philosophy on the benefits of speed to human well-being.
pp. 3–26, 'A great railway year'.

3870 W., A. Some statistics of our English express trains. *Windsor*, 1888. pp. 23, with tables of longest and fastest runs, etc.　BM

3871 CHAPMAN, S. A comparative analysis of English railway passenger traffic for the five years 1883–1887. *London*, 1889. pp. 30, with tables.　BR

*3872 FOXWELL, E. *and* FARRER, T. C. Express trains, English and foreign: being a statistical account of all the express trains of the world; with railway maps of Great Britain and Europe. *London*, 1889. pp. viii, 181, with 6 maps.   BM

part 1, pp. 5–77, Express trains in Gt. Britain; the 1888 races to Edinburgh. The maps were also issued separately.

3873 BIRD, C. H. Speed table. [*c.* 1890?]   IT
A large folding table for quick calculation of speeds of trains.

3874 STACKHOUSE, J. F. Our express trains. *London*, 1896. pp. 27.   BM
Twelve trains from twelve English railways, with twelve illustrations.

3875 BARBEY, C. Le Service actuel des trains rapides: Belgique, Angleterre, France, Suisse: notes de voyage 1897–98. *Paris*, 1899. pp. 70, with illus.   BR
pp. 10–34, British railways.

3876 ALEXANDER, J. T. B. Railway runs in three continents; being a short record of actual performances on some European, Canadian, Australian and American railways. *London*, 1900. pp. vi, 191.   BM
Seven out of the twenty-seven journeys described are on British railways.

3877 PHILLP, S. M. The manipulation of passenger traffic. *In* 'Modern railway working', edited by John Macaulay. vol. 1, 1912. pp. 157–68, with diagrams of station layouts.   BM

3878 JENKINSON, J. A., LAMB, D. R. *and* TRAVIS, C. Railway operation: the passenger station and signalling. *London*, 1914. pp. 173, with illus.   IT
A handbook.

3879 WIENER, L. Train speeds. *Westminster*, [1919.] pp. 57, with 56 tables & 51 maps & diagrams.   BM
Reprinted from the *Railway Gazette* of 1919.
A very detailed survey of contemporary scheduled runs on railways in various European countries, including Britain.

3880 RAILWAY CLEARING HOUSE. The Railway Companies' Book of Regulations relating to traffic by passenger train or other similar service. *London*, 1927. pp. viii. 77.   LSE

3881 WAY, R. B. Mixed traffic. *London: Nicholson & Watson*, 1937. pp. x, 160, with plates.   BM
Narratives of train working.

3882 DALBY, C. R. Some aspects of special traffic working by passenger train services, with special reference to excursion traffic. 1938. pp. 27. *Typescript*, with diagrams & tables taken from L.N.E.R. (GER) schedules.   LSE

3883 LONDON, MIDLAND & SCOTTISH RLY.— SCHOOL OF TRANSPORT. Passenger station working. *London*, 1938. pp. xi, 352, with 80 illus., diagrams, forms, charts, etc.   BR
'Not for publication.'

3884 RAILWAY posters and the War. *London: Railway Gazette*, 1939–1943. 6 parts.   BR
Reproductions of notices relating to alterations in services displayed to passengers, including, for comparison, some from the Great War, 1914–18.

3885 COZENS, L. Rail Speed Pocket Chart. *Sutton: the author*, [1950.] s.sh. (fold.).   BM
Quarter-mile timings in terms of miles per hour.

3886 BUCKLAND, W. R. Some statistical aspects of passenger transport planning. pp. xvi,
b   274; with 10 tables, maps, and a bibliography of systematic planning. (Thesis, Ph.D. (Applied Statistics) Univ. Lond. 1951.   UL
Statistical method and analysis of data applied to transport planning.

3887 NOCK, O. S. British railways in action. *London: Nelson*, 1956. pp. xi, 228, with 48 plates.   BM
Some train journeys described (with logs) and some modern problems of operation examined.

3888 RAILWAY CORRESPONDENCE & TRAVEL SOCIETY. A Midland Traffic Survey. [*Cheltenham*,] 1956. pp. 84, with many tables, 7 illus. & a map.   BR
A very detailed report on railway movement, from London to the North and from Bristol to Derby, observed within an area north of Market Harborough and Birmingham and south of Manchester and Leeds.

3889 BIEDENKOPF, W. Schienen-Schnellverkehr in Europa: die Entwicklung des Schienenschnellverkehrs in Europa bis 1959. Zweite, erweiterte Auflage. *Vevey*, [1960.] pp. 63, with tables.   BM
pp. 36–9, England, with 3 tables of fast journeys.

G4   RAILWAY ROAD SERVICES (Omnibus and Freight)

For cartage see also G 2

3890 BACHSCHMIDT, F. W. Die englische Eisen-
   b bahn-Kraftwagen-Politik von 1918 bis 1933.
      Heidelberg, 1934. pp. v, 96, with bibliogr.
      notes & bibliography.   BM
   Legislation bearing upon road transport by
   railways.

3891 LEE, C. E. Railway-owned omnibus services: a paper presented . . . to the Railway
   Club on Thursday September 10th, 1936.
   pp. 23[24]. *Typescript*.   RC
   Survey of the development of railway bus
   services generally and by individual railway
   companies.

3892 WALLACE, J. P. A history and survey of the
   road transport operations of the British
   railways. Thesis, M.A., University of
   Wales, 1947. pp. [15,] 340, with maps.
   Typescript.   NLW

3893 LEE, C. E. One hundred years of railway-
   associated omnibus services. January 1953.
   pp. 8. *Reproduced typescript*.   IT
   Address, as chairman, to the Omnibus
   Society, 8 Jan., 1937.

3894 CUMMINGS, J. M. The rise and decline of
   the railway bus. *London: Omnibus Society*,
   1958. pp. 15, with 8 illus.   IT

G5   RAILWAY WATER SERVICES

Docks, harbours, steamships, etc.—Train ferries and boat trains—
Canal and inland waterway services

3895 GRAHAME, T. Essays and letters on subjects conducive to the improvement and
   extension of inland communication and transport. *Westminster*, 1835. pp. 61.   BM
   pp. 59–60 refers to vessels used for conveying
   loaded railway coal wagons from the Monkland & Kirkintilloch Rly.

3896 COMMERCIAL docks on the southern coast
   of England. *London*, [1836.] pp. 35, with a
   fold. map & fold. plan of proposed railways
   from Southampton.   BM

3897 LEIGH, E. Plan for conveying railway trains
   across the Straits of Dover, showing the
   origin of the idea. *Manchester*, 1870. pp.
   8, with la. fold. plate.   BM
   A train ferry.

3898 OUGHT railway companies in the interests
   of the public and of their shareholders, to
   be steamboat proprietors? A question fully
   answered by the experience of the Great
   Eastern Railway Company in connection
   with their Harwich steamboat working. By
   a Late Shareholder. *London*, 1871. pp. 14,
   with 5 financial tables.   BM

3899 'PROGRESS.' Deep water railway docks in
   the Mersey, versus Manchester Ship Canal.
   By 'Progress'. *Edinburgh*, 1887. pp. 12, with
   3 diagrams.   BM
   Advantages of a railway dock in preference
   to the canal.

3900 WILLIAMSON, J. The Clyde passenger
   steamer: its rise and progress during the
   nineteenth century . . . *Glasgow*, 1904. pp.
   xv, 382.   BM
   pp. 81–98, Railway and steamer.

3901 BODINGTON, O. E. The Channel ferry.
   London, 1906. pp. 36.   BM
   'The transportation of trains across the
   channel in boats.'

3902 WOODWARD, W. H. The organization of
   the Docks and Marine Department. *In*
   'Modern railway working', edited by John
   Macaulay. vol. 2, 1912. pp. 71–94, with
   illus.   BM

3903 BODINGTON, O. E. The Channel ferry.
   In 'Jubilee of the Railway News, 1864–
   1914'. *London: Railway News*, [1914.]
   p. 211.   BM

3904 MACAULAY, J. The economics of dock
   administration. *In* 'Modern railway working', edited by John Macaulay. vol. 8, 1914.
   pp. 1–55, with illus.   BM

3905 RAILWAY companies' steamboat services.
   In 'Jubilee of the Railway News, 1864–1914'.
   London: Railway News, [1914.] pp. 133–6,
   with illus.   BM

3906 BOARD OF TRADE—CANAL CONTROL
   COMMITTEE. Handbook on Canals; containing information relating to controlled
   canals, lists of the towns served by them, and
   names and addresses of public carriers.

London, January 1918. pp. 27, with la. fold. map.   BM

—— 2nd edn. *London*, Nov. 1918. pp. 41, with a list of railway-owned canals, and la. fold. map.   BM

3907 MacQueen, A. Clyde river steamers of the last fifty years . . . *Glasgow & London*, 1923, with illus.   BM
pp. 37–43, Railway steamers, Caledonian Rly. and Glasgow & South Western Rly.

*3908 De Salis, H. R. Bradshaw's canals and navigable rivers of England and Wales: a handbook of inland navigation . . . *London*, 1904. pp. viii, 480.   BM
Railway-owned canals are listed under companies.
—— another edn. *London*, 1928. pp. vii, 455.   BM

3909 Parker, H. *and* Bowen, F. C. Mail and passenger steamers of the nineteenth century. The Macpherson Collection, with iconographical and historical notes. *London*, 1928. pp. xxvii, 324, with 170 illus. on plates & 16 colour plates.   BM
Alphabetically arranged.
Includes railway steamships.

3910 Bulkeley, G. Railway and seaport freight movement, with examples of British and American practice. *London*, 1930. pp. xiv, 221, with many illus. & diagrams.   BM
—— Students' edn. *London*, 1932. pp. xiv, 221.   IT

3911 Yates, S. R. The history and development of train ferries: lecture given to the Railway Club, London . . . 3 November, 1933. pp. 35[36]. *Typescript*.   RC

3912 Burtt, F. Cross Channel and coastal paddle steamers. *London: Richard Tilling*, 1934. pp. 440, with many plates & fold. diagrams.   BM
Individual steamers listed and described. Railway steamship services.

3913 Southern Rly. *and* London & North Eastern Rly. Through goods services to and from the Continent by train ferries. Dover – Dunkerque, Harwich – Zeebrugge. [*London*, 1937.] pp. 15, with illus., fold. map & fold. diagram of wagons.   BR
Cover title, *Train ferries for trade with the Continent*.

3914 Grasemann, C. *and* MacLachlan, G. W. P. English Channel packet boats.
c *London: Syren & Shipping*, 1939. pp. xviii, 205, with illus.   BM
Includes a chronological list and an index of vessels, including railway-owned steamships, engaged in regular cross-Channel service from 1790 to 1939.

3915 British Railways. Steamship services and register of shipping. *London*, Oct. 1948. pp. iii, 36[40].   BR
Tables. Corrections and additions in typescript were issued.

3916 Duckworth, C. L. D. *and* Langmuir, G. E. Railway and other steamers. *Glasgow: Shipping Histories*, 1948. pp. xii, 340.   BM
pp. 189–325, Fleet lists; with a 14 pp. index of ships.

3917 Thomas, J. British Railways steamers of the Clyde. *London: Ian Allan*, 1948. pp. 48, with illus.   BM

3918 British Railways (Scottish Region). Docks and inland waterways in Scotland owned by British Transport Commission. *Glasgow*, [1949.] pp. [16.]   BR
Accommodation and equipment; notes and illustrations.

3919 ABC, British Railways steamers. *London: Ian Allan*, 1953. pp. 46[47].   BM
Lists and illustrations.

3920 Duckworth, C. L. D. *and* Langmuir, G. E. West Coast steamers. *Prescot: T. Stephenson*, 1953. pp. ix, 195, with plates. BM
Includes descriptions of railway-owned steamships, with fleet lists and an index of vessels.

3921 Aickman, R. F. Know your waterways. *London: Coram Publications*, 1955. pp. 119, with illus.   BM
Includes brief histories of canals, with references to railway ownership.
—— [2nd edn.] *London*, [1956.] pp. 112. BM
—— [3rd,] *London*, 1959. pp. 119.   BM
—— [4th,] *London: Press Books*, [1961.] pp. 135.   BM

3922 British Transport Commission. Southampton Docks: Gateway to Britain. *London*, [1956.] pp. xxvi, 49, with illus., maps & plans.   BM

*3923 Farr, G. E. West Country passenger steamers. *London: Richard Tilling*, 1956. pp. 327, with plates.   BM
Includes steamships of the G.W.R., the L. & S.W.R. and other minor railways of the West and South-West.

3924 Bucknall, R. Boat trains and Channel packets: the English short sea routes.
b *London: Vincent Stuart*, 1957. pp. xi, 218, with col. frontis. & 108 illus. on 46 plates, maps & diagrams in text, & a bibliography (35 sources).   BM
The history of the boat services of the South Eastern, the London, Chatham & Dover, the South Eastern & Chatham, the Southern Railway and British Railways (Southern Region).

3925 Sprinks, N. W. Cross-Channel services, 1899 to 1959. pp. 8. *Typescript*.   RC
Paper, Railway Club, 24 March, 1959.

3926 British Transport Commission— Docks Division. Southampton Docks. Official handbook of rates, charges, and general information. *Southampton*, 1960.

pp. 102, with illus., fold. map & chron. table. BR

3927 CLEGG, P. *and* STYRING, J. S. Steamers of British Railways. *Prescot: T. Stephenson & Sons*, 1962. pp. viii, 140, with 16 illus. BM

3928 THORNTON, E. C. B. South Coast pleasure steamers. *Prescot: T. Stephenson & Sons*, 1962. pp. xi, 180, with 25 illus. on 16 plates. BM

Includes accounts of railway-owned steamers and services, with fleet lists.

G6 PUBLIC RELATIONS AND PUBLICITY
For pictorial advertising see also N

3929 JEWELL H. J. The Publicity Department. *In* 'Jubilee of the Railway News, 1864–1914'. *London: Railway News*, [1914.] pp. 213–20, with 17 reproductions of railway posters (12 in full colour). BM

3930 MEACOCK, D. H. F. Papers on railway advertising. pp. 45. *Typescript.* RC
Paper, Railway Club, 8 April, 1921, with MS. deletions.

3931 COURTENAY, J. W., LTD. Tramcar and motor bus advertising. *London*, [*c.* 1928.] pp. 13[15], with 4 illus., map & a table showing passengers per annum of tramway and omnibus services in 37 towns. PC

3932 LONDON PASSENGER TRANSPORT BOARD. A few facts about the Commercial Advertising Service of the L.P.T.B. *Westminster*, [1933.] pp. 33[34], with 22 illus. of advertising on vehicles and on fixed sites. LSE

3933 LONDON, MIDLAND & SCOTTISH RLY.— SCHOOL OF TRANSPORT. Salesmanship. *London*, 1938. pp. viii, 377, with tables, maps & diagrams. BR
'Not for publication.'

3934 DAVIES, A. Salesmanship and the railway. pp. 28. *Reproduced typescript.* IT
Paper, L.S.E. Railway Students' Association, 27 April, 1939.
Selling railway services.

3935 HARRISON, A. A. *and* FAWKNER, N. D. Selling the transport which the public wants. [*Felixstowe*, 1950.] pp. 27. BR
Paper, British Transport Commission Second Officers' Conference, Felixstowe, Second Session, 27 October, 1950. Printed but not published.

3936 SMITH, N. D. H. The presentation of road and rail passenger service information to the public. pp. 8. *Typescript.* IT
Paper, Institute of Transport, East Anglia Group, 8 December, 1950.

*3937 BRITISH TRANSPORT COMMISSION. Catalogue of the British Transport Film Library. *London*, 1954. pp. 40, with alphabetical & subject indexes. BR
Includes films and filmstrips made by the former railway companies.

3938 BRITISH RAILWAYS (LONDON MIDLAND REGION). Station display: a guide to station masters. *London*, 1955. pp. 11. BR
Railway advertising.

3939 ARKLE, E. W. Railway salesmanship. 1956. pp. 10. *Reproduced typescript.* IT
Paper, L.S.E. Railway Students' Association, 14 March, 1956.
The work of the Commercial Department.

3940 ELLIOT, J. Why should we mind what the public think? pp. 11. *Reproduced typescript.* IT
Paper, Institute of Public Relations 7th Annual Conference, 29 April, 1956.
Past experiences as P.R.O. for the Southern Rly. and description of present-day Public Relations & Publicity in London Transport.

3941 RAYMOND, S. E. Selling transport; with particular reference to British Railways. 1957. pp. 16. *Reproduced typescript.* IT
Paper, Institute of Transport, Scottish Section, 17 Dec., 1957.

3942 ROBBINS, R. M. Consulting the passenger. pp. 13. *Reproduced typescript.* IT
Paper, L.S.E. Railway Students' Association, 19 Feb., 1958.

G 7 ANCILLARY SERVICES

Hotels, catering, camping coaches and other special facilities—
Station kiosks and bookstalls

3943 [PHILLIPS, S.] The Literature of the Rail; republished . . . from 'The Times' of Saturday 9th August, 1851; with a preface. *London: John Murray,* 1851. pp. 23.　BM
Concern over the bad effects upon travellers of the trashy reading offered by station bookstalls (L. & N.W. excepted!). The result of a tour of investigation. Particular works and authors are mentioned and praise given to efforts by certain publishers to produce works of true merit in cheap editions to replace 'French novels in bright green covers'.

3944 TOWLE, W. Railway hotels, refreshment rooms, and dining cars. *In* 'Jubilee of the Railway News, 1864–1914'. *London: Railway News,* [1914.] p. 137.　BM

3945 VINCENT, W. Seen from the railway platform: fifty years' reminiscences. *London,* 1919. pp. 206.　BM
pp. 13–16, historical sketch of the rise of the station bookstall; followed by memoirs gathered from service on bookstalls at Tiverton Junction, Didcot, Taunton, Swansea, Reading and Euston.

3946 BEMROSE, H. H The House of Bemrose, 1826–1926. *Derby,* 1926. pp. xiv, 160, with plates.　BM
pp. 45–50, The printing of timetables.

3947 SMITH, W. H., & SON. W. H. Smith & Son: the romance of a great business. [*London,*] 1931. pp. 31.　LSE

3948 RAILWAY AIR SERVICES. [A collection of timetables and information booklets. Eight items, 1936–38.]　BR
Railway Air Services was the operating company formed by the four main line railway companies, Coast Lines Ltd., and Imperial Airways.

3949 MCCORQUODALE & COMPANY. A brief history of the rise of Cardington Street factory during one hundred years, 1846–1946. By G. W. S. *London,* [1946.] pp. 16, with illus.　pc
Railway printing, including a list of railways served.

3950 MCCORQUODALE & COMPANY. A survey of the foundation and growth of McCorquodale & Co., Ltd., during one hundred years. [*London,* 1946.] pp. [4.]　pc

3951 KOCHER, E. M. British railway catering.
b Thesis presented to the Faculty of Law & Economics of the University of Berne for obtaining the degree of Doctor rerum politicarum, [1956.] *Berne,* 1960. pp. 102, with bibliography.　BR
A, Historical; B, Catering under the 'Big Four'; C, Nationalised railway catering.

3952 TRAVEL refreshed: a pictorial review of the British Transport Hotels and Catering Services, and Pullman Car Co. *London: Ian Allan,* [1961.] pp. 40, with many illus. incl. 32 in colour.　BM

G 8 RESEARCH

3953 STAMP, J. C. Criticism, and other addresses. *London,* 1931. pp. 235.　BR
pp. 154–78, Scientific research in transport and the need for co-ordination.

3954 [LONDON, MIDLAND & SCOTTISH RLY.] Chemistry on the British main line railways. [*London,*] 1947. pp. 7.　BR
The place of chemistry in the development and maintenance of railways. Historical and descriptive.

3955 LONDON, MIDLAND & SCOTTISH RLY. The Scientific Research Department of the L.M.S. *Derby,* [1947.] pp. 23, with illus. BM

3956 BRITISH RAILWAYS. Memorandum on the services provided by the Railway Executive Research Department. *London,* January 1951. pp. 13.　BR

3957 HERBERT, T. M. Railway research. pp. 8. *Reproduced typescript.*　IT
Paper, L.S.E. Railway Students' Association, 12 March, 1958.

3958 UNITED KINGDOM RAILWAY ADVISORY SERVICE. United Kingdom Railway Advisory Service. Service de consultation britanniques des chemins de fer. El servico britanico de asesoramiento ferroviario. *London,* 1961. pp. 7.　BM
A brochure.

H RAILWAY LABOUR

Work and working conditions of railway servants and railway navvies and labourers—Pay, welfare, pensions and superannuation—Labour/management relations, labour questions and disputes, trade unions, strikes—Staff training—Safety of employees—Medical services—Memoirs of railway life

For railways and politics generally see **K**
For memoirs of railwaymen not entered here see under relevant railway in **L**

Marginal symbols: **b** bibliographies
　　　　　　　　 c chronologies
　　　　　　　　 l locomotivemen
　　　　　　　　 n navvies and labourers
　　　　　　　　 s safety, occupational hazards, prevention of accidents

Historical

3959 GRUNDY, F. H. Pictures of the past: memories of men I have met and places I have seen. *London*, 1879. pp. 375.　BM
　　pp. 140–62, The life of railway surveyors during the Railway Mania.
　　F. Grundy recalls acquaintanceships with many well-known railway personalities of the 1840's, including George Stephenson, to whom he was secretary for a time at Tapton House, George R. Stephenson, G. P. Bidder and George Hudson. Also, pp. 73–93, Patrick Branwell Brontë, including letters from Brontë to F. H. Grundy.

3960 VINCENT, C. B. An authentic history of railway trade unionism. By Charles Bassett Vincent, originator of the Amalgamated Society of Railway Servants, The Railway Servants' Orphanage, Derby, The Railway Clerks' Association, etc. *Derby*, 1902. pp. 66.　BM
　　Memoirs and observations on the development of railway trade unions from 1866. A highly autobiographical view, containing many exaggerated claims.

3961 MILLS, W. F. The Railway Benevolent Institution: its rise and progress from 1858 to 1897. *London*, 1903. pp. 182.　BR

3962 LANGDON, R. Life of Roger Langdon, told by himself; with additions by his daughter Ellen. *London*, [1908.] pp. 104.　BM
　　R. Langdon was station-master of Silverton, G.W.Rly., 1867–94.

3963 MUNBY, G. F. W. Former days at Turvey. *London*, 1908. pp. 96.　BM
　　pp. 79–85, 'The coming of the railway and its consequences'. The Bedford & Northampton Rly. (1872). Includes an account of the author's experience among navvies and labourers, and of their life and character.

3964 AMALGAMATED SOCIETY OF RAILWAY SERVANTS. Souvenir History, published on the occasion of the opening of the new offices, Unity House, Euston Road, N.W. September 17th, 1910. [*London*,] 1910. pp. 147, with plates, incl. portraits.　LSE

3965 KENNEY, R. Men and Rails. *London*, [1913.] pp. xiii, 263.　BM
　　'For a more rational treatment of railway problems in the hope that it will lead to a more humane treatment of railwaymen.' The history of relationships between railwaymen and their employers; their hardships, problems and endeavours for improvement; trade unions; the Railway Nationalisation Society.

3966 BAYLEY, G. B. Railway companies' provident funds. *In* 'Jubilee of the Railway News, 1864–1914'. *London: Railway News*, [1914.] pp. 184–7.　BM

3967 EDWARDS, W. R. The development of First Aid to the Injured amongst railway employees. *In* 'Jubilee of the Railway News, 1864–1914'. *London: Railway News*, [1914.] pp. 188–90, with illus.　BM

3968 MACGILL, P. Children of the Dead End: the autobiography of a navvy. *London*, 1914. pp. 305.　BM
n　　pp. [129]–145, & [245]–259, accounts of two periods of work as a railway platelayer in Scotland, late 19th century.

3969 The RAILWAY navvy. *In* 'Jubilee of the way News, 1864–1914'. *London: Railway*
n *News*, [1914.] pp. 26–8, with 8 illus.　BM

3970 COLE, G. D. H. *and* ARNOT, R. P. Trade unionism on the railways: its history and problems. *London: Fabian Research Department*, 1917. pp. 147. [*Trade Union Series*, no. 2.]　BM

3971 WEBB, S. J. *and* WEBB, B. The history of trade unionism. *London*, 1894. pp. xvi, 558. Includes railways.　BM
　　—— 2nd edn. *London*, 1896. pp. xvi, 558.　BM
　　—— new edn., *London*, 1920. pp. xviii, 784.　BM

3972 ALCOCK, G. W. The life of John H. Dobson, ex-organiser, National Union of Railwaymen. *London*, 1921. pp. 79.　BM

3973 RAYNES, J. R. Engines and men: the history
of the Associated Society of Locomotive
l Engineers and Firemen: a survey of organisation of railways and railway locomotive
men. *Leeds*, 1921. pp. xv, 302, with plates.
BM

3974 ALCOCK, G. W. Fifty years of railway trade
unionism. *London*, 1922. pp. xvi, 631, with
17 plates.   BM
The Amalgamated Society of Railway Servants.

3975 LABOUR   RESEARCH   DEPARTMENT.
Labour and capital on the railways. *London*, 1923. pp. 64. [*Studies in Labour and
Capital*. no. 4.]   LSE
pp. 42 to end, history and present position of
railway trade unions.

*3976 YOUNG, R. Timothy Hackworth and the
locomotive. *London*, 1923. pp. xxxii, 406.
l   BM
pp. 293–311, The first engine drivers. Working conditions and methods.

3977 STOKES, A. Fifty years on the railway:
yarns by a Methodist signalman . . . *Birmingham: the author*, 1936. pp. 74, with illus.
& some verse.   BR
A. Stokes was with the G.W.R. and worked
Solihull box from 1892 to 1936.

3978 NATIONAL UNION OF RAILWAYMEN.
Silver Jubilee Souvenir. General Secretary's
report to the Annual General Meeting,
Southport, July 1938. *London*, 1938. pp.
136, with illus.   NUR
pp. 1–22, historical account of railway trade
unionism.

*3979 KLINGENDER, F. D. Art and the Industrial
Revolution. *London: Noel Carrington*, 1947.
n pp. xiii, 232, with plates.   BM
pp. 136–41, The railway navvy. The plates
include reproductions of scenes of railway construction.

3980 MACKILLOP, N. The Lighted Flame: a
history of the Associated Society of Loco-
l motive Engineers and Firemen. *London:
Nelson*, 1950. pp. xiii, 402, with 18 plates,
& illus.   BM

3981 KINGSFORD, P. W. Railway labour, 1830–
1870. Thesis, Ph.D.(Econ.), University of
b London, 1951. pp. 333, with bibliogr.
notes & a bibliography. *Typescript*.   UL
Railway employment in England and Wales
(1) as an element in railway economy, and (2) as
a feature of the social life of the nation.

3982 STREET, J. W. I drove the Cheltenham
Flyer . . . *London: Nicholson & Watson*, 1951.
l pp. 154, with plates.   BM
An autobiography.

3983 HALVERSON, G. C. Development of labour
relations in the British railways since 1860.

b Thesis submitted for the Degree of Doctor
of Philosophy, University of London: London School of Economics & Political Science,
March 1952. pp. vii, 889. with a bibliography of 34 pages & bibliogr. notes.
Typescript.   UL
Includes the effect of nationalization on
labour relations.

3984 INTERNATIONAL TRANSPORT-WORKERS
FEDERATION. A brief survey of the history
and activities of the I.T.W.F. [*London*, 1952.]
pp. 48, with portraits of officials and delegates.   BM

3985 KINGSFORD, P. W. Labour relations on
the railways, 1835–1875. *In* 'Journal of
b Transport History', vol. 1, no. 2, November
1953. pp. 65–81, with 2 tables (strikes, &
railwaymen's petitions) & 50 bibliogr. notes.
BM

3986 LLOYD, R. Railwaymen's Gallery. *Lon-
n don: Allen & Unwin*, 1953. pp. 116.   BM
pp. 32–45, 'The old English navvy.'

3987 SALMON, J. L. A proud heritage: the
story of the Railway Convalescence Homes.
London: Railway Convalescence Homes,
1954. pp. 100, with 33 illus.   BM

3988 RANSOME-WALLIS, P. Men of the foot-
plate. *London: Ian Allan*, 1954. pp. 96, with
l 84 illus. on 33 plates.   BM
Collected memoirs of Walter T. Harris,
G.W.R.; Percy Cox, Southern; Albert Young,
L.M.S.; Charles H. Simmons, L.N.E.R.

3989 GRANT, J. S. Notes for lecture on development of Railway Medical Service. By Dr.
J. S. Grant. 1956. pp. 9. *Reproduced
typescript*.   BR
From 1847 to the present.

3990 BAGWELL, P. S. Early attempts at national
organization of the railwaymen, 1865–
b 1867. *In* 'Journal of Transport History',
vol. 3, no. 2, November 1957. pp. 94–102,
with 30 bibliogr. notes.   BM
Events leading up to the establishment of the
Amalgamated Society of Railway Servants in
1871.

*3991 PRIBIĆEVIĆ, B. The demand for workers'
control in the railway, mining and engineer-
b ing industries, 1910–22. Thesis, D.Phil.,
Oxford, 1957. pp. 724, with (pp. 706–24) a
bibliography. *Typescript*.
BODLEIAN LIBRARY, OXFORD

3992 BEALEY, F. *and* PELLING, H. Labour and
politics, 1900–1906: a history of the Labour
Representation Committee. *London: Macmillan & Co.*, 1958. pp. xi, 313.   BM
pp. 55–72, 'Taff Vale'; with bibliogr. notes.

3993 GUPTA, P. S. The history of the Amalgamated Society of Railway Servants, 1871–

b 1913. Thesis, D.Phil., University of Oxford, 1960. pp. vii, 537, with many bibliogr. notes, tables, and an extensive bibliography of primary and secondary material. *Typescript.*
NUR

3994 MACKILLOP, N. How I became an engine driver. *London: Nelson*, 1953. pp. ix, 116,
l with 7 plates, & illus.   BM
Norman MacKillop's career on the L.N.E.R.
—— 2nd edn. *London*, 1960. pp. ix, 116. BM

3995 PATMORE, J. A. A navvy gang of 1851. *In* 'Journal of Transport History', vol. 5,
n no. 3, May 1962. pp. 182–9, with 4 diagrams & 6 notes.   BM

3996 BAGWELL, P. S. The Railwaymen: the history of the National Union of Railwaymen.
b *London: George Allen & Unwin*, 1963. pp. 725, with col. frontis., 33 illus. on 16 plates, many bibliogr. notes, & a select bibliography of 90 items.   BM
An authoritative work.
pp. 671–95, 'Railwaymen and working-class education', by Frank Moxley.
pp. 698–701, Table of numbers of members, benefits paid, and total funds for each year, 1872 to 1961.

3997 BAGWELL, P. S. The National Union of Railwaymen, 1913–1963: a half-century of
c industrial trade unionism. *London: National Union of Railwaymen*, [1963.] pp.[46,] with 27 illus. (incl. 19 ports.), reproductions of posters & adverts., membership tables, & an outline chronology from 1872.   BM
Cover title, *N.U.R. Golden Jubilee Souvenir, 1913–1963.*
A concise review of railway trade unionism since 1872, based upon Dr. Bagwell's *The Railwaymen* (1963).

Contemporaneous

3998 SOCIETY OF FRIENDS. To the railroad excavators. 'My friends . . .' [*London, c.*
n 1838.] pp. 4. [*Tract Association of the Society of Friends. Publication* no. 101.]   BM

3999 MANCHESTER & LEEDS RLY. Accidents on railways, published by order of the direc-
s tors of the Manchester & Leeds Railway, for distribution among the company's servants. *Manchester*, 1840. pp. 42.   H
—— another edn. *Manchester*, 1841. pp. 19.   H

4000 CHADWICK, E. Papers read before the Statistical Society of Manchester on the
n demoralisation and injuries occasioned by
s the want of proper regulations of labourers engaged in the construction and working of railways . . . *Manchester*, [1846.] pp. iv, 51.   BM
Railway management should be responsible for protection from injury of its servants: pp. 9–17, a letter from John Robertson: pp. 45–51, a paper by Robert Rawlinson.

4001 MORAL and physical evils in connection with railway works . . . [*Manchester*, 1846.] pp. 10.   BM
From the *Manchester Guardian*, 7 & 11 March, 1846.
Considerations arising from Edwin Chadwick's pamphlet *Papers read before the Statistical Society of Manchester on the demoralisation and injuries occasioned by the want of proper regulations of labourers engaged in the construction & working of railways* (1846).

4002 NICHOLSON, T. Strictures on a pamphlet published at the request of the Manchester
n Statistical Society entitled 'Papers read before the Statistical Society of Manchester
s on the demoralisation & injuries occasioned by the want of proper regulations of labourers engaged in the construction & working of railways'. *Manchester*, 1846. pp. 24. LSE
Nicholson, a contractor for the Manchester & Sheffield Rly.'s Woodhead Tunnel, maintains that accidents are caused by the men's own carelessness and their disobedience to instructions. Cases cited. See *Great Central*, by George Dow. vol. 1 (1959), pp. 63–8.

4003 PARLIAMENT—HOUSE OF COMMONS. Railway labourers and labourers on public
n works. Report of a Select Committee of the House of Commons appointed to inquire into the condition of the labourers employed in the construction of railways and other public works . . . *London*, [1846.] pp. 44[45].   BM
A reprint of the official report.

4004 The NAVVIES. no. 1, Harry Johnson: a tale. (no. 2, Frank Meade: a tale.) *London,*
n 1847. pp. 94.   BM
pp. 87–94, Report of a trial for murder in a fight by railway labourers; from *The Times.*

4005 SEWELL, J. A complete set of rules and regulations for the practical management
l of a locomotive engine, and for the guidance of engine drivers. *London*, 1848. pp. 72. (Division A, Locomotive Engines, First Paper) *In* 'The principles and practice and explanation of the machinery of locomotive engines in operation on the several lines of railway . . .' by Thomas Tredgold.   BM
Qualifications, pay, and conditions of service; duties, including observations of signals; management of different kinds of trains under various conditions, etc., with 13 tables, and a glossary of terms.

4006 BRYDGES, C. J. Railway superannuation: an examination of the scheme of the General Railway Association for providing superannuation allowances to worn out and disabled railway employés. *London*, 1852. pp. 16.   BM

4007 BARBOUR, G. F. Letter to . . . Edward Cardwell, M.P., President of the Board of
s Trade, on the occasion of his Bill for the prevention of railway accidents . . . with appendix and documents. 1854. pp. 22.
NLC
Fatigue in railwaymen caused by the loss of their rest-day due to Sunday working of trains.

4008 The LEISURE hours of a railway labourer
. . . *Edinburgh*, 1855. pp. 96.   BM
n   Miscellaneous pieces, including satirical
verse arising from the author's work on the
North British Rly.

4009 FITZGERALD, J. The duty of procuring for
the labouring classes the earlier closing of
l   shops and the Saturday half-holiday. *London*, [1856.] pp. 75.   BM
pp. 49–56, 'The railway porters, engine
drivers, etc., deprived of religious observance on
Sundays'. Also a letter from Mark Huish on
L. & N.W. policy with regard to Saturday half-
holidays.

4010 [MARSH, C. M.] English hearts and English hands; or, The railway and the trenches.
n   By the author of 'Memorials of Captain
Hedley Vicars'. *London*, 1858. pp. xi, 356. BM
An account of the life of railway navvies
assembled to build the Crystal Palace at
Sydenham. The final chapter (pp. [347]–356) is
the most informative.
—— Das Pfarrhaus zu Beckenham. *Hamburg*, 1859.   BM

4011 [TREGELLES, A. R.] The ways of the line:
a monograph on excavators. *Edinburgh*,
n   1858. pp. 167.   BM

4012 PALK, W. A glance at the navvies. *London*,
n   1859. pp. 80.   BM
A record of observations: drink, the 'tommy
shops' and the tramp navvy.

4013 DEATH or Life; or, The story of my experience on 'the line': its partial successes
n   and its many failures, with some suggestions
as to their cause: being another appeal on
behalf of railway labourers; by one who has
known them for twenty years. *London:
Nisbet*, 1864. pp. 277.   LIVERPOOL PL
A record of missionary work.

4014 FLETCHER, J. O. Railways in their medical
s   aspects. *London*, 1867. pp. vi, 184.   BM
pp. 16–48, dangers to health in railway
work.

4015 MILLS, W. F. The railway service: its
exigencies, provisions and requirements.
s   *London*, 1867. pp. 141.   BM
A comprehensive work with a table showing
numbers and classification of railway employees, occupational hazards, insurance, wages,
provident societies, tables of accidents to railway
servants, superannuation systems, railway
building societies, the co-operative movement,
railway schools, benevolent institutions, friendly
societies, etc.

4016 [CONDER, F. R.] Personal recollections of
English engineers, and of the introduction of
n   the railway system into the United Kingdom.
By a Civil Engineer. *London*, 1868. pp. xvi,
432.   BM
Accounts of the work of surveyors, contractors and navvies, etc.

4017 BALLANTYNE, R. M. The Iron Horse; or,
Life on the line . . . *London*, 1871. pp. vi,
l   407, with illus.   BM
'A story founded largely on facts.'

4018 AMALGAMATED SOCIETY OF RAILWAY
SERVANTS. Full report of the First General
Meeting . . . together with a concise history
of the Union from its commencement. By
Edwin Phillips. *London*, 1872. pp. 46.   BM

4019 BRASSEY, T. Work and wages, practically
illustrated. *London*, 1872. pp. xvi, 296. BM
Includes examples of wages paid on various
railways.
—— 2nd edn. *London*, 1872. pp. xvi, 296.
        BM
—— 3rd, 'On work and wages'. *London*,
1872. pp. xvi, 296.   BM
—— [4th], 'On work and wages'. *London*,
1873. pp. xvi, 296.   BM

4020 [PHILLIPS, E.] A Voice from the Signal
Box; or, Railway accidents and their causes.
By A Signalman. *London*, 1874. pp. 48. BM
pp. 37–48 are adverts.
Introduced and presented by Edwin Phillips
to M. T. Bass, M.P., on behalf of an anonymous
signalman.

4021 AMALGAMATED SOCIETY OF RAILWAY
SERVANTS. Railway servants: an appeal to
s   Parliament and the public. (By Frederick W.
Evans.) *London*, [1878.] pp. 51.   LSE
'In support of the recommendations contained in the Report of the Royal Commission
on Railway Accidents, especially relating to
compensation to servants for injuries.'

4022 KIRKMAN, M. M. Railway service: trains
and stations; describing the manner of
operating trains, and the duties of train and
station officials. *New York*, 1878. pp. vii,
271.   BM
pp. 238–61, Regulations affecting employment and conditions on British railways and for
working the block system.

4023 GRIPPER, C. F. Railway tunnelling in
heavy ground. *London*, 1879. pp. 66, with 3
n   fold. plates.   BM
pp. 54–6, 'Beer versus work'.

*4024 [SIMMONS, H. A.] Ernest Struggles; or, The
comic incidents and anxious moments in
connection with the life of a station master.
By one who endured it. *London & Reading*,
[1879.] 2 vols. (pp. viii, 240: viii, 236.) BM
H. A. Simmons was at Windsor Station,
G.W.R., and had fifteen years' service on the
line.

4025 BARRETT, D. W. Life and work among the
navvies. 3rd edn. *London*, 1883. pp. xv, 162,
n   with illus.   BM

4026 EDDY, W. L'employé de chemins de fer; sa
condition en France et en Angleterre. *Paris*,
1883. pp. 56.   BM
A comparison of various aspects of railway
employment in France and in Britain.

4027 MACLEAN, J. L. The British railway system: a description of the work performed in
l   the principal departments. *London*, 1883.
pp. 103.   BM

4028 STRETTON, C. E. A few remarks on railway servants and the law. 4th edn. *Leicester*, 1883. pp. 8.   BM

4029 GARNETT, E. Our navvies, a dozen years
n   ago and today. *London*, 1885. pp. vi, 303.   BM
    Includes verses and anecdotes and an account of missionary work among navvies.

4030 HARFORD, E. Suggestions for safe railway working . . . *London: Amalgamated Society of*
s   *Railway Servants*, [1885.] pp. 71.   BM
    Twenty-three necessary requirements.

4031 MacGREGOR, D. Railway superannuation funds: their operation and suggested improvements. [*Edinburgh*, 1887.] pp. 16.

4032 REYNOLDS, M. Locomotive engine-driving: a practical manual for engineers in charge of
l   locomotive engines. *London*, 1877. pp. xiv, 225, with illus.   BM
    Includes advice concerning duties and technique; details of examinations and regulations.
   —— 2nd ed. *London*, 1878. pp. xiv, 225. BM
   —— 3rd, *London*, 1878. pp. xiii, 258.   BM
   —— 5th, *London*, 1882. pp. xiii, 258.   IT
   —— 6th, *London*, 1884. pp. xiii, 258.   BM
   —— 7th, *London*, 1885. pp. xiii, 258.   RC
   —— 8th, *London*, 1888. pp. xiii, 258.   IT

4033 SCOTTISH LEADER, *newspaper*. Slavery on Scottish railways. Reprinted from the Scottish Leader of June 4, 1888 and following dates. *Glasgow: Amalgamated Society of Railway Servants for Scotland*, 1888. pp. 16. [*Scottish Leader Specials* no. 2.]   LSE

4034 BAERNREITHER, J. M. English associations of working men. English edition, enlarged & revised. *London*, 1889. pp. xv, 473.   BM
    pp. 206–17, Railway company [friendly] societies.
   —— Die englischen Arbeiterverbände und ihr Recht. *Tübingen*, 1886.   BM

4035 RAILWAY CLEARING SYSTEM SUPERANNUATION FUND ASSOCIATION. Acts . . . and Deed Poll of the Railway Clearing System Superannuation Fund Association. *London*, 1890. pp. 44.   LSE
    Text of the Acts 36 & 37 Vic. ch. 88, and 47 & 48 Vic. ch. 6.

4036 FRITH, H. Biography of a Locomotive . . .
l   *London*, 1891. pp. 254.   BM
    Memoirs and short stories centred upon railway life and work.

4037 LIBERTY AND PROPERTY DEFENCE LEAGUE. Trade-unionism and free labour: speeches in the House of Lords by the Earl of Wemyss, Earl Fortescue, Lord Bramwell. *London: Hansard Publishing Union*, 1891. pp. 11.   LSE
    The Scottish railway strike. On the question of protection for unionists and non-unionists who are willing to work.

4038 MAVOR, J. The Scottish railway strike, 1891: a history and criticism. *Edinburgh*, 1891. pp. 66, with bibliogr. notes.   BM

4039 AMALGAMATED SOCIETY OF RAILWAY SERVANTS. Return of the hours of duty and rates of wages paid to railway servants on the principal lines in Great Britain, in operation May 1884 and May 1891. *London*, 1892.   LSE

4040 CHANNING, F. A. Overwork on railways and the remedy: draft report of the Select Committee on Railway Servants (Hours of Labour) proposed by F. A. Channing, M.P. *London*, [1892.] pp. 24.   LSE

4041 RAILWAYS and railway men. *London & Edinburgh*, 1892. pp. 128, with illus.   BM
    A popular description of the work of various classes of personnel.

*4042 REYNOLDS, M. Engine-driving life; or, Stirring adventures and incidents in the lives
l   of locomotive engine-drivers. *London*, 1881. pp. vi, 190.   BM
   —— 2nd edn. with additional chapters. *London*, 1889. pp. xi, 208.   IT
   —— 3rd, *London*, 1894. pp. xi, 208.   RC

4043 AMALGAMATED SOCIETY OF RAILWAY SERVANTS. Signalmen's hours of duty. Verbatim report of an interview of a deputation from the National Conference of Signalmen with . . . Charles T. Ritchie, M.P., President of the Board of Trade, February 14th, 1896. *London*, [1896.] pp. 16.   LSE

4044 PENNINGTON, M. Railways and other ways: being reminiscences of canal and railway life during a period of sixty-seven years; with characteristic sketches of canal and railway men, early tram roads and railways. *Toronto*, 1896. pp. 407, 48.   BM
    Railways of Canada and of Gt. Britain.

4045 RAILWAY EMPLOYEES' INTERCHANGE PRIVILEGE TICKET DELEGATION. The Railway Employee's Interchange Fares Book. *London*, 1896. pp. 105.
    A guide to interchange through bookings, arranged alphabetically under railways.

4046 [AMALGAMATED SOCIETY OF RAILWAY SERVANTS.] Labour's right to combine. The London & North Western-Railway Co. and its attitude towards its employés who are members of the A.S.R.S. Attempts at intimidation and how they were met and frustrated in December 1896. *London*, 1897. pp. 48.   LSE

4047 CROKER, E. J. Retrospective lessons on railway strikes, United Kingdom. *London & Cork*, 1898. pp. vi, 205.   BM
    Irish railway labour disputes, especially that of the Cork, Bandon & South Coast Rly., 1897–8. Criticism of trade unions.

4048 GORDON, W. J. Everyday life on the rail-
1 road. [*London*, 1892.] pp. 192, with illus.
                                   BM
    —— 2nd edn. *London*, 1898. pp. 192.   BM

4049 MacDONNELL, R. How to become a locomotive engineer: being advice to young
mechanical engineers passing through locomotive works. New edn. *London*, 1899. pp.
61.

4050 MINING ASSOCIATION OF GREAT BRIT-
AIN. Regulation of Railways Bill. Auto-
s matic couplings. Deputation to . . . C. T.
Ritchie, M.P. . . . *London*, 1899. pp. 45. BR
    Against the proposal to fit automatic coup-
lings to all wagons as a safety measure. 'Great
variation in dimensions of private owners'
wagons makes such modification impracticable. It will be sufficient to enforce the use of
the "coupling stick".'

4051 BELL, R. *and* SUNTER, T. Conference of
delegates of the Associated Society of Loco-
1 motive Engineers & Firemen and the Amalgamated Society of Railway Servants with
respect to federation; held at the Green
Dragon Hotel, Leeds, 3rd January, 1900.
Leeds, 1900. pp. 23.   NUR

4052 COOKE, C. J. B. British locomotives: their
history, construction and modern develop-
1 ment; with numerous illustrations . . . and
reproductions of official drawings and photographs. *London*, 1893. pp. xvi, 381.   BM
    pp. 341–76, Engine-drivers and their duties;
duties of drivers and firemen when working a
train.
    —— 2nd edn. *London*, 1894. pp. xvi, 381.
                                   RC
    —— 3rd, *London*, 1900. pp. xix, 422.   BM

4053 GENERAL RAILWAY WORKERS' UNION.
Manifesto to the railwaymen of the United
Kingdom. *London*, [*c.* 1900.] pp. [3.] LSE
'Join our trades union.'

4054 ORMEROD, C. The Driver's and Fireman's
Correspondent; or, How to make out appli-
1 cations and reports. *Plymouth*, 1895. pp. 71.
                                   BM
    —— another edn. *Plymouth*, 1900. pp. 84.
                                   BM

4055 AMALGAMATED SOCIETY OF RAILWAY
SERVANTS. The Taff Vale Case and the
injunction. *London*, Oct. 6 1902. pp. 55.
    'Private.'   LSE
    The LSE copy is followed by a letter dated 25
Nov., 1902, from Richard Bell to Mrs Sidney
Webb (Beatrice Webb), outlining the main
points.

4056 CAUSE and cure of railway labour disputes;
to railway shareholders and the men who
earn the dividends. By an experienced railway man . . . *London*, 1902. pp. 16.   BM

4057 OLIVER, T. Dangerous trades: the historical, social, and legal aspects of industrial
s occupations as affecting health, by a number
of experts. Edited by Thomas Oliver. *London*,
1902. pp. xxi, 891, with illus.   BM
    pp. 190–202, Railways.
    pp. 744–6, Underground railways. Vitiation
of air in Metropolitan Rly. tunnels.

4058 The TAFF VALE Railway Company v. The
Amalgamated Society of Railway Servants,
Richard Bell, James Holmes, Philip Hewlett,
George W. Alcock, and John Pilcher.
Heard before Mr. Justice Wills and a special
jury on the 15th December 1902. Judgement
of Mr. Justice Wills. pp. 18.   LSE
    Unpublished galley proof.

4059 BELL, R. *and* FOX, A. Conference of delegates of the Associated Society of Locomotive Engineers and Firemen and the
Amalgamated Society of Railway Servants
with respect to federation. held at the Leeds
Trades and Labour Hall, Leeds, 18th May
1903. *Leeds*, 1903. pp. 27.   NUR
    Includes the proposed scheme of federation.

4060 BOOTH, C. Life and labour of the people in
London. Second series: Industry, vol. 3.
London, 1903.   BM
    pp. 336–49, Railway service and railway
labour. Tables at end. Railways are shown on
the detailed maps which accompany this series.

4061 CHAPMAN, S. J. Work and wages, in continuation of Lord Brassey's 'Work and
wages' and 'Foreign work and wages'. Part
1, Foreign competition . . . *London*, 1904.
pp. xxxv, 301.   BM
    pp. 257–96, 'Railways'.

4062 RAILWAY BENEVOLENT INSTITUTION—
IRISH BRANCH. Tales of the Rail by Rail-
1 waymen . . . 1st edn. *Dublin*, 1904. pp. vii,
112.   BM
    A selection of anecdotes and short stories,
mostly humorous.

4063 AMALGAMATED SOCIETY OF RAILWAY
SERVANTS. Manifesto to railway servants.
Facts and figures for non-unionists. *London*,
February 1905. pp. 4. [*H.O.* no. 189.] LSE

4064 RIDGE, W. P. On Company's Service.
1 *London*, 1905. pp. viii, 251.   BM
    Stories of railway life.

4065 RIEBENACK, M. Railway provident institutions in English-speaking countries. *Philadelphia*, 1905. pp. 357, 31, [30,] with illus.
                                   LSE
    Welfare (insurance, relief, pension, super-
annuation, hospital funds, libraries, literary
institutes, loan clubs, etc.), arranged under
companies.

4066 BELL, R. Grievances of North Eastern railwaymen; submitted . . . for discussion on
23rd April, 1906. [1906.] pp. 18.

4067 The CONDITIONS of railway service and the 'National Programme'. *London*, [1906.] pp. 8.   LSE
Reprinted from the *Railway News*.
Trade union arguments refuted. Railway workers' conditions seen from the point of view of management. The effect of wage increases on dividends.

4068 SNOWDEN, K. The Railway Nerve: a day in the life of an engine driver; with 12 special
l photographs. *London*, 1906. pp. 14.   BR
Reprinted from the *Pall Mall Magazine*.

4069 AMALGAMATED SOCIETY OF RAILWAY SERVANTS. Facts and figures for locomo-
l tive-men. *London*, January 1907. pp. 4. [*H.O.* no. 235.]   LSE

4070 AMALGAMATED SOCIETY OF RAILWAY SERVANTS. The Railwaymen's Charter. Reply to criticisms; by Richard Bell. *London*, May 1907. pp. 24.   LSE

4071 AMALGAMATED SOCIETY OF RAILWAY SERVANTS. Re driver Gourlay, concerned
l in the Arbroath disaster on December 28, 1906. Report of proceedings taken by the A.S.R.S. for his protection and defence on the charge of manslaughter. *London*, May 1907. pp. 36, with letters, memorials & petitions. [*H.O.* no. 245.]   LSE

4072 AMALGAMATED SOCIETY OF RAILWAY SERVANTS. Summary statement of the results of the Census of Wages, Hours of Labour, etc., of men . . . employed on the railways of the United Kingdom. *London*, [1907.] pp. 11, with fold. chart & fold. map showing the location of branches.   LSE

4073 ASSOCIATED SOCIETY OF LOCOMOTIVE ENGINEERS & FIREMEN. Items of interest
l and extracts from 'Railway Service Gazette' and 'Railway Review', etc., 1877 onwards; showing that prior to the existence of the A.S.L.E. & F. the necessary protection was not provided. By A. Fox. [*Leeds*, 1907.] pp. 30.   TUC
Reasons for the separate existence of a locomen's trade union.

4074 GREAT WESTERN RLY. To the proprietors of the Great Western Railway. [*London*, 1907.] pp. 72.   LSE
Speeches, letters, and a reprint of Richard Bell's pamphlet *The Railwaymen's Charter* with point by point comments by the G.W.R.; correspondence between the G.W.R. General Manager and R. Bell, 1907, and between the G.W.R. and the Board of Trade on the Ebbw Vale Case, 1907.

4075 STANDARD, *newspaper*. The railway position with regard to labour questions. Extract from the Standard, June 13, 1907. [*London*, 1907.] pp. 8.   BM
The growing militance of trade unions and their threat to the stability of railway management and finance.

4076 ALFASSA, M. La Crise ouvrière récente des chemins de fer anglais: une solution nouvelle des conflits. *Paris*, 1908. pp. 100.

4077 AMALGAMATED SOCIETY OF RAILWAY SERVANTS. Report, giving statement of the results of the Census of Wages, Hours of Labour, etc. of men (in those grades referred to in the demands of the A.S.R.S.) employed on the railways of the United Kingdom. *London*, [January 1908.] pp. 135.   LSE
Comprehensive tables, the result of a referendum by means of a questionnaire, copies of which were sent to all branch secretaries in August 1907.

4078 BARING, E. Wages and Hours Arbitration. Award of the Earl of Cromer, 1st April, 1909. [Midland Rly.] pp. 35.   LSE
Printed but not published.

4079 GEDDES, E. C. Education and advancement of the railway clerk: paper read before the York Railway Lecture & Debating Society, 4th October, 1910. [*York*, 1910.] pp. 22.   LSE
E. C. Geddes was Chief Goods Manager, N.E. Rly.

4080 OSBORNE, W. V. Trade union funds and party politics: a statement of the case by Walter V. Osborne, Secretary, Walthamstow Branch, A.S.R.S. *Walthamstow*, 1910. pp. 16.   BM
Against a proposed alteration of Trade Union law to legalise levies upon members for the support of political parties.

4081 MACGILL, P. Gleanings from a navvy's
n scrap book. 1910.
The writer worked on the Caledonian Rly.
—— [2nd] edn. [1911.]

4082 MEMORANDUM on the Railway Conciliation Scheme of 1907 and its bearing on the recent railway disturbances: based on the Evidence given before the Royal Commission of Inquiry, August 28—October 3, 1911. pp. 28. *Typescript*.

4083 RAILWAY CLERKS' ASSOCIATION. The life of the railway clerk: a brief description of the main conditions of employment in the offices of British railway companies, and a statement of the case for higher scales of salary for all grades of railway clerical workers. Prepared by three experienced railwaymen . . . [*London*,] 1911. pp. 30[32].
With tables showing relationship of incomes to cost of living and to clerical salaries elsewhere.

4084 RAILWAY CLERKS' ASSOCIATION. Railway clerks and the National Insurance Bill: how exemption was secured. *London*, 1911. pp. 31.   LSE
Reprinted from the *Railway Clerk*, 15 November, 1911.

4085 SHANN, M. C. The lesson of the railway strike; or, The true method of co-partnership between labour and capital, particularly in the coming motor industry. [*London*, 1911.] pp. 7. LSE

4086 TAYLOR, G. The English railway strike and its revolutionary bearings. *Chicago*, 1911. pp. 15. [*City Club Bulletin* vol. 4, no. 19.] LSE
Paper, read 11 Oct., 1911. Also appeared in the *Survey*, 7 October, under the title 'England's revolutionary strike'.

4087 TILLETT, B. History of the London transport workers' strike, 1911. *London*, [1912.] pp. xii, 71. BM

4088 WATKINS, C. Conciliation or emancipation? (The question for railwaymen.) *In* 'Industrial Syndicalist', vol. 1, no. 11, May 1911. pp. 32. LSE

4089 BUREAU OF RAILWAY ECONOMICS [Washington]. A comparative study of railway wages and the cost of living in the United States, the United Kingdom and the principal countries of continental Europe. *Washington*, 1912. pp. 77. [*Bulletin* no. 34.] LSE

4090 LABOUR PARTY. Fighting the Government for a guinea a week! The Labour members' appeal for a minimum wage for underpaid railwaymen. *Westminster*, [1912.] pp. 15, with division list on J. H. Thomas's amendment on Railways (no. 2) Bill, Feb. 11, 1912. LSE

4091 LONDON MUNICIPAL SOCIETY—DE-PARTMENT OF SOCIAL ECONOMICS. Digest of official statistics: earnings and hours of labour in the railway service in 1907 and later. *London*, 1912. pp. 16. [*Statistical & Other Memoranda*, 2nd series, no. 3.] BM

4092 RAILWAY CLERKS' ASSOCIATION. The Railways (No. 2) Bill and railway labour questions. Victimisation and intimidation of clerks on the Midland Railway. Reprint of correspondence and general statement of the case, with details of evidence. [*London*, 1912.] pp. 11[12]. LSE

4093 [RAILWAY CLERKS' ASSOCIATION.] The Railway Bill again. [*London*, 1912.] pp. 2. LSE
Reprinted from the *Railway Clerk*, 15 December, 1912.
Dissatisfaction with the Bill, and the need for nationalization.

4094 FERGUSON, J. Experiences of a railway guard: thrilling stories of the rail. 2nd edn. *Dundee*, 1913. pp. 116. BR
Privately printed.
A series of nineteen sketches originally published in the *Weekly News*, and relating mostly to the Caledonian Rly.

4095 NATIONAL UNION OF RAILWAYMEN. Board of Trade inquiry into alleged victimisation of Midland Railway employees, January 1913. *London*, 1913. pp. 298. 'Confidential.'
Verbatim report of proceedings at Winchester House before J. R. Atkin.

4096 RAILWAY CLERKS' ASSOCIATION. The best thing for railway clerks and station-masters. [*London*, 1909.] pp. 2. LSE
—— 'The best thing for railway agents, station-masters and clerks.' [*London*, 1913.] pp. [4.] LSE

4097 RAILWAY CLERKS' ASSOCIATION. Permanency or dismissal? A question for You. 2nd edn. *Wolverhampton*, 1913. pp. 35. LSE
Cover title, 'The future of the railway service'.
Detailed reasons for supporting the R.C.A.

4098 RAILWAY CLERKS' ASSOCIATION. Railways (no. 2) Bill: memorandum as to amendments proposed by the Railway Clerks' Association. [*London*, 1913.] pp. [2.] LSE

4099 RAILWAY CLERKS' ASSOCIATION. Railways (no. 2) Bill: proposed two new clauses. [*London*, 1913.] pp. [2.] LSE
Suggested amendments: 1, to Annual Returns to the Board of Trade respecting grades, pay and hours; and 2, to protect trade union members from victimisation.

4100 SCOTT, J. Railway Romance, and other essays. *London*, [1913.] pp. viii, 291. BM
pp. [3]–137, Railway romance: ten essays, eight of which are on the fascination of railways and of railway life.

4101 CONDITIONS of railway service. *In* 'Jubilee of the Railway News, 1864–1914.' *London: Railway News*, [1914.] pp. 177–83, with illus. BM

4102 GATTIE, A. W. The advantages of economic transport to railway employees. *London: New Transport Co.*, 1914. pp. 27. LSE
Paper, S.E. & C. Rly. Research Association, 2 March, 1914.

4103 GREAT WESTERN RLY. The 'Safety' s Movement. [*London*,] 1914. pp. 47. BR

4104 OSBORNE, W. V. The Taff Vale judgement, and after. *In* 'Jubilee of the Railway News, 1864–1914.' *London: Railway News*, [1914.] pp. 192–4. BM

4105 RAILWAY CLERKS' ASSOCIATION. Forty reasons why you should join the Railway Clerks' Association. [*London*,] 1914. s.sh. LSE

4106 RAILWAY CLERKS' ASSOCIATION. Progress, combination and agreement amongst clerks. (The President's address at the 17th Annual Conference, 1914.) *London*, [1914.] pp. 15.   LSE
President, Herbert Romeril.

4107 RAILWAY conciliation boards. *In* 'Jubilee of the Railway News, 1864–1914.' *London: Railway News*, [1914.] p. 191.   BM

4108 The 'SAFETY' Movement. *Newcastle upon Tyne*, 1914. pp. 47, with illus.   PC
Hints for railwaymen.

4109 WILLIAMS, A. Life in a railway factory. *London*, 1915. pp. xiii, 315.   BM
Memories of twenty-three years at Swindon.

4110 RAILWAY CLERKS' ASSOCIATION. An open letter to a lady clerk. *London*, December 1916. pp. 31[32].   PC
Cover title, *To a lady clerk*.
Persuading women railway clerks to join the R.C.A.

4111 CONFERENCE OF RAILWAY TRADE UNIONISTS, New Earswick, 1917. Report of a conference of trade unionists and others on the industrial outlook on the railways, New Earswick, York, July 28 & 29, 1917. *Darlington*, [1917.] pp. 14.   LSE
'For private circulation only.'
An informal conference. The report is 'a summary of the consensus of opinion'.

4112 NATIONAL UNION OF RAILWAYMEN. Rules of the National Union of Railwaymen as amended in 1914, 1915 and 1916. *London*, 1917. pp. xiv, 80.   BM

4113 GREAT WESTERN RLY. The 'Safety' Movement: an interesting experiment for railwaymen. By Edward S. Hadley. [*London*,] 1918. pp. 7.   BR

4114 RAILWAY CLERKS' ASSOCIATION. Draft National Transport Services Bill, submitted by the Railway Clerks' Association. [*London*, 1918?] pp. 57.   TUC
Drafted by W. K. Southeard, solicitor. Includes schedules relating to superannuation.

4115 LABOUR RESEARCH DEPARTMENT. Report from the Labour Research Department to the National Union of Railwaymen on publicity work undertaken in connection with the recent strike, October 6, 1919. *London*, [1919.] pp. 5.   LSE
Signed, 'R. Page Arnot, Secretary'.

4116 MEMORANDUM in regard to management. [*London: Great Western Rly.*,] Dec. 1920. pp. 30. [*Great Western Pamphlets*, no. 3.]   BR
Management/labour relations. Includes extracts from exchanges during negotiations between the Railway Executive Committee and the railway trades unions in 1919.

4117 NATIONAL TRANSPORT-WORKERS' FEDERATION. Railway dispute, 1919. Report to the Labour movement of Great Britain, by the Committee appointed at the Caxton Hall (London) Conference, 1st Oct. 1919. [*London*, 1919.] pp. 13[14].   LSE
Chairman, Harry Gosling.

4118 ASSOCIATED SOCIETY OF LOCOMOTIVE ENGINEERS & FIREMEN. A further case for locomotive-men as put by the General Secretary and . . . witnesses from the Society before the National Railway Wages Board . . . May 18, 19, 20, & 27, 1920. Extract from the official report of the proceedings. *Leeds*, 1920. pp. 116.   TUC

4119 ASSOCIATED SOCIETY OF LOCOMOTIVE ENGINEERS & FIREMEN. National conditions of service of railway locomotive enginemen, firemen, motormen . . . *Leeds*, 1920. pp. 44.   TUC
A pocket book.

4120 COLE, G. D. H. Chaos and order in industry. *London*, 1920. pp. viii, 292.   BM
pp. 86–111, Nationalization of railways and railway trade unionism: guiding principles.

4121 LANCASHIRE & YORKSHIRE RLY. Hints to avoid injury. *Manchester*, [1920.] pp. 37[39].   BM
At the end is a detachable page for the recipient to return, acknowledging that he has received, carefully read, and retained the pamphlet.

4122 NATIONAL UNION OF RAILWAYMEN— KING'S CROSS NO. 2 BRANCH. The grade movement within the N.U.R. [*London, c.* 1920.] pp. 8.   LSE

4123 THATCHER, A. J. The 1919 railway strike and the settlement of January 1920. *London: National Labour Press*, [1920.] pp. 7, with tables of the new rates of pay.   LSE

4124 UNITED ADVISORY COUNCIL OF CO-OPERATORS & TRADE UNIONISTS. Trade unionism and Co-operation in action: a record of joint action during the railway dispute, 1919. *London*, 1920. pp. 14.   LSE

4125 AZCÁRATE FLÓREZ, P. de. La Guerra y los servicios publicos de carácter industrial. 1, El regimen ferroviario inglés y la guerra. *Madrid*, 1921. pp. 140, with bibliogr. notes.   BM
pp. 82–140, Tradeunionismo ferroviario en Inglaterra.

4126 COLE, G. D. H. Workers' Control for railwaymen. *London: National Guilds League*, [1921.] pp. 23. [*Workers' Control Series*, no. 3.]   BM
Reprinted from his *Chaos and order in industry* (1920).

4127 GREAT WESTERN RLY. The Railways Bill: a circular to shareholders by Churchill, Chairman. 18 May 1921. pp. 3.   LSE
Reporting on progress towards the compos-

ing of difficulties between the Railway Clerks' Association and the Government, and the assertion that the modifications now introduced into the Bill are the result of this.

4128 BROWNE, K. J. N. British railwaymen's wages: what are the facts? Pre-war concessions and post-war costs. *London: Great Western Rly.*, [1922.] pp. 8. (*Great Western Pamphlets* no. 9.)   LSE
Reprinted from the *Financial Times*, 26 June 1922.

4129 GREAT WESTERN RLY. Prevention of accidents: the 'Is it Safe?' pocket token.
s   [*London*,] 1922.   BR
A folder describing the use of a pocket talisman issued to employees in connection with the 'Safety First' campaign. A reminder, to promote personal safety.

4130 HADLEY, E. S. My railway and me: six of one and half-a-dozen of the other. *London: Great Western Rly.*, 1922. pp. 28.   BM
The need for economies by railwaymen.

4131 NATIONAL GUILDS LEAGUE. Towards a National Railway Guild. *London*, [1917.] pp. 16. [*Pamphlets of the N.G.L.*, no. 4.]   LSE
State ownership, but with control and management by railwaymen.

—— another edn. *London*, [1922.] pp. 15.   LSE

4132 ASSOCIATED SOCIETY OF LOCOMOTIVE ENGINEERS & FIREMEN. The financial position of British railways: a reply to the claim of the companies for a revision of the terms of service by our members. *London*, April 1923. pp. 18.   TUC
Reduction in wages unjustifiable.

4133 ASSOCIATED SOCIETY OF LOCOMOTIVE ENGINEERS & FIREMEN. Further case for
l   locomotivemen as put by the General Secretary before the National Railway Wages Board on November 13, 14, 15 & 16, 1923. Extracted from the official report of the proceedings. *London*, 1923. pp. 90.   TUC

4134 BROWNE, K. J. N. The Brown and other systems of railway discipline. *London*, 1923. pp. 67.   BM

4135 RATES of pay and conditions of service of railway operating staff, 1907–1922. *London: Great Western Rly.*, July 1923. pp. 42. [*Great Western Pamphlets*, no. 11.]   BR

4136 ASSOCIATED SOCIETY OF LOCOMOTIVE ENGINEERS & FIREMEN. Locomotive
l   Journal. Special Strike Issue, February 1924. *London*, 1924. pp. 94.   TUC
'The full history of the first official national railway strike of locomotivemen, Jan. 20–29, 1924.'

4137 CHAPPELL, H. Life on the Iron Road.
l   *London*, 1924. pp. viii, 207, with illus.   BM
Twenty essays on the work of various classes of railway personnel.

4138 INTERNATIONAL LABOUR OFFICE. Automatic couplings and the safety of rail-
s   way workers . . . *Geneva*, 1924. pp. 62. [*Studies & Reports*, Series F, section 2, no. 1.]   BM
Report on statistics of accidents due to coupling and uncoupling operations.

4139 INTERNATIONAL TRANSPORT-WORKERS' FEDERATION [Amsterdam]—RAILWAYMEN'S SECTION. Working conditions of railwaymen in different countries. *Amsterdam*, 1924. pp. 139.   TUC
pp. 65–98, Gt. Britain.

4140 LONDON, MIDLAND & SCOTTISH RLY. Prevention is better than cure: a few words
s   of advice regarding the cause and prevention of accidents, dedicated by the London, Midland & Scottish Railway Company to each member of the staff directly or indirectly engaged in the movement of traffic. *London*, 1924. pp. 54, with illus.   PC

4141 NATIONAL UNION OF RAILWAYMEN. Report of a Court of Inquiry into the application of Decision no. 728 of the Industrial Court to the London & North Eastern Rly. (Great Northern Section) with conclusions of the Industrial Court, April 15, 1924. *London*, 1924. pp. 159.   LSE

4142 TRIBUNAL FOR THE TRAMWAY INDUSTRY. Tramway industry, England, Wales, Scotland, Northern Ireland. Decision and report of the Tribunal for the Tramway Industry on Grouping, standardisation, increase in wages, stabilisation, and night work. (Chairman, Wm. H. Mackenzie.) *London*, 1st November, 1924. pp. 43.   LSE
Submitted to the Joint Industrial Council for the Tramway Industry. Contains schedules of recommended scales of pay.

4143 SIME, W. 'Repta' records: a brief history of the Railway Employees' Privilege Ticket Association. *Derby*, 1926. pp. 120.   LSE
Cheap travel facilities for railwaymen.

4144 GREAT WESTERN RLY. Safety and First
s   Aid. [*London*,] Dec. 1927. pp. 16.   BR

4145 NATIONAL JOINT INDUSTRIAL COUNCIL FOR THE TRAMWAY INDUSTRY. Objects, constitution and methods of procedure of the National Council, District Councils and Works Committees. *London*, January 1927. pp. 18.   LSE
Labour/management relations.

4146 NATIONAL UNION OF RAILWAYMEN. Rates of pay and conditions of service of conciliation grades. *London*, 1927. pp. 113.   LSE
Detailed information for each grade, with tables.

147 RAILWAY COMPANIES ASSOCIATION. The eight-hour day and forty-hour week as applicable to railwaymen. *London*, June 1927. pp. 51.   NUR
The Washington Draft Convention.

148 RAILWAYS STAFF CONFERENCE. National agreements in regard to railway staff, covered by negotiating machinery set up in accordance with Sections 62–66, part IV, of the Railways Act, 1921. Volume 1, June 1927. *London*, [1927.] pp. iv, 548.   LSE

149 [SAUNDERS, E.] The life story of the railwaymen's friend, Miss Emma Saunders of Clifton; or, The lady with the basket. Compiled by her niece. *Bristol*, May 1927. pp. 30[31], with illus., incl. portraits.   BR
Emma Saunders was entirely devoted to efforts of goodwill towards railwaymen.

150 INSTITUTE OF ACCIDENT PREVENTION. Accident prevention for permanent-way
s   men; presented by the Great Western Railway Company to each of their permanent-way employees. *London*, 1928. pp. 61, with illus.   BR

151 INTERNATIONAL TRANSPORT—WORKERS' FEDERATION. The dangers of the one-man locomotive and motor coach. *Amsterdam*, May 1928. pp. 16.   LSE
'Submitted to the Delegates of the XIth Session of the International Labour Conference, Geneva.'

152 JAMES, S. T. The railwayman: his work by night and day on the Iron Way. *London*, 1928. pp. 317, with plates.   BM

153 LEIGH, D. On the line. *Bungay*, [1928.] pp. 199.   BM
Sketches of life on the L.N.E.R.

154 RAILWAY CLERKS' ASSOCIATION. The R.C.A. and its path of progress. (By A. G. W[alkden].) *London*, [1928.] pp. 71.   LSE

155 RAILWAYMEN'S MINORITY MOVEMENT. The railwaymen's fight: that 2½% cut! Plain speaking by the Railwaymen's Minority Movement: facts and figures. *London*, 1929. pp. 14.   BM

156 BRATSCHI, R. Railway and motor transport. *Amsterdam: International Transportworkers' Federation*, 1930. pp. 40.   TUC
Reprint of a Paper, Madrid Conference of the ITF, 28 April–3 May, 1930.
Rail versus road competition as it affects the workers.

157 HADLEY, E. S. Railway thefts. To whom it may concern. *London*, 1922. pp. 23.   BM
Warnings to railwaymen. The folly of petty thieving.
—— 2nd edn. *London*, 1930. pp. 32.   BM

4158 HUNTER, G. B. Cost of labour on our railways. [*Newcastle*, 1930.] pp. [4.]   LSE
'Privately printed.'
'Present wages and conditions cannot be maintained without disaster.'
—— another edn. [*Newcastle*, 1930.] pp. [4.]   LSE

4159 PICK, F. Education for the railway service: a new standard of efficiency. *London: Modern Transport*, [1930.] pp. 7.   LSE
Reprint, *Modern Transport*, 8 & 15 Nov., 1930.
Presidential address, L.S.E. Railway Students' Association, 30 Oct., 1930.

4160 [RAILWAY COMPANIES ASSOCIATION.] Prevention of accidents to staff engaged in
s   railway operation. *London*, 1930. pp. 31, with illus. of various hazards.   BR

4161 ASSOCIATED SOCIETY OF LOCOMOTIVE ENGINEERS & FIREMEN. Statement sub-
l   mitted to the National Wages Board in support of the claims advanced by the Society [and] Reply to the proposals of the railway companies for a worsening of the conditions of service of our members. [*London*, Jan. 1931.] pp. 23.   TUC

4162 BELL, R. On a proper spirit of enterprise in railway work. pp. 15. *Reproduced typescript.*   IT
Paper, Railway Students' Association of Edinburgh, 16 October, 1931.

4163 BROCKWAY, A. F. Hands off the railmen's wages! A scathing exposure of the capitalist control of the railways, with a startling 'Who's Who' of the railway directors. *London: Independent Labour Party*, 1931. pp. 15.   BM

4164 INTERNATIONAL LABOUR OFFICE. Industrial Safety Survey, vol. VII, no. 4, July–August 1931. pp. [97]–113.   IT
'The one-man driving of self-propelled railway vehicles.'

4165 NATIONAL WAGES BOARD. Plan of negotiating machinery. [*London*, 1931.]   LSE
A wall chart showing the structure of levels of negotiation from the central organisation down to local branches.

4166 NATIONAL WAGES BOARD. Rates of pay and conditions of service: claims for modifications referred January 1931. *London*, 1931. pp. 132–88.   LSE

4167 RAILWAYS STAFF CONFERENCE. Evidence of the railway companies: statement of evidence on behalf of the railway companies by Mr. Kenelm Kerr, Assistant General Manager, L. & N.E. Rly., Chairman of the Railways Staff Conference. *London*, 1931. pp. 34.   LSE
For submission to the Royal Commission on Unemployment.

4168 FOX, W., *and others.* Ten years of railway finance: a study of the railways of Great Britain; their 'watered' capital, their directors, earnings, reserves and dividends, road transport interests and the position of the railway workers. *London: Labour Research Department,* 1932. pp. 23. BM
Proposed reduction in railwaymen's wages shown against an analysis of railway finances.

4169 LABOUR RESEARCH DEPARTMENT. Wages and profits on the railways. *London,* December 1932. pp. 15. [*Labour White Papers,* no. 46.] LSE

4170 RAILWAY CLERKS' ASSOCIATION. The case for safeguarding railway employment. Submitted by A. G. Walkden to the Railway Pool Committee . . . *London,* July 1932. pp. 119. LSE

4171 RAILWAY CLERKS' ASSOCIATION. Railway pooling proposals and joint working arrangements . . . Employees' case for safeguards as submitted to the Railway Pool Committee, October 31–November 2, 1932. (Mr. A. G. Walkden examined by Sir William Jowitt.) *London,* November 1932. pp. 63. LSE

4172 RAILWAY REVIEW. National Wages Board Meeting: Union's reply to companies' claim. *London,* 1932. pp. 8. TUC
Supplement to the issue of 16 December, 1932.

4173 RAILWAY REVIEW. National Wages Board Proceedings: companies' claims: cross-examination by Union representatives. *London,* 1932. pp. 8. TUC
Supplement to the issue of 9 December, 1932.

4174 RAILWAYS STAFF CONFERENCE. The case of the four Group railway companies for a reduction in railway labour costs. National Wages Board, November–December 1932. [*London,* 1933.] pp. 45, with tables. IT
The claim of the railway companies: trade union views: findings of the Board.

4175 BROWN, J. D., *and others.* Railway Labor Survey, prepared by J. Douglas Brown and associates. *New York: Social Science Research Council, Division of Industry & Trade,* 1933. pp. 153. *Reproduced typescript.* LC
A comparison, U.S.A., Canada, and Gt. Britain.

4176 GREAT WESTERN RLY. Claim by railway companies for reduction of salaries and wages. (Sir Ralph Wedgwood's final speech to the National Wages Board, January 1933.) *Paddington* (*London*), February 1933. pp. 6. LSE

4177 LABOUR RESEARCH DEPARTMENT. The National Wages Board and after. *London,* January 1933. pp. 15. [*Labour White Papers,* no. 47.] LSE

4178 [RAILWAY CLERKS' ASSOCIATION.] The London Passenger Transport Act, 1933: a summary of its main provisions with special articles on the negotiation machinery established to deal with salaries, wages and conditions of service . . .; also, particulars of the personnel of the new Board with terms and conditions of appointment and a two-page map of the Transport Board area. *London,* [1933.] pp. 12[13]. TUC
Reprint, *Railway Service Journal,* June and July 1933.

4179 IRISH TRANSPORT & GENERAL WORKERS' UNION. Three men and three days: a fight for Irish trade unionism. The story of the unsuccessful attempt of an English trade union operating in Ireland to deprive a number of Irish workers of their livelihood because they joined an Irish trade union. *Dublin,* [1934.] pp. 23. LSE
Press articles, letters and trade union circulars relating to a T. & G.W.U. demand for dismissal of three Dublin tramwaymen who joined the Irish T. & G.W.U.

4180 JONES, D. C. The Social Survey of Merseyside. *Liverpool: University of Liverpool,* 1934. 3 vols. BM
vol. 2, pp. 145–89, Inland transport; rail, road and canal: employment conditions of transport workers; with 15 tables and a map.

4181 FOX, W. Seven years of railway finance, 1928 to 1934; with three charts. *London: Labour Research Dept.,* 1935. pp. 31. BM
Railway finance in relation to railwaymen's wages. A revision of this author's *Ten years of railway finance* (1932).

4182 LONDON SCHOOL OF ECONOMICS. The New Survey of London Life and Labour. *London,* 1930–35. 9 vols. BM
vol. 8, London industries. pp. 106–46, and elsewhere, railway labour and conditions. Also, pp. 70–89, tramway and omnibus employment.
vol. 9, Life and leisure. pp. 393–413, Family life of railwaymen. (Reports on seven households.)

4183 NATIONAL WAGES BOARD—MACHINERY OF NEGOTIATION FOR RAILWAY STAFF. Memorandum of Agreement . . . [*London,* 1935.] pp. 35. LSE

4184 RAILWAY CLERKS' ASSOCIATION. Socialisation of transport. Special committee appointed . . . to prepare a scheme for a socialised transport industry. Reports to the Annual Conference at Folkestone, May 1935. (Agenda item no. 13, 'Workers' Control'.) [*London,* 1935.] pp. 22[23]. TUC
Majority and minority reports, and a diagram of proposed structure for national labour/management co-operation.

4185 RAILWAY STAFF NATIONAL TRIBUNAL —JOINT COMMITTEE ON MACHINERY OF NEGOTIATION FOR RAILWAY STAFF. Diagrams and summaries illustrating normal procedure . . . [*London*,] 1935. pp. 15.   TUC

4186 RAILWAY STAFF NATIONAL TRIBUNAL —JOINT COMMITTEE ON MACHINERY OF NEGOTIATION FOR RAILWAY STAFF. Explanatory minutes for Special Joint Committee. [*London*,] January 1935. pp. 5.   TUC

4187 RAILWAY STAFF NATIONAL TRIBUNAL —JOINT COMMITTEE ON MACHINERY OF NEGOTIATION FOR RAILWAY STAFF. Second [final] report . . . January 1935. [*London*, 1935.] pp. 35.   TUC

4188 RAILWAY STAFF NATIONAL TRIBUNAL —SPECIAL JOINT COMMITTEE ON MACHINERY OF NEGOTIATION FOR RAILWAY STAFF. Reports of the Special Joint Committee . . . 1933–34 [and January 1935]. [*London*, 1935.]   LSE

4189 ASSOCIATED SOCIETY OF LOCOMOTIVE ENGINEERS & FIREMEN. Full statement of the Society's claim . . . before the Railway Staff National Tribunal . . . December 7th–12th, 1936. [*London*,] 1936. pp. 254.   TUC

4190 COMMUNIST PARTY. Communism and the railways. [*London*, 1936.] pp. 13.   LSE
The railwaymen's position a result of railways being run for profit rather than as a public service.

4191 LONDON PASSENGER TRANSPORT BOARD. The training of drivers and conductors of buses, trams and trolley-buses. *London*, 1936. pp. 20, with illus.   LSE

4192 FAY, S. The War Office at war. *London: Hutchinson*, 1937. pp. 288.   BM
Includes references to railway labour problems during and after the War (1914–18).

4193 ASSOCIATED SOCIETY OF LOCOMOTIVE ENGINEERS & FIREMEN. Workmen's Compensation Bill. [*London*, 1938.] pp. 9.   TUC
To amend clauses in the 1928 Trades Union Congress Bill relating to workmen's compensation.

4194 MCCULLOCH, T. A. Working on the railway. *In* 'Seven shifts', edited by J. Common. *London*, 1938. pp. 247–71.   BM
His work as a fireman on the L.N.E.R.

4195 NATIONAL UNION OF RAILWAYMEN. The branch officer: a handbook for the information and guidance of branch officers of the N.U.R. [*London*, 1938.] pp. viii, 254.   BM

4196 EARL, L. A. Speeding north with the 'Royal Scot': a day in the life of a locomotive man . . . *London: O.U.P.*, 1939. pp. 143[160], with 28 illus. on 15 plates.   BM

4197 INTERNATIONAL TRANSPORT-WORKERS' FEDERATION [Amsterdam]. Working hours of railwaymen. Towards international regulation? *Amsterdam*, 1939. pp. 4. [*Editorial Supplement* no. 2, to '*Railwaymen*', 11 April 1939.]   TUC

4198 LABOUR RESEARCH DEPARTMENT. Justice for railwaymen: can the companies afford it? [*London*, Jan. 1939.] pp. 14[15].   LSE
Railwaymen overworked and underpaid in order to satisfy stockholders and industrialists.

4199 COMMUNIST PARTY. Clear the lines! *London*, [1943.] pp. 13.   LSE
Improvements in railway efficiency, conditions, training, etc. by unifying railway trade unions.

4200 ASSOCIATED SOCIETY OF LOCOMOTIVE ENGINEERS & FIREMEN. Post-war policy for railways: suggestions of the A.S.L.E. & F. for consideration. *London*, [1944.] pp. 15.   TUC
Outlines of a proposed policy for railway trade unions.

4201 CAMERON, M. A. Personnel management as a factor in transport efficiency. pp. 13. *Reproduced typescript.*   IT
Paper, Institute of Transport, Scottish Section, 24 April, 1944.

4202 CONFEDERATION OF SHIPBUILDING & ENGINEERING UNIONS. Rates of pay and conditions of service of railway workshop staff. *London*, 24 August, 1945. pp. 14[15].   LSE
Memorandum of agreement between the Railway Executive, the Amalgamated Engineering Union, the C.S.E.U. and the National Union of Railwaymen; with schedules.

4203 [WRIGHTSON, P.] Barnard Castle in war paint: a stationmaster's diary. *Barnard Castle: the author*, [1945.] pp. 11.   IT

4204 RAILWAY COMPANIES ASSOCIATION. Guide to juvenile employment on the main line railways. Issued by the Railways Staff Conference on behalf of the G.W., L.M.S., L.N.E. and S. railways, October 1946. [*London*, 1946.] pp. 16.   BR

4205 GREAT WESTERN RLY. Look out!: some hints for permanent-way men. *Paddington (London)*, 1947. pp. 19, with drawings.   PC

4206 BELL, F. E. The trade union in relation to transport. pp. 17. *Typescript.*   IT
Paper, Institute of Transport, Birmingham, 16 December, 1948.

4207 SKEGG, J. E. Transport staff welfare. pp. 13. *Reproduced typescript.*   IT
Paper, Institute of Transport, November 1948.

4208 WARD, S. G. Some aspects of railway staff administration. pp. 25. *Reproduced typescript.*   IT
Paper, L.S.E. Railway Students' Association, January 1948.

4209 BRITISH RAILWAYS. British Railways welcome you. *London,* [1949.] pp. 47, with illus.   BR
Addressed to new members of B.R. staff, describing organisation, work, conditions, welfare, etc.

4210 BRITISH TRANSPORT COMMISSION. Staff training and education: report of a committee appointed by the British Transport Commission. *London,* 1949. pp. vi, 26. TUC
A scheme submitted to, and approved by, the Minister of Transport.

4211 CLAY, H. Co-operation between staff and management. *London: British Transport Commission,* July 1949. pp. 20.   BR
Printed for private circulation.

4212 LANG, H. C. Staff negotiating machinery and consultative procedure. pp. 20. *Typescript.*   IT
Paper, British Railways (SR) Lecture & Debating Society, 8 Dec., 1950.

4213 NATIONAL UNION OF RAILWAYMEN. Rates of pay and conditions of service of railway salaried and conciliation staff. *London,* September 1950. pp. 167, with tables.   LSE

4214 PICKSTOCK, F. British Railways: the human problem: report of a Fabian Research Group. *London: Fabian Society,* 1950. pp. 36. [*Research Series,* no. 142.]   BM
The nature of the new structure and organisation of British Railways seen as a background to future trade union activity.

4215 SHARP, I. G. Industrial conciliation and arbitration in Great Britain. *London: Allen & Unwin,* 1950. pp. 466.   BM
pp. 238–69, The railway industry, with bibliogr. notes.

4216 ACTON SOCIETY TRUST. Training and promotion in nationalised industry. *London,* 1951. pp. 137.   BM
Includes British Railways and London Transport.

4217 BENSTEAD, J. Implementing the Transport Act of 1947, with special reference to labour relations. pp. 17. *Reproduced typescript.* LSE
Paper, L.S.E., 8 May, 1951.

4218 BRITISH RAILWAYS. Joint statement to the staff of British Railways, by the Railway Executive and the National Union of Railwaymen, the Associated Society of Locomotive Engineers & Firemen, the Railway Clerks' Association. What the Settlement means to you, and the part you are asked to play. [*London,*] March 1951. pp. 14[15].   BR
Issued to all B.R. staff, explaining the agreements made on 23 February, 1951, between the Railway Executive and the three unions.

4219 RAILWAY REVIEW. Court of Inquiry, January 1951. *London,* 1951. pp. iv. [*Railway Review Supplement,* no. 2.]   TUC
The N.U.R.'s reply to the Railway Executive.

4220 GILBERT, F. Transport staff relations: machinery of negotiation, joint consultation, training and education . . . *London: Pitman,* 1951. pp. xii, 260.   BM
After an historical introduction, the current arrangements in operation in individual transport undertakings are explained.
Appendix, pp. 121–257, Agreements, documents, reports and related legislation.

4221 HURCOMB, C. Address . . . to the Annual Conference of the Transport Salaried Staffs' Association . . . 30 May 1951. pp. 11. *Reproduced typescript.*   IT
Review of contemporary problems on British Railways. The need for good-will and co-operation between railwaymen.

4222 RAILWAY REVIEW. The wages settlement: full statement by the N.U.R. *London: Railway Review,* March 1951. pp. [2.] TUC
A supplement to the 2nd March issue.

4223 SHERRINGTON, C. E. R. The human spirit in the transport industry. pp. 16. *Typescript.*   PC
Paper, Institute of Transport, Southern Section, Southampton, November 14, 1951.

4224 TAYLOR, M. The engine-driver. *London: Educational Supply Association,* 1951. pp. 69, with illus. [*Information Books. People's Jobs.*]   BM

4225 GILBERT, F. Training for transport. pp. 11. *Reproduced typescript.*   IT
Paper, L.S.E. Railway Students' Association, 27 Feb., 1952.
A review of staff training in the British Transport Commission.

4226 AHERN, T. Right away for railway wages! *London: Communist Party,* [Oct. 1953.] pp. 7.   BM

4227 ASSOCIATED SOCIETY OF LOCOMOTIVE ENGINEERS & FIREMEN. Rates of pay and conditions of service of locomotive and electric trainmen: staff employed by the Railway Executive. *London,* April 1953. pp. 95.   IT

4228 LABOUR RESEARCH DEPARTMENT. Fair play for railwaymen. *London,* December 1953. pp. 7.   LSE

229 MINISTRY OF LABOUR & NATIONAL SERVICE. Industrial Relations Handbook: an account of the organisation of employers and workpeople in Great Britain: collective bargaining and joint negotiation machinery: conciliation and arbitration, and statutory regulation of wages in certain industries. *London*, 1944. pp. 260.   BM
   pp. 38–45 and elsewhere, Railways.
—— Supplement no. 3, Dec. 1949. 'Joint consultation in industry.' *London*, 1950.   BM
   pp. 95–8, Railways.
—— another edn. of main work. *London*, 1953. pp. iv, 284.   BM
   pp. 41–52, Railways. Contains an outline history of railway negotiation machinery.
—— rev. edn. *London*, 1961. pp. vi, 234. pp. 82–94, Railways.

230 NATIONAL UNION OF RAILWAYMEN. Rates of pay and conditions of service of railway workshop staff and railway electrical staff. 4th edn. *London*, March 1953. pp. 127.   IT

231 ROBERTSON, B. A message to every man and woman who works in British Transport. [*London*,] November 1953. s.sh.   BM
   An appeal for loyalty and co-operation, on taking up chairmanship of B.T.C.

232 C[AMERON], M. A. Profit motive and public interest in transport. 1954. pp. 16. *Typescript.*   IT
   Paper, Institute of Transport, Leeds, 11 Oct., 1954.
   Moral leadership by example the essential basis for practical worker/management co-operation in transport.

233 GILBERT, F. Industrial relations in transport. pp. 12. *Reproduced typescript.*   IT
   Paper, Institute of Transport, Merseyside & District Section, 7 Oct., 1954.

234 INTERNATIONAL LABOUR OFFICE. Causes of accidents in the coupling of railway vehicles and related operations, and measures for their prevention. *Geneva*, 1954. pp. 22, with illus.   IT

235 NATIONAL UNION OF RAILWAYMEN. Machinery of negotiation. [*London*,] 1954. pp. 81.   NUR
   Reproductions of some historical documents followed by (pp. 26 to end) 'Existing negotiation machinery'.

236 TRAIN, J. C. L. Planned productivity from the human angle. pp. 11. *Reproduced typescript.*   IT
   Presidential address, L.S.E. Railway Students' Association, 12 Oct., 1955.
   Work study.

237 BARNES, D. A railwayman looks at the railways. 2nd edn. *London: Independent Labour Party*, 1956. pp. 27.   BM
   A Socialist's views on present-day problems of the railways and of railwaymen, with a survey of their conditions under nationalization. There is an historical summary of the course of railway development under the control of private interests and of the growth of railway trade unionism.

4238 BRITISH RAILWAYS. Consultation between management and staff: to all members of the staff of British Railways. [*London*, 1956.] pp. 4.   LSE

4239 BRITISH RAILWAYS. Making joint consultation work. [*London*,] 1956. pp. 15.   TUC

4240 GILBERT, F. Some railway staff problems. *London: Institute of Transport*, 1956. pp. 9. *Reproduced typescript.*   IT
   Paper, Institute of Transport, Humberside Section, 21 Feb., 1956.

4241 GIRARD, J. M. La Productivité du travail dans les chemins de fer: Allemagne, États-Unis, France, Grande-Bretagne. *Paris: Centre d'Études et de Mesures de Productivité*, [1956.] pp. 139, with tables & charts.   IT

4242 LONDON TRANSPORT EXECUTIVE. Health in industry: a contribution to the study of sickness absence: experience in London Transport. *London*, 1956. pp. 177, with many statistical tables and charts.   BM

4243 MARLOW, N. Footplate and signal cabin. *London: Allen & Unwin*, 1956. pp. 222, with 15 plates.   BM
   An appreciation of railways, containing an account of the author's experiences as a wartime temporary signalman during university vacations; also, pp. 75–137, essays on practical and human aspects of locomotive driving, including extracts from the diaries of David Joy (1840's) and of the trips on broad gauge G.W. engines by A. H. Malan in 1891, followed by narratives of journeys undertaken by N. Marlow himself.

4244 TRANSPORT SALARIED STAFFS' ASSOCIATION. Rates of pay and conditions of service of British Railways salaried staffs. *London*, Sept. 1953. pp. 159.   IT
—— *London*, Dec. 1956. pp. 184, viii, & addenda.   IT

4245 WATKINS, J. W. Industrial and human relations. pp. 18. *Reproduced typescript.*   IT
   Presidential address, L.S.E. Railway Students' Association, 17 Oct., 1956.
   Management/labour co-operation.

4246 LEYLAND, E. A. Loco driver; illustrated by R. Barnard Way. *London: Edmund Ward*, 1957. pp. 94, with 10 illus. on 4 plates, & diagrams in text. [*Men of Action series*, no. 2.]   BM

4247 RAILWAY BENEVOLENT INSTITUTION. Report of the proceedings at a meeting held at the Railway Clearing House. *London*, 1958. pp. 15.   AU

4248 TAYLOR, M. Railways as a career. *London: Batsford*, 1959. pp. 127, with 15 illus. on 8 plates, & 10 illus. in text. [*Batsford Career Books.*]   BM

A guide for school leavers.

4249 WOOD, A. The engine-driver and the signalman. *London: Macmillan*, 1959. pp. 63, with illus.   BM

A career guide for boys.

4250 ALLEN, V. L. Trade unions and the Government. *London: Longmans*, 1960. pp. xii, 326.   BM

Includes railway trade unions.

*4251 CENTRAL YOUTH EMPLOYMENT EXECUTIVE. The railways. *London: H.M.S.O.*, 1960. pp. 47, with illus. [*Choice of Careers*, no. 88.]   BM

Outlines of various railway employments, conditions, etc.

4252 VINCENT, C. Railwayman: picture career book. *London: Lutterworth*, 1960. pp. [72,] with over 130 illus.   BM

General history and description of the working of railways, showing the railwayman's inheritance and the nature of his work today.

4253 MINISTRY OF TRANSPORT AND CIVIL AVIATION. Railway training in the United Kingdom: training facilities in the United Kingdom available for railway administrations in the region of the Economic Commission for Asia and the Far East. *London*, 1961. pp. v, 44, with 5 illus.   BM

K RAILWAYS AND THE NATION

Railways and their problems within the framework of national life—Fear of monopoly *vis-à-vis* the wastage of unbridled competition—The call for reform—Arguments for and against private ownership, and for and against government supervision, control, purchase, and state ownership—Railways and politics—Railways in relation to other forms of transport (road, canal, air, and coastwise shipping) as competitors and in co-operation—Integration of all forms of transport—Railway rating (taxation)—Railways and the future

For actual government participation in railway affairs see **K 6**
For actual nationalization see **B 9**

Marginal symbols: **b** bibliographies
c chronologies
ca canal and railway relationships
f future of railways (forecasts, and works having special emphasis on future needs)
s Socialism and railways

Historical

4254 DE SALIS, H. R. A Chronology of Inland
Navigation in Great Britain: being a record
c of the principal works and events connected
with inland navigation to the present time
ca ... *London*, 1897. pp. 133. BM
Includes events related to railway development, such as purchase and lease of canals.

4255 LAWSON, W. R. British railways: a financial
and commercial survey. *London*, 1913. pp.
xxxii, 320. BM
pp. 268–320, Railways and the state.

4256 BRICKWELL, A. J. A review of the rating of
railways since 1864. *In* 'Jubilee of the Railway News, 1864–1914.' *London: Railway
News*, [1914.] pp. 117–21. BM

4257 BUREAU OF RAILWAY ECONOMICS [Washington]. List of publications pertaining to
b government ownership of railways. *Washington*, 1914. pp. 74. [*Bulletin* no. 62.] LSE
pp. 34–41, 'Great Britain'. (Government
control.)

b —— rev. edn. *Washington*, 1917. pp. 100.
pp. 44–52, 'Great Britain'. LSE

4258 DAVIES, D. H. Nationalisation of railways:
historical aspects. *In* 'Jubilee of the Railway News, 1864–1914.' *London: Railway
News*, [1914.] pp. 163–5. BM

4259 JACKMAN, W. T. The development of
transportation in modern England. *Cam-*
b *bridge*, 1916. 2 vols., with many bibliogr.
ca notes & an extensive bibliography. BM
vol. 2, pp. 624–749, Competition between
railways and canals, up to 1850.
—— [Reprint] with a new introduction by
W. H. Chaloner. *London: Frank Cass*,
1962. pp. xxxviii, 820, with maps. BM

4260 MATSON, A. H. The co-operation and co-
ordination of road and rail transport in
Great Britain. [1921.] pp. 34. *Typescript*. LSE
Period, 1820–1921.

4261 KNOWLES, L. C. A. The industrial and
commercial revolutions in Great Britain
during the nineteenth century. *London*, 1921.
pp. xii, 420. [*Studies in Economic and
Political Science*, no. 61.] BM
pp. 253–90, Development of railways and
the problem of state control.
—— 2nd edn. *London*, 1922. pp. xii, 420. BM
—— 3rd, *London*, 1924. pp. xii, 416. BM

4262 SAYOUS, A. E. La Route contre le rail en
Angleterre. *Brussels*, 1930. pp. 41. BM
Reprint from *Revue Économique Internationale*, Feb. 1930.
Road-rail competition during the past twenty
years.

4263 GAMMONS, W. Forty years in transport.
London, 1931. pp. 163, with plates. LSE
The development of road haulage and of
industrial traffic management; road-rail relationship in the 1920's.

***4264** SHERRINGTON, C. E. R. A hundred years
of inland transport, 1830 to 1933. [*London*,]
1934. pp. 376. BM
Deals largely with the effect upon railways of
the introduction of later modes of transport.

4265 WICKWAR, W. H. The public services: a
historical survey. *London: Cobden-Sanderson*, 1938. BM
pp. 67–88, Railway traffic. (Competition and
government regulation.)
pp. 105–19, 'London Passenger Transport'.

4266 DAVIES, E. The State and the railways.
London: Fabian Society, 1940. pp. 24.
[*Research Series*, no. 51.] BM
A review of the relationship over the past
thirty years and the necessity for nationalization
and transport co-ordination following the War.

4267 MILLS, G. A Keith Lecture on transport, as delivered to the Royal Scottish Society of Arts, 15 Feb. 1941. *Edinburgh*, [1941.] pp. 19.   IT
Co-ordination.

4268 RIDLEY, G. The railways, retrospect and prospect. *London: Labour Party*, 1942. pp. 23. [*Between Two Wars*, no. 1.]   BM
Nationalization proposals, with an historical survey.

4269 OWEN, H. The truth about Britain's transport: monopoly v. the people. [*London: Reynolds News*, 1946.] pp. 24[25].   TUC
An historical review of railway ownership and finance, including the 'London Transport Monopoly'. The necessity for nationalization.

4270 CRUIKSHANK, R. J. Roaring Century. *London: Hamish Hamilton*, 1948. pp. xi, 280, with plates.   BM
pp. 42–61, The roar of railways, 1846–1946.

4271 BROWN, A. H. J. Twenty-five years of transport, 1924–1949. pp. 28[29]. *Reproduced typescript*.   IT
Paper, Institute of Transport, Northern Section, 21 Oct., 1949.

4272 MANCHESTER CORPORATION TRANSPORT DEPT. Souvenir Brochure on the occasion of the abandonment of the last tram service ... [*Manchester*, 1949.] pp. 31.   BM
Includes statistics of growth and decline of tramway services in relation to buses.

4273 DE MARE, E. The canals of England. *London: Architectural Press*, 1950. pp. 124,
ca with many illus.   BM
Historical and descriptive; includes fifteen references to railways.

4274 COURT, W. H. B. A concise economic history of Britain, from 1750 to recent times. *Cambridge: C.U.P.*, 1954. pp. viii, 368. BM
pp. 165–73 and elsewhere, railways.

*4275 HADFIELD, C. The canals of Southern England ... *London: Phoenix House*, 1955.
ca pp. 383, with 35 illus. incl. maps & plates. BM
pp. 264–336, 'The railways and after'. There are many other references to railways and tramroads in other parts of the text.

4276 WILKES, E. Why we had no Bloody Revolution. *London: Routledge & Kegan Paul*, 1955. pp. 16. [*Passport to Survival series*, no. 5.]   BM
Railways as an element of social and material progress in the nineteenth century.

4277 SAVAGE, C. I. Inland transport. *London: H. M. Stationery Office*, 1957. pp. xvii, 678, with tables & bibliogr. notes. [*History of the Second World War. United Kingdom Civil Series*.]   BM
A detailed record, including railways.

4278 WALKER, G. *and* SAVAGE, C. I. Inland carriage by road and rail. *In* 'The structure of British Industry: a symposium', edited by Duncan Burn. 1958. vol. 1, pp. 76–107, with bibliogr. notes.   BM
Transport related to general economic development, 1920–58.

*4279 HADFIELD, C. British canals: an illustrated
b history. *London: Phoenix House*, 1950.
ca pp. 259, with 8 plates, 44 illus., 17 maps, & a bibliography.   BM
The index has 84 entries relating to various railways.
pp. 177–92, 'War with the railways'.
——— 2nd edn. completely revised. *London*,
b 1959. pp. 291, with 8 plates, 44 illus., 17
ca maps, 139 bibliogr. notes, & a bibliography.
BM
pp. 196–227, 'Canals and railways'.

4280 HUGHES, J. R. T. Fluctuations in trade, industry and finance: a study of British economic development, 1850–1860. *Oxford: O.U.P.*, 1960. pp. xvi, 344, with tables & bibliogr. notes.   BM
pp. 184–206 and elsewhere, Railways.

*4281 SAVAGE, C. I. An economic history of
b transport. *London: Hutchinson*, 1959. pp. 216, with 7 tables, a bibliography of 87 items, & bibliogr. notes.   BM
The main theme covers the period from the beginning of the 19th century to 1939 and is concerned primarily with railways in the U.K. and their relationship to the State and to road competition.
b ——— new edn. *London*, 1961. pp. 216. BM

4282 STERN, W. M. Britain yesterday and today: an outline economic history from the middle of the eighteenth century. *London: Longmans*, 1962. pp. 294.   BM
pp. 129–57, 'Transport' (Railways, pp. 135–43 ... 155).

4283 GWILLIAM, K. M. Transport and public policy. *London: Allen & Unwin*, 1964. pp. 259, with bibliogr. notes. [*Minerva Series of Students' Handbooks*, no. 11.]   BM
Economic principles; comparative means of transport, past and present; history of government intervention; problems and implications of co-ordination of transport.

4284 PEARSON, A. J. The railways and the nation. *London: Allen & Unwin*, 1964. pp. 128. BM
An analysis of the present relationship and its problems, the 'Beeching Plan', and the future of railways within the general pattern of public transport.

Contemporaneous

4285 ARGUMENTS in support of the establishment of railroads, and to show the necessity of legislative sanction. *London*, 1825. pp. 32.   PO

4286 GRAY, T. Observations on a general iron rail-way, shewing its great superiority over all the present methods of conveyance, and claiming the particular attention of merchants, manufacturers, farmers, and indeed every class of society. *London*, 1820. pp. 22.   ICE

—— 2nd edn. *London*, 1821. pp. 60.   BM

—— 3rd, rev. & considerably enlarged. *London*, 1822. pp. xii, 131.   RC

—— 4th, considerably improved. *London*, 1823. pp. xii, 131.   BM

—— 5th, 'with maps and plans illustrative of the plan.' *London*, 1825. pp. xxiv, 233. BM

4287 BAADER, J. R. von. Huskisson und die Eisenbahnen: noch ein Wort zu seiner Zeit für eine gute Sache. *München*, 1830. pp. 36.   BM

4288 RAILWAY taxation considered, in a letter to . . . Lord Althorp, Chancellor of the Exchequer, etc., etc. *London*, 1833. pp. 15.   UL(GL)

Signed 'A Coach Proprietor'.
The unfair advantage enjoyed by railways in their exemption from tax. The Liverpool & Manchester Rly. chiefly criticised.

4289 'ARISTIDES.' Modern tyranny. *London*, 1835. pp. 57.   LSE

pp. 26–34, Monopoly by railway companies.

4290 CUNDY, N. W. Observations on railways, addressed to the nobility, gentry, clergy, agriculturists, merchants, manufacturers, ship owners & traders, particularly those situate on the line and connected with the Great Northern and Eastern Railroad. *Yarmouth*, 1834. pp. 55.   BM

The points raised are illustrated by records of interviews of persons representing these classes.

—— 2nd edn. *Yarmouth*, 1835. pp. 59. BM

4291 FAIRBAIRN, H. A treatise on the political economy of railroads; in which the new mode of locomotion is considered in its influence upon the affairs of nations. *London*, 1836. pp. xvi, 248.   BM

General survey of contemporary railways, with suggestions for improvements, including railways on turnpike roads, horse traction, and crossing of the English Channel and the Irish Sea by means of causeways.

4292 MORRISON, J. Railroads. Speech of James Morrison, Esq., M.P., in the House of Commons, 17th May 1836, on moving a resolution relative to the periodical revision of tolls and charges levied on railroads and other public works. *London*, 1836. pp. 23.   BM

4293 P, E. An essay to shew the advantages that will follow the progressive formation of railways throughout the Kingdom. *London*, 1836. pp. 44.   BM

4294 SMITH, H. Conjectures on the future effects of locomotion by steam: read at the conversazione of the Brighton Scientific & Literary Institution. *Brighton*, 1836. pp. 32.   H

4295 WHAT will Parliament do with the railways? *London*, 1836. pp. 16.   BM

Asking for more control over railway development, in the public interest.

—— 2nd edn. (reprint). *London*, 1836. pp. 16.   UL(GL)

4296 GODWIN, G. An appeal to the public on the subject of railways. *London*, 1837. pp. 45, with bibliogr. notes.   BM

General advantages of railways.

4297 JOHNSON, C. W. [*and* JOHNSON, G. W.] The advantages of railways to agriculture. By C. W. Johnson . . . Observations on the general importance of railways. By G. W. Johnson. *London*, [1836.] pp. 16.   BM

—— 2nd edn. *London*, 1837. pp. 16.   BM

4298 MUDGE, R. Z. Observations on railways, with a reference to utility and profit and the obvious necessity for a national system. *London*, 1837. pp. 73.   BM

4299 BERMINGHAM, T. Statistical evidence in favor of state railways in Ireland, with the speech of T. Bermingham . . . also an appendix containing above twenty statistical tables . . . with a map of Ireland shewing . . . the lines of the Irish Railway Commissioners, with additions recommended by the author. *Dublin*, 1841. pp. 22, xciv.   BM

4300 BOOTH, H. The carrying question stated in reference to railways and canals; also, considerations on the mode of levying the passenger tax on railways. *Liverpool*, 1841. pp. 32.   H

4301 The CARRIERS' case considered in reference to railways. *London*, 1841. pp. 36.   BM

Railways seek unfair advantage over carriers by 'oblique manœuvres': legislation needed to protect carriers.

4302 CONDER, F. R. Railway transit: a letter to . . . Henry Labouchere, M.P., President of the Board of Trade. *London*, 1841. pp. 32.   PO

'It is to Parliament alone that we can look for the due protection of the lives and interests of the public.'

4303 GORDON, A. Observations on railway monopolies, and remedial measures. *London*, 1841. pp. 57.   BM

Government control to offset monopolies.

4304 CHELTENHAM DISTRICT OF TURNPIKE ROADS—TRUSTEES. Road works on railways: a statement made by the Trustees of the Cheltenham District of Turnpike Roads to the trustees and persons interested in turnpike roads. *Cheltenham*, 1842. pp. 15.   BM

Railway bridges, etc., and existing roadways; the need for protective legislation.

4305 LANG, G. H. Letter to . . . Henry Goulburn, M.P. . . . on the unequal pressure of the Railway Passenger Tax. *Glasgow*, 1842. pp. 16.   BM
Small railways which ask low fares should have less tax to pay.

4306 RAILWAYS: their uses and management. *London*, 1842. pp. 65.   BM
Government control and supervision needed.

4307 HALY, W. T. The opinions of Sir Robert Peel, expressed in Parliament and in public. *London*, 1843.   BM
pp. 358–61, on railways generally, and in Ireland.

4308 PENFOLD, C. Rating of railways. *Croydon*, 1843. pp. 28.   BM
Originally printed in the *Railway Times*.

4309 [GALT, W.] Railway reform: its expediency and practicability considered; with a copious appendix containing a description of all the railways in Great Britain and Ireland, fluctuations in the prices of shares, statistical and Parliamentary returns . . . *London*, 1843. pp. 108.   BM
'A monopoly of means of transit by irresponsible individuals'.
—— 2nd edn. *London*, 1843. pp. 116.   BM
—— 3rd, *London*, 1844. pp. 116.
—— 'People's edn., printed textually from the 3rd edn., the appendix only being omitted.' *London*, 1844. pp. 76.   BM

4310 LANG, G. H. Letter to . . . W. E. Gladstone, M.P. . . . on the importance in a national point of view of railway extension . . . *London*, 1844. pp. 28.   ICE
Legislation for railway development in Britain compared with that in France and other countries.

4311 A LETTER to W. E. Gladstone, M.P., President of the Board of Trade, on railway legislation. *London*, 1844. pp. 57.   BM
The urgent need for reform by legislation and government control.

4312 MALLET, R. Report on the railroad constructed from Kingstown to Dalkey in Ireland upon the atmospheric system, and upon the application of this system to railroads in general. [*Paris*, 1844.] pp. 55, with 4 fold. plates.   UL(GL)
—— 'Rapport sur le chemin de fer établi suivant le système atmosphérique de Kingstown à Dalkey . . .' *Paris*, 1844. pp. 71, with plates.   PO

4313 [NASH, C. de Lacy.] Railway and land taxation, showing the origin, progress, law, operation and statistics of the poor and other rates and their injustice and impolicy with reference to railways . . . *London*, 1844. pp. 21.   BM
Written under a 'strong conviction of injustice'.

4314 OBSERVATIONS on the government measures as to railways: being extracts from the leading articles of the 'Railway Times.' *London: Railway Times*, [1845.] pp. 20.   LSE

4315 [ADAMS, W. B.] Railway improvement. [*London*,] 1845. pp. 34.   PO
From the *Westminster Review*, Sept. 1845.

4316 The DESTINY of railways. [1845.] pp. 3. BM
From the *Artizan*, March 1845.
Dangers of monopoly. Competition with some measure of government control to be encouraged.

4317 M'KENNA, J. N. A chapter on railways and railway schemes, considered with a view to their social and political effects; addressed to the people of England. *London & Dublin*, 1845. pp. 32.   RIA(H)

4318 PARLIAMENT and the railway schemes: suggestions for an improved method of railway legislation. *London*, 1845. pp. 30. BM
Proposes a Railway Board to relieve Parliament of some of its railway work and to ensure that railway promotion is in the public interest.

4319 ROBERTSON, J. Suggestions on railway legislation, from the Railway Review. [*London*, 1845.] pp. 8.   UL(GL)
Dated 14 November, 1845. (no title-page.)
A letter addressed to the editor of the *Morning Chronicle*.

4320 SPACKMAN, W. F. Analysis of the railway interest of the United Kingdom: embracing all companies registered to the 31st day of October 1845, shewing the defects of the present system of railway management, and the necessity for amendments in the law of provisional registration. *London*, 1845. pp. 54.   BM

4321 HARDING, W. Railways. The gauge question. Evils of a diversity of gauge, and a remedy . . . *London*, 1845. pp. 62, with a map.   BM
—— 2nd edn. *London*, 1845. pp. 62. UL(GL)
—— 4th, 'Uniformity of gauge. Railways. The gauge question. Evils of a diversity of gauge.' *London*, 1846. pp. viii, 53, 7. BM

4322 HUNT, T. The rationale of railway administration, with a view to the greatest possible amount of accommodation, cheapness and safety. *London*, 1846. pp. 74.   BM
General review of railways, their benefits, and the need for improvements.

4323 [MATHER, J.] Ships and railways. *London*, 1846. pp. 40.   BM
Advocating transport of coal by sea so as to provide a naval reserve.

4324 OBSERVATIONS on a proposed railway for supplying the Metropolis, and south and south-eastern counties, with excellent and cheap coal, coke, lime, and other products, from the counties of Derby, Leicester, and Warwick, with a few remarks on the coasting trade. *Liverpool*, [1846.] pp. 26.　　BM(MSS)

The BM copy is prefaced by a MS. letter from George Stephenson to Sir Robert Peel, dated 21 April, 1846, introducing the pamphlet which, he says, 'contains an explanation of my views.' The Prime Minister's reply is transcribed on to Stephenson's letter. He is unable to agree that the proposed railway would be so desirable but promises to read the pamphlet when he has time.

The construction and operation of the proposed line was to have been for goods only, at very low rates.

4325 ON the selection of projected lines, with description of the railway scale. *London*, [1846.] pp. 23.　　BM

Advocating a system of economic selection, and dissolution, of existing lines.

4326 TROUP, J. Railway reform and rights of shareholders and the public in the railway highways of the United Kingdom. *London*, 1846. pp. 39.　　BM

4327 WATSON, J. A paper on the present railway crisis; read at a meeting of the Literary & Commercial Society of Glasgow held on 26th March, 1846. *Glasgow*, 1846. pp. 22.　　BM

Calling for greater control by Government of railway promotion and expenditure.

4328 WILLIAMS, J. B. On the principles of railway management, and on the profitable increase in the traffic produced by great reductions in the charges. 1846. pp. 101–32.　　BM

An excerpt, *Journal of the Statistical Society*, vol. 9, 1846.

4329 ENTWISLE, W. Government railways. *London*, 1847. pp. 58.　　LSE

Reforms which would not restrict private enterprise. Existing railways to be purchased by Government; future railways to be under the control of a Government Board.

4330 WHITMORE, W. W. Letter to Lord John Russell on railways. *London*, 1847. pp. 22.　　BM

Condemning the control of railways by 'a set of gentlemen who look at the charge almost exclusively as a mercantile transaction.' Includes letters by G. Hudson, G. C. Glyn & C. Russell, protesting against Government interference.

4331 BANISTER, T. Memoranda relating to the present crisis as regards our colonies, our trade, our circulating medium, and railways. 2nd edn. *London*, 1848. pp. 8,[1.] BM

Advocates Government ownership of railways.

4332 BOYLE, T. Hope for the canals! showing the evil of amalgamations with railways . . .

ca *London*, 1848. pp. 43.　　BM

Introducing the 'Merchants & Manufacturers' Carrying Union' for sending goods via 'independent' canals.

4333 COOKE, L. Observations on renting and rating railways, on the depreciation of the moveable stock, and the mode of computing the tenant's profit, in a letter addressed to David Waddington, Esq., M.P. *London*, 1848. pp. 15.　　BM

Recommendations for principles of rating of railways founded upon Cooke's experience as land surveyor for the Eastern Counties Rly.

4334 MORRISON, J. The influence of English railway legislation on trade and industry; with an appendix of tracts and documents. *London*, 1848. pp. 187.　　BM

'In the history of no country has there been such a bare-faced sacrifice of the public interests for the benefit of private associations.'

4335 RAILWAY rescue: a letter addressed to the directorates of Great Britain. By 'A Traveller of Many Lands.' *London*, 1848. pp. 19.　　BM

Suggestions for reform.

4336 COTTERILL, C. F. The past, present and future position of the London & North Western and Great Western railway companies . . . with an inquiry how far the principle of competing lines in reference to railway undertakings is sound and defensible. *London*, 1849. pp. 56.　　BM

Criticism against misleading financial statements, with tables. Government control preferable to competition.

4337 GORDON, A. Past and present views of railways. *London*, 1849. pp. 20.　　ICE

'. . . the enormity of the deception' of railways as a means of communication. Objections to the financial methods and policies of railways. A review and re-affirmation of statements made in his earlier writings.

4338 HART, A. W. A letter to . . . Lord John Russell on the assumption of railways by government. *London*, 1849. pp. 23.　　BM

Suppression of monetary speculation, and protection of the public by a 'Government Railway Board'.

4339 LAING, S. Railway taxation. *Westminster*, 1849. pp. 23.　　BM

Unequal taxation a burden to railways; illustrating the case of the L.B. & S.C. Rly. of which Laing was Chairman.

4340 PENFOLD, C. The justice of rating railway companies to the relief of the poor considered: addressed to the owners of landed property and the ratepayers of England. *London*, 1849. pp. 21.　　UL(GL)

4341 RATING of railways: statement of the railway interest handed to Mr. Lewis. [*Manchester*, 1849?] pp. 7.　　LSE

To George C. Lewis, M.P. Complaints against unjust and excessive demands from railways for maintenance of the poor, highways, church, police, etc.

4342 REPORT of the public meeting of railway shareholders held in Liverpool, 16th of April, 1849, to consider the propriety of petitioning Parliament to amend the law in respect to the rating of railways. *Liverpool*, 1849. pp. 21.　　　　BRE

4343 WEBB, C. L. A letter to ... Henry Labouchere, M.P., President of the Board of Trade, etc., etc., on railways, their accounts and dividends, their progress, present position and future prospects, their effects on trade and commerce; with suggestions for Government assistance and the amendment of the General Railway Acts of 1845. *London*, [1849.] pp. 64, with fold. table.　　　　BM

4344 WHITEHEAD, J. Railway prostration: causes and remedies: letter to . . . Sir Robert Peel. *London*, 1849. pp. 25.　　BM
Warning against a too rapid expansion of railway development. Urges Government control.

*4345 LARDNER, D. Railway economy: a treatise on the new art of transport, its management, prospects and relations, commercial, financial and social . . . *London*, 1850. pp. xxiii, 528.　　　　BM
A very detailed work on railways in general and on specific aspects and problems.
—— another edn. *New York*, 1850. pp. xxiii, 442.

4346 RICHARDSON, J. A revised and complete report of the recent trial for libel, Richardson v[ersus] Wodson; with preliminary observations on the Railway Mania of 1845–6–7–8. Also, a biographical sketch of Mr. George Hudson . . . together with an appendix setting forth in detail the whole system of railway mismanagement and railway frauds pursued since the establishment of railways in the City of York. *London*, [1850.] pp. xvi, 27.　　　　BM

4347 HODGSON, H. J. Summary of the law as applied to the rating of railways and other undertakings extending through several parishes, with notes of all the cases hitherto decided by the Court of Queen's Bench on the subject of railway rating, and some observations on the practical mode of assessing a railway. *London*, 1851. pp. xii, 108.　　BM

4348 LAING, S. Audit of railway accounts: letter to the proprietors of the London, Brighton & South Coast Railway Company. [*London*, 1851.] pp. 16.　　　　LSE
Objection to Government interference with railway companies' accounts, the subject of two Bills presented in that Session.

4349 PENFOLD, C. A letter to Lord Campbell in reply to Mr. Smirke's letter to his lordship on the subject of rating of railways. *London*, 1851. pp. 19.　　　　LSE

4350 PENFOLD, C. Rating of railways: the Great Western Railway and Tilehurst parish: observations upon Lord Campbell's declaration of the necessity of Parliament fixing a rule for the assessment of railways; in a letter addressed to Henry Chase, Jun., of Reading, Berks., solicitor to the parish. *London*, 1851. pp. 16.　　　　LSE
Assessing railways for the relief of the poor.

4351 RIGHTWAY, L. Rail-ways, public-ways, and government-ways. *London*, 1851. pp. 11.　　　　BM

4352 SMIRKE, E. A letter to Lord Campbell on the rating of railways. *London*, 1851. pp. 26.　　　　BM
The inadequacies of railway law.

4353 BEAUMONT, G. D. B. Railway amalgamation by a scale. *London*, 1852. pp. 12.

4354 CRIPPS, H. W. How to rate a railway in accordance with the decisions of the Court of Queen's Bench. *London*, 1853. pp. vi, 85.　　　　BM

4355 MARSHALL, W. Railway legislation and railway reform considered with special reference to Scottish lines. *Edinburgh & London*, 1852. pp. iv, 111.　　BM
—— 2nd edn. *Edinburgh*, 1853. pp. 114. BM

4356 CASTLE, H. J. Contributive value a necessary element in the parochial principle of railway assessments; what it is and how it can be measured . . . with a brief history of railway rating. *London*, 1854. pp. 63. BM

4357 COATES, T. Notes on the present condition of railway legislation. *London*, 1854. pp. 28.　　　　BM
Condemning as impracticable, Cardwell's Bill for the introduction of an interchange system between railways in place of amalgamations.

4358 PARLIAMENTARY repudiation. [1854?] pp. 71.　　　　BM
No title page in BM copy.
A protest against *An Act to enable the Eastern Union Railway Company to redeem their preference shares, etc.* (16 & 17 Vict. cap. ccxxi) [20 August, 1853], and an exposure of corruption in the House of Commons with regard to Railway Bills generally.
Contains much detail on the affairs of the Eastern Union Rly., of Thomas Brassey the contractor-financier, the tyranny of railway promoters and the methods used to deceive investors and the public.

4359 SPENCER, H. Railway morals and railway policy: reprinted from the 'Edinburgh Review' with additions and a postscript by the author. *London*, 1855. pp. 116. [*Traveller's Library*, no. 89.]　　　　BM
Mismanagement, intrigue and corruption.

4360 BOTT, W. E. A letter to Lord Campbell, Lord Chief Justice of the Queen's Bench . . . suggesting alterations in the law of rating railways . . . *London*, 1856. pp. 15, with bibliogr. notes.   BM

4361 'CIVIS.' The railway question: practical suggestions for a fundamental reform of the railway system on a principle combining national benefits with the permanent interests of shareholders. *London*, 1856. pp. 50.
                                                  BM
Government control of future development (new lines) with dividends guaranteed.

4362 POOLE, B. The economy of railways as a means of transit . . . *London*, 1856. pp. 29.
                                                  BM
Excerpt, *Min. Proc. I.C.E.* vol. XI, 1852.
Suggests measures to reduce cost of transporting goods, and to add to safety of travel.

4363 HALL, J., *and others*. Memorial to Board of Trade: proposed remedies for railway grievances. [*London*,] 1857. pp. 8.   BM
Suggestions following a memorial 'lately presented'. Signed by 'John Hall' and six others.

4364 [VANCE, J. E.] Railway memorial to the Board of Trade. *London*, 1857. pp. 15. BM
Presented by 1000 subscribers, protesting against unjust legislation: with a report of the deputation and an extract from the *Observer* of 7th June, 1857.

4365 BOARD management: an address to shareholders in search of a dividend. *London*, 1858. pp. 20.   BM
Mismanagement and inefficiency of directors.

4366 LYNDALL, J. The highways of the nation: being a statement of the claims of railways upon the Government. *Carlisle*, 1858. pp. 36.
                                                  BM
The great benefits of railways, and the need for amalgamation and control by Government.

4367 [WILLIAMS, E. L.] Competition versus
ca monopoly. *Birmingham*, 1858. pp. 7.   ICE
Condemning railway control of canals.

4368 KINGDOM, W. Suggestions for improving the value of railway property and for the eventual liquidation of the National Debt. *London*, [1850.] pp. 15.   LSE
Government assistance to railway finance.
—— 2nd edn. 'Suggestions for the liquidation of the National Debt by means of railway property . . .' *London*, 1855. pp. 15. BM
—— 3rd, *London*, 1855. pp. 14.   BM
—— 4th, 'Suggestions for the increase of railway dividends and the liquidation of the National Debt.' *London*, 1859. pp. 12. BM
—— 7th, *London*, 1863. pp. 12.   BM

4369 WILSON, T. The railway system and its author, Thomas Gray . . . *London*, 1845. pp. 39.   BM
—— new edn. *London*, 1860. pp. vii, 63.
                                                  ICE
pp. 31–63, press opinions.

4370 YOUNG, C. F. T. The economy of steam power on common roads, in relation to agri-
ca culturists, railway companies . . . *London*, [1860.] pp. xii, 417[422], with plates.   BM
pp. 51–8, Railroads; pp. 89–113, Comparison of roads, railroads, and canals.

4371 [NASH, C.] Railway management, illustrated by the judgement in 'Hare versus the London & North Western' and other facts; with a retrospective glance at railways. By a Journalist. 2nd edn. *London*, [1861.] pp. 10. [*Public Companies Tracts*, no. 8.] BM
Extracts from *The Times* followed by general arguments in favour of reforms.

4372 MORRIS, T. A clue to railway compensation, the value of estates, and parochial assessment: a popular discussion of the subject, illustrated by tables and examples. *London*, 1863. pp. xi, 105.   BM

4373 [BRADFIELD, J. E.] Mileage duties. Case of the stage carriage proprietors. [*London*,] 1864. pp. 32, with fold. map.   LSE
Railway dues and omnibus dues compared.

4374 A., M. The Imperial Railway of Great Britain. By M.A., *Oxford & London*, 1865. pp. 12.   BM
A plan for a national system.
—— 2nd edn. *Oxford & London*, 1865. pp. 23.   BM

4375 CHADWICK, E. Address on railway reform. (On the economical principles of a reform of the legislation and administration for the conveyance of passengers and goods on railways.) *London: National Association for the Promotion of Social Science*, 1865. pp. 49.   BM

4376 CLIFFORD, F. The steam-boat powers of railway companies. *London*, [1865.] pp. 91.
                                              UL(GL)
An alleged impartial investigation into the growing control of steam-boat services by railway companies. pp. 87–91, Report of the Select Committee appointed to enquire into this subject, dated 18 March, 1864.

4377 GALT, W. Railway reform: its importance and practicability considered as affecting the nation, the shareholders and the government. *London*, 1864. pp. xxiv, 268.   BM
Urging government purchase.
—— another edn. *London*, 1865. pp. xliv, 405.

4378 [MITCHELL, J.] Plan for lessening the taxation of the country by the purchase and improved administration of the railways of Great Britain and Ireland, in a letter addressed to . . . W. E. Gladstone. By a Civil Engineer. *London*, 1860. pp. 37.   BM
—— rev. edn. 'Plan for lessening the taxation of the country by the assumption and

improved administration of the railways of Great Britain and Ireland by the state . . . By Jos[ep]h Mitchell.' *London*, 1865. pp. xi, 39.   BM

4379 [TENNANT, C.] Railway reform; in a letter to the . . . President of the Board of Trade: a plan for the systematic reform of the railways of the United Kingdom by legislative enactment. *London*, 1865. pp. 172.
Signed 'The Author of the People's Blue Book'.   IT
Uniformity of gauge; exemption of railways from taxation; a penny per mile maximum fare.
—— 2nd edn. 'Railways: in a letter . . .' *London*, 1865. pp. 172.   BM

4380 JACKSON, R. Hand Book of Irish Railway Reform; containing copy of memorial addressed to the Lords Commissioners of Her Majesty's Treasury by the people of Ireland, together with the resolutions passed at public meetings . . . and other data. Compiled by Robert Jackson. *Dublin*, 1866. pp. 63.   BM
Jackson was secretary to the Irish Railway Reform Committee.

4381 LIVESEY, W. A financial scheme for the relief of railway companies, submitted to directors, shareholders and the public, for their consideration. *London*, [1866.] pp. 40.   NLC
Proposes mutual control, under government supervision, of railway company finance, to end irregularities concerning borrowed capital.

4382 CONSOLIDATION of Irish railways: letter to the . . . Earl of Derby . . . *Dublin*, 1867. pp. 14.   BM (MSS)
Suggests the formation of one company under government supervision, for the whole of Ireland.

4383 ENGLAND, J. B. Railway accounts: a letter to Lord Redesdale. *London*, 1867. pp. 23.
                                                            BM
Criticism: the necessity for 'public audit' of railway accounts.

4384 MITCHELL, J. Railway finance: being suggestions for the resuscitation and improvement of the railway companies at present in financial difficulties; in a letter to . . . Benjamin Disraeli. *London*, 1867. pp. 27.   BM
Difficulties due to 'careless and indiscriminate granting of Bills' and to bad management. Urges government intervention to control all railways under Commissioners; with a letter from Lord Kinnaird.

4385 THOMAS, J. L. A letter on the present position of railways, addressed to railway shareholders. *London*, 1867. pp. 21.   BM
The evils of competing lines and the remedy in government assistance.

4386 WOOD, W. Railway management and accounts. *Edinburgh*, 1867. pp. 22.   BM

A criticism, urging, among other reforms, a 'gradual change in the direction.'(!)

4387 AYRES, H. The financial position of railways, and observations on the railway systems of accounts in the United Kingdom; showing the necessity for a more systematic and uniform plan of publishing railway accounts periodically under the authority of Parliament, the advantages to be derived from a complete system of registration for railway securities and the establishment of a special department of Government for the purpose of controlling the railway affairs of the country; with a variety of information respecting the railway property of the United Kingdom. *London*, 1868. pp. lxiii, 41.   BM

4388 B., F. Observations and suggestions on the railways of the United Kingdom, showing how the same may be immediately rendered more serviceable and beneficial to the public generally than they now are, and much more remunerative to their proprietors. *London*, 1868. pp. 12.

4389 DODDS, J. Railway reform a public necessity; with practical suggestions. *Belfast*, 1868. pp. 23, with fold. map.   BM
Government to undertake management of railways in Ireland.

4390 FAIRLIE, R. F. Observations on the construction of railway carriages, together with a paper on railways and their management. *London*, 1868. pp. 35.   ICE

4391 PICTET, F. The railways of England, Scotland and Ireland: a comprehensive scheme for the redemption of capital; a general reduction in the fares to uniform rates, and reform in management and expenses. *London*, [1868.] pp. 16, with fold. table of present & proposed fares.   BM
—— [2nd enl. edn.] *London*, 1868. pp. 16, 16.   BM

4392 RYDE, E. Rating of railways. (A handy book in a series of letters: letter VIII.) *London*, 1868. pp. 36.   LSE

4393 CASTLE, H. J. Practical remarks upon the Union Assessment Committee Act, 1862, showing how to apply the principles contained therein to the proper and uniform assessment of railway, gas, and water works . . . *London*, 1863. pp. viii, 128.   BM
—— 2nd edn. Practical remarks on the principles of rating as applied to the proper and uniform assessment of railways, gasworks, waterworks . . . . *London*, 1869. pp. xvii, 163[167].   BM

4394 JONES, G. W. G. W. Jones's plan of universal penny railways by the application of turnpikes to railways: a practical plan, suitable to the genius of the people and calculated to satisfy the locomotive requirements

of the country. *London*, 1869. pp. viii, 55. NLC
Government ownership, and a fares system based on sixteen-mile stages, with turnstiles at station entrances.

4395 HILL, J. The railway problem, 1870: a series of papers edited by J. Hill. *London*, 1870. pp. 70.   BM
Various proposed reforms.

4396 WATSON, J. H. British railway reform: a scheme for amalgamating the different railway companies in Great Britain: proving that uniform fares . . . would be profitable to the State; illustrated with a map showing proposed new central station for the Metropolis . . . *London*, 1870. pp. 32.   BM
Against monopoly and the abuse of power by railway directors; in favour of government control. Previous schemes by Galt and by Brandon considered.
—— abridged edn. *London*, 1870. pp. 16. BM

4397 WILLIAMS, A. J. The appropriation of the railways by the State: a popular statement; with a map. *London*, 1869. pp. xii, 140. BM
Map shows proposed nationalized railway system.
—— 2nd edn. *London*, 1870. pp. x, 140. BM

4398 BRANDON, R. Railways and the public: how to make railways remunerative to the shareholders, beneficial to the public and profitable to the State. *London*, 1868. pp. 22.   BM
Unification of railways. Any distance, same fare.
—— 2nd edn. *London*, 1869. pp. 31.   BM
—— 7th, *London*, 1870. pp. 15.   LSE
—— 8th, *London*, 1871. pp. 8.   BM

4399 EDWARDS, F. Y. Proposed government railway reforms: the Continental and English railway systems compared: a treatise on the foreign luxuries and home miseries of railway travel, with a notice of the state-managed lines of the Continent. *London: National Railway Assocn.*, 1870. pp. 15. LSE
Advantages of state control.
—— 2nd edn. *London*, 1871. pp. 15.   RC
—— 3rd, *London*, 1871. pp. 15.   BM

4400 LOW, W. *and* THOMAS, G. The proposed England and India Railway: a letter to . . . W. E. Gladstone, M.P., First Lord of the Treasury. *London*, 1871. pp. 36.   BM
A plan for a continuous line of railway from London to Karachi via the proposed Channel Tunnel. Includes descriptions of previous schemes for rail and sea routes to India.

4401 BENSON, R. The amalgamation of railway companies, or the alternative of their purchase by the State considered. *London*, 1872. pp. 30.   BM
For complete amalgamation or nationalization.

4402 GRAVES, S. R. Railway amalgamations, etc. *Westminster*, [1872.] pp. 25.   BM
pp. 11–25, advantages of state ownership.

4403 HAGGARD, F. T. Remarks upon the acquisition of railways by the State. *London*, 1872. pp. 16.   BM

4404 HAUGHTON, B. Railway amalgamation. *London*, 1872. pp. 26, with la. fold. map showing proposed four systems.   BM

4405 WATKIN, E. W. Railways and the State: observations by Sir E. W. Watkin at the meeting of the Manchester Chamber of Commerce on Monday May 13, 1872. *Manchester*, 1872. pp. 19.   LSE
His objections to government control.

4406 GROVER, J. W. Railways and their future development. Reprinted from the 'Quarterly Journal of Science', April 1873. *London*, 1873. pp. 20.   LSE
Mechanical and financial reforms urgently required.

4407 HAUGHTON, B. The railways amalgamated and grouped in competing systems. *London*, [1873.] pp. 48.   BM
'. . . so as to produce symmetry and order out of the seemingly chaotic mass.'

4408 LEA, T. The purchase of the railways by the State: speech of Mr. Lea in the House of Commons on Tuesday, May 20th, 1873. *London*, 1873. pp. 28.   NLC
In favour.

4409 OUGHT the State to buy the railways?: a question for everybody. Reprinted with additions from the 'British Quarterly Review.' By 'A Midland Shareholder.' *London*, 1873. pp. 44.   BM
Against government ownership.

4410 RAILWAY gauges; from 'The Times' of January 17, 1873. *London: Charles Whiting*, 1873. pp. 16.   NLC
A review of R. F. Fairlie's *Battle of the gauges: railways or no railways* (1872).

4411 JEVONS, W. S. The railways and the State. *In* 'Essays and addresses by professors & lecturers of the Owens College, Manchester', by B. Stewart & A. W. Ward. 1874. pp. 465–505.   BM
—— reprinted in his 'Methods of social reform.' 1883. pp. 353–83.   BM
Railways will be improved by legislative control and reform, not by state purchase.

4412 PORTER, J. N. The Railway Passenger Duty, its injustice and its repeal, considered together with the illegality of the recent judgment in the case of the Attorney-General v. the North London Railway Company. *London*, 1874. pp. 31.   BM

4413 ASSOCIATION FOR THE REPEAL OF THE PASSENGER DUTY ON RAILWAYS. Debate on the Railway Passenger Duty in the House of Commons, April 17th, 1877. *London*, 1877. pp. 87.   BM

4414 COLLET, C. D. The Railway Passenger Duty at the end of the Session 1877. 1, Mr. Knatchbull-Hugesson's Motion. 2, The Scandal of maintaining an obsolete law. 3, Tax on locomotion a public nuisance. Reprinted from the 'Industrial Review.' *London*, [1877.] pp. 16.   BM

4415 COLLET, C. D. Repeal of the tax on locomotion: syllabus of a lecture to be read by Mr. C. D. Collet . . . [*London*, 1877.] pp. 3.
BM

4416 COLLET, C. D. Reasons for the repeal of the Railway Passenger Duty . . . *London*, 1877. pp. 34.   BM

4417 The QUESTION of the age: how to avert the horrors of a general war. By a Cosmopolitan. *London*, 1877. pp. 32.   NLC
Includes a suggestion for co-operation between railway companies in Southern England and steam-boat services to improve communication between Paris and London, thereby improving political and commercial relations with France.

4418 HEDLEY, T. F. Local taxation . . . The rating of railways in England and Wales compared with the railways in Ireland, and the effects of the parochial principle of rating: observations on Mr. Goschen's Bill. *London*, 1878. pp. 136.   NLC
Addressed to W. E. Gladstone as Prime Minister.

4419 TRAVELLING TAX ABOLITION COMMITTEE. The tax on travelling: the laws as to its assessment set aside by the Board of Inland Revenue. *London*, 1879. pp. 8. LSE
Based on a paper prepared by the Committee's Secretary, C. D. Collet.

4420 WATHERSTON, E. J. Our railways: should they be private or national property? *London*, 1879. pp. 60.   BM
Historical survey of railways, with tables from 1854–1878, followed by description of individual Irish lines, with financial tables. State ownership desirable.

4421 CONDER, F. R. Report on the comparative cost of transport by railway and by canal; **ca** addressed, Feb. 14, 1882, to the President of the Wolverhampton Chamber of Commerce on the occasion of that Chamber proposing . . . a resolution relating to the 'emancipation of canals from the control of railway companies.' *London*, 1882. pp. 16. ICE

4422 DORNIG, A. Usi ed abusi delle forrovie: studi economici e sociali. *Milano*, 1883. pp. viii, 197, with bibliogr. notes.   BM
pp. 90–138, 'Inghilterra'.

4423 HEDLEY, T. F. Local taxation: observations on the rating of railways and suggestions for the amendment of the law. *Sunderland*, 1883. pp. 17.   BM

4424 BOON, M. G. How to construct free state railway and other national and municipal works of utility, without loans. *London*, 1884. pp. 52.   BRE

4425 'HERCULES.' British railways and canals in relation to British trade and government control. By 'Hercules.' *London*, [1884.] pp. 234.   BM
Reforms.

4426 GORDON, L. St. C. Railway federation. *Bristol*, [1885.] pp. 16.   BM
Consolidation under government supervision.

4427 SIMONS, W. Our railway system: a scheme for converting it into national property. *Cardiff*, 1885. pp. 31.   BM
'The whole country at the mercy of a few Boards. State purchase to remove the enormous burden to industry and trade of high rates and charges imposed by railways.'

4428 CARPENTER, E. A letter to the employees of the Midland, and other railway compan-
s ies. *Sheffield*, [1886.] pp. [3.]   LSE
Written on behalf of the Sheffield Socialist Party, concerning the economic dismissal of railway servants. Alternative —'lower the rate of dividend.' Urges nationalization.

4429 KEDDELL, F. The nationalisation of our railway system: its justice and advantages.
s *London*, [1886.] pp. 16.   BM
Reprinted from *Justice*.
A Socialist approach to railway reform.

4430 VENABLES, G. S. Railway and Canal Traffic Bill. Speech delivered . . . at a special meeting of Great Western Railway proprietors held at the Paddington Station on Monday April 5, 1886. *London*, 1886. pp. 15.
NLC
Protest against the Bill, which proposes Board of Trade control over the fixing of rates.

4431 HANDYSIDE, G. Reform of the land laws, and state protection withdrawn from railways: a cure for commercial distress and want of employment. *Newcastle on Tyne*, 1887. pp. 49.   BM

4432 JEANS, J. S. Railway problems: an inquiry into the economic conditions of railway
c working in different countries. *London*, 1887. pp. xxviii, 560.   BM
Financial and other current problems (administration, Irish railways, canal competition, accidents, state control, etc.); pp. 525–40, chronology of railway events and legislation in Gt. Britain, and tables.

4433 RAILWAY DEFENCE ASSOCIATION. Speeches in the House of Lords on second reading of the Railway and Canal Traffic Bill, March 14, 1887, by . . . Lord Grimthorpe . . . Lord Brabourne and . . . Lord Bramwell. *London*, [1887.] pp. 23. LSE
Board of Trade interference in the fixing of railway rates.

434 WARING, C. State purchase of railways. *London*, 1887. pp. xi, 204.　　　BM
　　Belgian, German and French railways followed by pp. 45–108, the English position: pp. 108–72, reprints from *Fortnightly Review*: pp. 174–203, State purchase of Irish railways.

435 TRAVELLING TAX ABOLITION COMMITTEE. When is a railway not a railway?: correspondence with the Solicitor of Inland Revenue. *London*, [1888.] pp. [450]–456.
　　　　　　　　　　　　　　　　　LSE
　　Should tramways be classed as railways for tax purposes?

436 COOPER, R. A. Free railway travel: a proposal that the State should acquire and maintain the railways, making them free to the public, like the highways. *London*, [1891.] pp. 31.　　　　　　　　　　　　LSE

437 DAVIDSON, J. M. Free rails and trams. *London: Free Railway Travel League*, [c. 1891–2.] pp. 14. [*Politics for the People* no. 4.]　　　　　　　　　　　　LSE
　　In support of the ideas of R. A. Cooper in his *Free railway travel*. Nationalization.
　　—— *also in his* 'Politics for the People: first series.' *London*, [1891.] pp. 105–16.　BM

438 JEFFERDS, M. R. Chart showing the railway mileage area, density of population, increase of railways since 1881, and the adequate railway service required for the principal countries of the world, as compared with Belgium. *London*, 1892. s.sh.　BM

439 PENFOLD, C. Principle and law of rating to the relief of the poor, railway, gas, water and other similar companies. *London*, 1847. pp. 96.　　　　　　　　　　　　BM
　　—— 2nd edn. 'Practical remarks upon the principle of rating railway, gas, water, and other similar companies...' *London*, 1849. BM
　　—— 3rd edn. *London*, 1857. pp. vii, 306. LC
　　—— 4th, *London*, 1860.　　　　　BM
　　—— 5th, *London*, 1869. pp. xii, 165.　BM
　　—— 6th, *London*, [1870.] pp. x, 304.　BM
　　—— 7th, *London*, 1884. pp. xvi, 349.　BM
　　—— 8th, *London*, 1893. pp. xlii, 554.　BM
　　The BM copies of the 4th and 5th editions were destroyed during the War and their pagination is not known.

440 LONDON REFORM UNION. The tramways. *London*, [c. 1894.] pp. [2.] [*Leaflet* no. 47.]
　　For public ownership.　　　　　　BM

441 ROBERTSON, J. M. Railway nationalisation. *Bradford: Truth Seeker Co.*, [1894?] pp. 7. [*Papers for the People* no. 11.] TUC
　　Political and social reasons in favour.

442 STANLEY, E. H. S. The purchase of railways by the State. *In his* 'Speeches and Addresses.' *London*, 1894. pp. 211–18. BM
　　Opposing.

*4443 BOLAS, T. An address to the members of the Railway Congress, London, 1895; together with a reprint of the Railway Reform Leaflets, 1 to 8. *London*, 1895. pp. [14.] BM
　　'The sole guiding principle of railway management is big dividends to the shareholders, the misery of others counting for nothing.' Urges a 'Railway Control Board'.

4444 BOLAS, T. Confiscation of all railway property as a leading step in solving the labour problem; also as a preliminary to the punishment of shareholders ... *London*, 1895. pp. 8.
　　　　　　　　　　　　　　　　　BM
　　Railways and Socialism.

4445 HOLE, J. National railways: an argument for state purchase. *London*, 1893. pp. xvi, 385, with bibliogr. notes.　　　　BM
　　—— 2nd edn. *London & Paris*, 1895. pp. xvi, 408.　　　　　　　　　　BM

4446 WOLFE, A. G. The nationalisation of the railway system. *London*, [1895.] pp. 31. [*Socialist Pamphlets*.]　　　　　BM

4447 BOLAS, T. Equitable nationalisation of railway property on a constitutional basis and without departure from existing legal usages, moreover with the very fullest justice for shareholders. *London*, 1895. pp. 12. LSE
　　'Half the total receipts of railways go to shareholders who do no work.'
　　—— another edn., *London*, 1898. pp. 8. LSE

4448 BOGLE, W. R. Nationalisation of railways: a reply to C. S. Dennis, General Manager, Cambrian Railways. [*Glasgow: Railway Nationalisation League*, 1898.] pp. 8　BRE
　　Reprinted from *The Buteman*, Rothesay, 5 February, 1898.

4449 MACAULAY, J. The nationalisation of railways. *Liverpool*, 1898. pp. 11.
　　From the *Railway News*, 27 November, 1897. Advantages.

4450 PERRIS, G. H. Railways for the nation. *London: Railway Nationalisation League*, 1898. pp. 43, with bibliogr. notes.　LSE
　　Reprinted from the *Co-operative Wholesale Societies' Annual* for 1898.

4451 CLODE, W. *and* CRIPPS-DAY, F. H. The law relating to the assessment and valuation of railways and stations for rating purposes. *London*, 1899. pp. 144.　　BM

4452 LABOUR REPRESENTATION COMMITTEE. Why our railways should be nationalised. *London*, [1899.] pp. 3. [*Leaflet* no. 12.] BRE

4453 BOGLE, W. R. Railway nationalisation: a paper read ... at an Industrial Conference in Glasgow, February, 1901. *Kingston-upon-Hull*, 1901. pp. 11.　　　　　LSE
　　In favour.

4454 SUTHERLAND, G. Twentieth century inventions: a forecast. *London*, 1901. pp. xvi,
f 286.   BM
pp. 91–121, road and rail.

4455 KEEN, F. N. Tramway companies and local authorities: being a collection of special provisions contained in Private Acts of Parliament of tramway companies and relating particularly to the interests of local authorities. *London*, 1902. pp. 295.   BM

4456 BEAVAN, A. H. Tube, train, tram and car; or, Up-to-date locomotion . . . *London*. 1903. pp. xviii, 291, with many illus.   BM

4457 SUTHERS, R. B. The truth about the trams. *London: Clarion Press*, 1903. pp. 16. [*Clarion Pamphlet* no. 39.]   LSE
The moral principle of public ownership of tramways.

4458 WILLIAMS, P. Our decrepit railway system: a word to the stockholder and the passenger. *London*, 1903. pp. 95.   BM
Criticisms and suggested reforms under twenty-four headings.

4459 HOBSON, S. G. Public control of electric power and transit. *London: Fabian Society*, 1905. pp. 15. [*Fabian Tract* no. 119.]   LSE

4460 CUNNINGHAM, W. Should our railways be nationalised? 2nd edn. *Dunfermline*, 1901. pp. 23.   LSE
The economics of nationalization.
—— [3rd edn.] *Dunfermline*, 1903. pp. 54.   LSE
—— 4th, much enlarged. *Dunfermline*, 1906. pp. 295.   BM

4461 PRATT, E. A. British canals: is their resuscitation practicable? *London*, 1906. pp. viii,
ca 159.   BM
Includes the railway versus canal question.

4462 BROWNE, J. H. B. The Railway and Canal Traffic Acts. [*London*, 1897.] pp. 21. [*London Chamber of Commerce Pamphlet* no. 22.]   LSE

4463 COOKE, W. G. Railway rating: an open letter addressed to boards of guardians, assessment committees and county councils. *London*, 1907. pp. 16.   BM
'For private circulation only.'

4464 EDWARDS, C. Railway nationalisation. *London*, 1898. pp. xii, 233.   BM
'a necessity and an advantage.'
—— 2nd edn. *London*, 1907. pp. xii, 243.   BM

4465 JOHNSTON, T. *and* ADAM, H. The railway difficulty and how to solve it. *Glasgow: For-*
s *ward Printing & Publishing Co.*, [1907.] pp. 16.   LSE
Nationalization: a Socialist view.

4466 LOCKWOOD, M. The nationalisation of British railways. *London*, 1907. pp. 16. [*Popular Financial Booklets*, no. 32.]
Reprint, the *Financial Review of Reviews*, Nov. 1907.

4467 PORTER, R. P. The dangers of municipal trading. *London*, 1907. pp. xii, 320.   BM
pp. 285–309, 'Nationalisation of railways.'

4468 PRATT, E. A. State railways: object lessons from other lands. *London*, 1907. pp. 107.   BM

4469 WILLETT, W. The waste of daylight. *London*, [1907.] pp. 16.   BM
'The success of the scheme depends very largely upon the railways.' The proposal to advance clock time by one hour during the summer months and ultimately introduced in May 1916.
—— 2nd to 14th editions. *London*, 1908–1914.   BM

4470 ACWORTH, W. M. The relation of railroads to the state: an address before the British Association for the Advancement of Science, at Dublin, Sept. 2, 1908. [*Philadelphia*, 1908.] pp. 14.   BRE
—— another edn. *London*, 1908. pp. 12.   BRE

4471 GIBB, G. S. Railway nationalisation: a paper read at the Quarterly Meeting of the Royal Economic Society, 10 November, 1908. [*London*, 1908.] pp. 30.   LSE
Arguments against.

4472 GREAT WESTERN RLY. Rating of railways. *London*, [1908.] pp. iii, 33[35], with tables & charts.   LSE
Reprinted with additions from the *G.W.R. Magazine*, Oct. 1906 to July 1907.
Principles and practice: methods of valuation.

4473 WARDLE, G. J. Nationalisation of railways. *London: Independent Labour Party*,
s 1908. pp. 14.   LSE

4474 BAZLEY, B. M. Should British railways be re-distributed? pp. 16. *Typescript*.   RC
Paper, Railway Club, Jan. 1909.
Division of the country into 'railway provinces' to avoid wasteful competition.

4475 BOLLAND, W. Railways and the nation: problems and possibilities. *London*, 1909. pp. 144.   BM
Varied aspects, including working expenses, competition, management, and social effects.

4476 THRELFALL, T. R. Shall the railways be nationalised? Plain words to railwaymen.
s *London: Anti-Socialist Publication Department*, 1909. pp. 11[12]. [*Anti-Socialist Tracts*, no. 15.]   LSE

4477 DAVIES, A. E. State purchase of railways: a practical scheme. *London: Fabian Society*, 1910. pp. 24. [*Fabian Tracts*, no. 150.]   BM

4478 PALMER, J. E. British canals: problems and
ca possibilities. *London*, 1910. pp. 254. BM
pp. 45–103, railways versus canals.

4479 PEASE, E. R. Railway nationalisation and
the railway workers. [*London*, 1910.] pp. 8.
LSE
Prospective advantages outlined.

4480 PRATT, E. A. Canals and traders: the argument pictorial as applied to the report of the
ca Royal Commission on Canals and Waterways. *London*, 1910. pp. xi, 123, with 43
illus. & 9 maps & diagrams. BM
Railway services compared with canals.

4481 RAILWAY NATIONALISATION SOCIETY.
Railway combinations and amalgamations.
London, [1910?] pp. 4. [*R.N.S. Leaflet*, no.
1.] LSE
Nationalization the only remedy for railway
problems.

4482 VROOMAN, C. S. American railway problems in the light of European experience;
or, Government regulation versus government operation of railways. *London*, 1910.
pp. vii, 376, with bibliogr. notes. BM
pp. 222–376, English railway corruption.

4483 DAVIES, A. E. The case for railway nationalisation. By Emil Davies. *London: National Labour Press*, [1911.] pp. 16. LSE

4484 DAVIES, A. E. The nationalization of railways. *London*, 1908. pp. 125. BM
A general survey of all aspects; pp. 113–25,
'How to nationalize the railways'.
—— 2nd edn. *London*, 1911. pp. 125. BM

4485 FABIAN SOCIETY. Manifesto on the rail-
s way situation. *London*, October 1911. pp.
[3.] LSE
The conflicting interests of shareholders,
workers, and traders. Solution—a nationalized
and unified railway system.

4486 FAY, S. Presidential address (London
School of Economics, Railway Students'
f Union, October 24, 1911). *London*, 1911.
pp. 8. LSE
The future of railways: a forecast.

4487 PRATT, E. A. Railway nationalisation and
its supporters. *London*, 1909. pp. 7. [*Anti-
s Socialist Union* no. 30.] BM
—— 2nd edn. 'Railway nationalisation.'
London, 1911. pp. 12. [no. 135.] BM

*4488 PRATT, E. A. Railways and nationalisation.
London: P. S. King, 1908. pp. vi, 455 BL
'Railway nationalisation . . . is unnecessary,
undesirable and impracticable.' Alternative
recommendations.

4489 DENT, F. H. Presidential address (London
School of Economics and Political Science
Railway Students' Association): delivered

22 October, 1912. [*London*, 1912.] pp. 11.
LSE
State purchase of the railways: a balanced
view presented to students.

4490 LASTEYRIE, C. de. La Nationalisation des
chemins de fer anglais. *Paris*, [1912.] pp. 30.
BM

4491 MUNICIPAL TRAMWAYS ASSOCIATION.
Light Railways Bill, 1912. Memoranda re
trackless trolley vehicles. (By Chris. J.
Spencer, Hon. Secretary.) [*Bradford*, May
1912.] pp. [4.] BM

4492 DAVIES, A. E. The case for railway nationalisation. *London & Glasgow*, [1913.] pp.
262, with bibliography. BM

4493 DUNN, S. O. Government ownership of
railways. *New York & London*, 1913. pp.
vii, 400. BM

4494 PRATT, E. A. The case against railway
nationalisation. *London*, [1913.] pp. 264.
BM

4495 RAILWAY NATIONALISATION SOCIETY.
Railways and the nation. [*London*, 1913?]
pp. 7[10]. [*R.N.S. Pamphlet*, no. 2.] LSE
—— another edn. [*London*, 1913?] pp.
7[14]. LSE

4496 RAILWAY NATIONALISATION SOCIETY.
What railway nationalisation would mean.
London, 1911. pp. 11. TUC
—— another edn. *London*, [1913.] pp. 12.
[*R.N.S. Pamphlet*, no. 1.] TUC

4497 RAILWAY NATIONALISATION SOCIETY.
Why the railways should be nationalised.
London, [1913?] s.sh. [*R.N.S. Pamphlet*, no.
1.] LSE

4498 ARNOLD, W. C. Royal railways with uniform rates: a proposal for amalgamation of
railways with the General Post Office and
adoption of uniform fares and rates for any
distance. *London*, 1914. pp. 61. BM

4499 BALLEN, D. Bibliography of Road-making
and Roads in the United Kingdom. *London*,
b 1914. pp. xviii, 281. BM
Includes works on road/rail relationships.

4500 CANE, A. B. The Railway Companies'
Association. *In* 'Jubilee of the Railway
News, 1864–1914.' *London: Railway News*,
[1914.] pp. 87–8. BM

4501 COX, H. Railway nationalisation. *In*
'Jubilee of the Railway News, 1864–1914.'
London: Railway News, [1914.] pp. 160–1.
BM

4502 DENT, F. H. The state acquisition of railways. *In* 'Jubilee of the Railway News, 1864–
1914.' *London: Railway News*, [1914.] p. 162.
BM

4503 GRIBBLE, T. G. Comparative economics of tramways and rail-less electric traction. *London*, 1914. pp. 36, with tables.   LSE
Excerpt *Min. Proc. I.C.E.*, Session 1913–14.

4504 LOMAS, A. D. Railway rating and valuation. *In* 'Modern railway working,' edited by John Macaulay. vol. 8, 1914. pp. 57–78, with tables.   BM

4505 RAILWAY NATIONALISATION SOCIETY. State ownership and operation of railways: memorandum submitted . . . to the Royal Commission on Railways, May 8, 1914. [*London*, 1914.] pp. 31. [*R.N.S. Pamphlet* no. 6.]   LSE

4506 STATE purchase of British railways. *In* 'Jubilee of the Railway News, 1864–1914.' *London: Railway News*, [1914.] pp. 167–75.   BM

4507 WELLS, H. G. Anticipations of the re-action of mechanical and scientific progress
f upon human life and thought. *London*, 1902. pp. 318.   BM
pp. 1–32, Locomotion in the twentieth century.
—— New & cheaper edn., with author's
f specially-written introduction. *London*, 1914. pp. xiii, 318.   BM

4508 RAILWAY NATIONALISATION SOCIETY. Railways and the War. *London*, [1915.] pp.
f [4.]   IT
Against a post-war return to private control.

4509 MURRAY, H. The Railway Swindle: a long-deferred exposure. *London*, 1916. pp. 160.   BM
An indictment of railway management methods.

4510 RADFORD, G. State services. *London*, 1916. pp. 142.   BM
pp. 108–26, Railways: reforms, and nationalization.

4511 RAILWAY NATIONALISATION SOCIETY. Fourth Annual Meeting, 8th June, 1916. Report of speeches by J. H. Thomas and Emil Davies. *London*, [1916.] pp. 15. [*R.N.S. Pamphlet*, no. 10.]   LSE

4512 RAILWAY NATIONALISATION SOCIETY. Report of proceedings at a conference on the terms of purchase of railways . . . 19 February, 1916 . . . *London*, [1916.] pp. 14[15]. [*R.N.S. Pamphlet*, no. 8.]   LSE

4513 RAILWAY NATIONALISATION SOCIETY. Three views on railway nationalisation: business, finance, labour. *London*, [1916.] pp. 14. [*R.N.S. Pamphlet*, no. 11.]   LSE
Reprinted from the *Daily Telegraph*, 12 Sept., 1916.

4514 WEBB, S. J. *and* FREEMAN, A. Great Britain after the War. *London*, Sept. 1916.
f pp. 80.   BM
pp. 64–7, How shall we re-organise the railways? The waste of competition and the tyranny of monopoly. Advantages of nationalization.

4515 The FUTURE of English railways. Reprinted from the 'Edinburgh Review,' Janu-
f ary, 1917. *n.p.* [1917.] pp. 84–103.   BM

4516 MACKENZIE, F. A. British railways and
f the War. *London*, 1917. pp. 31.   BM
Includes post-war problems.

4517 WEBB, S. J. How to pay for the War: being ideas offered to the Chancellor of the Ex-
ca chequer by the Fabian Research Depart-
f ment; edited by Sidney Webb. *Westminster: Fabian Society*, [1916.] pp. xv, 278, with bibliogr. notes.   BM
pp. 51–111, A public service of railway and canal transport.
—— 2nd edn. *London*, 1917. pp. xv, 278, xii.   BM

4518 [CRAMMOND, E.] The nationalisation of British railways. [*London*, 1918.] pp. 47.
f Reprint, *Quarterly Review*, Oct. 1909.   BRE

4519 GATTIE, A. W. How to solve the food problem. *London*, 1918. pp. 10,[2.]
Reprinted from *The Nineteenth Century and After*, April 1918.

4520 ASSOCIATION OF RAILROAD EXECUTIVES. Proposed English Ministry of Transportation: full text of the Bill submitted to Parliament by the English Cabinet, 1919. *New York*, [1919.] pp. 14.   BRE
Reprinted from the *The Times* Feb. 28, 1919. pp. 8–11, Power to purchase railways.

4521 GATTIE, A. W. Transport, the key industry of the Country . . . *London: New Transport Co.*, [1919?] pp. 15, with illus. & diagrams. [*Lecture* no. 1.]   BM
The wastefulness of steam; the steam locomotive, and the inefficient practice of shunting.

4522 GEDDES, E. Sir Eric Geddes' correspondence with Mr. A. Warwick Gattie on transport reform. *London: Transport Reform Society*, 1919. pp. 7.   BM

4523 HORNIMAN, R. How to make the railways pay for the War; or, The transport problem solved . . . *London*, 1916. pp. xx, 348, with 22 illus., plans & diagrams, & bibliogr. notes.   BM
The urgency of economic reforms and the need for a central clearing house in London.
—— 2nd edn. *London*, 1917. pp. xx, 340.   BM
—— 3rd, *London*, 1919. pp. xvi, 375.   BM

4524 RAILWAY NATIONALISATION SOCIETY. Nationalisation of Railways Bill. *London*, 1918. pp. 16. [*R.N.S. Pamphlet*, no. 14.] LSE
Introductory notes and text of the Bill.

—— another edn. *London*, 1919. pp. 15. TUC

4525 ACWORTH, W. M. Historical sketch of state railway ownership. *London*, 1920. pp. xv, 104.   BM
Review of nationalization in foreign countries and opinions on its application to British railways.

4526 BELFORT, R. Our bankrupt railways. *London*, 1920. pp. 72. [*Financial Empire* series, no. 2.]   BRE
Nationalization.

4527 BOLSHEVIK Boards. *London: Great Western Rly.*, 1920. pp. 3. [*Great Western Pamphlets*, no. 5.]   BR
Reprinted from the *Globe*, 14 Dec., 1920.
Blames railwaymen, not directors, for recent increases in fares, and an 'utter disregard of the public.'

4528 The COASTING trade: what must be done at once to keep the coasting services and the smaller ports going? 1920. pp. 6.   LSE
Railway rates must be raised to allow coastal traffic to compete on an equal footing.

4529 COLE, G. D. H. Chaos and order in industry. *London*, 1920. pp. viii, 292.   BM
pp. 86–111, Nationalization of railways, and railway trade unionism: guiding principles.

4530 DAVIES, A. E. The case for nationalization. *London*, [1920.] pp. 310.   BM
Including the draft of a 'Railway Nationalization Bill' prepared on behalf of the Railway Nationalisation Society in 1918.

4531 JENNINGS, H. J. Our insolvent railways. [*London: Great Western Rly.*, 1920.] pp. 15. [*Great Western Pamphlets*, no. 1.]   BR
Reprinted from the *Fortnightly Review*, Sept. 1920.
For the restoration of private company control.

4532 GREAT WESTERN RLY. Memorandum on the railway position. [*London*,] 1920. pp. 3.   LSE
An alternative amalgamation scheme, proposed by the Railway Companies Association, and addressed to the Minister of Transport.

4533 LONDON MUNICIPAL SOCIETY. State railways. *London*, Sept. 1913. pp. 19. [*Statistical & other Memoranda upon Political and Social Questions of the Day*, ser. 3, no. 5.]   LSE
—— another edn. *London*, Jan. 1920. pp. 19. [ser. 6, no. 1.]   LSE

4534 NATIONALISING the railways without paying for them. [*London: Great Western Rly.*, 1920.] pp. 16. [*Great Western Pamphlets*, no. 4.]   BR
Reprinted from the *Railway Gazette*, 10 Dec., 1920.

4535 RAILWAY nationalization, 1. *London*, June 1920. pp. 4. [*Oxford Tracts on Economic Subjects*, set 4, no. 26.]   BM
Points for and against, drawn from foreign experience of nationalization.

4536 ASSOCIATED SOCIETY OF LOCOMOTIVE ENGINEERS & FIREMEN *and* RAILWAY CLERKS ASSOCIATION. Railway re-organisation: memorandum on the proposals of the Minister of Transport as to the future organisation of transport undertakings in Great Britain and their relation to the State, as outlined in . . . Cmd. 787. *London*, 1921. pp. 7.   TUC

4537 BANBURY, F. G. Railways Bill: memorandum by the Chairman of the Great Northern Railway Co. *London*, 1921. pp. 4.   LSE
Addressed to all proprietors of the G.N.R. 'Railways should be handed back.' Amalgamations to be carried out, but by private arrangement between companies.

4538 BRITISH RAILWAY STOCKHOLDERS UNION. The case against the nationalisation of transport. [*London*, 1921.] pp. 12.   LSE
Speeches at a meeting at Caxton Hall, London, following the second reading of the Transport Bill.

4539 RAILWAY NATIONALISATION SOCIETY. Memorandum on the Railways Bill, 1921. *London*, [1921.] pp. 8. [*R.N.S. Pamphlet*, no. 17.]   LSE
Summary of the Bill's proposals, with observations and criticisms. Resolution, complete unification of the railways.

4540 THOMAS, J. H. The red light on the railways. *London*, 1921. pp. 143[144].   BM
The case for nationalization. Includes (pp. 138–44) the Ministry of Transport's outline of proposals as to the future organisation of transport.

4541 TIMES *newspaper*. Railway Number, August 15, 1921. (no. 42,799.) *London*, 1921. pp. xxiv.   LSE
The Grouping and the future of the railways.

4542 BROWNE, K. J. N. British railwaymen's wages: what are the facts? Pre-war concessions and post-war costs. *London: Great Western Rly.*, 1922. pp. 8. [*Great Western Pamphlets*, no. 9.]   BR
Reprinted from the *Financial Times*, 26 June, 1922.

4543 EASTWOOD, M. Behind the scenes in the railway world: public interest versus private capital. *Ripley: J. S. Reynolds & Co.*, [*c.* 1922.] pp. 15.   LSE
A Socialist viewpoint on nationalization, with revelations of harmful features of administration.

4544 HADLEY, E. S. My railway and me: six of one and half-a-dozen of the other. *London: Great Western Rly.*, 1922. pp. 28.   BM
The need for economies among railwaymen in face of growing road competition.

4545 NATIONAL GUILDS LEAGUE. Towards a National Railway Guild. *London*, [1917.]
s   pp. 16. [*Pamphlets of the N.G.L.*, no. 4.] LSE
State ownership, but with control and management by railwaymen.

—— another edn. *London*, [1922.] pp. 15.
LSE

4546 PRATT, E. A. Scottish canals and water-
ca   ways ... *London*, 1922. pp. xi, 299. BM

4547 TURNER, D. L. New York, London, Paris, & Berlin transit conditions compared. *New York*, Dec. 1922. *Reproduced typescript*. IT

4548 GRIFFITH, F. P. Notes on a convertible vehicle for use on railways and roads. *Dublin*, 1923. pp. 7, with 5 plates. BR
Interchangeable wheels.

4549 MANCHESTER CORPORATION TRAM-
WAYS. Report on the comparative utility of the motor'bus and tramcar. *Manchester*, July 1923. pp. 13, with 5 plates. IT

4550 SAMS, J. G. B. How to reform our railways: a discussion on cheapening transport. *London*, 1923. pp. 62. BM
Criticisms of the Grouping Scheme.

4551 SMITH, H. B. A. The re-organization of railways in Great Britain: its progress and prospects. *Washington: Government Printing Office*, 1923. pp. 28, with 12 tables of official statistics. [*Department of Commerce. Trade Information Bulletin*, no. 79.] BM
Supplement to *Commerce Reports*, issued by the Bureau of Foreign & Domestic Commerce.

4552 POLE, F. J. C. Cardiff and the Great Western Railway. *London: G. W. Rly.*, 1924. pp. 16. [*Great Western Pamphlets*, no. 12.]
BR
Read to Cardiff Business Club, 16 Oct., 1924.
The need for railways to be free from government control, and for railwaymen to work harder. Includes tables of receipts and expenditure of railways, 1913, and for the period of government control (during the War and after).

4553 COX, H. The failure of state railways. *London*, 1924. pp. 39. BM
Nationalized railways of other countries.

4554 DAVIES, A. E. British railways, 1825–1924: why nationalisation is inevitable. *London: Railway Nationalisation Society*, July 1924. pp. 39. [*R.N.S. Pamphlet*, n.s. no. 1.] LSE

4555 SHERRINGTON, C. E. R. Some economic results of the British 'Railways Act' of 1921. [1924.] pp. [227]–239. pc
Reprint, *American Economic Review*, vol. 14, no. 2, June 1924.

4556 FENELON, K. G. Economics of road transport. *London*, 1925. pp. 256. BM
Includes transport co-ordination.

4557 GOOD, E. T. Fair play for railways: some unacknowledged facts. *London: Great Western Rly.*, 1925. pp. 12. [*Great Western Pamphlets*, no. 14.] LSE
Reprinted from the *Financial Review of Reviews*, April–June 1925.
A defence against unfair and irresponsible criticism.

4558 JOHNSON, D. R. Some current transport problems. *Bristol: Bristol Incorporated Chamber of Commerce & Shipping*, 1925. pp. 24. IT
Address at Guildhall, Bristol, 25 Nov., 1925.
Costs of transport can be reduced by co-ordination.

4559 LAWLEY, F. E. Socialism and railways. *London: Independent Labour Party*, 1925.
s   pp. 40. [*Study Courses*, no. 9.] BM

4560 NEWBOLD, J. T. W. The railways, 1825–
s   1925 ... *London*, 1925. pp. 112. BM
Railways, Socialism, and nationalization.

4561 SHOWERS, F. W. Railways, local taxation, and road transport. *London: Great Western Rly.*, Dec. 1921. pp. 38. [*Great Western Pamphlets*, no. 7.] BR
—— another edn. *London*, April 1925. pp. 48.
BR

4562 BELL, R. The progress of railway transport in America and Great Britain. *London*, [1926.] pp. 19. IT
Paper, Newcastle & Sunderland Railway Lecture & Debating Society, Gateshead, 21 Oct., 1926.

4563 GREAT WESTERN RLY. General Strike, May 1926. *London*, [1926.] pp. 123. BR
A detailed record of the strike with reproductions of documents, correspondence, statements of various bodies, notices displayed by the G.W.R., and numerous statistical tables showing the effects of the strike on various aspects of G.W.R. traffic and working.

4564 GREAT WESTERN RLY. Memorandum in regard to railways and road transport. December, 1926. pp. 24. BR
'Private and confidential.'

4565 LAWLEY, F. E. Nationalise the railways. *London: Independent Labour Party*, [1926.]
s   pp. 15. BRE

4566 MOULTON, H. G. Waterways versus railways. *New York*, 1912. pp. xviii, 468.
ca   [*Hart, Schaffner & Marx Prize Essays*, no. 13.] LC
pp. [98]–145, Barge canals of Great Britain.

ca   —— another edn. *Cambridge, Mass.* 1914. pp. xviii, 468. (not in series.) LC

ca   —— another edn. *Boston & New York*, 1926. pp. xxviii, 468. [*H.S. & M. Prize Essays*, no. 13.] LC

4567 RAILWAY COMPANIES ASSOCIATION. Road motor competition: statement in support of letter from the Railway Companies' Association dated 4th February 1926. pp. 18. 'Secret.'
Includes the text of a letter to the Prime Minister—'. . . The railway companies are seriously concerned in regard to the unfair road motor competition to which they are being subjected. . . .'

4568 RAILWAYS and local rates. London: Great Western Rly., June 1926. pp. 10. [Great Western Pamphlets, no. 3, 1926.]   BR
The burden of local rates on railways, and the unfair basis upon which they are assessed.

4569 The RAILWAYS and the General Strike. Westminster: Railway Gazette, 1926. pp. 637–76, with 40 illus.   BR
A combined issue of nos. 19 & 20 of vol. 44, 1926.

4570 SOCIETY OF MOTOR MANUFACTURERS & TRADERS. Railways and road traffic: memorandum submitted to the Chancellor of the Exchequer and the Minister of Transport. [London, 1926.] pp. 3, with 2 fold. tables.   TUC
This follows upon the deputation to the Minister of Transport made by the Railway Companies Association, 10 March,1926.

4571 BELL, R. The lessons of our railway statistics. Manchester: Manchester Statistical Society, [1927.] pp. [57]–78.   PC
Paper, 14 Dec., 1927.

4572 BELL, R. The railway situation. London, 1927. pp. 16.   IT
Paper, Great Central Debating Society, Nottingham, 19 March, 1927.

4573 DAVENPORT, E. H. Railways versus roads. London, [July 1927.] pp. 23.   BM
The need for co-operation.
—— 2nd edn. London, August 1927. pp. 23.   RC

4574 EASTON, W. C. City local passenger transport. Glasgow, 1927. pp. 72.   IME
Reprint, Transactions of the Institution of Engineers & Shipbuilders in Scotland, vol. 71, Session 1927–28. (Paper, pp. 3–35, followed by discussion.)
The bus versus tram question in London, Glasgow and Manchester; underground railways and local steam services.

4575 GREAT WESTERN RLY. A few observations on railways. (By Felix J. C. Pole.) London, [1927.] pp. 21.   LSE
Railways and their difficulties during the Great War and since the amalgamations of 1921.

4576 GREAT WESTERN RLY. A Village Drama: reprinted from the G.W.R. Magazine, April 1927. (An allegory, with figures from the rate book.) By Hugh Mytton. London, 1927. pp. 8.   LSE
Rating. Illustrates in the style of a melo-

drama how the G.W.R. has to pay dearly to local councils on which it has no representation.

4577 GRIFFITHS, H. R. Problems of road and rail transport. London: Great Western Rly., 1927. pp. 14. [Great Western Pamphlets, no. 5.]   BR
Abstract of a Paper, Institute of Transport, Western Section, 4 Oct., 1927.

4578 GRIFFITHS, H. R. The railway position, January 1927. Bristol: Bristol Incorporated Chamber of Commerce & Shipping, [1927.] pp. 31, with 17 tables.   IT

4579 JOINT COMMITTEE OF MECHANICAL ROAD TRANSPORT ASSOCIATIONS. Railway shibboleths concerning road motor transport. London, May 1927. pp. 8[9].   BR

4580 LAWLEY, F. E. Railways of the world: the progress of nationalisation. London: Railway Nationalisation Society, June 1927. pp. 31. [R.N.S. Pamphlet no. 2.]   TUC

4581 SENTINEL WAGGON WORKS. Some railway problems of today and their solution. London, 1927. pp. 64, with illus. & diagrams.   BR
The branch line problem; light traffic on main lines; shunting economies; the carriage of small quantities at a profit.

4582 BELL, R. The railways in 1927. London, 1928. pp. 19.   IT
Paper, L.N.E.R. (Lond.) Lecture & Debating Society, 13 March, 1928.

4583 BROWN, A. The future of the railways . . .
f London, 1928. pp. v, 70, with a map.   BM
Reforms, including state control and amalgamation.

4584 BRUNNER, C. T. The problem of motor transport: an economic analysis. London, 1928. pp. 187.   BM
pp. 84–102, road versus rail.

*4585 GREAT WESTERN RLY. The railways and the roads: facts and figures. London, 1928. pp. 7.   BR
Circulated to the staff of the G.W.R.

4586 SMART, W. The railways and the nation. London: Railway Nationalisation Society, October 1928. pp. 11. [R.N.S. Pamphlet, n.s. no. 3.]   LSE

4587 BRUNNER, C. T. Road versus rail: the case for motor transport. London, 1929. pp. 128.   BM
A simplified version of his The problem of motor transport (1928).

4588 DAVIES, A. E. Nationalisation: some facts for Mr. Baldwin and others. London: Labour
s Party, 1929. pp. 16.   BRE

4589 FENELON, K. G. Transport co-ordination: a study of present-day transport problems. *London*, 1929. pp. 142, with 28 statistical tables.   BM

4590 KIDD, H. C. A new era for British railways: a study of the Railways Act, 1921, from an American standpoint, with special reference to amalgamation. *London*, 1929. pp. 158, with 4 maps in text.   BM

4591 LEAGUE OF NATIONS—ADVISORY COMMITTEE ON COMPETITION FOR COMMUNI-
ca   CATIONS AND TRANSIT. Report of the Special Committee on Competition between Railways and Waterways. *Geneva*, 1929. pp. 197.   BM

4592 MANCE, H. O. Some rail and road tendencies. *London*, pp. 12.   IT
Presidential Address, London school of Economics Railway Students' Association, 14 Nov., 1929. Privately printed.
Co-ordination.

4593 RAILWAY NATIONALISATION SOCIETY. The railways and the General Election. *London*, May 1929. pp. [4.]   LSE

4594 WALKDEN, A. G. A practical scheme for the nationalisation and co-ordination of public transport: memorandum submitted ... to the Royal Commission on Transport, together with extracts of his examination by the Commissioners. *London: Railway Clerks Association*, 1929. pp. 48.   LSE

4595 BELL, R. The influence of governments on transport. 1930. pp. 18. *Reproduced typescript.*   IT
Paper, York Railway Lecture & Debating Society, 28 January, 1930.
Post-war relationships in Britain and in the U.S.A.

4596 BRATSCHI, R. Railway and motor transport. *Amsterdam: International Transportworkers' Federation*, 1930. pp. 40.   TUC
Reprint of a paper read at the Madrid Conference of the ITF, 28 April–3 May, 1930.
Rail versus road competition as it affects the workers.

4597 GLEDHILL, A. H. The transition in road passenger transport, with special reference to the changes that have taken place between 1928 and 1930. *London: Municipal Tramways & Transport Association*, 1930. pp. 31, with 8 fold. charts.   pc
Paper, Annual Conference, M.T. & T.A., 1930.

4598 LONDON SCHOOL OF ECONOMICS—BRITISH LIBRARY OF POLITICAL SCIENCE. Road and rail transport: competition and co-ordination. *In* 'Bulletin of the British Library of Political Science', 1930. pp. 27–33. [*Select Bibliography*, no. 49.]   LSE

4599 BELL, R. Twelve months' changes in transport. pp. 15. *Typescript.*   IT
Paper, Hull (LNER) Lecture & Debating Society, 8 Dec., 1931.
Effect of the economic crisis upon railways, and the difficulties presented by increasing road competition.

4600 CO-OPERATIVE PARTY. Transport. [*London*, 1931.] pp. iv, 40, with illus. [*Britain Reborn*, no. 2.]   TUC
Plan for a National Transport Board, electrification of railways, etc.

4601 FARRAR, M. F. How to make the British railways pay: an economic survey. *London*, 1931. pp. xiv, 82.   BM
Proposed reforms.

4602 INTERNATIONAL UNION OF RAILWAYS. The main line railways of Great Britain, 1923–1930: a study by the Railway Research Service based on official figures. *Westminster*, 1931. pp. 46, with 57 tables.   BM
French and German translations appeared in *Bulletin* no. 4 of the I.U. of R., April 1931.
A detailed statistical survey of railway finance, mileage, operation, staff and accidents.

4603 MINISTRY OF TRANSPORT. Report of the Conference on Rail and Road Transport. (Chairman, Sir Arthur Salter.) *London: H.M.S.O.*, 1932. pp. 85.   BM
The 'Salter Conference'.

4604 ASSOCIATION OF COUNTIES OF CITIES IN SCOTLAND. Memorandum as to Report of Conference on Rail and Road Transport, dated 29 July, 1932. [*Edinburgh*,] 14 Oct. 1932. pp. 16.   IT
Twenty-four observations and recommendations.

4605 BELL, R. The railways and some Blue Books. *London*, October 1932. pp. 16.   pc
Paper, Middlesbrough District Railway Lecture & Debating Society, 18 Oct., 1932.
The railways in the present economic circumstances, and their future. Recent Government enquiries and measures.

4606 BROWN, A. The railway problem. *London*, 1932. pp. xvi, 143.   BM
Rail versus road.

4607 CONFERENCE OF MOTOR ORGANISATIONS. Memorandum to the Ministry of Transport in reply to the memorandum upon the position of the main line railway companies in relation to road transport competition. [*London*, 1932.] pp. 8.   LSE

4608 CONFERENCE OF NATIONAL ORGANISATIONS INTERESTED IN TRANSPORT. The case of trade and industry against the Report of the Conference on Rail and Road Transport ... *London*, 24 October, 1932. pp. 72.   TUC
Dissatisfaction expressed by sixty-six organisations, and the need for the Report to be reconsidered.

4609 JOLL, A. E. Railways (Valuation for Rating) Act, 1930. pp. 14. *Reproduced typescript.* IT
Paper, Incorporated Association of Rating & Valuation Officers, 17 Feb., 1932.
The end of 100 years' agitation for reform in the law of valuation of railways for rating.

4610 LABOUR PARTY. The national planning of transport. *London*, [1932.] pp. 20. [*Socialism*
s *in Action.*]   BM
Labour Party policy on transport.

4611 LABOUR RESEARCH DEPARTMENT. The London Traffic Combine: a study of the
s finances and ramifications of the London Traffic Combine . . . *London*, [1932.] pp. 16.   TUC

4612 MUNICIPAL TRAMWAYS & TRANSPORT ASSOCIATION. Report of the Conference on Rail and Road Transport. [*London*, 1932.] pp. 3.   LSE
A letter to members of the Association by the General Secretary, J. Beckett, including his reply to the Minister of Transport's request for observations on the Report.

4613 MUNICIPAL TRAMWAYS & TRANSPORT ASSOCIATION. Report of the Conference on Rail and Road Transport: observations and criticisms by the General Secretary, J. Beckett. *London*, 1932. pp. 16.   LSE
Opposition to the Salter Committee's Report. Its unfairness to road transport undertakings.

4614 NORTH WESTERN QUARRY OWNERS ASSOCIATION. Review of the Report of the Salter Rail & Road Commission. *Bacup*, 1932. pp. 7.   LSE
Road hauliers' grievances: sixty-eight points for consideration.

4615 [RAILWAY COMPANIES ASSOCIATION.] Fair play for the railways. [*London*, 1932.] pp. 15[16].   BM
Produced by the railway companies for general information.
New legislation wanted to remove unfair burdens.

4616 RAILWAY COMPANIES ASSOCIATION. Railways and road competition: the railway companies reply to criticisms. *Westminster*, 16 March, 1932. pp. 5.   LSE
Conditions of rail and road transport administration should be equalised.

4617 RAILWAY COMPANIES ASSOCIATION. Royal Commission on Transport: memorandum to the Minister of Transport upon the position of the main line railway companies in relation to road transport competition. *Westminster*, [1932.] pp. 7.   IT

4618 TIMES, *newspaper.* The railways: six special articles together with two leading articles, reprinted from 'The Times', May 12, 13, 14, 16, 17 & 18, 1932. *London*, [1932.] pp. 21.   BR
Current problems, especially road rivalry.

4619 TRANSPORT AND GENERAL WORKERS UNION—CONFERENCE ON RAIL AND ROAD TRANSPORT. Copy of a letter dated 17th December 1932, from the members of the Conference on Rail and Road Transport to the Minister of Transport. [*London*,] 1932. pp. 11.   LSE
Signed by Arthur Salter and others.

4620 TRANSPORT AND GENERAL WORKERS UNION—CONFERENCE ON RAIL AND ROAD TRANSPORT. Report of the Conference . . . Observations and criticisms of the T. & G.W.U., and record of the discussion . . . *London*, December 1932. pp. 18[19]. LSE
The 'Salter Conference'.

4621 BRITISH RAILWAY STOCKHOLDERS UNION. Your concern. *London*, [1933.] pp. 15.   BM
Road/rail relationships and national wellbeing.

4622 BRITISH ROAD FEDERATION. A statement by the British Road Federation supplemental to the case of trade and industry against what is known as 'The Salter Report'. *London*, 1933. pp. 7.   LSE
Road versus rail.

4623 DIMOCK, M. E. British public utilities and national development. *London*, 1933. pp. 349.   BM
pp. 63–117, The present position of railways; their problems and their future.

4624 INTERNATIONAL CHAMBER OF COMMERCE. Road and rail transport: introductory report submitted by the Committee of Independent Experts to the International Chamber of Commerce. *Paris*, Oct. 1933. pp. 15. [*Brochure* no. 85.]   IT

4625 KONSTAM, E. M. *and* ROWE, M. E. Railway rating: law and procedure; being the Railways Valuation for Rating Act, 1930; with an introduction and notes. *London*, 1933. pp. xix, 287, 15.   BM

4626 LLOYD, T. I. Roadway or railway? between Belfast and Bangor. *Belfast*, 1933. pp. 46, with map.
The Belfast & County Down Rly. should convert their line into a roadway with motor buses.

4627 MORRISON, H. Socialisation and transport: the organisation of socialised indus-
s tries with particular reference to the London Passenger Transport Bill. *London*, 1933. pp. xi, 312[313].   BM

4628 ROAD HAULAGE ASSOCIATION. Some observations on the road-rail problem. *London*, February 1933. pp. 4.   TUC

4629 TATTAM, C. R. Tramcars, trolley buses and petrol buses: some comparisons and contrasts: which for the future? *London*, June 1933. pp. 11.   IT
Paper, Municipal Tramways & Transport Assocn., Annual Conference, Blackpool, 1933.

4630 BRISTOW, F. G. The Road and Rail Traffic Act, 1933, as it affects commercial motor users. *London: British Road Federation*, [1934.] pp. 15.   BM

4631 BRITISH ROAD FEDERATION. Roads, railways and restrictions. *Westminster*, [1934.] pp. 18.   LSE
The freeing of railways from out-of-date regulations.

4632 DENNIS, A. G. *and* CORPE, T. D. Road and Rail Traffic Act, 1933: an explanatory handbook. *London*, 1934. pp. lxiv, 138.   BM
—— 2nd edn. *London*, 1934. pp. lxiv, 174.   BM

4633 DEPARTMENT OF COMMERCE [U.S.A.]— BUREAU OF FOREIGN AND DOMESTIC COMMERCE. Railway and highway transportation abroad: a study of existing relationships, recent competitive measures, and co-ordination policies. By W. Rodney Long. *Washington*, 1934. pp. ix, 426.   BM
pp. 99–140, Great Britain.

4634 GRUMBRIDGE, J. L. Railway pooling: the potentialities of the pooling agreements recently made between certain of the main line railway companies, both from the point of view of the public, and the railways themselves. 1934. pp. 53. *Typescript.*   LSE
Rosebery Prize Essay, London School of Economics.

4635 WESTCOTT, L. F. The potentialities of the pooling agreements recently made between certain of the main line railway companies, both from the point of view of the public, and of the companies themselves. 1934. pp. 65. *Typescript.*   LSE
Rosebery Prize Essay, London School of Economics.

4636 BRITISH ROAD FEDERATION. Road notes, Great Britain, 1934–35. *London*, [1935.] pp. 25.   BM
Basic statistics for road and rail, with notes, including legislation.

4637 DUNNAGE, J. A. Transport and the public. *London: Routledge*, 1935. pp. xii, 240.   BM
Includes railways.

4638 GLEDHILL, A. H. Co-ordination of road passenger transport and the formation of Transport Boards. *London: Municipal Tramways & Transport Association*, June 1935. pp. 54, with 4 fold. charts.   IT
Paper, Annual Conference, 1935.
The problems of co-ordinating transport.

4639 PONSONBY, G. J. An aspect of competition in transport. pp. 448–59.   IT
Reprinted from *Economica*, Nov. 1935.
Economic consequences of the protection of railways and tramways against competition from other forms of transport.

4640 WILLIAMS, S. C. S. *and* BROWN, A. Why not a National Transport Board? [*London*, 1935.] pp. 10.   TUC
Reprint *The Nineteenth Century and After*, vol. 117, 1935. pp. 330–9.

4641 WOHL, P. *and* ALBITRECCIA, A. Road and rail in forty countries: report prepared for the International Chamber of Commerce. *Oxford: O.U.P.*, 1935. pp. xix, 455, with 3 fold. tables.   BM
To be read in conjunction with brochure no. 85 of the International Chamber of Commerce—*Road and rail transport: introductory report*, 1933. (4624)

4642 WOOD, W. V. Are British railways over-capitalised?: the railway viewpoint: no substance in charge of 'watered' capital. *London: Modern Transport*, 1935. pp. 3–7.   IT
Reprint, *Modern Transport*, 23 Nov., 1935.

4643 [AUSTRALIA.] COMMONWEALTH OF AUSTRALIA GOVERNMENT. Report on transport investigation in Great Britain. *London*, 31 Dec., 1936. pp. 124.   IT
The system of administration set up to co-ordinate the various transport activities, and the action taken by the transport services themselves towards this end.

4644 'COMMERCIAL MOTOR.' Revelation of amazing Parliamentary blunder: vital clause in the Road and Rail Traffic Act 1933 nullified by important omission. [*London*, 1936.] pp. [3.]   TUC
Reprint, *Commercial Motor*, 24 Jan., 1936. Signed 'A.D.-J.'
Relating to the extent of permissible grounds for objection by railways to local road haulage facilities.

4645 DOWNTON, A. The London Transport scandal. *London: Communist Party*, June
s 1936. pp. 29.   LSE
Of L.T. workers' eight-hour day, three are worked for private profit of stockholders, whose names are secret. Transport should be 'socialized'.

4646 INDUSTRIAL TRANSPORT ASSOCIATION. The co-ordination of transport: papers presented at the Association's 1936 Congress . . . by Frederick A. Smith . . . and members of the Scottish Branch of the Association. *London*, [1936.] pp. 11.   IT
Road versus rail.

4647 PEARSON, A. J. The road and rail transport problem. 1936. pp. 26. *Typescript.*   IT
Lecture to Imperial Chemical Industries, Birmingham, 2 December, 1936.

4648 READER, E. R. The British coasting trade. *London: Institute of Transport*, 1936. pp. 19.   TUC
Historical review, and present position and problems, including railway relationships.

4649 SMITH, F. Blue print for transport. pp. 13. *Reproduced typescript.* IT
Paper, Industrial Transport Assoc., Sheffield Branch, 12 Oct., 1936.
Inadequacies of the Road and Rail Traffic Act (1933) and suggested reforms.

4650 COAL UTILISATION COUNCIL *and* BRITISH ELECTRICAL DEVELOPMENT ASSOCIATION. What about your trams? *London*, [c. 1937.] pp. 7. PC
Reasons for retaining electrically-propelled vehicles (trams and trolly-buses) rather than replacing them by motor-buses.

4651 LISSENDEN, G. B. The civilising influence of transport. *London: Stockwell*, [1937.] pp. 32, with 5 tables. BM
The relationship of transport to the growth and progress of civilisation.

4652 STAMP, J. C. Rail and road transport: Sir Josiah Stamp's speech at LMS Annual General Meeting, February 26, 1937. Road interests' comments on speech: Sir Josiah Stamp's replies. *London: Modern Transport*, [1937.] pp. 15. BM
Reprinted from *The Times*, 27 Feb., the *Financial Times*, 3 March, and *Modern Transport*, 13 March, 1937.

4653 BRITISH ROAD FEDERATION. The railways and road competition. *London*, Sept. 1938. pp. [4.] LSE

4654 MILLS, G. A square deal: railways ask for justice and freedom. *Edinburgh*, 1938. pp. [4.] IT
Reprinted from the *Edinburgh Evening News*, 28 December, 1938.

4655 NATIONALISATION of transport: an impartial review. *London: Modern Transport*, [1938.] pp. 75. LSE
Reprinted from a series of articles in *Modern Transport*, 1938.

4656 MORRISON, H. British transport at Britain's service. *London: Labour Party*, August 1938. pp. 11. BM
Proposed nationalization.

4657 RAILWAY COMPANIES ASSOCIATION. Clear the lines!: the railways ask for a square deal. *London*, [1938.] pp. 15. BM
Reform of railway legislation.

4658 STEVENS, W. J. The future of British railways: a plea for co-operation . . . *London: P. S. King & Son*, 1938. pp. xiii, 101. BM
Co-operation between all railway interests essential to ensure successful future for railways. pp. 62–end, financial position of the four mainline companies, with tables, 1929–36.

4659 TIMES, *newspaper*. Road and rail. *London*, 1938. pp. [2.] LSE
Leading article and letter reprinted from *The Times*, 24 November, 1938.

4660 WEDGWOOD, R. The railways' case. [*London*, 1938.] pp. 4. IT
Reprint from *The Spectator*, 16 Dec., 1938. The 'Square Deal'.

4661 BRITISH ROAD FEDERATION. Memorandum of evidence submitted by the British Road Federation to the Transport Advisory Council on the railway claim for freedom in rate fixing. *London*, January 1939. pp. 13. LSE
Railways should economize and re-organize instead of trying to oppose road haulage.

4662 BRITISH ROAD FEDERATION. Railway freight traffic and road competition. *London*, April 1939. pp. [4.] LSE
A reply to the complaint of the railways that loss of freight traffic is due to road competition.

4663 BRITISH ROAD FEDERATION. The spectre of monopoly. *London*, [1939.] pp. 12. LSE
An amendment to 1933 Road & Rail Traffic Act demanded, to remove restrictions imposed upon road hauliers. Fear of a monopoly of transport industry by railways.

4664 DALBY, A. W. Railways and the state: a report presented to the Swindon Education Committee . . . *Swindon*, 9 November, 1939. pp. 34. IT

4665 FENELON, K. G. British railways today. *London: Nelson*, 1939. pp. 187, with plates. [*Discussion Books*, no. 39.] BM
Railways and the public.

4666 GREAT WESTERN RLY. The railway position. *London*, February 1939. s.sh. LSE
Information to shareholders on the 'Square Deal' campaign.

4667 GRUMBRIDGE, J. L. Co-ordination of inland transport in Great Britain. Thesis,
f Ph.D.(Econ.) Univ. Lond., 1939. pp. 763, xix. *Typescript.* UL
Post-war developments (1918–39), present position, and the future. Competition versus nationalization as rival principles.

4668 LONDON, MIDLAND, & SCOTTISH RLY. The railway crisis. *London*, February 1939. pp. 2. LSE
An account of the 'Square Deal' campaign addressed to shareholders.

4669 RAILWAY COMPANIES ASSOCIATION. The railway crisis: the problem and its solution. *London*, 1939. pp. 17, viii. BM
Reform of railway legislation.

4670 RAILWAY COMPANIES ASSOCIATION. The railways ask for a square deal. *London*, [1939.] s.sh. LSE
Nine basic points of the Square Deal campaign.

4671 RAILWAY COMPANIES ASSOCIATION. A summary of the Report of the Transport Advisory Council upon the proposals of the railways with respect to the conveyance of merchandise by rail. *London*, [1939.] pp. 27. BM
Co-ordination of all transport services.

4672 SHERRINGTON, C. E. R. Transport conditions in Great Britain and the railways' campaign for a 'square deal'. pp. 16. PC
Paper, 49th Annual Meeting, Railway Accounting Officers, Toronto, 28 June, 1939.

4673 STAMP, J. The railways' case for altered conditions: address . . . to the members of the Manchester Chamber of Commerce . . . 18 January, 1939. *Manchester: Manchester Chamber of Commerce*, [1939.] pp. 20. LSE
'Square Deal' proposals.

4674 STAMP, J. The future of the railways: address by Lord Stamp . . . to the members of the Glasgow Chamber of Commerce . . . 15 February, 1939. *Glasgow*, [1939.] pp. 8. LSE
'Square Deal' campaign. Equality for all forms of transport.

4675 WILLIAMS, S. C. S. *and* SHORT, E. Railways, roads and the public. *London: Eyre & Spottiswoode*, 1939. pp. 157. BM
A detailed analysis of current problems; the causes of increasing expenditure and falling revenue; proposals for nationalization critically examined. pp. 63–88, 'What British railways do for passengers'. pp. 89–118, 'What the railways do for industry'. pp. 119–52, 'Railway stockholding'.

4676 WATERS, W. L. Rail and highway competition in England; presented before the American Society of Mechanical Engineers, Transportation Division, Metropolitan Section, New York, May 4, 1939. *New York*, 1939. pp. 10. LSE

4677 MANCE, H. O. The road and rail transport problem. *London: Pitman*, 1940. pp. xvi, 166. BM

4678 PARLIAMENTARY LAND VALUES GROUP. Half-a-crown an inch: railways are still paying for land bought 100 years ago. *London*, [1940.] s.sh. *Typescript*. LSE

4679 POWNALL, J. F. Transport reform in Great Britain, illustrated by a map: the bits and pieces character of British railways crystallised out . . . *London: the author*, [c. 1940.] pp. [4.]. BM
A large folding map illustrating a proposed re-alignment of the railways to enable the working of his 'railway hour' system.

4680 ADAM, W. W. A national fuel and transport programme . . . [*London*,] 1942. pp. 6, with illus. IME
Reprinted from the May 1942 issue of *Export*. Electrification as a basis for national reconstruction.

4681 RIDLEY, G. The railways, retrospect and prospect. *London: Labour Party*, 1942. pp. 23. [*Between Two Wars*, no. 1.] BM
Nationalization proposals; with an historical survey.

4682 JOHNSTON, K. H. Railway electrification and post-war reconstruction. *In* 'Creative demobilisation.' vol. 2, 'Case studies in national planning', by E. A. Gutkind. 1943. pp. 145–65. BM

4683 LABOUR PARTY. Post-war organisation of
f British transport. *London*, [1943.] pp. 23. LSE

4684 A NATIONAL transport programme: the approach to a long-term plan. *Westminster:*
f *Railway Gazette*, 1943. pp. 27. IT
Future of transport. Labour Party's proposals superficial, and made for political reasons only. Unification of all transport desirable but competition and enterprise in services should be preserved.

4685 [RAILWAY COMPANIES ASSOCIATION.] Memorandum: post-war policy. [*London*,]
f June, 1943. pp. 5. *Reproduced typescript*. BR
'Private and Confidential.'
The report of the general managers of the four main line railway companies on post-war policy.

4686 WOODCOCK, G. Railways and society.
s *London: Freedom Press*, 1943. pp. 31. BM
The control of the railways by the workers.

4687 ASSOCIATION OF BRITISH CHAMBERS OF COMMERCE. Post-war transport: a report
f of the Joint Committee of the Association of British Chambers of Commerce and Federation of British Industries. *London*, October 1944. pp. 13. BM
Recommendations from trade and industry for changes in the transport system: co-operation, reforms in organisation and working, and in legislation, as an alternative to nationalization.

4688 PARKINSON, H. Who owns the railways?: a series of articles . . . reprinted from the 'Financial News' of October 3, November 1, 2 & 3, 1944. [*London*, 1944.] pp. 14, with 2 fold. financial tables. LSE
Public ownership of railways: railways already publicly owned—by a large number of stockholders.

4689 [RAILWAY COMPANIES ASSOCIATION.] The rail-air plan, as presented in the House of Lords on the 12th October, 1944 by . . . Lord Balfour of Burleigh and . . . Earl Amhurst. *London*, [1944.] pp. 7. BR
Reprinted from *Parliamentary Debates* (Hansard).
Co-ordination of rail and air transport.

4690 AIMS OF INDUSTRY. The anatomy of nationalisation. *London*, [1945.] pp. 23.
s IT
Sees the proposed nationalization of transport as a political aim of the Labour Party.

4691 BRESSEY, C. Transport. *In* 'Homes,
f   towns, and countryside: a practical plan
    for Britain', edited by Gilbert and Elizabeth
    Glen McAllister. *London: Batsford*, 1945.
    pp. 60–66, with 12 illus. on plates.   BM
    The future; integration of transport.

4692 DAVIES, E. British transport: a study in
    industrial organisation and control. *Lon-*
f   *don: Fabian Society*, 1945. pp. 25.   LSE
    War-time control measures related to post-
    war problems.

4693 JOINT CONFERENCE OF THE INSTITUTE
    OF FUEL AND THE NATIONAL SMOKE
    ABATEMENT SOCIETY. Report of the
    Joint Conference . . . February 23, 1945.
    [*London*, 1945.]   IT
    pp. 24–31, 'Railway smoke', by M. G.
    Bennett.

4694 LABOUR RESEARCH DEPARTMENT. Rail-
    ways for the nation. *London*, [May 1945.]
    pp. 31, with bibliogr. notes.   LSE
    The case for a nationalised and co-ordinated
    transport system, including an historical record
    of railway ownership and finance.

4695 LIBERAL PARTY. The future of British
    transport: report of a Liberal committee
f   under the chairmanship of B. Seebohm
    Rowntree. *London*, [1945.] pp. 39[40].   BM
    Proposes that railways should be transferred
    to a public utility corporation.

4696 RAILWAY COMPANIES ASSOCIATION.
    The British main line railway companies:
    answers to questions and statements. *Lon-*
    don, June 1945. pp. 30.   IT
    Prepared for M.P.s and others. Forty-four
    common criticisms.

4697 RAILWAY COMPANIES ASSOCIATION.
    The railways: answers to questions and
    statements. *London*, June 1945. pp. 7. LSE
    Seven reasons why railways, labour and
    industry would do better to remain under
    private ownership.

4698 TRADES UNION CONGRESS. 4 T.U.C.
    documents approved by the Blackpool
    Congress, 1945. [*London*, 1945.] pp. 63. TUC
    pp. 19–41, The public operation of transport.

4699 WOOD, W. V. Railway and allied transport.
    In 'Post-war Britain', by J. Marchant.
f   1945. pp. 178–203.   BM
    Past experience and future needs.

4700 ASSOCIATION OF BRITISH CHAMBERS OF
    COMMERCE. Report on nationalisation of
    inland transport. *London*, [1946.] pp. 7. BM
    Opposition to nationalization from trade and
    industry.

4701 BOSCAWEN, A. G. The Government and
    transport. *London: Road Haulage Associa-*
    tion, [1946.] pp. [4.]   IT
    Reprinted from the *Sunday Times* 10 March,
    1946.
    Objections to nationalization.

4702 COLLIER, R. A. H. Railways and their
f   future. *London: Benn*, 1946. pp. 96.   BM
    Their past (especially their past mistakes)
    also reviewed. Based on his *Railways: their
    history and organisation* (1928).

4703 DUNNAGE, J. A. Transport plans and Bri-
    tain's future: some long-term aspects . . .
f   *London: Industrial Transport Publications*,
    1946. pp. 35.   BM
    Against nationalization. Suggested plan for
    general reforms.

4704 GORE, E. The case against nationalisation:
    what is best in the public interest? [*London*,
    1946.] pp. 8. *Reproduced typescript.*   BR
    Extract from an address at the A.G.M. of
    the Southern Rly., 7 March, 1946.

4705 LONDON & NORTH EASTERN RLY. The
    state and the railways: an alternative to
    nationalisation. *London*, 1946. pp. 8.   IT
    Government to buy railway property and
    then lease it (landlord and tenant scheme).

4706 LONDON MIDLAND & SCOTTISH RLY.
    State ownership and control of transport.
    [*Watford*, 1946.] pp. [4.]   BR
    A letter to stockholders asking their views,
    and an extract from the Chairman's speech at
    the Annual General Meeting, 1 March, 1946.

4707 RAILWAY CLERKS ASSOCIATION. On
    the way to greater service. *London*, 1946.
    pp. 22[23].   LSE
    Proposed shape and functions of a national-
    ised transport authority.

4708 RAILWAY COMPANIES ASSOCIATION.
    British railways and the future. *London*,
f   1946. pp. 20.   IT
    'The public interest will best be served by the
    existing organisation working under revised
    conditions.

4709 [RAILWAY COMPANIES ASSOCIATION.]
    The future of the railways: co-ordination
f   of transport. May 1946. pp. 33.   BR
    'Private & confidential.' Revised and re-
    issued as *British railways and the future* (1946).

4710 RAILWAY COMPANIES ASSOCIATION *and*
    ROAD HAULAGE ASSOCIATION. Co-
    ordination of road and rail freight transport:
    memorandum to the Minister of Transport,
    July 1946. [*London*,] 16 July 1946. pp. 8. IT

4711 RAILWAY COMPANIES ASSOCIATION *and
    the* ROAD HAULAGE ASSOCIATION. Why
    nationalise transport? [*London*, 1946.] pp.
    8.   LSE

4712 RAILWAY STOCKHOLDERS JOINT COM-
    MITTEE. Railway petition against the Trans-
    port Bill. [*London*,] 19 Dec., 1946. s.sh.
                                               BR
    'The Bill will deprive us of lawfully acquired
    properties . . . and will discourage the enterprise
    and sense of personal responsibility which is all
    important to industry.'

4713 SHORT, E. Railways and the state: the problem of nationalization. *London: British Railway Stockholders' Union*, [1937.] pp. iv, 56.   BM
An alleged impartial review of railway–state relationships in thirty-seven countries (principal trading nations).
—— another edn. 'Railways and the state: facts and factors of nationalization.' *London*, 1946. pp. iv, 84.   BM

4714 TEES-SIDE CHAMBER OF COMMERCE. Nationalisation of inland transport: report of the Transport Services Committee. [*Newcastle*,] Feb. 1946. pp. 11.   BR

4715 BIZERAY, C. R. Towards ideal transport in town planning and reconstruction. *London: Light Railway Transport League*, 1944. pp. 44, with 21 illus. on 15 plates.   BM
Tramways the ideal form of urban transport. Their comparative advantages over trolleybuses, motorbuses, and electric suburban railways.
—— 2nd edn. *London: L.R.T.L.*, 1947. pp. 52[54].   BM

4716 DAVIES, E. Nationalisation of transport. *London: Labour Party*, [1947.] pp. 19. [*Labour Discussion Series*, no. 10.]   BM

4717 JARY, J. Workers' Control. (Nationalisation
s of the railways.) [*London: the author*, 1947.] pp. 16.   IT
Suggested plan for a structure of local committees; their functions; management/worker relations.

4718 LABOUR PARTY. Transport for the nation: prepared for the Labour Party by the Fabian
s Society. *London*, January 1947. pp. [4.]
An illustrated folder giving outline rail and road statistics, and facts about the Transport Bill (1946).

4719 RAILWAY COMPANIES ASSOCIATION. Criticisms of the railways arising in Parliamentary Debates and in press and public discussion since the presentation of the Transport Bill, and the replies. [*London*, 1947.] 8 booklets.   BR
Section 1, Criticisms regarding the general structure and organisation of the railways. pp. 6.
Section 2, Criticisms regarding railway capital and finance. pp. 9.
Section 3, Criticisms regarding the physical assets of the railways. pp. 6.
Section 4, Criticisms regarding the operational efficiency of the railways. pp. 15.
Section 5, Criticisms regarding the services provided by the railways. pp. 5.
Section 6, Criticisms regarding the wages and conditions of railway workers. pp. 5.
Section 7, Criticisms regarding the road-rail co-ordination plan. pp. 5.
Contents, Summary and Index of Criticisms. pp. 22.

4720 RAILWAY COMPANIES ASSOCIATION. The Transport Bill. [*London*,] 1947. 7 booklets.   BR
1, Statement issued by the four main line companies. pp. 5.
2, Who owns the railways? pp. 3.
3, Co-ordination between road and rail. pp. 6.
4, How traders will be affected. pp. 6.
5, Advantages of transport operation under private ownership. pp. 7.
6, Organisation proposed for the future control of inland transport. pp. 9.
7, The 'dead hand' of Whitehall. pp. 11.

4721 SMITH, G. W. Q. The Transport Act, 1947, as it affects the road transport industry: a concise summary. *Birmingham: Morris Commercial Cars, Ltd.*, July 1947. pp. 34. BM

4722 WALKER, G. Road and rail: an enquiry into the economics of competition and state control. *London: Allen & Unwin*, 1942. pp. 236, with 4 fold. tables.   BM
Road-rail competition in England during the 1920's and 1930's.
—— 2nd edn. *London*, 1947. pp. 282, with 3 fold. tables.   BM

4723 BONAVIA, M. R. Inland transport. *In* 'The industrial future of Great Britain: a series of lectures arranged by the University of London, Centre for Courses in International Affairs, and the Institute of Bankers, November 1947 to March 1948.' *London: Europa Publications*, [1948.] pp. 92–113. BM

4724 HURCOMB, C. Progress towards the integration of transport. [*London*, 1948.] pp. 8.   TUC
Reprint, *Journal of the Institute of Transport.*

4725 BLEE, D. Co-ordination of transport. [*Felixstowe*, 1949.] pp. 39.   BR
Paper, British Transport Commission First Officers' Conference, First Session, 7 April, 1949. Printed but not published.

4726 HANCOCK, W. K. *and* GOWING, M. M. British war economy. *London: H.M. Stationery Office*, 1949. pp. xvii, 583, with bibliogr. notes.   BM
Includes railways.

4727 HURCOMB, C. Transport as an integrated public service. pp. 15. (Address, Western Region Lecture & Debating Society, 6 Oct. 1949.) *Reproduced typescript.*   TUC

4728 JOHNSTON, K. H. British Railways and economic recovery: a sociological study of the transport problem. *London: Clerke & Cockeran*, 1949. pp. 352, with plates & bibliogr. notes.   BM
A plan for more efficient railways. Electrification: British and foreign railways compared: the case against nationalization finally answered.

4729 LAUNDY, J. H. The problem of railway passenger fares and train services: a suggested plan for equalising passenger travel over both rail and road services. *London: Railway Gazette*, [1949.] pp. 18.   IT
Reprint, *Railway Gazette*, 28 Jan., 1949.

4730 BRITISH ELECTRICAL AND ALLIED MANUFACTURERS ASSOCIATION. Why trolleybuses? *London*, 1950. pp. [12.] LSE
Advantages of trackless vehicles. /

4731 BRITISH TRANSPORT COMMISSION. Integration of freight services by road and rail: a statement of policy. *London*, 1950. pp. 8.
TUC

4732 HURCOMB, C. W. An integrated transport system. *Manchester: Manchester Statistical Society*, 1950. pp. 17.   IT
Paper, 29 March, 1950.

4733 MENZLER, F. A. A. Rail and road statistics. [*London*, 1950.] pp. 352–75, with a bibliography.   BM
Reprint, *Journal of the Royal Statistical Society*, series A (general), vol. 113, part 3, 1950.
A survey of available sources for statistics.

4734 NORRIS, W. S. Railways: the object is to achieve the largest number of the cleanest, most comfortable, fastest and cheapest trains throughout the country. *West Byfleet: Fighting Fund for Freedom*, May 1950. pp. [4.]   TUC
A proposal to de-nationalise the railways and group them into ten units instead of the present five.

4735 ASSOCIATION OF BRITISH CHAMBERS OF COMMERCE. Integration of transport: memorandum submitted to the Minister of Transport. Integration of freight services by road, rail and inland waterway, June 1951. *London*, 1951. pp. 23.   BM
Cover title: Integration of transport by road, rail and inland waterway.
Includes the text of two statements of policy by the B.T.C. on this subject.

4736 BRITISH TRANSPORT COMMISSION. Electrification of railways. *London*, 1951. pp. xi, 94, with 10 tables & 7 maps.   BM
Survey of existing electrification systems and recommendations for future development.

4737 FORD, P. *and* BOUND, J. A. Coastwise shipping and the small ports. *Oxford: Blackwell*, 1951. pp. 52, with 18 tables. BM
Related to transport system generally and to the national economy.

4738 HUGHES, W. Integration of road and rail freight transport. 1951. pp. 13. *Typescript.*
IT
Paper, Institute of Transport, Leeds, 27 September, 1951.

4739 CARTER, C. F. The troubles of transport. 1952. pp. 7. *Reproduced typescript.*   IT
Paper, British Association, Belfast, Section F, 9 September, 1952.

4740 CONSERVATIVE PARTY. Transport Bill.
s [*Westminster*,] 15 Sept. 1952. pp. [4.] IT
Reply to the Labour Party and T.U.C. campaign against the Bill.

4741 LABOUR PARTY. Notes on Tory transport policy: Labour Party and Trade Union
s Campaign against the Transport Bill, 1952. [*London*, 1952.] pp. 15.   BM

4742 LABOUR RESEARCH DEPARTMENT. Transport robbery: exposure of Tory plan;
s with appendices on (1) railway profits before Nationalisation, (2) Transport Commission 1951 accounts, (3) plans of railway companies and hauliers before Nationalisation. *London*, 1952. pp. 11.   TUC
Based on legislation proposed to be introduced by the Conservative Party (Cmd. 8538).

4743 LIBERAL PARTY. Platform points: transport. *London*, October 1952. pp. 10. *Reproduced typescript.*
Railway problems and Liberal Party policy.

4744 POOLE, C. Job Lots for the Boys (A dramatic exposure of the Tory transport muddle). *London: The Tribune*, 1952. pp. 15. [*A Tribune Pamphlet.*]   BM

4745 VIAN-SMITH, H. S. Transport in the Modern Age. *London: Association of British Chambers of Commerce*, [1952.] pp. 15. IT
Paper, Oldham & District Chamber of Commerce, 4 Feb., 1952.
Includes railway and trader problems.

4746 CLEGG, H. A. *and* CHESTER, T. E. The future of nationalization. *Oxford: Blackwell*,
f 1953. pp. ix, 211.   BM
pp. 91–123 and elsewhere, Transport, including railways, and transport co-ordination.

4747 KARMEL, D. *and* POTTER, K. The transport Act, 1953, with general introduction and annotations. *London: Butterworth*, 1953. pp. 7, 333.   BM

4748 VIAN-SMITH, H. S. The Transport Act, 1953: an explanation for the transport user and operator . . . *London: Motor Transport*, 1953. pp. x, 157.   BM

*4749 SMITH, W. An economic geography of Great Britain . . . *London: Methuen*, 1949. pp. xv, 747, with 124 maps & diagrams, & bibliogr. notes.   BM
pp. 587–623 and elsewhere, Railways, and road/rail competition.
—— 2nd edn. *London*, 1953. pp. xv, 756.
BM

4750 LABOUR PARTY. British transport. *London*, [1954.] pp. 32. [*Challenge to Britain.*
s *Policy Pamphlet*, no. 1.]   BM
Labour Party transport policy, particularly with regard to the necessity to re-nationalise long-distance road haulage, returned to private ownership by the Conservative Government in 1952.

4751 ROBERTS, J. E. M. Relations with the passenger transport industry. pp. 20. *Reproduced typescript.*   IT
Paper, L.S.E. Railway Students' Association. 17 November, 1954.
The future of rail transport in relation to road, sea and air.

4752 SANDERSON, H. F. The railway branch line problem. 1954. pp. 18. *Typescript.* IT
Paper, Institute of Transport, Northern Section, 9 November, 1954.
Economic problems; with an historical review.

4753 EAVIS, P. M. A quicker way to London Airport: the advantages of rail transport. [*London*,] 1955. pp. 3, with map.   pc
Reprinted from the *Muck Shifter and Public Works Digest*, December 1955.
Three schemes: 1, Monorail; 2, Extension of the Piccadilly Line (Underground Railways); 3, A spur from the Southern Region line at Feltham. The third scheme thought to be the most practicable.

4754 MANCHESTER GUARDIAN *newspaper.* Planning for a new Railway Age [and other
f articles]. *Manchester*, 14 July 1955. pp. 7–14. (Supplement.)   LSE

4755 MASEFIELD, P. G. Air transport, the railways and the future. pp. 9, with tables.
f *Reproduced typescript.*   IT
Paper, Town & Country Planning Association Annual Conference, 1955.

4756 WILSON, R. For and against monopolies in transport; with special reference, in the main, to land transport in Great Britain. pp. 17. *Reproduced typescript.*   IT
Paper, Institute of Transport, Dublin, 22 Nov., 1955. (Final draft.)
Monopolies in private transport for private benefit; in public transport for public service: the necessity for control to provide a pattern of transport designed for maximum efficiency at lowest cost.

4757 BARNES, D. A railwayman looks at the railways. 2nd edn. *London: Independent
s Labour Party*, 1956. pp. 27.   BM
A Socialist's views on present-day problems of the railways and of railwaymen, with a survey of their conditions under nationalization. There is an historical summary of the course of railway development under the control of private interests and of the growth of railway trade unionism.

4758 MILNE, A. M. *and* LAING, A. The obligation to carry: an examination of the obligations owed to the public by British Railways. *London: Institute of Transport*, 1956. pp. 129, with bibliogr. notes.   BM

4759 MINISTRY OF TRANSPORT AND CIVIL AVIATION. Proposals for the railways; presented by the Minister of Transport and Civil Aviation to Parliament. *London: H.M. Stationery Office*, [1956.] pp. 43, with tables. [*Cmd.* 9880.]   BM
Present policy and future plans, with estimates.
pp. [9]–30, 'Review of policy and prospects, with special reference to the railways'.
pp. 31–9, 'The programme for railway modernisation'.

4760 ROBERTSON, B. B.T.C. future prospects: report to Minister of Transport. *London:
f British Transport Commission*, Oct. 1956. pp. 4. *Reproduced typescript.*   IT

4761 LLOYD, T. I. Twilight of the railways: what roads they'll make! Railway conversion as
f the cure for Britain's transport troubles. *London: Forster & Groom*, 1957. pp. 80. BM

4762 COMESKEY, F. G. The pattern of inland transport. 1958. pp. 35, with 7 tables.
f *Reproduced typescript.*   IT
Paper, Institute of Transport, South Wales and Monmouthshire Section, April 1958.
Planned integration for the future.

4763 SARGENT, J. R. British transport policy. *Oxford: O.U.P.*, 1958. pp. ix, 163.   BM
The Transport Act (1953) and the technical and economic improvement of transport.

4764 SHERRINGTON, C. E. R. The balance of transport components: air, rail, road, water. pp. 8. *Reproduced typescript.*   IT
Lecture, Institute of Transport, Humberside Section, April 1958.

4765 VALENTINE, A. B. B. The revolution on the railways in the freight field. 1958. pp. 20.
f *Reproduced typescript.*   IT
Presidential address, L.S.E. Railway Students' Association, 29 October, 1958.
The future of railways as part of an integrated transport organisation.

4766 'ENGINEER.' Railways into roadways?: leading articles and correspondence re-
f printed from 'The Engineer', 1958. *London*, 1959. pp. vi, 97.   BM
Seventy-eight items.

4767 WILSON, R. Economics of transport, with special reference to road-rail questions in the United Kingdom; presented to the British Association for the Advancement of Science, Sections F & G., York, 8th September 1959. *York*, 1959. pp. 41[42]. *Printed from typescript.*   BR

4768 ALLEN, V. L. Trade unions and the Government. *London: Longmans*, 1960. pp. xii, 326.   BM
Includes railway trade unions.

4769 DAVIES, E. Britain's transport crisis: a Socialist's view. *London: Road & Rail
s Association*, [1960.] pp. 29[32].   BM

4770 RAILWAY CONVERSION LEAGUE. Memorandum submitted on 18th June 1960 . . . to the Special Advisory Group on the British Transport Commission, under the chairmanship of Sir Ivan Stedeford, on the future of British Railways; being an outline of some relevant arguments for the conversion of the railway system into a system of reserved motorways. *Shanley Green*, 1960. pp. 22. BM
Text by M. J. Douglass.

771 WILSON, G. Britain's transport crisis: a Conservative's view. *London: Road & Rail Association*, [1960.] pp. 23.   BM

772 AHERN, T. The railways and the people: an appeal to the public and the workers. *London: Communist Party*, 1962. pp. 15.   BM
   An analysis of the present position, with an outline of Communist policy.

772a NATIONAL COUNCIL ON INLAND TRANSPORT. The road and rail crisis: memorandum to the Prime Minister . . . Harold Macmillan, M.P. *London*, September 1962. pp. 15.   BM
   Chairman, Lord Stonham.
   Proposed closures of unprofitable lines would be economically disastrous and socially intolerable. Instead, all forms of transport should be co-ordinated.

773 BRITISH RAILWAYS BOARD. The reshaping of British Railways. *London: H.M. Stationery Office*, 1963. pp. ii, 148, with 12[13] col. fold. maps in sep. folder.   BM
   The 'Beeching Report'. Proposals for rationalisation of the railways. Recommended reductions in services and closures of lines. Railways to be employed for classes of traffic for which they are most suited within the framework of transport as a whole. Produced under the chairmanship of Dr. Richard Beeching.

4773a HONDELINK, E. R. Review of Dr. Beeching's report, The Reshaping of British Railways. *Northwood: Great Central Association*, 1963. pp. 3. *Reproduced typescript.*   BM

4773b SITES, J. N. Quest for Crisis: a world-ranging search for clues to the transport future. *New York: Simmons-Boardman; London: Technical Press*, 1963. pp. xvi [xxiii], 223, with illus. & tables.   BM
   pp. 1–21, 'Turmoil in British transport'.
   pp. 22–35. 'Opposite trends in the two Irelands'.

4773c WALKER, P. R. J. The future pattern of transport in Britain. *Northwood: Great Central Association*, [1963.] pp. 4. *Reproduced typescript.*   BM

K 1 RAILWAYS AND SOCIETY

The effects of railways upon the life of the people—Opposition to railways from owners of property—Spoliation of land and of scenery—Displacement of the poor caused by railway development—Relief of poverty by means of employment in railway construction and by railway taxation—Objections to Sunday trains—Suburban development and the creation of new centres of population—The effects of increased facilities for travel and recreation made possible by railways—The effects upon railways of social change—Railways and public health—Workmen's trains

For this subject related to specific localities see C

Marginal symbols: **b** bibliographies
   c chronologies
   p railways and the poor: displacement of homes
   pr property and railway construction
   s Sunday trains; Sunday employment
   u urban and suburban development and railways
   w workmen's trains and fares

Historical

4774 FRANCIS, J. A history of the English railway: its social relations and revelations, 1820–1845. *London*, 1851. 2 vols.   BM
   Includes a detailed treatment of social background and related topics.

4775 [CONDER, F. R.] Personal recollections of English engineers and of the introduction of the railway system into the United Kingdom. By a Civil Engineer. *London*, 1868. pp. xvi, 432.   BM
   Effects of the coming of railways.

*4776 WILLIAMS, F. S. Our Iron Roads: their history, construction and social influences. *London*, 1852. pp. x, 390, with many illus.   BM
   Includes a table of accidents.

—— 2nd edn. [1883.] pp. xvi, 514.   BM
—— 3rd, 1883. pp. xvi, 514.   IME
—— 4th, 1883. pp. xvi, 514.   BM
—— 5th, 1884. pp. xvi, 514.   UL(GL)
—— 6th, 1885. pp. xvi, 514.   pc
—— 7th, 1888. pp. xvi, 514.   BM

4777 RUSKIN, J. The works of John Ruskin; edited by E. T. Cook and Alexander Wedderburn. *London*, 1912. 29 vols.   BM
The index (vol. 29) contains about 140 references to railways in his writings.

4778 GRAHAM, J. W. Harvest of Ruskin. *London*, 1920.   BM
pp. 248–52, an analysis of John Ruskin's attitudes to railways and locomotives.

4779 YOUNG, G. M. Early Victorian England, 1830–1865. *London*, 1934. 2 vols.   BM
Re-issued 1951.
Contains many references to railways, mostly relating to their social effects.

4780 ANDREWS, C. B. The Railway Age. *London: Country Life*, 1937. pp. xi, 145, with 82 plates & many illus.   BM
Mostly relating to the social aspects of railways, travelling conditions, and architecture.

4781 BRYANT, A. W. M. English Saga. *London: Collins*, 1940.   BM
pp. 79–83, 'Iron Horse'. Railways as a mainspring of social revolution in the 1840's.

*4782 KLINGENDER, F. D. Art and the Industrial Revolution. *London: Noel Carrington*, 1947. pp. xiii, 232, with plates.   BM
pp. 115–30, 'The Railway Age'.
The effects of railways on the work of contemporary artists. The social background of this period.

4783 CRUIKSHANK, R. J. Charles Dickens and Early Victorian England . . . with 64 illustrations in photogravure and 37 text illustrations in line and 14 . . . charts in colour. *London: Isaac Pitman*, 1949. pp. xii, 308. BM
pp. 91–100, Railways.

4784 HOUSE, H. The Dickens World. *London: O.U.P.*, 1941. pp. 231.   BM
pp. 137–52 and elsewhere, railways in Dickens' time and in his writings.

—— 2nd edn. *London*, 1942. pp. 231.   BM
—— Reprinted, *London*, 1950. [*Oxford Paperbacks*, no. 9.]   BM

4785 DYOS, H. J. Workmen's fares in South London, 1860–1914. *In* 'Journal of Transport History', vol. 1, no. 1, May 1953. pp.
w port History', vol. 1, no. 1, May 1953. pp.
b 3–19, with 99 bibliogr. notes.   BM

4786 DYOS, H. J. Railways and housing in Victorian London. *In* 'Journal of Transport
b History', vol. 2, no. 1, May 1955, pp. 11–21,
p with 59 bibliogr. notes; and vol. 2, no. 2,
pr November 1955, pp. 90–100, with 58 bibliogr. notes.   BM

4787 DYOS, H. J. Some social costs of railway building in London. *In* 'Journal of Trans-
p port History', vol. 3, no. 1, May 1957.
pr pp. 23–30, with plate, a table (pp. 25–9) of 'displacements of labouring classes by railways in London, 1853–1900' (61 instances) & 13 bibliogr. notes.   BM

4788 PIMLOTT, J. A. R. The Englishman's holiday: a social history. *London: Faber & Faber*, 1957. pp. 318.   BM
pp. 74–95, 'The threshold of the Railway Age'; and elsewhere.

4789 ROBBINS, M. The Railway Age. *London: Routledge & Kegan Paul*, 1962. pp. x, 227,
s with 12 plates (poster announcements),
b & a detailed · bibliography with notes (pp. 199–212).   BM
Essays on the social effects of railways in the nineteenth century.

4790 BROOKE, D. The opposition to Sunday rail services in north-eastern England, 1834–
b 1914. *In* 'Journal of Transport History', vol. 6, no. 2, November 1963. pp. 95–109, with 46 bibliographical & other notes.   BM

Contemporaneous

4791 The BURSTING of a Bubble; or, The birth of a new era: a national event hourly expected at no. 12 Westminster Hall. [*London*, 1826.] pp. 8.   BM
On the introduction of railways.

4792 EXTRACTS from the Evidence taken by the Select Committee of the House of Commons
s on Observance of the Lord's Day. [*Aberdeen*, 1832.] pp. 24.   AU

4793 RUELL, D. *and others*. Evidence given before the Select Committee of the House of
s Commons on Observance of the Lord's Day. By David Ruell, John Wontner, and Benjamin Baker. *London*, 1832. pp. 4.   AU

4794 HAMMOND, T. A few cursory remarks on railways, showing their beneficial tendency . . . *London*, 1835. pp. 32.   LSE
A lively retort to the anti-railway campaign of the *Morning Herald*.

4795 STEPHEN, G. Letter to . . . Lord John Russell on the probable increase of rural crime in consequence of the introduction of the new Poor Law and railroad systems. *London*, [1836.] pp. 51.   BM

4796 [STURGE, J.] Remarks on the regulation of railway travelling on Sundays, addressed to
s the directors and proprietors of the London & Birmingham Railway. By A Railway Director. *London*, 1836. pp. 25.   UL(GL)
—— 3rd edn. *London*, 1836. pp. 28.   ICE
Inscribed on the title page of the I.C.E. copy —'By the late John Sturge of Birm[ingham].'

4797 SOUTH EASTERN, BRIGHTON, LEWES & NEWHAVEN RLY. Evidence given before the Committee of the House of Commons on the London & Brighton Railways, on the subject of tunnels. Session 1837. *London: C. Roworth*, [1837.] pp. 24. BM

4798 The GHOST of John Bull; or, The Devil's Railroad: a marvellously strange narrative, dedicated—without , permission—to such Members of Parliament as may feel inclined to turn their coats, Poor Law Commissioners and railroad directors in particular. *London*, 1838. pp. 71. BM
An anti-railway satire.

4799 RAILROADIANA: a new history of England . . . First series, with a map and illustrations:
s London and Birmingham Railway. *London*, 1838. pp. 216. BM
pp. 200–10, Sunday travelling.

—— 2nd edn. *London*, 1838. pp. 212. BM

4800 STURGE, J. To the proprietors of the London & Birmingham Railway. *Birmingham*,
s January 26, 1838. pp. 2. BM
A printed letter asking shareholders not to allow trains on Sundays. The BM copy is followed by a MS. letter from Rev. James Yates [to the Secretary of the L. & B. Rly.?] opposing Sturge's request. (Exercise, change of scene and air, sick visiting, etc., are made possible by Sunday trains. Drinking and debauchery will be lessened by them.)

4801 BOWDLER, T. An appeal to the public on the subject of Sunday trains on railroads.
s *London*, 1839. pp. 20. BM

4802 POOH! Pooh!: a poem; by one of Job's Comforters. [*London*,] 1839. pp. 23. BM
pr Verses against the construction of railways in East Anglia by the 'squirearchy'. [By Henry Barrett?]

4803 RADCLIFFE, F. P. D. The noble science: a few general ideas on fox-hunting . . . *London*, 1839. BM
pp. 128–30, Railways and fox-hunting.

—— new edns., rev. by W. C. A. Blew. *London*, 1893 & 1911. BM

4804 NEWTON, W. L. Letters on the subject of Sunday travelling on railways, addressed
s to the late Dr. Arnold. *Derby*, [1840.] pp. 4. AU

4805 POLITICAL economy of the Sabbath; or, Reasons for cessation of work, and railway
s and other traffic, on the first day of the week. [*Edinburgh*, n.d.] pp. 2. AU

4806 DIMMICK, L. F. A discourse on the moral influence of rail-roads. *Newburyport*, 1841. pp. 125. P

4807 MACFARLAN, D. Railway travelling on the Lord's Day indefensible. *Glasgow*, 1841.
s pp. 32. AU

4808 HODGES, W. The law relating to the assessment of railways to the relief of the poor . . .
p *London*, 1842. pp. 31. BM

4809 [PEACE, J.] A descant upon railroads, by X.A.P. [J. Peace.] *London*, 1842. pp. 41. BM
Against railways.

4810 SYMINGTON, A. Speech at a meeting for protesting against the desecration of the
s Sabbath by running trains on the Edinburgh & Glasgow Railway on the Lord's Day, held in Glasgow, February 26th, 1842. Revised from the 'Scottish Guardian'. *Glasgow*, 1842. pp. 12. AU

4811 WORDSWORTH, W. Kendal & Windermere Railway: two letters re-printed from the 'Morning Post'; revised, with additions. *Kendal*, [1844.] pp. 23. BM
Prefaced by his sonnet 'On the projected Kendal & Windermere Railway'. Also includes his poem 'Steamboats and Railways'.

4812 An APPEAL to . . . the Lord Lieutenant on behalf of the labouring classes. *Dublin*,
p [1846.] pp. 54. LSE
Concerning the demolition of 'the bathing places of the poor' at Salt Hill, Kingstown, by the Kingstown & Dalkey Rly.

4813 CARLISLE LORD'S DAY ASSOCIATION. To the Chairman and directors of the
s Lancaster & Carlisle Railway Co. . . . by order of the Committee. Thomas A. Graham, Chairman. [*Carlisle*, 1846.] s.sh. LSE
A memorial asking that no trains be run on Sundays.

4814 EDINBURGH. The running of railway trains on the Sabbath: report of proceedings of
s a great public meeting of inhabitants of Edinburgh. *Edinburgh*, [1846.] pp. 15. AU

*4815 AGNEW, A. The Sabbath and railway trains: letter addressed to the Marquis of
s Breadalbane, Chairman, Scottish Central Railway Company. *Edinburgh*, 1847. pp. 12. AU

4816 BOOTH, H. Uniformity of time considered especially in reference to railway transit and the operations of the electric telegraph. *London*, 1847. pp. 19. H

4817 EDINBURGH & GLASGOW RLY. Sabbath passenger trains: authentic report of the great
s public meeting held in the City Hall, Glasgow, 20th January 1847, for the purpose of expressing approval of the conduct of the directors in discontinuing the running of passenger trains on the Lord's Day. *Glasgow*, 1847. pp. 32. AU

4818 'EDINENSIS'. Sunday railway travelling: the history and nature of the Sabbath as
s contained in writings of Calvin, Luther . . . by Edinensis. *Edinburgh*, 1847. pp. 16.
Against the closing of the Edinburgh & Glasgow Rly. on Sundays.

4819 GRAHAM, T. H. Discussion on Sabbath
trains at the Annual General Meeting of the
s Newcastle & Carlisle Railway Co. *New-*
castle, 1847. pp. 24,   LSE
See also item 716 in this volume, which is a
s.sh. announcement on the same subject dated
8 March, 1849.

4820 LETTER to shareholders, directors, and
others concerned in railway companies,
s on the evils of Sabbath traffic. *Newcastle*,
[n.d.] pp. 4.   AU

4821 The SABBATH and the railway. *Edinburgh*,
s [1847.] pp. 4.   BM
Reprinted from the *United Secession and*
Relief Magazine, January 1847.

4822 SPEECHES delivered at the Town Hall of
Manchester, January 23rd, 1847, at a meet-
s ing to promote better observance of the
Sabbath, and to adopt a memorial to the
directors of the Edinburgh & Glasgow Railway, in approbation of their conduct in
discontinuing passenger trains on the Lord's
Day. *Manchester*, [1847.] pp. 46.   AU

4823 STATISTICS of the Sabbath, with notes and
monitions 'to be thought on' by all concerned
s in the employment of their fellow-men on
the Lord's Day. Parts 1, 2, & 3. *London*,
1846–47. pp. 72.   BM
pp. 39–43, Sunday railway work, and railway
Sabbath desecration, with extracts from news
journals of the day.

4824 BRIDGES, J. The Sunday railways practically discussed: a letter to John James Hope
s Johnstone . . . Chairman of the Caledonian
Railway. *Edinburgh*, 1847. pp. 19.   BM
—— 4th edn. 'The Sabbath railway system
practically discussed.' *Edinburgh & London*,
1847. pp. 20.   H
—— 5th, *Edinburgh & London*, 1848. pp.
20.   H

4825 ETON SCHOOL. Speech of counsel on the
30th May, 1848, before a Select Committee
of the House of Commons, on behalf of the
head, lower, and assistant masters of Eton
against the Great Western Railway extension
from Slough to Windsor. [1848.] pp. 46. BM
'For private circulation only.'

4826 MOODIE, J. Railways, railway travelling
on Sunday, and prevention of its evil effects,
s and observations on railways generally:
principles and observations on speculations,
mining girls, sugar, slaves, East and West
Indies . . . *Edinburgh*, 1848. pp. 67.   PC

4827 ABERDEEN RLY. Debate on the running
of Sabbath trains . . . *Aberdeen*, [1849].
s pp. 18.   BM

4828 BREWSTER, P. Sunday trains defended.
By the Rev. Patrick Brewster of Paisley.
s *Paisley*, 1849. pp. 18.   UL(GL)
Report of a meeting in the Abbey Church, in
favour of Mr. Locke's Bill.

4829 HOPKINS, R. Railway compensation practice, with suggestions for its improvement:
pr a letter to the . . . Commissioners of Railways. *Westminster*, 1849. pp. 23.   BR
Compensation to owners of real property.

4830 LETTER to Joseph Locke, Esq., in reference
to his Bill 'to regulate Sunday travelling
s on railways.' By a Scotchman. *Glasgow*,
1849. pp. 16.   BM
'The Bill . . . is most obnoxious to the religious convictions of my countrymen.'

4831 LETTER to the Members of the House of
Commons on Mr. Locke's Bill. By a Rail-
s way Proprietor. *Edinburgh*, [1849.] pp. 8.
                    LSE
Opposing J. Locke's Bill for the provision of
passenger accommodation on Sunday mail
trains.

4832 LOW, W. Letter to . . . Lord John Russell
. . . explanatory of a financial system for
p extending railways in Ireland and for restoring confidence in railway property
generally. *London*, 1850. pp. 16.   BM
'. . . The relief of distress among the labouring classes in Ireland by promoting railways
[with the help of a loan fund].'

4833 SUNDAY trains may lawfully be used, and
Sunday letters may lawfully be written
s and delivered. By a Christian, but no fanatic.
London, 1850. pp. 24[25].   BM
Cover title—*The lawfulness of Sunday trains*
and Sunday letters.

4834 KNIGHT, C., *publisher.* Knight's Excursion
Companion: excursions from London, 1851.
London, [1851.] pp. [20, 24,] with maps. BM
Twenty excursions. Topographical, but con-
tains much railway information.

4835 EARDLEY, S. The Lord's Day: is it a holy
day or a holiday?: a letter to the Great
s Western Railway Company on their establishment of Sunday excursion trains from
Birmingham. 1853. pp. 15. BIRMINGHAM PL

4836 WIGRAM, J. C. An appeal to the better
feelings of the managers and directors of the
s railway and steampacket companies connected with the Port of Southampton on
behalf of their servants, and of the Christian
welfare of the town. *London*, 1853. pp. 35.
                    LSE
The growing popularity of Sunday excursion
trips, and the consequent 'desecration of the
Sabbath' and the keeping of railway servants in
a 'complete state of Sabbath slavery'. The
author writes as rector of St. Mary's, Southampton.

4837 KENNEDY, T. F. Correspondence on the
nuisance of smoke from locomotive engines
on railways. *London*, 1859. pp. 13.   BM
Letters to and from the Chairman of the
L. & N.W. Rly. concerning the interpretation
of 8 Vict. ch. 20, para. 114.

4838 COOK, T. Cook's Scottish Tourist Official Directory: a guide to the system of tours in Scotland under the direction of the principal railway, steamboat and coach companies commanding the Highland excursion traffic . . . with a series of new sectional maps . . . *London*, 1861. pp. 124, 22.   BM
  Contains much information and advice on travelling conditions. Appendix (pp. 1–22), two essays by Thomas Cook: 'Twenty years on the rails: excursions, tours and social science', and 'Physical, moral and social aspects of excursions and tours'.

4839 DENTON, W. Observations on the displacement of the poor by metropolitan railways
p and by other public improvements. *London*, 1861. pp. 40.   BM

4840 ADAMS, W. B. Roads and rails and their sequences, physical and moral. *London*, 1862. pp. xii, 372.   BM
  General and rather discursive observations.

4841 SEDGWICK, J. An essay on the rights of owners and occupiers of property required
pr by a railway company, to compensation, and the way to obtain it. *London*, 1862. pp. 10.   BM

4842 SUNDAY Excursion. *London*, [1863.] pp.
s 32. [*Household Tracts for the People*.] BM
  A story illustrating the moral (and physical) discomforts which attend Sunday trips to Brighton by rail.

4843 SUNDAY on 'the line'; or, Plain facts for working-men. *London*, [1863.] pp. 16, with
s engraved title-page.   BM
  A dialogue concerning the value of Sunday as a rest day. There is some reference to a memorial to the directors of the L.B. & S.C. Rly. asking for Sunday trains.

4844 WORDSWORTH, C. The law of compensations by arbitration and by jury under the
pr Lands and Railways Clauses Acts . . . *London*, 1863. pp. xiv, 159[164].   BM

4845 ROSS, W. A. Evil effects of Sabbath travelling proved by an appeal to facts, in a
s correspondence with the editor of the 'Scotsman' and a series of letters to the editor of the 'Daily Review.' *Edinburgh*, 1865. pp. 40.   AU

4846 ROSS, W. A. The Sabbath made for man: a sermon. 3rd edn. *Edinburgh*, 1865. pp.
s 16.   AU
  Includes objections to Sunday trains.

4847 SMITH, G. The Sunday question: a railway subject, quietly considered. *Edinburgh*,
s 1865. pp. 16.   AU
  Objection to the employment of railwaymen on Sundays.

4848 FREND, H. T. *and* WARE, T. H. Precedents of conveyances and other instruments

pr relating to the transfer of land to railway companies . . . *London*, 1846. pp. xiv, 452.   BM
—— 2nd edn., By D. Sturges and T. Ll. M. Browne. *London*, 1866. pp. xxx, 600. BM

4849 MASON, C. A. J. A sketch of the history of old St. Pancras Church and its graveyard, with an account of the recent desecration of the burial-ground attached thereto: a paper read by C. A. J. Mason . . . before the Waynflete Society on March 12, 1867. [*London*, 1867.] pp. 32.   BM
  pp. 17 to end, the Midland Railway's excavations in preparing the site for St. Pancras Station and its approaches 'allowing trains to be constantly flying past the very windows of the church and at the same time to be rumbling over the tombs of the hallowed dead.' A map in the text shows the areas affected.

4850 GREVILLE, F. The Rail and the Rod; or, Tourist-angler's guide to waters and quarters thirty miles around London. *London*, 1867–'71.   BM
  A series of guides to rail facilities for anglers. By 'F. Greville' (John Greville Fennell).
    no. 1, G.E.R. 1867. pp. vi, 72.
    no. 2, G.W.R. 1867. pp. vi, 70.
    no. 3, S.W.R. 1867. pp. vi, 82.
    no. 4, S.E.R. 1869. pp. iv, 76.
    no. 5, G.E.; L. & N.W.; M.R.; G.N. railways. 1871. pp. vi, 66.
    no. 6, G.E.; M.R.; L. & N.W.; G.N. railways. 1871. pp. iv, 84.

4851 SOCIETY FOR PROMOTING CHRISTIAN KNOWLEDGE. The Railway Ticket: a tract on infant baptism. *London*, 1872. pp. 16. [*Tract no.* 1646.]   BM
  'We cannot go without the ticket.'

4852 HOVENDEN, T. H. New railways and new streets: a few hints to those affected by
pr proposed public improvements. *London*, 1872. pp. 36.   BM
  Warnings to property owners regarding proposed new railways in London.
—— another edn. *London*, 1873. pp. 36. BM

4853 STAATS-FORBES, J. Reasons against the passenger duty on the Metropolitan District Railway. [*London*, 1876.] pp. 4.   LSE
  Large numbers of labourers carried at cheap rates.

4854 SOMERVELL, R. A protest against the extension of railways in the Lake District,
pr with articles thereon reprinted from the 'Saturday Review' etc., and a preface by John Ruskin . . . *Windermere*, [1876.] pp. 78.   BM
  Ruskin's preface runs to nine pages.

4855 RAILWAYS and commons: a Country Cockney's Blue Book (Session 1881).
pr Dedicated to both Houses of Parliament. *London*, [1881.] pp. 15.   BM
  Objections to the invasion of common land by railways. Signed 'A Country Cockney'.

4856 SPENCE, P. How the railway companies are crippling British industry and destroying the canals; with suggestions for reforming the whole system of railway charges and rescuing the water ways permanently for the nation . . . being the Evidence before the House of Commons Committee on Railway Rates, 1881–2. *Manchester*, [1882.] pp. 28.
ICE

4857 BUXTON, F. W. Workmen's trains and the passenger duty . . . *London: Travelling Tax*
w *Abolition Committee*, [1883.] pp. 7.   NLC
Reprinted from the *Fortnightly Review*, April 1883.

4858 [CAMBRIDGE.] UNIVERSITY OF CAM-BRIDGE—RESIDENT MEMBERS. Petition to
pr the House of Lords for the withdrawal of the Braithwaite & Buttermere Mineral Railway Bill, April 1883. pp. 3.   UL(GL)
The Bill was withdrawn before the petition could be presented.

4859 BOGLE, W. R. Cheap railway travelling: a solution of the problem of how to provide
w better houses for the working classes. *London*, 1884. pp. 11.   BM
Suburbs served by railways, with workmen's trains at reduced fares.

4860 FOXWELL, E. English express trains: two papers. *London*, 1884. pp. 128.   BM
1st paper, pp. 1–58, 'Apologetic.' The various beneficial effects of speed upon individuals and upon social well-being. 'Railways are incessantly persuading men into a disposition of more kindliness.' [!]
2nd paper, pp. 59–128, 'Statistical'. Tables and notes on long runs, gradients, etc.

4861 COOK, T. Temperance Jubilee Celebrations at Leicester and Market Harborough from November 13th to 18th, 1886. Arranged and compiled by Thomas Cook. *London: National Temperance League*, [1886.] pp. 78.
BM
p. 47, T. Cook's account of his arranging of the first public excursion train, 5 July 1841. (Also on pp. 22 and 27.)

4862 MACGOVERN, J. H. How to assess the value of property taken by railway and canal
pr companies and corporations. 2nd edn. *Manchester*, 1887–8. pp. 59.   BM

4863 MUNRO, W. On valuation of property. 2nd edn. *Edinburgh & London*, 1890. pp. 51.
BM
pp. 20–6, Valuation of railways and tramways.

4864 MAPLE, J. B. Cheap trains for London
w workers. [*London*,] 1891. pp. 47.   LSE
'A statement of what has been done up to the present . . . to obtain a reform of the London workmen's train system'. The Cheap Trains (London) Act, 1891.

4865 LONDON COUNTY COUNCIL—PUBLIC HEALTH AND HOUSING COMMITTEE. Re-
w ports of the Public Health and Housing Committee giving results of inquiries instituted by the Council with reference to the service of the workmen's trains provided by the thirteen railway companies having termini in the Metropolis. February and April, 1892. [*London*, 1892.] pp. 49, with tables.   BM

4866 ANTI SUNDAY-TRAVELLING UNION. Is it right to practise Sunday travelling? . . .
s [*London*, 1892.] s.sh.   BM
A tract.

4867 BECK, W. The Friends: who they are; what they have done. *London*, 1893. pp. 277.
BM
pp. 227–30, Friends (Quakers) and the railways.

4868 LONDON REFORM UNION. Workmen's trains: what the County Council has done to
w make the railway companies give us cheap trains. *London*, [1895.] pp. [2.]   BM

4869 LONDON COUNTY COUNCIL. Workmen's trains. Report of the Statistical Officer on
w the need for a general extension of the service of workmen's trains on metropolitan railways to 8 a.m. *London*, 1897. pp. 17, with tables.   UL(GL)

4870 LONDON COUNTY COUNCIL. Workmen's Trains Inquiry. Evidence prepared by the
w Statistical Officer of the London County Council in regard to the inquiry by the Board of Trade on the complaints of the London Reform Union as to the inadequate service of workmen's trains, London & North Western Railway. [*London*, 1899.] pp. 22, with tables.   BM
High cost of workmen's fares on the L.N.W.R.

4871 LONDON REFORM UNION. London Reform Union and workmen's trains: an
w account of the steps taken by the Union to secure an improved service of workmen's trains, with a verbatim reprint of the judgement in the case of the London Reform Union v. the Great Eastern Railway Company. *London*, 1899. pp. 15.   LSE

4872 BOOTH, C. Improved means of locomotion as a first step towards the cure of the housing
u difficulties of London. *London*, 1901. pp. 24.
LSE
'Browning Hall Conference' lectures. Includes recommendations for underground and tramway extensions.

4873 BROWNING HALL CONFERENCES ON HOUSING & LOCOMOTION. Report of
u Sub-Committee on Locomotion. [*London*, 1902.] pp. 14.   LSE
Proposed railway, tramway, and underground railway extension, around London.

4874 BRIGHT, C. The locomotion problem.
u *London*, 1905. pp. 75. BM
Problems and possibilities envisaged by the introduction of motor transport.
Urban transport problems. Railways have created large centres of population resulting in congestion. Rapid trains now required for adequate mobility. Relative merits of tramways, tube and electric railways, and motor cars.

4875 MACASSEY, L. The distribution of population by facilities of rapid transit. [*York: British Association*,] 1906. pp. 14. BR
u Suburban and inter-urban transport. L. Macassey was Secretary to the Royal Commission on London Traffic, 1905.

4876 BROWNING HALL CONFERENCES ON ·HOUSING & LOCOMOTION. Report of
u Sub-Committee on Housing and Locomotion in London, 1902–1907 . . . [*London*,] 1907. pp. 35. LSE

4877 HAZELL, A. P. Work for the unemployed! A national highway for military & motor
p traffic: a practical proposal for providing useful & productive work for the large number of professional, skilled and unskilled workers at present out of employment. *London: Twentieth Century Press*, [1908.] pp. 16. LSE
The highway to include rapid monorail transit.

4878 TAYLOR, T. F. The fallacy of speed. *London*, 1909. pp. 63. BM
'Whether the well-being of the world is enhanced by improved travelling facilities may be reasonably questioned.' Effects of speed on population, commerce and leisure.

4879 BOLLAND, W. State railways mean more employment. *London: Clarion Press*, [1910.] pp. 15. [*Pass On Pamphlets*, no. 28.] LSE

4880 LONDON COUNTY COUNCIL. Return of workmen's trains and other cheap morning
w trains between the London termini and each station in London and the neighbourhood, and of workmen's trams, giving times, fares, and distances, etc. [*London*,] November 1914. pp. 142. [*Publication* no. 45.] LCC

4881 STONE, H. W. D. The principles of urban
u traffic. *London*, 1917. pp. viii, 130. BM
pp. 77–96. 'Railways'. London suburban traffic problems.

4882 DULWICH COLLEGE. Dulwich College and L.C.C. opposition to tramway extension. [*London*, 1924.] s.sh. LSE
By J. Maitland, Chairman of the Estates Governors. A reprint from *The Times*, 5 January, 1924 concerning the proposed tramway from Gipsy Road to the Crystal Palace, through Dulwich College Estate.

4883 DAGGETT, S. Principles of inland transportation. *New York & London*, 1928. pp.
b xvii, 705, with bibliogr. notes & a bibliography. BM
pp. 565–90, The relations between the public and the railways in England.

4884 HURCOMB, C. W. The growth of passenger traffic in Great Britain, and some features of
u its regulation. *London: Municipal Tramways & Transport Association*, June 1933. pp. 35. IT
Paper, Annual Conference, 1933.

4885 OSBORN, F. J. Transport, town development, and territorial planning of industry.
u *London: New Fabian Research Bureau*, [October 1934.] pp. 35. [*Publication* no. 21.] BM
Railways and social problems, suburban development, and town planning.

4886 BRITISH RAILWAYS PRESS OFFICE. Notes about earlier holidays. *Westminster*, [*c.* 1937.] pp. 8. BR

4887 SCOTT, J. Salmon and trout rivers served by the London & North Eastern Railway. [*London:*] *L. & N.E.Rly.*, [1937.] pp. 156, with illus., 2 la. fold. maps, & a table (pp. 81–138). BM

4888 MADSEN, A. W. Why rents and rates are so high: land monopoly in town and country: 600 examples. *London: United Committee for the Taxation of Land Values*. 1938. pp. xx, 229 [232]. BM
pp. 23–6, Railway extensions around London. pp. 203–4, What railways had to pay [for land].

4889 WILLIAMS, S. C. S. *and* SHORT, E. Railways, roads, and the public. *London: Eyre & Spottiswoode*, 1939. pp. 157. BM
Road versus rail. Nationalization not the answer to the problem of stability of railways.

4890 LIEPMANN, K. K. The daily ebb and flow of labour between home and workplace in
u English industrial areas: a statistical and sociological study. Thesis for Ph.D. Degree, University of London, 1941. pp. 5, 281, with fold. charts & tables. *Typescript.* UL

4891 WILSON, R. Space and transport. 1943.
u pp. 20. *Reproduced typescript.* IT
Paper, L.S.E. Railway Students' Association, 27 October, 1943. Presidential address.
Problems of urban congestion on road and rail.

4892 LEE, C. E. Workmen's fares: survey of the provision of cheap daily conveyance of
u workmen between suburban homes and their
w places of business. *London*, [1944.] pp. 8. BM
Reprinted from the *Railway Gazette*, 30 June, 1944.

4893 LIEPMANN, K. K. The journey to work: its
significance for industrial and community
u   life . . . Illustrated with tables and plans.
b   London: Kegan Paul, 1944. pp. xii, 199, with
3 charts (2 of London & 1 of Birmingham) &
bibliogr. notes. [International Library of
Sociology & Social Reconstruction.]   BM
   General, social and economic survey with,
pp. 111–90, detailed statistical section, 'Past
and present statistical investigations', and
pp. 191 to end, 'Conclusions and recommendations'.

4894 NICHOLSON, L. M. R. The influence of
passenger transport on social conditions of
town and country. 1947. pp. 29. Typescript.
                                              IT
   Paper, Institute of Transport, 18 November,
1947.

4895 SMITH, P. H. The private car as a competi-
tor of the public transport undertakings,
with special reference to Birmingham: an
address to the Graduate and Student Society
of the Institute of Transport on November
13, 1947. pp. 22[25]. Typescript.   IT

4896 BRITISH TOURIST & HOLIDAYS BOARD.
Survey of holiday accommodation: a report
. . . London, [1949.] pp. 57, with detailed
tables & lists.   IT
   Requested by the Board of Trade to assist
the Ministry of Town & Country Planning and
local planning authorities in their development
plans under the Town & Country Planning Act,
1947.

4897 LATHAM, C. The social aspects of urban
travel: a speech made by Lord Latham,
u   Chairman, London Transport Executive, to
the Institute of Transport, 28 Feb., 1950.
[London: L.T.E., 1950.] pp. 7.   IT

4898 LONDON TRANSPORT EXECUTIVE. London Travel Survey, 1949. London, 1950. pp.
u   46, with 19 tables.   BM
   Survey of suburban travel patterns and of
traffic density, including railways.

4899 LONDON TRANSPORT EXECUTIVE. London's travelling public: an advertising
u   survey. London, 1950. 9 fold. tables.   IT
   An analysis of the 1949 Travel Survey
presented graphically, with a summary.

4900 ACTON SOCIETY TRUST. Relations with
the public. (Prepared by P. J. Saynor & J. H.
Smith.) London, 1953. pp. 38[39].   IT
   Nationalized industries, including railways:
findings of an enquiry.

4901 ARMSTRONG, J. The problem of workers'
uw   fares. pp. 13[14], with table. Typescript. IT
   Paper, Institute of Transport, March 1953.
   Arguments for and against, and the problem
of peak-hour travel and staggered hours.

4902 LONDON SCHOOL OF HYGIENE AND
TROPICAL MEDICINE. Report of the
study group on 'a London railway terminus'
by D. P. H. students, 1955–1956. (Chairman,
Dr. T. A. Evershed.) May 1956. pp. 36.
Reproduced typescript.   BR
   Waterloo Station and public health. Aspects
affecting railway personnel, the travelling public
and the non-travelling public who make use of
the station.
   The London School of Hygiene copy has 23
mounted photographs.

4903 LONDON TRANSPORT EXECUTIVE. London Travel Survey, 1954. London, 1956. pp.
u   63, with 19 tables.   BM
   Suburban travel patterns and traffic density,
including railways.

*4904 O'DELL, A. C. Railways and geography.
u   London: Hutchinson, 1956. pp. 198.   BM
   The influence of geographical factors on the
construction and operation of railways, including urban problems.

4905 CAMERON, M. A. Non-paying services: the
public's view. Reprinted from the 'British
Transport Review', vol. 4, April 1957, pp.
323–33.   SLS
   A survey of evidence given and views expressed before the Transport Users' Consultative Committees.

4906 MINISTRY OF TRANSPORT AND CIVIL
AVIATION. 'Crush hour' travel in Central
u   London: report of the first year's work of the
Committee for Staggering of Working Hours
in Central London. London, 1958. pp. 45,
with tables & map.   BM

4907 FREEMAN, T. W. The conurbations of
Great Britain . . . with a chapter on the
u   Scottish conurbations by Catherine P. Snod-
grass. Manchester: Manchester University
Press, 1959. pp. xii, 393, with 66 maps,
bibliographical notes, & 7 tables.   BM
   Includes railways in various geographical
regions.

4908 SALES, H. P. Travel and Tourism Encyclopaedia; with special reference to travel
agency operation. London: Travel World,
1959. pp. 760.   BM
   pp. 291–338, Railways.

K 2 RAILWAYS AND THE PASSENGER

Travelling conditions—Discomforts of early rail travel—Classes
of passenger accommodation—Passenger duty (Travelling tax)

For workmen's trains see **K 1**

Marginal symbols **cl** classes of passenger travel
tc travel conditions

Historical

4909 COLE, H. Fifty years of public work of Sir
Henry Cole, accounted for in his deeds,
speeches and writings. *London*, 1884. 2
vols.   BM
   vol. 2, pp. [147]–157, Break of gauge.

4910 WEYL, W. E. The passenger traffic of railways. *Philadelphia*, 1901. pp. 249. [*Publications of the University of Pennsylvania.
Series in Political Economy & Public Law*,
no. 16.]   BM
   pp. 90–111, Development of passenger
traffic in Gt. Britain.

4911 POPE, S. A. The Cheap Trains Act, 1883,
and its equitable interpretation as affecting
the Government, the public, and the English
railways. *London*, 1906. pp. 28.   LSE
   Paper, G. W. Rly., (London) Lecture &
Debating Society, 22 February, 1906.
   Railway passenger duty, including an
historical review of legislation relating to it.
Workmen's tickets.

4912 BURKE, T. Travel in England; from pilgrim
and pack-horse to light car and plane.
tc *London: Batsford*, 1942. pp. vi, 154, with
plates.   BM
   pp. 115–36, 'The Age of Steam'. Mainly on
conditions of travel.

4913 LEE, C. E. Passenger class distinctions.
London: Railway Gazette, 1946. pp. 76, with
cl 24 illus. & 9 tables.   BM
   The development and subsequent modification of classes of passenger accommodation on
British railways in relation to changes in social
and economic conditions.

4914 SIMMONS, J. Journeys in England: an
anthology edited by Jack Simmons. *London:
tc Odhams Press*, 1951. pp. 288.   BM
   Of ninety items, nos. 21, 24, 56, 57, 58, 59,
63, and 73 relate to railway travelling conditions.

Contemporaneous

4915 RAILWAY travelling and the toll question.
From no. LXXVII of the Westminster Review, for May 1843. *London*, 1843. pp. 15.
                                                        BM
   An examination and restatement of the substance of two pamphlets:
   1. 'Letter to H. Goulburn, Chancellor of the
Exchequer, on the unequal pressure of the
railway passenger tax.' By G. H. Lang
Glasgow, 1842.
   2. 'The toll question on railways exemplified
in the case of the Croydon and Greenwich
Companies.' By W. A. Wilkinson. *London*,
1841.

4916 [SALA, G. A.] Rain, Hail, Steam and Speed:
trifles for travellers dedicated to the world in
tc general and unprotected females in particular. By An Old Stoker. *London: Ackermann
& Co.*, [1845.] pp.[21.]   LSE
   'Practical exposition of Mr. J. M. W.
Turner's picture [*Rain, Steam and Speed; the
Great Western Railway* (1844)]. One shilling
plain, 2s. 6d., coloured.' Comic drawings on
the discomforts of rail travel in the 1840's.

4917 [COLE, H.] A few of the miseries of the
break of gauge at Gloucester which occasions
the shifting of passengers, luggage and goods
from one carriage to another. [1846.] s.sh.
                                                        LSE

4918 [COLE, H.] A railway traveller's reasons for
adopting uniformity of gauge: addressed to
I. K. Brunel. [1845.] pp. 24.   BM
—— 2nd ed. *London*, [1846.] pp. 24.   LSE
—— 3rd, *London*, [1846.] pp. 24.   BM
—— 4th, *London*, [1846.] pp. 24.   LSE
—— 6th, *London*, [1847?] pp. 31.   LSE
—— 7th, *London*, [1847.] pp. 31.   BM
—— 8th, *London*, [1847.] pp. 31.   BM

4919 SIDNEY, S. Speed on railways considered in
a commercial point of view. *London*, 1847.
pp. 22.   BM
   More slow trains at low fares wanted. Tables
of speeds.

4920 'VIATOR'. Speed of railways: the narrow
gauge faster than the broad gauge. By
Viator. *Cirencester*, [1847.] pp. 6, with
tables.   LSE
   Facts deduced from time-tables, of broad
and narrow gauge railways.

4921 LOCKE, J. Railway gauge: a letter to . . .
Lord John Russell, M.P. on the best mode of
avoiding the evils of mixed gauge railways
and the break of gauge. *London*, [1848.]
pp. 16, with fold. diagram.   LSE
   A scheme involving the adding of narrow-
gauge to broad-gauge from Oxford to Reading
and London, and from Reading to Basingstoke.

4922 [PHILLIPS, S.] The Literature of the Rail; republished . . . from 'The Times' of Saturday 9th August 1851; with a preface. *London: John Murray*, 1851. pp. 23.   BM
    The moral danger to railway travellers in the poor quality of the literature sold at station bookstalls, among which are 'French novels with bright green covers'. (L. & N.W. Rly. excepted!)

4923 HINTS to railway travellers and country visitors to London. By An Old Stager.
tc *London*, 1852. pp. vii, 51.   BM
    pp. 1–9, travelling by train.

4924 FACTS and strictures respecting the abuses and impositions of the Dover town porters on the passenger public and the public service. By A Looker-On. [*London*, 1856.] pp. 20.   UL(GL)
    Foreign visitors fleeced by porters between steam-boat and the station (S.E. Rly.).

4925 The INFLUENCE of railway travelling on public health. *London*, [June 1862.] pp. viii,
tc   152.   RC
    From *The Lancet*, Jan.–March, 1862.
    Medical opinions on the physiological and psychological effects of all aspects of railway travelling, including accidents.

*4926 The RAILWAY Traveller's Handy Book of Hints, suggestions and advice, before the
tc journey, on the journey, and after the journey. *London*, 1862. pp. iv, 154, 16.   BM
    Information on travelling conditions, and anecdotes.

4927 [BRADFIELD, J. E.] Mileage duties: case of the stage carriage proprietors. *London*, 1864. pp. 32, with fold. map.   NLC
    Railway and omnibus duties compared.

4928 BOND, R. Murray & Co's Book of Information for railway travellers and railway
tc officials, illustrated with anecdotes, etc. *London*, 1865. pp. vi, 203.   LSE
    R. Bond was Supt., Newport Stn., G.W. Rly.

4929 FLEMING, W. Railway Time-table and Speed Calculator, giving the time for running any distance at any speed, and the speed of any train [at sight]. 2nd edn. *Dublin*, [1868.] s.sh., with la. fold. table.   ICE

4930 HAVILAND, A. Hurried to death; or, A few words of advice on the danger of hurry
tc and excitement, especially addressed to railway travellers. *London*, 1868. pp. 56.   BM
    Reprinted from the *Medical Times & Gazette*, 22 Feb., 1868.

4931 JONES, G. W. G. W. Jones's plan of universal penny railways, by the application of
cl turnpikes to railways: a practical plan suitable to the genius of the people and calculated to satisfy the locomotive requirements of the country. *London*, 1869. pp. viii, 55.   NLC
    Government ownership, and a fares system

based on 16-mile stages at each of which 3rd class passengers would be required to get out of the train to go through a penny turnstile before continuing.

4932 HODGSON, W. A plea for justice to third-class passengers, with a few remarks on the
cl qualification of directors. 2nd edn. *London*, 1872. pp. 11.   BM
    Addressed to the Great Western Rly. 'Let 3rd class passengers travel by *every* train'.

4933 JONES, G. W. The million on the rail: a few statistics showing the expediency of encour-
cl aging the third class passenger to travel. *London*, 1874. pp. 19, with a table.   NLC
    An enlargement of his *Universal penny railways* (1869). A scheme for fares reform.

4934 MINOT, R. S. Railway travel in Europe and America; with 25 tables of recent and novel
tc statistics of journeys, speeds, fares, etc. for travellers and others. *Boston*, 1882. pp. 28.   BM
    pp. 5–13, American and European travelling conditions compared.

4935 REYNOLDS, J. R. Travelling: its influence on health. *In* 'The Book of Health', edited by Malcolm Morris. *London*, 1883. pp. [559]–588.   BM
    pp. 580–4, railway travelling.

4936 FOXWELL, E. English express trains: two papers. *London*, 1884. pp. 128.   BM
    1st paper, pp. 1–58, aspects of speed. 2nd paper, pp. 59–128, tables and notes.
    The beneficial effects of railway travel and of speed: a philosophy of rail travel.

4937 STRETTON, C. E. A paper on railway traffic, with summary of returns for year
cl 1883. *London*, [1884.] pp. 4.   BM
    Decline of 1st class and increase of 3rd.

4938 BAKER, T. A Battling Life. *London*, 1885. pp. viii, 447.   BM
tc An autobiography. pp. 105–9, discomforts of travel on the L. & S.W. Rly. The 'smoking' nuisance.

4939 GOODEVE, L. A. Railway passengers and railway companies: their duties, rights and liabilities. *London*, 1876. pp. xv, 149.   BM
—— 2nd edn. *London*, 1885. pp. xv, 158.   BM

4940 RAILWAY PASSENGERS PROTECTION ASSOCIATION. Railway and Canal Traffic Bill, 1886. Information for the Members of both Houses of Parliament. *London*, [1886.] pp. 12.   LSE
    Instances of unjust treatment of passengers by railway companies.

4941 GILES, R. W. Railway passenger traffic: a few words to railway passengers and railway
cl proprietors; by one of themselves. *London*, 1887. pp. 22.   BM
    Suggests a broader basis for passenger classes.

4942 [JENKINS, W. J.] Railway tyranny: a letter of appeal to the President of the Board of Trade against railway companies and their persistent disobedience to the law; by one who has defeated them five times. *London*, [1887.] pp. 16.　　　BM
Signed 'Justice' (W. J. Jenkins).

4943 MARSHALL, W. P. Modern railways and railway travelling. *Birmingham*, 1888. pp.
tc [183]–204.　　　ICE
Reprint, *Proceedings of the Birmingham Philosophical Society*, vol. 6, pt. 2.
Contemporary travelling conditions.

*4944 FOXWELL, E. *and* FARRER, T. C. Express trains, English and foreign; being a statistical account of all the express trains of the world; with railway maps of Great Britain and Europe. *London*, 1889. pp. viii, 181.　　　BM
pt. 1, pp. 1–73, Express trains in Gt. Britain.

4945 PARSONS, A. The liability of railway companies for negligence toward passengers. *London*, 1893. pp. xv, 196.　　　BM

4946 FINDLAY, G. On modern improvements of facilities in railway travelling. *In his* 'Work-
tc ing and management of an English railway.' 5th edn. *London*, 1894. pp. [377]–401.　　　BM

4947 HOLE, J. National railways: an argument for state purchase. *London*, 1893. pp. xvi,
cl 385.　　　BM
pp. 140–78, The third-class passenger.
—— 2nd edn. *London & Paris*, 1895. pp. xvi, 408.　　　BM

4948 KENNY, J. Railway law for the people: being the law as it affects railway passengers, treated in a popular way. *Manchester*, [1896.] pp. 46.　　　BM

4949 SCOTT, W. J. Mile-a-minute express trains, twentieth century. Reprinted from 'Cosmopolis,' August 1897, with emendations and additions. *London*, 1897. pp. 31, with 7 illus. & 2 tables.　　　BM
A forecast of possible achievements in near future train running.

4950 O'MOORE, M. Tips for travellers; or, Wrinkles for the road and rail . . . *London*,
tc 1899. pp. 158.　　　BM
pp. 41–66, for railway travellers.
—— Cheap edn. *London*, 1900. pp. 158.　　　BM

4951 EDALJI, G. E. T. Railway law for the 'man in the train,' chiefly intended as a guide for the travelling public on all points likely to arise in connection with the railways. *London*, 1901. pp. vi, 129.　　　BM

4952 LONDON COUNTY COUNCIL. Third class season tickets: report by the Statistical
cl Officer as to the issue of third class season tickets on railways having termini in Lon-
don; and return showing the comparative cost of season and ordinary return tickets of all classes issued between London railway termini and stations within 20 miles thereof. (By Edgar Harper, Statistical Officer.) *London*, May 1902. pp. xxvi, 81.　　　BM

4953 ANDERSON, H. D. *and* ARTHURTON, A. W. One, two or three classes: which is
cl most desirable? 1905. pp. 10.

4954 TEBB, W. S. The chemical and bacteriological condition of the air on the City & South London Railway. *London*, 1905. pp. 14.　　　BM
A report to Southwark Borough Council.

4955 LISSENDEN, G. B. The Railway Passenger's Handbook: a complete guide to railway
tc travelling. *London*, [1906.] pp. xi, 94.　　　pc
Points of law concerning passenger travel.

4956 ACWORTH, W. M. The rights of railway passengers in respect of unpunctuality. [*c.* 1910.] pp. 7.　　　LSE
Privately printed.
The legal position in Gt. Britain and in other countries.

4957 BIRCH, H. Penny railways: a practical rail-
cl way reform. *London*, [1917.] pp. 16.　　　BM
An enlarged version of an article in the *Manchester Guardian* of 12 August, 1917. Three classes of train—slow stopping, fast stopping, and non-stop. Passengers will pay more for time saved.

4958 LISSENDEN, G. B. Railway passengers and their luggage. *London*, 1928. pp. xii, 114. IT
'The relationship between us and the railway company after we have bought our ticket.'

4959 INSTITUTION OF AUTOMOBILE ENGINEERS. Comfort in travel. [*London*,] March
tc 1939. pp. 38, with 7 illus. & diagrams.　　　BR
Three Papers: 1, By road. Sidney Garcke; 2, By rail. Lord Stamp; 3, By air. E. W. Percival.

4960 WILLIAMS, S. C. S. *and* SHORT, E. Railways, roads and the public. *London:*
tc *Eyre & Spottiswoode*, 1939. pp. 157.　　　BM
pp. 63–88, 'What British railways do for passengers'.

4961 LIEPMANN, K. K. The journey to work: its significance for industrial and community
tc life . . . *London: Kegan Paul*, 1944. pp. xii, 199, with tables and plans. [*International Library of Sociology & Social Reconstruction.*]　　　BM
Problems of travelling conditions in urban areas. Results of a statistical investigation.

4962 THOMAS, G. O. Some thoughts on speed. *In his* 'Times may change.' *London: Epworth Press*, 1946. pp. [114]–117.　　　BM

4963 BUCKLAND, W. R. The 'cost' of travel to work. (Excerpt from the papers read before

tc the Health Congress of the Royal Society of
Health at Blackpool, 24–27 April, 1956.)
[*London*, 1956.] pp. [73]–77.   IT
No covers.

4964 NORMAN, L. G. The health of London's
travelling public. *London: Royal Society for*
tc *the Promotion of Health*, 1959. pp. 12.   IT
Paper, 11 March, 1959.

K3 SAFETY IN TRANSIT

Accidents and their prevention—Problems, theories and reforms
relating to signalling, brakes, passenger communication, safer
working of trains. Safety of the travelling public as a social aim

For safety engineering see E 15

Historical

4965 DAWNAY, A. D. A treatise upon railway
signals and accidents. *London*, 1874. pp.
123, with diagrams.   BM
Historical and descriptive. pp. 87–end,
Board of Trade requirements and recommendations.

4966 IRVING, J. The Annals of Our Time: a
diurnal of events social and political . . .
c from the accession of Queen Victoria . . .
London & New York, 1869. pp. vii, 742. BM
A chronology. Among many references to
railways are fifty brief accounts of accidents.

c —— New edn. *London*, 1871. pp. ix, 1033.
BM
c —— Supplement, 1871–4. *London*, 1875. pp.
169.   BM
c —— Supplement, 1874–9. *London*, 1879. pp.
152.   BM
The new edition with its two supplements
records about 100 accidents.

c —— another edn. '. . . 1871 to June 20,
1887.' *London*, 1889. pp. 987–1651.   BM
Sixty-two accidents.

4967 BENNETT, A. R. Historic locomotives and
'moving accidents' by steam and rail . . .
London, 1906. pp. 15, with 10 col. plates.
BM

4968 WILSON, H. R. The safety of British railways; or, Railway accidents—how caused
and how prevented, *London*, 1909. pp. viii,
240[242].   BM
An historical survey, with tables.

4969 WILSON, H. R. Railway accidents: legislation and statistics, 1825 to 1924. *London*,
c 1925. pp. xix, 39.   BM
Includes nine detailed tables of accidents,
including a 'list of all train accidents in which
passengers were killed'.

4970 THOMAS, J. Obstruction—Danger!: stories
of memorable railway disasters. *Edinburgh
& London: Blackwood*, 1937. pp. viii,
275[276].   BM

4971 ROBERTS, R. O. *and* GIBB, A. D. The law
of collisions on land. *London*, 1925. pp.
xxx, 280.   BM
pp. 88–117 and elsewhere, Running-down
accidents on railways.

—— 2nd edn. *London*, 1929. pp. xxxv, 308.
BM
—— 3rd, by A. D. Gibb. *London*, 1932. pp.
xxxv, 407.   BM
—— 4th, by A. D. Gibb. *London*, 1938. pp.
xli, 468.   BM

4972 RAILWAY   PASSENGERS   ASSURANCE
COMPANY. The oldest accident office in the
world: being the story of the Railway
Passengers Assurance Company, 1849–1949.
Compiled by F. Hayter Cox. [*London*,
1949.] pp. 67, with illus., incl. portraits. BR

4973 BLYTHE, R. Danger ahead: the dramatic
story of railway signalling . . . *London:*
b *Newman Neame*, 1951. pp. 132, with 31 illus.
(5 col.) & a bibliography.   BM

*4974 ROLT, L. T. C. Red for danger: a history of
railway accidents and railway safety pre-
b cautions. *London: Bodley Head*, 1955. pp.
c 225, with 11 illus. on 6 plates, a 3 p. chronology of accidents & a bibliography.   BM
—— 2nd edn. (not revised). *London: Pan
Books*, 1960. pp. 221, with 9 illus., chron.,
& bibliography.   BM

Contemporaneous

4975 PARKIN, T. A letter to George Glyn . . .
on railway accidents and other matters relative to railways, of great importance to the
public. *London*, 1840. pp. 16.   NLC

4976 BERMINGHAM, T. Statistical evidence in
favor of state railways in Ireland . . . also a
plan whereby collision on railways may be
altogether avoided . . . *Dublin*, 1841. pp. 22,
xciv.   BM

4977 CAYLEY, G. Essay on the means of promoting safety in railway carriages. [*London*,
1841.] pp. 16.   ICE
General consideration of problem of avoiding collision, with various suggestions, including signalling.

4978 GARVEY, M. A. The Patent Spondyloid
Life Train, . . . *London*, [c. 1845?] pp. 4,
with fold. diagram.   ICE
Shock of collision absorbed by pneumatic
compartments between carriages.

4979 OBSERVATIONS on the means of providing against the dangers and fatal accidents so much complained of in railway travelling, and of obtaining much greater power and economy by such improvements in the atmospheric system as will render iron rails and cylinders unnecessary. *London*, [1846.] pp. 59.   PO
The inherent dangers of conventional railways.

4980 RITCHIE, R. Railways: their rise, progress and construction, with remarks on railway accidents and proposals for their prevention . . . illustrated by numerous woodcuts. *London*, 1846. pp. viii, 444.   BM
Including reports of railway accidents.

4981 HAXBY, J. B. Signals upon railway trains: remarks upon the additional protection to passengers, and saving to railway companies, which must be effected in the prevention of accidents by the adoption of a more efficient mode of signalling upon railway trains. *London*, 1848. pp. 21.   PO
Communication between guards and drivers.

4982 ATKINSON, I. A. An effectual, simple, and scientific means (invented and patented by W. W. Sleigh) for preventing railroad accidents, whereby collisions between trains, and the serious effects of concussion, are obivated; with remarks by Mr. I. A. Atkinson, agent for the patentee. *London*, 1849. pp. 8. UCL
(1) an additional braking device to act upon rails from the rear carriage, and (2) safety straps for passengers.

4983 ROTCH, B. The objects of the Railway Passengers' Assurance Company considered with reference to existing railway interests and to the mode in which the business connected with passenger traffic is at present carried on. 1849. pp. 7.   PO

4984 The CASE of the railways considered, especially with reference to railway accidents and the operation of Lord Campbell's Act. By A Shareholder. *London*, 1852. pp. 50.   BM
Against an Act 'which imposes on railway companies heavy responsibilities in the event of accidents proving fatal'.

4985 RAILWAY PASSENGERS ASSURANCE COMPANY. Statement of claims and compensation awarded, to March 1851. *London*, [1851.] pp. 24.   BM
Fifty-nine cases, Nov. 1849 to March 1851.

—— another edn. *London*, [1852.] pp. 24. BM
139 accidents, with description of claimant, location and date.

4986 PETERS, W. Railway dangers and how to avoid them. *London*, 1853. pp. 64.   BM
Accident prevention; with letters reprinted from October 1853 issues of the *Daily News*.

4987 RAILWAY PASSENGERS ASSURANCE COMPANY. Table of premiums. 1853. s.sh.
UL(GL)
On reverse, Bradshaw's Map of Great Britain.

4988 BARBOUR, G. F. Letter to . . . Edward Cardwell, M.P., President of the Board of Trade, on the occasion of his Bill for the prevention of railway accidents . . . with appendix and documents. *London*, 1854. pp. 22.
NLC
Fatigue in railwaymen caused by the loss of their rest-day due to Sunday working of trains.

4989 BOOTH, H. A letter to Lord Campbell on 9 & 10 Victoria, cap. 93, being an Act for compensating the families of persons killed by accidents . . . showing the injustice of the measure and the propriety of its immediate repeal. *London*, 1854. pp. 38.   BM
The comparative safety of rail travel and the intolerable burden of liabilities placed upon railways by this Act.

4990 NEISON, F. G. P. Analytical view of railway accidents. [*London*, 1853.] pp. 49, with tables.   UL(GL)
From the *Journal of the Statistical Society of London*, December 1853.

—— Analytical view of railway accidents, continued. [*London*, 1854.] pp. 24, with tables.   UL(GL)
From the *Journal of the S.S.L.*, Sept. 1854.

4991 OGAN, A. Railway collisions prevented. *London*, 1855. pp. xx, 34.   BM
Tyer's electro-magnetic signals. Includes a general survey of the problems of safety.

4992 WILSON, G. On colour-blindness in relation to the danger attending the present system of railway and marine coloured signals. *Edinburgh*, 1855. pp. vi, 33.   NLC

4993 NEISON, F. G. P. Contributions to vital statistics . . . 3rd edn. *London*, 1857. pp. xliv, 630.   BM
pp. 230–301, Analytical view of railway accidents, based on Board of Trade figures, 1840–1853; with 41 tables and 28 lesser tables. (The 1st and 2nd edns. are much smaller and contain no railway information.)

4994 ACHARD, A. Public security on railways and in factories where steam power is applied by means of the 'embrayage electrique.' 1862. pp. 24.   ICE
French edn., 'La Securité publique sur les chemins de fer . . .' *Grenoble*, 1861.

4995 STEPHENSON, G. R. High speeds: a letter to . . . T. M. Gibson, M.P., President of the Board of Trade. *London*, 1861. pp. 35. ICE
Excessive speed the cause of most accidents. Examples given.

4996 SIMON, H. A. The law relating to railway accidents, including an outline of the liabilities of railway companies as carriers generally, concisely discussed and explained. *London*, 1862. pp. xii, 100.   BM

4997 MANBY, C. *and* FORREST, J. Railway accidents; comprising the following papers: 1, Railway accidents, their causes and means of prevention, by James Brunlees; 2, Railway accidents, showing the bearing which existing legislation has upon them, by Douglas Galton . . . Edited by C. Manby and J. Forrest. *London*, 1864. pp. 82.   BM
Excerpt, *Min. Proc. I.C.E.*, vol. 21, 1861/2.

4998 BOUTET, C. Prevention of railway accidents. *London*, 1865. pp. 38.   BM
Causes and types of accidents: pp. 30–8, 'opinions of scientific newspapers and others'.

4999 FLETCHER, J. O. Railways in their medical aspects. *London*, 1867. pp. vi, 184.   BM
Accidents: pp. 114–81, a table of 175 cases.

5000 HALL, J. C. Medical evidence in railway accidents. *London*, 1868. pp. 54.   BM

5001 PERCUSSION caps not dangerous, shown by experiments exhibited under the supervision of the Birmingham Chamber of Commerce on April 28, 1869. *Birmingham*, [1869.] pp. 18, with a mounted photograph at end.   PC
Shows that detonators cannot be exploded in bulk during transit.

5002 ADAMS, W. B. On the causes of railway axle fracture, and the remedy. *London*, 1870. pp. 11.   BM
Non-technical: urging mechanical reforms.

5003 WHAT system of communication between passengers, guards and drivers ought to be adopted on our railways? . . . By one who believes that a detached or independent system must in the end be adopted on all railways. *Manchester*, [1870.] pp. 32.   BM

5004 RHODES, C. E. P. The present railway travelling and the dangers thereof, and the millennium of railway travelling. *London*, 1871. pp. 16.   BM
pp. 14–16, an additional essay, 'The future of tramways'.

5005 WRIGLEY, T. Look before you leap: railway accidents, their cause and cure. *London*, 1871. pp. 56.   BM
For improved signalling.

5006 WATKIN, A. M. 'Don't leap in the dark': observations upon Mr. Wrigley's pamphlet on railway accidents entitled 'Look before you leap'. *Manchester*, 1871. pp. 12.   LSE
Friendly criticism of Wrigley. Describes block signalling system in operation on the South Eastern Rly.

5007 BRITTAIN, F. Railway management. *Sheffield*, [1872.] pp. 20.   LSE
Urging a Government enquiry into rail safety and the indifference of railway companies to accidents.

5008 DELL, B. Railway accidents and personal injuries: important questions for shareholders. *London*, 1873. pp. 16.   BM
The problem of excessive claims for damages.

5009 [EDINBURGH.] CHAMBER OF COMMERCE AND MANUFACTURES OF EDINBURGH. Report by Committee of the Chamber of Commerce and Manufactures of Edinburgh on railway accidents. (By David Maclaren, chairman.) [*Edinburgh*, 1873.] pp. 14.   BM
The misleading character of parliamentary returns on railway accidents. Causes analysed and suggestions made.

5010 The PRINCIPAL causes of railway accidents, with proposed remedies. By a railway servant of fifteen years' experience. *Edinburgh*, 1873. pp. 16.   BM
Under-staffing, mechanical, and other deficiencies.

5011 BAZAINE, A. G. Du controle de l'exploitation technique des chemins de fer anglais: analyse d'un mémoire du Capitaine Tyler, inspecteur-chef du 'Board of Trade'. [*Paris*, 1874.] pp. 25.
Extract from *Annales Industrielles*, livraisons des 13 et 30 décembre 1874.
Relating to a series of articles in the *Railway Times*, 6, 13, and 20 June, 1874, and H. W. Tyler's 'On simplicity as the essential element of safety and efficiency in the working of railways', *Min. Proc. I.C.E.*, vol. 37, 1873/4.

5012 GRAHAME, J. The safety of railway travelling in the United Kingdom, from 1861 to 1872 . . . *Glasgow*, 1874. pp. 16, with 8 tables of accident statistics.   BM

5013 MARTIN, S. M. Railway accidents; their causes and the means of prevention . . . *London*, [1874.] pp. 28.   BM

5014 [PHILLIPS, E.] A Voice from the Signal Box; or, Railway accidents and their causes. By A Signalman. *London*, 1874. pp. 48.   BM
Introduced and presented by E. Phillips on behalf of a signalman, and addressed to M. T. Bass, M.P.

5015 SMITH, J. C. On the prevention of railway accidents. *Dublin*, 1874. pp. 20.   ICE
A paper read at a meeting of the Institution of Civil Engineers of Ireland.

5016 TYLER, H. W. On simplicity as the essential element of safety and efficiency in the working of railways. *London*, 1874. pp. 35.   ICE
Excerpt, *Min. Proc. I.C.E.*, vol. 37, 1873/4.

5017 CONTINUOUS railway brakes; by a frequent railway traveller: a letter to . . . Sir Charles Adderley, President of the Board of Trade. *London*, [1875.] pp. 15.   BM

5018 HALL, J. C. Railway pathology: case of Harris versus the Midland Railway Company . . . *London*, 1875. pp. 14.   BM
Reprinted from the *British Medical Journal*, no. 780, 11 Dec., 1875. Accident claims.

5019 MCBRIDE. McBride's system for assuring to railway passengers compensation in the event of death or bodily injury from accident happening to the train by which they are travelling. *Leicester*, 1876. BM
Insurance tickets with counterfoils.

5020 ARMSTRONG, J. Railway accidents: the Royal Commission and human fallibility. *London*, 1877. pp. 32. BM
An essay on the conclusions of the Royal Commission on Railway Accidents.

5021 WOODS, E. On adequate brake-power for railway trains ... *London*, [1877.] pp. 14. ICE
Reports of his investigations for the Royal Commission on Railway Accidents of 1875.

5022 GALTON, D. Observations on the Report of the Royal Commission on Railway Accidents. [1878.] pp. 67–91. NLC
Extract from an unidentified periodical.

5023 ADAMS, C. F. Notes on railroad accidents. *New York*, 1879. pp. vi, 280. BM
Includes accounts of some British accidents.

5024 MORRIS, H. Communication between passenger and guard on railways; with an appendix containing a list of recent cases, proving its necessity ... *Manchester*, 1881. pp. 32. ICE

5025 STRETTON, C. E. A few remarks on railway accidents, their cause and prevention. 1st edn., 3rd issue (revised, & additional pages added). *Leicester*, 1881. pp. 34, with 3 fold. diagrams, 3 fold. plates, & tables. BM
—— 2nd edn. *Leicester*, 1882. pp. 36. SL
—— 3rd, *London*, 1882. pp. 35. BM
—— 3rd, rev. *London*, 1882. pp. 38. BM
—— 4th, *London*, 1882. pp. 38. (5 fold. plates.) RC

5026 STRETTON, C. E. A few remarks on railway permanent way. *London*, 1884. pp. 11, with 3 illus. (2 fold.). BM
The necessity for good permanent way to prevent accidents. The text of this and the following work are the same.

5027 STRETTON, C. E. A paper on railway permanent way ... *Leicester*, [1884.] pp. 11. BM
The text of this and the preceding work are the same.

5028 WHITTEN, H. Public danger and official delinquency on the North-Eastern Railway: an exposure. The East-Coast Route condemned. (Fifth edition.) *Newcastle-upon-Tyne*, 1885. pp. 16. NLC
A combined edition of four separate pamphlets issued between August and November 1884:
A Big Bad Monopoly; Half-a-day on the

North Eastern; Killing made easy; The Great Engine Scandal. Also an unheaded notice addressed to the directors concerning their disregard for safety.
'Only the baldest self-interest can drive the North Eastern Directorate into paying decorous attention to the safety of passengers.'

5029 MACDONALD, N. D. The railway companies and railway brakes. *Edinburgh*, 1890. pp. 62. PC
Reprinted from *The Scotsman*.
Articles and letters relating to accidents upon various railways caused by faulty brakes, or by inefficient types of brake.

5030 PAGE, H. W. Railway injuries; with special reference to those of the back and nervous system, in their medico-legal and clinical aspects. *London*, 1891. pp. ix, 148. BM

5031 STRETTON, C. E. Safe railway working: a treatise on railway accidents, their cause and prevention; with a description of modern appliances and systems. *London*, 1887. pp. x, 174. BM
—— 2nd edn. *London*, 1891. pp. viii, 214. BM
—— 3rd, *London*, 1893. pp. x, 230. BM

5032 BROWN, H. H. The procedure in accident inquiries and investigations, according to the law of Scotland. *Edinburgh*, 1897. pp. xi, 200. BM

5033 BOLAS, T. The Chiswick level crossing fatality. *Chiswick*, 1901. s.sh. BM

5034 FRASER, J. English railways statistically considered. *London*, 1903. pp. xii, 279, 12. BM
pp. 175–235, suggestions for increased safety; with illustrations.

5035 HAMILTON, A. M. Railway and other accidents with relation to injury and disease of the nervous system: a book for court use, with fifteen plates, two ... charts, and 36 illustrations. *London*, 1904. pp. xii, 351, with bibliography. BM

5036 JENKIN, F. C. J. C. The chief provisions of the law relating to railways and the safety of passengers and the public. *London: G.W.R. (London) Lecture & Debating Society*, 1909. pp. 16. LSE
Paper, 3 December, 1908.

5037 BYLES, C. B. The economics of safety. *London: G.W.R. (London) Lecture & Debating Society*, 1911. pp. 10. LSE
Paper, 19 January, 1911.

5038 NETTLESHIP, E. On cases of accident to shipping and on railways due to defects of sight. *London*, 1913. pp. 54, with bibliogr. notes. BM
Cover title, 'Accidents from defective sight'.

5039 PRATT, E. A. Train accidents and railway safety. December 1913. pp. 40, with tables. BR
'For private circulation.'
Analysis of the Accident Returns, of types of accidents, comparisons with foreign railways and comparative safety of rail and other forms of transport.

5040 [WILSON, J.] Railways. The prevention of accidents arising in connection with the doors of the carriages; locking and unlocking the doors. Manchester, 1914. pp. 48, with illus. LSE
Scheme for locking doors, with correspondence between the author and the Board of Trade.

5041 CARTER, C. F. Comparative safety on British and American railroads: an address . . . before the Safety Section of the American Railway Association. St. Louis, 1926. pp. 12. LSE
American railways much safer than British.

5042 CARPMAEL, R. Speed and safety on the railways. pp. 28. IT
Paper, Institute of Transport, London, 6 Feb., 1928, and Yorkshire Local Section, 2 March, 1928. Reprinted in the Journal of the Institute of Transport, 1928. pp. 270–303, with illus. and tables.

5043 INTERNATIONAL LABOUR OFFICE. Methods of compiling statistics of railway accidents. Geneva, 1929. pp. 82. [Studies & Reports, Series N, no. 15.] BM

5044 LONDON PASSENGER TRANSPORT BOARD. Safety on the Underground. Westminster, 1934. pp. 12, with illus. BM

5045 LEAGUE OF NATIONS. Signals at level crossings: report of the special committee of experts presented to the Council . . . Geneva, 1938. pp. 10. [Series VIII. 1938. 5.] LSE

K 4 RAILWAYS AND INDUSTRY, TRADE, AND AGRICULTURE

Railway facilities from the viewpoint of the distributor—Rates and charges reform—Private sidings and private wagon ownership

For rates and charges generally see F 1

Marginal symbols: **a** agriculture and railways
ct coal transport

Historical

5046 WILKINS, C. The South Wales coal trade and its allied industries, from the earliest
ct days to the present time. Cardiff, 1888. pp. v, xii, 405. BM
Includes railways.

5047 WAGHORN, T. Carriers and railway companies. London: Carriers Publishing Co., 1907. pp. 24. LSE
Reprint, World's Carriers & Contractors Review.
An historical survey of alleged misinterpretation of legislation by railways and their unfair monopoly of transport, both road and rail.

5048 USHER, A. P. An introduction to the industrial history of England. London, 1921. pp. xxii, 529, xxxiv. BM
pp. 431–58, The development of the railway.

5049 KNOWLES, L. C. A. The industrial and commercial revolutions in Great Britain during the nineteenth century. London, 1921. pp. xii, 420. [Studies in Economics & Political Science, no. 61.] BM
pp. 253–90, Development of railways and the problem of state control.
—— 2nd edn. London, 1922. pp. xii, 420. BM
—— 3rd, London, 1924. pp. xii, 416. BM

5050 CAMPBELL, C. D. British railways in boom and depression: an essay in trade fluctuations and their effects, 1878–1930. London, 1932. pp. 125, with bibliogr. notes. LSE

5051 CLAY CROSS COMPANY. A hundred years of enterprise: centenary of the Clay Cross
ct Company, Ltd. 1837–1937. Derby & London, [1937.] pp. 52, with illus., incl. portraits on plates. BR

*5052 CLAPHAM, J. H. An economic history of modern Britain: [vol. 1,] the Early Railway Age, 1820–1850. Cambridge: Cambridge University Press. 1926. pp. xviii, 623. BM
—— 2nd edn. Cambridge, 1930. pp. xvi, 623. BM
—— 2nd edn., repr. with corr., Cambridge, 1939 & 1950. BM

5053 ELSAS, M. Iron in the making: Dowlais Iron Company letters, 1782–1860. Edited by Madeleine Elsas. [Cardiff:] Glamorgan County Records Committee, 1960. pp. xix, 247. BM
pp. 148–52, Transport of iron by roads and tramroads.
pp. 166–70, Taff Vale Rly.
pp. 171–9, Rails for tramways and railways.

5054 SMITH, R. Sea-coal for London: history of
ct the coal factors in the London market.
London: Longmans, 1961. pp. xiv, 388. BM
Includes passages relating to the development of the railway coal market and its effects
upon the trade generally.

Contemporaneous

5055 WILKES, J. On the utility of iron rail-ways;
a from the second volume of 'Communications to the Board of Agriculture'. *In* 'The
Repertory of Arts and Manufactures', vol. 3.
London, 1800. pp. 167–71. BM

5056 ANDERSON, J. Recreations in agriculture,
a ... *London*, 1799–1802. 6 vols. BM
vol. 4, pp. 198–217, 'On cast-iron railways'.
pp. 473–7, 'Minutes to be observed on the
construction of railways'.
vol. 5, pp. 290–3, 'On iron rail-ways': a letter
by Bulstrode on the Surrey Iron Railway.

5057 DUMBELL, J. Mr. Dumbell's letter to Mr.
a Western. *London*, 1830. pp. 51. ICE
Addressed to Chas. C. Western, M.P.
Fears that the growing favour of locomotives
will mean fewer horses, and that farmers will
have no market for hay and corn.

5058 HOLMES, W. D. Report ... on the Midland
Grand Junction Railway, with some remarks
ct on the comparative facilities of the Midland
and the Northumberland and Durham coal
fields for the supply of sea-borne coals to
London. *London*, [1837.] pp. 23. H

5059 JOHNSON, C. W. [*and* JOHNSON, G. W.]
The advantages of railways to agriculture.
a By C. W. Johnson ... Observations on the
general importance of railways. By G. W.
Johnson. *London*, [1836.] pp. 16. BM
—— 2nd edn. *London*, 1837. pp. 16. BM

5060 DUNN, M. A historical, geological and
descriptive view of the coal trade of the
North of England, comprehending its rise,
progress, present state and future prospects
... *Newcastle upon Tyne*, 1844. pp. ix, 248,
with a chronology. BM
Includes many references to railways and
wagonways.

5061 HAIR, T. H. A series of views of the collieries in the counties of Northumberland and
ct Durham by T. H. Hair, with descriptive
sketches and a preliminary essay on coal and
the coal trade by M. Ross. *London*, 1844.
pp. 51. BM
Half title: 'Sketches of the coal mines in
Northumberland and Durham.'
Forty-two engravings of contemporary colliery scenes, mostly depicting rail transport.

5062 POOLE, B. Twenty short reasons for railway
companies being themselves the carriers of
goods, without any intervening parties existing between them and the public; on the
same principle as they are carriers of passengers. *Liverpool*, 1844. pp. 12. LSE

5063 POOLE, B. A dozen more short reasons why
railway directors should now dismiss those
middle-men who have intruded themselves
upon some lines of railway under the de-
nomination of 'railway and canal carriers'
upon toll, who usurp the profits belonging to
such railways and also injure the public; and
why such directors should take the collection
and delivery of all goods into their own company's hands. *Liverpool*, 1844. pp. 7. LSE

5064 SHIPTON, J. A letter addressed to railway
and canal directors on the subject of carrying
goods, being induced by the perusal of 'A
dozen more reasons' published by Mr. B.
Poole of Liverpool ... *Wolverhampton*, 1844.
pp. 12. LSE
Strong words about Poole and his 'rank and
deliberate falsehoods'. Upholds the principle of
independence of carriers.

5065 WILSON, H. Hints to railroad speculators,
together with the influence railroads will have
a upon society in promoting agriculture, commerce and manufacturers. *London*, 1845.
pp. 12. BM

5066 The AMALGAMATION of railways considered as affecting the internal commerce of
the country. *London*, 1846. pp. 16. BM
The evils of monopoly resulting from amalgamations; the benefits of free competition.

5067 OBSERVATIONS on a proposed railway for
supplying the Metropolis and south and
ct south-eastern counties with excellent and
cheap coal, coke, lime, and other products
from the counties of Derby, Leicester and
Warwick, with a few remarks on the coasting
trade. *Liverpool*. [1846.] pp. 26. BM(MSS)
The BM (Dept. of MSS.) copy, Add. MS.
40590, ff. 135–47, is prefaced by a holograph
MS. letter from George Stephenson to Robert
Peel containing 'an explanation of my views'.
From a literary standpoint it would seem
improbable that George Stephenson actually
wrote this pamphlet.

5068 An OLD CARRIER's petition to the directors of the Great Western Railway Company,
against the break of gauge at Gloucester.
London, 1846. pp. 12. LSE
Signed 'An Old Carrier'.
'The incredible evils attendant upon a trans-
position of goods from one waggon to another.'

5069 CARRYING question: remarks on the
memorial presented to the Railway Commissioners by some of the merchants of
Birmingham. *Manchester*, 1847. pp. 12.
LSE
Objections to the L. & N.W. doing its own
'carrying'.

5070 MORRISON, J. The influence of English
railway legislation on trade and industry;
with an appendix of tracts and documents.
London, 1848. pp. 187. BM

5071 SIDNEY, S. Railways and agriculture in
a   North Lincolnshire: rough notes of a ride
     over the track of the Manchester, Sheffield &
     Lincolnshire and other railways . . . *London*,
     1848. pp. xv, 103, with fold. map.   BM

5072 RAILWAY parcels and rates. *London*, 1849.
     pp. 8.
     An account of the case of Crouch v. the
     London & North Western Rly., Warwickshire
     Assizes, March 30, 1849, in the Common Pleas.
     Illegal overcharging, and opening, delaying,
     and separately despatching, of packages of small
     parcels by railways.

5073 ADAMS, W. B. Road progress; or, Amal-
a   gamation of railways and highways for
     agricultural improvement. *London*, 1850.
     pp. 76, with 3 fold. diagrams.   BM
     Railways on roads.

5074 PYM, J. The iron ways, bridges, rails and
     rolling stock, cheap transit combined with
     steam farming; or, Agriculture self-protected.
     By a Practician . . . *London*, 1850. pp. x, 45.
                                        BM
     Reprinted from the *Westminster & Foreign
     Quarterly Review* for January 1850.
     Running title—'Railway Progress.'
     Comments on railways and railway economy.

5075 PORT of Southampton on the banks of the
     Thames. By a Merchant. *London*, [1853.]
     pp. 14.   BM
     For increased wharf and warehouse accom-
     modation at Nine Elms, with the L. & S.W. Rly.
     an essential feature of the plan.

5076 HILL, C. Railway loans: a few words to the
     Chancellor of the Exchequer on this subject
     as a point of finance. *London*, 1854. pp. 15.
                                        BM
     'Preposterous to allow companies, with all
     money expended, to come annually into the
     market and borrow a sum exceeding all the
     Exchequer bills the Government has in circula-
     tion.'

5077 WESTLY, W. K. An account of the portable
a   farm railway. [1854.] pp. 3, with plate. ICE
     A cheap form of monorail post railway for
     farm purposes.

5078 WESTLY, W. K. On the uses and applica-
a   tions of the portable farm railway. [1854.]
     pp. 8.   ICE

5079 STOKES, H. P. Better canals, better trade:
     remarks on the carriage of heavy goods,
     etc. *Wolverhampton*, [1855.] pp. 23.
                                  BIRMINGHAM PL
     Railway rates.

5080 FORDYCE, W. Coal and iron: a history of
ct   coal, coke, coal fields . . . with numerous
     highly finished engravings. *London*, 1860.
                                        BM
     Issued in 16 monthly parts.
     Colliery railways are a prominent feature.

5081 ASSOCIATION OF CHAMBERS OF COM-
     MERCE. Report of committee appointed by
     the Association of Chambers of Commerce
     to consider the inequalities of railway rates.
     February 7th, 1872. *Wolverhampton*, 1872.
     pp. 12.   BM

5082 CUTHBERT, A. A. The carriage of explos-
     ives: letters to the Board of Trade by the
     British Dynamite Co. Ltd., regarding bye-
     laws proposed by the railway companies . . .
     under the Explosive Substances Act, 1876.
     Glasgow, 1876. pp. 16.   NLC
     'For private cirulation.'

5083 GUTTMANN, F. Der Gütertransport auf den
     Eisenbahnen Englands. *Bromberg*, 1876.
     pp. 116, with 30 fold. tables.   HRL

5084 REDMAN, J. H. A treatise on the law affect-
     ing railway companies as carriers of goods
     and live stock. 2nd edn. *London*, 1880. pp.
     xx, 204.   BM

5085 ROBERTS, S. Pleadings for reforms pub-
a   lished fifty years ago . . . A new edition, re-
     vised and enlarged. *Conway*, 1880. pp. 128.
                                        BM
     pp. 33–45, 'Railroads against sewers'.
     Proposal to convey sewerage for agricultural
     benefit.

5086 CONDER, F. R. The actual and the possible
     cost of conveyance between Manchester and
     Liverpool. *London*, 1882. pp. 29–44.   ICE
     A Manchester Statistical Society reprint.
     'Fifty years after the opening of the Liver-
     pool & Manchester Rly. it costs more to convey
     a bale of cotton . . . than it did in 1829.'

5087 RODWELL, J. K. Agricultural tramways.
a   *Bury St. Edmunds*, 1882. pp. 9.   LSE
     Suggested light feeder lines for cheap trans-
     port of farm produce.

5088 SHAW, T. The Railway and Carrier's Ready
     Reckoner, for ascertaining the charges of
     goods . . . *Dublin*, 1862. pp. 100.   BM
     —— another edn. 'The Railway Ready
     Reckoner.' *London*, 1883. pp. [72.]   BM

5089 BALLARD, S. Cheap railways for rural
a   districts. *Malvern*, 1884. pp. 11.   BM
     Light railways.

5090 HICKMAN, A. A paper on railway rates and
     canal dues, read by Alfred Hickman, presi-
     dent of the Wolverhampton Chamber of
     Commerce, and chairman of the South Staf-
     fordshire Railway Freighters Association, on
     September 20th, 1884, at the meeting of
     Social Science Congress in Birmingham.
     Wolverhampton, [1884.] pp. 8.   BM
     A reduction in rates essential to commerce.

5091 BRITISH IRON TRADE ASSOCIATION.
     Comparative statistics of English and foreign
     railways. *London*, 1885. pp. 26, with tables.
                                        LSE
     The threat of higher rates and charges, and
     the greater carrying capacity of British as
     compared with foreign railways.

5092 RAILWAY Rates and Charges Bills: three articles on the proposed railway legislation revised and reprinted from the 'Northern Echo'. *Darlington*, 1885. pp. 22. LSE
An explanation for the interest and help of traders.

5093 ASSOCIATION OF CHAMBERS OF COMMERCE. Railway and Canal Traffic Bill. Report of deputation representing the Association of Chambers of Commerce . . . to the President of the Board of Trade . . . 30 March, 1886. [*London*,] 1886. pp. 34. NLC

5094 BRITISH IRON TRADE ASSOCIATION. Iron and iron making materials: comparison of English and foreign railway rates. (Statistical report for 1885.) [1886.] pp. 33. NLC

5095 SAMUELSON, B. Report to C. M. Norwood, president of the Association of Chambers of Commerce of the United Kingdom, on the railway goods tariffs of Germany, Belgium and Holland compared with those of this country. *Birmingham*, [1886.] pp. 41. ICE
pp. 24–41, Tables of comparative rates.

5096 BOLTON CORPORATION. Railway rates and charges: a general statement concerning rates and charges in operation upon British railways, and of other matters relating thereto. *Bolton*, 1887. pp. 88. HRL

5097 RAILWAY (Carriage of Common Kinds of Fish) Rate Bill, 1888. [*London:*] *Railway News*, [1888.] pp. 8. LSE
Proposed cheap rates will injure shareholders and will not alter retail prices of fish.

5098 REMOVAL Contractors' and Furniture Dealers' ABC of Railway Rates . . . *London*, [1888.] pp. 62. BM

5099 GRAY, J. W. Facts and observations concerning railway rates, and practical suggestions relating to the proposed revised classification of merchandise traffic by the Board of Trade. *Shipley*, 1889. pp. 42. HRL

5100 MANSION HOUSE ASSOCIATION ON RAILWAY AND CANAL TRAFFIC. Preferential railway rates: copy of correspondence which has passed between the Executive Committee of the Mansion House Association and the South Eastern, and Chatham & Dover railway companies through the medium of the Board of Trade. [*London*,] 1889. pp. 19. LSE
Low rates for imported goods are unfair to home producer. Replies from the two companies, and tables.

5101 R., L. G. Is home trade in home productions worth having? [*London*, 1891.] pp. 8. LSE
Favourable rates for import and export traffic is ruining home trade. Examples quoted.

5102 COTSWORTH, M. B. The Railway and Traders' Calculator, showing at a glance by index, all rates . . . *York*, 1893. BM

5103 EXAMPLES of preferential railway rates given on foreign sugar imported into this country. Compiled by Sugar Trade, February 1893. *London*, [1893] pp. 11. LSE
Deputation to the President of the Board of Trade, Feb. 17, 1893, with eight tables from various railways.

5104 TAYNTON, H. J. An outline of the law relating to the private ownership of railway rolling stock. *London*, 1893. pp. 79. BM

5105 TECHNICAL CORRESPONDENCE AGENCY.
a Report on light railways for agricultural districts: presented to the Railway Department of the Board of Trade, December 1894. pp. 17. *Typescript*. LSE

5106 WILDMAN, J. R. The siding rent question.
ct *Leeds*, 1895. pp. 46. BM
J. R. Wildman was a coal merchant and this is a detailed record of his dispute with the Midland Rly., including letters, extracts from Acts, and a verbatim report of the proceedings in the Court of the Railway & Canal Commission.

5107 COLEMAN, T. J. Important hints to railway traders. [*London*, 1905.] pp. 24. BM

5108 EVANS, A. D. British railways and goods traffic: is the foreigner preferred? *Birmingham*, [1905.] pp. 56. BM
No. Preferential rates are *not* given to foreign produce.

5109 MIDLAND CHAMBERS OF COMMERCE. Railway companies and traders: owner's risk conditions. Report of the Standing Joint Committee of Midland Chambers of Commerce on Railway Matters, respecting their negotiations with the Great Western, the London & North Western, the Midland, and North Staffordshire railway companies, with regard to the interpretation of their 'owner's risk conditions' and the treatment of claims thereunder for loss, damage, or delay. *Birmingham*, [1905.] pp. 49. LSE

5110 NATIONAL FEDERATION OF FRUIT & POTATO TRADES ASSOCIATIONS OF GREAT BRITAIN & IRELAND. Conference of Fruit Growers 12 October, 1905. Discussion on 'railway grievances'. *London*, 1905. pp. 31. LSE
Rates.

5111 TAYLOR, J. S. Transit, trade and traffic in Ireland. *Dublin*, [1905.] pp. 16. LSE
A collection of views of manufacturers and traders expressing dismay at high railway rates.

5112 PRATT, E. A. The transition in agriculture.
a (Cheap edn.) *London*, 1906. pp. x, 354, with illus. BM
Includes the effect of railways upon agricultural marketing.

5113 WAGHORN, T. Agriculture and railway
rates. *London: Central & Associated Cham-*
a *bers of Agriculture,* 1906. pp. 46.   LSE
    Comparative rates for railway transport of
home and of foreign meat and fruit.

5114 PRATT, E. A. German versus British railways, with special reference to owner's risk
and traders' claims. *London,* 1907. pp. 64.
                                              BM
    Results of an investigation following D.
Lloyd-George's remark 'There is no such thing
as "owner's risk" in Germany', made to a
deputation of traders, Dec. 13, 1906.

5115 WAGHORN, T. Traders and railways. (The
trader's case.) *London,* 1907. pp. xi, 233.
                                              BM

5116 WILLIAMS, W. E. Transit over roadways,
waterways and railways in its relation to the
commercial development of the country,
with a special reference to the County of
Glamorgan. *Swansea,* 1907. pp. 95, with 18
illus.   BM
    Cover title, *Transit & Commerc.*
pp. 28–49, Transit by railways.

5117 PRATT, E. A. The organization of agriculture. *London,* 1904. pp. xi, 407.   BM
    pp. 1–11, The railways and agriculture.
    —— 2nd edn. *London,* 1905. pp. xii, 443
(pp. 1–11 & 327–63.)   BM
    —— 3rd, *London,* 1908. (chapters 1 & 25.)
                                              BM

5118 COCKBURN, J. H. Law of private railway
sidings and private traders' traffic. *London,*
1909. pp. xvii, 166.   BM

5119 GATTIE, A. W. How to improve London's
transport. *London,* [1910.] pp. 19, with 3
plates & illus. [*Lecture no.* 2.]   BM
    A central clearing house for goods.

5120 OSBORNE, H. Railway rebates from private
sidings traffic. *Liverpool,* 1910. pp. 32. BM

5121 GATTIE, A. W. Improvements in the transport and distribution of goods in London.
London, [1911.] pp. 27.   BM
    A goods clearing house for all London rail-
ways.

5122 PRIVATE owners' wagons; the bane of
English railways—a ban to progress . . .
London: Railway Engineer, 1911. pp. 16. BM
    Reprinted from the *Railway Engineer,* July
1911.

5123 ACWORTH, W. M. Railway policy from
the traders' point of view . . . *Birmingham,*
1912. pp. 20.   LSE
    Reprinted from the *Birmingham Chamber of
Commerce Journal,* 31 January, 1912.
    Railways and commerce: the improvement
of mutual interests.

5124 GATTIE, A. W. The economies and advantages to be obtained by the institution of

goods clearing houses suitably designed and
adequately equipped and approached: a
lecture . . . to the Great Central Railway
Debating Society. *Cardiff & London,* [1912.]
pp. 16, with 2 fold. plates, illus. & tables.
                                              BM
    —— another edn. *London,* [1912.] pp. 17.
[*Lecture no.* 6.]   BM

5125 GATTIE, A. W. How to cheapen transport.
London, [1912.] pp. 15. [*Lecture no.* 4.]
                                              BM
    A clearing house for goods from all London
railways.

5126 BATHURST, C. Railways: memorandum
a on agricultural grievances. pp. 7.   LSE
    Privately printed, House of Commons, 23
April, 1913.

5127 GATTIE, A. W. Economic transport and
the goods clearing house system. *London,*
[1913.] pp. 17, with plates & illus.   BM

5128 GATTIE, A. W. The great transport problem in its relation to labour unrest. *London:
New Transport Co.,* [1913?] pp. 11, with
illus. [*Lecture no.* 5.]   IME
    Paper, Royal Automobile Club, 17 April,
1912.
    Economy in goods transport, handling and
storing.

5129 GATTIE, A. W. A plea for more light on
railway administration. *London,* [1913.] pp.
31. [*Lecture no.* 7.]   BM
    pp. 10–31, detailed table of estimated traffic
from all London railways to and from a proposed goods clearing house.

5130 LISSENDEN, G. B. Pitman's railway (rebates) case law: a book of reference for
traders, railway officials, solicitors . . . containing the judgement of the court in every
rebate case submitted to the Commissioners.
London, [1913,] pp. vii, 453.   IT

5131 MOND, A. The railway position: memorandum by Sir Alfred Mond. April 1913.
pp. 4.   LSE
    'Privately printed.'
    The trader's position in the face of continu-
ing railway amalgamation and growing monopoly. Wider government control required.

5132 GATTIE, A. W. Goods transport reform.
pp. 4.   BM
    Galley proof of an address delivered in
Committee Room no. 12 of the House of Commons, to Members of all parties of both Houses
of Parliament, on 21 May, 1914.

5133 The GATTIE-SEAMAN system of goods
clearing house. *In* 'Jubilee of the Railway
News, 1864–1914.' *London: Railway News,*
[1914.] pp. 171–3, with 3 illus.   BM

5134 GRAY'S RAILWAY PUBLISHING CO.
Gray's Railway Traders' Compendium of
the regulations and conditions affecting the

transit of goods and merchandise in Great Britain and Ireland. *Manchester*, [*c.* 1914.] pp. 175. BM

5135 HARRIS, J. N. Railways and agricultural
a co-operation. *In* 'Jubilee of the Railway News, 1864–1914.' *London: Railway News*, [1914.] pp. 112–14. BM

5136 HARBEN, H. D. The railways and agri-
a culture. *London: Railway Nationalisation Society*, [1915.] pp. 9. [*R.N.S. Pamphlet* no. 4.] TUC
Reprinted from the Rural Reform Supplement to the *New Statesman*, 2 August, 1913.
Nationalization for lower rates, and the need for country bus services.

5137 PRATT, E. A. A London Transport Trust: criticism of an impracticable scheme. *London*, 1916. pp. 70. BM
Objections to A. W. Gattie's scheme for a 'central goods clearing house'.

5138 PRATT, E. A. Traders and tribunals: a digest of Evidence given before the Royal Commission on Railways concerning traders' grievances and their settlement. Extracted from the official report of June 25, 1914. *London*, [1916.] pp. ix, 111. LSE
The 'Loreburn Commission' of 1913.

5139 ASPINALL, J. A. F. Address . . . as President of the Institution of Civil Engineers, 5 November, 1918. *London*, 1918. pp. 25. ICE
Railways and the immediate future. Economies necessary if railways are to continue to serve trade and industry.

5140 ADVISORY COMMITTEE ON RAILWAY
a RATES. Minutes of Evidence, Tuesday, Nov. 25th, 1919. (Chairman, F. Gore-Brown.) pp. 47. *Typescript*. LSE
Agriculture and the proposed increase in railway rates.

5141 ASSOCIATION OF BRITISH CHAMBERS OF COMMERCE. Deputation on railway grievances. *London*, 1919. pp. 42. LSE
Verbatim report of an interview with Wm. F. Marwood, Permanent Secretary to the Board of Trade.

5142 HORNIMAN, R. How to make the railways pay for the War; or, The transport problem solved . . . *London*, 1916. pp. xx, 348, with 22 illus., plans & diagrams, & bibliogr. notes. BM
—— 2nd edn. *London*, 1917. pp. xx, 348. BM
—— 3rd, *London*, 1919. pp. xvi, 375. BM
Suggested reforms, including cartage problems, and Mr. Gattie's scheme.

5143 JACKSON, R. H. The economics of production and the Gattie system of cheap transport: an illustrated paper read . . . at the Caxton Hall, Westminster, 14 July, 1919. *London: New Transport Co.* [1919.] pp. 20,

with diagrams, including a sectional view of proposed Gattie wharf for the Albert Dock (London). LSE

5144 NEW TRANSPORT COMPANY. Preliminary estimate of revenue and expenditure and capital account, and wages schedule of the proposed Goods Clearing House for London . . . presented to the Board of Trade Committee appointed by Government to enquire into and report upon the 'Gattie' System. [*London*,] October 1919. pp. 14. LSE

5145 PRIVATELY owned wagons on railways: the case against state acquisition. [*London*, 1919.] pp. 15. LSE

5146 PRIVATELY owned wagons on railways: trading traffic and national reasons against their being interfered with. 1919. pp. 11. LSE
Against a government proposal to have all wagons under railway ownership.

5147 ASSOCIATION OF BRITISH CHAMBERS OF COMMERCE. Revision of railway rates: letter from Minister of Transport; letter to Minister of Transport submitting views of the Association; views of chambers. (Special report, March 1920.) *London*, 1920. pp. 67. LSE

5148 GATTIE, A. W. An open letter to Sir J. Fortescue Flannery. 1920. s.sh. LSE
Accusations of inaccuracies and misstatements in Flannery's committee report on Gattie's transport reform proposals.

5149 MODERN TRANSPORT. Limitations of the railways: need of a new standard loading gauge. [*London*, 1920.] pp. 10, with diagrams. BR
Reprinted from *Modern Transport*, 28 August, 1920.
A larger gauge for the transport of modern industrial equipment and products.

5150 NEW TRANSPORT COMPANY. Report of the Departmental Committee appointed to investigate Mr. A. W. Gattie's proposals for improving the method of handling goods and traffic . . . together with an analytical reply by the New Transport Co. *London*, 1920. pp. 39. BM
Showing that the Committee's report is 'based upon untruths'.

5151 LISSENDEN, G. B. Industrial traffic management. *London*, [1915.] pp. xv, 243. BM
Including the consignment of merchandise by rail; rates, charges and legal requirements.
—— 2nd edn. *London*, 1921. pp. xvi ,336 BM

5152 RAILWAY NATIONALISATION SOCIETY. Real rail cuts: British industry's most urgent need. *London* .[1922.] pp. 16. [*R.N.S. Pamphlet* no. 19.] LSE
Reprinted from the *Daily News* May and June 1922.

5153 KENYON, T. A. Railway service for the trader. *Widnes: Widnes Chamber of Commerce*, [1923.] pp. 16.   LSE
Reprint, *Widnes Weekly News*, Jan. 26, Feb. 2, 9 and 16, 1923.
Existing legislation prevents railways from competing on equal terms with road haulage. With press comments. T. A. Kenyon was an L.M.S. Rly. official.

5154 YOUR railway rates; by an expert. (A reference book for every trader.) *Leeds: Yorkshire Evening News*, [1923.] pp. 46.
IME
Relevant sections of the Railways Act (1921) simplified and explained.

5155 FRAAS, G. *and* BALDWIN, M. Railway claims explained; for the merchant, trader and shipper. *Manchester*, 1925. pp. 72. BM
Conditions applicable to 'owners risk' traffic, and regulations for the packaging and addressing of goods.

5156 IRVING, N. A Trader's Guide to the Railway Rates Revision. *Liverpool*, [1925.] pp. 51.   IT
Reprinted with additions from the *Monthly Journal of the Liverpool Chamber of Commerce*.

5157 BROADBENT, W. D. The standard terms and conditions of carriage uniformly applicable to the railways of Great Britain as approved by the Railway Rates Tribunal in accordance with the Railways Act, 1921. *Manchester: Iron & Steel Wire Manufacturers' Association*, [1926.] pp. 124.   LSE
A handbook for consigners of goods.

5158 GREAT WESTERN RLY. Miscellaneous information. *London*, Feb. 1926. pp. 11. [*Great Western Pamphlets*, no. 2, 1926.] BR
Remarks by the General Manager of the G.W.R. to Newport Chamber of Commerce, 11 Dec. 1925, and to Ealing Chamber of Commerce, 13 Jan., 1926, on the transport of goods by G.W.R.

5159 GREAT WESTERN RLY. A few observations on railways. (By Felix J. C. Pole.) *London*, [1927.] pp. 21. [*Great Western Information* no. 3.]   LSE
Lecture to Birmingham Chamber of Commerce, 6 Jan., 1927.
Railways and their difficulties during the Great War and since the 1923 amalgamations. Railways, traders and rates.

5160 HARTLEY, D. H. J. Guide to traders on exceptional rates and their continuation after the appointed day. *London*, [1927.] pp. 38.   BM

5161 ASSOCIATION OF PRIVATE OWNERS OF RAILWAY ROLLING STOCK. The compulsory acquisition of private wagons by (a) the railways, (b) the State. [*London*, 1928?] pp. 8.   LSE

5162 BELL, R. The trade and railway outlook. *Stratford: L.N.E. Rly.*, 1928. pp. 16.   IT
Paper, Newcastle & Sunderland Lecture & Debating Society, Gateshead, 18 October, 1928.
A call to railwaymen to do their best to meet the demands made upon railways for increased speed and efficiency. R. Bell was Assistant General Manager.

5163 [COMMITTEE OF THE REPRESENTATIVES OF THE OWNERS OF PRIVATE MINERAL RAILWAYS IN DURHAM & NORTHUMBERLAND.] Private mineral railways: memorandum dealing with the replies of the President of the Board of Trade to questions put to him on Thursday 8 November 1928. [*Newcastle upon Tyne*, 1928.] pp. [3.]   LSE
On the unfair exclusion of private mineral railways from freight transport rates relief.

5164 OLDHAM, W. The Grocers' and Allied Traders' Handbook on Railway Rates and Charges, containing particulars of the new system of standard rates and charges . . . [*London*,] 1928. pp. 207.   BM

5165 COMMITTEE OF THE REPRESENTATIVES OF THE OWNERS OF PRIVATE MINERAL RAILWAYS IN DURHAM & NORTHUMBERLAND. Private mineral railways. *Newcastle*, January 1929. pp. [3.]   LSE
Relief granted to public railways under the Rating & Valuation Act and the Local Government Bill should apply also to private railways. A circular letter asking for support to a plea for an amendment.

5166 PRIVATELY owned railway wagons: reasons for retention. [*Sheffield*,] 1929. pp. 41, with
ct   bibliogr. notes.   LSE
A case put forward by coal-trade interests.

5167 ARCHER, A. W. The handling of coal at a
ct   modern colliery. 1930. pp. 10. *Typescript.* IT
Paper, L.S.E. Railway Students' Association, Leeds, 4 July, 1930.
Railways, the coal industry, and the need for modern equipment to compete effectively with foreign markets.

5168 ATKINSON, G. L. The transport and ship-
ct   ment of coal. 1930. pp. 15. *Typescript.* IT
Paper, L.S.E. Railway Students' Association, Leeds, 4 July, 1930.

5169 DUNNAGE, J. A. Britain's new profession: industrial transport management. *London*, [1930.] pp. 60.   BM
pp. 36–9, Railway transport arrangements.

5170 HASTIE, A. Practical transport management. *London*, 1930. pp. xiii, 177.   BM
Industrial railway systems, and the use of public railways by industry and commerce.

5171 KENWORTHY, L. A. Private wagon ownership: facts versus fallacies. *London*, [1930.] pp. 22.   BM

5172 OLDHAM, W. A Guide to private siding problems, railway rates and charges, etc. *London*, 1930. pp. 90.   BM

5173 PRIVATE WAGON OWNERSHIP. Compulsory pooling of privately-owned wagons: comments on the recommendations of the Standing Joint Committee on Mineral Transport. *Rotherham*, [1930.] pp. 12.   IT

5174 ROBERTS, E. R. B. British railways and unemployment: how British railways can
a solve our greatest national problem . . . *London*, [1930.] pp. 65.   BM
    More efficient railway transport at lower cost will give movement to agriculture, trade and industry. Abolition of private wagon ownership called for.

5175 COMMERCIAL MOTOR USERS ASSOCIATION *and* SOCIETY OF MOTOR MANUFACTURERS & TRADERS. A fair chance for British industry. (A reply to a booklet issued by the Railway Companies Association entitled 'Fair play for the railways'.) *London*, 1932. pp. 12.   LSE
    Efficient and economic transport system needs freedom from restrictive legislation on railways and road haulage.

5176 BRITISH STEELWORK ASSOCIATION. Modern mineral transport. *London*, [c. 1934.] pp. 16, with 11 illus.   LSE
    The advantages of the new all-steel wagons for improved efficiency.

5177 CAREY, L. A. Modern railway practice, facilities and charges: a practical textbook written from the industrial viewpoint for all who send or receive goods by rail. *London: Industrial Transport Publications*, 1937. pp. 176.   LSE

5178 HALLSWORTH, H. M. Rail transport. *In* 'Britain in recovery.' British Association for the Advancement of Science, Economic Science & Statistics Section. *London*, 1938. pp. 283–98.   BM
    The part played by railways in the revival of industry and trade since 1932.

5179 LONDON, MIDLAND & SCOTTISH RLY. List of principal agricultural and horse etc. shows, 1931 . . . to and from which the L.M. & S. Rly carry either directly or in conjunction with other companies. *London*, 1931–38. 5 parts.   BM
    Parts 2 to 5 were probably published by the Railway Companies Association.

5180 RAILWAY COMPANIES ASSOCIATION. A summary of the report of the Transport Advisory Council upon the proposals of the railways with respect to the conveyance of merchandise by rail. *London*, [1939.] pp. 27.
                    TUC
    Reforms relating to classification of merchandise, rates and charges, and safeguards for industry and consigners of goods.

5181 WILLIAMS, S. C. S. *and* SHORT, E. Railways, roads and the public. *London: Eyre & Spottiswoode*, 1939. pp. 157.   BM
    pp. 89–118, 'What the railways do for industry.'

5182 BOND, S. A trader looks at transport. 1943. pp. 10. *Reproduced typescript.*   IT
    Paper, Institute of Transport, East Midlands Section, 17 December, 1943.
    What the trader requires from railways and other forms of transport.

5183 SMITH, F. Transport: the right use of communications. 1945. pp. 14. *Reproduced typescript.*   IT
    Paper, Swindon Economics Society, 30 January, 1945.
    The necessity for raising the pay-load and the speed of freight trains.

5184 LISSENDEN, G. B. Railway matters and how to deal with them: a vade mecum for merchants . . . *London: George Routledge*, 1946. pp. vii, 111.   BM

5185 NATIONAL UNION OF MANUFACTURERS. Nationalisation of transport. February 1946. pp. 3. *Reproduced typescript.*   IT
    Preferring the recommendations of the Transport Advisory Council in April 1939 to the proposed nationalization.

5186 HURCOMB, C. Speech . . . Mansion House Association in London . . . 25 March 1949. Improved rail facilities . . . *London: British Transport Commission*, 1949. pp. 9[10]. *Reproduced typescript.*   IT

5187 ASSOCIATION OF BRITISH CHAMBERS OF COMMERCE. Higher travel costs: a report on the Association's objections to the British Transport Commission (Passenger) Charges Scheme, 1951. *London*, Jan. 1952. pp. 33[36].   IT

5188 GILES, H. R. C. Transport in industry. *London: Pitman*, 1951. pp. vii, 122.   BM
    Relative cost, etc., of various forms of transport: pp. 11–58, railways.

*5189 ASSOCIATION OF BRITISH CHAMBERS OF COMMERCE. A.B.C.C. and the Transport Bill. (A selected analysis of press comments on the A.B.C.C.'s transport policy.) *Westminster*, 1952. pp. 12.   IT
    Cover title, *Transport policy: press comment.*

5190 VIAN-SMITH, H. S. Transport in the Modern Age: an address to the Oldham and District Chamber of Commerce, 69th Annual Meeting, 4th February, 1952. *London*, [1952.] pp. 15.   BM
    Changes in the economic concept of transport, and the interests of industry and commerce.

5191 ASSOCIATION OF BRITISH CHAMBERS OF
COMMERCE. Transport policy. *London*,
October 1952. pp. 24.   IT
A report to chambers of commerce on the
action taken by the Association regarding the
proposed amendment of the Transport Act,
1947.

5192 BRISBY, M. D. J. *and* EDDISON, R. T.
Train arrivals, handling costs, and the holding and storage of raw materials. *London*,
1952. pp. 171–83.   IT
Reprint, *Journal of the Iron & Steel Institute*,
vol. 172, 1952.

5193 [HARRISON, A. A.] The complementary use
of rail and road transport for freight traffic.
1952. pp. 8. *Reproduced typescript*.   IT
Paper, Institute of Transport, Metropolitan
Section, 7 January, 1952.

5194 HAVERS, E. The coal industry and the
ct railways. 1952. pp. 25[26]. *Typescript*. IT
Paper, Institute of Transport, Berks, Bucks &
Oxon Section, 29 September, 1952.

5195 NATIONAL COAL BOARD *and* BRITISH
RAILWAYS. Calverton Colliery, Notting-
ct hamshire. Official opening of the railway
branch line and of the colliery . . . 24 September 1952. pp. [13,] with illus. & map.   RC

5196 HULTGREN, T. Transport and the state of
trade in Britain. [By] Thor Hultgren, assisted by William I. Greenwald. *New York:
National Bureau of Economic Research*, 1953.
pp. xii, 114, with 40 tables & 28 charts.
[*Occasional Paper* no. 40.]   TUC
Mostly goods and passenger rail transport.

5197 SHERRINGTON, C. E. R. Railway services
as a function of national production. 1954.
pp. 20. *Typescript*.   PC
Lecture, London University Extra-Mural
Studies, 11 November, 1954.

5198 BURLEIGH, L. G. Some thoughts of a user
of transport. 1955. pp. 15. *Reproduced
typescript*.   IT
Paper, L.S.E. Railway Students' Association,
16 February, 1955.
Choice of means of transport depends upon
relative cost and efficiency.

5199 KELLY, W. L. Coal transport. 1956. pp. 11.
Typescript.   IT
Paper, Institute of Transport, South Wales &

Monmouthshire Section, 20 December, 1956.
The magnitude and complexities of present-
day coal transport, and the responsibilities of
the National Coal Board.

5200 SHAW, S. R. A study of the transport
facilities of the Nottinghamshire-Derbyshire
b coalfield. Thesis, M.A. (Geog.) University of
ct London. 1956. pp. 128, [39,] with 40 tables,
93 illus., maps, & a bibliography. *Typescript*.
                                           UL
Coal transport.

5201 BURLEIGH, L. G. 'Are the railways
finished?' asks a user. 1957. pp. 11. *Reproduced typescript*.   IT
Paper, Institute of Transport, Irish Section,
2 April, 1957.
Current trends in the development of transport, and a re-assessment of the part to be
played by railways.

5202 KELLY, W. L. Coal and transport. 1957.
ct pp. 8[9]. *Reproduced typescript*.   IT
Paper, L.S.E. Railway Students' Association,
18 December, 1957.

5203 ASSOCIATION OF BRITISH CHAMBERS OF
COMMERCE. Users' review of British Railways merchandise charges scheme. [*London*, 1958.] pp. [2.] *Reproduced typescript*. IT
Summary of replies to six questions sent to
700 firms.

5204 INTERNATIONAL CHAMBER OF COM-
MERCE. General transport policy in Europe
and the Treaty establishing the European
Economic Community: views of transport
users. *Paris*, [1958.] pp. 21[23]. [*Brochure
no. 194.*]   IT
Includes, at end, Title IV of the Treaty,
'Transport'.

5205 WILSON, R. Technical modernization and
new freight charges on British Railways.
[*London:*] *British Institute of Management*,
1958. pp. 25.   IT
Lecture at the B.I.M. National Conference,
1958, Section meeting F2.

5206 HONDELINK, E. R. Railway transport of
coal: constructive proposals for the more
ct economic handling of coal and other whole
load railway traffic without recourse to
excessive reliance upon concentration depots
and extensive uneconomic distribution by
road. *Northwood: Great Central Association*,
[1963.] pp. 2. *Reproduced typescript*.   BM

K5 RAILWAYS AND THE MONEY MARKET

Investment—The effects of over-speculation—The 'Railway Manias'

For railway finance generally see F

Marginal symbols: **b** bibliographies
c chronologies
gc government control

Historical

5207 [BRITISH railway finance, 1850–1914.] *In* 'Jubilee of the Railway News, 1864–1914.'
c *London: Railway News*, [1914.] pp. 29–39. BM
Articles and detailed tables.

5208 FIFTY years of British railway dividends. *In* 'Jubilee of the Railway News, 1864–1914.'
c *London: Railways News*, [1914.] pp. 29–31.
Tables. BM

5209 STEVENS, W. J. Who built our railways? Some interesting facts about railway development. *London: Great Western Railway*, 1925. pp. 11. LSE
In praise of shareholders.

5210 HYNDMAN, H. M. Commercial crises of the nineteenth century. *London*, 1892. pp. 174.
BM
pp. 54–62, 'The crisis of 1847'.

—— reprinted, 1902 & 1908. BM
—— 2nd edn. *London*, 1932. pp. 174. BM

5211 LAMBERT, R. S. The Railway King, 1800–1871: a study of George Hudson and the
b business morals of his times . . . *London: Allen & Unwin*, 1934. pp. 320, with illus. & a bibliography. BM

5212 EVANS, G. H. British corporation finance, 1775–1850. *Baltimore*, 1936. pp. 208, with tables & bibliogr. notes. BM
Includes railway investment and the history of the development of preference shares.

5213 LEWIN, H. G. The Railway Mania and its aftermath, 1845–1852: being a sequel to 'Early British railways'. *London: Railway Gazette*, 1936. pp. xx, 500, with 13 maps (5 fold.) & 15 tables. BM
Some alleged mis-statements are noted by M. D. Greville in *Journal of the Railway & Canal Historical Society*, vol. 2, no. 1, Jan. 1956 and in vol. 3, no. 3, May 1957.

5214 CRUIKSHANK, R. J. Charles Dickens and Early Victorian England . . . *London: Isaac Pitman*, 1949. pp. xii, 308, with 64 illus. BM
pp. 101–6, George Hudson.

5215 POPE-HENNESSY, J. Monckton Miles: the years of promise, 1809–1851. *London: Constable*, 1949. BM
pp. 198–201, 'Railway Boom'.

5216 POLLINS, H. The marketing of railway shares in the first half of the nineteenth century. [1953.] pp. 15, with 77 bibliogr. notes. *Typescript.* BR
Published in revised form in *Economic History Review*, vol. 7, no. 2, Dec. 1954.

5217 MARTIN, R. B. The impostume of much wealth: George Hudson and the Railway
b Mania. *In his* 'Enter rumour: four early Victorian scandals.' *London: Faber & Faber*, 1962. pp. 187–241, with port., plate, & a bibliography. BM

Contemporaneous

5218 CORT, R. Rail-road impositions detected; or, Facts & arguments to prove that the Manchester & Liverpool Railway has not paid one per cent nett profit; and that the Birmingham, Bristol, Southampton, Windsor, and other railways are, and must for ever be, only bubble speculations. (part 1.) *London*, 1834. pp. 64[72], with 3 fold. tables & notes. LSE
—— 2nd edn. (part 2.) *London*, 1834. pp. 195.
BM
Other contemporary railways analysed. A general and detailed criticism of railways.
—— German edn., 'Der Aufgedeckte Eisenbahnbetrug.' 1834.

5219 CORT, R. Rail-road impositions detected; or, Facts and arguments, being an exposé of the estimates for the Grand Northern Railway, submitted to public meetings at Norwich, Bury, Cambridge, etc. with disclosures and suggestions important to the canal interests of Great Britain. (part 3.) *London*, 1834. pp. 40. BM
At end of UL(GL) copy is a table: 'Proofs that the two best railways in the world are, and must for ever be, bubble speculations.' (The Liverpool & Manchester and the London & Birmingham.)

5220 CORT, R. The Anti-Railroad Journal; or, Rail-road impositions detected; contains an answer to the Edinburgh Review and

Mechanics Magazine, etc. (part 4.) *London*, 1835. pp. xii, 122[123].   BM

This is the fourth work of Richard Cort in his campaign against the conduct of railway promoters. The first three were entitled *Railroad impositions detected*, and in these the Liverpool & Manchester and the proposed Grand Northern are singled out as main objectives. Each work is in fact a detailed exposition of the financial roguery of, it would seem, all railway companies.

In the present work, Cort, writing now as Secretary of the 'Anti-Railroad Committee', re-emphasises his facts and repeats his testimonies and includes the text of a 'General Anti-Railroad Petition'. Included are indexes to all four works, and to a fifth, apparently never published.

In 1849, Cort's *Railway reform* appeared. This is again mainly concerned with the Liverpool & Manchester.

5221 HINTS to railway directors and shareholders on the subject of unpaid calls. *London*, 1837. pp. 12.   H

5222 A FEW general observations on the principal railways executed, in progress, and projected, in the midland counties & north of England, with the author's opinion upon them as investments . . . *London*, 1838. pp. xvi, 64, with maps.   BM

5223 GILBERT, J. Gilbert's Alphabetical List of Shareholders in Railways of two thousand pounds and upwards. *London: James Gilbert*, [c. 1840?]   PC

5224 LARDNER, D. The steam engine familiarly explained and illustrated; with plain maxims for railway speculation. 5th edn. *London*, 1836. pp. 357–69.   BM
—— 7th edn. *London*, [1840.]   BM

5225 WRIGHT, G. S. A letter to British capitalists upon the present and prospective advantages of investing capital in railway stock, with comparative details of the last and present year's receipts upon the Birmingham, Great Western, South Western, Blackwall, Brighton, Northern & Eastern, and Eastern Counties lines. *London*, 1842. pp. 12.   BM

5226 LIABILITIES of subscribers & shareholders in joint-stock and railway companies. [*Dublin*, 1844.] pp. 39.   RIA(H)
No title-page in RIA(H) copy.

5227 BRACE, G. 1845 national delirium; or, Hints on law and rail. *London*, 1845. pp. 15.   BM
The rage for speculation.

5228 HUTCHINSON, G. Observations intended to point out the only effectual means of
gc arresting the existing railway panic, and of preventing future gambling in projected railways. *Glasgow*, 1845. pp. 16.   RIA(H)
For government control of Bills.

5229 MULOCK, T. Railway revelations: being letters on the subject of the proposed Direct London & Manchester Railways. *London*, 1845. pp. 46.   ICE
The Railway Mania and the social evils resulting from uncontrolled enterprise. T. Mulock was Secretary to the proposed D.L. & M.
pp. 38–46, Supplement. 'Irish Railways.' A system of railways wanted for Ireland, not a series of 'schemes'.

5230 RAILTON, J. & SON. Circular to our friends. *Manchester*, August 30th, 1845. s.sh.
BM(MSS)
—— [Second Circular.] *Manchester*, September 6th, 1845. s.sh.   BM(MSS)
Bankers' warning against the dangers of speculation in railway shares.

5231 The RAILWAY Investment Guide. How to make money in railway shares: being a series of hints and advice to parties speculating in the shares of British, colonial and foreign railways. By One of the Initiated. *London*, [1845.] pp. 23.   BM
—— 2nd edn. 'By One of the Initiated behind the Scenes.' *London*, [1845.] pp. 23.
BM

5232 RUMINATIONS on railways: no. 1, Railway speculation. *London: John Weale*, 1845. pp. 15.   BM

5233 SPACKMAN, W. F. An analysis of the railway interest of the United Kingdom, embracing all companies registered to the 31st day of October 1845, shewing the defects of the present system of railway management, and the necessity for amendments in the law of provisional registration. *London*, 1845. pp. 54.   BM
Includes (pp. [21]–43) financial tables of 1428 railway projects—47 completed, 118 in course of construction, and 1263 schemes for new lines. Comments favourably on George Hudson's plans—'. . . a more honourable man does not exist . . . His word is a guarantee for everything that is good.'

5234 TERRELL, T. H. A treatise on the liabilities of a subscriber to a railway company incurred by signing the parliamentary contract. *London*, 1845. pp. 66.   BM

5235 TRUISMS. 'Fighting with the corn laws, lads . . .' *Bishopwearmouth: G. Garbett*, [1845.] s.sh.   BM
Seven verses in support of George Hudson, candidate for Sunderland in the Parliamentary Election of 1845.

5236 WILSON, H. Hints to rail-road speculators, together with the influence railroads will have upon society, in promoting agriculture, commerce and manufacturers. *London*, 1845. pp. 12.   BM

5237 À BECKETT, T. T. Railway litigation and how to check it; with remarks on the pro-

posed Railway Relief Bill, and suggestions for regulating the future conduct of railway enterprise. *London*, 1846. pp. 33.   BM
　Victimisation of investors by railway promoters.

5238 CLARK, G. D. Provisional railway code, with instructions to scripholders: being a summary of the legislative measures of this Session to protect scripholders, and facilitate the dissolution of railway companies. Compiled and arranged from Parliamentary Reports and official documents. *London*, 1846. pp. 24.   BM
　With a statement of the aims of the Railway Scripholders' Protection Society.

5239 CLARKE, H. Theory of investment in railway companies. *London*, 1846. pp. 37.   ICE

5240 COCHRANE, G. The way to make railroad shares popular. *London*, 1846. pp. 15.   BM
　Large number of small shares, with liabilities for debt laid upon a central committee.

5241 HARVEY, D. W. An address upon the law and liabilities of railway speculation, with hints for legislative interference. *London*, 1846. pp. 32.   BM
　D. W. Harvey writes as President of the Railway Mutual Protection Society.

5242 PEARSON, W. W. Suggestions for improved railway legislation at the present crisis in
gc Great Britain and Ireland; in a letter to the Committee of the House of Commons. *London*, 1846. pp. 8.   UL(GL)
　Measures to restore confidence to commercial interests and to afford relief to Ireland by railway promotion there, assisted by government finance.

5243 RAILWAY directors and investments. *Manchester*, 1846. pp. 23.   PO
　'The great injury done to railway property by the ignorance, incompetence and cupidity of railway directors.'

5244 RAILWAY MUTUAL PROTECTION SOCIETY. Rules and regulations. *London*, [1846.] pp. [4.]   H

5245 ROWCROFT, C. Currency and railways; being suggestions for the remedy of the pre-
gc sent railway embarrassments. *London*, 1846. pp. 24.   BM
　Suggests a special railway 'Exchequer bill' currency.

5246 SHAW, G. J. The law relating to allottees of shares in railway companies, containing a complete review of all the decisions which bear upon the subject, and an examination of the case of Woolmer v. Toby. *London*, 1846. pp. 12.   H

5247 SYMONS, J. C. Railway liabilities as they affect subscribers, committees, allottees and scripholders *inter se*, and third parties. *London*, 1846. pp. 79.   BM

5248 TEN minutes' advice to speculators in railway shares. By An Observer, a resident of Manchester. *London*, [1846.] pp. 14.   BM
　A warning 'to show, and prove, and expose the fallacy and folly, of the present rage for railway schemes'.

5249 AYTOUN, J. The railways and the currency as connected with the present monetary crisis. *Edinburgh*, 1847. pp. 36.   BM
　Five letters previously published in newspapers.

5250 COX, E. W. Railway liabilities: the liabilities of provisional committees as determined by the Court of Exchequer in the case of Reynell v. Lewis. *London*, 1847. pp. 54. BM

5251 SHORT and Sure Guide to Railway Speculation: a few plain rules how to speculate with safety and profit in railway shares. By a Successful Operator. *London*, 1845. pp. 8.   LSE
—— 6th edn. *London*, 1845. pp. 15.   LSE
—— 7th, *London*, 1845. pp. 15.   BM
—— 8th. 'A Short and Sure Guide to Permanent Investment in Railways.' *London*, 1846. pp. 28.   BM
—— 9th [title as 8th]. *London*, 1847. pp. 24.   BM

5252 WARD, J. Railways for the many and not for the few; or, how to make them profitable to all. *London*, 1846. pp. 34.   BM
　Proposes small shares.
—— 2nd edn. *London*, 1847. pp. xi, 57. BM

5253 The NATIONAL distress, its financial origin and remedy; with the proposal of a common principle of union amongst the promoters of an equitable adjustment of the currency and a vindication of the railways. *London*, 1848. pp. 260, 8.   H

5254 PHIPPS, E. The adventure of a £1000 note; or, Railway ruin reviewed. *London*, 1848. pp. 32.   BM
　The nature and effects of investment explained in an imaginary 'narrative' of a banknote.

5255 The SCOTTISH Railways and Shareho'ders' Companion. By an Accountant. *Perth & London*, 1848. pp. 90, with fold. map.   H

5256 SMITH, A. The Bubble of the Age; or, The fallacies of railway investments, railway accounts and railway dividends. *London*, 1848. pp. 56.   LSE
　An analysis of the finances of all main line companies.
—— 2nd edn. *London*, 1848. pp. 63, with fold. tables.   BR
—— 3rd edn. *London*, 1848. pp. 83.   BM
　pp. 65–83, 'An appendix to the second edition of *The Bubble of the Age* . . . no. 1, The London & North Western Co.'

5257 SUGGESTIONS for the relief of the railway
gc interest. *Gloucester*, 1848. pp. 14.   BM
　Remedy—to convert a portion of capital into 'government railway stock'.

5258 TUCK, H. The Railway Shareholder's Manual; or, Practical guide to the railways of Great Britain, completed, in progress, and projected, forming an entire railway synopsis, indispensable to all interested in railway locomotion. *London*, 1845. pp. 112.
                                                                    BM
—— 2nd edn., *London*, 1845. pp. 112.   H
—— 3rd, *London*, 1845. pp. 117.   H
—— 4th, *London*, 1845. pp. 140.   H
—— 5th, *London*, 1845. pp. 147[154].   H
—— 6th, *London*, 1845. pp. 244[249].   H
—— 7th, *London*, 1846. pp. 297.   H
—— 8th, *London*, 1847. pp. 412.   BR
—— 9th, *London*, 1848. pp. 491.   BR
There are variants in some editions.

5259 WOODHOUSE, T. Railway property as it is and railway property as it should be; or, an examination into the causes of its depression, and the means necessary to retrieve it. *London*, 1848. pp. 16.   ICE
—— 2nd edn. *London*, 1848. pp. 16.   BM

5260 CORT, R. Railway reform; in a letter to William Chaplin Esq., M.P., Chairman of the L. & S. W. Rly. Co., showing that the Liverpool & Manchester Rly. Co. has not paid a single dividend except out of borrowed money, and that all other railways are, & must be, in the same predicament; with an appendix containing the published accounts of the L. & M. Rly. Co. . . . *London*, 1849. pp. 109.   BM

5261 EVANS, D. M. The commercial crisis, 1847–48: being facts and figures illustrative of the events of that important period considered in relation to the three epochs of the Railway Mania, the Food and Money Panic, and the French Revolution . . . *London*, 1848. pp. viii, 151, lxxx.   BM
pp. 1–52, The Railway Mania.
—— 2nd edn. *London*, 1849. pp. xi, 155, ci.   BM

5262 HARVEY, T. S. What shall I do with my money?; or, Thoughts about safe investments. (2nd edn.) *London*, 1849. pp. 31. BM
pp. 8–16, 'Railways'.

5263 MARTIN, R. M. Railways, past, present and prospective. *London*, 1849. pp. 82.   BM
—— 2nd edn. *London*, 1849. pp. 82.   BM
Finance of railways; addressed to investors. Statistics.

5264 [NASH, C.] Railways and shareholders; with glances at railway transactions, shareholder's powers, accounts and audits, railway meetings, defective legislation, etc., etc. By an Edinboro' Reviewer. 2nd edn. *London*, 1849. pp. 20.   BM
A vigorous appeal for parliamentary investigation into alleged widespread corruption in railway management.

5265 CROWQUILL, A. How he reigned and how he mizzled: a railway raillery. *London*, 1849. pp. 8.   BM
Twenty-six satirical drawings on George

Hudson. Inserted in the BM copy is a holograph letter from G. Hudson—
'Sir, I have no recollection of such a person as you name ever being in my service. London, Feb. 12, 1852'.

5266 HUDSON, G. Report of the evidence of G. Hudson, Esq., M.P. on the trial of the cause of Richardson versus Wodson, York Summer Assizes, 1850. Edited by a barrister. *London*, [1850.] pp. 44[45].   BM
A collection of press reports of the trial with notes 'to do justice to a deeply injured individual' [Hudson]. A verbatim record of questions and answers.

5267 RICHARDSON, J. A revised and complete report of the recent trial for libel, Richardson v. Wodson; with preliminary observations on the Railway Mania of 1845-6-7-8; also a biographical sketch of Mr. George Hudson, M.P. for Sunderland, together with an appendix setting forth in detail the whole system of railway mismanagement and railway frauds pursued since the establishment of railways in the City of York. *London*, [1850.] pp. xvi, 27.   BM

5268 SMITH, A. The railway returns made to the special orders of the House of Lords, 1849–1850, prefaced with the results of previous returns, with a view to the complete comprehension of the nature of railway investment and the restoration of confidence by the adoption of a sound policy and management. *London*, 1850. pp. ii, [48.]   BM
To encourage investment rather than speculation. Mainly L. & N.W. and L. & S.W.

5269 WHITEHEAD, J. Railway and government guarantee: which is preferable? . . . Second
gc edition with additions . . . *London*, 1847. pp. 55.   BM
—— 4th edn. *London*, 1847. pp. 55.   LSE
—— 6th, *London*, 1849. pp. 50[56].   BM
—— 7th, *London*, 1850. pp. 54.   BR

5270 SCRIVENOR, H. The railways of the United Kingdom statistically considered in relation to their extent, amalgamations, debentures, financial position . . . concisely arranged from solely authentic documents; together with the railway accounts, rendered upon a uniform plan. *London*, 1849. pp. xii, 733, 106, with tables.   BM
A reference work for investors.
—— 'Supplemental part.' *London*, 1851. pp. viii, 159.   BM

5271 SLAUGHTER, M. Railway Traffic Tables, 1849, 1850, 1851 & 1852, intended as a ready means of comparing the gross traffic receipts of sixteen principal lines in 1849 and 1850 with those current and to come. Compiled from official sources. *London*, 1851. pp. 63.   BM
A reference work for investors, arranged under railways.

5272 SMILES, S. Railway property, its condition and prospects. *London*, [1849]. pp. 64, with bibliogr. notes.   BM
—— 2nd edn. *London*, [1851.] pp. 64.   BM

5273 VATES. Vates' railway prospects for 1851 investigated. *London*, [1851.] pp. 8.   BM
Criticisms.

5274 ALCOCK, T. Observations upon railway management. *Dover: W. Batchelor*, 1852. pp. 39.   NLC
Privately issued. The L. & N.W. Rly. and George Hudson.

5275 PARKE, G. A letter on railway dividends, with important suggestions on debentures. *Whitby*, 1853. pp. 20.   LSE

5276 RAILWAY Equation Table, shewing the relative value of the several railway stocks to each other according to the dividends they pay. *London: Effingham Wilson*, [1853.] s.sh.   BM

5277 HILL, C. Railway loans: a few words to the Chancellor of the Exchequer on this subject as a point of finance. *London*, 1854. pp. 15.   BM
'Preposterous to allow companies, with all money expended, to come annually into the market and borrow a sum exceeding all the Exchequer bills the Government has in circulation.'

5278 The RAILWAY Meeting: a satire dedicated to the pillaged and plundered shareholders of Great Britain. By a Lancashire Victim. *London*, 1856. pp. vi, 137.   BM
Verses (from p. 53 to end, not confined to railways).

5279 LISTER, J. Suggestions for the improvement of railway property; in a letter to . . . the Chancellor of the Exchequer. *Edinburgh*, 1858. pp. 16.   BM

5280 The TRUE remedy for the distress of the railway interest. 1858. pp. 13.
An anonymous pamphlet addressed to Col. J. W. Patten and signed 'A Railway Shareholder'.

5281 WRIGLEY, T. Railway management—the official view refuted; being a reply to
gc objections urged against a plan for the government and working of a railway. *London*, 1858. pp. 44.   BM
On the misapplication of capital to revenue expenses. More control by shareholders urged.

5282 RAILWAY management; or, How to make ten per cent. *London*, 1860. pp. 24.   BM
Reforms in railway economy. The BM has two copies, one of which (C.T. 310(2)) is considerably altered in ink.

5283 N., M. No more interest to pay upon debenture debts and greatly improved

dividends from British railways. 2nd edn. [*London*,] 1861. pp. 7.   BM
Amalgamation for better economy among London termini railways.

5284 COLES, J. A few remarks on railway debentures. *London*, 1866. pp. 19, with tables.   BM
—— 2nd edn. *London*, 1866. pp. 19.   BM

5285 ELPHINSTONE, H. W. On the borrowing powers of railway companies. 1866. pp. 16.
gc   LSE
'Printed for private circulation.'
Asks for legal reform for the protection of debenture holders.

5286 The PROFITS of panics, showing how financial storms arise, who make money by them, who are the losers, and other revelations of a city man. By the author of 'The Bubbles of Finance'. *London*, 1866. pp. 108.   BM
pp. 45–67, Railway construction.

5287 CHILD, J. G. T. Railway debentures secured by a scheme for the establishment of a railway debenture insurance association; in a letter to Sir Daniel Gooch. *Manchester*, 1867. pp. 12.   BRE

5288 [KEPPEL, W. C.] Facts for the times!: no. 2, Railway finance; reprinted from 'The Pall
gc Mall Gazette'. By 'B.' *London*, 1867. pp. 32.   BM
By Lord Bury, 7th Earl of Albemarle [William Coutts Keppel].
The nature and extent of legislation required to restore confidence to railway shareholders and soundness to railway finance.

5289 RAILWAY debentures and how to deal
gc with them. *London*, 1867. pp. 14.   BM
Proposes an issue of government stock in exchange for debenture stock.

5290 BAXTER, R. D. Private Bill legislation and
gc competition. *London*, 1868. pp. 15.   NLC
Mostly on railway Bills. Warns against reform which would destroy confidence in investments, 'now a well-established edifice of our national wealth'.

5291 LAING, J. The railway dilemma; respectfully addressed to railway proprietors. *London*, 1868. pp. 28.   BM
Reprinted, with some additions, from the author's *Theory of business* (1867; 2nd, 1868). Analyses causes of depreciation of railway investments, and suggests remedies.

5292 RAILWAY SHAREHOLDERS ASSOCIATION. Report of the proceedings at the National Conference of Railway Shareholders held at Town Hall, Manchester . . . April 14th & 15th, 1868. *Manchester*, [1868.] pp. 69.   BM
Financial reforms.

5293 WRIGLEY, T. Railway reform: a plan for the effectual separation of capital from revenue. *Bury*, [1868.] pp. 23.   BM
A re-statement of his *Railway management* (1858).
—— another edn. *London*, 1868. pp. 23. BM

5294 REYNOLDS, J. J. A Commercial Pamphlet . . . *London*, [1869.] pp. 68.   BM
Advice to investors, including (pp. 32–41) 'Railways'. Historical summaries of rates of dividend for Caledonian; Bristol & Exeter; G.W.; G.N.; L. & Y.; L. & N.W.; Midland; N.B.; and N.E. railways.

5295 RAILWAY prospects in 1870: being remarks on the present and prospective values as investments of the principal railways stocks most largely dealt in on the British stock exchanges . . . *London*, [1870.] pp. 26. BRE
Reprinted from *Railway News*, Jan 1, 1870.

5296 CARTER, S. Railway legislation: a letter to shareholders and holders of debentures and debenture stock in railways on certain threatened legislation. [*Westminster*, 1874.] pp. 8.   BM
Against a proposal to permit the Railway Commissioners to interfere in the fixing of rates for through traffic.

5297 SCHULTZ, C. W. H. The forthcoming British railway dividends. *London*, 1875. pp. 15.   BM
Advice to would-be investors as to which railways are the most progressive and profitable, with short statements on the financial state of each railway.

5298 CARTER, S. Railway debentures and the Railway Commissioners . . . *Westminster*, 1877. pp. 18.   BM

5299 PHILLIPS, E. The railway autocracy: a question of vital importance to shareholders and directors hitherto overlooked; prefaced by a communication from M. T. Bass, M.P. *London*, 1877. pp. 21.   BM
'. . . the helplessness of railway shareholders controlling the election of directors and their policies.'

5300 RAILWAY SHAREHOLDERS ASSOCIATION. Circular letter to the proprietors of the London & South Western, Great Western, Great Northern, Great Eastern, and other railways. *London*, [1882.] pp. [4.] ICE

5301 WATHERSTON, E. J. Our railways: rates and fares: a plea for unity of administration. *Edinburgh*, 1833. pp. 19.   BM
With three tables showing rates per cent of dividends paid, 1880–1882. Low dividends, but high fares and rates.

5302 DUNSFORD. Dunsford's glance prices and dividends of the principal railways for 15 years . . . the lowest and highest prices; also the dividends for every year during that period. *London*, 1890. pp. 28.   BM

5303 MATHIESON, F. C. & SON. Dividends paid, and highest and lowest prices, 1875–90, of British railways. *London*, 1891. s.sh.   BM

5304 COUCHMAN, E. & CO. Transfer arrangements of the chief railways of the United Kingdom, including an accurate description of the stocks, amounts transferable, charges, etc., etc. *London*, 1893. pp. 29.   BM
—— 2nd edn. *London*, 1893. pp. 29.   BM

5305 BOLAS, T. Confiscation of all railway property as a leading step in solving the labour problem; also as a preliminary to the punishment of shareholders . . . *London*, 1895. pp. 8.   BM
Railways and Socialism.

5306 STEVENS, W. J. Home railways as investments. *London*, 1896. pp. vii, 204, with 11 tables.   BM
Each railway's financial state examined.
—— 2nd edn. *London*, 1897. pp. xi, 237, with 13 tables.   BM

5307 HAGGARD, F. T. Our railways. [*Tunbridge Wells*, 1900.] pp. 10.   BR
Railways conducted more to the interests of the travelling public than is fair to shareholders.

5308 STEVENS, W. J. Investment and speculation in British railways. *London*, 1902. pp. vi, 262, with 13 tables.   BM
The financial position of individual railways. (See footnote to the entry for his *British railway outlook*, 1906.)

5309 WALL, W. W. British railway finance: a guide to investors. *London*, 1902. pp. xii, 410.   BM
An analysis of the financial state of each of the main-line railways.
—— 2nd edn. 'How to invest in railways.' *London*, 1903. pp. xii, 410.   BM

5310 STEVENS, W. J. The British railway outlook. *London*, 1906. pp. 64.   BM
'The present and prospective advantages to shareholders arising from reforms in railway management and finance.' Written to explain the changed circumstances which the author believes have come about since the publication of his previous pamphlet, *Investment, and speculation in British railways*, in 1902, when he described the outlook as 'dark and uncertain'.
—— another edn. *London*, 1906. pp. 64. BM

5311 LAWSON, W. R. For and against home railways. *London*, [1911.] pp. 18. [*Popular Financial Booklets*, no. 63.]   LSE
Reprint, *Financial Review of Reviews*, March 1911.
A guide to investors.

5312 ANTI-SOCIALIST UNION OF GREAT BRITAIN. Nationalisation of railways: . . . Report of the Special Railway Committee of the Anti-Socialist Union of Great Britain appointed to protect the interests of railway shareholders. *Westminster*, [February 1913.] pp. [4.]   BM

5313 MATHIESON, F. C. & SONS. Investors' Handbook of Railway Statistics, 1877–1893(–1878–1900) [continued as] Twenty years' railway statistics, 1892 (–1914.) *London*, 1893–1914.   BM
Various editions.

—— German edn. 'Amerikanische u. englische Bahnen, 1894 bis 1914. *Berlin*, 1914. pp. 247.   BM

5314 The STOCK EXCHANGE home railway market. *In* 'Jubilee of the Railway News, 1864–1914.' *London: Railway News*, [1914.] pp. 129–30.   BM

5315 SCOTTISH RAILWAY STOCKHOLDERS PROTECTION ASSOCIATION. Your railway dividends in danger: why? [*Glasgow*, 1918.] pp. [12.]   RC
gc
The possible imminent purchase of railways by the State.

5316 MARSHALL, A. Industry and trade: a study of industrial technique and business organisation and of their influences on the conditions of various classes and nations. *London*, 1919. pp. xxiv, 875.   BM
pp. 423–506, Competition and monopoly in transport. (Railways, pp. 445–506.)

—— 2nd edn. *London*, 1919. pp. xxiv, 874.
                                                        BM

5317 CENTRAL COUNCIL OF ENGLISH, SCOTTISH AND IRISH RAILWAY STOCKHOLDERS PROTECTION ASSOCIATIONS. Danger ahead!: a statement of the railway stockholders' case. *London*, [March 1921.] pp. 63.
                                                        BM
De-control and the question of just compensation to stockholders in view of arrears of maintenance and replacements. Settlement needed before the termination of Government control (August 15th).

5318 BETTS, F. C. Railways and railway securities: a study of all the railway companies whose securities are quoted on the Stock Exchange, London; with details concerning capital and resources. *London*, 1922. pp. 446.   BM
pp. 7–84, 'Home railways'. Summarises the history, routes, rolling stock and finance of British railway companies.

5319 FINANCIAL TIMES. Special Railway Supplement, 1st January 1923. pp. 36.   RC
Articles on the current railway financial situation.

5320 MATHIESON, F. C. & SONS. The new railway groups: amounts available for dividends according to the 1922 earnings of the amalgamated companies compared with 1913 earnings. *London*, [1923.] pp. [7.]   BM

5321 MATHIESON, F. C. & SONS. Railway amalgamations (& absorptions) up to date. *London*, 1922–23. 7 parts.   BM
A guide to investors, with tables of constituent and subsidiary companies amalgamated under the Railways Act (1921).

5322 MATHIESON, F. C. & SONS. Railway stocks officially quoted on the Stock Exchange on the last day of 1922; with prices, yields, highest and lowest for two years, dividends, etc. *London*, 2 January, 1923. pp. [4.]   BM

5323 RAILWAY stock changes under the Railways Act, 1921. *London: Effingham Wilson*, 1923. pp. 29.   BM
A guide for investors. 'If I hold £100 of any home railway stock, what do I receive in exchange?' Tables of amalgamations and absorptions.

5324 SOMMERFIELD, V. The Railway Grouping Scheme: a handbook for stockholders and investors. *London: Financial News*, [1923.] pp. 36.   BM
Tables showing constituent and subsidiary companies with their joint undertakings and principal officers.

5325 SPENS, N. The capital expenditure of British railways: its conditions and its critics: being a paper read before the Scottish Society of Economists on 8 February, 1927. *London*, 1927. pp. 24.   BM
The rights of shareholders under the Railways Act (1921).

5326 PARKER, J. W. Traders' rail charges up to date: a concise and practical guide to the new system, written from the trader's point of view. *London*, 1928. pp. vii, 128.   LSE

5327 BRITISH railway securities, 1928. *Cardiff: Business Statistics Co.*, [1928.] pp. [31.] BM
Financial tables, 1923–7.
—— British railway securities, 1929. *Cardiff*, [1929.] pp. [35.]   BM

5328 COLLIN, T. W. Railway finance in the light of the Railways Act, 1921. pp. 16, with an errata slip.   IT
Reprint, *The Accountant*, Jan. 1932.

5329 DAILY EXPRESS—FINANCIAL INFORMATION BUREAU. British railway stocks and the investor. *London*, [1932.] pp. 33. [*Daily Express Aids to Investors*.]   BM
An outline of the financial state of British railways with a review of economic factors which have caused a decline; the present position and future prospects. With financial tables of the main-line companies for 1929, 1930 and 1931.

5330 B., J. H. Apathy or action? *London: British Railway Stockholders Union*, [1934.] pp. 15.   ICE
Calling upon stockholders to protect and promote their interests by joining the Union.

5331 WILLIAMS, S. C. S. *and* SHORT, E. Railways, roads and the public. *London: Eyre & Spottiswoode*, 1939. pp. 157.   BM
pp. 119–52, 'Railway stockholding'.

5332 GLOVER, K. F. The recent course of gross investment in inland transport in Great

Britain and the influence of government action upon it. pp. 152, with 47 statistical tables.   UL
Thesis, M.Sc.Econ., Univ. Lond., 1949.

5333 WILSON, H. The financial problem of British transport. [*London*, 1951.] pp. 43. *Reproduced typescript.*   TUC
Compensation to stockholders upon nation-

alisation; financial results of transport in general since 1948; conclusions and recommendations.
Appendix contains a schedule of valuations on stock of pre-1948 railway companies; a summary of the Debate on the Financial Provisions of the Transport Bill, March–May 1947; the principal provisions in the Transport Act (1947) relating to compensation; and a summary of the main increases in transport costs, 1948–51.

K 6 GOVERNMENT CONTROL AND INSPECTION

Parliament and the Railways—Legislation—Select Committees—
Procedure—Standing Orders—Railway Department of the Board
of   Trade — Railway   Commission — Railway   Inspectorate —
Ministry of Transport

Marginal symbols: **b** bibliographies
c chronologies

Historical

5334 MORRISON, J. The influence of English railway legislation on trade and industry; with an appendix of tracts and documents. *London*, 1848. pp. 187.   BM
Includes a history of railway legislation.

5335 COHN, G. Untersuchungen über die englische Eisenbahnpolitik. *Leipzig*, 1874–75. 2 vols. pp. xiii, 3   ; xii, 646.   BM
Bd. 1, Die Entwickelung der Eisenbahngesetzgebung in England.
Bd. 2, Zur Beurteilung der englischen Eisenbahnpolitik.
A very detailed work. This author's *Die englische Eisenbahnpolitik der letzten zehn Jahre, 1873–1883* (1883) incorporates a revision of part of this work and has an index for all three volumes.

5336 GRAHAME, J. Mr. Mundella's Bill for the better regulation of railway and canal traffic: a digest of the opinion of Parliament on the powers and management of railways and canals as expressed by Select Committees and Royal Commissions between 1839 and 1886; with map of lines excepted from state interference by the Act of 1844. *Glasgow*, 1886. pp. 30.   ICE
'Written as a general collection of parliamentary thought in regard to railways.' A. J. Mundella's Bill was withdrawn.

5337 CLIFFORD, F. History of Private Bill legislation. *London*, 1885–87. 2 vols.   BM
vol. 1, pp. 43–193, Railways; tramways.

5338 IVATTS, E. B. Origin of the train staff. [*Dublin*, 1888.] pp. 10.   ICE
Reprint, *Railway Herald*, 15 & 22 Dec., 1887.
History of its use, and an historical account of government inspection of new lines.

5339 PORTER, W. History of the Corps of Royal Engineers. *London*, 1889. 3 vols.   BM
vol. 2, pp. 326–40, Civil railway and telegraph work. The Corps and the Board of Trade. pp. 282–5, Biography of Capt. Sir Douglas S. Galton.

5340 UNITED STATES OF AMERICA—LIBRARY OF CONGRESS. Select List of Books on
b railroads in foreign countries: government regulation, etc. *Washington*, 1905. pp. 72. BM
pp. 16–29, Great Britain.

5341 POTTER, F. The Government in relation to the railways of the country. *London*, 1909. pp. 40.   LSE
Paper, G.W. Rly. (London) Lecture & Debating Society, 11 Feb., 1909.
A concise historical review of Acts, Select Committees, Commissions, and other instances whereby Government has exercised its influence upon railways. The text is arranged under subjects.

5342 EYRE & SPOTTISWOODE, LTD. Acts of Parliament, reports of Commissions, and periodical returns relating to railways. *In* 'Jubilee of the Railway News, 1864–1914.' *London: Railway News*, [1914.] pp. 221–3. BM
Arranged under classified headings.

5343 MACASSEY, L. A century of railway Private Bill legislation. *In* 'Jubilee of the Railway News, 1864–1914.' *London: Railway News*, [1914.] pp. 99–112.   BM

5344 POTTER, F. Railways and the Legislature. *In* 'Jubilee of the Railway News, 1864–1914.' *London: Railway News*, [1914.] pp. 39–42.
                                            BM

5345 ACWORTH, W. M. Historical sketch of government ownership of railroads in foreign countries. Presented to the Joint Committee of Congress on Interstate Commerce, May 1917. *Washington*, 1917. pp. 63. LSE.

Includes consideration of measures of government control over railways in U.K. and of progress and inventiveness being the fruits of free enterprise.

5346 USHER, A. P. An introduction to the industrial history of England. *London*, 1921. pp. xxii, 529, xxxiv. BM

pp. 439–74, The Government and the railways.

5347 SHERRINGTON, C. E. R. The economics of rail transport in Great Britain. *London*, 1928. 2 vols. BM

vol. 1, pp. 223–66, 'Growth of government regulation'.

5348 SMITH, H. L. The Board of Trade. *London & New York*, 1928. pp. 288. BM

pp. 124–46, 'The Board of Trade and railways'.

5349 SHERRINGTON, C. E. R. Government interference with the free play of economic forces. *Fitchburg, Mass.*, [1930.] pp. 47. PC

The history and present position on the railways of Great Britain. Prize-winning essay in the ninth Alva T. Simonds Economic Contest, 1930.

5350 HYDE, F. E. Mr. Gladstone at the Board of Trade. *London: Cobden-Sanderson*, 1934. pp. xxviii, 256. BM

pp. 129–81, problems affecting the growth of the early railways; the Railway Age.

5351 LEWIN, H. G. The Railway Mania and its aftermath, 1845–1852: being a sequel to 'Early British railways'. *London: Railway Gazette*, 1936. pp. xx, 500. BM

Government measures for control of railways during this period. (Some alleged mis-statements are noted by M. D. Greville in *Journal of the Railway & Canal Historical Society*, vol. 2, no. 1, Jan. 1956; and in vol. 3, no. 3, May 1957.)

5352 FAY, S. The War Office at war. *London: Hutchinson*, 1937. pp. 288. BM

Includes accounts of the work of the Railway Executive Committee, 1912–21.

5353 CENTENARY of railway inspection. *Lon-*
c *don: Railway Gazette*, 1940. pp. 20. IT

Reprinted from the *Railway Gazette*, 12 July, 1940.

A review of government supervision over railway working, with a chronological list of Inspecting Officers.

5354 RAILWAY inspection. *London: Railway*
c *Gazette*, 1946. pp. 24. BM

An historical account of the work of the Board of Trade and Ministry of Transport Inspecting Officers from 1840, with a list of officers.

5355 WILLIAMS, O. C. The historical development of Private Bill procedure and Standing Orders in the House of Commons. *London: H.M.S.O.*, 1948–49. 2 vols. pp. x, 340; xiii, 283. BM

Contains much detail on Parliamentary arrangements relating to railways and Railway Bills.

5356 PROUTY, R. The transformation of the Board of Trade, 1830–1855: a study of administrative reorganisation in the heyday of *laissez-faire*. *London: Heinemann*, 1957. pp. viii, 123. BM

pp. 9–14, Legislation for railways.

5357 WILSON, G. R. S. The Railway Inspectorate. *London: Railway Students Association*, 22 Jan. 1958. pp. 14. *Reproduced typescript.* IT

The Government and railway safety; with historical introduction.

5358 JENKINS, T. G. The Ministry of Transport and Civil Aviation. *London: George Allen & Unwin*, 1959. pp. 231. [*New Whitehall Series.*] BM

pp. 33–6, History of railway control by the Board of Trade and the Ministry of Transport. Road and rail competition and co-ordination.

5359 PARRIS, H. W. The regulation of railways
b by the Government in Great Britain: the work of the Board of Trade and the Railway Commissioners, 1840–1867. Thesis, Ph.D., Dept. of History, University of Leicester, 1959. pp. xi, 297, with charts and a bibliography. *Typescript.* LEICS. UNIV.

5360 ROOS, I. The railway system of Great Britain in British legislation. Diplomarbeit zur Erlangung des akademischen Grades eines Diplom-Übersetzers der Ruprecht-Karl-Universität, Heidelberg. 1960. pp. 84. *Typescript.* BR

5361 ALDCROFT, D. H. The decontrol of British
b shipping and railways after the First World War. *In* 'Journal of Transport History', vol. 5, no. 2, November 1961. pp. 89–104, with 115 bibliogr. notes. BM

5361a PARRIS, H. W. Pasley's Diary: a neglected source of railway history. *In* 'Journal of
b Transport History', vol. 6, no. 1, May 1963. pp. 14–23, with 43 bibliogr. notes. BM

An analysis of Major-General Sir Charles Pasley's activities as Inspector-General of Railways, 1841–6, recorded in his diary (Brit. Mus. Additional MSS. 41989–41992).

An earlier version entitled 'A Civil Servant's Diary, 1841–46' appeared in the Winter, 1960 issue of *Public Administration*, pp. 369–80, with 29 bibliogr. notes.

Contemporaneous

5362 GIBBS, J. Some observations relative to the introduction of railway Bills into Parliament, respectfully addressed to the considera-

tion of the Members of both Houses. *London*, [1836.] pp. 14.   BM
Proposes a Government committee to investigate the merits of every proposed railway.

5363 GRAHAME, T. A letter on the present system of legislation which regulates internal intercourse in Great Britain; with strictures on the new principles rapidly being introduced in this department of British policy. *Westminster*, 1836. pp. 20.   H

5364 WHAT will Parliament do with the railways? *London*, 1836. pp. 16.   BM
Asking for greater control over railway development.
—— 2nd edn. (reprint). *London*, 1836. pp. 16.   UL(GL)

5365 'CAUTUS.' Some words on railway legislation in a letter addressed to Robert Peel. *London*, 1837. pp. 16.   BM
Pointing out alleged defects in legislation, with suggestions for reform.

5366 'CAUTUS.' A second letter to Sir Robert Peel on railway legislation. *London*, 1837. pp. 23.   BM
Urging support for a proposal by E. Pease for a parliamentary enquiry into varying gauges, and other reforms.

5367 REMARKS on the Standing Orders and Resolutions of the last Session of Parliament relating to railways, with practical instructions for their amendment. By a Parliamentary Agent. *London*, 1837. pp. iv, 168.   BM

5368 POUSSIN, G. T. Examen comparatif de la question des chemins de fer en 1839 en France et à l'étranger, et de l'intervention du gouvernement dans la direction et l'exécution des travaux. *Paris*, 1839. pp. xvi, 167.   H

5369 GALE, C. J. A letter to . . . the Earl of Dalhousie, President of the Board of Trade, on railway legislation. *London*, 1844. pp. 32. BM

5370 REPORTS of Select Committees of the House of Commons upon questions connected with general railway legislation, general railway Acts, and minute of the Board of Trade . . . *London: W. Clowes & Sons*, 1844. pp. iv, 135.   NLC

5371 BIGG, J. & SON. Special reports of Committees on Railway Bills relating to the adoption or rejection of the recommendations of the Board of Trade, Session 1845; with general index. *Westminster*, 1845. pp. 68.   BM
A summary of all special reports of this Session.

*5372 BIGG, J. & SON. The Standing Orders of the House of Lords relative to Private Bills, as amended the 7th of August 1845; with an abstract of the orders respecting Railway Bills, arranged in the order of the proceedings thereon, and a copious index. *Westminster*, 1845. pp. 98.   UL(GL)

5373 The BOARD of Trade and the Kentish railway schemes. *London*, 1845. pp. 41.   BM
'Their duty to advise and assist Parliament, not to decide.'

5374 MENCE, R. M. Remarks upon the General Railway Acts printed and to be proposed in the approaching Session, with suggestions for more efficient restraint on the arbitrary powers of the railway companies. By a small landowner. *London*, 1845. pp. 14.   BRE

5375 RAILWAYS and the Board of Trade. *London*, 1845. pp. 32.   LSE
'Interference' of the Railway Department of the Board of Trade.
—— 2nd edn. *London*, 1845. pp. 40.   H
—— 3rd, *London*, 1845. pp. 40.   BM

5376 RUMINATIONS on railways, no. 2, The Railway Board of Trade. *London: John Weale*, 1845. pp. 32.   BM

5377 The GUIDE for passing Railway Bills through Parliament, in which the Standing Orders of both Houses relating to Railway Bills to be complied with by the promoters are arranged in their order of proceeding, with directions for proofs before the Standing Orders, Committees . . . *London: Reid & Son*, 1845. pp. 48.
By J. J. Scott (?)

5378 WALLACE, R. [Petition for the repeal of Gladstone's Railway Act, 1844.] To the Honourable the Commons of Great Britain and Ireland in Parliament assembled, the petition of Robert Wallace, Esquire, lately a Member of your Honourable House. [1845.] pp. [2.]   BM(MSS)
Printed. (In lists of 10 May.)

5379 BIGG, J. & SON. The Railway Bill Register; containing a list of Railway Bills in progress through Parliament, with a statement in each case of . . . the lines proposed to be amalgamated . . . and also, the proceedings on each Bill in both Houses . . . *Westminster*, 1846. pp. xxiv, 167.   BM

5380 COLLINS, C. J. The projected new railways: an epitome of the new lines of railway in England which Parliament will probably sanction, with reasons for their doing so. *London*, 1846. pp. 32.   BM

5381 GREAT WESTERN RLY. Observations on the report of the Gauge Commissioners presented to Parliament. *Westminster*, [1846.] pp. 45 [47].   BM
Appendix—G.W. Rly. reports to the Gauge Commission.

5382 MORRISON, J. Observations illustrative of the defects of the English system of railway legislation and of its injurious operation on the public interests, with suggestions for its improvement. *London*, 1846. pp. 44. BM

5383 RIDDELL, H. Railway Parliamentary practice; with an appendix containing the Standing Orders of both Houses of Parliament relating to railways, etc., to which is added a treatise on the rights of parties to oppose the preamble and clauses of a Railway Bill, and to the insertion therein of protective and compensatory clauses. *London*, 1846. pp. xxii, 223, cvi[cviii], 16, with a fold. plan specifying the required style of map and section to accompany a Railway Bill.   BM

5384 SCOTT, J. J. Railway practice in Parliament: the law and practice of railway and other Private Bills . . . *London*, 1846. pp. xix, 258, 404.   BM

5385 BEAVAN, E. *and* WALFORD, F. Parliamentary cases relating to railways . . . determined by the Select Committees of the Houses of Parliament in the Session 1846. *London*, 1847. vol. 1, pts. 1 & 2. pp. vii, xxiv, 134.   BM
No more published.

5386 LAING, S. Observations on Mr. Strutt's amended Railway Regulation Bill now before Parliament. *Westminster*, 1847. pp. 32.   BM
Objections to the Bill.

5387 OBSERVATIONS on Mr. Strutt's Railway Bill. *Westminster: James Bigg & Son*, 1847. pp. 56.   BM

5388 SALOMONS, D. Railways in England and France; being reflections suggested by Mr. Morrisons's pamphlet and by the report drawn up by him for the Railway Acts Committee. *London*, 1847. pp. 79.   BM

5389 SHAEN, S. Review of railways and railway legislation at home and abroad. *London*, 1847. pp. 103, with bibliogr. refs. to British Parliamentary Papers.   BM
pp. 72–103, suggested legislative reforms.

5390 DOULL, A. Random hints on railways and railway legislation. *London*, 1848. pp. 43.   BM
Largely concerning Mr. Strutt's Railway Regulation Bill, and railway construction law.

5391 SCRIVENOR, H. Government intervention in railway affairs: a letter to H. Labouchere, M.P., President of the Board of Trade, upon the right, necessity and duty of government interference in railway affairs; with especial reference to the establishing of a uniform system of railway accounts and an independent audit of such accounts as an effectual remedy for existing evils. *London*, 1849. pp. 61, with a proposed form for statements of accounts, on 2 fold. plates.   BM

5392 LANG, G. H. Reasons for the repeal of the railway passenger tax. *London*, 1851. pp. 47.   BM

5393 GRAHAME, T. Correspondence between the Board of Trade and T. Grahame on railway and canal combination. *London*, 1852. pp. 43.   BM
'. . . calling attention to a system of legislation equally hostile to the agricultural, manufacturing and mercantile interests of the country.'

5394 PARLIAMENT—HOUSE OF COMMONS. Proceedings of the General Committee and Sub-Committees on Railways, selected from the Standing Orders. 1854. pp. 27.   BM

5395 COATES, T. Railway deposits discussed in a letter to the chairman of the Committee. *London*, 1864. pp. 23.   BM
'The passage of an Act should not be impeded by financial difficulties arising from construction expenses. Money should be deposited and impounded until Act is passed.' Addressed to J. H. Scourfield, Select Committee on Standing Orders (Parliamentary Deposits).

5396 COATES, T. Railways and the Board of Trade again discussed. (Railways construction facilities; Railway companies' powers; Bills.) *London*, 1864. pp. 16.   BM
Objection to Board of Trade control over railway promotion.

5397 MAYNE, H. B. Railway schemes: Parliamentary deposits . . . *Westminster*, 1864. pp. 20.   BM
'For private circulation only.'
A defence by the Public Bill Office, House of Commons, against accusations of misuse of legislation.

5398 CRAWFORD, R. W. Railway legislation: speech delivered by R. W. Crawford, Esq., in the House of Commons on Tuesday April 2nd, 1867; together with the debate and opinions of the press. *London*, 1867. pp. 87.   BM

5399 FRANCE, R. S. Lord Redesdale and the new railways: a review of his lordship as a railway legislator, in a letter by R. S. France. *London*, 1867. pp. 24.   LSE
Alleged obstruction by Redesdale of a Bill concerning the Mold & Denbigh Junction Railway, to which R. S. France was a contractor.

5400 FRANCE, R. S. Lord Redesdale and the new railways: correspondence between his lordship and Mr. France. *London*, 1867. pp. 18.   LSE
Relating to alleged obstruction by Redesdale of a Bill concerning the Mold & Denbigh Junction Railway, to which R. S. France was a contractor.

5401 FRANCE, R. S. Mr. France's pamphlet, 'Lord Redesdale and the new railways.' Lord Redesdale's control over the legislation of both Houses. *London*, 1867. pp. 16.   BM
The case of the Mold & Denbigh line; Redesdale's support of the L. & N.W. Rly. and his 'back-stairs' methods in opposing the Bill.

5402 MORTIMER, C. S. Unfair legislation for railway companies. *London*, 1872. pp. 6.
Passenger duty.   NLC

5403 CARTER, S. Railway legislation: letters on the subject of proposed transfer to Railway Commissioners of the power of fixing rates on railways, and correspondence relating thereto. *Westminster*, 1874. pp. 34.   LSE

5404 CARTER, S. Railway legislation: the railway companies and the Railway Commissioners. Proposed transfer to the Commissioners of the power of fixing rates on railways, and repeal of existing Parliamentary rates: letters and correspondence. *Westminster*, 1874. pp. 34.   BM

5405 DAWNAY, A. D. A treatise upon railway signals and accidents. *London*, 1874. pp. 125.   BM
History and description. pp. 87 to end, 'Extracts from the requirements and recommendations of the Board of Trade issued in February 1872'.

5406 JEVONS, W. S. Railways and the state. *In* 'Essays and addresses by professors and lecturers, Owens College, Manchester'. *London*, 1874. pp. 465–505.   BM
—— Reprinted in his 'Methods of social reform'. 1883. pp. 353–83.   BM
Railways will be improved by legislative control and reform, not by state purchase.

5407 JUNNER, R. G. The practice before the Railway Commissioners under the Regulation of Railways Act, 1873 . . . *London*, 1874. pp. xxxvi, 216.   BM

5408 ADAMS, C. F. The railroad problem. *New York*, 1875. pp. 19.   BM
The control of railway development by government regulation, with special reference to England.

5409 The RAILWAY Passenger Duty. Public meeting at the City Terminus Hotel, Cannon Street, London, March 16, 1875 . . . [*London*, 1875.] pp. 43.   BM
Reprinted from the *Railway News*. Proposals to remove the passenger duty.

5410 BROWNE, J. H. B. The practice before the Railway Commissioners under Regulation of Railways Acts, 1873 and 1874, with notes of their decisions . . . *London*, 1876. pp. xii, 319.   BM

5411 CARTER, S. Railway debentures and the Railway Commissioners: statement for the consideration of holders of debentures, or debenture stock, and railway shares. *Westminster*, 1877. pp. 18.   BM
Concerning the Act of 1873 for government control over fixing of rates for through traffic by Railway Commissioners. This pamphlet is discussed in *Observations upon the working of the Regulation of Railways Act, 1873*(1878).

5412 OBSERVATIONS upon the working of the 'Regulation of Railways Act, 1873' and of the Court of the Railway Commissioners. *Manchester*, 1878. pp. 48.   BM
Criticism of the interpretation of the Act by the Court of Railway Commissioners, and suggested reforms. Discusses S. Carter's pamphlet, *Railway debentures and the Railway Commissioners* (1877).

5413 FRANQUET DE FRANQUEVILLE, A. C. L'État et les chemins de fer en Angleterre. *Paris*, 1880. pp. 32.   BM
A review of the work of the Railway Commissioners.
—— German edn. 'Eisenbahn-Konkurrenz und Eisenbahn-Fusionen in England.' *Wien*, 1875.

5414 TRAVELLING TAX ABOLITION COMMITTEE. Usurpation of the functions of Parliament by the Board of Inland Revenue. *London*, June 1880. pp. 8.   BR

5415 BOARD OF TRADE. Documents to be sent to the Railway Department, Board of Trade, previously to the second notice of the intention to open a railway being given. *London*, 1877. pp. 7.   ICE
—— another edn. *London*, 1881. pp. 8.   ICE

5416 FRANQUET DE FRANQUEVILLE, A. C. La Commission des Chemins de Fer en Angleterre: réponse à un article inséré dans les Annales des Ponts et Chaussées, août, 1880. *Paris*, 1881. pp. 39.   BM

5417 HAGGARD, F. T. Railways in the United Kingdom. Third class passenger traffic and the difficulties of conducting it. *London*, 1881. pp. 22.   BR
Dated 4 October, 1881.
Freedom from passenger duty on third-class fares.
—— 'Supplement to Pamphlet dated 4 October 1881,' November 1881. pp. 8.   BR

5418 BECKETT, E. Speech of Sir Edmund Beckett on the Bill for extending the power of the Railway Commissioners, at a meeting of shareholders . . . 5 June, 1884. *London: Association of Railway Shareholders*, [1884.] pp. 16.   LSE
Reasons for opposing the Bill.

5419 RAILWAY Rates and Charges Bills: three articles on the proposed railway legislation . . . *Darlington*, 1885. pp. 22.   LSE
Revised and reprinted from the *Northern Echo*. An analysis of the Bills proposed for the 1885 Session.

5420 TRAVELLING TAX ABOLITION COMMITTEE. Exemption of street railways, called tramways, from the railway passenger duty. *London*, February 1885. pp. [4.]   BR

5421 [JENKINS, W. J.] Railway tyranny: a letter of appeal to the President of the Board of Trade against railway companies and their persistent disobedience to the law. By one who has defeated them five times. *London*, [1887.] pp. 16. Signed 'Justice'. (W. J. Jenkins.)   BM

5422 RAILWAY DEFENCE ASSOCIATION. Speeches in the House of Lords on second reading of the Railway and Canal Traffic Bill, March 14, 1887, by . . . Lord Grimthorpe . . . Lord Brabourne and . . . Lord Bramwell. *London*, [1887.] pp. 23.   LSE
Objections to Board of Trade interference in the fixing of railway rates.

5423 STERNE, S. Report to the Hon. Thomas F. Bayard, Secretary of State, on the relations of the governments of the nations of Western Europe to the railways. *Washington: Government Printing Office*, 1887. pp. 45. [*U.S. 49th Congress, 2nd Session. Senate Miscellaneous Documents*, no. 66.]   BM
pp. 2–20, England.

5424 ADAMS, C. F. Railroads; their origin and problems. *New York*, 1878. pp. 216.   BM
pp. 80–94, the difficulties of adapting existing legislation to deal with the new problems brought by railways in Gt. Britain.

—— rev. edn. *New York & London*, 1886.   RC

—— rev. edn. *New York & London*, 1888.   PO

5425 The RAILWAY and Canal Traffic Acts, 1854, 1873, and 1888, and other statutes; with the general rules (of February 1889) and schedules of forms and table of fees made in pursuance of the Railway and Canal Traffic Act, 1888 (51 & 52 Vic. cap. 25). *London*, 1889. pp. 74.   BM

5426 WHITE, W. N. Railway and Canal Traffic Act, 1888: copy of correspondence that has taken place on this question which has appeared in 'The Times' between W. N. White of Covent Garden Market, and Henry Oakley . . . Hon. Sec. to the Railway Association. [*London*, 1889.] pp. 22.   NLC

5427 WAGHORN, T. *and* STEVENS, M. Railway and Canal Traffic Act, 1888. Report upon the proceedings at the enquiry held by the Board of Trade, 1889–90; with an appendix containing tables, diagrams, digest of Evidence, etc. *Manchester*, 1890. 2 pts. pp. 158,[205].   BM

5428 BOARD OF TRADE. Requirements of the Board of Trade in regard to the opening of railways, and recommendations in reference to their working. *London*, 1892. pp. 13. PO

5429 ACWORTH, W. M. Government interference in English railway management. *In* 'Compendium of Transportation Theories',

by C. C. MacCain. Kensington Series: first book. *Washington*, 1893. pp. 267–76.   BM

5430 CROWTHER, F. J. Provisional Orders of the Board of Trade in reference to gas and water, tramway, pier and harbour, and electric light undertakings. *London*, 1893. pp. viii, 48.   BM

5431 TODD, M. Railways of Europe and America; or, Government ownership; with notes from official sources. *Boston*, 1893. pp. 293. BM
pp. 207–16, 'England's Royal Commission' [on Railways, appointed March 1865]. 'Gladstone and Peel on government railways.'

5432 ACWORTH, W. M. The state in relation to railways. *In* 'A policy of free exchange: essays by various writers . . .' edited by T. MacKay. *London*, 1894. pp. 163–210. BM

5433 HINES, W. D. Railway regulation: the English system contrasted with the demands of the Interstate Commerce Commission. *Louisville*, 1898. pp. 8.   LSE

5434 HENDRICK, F. Railway control by Commissions. *New York*, 1900. pp. 161.   BM
pp. 63–91, Railway regulation in England, with bibliogr. notes.

5435 UNITED STATES OF AMERICA—SENATE—COMMITTEE ON INTERSTATE COMMERCE. Hearings, May 8 to May 17, 1905. vol. 3. *Washington*, 1905. pp. 1843–70.   BM
Government regulation of railways in the United Kingdom.

5436 WEDGWOOD, R. L. State control of railways in England. *London*, 1908. pp. 31. LSE
Paper, York Railway Debating Society, 28 Jan., 1908.
Some misconceptions righted.

5437 WHITTEN, R. H. Supervision of street railways in England and Prussia. *Albany*, 1909. pp. 76.   LSE
Reprint from the *Annual Report of the Public Service Commission for the First District of the State of New York*, 1908.
pp. 9–34, England. Board of Trade supervision, and the purchase, control and operation of tramways.

5438 ROYAL ECONOMIC SOCIETY. The state in relation to railways: papers read at the Congress of the Royal Economic Society, January 11, 1912. *Westminster*, 1912. pp. 100.   BM
pp. 5–11, The state in relation to railways in England. W. M. Acworth.
pp. 12–18, State control of British railways. W. T. Stephenson.
pp. 19–27, Parliament and the railways. E. C. Stevens.

5439 GATTIE, A. W. A statement made by Mr. A. W. Gattie to the Select Committee of the House of Commons appointed to examine into the conditions of transport in the United Kingdom (to which is appended a list of defects and inaccuracies of the Board of Trade Railway Returns for . . . 1913, with notes). *London: Transport Reform Society*, 1918. pp. 17.   BM

5440 MACLEAN, S. J. The English Railway and Canal Commission of 1888. *In* 'Railway problems' [a collection of reprints] by William Z. Ripley. *Boston*, 1907. pp. 602–49. BM
—— another edn. *Boston*, 1913. (pp. 745–94.)   BM

5441 WILLIAMS, E. E. G. Manual of the Law and Practice of the Railway and Canal Commissioners' Court. *London*, 1913. pp. xxi, 292, 13.   BM

5442 BROWNE, J. H. B. The Railway Commission. *In* 'Jubilee of the Railway News, 1864–1914.' *London: Railway News*, [1914.] pp. 49–52.   BM

5443 WILLIAMS, E. E. Railways and the Board of Trade. *In* 'Jubilee of the Railway News, 1864–1914.' *London: Railway News*, [1914.] pp. 45–9.   BM

5444 BUREAU OF RAILWAY ECONOMICS [Washington]. Experience of British railways under war control. *Washington*, 1917. pp. 3. *Leaflet* no. 34, April 26, 1917.] LC

5445 The RAILWAY and Canal Traffic Acts, 1854, 1873, 1888, and 1894, and other statutes, with the general rules of the Railway and Canal Commission. *London: H.M.S.O.*, 1899. pp. 91.   BM
—— *London*, 1907. pp. 95.   BM
—— *London*, 1910. pp. 95.   BM
—— *London*, 1913. pp. 95.   BM
—— *London*, 1914. pp. 95.   BM
—— *London*, 1918. pp. 94.   BM

5446 DIXON, F. H. *and* PARMELEE, J. H. War administration of the railways in the United States and Great Britain. *New York*, 1918. pp. x, 155. [*Carnegie Endowment for International Peace. Preliminary economic studies of the war.*]   BM
pp. 71–127, and supplementary chapters, 'Great Britain'.
—— another edn. *New York*, 1919. pp. vi, 203.   LSE

5447 GEDDES, E. The new Ministry of Transport: Sir Eric Geddes on the need for reform. *London: Railway Nationalisation Society*, [1919.] pp. 4. [*Pamphlet*, no. 3.]   LSE

5448 GATTIE, A. W. An open letter to Sir J. Fortescue Flannery. 1920. s.sh.   LSE
Accusing Flannery of 'inaccuracies and misstatements' in his Committee Report on Gattie's transport reform proposals. 'A copy forwarded to every Member of the House of Commons.'

5449 NEW TRANSPORT COMPANY. Report of the Departmental Committee appointed to investigate Mr. A. W. Gattie's proposals for improving the method of handling goods and traffic . . . together with an analytical reply by the New Transport Co. *London*, 1920. pp. 39.   BM
Showing that the Committee's report is 'based upon untruths'.

5450 CENTRAL COUNCIL OF ENGLISH, SCOTTISH AND IRISH RAILWAY STOCKHOLDERS PROTECTION ASSOCIATIONS. Danger ahead!: a statement of the railway stock-holders' case. *London*, [1921.] pp. 63.   BM
Warnings concerning the imminent cessation of government control of railways.

5451 KENYON, T. A. Railway statistics in Great Britain. *Manchester: Manchester Statistical Society*, 1922. pp. 63–89, 15, with 15 statistical diagrams for 1921.   BM
An outline of the broad features of the statistical returns submitted by railway companies to the Board of Trade.

5452 JAGTIANI, H. M. The role of the state in the provision of railways. *London*, 1924. pp. ix, 146. [*Studies in Economics & Political Science*, no. 73.]   BM
pp. 14–44, 'England' (i.e. Gt. Britain).

5453 SECTIONS of the Railway and Canal Acts and of the other statutes conferring jurisdiction upon the Railway and Canal Commission Court, together with the general rules authorised by the Commissioners, and forms of procedure and Fees Order. *London: H.M.S.O.*, 1925. pp. viii, 225.   BM

5454 RAILWAY CLEARING HOUSE. Instructions for the compilation of statistics rendered to the Minister of Transport by the railway companies in Great Britain in accordance with the Railway Act, 1921 . . . and the Railway Companies' Road Transport Acts, 1928. *London*, Dec. 1928. pp. 118, with specimen forms.   LSE
'Private and not for publication.'

5455 SPARKE, H. C. An outline of the state control of English railway rates and facilities. *Calcutta*, 1930. pp. 105.   IT

5456 KIRKUS, A. E. An outline of the functions of the Ministry of Transport. pp. 28. *Reproduced typescript.*   IT
Paper, York Railway Lecture & Debating Society, 16 March, 1937.

*5457 ADIE, K. S. The scandal of the British railways. *London: the author*, 1944. pp. 19.   LSE
Government robbing the railways and railway investors by enforcement of the Railway Control Agreement of 1941, and of the Second Agreement of 1944.

K7 RAILWAY LAW

Manuals and treatises on statute and case law relating to railways—Collections of Acts—Legal obligations of railways and of
passengers and consignors of goods

For law relating to lesser subjects see under those subjects

5458 GUILLAUME, A. De la législation des rail routes ou chemins de fer, en Angleterre et en France. *Paris*, 1838. pp. 223, 191, with 4 fold. plates. BM

5459 HODGES, W. The statute law relating to railways in England and Ireland. *London*, 1845. pp. viii, 234. BM

5460 LEWIS, G. H. The liabilities incurred by the projectors, managers, and shareholders of railway and other joint-stock companies considered . . . *London*, 1845. pp. 79. NLC

5461 BIGG, J. & SON. A collection of the special Acts authorizing the construction of railways, passed in the eighth and ninth year of the reign of Her Majesty Queen Victoria; with tabular abstract, introduction, and indexes. In two volumes. *Westminster*, 1846. pp. 1, 599; 600–1240. BM
Text of 120 Acts for incorporation, amalgamation, leasing, and further financing of railways in 1845.

5462 NICHOLL, H. I., HARE, T. *and* CARROW, J. M. Cases relating to railways and canals, argued and adjudged in the Courts of Law and Equity, 1835 to 1840 (1840–42, 1842–46). *London*, 1840, 1843, 1846. 3 vols. BM
At end of vol. 3 is an appendix of eighty-eight pages containing a digest of railway cases before 1835.

5463 WALFORD, F. A summary of the law of railways . . . *London*, 1845. pp. xxviii, 344, 237. BM
—— 2nd edn. *London*, 1846. pp. xxviii, 424, ccccx. BM

5464 BIGG, J. & SON. An abstract of the special Acts authorizing the construction of railways, passed in the ninth and tenth ([and] tenth and eleventh) year of the reign of . . . Queen Victoria; with introduction and index . . . *Westminster*, 1847, 48. 2 vols. pp. xlviii, 1050; xlviii, 660. BM
Acts of incorporation, etc., of railway companies, 1846 and 1847.

5465 COLLIER, R. P. The Railway Clauses, Companies' Clauses, and Lands' Clauses Consolidation Acts . . . *London*, 1845. pp. xii, 285, 60, cxxii*, 30. BM
—— 2nd edn. *London*, 1847. pp. xvii, 288, 104, cxlvii, 32. BM

5466 HODGES, W. The law relating to railways and railway companies, with all the cases . . . decided in the Courts of Law and Equity . . . *London*, 1847. pp. xxviii, 721, 278. BM

5467 CHAMBERS, T. *and* PETERSON, A. T. T. A treatise on the law of railway companies . . . *London*, 1848. pp. xl, 804. BM

5468 WORDSWORTH, C. F. F. The law relating to railway, bank, insurance, mining, and other joint-stock companies; with an appendix containing statutes, cases at law and in equity, resolutions of the Houses of Parliament as to railway and other Bills, forms of deeds, etc. Second edn. *London*, 1837. pp. xxiii, 192, 363. BM
—— 3rd edn. 'The law of joint stock companies.' *London*, 1842. pp. xix, 397, 200. BM
—— 4th, *London*, 1845. pp. lii, 408, 280. BM
—— 5th. 'The law of railway, banking, mining, and other joint stock companies.' *London*, 1845. pp. xxxviii, 438, 594. BM
—— 6th. 'The law of railway, canal, water, dock, gas, and other companies.' *London*, 1851. pp. xxvi, 533, 623. BM

5469 EVANS, G. A treatise on the Railway & Canal Traffic Act, 1854 (17 & 18 Vict., ch. 31); with the act and regulæ generales made pursuant thereto. *London*, 1859. pp. v, 54. BM

5470 MOORE, A. A Hand-book of Railway Law; containing the Public General Acts from 1838 to 1858 inclusive, and statutes connected therewith, with an introduction containing statistical and financial information . . . *London*, 1859. pp. cxvi, 404. BM
—— 2nd edn. *London*, 1860. pp. cxvi, 488. LSE

5471 BIGG, J. & SON. A Collection of the Public General Acts relating to railways in Scotland, including the Companies, Lands, and Railways Clauses Consolidation (Scotland) Acts, 1838–1845; with general index. *Westminster*, 1845. pp. 200. BM
—— another edn. '1838–1846.' *Westminster*, 1847. pp. 232. IT
—— 5th edn. '1830–1861.' *Westminster*, 1862. pp. viii, 292. BM

5472 MANNING, W. T. Railway abandonment: the Acts relative to the abandonment of railways, with introduction and forms of procedure. *London*, 1867. BM

5473 SHELFORD, L. The law of railways, including the three consolidated Acts, 1845, and other general Acts for regulating railways in England and Ireland . . . *London,* 1845. pp. xxxii, 614.   BM
—— 2nd edn. *London,* 1846. pp. xxxviii, 723.   BM
—— 3rd, *London,* 1853. pp. xlii, 826. BM
—— 4th, *London,* 1869. 2 vols. lxxxviii, 724; xxxi, 909.   BM

5474 BAKER, G. S. A Handy Book on the Law of Railway Companies for the use of railway travellers, consignors and consignees of goods, and railway officials. *London,* 1873. pp. iv, 93.   BM

5475 FRANQUET DE FRANQUEVILLE, A. C. Du régime des travaux publics en Angleterre. *Paris,* 1874. 4 vols., with 4 fold. plates.
Largely concerned with British railways and their legislation.
—— 2nd edn. *Paris,* 1875. 4 vols.   BM

5476 IVATTS, E. B. Carriers' law, relating to goods and passenger traffic on railways, canals and steam ships; with cases. *London,* 1883. pp. xxvii, 1132.   BM

*5477 HADLEY, A. T. Railroad transportation, its history and its laws. *New York & London,* 1885. pp. v, 269.   RC
pp. 146–86, 'English railroad legislation.'
—— *New York & London,* 1886. pp. 269.   BM
—— 15th impr. *New York & London,* 1903.   LSE
—— 'Le Transport par les chemins de fer: histoire, législation.' *Paris,* 1887. pp. xvii, 391.   IT

5478 HODGES, W. Treatise on the law of railways, railway companies, and railway investments. 2nd edn. *London,* 1855. pp. xxxviii, 768, 295.   BM
—— 3rd edn. By C. M. Smith. *London,* 1863.   BM
—— 4th, *London,* 1865. pp. xxxvi, 624, 346. BM
—— 5th, *London,* 1869. pp. xxxviii, 675, 401.   BM
—— 6th, *London,* 1876.   BM
—— 7th, by J. M. Lely. *London,* 1888, 1889. 2 vols.   BM

5479 DARLINGTON, H. R. The Railway and Canal Traffic Acts, 1854 to 1888 . . . *London,* 1889. pp. xl, 486.   BM

5480 WOODFALL, R. New law and practice of railway and canal traffic. *London,* 1889. pp. xv, 221.   BM

5481 BEACH, C. F. The modern law of railways as determined by the courts and statutes of England and the United States. *San Francisco,* 1890. 2 vols.   BM

5482 PRESTON, F. M. Manual of Railway Law. *London,* 1892. pp. x, 318.   BM

5483 DAVIES, J. Railway rates, charges and regulations of the United Kingdom; being a summary of the Railway Rates and Charges (Order Confirmation) Acts, 1891 and 1892, and of the Acts passed from 1854 to 1888 for the general regulation of railways . . . *London,* [1893.] pp. 234.   BM

5484 FERGUSON, J. Five year's railway cases, 1889–93. *Edinburgh,* 1894. pp. 124.   BM

5485 EASTON, R. S. Railway law for passengers and goods. *London,* [1896.] pp. vi, 28. [*Easton's Handy Series of Popular Handbooks,* no. 1.]   BM

5486 DEAS, F. The law of railways applicable to Scotland. *Edinburgh,* 1873. pp. xi, 593, cccxvi.   BM
—— enl. edn. by J. Ferguson. *Edinburgh,* 1897. pp. lx, 1002.   BM

5487 FERGUSON, J. Public statutes relating to railways in Scotland. *Edinburgh,* 1898. pp. xvi, 493, lvii.   BM

*5488 BOYLE, E. *and* WAGHORN, T. The law relating to traffic on railways and canals. *London,* 1901. 3 vols.   BM

5489 STEPHENS, J. E. R. Law of carriage. *London,* [1909.] pp. xvi, 324.   BM

5490 LISSENDEN, G. B. The Railway Clerk's Assistant. *London,* 1910. pp. ix, 101.   IT
A simple guide to railway law.

*5491 BIGG, J. & SON. A collection of the Public General Acts for the regulation of railways; including the Companies, Lands, and Railway Clauses Consolidation Acts, 1838–1845. *Westminster,* 1845. pp. 207.   BM: BR
—— '1838–1846.' 1846. pp. 245.
—— '1838–1847.' 1849. pp. 251.
—— '1838–1851.' 1852. pp. vi, 301.
—— '1838–1854.' 1855. pp. vi, 314.
—— '1838–1859.' 1860. pp. viii, 302.
—— 9th edn. '1838–1860.' 1861. pp. viii, 310.
—— 10th, '1830–1863.' 1864. pp. viii, 404.
—— 11th, '1830–1864.' 1865. pp. xi, 473.
—— 12th, '1830–1866.' 1866. pp. xii, 525.
—— 13th, '1830–1874.' 1875. pp. xii, 689.
—— Suppl. to 13th, '1875–1883.' 1883. pp. 611–721.
—— 14th, '1830–1884.' 1885. pp. xv, 823.
—— 15th, '1830–1898.' 1898. pp. xviii, 951.
—— 16th, '1830–1911.' 1912. pp. xx, 1141.   BM: BR (all editions)

5492 MILEHAM, E. C. The law relating to railways. *In* 'Modern railway working,' edited by John Macaulay. vol. 1, 1912. pp. 127–56.   BM

5493 STERNE, S. Railways in the United States: their history, their relation to the state, and an analysis of the legislation in regard to

their control. *New York & London*, 1912.
pp. xiii, 209. BM
  pp. 63–88, Railway legislation in England
after 1839.

5494 AMERICAN and English railroad cases:
a collection of all the railroad cases in the
courts of last resort in America and England.
Northport: Edward Thompson, [1883–95.]
61 vols. BM
—— Digest of the cases reported . . . and
index to the notes . . . vol. 1 to 35 (36 to
45) . . . By William M. McKinney. *Northport*, 1890, 1891. 2 vols. BM
—— new series. Cases decided by the
courts of appellate jurisdiction in the United
States, England and Canada. *Northport*,
[1895–1902.] 23 vols. BM
—— Railroad reports, vols. 24–68. *Charlottesville: Mickie & Co.*, 1902–13. 45 vols.
BM
—— Digest of the cases reported in volumes
1 to 10 [and] Indexes to notes in volumes
11 to 20 [and] Index-digest of the cases
reported in volumes 1 to 30. *Charlottesville*,
1899–1909. 4 vols. BM

5495 FERGUSON, J. Railway cases, 1897–1912,
and railway statutes, 1898–1912. *Edinburgh*,
1913. pp. xxviii, 218. BM

5496 CLARKE, S. W. The law relating to the
carriage by land of passengers, animals and
goods. *London*, 1915. pp. xxv, 323. BM

5497 CHAPMAN, A. E. The Student's Guide to
Railway Law: a manual of information for
traders, passengers and railway students.
London, [1913.] pp. vi, 196. BM
—— 2nd edn. Guide to Railway Law: a
manual of information for traders, passengers and railway students. *London*, 1921.
pp. xii, 227. BM

5498 WILLIAMS, E. E. G. Epitome of Railway
Law. *London*, 1912. pp. xxviii, 240. BM
—— 2nd edn. *London*, 1921. pp. xxiv, 271.
BM

5499 MACNAMARA, W. H. A digest of the law
of carriers of goods and passengers by land
and internal navigation. *London*, 1888.
pp. xxxi, 580. BM
—— 2nd edn. 'Law of carriers of merchandise and passengers by land.' *London*,
1908. pp. xxxvii, 672. BM
—— 3rd [same title], by W. A. Robertson
and A. Safford. *London*, 1925. pp. xxviii,
682. BM

5500 LESLIE, A. The law of transport by railway. *London*, November 1920. pp. xcvi,
579. BM
—— another edn. '. . . with a supplement
dealing with changes effected by the Railways Act, 1921.' *London*, 1925. pp. xcvi, 24,
579. BM
—— 2nd edn. *London*, 1928. pp. lxx, 852. BM

5501 LIPSETT, L. R. *and* ATKINSON, T. J. D.
The law of carriage by railway in Great
Britain and Ireland. *London*, 1928. pp.
xxiv, 942. BM

5502 WILLIAMS, E. E. G. Modern railway law:
being a collection of Public Acts and rules
relating to railway companies, with notes
of cases decided thereon. *London*, 1928.
pp. xvi, 407. BM

5503 DISNEY, H. W. The law of carriage by
railway. *London*, 1905. pp. xv, 232. BM
  A non-technical manual.
—— 2nd edn. *London*, 1909. pp. xvi, 266. BM
—— 3rd, *London*, 1912. pp. xix, 277. BM
—— 4th, *London*, 1915. pp. xix, 287. BM
—— 5th, *London*, 1921. pp. xx, 288. BM
—— 6th, *London*, 1923. pp. xix, 332. BM
—— 7th, *London*, 1927. pp. xxi, 330. BM
—— 8th, *London*, 1929. pp. xxiii, 356. BM

5504 HUGHES, J. D. I. The law of transport by
rail. *London*, 1931. pp. xvi, 176. BM

5505 DAVIES, H. B. F. The rights and duties of
transport undertakings. *London*, 1926. pp.
xii, 123. BM
—— 2nd edn., by H. B. F. Davies and F. M.
Landau. *London*, 1932. pp. xxiii, 283. BM

5506 GUNN, W. H. Law of inland transport.
London, 1932. pp. xviii, 314. BM

5507 HOLDSWORTH, M. E. The law of transport.
London, 1932. pp. xxiv, 201, 11. BM

5508 MAHAFFY, R. P. *and* DODSON, G. Road
and rail traffic law, 1934. *London*, 1934.
pp. xli, 319, 36. BM

5509 WOODWARD, E. G. The Road and Rail
Traffic Act, 1933; the complete text as
passed by Parliament, edited, with an introduction, explanatory notes, tables of
cases and statutes, and a complete index, by
E. G. Woodward. *London*, 1934. pp. xi, 188.
BM

*5510 STATUTE LAW COMMITTEE. Index to
Local and Personal Acts, consisting of classified lists of the local and personal and private
Acts and Special Orders and Special Procedure Orders, 1801–1947. *London:
H.M.S.O.*, 1949. pp. viii, 1140. BM
  pp. 85–253, Railways (including light railways).
  pp. 257–81, Tramways.
—— a previous edition, 'Index to Local
Acts, 1801–1899'. *London*, 1900. pp. viii,
807. BM

5511 KARMEL, D. *and* POTTER, K. The Transport Act, 1953, with general introduction
and annotations by D. Karmel and K. Potter. *London: Butterworth*, 1953. pp. 7,
333. BM
  pp. 1–50, Introduction.
  pp. 51–305, Transport Act, 1953, and Appendices.

*5512 KAHN-FREUND, O. Law of carriage by inland transport; founded on Disney's 'Law of carriage by railway'. *London: Stevens & Sons*, 1939. pp. xxiii, 424.   BM

Disney's 8th edn., re-written.

—— 2nd edn. *London*, 1949. pp. xxv, 357.   BM

—— 3rd, *London*, 1956. pp. xxxii, 472.   BM

K 8 RAILWAYS AND CRIME

Offences against railways or committed upon railway property

5513 [NASH, C.] The railway robberies. *London*, 1846. pp. 21.   BM
> From the *Railway Record*, 5 Dec., 1846.
> The case of Wareham v. Prance, Collard and Nash.

5514 RAILWAY robberies: the summing up of Chief Justice Wilde; notes of the trial, December 1846, Wareham v. Prance, Nash and Collard; original documents and correspondences, confessions of the depredators, the evidence of Garratt and Maynard, with summary of remarks on the cases of Garratt, Maynard, Farr, etc., etc. [*London*,] 1847. pp. 104.   BM

*5515 EVANS, D. M. Facts, failures, and frauds: revelations financial, mercantile, criminal. *London*, 1859. pp. viii, 727.   BM
> pp. 6–73, The rise and fall of George Hudson.
> pp. 432–83, The G.N.R. frauds and forgeries of Leopold Redpath.

pp. 484–595, The bullion robbery by Pierce, Agar and Burgess on the S.E.Rly., 19 May, 1855.

5516 WALKCE, G. S. Crime and the Iron Road. pp. [14.] *MS*.   RC
> Paper, Railway Club, 4 March, 1929.

5517 WHITBREAD, J. R. The railway policeman: the story of the constable on the track . . . *London: Harrap*, 1961. pp. 269, with 36 illus. on 15 plates.   BM

5518 [The Great Mail Train Robbery of 8th August, 1963, near Cheddington, Buckinghamshire.]
> Among newspaper accounts of the operation which appeared at the close of the first trials in March 1964, two are noteworthy: 'The diary of a master-crime' by Eric Clark, in the *Guardian*, 28 March, and 'On time with the train robbers' by Roy Perrott, in the *Observer*, 29 March.

K 9 RAILWAYS AND THE POST OFFICE

Travelling Post Offices—Post Office Underground Railway—Railway letter stamps

Historical

5519 BAINES, F. E. Forty years at the Post Office: a personal narrative. *London*, 1895. 2 vols. pp. vii, 337, 2: 345.   LSE
> Includes railways and the Post Office, and T.P.O.'s.

5520 EWEN, H. L'Estrange. Reference List of Railway Letter Post Stamps: first edition, 1898–1899. *Norwood*, 1898. pp. 33, with 24 illus.   BM

5521 EWEN, H. L'Estrange. A history of railway letter stamps, describing all varieties issued by the railway companies of Great Britain and Ireland . . . *London*, 1901. pp. vii, 430, with illus.   BM
> The author's collection of approximately 40,000 stamps in 32 volumes now forms part of the British Museum Stamp Collection.

5522 EWEN, H. L'Estrange. Priced Catalogue of the Railway Letter Stamps of the United Kingdom. (Railway letter stamps of the United Kingdom.) *Norwood*, 1903–6.   BM
> no. 1, '. . . from February 1st, 1891 to end of April, 1903. 1st edition'. 1903. pp. iii, 46, with illus.
> no. 2, '. . . from February 1st, 1891 to October, 1904. 2nd edition'. 1904. pp. iii, 55, with illus.
> no. 3, part 1, 'Railway companies of England and Wales, 1891–1905. 3rd edition'. 1905. pp. v, 96, with illus.
> no. 4, part 2, 'Railway companies of Scotland and Ireland, 1891–1906'. 1906. pp. xxv, 63, with illus.
> The preface to no. 4 was also issued separately.

5523 EWEN, H. L'Estrange. Railway newspaper and parcel stamps of the United Kingdom issued from 1855 to October 1906. First edition. *London*, 1906. pp. viii, 152.   BM
> Contains many reproductions of stamp impressions.

5524 GENERAL POST OFFICE. The Post Office: an historical summary. *London*, August 1911. pp. 139.   RC
> pp. 33–5, Railway letter service.
> pp. 44–6 Travelling Post Office.

5525 BENNETT, E. The Post Office and its story
. . . *London*, 1912. pp. 355, with 31 illus. BM
pp. 69–82, The Travelling Post Office; with
6 illus. on 3 plates.

*5526 SHERRINGTON, C. E. R. A hundred years
of inland transport, 1830–1933. [*London*,]
1934. pp. 376. BM
Includes a section on railways and the Post
Office.

5527 GENERAL POST OFFICE. T.P.O. Centenary of the Travelling Post Office. [*London*,
1938.] pp. [24,] with illus. RC
A graphic history and description, including
W. H. Auden's poem 'Night Mail'.

5528 WARD, C. W. Irish T.P.O's; their history
and postmarks. *Croydon: C. A. Cook*,
[1938.] pp. 16, with reproductions of postmarks. BM

5529 RANDELL, W. L. Messengers for mankind.
London: Hutchinson, [1940.] pp. 240.
[*Hutchinson's Illustrated Library of Modern
Knowledge*, no. 5.] BM
pp. 40–51, The Travelling Post Office; with
illus.
pp. 51–5, The Post Office Underground
Railway; with illus. and map.

5530 WARD, C. W. Scottish T.P.O's; their history and postmarks. *Croydon: Cook's
Printing Works*, 1947. pp. 27, with reproductions of postmarks. BM

5531 HARAM, V. S. Centenary of the Irish Mail.
*1848–1948. London: British Railways (Lon-
don Midland Region)*, 1948. pp. 31, with 16
illus. on 8 plates, & a map. BM

5532 ECCLESTONE, A. J. *and* TURNER, S. R.
The railway letter stamps of Great Britain,
1891–1941. Cheam: the authors, 1946, 1949.
2 pts. (pp. 40, 63), with 95 reproductions. BM
Descriptions arranged chronologically under
companies.

5533 WARD, C. W. English T.P.O's; their history and postmarks. *Croydon: C. A. Cook's
Printing Works*, [1949.] pp. 106, with illus.,
maps & numerous reproductions of postmarks. BM

5534 KAY, F. G. Royal Mail: the story of the
posts in England from the time of Edward
IVth to the present day. *London: Rockliff*,
1951. pp. ix, 198. BM
pp. 61–5, Royal Mail by rail.
pp. 112–17, the T.P.O.

5535 ENCYCLOPAEDIA of British Empire Postage
Stamps, 1661–1947. vol. 1, Great Britain
and the Empire in Europe. *London: Robson
Lowe*, March 1948. BM
pp. 206–11, Railway letter stamps. By
George Brumell.
—— 2nd edn. *London*, 1952. BM
(pp. 308–26.)

pp. 299–300, Railway newspaper and parcel
stamps, 1855–1906.
pp. 308–26, Railway letter stamps.

5536 WATSON, J. M. C. Stamps and railways.
London: Faber, 1960. pp. 142, with 17
illus. BM

Contemporaneous

5537 CORRESPONDENCE between the Manchester & Birmingham Railway Company
and the General Post Office with reference
to the conveyance of the mails between
Manchester and Crewe. [*Manchester*, 1843.]
pp. 36. LSE
Forty-three letters.

5538 REMARKS on Post Office arrivals and
departures to the north of Perth. *Aberdeen*,
1849. pp. 12. AU
Advocating the extension of the T.P.O.
service beyond Perth to Aberdeen.

5539 POSTCRIPT to 'Remarks on Post Office
arrivals and departures to the north of Perth'.
Aberdeen, 1849. pp. 11. AU
Further points on the same theme.

5540 REMARKS on the conveyance of the mails
between London and Paris, shewing the
advantages that would result by adopting
the shortest route, by Folkestone and
Boulogne. *London*, 1850. pp. 28. BM
Via South Eastern Rly.

5541 LEWINS, W. Her Majesty's Mails: an
historical and descriptive account of the
British Post Office. *London*, 1864. pp. ix,
358. BM
pp. 213–29, The T.P.O.'s: pp. 342–3, table
showing the cost of the conveyance of mails on
various railways, 1863–4.
—— 2nd edn. *London*, 1865. pp. xii, 339. BM

5542 GALT, W. Acceleration of the Irish mail
trains: a general review of the present
state of the mail service throughout Ireland
and in connection with England; with suggestions for its improvement. [*Dublin*?]
1884. pp. 20. ICE

5543 TOMBS, R. C. The Bristol Royal Mail: post,
telegraph and telephone. *Bristol*, [1899.]
pp. 295. BM
pp. 49–67, 'Mail transport by railway'.

5544 GENERAL POST OFFICE. Wayleaves. [*London*, 1912.] RC
Pages un-numbered.
Construction and maintenance of telegraph
lines on railways. Arrangements with the various railway companies.

5545 ARNOLD, W. C. Royal railways with uniform rates: a proposal for amalgamation of
railways with the General Post Office . . .
London, 1914. pp. 61. BM

5546 EVANS, E. The Post Office (London) Railway: its equipment and operation: a paper read at meetings of the 'Underground' staff on the 20th November & 14th December, 1928. *London*, 1929. pp. 39, with 26 illus., incl. maps.   LSE
'For private circulation only.'

5547 INTERNATIONAL POSTAL CONGRESS [London, 1929]. Souvenir of a banquet given by the Associated Railway Companies of Great Britain to the delegates, at the Savoy Hotel, London, 18 June, 1929. *London*, 1929. pp. 14, with 11 illus.   LSE
The text is an essay by Cecil J. Allen, entitled *British railways and the Post Office*.

—— 'Souvenir d'un banquet offert par les compagnies réunies de chemins de fer de la Grande Bretagne . . .' (*Les chemins de fer anglais et l'administration des postes*.) *London*, 1929. pp. 14. (11 illus.)   LSE

5548 GENERAL POST OFFICE. The Travelling Post Office. *London*, Sept. 1936. pp. 16, with 12 illus. & a map.   IT

5549 ROWDEN, J. J. C. The Travelling Post Office. *London: G.P.O.*, 1936. pp. 14, with 12 illus. [*Post Office Green Papers*, no. 24.]   RC

5550 CARTER, W. G. Post Office (London) Railway. *London: G.P.O.*, Sept. 1937. pp. 21, with 22 illus., diagram & map. [*Post Office Green Papers*, no. 36.]   BM

5551 GENERAL POST OFFICE. Night Mail: the Travelling Post Office. [*London*,] April 1939. pp. 15. [*Series PL*, no. 21.]   BM
Illustrated by Pat Keeley.

5552 STEVENS, F. L. Under London: a chronicle of London's underground life-lines and relics. *London: Dent*, 1939. pp. 204.   BM
pp. 61–9, Post Office Underground Rly.

*5553 GENERAL POST OFFICE. The Post Office Railway, London. *London*, March 1936. pp. 7, with 7 illus. & map.   IT
—— another edn. *London*, October 1948. pp. [4,] with 6 illus. & map.   RC

5554 HOWSON, F. H. Narrow gauge railways of Britain. *London: Ian Allan*, 1948. pp. 79, with illus.   BM
Includes the Post Office tube railway, London.

5555 ASHDOWNE, H. A. Transportation of mails. pp. 18. *Typescript*.   IT
Paper, Institute of Transport, Northwest Section, 2 Feb., 1954.
T.P.O.'s.

5556 GENERAL POST OFFICE. The Post Office Railway. [*London*,] Sept. 1952. pp. [6,] with 7 illus. [*Series PL*, no. 4.]   BM
—— another edn. [*London*,] 1957. pp. [6.] [*Series PL*, no. 110.]   BM

K 10   RAILWAYS AND NATIONAL DEFENCE

The use of public railways for movements of troops and equipment

For military railways see **K 11**
For fears of invasion via the Channel Tunnel see **C 8**

5557 TYLER, H. W. Railways strategically considered. [*London*, 1864.] pp. 23, with a map.   BM
From the *Journal of the Royal United Service Institution*, vol. 8.

5558 ARMY. Regulations for the transport of troops by railway. Quartermaster-General's Office, Horse Guards, 28th February 1867. *London: H.M.S.O.*, [1867.] pp. 7.   BM

5559 LONGMORE, T. A treatise on the transport of sick and wounded troops; illustrated by nearly two hundred wood-cuts. *London: H.M.S.O.*, [1869.] pp. xxvi, 514.   BM
Cover title, *Treatise on ambulances*.
pp. 443–88, 'Conveyances moved by steam power on railways'.

5560 WEBER, M. M. von. Our railway system viewed in reference to invasion; being a translation of a memoir entitled 'The training of railways for war in time of peace' with an introduction and notes by Robert Mallet. *London*, 1871. pp. 110.   BM
A translation of M. M. von Weber's *Die Schulung der Eisenbahnen für den Krieg im Frieden*.
In his introduction (pp. 1–60), Robert Mallet applies the subject to the British Isles.

5561 GIROUARD, E. P. C. The use of railways for coast and harbour defence. *London: Royal United Service Institution*, 1891. pp. 20, with fold. map.   ICE
'For private circulation only.'
Girouard was Railway Traffic Manager at the Royal Arsenal, Woolwich.

5562 SCHEME for the mobilisation of Royal Naval Reserve: timetable of special trains and ordinary train routes. December 1897. pp. 24.   BR
Arranged under Portsmouth, Sheerness and Chatham, and Devonport Commands.

5563 FINDLAY, G. The working and management of an English railway; with numerous illustrations. 4th edition. *London*, 1891. pp. vi, 354.   BM
—— 5th edn. *London*, 1894. pp. 412.   BM
—— 6th, *London*, 1899. pp. 412.   BM
   Only the 4th, 5th, and 6th editions have a substantial section on railways and national defence.

5564 HAZELL, A. P. Work for the unemployed! A national highway for military & motor traffic: a practical proposal for providing useful & productive work for the huge number of professional, skilled and unskilled workers at present out of employment. *London: Twentieth Century Press*, [1908.] pp. 16. LSE
   Includes mono-rail for rapid transport of troops in case of invasion.

5565 PRATT, E. A. The rise of rail power in war
b   and conquest, 1833 to 1914; with a bibliography. *London*, 1915. pp. xii, 405.   BM
   The military use of railways.

5566 WAR OFFICE. Manual of Movement (War). *London: H. M. Stationery Office*, 1923. pp. 218.   BM
   Subsequently issued as part VI of *Instructions in Military Engineering*.

K 11   MILITARY RAILWAYS

Systems owned, operated, and maintained by military authorities

5567 RAILWAYS and their future improvements, especially in a military point of view: an essay recently submitted to, and approved by, the Prussian Government. *London*, 1845. pp. 40.   BM

5568 FELL, J. B. Lecture delivered at a meeting of the United Service Institution at Plymouth . . . on the use of improved narrow gauge railways in the operations of war . . . *Aldershot*, 1873. pp. 30.   ICE

5569 FELL, J. B. Military field railways . . . *Ulverston*, 1876. pp. 10.   ICE

5570 [FELL, J. B.] Reports of the Royal Engineers Committee and correspondence with the Secretary of State for War, on the experiments made at Aldershot with Mr. J. B. Fell's system for the rapid construction of military field railways. *Ulverston*, 1876. pp. 19.   ICE

5571 HADDAN, J. L. Military railways . . . *London*, [1878.] pp. 34.   BM
   'For private circulation only.'

5572 ARMY—ROYAL ENGINEERS. Manual of Military Railways. *London*, 1889. pp. 95, with 17 plates & tables.   BM
   Field railways and trench tramways, with sections on engine driving and maintenance, and platelaying.

5573 FINDLAY, G. On the transport of troops by rail within the United Kingdom. [1890.] pp. 25, with 2 plates.   pc
   'For private circulation.'

5574 MANCE, H. O. Armoured trains. *Chatham*, 1906. pp. 52, with 9 plates. [*Royal Engineers. Professional Papers, Fourth Series*, vol. 1, no. 4.]   BM

5575 ARMY—ROYAL ENGINEERS—20TH LIGHT RAILWAY TRAIN CREWS COMPANY. With the British Expeditionary Force, 1917–1919. *Bath*, [1919.] pp. 52, with illus.   BM
   Edited by Sapper J. Helliwell Laytham.

5576 REDMAN, A. S. Transportation in war, course of 5 lectures given to the Army Class, London School of Economics, Lent Term 1925. *London*, 1925. pp. 50, with fold. table.   IT

5577 HENNIKER, A. M. Transportation on the Western Front, 1914–1918. *London: H.M.S.O.*, 1937. pp. xxxiv, 531, with 17 sketch maps in text & 14 la. fold. maps in separate case. No illus. [*History of the Great War* Series.]   BM

5578 LANGLEY, C. A. Longmoor Military Railway. *Westminster*, 1946. pp. 22, with 19 illus. & a map.   BM
   Reprinted from the *Railway Gazette*, 5 July, 1946.
   An address by the Commandant.

5579 MACCREARY, R. *and* CHARLESWORTH, R. L. Railways in the N.W. Europe Campaign. *Belfast: Belfast Association of Engineers*, [1950.] pp. 22.   SLS
   Lecture, 11 January, 1950.
   Includes activities of British Army Railway Construction & Operating Groups.

5580 ARMY—ROYAL ENGINEERS—TRANSPORTATION TRAINING CENTRE, LONGMOOR. 'At Home', 3rd September, 1947: souvenir programme. *Aldershot: Gale & Polden*, [1947.] pp. 15, with 8 illus., map & plan.
                                          BM
—— 'Public Day, Saturday, 3rd September, 1949: souvenir programme.' *Aldershot*, 1949. pp. 15, with 5 illus., map & plan. pc
—— 'Public Day, 5 September, 1953. Jubilee souvenir programme.' [*Guildford*, 1953.] pp. 16, with illus.   IT

5581 COOPER, F. W. The Calshot 'Express': a history of the narrow-gauge railway at the Royal Air Force Station, Calshot, Southampton. *Lingfield: Oakwood Press*, 1963. pp. 28, with 9 illus. on 4 plates, map in 3 sections, diagrams, & tables of locomotives.
                                          BM
   Cover title, *The Calshot R.A.F. Railway*.

The history and description of individual lines, including accounts of their locomotives, etc. Collective works followed by an alphabetical arrangement of railway 'families' (see note below).

For 'British Railways' see **B 10**
For railways, tramways, and underground railways owned and operated by local authorities see **C**

Note on the arrangement:
British railway history is largely the history of its amalgamations. In order to embrace this continual change and to present an arrangement of railway companies representing their history as a whole, it is necessary to intercept the process at some stage where, if possible, the whole scene may be brought into view.

Undoubtedly the most favourable vantage point is to be found in the decade preceding the 'Big Four' amalgamations of 1st January, 1923 (Railways Act, 1921). By this time the companies had formed themselves into what may be regarded as their natural family groups, with individualities and traditions of their own making. Here, past and present can be photographed and fixed with everything in focus.

The following is an alphabetical arrangement of these railway families, in so far as they or their members claim a place in this Bibliography as subjects of monographs. To this is added the companies formed in 1923—Southern, Great Western (although this was virtually the old company unchanged), London, Midland & Scottish, and the London & North Eastern, and a few small companies formed since.

Lists of companies amalgamated under the Railways Act, and of undertakings nationalized under the Transport Act (1947), and four genealogical tables, are included as Appendices.

Marginal symbols: **b** bibliographies
c chronologies

Additional symbols are used to identify works relating to the main constituent companies within each group (e.g. under Great Eastern Railway, EC for Eastern Counties Railway).

COLLECTIVE WORKS

5582 CORT, R. Rail-road impositions detected; or, Facts and arguments to prove that the Manchester & Liverpool Railway has not paid one per cent nett profit, and that the Birmingham, Bristol, Southampton, Windsor, and other railways are, and must for ever be, only bubble speculations. *London,* 1834. pp. 64 [72], with tables & notes.   LSE
   Liverpool & Manchester; London & Birmingham; Great Western; London & Southampton; Midland Counties; London & Greenwich.
—— 2nd edn. *London,* 1834. pp. 195.   BM

5583 WHISHAW, F. Analysis of railways, consisting of a series of reports on the twelve hundred miles of projected railways in England and Wales now before Parliament, together with those which have been abandoned for the present Session, to which are added a table of distances from the proposed London termini to eight well-known places in the Metropolis . . . and other useful information. *London,* 1837. pp. xv, 296.   BM
   Eighty railways.
—— 2nd edn., with additions & corrections. *London,* 1838. pp. xv, 298.   ICE

*5584 WHISHAW, F. The railways of Great Britain and Ireland, practically described and illustrated. *London,* 1840, 1841. pp. xxvi, 500; lxiv, with 17 fold. plates.   BM
   Detailed accounts of fifty-eight railways, with tables compiled from results of experimental runs extending to 7000 miles, and tables relating to the performances of 630 locomotives. Also, Standing Orders of the House of Commons relating to Railway Bills.
—— 2nd edn. '. . . with some additional useful plates.' *London,* 1842. pp. xxvi, 500; lxiv, with fold. map & 19 plates.   LSE

5585 [GALT, W.] Railway reform: its expediency and practicability considered; with a copious appendix containing a description of all the railways in Great Britain and Ireland. *London,* 1843. pp. 108.   BM
—— 2nd edn. *London,* 1843. pp. 116.   BM
—— 3rd edn. *London,* 1844. pp. 116.   H
—— People's edn. *London,* 1844. pp. 76.   BM

5586 BRITISH MUSEUM—DEPARTMENT OF PRINTED BOOKS. [Documents relating to railways in Great Britain and Ireland. A collection of prospectuses, reports, maps, pamphlets, etc. concerning 341 railway companies under formation between 1829 and 1875, arranged alphabetically in 7 volumes, with an index.]   BM(MAPS)

5587 STRETTON, C. E. Locomotive development. *Leeds: Associated Society of Locomotive Engineers & Firemen*, [1889.] pp. 40. ICE
Special number of the Society's *Locomotive Engineer's & Fireman's Monthly Journal.*
Arranged under railways.

5588 PATTINSON, J. P. British railways; their passenger services, rolling stock, locomotives, gradients and express speeds . . . *London*, 1893. pp. xiv, 249, with 35 plates.
BM

5589 ROUND the works of our great railways; by various authors . . . *London*, [1893.] pp. vii, 232, with illus.   BM

The London & North Western Railway Works at Crewe. C. J. B. Cooke.
The Midland Railway Works at Derby. C. H. Jones.
The Great Northern Railway Works at Doncaster. A. J. Brickwell.
The North Eastern Railway and its engines. W. Worsdell.
The Great Eastern Railway Works at Stratford. A. P. Parker.
The Great Western Railway Works at Swindon. A. H. Malan.
Old broad gauge engines and their successors. A. H. Malan.
The North British Railway Works at Cowlairs. A. E. Lockyer.

5590 GORDON, W. J. The story of our railways. *London*, [1896.] pp. 159, with illus.   BM
General railway history, and histories of individual lines.

*5591 ACWORTH, W. M. The railways of England . . . *London*, 1889. pp. xvi, 427, with 56 illus.   BR
Historical accounts of main-line companies.
—— 2nd edn. *London*, 1889. pp. xvi, 427. UL
—— 3rd, *London*, 1889. pp. xvi, 427.   BM
—— 4th, *London*, 1890. pp. xvi, 427.   IT
—— 5th, *London*, 1900. pp. xxiv, 480, with 67 illus.   BM

5592 STRETTON, C. E. [A collection of cuttings from local newspapers, and pamphlets; being reports of lectures given by Clement E. Stretton on the history of various railways. About 100 items.] 1867–1904. 7 vols.   BM
The reports are mostly verbatim and in length may average between two or three columns. The place and date of each lecture are usually added in MS. and show that most of Stretton's visits were made to centres in the Midlands and North of England between 1867 and 1904. Some items are marked 'Railway Club Paper'; others were addressed to gatherings of the Permanent Way Institution or the Amalgamated Society of Railway Servants.
Stretton reproduced some of these lectures

as pamphlets, and in this form they appear as 'second [etc.] edition'. Examples are found in vol. 6 of this collection.
As sources of information these popular lectures are incomplete and unreliable.

vol. 1. The history of the South Leicestershire Railway. 1867.
The history of the Nuneaton & Hinckley, afterwards the South Leicestershire Railway. 1868.
—— another edn. 1886.
The history of the Belvoir Castle Railway. 1869.
—— another edn. *n.d.*
The history of the Loughborough & Nanpantan Railway. 1869.
—— another edn. *n.d.*
The history of the Leicester & Burton line. 1870.
The history of the South Midland, afterwards the Leicester & Hitchin line. 1872.
The history of the Coleorton Railway. 1872.
The history of the Bolton & Leigh and the Kenyon & Leigh Junction railways. 1878.
The history of the Liverpool & Manchester Railway. 1880.
The history of the Wigan Branch Railway. 1882.
The history of the Preston & Wigan Railway.
The history of the Birmingham & Gloucester Railway. 1884.
The history of the Ashby & Nuneaton Joint Railway. 1884.
The history of the Ashby Canal and Outram roads. 1885.

vol. 2. The history of the Mansfield & Pinxton outram-way.
The history of the South Midland, afterwards the Leicester & Hitchin line. 1885.
The history of the Leicester & Hitchin line. 1885.
The history of the Stour Valley Railway. 1885.
The history of the North Midland Railway. 1885.
The history of the Birmingham & Derby Junction Railway. 1885.
The history of the Mansfield & Pinxton outram-way. 1887.
The history of the Settle & Carlisle line. 1886.
—— another edn. 1886.
The history of the Sheffield & Rotherham Railway. 1888.
—— another edn. [after 1897.]

vol. 3. The history of the Leeds & Bradford Railway. 1886.
The history of the North Western Railway. 1886, 1887.
—— another edn. *n.d.*
The history of the Rowsley, Buxton & New Mills (Midland line). 1887.
The history of the Manchester, Buxton, Matlock & Midlands Junction Railway. 1887.

—— another edn. 1887.

The history of the Grand Junction Railway. 1887.

The history of the Bristol & Gloucester Railway. 1887.

The history of the North Union Railway Company. 1888.

The history of the Birmingham & Derby Junction Railway. 1889.

The history of the North Midland Railway. 1890.

The history of the Lancaster & Preston Junction Railway. 1890.

vol. 4. The history of the Pinxton & Leicester, afterwards Midland Counties Railway. 1890.

The history of the Preston & Wyre Railway. 1890.

The history of the Coleorton Railway. 1892.

The history of the Leicester & Swannington Railway. 1892.

The history of the canals, edge-railways, outram-ways, and railways in the county of Leicester. pts. 1, 2, & 3. 1894.

The history of the Irish Mail route. 1893.

Early locomotive engines and their work. 1893.

The early locomotive firm, Messrs. Nasmyth & Co. 1893.

Locomotives built by Messrs. Mather, Dixon & Co. 1893.

vol. 5. The Midland Railway Company: a summary. 1893.

The history of the Sheffield & Rotherham Railway. 1893.

The history of the Mansfield & Pinxton outram-way. 1893.

The Midland Railway Company. [Duplicate of the first item in this volume.] 1894.

The history of the Bristol & Gloucester Railway. 1894.

The history of the London & North Western Railway. 1896.

The history of the Lancaster & Carlisle Railway. 1896.

The history of the Kendal & Windermere Railway. 1897.

The history of the Trent Valley Railway. 1897.

The history of the Portpatrick & Wigtownshire Joint line. 1897.

The history of the Chester & Holyhead Railway. 1898.

The history of the Syston & Peterborough line. 1898.

The history of the Conway Tubular Bridge. 1898.

The history of the Larne & Stranraer (boat) route. 1898.

The history of the Holyhead & Greenore route to Ireland. 1898.

The history of the Fleetwood & Belfast service. 1898.

vol. 6. The history of the Holyhead mail route to Ireland. 1898.

Derbyshire railway history. pts. 1, 2, & 3. 1899.

The history of the Britannia Tubular Bridge. 1900.

Railway history at the Leicester Museum [with illus.]. 1901.

The history of the various routes from Leicester to London. 1901.

The canals, edge-rail-ways, outram-ways, and railways in the county of Leicester. pt. 4. 1901.

The history of the Holyhead & Dublin railway boat service. 1902.

The history of the Birmingham & Gloucester, and Bristol & Gloucester railways. 2nd edn. Leeds, 1902. pp. 19.

The history of the South Leicestershire Railway. 3rd edn. Leeds, 1902. pp. 9.

The history of the Ashby & Nuneaton Joint Railway [and] The history of the Sheffield & Rotherham Railway. In 'Locomotive Engineer's & Fireman's Monthly Journal', vol. 15, no. 5, May 1902. pp. [193]–200.

The history of the London & North Western Railway. 3rd edn. Leeds, 1902. pp. 17.

The history of the London & North Western Railway: a summary. 1896.

—— 3rd edn. 1902.

List of railway rails presented to the Leicester Museum by C. E. and C. Stretton. MS. title. 1904.

The Compulsory Metric System Bill. 1907.

vol. 7. The history of the Dundee & Newtyle Railway. 1881.

The history of the canal and railway communication with Loughborough. 1883.

The history of the Manchester & Birmingham Railway. 1886.

The history of the Kendal & Windermere Railway. 1886.

The history of the Lancaster & Preston Junction.

Stretton Collection, Chicago Exhibition, 1893. Details of English plates, rails, etc. 1893.

The history of the Syston & Peterborough line. 1893.

The Loughborough & Nanpantan edge railway. 1893.

The history of St. George's Harbour & Chester Railway. 1898.

The history of the railway companies' boat service between Holyhead and North Wall. 1898.

The history of the Blackpool & Lytham Railway. 1903.

The history of railway permanent way [with illus.]. 1904.

Bradford's first railway.

The history of the Pinxton & Leicester, afterwards Midland Counties Railway. 1904.

The history of railway permanent way.

The history of the Great Western Railway. [Four instalments from the Gloucester Journal, August 1, 8, 15, & 22, 1903.]

The history of the Pinxton & Leicester, afterwards the Midland Counties Railway. 1904.

5593 GORDON, W. J. Our home railways: how they began and how they are worked; with 36 original coloured plates by W. J. Stokoe and 300 illustrations from photographs. *London*, 1910. 2 vols. pp. xvi, 268; x, 248.   BM
Also issued in 12 parts.
The main-line railways. Three coloured plates for each railway illustrate its coat of arms, a locomotive and a carriage.

—— reprint, *London: Ian Allan*, 1962. 2 vols.   BM
Plates in monochrome.

5594 DEFRANCE, P. Les Chemins de fer de la Grande-Bretagne et de l'Irlande: étude au point de vue commercial et financier. *Bruxelles & Paris*, 1911. pp. 292, with 61 illus.   BM
pp. 13–142, History and description of individual railways.

5595 PRATT, E. A. British railways and the Great War . . . *London*, 1921. 2 vols. (pp. x, 1194.)   BM
Sixteen of the seventy-four chapters deal with individual railways.

5596 LOCOMOTIVE, RAILWAY CARRIAGE & WAGON REVIEW. Railway Centenary Supplement . . . *London*, June 30, 1925. pp. 124, with 28 plates (7 col.).   PO
Historical essays by various writers on each of the components of the main-line companies and the Underground Railways of London, including their locomotive history.

5597 HOME, G., TODD, G. E., *and* MITTON, G. E. The railways of Britain: G.W.R., L.M.S., L.N.E.R., & S.R., with 32 coloured plates and many line illustrations. *London*, [1926.]   BR
A combined edition of four works:
The Great Western Railway, by Gordon Home. 1926. pp. 89.
The London, Midland & Scottish Railway, by G. Eyre Todd. 1926. pp. 91.
The London & North Eastern Railway, by Geraldine E. Mitton. 1925. pp. 91.
The Southern Railway, by G. E. Mitton. 1925. pp. 91.
These works are for general reading and are mainly concerned with the topography of the areas served. Their railway information is very limited.

5598 JACKSON, G. G. British locomotives; their evolution and development. *London*, [1929.] pp. x, 246, with many illus. on plates.   BM
Arranged under companies.

5599 LONDON SCHOOL OF ECONOMICS— BRITISH LIBRARY OF POLITICAL AND ECONOMIC SCIENCE. Early British railways: a collection, chiefly of press cuttings, maps, & other printed matter, also of manuscript letters, maps and plans, illustrating the rise and progress of some early British railways from 1795 to 1850, and the victory of railway over canal. Compiled by Septimus Bell . . . between 1848 & 1850. 1943. 8 vols, with typescript introduction & detailed indexes.   LSE
Blaydon, Gateshead & Hebburn, vol. IV.
Brandling Junction, vol. IV.
Durham & Sunderland, vol. IV.
Grand Eastern Union, vol. VIII.
Great North British, vol. VIII.
Great North of England, vol. VI.
Great Western, vol. V.
London & Birmingham, vol. V.
Lancaster & Carlisle, vol. VIII.
London & Greenwich, vol. VI.
Liverpool & Manchester, vol. IV.
Liverpool, Manchester & Newcastle, vol. IV.
Newcastle & Berwick, vol. VIII.
Newcastle & Carlisle, vols. I–III.
Newcastle & Darlington Junction, vol. VIII.
Newcastle, Edinburgh & Glasgow, vol. VII.
South Eastern and some lesser railways, vol. VI.

5600 COMING of age of Railway Grouping: G.W.R., L.M.S.R., L.N.E.R., S.R. *London: Railway Gazette*, 1944. pp. iii, 64, with portraits of senior railway officials.   BM
A review of British railways since 1921.

*5601 BUCKNALL, R. Our railway history; illustrated. *London*, 1944. pp. 140, in 3 parts issued separately.   BM
Published by the author.
pt. 1, London & North Western; Great Western; Midland; North Eastern; Great Northern.
pt. 2, Great Eastern; Lancashire & Yorkshire; Great Central; London & South Western; London, Brighton & South Coast; South Eastern & Chatham.
pt. 3, North British; Caledonian; Glasgow & South Western; Highland; Great North of Scotland.

—— 2nd edn., rev. & enl. *London*, 1945. pp. 148. in one vol., with la. fold. map & 122 illus.   BM

5602 The LOCO Book, 1947. *Huddersfield: Quadrant Publications*, [1947.] pp. 48[49].   BM
Lists of the locomotives of the main-line companies.

5603 GREENLEAF, H. Britain's Big Four: the story of the London, Midland & Scottish, London & North Eastern, Great Western, and Southern railways. *London: Winchester Publications*, 1948. pp. 228, with many illus. (come col.).   BM

5604 ELLIS, C. H. Four main lines. *London: Allen & Unwin*, 1950. pp. 225, with 78 illus. on 32 plates (8 col.).   BM
The story of the evolution of the L.M.S., L.N.E.R., G.W.R., and L. & S.W.R.

5605 AHRONS, E. L. Locomotive and train working in the latter part of the nineteenth century. Edited by L. L. Asher . . . *Cambridge: Heffer*, 1951–4. 6 vols.   BM
Previously published in the *Railway Magazine* between 1915 and 1926. Each volume has forty-eight illustrations of locomotives.
vol. 1, Great Northern; Manchester, Sheffield

and Lincolnshire; North Eastern; Great Eastern; Midland & Great Northern; Hull & Bansley.

vol. 2, London & North Western; Lancashire & Yorkshire; Midland; North Staffordshire; Furness; Maryport & Carlisle; North London.

vol. 3, Glasgow & South Western; Caledonian; Highland; North British; Great North of Scotland.

vol. 4, Great Western; Cambrian; Brecon & Merthyr; Taff Vale; Rhymney; Barry; Midland & South Western Junction.

vol. 5, South Eastern; London, Chatham & Dover; London, Brighton & South Coast; Somerset & Dorset Joint; Metropolitan; Metropolitan District.

vol. 6, [Ireland.] Great Southern & Western; Waterford, Limerick & Western; Dublin, Wicklow & Wexford; Midland Great Western; Great Northern (I).

5606 CARTER, E. F. An historical geography of
c   the railways of the British Isles. *London*,
1959. pp. x, 637.   BM
A chronological (not geographical) record of railway company history, with much detail concerning openings, extensions, closures, etc., of lines. The work contains many errors and omissions. (See reviews in *Journal of Transport History*, vol. 4, no. 3, May 1960; and *Railway Magazine*, February 1960.)

5607 STEPHENSON LOCOMOTIVE SOCIETY. Railway progress, 1909–1959. Jubilee Year publication, volume one. *London*, [1960.] pp. 139, with 65 illus. on 24 plates.   pc
Locomotive development on various railways.

*5608 OTTLEY, G. Railway company prospectuses in the British Museum Library: a handlist. *In preparation.*

INDIVIDUAL RAILWAYS

Aberdeen, Banff & Elgin Railway

5609 ABERDEEN, BANFF & ELGIN RLY. Statements, etc. connected with the proposed railway. *Aberdeen*, 1846. pp. [iv,]44.   AU

Alexandra (Newport & South Wales) Docks and Railway

5610 ALEXANDRA DOCKS & RLY. CO. Alexandra Docks and Railway Company. *Newport, Mon.*, 1903. pp. 86, with 35 illus. & 2 fold. maps.   BM
A descriptive handbook.

5611 ALEXANDRA DOCKS & RLY. CO. Tables of Rates . . . general information . . . *Newport, Mon.* 1910. pp. 72.   BM
—— another edn. 'Newport Docks . . .: book of rates and general information.' *Newport, Mon.*, 1919. pp. 77.   NEWPORT PL

Alford & Sutton Tramway

5612 DOW, G. The Alford and Sutton Tramway. *Chislehurst: Oakwood Press*, 1947. pp. 20, with illus., diagrams & maps. [*Locomotion Papers*, no. 1.]   BM
Reprinted from *Locomotion*, vol. XI, no. 35, July 1947.

Ashover Light Railway

5613 GOTHERIDGE, I. *and* K. P. PLANT. The Ashover Light Railway. *London: the authors*, [1956.] pp. 26, with illus. & maps. *Reproduced typescript.*   RC

Axholme Joint Railway

5614 OATES, G. The Axholme Joint Railway. *Lingfield: Oakwood Press*, 1961. pp. 26, with 12 illus., map, & a chronology. [*Locomotion Papers*, no. 16.]   BM

Barry Dock and Railway

5615 ROBINSON, J. Description of the Barry Dock and Railways. *London*, [1888.] pp. 17, with 7 fold. plates of plans & diagrams.   BM
Paper, South Wales Institute of Engineers, Cardiff, 26 July, 1888.

5616 BARRY RLY. Barry Dock and Railways: description of the undertaking. *Cardiff*, 1889. pp. 20, with fold. map.   BR
—— another edn. *Cardiff*, 1906. pp. 17. BR
—— another edn. '. . . with tables of rates & general information.' *Cardiff*, [1911.] pp. 65.   BR
—— another edn. '. . . Compiled & arranged by H. N. Appleby.' *Barry Docks*, 1919. pp. 148.   BR

5617 RIMELL, R. J. History of the Barry Railway Company, 1884–1921. *Cardiff*, 1923. pp. 131, with fold. map.   BM

5618 DAVIES, L. N. A. The history of the Barry Dock & Railways Company in relation to the development of the South Wales coalfield. Thesis, M.A., University of Wales, 1938. pp. 193, 10, with maps (some printed), mounted photographs (cuttings), and diagrams, including a graph. *Typescript.* NLW

5619 ALLCHIN, M. C. V. Locomotives of the Cambrian, Barry and Rhymney railways: types, building dates, etc. *Fareham: the author*, [1942.]. pp. 12.   BM
—— rev. edn. *Fareham*, [1943.] pp. 12. BM

*5619a BARRIE, D. S. The Barry Railway. *Lingfield: Oakwood Press*, 1962. pp.[151]–213, with 31 illus. on 12 plates, 2 maps, & 3 tables relating to locomotives. [*Oakwood Library of Railway History*, no. 57.]   BM

Basing & Bath Railway Company
[not incorporated]

5620 GILES, F. *and* BRUNTON, W. Plan of the intended Basing and Bath Railway. 1834, with 12 large scale plans of the route.   BM

5621 REPORT of the proceedings of a meeting held at the White Hart Inn, Bath, on Friday

12 September, 1834, for the purpose of affording explanations respecting a projected railway between that City and Basing (Basing, Bath & Bristol Rly.). *Bristol*, [1834.] pp. 15.   LSE

Copied from the *Bath Guardian* of September 13, 1834.

Basingstoke & Alton Light Railway

5622 GRIFFITH, E. C. The Basingstoke and Alton Light Railway, 1901 to 1936. *Farnham: E. W. Langham*, 1947. pp. 28, with 19 illus., map & timetables.   BM

Berwick & Kelso Railway

5623 CALCULATIONS of the probable benefit to the neighbouring country and to the proprietors, of an iron rail way from Berwick to Kelso, passing by the coal pits and lime works in the North Bishopric of Durham. *Kelso*, 1809. pp. 20.   UL(GL)

An interim publication circulated while awaiting the report of a survey by John Rennie. Only a few copies printed.

5624 RENNIE, J. Report by Mr. John Rennie, engineer, respecting the proposed railway from Kelso to Berwick, 14 November 1809. *Edinburgh*, 1824. pp. 16, with fold. map.   UL(GL)

A reprint of a report originally published in Kelso, 1810.

Bideford, Westward Ho! & Appledore Railway

*5625 STUCKEY, D. The Bideford, Westward Ho! & Appledore Railway, 1901–1917. *Stoke-on-Trent: Clarion Printers*, 1962. pp. 18, with 8 illus. on 4 plates, tables, & a map & 2 plans on covers. [*West Country Handbooks*, no. 1.]   BM

Bishop's Castle Railway

5626 FRASER, J. Bishop's Castle Railway. Mr. Fraser's report, March 1875. pp. 18, with fold. map.   BR

No title-page in BR copy.

Report on the company's position and affairs, submitted by J. Fraser as chairman of the meeting of debenture holders held 4 May, 1874. Includes a financial history of the line.

*5627 GRIFFITH, E. C. The Bishop's Castle Railway, Shropshire, 1865–1935. *Farnham: E. W. Langham*, 1949. pp. 54, with 32 illus. & 2 maps.   BM

Bluebell Railway

(part of the Lewes and East Grinstead Branch, London, Brighton & South Coast Railway)

5628 BLUEBELL RAILWAY PRESERVATION SOCIETY. The Handbook of the Bluebell Line. *Tunbridge Wells*, [1960.] pp. 19, with 10 illus. & a map.   BM

—— another edn. *Tunbridge Wells*, [1962.] pp. 32, with 16 illus., tables & map.   BM

5629 BLUEBELL RLY. Introducing the Bluebell Railway in pictures. *Uckfield*, [1964.] pp. [32,] with 50 illus., map, & cover illus. in col.   BM

Brecon & Merthyr Tydfil Junction Railway (Brecon & Merthyr Rly.)

5630 BARRIE, D. S. The Brecon & Merthyr Railway. *Lingfield: Oakwood Press*, 1957. pp. [95]–150, with 19 illus. on 8 plates; maps & tables of locos. in text. [*Oakwood Library of Railway History*, no. 13.]   BM

Caledonian Railway
Historical

5631 GRAHAM, G. The Caledonian Railway: account of its origin and completion, largely composed of extracts from information got from the original promoters. *Glasgow & London*, 1888. pp. 96[97], with portraits & a map.   LSE

'Printed for private circulation and not for publication.'

5632 'N'OUBLIEZ.' Print of cuttings from newspapers relative to the Caledonian Railway and its originators. [By] N'Oubliez. *Glasgow*, 1890. pp. 48.   ICE

Privately printed. Cover title, *The Caledonian Railway & its originators*.

5633 LONDON, MIDLAND & SCOTTISH RLY. Centenary of the Caledonian Railway, 1847–1947. *London*, Sept. 1947. pp. 32, with 16 illus. on 8 plates, & 2 maps inside covers.   BM

5634 STEPHENSON LOCOMOTIVE SOCIETY. Caledonian Railway Centenary, 1847–1947. *London*, Sept. 1947. pp. 76, with 65 illus. on plates, fold. maps & plans.   IT

5635 MACLEOD, A. B. The McIntosh locomotives of the Caledonian Railway, 1895–1914. *Staines: Ian Allan*, 1944. pp. 41, with illus. & tables.   BM

—— another edn. *London*, 1948. pp. 48. BM

5636 NOCK, O. S. The Caledonian Railway. *London: Ian Allan*, [1962.] pp. 190, with col. frontis., 32 plates (incl. portraits) & illus., maps, plans, tables & diagrams.   BM

Contemporaneous

5637 GRAINGER, T. *and* MILLER, J. Report and estimate of the probable expense of the proposed extension of the Garnkirk & Glasgow Railway to Port Dundas. *Edinburgh*, 1829. pp. 8, with fold. map.   ICE

5638 HILL, D. O. Views of the opening of the Glasgow & Garnkirk Railway. *Edinburgh*, 1832. pp. 11, with 5 plates & illus.   H

5639 BLACKADDER, W. Report relative to the Strathmore Railway, being the extension of Dundee & Newtyle Railway from Newtyle

along Strathmore between Coupar and Forfar. *Dundee*, 1833. pp. 26, with 3 fold. maps.
LSE

5640 [ARBROATH & FORFAR RLY.] Proceedings in regard to the projected Arbroath & Forfar Railway. *Arbroath*, 1835. pp. 8. ARBROATH PL

5641 FINDLATER, J. R. Report relative to the formation of a railway between the towns of Dundee and Perth, passing through the districts of the carse of Gowrie; submitted to a meeting of the promoters of that undertaking . . . Supplementary report by George Buchanan. *Dundee*, 1835. pp. 24, 11, with fold. map.   H

5642 GRAINGER, T. *and* MILLER, J. Report relative to the proposed railway from Arbroath to Forfar, drawn up for the consideration of a meeting to be held at Arbroath on 7 August 1835. *Edinburgh*, 1835. pp. 17.   ARBROATH PL

5643 DUNDEE & NEWTYLE RLY. Vidimus of the state of the affairs and prospects of the Dundee & Newtyle Railway Company. *Dundee*, 1836. pp. 14.   H

5644 [DUMFRIES.] PROVISIONAL COMMITTEE FOR PROMOTING THE RAILWAY FROM CARLISLE THROUGH THE VALE OF EVAN TO EDINBURGH & GLASGOW. Reports on the proposed line of railway from Carlisle to Glasgow and Edinburgh by Annandale. [*Dumfries*,] 1838. pp. 11[12.]   BM
pp. 9–11, A report from J. Locke reprinted for the subscribers, with an additional report from the Committee.

5645 WARDEN, J. The Glasgow & Ayr and Glasgow & Greenock Railway Companion; containing a description of the railroads . . . *Glasgow*, 1841. pp. 134.   LSE

5646 ADAMSON, R. Report by the Committee of Management of the Dundee & Arbroath Railway Company to the Annual General Meeting of the Company, held 1st day of June, 1842. *Dundee*, 1842. pp. 14.   LSE
In the LSE copy, pp. 11 and 12 are missing.

5647 KENDAL RAILWAY COMMITTEE. Caledonian Railway. Relative advantages of the Kendal line and the Lune line to their junction at Borrow Bridge considered. *Kendal*, 1842. pp. 12.   BM
Signed 'on behalf of the Kendal Railway Ctte., Cornelius Nicholson, Secretary'.

5648 ATKINSON, R. Thoughts on the subject of the proposed Caledonian Railway, by the Valley of the Lune, or by Kendal; with observations on a pamphlet published on behalf of the Kendal Railway Committee by their secretary, Mr. C. Nicholson. *Kirby Lonsdale*, 1842. pp. 16.   H

5649 [CALEDONIAN RLY.] Remarks on the Caledonian Railway and other railway projects

for completing the railway communication between England and Scotland. *Edinburgh*, 1845. pp. 16.   BM
Reasons for supporting the Caledonian.

5650 BRIDGES, J. The Sunday railways practically discussed: a letter to J. J. H. Johnstone . . . Chairman of the Caledonian Railway Company. *Edinburgh*, 1847. pp. 19.   BM
—— 4th edn. *Edinburgh & London*, 1847. pp. 20.   H
—— 5th edn. *Edinburgh & London*, 1848. pp. 20.   H

5651 ABERDEEN RLY. Debate on the running of Sabbath trains . . . *Aberdeen*, [1849.] pp. 18.
BM

5652 ABERDEEN RLY. Report of a discussion on Sabbath trains at a meeting held at Radley's Hotel, London, 24th October 1850. Extracted from the 'Aberdeen Banner'. [*Aberdeen*, 1850.] pp. 11.   AU
Sunday trains on the Aberdeen Rly.

5653 TAYLEUR & CO. Specification for the passenger engines on the Caledonian Railway. *In* 'The principles and practices and explanation of the machinery of locomotive engines in operation on the several lines of railway' by T. Tredgold. (Division A, Locomotive engines; 7th paper.) *London*, 1850. pp. 12, with tables & 6 plates.   BM

5654 'JUDEX.' The Hawick & Carlisle railways: the case stated and the best route indicated. By Judex. *Carlisle*, 1858. pp. 38.   BM
Arguments against the Caledonian and in favour of the North British Hawick & Carlisle Junction Rly. Bill. Appendix—The Silloth Rly. & Dock.

5655 MEASOM, G. The Official Illustrated Guide to the Lancaster & Carlisle, Edinburgh & Glasgow and Caledonian railways . . . *London*, 1859. pp. 384, 184, 8, 8, with 150 engravings.   BM

5656 SCOTTISH NORTH EASTERN RLY. Railway station at Perth: explanatory statement by directors, Aberdeen, August 1859. *Dundee*, [1859.] pp. 35.   AU

5657 CALEDONIAN RLY. Standing Orders, based on the rules and regulations of the Company, and to be observed by the officers and men in the Superintendent's Department of the Company's service. *Glasgow*, February 1863. pp. 50.   LSE

5658 The CALEDONIAN Railway: a review of its financial position. By a Public Accountant. *London*, 1867. pp. 24.   BM

5659 The CALEDONIAN Railway: a further review of its financial position . . . By a Public Accountant. *London*, 1867. pp. 32.   BM
Written following criticism of his earlier pamphlet, *The Caledonian Railway: a review of its financial position* (1867).

5660 GRAHAME, J. Financial Fenianism and the Caledonian Railway. *Glasgow*, 1867. pp. 31.
BM
A defence of the Caledonian against an attack upon it in the *Pall Mall Gazette*.
pp. 21–8, tables comparing the Caledonian with the L. & N.W. Rly.
pp. 29–31, 'Caledonian accounts'.

5661 CALEDONIAN Railway: third pamphlet. By a Public Accountant, with opinion on the position of the company by the professional accountants of the London & North Western, Brighton, and other railways. (Second edition.) *London*, 1868. pp. 28. BM

5662 MACLEAN, J. L. The British railway system: a description of the work performed in the principal departments. *London*, 1883. pp. 103. BM
Exemplified by Caledonian Railway practice.

5663 CALEDONIAN RLY. The proposed transfer of the Glasgow & South Western Railway: the Caledonian Railway Company's proposal. *Westminster*, 1889. pp. 54. LSE
Explaining two Bills proposing dissolution of the G. & S.W. and the transfer of its property and working (1) to the North British, and (2) to the Caledonian.

5664 BOGLE, W. R. Our railways and the zone system fully explained and practically illustrated as applied to the Caledonian Railway Company. *London*, 1891. pp. 8. LSE
Reprinted from *Tinsley's Magazine*, July 1891.
Centralization of railway management.

5665 MACKENZIE, HOLLAND & WESTINGHOUSE POWER SIGNAL COMPANY. The signalling of the Glasgow Central Station, Caledonian Railway. *London*, [1908.] pp. 16, with 7 illus. & a diagram. SLS

5666 MASON, T. Caledonian Railway Budget . . . *Glasgow*, 1893–1908. BM
Various editions.
A small pocket-book for travellers, with timetables.

5667 BRITISH RAILWAYS (SCOTTISH REGION). Caledonian Railway Company locomotive no. 123. *Glasgow*, March 1958. pp. 3, with col. plate (cover). BR
The special run from Perth to Edinburgh, 18 March, 1958.

Caledonian, West Cumberland & Furness Railway Company
[not incorporated]

5668 HAGUE, J. Caledonian, West Cumberland & Furness Railway. Report . . . on embanking the estuaries of Morecambe and the Duddon, for the purpose of forming a railway communication from Lancashire to Glasgow. *Whitehaven*, 1838. pp. 15, with fold. map. BM

Cambrian Railways

5669 OSWESTRY & NEWTOWN RLY. Rules and regulations to be observed by all officers and servants . . . *Oswestry*, 1860. pp. xiv, 120 [121]. UL(GL)

*5670 GASQUOINE, C. P. The story of the Cambrian: a biography of a railway. *Wrexham & Oswestry*, 1922. pp. ix, 157, with plates, map & timetables. BM

5671 ALLCHIN, M. C. V. Locomotives of the Cambrian, Barry, and Rhymney railways: types, building dates, etc. *Fareham: the author*, [1942.] pp. 12.
—— rev. edn. *Fareham*, [1943.] pp. 12.
BM

5672 KIDNER, R. W. The Cambrian Railways. *South Godstone: Oakwood Press*, 1954. pp. 45, with 34 illus. on 12 plates, drawings, tables, maps, gradient profiles & a bibliography. [*Oakwood Library of Railway History*, no. 55.] BM

5673 COZENS, L. The Llanfyllin Railway. *Highgate: the author*, [1959.] pp. 56, with illus. & a map. BM

Cheshire Junction Railway Company
[not incorporated]

*5674 CHESHIRE JUNCTION RLY. Addenda to the 'Extracts from the Minutes of Evidence given in support of the Cheshire Junction Railway Bill . . .' *Manchester*, 1836. pp. 29. LSE

5675 A FEW reasons for postponing the Bill brought in by the Cheshire Junction Railway Company. (8 March 1836.) [*London*, 1836.] pp. 2. BM
Advantages of an alternative line, not named.

5676 MANCHESTER SOUTH UNION RLY. Case of the Manchester South Union Rly. Co. and the Cheshire Junction Rly. Co. *Manchester*, [1842.] pp. [4,] with map. BM
A comparison, favouring the M.S.U.

Cheshire Lines Committee

*5677 GRIFFITHS, R. P. The Cheshire Lines Railway. *South Godstone: Oakwood Press*, 1947. pp. iv, [4,]57, with 13 illus. on plates, & 6 maps. [*Oakwood Library of Railway History*, no. 5.] BM
—— 2nd edn. [*Lingfield*, 1958.] pp. 54, with 16 illus. & 4 maps. BM

Cleator & Workington Junction Railway

5678 CLEATOR & WORKINGTON JUNCTION RLY. History of the Railway. *Workington*, January 1901. pp. 37. PC
'For directors' information only.'
Financial and legal information, and texts of agreements; but no written history.

5679 CLEATOR & WORKINGTON JUNCTION RLY. Future of railways: report for the information of the directors; including the general history of the Railway, its financial and trading position, Engineer's report, particulars of agreements and other details summarised in connection with the proposed absorption of the Cleator & Workington Junction Railway Company under the Railways Act, 1921 . . . By James A. Haynes, Secretary & General Manager. Workington, 7 July, 1921. pp. 34, with map.   UL(GL)
'Private & confidential.'

5680 GRADON, W. M. The Track of the Ironmasters: a history of the Cleator & Workington Junction Railway. *Altrincham: the author*, 1952. pp. 70, with 14 illus., map, gradient profiles, timetables & some verse. IT

Cleobury Mortimer & Ditton Priors Light Railway

*****5681** PRICE, M. R. C. The Cleobury Mortimer & Ditton Priors Light Railway. *Lingfield: Oakwood Press*, 1963. pp. 27, with 16 illus. on 8 plates, map, station diagrams & a bibliography. [*Locomotion Papers*, no. 21.]
BM

Cockermouth, Keswick & Penrith Railway

5682 GRADON, W. M. A history of the Cockermouth, Keswick & Penrith Railway. *Altrincham: the author*, [1948.] pp. 35, with illus., maps & diagrams.   BM

Colne Valley & Halstead Railway

5683 WHITEHEAD, R. A. *and* SIMPSON, F. D. The story of the Colne Valley. *Brentwood: Ridgway*, 1951. pp. xi, 82, with 49 illus. on plates, a fold. plan of stations, & maps inside covers.   BM

Corris Railway

*****5684** COZENS, L. The Corris Railway. *Sutton: the author*, 1949. pp. 40, with 20 illus., 4 maps & diagrams & bibliography.   BM

Denburn Valley Junction Railway

5685 ABERDEEN ROYAL INFIRMARY. Denburn Valley Junction Railway as affecting Aberdeen Royal Infirmary. 'Extracted from Minute and Letter Books of Infirmary, Aberdeen, 16 March 1864.' [*Aberdeen*, 1864.] pp. 18.   AU

Derwent Valley Light Railway

5686 BRANCH LINE SOCIETY. Derwent Valley Light Railway Tour, May 17th, 1958. Itinerary. 1958. pp. 3[4], with map. *Reproduced typescript.*   BR

Durham & Sunderland Railway

5687 DAY, J. Observations on the railway now in progress between Durham and Sunderland, shewing the utility of making it a public locomotive railway. *Sunderland*, 1836. pp. vii, 100[102].   LSE
A detailed explanation of the difficulties encountered by James Day as superintendent of the masonry on account of the 'discreditable behaviour of the engineer' [John Blenkinsop].

East London Railway
(The London, Brighton & South Coast, South-Eastern, Great Eastern, Metropolitan, and Metropolitan District Joint Railway)

5688 THAMES TUNNEL COMPANY. [A collection of documents, reports, manuscript letters, Acts of Parliament, prints, and pamphlets, relating to the Thames Tunnel, 1822–1853.]   BM
About eighty items, including some holograph letters from M. I. Brunel and Thomas Jevons.

5689 EAST LONDON RLY. Reasons for the immediate completion of the East London Railway (Thames Tunnel line). *London*, 1864. pp. 8, with fold. map.   BR
Signed 8 February, 1864.

5690 GRANT, A. Mr. A. Grant's reply to Sir Edward Watkin's circular to the proprietors of the East London Railway Co. [*London*, 1878.] pp. 23.   ICE
Watkin had made accusations against Grant, who now replies to them, following this with (pp. 8–17) a counter-attack on Watkin.

5691 BRITISH TRANSPORT COMMISSION. I. K. Brunel and the Thames Tunnel. [1959.] pp. 8[10]. *Reproduced typescript.*   IT

East Lothian Railway Company
[not incorporated]

5692 STEVENSON, R. Report of a survey for the East Lothian Railway. *Edinburgh*, 1825. pp. 16, with fold. section at end.   ICE

Edge Hill Light Railway

5693 TONKS, E. S. The Edge Hill Light Railway: the story of an unfortunate line. *Birmingham: the author*, 1948. pp. 44, with 23 illus., map & 3 diagrams.   BM

Edinburgh, Leith & Newhaven Railway

5694 NEILL, P. Considerations regarding the Edinburgh, Leith & Newhaven Railway. Addressed to the Commissioners of Improvements, the inhabitants of the Eastern Divisions of Princes Street . . . and to the shareholders of the railway company. *Edinburgh*, 1837. pp. 40.   BM

—— 3rd edn. '. . . with additional important documents in Appendix.' *Edinburgh*, 1837. pp. 48.   BM
—— 'Further considerations . . . submitted to the subscribers.' *Edinburgh*, 1837. pp. 7. H
—— 2nd edn. *Edinburgh*, 1837. pp. 12.   H

5695 NEILL, P. Remarks on the progress and prospects of the Edinburgh, Leith and New-haven Railway in January 1839 . . . with an appendix of documents. *Edinburgh*, 1839. pp. 36.   BM

5696 EDINBURGH, LEITH & NEWHAVEN RLY. Reply for the directors of the Edinburgh, Leith & Newhaven Railway Company to certain 'Remarks on the progress and pros-pects' of that company by Dr. Neill, Canon-mills. *Edinburgh*, 1839. pp. 26.   H

5697 NEILL, P. An examination of the 'Reply for the directors of the Edinburgh, Leith & Newhaven Railway Company, March 1839'. *Edinburgh*, 1839. pp. 32.   BM

Festiniog Railway

5698 SPOONER, C. E. A descriptive account of the construction and working the Festiniog Railway, together with description and par-ticulars of the most practical narrow gauge railway, and suitable rolling stock, for work-ing the same. Written at the request of and for . . . Count Alexis Bobrinskoy, President of the Imperial Russian Commission ap-pointed to investigate the Fairlie system working in England. *London*, 1870. pp. 26, with tables, maps, drawings & gradient profiles.   PO
Includes an historical account.

5699 VIGNES, E. Étude technique sur le Chemin de fer Festiniog et quelques autres chemins de fer à voie étroite de l'Angleterre. *Paris*, 1878. pp. v, 180, with tables, & atlas of 11 plates.   BRE. Photocopy LU(THC)

5700 SPOONER, C. E. Narrow gauge railways. *London*, 1871. pp. 128.   BM
pp. 10–57, Festiniog Rly, with fold. diagrams incl. map, gradient profiles, and tables.

—— 2nd edn. *London*, 1879. pp. 128.   BM

5701 RICHARDS, W. M. Dissertation on the
b history of Traeth Mawr and the industrial results of the formation of the Embankment. Thesis, M.A., University of Wales, April 1925. pp. [532,] with 3 graphs, a roll of maps & a bibliography. *Typescript*   NLW
'History of the railways' occupies 17 pp. (5 pp. are on the Welsh Highland Rly.).

5702 JONES, J. G. The social and historical geo-graphy of the Ffestiniog slate industry. Thesis, M.A., University of Wales, 1939. 2 vols. (pp. 322: 70 maps). *Typescript*. NLW
pt. 2, ch. 2, The transport of slates,

5703 RICHARDS, W. M. Some aspects of the Industrial Revolution in South Caernarvon-shire: part 2, Portmadoc. *In* 'Transactions of the Caernarvonshire Historical Society', vol. 5, 1944. pp. 71–5.   BM
Origins of the Festiniog Rly. (In the con-tents list to this volume the title of this essay is given as 'Some aspects of the Industrial Revo-lution in South East Caernarvonshire'.)

5704 BOYD, J. I. C. Narrow-gauge rails to Port-madoc: a historic survey of the Festiniog–Welsh Highland Railway and its ancillaries; with drawings by R. E. Tustin. [*South Godstone*:] *Oakwood Press*, 1949. pp. iii, 158, with plates, illus. in text, & map.   BM

5705 HOLLAND, S. The memoirs of Samuel Holland, one of the pioneers of the North Wales slate industry. [*Dolgelly*, 1952.] pp. vii, 32, with portrait. [*Merioneth Historical & Record Society. Extra Publications*, series 1, no. 1]   BM
Formation and early history of the Festiniog Railway.

*5706 FESTINIOG RLY. Festiniog Railway Guide. *Portmadoc*, [1956.] pp. 24, with 19 illus., map, & lists tables.   BM
pp. 3–9, an historical account.
—— another edn. [*Portmadoc*, 1957.] pp. 32.   BM
pp. 7–19, historical and descriptive account of the line.
—— another edn. 'Guide Book.' [*Port-madoc*, 1959.] pp. 32, with the addition of 8 route diagrams.
—— another edn. [*Portmadoc*, 1960.] pp. 36.

*5707 FESTINIOG RLY. A Pictorial History of the Festiniog Railway. *Portmadoc*, [1958.] pp. 22[25], with 62 illus. & a map.   BM

*5708 BOYD, J. I. C. The Festiniog Railway: a
b history of the narrow gauge railway con-necting the slate quarries of Blaenau
c Festiniog with Portmadoc, North Wales. In two volumes . . . with drawings by J. M. Lloyd and R. E. Tustin. *Lingfield: Oakwood Press*, 1956, 1959. pp. 448.   BM
vol. 1, '1800–1889'. pp. 194, with 5 fold. plates, illus., maps, diagrams, and tables.
vol. 2, '1890–1959'. pp. 201–448, with illus., maps, diagrams, tables, and 21 appendices, including a chronology and a bibliography.
—— 2nd edn. *Lingfield*, 1960, 62. 2 vols. pp. 449.   BM
A revision, embodying some new research.

*5709 FESTINIOG RAILWAY SOCIETY—LONDON AREA GROUP. Volunteers' Manual. Edited by Roy Cunningham. *Welling*, [1960]. pp. 14. *Reproduced typescript.*   BM
A maintenance handbook for members.

5710 FESTINIOG RLY. Stock Book of Locomo-tives, Carriages & Wagons. *Portmadoc*, 1962. pp. 20. (21 illus. & 3 tables.)   BM

5711 WHITEHOUSE, P. B. Festiniog Railway revival. *London: Ian Allan*, 1963. pp. 84, with col. frontis., 56 illus., la. fold. map and layout plans.   BM
The history of the line, its renaissance, and present prosperity.

*5712 FESTINIOG RLY. The Festiniog Railway in pictures, 1951–1961. *Portmadoc*, 1962. pp. 20, with 59 illus. & a map.   pc

5713 BAILEY, T. Festiniog Railway Guide Book. *London: Ian Allan*, [1963.] pp. 56, with 37 illus. & a map.   BM

Fordell Railway
[industrial railway]

5714 INGLIS, J. C. *and* INGLIS, F. The Fordell Railway. *Perth: the authors*, 1946. pp. 32, with illus. & fold map.   BM

Furness Railway

5715 LINTON, J. A Handbook of the Whitehaven & Furness Railway: being a guide to the Lake District of West Cumberland and Furness . . . *London*, 1852. pp. 134, with a map. & 12 engravings.   BM
pp. 2–6 describes the railway.

5716 GRADON, W. M. Furness Railway; its rise and development, 1846–1923. [*Altrincham*:] *James Collins*, 1946. pp. 109, with illus., maps, & timetables.   BM

5717 POLLARD, S. *and* MARSHALL, J. D. The
b   Furness Railway and the growth of Barrow. *In* 'Journal of Transport History', vol. 1, no. 2, November 1953. pp. 109–26, with map, 2 tables, & 87 bibliogr. notes.   BM

5718 MARSHALL, J. D. Furness and the Indus-
b   trial Revolution: an economic history of Furness, 1711–1900, and the town of Barrow, 1757–1897; with an epilogue. *Barrow-in-Furness: Central Library*, 1958. pp. xxii, 438, with illus., 34 tables & many bibliogr. notes.   BM
The Furness Rly. is prominent in this survey.

Garstang & Knott End Railway

5719 RUSH, R. W. *and* PRICE, M. R. C. The Garstang & Knott End Railway. [*Lingfield*:] *Oakwood Press*, 1964. pp. 70, with 13 illus. on 6 plates, with numerous diagrams, map, & table of locomotives. [*Locomotion Papers*, no. 23.]   BM
Includes the Knott End Rly.

Glasgow & Berwick Railway
[not incorporated]

5720 TELFORD, T. Report by Mr. Telford relative to the proposed railway from Glasgow to Berwick-upon-Tweed, with Mr. Jessop's opinion thereon, and minutes of a meeting of the General and Sub-Committees, 4 April, 1810. *Edinburgh*, 1810. pp. 36, 9. BM
The proposed Glasgow & Berwick Rly. pp. 21–36, Book of Reference.

Glasgow & South Western Railway

5721 IRVINE RLY. Rules and regulations of the Irvine Railway Company. *Irvine*, 1835. pp. 14.   NLC

5722 GLASGOW, PAISLEY, KILMARNOCK & AYR RLY. Proceedings of the First General Meeting of the shareholders . . . held in the hall of the Black Bull Inn, Glasgow, on Wednesday November 9th, 1836. *Glasgow*, 1836. pp. 16.   NLC

5723 LOCKE, J. London & Glasgow Railway, through Lancashire; to the directors of the Grand Junction Railway Co. [*Liverpool*,] 1836. pp. 3.   BM
Report of a survey for a line between Preston and Glasgow.

5724 McCORMICK & GEMMELL, *publishers*. Guide to the Glasgow & Ayrshire Railway, with descriptions of the Glasgow & Edinburgh and Glasgow & Greenock railways . . . *Ayr*, 1841. pp. 110.   BR
pp. [1]–12, Origin and progress of the Glasgow & Ayrshire Rly.

5725 WARDEN, J. The Glasgow & Ayr and Glasgow & Greenock Railway Companion; containing a description of the railroads . . . *Glasgow*, 1841. pp. 134.   LSE

5726 DALRYMPLE, J. M. Correspondence between Viscount Dalrymple, Chairman of the Portpatrick Rly. Co. and Sir Andrew Orr, Chairman, & James White Esq., Deputy Chairman, of the Glasgow & South Western Rly. Co. relative to a contribution of £40,000 from the G. & S.W. Rly. Co. to the Portpatrick Co. *Stranraer*, 1861. pp. 16.   BM

5727 GLASGOW & SOUTH WESTERN RLY. St. Enoch Station Hotel. Guide to Glasgow and the Clyde, with illustrations: a souvenir presented to visitors. By E. W. Thiem, manager. *Glasgow*, 1880. pp. 53, with illus., incl. 3 of the hotel, in colour.   pc

5728 M'ILWRAITH, W. The Glasgow & South-Western Railway; its origin, progress and present position. *Glasgow*, 1880. pp. viii, 186.   BM

5729 CALEDONIAN RLY. The proposed transfer of the Glasgow & South Western Railway. The Caledonian Railway Company's proposal. *Westminster*, 1889. pp. 54. LSE
Explaining two Bills proposing dissolution of the G. & S.W. and the transfer of its property and working (1) to the North British Rly., and (2) to the Caledonian Rly.

5730 AITKEN, W. Songs from the 'South-West' and bits for the bairns. By Inspector Aitken. *Glasgow*, 1913. pp. 194, with plates.   BR
With a preface (pp. [5]–8), 'Biographical sketches of the author' from *Poets and poetry of the Land of Burns* by A. B. Todd, and 'Nights wi' famous Scots' in *Weekly News* and dedicated to David Cooper, General Manager, Glasgow & South Western Rly., with portrait and poem.

731 AITKEN, [W.] The old South-Western, 1839–1922. [*Glasgow*, 1923.] s.sh.   BR
Five verses.

732 MACADAM, W. The birth, growth and eclipse of the Glasgow & South Western Railway. *Glasgow*, 1924. pp. 64, with illus. & fold. map.   BR

733 TATLOW, J. Fifty years of railway life in England, Scotland and Ireland. *London*, 1920. pp. vi, 223.   BM
J Tatlow was with the Belfast & County Down, Midland, Glasgow & South Western, Midland Great Western of Ireland, and the Dublin & Kingstown railways. Several well-known railwaymen are mentioned.
—— 2nd edn. *London*, 1948. pp. 223, with a biographical introduction by Charles E. Lee.   BM

734 MACGREGOR, C. Chronology of the Glasgow & South Western Railway. pp. 29
c [33]. [*c.* 1950.] *Reproduced typescript.*   BR

735 STEPHENSON LOCOMOTIVE SOCIETY. The Glasgow & South Western Railway, 1850–
c 1923 . . . *London*, 1950. pp. 60, with illus. on plates; tables & (pp. 5–22) a chronology.   BM

736 SMITH, D. L. Tales of the Glasgow & South Western Railway. *London: Ian Allan*, 1962. pp. 96, with col. frontis. & 51 illus. on 16 plates.   BM
Memoirs. A unique feature is the inclusion of a glossary of G. & S.W. vernacular.

Glyn Valley Tramway

737 DAVIES, D. Ll. The Glyn Valley Tramway. *Lingfield: Oakwood Press*, 1962. pp. 61, with 24 illus., 3 maps, diagrams, gradient profile, lists & tables. [*Locomotion Papers*, no. 18.]   BM

Grand Northern Railroad Company
[not incorporated]

738 CUNDY, N. W. Inland transit; the practicability, utility and benefit of railroads: the comparative attraction and speed of steam engines on a railroad, navigation, and turnpike road . . . Also, the plans, sections and estimates of the projected Grand Southern and Northern railroads. *London*, 1833. pp. iv, 161, with charts & a plate.   BM
—— 2nd edn. *London*, 1834. pp. iv, 161.   BM

739 CORT, R. Rail-road impositions detected; or, Facts and arguments, being an exposé of the estimates for the Grand Northern Railway . . . with disclosures and suggestions important to the canal interests of Great Britain. *London*, 1834. pp. 40.   BM

Grand Northern & Eastern Railway Co.
[not incorporated]

740 [BARRETT, H.] Observations on railways, addressed to the nobility, gentry, clergy, agriculturists . . . particularly to those situate on the line and connected with the Grand Northern and Eastern Railroad, projected by N. W. Cundy. *Yarmouth*, 1834. pp. 55.   BM
—— 2nd edn. *Yarmouth*, 1835. pp. 59. BM
The BM copy of the 2nd edn. is inscribed 'With the Compiler's compliments. Henry Barrett.'

Grand Southern Railroad Company
[not incorporated]

741 CUNDY, N. W. Inland transit; the practicability, utility and benefit of railroads: the comparative attraction and speed of steam engines on a railroad, navigation and turnpike road. . . . Also, the plans, sections, and estimates of the projected Grand Southern and Northern railroads. *London*, 1833. pp. iv, 161, with charts and a plate.   BM
—— 2nd edn. *London*, 1834. pp. iv. 161. BM

Great Central Railway

Historical

742 GREAT CENTRAL RLY. Dates of openings of various portions of the system, including
c joint railways. January 1909. pp. 12.   BR
Privately printed.

743 DOW, G. The first railway between Manchester and Sheffield. Issued by the London & North Eastern Railway to commemorate the opening of the Sheffield, Ashton-under-Lyne & Manchester Railway one hundred years ago. *London: L.N.E.R.*, 1945. pp. 44, with fold. table of locos., illus., maps & plans. BM

744 ALDRICH, C. L. The Robinson locomotives of the Great Central Railway, 1900 to 1923. *London: E. V. Aldrich*, 1946. pp. 46[47], with 20 illus., tables.   BM
—— new edn. '. . . with their subsequent LNER history to 1947.' *London*, 1948. pp. 55, with 27 illus., tables.   BM

745 SIMMONS, J. Parish and Empire: studies and sketches. *London: Collins*, 1952. pp. 256.   BM
pp. 155–65, 'The building of the Woodhead Tunnel'; with bibliogr. notes.

746 DOW, G. The third Woodhead Tunnel. Issued by British Railways, London Midland Region, to commemorate the formal opening of the new Woodhead Tunnel . . . 1954. *London*, 1954. pp. 27, with illus., map & diagrams.   BM

747 DUNN, J. M. The Wrexham, Mold & Connah's Quay Railway. *Lingfield: Oakwood Press*, 1957. pp. 32, with 21 illus. on 8 plates, maps & table. [*Oakwood Library of Railway History*, no. 14.]   BM

5748 ABBOTT, R. D. The building of the Great
Central Railway. *In* 'Journal of Transport
History', vol. 4, no. 2, November 1958.
pp. 81–4.   BM
   Seven illustrations on four plates, with
explanatory text, from the collection of photo-
graphs by S. W. A. Newton in the Leicester
Museum & Art Gallery.

5749 DOW, G. Great Central. *London: Locomotive Publishing Co.*, 1959– . 3 vols. BM
   A very detailed history of the G.C.R., with
many illus., maps, lists and tables.
   vol. 1, The Progenitors, 1813–1863. 1959.
pp. xi, 298.
   vol. 2, Dominion of Watkin, 1864–1899.
1962. pp. vii, 422.
   [vol. 3, not yet published.]

5750 POLLINS, H. The last main railway line
 b   to London. *In* 'Journal of Transport
     History', vol. 4, no. 2, November 1959.
pp. 85–95, with map & 24 bibliogr. notes. BM

*5751 LEICESTER MUSEUM. The last main line:
photographs by S. W. A. Newton; edited
by R. D. Abbott. *Leicester*, 1961. pp.
[26,] with a map.   BM
   Thirty-seven photographs of the building of
the Great Central, selected from the Newton
Collection at the Leicester Museum.

*5752 COSSONS, N. Contractors locomotives,
G.C.R. By N. Cossons; photographed by
S. W. A. Newton. *Leicester: Leicester Museums*, 1963. pp. 36, with 24 photographs, &
12 line illus., with historical notes and
dimensions.   BM

Contemporaneous

5753 SANDERSON, H. Considerations on the
proposed communication by a navigable
canal between the town of Sheffield and the
Peak Forest Canal; with remarks and calculations tending to prove the superiority of
an edge-railway for passing over a moun-
tainous district, and a comparative account
of the several practicable lines which have
hitherto been pointed out by Henry Sanderson, land surveyor. *Sheffield*, [1826.] pp.92.
                                   UL(GL): DERBY PL
   This pamphlet is described, with excerpts, in
Great Central, by George Dow, vol. 1, 1959.
pp. 3–6.

5754 SANDERSON, H. Description of the intended line of the Sheffield & Manchester
Railway; with some observations thereon, by
Henry Sanderson of Sheffield, the surveyor
appointed to take the levels by George
Stephenson, civil engineer. *Sheffield*, 1831.
pp. 19, with plate.   DERBY PL
   This contains a full description of Stephenson's proposed route, of which Sanderson was
critical. See *Great Central* by George Dow,
vol. 1, 1959, p. 7.

5755 SANDERSON, H. An Appendix to the 'Description of the intended line of the Sheffield
& Manchester Railway', containing an
abstract of the Act of Parliament (omitting
those clauses which relate to legal formalities
and technicalities), a comparison of this
line with the Liverpool & Manchester line
of railway in sundry important particulars,
and a statement of the actual expenditure on
the one, with the probable expenditure on the
other line, arranged under the same separate
heads and departments, with further observations by Henry Sanderson of Sheffield,
surveyor. *Sheffield*, [1831.] pp. 16. DERBY PL
   This work is described on pp. 14 and 15 of
Great Central, vol. 1, by George Dow (1959).

5756 SHEFFIELD & MANCHESTER RLY. Report of the Provisional Committee of the
Sheffield & Manchester Railway appointed
for obtaining the Act of Parliament. *Liverpool*, 1831. pp. 11, 52, with map.   LSE

5757 SHEFFIELD & MANCHESTER RLY. Appendix to the report of the Provisional
Committee of the Sheffield & Manchester
Railway to the Company of the Proprietors
at their First General Assembly to be held
October 29, 1831 . . . *Liverpool*, [1831.]
pp. 52, with fold. map.   UL(GL)
   Includes George Stephenson's 'Report upon
the practicability of making the line' (pp. 1–22).

5758 SANDERSON, H. The line of the Sheffield &
Manchester Railway compared with another
and better line by Saltersbrook, and observations on Mr. Stephenson's report,
dated 30 September, 1831; respectfully
addressed to the individual attention of the
holders of shares in this important undertaking. By Henry Sanderson, surveyor.
Sheffield, 1833. pp. 29.   LEEDS PL

5759 HOMERSHAM, S. C. Report to the directors
of the Manchester, Sheffield & Lincolnshire
Railway Co., comparing the quantity,
quality and price of the water that can be
supplied to the inhabitants of Manchester
and Salford by means of the Surplus Water
Act obtained last Session by the M.S. &
L. Rly. Co., with that of the water works
scheme promoted by the Corporation of
Manchester . . . *London*, 1848. pp. 88, 12,
with 3 plates.   BM

5760 SIDNEY, S. Railways and agriculture in
North Lincolnshire: rough notes of a ride
over the track of the Manchester, Sheffield &
Lincolnshire, and other railways. *London*,
1848. pp. xv, 103, with fold. map.   BM

5761 MANCHESTER, SHEFFIELD & LINCOLN-
SHIRE RLY. A description of the new docks
at Great Grimsby . . . and of the Manchester,
Sheffield & Lincolnshire Railway and other
railways in direct connection; with a plan

of the docks and a map of the railways in connection. *Manchester*, [1852.] pp. 24. BR

5762 MINUTES and correspondence between the London & North Western, Midland, and Manchester, Sheffield & Lincolnshire companies, and the Great Northern Railway Company. *London*, 1856. pp. 47. BM

5763 LONDON & NORTH WESTERN RLY. Report of the directors to the shareholders on the subject of the Manchester, Sheffield & Lincolnshire Company's breach of their agreement. *London*, 15 July, 1857. pp. 20.
BM
—— Further correspondence in continuation of the report of the directors ... *London*, August 1857. pp. 6. BM

5764 HANDYSIDE, G. Review of the Manchester, Sheffield and Lincolnshire Railway. *Newcastle-upon-Tyne*, 1863. pp. 34. BM
Criticisms and suggestions

5765 LANCASHIRE, DERBYSHIRE & EAST COAST RLY. Memorandum. *Chesterfield*, 1891. pp. 10. LSE
—— another edn. [*London*, 1891.] pp. 11.
LSE

5766 LANCASHIRE, DERBYSHIRE & EAST COAST RLY. Descriptive statement. (A great central railway of 170 miles running from sea to sea, traversing the great Midland coalfield for 50 miles, with shipping facilities at either end.) [*Westminster*, 1892?] pp. 11, with 6 maps in text. LSE
A proposed railway (54 & 55 Vic. c. 189).

5767 GREAT CENTRAL RLY. Illustrated description of the Great Central Railway, prepared in connection with the inaugural opening of the new extension line to London on March 9th, 1899 by ... C. T. Ritchie, M.P., President of the Board of Trade. *Manchester*, 1899. pp, 39, with 10 maps & plans (some fold.), & 38 illus. BM
No title-page.

5768 GREAT CENTRAL RLY. Programme of arrangements for the ceremony of opening the Extension to London Railway at Marylebone Station, March 9th, 1899. [*Manchester*, 1899.] pp.[4.] BM
An illustrated folder.

5769 SHEFFIELD DISTRICT RLY. Opening of the Sheffield District Railway by the Duke of Portland on Monday May 21st, 1900. [*Sheffield*,] 1900. pp. [6.] PC
A brochure.

5770 HOLMES, F. A. The Great Central Railway: an enterprising company. *Leeds*, 1904. pp. 11, with 6 illus. (2 on front cover). RC

5771 GREAT CENTRAL RLY. Per rail. *London*, 1913. pp. 238, li, with 3 la. fold. maps (col.) & many illus. BM
A topographical survey designed to show the G.C.R. as the servant of industry. Inserted at the end (pp. li) is a list of stations served. No historical or descriptive account is given.

Great Eastern Railway
Eastern Counties Railway: EC

Historical

5772 [GREAT EASTERN RLY.] Extracts from Tuck's Railway Shareholders' Manual, 1847, relating to certain railways in Middlesex, Essex, Hertford, Cambridge, Suffolk, and Norfolk, many of which now form a portion of the Great Eastern Railway; also the Blackwall Railway. *Stratford*, 1899. pp. 14.
PC

5773 GREAT EASTERN RAILWAY MAGAZINE. Special Number, Great Eastern Railway Jubilee, 1862–1912. (vol. 2, no. 20, pp. 219–80.) [*London*,] August 1912, with many illus. & 3 col. plates. PC

5774 LOWE, A. C. W. The Great Eastern Railway: its history, features and rolling stock. pp. 12. *Typescript*. RC
Paper, Railway Club, 11 April, 1924.

5775 BROWN, K. A derelict railway: being the history of the Newmarket & Chesterford Railway. [*Cambridge*,] 1931. pp. 16, with 6 plates, illus. & map. BM
From the Cambridge Antiquarian Society's *Communications*, vol. 31, 1931.

*5776 LAMBERT, R. S. The Railway King, 1800–1871: a study of George Hudson and the
EC business morals of his times ... *London: Allen & Unwin*, 1934. pp. 320, with illus. BM
Contains much information relating to the railways with which Hudson was associated, including the Eastern Counties Rly.
—— reprinted, *London: Allen & Unwin*, 1964. BM

5777 DOBLE, E. History of the Eastern Counties Railway in relation to economic develop-
EC ment. (Thesis submitted for the Degree of
b Ph.D. in the University of London, May 1939.) pp. 379, with 31 tables, 4 maps, bibliogr. notes & a bibliography. *Typescript*.
UL
Period, 1835–1870.

5778 HILTON, H. F. The Eastern Union Railway, 1846 to 1862 ... [*London: L.N.E.Rly.*,] 1946. pp. 42, with fold. tables, illus. & maps. BM

5779 DOW, G. The first railway in Norfolk. *London: L.N.E.R.*, 1944. pp. 19[22], with illus., maps & tables. ICE
The Yarmouth & Norwich, and the Norfolk Rly.
—— 2nd edn. *London*, 1947. pp. 31, with a table of locos. inserted at end. BM

5780 BURTT, F. Steamers of the Thames and
Medway. *London: Richard Tilling*, 1949.
pp. 192.   BM
    pp. 53–5, The London & Blackwall Rly. Co.'s
    steamships.

5781 CLARK, R. H. Steam engine builders of
Suffolk, Essex and Cambridgeshire. *Norwich: Augustine Steward Press*, 1950. pp.
141.   BM
    pp. 109–13, Stratford G.E.R. Works.

5782 SKEAT, W. O. The Decapod locomotive of
the Great Eastern Railway. pp. 169–85, with
12 illus. on 4 plates, & 6 diagrams (1 fold.).
                                            SLS
    Excerpt, *Transactions of the Newcomen
    Society*, vol. 28, 1951–2, and 1952–3. Read
    10 December, 1952.

5783 PROUD, P. The Great Eastern Railway
0–6–0 T's. [*London:*] *Railway Correspondence
& Travel Society*, [1945.] pp. 12, with 18
illus. & a history chart.   BM

*5784 ALDRICH, C. L. G.E.R. locomotives,
1900–1922: a brief outline of types existing
at the close of 1922, post-grouping additions
and L.N.E.R. rebuilds, together with a short
description of the famous 'Decapod'.
Brightlingsea, 1942. pp. 40, with 30 illus. RC
—— another edn. 'G.E.R. Detailed Loco
Stock List as at 1st April 1921, with subsequent and post-Grouping additions of G.E.
types. Compiled from an official Stratford
register.' *Cricklewood: Fowler & Son*, 1944.
pp. 35.   BM
—— new & rev. edn. 'G.E.R. locomotives,
1923, with additions & rebuilds to 1943: a
brief descriptive souvenir of types existing
at the close of 1922, post-grouping additions
& L.N.E.R. rebuilds, together with a short
description of the famous "Decapod" & the
last G.E. "singles".' *Brightlingsea*, 1944.
pp. 54[55], with illus.   LSE
—— another edn. 'Great Eastern locomotives past & present, 1862 to 1944.' *Brightlingsea*, 1944. pp. 80, with 56 illus.   BM
—— Victory edition. *Brightlingsea*, 1945.
pp. 112, with 63 illus.   BM
—— 6th edn. 'The locomotives of the
Great Eastern Railway, 1862 to 1954 . . .'
Wickford, 1955. pp. 127, with 66 illus.   BM

5785 ALLEN, C. J. Great Eastern. *London:
Ian Allan*, [1959.] pp. 64, with illus.   BM
    History, description, and recent progress
    with electrification and improved services.

5786 DEWES, S. The 'Hadleigh Express'. *In
his* 'A Suffolk childhood.' *London: Hutchinson*, 1959. pp. 11–23.   BM
    Recalling a footplate journey from Hadleigh
    to Bentley, *c*. 1916.

5787 PROUD, P. The Great Eastern 'Claud
Hamilton' class. *Birmingham: Railway
Travel & Correspondence Society*, 1959. pp.
17[22], with 22 illus. & detailed lists.   BR

*5788 ALLEN, C. J. The Great Eastern Railway.
London: Ian Allan, 1955. pp. 222, with
c col. frontis., 96 illus. on 32 plates, 2 maps,
9 tables & a 6-page chronology.   BM
c —— 2nd edn. *London*, 1956. pp. 221.   BM
c —— 3rd, *London*, 1961. pp. 241, with fold.
map but no col. frontis.   BM

Contemporaneous

5789 DIMES & BOYMAN. Eastern Counties
Railway. To the editor of the Essex Stan-
EC dard. *Chelmsford*, [1834.] s.sh.   ICE
    Off-print of two columns. Repudiation of an
    assault by 'Verax' on Dimes & Boyman,
    E.C. Rly. solicitors, for 'empty assertions and
    fallacious promises'.

5790 COMMERCIAL ROAD [London]—TRUS-
TEES. Report . . . to the proprietors, affording a comparative view of the capabilities of
the Commercial and East India Dock Roads,
with reference to the projected rail-ways to
the East and West India Docks and Blackwall. *London*, 1835. pp. 13.   ICE
    Signed 'W. Baker, Clerk'.
    Advantages of the Commercial Road over
    the projected London & Blackwall Rly.

5791 COMMERCIAL RLY. General plan shewing
the River Thames with the line of the Commercial Railway from London to Blackwall,
with its terminus at Brunswick Wharf.
[*London, c.* 1836,] with fold. plan.   ICE

5792 EASTERN COUNTIES RLY. Proceedings of
the First General Meeting of the Eastern
EC Counties Railway Company incorporated
by Act of Parliament July 4, 1836, held at
the London Tavern, Bishopsgate Street,
Monday 26th September, 1836. *London*,
[1836.] pp. 43, with la. fold. map.   BM

5793 'CITIZEN.' Observations upon the proposed extension of the Commercial Railway
from the Minories to Leadenhall Street.
London, 1837. pp. 35.   BM
    Objections.

5794 LONDON & BLACKWALL RLY. A brief
statement of the advantages which will result
to the public from the establishment of a
communication by railroad between London
and Blackwall, with an estimate of the probable return to the subscribers. *London*, 1837.
pp. 42.   G
    Includes Wm. Cubitt's Report (pp. 34–42).

5795 ROBERTSON, J. C. Letter to Henry North-
cott Ward, Esq., on the progress and pros-
EC pects of the Eastern Counties Railway Company. *London*, 1837. pp. 29.   H

5796 MANSELL, G. Eastern Counties Railway
Guide, with the fares, and times of starting to
EC the Stratford, Ilford, Romford, and Brentwood stations. *Borough* [*London*], 1838. pp.
12, with 3 diagrams of stations & a fold.
frontis.   PC
    Reprinted from the *Stratford Express*.

5797 The MONSTROUS delusion of the Eastern
Counties Railway. [*London*, 1838.] pp. 32,
EC with tables.   H

5798 STEPHENSON, G. *and* BIDDER, G. P.
London & Blackwall Commercial Railway.
Report. [1838.] pp. 22.
Dated January 6th, 1838.
The mode of constructing and working the
London & Blackwall Rly. (opened 4 July, 1840).

5799 EASTERN COUNTIES RAILWAY. The
Eastern Counties Railway Guide: a descrip-
EC tion of the First Grand Opening, particulars
of the whole line of railway with the fares
and time of starting. *London*, 1839. pp. 12.
H

5800 NORRIS, J. T., *printer*. A Guide to the Eastern Counties Railway, containing an ac-
EC count of the rise and progress of the company, a description of the works . . . with
engravings of the bridges, etc. with correct
time, distance and fare tables. *London*,
1839. pp. 54.   LSE

5801 RAILWAY Rhymes; or, The scenery versi-
fied from London to Brentwood. By the
Essex Rhymer. 1840.   CHELMSFORD PL

5802 PERRY, S. A letter on the Eastern Counties
Railway, addressed to . . . William Lord
EC Petre . . . *London*, 1842. pp. 46, with engr.
frontis.   CHELMSFORD PL
p. 32 to end are taken up with other concerns of Samuel Perry quite unconnected with
the E.C. Rly.

5803 BUTLER, C. The First Trial, on the opening
of the Eastern Counties Railway, 27th
EC February 1843. s.sh. *Typescript*
CHELMSFORD PL
A modern transcript of a poem written in
1843. 'Dear Charles, I told you I would tell
the tale . . .'

5804 HOSKINS, W. Harwich Railway: the
Engineer's report . . . *London*, 1844. pp. 16.
ICE

5805 STEVENSON & MATCHETT, *publishers*.
A Guide to the Norfolk Railway, from
EC Yarmouth to Ely, and to the Eastern Coun-
ties Railway, Cambridge Line, from Ely to
London. *Norwich*, August 1845. pp. 94,
with fold. map.   pc
Reprinted from the *Norfolk Chronicle*.
Contains details of station architecture.

5806 BIDDER, G. P. Account of the swing bridge
over the River Wensum at Norwich, on the
. . . Norfolk Railway. *London*, 1846. pp. 7,
with fold. diagram.   ICE
Excerpt, *Min. Proc. I.C.E.*, vol. 5, 1846.

5807 SMITH, A. The Eastern Counties Railway
viewed as an investment; with statistical
EC information . . . *London*, 1847. pp. 24, with
b   many bibliogr. notes relating to Parliamentary Papers.   BM

5808 STEVENSON & MATCHETT, *publishers*. A
Guide to the branch railway from the
EC Eastern Counties line at Ely to Peterborough,
comprising a description of the line . . .
Norwich, [1847.] pp. 21, with fold. map.   BM

5809 STEVENSON & MATCHETT, *publishers*. A
Guide to the Eastern Counties Railway
EC (Cambridge Line), from London to Brandon;
of the Norfolk Railway, from Brandon by
Norwich to Yarmouth; and of the Brox-
bourne & Hertford Branch; with historical
and topographical notices of the parishes
and towns etc. 2nd edn. *Norwich*, [1847.]
pp. 115, with fold. map.   BM
Map missing from BM copy.

5810 EASTERN COUNTIES RLY. Signals and
EC regulations, 20 December 1846. pp. 51. pc
—— another edn. 1849. pp. 52.   LSE

5811 EASTERN COUNTIES RLY. Report of the
Committee of Investigation to the shareholders
EC of the Eastern Counties Railway Company.
London, 1849. pp. 31, xv, 22.   BM
'Past management, present position and the
future prospects of your Company.' With
financial tables, statements, accountant's re-
port, and extracts from accounts.

5812 EASTERN COUNTIES RLY. [Report to the
shareholders on the Report of the Commit-
EC tee of Investigation, 1849.] [*London*, 1849.]
pp. 14.   BM
No title-page to BM copy.

5813 To the SHAREHOLDERS of the Eastern
EC Counties Railway. *London*, 1849. pp. 15
NLC
Dated '30.4.1849', and signed 'A Shareholder
in the Eastern Counties Rly.'
On the report of the Investigation Com-
mittee.

5814 SECOND edition of a letter addressed to
shareholders of the Eastern Counties Rail-
EC way Company, on the subject of the proposed amalgamation with the Norfolk
Company; to which is now appended
'Remarks and statements proposed since the
report of the committee on Eastern Counties
affairs has been circulated'. By a Shareholder. *London*, 1849. pp. 32.   LSE

5815 'VERAX' *pseud*. Hudson versus Wadding-
ton . . . a few words addressed to the share-
EC holders of the Eastern Counties Railway.
By 'Verax'. *London*, 1849. pp. 12.   LSE
George Hudson and David Waddington.

5816 BAGSHAW, J. A short account of transactions in the affairs of the Harwich Railway
and Pier, with an appendix. *London*, 1850.
pp. 40, ii, with bibliogr. notes.   BM

5817 FREWEN, C. H. To the shareholders [of the
Eastern Counties Railway]. [*London*,] 1850.
EC pp. 2.   HRL
A circular letter, dated Feb. 16, 1850.

5818 CASTLE, H. J. A few words to the shareholders of the Eastern Counties Rly. Co.
EC *London*, [1851.] pp. 24.   BM
    Urging amalgamation of the Eastern Coun-
ties, Eastern Union, and Norfolk Rly. to gain
control of East Anglia before the Great
Northern Rly.

5819 DUNCAN, J. Observations on the affairs and
policy of the Eastern Counties Railway
EC Company. *London*, [1851.] pp. 51.   BM
    An exposure of the financial circumstances
of the E.C. Rly., with correspondence between
the Secretary and J. Duncan, who had been
solicitor to the company for fifteen years.

5820 EASTERN COUNTIES RLY. The Eastern
Counties Railway Illustrated Guide. *Lon-*
EC *don*, 1851. pp. 64.   UL(GL)
    The Introduction summarises the financial
position of the E.C. Rly. on 4 Jan., 1850.

5821 SAUNDERS, J. F. Railways in the Eastern
Counties' district: the mode by which a fair
fusion of railway interests eastward of the
EC Great Northern Railway may be effected, the
lines not yet under agreement with the Eastern Counties Company be placed under their
control, and the injury to all that has
ensued from competition be arrested. Recommended to the consideration of all
shareholders in the above district. *London*,
[1852.] pp. 11.   BM

5822 BELL, STEWARD & LLOYD, *solicitors*.
Eastern Union Railway Bill. Opponents'
observations on Special Report, 22 July,
1853. *London*, 1853. pp. 19.   BM

5823 BELL, STEWARD & LLOYD, *solicitors*.
Eastern Union Railway. Repudiation of
£300,000 preference shares. Opponents'
statement. [*London*,] 1853. s.sh.   BM

5823a PARLIAMENTARY repudiation [1854?]. pp.
71.   BM
    A protest against *An Act to enable the Eastern
Union Railway Company to redeem their Preference Shares, etc.* (16 & 17 Vic., cap. ccxxi)
[20 August, 1853], and an exposure of corruption
in the House of Commons with regard to Railway Bills.
    Contains much detail on the affairs of the
Eastern Union Rly., of Thomas Brassey the
contractor-financier, the tyranny of railway
promoters and the methods used to deceive
investors and the public.

5824 WASON, R. A letter to the inhabitants of
Ipswich, upon the injustice of Mr. Justice
Cresswell's summing up in the case of Ayres,
Secretary to the Eastern Union Company,
v. Wason. *London*, 1854. pp. 25.   BM

5825 EASTERN COUNTIES RLY. Report of the
Committee of Investigation and minutes of
EC evidence taken before the Committee, together with the documents in relation thereto. *London*, 1855. pp. xi, 107, with tables. BM
    Results of an inquiry into the affairs of the
company.

5825a HAWKES, H. Henry Hawkes, Esq., v. the
Eastern Counties Railway Company. Re-
EC port of the above case, from the short-hand
writer's notes, including the proceedings in
the High Court of Chancery, and in the House
of Lords. J. R. Carter & Son, solicitors for
the plaintiff; Gregory, Gregory, Skirrow &
Rowcliffe, agents. *London*, 1855. pp. iii,
78, 28, 79–127, 28, 26, 42, with fold. plates.
                      BODLEIAN LIBRARY, OXFORD
    Privately printed.
    A successful action for breach of a contract to
purchase the plaintiff's land in Spalding for a
line which was never constructed.

5826 WADDINGTON, D. Eastern Counties Railway: the Chairman's answer to the report
EC of the Committee of Investigation [of the
shareholders]. 1855. *London*, 1855. pp. 107.
                                           BM

5827 EASTERN COUNTIES RLY. Observations
of the Investigation Committee on Mr.
EC Waddington's answer to the report adopted
by the shareholders on December 7th 1855.
London, 1856. pp. 47.   ICE
    The official view, with explanation of various
projects undertaken.

5828 EASTERN COUNTIES RLY. The Chairman's final answer to the report and ob-
EC servations of the Committee of Investigation
[dated 23 January 1856]. [*London*, 1856.]
pp. 4.   ICE

5829 HOY, George, *pseud*. [G. Wilson Ancell.]
[Satirical notices relating to the Eastern
EC Counties Railway.] *Bethnal Green* [*London*],
1856–7.   BM
    A series of 19 single or double sheets issued
'for general distribution amongst railway
passengers'.
    1. A Challenge!!!
    2. The Eastern Counties Railway offers the
following advantages to nervous persons.
    3. Hoy's donkey's lament.
    4. The new 'reader' for the Eastern Counties
Rly. Co.: The old donkey's ditty.
    5. Hoy's donkey wanted again!!!
    6. Remonstrance of the engine drivers on
the Eastern Counties Rly.
    7. Petition of shareholders to the Eastern
Counties Board.
    8. The Eastern Counties Rly. Co. versus
speed and economy. Nuts to crack.
    9. Notice to the passengers on the E.C. Rly
    10. Oh, what shall we do with the crest?
    11. Three cheers for Hoy's donkey!!!
    12. The Hertford Blue-coat Boys' song of
rejoicing . . .
    13. Hoy's donkey wanted at Sudbury.
    14. Railway excitement at Sudbury.
    15. Another wrong move by the notorious
Eastern Counties Rly. Board.
    16. Remonstrance of the Tottenham pas-
sengers.
    17. Great trial of speed! The Eastern
Counties Rly. versus Hoy's donkey.
    18. The poor man's complaint against the
Eastern Counties Rly. Co.
    19. Modest requirements!!!
    G. W. Ancell's series of leaflets was directed
against the slowness and unpunctuality of

trains on the E.C. Rly. 'The only fast trains on this line', he says, 'are those that are stuck fast'. His campaign began with a challenge to beat some of their business trains on his old donkey, and in his later notices he claims to have done so. He also complains of high fares and there are recurrent references to the excellence of the services run by the Great Northern. Some of the issues are in verse and some are illustrated. Ancell also published a 'prospectus' for a 'Donkey Express Company' under the pseudonym of 'Mangold Wurzel, Esq.' (7708).

5830 PETOVIA; being a review of the scheme for a railway from Pitsea to Colchester and an
EC exposure of the motives which prompted it, the absurdities which characterise it, and the inevitable failure which awaits it. Dedicated to its promoters and their victims. By 'A Tooth of the Dragon.' *London*, 1857. pp. 63.   BM
    A proposed branch of the Eastern Counties Rly. to be called the Pitsea, Maldon & Colchester Railway. The writer attacks the prospectus —'a mass of deception'—and the promoter/contractor, Sir M. Peto—'the hapless victim of greed or of desparation'. The line was never built.

5831 WALLEN, J. The Eastern Counties Railway and district: their capabilities for yielding
EC good dividends to the shareholders of the former: a letter to the proprietors. *London*, 1857. pp. 10[12].   BM
    The E.C. Rly. compared with the London, Tilbury & Southend Rly.

5832 EAST SUFFOLK RLY. Banquet at the Royal Hotel, Lowestoft on Tuesday 14th of June 1859. pp. 12.   BR
    Programme of vocal items in a concert held to celebrate the extension to Lowestoft.

5833 The EASTERN Counties Railway: why does it not pay? . . . *London*, 1859. pp. 114, with
EC a map.   LSE
    Horatio Love's chairmanship ruinous to the company. Addressed to the proprietors.
    —— 7th edn. *London*, 1860. pp. 114. UL(GL)

5834 EASTERN COUNTIES RLY. A few facts and figures omitted from 'Why does it not
EC pay?' being an exposure of the palpable misrepresentations and falsehoods contained in that pamphlet. *London*, 1860. pp. 55. LSE

5835 A WORD or two about 'E.U.', being an appeal to the President of the Board of
EC Trade. By An Old Acquaintance. *London*, 1860. pp. 51.   BM
    The early history of the Eastern Union Rly., its amalgamation with the Eastern Counties Rly , and how the E.U. has suffered from this association owing to the E.C. Rly. evading the terms of agreement. Urging independence of E.U. Rly.

5836 COCKBURN, A.J.E. The short-hand writer's notes of the summing up of Lord Chief
EC Justice Cockburn in the case of Stokes and others versus the Eastern Counties Railway

Company, arising out of an accident which occurred near the Tottenham Station on February 20, 1860. *Stratford*, 1861. pp. 44.
                                              LSE

5837 EMERSON, G. R. Guide to the Great Eastern Railway; with historical, topographical, statistical and descriptive notes. *London*, [1864.] pp. viii, 96, & 23 pp. adverts.   pc
    pp. 1–3, history and description of the G.E.R.

5838 GREAT EASTERN RLY. Statement of the Board of Directors of the Great Eastern Railway Company in reference to the G.E. Northern Junction Railway Bill, accompanied by a map of the G.E. Rly. system, showing the proposed new line to the North of England, the communications with the docks of London, and the Metropolitan districts to be served. *London*, 1864. pp. 29.   BM

5839 GREAT EASTERN RAILWAY SHAREHOLDERS ASSOCIATION. Report of the Committee of the Great Eastern Railway Shareholders' Association. [*London*, 1867.] pp. 16.   BM
    Concern over large outlays of money for suburban extensions.

5840 MITCHELL, J. Railway finance: being suggestions for the resuscitation and improvement of the railway companies at present in financial difficulties; in a letter addressed to . . . Benjamin Disraeli, H.M. Chancellor of the Exchequer. *London*, 1867. pp. 27.   BM
    pp. 19–23, estimates of revenue and dividends of the Great Eastern Rly., 1867–1876.

5841 OUGHT railway companies, in the interests of the public and of their shareholders, to be steamboat proprietors? A question fully answered by the experience of the Great Eastern Railway Company, in connection with their Harwich steamboat working. By a Late Shareholder. *London*, 1871. pp. 14, with 5 financial tables.   BM

5842 WATKIN, E. W. Great Eastern Railway. December 1872. pp. 27.   BR
    'Private and Confidential.'
    'I have written this confidential paper at the wish of some friends who think they ought to know the circumstances of my association with the Great Eastern Railway, which began in 1867 and ended last Summer.'

5843 PHILP, R. K. The Great Eastern Railway Panoramic Guide. *London*, [1874.] pp. 48, with maps.   BM

5844 BASS, M. T. A Circular from M. T. Bass, M.P., to Great Eastern shareholders, with a financial report. *London*, 1876. pp. 34. BM
    Inefficient management: a call for an enquiry into 'the causes of the excessive cost of working the line'. The financial report is by J. P. Lythgoe. Appendix contains ten tables.

5845 BASS, M. T. Second Circular from M. T. Bass, M.P., to the shareholders of the Great Eastern Railway, in reply to the directors' special report, July 21st, 1876. *London*, 1876. pp. 14.   BM
  This contains (pp. 5–14) a second report from J. P. Lythgoe to M. T. Bass following upon the directors' reply to Lythgoe's first report in Bass's first circular.

5846 CRORY, W. G. East London industries. *London*, 1876. pp. vi, xi, 279.   BM
  pp. [208]–220, Locomotion. The locomotive and carriage and wagon works of the North London Rly. and of the Great Eastern Rly.

5847 MR. BASS and his agent; from the Retford Times of May 13th, 1876. [1876.] pp. [2.]
                                           BM
  G.E. Rly. affairs. The agent is Edwin Phillips.

5848 MR. BASS and his editor; from the Retford Times of May 13th, 1876. [1876.] pp. [2.]
                                           BM
  G.E. Rly. affairs. The 'editor' is Edwin Phillips.

5849 PHILLIPS, E. A report to M. T. Bass, M.P., on the Great Eastern Railway. *London*, 1876. pp. 29.   BM
  Criticism of management and working; pp. 25–9, 'The Great Eastern Half-Yearly Meeting' from the *Railway Service Gazette*.

5850 THETFORD & WATTON RLY. Rules and regulations for the guidance of the officers and men in the service of the Thetford & Watton Railway Company. July 1876. *London*, [1876.] pp. 131.   PC

5851 WATKIN, E. W. To the shareholders of the Great Eastern Railway Company who elected me a director in August last. *London*, [Oct. 1876.] pp. 15.   BR
  On his difficulties with the Board over the question of incompetent administration.

5852 GREAT EASTERN RLY. To the shareholders of the Great Eastern Railway. [1877.] pp. 2[4].   BM
  Circular letter from the Board suggesting that Edwin Phillips be nominated auditor. Dated 23 July, 1877. Enclosed is a form 'to be signed at once'. (Closing date 27 July.)

5853 The POOR and the High Beach Railway. *London*, [c. 1880.] pp. 19.   BM
  Support for the proposed extension from Chingford.

5854 GREAT EASTERN RLY. Railway & Canal Traffic Act, 1888. Estimated annual losses ... [*London*, 1890.] pp. 13.   LSE
  Tables.
  —— Appendix. pp. 17.   LSE

5855 GREAT EASTERN RLY. The Yarmouth and Lowestoft express trains: annotated time tables. [*London*, c. 1890.] pp. 14, with 1 illus.   PC

*5856 GREAT EASTERN RLY. Memoranda connected with the Locomotive and Carriage Works at Stratford, and the Wagon Works at Temple Mills. *Stratford*, June 1903. pp. 45, with illus., 2 fold. plans of works & 14 diagrams of locomotives.   IME

5857 GREAT EASTERN RLY. Wages and Hours Arbitration, 1909. Award of Lord Gorrell of Brampton, P.C. [1909.] pp. 25.   LSE
  'Privately printed.'
  'I make no award upon any of the claims.'

5858 GREAT EASTERN RLY. A lecture on tickets and ticket holders and the method of dealing with them; delivered in the Essex Room of the Great Eastern Hotel, Liverpool Street, on June 12, 1917. . . . By A. W. Brenes, Chief Traffic Manager's Dept. *Stratford*, [1918.] pp. 19.   LSE
  'For official use only.'

5859 GREAT Eastern Railway. The last word in steam-operated suburban train services. *London: Railway Gazette*, [1920.] pp. 31, with 34 illus., plans (1 fold.) & tables.   BM
  Reprint, *Railway Gazette*, 1 Oct., 1920.

5860 FREEMAN, A. V. Great Eastern Railway suburban system scandals. *Witherby*, [1913?] pp. 16.   BM
  Overcrowding, mismanagement at stations, unpunctuality, etc.

5861 GREAT EASTERN TRAIN FERRIES, LTD. Harwich-Zeebrugge train ferry service: a new link with the Continent. (Souvenir of the opening . . . 24 April, 1924.) [*London*, 1924.] pp. 11, with illus.   RC

5862 WHITE, B. R. Great Eastern Section suburban services of the London & North Eastern Railway. pp. 18. *Typescript.*   RC
  Paper, Railway Club, 26 May, 1938.

Great Eastern Northern Junction Rly. Co.
[not incorporated]

5863 HALF an hour on the Great Eastern Northern Junction; by a Norfolk Man. *Norwich*, 1864. pp. 21.   NORWICH PL
  A vindication of the G.E. Rly. Co. against its detractors who the author suggests have saddled it with the bad reputation of its parent companies. Improvements made, and proposals for a northern extension to convey Norwich market produce and to bring in coal.

5864 BURKE, J. ST. G. Speech of J. St. George Burke in opening the case of the promoters of the Great Eastern Northern Junction Railway Bill, and in answer to that of the Great Northern Railway Company, before the Select Committee of the House of Commons, May 4, 1864. *London*, 1864. pp. 72.
                                           BM

Great North of Scotland Railway

5865 NOTMAN, R. R. Deeside Railway: letter to the landed proprietors of Deeside. *Aberdeen*, 1850. pp. 38.   AU
In favour of the railway.

5866 MEASOM, G. Measom's Official Illustrated Guide to the North Eastern, North British, Edinburgh & Glasgow, Scottish Central, Edinburgh, Perth & Dundee, Scottish North Eastern and Great North of Scotland railways . . . *London*, 1861. pp. 447, 224, with 200 engravings.   BM

5867 ANDERSON, W. Guide to the Formartine & Buchan Railway . . . *Peterhead*, 1862. pp. 60.   BM

5868 The PAST and present policy of the directors and the future prospects of the Great North of Scotland Railway Company: a letter to the shareholders by one of themselves. *Aberdeen*, [1862.] pp. 26.   EDINBURGH UL

5869 FERGUSON, W. The Great North of Scotland Railway. *Edinburgh*, 1881. pp. 174. BM
A guide to places served.

5870 REID, G. Twelve sketches of scenery and antiquities on the line of the Great North of Scotland Railway, with illustrative letterpress by W. Ferguson of Kinmundy. *Edinburgh*, 1883. pp. 115.   BR

5871 SCOTT, W. J. Little and good: a study of the Great North of Scotland Railway and its train service. *Aberdeen*, 1898. pp. 62, with illus., maps, diagrams & tables.   RC

5872 GREAT NORTH OF SCOTLAND RLY. Report by the General Manager to the Chairman and directors. Railway motor cars. *Glasgow*, 1904. pp. 20.   BR
'Private.'
Steam rail-cars.

5873 DUNBAR, B. G. Locomotives of the G.N.S.R. as at 31st December, 1922, with alterations to date. *Glasgow*, 1931. pp. [7.]
A list.   BM

5874 HARVEY, C. M. B. A history of the Great North of Scotland Railway. *London: Locomotive Publishing Co.*, 1940. pp. viii, 222, with 44 illus. on plates (col. frontis.) & illus. in text.   BM
—— 2nd edn. *London*, 1949. pp. 231, with
c a chronology of openings, etc.   BM
A photo-lithograph version of the 2nd edn., without col. frontis. was printed in Belgium and published in 1962.

5875 ALLCHIN, M. V. C. Locomotives of the Great North of Scotland Railway, illustrated: types, building dates, etc. *Southsea: Railway Hobbies*, 1950. pp. 21.   BM

5876 STEPHENSON LOCOMOTIVE SOCIETY. Great North of Scotland Railway, 1854–
c 1954. *London*, 1954. pp. 277–320, with 26 illus. on 12 plates, lists & descriptions of locomotives, and a detailed chronology, 1793–1915. [*Journal of the Stephenson Locomotive Society*, vol. 30, no. 352, September 1954.]   BM

Great Northern Railway

Historical

5877 GRINLING, C. H. The history of the Great Northern Railway, 1845–1895. *London*, 1898. pp. vi, 429, with illus. & map.   BM
—— [2nd edn.] The history of the Great Northern Railway, 1845–1902 . . . a new issue with an introduction and an additional chapter. *London*, 1903. pp. xviii, 463, with illus. & maps.   BM

5878 SEKON, G. A. Notes on the railways: no. 1,
c Great Northern Railway. [1904.] pp. 16.
                                              BM
History, with a five-page chronology.

5879 BIRD, G. F. The locomotives of the Great Northern Railway, 1847–1902; with 8 full-page illustrations & 112 illustrations in the text, by the author. *London*, 1903. pp. xi, 203, with lists.   RC
—— new edn. '1847–1910.' *London*, 1910. pp. xi, 228, with 8 plates, 121 illus., & lists.
                                              BM

5880 'ENGINEER.' The Great Northern Railway. *London: The Engineer*, 1913. (Supplement to the issue of 28 November.) pp. xv, with 29 illus., 2 maps, 9 tables, numerous diagrams showing locomotive development, 2 la. fold. diagrams of locomotives, 3 photogravure plates of 6 G.N.R. scenes and a timetable.   BM

5881 GREAT NORTHERN RLY. Workmen's tickets: a resumé of the practices governing the issue of workmen's tickets on the Great Northern Railway from the commencement of their issue on March 1st 1871, to September 1920. [1920.] pp. 9[11]. *Typescript*.
                                              LSE

5882 BACK, W. N. R. J. London & North Eastern Railway: history of the Great Northern section.   RC
MS. Papers, Railway Club, March 1925, 1926 and 1927.
pt. 1, From inception until 1867. pp. 54 + pp. xxv (tables).
pt. 2, 1867 to 1884. pp. 46 + xxiv (tables).
pt. 3, Conclusion. pp. [47.]

*5883 LAMBERT, R. S. The Railway King, 1800–1871: a study of George Hudson and the

business morals of his times . . . *London: Allen & Unwin*, 1934. pp. 320, with illus.
BM

Contains much information on the railways with which Hudson was associated, including the London & York.
—— reprinted, *London: Allen & Unwin*, 1964.
BM

*5884 WEIGHT, R. A. H. Great Northern locomotives, 1847–1947: Bury, Sturrock, Stirling, Ivatt, Gresley: personal narratives: the story of the famous 'Atlantics': numbers, dates, dimensions & classes, drawings & illustrations. *Hastings: the author*, 1947. pp. 78 [79], with plates.
IT

5885 BRITISH RAILWAYS (EASTERN REGION). Great Northern Railway: historical information. [*London, c.* 1950?] pp. 7. *Reproduced typescript.*
BR

5886 WEIGHT, R. A. H. The Great Northern Railway. *London: Ian Allan*, [1952.] pp. 32. [*Railways before the Grouping.*]
BM
Cover title, *Great Northern*.
Illustrations, with brief history and description of services between 1909 and 1922.

5887 KLAPPER, C. F. From King's Cross to Kingstown, and other railway might-have-beens: a paper presented to the Railway Club, 3 June, 1955. pp. 30. *Typescript.* RC
The G.N.R. and its intended through route to Porthdinllaen over the Potteries, Shrewsbury & North Wales Rly., and other abortive schemes of various railways.

5888 FERRIDAY, P. Lord Grimthorpe, 1816–1905. *London: J. Murray*, 1957. pp. xiii, 230.
BM
pp. 1–7 and elsewhere, Edmund Denison, father of Lord Grimthorpe, and Chairman of the Great Northern.

5889 NOCK, O. S. The Great Northern Railway. *London: Ian Allan*, 1958. pp. 192, with 72 illus. on 33 plates (col. frontis.), maps & tables.
BM

5890 PERRIN, R. The history of New England. [*Peterborough*, 1958.] pp. 44, with 6 illus. PC
Privately issued to commemorate the New England School Old Boys' Reunion and the centenary of the G.N. Rly. New England School, 1857–1957.

5891 ALLEN, C. J. Great Northern. *London: Ian Allan*, [1961.] pp. 56, with illus.
BM

5892 PERRIN, R. G.N.R. schools: the history of the old railway church schools, 1856–1911. [*Peterborough*, 1961.] pp. 51, with 16 illus., incl. portraits of groups.
PC
Privately issued to members of the New England Old Boys' Association.

5893 GREAT NORTHERN RLY. [A collection of documents.]   UL(GL)
1, Act of Incorporation.
2, Reports of Meetings, 1846 to 1852.
3, Reports of Royston & Hitchin Rly.
4, Reports of East Lincolnshire Rly.

Contemporaneous

5894 GIBBS, J. Report of Joseph Gibbs, civil engineer, upon the Great Northern Railway. [*London*,] 1835. pp. 23.   ICE
A proposed line from Whitechapel (London) via Dunmow, Saffron Walden, Cambridge and Lincoln to York. The Bill was defeated.

5895 WELLS, S. A letter to John Fryer . . . on the lines proposed by Messrs. Walker & Gibbs, civil engineers, for a railway from London to York, and a branch to Norwich, etc., with a letter from Earl Fitzwilliam, and the reports of Messrs. Walker & Gibbs. 2nd edn. *London*, 1835. pp. 58.   BRE

5896 DIRECT NORTHERN RLY. The following is an accurate description of the route of this railway . . . [1844.] s.sh.   BM

5897 DIRECT NORTHERN RLY. Statement of the case and merits of the Direct Northern Railway from London to York, by Lincoln. [*London*, 1844.] pp. 3.   BM

5898 LOCKE, J. The following correspondence will not be without interest to shareholders in the York lines. [1844.] pp. 4.
Letters, mostly between Joseph Locke and the Secretary of the London & York concerning his resignation as Engineer.

5899 BOARD OF TRADE—RAILWAY DEPARTMENT. Report of the Railway Department of the Board of Trade on the schemes for extending railway communication between London and York . . . *London*: printed by *Jones & Causton*, [1845.] pp. 61.   BM
p. 41 ' . . . the Direct Northern . . . affords decidedly the best means of communication to York'. A private reproduction of the official report issued by the Direct Northern directors.

5900 DIRECT NORTHERN RLY. Comparative distances by Direct Northern, and London & York Railways. *London*, January 1845. s.sh.   BM
A table in two columns showing the D.N.'s shorter distances.

5901 DIRECT NORTHERN RLY. Distances by Eastern Counties Extension from Cambridge . . . *London*, January 1845. s.sh. BM
Tables.

5902 DIRECT NORTHERN RLY. Distances by Eastern Counties, proposed Cambridge & Lincoln, Lincoln, York & Leeds District & Independent. *London*, January 1845. s.sh.
Tables.   BM

5903 DIRECT NORTHERN RLY. Memorial of the Provisional Committee [to the Board of Trade]. [*London*, 1845.] pp. 15. BM
Submitting a 'full and complete exposition of their scheme'.

5904 DIRECT NORTHERN RLY. [A printed letter addressed to 'My Lord Duke' concerning the necessity for the D.N.Rly. to cross the Don Navigation by means of a fixed (and not a swing) bridge.] *London*, 5 March 1845. pp. [4.] BM

5905 [LONDON & YORK RLY.] Select Committee on London & York Railway Bill . . . Tuesday 29th April, 1845; Lord Courtenay in the chair. pp. 54. NLC
—— Reply. Monday 21 July, 1845. pp. 68. NLC

5906 MILLER, J. To the Provisional Committee of the Direct Northern Railway. *London*, 1 September, 1845. pp. 2. BM
The report of his survey.

5907 DIRECT Northern Railway Company, from London to York. *Westminster*, 1846. pp. 11, with map. H

5908 CUBITT, L. Schedule of prices and terms of contract intended to be applied to the execution of the several works which may be directed by the architect to be performed in the buildings or other constructions forming the London permanent goods and temporary passenger station for the Great Northern Railway Company on their land north side of the Regent's Canal, Maiden Lane, King's Cross, London. *London*, 1850. pp. 51[55]. *Lithograph.* BM
Specification for circulation to would-be contractors. Includes detailed estimates of expenses (materials and wages), precise requirements relating to structures and fittings, and a 'tender for works' to be completed and returned to the Secretary of the G.N.R.

5909 FREEBODY, W. Y. Statement of the position of the Great Northern Railway in relation to the actual (and estimated) outlay and the real (and probable) profit. *London*, February 1850. pp. 16. IT
'For private circulation.'
Includes ten letters between Freebody and the G.N.R. concerning his request for more information for shareholders regarding expenditure on works.

5910 SOME of the reasons why the Great Northern Railway is likely, at its present market price, to yield the largest percentage return ever paid by any railway in the Kingdom. By a Shareholder. (To the shareholders of the G.N. Rly.) *London*, 1850. pp. 14. BM

5911 MILNES, R. M. Answer from R. M. Milnes to Robert Baxter on the South Yorkshire Isle of Axholme Bill. 3rd edn. *Pontefract*, 1852. pp. 10. BM
Concerning the proposed line by the G.N.R.

5912 BERTIE, G. A. F. A. The Earl of Lindsey versus the Great Northern Railway Company: judgement of the Vice-Chancellor, Sir W. Page Wood, March 22, 1853. *London*, 1853. pp. 33. NLC

5913 MACKIE, C. Itinerary of the Great Northern Railway from London to York . . . *London*, [1852.] pp. 96, with map. BM
—— new edn. *London*, [1854.] pp. 122.

5914 MINUTES and correspondence between the London & North Western, Midland, and Manchester, Sheffield & Lincolnshire companies, and the Great Northern Railway Company. *London*, 1856. pp. 47. BM

5915 GREAT NORTHERN RLY. Report of the proceedings on the trials of Leopold Redpath and Chas. James Comyns Kent, for forgery, at the Central Criminal Court on Friday 16th January 1857, before Mr. Baron Martin and Mr. Justice Willes. *London*, [1857.] pp. 47. BR

5916 MOWATT, J. R. The Great Northern Railway Company: a letter to the shareholders from Mr. Mowatt, late Secretary of the Company. *London*, 1858. pp. 20. BM
'For private circulation amongst the shareholders.'
His explanation of the reasons for his dismissal from office, refuting charges made against him and making accusations against the Chairman, Edmund Denison.

5917 GREAT NORTHERN, HOLBORN & CITY EXTENSION RLY. Statement of the directors of the Great Northern, Holborn & City Extension Railway, submitted for the consideration of the Great Northern Railway Company. *London*, 1860. pp. 14, with a fold. map. BR
Proposed City extension branching off from the G.N.R. south of Copenhagen Tunnel.

5918 MEASOM, G. Measom's Illustrated Guide to the Great Northern Railway; including the Manchester, Sheffield & Lincolnshire, and Midland Railways . . . *London*, 1857. pp. 200, with 250 engravings. BM
—— another edn. *London*, 1861. pp. 544. BM

5919 SHEARDOWN, W. The Great North Road and the Great Northern Railway; or, Roads and rails. *Doncaster*, [1863.] pp. 43. LEEDS PL
From the *Doncaster Gazette*, August 14, 21, 28, and September 4, 1863.
Includes ancient British and Roman roads, packhorse roads, turnpike roads, coaches, and a history of the development of the railway.

5920 BURKE, J. St. G. Speech of J. St. George Burke in opening the case of the Great Eastern Northern Junction Railway Bill, and in answer to that of the Great Northern Railway Company, before the Select Committee of the House of Commons, May 4, 1864. *London*, 1864. pp. 72. BM

5921 'THERE'S a good deal in that!' A reply to the attacks of Mr. Lythgoe and others on the Great Northern Railway Company. Magna est veritas. *London*, 1878. pp. 31. NLC

5922 ADDY, J. Proposed Nottingham, Stamford & Huntingdon Railway. *Stamford*, 1882. pp. 12. ICE
A loop from Huntingdon on the Gt. Northern Rly. to provide a shorter journey from Nottingham to London.

5923 GREAT NORTHERN RLY. Revised classification of merchandise traffic and revised schedule of maximum rates and charges applicable thereto, proposed to be charged by the Great Northern Rly. Co. Submitted to the Board of Trade in pursuance of the provisions of the Railway & Canal Traffic Act, 1888. *London*, 1889. pp. 23. LSE

5924 SCOTT, W. J. Great Northern speeds; or, The fastest travelling in the world: being a study of Great Northern (& M. S. & L.) quick-running trains, according to the time-tables for the Summer, 1888 . . . with some notes on the fastest trains of other English lines. *London*, [1888.] pp. 22. BM
—— 2nd edn. '. . . for the Summer, 1889.' *London*, [1889.] pp. 32. LSE

5925 GREAT NORTHERN RLY. Railway & Canal Traffic Act, 1888. Summary of estimated losses for 12 months on mineral goods, perishable, and live stock traffic, upon comparing the existing charges with the maximum rates and charges proposed by the Board of Trade. *London*, 1890. pp. 27. LSE

5926 PETITION of delegates appointed by goods guards, brakesmen, foremen shunters, shunters, assistant shunters and porter shunters, on the Great Northern Railway, to H. Oakley, General Manager . . . with subsequent correspondence referring to the matters contained therein. [*London*,] 1890. pp. 7. LSE

5927 DICK, KERR & CO. Scheme for the substitution of electricity for steam traction on the suburban lines of the Great Northern Railway Company. June 29th, 1903. pp. 16, with diagrams, illus. & charts on 22 plates. BR
Includes a proposed timetable for an electric train suburban service, 8–10 a.m.

5928 HOPWOOD, H. L. The London suburban services of the Great Northern Railway. pp. 34. *Typescript*. RC
Paper, Railway Club, 14 Sept., 1905.

5929 GREAT NORTHERN RLY. Indenture declaring the rules and regulations of the Superannuation Fund. [*London*, 1906?] pp. 26. LSE
Printed reproduction in booklet form.

Great Western Railway

For a genealogical table of the Great Western see Appendix IIIa.

Historical

*5930 BOURNE, J. C. The history and description of the Great Western Railway . . . from drawings taken expressly for this work and executed in lithography by John C. Bourne. *London*, 1846. pp. iv, 76, with engr. t.-p. & 50 plates. BM

5931 OSLER, E. History of the Cornwall Railway. *Truro*, 1846. pp. 48. BM
Reprinted from the *Cornwall Gazette*.
An account of early schemes, 1833 to 1846.

*5932 BRUNEL, I. The life of Isambard Kingdom Brunel, civil engineer. *London*, 1870. pp. xxviii, 568, with 5 plates, illus., & bibliogr. notes. BM
Contains many reports and letters.

5933 SLOUS, F. L. Stray leaves from the scrape book [*sic*] of an awkward man; reprinted in June 1881 from the edition of 1843, with additions and subtractions by the author. *London*, 1881. pp. 203. BM

5934 ARROWSMITH, F. W. The Coleford Railway. *Bristol*, 1883. GLOUCESTER PL

*5935 GOOCH, D. Diaries of Sir Daniel Gooch. *London*, 1892. pp. xxiv, 254. BM
Extracts selected by his widow and friends.

5936 GREAT WESTERN RLY. The town and works of Swindon, with a brief history of the broad gauge. *Swindon*, 1892. pp. 47, with portraits of I. K. Brunel and D. Gooch. PC

*5937 SEKON, G. A. History of the Great Western Railway; being the story of the broad gauge . . . *London*, 1895. pp. xvi, 373, with frontis. & 15 illus. BM

5938 BIRD, G. F. The broad gauge locomotives of the Great Western Railway, 1837–1892; reproduced from drawings by Geo. Fredk. Bird. *London: Locomotive Publishing Co.*, [*c.* 1903.] la. fold. s.sh. RC
Fifty-three drawings reprinted from the *Locomotive Magazine*, 1901–3, with marginal lists.

5939 BURROWS, G. H. Great Western Railway locomotives. *London: GWR (London) Lecture & Debating Society*, 1905. pp. 8, with diagrams. BR

5940 SCOTT, W. J. Great Western train speeds, 1845–1905. *London: GWR (London) Lecture & Debating Society*, 1905. pp. 9. BM

5941 LANGDON, R. Life of Roger Langdon, told by himself; with additions by his daughter Ellen. *London*, [1908.] pp. 104.   BM

R. Langdon was station-master of Silverton, G.W. Rly., 1867–94.

*5942 GIBBS, G. H. Extracts from the Diary of Mr. George Henry Gibbs. [*London, c.* 1910.] pp. 68.   BM

Reprinted from *G.W. Rly. Magazine*, 1909–10. Relating to G.W.R. affairs during his period as a director, March 1836 to May 1840.

5943 POLE, F. J. C. The conversion of the gauge of the Great Western Railway main-line. *In* 'Engineering wonders of the world', edited by Archibald Williams. *London*, 1909–10. vol. 1, pp. 108–18, with illus.   BM

5944 'ENGINEER.' The Great Western Railway. *London: The Engineer*, 1910. (Supplement to the issue of 16 December.) pp. xxiv, with 26 illus., a table, and numerous drawings of broad gauge engines, la. fold. plate reproducing four of J. C. Bourne's drawings of G.W.R. scenes, and 2 la. fold. diagrams of G.W.R. locomotives.   BM

*5945 WILLIAMS, A. Life in a railway factory. *London*, 1915. pp. xiii, 315.   BM

Memories of twenty-three years at Swindon.

5946 LEVIEN, D. V. Great Western heirlooms: being a lecture on some treasures (hidden and unearthed) and odds and ends in the Company's archives at Paddington Station. pp. vi, 52. *Typescript*, with MS. alterations.   BR

Paper, G.W.R. Lecture & Debating Society, 9 Feb., 1922.

5947 RALPH, H. Railway days and railway ways: being the reminiscences of a Great Western Railway man. *Reading*, [1922.] pp. 38, with fold. plate & many illus.   RC

Reprinted from the *Reading Standard* of December 1921—April 1922.

*5948 CHAPMAN, W. G. The 10-30 Limited . . . *London: G.W. Rly.*, 1923. pp. 118, with many illus.   BM

A history and description of the G.W.R.

—— 2nd edn. *London*, 1923. pp. 124.   BM
—— 3rd, *London*, 1923. pp. 124.   IT
—— 4th, *London*, 1923. pp. 131.   BM

*5949 CHAPMAN, W. G. Caerphilly Castle . . . *London: G.W. Rly.*, 1924. pp. 199, with illus.   BM

A history and description of the G.W.R.

5950 [GREAT WESTERN RAILWAY.] Common seals of railway, canal and road motor companies now vested in the organisation of the Great Western Railway Company. [*c.* 1924?]   BR

A typed list of about 250 items, with photographs of seals.

5951 GREAT WESTERN RLY. List of collieries on or connected with the Great Western Railway. [*London*.] 1924. pp. 76, with 2 fold. maps.   BM

Includes a history and description of ports owned by the G.W.R.

5952 GREAT WESTERN RLY. The romance of a railway: the Great Western Railway. *London*, [1925.] pp. 40, with illus. & map.   BR

*5953 WILLIAMS, A. Brunel and after: the romance of the Great Western Railway . . . *London; G.W. Rly.*, 1925. pp. vii, 205, with 78 illus., chronology & a fold. map.   BM

5954 GALE, P. R. The Great Western Railway, including the railways built under the Act of Incorporation, the railways since promoted by the Great Western Railway Co., the railways absorbed prior to the passing of the Railways Act, 1921, and the railways amalgamated therewith by virtue of the Railways Act, 1921 . . . [*London: Great Western Rly.*], 1926. pp. 142, with map.   BR

Printed for G.W.R. use; not published.

G.W.R. components from 1792–1926 in a series of detailed tables. The large folding map is coloured and is related to the tables by numbers which indicate the location of each line.

5955 HOME, G. The Great Western Railway . . . *London*, 1913. pp. iv, 91, with 8 plates & 21 illus. [*Peeps at Great Railways.*]   BM

History and description. Introductory.

—— 2nd edn. *London*, 1926. pp. vi, 89.   BM

5956 GREAT WESTERN RLY. General statistics, 1913–1927. *Paddington* (*London*), April 1928. pp. 67.   LSE

Fifty tables relating to the G.W.R., including comparisons with other railways.

5957 GREAT WESTERN RLY. A silver anniversary: the Cornish Riviera Express, 1904–1929. *London*, July 1929. pp. 19, with illus. & tables.   RC

*5958 MACDERMOT, E. T. History of the Great Western Railway. *London: Great Western Rly.*, 1927–31. 2 vols. in 3, with many illus., tables, lists, maps, & chronology. (vol. 1, pt. 1, pp. xv, 456; pt. 2, pp. x, [457]–902: vol. 2, pp. xii, 654.)   BM

A detailed, authoritative work, founded upon records made by Albert Robert Burnell, a G.W.R. clerk, between 1874 and 1908. Full accounts are given of all component companies and the 'Gauge War'.

A complete revision is now (August 1964) in preparation by C. R. Clinker. This includes corrections to all known factual errors and will continue MacDermot's account in a third volume by C. R. Clinker, covering the final years of the G.W.R., from 1921 to 1947.

—— rev. edn. By C. R. Clinker. *London: Ian Allan*, 1964– . 3 vols.   BM

vol. 1, 1833–1863. *London*, 1964. pp. xii, 490, with frontis., 58 illus. on 32 plates, many diagrams & tables, lists, & a chronology.

*5959 TORR, C. Small talk at Wreyland. *Cambridge*, 1918, 21, 23. 3 vols., with plates. BM
—— abridged edn. *Cambridge*, 1926. pp. 352, with 9 plates & a map. BM
—— further abridgement. *Cambridge*, 1932. pp. 216, with 9 plates & a map. [*Cambridge Miscellany*, no. 1.] BM
A record mostly of local events drawn from letters written by the author's father and grandfather, and from personal observations. Contains some contemporary accounts of the coming of the South Devon Rly. (Newton to Moreton branch) and has several references to social aspects of early railways.
Only the 1926 edition is indexed.

*5960 CHAPMAN, W. G. The Cheltenham Flyer: a new railway book for boys of all ages. *London: G.W. Rly.*, 1934. pp. 232, with illus. BM
The G.W.R.

5961 FINANCIAL TIMES. Special G.W.R. Centenary Review. *London*, 31 August 1935. pp. IV, with illus. (Supplement.) LSE

*5962 GREAT WESTERN RLY. Great Western progress, 1835–1935. [*London*, 1935.] pp. 180, with illus. & map. BR
Reprinted from the G.W. Rly. Centenary number of *The Times. See* 5967.

5963 GREAT WESTERN RLY. Great Western Railway Centenary, 1835–1935. Commemorative luncheon in the Great Hall, Bristol University, August 31st 1935. pp. 24, with mounted plates, & maps. RC
pp. 2–24, Bristol and its association with the G.W.R., 1835–1935.

5964 GREAT WESTERN RAILWAY MAGAZINE. G.W.R. Centenary Number, September, 1935. vol. XLVII, no. 9. pp. 439–500. BM
G.W.R. history, with many illustrations.

5965 GREAT WESTERN RLY. Indexes to Brunel's Reports, 1835–1842. Daniel Gooch's Diaries, 1816–1889. Gibbs' Diary, 1836–1840. pp. 13, 5, 3. *Typescript*. BR

5966 RAILWAY GAZETTE. G.W.R. Special Centenary Number, 30 August 1935. pp. 52 & adverts, with many illus. & maps. IT

5967 TIMES *newspaper*. Great Western Railway Centenary Number. *London*, 31 August 1935. pp. xxviii, with many illus. (Supplement to issue no. 47157.) LSE
Contains much historical and descriptive information.

*5968 CHAPMAN, W. G. Loco's of 'The Royal Road.' *London: G.W. Rly.*, 1936. pp. 232, with many illus. of G.W.R. locomotives, past & present. BM

5969 FELLOWS, R. B. London to Bristol: a Great Western Railway monopoly. pp. 25. *Typescript*. RC
Paper, Railway Club, 5 May, 1938.

5970 NOBLE, C. B. The Brunels, father and son. *London: Cobden-Sanderson*, 1938. pp. xi, 279, with plates. BM
pp. 101–260, I. K. Brunel.

*5971 CHAPMAN, W. G. Track topics: a book of railway engineering for boys of all ages . . . *London: G.W. Rly.*, 1935. pp. 260, with illus. BM
pp. 15–114, G.W.R. history.
—— 2nd edn. *London*, 1935. pp. 260. RC
—— 3rd, *London*. May 1939. pp. 259. RC

5972 ST. MARK'S PAROCHIAL CHURCH COUNCIL [Swindon]. Saint Mark's, Swindon, 1845–1945. *Swindon*, 1945. pp. viii, 120, with illus. BR
pp. 1–10, The G.W.R. and St. Mark's.

5973 WEBB, B. Locomotive engineers of the G.W.R. *London: Ian Allan*, 1946. pp. 31, with illus., incl. portraits. BM
D. Gooch; J. Armstrong; W. Dean; G. J. Churchward; C. B. Collett; F. W. Hawksworth.

5974 GREY, R. L. Great loco story: Churchward's work on the G.W.R. *Huddersfield: Quadrant Publications*, 1947. pp. 56, with 31 diagrams & 4 tables. BM

5975 PEACOCK, T. B. Monmouth to Coleford by rail. *Halstead: the author*, 1947. pp. 16, with fold. map & 10 illus. pc
The Coleford Rly. This essay also appears in his *Musing on railways* (1948) and in a revised form in his *Railways to Tintern and Coleford* (1952).

*5976 PEACOCK, T. B. Great Western suburban services . . . a history of the passenger services in the London district which were operated by the Great Western . . . *Halstead, the author*, 1948. pp. 51, with fold. map. BM

5977 PEACOCK, T. B. A trip by the Wye Valley train. *Halstead: the author*, 1948. pp. 20, with 2 fold. maps & 5 illus. pc
The Tintern Wireworks Tramway and the Wye Valley Rly. This essay also appears in his *Musing on railways* (1948) and in a revised form in his *Railways to Tintern and Coleford* (1952).

5978 BUCKLEY, S. E. Isambard Kingdom Brunel. *London: Harrap*, 1949. pp. 64, with illus. [*Harrap's Great Engineers Library*.] BM

5979 TOYNE, S. M. A great engineer: I. K. Brunel. [*London*, Oct. 1949.] pp.[44,] with illus. [*Common Ground Books*.] IT

5980 COOK, K. J. The late G. J. Churchward's locomotive development on the Great Western Railway. [*Southampton:*] *Railway Correspondence & Travel Society*, 1950. pp. 40 [41], with frontis. (portrait), 47 illus. (3 fold.) & 4 tables. [*Railway Observer Supplement*, no. 12.]

Paper, Institution of Locomotive Engineers, 22 March, 1950.

5981 GREAT WESTERN RLY. Swindon Works and its place in Great Western history. *London*, 1935. pp. 56, with many illus. & a la. fold. plan of the works.   BR
—— another edn. *London*, 1947. pp. 64.   BM
—— another edn. 'Swindon Works and its place in British railway history.' *London: British Railways (WR)*, 1950. pp. 64.   BM

5982 NOCK, O. S. The Great Western Railway: an appreciation. *Cambridge: Heffer*, 1951. pp. xii, 185, with 32 plates & 7 drawings & 2 maps.   BM

5983 MEYNELL, L. Builder and dreamer: a life of I. K. Brunel. *London: J. Lane*, 1952. pp. 192, with 4 plates & 8 drawings.   BM
For young readers.

5984 PEACOCK, T. B. Railways to Tintern and Coleford. *London: Locomotive Publishing Co.*, 1952. pp. 65, with 24 illus., 5 maps, 3 diagrs., bibliography & chronology.   BM
Extracted from his *Musing on Railways*.

5985 SIMMONS, J. Parish and Empire: studies and sketches. *London: Collins*, 1952. pp. 256.   BM
pp. 166–79, 'The end of the Great Western Railway'; with 2 plates & bibliogr. notes.
An appreciation, with references to the G.W.R. in English literature.

5986 HOLCROFT, H. The Armstrongs of the Great Western: their times, surroundings & contemporaries. *London: Railway World*, 1953. pp. 140, with 52 illus. on 34 plates (1 col.), incl. portraits, 28 illus. & diagrams, 16 maps & plans, & a genealogy.   BM

5987 GARNETT, E. The master engineers . . . [*London:*] *Hodder & Stoughton*, 1954. pp. 223, with illus.   BM
For young readers. An account of early 19th-century railways, particularly the G.W.R., and of I. K. Brunel and D. Gooch.

*5988 NOCK, O. S. Fifty years of Western express running. *Bristol: Everard*, 1954. pp. xi, 353, with 87 illus. on plates (8 in col.) & illus. in text; 7 fold. tables of gradients.   BM
The G.W.R.

5989 POLE, E. R. Little Bedwyn School Centenary, 1854–1954, and Supplement to the memory of Sir Felix J. C. Pole. *Reading*, [1954.] pp. 32, with illus. & obituary notice.   BR
A few copies only privately printed.
F. J. C. Pole was associated with the school.

*5990 POLE, F. J. C. Felix J. C. Pole: his book. Christmas 1954. pp. 235, with plates.   BM
'For private circulation only.'
Reminiscences and comments, chiefly con-

cerning the G.W.R. of which he was General Manager, 1921–9: also on railways and their problems generally.

5991 MEYNELL, L. W. Isambard Kingdom Brunel. *London: Newnes*, 1955. pp. 48, with illus.   BM
For young readers.

*5992 EVERSLEY, D. E. C. The Great Western Railway and the Swindon Works in the
b   Great Depression. pp. [167]–190 + 2 tables & 59 bibliogr. notes. Reprint, *University of Birmingham Historical Journal*, vol. 5, no. 2, 1957.   BR
The continuing progress of Swindon in a period of general economic depression (1873–96).

5993 HOLCROFT, H. An outline of Great Western locomotive practice, 1837–1947. *London: Locomotive Publishing Co.*, 1957. pp. viii, 168, with col. frontis., 96 illus. on 32 plates, & diagrams.   BM

5994 STEPHENSON LOCOMOTIVE SOCIETY— MIDLAND AREA. Leominster & Kington Railway Centenary Rail Tour, July 27th, 1957. Notes. pp. [3.] *Reproduced typescript*, with a Supplement (2 pp.), 'Historical notes for a visit to the railways of West Herefordshire,' by C. R. Clinker.   SLS

5995 CAMPBELL, J. M. Some new Brunel letters. *In* 'Journal of Transport History,' vol. 3, no. 4, November 1958. pp. 201–204.   BM
Includes six excerpts relating to the building of the Royal Albert Bridge, Saltash, Cornwall Rly.

*5996 TUPLIN, W. A. Great Western Steam. *London: Allen & Unwin*, 1958. pp. xiv, 193, with 44 illus. on 16 plates, & 6 tables.   BM
A review of G.W.R. locomotive history and performance, including records of some journeys.

5997 BRITISH RAILWAYS (WESTERN REGION). Centenary of Royal Albert Bridge, Saltash, and opening of Cornwall Railway from Plymouth to Truro (1859–1959). *Paddington (London)*, [1959.] pp. [8,] with illus.   BR

5998 EVERSLEY, D. E. C. The Great Western Railway Works, Swindon. *In* 'A history of
b   Wiltshire.' *London: O.U.P.*, 1959. vol. 4, pp. 207–19, with 2 plates & 119 bibliogr. notes. [*Victoria History of the Counties of England.*]   BM

5999 SIMMONS, J. South Western v. Great Western: railway competition in Devon and
b   Cornwall. *In* 'Journal of Transport History,' vol. 4, no. 1, May 1959. pp. 13–36, with map, table, & 54 bibliogr. notes.   BM

6000 WOODFIN, R. J. The centenary of the Cornwall Railway. *Ely: W. Jefferson & Son,* [1960.] pp. xiii, 193, with fold. map (frontis.), & 13 plates.   BM

6001 ROLT, L. T. C. Isambard Kingdom Brunel: a biography. *London: Longmans,* 1957. pp. xiv, 345, with 30 illus. on 16 plates, & a bibliography.   BM
——*London: Arrow,* Feb. 1961. pp. 343, with 8 plates. [*Grey Arrow Books.*]   BM
Paperback, unabridged.

6002 ALLEN, C. J. Great Western. *London: Ian Allan,* [1962.] pp, 72, with 41 illus.   BM
A concise history.

6003 HOLCROFT, H. Locomotive adventure: fifty years with steam. *London: Ian Allan,* [1962.] pp. 216, with 77 illus. on 32 plates, & detailed tables.   BM
Memoirs, G.W.R., S.E. & C. Rly., and Southern Rly.

6004 NOCK, O. S. The Great Western Railway in the nineteenth century. *London: Ian Allan,* 1962. pp. 200, with col. frontis., 66 illus. on 32 plates, diagrs., tables & 2 maps.   BM

*6005 RAILWAY CORRESPONDENCE AND TRAVEL SOCIETY. The locomotives of the Great Western Railway. [*Cheam, etc.*] 1951– . *In progress.*   BM
A series in 12 parts with supplements, by various authors.
1, Preliminary survey. 1951. pp. 62, with 82 illus. and col. frontis.
2, Broad gauge. 1952. pp. 56, with 108 illus.
3, Absorbed engines, 1854–1921. pp. 101, with 203 illus. and map.
4, Six-wheeled tender engines. 1956. pp. 93, with 160 illus.
5, Six-coupled tank engines. 1958. pp. 96, with 147 illus.
6, Four-coupled tank engines. 1959. pp. 50, with 101 illus. and col frontis.
7, Dean's larger tender engines. 1954. pp. 53, with 99 illus.
8, Modern passenger classes. 1953. pp. 40, with 68 illus.
—— 2nd edn. 1961. pp. 40.
9, Standard two-cylinder classes. 1962. pp. 56, with 199 illus.
10, Absorbed engines, 1922–1947.*
11, The Rail motor vehicles and internal combustion locomotives. 1952. pp. 24, with 36 illus.
—— 2nd edn. 1956. pp. 25, 36 illus.
12, Chronological and statistical survey.*
     * Not yet published (August 1964).

6006 ROLT, L. T. C. The Great Western Railway Museum, Swindon. *London: British Railways Board,* 1963. pp. 31, with 28 illus.   BM
A general historical guide to the Museum.

6007 LEECH, K. H. The 'Castle' saga. (The 'Castles' of the Great Western Railway.) *Birmingham: Stephenson Locomotive Society,* 1963. pp. 27, with 28 illus. & a list of the 171

locomotives of this class.   BM
A supplement to the September 1963 issue of the *Journal of the S.L.S.*

6008 NOCK, O. S. The Great Western Railway in the twentieth century. *London: Ian Allan,* 1964. pp. 212, with col. frontis., 73 illus. on 32 plates, diagrams & tables.   BM

Contemporaneous

6009 BRITTON, J. Lecture on the road-ways of England, pointing out the peculiarly advantageous situation of Bristol for the commerce of the West, with remarks on the benefits likely to arise from a rail-road between that port and London. *Bristol,* [1833.] pp. 14.   BM

6010 GREAT WESTERN RLY. Extracts from the Minutes of Evidence on the London & Birmingham Railway Bill together with abstracts from Acts of Parliament, etc., etc. *London,* 1833. pp. 50.   LSE
Circulated as a guide to general knowledge of the advantages of the railway system, and possibly to encourage investment in the G.W.R.

6011 The GREAT Western Railway Bubble, now before Parliament. [March, 1834.] pp. [2.]   BM
A pamphlet, criticising the proposed railway. (Reproduced on pp. 454–5 of the *Great Western Railway Magazine* Centenary Number, September 1935.)

6012 GREAT WESTERN RLY. An account of the proceedings of the Great Western Railway Company, with extracts from the Evidence given in support of the Bill before the Committee of the House of Commons in the Session of 1834. *London,* 1834. pp. 68, 51.   BM
pp. 20–64, Bristol & London Railway: an account of a public meeting at Bristol, 30 July, 1833.

6013 GREAT WESTERN RLY. Extracts from the Minutes of Evidence given before the Committee of the House of Commons on the Great Western Railway Bill. *Bristol,* 1834. pp. iv, 51.   BM
Addressed to the subscribers and the public to 'convince them of the advantages of the undertaking'.

6014 GREAT WESTERN RLY. Great Western Railway: case of the promoters of the Bill. [*London,* 1834.] pp. 20.   BM
Opposing the London & Southampton's plans for extensions westward.

*6015 CHELTENHAM & GREAT WESTERN UNION RLY. An address from the directors of the Cheltenham & Great Western Union Rly. Co. to the shareholders. *Cirencester,* 1836. pp. 22.   ICE
On the opposition from the London & Birmingham's proposed line from Cheltenham to Tring.

6016 GREAT Western Railway. Case of the village of East Acton. [1836.] pp. [4,] incl. map.   H

6017 [GREAT WESTERN RLY.] An account of the proceedings of the Great Western Railway Company in the Session of 1835. *London*, [1836.] pp. 24[25], with fold. table.   BM

6018 GREAT Western Railway: capital £2,500,000: date of the royal assent, August 31, 1835. *Bristol*, [1836.] pp. 7.   BM
Reprint from *Herapath's Railway Magazine*. Description of the proposed railway, with financial details.

6019 A VOICE from Cheltenham, addressed to all whom it may concern, and in particular to the shareholders in the Cheltenham & Oxford and London & Birmingham Union Railway Company; by One of Themselves. *London*, [1836.] pp. 46.
Signed 'A Shareholder in the Tring Co.' and dated 5 Nov., 1836.
'We have been grossly misled and deluded.'

6020 THAMES & SEVERN CANAL NAVIGATION CO. Case of the Thames & Severn Canal Navigation Company, opposing the Cheltenham & Great Western Union Railway Bill. [1837.] pp. 2[3].   BM
Arguments against the Bill. Traffic insufficient for both canal *and* railway.

6021 GREAT WESTERN RLY. [Reports of John Hawkshaw, I. K. Brunel and Nicholas Wood to the directors of the Great Western Railway, 1838, with an 'introductory letter' by Nicholas Wood.]   BM
1, Report of John Hawkshaw, dated 4 Oct., 1838. pp. 31.
2, Report of I. K. Brunel [commenting on Hawkshaw's Report], dated 13 Dec. pp. 34.
3, Report of Nicholas Wood [supplementing his 'letter to the directors' of 5 Oct.], dated 10 Dec. pp. 82. (See 6024).
4, Report of I. K. Brunel [commenting on N. Wood's Report of 10 Dec.], dated 27 Dec. pp. 22.

6022 HAWKSHAW, J. Report of John Hawkshaw . . . to the directors of the Great Western Railway. [1838.] pp. 31.   BM
Text dated 4 Oct., 1838.
His opinions on working costs, gradients, the broad gauge, locomotives, and the bridge at Maidenhead.
—— German version, 'Die Resultate der Experimente mit Dampfwagen auf der "Grossen Westlichen" und anderen englischen Eisenbahnen.' *Hamburg*, 1838. pp. 44.   H

6023 A LETTER to the shareholders of the Great Western Railway. By a Proprietor. *London*, 1838. pp. 57.   LSE
A reply to a 'malicious attempt made by certain parties to depreciate the value of your property'. Re-assurance on the state and prospects of the G.W.R.

6024 WOOD, N. Introductory letter of Nicholas Wood . . . to the directors of the Great Western Railway. [1838.] pp. 17.   BM
The report of his survey of the line from Paddington to Maidenhead, dated Oct. 5, 1838.

6025 BREES, S. C. Appendix to Railway Practice, containing a copious abstract of the whole of the Evidence given upon the London & Birmingham and Great Western Railway Bills . . . *London*, 1839. pp. vii, 373.   BM

6026 [GREAT WESTERN RLY.] A Guide Book to the Great Western Railway, containing some account of the construction of the line, with notices of the objects best worth attention upon the course, with tables of distances, time and fares, of the trains, and Hackney Coach and cab fares, together with the proceedings of the Great Western Steamship Company. (By G. T. Clark?) *London: Smith & Ebbs*, 1839. pp. 72, 19–22.   BM
The BM copy is inscribed 'By G. T. Clark.'
Includes bye-laws, orders and regulations.

6027 WYLD, J. The Great Western, Cheltenham & Great Western, and Bristol & Exeter Railway Guides . . . *London*, 1839. pp. xxxvi, 284.   BR
pp. ix–xxxvi, Account of the G.W.R.

6028 FREELING, A. The Great Western Railway Companion . . . *London*, [1840.] pp. viii, 54, 78. with illus. & 2 fold. maps.   LSE

6029 RENDEL, J. M. Report of a proposed line of railway from Plymouth, Devonport, and Stonehouse, to Exeter, over the Forest of Dartmoor, with a branch to Tavistock. *Plymouth*, [1840.] pp. 26, with fold. map.   H

6030 GRAVATT, W. A letter to the shareholders of the Bristol & Exeter Railway. *London*, 1841. pp. 29.   ICE
'What a state we are in!'

6031 NIXON, C. Description of the tunnels situated between Bristol and Bath, on the Great Western Railway, with the method adopted for executing the works. *London*, 1842. pp. 6.   BM
Excerpt, *Min. Proc. I.C.E.*, vol. 2, 1842.

6032 [HESTER, G. P.] Oxford & Didcot Railway Bill. Copy of the Evidence taken before a Committee of the House of Commons [March 1843]. *Oxford*, [1843.] pp. 33.   BM
'Printed by the order of George Parsons Hester, agent for the petitioners against the Bill, for the private use of the petitioners.'

6033 RUTTER, J. A New Guide to Weston-Super-Mare . . . (including a descriptive account [pp. 9–12] of the Bristol & Exeter Railway with its stations, etc.). *Weston-Super-Mare*, [1843.] pp. 56.   BM

6034 BLEWITT, R. J. New Monmouthshire railway from Newport to Nanty-Glo and Blaenafon through Pontypool. [*London*,] 1844. pp. 31.   BM
Objects of the proposed line, addressed to the Board of Trade.

6035 [GREAT WESTERN RLY.] Great Western & Newbury, and South Western & Newbury Railway Bills. The case of the promoters of the Great Western & Newbury Bill. (In the words of Mr. Austin.) *London*, 1844. pp. viii, 61.   LSE

6036 MOGG, E. Mogg's Great Western Railway and Windsor, Bath & Bristol Guide, accompanied by a large official map of the line, an account of the Bristol & Exeter Railway and notice of the Cheltenham & Great Western Union Railway . . . *London*, 1841. pp. 48.
                                               LSE
—— another edn. *London*, 1842. pp. 50.
                                               LSE
—— another edn. *London*, 1844. pp. 52. BR

6037 OBSERVATIONS on the navigation of the River Severn and the proposed South Wales Railway. *Gloucester*, 1844. pp. 12.   BM
   Arguments against the proposal to alter the proposed eastern terminus of the railway from Gloucester, to Standish, where it would connect with the G.W. Rly.

6038 COCKBURN, A. J. E. Oxford, Worcester & Wolverhampton, Oxford & Rugby, and the London, Worcester & South Staffordshire Railway Bills. Mr. Cockburn's speech before the Select Committee. *London*, 1845. pp. 78.   LSE

6039 CORNWALL Railway. Extracts from the Evidence given before the Committee of the House of Commons, touching the Passage of Hamoaze, and the engineering incapabilities which preclude speed, punctuality, economy, and safety, on this railway. [1845.]   NLC
   Dated 3 June, 1845.

6040 STATEMENT of facts respecting the Cornwall Railway, from Plymouth to Falmouth. [1845.] pp. 8.   NLC
   Reasons why the proposed railway (broad gauge) should not be supported. In favour of the Central Direct, from Exeter to Falmouth (narrow gauge).

6041 WALKER, J. South Wales Railway: Mr. Walker's report to the Lords Commissioners of the Admiralty as to the crossing the River Severn. *London*, 1845. pp. 17.   ICE
   No title-page. Text headed 'River Severn and South Wales Railway'.

6042 BRISTOL & EXETER RLY. Special report of the directors to the proprietors of the Bristol & Exeter Railway. *Bristol*, [1846.] pp. 20.
                                               BR
   Signed 'James Gibbs, Chairman, 18th February, 1846'.
   On the proposed transfer of the B. & E. to the Great Western.

6043 The BROAD and the narrow gauges: remarks on the trial trip on the Great Western Railway, from the 'Morning Post'. *London*, [1846.] pp. 4.   BM

6044 The BROAD gauge proved the one best adapted to the commercial wants of the nation . . . *London*, 1846. pp. 32.   BM

6045 The BROAD gauge the bane of the Great Western Railway Company, with an account of the present and prospective liabilities saddled on the proprietors by the promoters of that peculiar crotchet. By 'L.s.d.' *London*, 1846. pp. 57.   LSE
—— 3rd edn. *London*, 1846. pp. 57. UL(GL)
—— 4th, *London*, 1846. pp. 57.   BM
—— 5th, *London*, 1846. pp. 57.   BR
—— 7th, *London*, 1846. pp. 57.   BM

6046 CHAPLIN, W. J. Letter by the Chairman of the London & South Western Railway Company to the shareholders in that company, on the pending differences between the London & South Western and the Great Western railway companies. *London*, 1846. pp. 76.   BM
   Appendix contains correspondence with the Southampton & Dorchester Rly. and Great Western Rly. and extracts from the proceedings before the Committee of Peers on the Wiltshire, Somerset & Weymouth Rly.

6047 CLARKE, H. Two articles on the ga[u]ge question, and on the performance of the Great Western leviathan locomotive. *London*, 1846. pp. 28.   ICE

6048 ETON COLLEGE. [Petition of Eton College to the Commons against the Windsor, Slough & Staines Atmospheric Railway Bill, 1846.] To the Honourable the Commons of the United Kingdom of Great Britain and Ireland in Parliament assembled. The humble petition of the Provost and College Royal of the Blessed Mary of Eton, near unto Windsor in the County of Bucks. 1846. pp.[4.] Printed.   BM(MSS)
   Objection to the G.W.R. making a line through College lands and over ground adjoining the playing fields. The BM copy is preceded by a MS. letter from the Provost to Sir Robert Peel, dated 19 Feb., 1846.

6049 EXPERIMENTAL trip of the 'Great Western' new locomotive passenger engine, made on the 13th June 1846. Extracted from the 'Morning Herald' of the 15th June. *London*, [1846.] pp. 16.   BM
   Written on behalf of broad-gauge interests (G.W.R.).

6050 A FEW plain reasons why the Gauge Commissioners' Report should receive legislative sanction, illustrated with drawings of ordinary and monster engines for both gauges, shewing the capability of the narrow gauge both in power and speed and why the public cannot be called upon to pay compensation to the Great Western Railway. By One of the Public. *London*, 1846. pp. 45, 24, with tables and appendix.   BM

6051 GREAT WESTERN RLY. Communication to the proprietors of the Great Western Railway, submitting a few words of peaceful caution and reviving the question, whether we have been benefited by adopting the broad gauge. By One of Yourselves. [*London*, 1846.] pp. 4.   BRE

6052 A LETTER to the directors of the Great Western Railway Company shewing the public evils and troubles attendant upon their break of gauge and pointing out the remedy. By An Old Carrier. *Manchester*, 1846. pp. 7.   ICE
    Urging the G.W.R. to reduce its gauge to 'narrow' [i.e. standard gauge].

6053 The NEW lines of railway between Cheltenham and London promoted by the London & North Western and Great Western companies respectively, considered in reference to the interests of Gloucester and the neighbourhood. By a Gloucester Man. *Gloucester*, 1846. pp. 16.   BR
    In support of the L. & N.W.R.

6054 A FEW observations on a pamphlet entitled 'The new lines of railway between Gloucester and London promoted by the London & North Western and Great Western companies, etc.' By Another Gloucester Man. *Gloucester*, 1846. pp. 12.   BR
    In support of the G.W.R. The pamphlet referred to is in fact entitled 'The new lines of railway between Cheltenham and London, *etc.*' By a Gloucester Man. 1846. (6053)

6055 [GREAT WESTERN RLY.] Observations on the Report of the Gauge Commissioners, presented to Parliament. *Westminster*, [1846.] pp. 45[47].   BM
    Appendix, G.W.R. reports to the Commissioners.

6056 [GREAT WESTERN RLY.] Supplemental observations on the published Evidence and Appendix of the Gauge Commission. *Westminster*, 1846. pp. 33.   BM
    Appendix, Letters to and from the G.W.R. and tables of experiments on broad and narrow gauge lines.

6057 REPLY to 'Observations' of the Great Western Railway Company on the Report of the Gauge Commissioners. *London*, 1846. pp. 75.   BM
    Survey of the gauge controversy, the Inquiry, and the attitude of the G.W. Rly. to its findings, etc.

6058 GREAT WESTERN RLY. Report of the directors of the Great Western Railway Co. to the proprietors, 17 December 1846. *London*, [1846.] pp. 69.   BM
    Vindication of charges, of reckless competition, and a policy designed to injure the L. & N.W.R. and the L. & S.W.R.
    Appendix, pp. 33–69, Letters between L. & N.W.R. and G.W.R. and by Brunel, Huish, Glyn, Russell and Saunders.

6059 An OLD carrier's petition to the directors of the Great Western Railway Company, against the break of gauge at Gloucester. *London*, 1846. pp. 12.   LSE
    Signed 'An Old Carrier'.
    'The incredible evils attendant upon a transposition of goods from one waggon to another.'

6060 OXFORD, WORCESTER & WOLVERHAMPTON *and* OXFORD & RUGBY RLY. Oxford, Worcester & Wolverhampton, and Oxford & Rugby Railway Bills: statement of the promoters. [*London?, c.* 1846.] pp. 8, with fold. map.   BM
    Questions of gauge, and opposition to London & Birmingham Rly., with comparisons.

6061 TALBOT, J. C. Exeter Great Western Railway. Mr. Talbot's speech before the Select Committee. *Westminster*, 1846. pp. 57.   BR
    Select Committee on Railway Bills, Group no. 18, Thursday, 28 May, 1846. The Great Western from Yeovil to Exeter.

6062 'VIGIL,' *pseud.* [Henry Cole.] Railway eccentrics: inconsistencies of men of genius exemplified in the practice and precept of Isambard Kingdom Brunel, Esq., and in the theoretical opinions of Charles Alexander Saunders, Esq., Secretary of the Great Western Railway. *London*, 1846. pp. 30. BM
    Criticism of Brunel and of Saunders, with extracts from official reports.
—— 2nd edn. *London*, 1846. pp. 30.   BR
—— 4th, *London*, 1846. pp. 30.   BM

6063 BROWN, J. The present state and future prospects of the Monmouthshire Canal Company considered, in a letter addressed to the Committee of Management. *London*, 1847. pp. 37.   BM
    Urges adoption of edge rails of standard gauge to replace tram plates.

6064 'OXONIENSIS.' Remarks on the position and prospects of the Great Western Railway Company. *London*, 1847. pp. 14.   BR
    'The tide of fortune is turning.' Break of gauge ruinous. Modifications and reforms proposed. The G.W.R. should be at peace with its neighbours and show liberality towards the public.

6065 COURT, M. H. A digest of the realities of the Great Western Railway. *London*, 1848. pp. 17[23], with 6 financial tables relating to the G.W.R. since 1841.   BM
    Encouragement to shareholders.

6066 ETON COLLEGE. Speech of counsel on the 30th May, 1848, before a Select Committee of the House of Commons, on behalf of the head, lower and assistant masters of Eton against the Great Western Railway extension from Slough to Windsor. [1848.] pp. 46.   BM
    'For private circulation only.'

6067 GILL, T. Address to the proprietors of the South Devon Railway, by the Chairman of the Board of Directors. *London*, 1848. pp. 59, with tables. BR
　　Contains the Engineer's reports on the atmospheric system, and financial statements. T. Gill defends excessive expenditure on the atmospheric experiment.

6068 JENKINSON, R. *and* BRIGHT, J. The contest between the blind basket-maker and his amanuensis, with [sic] the directors of the Birmingham & Oxford Railway Company. *Birmingham*, 1848. pp. 16. BIRMINGHAM PL
　　Correspondence between Richard Jenkinson on behalf of John Hooper, and John Bright, M.P. for Birmingham, on the threat to John Hooper's livelihood by the proposal of the B. & O. Rly. to demolish his home and workplace. Followed by a petition.

6069 [SMITH, A.] Railways as they really are; or, Facts for the serious consideration of railway proprietors: no. 5, The Great Western Railway and all broad gauge lines. *London*, 1848. pp. 83. BM

*6070 WATERMAN, J. The Great Western Railway: its form and pressure. (By Rear Admiral Waterman.) *London*, [1848?] pp. 16. PO
　　An appraisal, with various criticisms.

6071 COTTERILL, C. F. The past, present and future position of the London & North Western and Great Western Railway companies . . . with an inquiry how far the principle of competing lines in reference to railway undertakings is sound and defensible. *London*, 1849. pp. 56. BM
　　Criticism against misleading financial statements, with tables. Government control preferable to competition.

6072 PARRY, E. The Railway Companion from Chester to Shrewsbury . . . with a new map of England and Wales, with the railways. *Chester*, [1849.] pp. 138. BM
　　pp. 5–13, a descriptive and historical account of the line.

6073 STATEMENT of the position of the South Wales Railway Company in reference to its relations with the Great Western Railway Company. *London*, 1849. pp. 37. BR
　　Warning to South Wales shareholders. A committee required to safeguard their interests.

6074 CHELTENHAM & OXFORD RLY. [Collection of about seventy-five newspaper cuttings, handbills, notices, maps and prospectuses issued in 1845 and 1846.] LSE

6075 BRISTOL & EXETER RLY. Answer to the report of the Committee of Investigation appointed at the General Meeting of the Company . . . 5 & 6 March, 1850. *Exeter*, 1850. pp. 23. LSE
　　Addressed to the shareholders.

6076 GREAT WESTERN RLY. [Shareholders]. Report of the Committee of Consultation appointed by the proprietors of the Great Western Railway, September 20, 1849. [1850.] pp. 20. BR
　　Recommendations as to future expenditure. pp. 17–20, I. K. Brunel's report on depreciation of railway plant, 9 Jan., 1850.

6077 TYRRELL, T. To the directors of the Great Western Railway Company. May 10, 1850. pp. 9[16], with 3 tables. BR
　　Accusations of irregularities in the presentation of accounts at General Meetings. Shareholders prevented from inspecting them.

6078 WHITEHEAD, J. The key to railway investments: part I, The Great Western Railway; illustrated by a map of the district. *London*, 1850. pp. 20. BR

6079 PROTHERO, T. Mr. Prothero's letter to the Monmouthshire Railway & Canal Company, in reply to the Report of the Investigation Committee, read at the Adjourned Special General Meeting held April 2, 1851, at the Canal House, Newport. *Newport*, 1851. pp. 11. BM

6080 MEASOM, G. The Illustrated Guide to the Great Western Railway, embellished with fifty illustrations from original drawings. *London*, 1852. pp. 64. IT
　　Twenty-two of the illustrations are of scenes on the railway.

6081 WORCESTER & HEREFORD RLY. Worcester & Hereford Railway Bill: case of the promoters on the Second Reading (27 February 1852). *London*, 1852. pp. 2. BM

6082 OXFORD, Worcester & Wolverhampton Railway: documents bearing on the question of gauge. [c. 1855.] pp. 29. ICE

6083 FLETCHER, L. E. Description of the Landore Viaduct on the line of the South Wales Railway. *London*, 1856. pp. 17, with fold. diagram. ICE
　　Excerpt, *Min. Proc. I.C.E.*, vol. 14, 1854/5.

6084 GREAT WESTERN RLY. Presentation of a testimonial to Charles Alexander Saunders, Secretary & General Superintendent of the Great Western Railway Company, at Paddington on Saturday April 19, 1856. *London*, 1856. pp. 21, 8. BR
　　Accounts of the proceedings, speeches, etc., and a list of subscribers.

6085 'INVESTIGATOR.' The Great Western Railway Company: what next? and next? *London*, 1856. pp. 16. BM
　　An 'analysis of the position and prospects of the Company'. Criticisms and suggestions include the broad gauge, and Paddington Station.

6086 BAYLEY, R. Statement and correspondence relative to an agreement made by the directors with the Ruabon Coal Company. *London*, 1857. pp. 28. HRL
　　The G.W.R.

6087 GREAT WESTERN RLY. Reports of the deputation of shareholders appointed at the Half-Yearly Meeting held at Bristol . . . 15 August, 1856, and of the directors in reply, dated 13 January, 1857, with an appendix. [*London*, 1857.] pp. 90.   LSE
Concerning proposed changes in the constitution of the Board of Directors.

6088 A CRITICAL examination of the report of the deputation of shareholders, and of the directors in reply. By a Shareholder. (Great Western Railway.) *London*, 1857. pp. 54.   BM
Addressed 'to the proprietors of the G.W.R. Co. . . . "to implore you not to peril our future career of prosperity by encouraging cabal against our Board and against ourselves . . .".'

6089 MALINS, W. Two letters to Lord Barrington, Chairman of the Great Western Railway: first, on continuing the 'narrow gauge' from Reading to Paddington; and secondly, on Great Western affairs generally. *London*, 1857. pp. 23.   BM
1, urging 'mixed' gauge, and 2, suggesting reforms.

6090 HOLDSWORTH, A. H. A letter to the inhabitants of Dartmouth on the subject of the railway from Torquay to Dartmouth. *London*, 1858. pp. 16.   BM
The Dartmouth & Torbay Rly.

6091 WILLIAMS, E. L. Reasons why the Oxford, Worcester & Wolverhampton Railway Company should neither be allowed to abandon their Diglis branch nor obtain the control of the Worcester and Birmingham Canal. *Worcester*, [1858.] pp. 4.   ICE

6092 COURT OF COMMON PLEAS. In the Court of Common Pleas, the case of Nicholson v. The Great Western Railway Company, on the subject of the Ruabon coal traffic . . . with map of the railway. *London: Effingham Wilson*, [1859.] pp. 54, 26.   UL(GL)

6093 HISTORY of the Royal Albert Bridge for the Cornwall Railway, across the River Tamar at Saltash . . . *Devonport*, [1859.] pp. [5,] with 2 illus.   BM

6094 MEASOM, G. Measom's Guide to the Great Western Railway, including Oxford, Worcester & Wolverhampton, Chester & Holyhead Line, and Isle of Man. *London*, 1860. pp. 872.   BM

6095 MEASOM, G. The Official Illustrated Guide to the Bristol & Exeter, North and South Devon, Cornwall, and South Wales railways . . . 2nd edn. *London*, [1861.] pp. 280, 208, 8, with 270 engravings.   UL(GL)

6096 MEASOM, G. The Official Illustrated Guide to the Great Western Railway, including the amalgamated West Midland Line and the Chester & Holyhead Line; also the Isle of Man . . . 2nd edn. *London*, [1861.] pp. 800, with 350 engravings.   UL(GL)

6097 CASE of the Cheltenham petitions against the Bill. Minutes of Evidence before the Select Committee of the House of Lords on the East Gloucestershire Railway. *Cheltenham*, 1862. pp. 48.   GLOUCESTER PL

*6098 RANDALL, J. Handbook to the Severn Valley Railway . . . *London*, 1863. pp. 50. BM
Includes some brief notes on the railway.

6099 GREAT WESTERN RLY. Presentation of a testimonial to Walter Stevenson on retiring from the Financial Secretaryship of the Great Western Railway Company. *Paddington*, 1867. pp. 15.   BR
Speeches and a list of subscribers.

6100 HODGSON, W. A plea for justice to third-class passengers, with a few remarks on the qualification of directors. 2nd edn. *London*, 1872. pp. 11.   BM
Addressed to the G.W. Rly. 'Let third-class passengers travel by *every* train.'

6101 SEVERN BRIDGE RLY. Minutes of Evidence taken before the Select Committee of the House of Lords on the Severn Bridge Railway Bill, 7–19 June, 1872. [1872.] pp. 402.   GLOUCESTER PL

6102 PHILP, R. K. The Great Western Railway Panoramic Guide. *London*, [1876.] pp. 64, with la. fold. map.   BM
A route chart.

6103 [MACAULAY, J. B.] Guide Book for the use of visitors to the Precelly Range, Pembrokeshire; with notes on the Maenclochog Railway and line of route . . . *Carmarthen: W. J. Morgan, 'Welshman' Office*, [1879.] pp. 13[17], with 4 col. illus.   BM
pp. [3]–6, Description of a journey.

6104 BROWN, J. Facts worth thinking about and dealing with: an exposition of the glaring anomalies in the G.W.R. Co's traffic and charges for the conveyance of passengers. *Newport*, 1880. pp. 8.   NEWPORT PL
—— Further facts worth thinking about . . . *Newport*, 1880. pp. 10.   NEWPORT PL

6105 COLBORNE, T. The Monmouthshire Railways and the Monmouthshire freighters: notes for the freighters on the Monmouthshire Railways. *Newport & Cardiff*, 1890. pp. 63.   BM

6106 GREAT WESTERN RLY.—PRINTING OFFICE. Specimens of type. [*London*,] August 1898. pp. [6.]   BR
Fifty-four type faces used in G.W.R. publications.

6107 PORT TALBOT RLY. Port Talbot Railway and Docks. (General information as to facilities, rates, tolls, etc., together with a description of the Undertaking . . . by Albert Haverlock Case . . .) *London*, [1898.] pp. 19, with la. fold. illus. & la. fold. map.   RC

6108 VINTER, P. J. Great Western expresses: being an account of the express trains on the various portions of the Great Western Railway for the year 1894. *Plymouth*, 1894. pp. 37, with 8 gradient sections.   BM

Details of express speeds and of difficulties which G.W.R. engines have to overcome.

—— another edn. *London*, 1898. pp. 36. LSE

—— 'Great Western expresses: an account of some Great Western expresses and trains'; with 21 illustrations and 9 gradient sections. *London*, 1901. pp. 47, with col. frontis. RC

6109 G., A. 'Tim': G.W.R. collecting dog at Paddington Station, London. By 'A. G.' [*c*. 1903?]   BR

A poem (7 verses) to commemorate the services of Inspector Bush's dog, which between 1892 and 1902 collected over £300 for the G.W.R. Servants' Widows & Orphans Fund.

*6110 SCOTT, W. J. The great Great Western: a study of Great Western train services from 1889 to 1902 inclusive, with notes on engines, coaches and gradients. *London*, [1903.] pp. 86[88], with 3 fold. gradient profiles inserted.   BR

6111 GREAT WESTERN RLY. To the proprietors of the Great Western Railway. [*London*, 1907.] pp. 72.   LSE

Speeches, letters, and a reprint of Richard Bell's pamphlet, *The Railwaymen's Charter*, with comments point by point by G.W.R.; correspondence between the G.W.R. General Manager and R. Bell, 1907, and between the G.W.R. and the Board of Trade on the Ebbw Vale Case, 1907.

6112 GREAT WESTERN RLY. List of towns & places to and from which the Great Western Railway Company carry goods from and to London. *London*, 1909. pp. 89, with 2 la. fold. maps.   PC

The 'commercial' map shows the G.W.R. connections with ports, coalfields, china clay, salt, mineral, and slate-producing areas, in colours.

The 'G.W.R. London Suburban map' shows goods stations and depots.

Includes scales of charges for small parcels by merchandise trains.

*6113 GREAT WESTERN RLY. Names of engines. *London*, 1911. pp. 21.   BM

A list with twelve illustrations.

6114 GREAT WESTERN RLY. Suggested questions, with appropriate answers, for the use of officers when examining the staff engaged in the Traffic Department. [*London*,] Feb. 1912. pp. 67.   RC

'Private and not for publication.'

6115 MACKENZIE, HOLLAND & WESTINGHOUSE POWER SIGNAL COMPANY. Electro-pneumatic power signalling installation at Slough, Great Western Railway. By H. E. Cox. *London*, [1914.] pp. 15, with 7 illus. & a diagram.   SLS

Reprinted from the *Great Western Railway Magazine*, Dec. 1913.

6116 GREAT WESTERN RLY. War reports of the General Manager to the Board of Directors, 1914–1919. Jan. 1920. pp. 300.   RC

Reports by Frank Potter.

6117 MACKENZIE, HOLLAND & WESTINGHOUSE POWER SIGNAL COMPANY. The signalling of the Ealing & Shepherd's Bush Railway. *London*, [1920.] pp. 23, with 14 illus. & fold. diagram.   SLS

Reprinted from the *Railway Gazette*, 29 October, 1920.

The first installation in Gt. Britain of three-position automatic signalling.

6118 PRATT, E. A. War record of the Great Western Railway. *London*, 1922. pp. 52. BM

From his *British railways and the Great War* (1921) with additional matter in the Appendix.

6119 SCOTT, W. J. Restored (pre-war) train speeds on the G.W.R. October . . . 1921. (Winter of 1921–22) etc. *London*, [1922.] pp. 9.   RC

Records of six runs.

6120 GREAT WESTERN RLY. Commerce and the Great Western Railway. *London*, April 1924. pp. 31, with plates.   BR

G.W.R. facilities, with lists of commodities and places served.

6121 GREAT WESTERN RLY. The docks of the Great Western Railway. *London*, [1924.] pp. 58, with 15 illus. & 8 fold. maps at end.   BM

6122 GREAT WESTERN RLY. Souvenir of the Great Western Railway (British Empire Exhibition, Wembley, 1924). *London*, [1924.] pp. 20, with 12 plates (4 col., mounted). BR

A brief account of the history, organisation, and holiday facilities of the G.W.R.

6123 GREAT WESTERN RLY. Visit of . . . the King and Queen to Swindon, April 28th 1924. [*London*, 1924.] pp. 15, with illus. & fold. plates.   SLS

6124 GREAT WESTERN RLY. Visit of the Institute of Transport to Swindon, May 30th, 1924. [*London*, 1924.] pp. 10, with 10 plates & fold. plan.   RC

6125 POLE, F. J. C. Cardiff and the Great Western Railway. [*London: G.W. Rly.*,] 1924. pp. 16. [*Great Western Pamphlets*, no. 12.]   LSE

A lecture by F. J. C. Pole, as General Manager of the G.W. Rly., to Cardiff Business Club, October 16, 1924. Co-operation, to revive trade and ensure prosperity.

6126 GREAT WESTERN RLY. Great Western Railway of England: handbook for travellers from overseas. *London*, 1924. pp. 72, with illus. & a fold. map.   BR

—— another edn. *London*, 1925. pp. 72. BR

6127 GREAT WESTERN RLY. A Great Western Railway signal box: souvenir of the exhibit at the British Empire Exhibition, Wembley, 1925. *London*, [1925.] pp. 30, with illus., & fold diagram.　　BR

6128 GREAT WESTERN RLY. General Strike, May 1926. *London*, [1926.] pp. 123.　　BR
A detailed record of the strike, with reproductions of documents, correspondence, statements of various bodies, notices displayed by the G.W.R. and numerous statistical tables showing the effects of the strike on various aspects of G.W.R. traffic and working.

6129 [CHAPMAN, W. G.] Twixt rail & sea: a book of docks, seaports, and shipping, for boys of all ages. *London, G.W. Rly.*, [1927.] pp. 148, with 84 illus. & plans.　　BR

6130 GREAT WESTERN RLY. Great Western Railway of England, 1837–1927: the quickest route, New York to London via Plymouth. Souvenir published by the Great Western Railway of England in connection with the Centenary Exhibition & Pageant of the Baltimore & Ohio Railroad, Baltimore, Maryland, U.S.A., September 24th—October 8th, 1927. *London*, [1927.] pp. 23[24], with illus. & fold. map.　　BM
Issued to attract tourists; contains little historical information.

6131 PALMER, A. The Engine Driver. *In his* 'Straphangers.' *London*, 1927. pp. 129–37.　　BM
Description of the work of a G.W.R. driver.

6132 CHAPMAN, W. G. The 'King' of railway locomotives . . . *London: G.W. Rly.*, 1928. pp. 149, with illus.　　BM
pp. 8–42, 'The evolution of the "Kings".'

6133 TODD, J. S. The future of Paddington Station. *Paddington* (*London*), Sept. 1928. pp. 52, with tables & 14 la. fold. maps in colour. *Reproduced typescript.*　　BR
Submitted to the G.W.R.

6134 GREAT WESTERN RLY. The Swindon Works of the Great Western Railway. *Paddington* (*London*), 1929. pp. 54, with illus. & fold. plan.　　SLS

6135 GREAT WESTERN RLY. Warehousing facilities, railhead distribution, goods train transits and other matters affecting the trader's transport problems. *London*, [1929.] pp. 100.　　BR
Cover title, *Speed in transport*.
pp. 29–100, list of transits between G.W.R. stations and stations on other lines to which direct wagons are sent daily.

6136 GREAT Western Railway 4-6-0 four-cylinder express locomotive; C. B. Collett, Chief Mechanical Engineer. *London*, [*c.* 1930.] la. fold. s.sh.　　BM
Coloured sectional drawing of a King class locomotive, with an identification list of 250 parts.

6137 GREAT WESTERN RLY. Locomotives of the Great Western Railway: 12 photogravure plates of G.W.R. engines. London, 1930. BM

6138 GREAT WESTERN RLY. Railhead distribution. *London*, [*c.* 1930.] pp. 19, with lists & maps of places served.　　BR
Road transport services.

6139 GREAT Western Railway. Development works costing approximately £8,000,000. *London: Railway Gazette*, 1933. pp. 66.　　IT
Supplement, *Railway Gazette*, 8 December, 1933.

6140 SMITH, N. R. Pilgrim from Paddington: the record of an experiment in travel . . . between August 22, 1932 & July 20, 1933. *London*, [1933.] pp. 347.　　BM
Accounts of pleasure journeys on the G.W.R.

6141 GREAT WESTERN RLY. The Streamline Way: inauguration of express streamlined rail car service between Birmingham and Cardiff, July 1934. *London*, [1934.] pp. 35, with illus. & a map.　　BR

6142 GREAT WESTERN RLY. Camping holidays on the G.W.R. *London*, 1923–1936. BR
Various editions. Includes lists of sites.

6143 CHAPMAN, W. G. By Cornish Riviera Limited. *London: G.W. Rly.*, 1936. pp. xiv, 136, with plates & diagrams.　　BM
The journey from Paddington to Penzance described.

6144 GREAT WESTERN RLY. Guide to economical transport. *London*, 1936. pp. 142, with illus. & 2 fold. maps.　　BR
Freight transport facilities: pp. 45–142, examples of one-day transits.

* 6145 GREAT WESTERN RLY. Hotels and catering services of the G.W.R. *London*, 1931. pp. 67, with 25 illus.　　BR
—— another edn. *London*, 1938. pp. 43, with 34 illus. on 29 plates.　　BR

6146 KNOX, C. The Un-beaten Track. *London: Cassell*, 1944. pp. 199, with plates.　　BM
The G.W.R. during the War: pp. 184–99, Lists of awards to staff; officials of the G.W.R.

6147 BROWN, A. Dunkirk and the Great Western: a plain and authentic account of the experiences of some Great Western steamships during the evacuation of the Expeditionary Force from Dunkirk and Western France. *London: G.W. Rly.*, [1945.] pp. 39, with illus., map & a list.　　BM

6148 The ABC of Great Western locomotives. *London: Ian Allan*, 1943–6.　　BM
Various editions of a booklet of between 24 and 48 pages, containing lists and illustrations.

6149 CRESWELL, A. J. Names and numbers: GWR & SR: over 5000 engines recorded and classified. *Huddersfield: Quadrant*, 1946. pp. 20.　　BM

* 6150 GREAT Western Railway engines (G.W.R. Engine Book): names, numbers, types and

classes. *London: Great Western Rly.*, 1921.
pp. 48, with illus.   BM
—— 1922. pp. 45.   BM
—— 1925. pp. 47.   BM
—— 1928. pp. 64.   BM
—— 1929. pp. 64.   PC
—— 1932. pp. 72.   BM
—— 1938. By W. G. Chapman. pp. 112. BM
—— 1946. By W. G. Chapman. pp. 108. BM

6151 TITANS of the Track: Great Western
Railway. *Staines: Ian Allan,* 1945. pp. [32.]
                                                   BM
   Photographs, with historical notes.

—— 2nd edn. *Staines,* [1946.] pp. 32.   BM

*6152 BARMAN, C. Next Station: a railway plans
for the future. *London: Allen & Unwin,* 1947.
pp. vi, 113.   BM
   A contemporary account of the G.W.R.

6153 GREAT WESTERN RLY. Ships of the
G.W.R. [*London,* 1947.] pp. 32, with 15
illus. & maps on inside covers.   BR

*6154 NOCK, O. S. The 'Kings' and 'Castles' of the
Great Western Railway. *London: Ian Allan,*
1949. pp. 72, with plates, tables, lists and
drawings.   BM

6155 STREET, J. W. I drove the Cheltenham
Flyer; illustrated by R. Barnard Way.
London: Nicholson & Watson, 1951. pp. 154,
with plates.   BM
   An autobiography of a G.W.R. engine-
driver.

6156 WRIGHT, J. S. B. The King George V,
described by John S. B. Wright. *London &
Glasgow: Collins,* [1952.] pp. 22, with diagrams & a Transart section by Thomas Forman showing interior of loco in 6 layers. BM

6157 STEPHENS, T. C. The Severn Tunnel and its
pumping engines. *Swindon: Swindon Engineering Society,* 1954. pp. 26, with 8 illus.,
3 diagrams & a map. [*Pamphlet no.* 225.]
                                                   SLS
   Excerpt from *Transactions,* 1951–4.

6158 THOMAS, G. O. Temple Meads. *In his* 'Window in the West.' *London: Epworth Press,*
1954. pp. [19]–25.   BM
   Thoughts on the fascination of railways,
locomotives, and the life of stations, with a
personal tribute to Bristol (Temple Meads),
G.W.R.

6159 WRIGHT, J. S. B. The steam engine, described by John S. B. Wright; illustrated by
the Techni-View method. *London: Cassell,*
1954. pp. 32, with 10 diagrams & 4 superimposed layer diagrams in colour, showing
interior of a County class locomotive,
G.W.R.   BM

Great Western and Great Central Joint Railway

6160 [JACKSON, A. S.] G.W. & G.C. Joint Railway: 50 years of the 'Joint Line', 1906–1956.
High Wycombe: Chiltern Railway Society,
[1956.] pp. 11.   BM

Highland Railway

6161 ANDERSON, G. *and* ANDERSON, P.
Handbook to the Inverness & Nairn Railway, and scenes adjoining it; with the time
tables, list of fares, and regulations of the
line. *Inverness,* 1856. pp. 32, 8.   BM

6162 ANDERSON, G. *and* ANDERSON, P. Hand-
book from Perth to Forres, Inverness and
Bonar Bridge, by Inverness & Perth, and
Inverness & Aberdeen Junction railways.
Edinburgh, [1864.] pp. 63, with fold map. AU

6163 'INVERNESS ADVERTISER.' Sixpenny Guide
to the Skye Railway, with excursions to
Lochs Maree and Torridon, Gairloch,
Skye, etc. *Inverness,* [1870.] pp. 28, with
map of the Highland Rly.   BM

6164 ANDERSON, G. *and* ANDERSON, P. Handbook to the Highland Railway system from
Perth to Forres, Keith, Inverness and Bonar
Bridge. *Edinburgh,* 1865. pp. 91, with plate
& fold. map.   BM
—— another edn. *Edinburgh,* [1868.] pp.
117.
—— 5th edn. *Inverness,* [1890.] pp. 204.
—— 9th edn. *Inverness,* [1890.] pp. 223, 28,
lxiv.   BM

6165 'SCRUTATOR.' Behind the Highland engines. By 'Scrutator'. *Inverness,* 1913. pp.
16.   BR
   Highland train working related to the difficulties of gradients and of connecting delays at
Perth, with examples.

6166 ELLIS, C. H. Highland engines and their
work. *London,* 1930. pp. 117, with 35 plates;
illus. & diagrams.   BM

*6167 ALLCHIN, M. C. V. A history of Highland
locomotives. *Southsea: Railway Hobbies,*
1947. pp. 72, with 84 illus., 21 diagrams,
tables, & a genealogical chart of the Highland Rly.   BM
   Includes locomotives of constituent railways.

6168 The HIGHLAND Railway. pp. [3.]   BR
   Genealogical table, fold. chart and diagram.

6169 STEPHENSON LOCOMOTIVE SOCIETY. The
Highland Railway Company and its con-
c stituents and successors, 1855 to 1955.
London, 1955. pp. 121, with 12 plates &
map, & over 60 pages in chronologies of the
Highland & its locomotives.   BM

6170 STEPHENSON LOCOMOTIVE SOCIETY—
SCOTTISH AREA. Excursion from Glasgow
to Blair Atholl, 21st November 1959: engine,
Highland Railway 4-6-0 no. 103. [*Glasgow,*
1959.] pp. [2.] *Reproduced typescript.*   PC
   Brief itinerary followed by an historical and
descriptive account of the 'Jones Goods' class.

*6171 VALLANCE, H. A. The history of the High-
land Railway. *London: A. H. Stockwell,*

1938. pp. 224, with maps, tables, & many illus.   BM

—— 2nd 'revised & extended' edn. 'The Highland Railway.' *Dawlish: David & Charles; London: Macdonald,* 1963. pp. 182, with 46 illus. on 16 plates, tables, & 8 maps.   BM

Hull & Barnsley Railway
(Hull, Barnsley & West Riding Junction Railway & Dock)

6172 The PROPOSED new railway for Hull: report of proceedings at Town's meeting, July 14th 1879; reprinted from the 'Eastern Morning News', July 15, 1879. *Hull,* 1879. pp. 20.   ICE
The Hull & Barnsley Rly.

6173 HULL, BARNSLEY & WEST RIDING JUNCTION RAILWAY & DOCK COMPANY. Preliminary Official Programme of the great procession and demonstration on the occasion of Lt. Col. Gerard Smith turning the first sod of the new railway and dock on Saturday, January 15th, 1881. [*Hull,* 1881.] pp. [8.]   BM

6174 COLE, E. M. Notes on the geology of the Hull, Barnsley & West Riding Junction Railway & Dock. *Hull,* 1886. pp. 60, with fold. map.   BM

6175 SHELFORD, A. F. The life of Sir William Shelford, by his daughter. *London,* 1909.   BM
Printed for private circulation.
pp. 67–76, Wm. Shelford's work in promoting and constructing the Hull & Barnsley Rly.

6176 PARKES, G. D. The Hull & Barnsley Railway. *Chislehurst: Oakwood Press,* 1946. pp. 25, with 9 illus. & maps on 5 plates. [*Oakwood Library of Railway History,* no. 3.]   BM
—— another edn. *South Godstone,* 1948. pp. 25, with 11 illus. & 2 maps on 7 plates. BM

Hundred of Manhood & Selsey Tramway
(later 'West Sussex Railway')

*6177 GRIFFITH, E. C. The Hundred of Manhood & Selsey Tramway, later known as the West Sussex Railway, 1897–1935. *Farnham: E. W. Langham,* 1948. pp. 42, with 28 illus., map, & timetables.   BM

Inverness & Glasgow Railway Company
[not incorporated]

6178 MACBEAN, S. Proposed Inverness & Glasgow Railway. *Westminster,* 1874. pp. 20.
An account of the plans of the promoters.

—— 'No. 2.' [*London,* 1875.] pp. 26.
Modified version, including map & (pp. 17–26) press opinions.

Kelvedon, Tiptree & Tollesbury Light Railway

6179 THOMAS, G. O. Calm Weather. *London,* 1928.   BM
pp. 67–74, A Corner of Essex. (Tollesbury Light Railway.)

Kent & East Sussex Railway
(The 'Rother Valley Railway')

6180 FINCH, M. L. The Rother Valley, later the Kent and East Sussex Railway, 1896–1948. *Sevenoaks: the author,* 1949. pp. 80, with illus., maps, diagrams & tables.   BM

6181 [COLE, D.] The Kent & East Sussex Railway. *London: Union Publications,* 1963. pp. 35, with 22 illus., map & tables.   BM

King's Lynn Docks and Railway

6182 KING'S LYNN DOCKS & RAILWAY CO. [Brochure, announcing increased facilities resulting from widening of the lock entrance, and other improvements.] *King's Lynn,* [March 1935.] pp. [8], with 9 illus. & a plan of the docks & railway.

Lampeter, Aberayron & New Quay Light Railway

6183 COZENS, L. Aberayron transport. *Highgate: the author,* [1957.] pp. 92, with illus. & maps.   BM
The Lampeter, Aberayron & New Quay Light Rly.

Lancashire & Yorkshire Railway
Historical

6184 NORMINGTON, T. The Lancashire & Yorkshire Railway: being a full account of the rise and progress of this railway, together with numerous interesting reminiscences and incidents on the line. *London,* 1898. pp. 375, with illus. & tables.   BM

6185 CLARKE, S. Clitheroe in its railway days ... *Clitheroe,* 1900. pp. vl, [310,] with illus.   BM
pp. 9–50, a detailed record of events and personalities connected with the Blackburn & Clitheroe Rly. Reprinted as the second part of the 2nd edn. of *Clitheroe in its old coaching and railway days* (1929).

6186 RUSH, R. W. The Lancashire & Yorkshire Railway and its locomotives, 1846–1923. *London: Railway World,* 1949. pp. 154, with fold map. many illus., & lists of locos.   BM

6187 CHADWICK, S. Gateway to the South: the centenary of the Huddersfield & Sheffield Junction Railway, Penistone & Holmfirth. *Huddersfield: the author,* 1950. pp. 12, with 3 illus. (2 on inside covers.)

6188 MASON, E. The Lancashire & Yorkshire Railway. *London: Ian Allan*, [1953.] pp. 32. [*Railways before the Grouping*, no. 3.]   BM
Cover title, *The Lancashire & Yorkshire*.
Illustrations accompanied by a brief history and a description of services.

6189 BROADBRIDGE, S. A. The finances of the Lancashire & Yorkshire Railway, 1835–1873.
b (Thesis for Ph.D.(Econ.) Univ. Lond., 1957.) pp. vii, 425, with 28 tables, 3 maps, bibliogr. notes & a very full bibliography, including, among primary sources, some MS. items.   UL

6190 RAILWAY CORRESPONDENCE AND TRAVEL SOCIETY—LANCASHIRE AND NORTH WESTERN BRANCH. Itinerary of the Roses Rail Tour, 8th June, 1958. pp. [4], map & schedule. *Printed.*   pc
—— The Roses Rail Tour, Lancashire & Yorkshire, June 8th, 1958. Itinerary and notes. pp. 6. *Reproduced typescript.*   pc

*6191 MASON, E. The Lancashire & Yorkshire Railway in the twentieth century. *London: Ian Allan*, 1954.   pp. 236, with col. frontis., 96 illus. on 32 plates, fold. map, & diagrams, maps, tables (incl. 7 gradient profiles) in text.   BM
Personal observations and records made between 1906 and 1922.
—— 2nd impr., *London*, 1961.   BM
A revised text.

Contemporaneous

6192 'INVESTIGATOR.' On tunnels and inclined planes as forming parts of railways. [*Manchester*, 1830?] s.sh.   ICE
Reprinted from the *Manchester Guardian*.
Objections to tunnels and inclines on the proposed Manchester & Leeds Rly.

6193 'OBSERVER.' Thoughts on railways and projected railways. By 'Observer'. *Liverpool*, 1833. pp. 15.   ICE
Reasons against the proposed extension of the Manchester, Bolton & Bury Rly. to the north end of Liverpool, and against a rival line to the Liverpool & Manchester Rly.

6194 BUTTERWORTH, E. An historical sketch of the Manchester & Leeds Railway as far as completed; with descriptive notes on the most remarkable objects near the line. *Rochdale*, 1839. pp. 28.   LEEDS PL
The remarkable objects referred to are places of topographical and historical interest, and are not the skeletons, etc. which are reported to have been unearthed when the line was built. (See 7687.)

6195 CLEATHER, E. J. Manchester & Leeds, and Manchester & Birmingham Railway. *Manchester*, 1843. s.sh.   LSE
Dispute arising from a statement by the

M. & L. in the *Manchester Guardian*, 7 March. The author writes 'By order of the M. & B. Board'.

6196 GREIG, T. The Manchester & Leeds, and Manchester & Birmingham Railway companies: an elucidation of the conduct of the directors of these companies in the matter of the Hunt's Bank Junction, with copies of their letters . . . *Manchester*, 1843. pp. 22.   BM
With extracts from reports and newspapers. An alleged breach of agreement by the M. & L. directors.

*6197 TAIT, A. F. Views on the Manchester & Leeds Railway, drawn from nature and on stone by A. F. Tait, with a descriptive history by Edwin Butterworth. *London*, 1845. pp. 34, with frontis. & 19 plates. la. 4°.   BM

6198 [SMITH, Arthur.] Railways as they really are; or, Facts for the serious consideration of railway proprietors: no. 7, Lancashire & Yorkshire Railway. 2nd edn. *London*, 1847. pp. 40.   BM
pp. 5–13, 'Observations on the past and coming crisis'.

6199 COPLEY, G. F. An Historical and Descriptive Guide to the Wakefield, Pontefract and Goole Railway. *Pontefract*, [1848.] pp. 83.   BM
pp. 7–10, 79–83 are about the railway; the remainder describes places en route.

6200 RAWSON, W. An address to the shareholders of the Lancashire & Yorkshire Railway Co., on the present crisis in their affairs, with a view to demonstrate the irreparable injury their property will sustain by any further expenditure on the useless lines already begun or to be hereafter executed; with a map of the objectionable lines. *London*, [1848.] pp. 34.   BM

6201 HAWKSHAW, J. Lancashire and Yorkshire Railway: Mr. Hawkshaw's report on the rolling stock and permanent way . . . *Manchester*, 1850. pp. 12.   ICE
Detailed statistical tables at end.

6202 EAST LANCASHIRE RLY. Bye-laws, rules and regulations to be observed by the officers and men in the service of the East Lancashire Railway Company, October 1856. *Manchester*, 1856. pp. 89.   LSE

6203 LANCASHIRE & YORKSHIRE RLY. Distance tables in miles and yards, January 1869. *London*, [1869.] pp. 240.   BM

6204 JOHNSON, W. B. Lancashire & Yorkshire Railway: correspondence between Joshua Radcliffe, Deputy-Chairman and W. B. Johnson, C.E. *Manchester*, August 1879. pp. 28.   BM
Addressed to shareholders, concerning the folly of the company's 'autocratic, expensive and inefficient' policy of management. W. B. Johnson writes as Secretary of the L. & Y.

6205 The 'LANGUISHER and Yawner Railed-at Company'; or, The railroad to ruin. By a Wide-awake Cuss. [1883?] pp. 12.   LSE
A rich satire on the L. & Y. Rly., the 'Languisher & Yawner' being 'the most fitting name for a company in possession of so many old sleepers'.

6206 LANCASHIRE & YORKSHIRE RLY. Workshops of the Lancashire & Yorkshire Railway Company, Horwich, Lancashire. *Horwich*, September 1903. pp. 27, with 6 illus. & la. fold. plate.   SLS

6207 DICK, KERR & CO. Electric traction on the Lancashire & Yorkshire Railway. [*London*, 1906.] pp. 48, with illus., map, charts & comparative timetables (steam & electric services).   IT

6208 LANCASHIRE & YORKSHIRE RLY. Description of the Liverpool, Southport & Crossens Electric Section. *Manchester*, [1906.] pp. 16, with illus. & 8 fold. diagrams; maps & plans.   LSE

6209 LANCASHIRE & YORKSHIRE RLY. Twentieth century development of the Lancashire & Yorkshire Railway. *London*, [1913.] pp. 48, with many illus. & a fold. plate.   pc
Reprinted from *Railway & Travel Monthly*.

6210 ENGLISH ELECTRIC COMPANY. The 1,200 volt direct-current electrification of the Manchester–Bury Section, Lancashire & Yorkshire Railway. *London*, [1915.] pp. 35, with many illus. & diagrams.   pc

6211 ELECTRIFICATION of the Manchester to Bury Section of the Lancashire & Yorkshire Railway. *London: Railway Gazette*, [1916.] pp. 35, with 59 illus., diagrams, and a map.   BR
Reprinted from the *Railway Gazette*, 14 Jan. to 4 Feb., 1916.

6212 GOBEY, F. E. British and Continental ambulance trains supplied to the War Office by the Lancashire & Yorkshire Railway. *Horwich: Horwich Railway Mechanics' Institute Engineering & Scientific Club (L. & Y. Rly.)*, [1916.] pp. 45, with 23 plates. BR
Lecture, 11 January, 1916.

6213 LANCASHIRE & YORKSHIRE RLY. Electrification of line, Manchester to Bury, via Prestwich. *Manchester*, 1916. pp. 15, with illus.   LSE

6214 MACKENZIE, HOLLAND & WESTINGHOUSE POWER SIGNAL COMPANY. The Re-signalling of Southport Station, Lancashire & Yorkshire Railway. *London*, [1919.] pp. 26[27], with 12 illus. & fold. diagram. SLS
Reprinted from the *Railway Gazette*, 23 May, 1919.

6215 REGULATION of high-density passenger traffic on the Lancashire & Yorkshire Railway. *London: Railway Gazette*, [1920.] pp. 31, with fold. map, illus. & tables.   pc
Reprinted from the *Railway Gazette*, 2 July, 1920.

6216 WATSON, A. A survey of the comprehensive control system operating on the Lancashire & Yorkshire Railway, opened August 1915. [*Manchester*,] January 1921. pp. 51, with many illus., diagrams (some col.) & specimen forms.   BR
Cover title: *Lancashire & Yorkshire Railway: train control arrangements*.
Movement and control of freight trains.

—— another edn. *Manchester*, [*c.* 1921.] pp. 30.   BR

6217 WATSON, A. Some advantages of control as applied to traffic on railways. [*London*, 1921.] pp. 22, 51.   LSE
Paper, Institute of Transport, April 18, 1921. Train control. The address is followed by a copy of the work described in the preceding entry (6216).

Lee Moor Tramway

6218 HALL, R. M. S. The Lee Moor Tramway. *Lingfield: Oakwood Press*, 1963. pp. 15, with 11 illus., map & 6 diagrams. [*Locomotion Papers*, no. 19.]   BM

Leeds, York & Midland Junction Railway Co.
[not incorporated]

6219 WILKINS, C. Leeds, York & Midland Junction Railway, House of Commons, Session 1846: speech of Mr. Serjeant Wilkins as counsel on behalf of the promoters on Thursday and Friday, March 14 and 15, 1846 ... *London*, 1846. pp. 34.   BM

Leek & Manifold Light Railway
(incorporated as the Leek, Caldon Low & Hartington Light Railway)

*6220 'MANIFOLD'. The Leek & Manifold Valley Light Railway. *Ashbourne: Henstock*, 1955. pp. 66, with 22 illus. on 13 plates, maps, & gradient profile.   BM

Liverpool Overhead Railway

6221 ELECTRIC CONSTRUCTION CORPORATION. Liverpool Overhead Railway. *Wolverhampton*, [1893.] pp. [15], with 6 illus., grad. profile, & diagrams on 9 plates.   pc
Description of the plant, and report of a trial trip, 7 January, 1893.

6222 GREATHEAD, J. H. *and* FOX, F. The Liverpool Overhead Railway ... ; and, The electrical equipment of the Liverpool Overhead, Railway, by Thomas Parker; with an abstract of the discussion upon the papers. *London*, 1894. pp. 36, with 3 fold. plates. LSE
Excerpt, *Min. Proc. I.C.E.*, vol. 117, 1893–4, pt. iii.

6223 COTTRELL, S. B. Liverpool Overhead Railway. *Liverpool*, 1896. pp. 15, with 2 fold. maps & 2 fold. diagrams.   ICE

6224 HALDANE, J. W. C. Railway engineering, mechanical and electrical. *London*, 1897. pp. xx, 562, with plates & illus.   BM
Contains passages relating to the Liverpool Overhead Rly.

6225 LIVERPOOL OVERHEAD RLY. Description and views of the Liverpool Overhead Railway . . . [*Liverpool*, 1897.] pp. 56.   BR

6226 NEACHELL, E. J. Notes on the Overhead Railway. *Liverpool*, 1915. pp. 9.
Paper, Liverpool Engineering Society, 1 Dec., 1915. Excerpt, *Transactions, L.E.S.*, vol. 37.

6227 The RE-SIGNALLING of the Liverpool Overhead Railway with daylight colour-light signals. *London*, [1922.] pp. 12, with 9 illus. & a diagram.
Reprinted from the *Engineer*, 4 Nov., 1921.

6228 ROSTRON, H. M. The Liverpool Overhead Railway: a pioneer in rapid transit. *Liverpool*, 1952. pp. 24, with 8 illus. & map.   IT
Excerpt, *Transactions, Liverpool Engineering Society*, vol. 73.

6229 BOX, C. E. Liverpool Overhead Railway, 1893–1956. *London: Railway World*, 1959. pp. 189, with 84 illus., 28 maps, drawings & diagrams, timetables, etc.   BM

6230 BETT, W. H. The tickets of the Liverpool Overhead Railway. *Sidcup: Electric Railway Society*, in association with the *Ticket & Fare Collection Society*, 1963. pp. 22[24], with reproductions of 6 tickets on fold. plate. [*Electric Railway Society Monograph Series*.]
                    BM

Llandudno & Colwyn Bay Electric Railway

6231 LAWSON, R. *and* MORRIS, G. C. J. The Llandudno & Colwyn Bay Electric Railway. *Cricklewood (London): Light Railway Transport League*, [1956.] pp. 12, with 5 illus. & a map.   pc
Reprinted from the *Modern Tramway*.

London & Exeter Railway Company
[not incorporated]

6232 COLOMBINE, D. E. Exposition of the circumstances attending the promotion and general management of the Direct London & Exeter Railway, shewing its present condition and prospects. *London*, 1846. pp. 52.   BM

London & North Eastern Railway
Historical

6233 LONDON & NORTH EASTERN RLY. The evolution of L.N.E.R. locomotives. [*London*, 1924.] pp. 16.
Thirteen illustrations of locomotives, with details.

6234 LONDON & NORTH EASTERN RLY. List of lines, not including those jointly owned, with the Acts of Parliament authorizing them and the dates of opening. By Sir Francis Dunnell, Chief Legal Adviser. 1926. pp. 38, 18, 15, 8.   BR
Not published.

6235 ALLCHIN, M. C. V. Locomotives of the London & North Eastern Railway. 2nd edn. *Southsea: the author*, 1935. pp. [32.] *Reproduced typescript.*   BM

6236 LONDON & NORTH EASTERN RLY. List of works, other than railways, with the Acts of Parliament authorizing them. By I. Buchanan Pritchard, Chief Legal Adviser. 1930. pp. 112.   BR
Not published.

*6237 LONDON & NORTH EASTERN RLY.—The 'Flying Scotsman', the world's most famous express. *London*, 1925. pp. 129, with illus.   pc
History, description, and itinerary.
—— 2nd edn. *London*, 1927. pp. 129.
—— 4th edn. *London*, 1931. pp. 130.   pc

6238 BAINBRIDGE, F. F. Centenary of Shildon (London & North Eastern Railway) Institute: a record of its rise, progress and activities. [1933.] pp. 44, with illus.   BR

6239 LOCOMOTIVES of the L.N.E.R., past and present. *London*, [1929.] pp. 48, with 33 illus.   BM
'Published with the authority of the L.N.E.R.'
An outline history with a list of all named engines.
—— another edn. 'Past and present locomotives of the L.N.E.R.' *London*, [1935.] pp. 50.   BM
Cover title, *Locomotives of the L.N.E.R. past and present*.

6240 PRENTICE, K. R. *and* PROUD, P. The locomotives of the L.N.E.R., 1923–1937. [*London: Railway Correspondence & Travel Society*, 1941.] pp. 136, with illus.   SLS
Detailed lists and notes.

6241 NOCK, O. S. The locomotives of Sir Nigel Gresley . . . *London: Longmans*, 1945. pp. 180, with 147 illus. (2nd impr. 1946.)   BM

6242 LONDON & NORTH EASTERN RLY. A brief history of the L.N.E.R. [*London*,] September, 1946. pp. 9.   BR

6243 WEBB, B. Locomotive engineers of the L.N.E.R. and its constituent companies. *London: Ian Allan*, 1946. pp. 76, with illus., incl. portraits.   BM
G.N. Rly. Patrick Stirling; H. A. Ivatt.
N.E. Rly. E. Fletcher; T. W. Worsdell; Wilson Worsdell; V. L. Raven.

G.E. Rly. James Holden; S. D. Holden; A. J. Hill.

G.C. Rly. Harry Pollitt; J. G. Robinson.

H. & B. Rly. Matthew Stirling.

N.B. Rly. M. Holmes; W. P. Reid.

G.N. of S. Rly. W. Pickersgill; T. E. Heywood.

G.N.R. and L.N.E.R. Nigel Gresley.

L.N.E.R. E. Thompson; A. H. Peppercorn.

6244 WETHERSETT, E. R. *and* ASHER, L. L. Locomotives of the L.N.E.R.: a pictorial record . . . with . . . a renumbering supplement . . . *Cambridge: Heffer*, 1947. pp. ix, 122, with many illus.   BM

6245 NEWSOME, N. The development of L.N.E.R. carriage and wagon design, 1923–1941. *Westminster: Institution of Locomotive Engineers*, 1948. pp. 54, with 45 illus. & diagrams (some fold.).   BR

6246 ALLEN, C. J. The Gresley Pacifics of the LNER. *London: Ian Allan*, 1950. pp. 127, with plates & tables. [*Famous Locomotive Types*, no. 6.]   BM

6247 DOW, G. East Coast route. *London: Locomotive Publishing Co.*, 1951. pp. 64, with 46 illus. on 32 plates, & 2 maps.   BM
History; detailed description of features en route, King's Cross to Aberdeen, and (pp. 53–60) 'Some famous East Coast expresses'.

6248 BRITISH RAILWAYS. Centenaries Exhibition, 1852–1952: historical brochure. *London*, 1952. pp. 8, with 8 illus., map, & a chronology of the GNR–LNER.   IT
Inserted in the IT copy are 4 pages of additional notes on King's Cross Station issued in reproduced typescript by B.R.(ER).

6249 WEBSTER, H. C. 2750: legend of a locomotive. *London: Nelson*, 1953. pp. xii, 209.   BM
An account of the life of an L.N.E.R. A3 Pacific of the 1920–40 period and her crew.

*6250 MACKILLOP, N. Enginemen Elite. *London: Ian Allan*, 1958. pp. 154, with 40 illus. on 16 plates.   BM
'Highlights of memory' selected from forty years on the North British and the L.N.E.R

6251 MACKILLOP, N. How I became an engine driver. *London: Nelson*, 1953. pp. ix, 116, with 7 plates & illus.   BM
Norman MacKillop's career on the L.N.E.R.
—— 2nd edn. *London*, 1960. pp. ix, 116.   BM

6252 BROWN, F. A. S. Nigel Gresley, locomotive engineer. *London: Ian Allan*, 1961. pp. 256, with illus. on 32 plates.   BM

6253 ARKLE, E. W. The L.N.E.R. and British Railways. *In* 'Journal of Transport History', vol. 5, no. 3, May 1962. pp. 139–45.   BM

6254 BELL, R. The London & North Eastern Railway: sixteen years, 1923–38. *In* 'Journal of Transport History', vol. 5, no. 3, May 1962. pp. 133–9.   BM

6255 ELLIS, C. H. The Flying Scotsman, 1862–1962: portrait of a train. *London: Allen & Unwin*, 1962. pp. 47, with 27 illus. on 16 plates, & map.   BM

*6256 RAILWAY CORRESPONDENCE AND TRAVEL SOCIETY. Locomotives of the L.N.E.R. 1963– . *In progress*.   BM
A series in ten parts, by various authors.
1, Preliminary survey. 1963. pp. 120,[1,] with col. frontis., 171 illus. on 32 plates, & detailed lists, incl. (pp. 104–120) an 8-column list of locomotives.

Contemporaneous

6257 LONDON & NORTH EASTERN RLY. The Port of Hull and its accommodation and arrangements . . . *York*, 1924. pp. 24, with illus. & fold. map.

6258 LONDON & NORTH EASTERN RLY. London & North Eastern Railway: commercial geography. *London*, 1925. pp. 178, with maps (2 fold.) & diagrams in text.   IT
For the use of staff preparing for examinations. Areas of supply and demand, the L.N.E. Rly's. terrain; commercial aspects, coalfields, ports and industries.
—— L.N.E.R.: commercial geography. Revision sheets for booklet, dated March 1925. *York*, September, 1931. pp. 26. UL(GL)

6259 LONDON & NORTH EASTERN RLY. The London & North Eastern Railway presents this souvenir to the members of the International Hotel Alliance on the occasion of their visit to Great Britain, April 1926. *London*, [1926.] pp. [42,] with 20 plates & illus. in colour, incl. reproductions of L.N.E.R. posters.
Contains information on L.N.E.R. hotel facilities, etc.

6260 LEIGH, D. On the line. *Bungay*, [1928.] pp. 199, with plates.   BM
Sketches of contemporary railway life on the L.N.E.R.

6261 LONDON & NORTH EASTERN RLY. 'Queen of Scots' new Pullman-de-luxe all steel trains, commencing Monday July 9th, 1928. [1928.] pp. 15, with illus.
Brochure.

6262 WHITEMOOR Marshalling Yard, L.N.E.R. [*Westminster:*] *Railway Gazette*, [1929]. pp. 20, with illus. & diagrams.   PC
Reprinted from the *Railway Gazette*, 20 September, 1929.

6263 LONDON & NORTH EASTERN RLY.— SOUTHERN AREA. Organization of Passenger Manager's Headquarters Office. [*London*,] January 1930. pp. 9. *Typescript*. LSE
For the information of staff.

6264 'VOYAGEUR.' Gradients of the London & North Eastern Railway. *London: Railway Publishing Co.*, [1930.] pp. 48, with 24 detailed gradient profiles.   IT

6265 LONDON & NORTH EASTERN RLY. How the L.N.E.R. carries exceptional freight loads. *London*, 1929. pp. 43, with illus., diagrams & tables of various special wagons.
—— 2nd edn. *London*, 1931. pp. 59.

6266 LONDON & NORTH EASTERN RLY.— ELECTRIFICATION COMMITTEE. Proposed electrification of a portion of the Great Eastern suburban lines. (Chairman, C. J. Selway.) [1931.] pp. 29, with tables. *Reproduced typescript.*   BR

6267 LONDON & NORTH EASTERN RLY. On either side: features of interest seen from the train between London (Liverpool Street) and East Anglia. *London*, [1932.] pp. 41. BR

6268 LONDON & NORTH EASTERN RLY. The Silver Jubilee: Britain's first streamline train. [*London*,] 1935. pp. 15.
Description and timetables.

*6269 LONDON & NORTH EASTERN RLY. Doncaster Locomotive and Carriage Plant Works. [*London*, 1936.] pp. 16, with illus. & fold. plan.

6270 LONDON & NORTH EASTERN RLY. London Passenger Transport Pool: report on proposed electrification of L.N.E.R. suburban lines, Liverpool Street and Fenchurch Street to Shenfield. March 1936. (Chairman, Electrification Committee, C. J. Selway.) pp. 22, with tables. *Reproduced typescript.*   BR

6271 WESTINGHOUSE BRAKE & SIGNAL CO. Bethnal Green—Enfield colour light signalling, L.N.E.R. *London*, [1936.] pp. 7, with illus., diagrams & map.   BR
Reprinted from the *Railway Gazette*, 21 February, 1936.

6272 LONDON & NORTH EASTERN RLY. 'The Coronation': the first streamline train, King's Cross for Scotland. *London*, 1937. pp. 16.
A descriptive brochure.

6273 LONDON & NORTH EASTERN RLY.— On either side . . . King's Cross to Edinburgh. *London*, 1925.   BR
A route chart.
—— another edn. *York*, 1935. pp. 72[75].   BR
—— another edn. [*London*, 1937.] pp. 72 [74].   BR

6274 WAY, R. B. North with the Flying Scotsman. *In* 'The Romance of reading'; second series, edited by Rodney Bennett. Book 4, 'Mixed cargoes'. *London*, 1937. pp. 62–74. BM

6275 WESTINGHOUSE BRAKE & SIGNAL CO. Electro-pneumatic point operation and colour-light signalling at Leeds New Station, London & North Eastern Railway. *London*, June 1937. pp. 20, with illus. & a fold. diagram.   LSE

6276 ALLEN, C. J. The 'Coronation' and other famous L.N.E.R. trains. *London: Nicholson & Watson*, 1937. pp. 175, with many illus.
—— 2nd edn. *London*, 1938. pp. 185.   BM

6277 LONDON & NORTH EASTERN RLY. Notes and running times for passengers by restaurant car trains between London and West Riding, Hull, Newcastle and Scotland, 4 July to 25 September, 1938. *London*, [1938.] pp. 35.
Cover title: *Notes for L.N.E.R. passengers.*
Selected timetables. pp. 23–34 have a perforated inner margin for detachment.

6278 LONDON & NORTH EASTERN RLY. The ports of Grimsby and Immingham. *Leeds*, 1938. pp. 15, with illus. & 2 fold maps.

6279 LONDON & NORTH EASTERN RLY. Ports of the London & North Eastern Railway. *London*, 1927–38.   BR
Various editions. A book of reference giving particulars of facilities, with plans of each port.

6280 MODERN locomotives of the L.N.E.R. *London: Locomotive Publishing Co.*, [1938.] pp. 48[49], with illus.   RC
Cover title: *L.N.E.R. locomotives, 1938.*

6281 WESTINGHOUSE BRAKE & SIGNAL COMPANY. Route relay interlocking and re-signalling at Paragon Station, Hull, L. & N.E. Rly. *London*, [1938.] pp. 16, with illus. & diagram.   SL

6282 LONDON & NORTH EASTERN RLY. Equipment of the 'Shenfield lines' for electric working. [*London*,] May 1939. pp. [6,] with 6 illus. & a map of LNER electrification and Central Line tube extension.   BR

6283 THE TYNESIDE electrified lines of the L.N.E.R.: the present-day equipment and operation of one of the earliest English steam railways to be electrified . . . *Westminster: Railway Gazette*, 1939. pp. 15, with illus., diagrams & fold. plan.   PC
Reprint, *Railway Gazette*, 13 October, 1939.

6284 CRESWELL, A. J. Names and numbers, LMS & LNE: over 14000 engines recorded and classified. *Huddersfield: Quadrant Publications*, 1946. pp. 32.   BM

6285 CRESWELL, A. J. Stock changes, LMS, GWR, SR, LNER. New numbers, names & classes: old from new & new from old. LNER conversion tables. *Huddersfield: Quadrant Publications*, 1946. pp. viii, 28. BM
Mainly L.N.E.R.

6286 DUCKWORTH, C. L. D. *and* LANGMUIR, G. E. Clyde River and other steamers. *Glasgow: Collingridge*, 1937. pp. xii, 254, with plates. BM
pp. 73–91, L.N.E.R. steamers.

—— 2nd edn. *Glasgow*, 1946. pp. xi, 260. BM

6287 LONDON & NORTH EASTERN RLY. Forward: the L.N.E.R. Development Programme. [*London*, 1946.] pp. 25, with illus. Post-war recovery and future plans.

6288 LONDON & NORTH EASTERN RLY. Sign standards: letters, totem, figures, arrow. Rev. edn. *London*, October 1946. pp. 12. PC

6289 LONDON & NORTH EASTERN RLY. Station improvements: a code of practice for the guidance of the Station Improvements Committees. [*London*, Jan. 1946.] pp. 18.

6290 WESTINGHOUSE BRAKE & SIGNAL COMPANY. Northallerton to Darlington resignalling, L.N.E.R. *London*, [1946.] pp. 11, with illus. & fold. diagram. SL

6291 TITANS of the Track: London and North Eastern Rly. *London & Staines: Ian Allan*, 1946–7. BM
Illustrations with historical notes.

6292 CRESWELL, A. J. On the footplate. *Huddersfield: Quadrant Publications*, [1947.] pp. 40. BM
A trip on the 'West Riding Ltd.', and various other short essays on locomotives.

6293 CRUMP, N. By rail to victory: the story of the L.N.E.R. in wartime. [*London:*] *L. & N. E. Rly.*, 1947. pp. xii, 196, with plates & a map. BM

6294 GILL, E. Letters of Eric Gill; edited by Walter Shewring. *London: Jonathan Cape*, 1947. BM
pp. 269–74, 'On the "Flying Scotsman".' King's Cross to Grantham on no. 2582.

6295 GODDARD, M. N. Report . . . on goods, passenger and parcels traffic on the London & North Eastern Railway, and modern goods shed operation on the London, Midland & Scottish Railway. pp. 28. *Typescript*. IT
Paper, Institute of Transport, April 1947.

6296 LAKE, G. H. British Trains Album: no. 1, LNER. *London & Bedford: W. P. Griffith*, [1947.] pp. 24. BM
No more published.
Twenty-nine illustrations of contemporary trains, with descriptions.

6297 LONDON & NORTH EASTERN RLY. S.S. 'Arnhem'. [*London*, 1947.] pp. [12.] BR
Description of the ship, with illustrations.

6298 NOCK, O. S. Locomotives of the L.N.E.R.: standardisation and renumbering. *London: L.N.E. Rly.*, 1947. pp. 68, with illus., diagrams, tables & lists. BM

6299 PIKE, S. N. Mile by mile on the L.N.E.R.: King's Cross edition. *London: Atlas Publishing Co.*, 1947. pp. 40. BM
A route chart with notes on features of railway interest to be seen from the train.

6300 A B C of L.N.E.R. locomotives. *London: Ian Allan*, 1943–48. BM
Various editions of a booklet of between 64 and 80 pages, containing lists and illustrations.

6301 STEPHENSON LOCOMOTIVE SOCIETY. Ivatt Atlantic Special, King's Cross to Doncaster, Sunday 26 November 1950. Last run of last Ivatt Atlantic, no. 62822. [*London*, 1950.] pp.[8,] with 7 illus. & logs of journeys. SLS

London & North Western Railway

Grand Junction Railway: GJ
Liverpool & Manchester Railway: LM
London & Birmingham Railway: LB
Chester & Holyhead Railway: CH

For a genealogical table of the London and North Western see Appendix IIIb.

Historical

6302 LIVERPOOL & MANCHESTER RLY. Reports of the Liverpool & Manchester Railway as published by order of the proprietors at their General Meetings. *London*, 1837. pp. 28, 6–100. UL(GL)
Complete set, from 7 May, 1826 (the date of incorporation) to 27 July, 1836. Republished 'for the convenience of the public'.

6303 LECOUNT, P. The history of the railway connecting London and Birmingham, containing its progress from the commencement; to which are added a popular description of the locomotive engine and a sketch of the geological features of the line. *London*, [1839.] pp. 118, with illus. BM

6304 ROSCOE, T. *and* LECOUNT, P. The London & Birmingham Railway, with the home and country scenes on each side of the line, assisted in the historical details by Peter Lecount . . . with a map of the line, eighteen fine steel plates and numerous wood engravings. *London*, [1839.] pp. 192[196], with col. fold. map. BM
Also issued serially as *History and description of the London & Birmingham Railway* (1839).

6305 TRENT VALLEY RLY. Trent Valley Railway: origin and progress of the undertaking; compiled from official documents. *Manchester*, 1845. pp. 20. LSE
—— *Manchester*, 1845. pp. 46. BM
—— *Manchester*, 1845. pp. 82. PC

6306 HISTORICAL and descriptive account of the Lancaster & Carlisle Railway, illustrated with wood engravings. [*Kendal*, 1847.] pp. 24.   LSE
Reprinted from the *Kendal Mercury* of 12 December, 1847.

6307 ROSCOE, T. Illustrated history of the London & North Western Railway from London to Birmingham, Liverpool and Manchester. *London*, 1847. 2 pts. in 1 vol. (pp. 192:154), with 25 plates & 29 illus.   HRL

6308 BAINES, T. History of the commerce and town of Liverpool . . . *London*, 1852. pp.
LM xvi, 844, 13.   BM
pp. 591–622, formation of the L. & M. Rly., 1825–30.

*6309 [HEAD, F. B.] Stokers and Pokers; or, The London & North Western Railway, the electric telegraph, and the Railway Clearing House. By the author of 'Bubbles from the Brunnen of Nassau'. *London*, 1849. pp. 208.
BM
—— 2nd edn. *London*, 1850. pp. 224.   IT
—— new edn. *London*, 1855. pp. 224.   BRE
—— another edn. *London*, 1861. pp. 224.
LSE

*6310 JEAFFRESON, J. C. The life of Robert
LB Stephenson, . . . *London*, 1864. 2 vols.   BM
vol. 1, pp. 184–237, The London & Birmingham Rly.
vol. 1 also contains details on the Liverpool & Manchester not found in S. Smiles' *Lives of G. & R. Stephenson*.

6311 LONDON & NORTH WESTERN RLY. [Documents relating to the London & North
LB Western Railway, 1832–1865. 245 items consisting of reports, letters to shareholders, maps, pamphlets and newspaper cuttings, chronologically arranged.]   BM
Items 1–51 issued by the London & Birmingham Rly.
Items 54–6, 59–71 issued by the Buckinghamshire Rly.

6312 POLLINS, H. Railway auditing: a report of 1867. pp. 22.   BR
Reprint, *Accounting Research*, vol. 8, no. 1, Jan. 1957.
L. & N.W. Rly.

6313 [CONDER, F. R.] Personal recollections of English engineers, and of the introduction of
LB the railway system into the United Kingdom. By a Civil Engineer. *London*, 1868. pp. xvi, 432.   BM
pp. 28–44, The extension of the L. & B. Rly. from Camden Town to Euston Square.

6314 ROBINSON, H. C. Diary. *London*, 1869.
LM 3 vols.   BM
vol. 3, pp. 26–8, account of a journey on the L. & M. Rly.

6315 SMILES, R. Memoir of the late Henry Booth of the Liverpool & Manchester, and
LM afterwards of the London & North Western Railway. *London*, 1869. pp. 117.   BM

6316 HARE, A. J. C. Memorials of a quiet life
LM . . . *London*, 1872. 2 vols.   BM
vol. 1, pp. 280–3, account of a visit to the L. & M. in December 1829.

6317 WATKIN, E. W. Debates in the House of Commons on the Liverpool & Manchester
LM Railway Bill, 2 March 1825 and 6 April 1826. *London*, 1872. pp. 24.   BR
Reprinted from *Hansard*.

6318 GREVILLE, C. C. F. The Greville Memoirs.
LM *London*, 1874. 3 vols.   BM
vol. 2, pp. 47–51, an account of the accident to Wm. Huskisson. (Also to be found in other editions.)

6319 DAWSON, G. J. C. A brief sketch of the introduction of railways into this country, and the wonderful results thereof. *Tamworth*, [1875.] pp. 22.   ICE
Reprinted with revision from the *Nuneaton Chronicle* of 17 Feb., 1872.
pp. 15–22, an account of the opening of the Trent Valley Rly.

6320 KEMBLE, F. A. Record of a Girlhood . . .
LM *London*, 1878. 3 vols.   BM
vol. 2, pp. 187–97, Opening of the L. & M., and the accident to Huskisson.
—— 2nd edn. *London*, 1879.   BM
vol. 2, pp. 187–97.

6321 SLUGG, J. T. Reminiscences of Manchester fifty years ago. *Manchester*, 1881.
LM pp. vi, 355.   BM
pp. 227–34, Opening of the railway to Liverpool.

6322 PIKE, R. Romance of the Liverpool & Manchester Railway, as described by Fanny
LM Kemble . . . C. F. Adams . . . *Manchester*, [*c.* 1887.] pp. 36.   LSE

6323 BAILEY, W. H. Chat Moss and a new chapter in the history of the Manchester &
LM Liverpool Railway . . . *Manchester*, 1889. pp. 17.   ICE
—— another edn. 'A new chapter in the history of the Manchester & Liverpool Railway . . . *Manchester*, 1889. pp. [23]–30.
Paper, Manchester Association of Engineers, 26 January, 1889.
The draining and cultivating of Chat Moss by William Roscoe, with the aid of light wagonways supplied by Robert Stannard, 1816.

6324 LONDON & NORTH WESTERN RLY. London & North Western Railway, illustrated: fifty years of successful railway enterprise. *London*, [*c.* 1890.] pp. 280.   RC
Produced to publicise facilities.

6325 NICHOLSON, C. A well-spent life: memoir of Cornelius Nicholson; with a selection of his lectures and letters. *Kendal*, 1890. pp. 289, with portrait & a facs. holograph letter & envelope inserted at end.   BM
pp. 15–42, Cornelius Nicholson's part in the struggle for a trunk line from London to Scotland via Kendal (Lancaster & Carlisle Rly.), 1844, including, pp. 17–40, an article from the *Kendal Mercury* on the opening of the line, 21 Sept., 1846.
pp. 69–88, Kendal & Windermere Rly. An

article from the *Westmorland Gazette*, 24 April, 1847. On pp. 119–39 is a reprint of *The London & Glasgow Railway: the interests of Kendal considered* (1837) by C. Nicholson.

6326 STRETTON, C. E. The history of the Chester & Crewe Railway . . . *Chester*, 1890. pp. [5.]   BM

6327 STEVENSON, D. Fifty years on the London & North Western Railway, and other memoranda in the life of D. Stevenson. Edited by Leopold Turner. *London*, 1891. pp. 153.   BM
   pp. 5–46, Memoirs of LNWR life, 1838–1890.

6328 [BURROWS, E.] The Triumphs of Steam; or, Stories from the lives of Watt, Ark-
LM wright and Stephenson. *London*, 1859. pp. viii, 263.   BM
   pp. 83–263 relate to G. Stephenson and to the L. & M. Rly.
   —— another edn. By H. Frith. *London*, 1892. pp. xii, 263.   BM

6329 STRETTON, C. E. The history of the Birmingham, Wolverhampton & Stour Valley Railway . . . 1893. pp. [21.]   BM

6330 LONDON & NORTH WESTERN RLY. The London & North Western Railway Company's fleet of Channel steamers. [*London*, Dec. 1897.] pp. 8, with illus. of the 'Cambria'.   BR
   An historical account of L. & N.W. steamships, issued in connection with the trial trip of the 'Cambria'.

6331 FOWLER, J. K. Records of old times, historical, social, political, sporting and agricultural . . . *London*, 1898. pp. xix, 238.   BM
   pp. 186–95, The Buckinghamshire Railway.

6332 STRETTON, C. E. The history of the Chester & Holyhead Railway: a lecture de-
CH livered at Bangor on the occasion of the Jubilee of the opening of the railway from Chester to Bangor, 1st May, 1898. *Bangor*, 1898. pp. [14.]   BM
   —— another edn. '. . . on the occasion of the Jubilee of the opening of the railway between Llanfair and Holyhead, 1st August, 1898.' *Holyhead*, 1898. pp. [19.]   BM

6333 STRETTON, C. E. The history of the Conway Tubular Bridge: a paper read at the
CH bridge on the occasion of the Jubilee of the opening . . . *Conway*, 1898. pp. 8.   BM

6334 STRETTON, C. E. The history of the amalgamation and the formation of the London & North Western Railway Company . . . *Leeds*, 1901. pp. 5.   BM

6335 STRETTON, C. E. The history of the Bolton & Leigh, and the Kenyon & Leigh Junction railways. *Leeds*, 1901. pp. 16.   BM

6336 STRETTON, C. E. The history of the Grand
GJ Junction Railway . . . *Leeds*, 1901. pp. 13.   BM

6337 STRETTON, C. E. The history of the Holy-
CH head Railway boat service. 2nd edn. *Leeds*, 1901. pp. 19.   BM
   —— 2nd edn. enl. *Leeds*, 1901. pp. 19.   BM

6338 STRETTON, C. E. The history of the Lancaster & Preston Junction, Lancaster & Carlisle, and Kendal & Windermere railways. 2nd edn. *Leeds*, 1901. pp. 21.   BM

6339 STRETTON, C. E. The history of the Liverpool & Manchester Railway. 3rd edn.
LM [1901.] pp. 15.   BM
   Reprinted from the *Lancaster Observer*, 14 June, 1901.

6340 STRETTON, C. E. The history of the London & Birmingham Railway. 2nd edn.
LB *Leeds*, 1901. pp. 12.   BM

6341 STRETTON, C. E. The history of the Manchester & Birmingham Railway . . . 2nd edn. *Leeds*, 1901. pp. 5.   BM

6342 STRETTON, C. E. The history of the South Staffordshire Railway . . . [*Leicester*, 1901.] pp. [4.]   BM
   Reprinted from the *Staffordshire Chronicle*, 15 June, 1901.

6343 STRETTON, C. E. The history of the Trent Valley Railway . . . 2nd edn. *Burton-on-Trent*, 1901. pp. 7.   BM

6344 STRETTON, C. E. The history of the Warrington & Newton Railway . . . 3rd edn. *Leeds*, 1901. pp. 12.   BM

6345 STRETTON, C. E. The history of the London & North-Western Railway. 3rd edn. *Leeds*, 1902. pp. 17.   BM

6346 STRETTON, C. E. The history of the South Leicestershire Railway. 3rd edn. *Leeds*, 1902. pp. 9.   BM

6347 ASHBURY, T. The early history of the Liverpool & Manchester Railway: a paper
LM read before the Manchester Association of Engineers, Employers, Foremen & Draughtsmen . . . February 28, 1880. *Manchester*, 1880. pp. 52. *In his* 'Miscellaneous Papers.' [*Manchester*, 1904.]   LSE
   Based upon extracts from newspapers, 1824 to 1830. Two prospectuses are reproduced.

*6348 NEELE, G. P. Railway reminiscences: notes and reminiscences of half-a-century's progress in railway working and of a railway superintendent's life, principally on the London & North Western Railway . . . *London*, 1904. pp. vi, 544, with portraits & (pp. 533–6) a list of royal journeys.   BM
   Some account of his early career with the Eastern Counties, and with the South Staffordshire, is also given.

6349 The LONDON & North Western Railway Diamond Jubilee Album, 1846–1906. *London: Railway News*, [1906.] pp. 32, with many illus. BR
Reprinted from the *Railway News* of 14 July, 1906.

6350 'ENGINEER.' The London & North Western Railway and Crewe Works. *London*, 1908. pp. xvi, with 20 illus., 4 diagrams, incl. one of 18 drawings depicting development in L.N.W.R. locomotive design, 2 la. fold. plates & 4 col. plates and a table of locomotive development on the L.N.W.R. BM
Supplement to *The Engineer*, 11 December, 1908.

6351 LONDON & NORTH WESTERN RLY. The L. & N.W. Railway from 1830 to the present time. Reproduced from the L. & N. W. series of pictorial postcards. *London*, 1909. pp. 49, with fold. map. BR

6352 LONDON & NORTH WESTERN RLY. Chronological and Alphabetical List of
c the leading events in the history of the London & North Western Railway, together with the names of the chairmen and principal officers, and their terms of office, etc. pp. [200.] *Typescript*, with an index & a supplementary list at end. BR
Period 1845–1914.

6353 STEEL, W. L. The history of the London & North Western Railway . . . *London*, 1914. pp. xii, 502, with 100 illustrations. BM

6354 DENDY MARSHALL, C. F. The Liverpool & Manchester Railway. [*London*, 1923.] pp.
LM 33, with 13 plates, a descriptive bibliography
b (pp. 24–31), bibliogr. notes, descriptive lists of prints and commemorative medals, etc., and a list of locomotives. BM

6355 FUERST, A. Die hundertjährige Eisenbahn: Wie Meisterhände sie schufen: mit vielen
LM Abbildungen. *Berlin*, 1925. pp. 308. BM
pp. 124–67, 'Das grösste Wunderwerk unserer Zeit'. (The L. & M.)

6356 GREVILLE, C. C. F. The Greville Diary, including passages hitherto withheld from
LM publication. Edited by Philip Whitwell Wilson. Illustrated. *London*, 1927. 2 vols. BM
vol. 1, pp. 318–22, the accident to Huskisson. This is recorded in all complete editions. Other entries on railways appear elsewhere in this work.

6357 VEITCH, G. S. Huskisson and Liverpool . . . [*Liverpool*, 1929.] pp. 54, with bibliogr.
LM notes. BM
Reprinted from the *Transactions of the Historic Society of Lancashire and Cheshire*, 1929.
pp. 45–9, Huskisson and the promotion of the L. & M. Rly.

6358 LIVERPOOL & MANCHESTER RAILWAY CENTENARY. The Book and Programme of
LM the Liverpool & Manchester Railway Centenary: LMR 1830 to LMS 1930. (Edited by Matthew Anderson.) *Liverpool*, [1930.] pp. 124, with plates & illus. BM
Includes a short history of the L. & M.

6359 LIVERPOOL AND MANCHESTER RAILWAY CENTENARY. Catalogue of the ex-
LM hibition of literature, portraits, maps, plans and drawings . . . in commemoration of the opening on 15 September 1830 of the Liverpool and Manchester Railway. *Liverpool*, 1930. pp. 56. pc

6360 LIVERPOOL PUBLIC LIBRARIES. The Centenary of the Liverpool & Manchester
LM Railway, 1830 to 1930: a list of printed and illustrated material in the Reference Library. (Compiled by W. A. Phillips.) *Liverpool*, 1930. pp. 35. BM

6361 DENDY MARSHALL, C. F. Centenary history of the Liverpool & Manchester Railway,
LM to which is appended a transcript of the relevent portions of Rastrick's 'Rainhill Notebook'. *London*, 1930. pp. ix, 192, with 28 plates (20 col. & 1 fold.), illustrations, map, & pp. (140–51), annotated bibliography. BM
A full account, including such detail as reproductions of commemorative medals and pottery, etc. In his *One hundred years of railways* (1930), C. F. D. Marshall adds further information on the L. & M.

6362 VEITCH, G. S. The struggle for the Liverpool and Manchester Railway. *Liverpool*,
LM 1930. pp. 68, with plates. BM
The conception and formation of the L. & M. Rly.

6363 LEVIEN, D. V. A short history of the Birmingham, Bristol & Thames Junction Railway Company, incorporated in 1836, which changed its name in 1840 to The West London Railway Company. August 1933. pp. A–G, 86. *Typescript*. BR
The West London ('Punch's Railway') and West London Extension railways, with some notes on the Kensington Canal, Pinkus's Pneumatic Rly., Clegg & Samuda's atmospheric railway system, Prosser's new wooden guidewheel railway, Victoria & Pimlico Rly.

6364 ROBINSON, E. E. The Crewe locomotives of the L. & N.W.R., 1845–1858. *Westminster*, [c. 1934.] pp. 41. BR

6365 ROBINSON, E. E. The L. & N. W. R. 4-cylinder 4–4–0 compound passenger engines & the 2-cylinder 'Renown' class simples. (LMS locomotives, Handbook no. W1.) *Egham: the author*, [1934.] pp. 13. BM

6366 LONDON, MIDLAND & SCOTTISH RLY.
LB A century of progress: London–Birmingham, 1838–1938. (Souvenir of the Centenary
of the London & Birmingham Railway,
September 1938.) [*London*, 1938.] pp. 43,
with maps & illus. on plates.   BM

6367 SMITH, G. R. Old Euston: an account of
the beginning of the London & Birmingham
LB Railway and the building of Euston Station.
London: L.M.S. Rly., 1938. pp. xi, 67[70,]
with 6 plates; illus. in text.   BM
A centenary publication.

6368 KEMBLE, F. A. Fanny Kemble's ride on the
Liverpool & Manchester Railway. *New
LM York: Valve Pilot Corporation*, [1939.] pp.
11, with 2 portraits & a map.   BR
Extracts from her diary.

6369 DUNN, J. M. The Chester & Holyhead
Railway. *South Godstone: Oakwood Press*,
CH 1948. pp. 60, with plates, gradient profiles,
tables & chronology.   BM

6370 LIVESEY, H. F. F. The locomotives of the
L.N.W.R. *London*, 1948. pp. 100, with
c illus.   BM
A chronological arrangement.

6371 CHADWICK, S. 'All stations to Manchester!' The Centenary of the Huddersfield
& Manchester Railway and Standedge
Tunnel. *Huddersfield: the author*, 1949. pp.
23, with 2 illus. on inside covers.   SLS

6372 CHALONER, W. H. The social and economic development of Crewe, 1780–1923.
GJ *Manchester: Manchester University Press*,
1950. pp. xx, 326.   BM
pp. 1–83, The transformation and development of Crewe by the Grand Junction Rly. and,
from 1846, the L.N.W.R.

6373 GREGORY, J. R. The L.N.W.R. eight-
coupled goods engines. [*Leamington Spa:
c Railway Correspondence & Travel Society*,
1950.] pp. 23, with 26 illus. on 8 plates,
a chron. table of annual totals, 1892–1949,
and detailed lists compiled by W. T. Stubbs
and D. R. Pollock.   BM

6374 NOCK, O. S. The Premier Line: the story
of London & North Western locomotives.
London: Ian Allan, 1952. pp. 239, with 94
illus. on 36 plates (4 col.).   BM
—— Locomotives of the Premier Line in
pictures: a reprint of the illustrations from
'The Premier Line' . . . by O. S. Nock.
London: Ian Allan, [1952.] pp. 40, with 95
illus. (3 col.).   BM

6375 POLLINS, H. The finances of the Liverpool
& Manchester Railway. (Reprinted from
LM 'The Economic History Review', Second
Series, vol. 5, no. 1, 1952.) pp. 90–7, with
bibliogr. notes & tables.   pc

*6376 BASNETT, L. The history of the Bolton &
Leigh Railway, based on the Hulton Papers,
1824–1828. *Manchester: Lancashire & Cheshire Antiquarian Society*, 1953. pp. 157–76,
with diagrams.   BM
Reprint, *Trans. Lancs. & Ches. Antiq. Soc.*
vol. 62, 1950/51.

6377 FULFORD, R. Glyn's, 1753 to 1953 . . .
London: Macmillan, 1953. pp. xvi, 266, with
plates (some col.).   BM
App. IV, Railways which had accounts with
Glyn's (including L. & N.W.R.).

6378 LLOYD, R. Railwaymen's Gallery. *London:
Allen & Unwin*, 1953. pp. 166, with plates.
          BM
pp. 46–93, The decline and fall of the Euston
Empire, 1848–1858.
pp. 94–118, The railway towns (Crewe and
Swindon).
pp. 136–48, Behind the Christmas scenes at
Crewe.

6379 GROCOTT, F. W. The story of New Street;
issued by British Railways, London Midland
Region, to commemorate the centenary of
the opening of Birmingham New Street
Station, 1st June, 1854. [*London*, 1954.] pp.
16, with 15 illus. & a map.   BM

*6380 HOLT, G. O. A short history of the Liver-
pool & Manchester Railway. *Bingley:
LM Railway & Canal Historical Society*, September 1955. pp. 21[22], with a map. *Reproduced typescript.*   BR

*6381 RIMMER, A. The Cromford & High Peak
Railway. *Lingfield: Oakwood Press*, 1957.
pp. 36, with illus., maps, & gradient profile.
[*Locomotion Papers*, no. 10.]   BM
—— rev. edn. *Lingfield: Oakwood Press*,
1962. pp. 36.   BM

6382 RICHARDS, P. S. Some geographical aspects of the construction of the London &
LB Birmingham Railway and its influence on the
b growth of towns along the route. M.A.
Thesis, Univ. Lond., 1957. pp. 265, xvi,
with a bibliography. *Typescript.*   BR

6383 CLARKE, M. L. Britannia Park. *Caernarvon: Caernarvonshire Historical Society*,
CH [1958.] pp. 54–60, with 33 bibliogr. notes &
a map.   BR
Reprint, *Trans. C.H.S.*, 1958, vol. 19.
The Chester & Holyhead's plan for the
creation of a ninety-acre residential estate.

6384 STEPHENSON LOCOMOTIVE SOCIETY—
MIDLAND AREA. Photographic Souvenir and
historical notes in connection with the last
train on the Abergavenny–Merthyr Line . . .
5th January 1958. *Birmingham*, [1958.] pp.
[12,] with illus., map, & gradient profile. SL

6385 [CLINKER, C. R.] The Cromford & High
Peak Railway. *Rugby*, May 1959. pp. 4[5].
Reproduced typescript.   pc
Historical notes produced for a tour by the
Railway & Canal Historical Society.

6386 NOCK, O. S. The London & North Western Railway. *London: Ian Allan,* 1960. pp. 232, with col. frontis., 64 illus. on 30 plates, maps & tables. BM

By mischance, the index and inserted map were omitted from the first issues.

6387 CLINKER, C. R. London & North Western Railway: a chronology of opening and closing
c dates of lines and stations, including joint, worked and associated undertakings, 1900–1960. Compiled by C. R. Clinker. *Dawlish: David & Charles,* 1961. pp. 32. BM

6388 GREVILLE, M. D. *and* HOLT, G. O. The Lancaster & Preston Junction Railway. *Dawlish: David & Charles,* 1961. pp. 64, with 3 illus. & a map on 4 plates. BM

6389 STEPHENSON LOCOMOTIVE SOCIETY— NORTH WEST AREA *and* MANCHESTER LOCOMOTIVE SOCIETY. High Peak Rail Tour Itinerary, Saturday, 22nd April, 1961. pp. 7, with map. *Reproduced typescript.* PC

Historical and descriptive notes by G. J. Aston.

6390 STEPHENSON LOCOMOTIVE SOCIETY— NORTH WEST AREA *and* MANCHESTER LOCOMOTIVE SOCIETY. The High Peak Railtour, Saturday 30th September, 1961. Itinerary and historical notes (by G. J. Aston). pp. 8. *Reproduced typescript.* PC

6391 ATKINSON, F. G. B. *and* ADAMS, B. W. London's North Western Electric: a jubilee history. *Sidcup: Electric Railway Society,* 1962. pp. 48, with 16 illus. on 4 plates, lists, map & plan. [*E.R.S. Monograph series,* no. 1.] BM

General history and a detailed analysis of rolling stock, liveries, numberings, etc.

6392 GADSDEN, E. J. S. The Aylesbury Railway. [*Pinner:*] *Bledlow Press,* 1962. pp. 36[38], with 10 illus. & a map. *Reproduced typescript.* BM

6393 HARMAN, R. G. The Conway Valley Railway. *Teddington: Branch Line Handbooks,* 1963. pp. 25[27], with 5 illus., 4 diagrams, & 2 maps. *Reproduced typescript.* [*Branch Line Handbooks,* no. 17.] BM

6393a HODGKINS, D. J. The origins and in-
b dependent years of the Cromford & High Peak Railway. *In* 'Journal of Transport History', vol. 6, no. 1, May 1963. pp. 39–55, with 42 bibliogr. notes. BM

6393b TUPLIN, W. A. North Western Steam. *London: Allen & Unwin,* 1963. pp. 251, with frontis., 58 illus. (incl. 42 on 16 plates) & 4 tables. BM

Contemporaneous

6394 LIVERPOOL & MANCHESTER RLY. Proceedings of the Committee of the House of
LM Commons on the Liverpool & Manchester Railroad Bill, Session 1825. *London,* [1825.] pp. xi, 772, with fold. maps & plans. BM

Minutes of Evidence and cases of petitioners.

6395 LIVERPOOL & MANCHESTER RLY. A synopsis of the proceedings necessary in
LM soliciting the Bill; with observations. *Liverpool,* [c. 1825.] pp. 24. LSE

6396 SANDARS, J. A letter on the subject of the projected rail road between Liverpool and
LM Manchester, pointing out the necessity for its adoption and the manifest advantages it offers to the public; with an exposure of the exorbitant and unjust charges of the water carriers. *Liverpool,* [1824.] pp. 32. ICE
—— 2nd edn. *Liverpool,* [1824.] pp. 32. ICE
—— 3rd, *Liverpool,* [1825.] pp. 46. BM
—— 5th, *Liverpool,* [1825?] pp. 46. BM

6397 A SHORT statement of the advantages offered to the public by the proposed railroad
LM between Liverpool and Manchester. *Liverpool,* 1825.

A broadside, with map.

*6398 SYLVESTER, C. Report on rail-roads and locomotive engines, addressed to the Chair-
LM man of the Committee of the Liverpool & Manchester projected Rail-Road. *Liverpool,* 1825. pp. 39. LSE

Findings of 'an examination of the locomotive engines of the Killingworth and Hetton collieries'.

—— 2nd edn. *Liverpool,* 1825. pp. 39. BM

6399 DESCRIPTION of the tunnel of the Liverpool & Manchester Railway . . . *Liverpool: T.*
LM *Bean,* [1829.] pp. 11. BM

Reprinted from the *Albion,* 20 July, 1829.

6400 HILL, T. A supplement to the short treatise on railroads generally, explaining particu-
LM larly the Liverpool and Manchester, also the Leeds, Selby and Hull rail-roads; the consequent great change that will be effected by them . . . and which will shew that horse-power is cheaper, preferable & more expeditious than locomotive engines . . . *Leeds,* 1829. pp. 16, with 2 diagrams & a map. ICE

6401 TELFORD, T. Liverpool & Manchester Railway. Mr. Telford's report to the Com-
LM missioners for the Loan of Exchequer Bills; with observations in reply by the directors of the said rail-way. *Liverpool,* 1829. pp. 16, with plans. ICE

Describes terrain and engineering works.

6402 WALKER, J. *and* RASTRICK, J. U. Liverpool & Manchester Railway. Report to the
LM directors on the comparative merits of locomotive and fixed engines as a moving power. *Liverpool,* 1829. pp. 80, with diagrams. BM

In favour of fixed engines. As a result of the Rainhill Trials, locomotives were, however, adopted. (See *Observations on the comparative merits of locomotive and fixed engines as applied to railways, being a reply to the report of Mr.*

James Walker to the directors of the Liverpool & Manchester Rly., by R. Stephenson & J. Locke (1830).)

—— 2nd edn. By J. Walker. *London.* 1829. pp. vii, 50.   UL(GL)

—— 2nd edn. By J. U. Rastrick. *Birmingham*, 1829. pp. vii, 46.   ICE

—— another edn. By J. Walker, with 'Observations on the comparative merits . . .', by R. Stephenson & J. Locke, and 'An account of the Liverpool & Manchester Railway' by Henry Booth. *Philadelphia*, 1831. pp. 206, with frontis., plates and plan.   LSE

6403 BETHELL, W. History of the origin, rise, and progress of the Liverpool & Manchester
LM Railway. (Bethell's Broad Sheet, no. 1.) *Liverpool*, [1830.] s.sh.   BM

*6404 BOOTH, H. An account of the Liverpool & Manchester Railway, comprising a history
LM of the parliamentary proceedings preparatory to the passing of the Act, a description of the railway in an excursion from Liverpool to Manchester, and a popular illustration of the mechanical principles applicable to railways; also, an abstract of the expenditure from the commencement of the undertaking, with observations on the same. *Liverpool*, [1830.] pp. 104, with frontis., 8 plates & a fold. map.   BM

—— 2nd edn. *Liverpool*, 1831. pp. 104, with frontis., fold. map & 1 fold. plate. ICE

—— another edn. with 'Report to the directors of the Liverpool & Manchester Railway' by James Walker. *Philadelphia*, 1831. pp. 123, 98.   LSE

—— Chemin der fer de Liverpool à Manchester: notice historique. *Paris*, 1831. pp. 92.

—— Eight views illustrating the Liverpool & Manchester Railway and the engines and carriages employed upon it. [*Chester*, 1830.] 8 plates, each referring to the relevant page in H. Booth's text.   SL

6405 CORDIER, M. J. Considérations sur les chemins de fer . . . *Paris*, 1830. pp. lxxvi, 191,
LM with tables, maps and diagrams.   BM
pp. 1–146, 'Considérations sur le chemin de fer de Liverpool à Manchester'.

6406 COSTE, L. *and* PERDONNET, A. Mémoire sur les chemins à ornières. *Paris*, 1830. pp.
LM 200, with 3 fold. plates.   BM
Reprinted, with additions, from *Annales des Mines*, 2me. série, tom. VI, 1829.
Railways generally, the Rainhill Trial, and the L. & M. Rly.

6407 [LONDON & BIRMINGHAM RLY.] Considerations as to the proposed rail road be-
LB tween London and Birmingham, there to communicate with the intended Birmingham & Liverpool Rail Road. [*London*, April 7, 1830.] s.sh. *Reproduced from hand-writing.*

6408 A GUIDE to the Liverpool & Manchester

LM Railway, with a history of the work, and an estimate of its expense; with a map of the railway. *Liverpool*, 1830. pp. 15, with a plate.   BM

—— 3rd edn. *Liverpool*, 1830. pp. 16. LSE

6409 STEPHENSON, R. *and* LOCKE, J. Observations on the comparative merits of locomotive
LM and fixed engines as applied to railways: being a reply to the report of Mr. James Walker to the directors of the Liverpool & Manchester Railway, compiled from the reports of Mr. George Stephenson; with an account of the competition of locomotive engines at Rainhill in October 1829, and of the subsequent experiments. *Liverpool*, [1830.] pp. viii, 83, with frontis.   LSE
A reply to the reports of J. Walker and J. U. Rastrick, who both favoured fixed engines.

6410 Das GRÖSSTE Wunderwerk unsere Zeit; oder, Die Eisenbahn für Dampfwagen zwi-
LM schen Liverpool und Manchester, in England. *Nuremberg*, 1831. pp. 8, with 13 plates. PO

6411 HUSKISSON, W. The speeches of . . . William Huskisson; with a biographical
LM memoir . . . *London*, 1831. 3 vols.   BM
vol. 1, pp. 223–50, an account of his fatal accident.

6412 'INVESTIGATOR.' Remarks on the proposed railway between Birmingham and London,
LB proving by facts and arguments that that work would cost seven millions and a half, that it would be a burden upon the trade of the Country, and would never pay. *London*, 1830. pp. 116.   UL(GL)

—— 2nd edn. 'Beware the Bubbles!!!: remarks on proposed railways . . .' *London*, 1831. pp. viii, 116.   LSE

6413 CAPPER, C. H. Observations on 'Investiga-
LM tor's' pamphlet, relative to railways. *London*,
LB 1831. pp. iv, 28, with tables.   BM
A reply to *Remarks on the proposed railway between Birmingham & London*, by 'Investigator', upholding the merits of railways and accusing 'Investigator' of misrepresenting the L. & M. Rly.

6414 KIRWAN, J. A descriptive and historical account of the Liverpool & Manchester
LM Railway from its first projection to the present time, containing all the facts and information that have yet appeared on the subject, with numerous interesting and curious original details, estimates of expenses, etc., etc. *Glasgow*, 1831. pp. 32, with illus., tables & charts.   BM

—— 2nd edn. *Glasgow*, 1831. pp. 32. ICE

6415 OBSERVATIONS on railways, particularly on the proposed London & Birmingham Rail-
LB way. *London & Birmingham*, 1831. pp. 20.
                                          BM

6416 The PROBABLE effects of the proposed railway from Birmingham to London considered.
LB *London*, 1831. pp. 50.   BM
Warnings: canals preferable.

6417 REMARKS upon the pamphlet by 'Investigator' on the proposed railway between Birmingham and London. By a Subscriber to the Railway. *London*, 1831. pp. 32. BM
LB
In support of the L. & B. Rly.

6418 LONDON & Birmingham Railway: address of a shareholder to owners and occupiers of land upon the proposed line. 1831. pp.[4.]
LB
BIRMINGHAM PL

* 6419 SHAW, I. Views of the most interesting scenery on the line of the Liverpool & Manchester Railway, and of other objects of public interest connected with it; from drawings taken on the spot expressly for this work and engraved by I. Shaw . . . *Liverpool*, 1831. pp. 12. BM
LM
pp. 5–8, 'Historical epitome of the L. & M. Rly.'
pp. 9–12, Description of the plates.

* 6420 BURY, T. T. Six coloured views on the Liverpool & Manchester Railway, with a plate of the coaches, machines, etc.; from drawings made on the spot by Mr. T. T. Bury. *London: R. Ackermann*, 1831.
LM
—— another edn. 'Coloured views on the Liverpool & Manchester Railway, with plates of the coaches, machines, etc. . . .; with descriptive particulars, serving as a guide to travellers on the railway.' *London*, 1831. pp. 8, with 15 col. plates (2 fold.). BM
—— another edn. *London*, 1832. pp. 8, with 6 plates.
—— another edn. *London*, 1832. pp. 8, with 13 plates. BM
—— another edn. *London*, 1833. pp. 8, with 13 plates. LSE
—— another edn. 'Six coloured views . . .' *London*, 1837. 6 plates. G
For a detailed analysis of editions and variants, see *The Liverpool & Manchester Railway* by C. F. Dendy Marshall. (*Transactions of the Newcomen Society*, vol. 2, 1921–2.)

6421 A HISTORY and description of the Liverpool & Manchester Railway (to which is prefixed a lithographic sketch of the engines & carriages, with a section of the line of railway from Liverpool to Manchester). *Liverpool: T. Taylor*, 1832. pp. 71, with fold. diagram. BM
LM

6422 LIVERPOOL & MANCHESTER RLY. Answer of the directors to an article [by Dr. D. Lardner] in the 'Edinburgh Review' for October 1832. *Liverpool*, 1832. pp. 32. PC
LM
Signed 'Charles Lawrence, Chairman'.
pp. 18–32, Letter from Hardman Earle, a director, to D. Lardner.

* 6423 LONDON & BIRMINGHAM RLY. Extracts from the Minutes of Evidence given before the Committee of the Lords on the London & Birmingham Railway Bill. *London*, 1832. pp. viii, 65, with la. fold. map. BM
LB

6424 LONDON & BIRMINGHAM RLY. Meeting of Peers, Members of the House of Commons, and other persons favourably disposed to the undertaking, held at the Thatched House Tavern . . . 13 July 1832 . . . Lord Wharncliffe in the chair. *London*, 1832. pp. 3.
LB

6425 LONDON & BIRMINGHAM RLY. Observations on the proposed railway from London to Birmingham. (Observations explanatory of the plan.) *London*, February 1832. pp.[4.
LB

* 6426 WALKER, J. S. An accurate description of the Liverpool & Manchester Railway: the tunnels, the bridges, and other works throughout the line . . . *Liverpool*, 1830. pp. 46, with fold. plan (frontis.). BM
LM
This first edition is dated 13th Sept. The line was opened on the 15th.
—— 2nd edn. '. . . with an account of the opening of the railway and the melancholy accident which occurred; a short memoir of the late . . . Wm. Huskisson and particulars of the funeral procession . . .' *Liverpool*, 1830. pp. 52. LSE
—— 3rd, *Liverpool*, 1831. pp. 52. BM
—— 3rd, '. . . [with a description of] the branch railways to St. Helens, Warrington, Wigan, and Bolton.' *Liverpool*, 1832. pp. 53. BM
The author, James Scott Walker, is not James Walker, the engineer who with J. U. Rastrick had recommended fixed engines and cable haulage in preference to locomotives for the railway. Some comment on J. S. Walker and this present work may be found in *Lancashire authors and orators*, by John Evans (1850).

6427 CUCHETET, C. Voyage de Manchester à Liverpool par le raill-way et la voiture à vapeur, extrait d'un voyage en Angleterre pendant l'anneé, 1831. *Louviers*, 1833. pp. 23.
LM

6428 LIVERPOOL & MANCHESTER RLY. Rules and regulations to be observed by enginemen, guards, policemen, and other servants of the company. March 1833. pp. 10.
LM

6429 MOREAU, P. *and* NOTRÉ, A. Description raisonnée et vues pittoresques du chemin de fer de Liverpool à Manchester, publiées par P. Moreau, . . . d'après son examen sur les lieux, les renseignemens fournis par M. Stephenson, . . . et les documens tirés des ouvrages de ce dernier, de M. Wood, etc., et mis en ordre par Auguste Notré. *Paris*, 1831. pp. 98, with 12 plates (2 fold.) & fold. map. LSE
LM
—— Eng. trans. by J. C. Stocker. 'Description of the railroad from Liverpool to Manchester . . .' *Boston, Mass.*, 1833. pp. 94.

6430 'OBSERVER.' Thoughts on railways and projected railways. By Observer. *Liverpool*, 1833. pp. 15. ICE
Reasons against the proposed extension of

the Manchester, Bolton & Bury Rly. to the north end of Liverpool and against a rival line to the Liverpool & Manchester Rly.

6431 The RAILWAY Companion, describing an
LM excursion along the Liverpool line, accompanied with a succinct and popular history of the rise and progress of rail-roads, illustrated by several lithographic views. By a Tourist. *London*, 1833. pp. 46, with 5 fold. plates.
BM

6432 CORT, R. Rail-road impositions detected;
LM or, Facts and arguments to prove that the Manchester and Liverpool Railway has not paid one per cent nett profit, and that the Birmingham, Bristol, Southampton, Windsor and other railways are, and must for ever be, only bubble speculations. (part 1.) *London*, 1834. pp. 64[72], with tables & notes.   LSE
—— 2nd edn. (part 2.) *London*, 1834. pp. 195.   BM
    pp. 9–60, The L. & M. Rly.

—— German edn. 'Der Aufgedeckte Eisenbahnbetrug . . .' 1834.

6433 DESCRIPTIVE Catalogue of the padorama
LM [panorama] of the Manchester & Liverpool Road, containing 10,000 square feet of canvass [sic], now exhibiting at Baker Street, Portman Square, illustrated with twelve lithographic views taken on the spot by artists of acknowledged talent. *London*, 1834. pp. 16.   LSE

6434 EVERETT, J. Panorama of Manchester and Railway Companion. *Manchester*, 1834.
LM pp. viii, 258.   BR
    pp. 188–211, The L. & M. Rly.

6435 GRAHAME, T. A letter to the traders and carriers on the navigations connecting Liver-
LM pool and Manchester, showing the easy means they possess of establishing, on the navigations between these towns, an elegant and comfortable conveyance for passengers at the rate of ten miles an hour, at fares only one-fourth of those on the railway, and the means they possess of conveying goods between Liverpool and Manchester with despatch equal to that of the railway, at a charge lower than the bare railway outlays. *Glasgow*, 1833. pp. 29.   H
—— 2nd edn. *Glasgow*, 1834. pp. 36.   BM

6436 BARLOW, P. Experiments on the transverse strength and other properties of malleable
LB iron, with reference to its uses for railway bars, and a report founded on the same addressed to the directors of the London & Birmingham Railway Company. *London*, 1835. pp. 97.   ICE
—— French edn. Expériences sur la force transversale et les autres propriétés du fer maléable dans son application aux chemins de fer . . . *Paris*, 1838. pp. 151.   BM

6437 CUNDY, N. W. Observations on railways
LM . . . *Yarmouth*, 1834. pp. 55.   BM
    The L. & M. Rly. discussed.
—— 2nd edn. *Yarmouth*, 1835. pp. 59. BM

6438 VIGNOLES, C. B. *and* LOCKE, J. Two reports addressed to the Liverpool & Man-
LM chester Railway Co., on the projected north line of railway from Liverpool to the Manchester, Bolton & Bury Canal, near Manchester; with estimates . . . *Liverpool*, 1835. pp. 32.   ICE

6439 BIRMINGHAM, BRISTOL & THAMES JUNCTION RLY. Observations upon and answers to certain erroneous statements circulated against the proposed Birmingham, Bristol & Thames Junction Railway. (March 21, 1836.) *London*, [1836.] pp. 3.
BM
    Signed by William Gunston, chairman of the Provisional Committee.

6440 BOOTH, H. A letter to His Majesty's Commissioners on Railways in Ireland, in reply
LM to a communication from H. D. Jones, Esq., Secretary to the Commissioners. *Liverpool*, 1836. pp. 12.   UL(GL)
    Advice based on experience of six years' working of the L. & M., and an invitation to the Commissioners to come to see the line for themselves.

6441 FREELING, A. Lacey's Railway Companion and Liverpool and Manchester Guide, des-
LM cribing all the scenery on, and contiguous to, the rail-way . . . *Liverpool*, [1836.] pp. 70.
LSE

6442 STEVENSON, D. Observations on the Liverpool & Manchester Railway, with remarks
LM on the Dublin & Kingstown Railway. [*Edinburgh*,] 1836. pp. 16, with 3 plates. ICE
    From *Transactions of the Society of Arts for Scotland*, as published in the *Edinburgh New Philosophical Journal*, March 1835.
    Descriptions of both railways (pp. 1–10, L. & M.; pp. 11–16, D. & K.).

6443 A VOICE from Cheltenham, addressed to all whom it may concern, and in particular to the shareholders in the Cheltenham & Oxford and London & Birmingham Union Railway Company. By One of Themselves. *London*, [1836.] pp. 46.   ICE
    Signed 'A Shareholder in the Tring Co.' and dated 5 Nov., 1836.
    'We have been grossly misled and deluded.' Relating to a proposed railway from Cheltenham to London via Tring.

6444 BARLOW, P. Second report addressed to the directors and proprietors of the London
LM & Birmingham Railway Company, founded
LB on an inspection of, and experiments made on, the Liverpool & Manchester Railway. *London*, 1835. pp. 67, 82–116, with illus., tables & diagrams.   ICE
    A technical report on the permanent way of the L. & M. Rly.

—— 2nd edn. 'Report on the weight of

rails, the description of chairs and fastenings, the distance of the support and the size
of blocks, of the Liverpool & Manchester
Railway.' *London*, 1837. pp. 116.   ICE

6445 A CTS relating to the London & Birmingham
Railway . . . with a general index. *London:
Eyre & Spottiswoode*, 1837. pp. 440. UL(GL)
Reprints of three Acts.

6446 FREELING, A. The London & Birmingham
Railway Companion . . . *London*, [1837.] pp.
LB   xi, 204, 32, with fold. map.   H

6447 GRAND JUNCTION RLY. Case of the Grand
Junction Railway Company as opponents of
GJ   the South Union Company. [*Liverpool*,
1837.] pp. [3,] with map.   H

6448 GARNETT, W. Answer to the 'Case of the
Grand Junction Railway Company as op-
GJ   ponents of the Manchester South Union
Railway Company'. *London*, 1837. pp. 15.
LSE
W. Garnett was chairman of the M.S.U. Rly.

6449 BOOTH, H. An account of the Liverpool
& Manchester Railway. *In* 'Remarks on the
LM   comparative merits of cast metal and malleable iron railways', by Michael Longridge
and John Birkinshaw. [2nd] edn., 1832. BM
—— [3rd] edn., 1838.   BM

6450 BOOTH, H. Liverpool & Manchester Rail-
way. Extracted by permission from 'An
LM   account of the Liverpool & Manchester
Railway' by Henry Booth . . . [1838.] pp. 38.
BM

*6451 COGHLAN, F. The Iron Road Book and
Railway Companion from London to Birm-
GJ   ingham, Manchester and Liverpool . . .
LB   times of arrival and departure of the trains
. . . illustrated with maps of the entire line.
London, 1838. pp. 180.   BM
—— 2nd edn. '. . . corrected to the opening
of the entire line.' *London*, [1838.] pp. iv,
64, 104, 18, with frontis., 6 maps & table.
BM

*6452 CORNISH, J. The Grand Junction and
Liverpool & Manchester Railway Compan-
GJ   ion, containing . . . the company's charges
LM   from one station to another, with their regulations, time of departure & arrival of each
train. *Birmingham & London*, 1837. pp. 110,
with fold. map & fold. table.
—— 2nd edn. *Birmingham & London*, 1837.
pp. 172.   BM
—— 3rd edn. *London*, 1838. pp. 216.   BM

*6453 DRAKE, J. Drake's Road Book of the
Grand Junction Railway from Birmingham
GJ   to Liverpool and Manchester. *Birmingham*,
[1837.] pp. xvi, 184, with fold. map. (pp.
109–84, adverts.)   BM
—— 2nd edn. *London*, [1838.] pp. vi, 147,

with engravings of scenes on the line, & a
fold. table of fares, distances & regulations.
LSE

6454 FREELING, A. Freeling's Railway Companion from London to Birmingham, Liver-
GJ   pool and Manchester . . . and fare tables . . .
LB   *London*, [1838.] pp. 36, 200, 36, with fold.
map of the G.J. Rly.   BM
—— another edn. *London*, [1838.] pp. vii,
36, 204.   BM
—— new edn. *London*, 1838. pp. 192.   BR

6455 FREELING, A. The Grand Junction Railway Companion to Liverpool, Manchester
GJ   and Birmingham . . . including a complete
description of every part of the rail-road . . .
Liverpool, 1837. pp. iv, 228, viii, with fold.
map.   H
—— another edn. '. . . containing narrative
of the parliamentary history of the project.'
London, 1838. pp. 192, 32[36].   LSE

6456 GRAND JUNCTION RLY. [Correspondence
between the Grand Junction Railway and
GJ   the directors of the Manchester & Birmingham Railway.] *Liverpool*, [1838.] pp. 48.
ICE

6457 LOCKE, J. London & Glasgow Railway by
Penrith . . . Mr. Locke's report to the provisional committee of the proposed railway
from Lancaster to Carlisle. *Penrith*, 1838.
pp. 8.

6458 LONGRIDGE, M. [*and* BIRKINSHAW, J.]
Remarks on the comparative merits of cast
LM   metal and malleable iron rail-ways, and an
account of the Stockton & Darlington Rail-
way and the Liverpool & Manchester Rail-
way. *Newcastle*, 1832. pp. 26, 39, 38.   PO
The section on the L. & M. Rly. is by Henry
Booth.

—— another edn. *Newcastle*, 1838. pp. 32,
38, 38.   SL

6459 RAILROADIANA; a new history of England;
or, Picturesque, biographical, historical,
LB   legendary and antiquarian sketches, descriptive of the vicinity of the railroads. First
series, with a map and illustrations. London
and Birmingham Railway. *London*, 1838.
pp. 216, with 8 plates & fold. map in pocket.
BM
—— 2nd edn. *London*, 1838. pp. 212.   BM

6460 STURGE, J. To the proprietors of the
London & Birmingham Railway. *Birming-
LB   ham*, January 26, 1838. pp. 2.   BM
Asking shareholders not to allow trains to
run on Sundays.

6461 WALLIS, E. *publisher*. The London, Birm-
ham, Liverpool and Manchester railways
. . . Sketch of the origin and progress of the
railways. *London*, [1838.] s.sh. fol., with 10
illus.   BM (P & D)

6462 WYLD, J. Wyld's Guide to the Grand
GJ Junction and Liverpool & Manchester Rail-
LM ways, containing a complete map and
description of the routes, and rules, regulations, fares, times of departure and arrival
. . . *London*, [1838.] pp. 36, viii, xiii, 179,
with fold. map. UL(GL)

6463 W[YLD], J. W. The London & Birmingham
Railway Guide, and Birmingham & London
LB Railway Companion; containing a minute
description of the railroad . . . By J. W. W.
London, 1838. pp. viii, xiii, 179, with illus.
& fold. maps (incl. frontis.). BM

6464 ARMENGAUD, J. E. *and* C. L'Industrie des
chemins de fer; ou, Dessins et descriptions
LM des principales machines locomotives . . .
wagons de transports . . . en usage sur les
routes en fer de la France, d'Angleterre . . .
Paris, 1839. pp. 174. BM
Includes the L. & M. Rly.

6465 BOURNE, J. C. Drawings of the London &
Birmingham Railway . . . with an historical
LB and descriptive account by John Britton . . .
London, 1839. pp. 26. BM
Thirty plates and many important notes.

6466 BREES, S. C. Appendix to Railway Prac-
tice, containing a copious abstract of the
LB whole of the Evidence given upon the
London & Birmingham and Great Western
Railway Bills . . . *London*, 1839. pp. vii, 373.
BM

6467 CORNISH, S. & Co. Cornish's Guide and
Companion to the London & Birmingham
LB Railway, containing . . . the company's
charges for conveyance, time of starting each
train, etc., etc. *London*, 1839. pp. v, 18, 65–
72, 6–90, 12. BM

6468 GROOMBRIDGE, R., *publisher*. A Handbook for Travellers along the London and
LB Birmingham Railway . . . embellished with
twenty-five fine engravings on wood, and a
map of the line . . . *London*, [1839.] pp. 147,
with 23 plates. BM

6469 LIVERPOOL & MANCHESTER RLY. The
Treasurer's report to the directors on the
LB comparative disbursements of the London &
LM Birmingham and Liverpool & Manchester
railways. *Liverpool*, 1839. pp. 21[23].

6470 LONDON & BIRMINGHAM RLY. Tables of
fares and rates, distances and regulations
LB . . . with a map of the line. *London*, 1838.
pp. 32. BM
—— new edn. *London*, August, 1839. pp. 32.

6471 MANCHESTER & BIRMINGHAM RLY. Correspondence between the Manchester &
GJ Birmingham and the Grand Junction railway companies . . . [*Manchester*, 1839.]
pp. xvi, 58. LSE
Introduction by Thomas Ashton, Chairman.

6472 MANSELL, G. The London, Birmingham,
Liverpool & Manchester Railway Guide,
LB giving a description of the entire route from
London to Birmingham, with the fares &
rates, and time of starting from London to
Birmingham. *London*, [1839.] pp. 9[12].
UL(GL)
London to Birmingham only described.

6473 ON the opening of the Grand Junction
Railway between Birmingham and Man-
GJ chester, July 20, 1837. *In* 'Essays critical and
miscellaneous, with extracts from a tourist's
journal' by the author of 'Essays on subjects of general interest'. *London*, 1839. pp.
164–70. BM
Dated Paris, July 25, 1837.

6474 'PUBLICOLA.' A letter to a Member of
Parliament on the subject of the proposed
Manchester & Birmingham Extension Rail-
way. *London*, [May 1839.] pp. 33. PC
Opposing the construction of fifty-four miles
of new railway to shorten the journey from
Manchester to London by twelve miles.

6475 ROSCOE, T. The Book of the Grand Junction Railway: being a history and descrip-
GJ tion of the line from Birmingham to Liverpool and Manchester; with sixteen engravings and four maps. *London*, 1839. pp.
154[157], with fold. frontis., plates & maps.
BM

6476 [ROSCOE, T.] Home and country scenes
on each side of the line of the London &
GJ Birmingham, and Grand Junction railways;
LB with steel plates and numerous wood en-
gravings. *London*, [1839.] pp. 104, 136. LSE
The two parts were also issued separately.

6477 REMARKS on the construction put on certain
clauses of the London & Birmingham Rail-
LB road Act [3 Will. IV, *c.* 36, 1833]. 1839.
pp. 16. BIRMINGHAM PL

6478 SHARPE, E. Correspondence between Ed-
mund Sharpe, Esq., and the directors of the
Lancaster and Preston Junction Railway
Company. *Lancaster*, 1839. pp. 31. H

6479 STEPHENSON, G. Report . . . on the com-
parative merits of the railway from Chester
CH to Holyhead, and of that from Wolverhamp-
ton to Porthdynllaen. *Chester*, 1839. pp. 8.
BM
Addressed to the directors of the Chester &
Crewe Rly. and preferring the Chester to Holy-
head route.

6480 THOMAS, J., *publisher*. Railroad Guide
from London to Birmingham, containing
LB picturesque, historical, legendary and statistical sketches of its vicinity. 3rd edn. *London*,
1839. pp. 236, with 8 plates & map. H

6481 CORNISH, S. & Co. Cornish's Stranger's
Guide through Liverpool and Manchester,

LM with the Traveller's Companion on the Rail-road, and an accurate engraving of the line of road, a section of the line . . . *London*, [1840.] pp. 108.   BM

6482 DRAKE, J. Drake's Road Book of the London & Birmingham, and Grand Junction
GJ   railways, . . . *London*, [1839.] pp. vi, 112,
LB   with illus., 2 fold. maps (col.) & fold. time-table.   BM
—— another edn. *London*, [1840.] pp. vi, 147.   BR

6483 OSBORNE, E. C. *and* OSBORNE, W. Osborne's Guide to the Grand Junction, or
GJ   Birmingham, Liverpool & Manchester Rail-way . . . *London*, 1838. pp. iv, 378, with map.
                                            BM
     Contains history, regulations, etc., of the G.J. Rly.
—— 2nd edn. *Birmingham*, 1838. pp. iv, 347.   BM
—— 3rd, *Birmingham*, 1840. pp. viii, 252.
                                            BM

6484 OSBORNE, E. C. *and* OSBORNE, W. Osborne's London & Birmingham Railway
LB   Guide; illustrated with numerous engrav-ings and maps. *Birmingham*, [1840.] pp. viii, 270.   BM
     Contains much railway information.

6485 BROOKS, R. The London & Birmingham Railway Pocket Book . . . *London*, 1841. pp.
LB   128.   BM

6486 The CARRIERS' case considered in reference
GJ   to railways. *London*, 1841. pp. 36.   BM
     The G. J. Rly. attempting to monopolise carriers: protective legislation called for.

6487 The RIVAL Rails; or, Reply to the 'Remarks on the proposed railway between England and Scotland'. *Carlisle*, 1841, pp. 40, with tables.   LSE
     Clydesdale route, Lancaster via Carlisle to Edinburgh, preferable to East Coast Route: (pp. 35–40, reports of meetings).

6488 SKEY, R. S. Report to the Committee of the Birmingham & Liverpool Junction Canal,
GJ   on the present state of the competition be-tween the canal carriers using that line and the Grand Junction Railway Company, with suggestions for a more economical working of the canal. *Westminster*, 1841. pp. 25. BM

6489 CLEATHER, E. J. Manchester & Leeds, and Manchester & Birmingham Railway. *Man-chester*, 1843. s.sh.   LSE
     A dispute arising from a statement by the M. & L. in the *Manchester Guardian*, 7 March. The author writes 'by order of the M. & B. Board'.

6490 CORRESPONDENCE between the Man-chester & Birmingham Railway Company and the General Post Office with reference to the conveyance of the mails between Man-chester and Crewe. [*Manchester*, 1843.] pp. 36.   LSE
     Forty-three letters.

6491 CORRESPONDENCE between the Man-chester & Birmingham Railway Company and Thomas Grimsditch, M.P. for the Borough of Macclesfield. [*Manchester*, 1843.] pp. 12.   LSE

6492 FITZWILLIAM, C. W. W. Two letters by . . . Earl Fitzwilliam on the railway from Blisworth to Peterborough, containing also his . . . opinion upon the advantages of an extension of the Northern & Eastern Rail-way. *London*, 1843. pp. vi, 12.

6493 GREIG, T. The Manchester & Leeds and Manchester & Birmingham railway com-panies: an elucidation of the conduct of the directors of these companies in the matter of the Hunt's Bank Junction; with copies of their letters . . . *Manchester*, 1843. pp. 22.
                                            BM
     With extracts from reports and newspapers. An alleged breach of agreement by the M. & L. directors.

6494 NORTHAMPTON & Peterborough Railway: reply to the allegations of a petition circu-lated by the opponents of the measure. *Lon-don*, [1843.] pp. 12.   NORTHAMPTON PL

6495 REMARKS on the proceedings in the Com-mittee on the Northampton & Peterborough Railway Bill. *London*, [1843.] pp. 39, with map.   NORTHAMPTON PL

6496 The WONDERFUL effects of the Peter-borough & Northampton Railway; or, The pleasure of travelling by hot water. *North-ampton*, [1843.] s.sh.   NORTHAMPTON PL
     A poem.

6497 CHESTER & HOLYHEAD RLY. Details of
CH   bridges and other works. 1844. obl. fol. BM
     Thirty-four plates.

6498 LONDON & BIRMINGHAM RLY.—CREED TESTIMONIAL FUND. Report of the Com-
LB   mittee for conducting the Creed Testimonial Fund, and list of the subscribers. August, 1844. *London*, 1844. pp. 26.
     Richard Creed had been Secretary for four-teen years: 965 contributors gave 2100 guineas.

6499 WORDSWORTH, W. Kendal & Winder-mere Railway: two letters re-printed from the Morning Post; revised, with additions. *Kendal*, [1844.] pp. 23.   BM
     Prefaced by his sonnet 'On the projected Kendal & Windermere Railway'. Also in-cludes his poem, 'Steamboats and Railways'.

6500 A DESCRIPTION of objects occurring on the Northampton and Peterborough Rail-Road. [Cover title.] *Northampton*, 1845. pp. 8.
                              NORTHAMPTON PL

6501 HUGHES, T. Description of the method employed for draining some banks of cut-
LB tings on the London & Croydon, and London & Birmingham railways, and a part of the retaining wall of the Euston incline, London & Birmingham Railway. *London,* 1845. pp. 11. ICE
Excerpt, *Min. Proc. I.C.E.*

6502 CHESTER & HOLYHEAD RLY. Engineer's Report. [By] Robert Stephenson. 9 Febru-
CH ary 1846. [1846.] pp. 2. BM

6503 CHESTER & HOLYHEAD RLY. Statistical memoranda of the Chester & Holyhead
CH Railway: April, 1846. *London,* 1846. pp. 16. BM
'Private and confidential.'
Description of line, gradients, and equipment.

6504 HOPE, *Mr.* Speech of Mr. Hope on behalf of the Huddersfield & Manchester Railway Company, in the Select Committee of the House of Commons on the Huddersfield & Manchester Company's Bradford branch, and on the West Riding Union Railways, on Wednesday 1st July 1846 . . . *Huddersfield,* [1846.] pp. 8. UL(GL)

6505 LETTER to George Carr Glyn [Chairman of the London & Birmingham Railway] on
LB the jeopardy to which the interests of that line are exposed by the parliamentary resolutions of the House of Commons reversing the Gauge Commissioners' Report. By a Proprietor of the London & Birmingham Railway. *London,* 1846. pp. 16. H

6506 MAIR, F. H. The Railway Hand Book; or, The traveller's descriptive guide and companion to the Blisworth, Northampton & Peterboro' Railway. *London,* 1846. pp. 48. BM

6507 The NEW lines of railway between Cheltenham and London promoted by the London & North Western and Great Western companies respectively, considered in reference to the interests of Gloucester and the neighbourhood. By a Gloucester Man. *Gloucester,* 1846. pp. 16. BR
In support of the L. & N.W. Rly.

6508 A FEW observations on a pamphlet entitled 'The new lines of railway between Gloucester and London promoted by the London & North Western and Great Western companies . . .' By Another Gloucester Man. *Gloucester,* 1846. pp. 12. BR
In support of the G.W.R. The pamphlet referred to is, in fact, entitled *The new lines of railway between Cheltenham and London . . . By a Gloucester Man* (1846).

6509 NEWTON, W. E. Notes of the cause tried at the Liverpool Summer Assizes, 1845, between W. E. Newton and the Grand Junction Railway Company for an infringement of Letters Patent for improvements in the construction of boxes for the axeltrees of locomotive engines and carriages . . . *London,* 1845. pp. 186[187]. BM
Includes evidence of several well-known railway engineers.

—— Notes of the hearing and judgement . . . January 29th, 1846. *London,* 1846. pp. 78. BM

6510 REPLY to 'Observations' of the Great Western Railway Company on the Report
LB of the Gauge Commissioners. *London,* 1846. pp. 75. BM
Survey of the gauge controversy; the Inquiry, and attitude of the G.W.R. to its findings; comparative merits of both gauges; the races; and, pp. 61–75, reports to the London & Birmingham Rly.

6511 STEEL, J. Steel's Guide to the Lancaster & Carlisle Railway . . . with time tables . . . *Carlisle,* 1846. pp. 64. BM

6512 STEPHENSON, R. Reports of Mr. Robert Stephenson, Mr. Wm. Fairbairn and Mr. E.
CH Hodgkinson, upon the experiments made to ascertain the practicability of erecting a tubular bridge across the Menai Straits, for the passage of railway trains. *London,* 1846. pp. 20. BM

6513 CARRYING question: remarks on the memorial presented to the Railway Commissioners by some of the merchants of Birmingham. *Manchester,* 1847. pp. 12. LSE
Objections to the L. & N.W. doing its own 'carrying'.

6514 A HISTORY of the Holyhead harbour of refuge, showing the circumstances under
CH which these works originated, their present progress, their probable cost, and questionable utility when completed. Compiled from parliamentary records. [*Liverpool*?] 1847. pp. 32, with map. RIA(H)

6515 SCOTT & BENSON, *publishers.* Handbook to the Lancaster & Carlisle Railway; numerous illustrations and a map of the line. *Carlilse,* 1847. pp. 36. LSE

6516 WILLIAMS, C. W. Remarks on the proposed asylum harbour at Holyhead and the
CH monopoly contemplated by the Chester & Holyhead Railway Co. in a letter addressed to Lord Viscount Sandon. [*London,*] 1847. pp. 46, with 3 la. fold. plates. BM

6517 WILLIAMS, C. W. Further remarks on the proposed asylum harbour at Holyhead and
CH the monopoly contemplated by the Chester & Holyhead Railway Co., in a second letter to Lord Viscount Sandon. [*London,*] 1847. pp. 40, with 3 la. fold. plates. BM

6518 WILLIAMS, C. W. Holyhead Harbour.
CH [*London*, 1847.] pp. 3.   RIA(H)
A letter explaining objections to the Chester & Holyhead Railway's plan for a pier and harbour at Holyhead. Written on behalf of the Steam Ship-Owners Association.

6519 KING, G. Holyhead Harbour. Reply to a letter addressed by Charles Wye Williams
CH to . . . Viscount Sandon, M.P. [*London*,] 1847. pp. 19.   BM

6520 CLEVELAND, R. F. The London & North Western Railway: are railways a good investment? The question considered by an examination of the last half-yearly statements of the six leading companies. *London*, 1848. pp. iv, 53, with financial tables of L.N.W. Rly. for half-year ending 30 June, 1848.   BM
The L. & N.W. only dealt with.

6521 LONDON & NORTH WESTERN RLY. Report of the Rating Committee of the London & North Western Railway Company on the general question of railway rating, and on alterations in the law which are required to protect railway interest. *London*, [1848.] pp. 14.   BR
Dated 27 October, 1848. Privately distributed.

6522 WHITEHEAD, J. Railway management: letter to George Carr Glyn . . . Chairman of the London & North Western Railway Company. 2nd edn. *London*, 1848. pp. 23.   BM
Dated 15 Nov., 1848. Suggested reforms. See 3693.

6523 HUISH, M. Letter to George Carr Glyn . . . Chairman of the London & North Western Rly. Co. on some points of railway management: in reply to a late pamphlet [by John Whitehead] . . . By Mark Huish, General Manager of the L. & N.W. Rly. *London*, 1848. pp. 22.   UL(GL)
See 3693.

6524 WHITEHEAD, J. Railway management: a second letter to George Carr Glyn . . . in reply to Capt. Huish's letter. *London*, 1848. pp. 17.   BM
See 3693.

6525 RAILWAY policy: a letter to George Carr Glyn . . . Chairman of the London & North Western Railway Company, on the correspondence addressed to him by Captain Huish and Mr. John Whitehead. From a Sufferer. *London*, 1848. pp. 12.   BM
See 3693.

6526 CORT, R. Railway reform; in a letter to William Chaplin, Esq., M.P., Chairman of
LM the London & South Western Railway Co., showing that the Liverpool & Manchester Railway Company has not paid a single dividend except out of borrowed money, and that all other railways are, and must be, in the same predicament; with an appendix containing the published accounts of the Liverpool & Manchester Railway Company . . . *London*, 1849. pp. 109.   BM

6527 COTTERILL, C. F. The past, present and future position of the London & North Western, and Great Western Railway companies . . . with an inquiry how far the principle of competing lines in reference to railway undertakings is sound and defensible. *London*, 1849. pp. 56.   BM
Criticism against misleading financial statements, with tables. Government control preferable to competition.

6528 GENERAL description of the Britannia and Conway tubular bridges on the Chester &
CH Holyhead Railway . . . By a Resident Assistant. [Edwin Clark?] *London*, 1849. pp. 34.   BM

6529 GORDON, A. Past and present views of
LM railways. *London*, 1849. pp. 20.   ICE
'. . . the enormity of the deception' [of railways as a means of communication]. Objections to financial methods and policies of railways. A. Gordon reviews and re-affirms statements made in his earlier writings, using the Liverpool & Manchester Railway as an example of financial deception (similar to the more detailed condemnation by Richard Cort in his *Railroad impositions detected* (1834)).

6530 [HEAD, F. B.] Highways and Dry-ways; or, The Britannia and Conway tubular bridges;
CH by the author of 'Stokers and Pokers'. *London*, 1849. pp. 83.   BM
Criticism of Thomas Fairbairn.

6531 HUISH, M. On deterioration of railway plant and road, in two reports to the directors of the London & North Western Railway Company, with prefatory remarks by Mark Huish, General Manager, London & North Western Railway. *London*, 1849. pp. viii, 64.   SL
pp. 3–26, Report to the directors . . . on the present condition of their moveable stock. *London*, June 1848.
pp. [29]–64, Report to the General Works Committee on the present condition of the permanent way . . . *Manchester*, April 1849.

6532 LONDON & NORTH WESTERN RLY. Report upon the cattle traffic on the London & North Western Railway for the year 1849. Printed by order of the Committee. (Private.) [*London*, 1849.] pp. 40.   SL
Addressed to Capt. Huish, General Manager, and signed 'Fisher Ormandy, Manager of Cattle Traffic'. The report has (pp. 34–40) a series of very detailed tables showing the extent of cattle traffic at each station.

6533 LONDON & NORTH WESTERN RLY. Roll of the directors and principal officers of the company, with the various committees and days of meeting. 1849. pp. 11.   BM

6534 MARTIN, R. M. Railways past, present and prospective. *London*, 1849. pp.82.   BM
Railway finance explained to investors; the L.N.W.R. taken as an example.
—— 2nd edn. *London*, 1849. pp. 82.   BM

6535 MORGAN, W. The Chester & Holyhead Railway and its prospects. By W. Morgan, a
CH shareholder. *London,* [1849.] pp. 11.   BM
Urging shareholders not to part with their shares.

*6536 PARRY, E. The Railway Companion from Chester to Holyhead. *London,* 1848. pp.
CH 154.   BM
—— 2nd edn. *London,* [1849.] pp. 158.   BM

6537 POOLE, B. A report to the Road and Traffic Committee of the Northern Division of the Directors of the London & North Western Railway Company on Coal Traffic, ordered 15th June, 1849. [*Liverpool,*] 1849. pp. 21.
BM
The possibilities of increasing coal traffic from Lancashire coalfields.

—— Extracts from a report to the Road & Traffic Committee. [*Liverpool,*] 1849. pp. 11.
BM

6538 WHITEHALL, C. The Buckinghamshire Railway. *Buckingham,* 1849. pp. 36.   BM
A poem.

6539 WHITEHEAD, J. Railway management: the proof! A third letter to George Carr Glyn . . . *London,* 1849. pp. 48.   BM
See 6522–5.

6540 FAIRBAIRN, T. Britannia and Conway tubular bridges. Truths and tubes on self-
CH supporting principles: a few words in reply to the author of 'High-ways and Dry-ways'. [F. B. Head.] *London,* 1849. pp. 62.   BM
A refutation of allegations made against him by F. B. Head. See 6530.

—— 2nd edn. *London,* 1850. pp. 63.   IT

6541 A LETTER addressed to the shareholders in the Chester & Holyhead Railway Company
CH and the London & North Western Railway Company, on the doings of directors in the case of the Chester & Holyhead Railway and the Mold Railway. By a Shareholder. *London,* [1850.] pp. 24, 18–40.   BM
pp. 18–40 at end consists of half-yearly reports nos. 1–11 of the C. & H., 1844–1849, and part of the text is a critical analysis of these, showing how the directors have deceived the shareholders. The author advises against purchasing the Mold Railway.

6542 STEAM SHIP OWNERS ASSOCIATION. Reasons against conceding to the Chester &
CH Holyhead Railway Company power to become a steam ship company with limited liability. [*London,* 1850.] pp. 8.   BM

6543 TURNER, R. Suggestions respectfully submitted by R. Turner of Dublin for the improvement of the Euston Station, London.. *London,* [1850?] pp. 8, with 4 la. fold. plans..   ICE

6544 A FEW words to the shareholders of the North Staffordshire Railway Company, on the true policy of that company, especially in relation to the London & North Western Railway Company. By One of Themselves. *London,* 1851. pp. 18.   BM

*6545 SIDNEY, S. Rides on railways leading to the lake and mountain districts of Cumberland, North Wales, and the dales of Derbyshire; with a glance at Oxford, Birmingham, Liverpool, Manchester, and other manufacturing towns, illustrated by 24 engravings . . . with a correct map of the North Western Railway & its branches. *London,* [1851.] pp. 254.
BM

6546 ALCOCK, T. Observations upon railway management. *Dover: E. Batchelor,* 1852. pp. 39.   NLC
Privately issued.
The L. & N.W. Rly. and George Hudson.

6547 CHESTER & HOLYHEAD RLY. [A printed circular letter announcing 'special tourist
CH facilities & accommodation to persons desirous of visiting Ireland during the present Summer.'] *Dublin,* May 1852. pp.[4,] with map on centre pages.   BM
Signed 'C. P. Roney'.

6548 BROWN, H. Railway accidents, railway amalgamation and railway management, in a series of letters to 'The Morning Chronicle' by 'A Gloucestershire M.P.' *London,* 1853. pp. 45.   BM
Seven letters criticising railway administration generally and the L. & N.W. in particular.

6549 CHESTER & HOLYHEAD RLY. Rules and regulations for the conduct of the traffic and
CH for the guidance of the officers and men in the service of the C. & H. Rly. Co. Revised and corrected to February, 1853. *London,* 1853. pp. 90[91].   LSE

6550 L. & N.W. RLY. [A collection of private and confidential reports, circulated to directors, 1838–1853.]   SL
[1] On deterioration of railway plant and road; or, Two reports to the directors of the London & North Western Railway Company, with prefatory remarks. By Mark Huish. *London,* May 1849. pp. viii, 64.
[a] Report to the directors of the L. & N.W. Rly. Co. on the present condition of their moveable stock. *London,* June 1848 (1849). pp. 26.
[b] Report to the General Works Committee on the present condition of the permanent way . . . *Manchester,* 1849. pp. [29]–64.
[2] Report on the passenger traffic of the L. & N.W. Rly. Co., prepared by order of the Road and Traffic Committees. By Mark Huish. *London,* April 1850. pp. 47, with detailed tables.
[3] Three reports addressed to the General Manager of the L. & N.W. Rly. on the merchandise (1853) traffic of the town and port

of Liverpool. By Braithwaite Poole. *London*, 1853. pp. 33, with map.

[4] Report to the General Locomotive Committee (L. & N.W. Rly.), 5th April 1853. By Edward Woods and William P, Marshall. *London*, 1853. pp. 21, with 8 tables & a fold. table of comparative experiments with engines of the Southern & Northern Divisions, Feb. & March 1853.

[5] Report to the Locomotive Committee on the engines for Southern Division. By J. E. McConnell, Wolverton. *London*, May 1853. pp. 29[30], with tables.

[6] Second report to the General Locomotive Committee, by E. Woods and W. P. Marshall. *London*, May 1853. pp. 22.

[7] Coke. Two reports to the Locomotive Sub-Committee of the Southern Division, 1849 and 1853. By Messrs. Watkin and M'Connell. *London*, 1853. pp. 16.

[8] Report to the Permanent Way Committee on the Renewal Fund. *London*, 1853. pp. 42.

6551 SHAREHOLDER's key to the L. & N.W. Rly., containing full particulars of all the subsidiary and other lines in which the proprietors of the L. & N.W. Rly. are interested. By a member of the Stock Exchange. *London*, 1853. pp. 48, with la. col. map of the railway.
LSE

6552 CLARK, E. Letter to Captain Huish as to proposed improvements in the electric telegraph system for the service of the London & North Western Railway Company. *London: Electric Telegraph Co.*, March 1854. pp. 32, with tables.   BR

6553 MINUTES and correspondence between the London & North Western, Midland, and Manchester, Sheffield & Lincolnshire companies, and the Great Northern Railway Company. *London*, 1856. pp. 47.   BM

6554 A REVIEW of the London & North Western Railway accounts for the last ten years. By a Manchester Shareholder. *Manchester*, 1856. pp. 37.   BM
A detailed critical analysis.

6555 LONDON & NORTH WESTERN RLY. Report of the directors to the shareholders on the subject of the Manchester, Sheffield & Lincolnshire Company's breach of their agreement. *London*, 15 July 1857. pp. 20.BM
—— Further correspondence in continuation of the Report . . . *London*, August 1857. pp. 6.   BM

6556 RAWSON, W. Diary of a director: notes and recollections made during the last fourteen years by W. Rawson . . . late a director of the L. & N.W. Rly. Co. Part 1, addressed to H. W. Wickham, Chairman, & to the shareholders of the Lancashire & Yorkshire Rly. Co. *London*, 1857. pp. 54.   BM
'It shall be the aim of this volume to build up

and not to pull down, to narrate facts connected with the leading mischief to be remedied, and to open a discussion . . .' The Appendix contains a reply from Wickham and an answer to this from Rawson.

* 6557 MEASOM, G. The Official Illustrated Guide to the Lancaster & Carlisle, Edinburgh & Glasgow, and Caledonian railways . . . *London*, 1859. pp. 384, 184, 8, 8, with 150 engravings.   UL(GL)

* 6558 MEASOM, G. The Official Illustrated Guide to the North-Western Railway, including the CH Chester & Holyhead line and all their branches . . . *London*, [1859.] pp. 574, with 300 engravings.   UL(GL)

6559 BURY, E. Recollections of Edward Bury . . . LB by his widow. *Windermere*, [1860?] pp. 24.
    BM
Edward Bury was Locomotive Superintendent of the London & Birmingham Rly.

6560 IMPORTANT facts for the consideration of the shareholders of the London & North Western Railway, from which it is shewn that the dividend for this half-year should be six per-cent instead of five per cent per annum. [1860.] pp. 2.   BM
Signed 'A Shareholder, August 14, 1860'.

6561 LANGLEY, J. B. The dangers of the North British Railway policy; or, A question for the consideration of the inhabitants of Newcastle and the surrounding towns, candidly stated and impartially discussed. Second edn. *Newcastle*, [1861.] pp. 16.   BM
Anti-N.B., pro- L. & N.W.

6562 LONDON & NORTH WESTERN RAILWAY SHAREHOLDERS ASSOCIATION. Reply . . . to the circular letter of Mr. R. Moon and Mr. J. P. Brown-Westhead. 29 October, 1862. pp. 2[3].   BM
On the recently published letter from the Chairman and Deputy-Chairman of the L. & N.W.R., calling upon shareholders not to join the Shareholders' Association.

6563 WRIGLEY, T. London & North Western Railway: Mr. Thomas Wrigley's reply to the letter of Mr. Richard Moon & Mr. J. P. Brown-Westhead, in answer to the report of their proceedings, circulated by the L. & N.W. Shareholders' Association. Published under the authority & with the sanction of the L. & N.W. Shareholders' Association. *Manchester*, [1862.] pp. 16.   BM

6563a LONDON & NORTH WESTERN RLY. Statement read at the conferences held at Euston Station, London, on the 5th & 6th November 1862. *London*, 1862. pp. 14. BM
Signed 'Charles E. Stewart, Secretary', and dated 4 Nov., 1862.
Thos. Wrigley's proposals for re-organising the management of the L. & N.W., examined and found to be based on false reasoning and wrong information.

6564 ENTWISLE, W. To the shareholders of the London & North Western Rly. Co. *Torquay*, April 13, 1863. BM
Complaint that shareholders, while professing to agree with the principles and recommendations of the Shareholders' Association, ignore these in practice and support expanding commitments and risks.

6565 LONDON & NORTH WESTERN RAILWAY SHAREHOLDERS ASSOCIATION. Address to the proprietors by the Committee of the London & North Western Shareholders' Association. *Bury*, [1863.] pp. 32. BM
Criticising the policy of the directors. Tables of accounts and mileage, 1846–62.

6566 FRANCE, R. S. Lord Redesdale and the new railways: a review of his lordship as a railway legislator, in a letter by R. S. France. *London*, 1867. pp. 24. LSE
Alleged obstruction by Redesdale of a Bill concerning the Mold & Denbigh Junction Railway, to which R. S. France was a contractor.

6567 FRANCE, R. S. Lord Redesdale and the new railways: correspondence between his lordship and Mr. France. *London*, 1867. pp. 18. LSE
Relating to alleged obstruction by Redesdale of a Bill concerning the Mold & Denbigh Junction Railway, to which R. S. France was a contractor.

6568 FRANCE, R. S. Mr. France's pamphlet 'Lord Redesdale and the new railways'. Lord Redesdale's control over the legislation of both Houses. *London*, 1867. pp. 16. BM
Redesdale's support of the L. & N.W. Rly. in opposing the Bill for the Mold & Denbigh line.

6569 GRAHAME, J. Financial Fenianism and the Caledonian Railway. *Glasgow*, 1867. pp. 31. BM
pp. 21–8, tables comparing the Caledonian with the L. & N.W. Rly.

6570 DOUGLAS, J. P. A run through South Wales via the London & North Western Railway. *Shrewsbury*, 1868. pp. 80. BM
Contains some information on the Knighton, the Central Wales, and the Central Wales Extension railways.

6571 LONDON & NORTH WESTERN RLY. Instruction to audit inspectors. 1871. pp. 20. PC

6572 THOMPSON, H. To the Chairman and directors of the London & North Western Railway Company. *Bangor*, [1872.] pp. 8, with fold. plate. NLC
On the Holyhead Old Harbour improvements.

6573 PHILP, R. K. The London & North Western Railway Panoramic Guide. *London*, 1874. pp. 54. BM
Route book, with maps.

6574 BRADBURY, E. In the Derbyshire highlands: highways, byeways, and my ways in the Peake Countrie. *Buxton*, 1881. pp. ix, 274. PC
pp. [104]–120, Over the High Peak Railway.

6575 INVESTORS PROTECTION ASSOCIATION. An inflated security: the London & North Western Railway. *London*, 1883. pp. 11. BM
Stockholders advised to sell 'before the crash comes'.

6576 LONDON & NORTH WESTERN RLY. Facts and information for visitors to the exhibitions in London, Liverpool and Edinburgh as to travelling in England, Scotland and Wales. *London*, 1886. pp. 40. BM
General information and timetables.

6577 FINDLAY, G. Report of a lecture delivered . . . at the School of Military Engineering, Chatham, 8 March, 1888. Subject, 'The working of an English railway'. *London*, 1888. pp. 37. ICE
As exemplified by the L. & N.W. Rly.

6578 TAYLOR, P. Autobiography of Peter Taylor. *Paisley*, 1903. pp. 244. BM
Includes (pp. 92–120) an account of his work on locomotive maintenance at Kilmarnock, Glasgow & South Western Rly., and two letters from Charlie Dick, Works Manager at Crewe Works, London & North Western Rly. in the 1880s (pp. 179–87) containing observations on working conditions there.

6579 FINDLAY, G. The working of an English railway: a lecture . . . City of London Young Men's Christian Association. [*London*, 1890.] pp. 22. BR
Read 10 December, 1890.
The L. & N.W. Rly. G. Findlay was General Manager.

6580 The FROZEN Vacuum Brake; in a series of eight articles reprinted from the Saturday Review; with especial reference to the accident to the London & North Western train at Carlisle Station on the 4th March, 1890. [*London*,] 1890. pp. 59. BR

6581 LONDON & NORTH WESTERN RLY. Railway & Canal Traffic Act, 1888. Particulars of the reduction in revenue which would be entailed by the revised classification of merchandise traffic and schedule of maximum rates & charges applicable thereto . . . *London*, 1890. 3 pts. in 1. LSE

6582 COOKE, C. J. B. London & North Western Railway Works at Crewe. *In* 'Round the works of our great railways.' 1893. pp. 1–34. BM

*6583 FINDLAY, G. The working and management of an English railway . . . *London*, 1889. pp. vi, 270, with many illus. BM
The L. & N.W. Rly.

—— 2nd edn. *London*, 1889, pp. vi, 300. BM

—— 3rd, *London*, 1890. pp. vi, 300.   BM

—— 4th, *London*, 1891. pp. vi, 354.   BM

—— 5th, with a biographical sketch of G. Findlay. *London*, 1894. pp. 412.   BM

6584 PHILLP, S. M. [Biographical sketch of George Findlay.] *In* 'The working and management of an English railway', by G. Findlay. 5th edn. 1894. pp. 1–36.   BM

6585 INTERNATIONAL RAILWAY CONGRESS, London, 1895. Visit to the Edge Hill gridirons, Liverpool, London & North Western Railway, on the 28th June 1895. By Harry Footner. 1895. pp. 9, with 9 illus & 4 maps.   IT

6586 INTERNATIONAL RAILWAY CONGRESS [London, 1895]. Visite du Congrès International des Ingénieurs des Chemins de Fer aux chantiers de Crewe. Description des chantiers de construction de locomotives de la Compagnie des Chemins de Fer du Nord-Ouest d'Angleterre (London & North Western) à Crewe, juin 1895. *Londres*, 1895. pp. 19, with fold. plan of Works and 4 plates (loosely inserted).   BR

6587 WILLIAMS, R. P. Railway rates and terminal charges. *London*, 1896. pp. 44. ICE
Reprinted from the *Journal of the Royal Statistical Society*, vol. 59, pt. 3, September 1896.
Contains many tables and charts relating to income, expenditure and traffic on the L. & N.W. Rly.

6588 [AMALGAMATED SOCIETY OF RAILWAY SERVANTS.] Labour's right to combine. The London & North Western Railway Co. and its attitude towards its employees who are members of the A.S.R.S.: attempts at intimidation and how they were met and frustrated in December 1896. *London*, 1897. pp. 48.   LSE

6589 HALDANE, J. W. C. Railway engineering, mechanical and electrical . . . *London*, 1897. pp. xx, 562, with many plates and illus. BM
Includes Crewe Works.

6590 COTTERELL, S. *and* WILKINSON, G. H. The London & North Western locomotives, simple and compound. *Birmingham*, 1899. pp. [x,] 129, with fold. frontis. & illus.   BM
Issued serially, in eight parts.

6591 DEARDEN, G. A. Observations on the Teutonics, Greater Britains, and four-cylinder compounds, L. & N.W.R. *Birmingham*, [1899.] pp. 14.   BM

6592 CHARLEWOOD, R. E. Preston and Carlisle express services, 1900–1. *London*, 1901. pp. 17[24], with tables. [*Railway Club Library*, no. 2.]   BM

6593 THOMAS, J. H. *and* BROMLEY, J. The truth about the Shrewsbury disaster . . . Verbatim report of the debate held in the Tredegar Hall, Newport, on Sunday, June 14th, 1908. [*London*:] *Amalgamated Society of Railway Servants*, [1908.] pp. 24.   LSE

6594 [WILLIAMS, C.] List of all the named engines now in use on the L. & N.W. Railway. *Crewe*, 1907. pp. 18.   BM

—— another edn. 'A list of named engines now running on the L. & N.W. Rly.' *Crewe*, 1909. pp. 19.   BM

*6595 WILLIAMS, C. A Register of all the locomotives now in use on the London & North Western Railway. *Birmingham*, 1899. pp. 38.

—— another edn. *Crewe*, 1912. pp. 67.   BM
'Revised down to December 1st, 1911.'
3089 engines listed, with a section on named engines.

—— Supplementary list, with corrections. *Crewe*, 1918. pp. 20.   BM

6596 LONDON & NORTH WESTERN RLY. Description of the London & North Western Railway Company's locomotive works at Crewe. [*Crewe*,] April 1913. pp. 31, with illus. & fold. plan of works.   BR
Cover title, *Locomotive Works, Crewe*.

6597 MODERN railway working. (Locomotive engine: railway carriage.) *London: Gresham Publishing Co.*, 1913. obl. 4°.   BM
Two folding diagrams arranged to show interiors of a contemporary L. & N.W. locomotive and carriage.

6598 DARROCH, G. R. S. Deeds of a great railway: a record of the enterprise and achievements of the L. & N.W.R. Co. during the Great War . . . *London*, 1920. pp. xvi, 217, with 18 plates & 22 illus.   BM

6599 LONDON & NORTH WESTERN RLY. London & North Western Railway Company's Roll of Honour, gratefully dedicated to the memory of London & North Western Railwaymen who lost their lives whilst serving their country during the Great War, 1914–19. [*London*, 1921.] pp. 72.   BM

6600 LONDON & NORTH WESTERN RLY. Opening of Euston and Watford electric line, July 10, 1922. [*London*, 1922.] pp. 21, with illus. & fold. map of line.   RC

6601 PRATT, E. A. War record of the London & North Western Railway . . . *London*, 1922. pp. 70.   BM
Extracted from *British railways and the Great War*, by E. A. Pratt (1921).

6602 WALSH, A. ST. G. Passenger train formation on the L. & N.W.R. pp. 16. *Typescript*. RC
Paper, Railway Club, 10 March, 1927.

London & North Western and Great Central Joint Railway

603 MANCHESTER SOUTH JUNCTION & AL-TRINCHAM RLY. The Manchester South Junction & Altrincham Railway: its inception and development; with maps. Jubilee, 1849–1899. *Manchester & London*, 1899. pp. 24[29], with illus., reprints of timetables, & 2 fold. maps.   BM

604 HEYWOOD, J. LTD., Manchester South Junction & Altrincham Railway Co., 1849–1931. *Manchester*, [1931.] pp. 20, with illus.   RC
Souvenir of Manchester to Altrincham electric train service, commenced 11 May, 1931.

London & North Western and Lancashire & Yorkshire Joint Railway

605 STRETTON, C. E. The history of the Preston & Walton Summit plate-way: a paper read at Walton Summit on the occasion of the eightieth anniversary of the opening of the line, 1st June, 1883. [1883.] pp. [9.]   BM
'Printed for Chicago Exhibition, 1893.'

606 STRETTON, C. E. The history of the Wigan Branch, and the Preston & Wigan railways, afterwards the North Union Railway . . . 2nd edn. *Leeds*, 1901. pp. 15.   BM

London & South Western Railway
(formerly London & Southampton Railway)

Historical

607 RUEGG, L. H. The history of a railway. *Sherborne*, 1878. pp. 66.   BM
—— The Salisbury & Yeovil Railway: a centenary reprint of 'The History of a railway'. *Dawlish: David & Charles*, 1960. pp. [4,] 66.   BM
The Introduction is by David St. John Thomas.

608 FAY, S. A Royal Road; being the history of the London & South Western Railway from 1825 to the present time. *Kingston-on-Thames*, 1882. pp. 138, with 4 plates.   pc
Includes biographical sketches of officials.
—— Reprinted, 1883.   BM

609 SEKON, G. A. The London & South-Western Railway: half a century of railway progress. *London*, 1896. pp. iv, 96.   BM

610 WILLIAMS, H. W. Some reminiscences, 1838 to 1918. *Penzance*, 1918. pp. 112. BM
Includes episodes during service with the L. & S.W. Rly., 1856–78.

611 LONDON & SOUTH WESTERN RLY. The
c   South Western Railway: 88 years of progress. Report of the proceedings at the final Annual Meeting of the Shareholders of the Company held at Waterloo Station on the 16th February 1923. pp. [16], with 5 illus., chronology, & a list of directors & chief officers.   BR

6612 B[UCKMASTER], W. Railway reminiscences: L. & S.W.R., 1875 to S.R., 1925. By W. B. *London: the author*, 1937. pp. 32, with 7 plates.   BR
A record of service.

6613 LEE, C. E. Aldershot & District Traction Co. Ltd. *London: Omnibus Society*, 1938. pp. 12, with illus. & time-table.   BM
pp. 3–6, L. & S.W. Rly. bus services between Farnham & Haslemere.

6614 SOUTHERN RLY. Centenary of the opening, on May 5th 1845, of the London & South Western Railway from Woking to Guildford. Exhibition at . . . Guildford, May 5th–19th 1945. [*London*, 1945.] pp. 8.   BR
Description of 113 exhibits and (pp. 6–8) 'Guildford's Railway Centenary'.

6615 [ALLCHIN, M. C. V.] The duplicate locomotives of the London & South Western Railway; illustrated. Types, building dates, etc. *Southsea: Railway Hobbies*, [1946.] pp. 16.   BM

*6616 BURTT, F. L. & S.W.R. locomotives, 1872–1923. *London: Ian Allan*, [1949.] pp. 96, with plates.   BM
Descriptions and lists.

6617 CLINKER, C. R. The Bodmin & Wadebridge Railway, 1834 to 1950. *Padstow: the author*, 1951. pp. 19[29], with maps, tables & extracts from documents. *Reproduced typescript.*   BM

6618 COZENS, L. The Axminster & Lyme Regis Light Railway, with complementary road passenger services. *Highgate: the author*, 1952. pp. 44, with 14 illus., maps & diagrams.   BM

6619 ST. THOMAS SCHOOL RAILWAY CLUB. LSWR and Salisbury, 1847–1952. [*Salisbury*,] 1952. pp. 16[17]. *Reproduced typescript*, with 9 mounted photographs & a map.   pc

6620 ELLIS, C. H. The South-Western Railway: its mechanical history and background. 1838–1922, *London: Allen & Unwin*, 1956. pp. 256, with 71 illus. on 35 plates (col frontis.) & a fold. map.   BM

6621 CARR, K. G. The beginning of the London & Southampton Railway: a paper read to the Railway Club on Friday 3rd May 1957. pp. [56.] *Typescript*.   RC

6622 MORRIS, P. H. Southampton in the early
b   dock and railway age, 1830–60. Thesis, M.A., Southampton, 1957. pp. 228, with map & bibliography of 150 items, incl. primary sources.

6623 SIMMONS, J. South Western *v.* Great
b   Western: railway competition in Devon and Cornwall. *In* 'Journal of Transport History', vol. 4, no. 1, May 1959. pp. 13–36, with map, table, & 54 bibliogr. notes.   BM

6624 SHERBORNE HISTORICAL SOCIETY. Railway Centenary Exhibition, to commemorate the opening of the Salisbury & Yeovil Railway to Sherborne, May 7th, 1860. [*Sherborne*, 1960.] pp. 11, with 2 plates & a map.   pc
pp. 1–11, Historical notes, by F. Haythornthwaite.

Contemporaneous

6625 STEPHENS, E. L. A report to the committee for establishing a company to form a railway from Southampton to London, with docks at Southampton. *Southampton*, 1831. pp. 28, with fold. map of Southampton area.   BM

6626 STEPHENS, E. L. Statement of the local and national benefits which will be produced by the Southampton & London Railway. *London*, 1831. pp. 33, with fold. map, and fold. table showing returns (passengers & revenue) of road coaches, Southampton, Basingstoke and London, October 1830. PO

6627 The ADVANTAGES and profits of the Southampton Railway analysed. *London*, 1834. pp. 58.   BM
Criticisms of F. Giles' scheme, written after the passing of the Bill.

6628 GREAT WESTERN RLY. Great Western Railway. Case of the promoters of the Bill. [*London*, 1834.] pp. 20.   BM
Opposing the plans of the L. & S. Rly. for extensions westward.

6629 [LONDON & SOUTHAMPTON RLY.] Extracts from the Evidence given on the London and Southampton Railway Bill, as printed by order of the House of Lords. [*London*, 1834.] pp. 68.   BM

6630 OPPOSITION to the London & Southampton Railway. [*London*, 1834.] pp. 14.   H

6631 FREELING, A. The London & Southampton Railway Companion . . . *London*, 1838. pp. 204, with map & illus.   H
—— another edn. *London*, 1839. pp. 216. BM

6632 LONDON & SOUTHAMPTON RLY. Southampton Railway Guide; with an accurate map of all the railroads in England. *London*, [1839.] pp. 4.   BM

6633 WYLD, J., *publisher*. The London & Southampton Railway Guide . . . *London*, 1839. pp. xi, 197, with fold. map.   BM
Contains (pp. 1–23) an account of the L. & S. and of general methods of railway promotion and construction.

6634 FAIRBAIRN, H. A letter to the shareholders of the Southampton Railway on the practicability and expediency of carrying merchandise by horse power without impeding the present arrangements of the steam locomotive passenger trains. *London*, 1840. pp. 28.   UL(GL)
Sidings, with stables, at twenty-five-mile intervals; horse trains to travel at night.

6635 MOGG, E. Mogg's Southampton Railway and Isle of Wight Guide, accompanied by an official map of the line . . . time and fare table, and latest regulations of the company. *London*, [1841.] pp. 36[38].   LSE

6636 CARROW, J. M. Report of the case of the Queen against the South Western Railway Company; decided in the Court of Queen's Bench, June 4th, 1842. *London*, 1842. pp. 32.   BM
An appeal by the L. & S.W. Rly. against the rating assessment for poor relief in Mitcheldever parish. Concluded in favour of the parish. General principles of the rating of railways are discussed in the light of the Parochial Assessment Act.

6637 ROSCOE, T. Summer tour in the Isle of Wight, including Portsmouth, Southampton, Winchester, the South Western Rly., etc. [*London*,] 1843. pp. 158, with 33 plates. BM
Contains two engravings of railway station exteriors—Southampton, and Gosport.

6638 BLANCHARD, E. L. L. Bradshaw's Descriptive Guide to the London & South Western Rly. *London: W. J. Adams; Manchester: Bradshaw & Blacklock*, 1845. pp. 97. UL(GL)

6639 COLOMBINE, D. E. Letter addressed to the Right Hon. Lord Carteret . . . Lord Vivian, Sir William L. S. Trelawney . . . Francis Rodd . . . and the chief magistrates, landowners and merchants of the County of Cornwall. *London*, 1845. pp. 10, with fold. map.   BM
The claims of the proposed London & Exeter Rly. in preference to the Exeter, Yeovil & Dorchester Rly., the Salisbury & Yeovil Rly. and the L. & S.W. Rly.

6640 LONDON & SOUTH WESTERN RLY. Rules to be observed by enginemen & firemen . . . [*London*,] 1845. pp. 36.   LSE

6641 CHAPLIN, W. J. Letter by the Chairman of the London & South-Western Railway Company to the shareholders in that company on the pending differences between the London & South-Western and the Great Western railway companies. *London*, 1846. pp. 76.   BM
Appendix contains correspondence with the Southampton & Dorchester Rly. and Great Western Rly., and extracts from the Proceedings before the Committee of Peers on the Wilts., Somerset & Weymouth Rly.

6642 MORGAN, A. [A letter to George Richard Corner, Vestry Clerk of S. Olave, Southwark, as to the proposed extension of the London & South Western Railway to London Bridge.] *London*, 1846.   G

6643 TALBOT, J. C. House of Lords Select Committee on the London & South-Western

(Basingstoke & Salisbury Extension) Railway Bill; the London, Salisbury & Yeovil Railway Bill, and the Exeter, Yeovil & Dorchester Railway Bill. Mr. Talbot's speech against the Bills. *Westminster*, 1846. pp. 64.　　　　　　　　　　　　　　BM

6644 COCKBURN, A. J. E. Speech of Mr. Cockburn on behalf of the Salisbury & Yeovil; Exeter, Yeovil & Dorchester; Exeter & Exmouth; and Blandford & Bruton lines, on the 30th of June and 1st & 2nd of July, 1847. [*London*, 1847.] pp. 175.　　　BM
The case for the South Western Rly.

6645 T., R. R. The projected Windsor railways considered, with suggestions for adjusting the differences arising out of the conflicting interests affected by those schemes. [*Windsor*,] 1847. pp. 11.　　　　　　　　H
Signed, 'R. R. T.'

6646 An APPEAL on behalf of the farmers and miners of Devon and Cornwall against the last decision of an ex-Commissioner of Railways. *London*, 1848. pp. 244(?)　NLC
(NLC copy incomplete.)
Against Edward Strutt's decision to construct the Taw Valley Extension to Crediton on broad gauge.

6647 TAW VALLEY RLY. An appeal to Parliament from an Order of the Commissioners of Railways with reference to the gauge of the Taw Valley line; by the directors of that railway. *London*, 1848. pp. 43.　　BM
An appeal against the decision to construct an extension on broad gauge; a table of comparative fares on broad and on narrow gauge lines; a reprint of the prospectus for the proposed extension.

6648 WINDSOR, STAINES & SOUTH WESTERN RLY. Statement of the directors . . . respecting their arrangements with the Commissioners of Her Majesty's Woods, etc. as to the Windsor, Staines & South-Western Railway and the contemplated Windsor improvements, and the recent argument between the Commissioners and the Great Western Railway Company as to their proposed branch railway from Slough to Windsor. [1848.] pp. 23, xlii.　　　LSE
Appendix—Extracts from Evidence before the Committee of the House of Commons on the Great Western Windsor Branch Bills, 1847 and 1848, and from the Evidence on the Windsor, Staines & South-Western Railway Bill, 1847; and agreements between H.M. Commissioners of Woods and the W.S. & S.W. Rly. and with the G.W. Rly.

6649 LONDON & SOUTH WESTERN RLY. Regulations and charges for goods, cattle, etc. January 1850. *London*, [1850.] pp. 61, with fold. tables.　　　　　　IT

6650 WHITEHEAD, J. The key to railway investments. Part 3, The London & South Western Railway; illustrated by a map of the district. *London*, 1850. pp. 14.　　BM

6651 PORT of Southampton on the banks of the Thames. By a Merchant. *London*, [1853.] pp. 14.　　　　　　　　BM
For increased wharf and warehouse accommodation at Nine Elms. The L. & S. W. Rly. an essential feature of the plan.

6652 WIGRAM, J. C. An appeal to the better feelings of the managers and directors of the railway and steam-packet companies connected with the Port of Southampton on behalf of their servants, and of the Christian welfare of the town. *London*, 1853. pp. 35.　　　　　　　　　LSE
Popularity of Sunday excursion trips to Crystal Palace and to Southampton and other places on the L. & S.W. and the consequent 'desecration of the Sabbath' and the keeping of railway servants in a 'complete state of Sabbath slavery'. Author was rector of St. Mary's, Southampton.

6653 WREFORD, R. A letter to local capitalists on the subject of the Exeter & Exmouth Railway. *Exeter*, 1855. pp. 26.
'This undertaking cannot fail to pay at least 5 per cent.'

6654 FOTHERGILL, B. Report on the coal and coke burning engines on the London & South Western Railway. *Manchester*, March 1856. pp. 7, with 29 pages of tables entitled 'Detailed report of experimental trips'. IME
Addressed to directors of the L. & S.W. Rly.

6655 MANGLES, C. E. To the shareholders in the London & South Western Railway. *London*, 1859. pp. 44[45], with fold. map.　　BM
No title-page in BM & LSE copies.
Relations with the L. B. & S. C. Rly., and a proposed course of action.

6656 LONDON & SOUTH WESTERN RLY. Rules and regulations for the guidance of the officers and servants of the L. & S. W. Rly. Co. *London*, 1864. pp. 302.　　UL(GL)

6657 PHILP, R. K. London & South Western Railway Panoramic Guide. *London*, 1874. pp. 54.　　　　　　　　BM
A route book, with maps.

6658 CLARKE, J. F. M. The geology of the Bridgwater Railway: a brief account of lias cuttings through the Polden Hills in Somersetshire. *Bath*, 1891. pp. 10.　　ICE
Read before Bath Natural History & Antiquarian Field Club.

6659 CORRESPONDENCE etc. between the South Eastern and London & South Western railway companies, as to the Charing Cross Railway, from 1861 to 1868. *London*, 1892. pp. 64.　　　　　　BR

6660 SZLUMPER, A. W. The signalling at the Waterloo terminus of the London & South Western Railway. *London: Institution of Civil Engineers*, 1892. pp. 29, with 2 fold. plates.　　　　　　　　BR
Excerpt, *Min. Proc. I.C.E.,* vol. 111, Session 1892–3, pt. 1.

6661 HAY, H. H. D. The Waterloo & City Railway, by Harley Hugh Dalrymple Hay; and The electrical equipment of the Waterloo & City Railway, by Bernard Maxwell Jenkin . . . *London*, 1900. pp. 158, with 6 plates of detailed diagrams.   UL(GL)
      Excerpt, *Min. Proc. I.C.E.*, vol. 139, pt. 1.

6662 LONDON & SOUTH WESTERN RAILWAY SERVANTS ORPHANAGE. Souvenir to commemorate the opening of the London & South Western Railway Servants' Orphanage at Woking . . . July 5, 1909 . . . Edited by George Kellow. *London*, 1909. pp. 22.   BM

6663 FELTHAM Concentration Yard, London & South Western Railway. *London: Railway Gazette*, [1922.] pp. 8, with illus. & diagrams (1 la. fold.).   RC
      Reprint, *Railway Gazette*, 12 May, 1922.

6664 LONDON & SOUTH WESTERN RLY. London's largest railway station: some interesting facts concerning the reconstruction of Waterloo Station, and war record of the London & South Western Railway. *London*, March 1922. pp. 16, with illus.   BR
      Cover title, *The new Waterloo Station. Opening by . . . the King and Queen on Tuesday March 21st, 1922.*

6665 METROPOLITAN-VICKERS ELECTRICAL COMPANY. London & South-Western Railway electrification. *Manchester*, 1922. pp. 31, with 34 illus. & la. fold. map of electrified sections.   SLS
      Cover title, *Electrification on the L. & S.W. Rly.*

6666 The NEW Waterloo Station, London & South Western Railway. *London: Railway Gazette*, 1922. pp. 40, with 40 illus. & diagrams, & fold. plan.   IT
      Reprint, *Railway Gazette*, June 9, 1922.

6667 FROUD, W. H. The through services between the L.S.W.R. and the North. pp. 12 [15]. MS.   RC
      Paper, Railway Club, 13 April, 1923.

*6668 REJUVENATION of the Waterloo & City Tube, Southern Railway . . . *Westminster: Railway Gazette*, 1940. pp. 16, with illus.   PC
      Reprinted from the *Railway Gazette*, 15 November, 1940.

London & South Western and Midland Joint Railway

6669 ALLCHIN, M. C. V. Locomotives of the Somerset & Dorset Joint Railway and the Irish narrow gauge railways; illustrated: types, building dates, etc. *Fareham: the author*, 1944. pp. 12.   BM

*6670 BARRIE, D. S. M. *and* CLINKER, C. R. The Somerset & Dorset Railway. *South God-stone: Oakwood Press*, 1948. pp. 73, with 37 illus. & maps on 15 plates; tables. [*Oakwood Library of Railway History*, no. 6.]   BM

6671 ATTHILL, R. The curious past: West Country studies. *Taunton: Wessex Press*, 1955. pp. ix, 94, with 5 illus.   BM
      pp. 29–35, 'The Somerset & Dorset'. An essay in praise of the S. & D. Rly.

6672 BARBER, L. H. A family and a railway: Centenary (1854–1954), Somerset Central Railway. *Street: C. & J. Clark*, 1955. pp. 48, with 23 illus. and a 3 pp. addendum inserted.   BM
      The Clarks of Street: James Clark and his descendants.

6673 [SLADEN, M.] The Somerset & Dorset Railway. *London: Branch Line Re-invigoration Society*, 1962[1963]. pp. 19, with 4 maps & 8 tables. *Reproduced typescript.* BM
      A detailed affirmation of its present and potential utility set out as an argument against threatened closure, with practical suggestions for modifications which it is believed would ensure economic working of the line.

London, Brighton & South Coast Railway

Historical

6674 BUCKLAND, F. T. Curiosities of natural history. *London*, 1871.   BM
      p. 102, Rats in the Croydon Atmospheric. (Also to be found in other editions of this work.)

6675 SLOUS, F. L. Stray leaves from the scrapebook [*sic*] of an awkward man. Reprinted in June 1881 from the edition of 1843, with additions and subtractions by the author. *London*, 1881. pp. 203.   BM
      pp. 47–50, A dialogue between the Croydon railroad and the Croydon Canal. 1840. (11 verses.)

6676 BANISTER, F. D. Historical notes in reference to the lines of railway between Redhill and London by means of which the L.B. & S.C. and South Eastern railway companies obtain access to the London Bridge Station of both companies. *London*, 1888. pp. 18, with 6 diagrams.   ICE

6677 LONDON, BRIGHTON & SOUTH COAST RLY. Agreements between the L.B. & S.C.R. and the South Eastern Railway Company relating to the use of the London and Redhill lines (1839–1898) with historical notes in reference to the lines of railway between Redhill and London by means of which the L.B. & S.C. and S.E. railway companies obtain access to the London Bridge stations of both companies, by Fred D. Banister. [1898.] pp. 81, with maps.   SLS
      'Private.'

6678 [BURTT, G. F.] The locomotives of the London, Brighton & South Coast Railway,
c 1839–1903 . . . *London*, 1903. pp. 245, with 8 plates & 146 illus.   BM
   pp. 1–20, an historical survey of the L.B. & S.C. Rly., with a chronology.
   This work first appeared as a series of articles in *Moore's Monthly Magazine*, March–December 1896, and in its successor, the *Locomotive Magazine*, January–December 1897, February–December 1898, January, March, May, June, July and September 1899, under the pseudonym 'F. S. Hollandsche'. The author, G. F. Burtt, was an employee at the company's Brighton Works, and the locomotive superintendent, Robert John Billinton, in obedience to the company's policy, forbade him to disclose his authorship. The choice of pseudonym is capricious. Mr. John Pelham Maitland, a modern authority on the L.B.S.C. Rly., understands that G. F. Burtt adopted the name from a cigar box labelled 'Hollandsche Sigaren Fabriek', with the initial letters of the second and third words used in reverse order.
   —— Adjustments and amplifications, by John Pelham Maitland. 1963. pp. 9. *Reproduced typescript*.   BM
   About 150 items, with additional notes.

6679 MITTON, G. E. The South-Eastern & Chatham, and London, Brighton & South Coast railways . . . *London*, 1912. pp. vii, 87.   BM
   Brief histories of these railways form an introduction to an historical topography of the areas served.

6680 CAREY, A. Sir Waterloo: fragments of the biography of a Sussex lad. *London*, 1920. pp. 320.   BM
   pp. 93–7 and elsewhere, the parliamentary background to the birth of the London & Brighton Rly., and social aspects of prospecting.

6681 LONDON, BRIGHTON & SOUTH COAST RLY. The London, Brighton & South Coast Rly. Co., 1846–1922. *London*, 1923. pp. 16, with 10 illus.   BM

6682 MASKELYNE, J. N. The locomotives of the London Brighton & South Coast Railway, 1903–1923. *London*, 1928. pp. 155, with plates (some col.) & illus.   BM
   —— Corrections and augmentations, by John Pelham Maitland. 1961. pp. 9. *Reproduced typescript*.
   156 items.

6683 SOUTHERN RLY. Centenary of the opening of the Shoreham branch and Brighton Station, London & Brighton Railway, May 11th 1840. [*London*, 1940]. pp. 12.   pc
   Description of seventy exhibits and (pp. 8–12) an historical account of the L. & B. Rly.

6684 SOUTHERN RLY. Centenary of the opening, on November 24th, 1845, of the London & Brighton Railway from Shoreham to Worthing. Exhibition at . . . Worthing, November 24th—December 8th, 1945. [*London*, 1945.] pp. 12.   BR

Description of 130 exhibits and (pp. 8–12) 'How the railway came to Worthing'.

6685 BURTT, G. F. L.B. & S.C.R. locomotives: an up-to-date survey from 1870. *Staines: Ian Allan*, 1946. pp. 57.   BM
   Descriptions, lists and illustrations.

6686 SOUTHERN RLY. Centenary of the opening, on March 15th 1847, of the London, Brighton & South Coast Railway from Chichester to Havant. Exhibition at . . . Havant, March 15th to March 22nd 1947. [*London*, 1947.] pp. 8.   BR
   Description of 124 exhibits and (pp. 5–8) 'Havant Railway Centenary'.

6687 BRITISH RAILWAYS—SOUTHERN REGION. Centenary of the opening, on February 14th 1848, of the London, Brighton & South Coast Railway from Three Bridges to Horsham. Exhibition at . . . Horsham, February 13th to February 19th, 1948. [*London*, 1948.] pp. 8.   BR
   Description of ninety-nine exhibits and (pp. 5–8) 'How the railway came to Horsham'.

6688 MORRIS, O. J. L.B. & S.C.R. *London: Ian Allan*, [1952.] pp. 32. [*Railways before the Grouping*, no. 1.]   BM
   Illustrations with a brief history and a description of services.

6689 RAILWAY CORRESPONDENCE & TRAVEL SOCIETY. Itinerary of the Brighton Works Centenary Special, 5th October 1952. *Leamington Spa*, [1952.] pp. 7[8], with gradient profile & route diagram.   BR

6690 TYLER, E. J. The Brighton Railway in Mr. Craven's time. pp. 29. *Typescript*.   RC
   Paper, Railway Club, 6 June, 1952.

6691 BROOKFIELD, H. C. Three Sussex ports, 1850–1950. *In* 'Journal of Transport
b History', vol. 2, no. 1, May 1955. pp. 35–50, with 4 tables & 48 bibliogr. notes.   BM
   Littlehampton, Shoreham, and Newhaven. Includes railway development (L.B. & S.C. Rly.).

6692 COLE, D. Mocatta's stations for the Brighton Railway. *In* 'Journal of Transport
b History', vol. 3, no. 3, May 1958. pp. 149–57, with plate (2 illus.), 3 diagrams, & 48 bibliogr. notes.   BM

*6693 ELLIS, C. H. The London, Brighton & South Coast Railway: a mechanical history of the London & Brighton, the London & Croydon, and the London, Brighton & South Coast railways, from 1839 to 1922. *London: Ian Allan*, 1960. pp. 271, with col. frontis,. 79 illus. on 32 plates, lists, a map, & a chart (on 7 pp.) of engine head codes. Index of 17 pp.   BM
   —— Corrections and addenda by J. Pelham Maitland, Nov. 1961. pp. 15. *Reproduced typescript*.   BM
   About 200 items, mostly augmenting statements in the text, with a few corrections added.

6693a HARMAN, R. G. The Hayling Island Railway. *Teddington: Branch Line Handbooks*, 1963. pp. 26[30], with 12 illus., map & 2 diagrams. [*B.L.H.*, no. 18.] *Reproduced typescript.* BM

Contemporaneous

6694 FORTUNE, F. London and Brighton Junction Rail Road as suggested to Government by F. Fortune in 1825. *London*, [1825.] pp. 16, 2, 2. UL(GL)
pp. 11–16, A letter to the *Nottingham Review* by Thomas Gray on railroads.
The main work is followed by two leaflets: *Junction Rail Road*, pp. 2, and *London & Brighton Rail Road*. pp. 2.
Appended to the UL(GL) copy are other works of the same format, paper and type: pp. [3]–9, 'Liverpool & Manchester Rail Road'; pp. 9–10, 'An Account of Dick's Suspension Railway'; pp. 11–16, 'Fortune's General Junction Rail Road through England as laid before Government in 1825, with locomotive engines'; p. 16, 'Opening of the Canterbury & Whitstable Rail Road. Report.'

6695 STEPHENSON, R. Report on the two proposed lines of railway from London to Brighton, to the Committee of the London & Brighton Railway Company. [*London*, 1835.] pp. 8. LSE

6696 GIBBS, J. Report of Mr. Gibbs, civil engineer, upon the several proposed lines for a Brighton Railway. *London*, [1836.] pp. vii, 91, with gradient tables & a fold. map showing the six proposed lines. BM
—— 2nd edn. *London*, [1836.] pp. vii, 91. IT

6697 HILL, M. D. Speech . . . before a Committee of the House of Lords in summing up the Engineering Evidence on the Brighton Railway without a Tunnel. [*London*, 1836.] pp. 36. H

6698 JOY, H. H. The Direct London & Brighton Railway . . . Speech of H. H. Joy on the summing up of the Evidence given before the Committee of the House of Commons, in support of Sir John Rennie's, or the Direct, Line. *London*, 1836. pp. 70. NLC

6699 JOY, H. H. Sir John Rennie's line: speech . . . before the Committee of the House of Commons, May 19, 1836. *Brighton*, [1836.] pp. 20. BM
On behalf of the London & Brighton Rly.

6700 [LONDON & BRIGHTON RLY.] Minutes of Evidence taken before the Committee on the London & Brighton Railway Bills (House of Commons). Engineering Evidence, Robert Stephenson, George P. Bidder, Sir John Rennie, Joseph Locke. Copy from Mr. Gurney's short-hand notes. *London*, [1836.] pp. 454.

6701 PEARSON, C. Brighton Railroad . . . The substance of a speech . . . before the Committee of the House of Lords on the 1st of August, in opposition to Stephenson's Railroad Bill, and in favour of a line without a tunnel; to which is appended the Evidence of . . . medical witnesses stating the inconvenience and danger to be apprehended by invalids and persons of delicate constitution from the sudden changes of temperature in travelling through tunnels. *London*, 1836. pp. iv, 72. LSE

6702 POLLOCK, D. The Direct London & Brighton Railway, Session 1836. Speech . . . on the summing up of the Evidence of traffic given before the Committee of the House of Commons in support of Sir John Rennie's, or the Direct Line. *London*, 1836. pp. 48. H

6703 RAILROADS: statements and reflections thereon, particularly with reference to the proposed railroad without a tunnel and the competition for the line between London and Brighton. By a Shareholder, at the request of other shareholders. *London*, 1836. pp. 59, 10. BM
—— Addenda: 'London, Shoreham & Brighton Railway without a Tunnel.' *London*, 1836. pp. 3. BM
Both works stress the advantages of Cundy's line over Stephenson's.

6704 TALBOT, J. C. The Hon. Mr. Talbot's address to the Committee of the House of Commons on behalf of Stephenson's line of railroad from London to Brighton. *Brighton*, 1836. pp. 24. LSE
'To the Inhabitants of Brighton.'

6705 TALBOT, J. C. Stephenson's London & Brighton Railway. Speech of . . . J. C. Talbot on summing up the Engineering Evidence given in support of Stephenson's line, before the Hon. Committee of the House of Commons, 17th May, 1836. *Westminster*, 1836. pp. 41. BM
To the Committee on London & Brighton Railway Bills.

6706 STATEMENT of the public proceedings which have occurred at Brighton relative to a railway; printed for the Committee appointed at a town meeting held 18th February 1836, to promote the line projected by Sir John Rennie. *Brighton*, [1836.] pp. 8. ICE

6707 WOOD, W. P. H. Stephenson's London and Brighton Railway: speech of W. P. Wood on summing up the Engineering Evidence given in support of the Bill for Stephenson's line of railway before the . . . Committee of the House of Lords, 22 July, 1836. *Westminster*, 1836. pp. 31. BM

6708 ALEXANDER, W. J. Speech of W. J. Alexander for the South Eastern, Brighton, Lewes & Newhaven Railway . . . April, 7th, 1837. London, [1837.] pp. 45. BM
To the House of Commons Committee on the Brighton railways.

6709 EVIDENCE given before the Committee of the House of Commons on the London & Brighton railways on the subject of tunnels: Session 1837. *London: Rowarth & Sons*, [1837.] pp. 24. BM

The South Eastern, Brighton, Lewes & Newhaven Rly.

6710 LONDON & Brighton Railways. Answer to 'Observations on the result of the Evidence given before the Committee on the Bills'. *London*, 1837. pp. 8.

Pointing out mis-statements and omissions. The advantages of a proposed common line with the South Eastern from London Bridge to Reigate.

6711 MILLS, J. Two reports from Mr. Mills to the directors of the London and Brighton Railway without a Tunnel . . . *London*, 1837. pp. 12, with a petition to the Lords. BM

6712 STEPHENSON, R. Report from Mr. Stephenson to the directors of the Western London & Brighton Railway Company. *London*, 1837. pp. 7. PO

6713 ALDERSON, R. Report on the several proposed lines of railway between London and Brighton. *In* 'Papers on subjects connected with the duties of the Corps of Royal Engineers', vol. 2. *London*, 1838. pp. 105–13, with map. BM

6714 STEPHENSON, R. London & Brighton Railway: Mr. Robert Stephenson's reply to Capt. Alderson. *London*, 1837. pp. 16, with map. IME

Alderson's 'Report on the various lines of railway to Brighton' is reproduced in full length in the margins.

6715 LONDON & CROYDON RLY. London & Croydon Railway Companion, containing a complete description of everything worthy of attention on or near the line; with correct time and fare tables, and a coloured map. 2nd edn. *London*, 1839. pp. 46. H

6716 [TROTTER, W. E.] The Croydon Railway and its adjacent scenery; illustrated with six views, elevations of all the bridges, plans of the various stations, and a map and section of the line, together with its continuation to Merstham by the Brighton Railway now in progress. By the author of 'Illustrated topography of thirty miles around London'. *London*, [1839.] pp. 57, with la. fold. col. map showing 18 bridges & 6 station plans. ICE

pp. 1–10, a history of the railway; pp. 10–23, description of a journey, with four engravings showing the railway.

6717 AUSTIN, C. Committee on the Greenwich Railway Bill and Station Bill, and on the Croydon Railway and Station Bill. Speech of Mr. Austin. (House of Commons, 7 April, 1840.) *London*, [1840.] pp. 46. BERMONDSEY PL

On behalf of the L. & C. Rly.

6718 RAILWAY TIMES. The London & Brighton Railway Guide, containing a correct description of the railway . . . and the official map and section of the line . . . *London*, [1840.] pp. 57[60], with time-tables. PC

6719 To the SHAREHOLDERS of the Croydon, Greenwich, Brighton, and South Eastern railways. [*London*,] 1840. pp. 11. BM

By 'A Shareholder in more than one railway'. A reply to a pamphlet by W. A. Wilkinson, Chairman of the London & Croydon Rly.

6720 JOBBINS, J. R. The London & Brighton Railway Guide, containing a correct description of the railway, . . . and the official map and section of the line. *London*, [1841.] pp. 57. H

—— 2nd edn. *London*, 1841. pp. 54. LSE

6721 LONDON & BRIGHTON RLY. Regulations. 1841. pp. 41. H

6722 MOGG, E. Mogg's Brighton Railway and Brighton, Shoreham & Worthing Guide, accompanied by an official map of the line and an account of the Shoreham Branch Railway, to which is added the time and fare table with the latest regulations of the Company. *London*, 1841. pp. 26. LSE

6723 WILKINSON, W. A. The toll question on railways exemplified in the case of the Croydon and Greenwich Companies. *London*, 1841. pp. 16. BM

This pamphlet is discussed in *Railway travelling and the toll question* (anon.), 1843.

6724 RAILWAY travelling and the toll question. *London*, 1843. pp. 15. BM

From no. 77 of the *Westminster Review* for May 1843.

Particularly with regard to the toll exacted by the London & Greenwich Rly. from L. & C. passengers. The substance of two pamphlets is re-stated: 1, *Letter to H. Goulburn on the unequal pressure of the Railway Passenger Tax*, by G. H. Lang (1842); and 2, *The toll question on railways exemplified in the case of the Croydon and Greenwich companies*, by W. A. Wilkinson (1841).

6725 BLANCHARD, E. L. L. Bradshaw's Descriptive Guide to the London & Brighton Railway . . . *London: Bradshaw & Blacklock*, 1844. pp. 49. ICE

6726 GREGORY, C. H. On railway cuttings and embankments, with an account of some slips in the London clay on the . . . London & Croydon Railway. *London*, 1844. pp. 40, with diagrams. ICE

Excerpt, *Min. Proc. I.C.E.*

6727 LONDON & CROYDON RLY. Statement of the directors of the Croydon Railway Company and their correspondence with the directors of the South-Eastern Railway Company, on the projected lines to North

Kent, and on the leasing to them of the loco-motive portion of the Croydon Railway. For circulation among the proprietors of the Croydon Railway. *London*, 1844. pp. 43. NLC

6728 OGLE, H. A. Brighton, Lewes & Hastings Railway. Copy of a letter addressed to Arthur R. Briggs, solicitor at Lewes, for the Brighton, Lewes & Hastings Railway. [*Eastbourne*, 1844.] pp. 10. LSE
Signed 'Harriet Anne Ogle, proprietor of freehold land and of houses at the seaside'.
The advantage of a line to Eastbourne.

6729 [SMITH, A.] Railways as they really are; or, Facts for the serious consideration of railway proprietors: no. 1, London, Brighton & South Coast Railway. *London*, 1847. pp. 39. BM

6730 MILLER, J. Statistics of railways: no. 1, London and Brighton Railway, from its commencement to its amalgamation with the London and Croydon line . . . 1846. *London*, 1848. pp. 8. BM
Financial statistics.

6731 MILLER, J. Statistics of railways: no. 2, London and Croydon Railway, from its commencement to its amalgamation with the London and Brighton line . . . 1846. *London*, 1848. pp. 11–18. BM
Financial statistics.

6732 LAING, S. Railway taxation. *Westminster*, 1849. pp. 23. BM
Unequal taxation a burden to railways, illustrating the case of the L.B. & S.C. Rly., of which Laing was Chairman.

6733 WHITEHEAD, J. The key to railway in-vestments: part 2, The London & Brighton Railway; illustrated by a map of the dis-trict. *London*, 1850. pp. 12. BM

6734 BRIGHTON RAILWAY SHAREHOLDER. Address to the London, Brighton & South Coast Railway proprietary, on the project for removing the 'Crystal Palace' to Syden-ham, in connection with their railway. *London*, 1852. pp. 16. UL(GL)
Signed 'A Brighton Railway Shareholder'.
'Have nothing to do with it!'

6735 LAING, S. Letter to the working men in the employment of the London, Brighton & South Coast Rly. Co. on the present contest between the Amalgamated Society of En-gineers and the employers, from S. Laing, Chairman of the Company. *London*, 1852. pp. 31. BM

6736 NAUTICAL MAGAZINE. The harbours of Portsmouth and Langstone, with the pro-posed Hayling Docks and Railway. *London*, [1855.] pp. 7, with map. NLC
From the *Nautical Magazine*, March 1855.
A commercial harbour.

6737 LONDON, BRIGHTON & SOUTH COAST RLY. Bye-laws, rules and regulations to be observed by the officers and servants of the London, Brighton & South Coast Railway Company. 1st January 1857. *London*, [1857.] pp. 164. PC
Contains extracts from Acts of Parliament relating to the L.B. & S.C. Rly.

6738 MANGLES, C. E. To the shareholders in the London & South Western Railway. *London*, 1859. pp. 44[45], with fold. map. BM
No title page in BM and LSE copies.
Relations with the L.B. & S.C., and a pro-posed course of action.

6739 RELATIONS of the Brighton and South-Eastern companies: a compilation of agree-ments and correspondence. *London*, 1860. pp. 95, 7. BM
Correspondence includes exchanges con-cerning the Caterham Rly. (22 letters); Ports-mouth Rly. (4 letters); proposed Uckfield & Tunbridge Wells Rly. (11 letters with 10 more in an addenda of 'further correspondence'); and proposed Eastbourne & South-Eastern Rly. (3 letters).

6740 SOUTH EASTERN RLY. Report of the General Manager and Secretary on the re-lations of the South Eastern and Brighton Companies. *London*, 1863. pp. 31. LSE
Signed 'C. W. Eborall & S. Smiles'.

6741 LONDON, BRIGHTON & SOUTH COAST RLY. Report of the Committee of Investi-gation. [*London*, 1867.] pp. 41, with tables & correspondence. LSE
Finding that there had been a 'reckless dis-regard of shareholders' interests for many years'. A new Board to be set up.

6742 BLUNDELL, J. W. The financial prospects of the London, Brighton & South Coast Rly. Co. *London*, 1871. pp. 11. BM

6743 PHILP, R. K. The London, Brighton & South Coast Railway Panoramic Guide. *London*, [*c.* 1874.] pp. 44. BM
A route book, with maps.

6744 VINE, J. R. S. The Iron Roads Dictionary and Travellers' Route Charts . . . The Lon-don, Brighton & South Coast Railway . . . *London*, 1881. pp. xxiv, 124, with maps. BM
Includes an historical sketch.

6745 DOUGLAS, J. M. The truth about the Lon-don, Brighton & South Coast Railway; its accounts, its working, and its assailants. 2nd edn., 'with notes in reply to criticisms . . .' *London*, 1882. pp. 16. BM

6746 [LYTHGOE, J. P.] The London, Brighton & South Coast Railway Company: being a critical review of its financial position from 1868 to 1881. By A Railway Accountant. *London*, 1882. pp. 24. BR

5747 LYTHGOE, J. P. The London, Brighton & South Coast Railway Company: being a further critical review of its financial position. *London*, 1882. pp. 16.   BR

5748 FRASER, J. Who's right, company or critics? The case against the Brighton Railway, with proofs, being the facts and figures disclosed in the company's official statements. *London*, [1883.] pp. 30, with tables.   NLC
Relating to 'The true position and prospects of the L.B. & S.C. Rly.' and calling for an investigation into the company's affairs by an auditor appointed by the Board of Trade.

5749 LONDON, BRIGHTON & SOUTH COAST RLY. Daily traffics for 1882 and 1883, with monthly statements, etc. *London*, 1884. pp. 72.   BM
Abstracts of financial statistics.

5750 STROUDLEY, W. The construction of locomotive engines, with some results of the working of those on the London, Brighton & South Coast Railway; with an abstract of the discussion on the Paper. *London: Institution of Civil Engineers*, 1885. pp. 93, with 8 tables & fold. plate.   ICE
Excerpt, *Min. Proc. I.C.E.*, vol. 81, pt. 3.

5751 LONDON, BRIGHTON & SOUTH COAST RLY. The Speculator's Companion, shewing the traffic receipts for 1887 together with the weather report and closing price of the deferred stock for every day throughout the year. Compiled from official sources. *London*, 1888. pp. 31.   BM

5752 LAWSON, W. R. The Brighton Railway: its resources and prospects. *London: Financial Times*, 1891. pp. 92, with tables.   LSE
Detailed survey of the financial position and future prospects of the L.B. & S.C. Rly. with (pp. 19–24) early history of the lines. The author believes the 'Brighton' offers the best investment of all British railways.

5753 [PATTINSON, J. P.] The London, Brighton & South Coast Railway, its passenger services, rolling stock, locomotives, gradients, and express speeds. By the author of 'British railways'. *London*, 1896. pp. x, 56, with many tables & 2 plates.   BM
Includes nearly 200 instances of actual train performances.

5754 WINTER, J. B. The principal head boards and lights of the L.B. & S.C. Ry.; compiled and arranged by J. B. Winter. For private circulation only. *Brighton: printed by J. Farncombe, Eastern Road*, 1897. pp. [116.] 2″ × 1¼″, gilt edges.   pc
A pocket guide to the identification of train destinations.

5755 FRASER, J. English railways statistically considered. *London*, 1903. pp. xii, 279, 12.   BM
Criticism of railway accounting methods and management, especially relating to the L.B. & S.C. Rly.; with tables of L.B. & S.C. and Midland Rly. accounts for 1900.

6756 BLACKWELL, R. W. The London, Brighton & South Coast Railway electrification. *London*, 1912. pp. 24. la. 4°. in triple column, with 86 illus., diagrams, gradient profiles & plans.   BR
Reprinted from *Engineering*.

6757 LONDON, BRIGHTON & SOUTH COAST RLY. Extension of the elevated electric, London Bridge to Tulse Hill, Crystal Palace, Streatham Hill, Balham, etc. *London*, June 1912. pp. 13, with map.   pc

6758 LONDON, BRIGHTON & SOUTH COAST RLY. Report by Philip Dawson on proposed substitution of electric for steam operation for suburban, local and main line passenger and freight services. [*London*,] January 1921. pp. xxiii, with an accompanying volume of blue-print maps.   BR

6759 TILLING, W. G. The locomotives of the London, Brighton & South Coast Railway, June 1920. *London*, 1920. pp. 44[47].   BM
Lists, notes and illustrations.
—— another edn. *London*, [1923.] pp. 56.   IT
—— 3rd, *London*, [c. 1925.] pp. 56.   RC

London Canal and Railroad Company
[not incorporated]

6760 TATHAM, W. London Canal and Rail-Road! Explanatory remarks on the projected London Canal and Railroad, addressed to the public interests of the metropolis and to the consideration of the nobility, gentry and others, convened at the Crown and Anchor on the invitation of the New River Company. By William Tatham, one of the Sufferers. *London*, 1803. pp. 21.   ICE

London Grand Junction Railway Company
[not incorporated]

6761 MACWILLIAM, R. London Grand Junction Railway: letter to Robert Hay Graham, M.D. *London*, 1836. pp. 23.   PO
Reasons for opposing the railway.

6762 LONDON GRAND JUNCTION RLY. London Grand Junction Railway: a review of its prospects and utility. By a Proprietor. 2nd edn. *London*, 1837. pp. 28.   BM
Advantage of the L.G.J.'s proposed terminus near Euston.

6763 MACWILLIAM, R. London Grand Junction Railway and Sir Samuel Whalley, M.P.: letter to Robert Hay Graham, M.D. (3rd edn.) *London*, 1837. pp. 23.   BM
Reasons for opposing the proposed railway, expressed with heavy sarcasm against Graham.

6764 MacWilliam, R. London Grand Junction Railway, surnamed The Humbug: second letter to Robert Hay Graham, M.D. *London*, 1837. pp. 54.   BM

6765 MacWilliam, R. London Grand Junction Railway, surnamed The Humbug: a letter to . . . John, Duke of Bedford . . . John, Marquis Camden . . . Charles, Lord Southampton . . . George, Lord Calthorpe. *London*, 1838. pp. 52.   BM

6766 MacWilliam, R. London Grand Junction Railway: second letter to . . . John, Duke of Bedford . . . John, Marquis Camden . . . Charles, Lord Southampton . . . George, Lord Calthorpe. *London*, 1838. pp. 43.   LSE

London, Midland & Scottish Railway

Historical

6767 London Midland & Scottish Rly. Historical sketch showing the evolution of the London, Midland & Scottish Railway with a track mileage of upwards of 20,000 miles, from the Liverpool & Manchester Railway with a track mileage of 31½ miles. [*London*,] 1925. pp. 34, with 8 plates.   BM
Cover title, *Centenary of railways*.

6768 Mais, S. P. B. Royal Scot and her forty nine sister engines. *London*, [1928.] pp. 64, with illus.   BM
pp. 11–38, 'The pioneer engines', describing locomotives prior to 1858 of lines which became part of the L.M.S. system.

6769 Vallance, H. A. The Highland section of the L.M.S. Railway. pp. 25. *Typescript.*   RC
Paper, Railway Club, 4 November, 1929.

6770 Dendy Marshall, C. F. One hundred years of railways: from Liverpool & Manchester to London, Midland & Scottish. *London: LMS. Rly.*, 1930. pp. vi, 62, with frontis., 3 plates (1 fold.), and 20 illus. & facsimiles.   BM
Contains details of the L. & M. supplementary to his *Centenary history of the Liverpool & Manchester Railway* (1930).

6771 London, Midland & Scottish Rly. Locomotives of the L.M.S., past and present. *London*, [1931.] pp. 51, with 80 illus. of locomotives (8 col.).   BM

6772 Gardner, J. W. F. London, Midland & Scottish Railway: origin and subsequent development of the railways in Scotland. *Glasgow: the author*, 1934. pp. 75, with plates.   LSE
Cover title, *Railway enterprise*.

6773 London, Midland & Scottish Rly. The story of the Irish Mail, 1848–1934.

[*London*, 1934.] pp. 20. [*LMS Book of the Train*, no. 2.]   BM

6774 London, Midland & Scottish Rly. Constituent and subsidiary companies forming the L.M.S. [*c.* 1936.] pp. 21.   BR
pp. 1–14, Railways.
pp. 15–17, Canals, steamship services, harbours, etc.
pp. 18–21, Joint railways.

6775 Vale, E. Ships of the narrow seas. *London: L.M.S. Rly.*, [1936.] pp. 59, with illus.   BR
L.M.S. ships. Historical and descriptive.

6776 'Economist' *newspaper*. London, Midland & Scottish Railway. *London*, 1938. pp. 15, with tables. (*L.M.S. Supplement.*)   LSE
Histories of the constituent companies of the L.M.S. Rly.

*6777 LMS Centenary of opening of first main-line railway. (Supplement to 'Railway Gazette', Sept. 16, 1938.) *London: Railway Gazette.* pp. 84, with many illus., maps & diagrams.   IT

6778 London, Midland & Scottish Rly. A Century of Progress: London-Birmingham, 1838–1938. (Souvenir of the Centenary of the London & Birmingham Railway, September, 1938.) [*London*, 1938.] pp. 43, with 26 illus., 10 portraits of chairmen, & 2 maps (1 la. col.).   BM

6779 'Times' *newspaper*. London, Midland & Scottish Railway Centenary; reprinted from the L.M.S. Rly. Centenary Number of The Times . . . September 20, 1938. *London*, 1938. pp. 199, with frontis., & 40 illus. on 23 plates.   BM

6780 Willis, R. C. My fifty-one years at Euston. *London: Bell*, 1939. pp. vii, 208.   BM
R. C. Willis was Registrar of the L.M.S. Rly. The work is mainly concerned with his private activities.

6781 London, Midland & Scottish Rly. Centenary of Crewe Locomotive Works, 1843–1943. [*Crewe*, 1943.] pp. 24, with 7 illus. on 4 plates. *Reproduced typescript.*   BR

6782 Chadwick, S. Through the Backbone of England: a complete account of the canal and railway tunnels at the Standedge, Yorkshire. [*Huddersfield: the author*, 1944.] pp. [8.]   SLS

6783 Chadwick, S. Through the Backbone of England. Woodhead Railway Tunnel Centenary; with a complete account of the canal and railway tunnels at the Standedge, Yorkshire. 2nd edn. *Huddersfield: the author*, [1945.] pp. 15.

6784 FISHER, F. H. Notes on the historical background and industrial economy of the South, West and Central Wales district of the L.M.S. *Swansea: L.M.S. District Goods & Passenger Manager's Office*, July, 1945. pp. 23. *Reproduced typescript with printed cover.*   BR

6785 BISHOP, F. C. Queen Mary of the Iron Road: the autobiography of an engine-driver. *London: Jarrolds*, 1946. pp. 150.   BM
His career generally, and with the 'Royal Scot' and 'Coronation Scot' locomotives. Includes an account of the L.M.S. in war-time.

6786 CRESWELL, A. J. Names and numbers, LMS & LNE: over 14,000 engines recorded and classified. *Huddersfield: Quadrant Publications*, 1946. pp. 32.   BM

6787 LONDON, MIDLAND & SCOTTISH RLY. A record of large-scale organisation and management, 1923–1946. *London*, 1946. pp. 20, with 8 statistical tables on 2 fold. sheets.   LSE

6788 COX, E. S. A modern locomotive history: ten years' development on the LMS, 1923–1932: a paper read ... before the Institution of Locomotive Engineers on 2nd January, 1946. *[Leamington Spa:] Railway Correspondence & Travel Society*, 1946. pp. 44, with illus., diagrams, & 10 tables of locomotives, 1923–32. [*Railway Observer Supplement*, 1946, no. 6.]   BM

6789 TITANS of the Track: London, Midland & Scottish Railway. *London & Staines: Ian Allan*, [1945.] pp. [32.]   BM
Photographs.
—— another edn. 1946. pp. 64, with an historical summary on verso pages.   BM

6790 BARRIE, D. S. [M.] The Euston & Crewe c Companion. *South Godstone: Oakwood Press*, 1947. pp. 42, with plates, 4 fold. sections, chronology & bibliography.   BM
History and description of the L.M.S. Rly.

6791 LONDON, MIDLAND & SCOTTISH RLY. Locomotives old and new: some of the engines built by the L.M.S. and its constituent companies, 1829–1947. *London*, 1947. pp. 62.   BM
Illustrations with descriptions.

6792 HARAM, V. S. Centenary of the Irish Mail, 1848–1948. [*London:*] *British Railways(LMR)*, [1948.] pp. 31, with 16 illus. on 8 plates & a map.   BM

6793 LLOYD, R. Railwaymen's Gallery. *London: Allen & Unwin*, 1953. pp. 166, with plates. BM
pp. 119–35, The Highland Railway at war, 1939–45.

6794 TOMKINS, R. M. The Midland Railway 4–4–0 three-cylinder compound locomotives

and later developments. [*London:*] *Stephenson Locomotive Society*, [1954.] pp. 9[10].   BR
Reprint, *S.L.S. Journal*, June 1954.
pp. 5–10, List of compound locos, Midland Rly. and L.M.S. Rly.

6795 'RIVINGTON.' My life with locomotives: a retired locomotive engineer looks back. *London: Ian Allan*, 1962. pp. 168, with 48 illus. on 20 plates, drawings in text, & 2 fold. plans at end.   BM
Forty-five years with the Lancashire & Yorkshire, London & North Western, and the L.M.S. Rly.

*6796 NOCK, O. S. William Stanier: an engineering biography. *London: Ian Allan*, 1964. pp. 190, with 71 illus. on 32 plates, diagrams & tables.   BM
William Stanier was Chief Mechanical Engineer of the L.M.S. from 1932 to 1944.

Contemporaneous

6797 LONDON, MIDLAND & SCOTTISH RLY. Travel LMS—the best way. [*London*, 1924.] pp. 23, with illus.   BR
Outline statistics of the L.M.S.
—— another edn. Britain's greatest railway: London, Midland and Scottish Railway. [*London*, 1925.] pp. 23, with illus.   BR

6798 LEIGH, D. Golf at its best on the L.M.S. *London: L.M.S. Rly.*, 1925. pp. 117, with illus. & fold map.   BR
Includes (pp. 100–17) a list of 550 golf courses which may be reached by the L.M.S. Rly.

6799 LONDON, MIDLAND & SCOTTISH RLY. Gleneagles Hotel: the story of Scotland's great caravanserai. [1925.] pp. 88, with illus.   BR

6800 LONDON, MIDLAND & SCOTTISH RLY. LMS control: the magic wand of transport: the brains behind railway traffic management: the 'all-seeing eye': British Empire Exhibition, Wembley, 1925. *London*, 1925. pp. 35, with illus. & diagrams.   BR
Guide to an exhibit designed to show how trains are controlled.

6801 LONDON, MIDLAND & SCOTTISH RLY. Particulars of steamers, tugs, dredgers and other craft employed on various services. [*London*, 1925.] 10 detailed tables.   BR
Compiled for official use.

6802 LONDON, MIDLAND & SCOTTISH RLY. Description of the London, Midland & Scottish Railway Company's Locomotive Works at Crewe. [1926.] pp. 9. *Reproduced typescript.*   BR

6803 LONDON, MIDLAND & SCOTTISH RLY. The L.M.S.; its railways and its hotels: souvenir of a visit of the International Hotel Alliance to the Adelphi. [*London*, 1926.] pp.[28.]   BR
A brochure, with reproductions of four historic documents.

6804 LONDON, MIDLAND & SCOTTISH RLY.
Some interesting statistics of the LMS and
photos illustrating modern methods in railway carriage and locomotive building.
[*London*, 1923.] pp. 40, with illus.   BR
—— another edn. [*London*, 1927.] pp. 23.
                                               BR

6805 BEAMES, H. P. M. The re-organization of
Crewe Locomotive Works. *London: Institution of Mechanical Engineers*, 1928. pp. 245–
88, with illus.   BR
Excerpt, *Min. Proc. I.M.E.*, meetings, 16 and
22 March, 1928.

6806 LONDON, MIDLAND & SCOTTISH RLY.
LMS railhead storage and distribution, and
other services. *London*, [*c.* 1928.] pp. 35,
with illus.   BR

6807 A PROGRESSIVE system of railway wagon
building. [*London:*] *Railway Engineer*, [1928.]
pp. 13, with illus.   BR
Reprinted from the *Railway Engineer*, April
1928.
The re-organisation of the Earlestown Works
of the L.M.S. and the resulting increased output
of wagons.

6808 LONDON, MIDLAND & SCOTTISH RLY.
Distribution: a vital factor in sales. The new
L.M.S. plan for warehousing and distribution in Great Britain. *New York*, [1929.]
pp. 19.   BR

6809 LONDON, MIDLAND & SCOTTISH RLY.
List of the principal towns and places to
which the London, Midland & Scottish
Railway Company convey goods from
London. *London*, 1929. pp. 99, with fold.
map.   BM

6810 RE-ORGANISATION of Crewe Locomotive
Works, London, Midland & Scottish Railway . . . *London: Railway Engineer*, 1929.
pp. 118, with 5 fold. plates & many illus. &
diagrams in text.   BM

6811 TRAFFIC control on the L.M.S.R. . . .
Westminster: Railway Gazette, [1929.]
pp. 20, with illus., maps & diagrams.   BM

6812 LONDON, MIDLAND & SCOTTISH RLY.
Ports owned and served by the London,
Midland & Scottish Railway. Compiled &
arranged by H. N. Appleby. *London*, [1932.]
pp. lv, 128, with illus. & fold. maps & plans.
                                               BM
A handbook relating to facilities and accommodation at L.M.S. docks, harbours, wharves
and piers.

6813 'MODERN TRANSPORT.' Modern development on LMS Railway: rationalisation; scientific research; costing. *London*,
1932. pp. 30, with 4 fold. tables showing
details of costing methods on the LMS.   IT
Reprint, *Modern Transport*, 28 June; 4 and
1 July, 1932.

6814 LONDON, MIDLAND & SCOTTISH RLY.
LMS country lorry services; list of stations
and schedules of charges: door-to-door
service between producer and consumer.
[*London*, June 1933.] pp. 24, with illus. &
map.   BR

6815 LONDON, MIDLAND & SCOTTISH RLY.
The story of the Royal Scot: Souvenir of the
visit of the train to the North American
Continent and the Century of Progress Exposition, Chicago, 1933. *London*, [1933.]
pp. 31, with 23 illus., incl. a portrait of Sir
Josiah Stamp, Chairman, L.M.S. Rly.   BR

6816 LONDON, MIDLAND & SCOTTISH RLY.—
ELECTRICAL ENGINEERS' DEPARTMENT.
Stonebridge Park Generating Station and
Repair Shop. [1933.] pp. [14,] with 17
mounted photographs. *Reproduced type-
script.*   BR

6817 WILLIAMSON, J. W. A British railway behind the scenes. *London: Benn*, 1933. pp. ix,
213, with 32 illus. on plates.   BM
The L.M.S. Rly.

6818 LONDON, Midland & Scottish Railway
4-6-0 two-cylinder mixed traffic locomotive;
W. A. Stanier, Chief Mechanical Engineer.
London, [1934.] la. fold. s.sh.   BM
Coloured sectional drawing of a Class 5
locomotive, with an identification list of 162
parts.

*6819 LONDON, MIDLAND & SCOTTISH RLY.
The triumph of the Royal Scot, 1933: North
American tour of the Royal Scot train.
London, [1934.] pp. 36, with illus.   BM

6820 LONDON, MIDLAND & SCOTTISH RLY.—
CHIEF COMMERCIAL MANAGER'S DEPART-
MENT. A commercial survey of a rural area
on the London, Midland & Scottish Railway.
Euston (*London*), March 1934. pp. 89.   BR
Very detailed findings of social and industrial
conditions, and transport facilities (goods and
passenger) in the vicinity of Ashchurch, near
Bristol. Presented by S. Scarisbrick and
P. H. D. West; with 13 appendices.

6821 ROBINSON, E. E. The Claughton and Baby
Scot classes (LMS locomotives, Class Book
no. 1.) *Egham*, [1934.] pp. 10, with illus.
                                               BM
Privately printed.
—— Supplement. [1934.] pp. [3.]   BM

6822 LONDON, MIDLAND & SCOTTISH RLY.—
LABOUR AND ESTABLISHMENT DIVISION.
Scheme of machinery of negotiation for rail-
way staff. *London*, May 1935. pp. 32, 35. LSE

6823 LONDON, MIDLAND & SCOTTISH RLY.
—RESEARCH LABORATORY, DERBY. LMS
Research Laboratory, Derby. Official opening
ceremony . . . December 10th, 1935. [*Derby*,
1935.] pp. [12,] with illus.   BR

6824 BELL, W. J. Recent locomotives of the London, Midland & Scottish Railway. *London: Virtue & Co.*, [1936.] pp. 35, with illus. & diagrams. BM

6825 BARRIE, D. S. [M.] Modern locomotives of the L.M.S. *London: L.M.S. Rly.*, [1937.] pp. 34, with 29 illus. on 16 plates. BM

6826 The CORONATION Scot (London, Midland & Scottish Railway). *London: Railway Gazette*, [1937.] pp. 16, with 23 illus. & diagrams of the locomotive 'Coronation' and of the coaches of the train.
Reprinted from the *Railway Gazette*, 28 May, 1937.

*6827 DUCKWORTH, C. L. D. *and* LANGMUIR, G. E. Clyde River and other steamers. *Glasgow: Collingridge*, 1937. pp. xii, 254, with plates. BM
pp. 1–71, L.M.S. Rly. steamers.
pp. 73–91, L. & N.E. Rly. steamers.
—— 2nd edn. *Glasgow*, 1946. pp. xi, 260. BM

6828 LONDON, MIDLAND & SCOTTISH RLY. Reorganisation of the Motive Power Department. *London: Railway Gazette*, [1937.] pp. 27, with illus. & diagrams (2 fold.) RC
Reprinted from *Railway Gazette*, 16, 23 and 30 April, 1937.

6829 LONDON, MIDLAND & SCOTTISH RLY. The track of the Coronation Scot. [*London*, 1937.] pp. 27. [*LMS Book of the Train*, no. 3.] BM
A route chart.

6830 LONDON, MIDLAND & SCOTTISH RLY. —CHIEF MECHANICAL ENGINEER'S OFFICE. Description of coaching stock for 'The Coronation Scot' trains. *Euston (London)*, May 1937. pp. 3, with 7 mounted photographs & a fold. diagram. *Reproduced typescript.* BR

6831 LONDON, MIDLAND & SCOTTISH RLY. —CHIEF MECHANICAL ENGINEER'S OFFICE. Description of new 4–6–2 streamlined locomotive 'Coronation'. *Euston (London)*, May 1937. pp. 6, with mounted photographs & diagram. *Reproduced typescript.* BR

6832 MODERNISING goods depots on the L.M.S.R. *Westminster: Railway Gazette*, [1937.] pp. 12, with illus. PC
Reprinted from the *Railway Gazette*, 5 March, 1937.

6833 LONDON, MIDLAND & SCOTTISH RLY. LMS School of Transport, Osmaston Park, Derby. Official opening ceremony, etc. [*Derby*,] 1938. pp. 16, with plan & 7 illus. BR

6834 LONDON, MIDLAND & SCOTTISH RLY. The track of the Royal Scot: a running commentary on the journey from London to Glasgow & Edinburgh by the West Coast route. *London* [1938.] pp. 31. [*LMS Book of the Train*, no. 4.] BR
A combined edition of *L.M.S. Route Books*, nos. 3 and 4 of 1928.

6835 EARL, L. A. Speeding north with the 'Royal Scot': a day in the life of a locomotive man ... *London: O.U.P.*, 1939. pp. 143[160], with 28 illus. on 15 plates. BM

6836 MECHANISATION of Toton Down Marshalling Yard, L.M.S.R.: introduction of rail-brakes, power-operated points, and other modern equipment. [*Westminster:*] *Railway Gazette*, [1939.] pp. 27, with illus. PC
Reprinted from the *Railway Gazette*, 18 April, 1939.

6837 FAIRBURN, C. E. The electrification of the Wirral lines of the London, Midland & Scottish Railway. *London: Institution of Civil Engineers*, 1944. pp. 52, with illus. & diagrams (some fold.). BR

6838 RUDGARD, H. L.M.S.R. locomotive casualty report system: methods used for reporting and dealing with engine failures. *London: Railway Gazette*, 1944. pp. 7.

6839 STATION design: a modern L.M.S.R. example. *Westminster: Railway Gazette*, 1944. pp. 4, with 6 illus. BM
Luton Station.

6840 LONDON, MIDLAND & SCOTTISH RLY. Reconstruction of Lawley Street Goods Depot, Birmingham. Official opening of new goods shed ... 29 October, 1945. [*London*,] 1945. pp. 20, with 10 illus. & diagram. BR

6841 STOCKTON, V. C. Sectioned perspective view of locomotive front end: a notable drawing of L.M.S.R. Class '7P' 4–6–2 locomotive of the latest type. *Westminster: Railway Gazette*, 1945. pp. 3. BM
A large folding diagram by V. C. Stockton, with descriptive text.

6842 LONDON, MIDLAND & SCOTTISH RLY. LMS getting back to normal. [*London*,] January 1946. pp. 16, with illus. BR
The return to carriage construction: post-war difficulties. A brochure issued to passengers.

6843 LONDON, MIDLAND & SCOTTISH RLY. What you did. [*London*, 1946.] pp. 11. BR
A record of the war work of L.M.S. staff, 1939–45.

6844 LONDON, MIDLAND & SCOTTISH RLY. —CHIEF MECHANICAL AND ELECTRICAL

ENGINEER'S OFFICE. History of the War. [1946.] pp. 128, with many illus. on plates. *Reproduced typescript.* BR

Activities of the Department, including the manufacture of war supplies.

6845 NASH, G. C. The LMS at war. *London: L.M.S. Rly.,* 1946. pp. 87, with plates (some col.). BM

6846 GODDARD, M. N. Report . . . on goods, passenger and parcels traffic on the London & North Eastern Railway, and modern goods shed operation on the London, Midland & Scottish Railway. pp. 28. *Typescript.* IT

Paper submitted to Institute of Transport, April 1947.

6847 L.M.S.R. modernised traffic control organisation . . . *Westminster: Railway Gazette,* [1947.] pp. 12. LSE

Reprinted from the *Railway Gazette,* 9 May, 1947.

6848 LONDON, MIDLAND & SCOTTISH RLY. Carlisle Citadel Station Centenary. [*Carlisle,*] September 1947. pp. 12. BR

Four essays by local railway officials on historical background and present facilities.

6849 LONDON, MIDLAND & SCOTTISH RLY. LMS locomotives in colour. [*c.* 1947.] BR

Six coloured postcards.

6850 LONDON, MIDLAND & SCOTTISH RLY. The LMS Works Training School: Derby Locomotive Works. [*Derby,*] 1947. pp. 24, with illus. & diagrams. BR

6851 LONDON, MIDLAND & SCOTTISH RLY. Locomotive Spotters' Book. [*London,*] 1947. pp. 312. BM

Lists and illustrations of L.M.S. locomotives, followed by (pp. 69 to end) a log for entering spotted locomotives (!).

6852 LONDON, MIDLAND & SCOTTISH RLY. The Scientific Research Department of the L.M.S. *Derby,* [1947.] pp. 23, with illus. BM.

6853 PIKE, S. N. Mile by mile on the L.M.S: the route described in detail through 188 main line stations on the L.M.S. *Worthing,* [1947.] pp. 40. BR

Published by the author. A route chart.

6854 VALE, E. Along the Viking Border . . . *London,* 1928. pp. xxiii, 41. [*Who runs may read. LMS Route Book,* no. 2.] BM

A route chart and itinerary for passengers.

—— another edn. *London,* 1947. pp. xxviii, 51. BM

6855 VALE, E. The track of the Irish Mail . . . *London,* [1928.] pp. xxiv, 72. [*Who runs*

may read. LMS Route Book, no. 1.] BM

A route chart and itinerary for passengers.

—— another edn. *London,* 1947. pp. xxxii, 68. BM

6856 VALE, E. The track of the Twenty Fives, St. Pancras to Manchester . . . *London,* [1929.] pp. xxiv, 51. [*Who runs may read. LMS Route Book,* no. 5.] BM

The expresses which leave St. Pancras at 8.25, 10.25, 12.25, 2.25, 4.25, 6.25 and 8.25 daily.

—— another edn. The track of the Peak Expresses. *London,* Dec. 1947. pp. xxiv, 51. [*LMS Route Book,* no. 5] BM

6857 VALE, E. The track of the Royal Scot. Part 1, Euston to Carlisle . . . Pen and ink sketches . . . *London,* [1928.] pp. xxx, 76. [*Who runs may read. LMS Route Book,* no. 3.] BM

A route chart and itinerary for passengers.

—— another edn. *London,* 1947. pp. xxxvi, 75. BM

6858 VALE, E. The track of the Royal Scot. Part 2, Carlisle to Edinburgh and Glasgow . . . *London* [1928.] pp. xxiv, 48. [*Who runs may read. LMS Route Book,* no. 4.] BM

A route chart and itinerary for passengers.

—— another edn. *London,* 1947. pp. xviii, 40[41]. BM

6859 ALLAN, I. *and* MACLEOD, A. B. The ABC of L.M.S. locomotives. *London: Ian Allan,* 1943–8. BM

Various editions of a booklet containing lists and illustrations.

6860 ALLEN, C. J. The Stanier Pacifics of the L.M.S. *London: Ian Allan,* 1948. pp. 64, with illus. [*ABC Locomotive Series. Famous Locomotive Types,* no. 3.] BM

6861 SYKES, R. P. L.M.S.R. Locomotive Reference Book. *Bristol: British Locomotive Society,* September 1946. BM

—— 2nd edn. *Bristol,* June 1947. pp. 97. BM

—— 3rd edn. 'L.M.R. Locomotive Reference Book, including the ex-L.M.S.R. engines of Scottish Region.' *Bristol,* December 1948. pp. 98. BM

—— 4th edn., by H. R. Christian & R. P. Sykes. *Bristol,* May 1950. pp. 95. BM

6862 ALDRICH, C. L. Fowler and Stanier locomotives of the L.M.S.: a brief descriptive illustrated souvenir of types. *London: E. V. Aldrich,* 1947. pp. 71. BM

—— new edn. 'Fowler, Stanier and Ivatt locomotives of the L.M.S. . . . 1923–1950.' *Brightlingsea,* 1951. pp. 80. BM

6863 RANSOME-WALLIS, P. On railways, at home and abroad. *London: Batchworth Press,* 1951. pp. 299, with frontis. & 100 illus. on 40 plates. BM

—— 2nd edn. *London: Spring Books,* 1960. pp. 300. BM

pp. 75–81, A day on the Lickey Incline.
pp. 81–113, Some modern locomotive work in Great Britain. (Southern and L.M.S.)

London, Tilbury & Southend Railway

6864 THAMES HAVEN DOCK & RAILWAY. Thames Haven Railway, with observations on its anticipated advantages. *London*, 1835. pp. 27. BM

A proposed railway from the Eastern Counties Rly. at Romford, via Hornchurch, Upminster, Orsett and Horndon to Shell Haven.

—— another edn. *London*, 1836. pp. 26. BM

—— another edn. 'Thames Haven Dock & Railway, incorporated by Act of Parliament; with observations on their anticipated advantages.' *London*, 1836. pp. 44. BM

—— another edn. *London*, 1841. pp. 86. BRE

—— another edn. *London*, 1842. pp. 94[96]. LSE

6865 THAMES HAVEN DOCK & RAILWAY. Estimated revenue of the Thames Haven Tide-Dock & Railway as laid before Parliament, and an extract from the 'Public Ledger' of August 2, 1836. *London*, [1836.] pp. 3[4]. BM

6866 MACCRACKEN, N. The London, Tilbury & Southend Railway, from its inception to its absorption by the Midland Railway in 1912. pp. 27. *Typescript*. RC
Paper, Railway Club, 6 May, 1937.

6867 ALLCHIN, M. C. V. Locomotives of the North Staffordshire and the London, Tilbury & Southend railways: types, building dates, etc. *Fareham: the author*, [1943.] pp. 11. BM

6868 ALDRICH, C. L. London, Tilbury and Southend locomotives, past and present, 1880 to 1944. [*London:*] *E. V. Aldrich*, 1945. pp. 39, with 14 illus., lists and notes. BM

—— new edn., *London*, 1946. pp. 48, with 19 illus. BM

6869 WELCH, H. D. The London, Tilbury & Southend Railway. *South Godstone: Oakwood Press*, 1951. pp. 38, with 12 illus. & 2 maps on 7 plates; table of locos. [*Oakwood Library of Railway History*, no. 8.] BM

—— rev. edn. *Lingfield*, 1963. pp. 38. BM

6870 BRITISH RAILWAYS—EASTERN REGION. London, Tilbury & Southend Railway Centenary, 1856–1956. *London*, 1956. pp. [6,] with 11 illus. RC
Commemorative folder.

6871 GOTHERIDGE, I. The Corringham Light Railway. [1958.] pp. 4, with map & illus. *Reproduced typescript*. BM
From *Branch Line News*, December 1957.

Loughborough & Nanpantan Railway

6872 STRETTON, C. E. The history of the Loughborough & Nanpantan edge-rail-way. [1889.] pp. [3.] BM

Lynton & Barnstaple Railway

6873 CATCHPOLE, L. T. The Lynton & Barnstaple Railway, 1895–1935. *Sidcup: Oakwood Press*, March 1936. pp. 62, with col.

frontis., 48 illus., maps & gradient profile on 24 plates, and diagrams and tables in text. BM
The Appendix contains reprints of articles and letters from the local Press.

—— 2nd edn. *Sidcup*, July 1936. pp. 67. IT

—— 3rd, *Sidcup*, 1937. pp. 67. BM

—— 4th, *South Godstone*, 1949. pp. 35. BM

—— 5th, *South Godstone*, 1954. pp. 35. BM
Reprinted, April 1960.

6874 BROWN, G. A. The operation of the Lynton & Barnstaple Railway, 1898 to 1935. *Glasgow*, February 1960. pp. 34, with tables & diagrams. *Reproduced typescript*. BM

Manchester & Cheshire Junction Railway Co.
[not incorporated]

6875 MANCHESTER & CHESHIRE JUNCTION RLY. Report by J. U. Rastrick, 10 October 1836. *Manchester*, 1836. s.sh. BM
His survey.

6876 BELLASIS, E. Speech of E. Bellasis, Esq., before the Committee of the Manchester & Cheshire Junction Railway, in summing up the case on the part of the Manchester South Union Railway Co., Monday, May 9th, 1836. *London*, 1836. pp, 48, with 6 maps. BM

6877 MEREWETHER, H. A. Manchester & Cheshire Junction Railway: speech of Mr. Serjeant Merewether in summing up the case for the Bill, July 22nd 1836. *London*, [1836.] pp. 38. H

6878 MANCHESTER & CHESHIRE JUNCTION RLY. Comparative statement of population, etc. on the lines of the Manchester South Union and Manchester & Cheshire Junction railways. *London*, [1837.] pp. 4. H

Manchester South Union Railway Co.
[not incorporated]

6879 BELLASIS, E. Speech of E. Bellasis, Esq., before the Committee of the Manchester & Cheshire Junction Railway, in summing up the case on the part of the Manchester South Union Railway Co., Monday, May 9th, 1836. *London*, 1836. pp. 48, with 6 maps. BM

6880 GARNETT, W. Answer to the 'Case of the Grand Junction Railway Company as opponents of the Manchester South Union Railway Company'. *London*, 1837. pp. 15. LSE
W. Garnett was chairman of the M.S.U. Rly.

6881 MANCHESTER & TAMWORTH RLY. Report of the debate in the House of Commons, Friday 24th February 1837, on the second reading of the Bill. *London*, 1837. pp. 19. UL(GL)

6882 The SOUTH Union, or Manchester & Tamworth Railway: debate in the House of Commons on the second reading of the Bill, Friday 24 February, 1837. *London*, [1837.] pp. 20.   LSE

6883 MANCHESTER SOUTH UNION RLY. Case of the Manchester South Union Rly. Co. and the Cheshire Junction Rly. Co. [*Manchester*, [1842.] pp. [4,] with map.   BM
A comparison, favouring the M.S.U. Rly.

Maryport & Carlisle Railway

6884 MARYPORT & CARLISLE RLY. Exposition of the traffic, actual and prospective, on the line of the Maryport & Carlisle Railway . . . *Carlisle*, 1837. pp. 16, with a list of committee members, and George Stephenson's report. (By George Gill Mounsey and Edward Tyson, solicitors to the company.) BM

6885 PAPE, F. J. The 'Borough' Guide to the Maryport & Carlisle Railway. *Cheltenham*, [1911.] pp. 56, with illus. & 2 maps.   BM

6886 SIMMONS, J. The Maryport & Carlisle Railway. *Chislehurst: Oakwood Press*, 1947.
b   pp. 34[37], with 11 illus., on 5 plates, maps, tables & many bibliogr. notes. [*Oakwood Library of Railway History*, no. 4.]   BM

Mawddwy Railway

*6887 COZENS, L. The Mawddwy Railway, with the Hendre-Ddu Tramway. *Highgate: the author*, 1954. pp. 64, with 18 illus., 2 maps & a bibliography.   BM

Mersey Railway

6888 Fox, C. D. The Mersey Railway . . . [*London*,] 1883. pp. 8.   ICE
Reprinted from *Contract Journal*, 3 and 10 October, 1883.

6889 Fox, F. The Mersey Railway: comprising the following papers: The Mersey Railway, by Francis Fox; the hydraulic passenger lifts at the underground stations of the Mersey Railway, by William Edmund Rich; with an abstract of the discussion upon the papers. *London: Institution of Civil Engineers*, 1886. pp. 82, with 3 fold. diagrams.   ICE

6890 BRITISH WESTINGHOUSE ELECTRIC AND MANUFACTURING COMPANY. The electrification of the Mersey Railway. *London*, [1903.] pp. 15, with 22 illus., map & gradient profile. [*Special Publication*, no. 7006.]   BR
Reprinted from *The Tramway & Railway World*, 9 April, 1903.

6891 MERSEY RLY. A few facts about the Mersey Railway. *Liverpool*, 1903. pp. 25, with illus. & 3 maps.   RC
History and description.

6892 BRITISH WESTINGHOUSE ELECTRIC AND MANUFACTURING COMPANY. The Mersey Railway of today; being a souvenir of the introduction of electric power on the Mersey Railway, May 1903. *London & Manchester*, 1903. pp. 42[46], with 28 illus., gradient profile & map.   BM

Middleton Colliery Railway

6893 EMSLEY, W. Hunslet Moor: the four Acts of Parliament passed in 1758, 1779, 1793 and 1803, giving powers to the owners of the Middleton Collieries upon certain conditions, to make and use a waggon road over Hunslet Moor to Leeds, with observations thereon. *Leeds*, 1877.   BM

6894 RAILWAY CORRESPONDENCE & TRAVEL SOCIETY *and* RAILWAY & CANAL HISTORICAL SOCIETY. Middleton Colliery Railway Bicentenary Rail Tour, Saturday, 7th June, 1958. Notes and information for passengers. pp. 8, 2, with la. fold. map. *Reproduced typescript*.   PC
Historical notes by David Garnett.

*6895 MIDDLETON RAILWAY PRESERVATION SOCIETY. The Middleton Colliery Railway, Leeds. *Leeds*, April 1960. pp. 16. By David Garnett, with additional notes by York Railway Museum and the Leeds University Railway Society. *Reproduced typescript*. BM
—— 2nd edn. *Leeds*, Dec. 1960. pp. 18, with map.   BM

Midland Railway

For a genealogical table of the Midland see Appendix IIIc

Historical

*6896 [WRIGHT, W.] Th' history o' Haworth Railway fro' t'beginnin' t' th'end. *Keighley*, 1866. pp. 32.   BM
Partly in verse. An account of the construction of the Keighley & Worth Valley Rly in 1862, absorbed by the Midland Rly in 1881.
—— 3rd edn. *Keighley*, 1867. pp. 16.   BM

6897 STRETTON, C. E. The history of the Nottingham & Lincoln line: a paper read at Nottingham on the occasion of the Newark brake trials being held on this branch of the Midland Railway. [*Nottingham*,] 1875. pp.[8.]   BM

6898 STRETTON, C. E. History of the South Midland, afterwards the Leicester & Hitchin line: a paper read at Bedford on the occasion of the eighteenth anniversary of the formal opening of the line. 1875. pp. [12.]   BM

6899 STRETTON, C. E. A few notes on the Leicester & Swannington Railway, compiled principally from the company's books and documents . . . *London*, [1885.] pp. 8.   BM

6900 WILLIAMS, F. S. The Midland Railway, its rise and progress: a narrative of modern enterprise. *London*, [1876.] pp. xii, 700, with 123 illus. & 7 maps.　　　BM
—— 2nd edn., a re-issue, with Press comments appended. *London*, [1876 or 1877.] pp. xii, 700, 4.　　　BM
—— 3rd, *London*, 1877. pp. xvi, 681.　　　BM
—— 4th, *London*, 1878. pp. xvi, 687.　　　BM
—— 5th, *London*, 1888. pp. xvi, 510.　　　BM

6901 STRETTON, C. E. Notes on the Leicester & Swannington Railway. *Leicester*, 1891. pp. 18, with illus.　　　ICE

6902 STRETTON, C. E. The history of the North-Western Railway: a paper read at the North-Western Hotel, Morecambe, on the occasion of the termination of the company, 1st Janaury, 1871. *Leicester*, [1893,] pp.[13.]　　　BM

6903 STRETTON, C. E. The history of the Leeds & Bradford Railway. *London*, 1901. pp. 8.　　　BM
—— 2nd edn. 'The history of the Leeds & Bradford, and Leeds & Bradford Extension railways. 2nd edn. combined.' *Leeds*, 1901. pp. 18.　　　BM

6904 STRETTON, C. E. The history of the Midland Railway . . . with one hundred illustrations and six diagrams. *London*, 1901. pp. xii, 358.　　　BM

6905 STRETTON, C. E. The history of the Birmingham & Gloucester and Bristol & Gloucester railways. 2nd edn. *Leeds*, 1902. pp. 19.

6906 BEMROSE & SONS, LTD. Midland Railway: scenery, industries, history. *London*, 1902. pp. 324.　　　BM
An illustrated guide containing (pp. 51–100) 'A short history of the Midland Railway'. This work, known as the 'Midland Railway Carriage Book', was placed in carriages for the information of passengers.
pp. 53–99, 'Historical notes of the Midland Railway'.
—— 2nd edn. *London*, 1903. pp. 332.　BM

6907 STRETTON, C. E. The history of the Erewash Valley and the Erewash Valley Extension railways: papers read at the Leicester section of the Permanent Way Institution. 1904. pp. [10.]　　　BM

6908 STRETTON, C. E. The history of the Groby granite (private) railway: report of the meeting of the Permanent Way Institution . . . *Groby*, 1904. pp. [8.]　　　BM
A private line forming a branch to the Leicester & Swannington Rly.

6909 STRETTON, C. E. The history of the Ibstock Colliery (private) railway: a paper read at the Ibstock meeting of the Permanent Way Institution. *Ibstock*, 1904. pp. [5.] BM
A private branch line from the Leicester & Swannington Rly.

6910 STRETTON, C. E. The history of the Pinxton & Leicester, afterwards Midland Counties, Railway. [1904.]　　　BM
Offprint from a local newspaper; 10 columns on 5 galleys.

6911 STRETTON, C. E. The history of the Snibston no. 2 Colliery (private) railway: a paper prepared for the Coalville meeting of the Permanent Way Institution. *Coalville*, 1904. pp. [3.]　　　BM
A private branch line from the Leicester & Swannington Rly.

6912 STRETTON, C. E. The history of the Whitwick Colliery (private) railway: a paper prepared for the Coalville meeting of the Permanent Way Institution. *Coalville*, 1904. pp. [2.]　　　BM
A private branch line from the Leicester & Swannington Rly.

6913 STRETTON, C. E. The history of the Nottingham & Mansfield line: a paper read before the Leicester section of the Permanent Way Institution. *Leicester*, 1905. pp. [5.]　　　BM
A branch from the Midland Rly.

6914 STRETTON, C. E. Notes for the information of the members of the Railway Club acting as guides on the occasion of the visit of the British Association for the Advancement of Science to the Leicester & Swannington Railway, August 3rd, 1907. [*Leicester*, 1907.] pp. 16, with map & illus.　　BM
Itinerary, with historical notes.

6915 MUNBY, G. F. W. Former days at Turvey. *London*, 1908. pp. 96.　　　BM
pp. 79–85, 'The coming of the railway and its consequences'. The Bedford & Northampton Rly. (1872).

6916 MIDLAND RLY. The history of a great enterprise: published as a souvenir of a great extension scheme, 1914. [*Derby*, 1914.] pp. 95.　　　BR
A brochure with coloured illustrations issued to commemorate the re-opening of the Adelphi Hotel, Liverpool.

6917 MIDLAND Railway. Dates on which various lines and branches were opened. pp. [9.]
c　*Typescript.*　　　BR

6918 PRATT, G. J. Midland Railway memories: personalities of other days: lights and shadows of the railway service . . . *Derby*, 1924. pp. 32.　　　DERBY PL
Reprinted from the *Derby Daily Telegraph*.
Mostly personalities, but has some interesting sidelights on railway working in the Derby area.
—— Second series. *Derby*, 1924. pp. 76.　　　DERBY PL

*6919 LAMBERT, R. S. The Railway King, 1800–1871: a study of George Hudson and the

business morals of his times . . . *London: Allen & Unwin*, 1934. pp. 320, with illus. BM

Contains much information relating to the railways with which Hudson was associated, including the Midland and North Midland.

—— reprinted, *London: Allen & Unwin* 1964. BM

*6920 HOUGHTON, F. W. The story of the Settle-Carlisle line; (told by F. W. Houghton from an idea by W. H. Foster). *Bradford: Norman Arch Publications*, 1948. pp. 113, with fold. map & 41 illus. BM

6921 TATLOW, J. Fifty years of railway life in England, Scotland and Ireland. *London*, 1920. pp. vi, 223. BM

J. Tatlow was with the Belfast & County Down, Midland, Glasgow & South Western, Midland G.W. of Ireland and the Dublin & Kingstown. Several well-known railwaymen are mentioned.

—— 2nd edn. *London*, 1948. pp. 223, with a biographical introduction by Charles E. Lee. BM

*6922 CLINKER, C. R. The Leicester & Swan-
b nington Railway . . . *Leicester*, 1954. pp. 59–114, with 6 plates, illus., map, tables, 52 bibliogr. notes & a bibliography of 25 items. BM

Reprinted from the *Transactions of the Leicester Archaeological Society*, vol. 30, 1954.

6923 ELLIS, C. H. The Midland Railway. *Lon-
c don: Ian Allan*, 1953. pp. viii, 192, with 90 illus. on plates & a chronology. BM

A history, mainly of Midland locomotives.

—— 2nd edn. *London*, 1955. pp. viii, 192.

6924 CLINKER, C. R. The Birmingham & Derby
b Junction Railway. *Oxford: Dugdale Society*, 1956. pp. 27, with illus., map, & 54 bibliogr. notes. [*Occasional Papers*, no. 11.] BM

6925 DERBY MUSEUM & ART GALLERY. Illus-trated Guide to the Midland Railway Ex-hibit, with description of methods used in its construction. *Derby*, March 1955. pp. 16, with 15 illus. PC

Describing a working model of a section of the Midland Rly., *c.* 1900.

—— 2nd edn. *Derby*, 1957. pp. 20. BM

6926 LEICESTER MUSEUMS & ART GALLERY. Leicester and the Midland Railway. *Leices-ter*, 1957. pp. 15, with 7 illus. BM

Catalogue describing ninety-eight items ex-hibited June–July 1957, with an historical introduction (pp. 4–8) by Jack Simmons.

6927 CLINKER, C. R. The Hay Railway. *Daw-lish: David & Charles*, 1960. pp. 61, with 12 illus. on 8 plates, map, & a reproduction in full of the bye laws, orders & regulations of the company in 1816. BM

6928 ROBBINS, [R.] M. The North Midland Rail-
b way and its enginemen, 1842–3. *In* 'Journal of Transport History', vol. 4, no. 3, May 1960. pp. 180–6, with 22 bibliogr. notes. BM

*6929 POVEY, R. O. T. The history of the Keighley & Worth Valley Railway. *Keighley: Keighley & Worth Valley Railway Preservation Society*, 1963. pp. [34,] with 13 illus. & a plan. BM

Contemporaneous

6930 MIDLAND COUNTIES RLY. Midland Counties Railway. Prospectus of the pro-jected railway from Pinxton to Leicester, with reports on the estimated cost of that undertaking, and on the application of loco-motive steam power to railways generally. *Alfreton*, 1833. pp. 42, with la. fold. map. ICE

Includes Wm. Jessop's report on the altered course of the line and Joseph Glynn's opinions on locomotives.

6931 RENNIE, G. Report of George Rennie on the Midland Counties Railway, to the pro-visional committee. *Leeds*, Nov. 27, 1833. s.sh. LSE

6932 BABINGTON, M. A letter in reply to ob-servations on the subject of the Midland Counties Railway by N. W. Cundy. *Leices-ter*, [1835.] pp. 14. LEICESTER PL

6933 REASONS for altering the line of the Midland Counties Railway so as to pass through the towns of Northampton and Harborough instead of the proposed line by Rugby. *Northampton: Weaver*, [1836.] s.sh. BM

*6934 ALLEN, R., *publisher*. The Nottingham & Derby Railway Companion, beautifully illustrated. *London*, 1839. pp. 47[49]. LSE

6935 DRAKE, J. Drake's Road Book of the Nottingham & Derby and Derby Junction railways . . . *London*, [1839.] pp. 60, with fold. map. LSE

6936 ALLEN, E., *publisher*. The Midland Coun-ties Railway Companion, with topographical descriptions of the country through which the line passes, and time, fare, and distance tables, corrected to 24 August; also, com-plete guides to the London & Birmingham and Birmingham & Derby Junction rail-ways . . . *Nottingham*, 1840. pp. 135, 166, with many illus. BM

6937 DRAKE, J. Road Book of the Sheffield & Rotherham Railway . . . *London*, 1840. pp. vi, 74, with frontis. & map. LSE

pp. 1–6, an historical account of the railway. Also contains 'Stanzas on the opening of the Sheffield & Rotherham Railway'. By Ebenezer Elliott. 'They come! the shrieking steam as-cends . . .'

6938 TEBBUTT, R. A Guide or Companion to the Midland Counties Railway, containing its parliamentary history, engineering facts . . . fare and time tables; with a plan and section of the gradients and numerous pic-torial illustrations. *Leicester*, 1840. pp. 110. LSE

6939 HOLT, G. A sketch of the principal and most interesting objects observed in a tour along the railway from Birmingham to Derby . . . and a continuation of the tour along the North Midland Railway to Belper to Amber Gate . . . *Birmingham*, [1841.] pp. 16, 17. BM

6940 TEBBUTT, R. A Guide to the North Midland, Midland Counties, and London & Birmingham railways, with correct time and distance tables; and illustrated with a map and numerous engravings. An improved edition. *Leicester*, 1842. pp. 122. BM
The earlier edition was *Guide or Companion to the Midland Counties Railway* (1840).

6941 [BIRMINGHAM & GLOUCESTER RLY.] Travellers between Birmingham and Bristol who would prefer not to have to change the carriage at Gloucester are informed that the following petition lies for signature at the stations on the line . . . [1846.] s.sh. LSE
A petition addressed to the House of Commons asking that the recommendations of the Gauge Commission should be adopted, establishing a national uniform gauge. This was part of the campaign of the Birmingham & Gloucester against the broad gauge Bristol & Gloucester.

6942 DRURY, J. *publisher.* The Traveller's Handbook for the Lincoln & Nottingham Railway, describing in an attractive and pleasing form the towns, villages, scenery, etc. during the rapid ride. *Lincoln*, [1846.] pp. 48. BM

6943 DERBY MERCURY. Derby Mercury Extraordinary . . . with a supplement, Wednesday August 15, 1849 . . . Report of the Committee of Investigation to the shareholders of the Midland Railway Company. *Derby*, 1849. pp. 132, with tables. DERBY PL
This report on the administration and accounts of the Midland followed criticism of the conduct of directors in October 1848 and February 1849. (See *The Midland Railway*, by F. S. Williams, 2nd edn., 1877. pp. 123–8.)

6944 NORTH WESTERN RLY. Rules and regulations to be observed by officers and men on the North Western Railway, October 1849. *Settle*, 1849. pp. 52. UL(GL)

6945 A LETTER to John Ellis, Esq., M.P., chairman of the Midland Railway Company, on the Leeds and Bradford lease. *London*, 1851. pp. 56. BM
Criticisms of Ellis, George Hudson and others.

6946 MINUTES and correspondence between the London & North Western, Midland, and Manchester, Sheffield & Lincolnshire companies, and the Great Northern Railway Company. *London*, 1856. pp. 47. BM

6947 A WORD to the shareholders. *London*, 1867. pp. 8. BM
Criticising the policy of the directors of the Midland; dated 18 June, 1867.

6948 The MIDLAND Railway: another word to the proprietors. By a large shareholder. *London*, 1867. pp. 8. BM
Reassuring shareholders of the sound financial position of the company. This is in reply to *A Word to the shareholders*. Dated 3 July, 1867.

6949 BASS, M. T. Overtime, etc. on the Midland Railway: correspondence between M. T. Bass and W. R. Price, Chairman of the Midland Railway. 1871. pp. 17. NLC
See *A Life for Unity*, by Gregory Blaxland (1964). pp. 25–6.

6950 BAZAINE, A. G. Concurrence entre les compagnies de chemins de fer en Angleterre. De la suppression de la 2e classe sur le réseau du Midland, novembre 1874. [*Paris*, 1874.] pp. [27]–40.
Extrait des *Annales Industrielles*, livraison du 27 décembre, 1874.

6951 JONES, G. W. The million on the rail: a few statistics showing the expediency of encouraging the third class passenger to travel. *London*, 1874. pp. 19. NLC
An enlargement of the theme of his *Universal penny railways* (1869). Replies to criticism by James Allport of the Midland of his scheme for fares reform, and analyses the Midland's affairs in the process.

6952 PHILP, R. K. The Midland Railway Panoramic Guide. *London*, 1873. pp. 56. BM
A route book, with maps.
—— new edn. *London*, 1874. pp. 56. BM

6953 'STREPHON' *pseud.* [Edward Bradbury.] Midland Railway sketches: reprinted from The Sheffield Daily Telegraph. *London: Bemrose & Sons*, [1876]. pp. 52. BM
1, 'The Midland Railway at Derby' [station and works]; 2, 'Over the Settle & Carlisle line'; 3, 'On the engine of the Midland midnight express'.

6954 STOKES, E. P. The Barrow route to the Isle of Man. *London: Midland Rly.*, [1883.] pp. 143, with maps & illus. BM
The Midland Rly. and its route from St. Pancras to Barrow described.

6955 MIDLAND RLY. Railway & Canal Traffic Act, 1888. Summary of estimated losses for 12 months on mineral and goods traffic . . . [*Westminster*, 1890.] pp. 6[11], 5[7], with tables. LSE

6956 BRADBURY, E. The Dore & Chinley Railway: the Sheffield Independent's gossiping guide to the district, with map and illustrations of local scenery. *Sheffield*, 1894. pp. 48.
pp. 7–10, The Railway. BM

6957 MIDLAND RLY. A problem and its solution. [*Derby*, 1903.] pp. 56[59], with 29 illus. BR
The heating and ventilation of the Midland Hotel, Manchester.

6958 MEREDITH, W. L. The administrative organization of the Midland Railway Engineering Department ... written 26/12/1883. *Gloucester*, [1904.] pp. 15. BM

Printed for private circulation. 'This descriptive, or biographical outline ... was originally prepared for the information of the Great Western Engineering Committee'.

6959 The COMPLETE Railway Traveller ... [*London*, 1906.] pp. 41, with 19 illus. & 2 maps. BM

Articles from *The Times* of 21 and 28 November, 5, 12 and 19 December, 1905, and 2 January, 1906. A record of a 2000-mile investigation by a member of the staff of *The Times*, in which the 'enterprise and magnitude of the operations of the Midland' are described. The account is given entirely from the aspect of the traveller, and although it is introduced as the result of independent investigation, praise for the Midland is the theme from beginning to end.

6960 COOKE, W. G. Railway rating: an open letter addressed to boards of guardians, assessment committees and county councils. *London*, 1907. pp. 16. BM

'For private circulation only.'
On the appeal by the Midland against assessment of their line and stations at Hampstead.

6961 STRETTON, C. E. Souvenir of the visit of the Railway Club to the Leicester & Swannington Railway, Saturday August 3rd, 1907. [*London: Railway Club*, 1907.] pp. 16, with illus., diagrams & map. RC

6962 MIDLAND RLY. Electrification of the Heysham, Morecambe and Lancaster lines. *London*, 1908. pp. 16, with 16 illus., 11 diagrams & a map. BR

Reprinted from the *Railway Gazette*, 12 and 19 June, 1908.
The first single-phase line in Gt. Britain.

6963 LEAROYD, J. I. Mr. Learoyd's record: travels 1000 miles on British railway in a day ... [*Halifax*, 1910.] pp. 3. BM

From the *Halifax Courier*, 23 July, 1910.
St. Pancras–Leeds–St. Pancras–Carlisle–St. Pancras.

6964 LEAROYD, J. I. Unique trip by train: 1000 miles in twenty hours. Mr. J. I. Learoyd's experiences ... [*Halifax*, 1910.] pp. [7.] BM

Reprinted from the *Halifax Guardian*, 23 July, 1910.

6965 MIDLAND RLY.—MIDLAND GRAND HOTEL, LONDON. [A collection of circulars and instructions issued to staff on the running of the hotel between 1898 and 1911.] BR

About 150 items mounted in a guard book.

6966 MERZ AND MACLELLAN. Midland Railway: report upon the development of suburban traffic by electric traction. *London*, 1913. pp. v, 37, with 8 tables, 4 diagrams & 5 plates. BR

'Private and confidential.' (Two further tables and a typescript letter are inserted at the end of the BR copy.)
Estimated effects of electrification.

6967 MIDLAND RLY. 'Undeniably perfect.' [*Derby*,] 1914. pp. 30. BR

A brochure, with coloured illustrations, issued to commemorate the opening of the new extension to the Adelphi Hotel, Liverpool.

6968 MIDLAND RAILWAY. For King and Country, 1914–1919. [*Derby*, 1921.] pp. vii, 72. BR

A record of the unveiling of the Midland Railway War Memorial at Derby, 15 December, 1921, with a list of 2941 men of the Midland who lost their lives, and other statistical tables of war service.

6969 MIDLAND traffic working: the train control system of the Midland Railway ... *London: Railway Gazette*, 1921. pp. 53, with illus. & diagrams. BM

Reprinted from the *Railway Gazette*, 8 July, 1921.

6970 MIDLAND Railway Carriage and Wagon Works at Derby. [*London:*] *Railway Engineer*, [1922.] pp. 40, with illus. & diagrams. IME

Reprinted from the *Railway Engineer*.

Midland & Great Northern Joint Railway

6971 MIDLAND & GREAT NORTHERN JOINT RLY. Eastwood Ho! via the Royal Route: a guide to the Midland & Great Northern Joint Rly. [1900.] pp. 95, with fold. map. BM

6972 CASSERLEY, H. C. The Midland & Great Northern Railway. *In* 'Regional rounds. No. 1, Eastern and North Eastern Regions' by G. F. Allen. *London*, 1949. pp. 33–9, with illus. BM

6973 BROWN, K. The Eastern & Midlands Railway: a paper read to the Railway Club on 6th February 1953. pp. 25. *Typescript*. RC

6974 MIDLAND & GREAT NORTHERN RAILWAY PRESERVATION SOCIETY. Prospectus. *Ilford*, 1959. pp. 11. RC

The case for preserving the line, recently closed, and recommencing a train service.

6975 MIDLAND & GREAT NORTHERN RAILWAY PRESERVATION SOCIETY. Rail tour, 21st May, 1960. Itinerary. [*Ilford*, 1960.] pp. 5, with 2 illus. & a map. PC

6976 MIDLAND & GREAT NORTHERN RAILWAY PRESERVATION SOCIETY. M. & G.N., and Waveney Valley rail tour, Saturday 8th October 1960. Itinerary. [*Ilford*, 1960.] pp. 7, with 4 illus. & a map. PC

Midland & South Western Junction Railway

6977 TALBOT, J. C. Manchester & Southampton Railway Bill. Mr. Talbot's speech on behalf of the opposing landowners against the Bill, in the House of Lords, 20th August, 1846. *Westminster*, 1846. pp. 59. BM

5978 ALLCHIN, M. C. V. Locomotives of the smaller Welsh railways and of the Midland & South Western Junction Railway: types, building dates, etc. *Fareham: the author,* [1943.] pp. 12.   BM

5979 SANDS, T. B. The Midland & South Western Junction Railway. *Lingfield: Oakwood Press,* 1959. pp. 58, with 20 illus. on 9 plates. [*Oakwood Library of Railway History,* no. 16.]   BM

Mid-Suffolk Light Railway

5980 COMFORT, N. A. The Mid-Suffolk Light Railway. *Lingfield: Oakwood Press,* 1963. pp. 31, with 12 illus. & map on 8 plates, & a bibliography. [*Locomotion Papers,* no. 22.]   BM

Mistley, Thorpe & Walton Railway

5981 PEACOCK, T. B. The Mistley, Thorpe & Walton Railway. *Halstead: the author,*1946. pp. 23, with 10 illus. & map.   BM
This essay also appears in his *Musing on railways* (1948).

North British Railway
Historical

5982 HISTORICAL sketch of the Carlisle & Silloth Bay Railway & Dock Company, dedicated to the shareholders. *Birmingham,* [1871.] pp. 8.   CARLISLE PL
Deals with financial and parliamentary matters only. The last date mentioned in the text is 20 June, 1871.

5983 VALLANCE, H. A. The story of a railway waif: the Invergarry & Fort Augustus Railway. pp. 13. *Typescript.*   RC
Paper, Railway Club, 9 January, 1936.

5984 DOW, G. The first railway across the Border. Issued by the London and North Eastern Railway to commemorate the opening of the North British Railway one hundred years ago. [*London,*] 1946. pp. 43, with illus., tables & fold. map.   BM

5985 [DOW, G.] The story of the West Highland. *London: L.N.E. Rly.,* August 1944. pp. 44, with illus., map & 4 fold. diagrams.   IT
—— 2nd edn. [*London,*] 1947. pp. 63, with a table added.   BM

5986 ELLIS, C. H. The North British Railway. *London: Ian Allan,* 1955. pp. viii, 232, with col. frontis., 92 illus. on 32 plates, & a list of locomotives in 1922.   BM
—— rev. edn. *London,* 1959. pp. viii, 230, with fold. map but no frontis.   BM

5987 STEPHENSON LOCOMOTIVE SOCIETY— SCOTTISH AREA. 'Festival Special', 29th August 1959. pp. 6, with map. *Reproduced typescript.*   SLS
Rail tour itinerary.

5988 STEPHENSON LOCOMOTIVE SOCIETY— SCOTTISH AREA. The White Cockade [Rail Tour]. [*Glasgow,* 1960.] pp. [14.] *Reproduced typescript.*   PC
Itinerary, West Highland Rly., Glasgow–Fort William–Glasgow.

Contemporaneous

5989 GRAINGER, T. Report to the subscribers for a survey of a railway from the Monkland & Kirkintilloch Railway to that part of the Monkland coal field situated north east of Airdrie. *Edinburgh,* 1825. pp. 14, with fold. map & section.   PO

5990 EDINBURGH & GLASGOW UNION CANAL Co. Report relative to railways between Edinburgh and Glasgow. By a special committee appointed by the directors of the Edinburgh & Glasgow Union Canal Company. *Edinburgh,* 1830. pp. 44.   PO

5991 GRAINGER, T. *and* MILLER, J. Observations on the formation of a railway communication between the cities of Edinburgh and Glasgow, with branches to the Frith [*sic*] of Forth at Leigh, and the River Clyde at Glasgow. *Edinburgh,* 1830. pp. 10, 4, with map & illus.   PO

5992 EDINBURGH & GLASGOW RLY. Reports by Mr. George Stephenson of Liverpool and Messrs. Grainger and Miller of Edinburgh, civil engineers. Submitted to the subscribers and to the communities of Edinburgh, Glasgow and Leith by the Committee of Management, November 1831. *Edinburgh,* 1831. pp. 28, with la. fold. map & section.   BM

5993 CRICHTON, D. M. M. Defence of the proprietors and tenantry of Fife from the charge of resisting reasonable terms and forcing the Edinburgh & Northern Railway Company into litigation. [*Edinburgh,* 1840?] pp. 4.   H

5994 GRAINGER, T. Observations addressed to the Committee of the Chamber of Commerce of the City of Edinburgh relative to the proposed railway from the north shore of the Firth of Forth . . . to the shore of the River Tay . . . to be called the Edinburgh, Dundee and Northern Railway; with remarks on the proposed line . . . called the Forth & Tay Western line of railway. *Edinburgh,* 1841. pp. 32, with maps & tables.   LSE

5995 WILLOX, J. Guide to the Edinburgh & Glasgow Railway . . . *Edinburgh,* 1842. pp. viii, 136, with 3 fold. maps.   BM

5996 FRASER & CO. Fraser's Companion for the Edinburgh & Glasgow Railway . . . *Edinburgh,* [1845.] pp. 4.   LSE
Map and sections, time-tables and description of the line, folded into a wallet.

6997 AYTOUN, J. Speech . . . on the Sunday trains question, Edinburgh & Glasgow Railway. *Glasgow*, 1847. pp. 8.

6998 EDINBURGH & GLASGOW RLY. Sabbath passenger trains: authentic report of the great public meeting held in the City Hall, Glasgow, on Wednesday evening, 20th January 1847, for the purpose of expressing approval of the conduct of the directors of the Edinburgh & Glasgow Railway in discontinuing the running of passenger trains on the Lord's Day. *Glasgow*, 1847. pp. 32. AU

6999 EDINBURGH & GLASGOW RLY. Withdrawal of Sabbath passenger trains neither a violation of contract with the Government nor an infringement of rights of conscience. *Glasgow*, 1847. pp. 16.   AU

7000 MONKLAND & KIRKINTILLOCH RLY. Rules, bye-laws and orders of the Monkland & Kirkintilloch Railway, the Ballochney Railway, and the Slamannan Railway. *Glasgow*, 1847. pp. 57.   LSE

7001 BRUCE, J. Tullis's Guide to the Edinburgh & Northern Railway . . . *Cupar*, 1848. pp. 37.
                    BM

7002 'ARGUS' *and others.* Letters of Argus, Civis, and Master Mariner, exposing the folly of the project of railway from Drumburgh to Silloth Bay; with an Appendix containing the reports of Messrs. Hartley, Robinson and Blyth. [*Carlisle*,] 1853. pp. 32.   BM
    Letters to the *Carlisle Patriot* and the *Carlisle Journal.*

7003 [CHAMBERS, W. & R.] Peebles and its neighbourhood, with a run on Peebles Railway. *Edinburgh*, 1856. pp. 96, with illus.   BM
    pp. 8–28, History and description of the line

7004 'JUDEX.' The Hawick and Carlisle railways: the case stated and the best route indicated. By Judex. *Carlisle*, 1858. pp. 38.   BM
    Arguments in favour of the North British, Hawick & Carlisle Junction Railway Bill and against the Caledonian Railway's plans. Appendix, 'The Silloth Railway & Dock'.

7005 MEASOM, G. The Official Illustrated Guide to the Lancaster & Carlisle, Edinburgh & Glasgow, and Caledonian railways . . . *London*, 1859. pp. 384, 184, 8, 8, with 150 engravings.   UL(GL)

7006 LANGLEY, J. B. The dangers of the North British Railway policy; or, A question for the consideration of the inhabitants of Newcastle and the surrounding towns, candidly stated and impartially discussed. 2nd edn. *Newcastle*, [1861.] pp. 16.   BM
    The London & North Western preferred to the N.B. Rly.

7007 MEASOM, G. Measom's Official Illustrated Guide to the North Eastern, North British, Edinburgh & Glasgow, Scottish Central, Edinburgh, Perth & Dundee, Scottish North Eastern, and Great North of Scotland railways . . . *London*, 1861. pp. 447, 224, with 200 engravings.   BM

7008 LEES, H. The North British Railway: its past and future policy; with remarks on the duties and responsibilities of directors in reference to accounts. *Edinburgh*, 1866. pp. 18.   BM

*7009 [WEST HIGHLAND RLY.] Mountain, moor and loch illustrated by pen and pencil on the route of the West Highland Railway . . . *London*, 1894. pp. 180, with 230 illus. & a map of the railway.   BM
    Some W.H. Rly. scenes are included.

7010 NORTH BRITISH RLY. Souvenir of the opening of the North British Station Hotel, Edinburgh, 15th October 1902. Contents, Old and New Edinburgh; North British Station Hotel; North British Railway. By John Geddie. *Edinburgh*, [1902.] pp. 89, xxi, with illus. & fold. map.   BR

North Devon & Cornwall Junction Railway

*7011 WHETMATH, C. F. D. *and* STUCKEY, D. The North Devon & Cornwall Junction Light Railway and the Marland Light Railway. (Torrington to Halwill.) *Lingfield: Oakwood Press*, 1963. pp. 24, with 15 illus. on 8 plates, map, & 3 diagrams. [*West Country Handbooks*, no. 3.]   BM

North Eastern Railway

Newcastle & Carlisle Railway: NC
Stockton & Darlington Railway: SD

Historical

7012 NEWCASTLE & CARLISLE RLY. [Reports of the directors, of the Managing Committee, and of Francis Giles, Engineer, 1823–1845.]   BM
NC

7013 MACNAY, T. A lecture on our roads and railways, delivered at the Mechanics' Hall, Darlington, on Friday, February 1st, 1861. *Darlington*, 1861. pp. 24.   LSE
SD   On the S. & D. and on railway development generally. Edward Pease presided at this meeting.

7014 MEWBURN, F. Memoir of Francis Mewburn, Chief Bailiff of Darlington and first railway solicitor. By his son. [*Darlington*,] August, 1867. pp. 82.   BM
SD   F. Mewburn and his work as solicitor for the S. & D. and for the Auckland & Weardale, Wear Valley, Middlesbrough & Redcar, Great North of England and the Middlesbrough & Guisbrough. Edward Pease.

7015 TWEDDELL, G. M. The history of the Stockton & Darlington Railway and its various branches, from its commencement
SD

to the present time. *Stokesley*, 1869–70. pp. 72. BM
Six parts only of an intended twelve, published serially.

7016 JOSEPH PEASE: a memoir . . . *London & Darlington*, [1872.] pp. 38, with an Ap-
SD pendix. BM
Reprinted from the *Northern Echo*, 9 February, 1872.

7017 CLEPHAN, J. The story of Stockton Bridge, with also, the canal and the railroad (Stock-
SD ton & Darlington) and the steamboat on the Tyne. *Newcastle-upon-Tyne*, 1875. pp. 58. BM
'Printed for private circulation.'
pp. 27–50, an account, in part memoirs of the author, of the events and personalities con-concerned with the formation of the S. & D. Rly.

7018 JEANS, J. S. Jubilee Memorial of the Rail-way System: a history of the Stockton & Darlington Railway and a record of its
SD results. *London*, 1875. pp. xvii, 315, with 6 plates. BM
Very detailed. pp. 191–269, biographical accounts of E. Pease, J. Backhouse, G. Stephenson, J. Pease, T. Meynell, H. Pease, F. Mewburn, J. Dixon, T. Hackworth, and a list of original shareholders.

7019 MEWBURN, [F.] The Larchfield Diary: extracts from the diary of the late Mr. Mew-
SD burn, first railway solicitor. *London*, 1876. pp. 224. PC
Period, 1825–1867. Contains much information on railway affairs and personalities, especially relating to the S. & D. and other railways in the Darlington area.

7020 [RICHARDSON, T.] History of the Darling-ton & Barnard Castle Railway; with notices
SD of the Stockton & Darlington, Clarence, West Hartlepool, and other railways and companies in the district. By 'An Inhabitant of Barnard Castle'. *London*, 1877. pp. iv, 93. BM

7021 STOCKTON & DARLINGTON RLY. [A collection of letters, cuttings, etc., relating
SD to the early history of railways, and especi-ally to the Stockton & Darlington Railway. Period, 1818–1881. Compiled by William Weaver Tomlinson.] 5 vols. NEWCASTLE PL

7022 JUBILEE of the world's first public railway, the Stockton & Darlington, 1875: a chapter
SD in the history of railway locomotion, and a memoir of Timothy Hackworth, the father of locomotives; with a portrait and a list of some of his principal inventions. *Leam-inton Spa*, [1893.] pp. 36. BM
pp. 3–13, 'A chapter in the history of railway locomotion', reprinted from the *Practical Mechanics Journal*, 1851.
pp. 14–20, 'Memoir of Timothy Hackworth',

reprinted from the *Practical Mechanics Journal*, 1851.
pp. 22–3, Appendix, 'Timothy Hackworth's inventions', by John Wesley Hackworth.

7023 HARRISON, C. A. Presidential address delivered to the Newcastle upon 'Tyne As-sociation of Students of the Institution of Civil Engineers, October 24, 1894. [*New-castle upon Tyne*, 1894.] pp. 13. BR
Review of progress of railway civil engineer-ing, especially on the North Eastern.

7024 MACLEAN, J. S. The locomotives of the North Eastern Railway, 1854–1905: intro-duced by a sketch of the formation of the company and an account of some of the early famous locomotives on the lines now merged in its system. *Newcastle-on-Tyne*, [1905.] pp. 142, with 62 illus., diagrams & tables. BM

*7025 POTTER, G. W. J. History of the Whitby & Pickering Railway . . . 2nd edn. *London*, 1906. pp. vi, 81, v, with 40 illus. & 2 maps. BM

7026 HEAVISIDES, M. The history of the first public railway, Stockton & Darlington: the
SD opening and what followed. *Stockton-on-Tees*, 1912. pp. 95, with illus. BM

7027 PROGRESS on the North Eastern. *In* 'Jubi-lee of the Railway News, 1864–1914.' *London: Railway News*, [1914.] pp. 124–8, with illus. BM

*7028 TOMLINSON, W. W. The North Eastern Railway: its rise and development. *New-
c castle-upon-Tyne*, [1915.] pp. xvi, 820, with many illus. & maps; chronology (1904–
SD 1914); lists of officials; bibliographical notes. BM
'Written with full access to official docu-ments.'
Includes a detailed history of the Stockton & Darlington Rly.

*7029 YOUNG, R. Timothy Hackworth and the
SD locomotive. *London*, 1923. pp. xxxii, 406. BM
Includes the S. & D. Rly.

7030 WILKINSON, E. F. History of the North Eastern Railway Company's coat of arms; illustrated by J. Foster Stackhouse. *Leeds*, [1924?] pp. 17[19]. BR

7031 DAVIES, R. The Railway Centenary: a retrospect. *London: London & North Eastern
SD Rly.*, [1925.] pp. 49, with 18 illus. on plates (3 col.). BM
pp. 4–41, the Stockton & Darlington scheme, the Rocket, and the opening ceremony.

7032 D[IXON], W. Intimate story of the origin of railways. By 'W. D.' *Darlington*, 1925.
SD pp. 22, with illus. & maps. BM
Personal boyhood reminiscences of acquain-tanceship with early pioneers, including George Stephenson and Edward Pease.

*7033 'NORTHERN ECHO.' Railway Centenary Supplement. *Darlington*, 1925. pp. 80, with
SD many illus. IME
The S. & D. and subsequent railway development in North-east England.

7034 STOCKTON-ON-TEES RAILWAY CENTENARY COMMITTEE. The centenary of
SD public railways at their birthplace, Stockton-on-Tees, with a brief history of the town prior to and since 1825. *Stockton-on-Tees*, 1925. pp. 105[107], with illus. RC
pp. 22–83, Early railway and locomotive history, and the Stockton & Darlington Rly.

*7035 LAMBERT, R. S. The Railway King, 1800–1871: a study of George Hudson and the business morals of his times . . . *London: Allen & Unwin*, 1934. pp. 320, with illus. BM
Contains much information relating to the railways with which Hudson was associated, including the Newcastle & Berwick, and the York & North Midland.
—— reprinted, *London: Allen & Unwin*, 1964. BM

7036 MACLEAN, J. S. The locomotives of the North Eastern Railway, 1841 to 1922. *Newcastle-on-Tyne*, [1925.] pp. 120, with 129 illus. BM
—— 'War-time Emergency edn.' *London*, 1944. pp. 120. BM

7037 [TAYLOR, E. H.] Weardale Railway Centenary, 1847 [to] 1947. *Bishop Auckland: J. Lingford*, 1947. pp. 24, with illus. & a map in text. BM
pp. 2–6, 'A century of wheels: the railway in Weardale' by S. W. M. Hind.

7038 MACLEAN, J. S. The Newcastle & Carlisle Railway, 1825—1862; compiled from
NC official reports, documents and records. *Newcastle upon Tyne: R. Robinson*, 1948. pp. vi, 121, with 46 plates, 39 illus. & 2 fold. diagrams. BM
Includes biographies.

7039 METCALFE, A. J. An interesting record of railway life: over 100 years link with 3
SD railways: S. & D.R., N.E.R., L.N.E.R. [*c.* 1950] pp. [12,] with 5 illus., mounted. *Typescript.* BR
John Metcalfe, first railway policeman [?], S. & D. Rly., 1846, and other members of the Metcalfe family in railway service.

7040 BELL, R. Twenty-five years of the North Eastern Railway, 1898–1922. *London: Railway Gazette*, 1951. pp. 87. BM
R. Bell was General Manager of the N.E.R. and the L.N.E.R., 1922–1943. A 'sketch in lighter vein' to supplement Tomlinson's official history of the North Eastern Rly.

7041 JONES, C. M. J. The North Eastern Railway: a centenary story. [*York*:] *British Rlys. (N.E. Region)*, 1954. pp. 31, with 19 illus. & 2 maps. BM

7042 NOCK, O. S. Locomotives of the North Eastern Railway. *London: Ian Allan*, 1954. pp. viii, 200, with col. frontis. & 82 illus. on 35 plates (some col.). BM

7043 ARMSTRONG, J. W. *and* HARROP, G. The Tees-Tyne rail tour (Manchester Locomotive Society and Stephenson Locomotive Society, North Western Area). Descriptive notes. *Manchester*, August 1956. pp. 14. *Reproduced typescript.* PC
The N.E. Rly. in Durham. Historical and descriptive.

7044 HOOLE, K. The B 16 4–6–0 locomotives [of the North Eastern Railway]. pp. 3. *Reproduced typescript.* PC
Issued as a Supplement to the Itinerary of the Tees–Tyne rail tour, 2 September, 1956, Manchester Locomotive Society and the Stephenson Locomotive Society, N.W. Area.

7045 PARRIS, H. W. Northallerton to Hawes: a study in branch-line history. *In* 'Journal
b of Transport History', vol. 2, no. 4, November 1956. pp. 235–48, with map, 3 tables & 77 bibliogr. notes. BM
N.E. Rly.

7046 BRITISH TRANSPORT COMMISSION— HISTORICAL RECORDS. Stockton & Dar-
SD lington Railway: a summary of the letters and other documents, 1818–1825, in the classified collection of the British Transport Commission Historical Records at York. *York*, July 1957. pp. 8. *Typescript.* BR

7047 WHESSOE, LTD. The history of Whessoe. *Darlington*, [1958.] pp. 26[27], with illus.
SD BM
William & Alfred Kitching and their foundry work for the S. & D. Rly.

7048 HOOLE, K. The North Eastern electrics. *Lingfield: Oakwood Press*, 1961. pp. 58, with 18 illus., map, chronology & distance chart. BM

7049 ELLIS, C. H. Lewin papers concerning Sir George Gibb. *In* 'Journal of Transport History', vol. 5, no. 4, November 1962. pp. 226–32. BM
George Stegmann Gibb and the North Eastern Rly. Contains a memorandum by Henry Grote Lewin on his career with the N.E. Rly., and details of the work of E. C. Geddes and Philip Burtt.

*7050 ALLEN, C. J. The North Eastern Railway. *London: Ian Allan*, 1964. pp. 240, with 125 illus. on 48 plates, 13 maps & 5 diagrams. BM

Contemporaneous

7051 [CHAYTOR, W.] Observations on the proposed rail-way or tramroad from Stockton to
SD the collieries by way of Darlington. *Durham*, 1818. pp. 23, with tables.
The report to the provisional committee appointed by the subscribers.

7052 A REPORT relative to the opening a communication by a canal or a rail or tramway,
SD from Stockton, by Darlington, to the collieries. *Stockton*, 1818. pp. 16.   BM
Issued by a committee appointed to consider the opening of a line of communication between Stockton and the collieries by Darlington. (Chairman, Thomas Meynell.) The report is based upon the survey made by George Overton and the advice of John Rennie.

7053 The FOLLOWING objections to the proposed railway between Stockton and Darling-
SD ton and the collieries by Darlington having been circulated it is deemed necessary to expose their fallacy. *Darlington*, [1819.] s.sh.   DARLINGTON PL

7054 STOCKTON & DARLINGTON RLY. A further report on the intended rail or
SD tram road from Stockton by Darlington to the collieries, with a branch to Yarm. *Darlington*, 1821. pp. 22.   ICE

7055 CHAPMAN, W. A report on the cost and separate advantages of a ship canal and of a
NC railway from Newcastle to Carlisle, published by order of and addressed to the Committee of Enquiry. *Newcastle*, 1824. pp. 21.   BM
—— 2nd edn. *Newcastle*, 1824. pp. 21, BM

7056 CHAPMAN, W. Observations on the most advisable measures to be adopted in form-
NC ing a communication for the transport of merchandise and the produce of land to or from Newcastle and Carlisle or the places intermediate . . . *Newcastle*, 1824. pp. 10. BM
A railway preferred.

7057 JESSOP, J. Report of Josias Jessop . . . civil engineer, drawn up by order of and
NC addressed to, the committee of enquiry into the most desirable mode of improving the communication between Newcastle and Carlisle. *Butterley Hall*, 1825. pp. 2.   LSE
A railway preferable to a canal.

7058 THOMAS, W. Observations on canals and railways, illustrative of the agricultural and
NC commercial advantages to be derived from an iron rail-way adapted to common carriages between Newcastle, Hexham and Carlisle, with estimates of the presumed expense, tonnage and revenue. Also, Second edition, a report of Barrodall Robert Dodd . . . on a proposed navigable canal between Newcastle and Hexham, with Appendix containing remarks on the great utility of a proposed junction canal or railway uniting Newcastle . . . and Carlisle with Liverpool, Manchester, Hull, Derby, Shef-

field, Birmingham, Bristol and London. *Newcastle-upon-Tyne*, 1825. pp. 52.   BM
Printed from a copy of the paper read to the Literary & Philosophical Society of Newcastle in 1805.

7059 ADAMSON, J. Sketches of our information as to railroads; also, An account of the
SD Stockton & Darlington Rail-Way. *Newcastle*, 1826. pp. 60.   BM
pp. 30–60, Stockton & Darlington Rly.

7060 An ACCOUNT of the opening of the Stockton & Darlington Railway, and extracts
SD from the report of the Committee to the proprietors at their annual meeting held at Yarm on Tuesday the 10th day of July 1827. *Newcastle*, 1827. pp. 10.   BM
Reprinted from the *Newcastle Courant*, 1st October, 1825.

7061 HILL, T. A treatise upon the utility of a railway from Leeds to Selby and Hull . . . *Leeds*, 1827. pp. 32, with 3 plates. ICE
The proposed Leeds & Hull Rly.

7062 OBSERVATIONS on the practicability and advantages of the continuation of the Stock-
SD ton & Darlington Railway from Croft Bridge to the City of York, and by means of collateral branches to effect a speedy, cheap and direct communication between the counties of Northumberland and Durham, the ports of Newcastle and Stockton, and the agricultural districts of the North Riding of Yorkshire and the manufacturing and commercial districts of Yorkshire and Lancashire, etc. *Ripon*, 1827. pp. 18.   BM
Signed 'A Practical Farmer'.
pp. 13–18, 'Railway from Croft Bridge to the City of York'. Addressed to the editor of the *York Herald* and signed 'A Constant Reader'.

7063 CLARENCE RLY. Reasons in support of the Bill. April 1829. [*London*, 1829.] pp. 3. BM

7064 HILL, T. A supplement to the short treatise on railroads generally, explaining particularly the Liverpool and Manchester, also the Leeds, Selby and Hull rail-roads & the consequent great change that will be effected by them . . . & which will show that horsepower is cheaper, preferable & more expeditious than locomotive engines . . . *Leeds*, 1829. pp. 16, with 2 diagrams & a map.   ICE

7065 [NEWCASTLE & CARLISLE RLY.] Copy of the Evidence taken before a Committee
NC of the House of Commons on the Newcastle & Carlisle Railway Bill . . . taken from the short hand notes of Mr. Gurney; to which is added the Report of Mr. Leather on the projected line of railway. *Newcastle-upon-Tyne*, 1829. pp. 229.   LSE

7066 WALKER, J. Report to the Committee of the proposed railway from Leeds to Selby, July 18, 1829. *London*, 1829. pp. 24, with fold. map & fold. plan.   ICE

7067 GILES, F. Newcastle & Carlisle Railway. Report on the comparative qualities of a NC line between Scotswood and Crawcrook Mill by way of Blaydon . . . and between those points by way of Lemington. *Newcastle*, 1830. pp. 12. BM

7068 GILES, F. Report on improvement in the line of railway between Scotswood and NC Ryton so as to pass it through Lemington and Newburn instead of through Blaydon. *Newcastle*, 1830. pp. 7. BM

7069 GILES, F. Report on the parliamentary line of railway from Newcastle to Carlisle. NC May 1829. *Newcastle*, 1830. pp. 7. BM

7070 GILES, F. Second report on the line of railway from Newcastle to Carlisle, with NC estimate of the cost thereof, August 19, 1829. *Newcastle*, 1830. pp. 32, with tables. BM
Addressed to the directors of the Newcastle & Carlisle Rly.

7071 HUGILL, J. An address to the inhabitants of Whitby and its vicinity . . . on extending our commerce by constructing a railway to Pickering and Malton. *Whitby*, 1830. pp. 70. BM

7072 GILES, F. Report of Francis Giles . . . Engineer for the Newcastle & Carlisle NC Railroad, read to the shareholders at their Annual Meeting, March 28, 1832. *Newcastle*, [1832.] pp. 4. LSE

7073 GILES, F. Mr. Giles' report to the directors of the Newcastle & Carlisle Railway NC Co., read to the shareholders at their Annual Meeting, March 27, 1833. *Newcastle*, 1833. pp. 2. BM

7074 THOMPSON, W. The Whitby & Pickering Railway: its probable traffic and revenue. *Whitby*, 1833. pp. 15. BM

7075 G., J. A Guide to Croft, Dinsdale, Middleton, Darlington, etc., comprising analysis SD of the mineral waters, and a detailed account of the Stockton & Darlington Railway. *Darlington*, 1834. pp. 105, with frontis. & plates. H

7076 RICHARDSON, J. Observations on the proposed railway from Newcastle upon Tyne to North Shields and Tynemouth. *Newcastle-upon-Tyne*, 1831. pp. iv, 48, with tables. ICE
Newcastle, North Shields & Tynemouth Rly.
—— 2nd edn. *London*, 1834. pp. 72. H

7077 [STANHOPE & TYNE RLY.] Opening of the Stanhope & Tyne Railway . . . *Newcastle-upon-Tyne*, 1902. pp. 18. BM
Reprinted from the *Newcastle Journal*, 13 September, 1834.

7078 WALKER, J. *and* BURGES, A. Report to the subscribers for a survey of the part of the Leeds & Hull Junction Railway between Hull and Selby. *Hull*, 1834. pp. 8. ICE

*7079 BRANDLING JUNCTION RLY. Brandling's Junction Railway, to connect the towns of Gateshead, South Shields, and Monk Wearmouth, to facilitate the communication between the adjacent towns of Newcastle-upon-Tyne, North Shields, Bishop Wearmouth, and Sunderland, and to join the Newcastle & Carlisle, Springwell, Tyne & Stanhope, and Durham Junction railways. *London*, 1835. pp. 18. BM
A prospectus.

7080 G., J. Newcastle & Carlisle Railway: a new song; tune, 'Patrick O'Neell'. 'On NC the ninth day of March in the year thirty-five . . .' *Newcastle: W. Boag*, [1835.] s.sh. LSE
Nine verses.

7081 MALAM, J. Considerations on railways, proving their utility, with explanatory remarks demonstrating great advantage to the agricultural, commercial and manufacturing interests from the projected line between Hull and Selby. *Hull*, [1835.] pp. 15, with tables. H

7082 PARSONS, E. The Tourist's Companion; or, The history of the scenes and places on the route by the rail-road and steam-packet from Leeds and Selby to Hull. *London*, 1835. pp. vii, 243. BM
pp. 53–84, The Railroad (the Leeds & Selby, and the Hull & Selby railways).

7083 BRANDLING JUNCTION RLY. Prospectus of the Brandling Junction Railway, to connect the towns of Gateshead, South Shields, and Monkwearmouth, to facilitate the communication between the adjacent towns of Newcastle-upon-Tyne, North Shields, Morpeth, Bishopwearmouth, and Sunderland, to join the Stanhope & Tyne, and Durham Junction, the Newcastle & Carlisle, and Great North of England railways, and to complete the communication between the east and west seas. [*Newcastle-upon-Tyne*, 1836.] pp. 28. PO

7084 BROOKE, H. Sketch of the railroad from Carlisle to Greenhead; with a description of NC the scenery along the line, taken Wednesday, July 13th, 1836. *Carlisle*, 1836. pp. 15. BM
Notes of a journey made on the N. & C. a few days before its opening.
—— 2nd edn. *Carlisle*, 1836. pp. 15. BM

*7085 DODGSON, G. Illustrations of the scenery on the line of the Whitby and Pickering Railway in the North Eastern part of Yorkshire; from drawings by G. Dodgson; with a short description of the district and undertaking by Henry Belcher. *London*, 1836.

pp. viii, 115, with engr. t.-p., 12 plates, & illus. in text.   BM

pp. 107–15, 'The account of the opening of the railway'.

7086 HULL & SELBY RLY. Hull & Selby Railway, connecting Liverpool with Hull, through Manchester and Leeds, making a complete railway communication from the Irish Sea to the German Ocean: report of the directors . . . laid before the proprietors at their First General Meeting on Wednesday the 31st of August 1836; with an Appendix. *Hull*, 1836. pp. 30, with fold. map & section.   PO

7087 LEEDS & SELBY RLY. Case of the Leeds and Selby Railway Company, petitioners against the York and North Midland Railway Bill. April 1836. *London*, [1836.] pp. [2.]   H

7088 STOREY, T. Report on the Great North of England Railway connecting Leeds and York with Newcastle-upon-Tyne. *Darlington*, 1836. pp. 25, with fold. plan of G.N. of E. Rly. & fold. chart showing sections.   PO

Addressed to the Central Provisional Committee of the G.N. of E. Rly.

7089 NEWCASTLE, EDINBURGH & GLASGOW RLY. An account of the public meetings holden in the several towns in Scotland through or near which the railway from Newcastle to Edinburgh and Glasgow is proposed to go, with the resolutions passed at the meetings, together with the general report on the line by Joshua Richardson; with a coloured map of the railway, engraved by Collard. *Newcastle-upon-Tyne*, 1837. pp. viii, 60.   BM

This work has a secondary title-page, 'Report of the proceedings of several meetings held for the purpose of considering the expediency of forming a railway betwixt Newcastle, Edinburgh & Glasgow, through Jedburgh. From the Kelso Chronicle.' *Kelso*, 1836.   BM

7090 RAILWAY from Hull to Selby. By a shareholder . . . *London*, 1837. pp. 12.   ICE

From the *Railway Magazine*, June 1837.

7091 RICHARDSON, J. The second General Report on the Newcastle-upon-Tyne, Edinburgh & Glasgow Railway. Addressed to the provisional committees, 22nd June, 1837. *Newcastle-upon-Tyne*, 1837. pp. 32, 13, with fold. map & section.   BM

The report is wrongly dated 1836 at end. The Appendix is a selection of letters from Scottish newspapers.

7092 BLACKMORE, J. Great Inland Junction Railway; or, Inland line of railway from NC Newcastle-upon-Tyne to Edinburgh. To the directors of the Newcastle-upon-Tyne & Carlisle Railway. *Newcastle-upon-Tyne*, 1838. pp. 4.   BM

7093 DIBDIN, T. F. A bibliographical, antiquarian and picturesque tour in the northern NC counties of England and in Scotland. *London*, 1838. 3 vols.   BM

vol. 1, pp. 402–6, Newcastle & Carlisle Rly.

7094 LONGRIDGE, M. [*and* BIRKINSHAW, J.] Remarks on the comparative merits of cast SD metal and malleable iron rail-ways, and an account of the Stockton & Darlington Railway . . . *Newcastle*, 1827. pp. iv, 22, 39.   PO

—— another edn. '. . . and the Liverpool & Manchester Railway, by Henry Booth.' *Newcastle*, 1832. pp. 26, 39, 38.   PO

—— another edn. *Newcastle*, 1838. pp. 32, 38, 38, with two lithograph letters.   SL

A collection of correspondence, newspaper extracts, reports from railway companies, etc., brought together by Michael Longridge and John Birkinshaw of Bedlington Iron Works.

Also issued with an additional work bound in: *Sketches of our information as to railroads*, by James Adamson. [*Newcastle*, 1826.] pp. 26.   PO

7095 MITCHELL, W. & M., *printers*. A Guide to the Newcastle & Carlisle Railway, contain- NC ing a descriptive account of the Grand Opening on the 18th June, 1838. *Newcastle*, 1838.

*7096 CARMICHAEL, J. Views on the Newcastle & Carlisle Railway, from original drawings NC by J. W. Carmichael, with details by J. Blackmore. *Newcastle*, 1836. pp. [23.] BM Twenty-three engravings, with descriptions.

—— another edn. *Newcastle*, 1839.   BR Fifteen engravings.

7097 SCOTT, H. Scott's Railway Companion, describing all the scenery on and contiguous NC to the Newcastle & Carlisle Railway; with a short sketch of Carlisle and Newcastle. *Carlisle*, [1837.] 2 parts. pp. vii, 105, with fold. map.   UL(GL)

Includes plans and sections of a surveyed route. This work is fully described in Francis Whishaw's *Analysis of railways* (1837 & 1838).

—— 2nd edn. *Carlisle*, 1839. pp. xv, 111.   LSE

7098 BRANDLING, R. W. A short account of the formation of the Brandling Junction Railway, with two plans, one showing the general line of it, and the other the proposed mode of carrying it across the River Tyne and extending it to the Forth and the North Shields Railway, and through the town of Newcastle-upon-Tyne. *Newcastle-upon-Tyne: printed at the Journal Office by John Hernaman*, 184–. pp. 7, with fold. map & fold. plan.   NEWCASTLE PL

7099 HAWTHORN, R. & W. Experiments by R. and W. Hawthorn of two locomotive NC engines, the 'Sun' and 'Star', upon the Newcastle-upon-Tyne & Carlisle Railway, as to the consumption of coke and water. *Newcastle-upon-Tyne*, 1840. pp. 71, with tables.   ICE

7100 KNOWLES, G. Railroads. Observations on the expediency of making a line of railroad from York to Scarborough. *Scarborough*, 1841. pp. 8.   BM

Reasons against a proposal by the York & North Midland Rly.

7101 BELCHER, H. The Stranger's Guide for a summer day's excursion from Scarborough to Pickering, and thence by the railway to Whitby . . . *Scarborough*, 1843. pp. 30.

SCARBOROUGH PL

The course of the Whitby & Pickering Rly. described.

7102 BRANDLING JUNCTION RAILWAY SHAREHOLDERS COMMITTEE. The Report of the Committee of Investigation of the affairs of the Brandling Junction Railway Co., appointed at a meeting of the shareholders held the 6th May 1842. *Newcastle*, 1843. pp. 34, [57,] 65, 70.   LSE

A very detailed report produced in the style of a Parliamentary Paper. The third section has a separate title-page worded 'Capital Account, with schedules prepared by the Committee of Investigation, and miscellaneous papers . . .' *Gateshead*, 1843.

7103 BRANDLING JUNCTION RLY. The reply of the directors of the Brandling Junction Railway Co., to the report of the Committee of Investigation of the affairs of that company, appointed at a meeting of shareholders, May 6, 1842. *Gateshead*, 1843. pp. 25.   LSE

Signed 'George Johnson, Chairman'.

7104 JOHNSON, G. W. *and* WOOD, N. Report of Messrs. Johnson and Wood on a central line of railway into Scotland made by them to the directors of the Newcastle-upon-Tyne & Carlisle Railway Company. *Newcastle-on-Tyne*, 1843. pp. 16, with fold. map showing proposed extension.   SL

Dated 19 November, 1843.

7105 GANDELL, J. H. *and* BRUNTON, J. Report on the practicability of forming the trunk line of railway from Newcastle to Berwick by way of Alnwick. *Alnwick*, 1845. pp. 8.   BM

7106 GREEN, R. To the proprietors of the Newcastle & Darlington Railway. *Longhorsely*, 1845. pp. 4.   BM

Concerning 'a most false and scandalous charge brought against me by Mr. Hudson . . . respecting my shares in the Brandling Railway'.

7107 NEWCASTLE & Carlisle Railway abuses, and the remedies: a letter to M. Plummer Esq., chairman of the directors . . . by an Impartial Observer. 2nd edn. *Carlisle*, 1845. pp. 26.   LSE

NC

Exorbitant rates and fares. The Preface contains a reference to the first edition, pub-

lished a few weeks earlier. The writer suspects that most copies were intercepted and destroyed.

7108 TOURIST'S Companion; or, The history and description of the scenes and places on the route by railway from York to Scarborough. 2nd edn. *York*, 1846. pp. 32.   PC

Includes 'Origin and progress of the Railway'. (York & Scarborough branch of the York & North Midland.)

7109 TO THE SHAREHOLDERS of the Newcastle-upon-Tyne & Carlisle Railway Company. *London*, May 11, 1846. s.sh.   LSE

NC

Calling for explanations by the directors concerning the condition of the company's affairs.

7110 LEEDS & THIRSK RLY. Leeds & Thirsk Railway, Durham and Leeds extension: Great Northern Railway, Leeds and Wakefield extension. Resolutions at a public meeting in Stockton-upon-Tees on 17th April 1847. In favor [of both schemes]. John Crosby (Mayor) in the chair. [*Stockton*, 1847.] pp. 2.   BM

7111 LEEDS & THIRSK RLY. Rules and regulations for the guidance of the officers and men in the service of the company, May 1849. *Leeds*, 1849. pp. 64.   LEEDS PL

7112 GRAHAM, T. H. Discussion on Sabbath trains at the Annual General Meeting of the Newcastle & Carlisle Railway Company. [25 March, 1847.] *Newcastle* 1847. pp. 24.   LSE

NC

7113 RICHARDSON, G. B. A Guide to the Newcastle & Berwick Railway. *Newcastle*, [1847.] pp. 26.   H

7114 STOCKTON & HARTLEPOOL RLY. Stockton & Hartlepool, and Clarence railways. Rules and regulations to be observed by the company's servants. *Stockton*, 1847. pp. 28, with table.   H

7115 EVIDENCE concerning the High Level Bridge over the Tyne at Newcastle, taken at the Guildhall in that town on the 2nd of August, 1848, before Captain Washington, R.N. of the Harbour Department of the Admiralty. *Newcastle*, 1848. pp. 24.   BM

Obstruction to river traffic. Complaints by keelmen and watermen against the York, Newcastle & Berwick Rly.'s erections in the river.

7116 YORK & NORTH MIDLAND RLY. [Shareholders.] Report of the Committee of Investigation. *York*, 1849. pp. 10[11], with tables from January to April 1849.   UL(GL)

An enquiry by shareholders on the management and affairs of the company.

—— Second Report. *York*, 1849. pp. 58. BM
—— First part of the Third Report. *York*, [1849.] pp. 8.   UL(GL)
—— Conclusion of the Third Report. *York*, 1849. pp. 60, xxi[xxiii], with tables & fold. map.   UL(GL)

—— Fourth and Final Report. *York*, 1849. pp. 12, xxv, with detailed financial tables.   UL(GL)

*7117 S., H. U. Handbook to the Newcastle & Carlisle Railway, by H. U. S., with a visit NC to the Roman Wall. *Newcastle*, 1851. pp. iii, 85, with a map.   PC

7118 An ADDRESS to the shareholders of the Leeds Northern Railway Company; by an old railway director and ex-chairman, but not of the Leeds Northern line. *London & Peterborough*, 1853. pp. 12.   LEEDS PL
A discussion of the financial aspects of the amalgamation of the Leeds Northern with the York, Newcastle & Berwick, and York & North Midland, with the text of a resolution on amalgamation adopted by shareholders of the Leeds Northern on 16 December, 1852, signed by S. Smiles, Secretary.

7119 COLEMAN, B. [Letter] to the preference share, stock and bond holders of the West Hartlepool Dock & Railway Company. *London*, 1859. pp. 10.   UL(GL)
No title-page in UL(GL) copy.
—— Second letter from Mr. Benjamin Coleman to the proprietors of the West Hartlepool Dock & Railway Company. pp. 14.   UL(GL)
No title-page in UL(GL) copy.

7120 JACKSON, R. W. Letter from Ralph Ward Jackson, Chairman, to the proprietors, 18 January, 1859. (West Hartlepool Harbour & Railway Co.) *London*, 1859. pp. 8.   BM
Reply to a personal attack by Benjamin Coleman concerning a 'private family matter'.

7121 The PAST and present financial and commercial position of the West Hartlepool Harbour & Railway Company considered. *London*, [1859.] pp. 34, with tables of accounts.   BM
A criticism.

7122 The PRESENT financial and commercial position of the West Hartlepool Harbour & Railway Company considered. *London*, 1860. pp. iv, 34, with tables of accounts. BM
The criticism extended. '. . . great discrepancies between the company's published accounts and the Returns to the Board of Trade.'

7123 COLEMAN, B. A reply to the proceedings of a meeting held at West Hartlepool on the 28th June 1860, addresssed to the share and debenture holders of the West Hartlepool Harbour & Railway Company. *London*, [1860.] pp. 39.   BM
Concerning alleged misdealings by R. W. Jackson and Edwin Jackson. pp. 21–3 are blank, having been 'expunged by order'.
—— 2nd edn. 'An address to the proprietors . . .' *London*, [1860.] pp. 84.   BM
Further allegations.

7124 JACKSON, R. W. Correspondence between R. W. Jackson . . . and Mr. Benajamin Cole-

man of London; addressed to the preference share, stock and bond holders of the West Hartlepool Dock & Railway Co. *London*, 1860. pp. v, 60.   BM
Vigorous exchanges.

7125 FAWKES, F. H. North Eastern Railway: an address to the landowners of Wharfedale. *Otley*, 1861. pp. 15.   BM
The proposed line of the Leeds & Thirsk Rly. considered in relation to the plan of the North Eastern and the Midland Rly. for a line between Otley and Ilkley. Appendix, five letters between F. H. Fawkes and the N.E. Rly.

7126 GARNETT, J. North Eastern Railway: a reply to Mr. Fawkes' remarks on the Wharfedale Railway. *Otley*, 1861. pp. 7.   BM
Criticising Fawkes' opposition to a railway between Otley & Arthington.

7127 MEASOM, G. Measom's Official Illustrated Guide to the North Eastern, North British, Edinburgh & Glasgow, Scottish Central, Edinburgh, Perth & Dundee, Scottish North Eastern and Great North of Scotland railways . . . *London*, 1861. pp. 447, 224, with 200 engravings.   BM

7128 REVELATIONS in Parliament, with the true state of the West Hartlepool Harbour & Railway Company's capital account, and shorthand notes of the decision of the committee, addressed to the shareholders. *London*, [1861.] pp. 5.   HRL

7129 LANGLEY, J. B. The Illustrated Official Guide and Tourist's Hand Book to the North Eastern Railway and its branches. *Newcastle-upon-Tyne*, 1863. pp. 231.   BR

7130 WEST HARTLEPOOL HARBOUR & RAILWAY CO. Debenture stock no security, an Act of Parliament no protection. *London*, 1863. pp. 16.   BM
Following upon the decision of the House of Commons Select Committee on the West Hartlepool Harbour & Railway Bill. With seven pages of press opinions issued before and after the passing of the Bill.

7131 TROTTER, H. J. North Eastern Railway Company: the recent correspondence on this subject and a full annotated report of the proceedings at the special meeting at York on November 19, 1867, with some further remarks on the financial position of the company. *London*, 1867. pp. 83.   RC
Differences with the Chairman on the management of the company and its financial policy in expending large sums on maintenance and replacements. (See W. W. Tomlinson's *The North Eastern Rly.* pp. 630–2.)

7132 LYTHGOE, J. P. North Eastern Railway: its position and prospects. *London*, 1870. pp. 15.   RC
For shareholders.

7133 ABRATH, G. A. In the House of Lords. On appeal from Her Majesty's Court of Appeal (England) . . . between G. A. Abrath . . . Appellant, and the North Eastern Railway Company . . . Respondents. Appellant's case. *London*, [1886.] pp. iv, 522.   BM

7134 EGGLESTONE, W. M. The projected Weardale Railway . . . A paper prepared for the Weardale Railway Committee and laid before the directors of the North Eastern Railway Co. at York on the occasion of the visit of the deputation from the said committee, June 17th, 1887. *Darlington*, 1887. pp. 31.   BR
'The benefits which might accrue commercially to the inhabitants and others if the Wear Valley Railway was extended from Stanhope to Wearhead.'

7135 BRECKON, J. R. North Eastern Railway
c Company: an analysis of the capital expended from 1868 to 1889, showing the annual outlay upon the numerous works constructed during that period . . . *Newcastle-upon-Tyne*, 1890. pp. 38.   BM
Eleven very detailed tables and seven further schedules and correspondence in an Appendix (pp. 25–38).

7136 NORTH EASTERN RLY.—LOCOMOTIVE DEPARTMENT. Report with reference to the working of compound engines compared with the working of other classes of engines on the North Eastern Railway, November 1893. (By Vincent Raven and Ramsey Kendal.) pp. 20, with 23 tables & 12 mounted photos. of locos.   BR
'Private & confidential.'

7137 NORTH EASTERN RLY. Wages of signalmen. *Leeds*, 1895. pp. 34.   LSE
A detailed list of the complete signal-cabin staff of the N.E. Rly., with the number of hours worked and wages paid in each cabin.

7138 NORTH EASTERN RLY. Hours and Wages Arbitration. Before . . . Lord James of Hereford. Award dated 9 August 1897. [*Leeds*,] 1897. pp. 58.   LSE
A schedule of proposals by the Amalgamated Society of Railway Servants; statement by N.E. directors and detailed tables of proposed changes in wages, hours and grading.

7139 NORTH EASTERN RLY. Instructions applicable to men and lads employed in the Passenger Department. *York*, 1 October 1898. pp. 25.   LSE
Re-arrangement of wages, hours and grading.

7140 NORTH EASTERN RLY. Principal classes of locomotive engines. *Gateshead*, June 1899. pp. 29, with plates.   BR
Photographs, with descriptions.

7141 NORTH EASTERN RLY. Hours, wages, and conditions of service: regulations affecting men and lads employed in the Superinten-

dent's Department, applicable on and from 1st December 1900. *York*, 1900. pp. 35.   LSE

7142 ELECTRIC traction on the North Eastern Railway: equipment of the Newcastle local lines. *London: Tramway & Railway World*, 1904. pp. 17, with 15 illus., 16 diagrams & a map.   BR
Reprinted from the *Tramway & Railway World*, 14 January, 1904.

7143 MERZ, C. H. *and* MACLELLAN, W. The use of electricity on the North Eastern Railway and upon Tyneside. [*Cambridge*, 1904.] pp. 19, with 12 illus. (2 fold.), 2 maps & 9 diagrams.   BR
Reprinted from the *Engineer*. Paper, British Association, Cambridge meeting, 22 August, 1904.

7144 NORTH EASTERN RLY. Specifications of uniforms worn by staff, and regulations applicable to the supplying of same. *Leeds*, 1905. pp. 126, with many illus.   BR
A complete range.

7145 NORTH EASTERN RLY. Visit to the Carriage & Wagon Works, North Eastern Railway, Holgate, York. [*Holgate*, 1906.] pp. 11, with 12 illus., diagram & 2 fold. plans.   PC

7146 ROBINSON, J. North Eastern Railway: recent dock extension works at Middlesbrough. *Barry Docks*, 1906. pp. 39, 11.   BM
pp. 1–11 at end, Historical and descriptive notices of former dock works at Middlesbrough.

7147 NORTH EASTERN RLY. Memo on organisation of Traffic Department. *York*, July 1907. pp. 9.   LSE

7148 NORTH EASTERN RLY. Summaries of freight traffic statistics, 1902 to 1907. [*York*], 1908. pp. 11.   LSE
In the LSE copy, entries for 1908 and 1909 have been added in ink.

7149 HALLSWORTH, H. M. The elements of railway operating. [*Newcastle on Tyne*, 1914.] pp. 350.   BM
Printed and issued for private circulation by the N.E. Rly.

7150 MARTINDALE, F. W. Alice in Holidayland: a parody in prose, verse and picture. [*York:*] *North Eastern Rly.*, [1914.] pp. 47.   BM
—— 2nd edn. [1914.] pp. 47.   BM

7151 NORTH EASTERN RLY. Roll of Honour and List of N.E.R. men serving in the Navy and Army. May, 1915. pp. 117[118].   BM
A supplementary list (pp. 119–129[130]) was issued on July 1st, 1915.

7152 The FIRST electrified mineral line in England: the Shildon–Newport electrification, North Eastern Railway. *London: Railway Gazette*, 1916. pp. 24, with 31 illus., diagrams (1 fold.) & map.   BR
Reprinted from the *Railway Gazette*, 26 May and 2 June, 1916.

7153 MERZ AND MACLELLAN. The electrification of the Shildon-Newport branch of the North Eastern Railway. [*London*, 1916.] pp. 16. la. 4° in triple column, with 46 illus., diagram & map. BR
Reprinted from *Engineering*, 26 May and 2 June, 1916.

7154 MERZ AND MACLELLAN. Memorandum, North Eastern Railway extension of electrification. *London*, June 1919. pp. 12, with illus., diagrams & a map on 10 plates. BR

7155 NORTH EASTERN RLY. Report on proposed electrification of main line, York to Newcastle, with intermediary feeders. *Darlington*, October 1919. pp. 18, with tables, map, & diagram of Thirsk Junction. BR

*7156 NORTH EASTERN RLY. Trade and commerce of the North Eastern Railway district. *York*, Oct. 1921. pp. 80. UL(GL)
'Private.' Commercial geography, with an added chapter on railway geography by C. B. Fawcett of Leeds. A revised edition of a work first issued in 1912 for the use of clerks preparing for examinations.

7157 SHAKESPEAR, J. A record of the 17th & 32nd Service Battalions, Northumberland Fusiliers (North Eastern Railway Pioneers), 1914–1919. *Newcastle upon Tyne*, 1926. pp. xv, 183, with 29 plates & 5 maps and (pp. 109–65) lists of men who served. BM

North London Railway

(incorporated as East & West India Docks & Birmingham Junction Railway)

7158 NORTH LONDON RLY. [A collection of directors' reports, 1853–1865.] BM

7159 CRORY, W. G. East London industries. *London*, 1876. pp. vi, xi, 279. BM
pp. [208]–220, Locomotion. The locomotive and carriage and wagon works of the North London Rly. and of the Great Eastern Rly.

7160 NORTH LONDON RLY. Judgement delivered in the House of Lords on Tuesday the 22nd February 1876, in the case of the North London Railway Company *v.* the Attorney-General. *London*, 1876. pp. 19. NLC
Appeal dismissed.

7161 CHISHOLM, A. J. The North London Railway . . . *London*, 1902. pp. 27, with illus. BM

7162 ROBBINS, R. M. The North London Railway. *Sidcup: Oakwood Press*, 1937. pp. 24, with 5 illus. & map on 4 plates. [*Oakwood Library of Railway History*, no. 1.] BM
—— 2nd impression, 1938. PC
—— 3rd edn. *Chislehurst*, 1946. pp. 29. IT
—— 4th edn. *South Godstone*, 1953. pp. 29, with 11 illus. & 2 maps on 8 plates. BM

North Metropolitan Railway & Canal
(later Regent's Canal and Dock)

7163 PEASE, J. W. Speech on the second reading of the Regent's Canal—City & Docks—Railway Bill, delivered in the House of Commons, Friday May 1, 1885. Extracted from Hansard . . . *London*, 1885. pp. 8. BM

North Staffordshire Railway

7164 ALLBUT, SON, AND HOBSON, *publisher*. Descriptive Guide to the North Staffordshire Railway; with a map of the lines. *Hanley*, [1850.] pp. 46. BM

7165 A FEW words to the shareholders of the North Staffordshire Railway Company on the true policy of that company, especially in relation to the London and North Western Railway Company. By One of Themselves. *London*, 1851. pp. 18. BM

7166 NORTH STAFFORDSHIRE RLY. Index of the North Staffordshire Railway and other Acts affecting the company. 1900. pp. 50. BR
Privately printed.

7167 ALLCHIN, M. C. V. Locomotives of the North Staffordshire and the London, Tilbury & Southend railways: types, building dates, etc. *Fareham: the author*, [1943.] pp. 11. BM

7168 'MANIFOLD.' The North Staffordshire Railway: a history of the line and its locomotives. By 'Manifold' [J. R. Hollick & others]. *Ashbourne: Henstock*, 1952. pp. 182, with 130 illus. on plates (col. frontis.), maps, gradient profiles & time-tables. BM

7169 HOLLICK, J. R. The workings of the locomotives and trains of private firms over the North Staffordshire Railway. 1958. pp. 24, with 2 pp. addenda & fold. map. *Reproduced typescript*. BR

7170 BRITISH RAILWAYS. Souvenir Programme, City of Stoke-on-Trent Golden Jubilee Celebrations . . . 1910–1960. Railway exhibition at London & North Western Yard, Stoke-on-Trent, May 11th–24th, 1960. [*London*,] 1960. pp. 8. BR
Folder with 5 illus. and map.
The North Staffordshire Rly.

North Wales Railway
[Porth Dynllaen to Bangor. Authorised but not constructed]

7171 ARCHER, H. The Black Book with a White Cover; or, The proceedings of the North Wales Railway directors turned inside out for the timely enlightenment of the shareholders. *Caernarvon*, [1846.] pp. 50. NLC

Northumberland Railway Company
[not incorporated]

7172 DUNN, M. Prospectus of a railway from Newcastle to Morpeth, to be called the Northumberland Railway . . . *Newcastle upon Tyne*, 1835. pp. 14.   BM

Park Mile Railway

7173 BROWN, J. The Park Mile: is it rateable? [*Newport (Monmouthshire)*,] 19 October, 1883. pp. 3.   NEWPORT PL

The Park Mile Rly. was a section of the Monmouthshire Canal Co.'s tramroad running through the Tredegar Estate, near Newport. It was privately owned and maintained by the Morgan/Tredegar family, to whom tolls were paid from its opening (1805?) until its incorporation into the Great Western Rly. in 1923.

Pentewan Railway

7174 LEWIS, M. J. T. The Pentewan Railway, *1829–1918. Truro: D. B. Barton*, 1960. pp. 58, with 16 illus., diagrams & maps on 10 plates.   BM

Perth & Inverness Railway Company
[not incorporated]

7175 FRASER, J. B. The Perth & Inverness Railway: its importance as a national and commercial enterprise. *London*, 1846. pp. 28.   AU

Plymouth & Dartmoor Railway

7176 TYRWHITT, T. Substance of a statement made to the Chamber of Commerce, Plymouth, on Tuesday the 3rd day of November 1818, concerning the formation of a railroad from the Forest of Dartmoor to the Plymouth lime quarries, with additional observations and a plan of the intended line. *Plymouth Dock*, [1819.] pp. 29, with 2 fold. maps.   BM

To be worked by horses.

7177 CARRINGTON, N. T. Dartmoor: a descriptive poem. 2nd edn. *London*, 1826. pp. xix, 206.   BM

pp. 127–9, 'Plymouth & Dartmoor Railway', with informative notes.

Plynlimon & Hafan Tramway

7178 COZENS, L. The Plynlimon & Hafan Tramway. *Highgate: the author*, 1955. pp. 36, with 10 illus. & a map.   BM

Portpatrick & Wigtownshire Joint Railway

7179 DALRYMPLE, J. H. Correspondence between Viscount Dalrymple, Chairman of the Portpatrick Railway Company, and Sir Andrew Orr, Chairman and James White, Esq., Deputy Chairman of the Glasgow & South Western Railway Company, relative to a contribution of £40,000 from the Glasgow and South Western Railway Company to the Portpatrick Company. *Stranraer*, 1861. pp. 16.   BM

Ravenglass & Eskdale Railway

7180 GREENLY, H. The Ravenglass & Eskdale Narrow Gauge Railway: the smallest railway in the world: an illustrated history and description of the line, its locomotives and equipment. [*Ravenglass*,] 1923. pp. 26, with illus., maps & diagrams of locomotives. BR

7181 GRADON, W. M. 'Ratty': a history of the Ravenglass and Eskdale Railway. *Altrincham: the author*, [1947.] pp. 63, with illus., diagrams & maps.   BM

*7182 RAVENGLASS & ESKDALE RLY. Ravenglass & Eskdale Railway Handbook. [*Ravenglass*,] 1962. pp. 32, with 6 illus., map in 7 sections, a plan, & lists of stock.   BM

History and description.

Redruth & Chasewater Railway

*7183 BARTON, D. B. The Redruth & Chasewater Railway, 1824–1915. *Truro: Truro Bookshop*, 1960. pp. 56, with 7 illus. & 2 maps.   BM

Rhymney Railway

7184 ALLCHIN, M. C. V. Locomotives of the Cambrian, Barry, and Rhymney railways: types, building dates, etc. *Fareham: the author*, [1942.] pp. 12.   BM

—— rev. edn. *Fareham*, [1943.] pp. 12. BM

7185 BARRIE, D. S. The Rhymney Railway. *South Godstone: Oakwood Press*, 1952, pp. [47]–92, with 19 illus. on 8 plates; maps & tables in text. [*Oakwood Library of Railway History*, no. 9.]   BM

Romney, Hythe & Dymchurch Railway

*7186 The ROMNEY, Hythe & Dymchurch Railway. *London*, [1927.] pp. 26, with illus. & map.   BM

*7187 MORRIS, O. J. The world's smallest public railway. *London: Ian Allan*, 1946. pp. 64, with 49 illus., station diagrams & map. BM

7188 ROMNEY, HYTHE & DYMCHURCH RLY. Exhibition of locomotive 'Southern Maid' at Waterloo Station, London . . . January 4th–18th, 1947, to celebrate the coming of age of the smallest public railway in the world. *London*, [1947.] pp. 5, with illus.   T

*7189 ROMNEY, HYTHE & DYMCHURCH RLY. Romney, Hythe & Dymchurch Railway: Guide and Timetable. *London: Ian Allan*, 1946. pp. 20, with illus.   BM

—— *London*, 1946. pp. 28. By C. J. Allen.   BM

—— *London*, [1947.] pp. 52. By O. J. Morris.   BM

—— *London*, [1949.] pp. 28.   BM

—— *London*, [1951.] pp. 28.   BM

*7190 ROMNEY, HYTHE & DYMCHURCH RLY. The Line that Jack built: the Romney, Hythe & Dymchurch Railway: a pictorial history

of the world's smallest public railway. *London*, [1947.] pp. [32.]   BM

—— *London*, [1950.] pp. 29.   BM
—— *London*, [1954.] pp. 28.   BM
—— *London*, [1956.] pp. 28.   BM

*7191 RANSOME-WALLIS, P. The world's smallest public railway: the Romney, Hythe & Dymchurch. *London: Ian Allan*, [1957.] pp. 60[61], with illus. & diagrams.   BM
History and description.

—— another edn. *London: Ian Allan*, [1962.] pp. 60, with 59 illus., map, tables, & route diagrams.   BM

Roxburgh & Selkirk Railway Company
[not incorporated]

7192 STEVENSON, R. Report [to the Duke of Roxburgh and others on a survey for a railway between the coalfields of Mid-Lothian to the Tweed and Leader]. (Roxburgh & Selkirk Rly.) *Edinburgh*, 1821. pp. 16.   UL(GL)

Shropshire & Montgomeryshire Railway

7193 ROBERTS, S. Pleadings for reforms published fifty years ago . . . A new edition, revised and enlarged. *Conway*, 1880. pp. 128.   BM
pp. 75–80, 'Railways. The Montgomeryshire Railway.'

7194 LUCY, H. W. Sixty years in the wilderness: some passages by the way. *London*, 1909. pp. x, 450.   BM
pp. 56–62, R. S. France and the Potteries, Shrewsbury & North Wales Rly.

7195 SHROPSHIRE & MONTGOMERYSHIRE RLY. Handbook to Shropshire & Montgomeryshire Railway. *Shrewsbury*, [c. 1920.] pp. 37, with illus.   PC
General and topographical guide.

—— another edn. By 'R.D.' *Shrewsbury*, [1925.] pp. 36[37], with illus., map & current time-table.   SLS
Contains a short historical account.

7196 TONKS, E. S. The Shropshire & Montgomeryshire Railway. *Birmingham: the author*, 1949. pp. 70, with 39 illus., map & 2 diagrams.   BM

Snailbeach District Railways

7197 TONKS, E. S. The Snailbeach District Railways. *Birmingham: the author*, 1950. pp. 32, with 18 illus., map & 4 diagrams.   BM

Snowdon Mountain Railway
(originally Snowdon Mountain Tramroad and Hotels Co.)

7198 MORRIS, O. J. The Snowdon Mountain Railway. *London: Ian Allan*, [1951.] pp. 48,

with 29 illus., maps, sections & tables.   BM
History and description, with details of the Abt system and its locomotives.

—— another edn. *London*, [1960.] pp. 48.   BM

—— 3rd edn. By P. Ransome Wallis. *London*, 1964. pp. 48   BM

'South Eastern & Chatham Railway'

The South Eastern Railway, 1836–1898; the London, Chatham & Dover Railway, 1859–1898 (1852–1859 as the East Kent Railway); and the South Eastern & London, Chatham & Dover Managing Committee, 1899–1922

London & Greenwich Railway: LG
London, Chatham & Dover Railway: LCD

Historical

7199 BANISTER, F. D. Historical notes in reference to the lines of railway between Redhill and London, by means of which the London, Brighton & South Coast, and South Eastern Railway companies obtain access to the London Bridge stations of both companies. *London*, 1888. pp. 18, with 6 diagrams.   ICE

7200 HOWELL, G. O. Kentish Note Book. *London*, 1894.   BM
vol. 2, pp. 319–22, 'The Genesis of the Gravesend Railway': transcript of a petition against a Bill for making a railway from Greenwich to Gravesend, 1836. (North Kent line.)

7201 SEKON, G. A. The History of the South Eastern Railway. *London*, 1895. pp. 40.   BM

7202 LONDON, BRIGHTON & SOUTH COAST RLY. Agreements between the L.B. & S.C.R. and the S.E.R. Co. relating to the use of the London and Redhill lines (1839–1898) with historical notes in reference to the lines of railway between Redhill and London by means of which the L.B. & S.C. and S.E. Rly. companies obtain access to the London Bridge stations of both companies, by Fred D. Banister. [1898.] pp. 81, with maps.   SLS
'Private.'

7203 SMILES, S. The Autobiography of Samuel Smiles. Edited by Thomas Mackay. *London*, 1905. pp. xiii, 452, with 2 portraits.   BM
S. Smiles was Secretary of the S.E. Rly., 1854–1866.

7204 MITTON, G. E. The South-Eastern & Chatham and London, Brighton & South Coast Railways . . . *London*, 1912. pp. vii, 87. [*Peeps at Great Railways.*]   BM
Brief histories of these railways form an introduction to the topographical history of the areas served.

7205 SOUTH EASTERN & CHATHAM RLY. Coronation Souvenir of the Continental

Express and the South Eastern and Chatham Railway. [*London*,] 1911. pp. 96.   BM
pp. 28–55, History of the S.E. & C.R.
pp. 56–60, The Rise of the [S.E. Rly.] locomotive.

*7206 BENNETT, A. R. The first railway in London: being the story of the London & Greenwich Railway from 1832 to 1878. *London*, 1912. pp. 48, with 47 illus., chronology, & historical summary. [*Locomotive Magazine Souvenir*, no. 21.]   BM
LG

7207 WATKIN, A. Absalom Watkin: extracts from his Journal, 1814–1856, edited by his great-grandson, A. E. Watkin. *London*, 1920. pp. 332.   BM
Includes entries relating to Edward W. Watkin, *b.* 1819.

7208 HUNT, C. A. South Eastern & Chatham Railway considered as the earliest railway group, with some notes on Continental boat trains. pp. 12[14]. *Reproduced typescript*.   RC
Paper, Railway Club, 9 June, 1922.

7209 VALLANCE, H. A. The Canterbury & Whitstable Railway. pp. 11. *Typescript*. RC
Paper, Railway Club, 17 January, 1927.

7210 VALLANCE, H. A. The London & Greenwich Railway. pp. 17. *Typescript*.   RC
LG
Paper, Railway Club, 14 November, 1927.

7211 FELLOWS, R. B. History of the Canterbury & Whitstable Railway: an account of the construction, opening and working of the first passenger railway in the South of England. *Canterbury*, 1930. pp. 94, with frontis., 10 plates, 8 maps, plans & sections, & many bibliogr. notes.   BM
b
Appendix contains extracts from the company's Letter Book, 1825–8, and a list of Acts.

7212 SOUTHERN RLY. Centenary of the opening of the London & Dover (via Tonbridge) Railway. (Exhibition held at . . . Dover, from February 7th to February 12th, 1944.) [*London*, 1944.] pp. 12.   BR
Description of eighty-two exhibits and (pp. 8–12) 'The London & Dover Railway: centenary of the opening to Dover'.

7213 SOUTHERN RLY. Centenary of the opening of the South Eastern Railway to Maidstone from Paddock Wood, September 25th 1844. [*London*, 1944.] pp. 8.   BR
Description of an exhibition of seventy-eight items and (pp. 5–8) 'Maidstone's Railway Centenary'.

7214 SOUTHERN RLY. Centenary of the opening, on September 20th, 1845, of the South Eastern Railway from Tonbridge to Tunbridge Wells. Exhibition at . . . Tunbridge Wells, September 20th–October 6th 1945. [*London*, 1945.] pp. 8.   BR
Description of eighty exhibits and (pp. 5–8) 'How the railway came to Tunbridge Wells'.

7215 TOMS, A. H. Folkestone Warren landslips: research carried out in 1939 by the Southern Railway Company. *London: Institution of Civil Engineers*, 1946. pp. 44, with 27 illus. & diagrams, incl. 4 plates.   BR
Paper, 1 January, 1946.

7216 BURTT, F. S.E. & C.R. locomotives, 1874–1923. *London: Ian Allan*, 1947. pp. 48.   BM
Descriptions, lists and illustrations.

*7217 KIDNER, R. W. The London, Chatham and Dover Railway. *South Godstone: Oakwood Press*, 1952. pp. 42, with 27 illus. on 12 plates, maps, tables, & bibliography. [*Oakwood Library of Railway History*, no. 52.]   BM
LCD

7218 SPENCE, J. The Caterham Railway: the story of a feud and its aftermath. *South Godstone: Oakwood Press*, 1952. pp. x, 84, with 17 illus. on 8 plates, 2 maps (1 col., 1 fold.), plan, gradient section, and many bibliogr. notes.   BM
b
A detailed account of the relationship of this railway with the L.B. & S.C.R. and the S.E.R. and its subsequent history as part of the Southern Rly.

*7219 KIDNER, R. W. The South Eastern Railway, and the S.E. & C.R. *South Godstone: Oakwood Press*, 1953. pp. 51, with 32 illus. on 12 plates, 2 maps & gradient profile. [*Oakwood Library of Railway History*, no. 53.]   BM

7220 WAKEMAN, N. The South Eastern & Chatham Railway Locomotive List, 1842–1952: a numerical list of the S.E.R., L.C. & D.R., S.E. & C.R., S.R. (Eastern Section). *South Godstone: Oakwood Press*, 1953. pp. 50, with many illus.   BM

7221 COURSE, E. A. The Bexleyheath Railway, 1883–1900. *Woolwich: Woolwich and District Antiquarian Society*, 1954. pp. 15, with 2 illus., 2 maps and 23 bibliogr. & other notes.   BM
From the Woolwich and District Antiquarian Society's *Proceedings*, vol. 30.

7222 BAGWELL, P. S. The rivalry and working union of the South Eastern, and the London, Chatham & Dover railways. *In* 'Journal of Transport History', vol. 2, no. 2, November 1955. pp. 65–79, with map, 2 tables & 70 bibliogr. notes.   BM
b
LCD

7223 CATERHAM RAILWAY CENTENARY COMMITTEE. Souvenir Programme of the Commemoration of the first centenary of the opening of the Caterham Railway, 1856–1956. [*Caterham*, 1956.] pp. 19, with illus.   PC
pp. 11–19, 'The Caterham Railway' by J. Spence.

7224 RANDALL, F. O. The Hundred of Hoo Railway: a study in railway history and geography. *London*, January 1956. pp. 45, with map & tables. *Reproduced typescript*.   BR
A detailed account.

7225 CURRIE, A. W. Sir Edward Watkin: a
b   Canadian view. *In* 'Journal of Transport
    History', vol. 3, no. 1, May 1957. pp. 31–40,
    with plate (port.) & 39 bibliogr. notes.   BM

*7226 BRADLEY, D. L. The locomotives of the
    London, Chatham & Dover Railway.
LCD *[Cheltenham:] Railway Correspondence &
    Travel Society*, 1960. pp. 48[50], with 85
    illus., 2 maps & lists.   BM

7227 RANSOME-WALLIS, P. On railways, at
    home and abroad. *London: Batchworth Press*,
    1951. pp. 299, with plates.   BM
    pp. 66–9, East Kent swan song.

    —— 2nd edn. (reprint). *London: Spring
    Books*, [1960.] pp. 300.   BM

7228 BRADLEY, D. L. The locomotives of the
    South Eastern & Chatham Railway. [*South-
    ampton: Railway Correspondence & Travel
    Society*, 1961. pp. 79[80], with 83 illus. &
    diagrams on plates, & lists.   BM

7229 CROMBLEHOLME, R. The Hawkhurst
    Railway. *New Malden: Narrow Gauge &
    Light Railway Society*, 1961. pp. 47, with
    14 illus. on 6 plates & cover, map & dia-
    grams. *Reproduced typescript.*   BM

*7230 NOCK, O. S. The South Eastern & Chatham
    Railway. *London: Ian Allan*, [1962.] pp.
    198, with col. frontis., 71 illus. on 32 plates,
    19 tables, 3 maps, and diagrams.   BM

Contemporaneous

7231 The ADVANTAGES of railways with loco-
    motive engines, especially the London and
LG Greenwich Railway or Viaduct, . . . 2nd
    edn. *London*, 1833. pp. 16.   BM

7232 [LONDON & GREENWICH RLY.] Extracts
    from various reviews and publications on the
LG London & Greenwich Railway. [*London:
    Brown & Syrett*, 1834.] pp. 24, with fold.
    frontis. map & diagram.   SL
    Reprints of laudatory accounts from news-
    papers and from *Northcroft's Parliamentary
    Chronicle.*

7233 [COCHRANE, T.] The examination exam-
    ined; or, Testimony on oath, proving a
LG failure in the peers to support the London
    and Greenwich Railway . . . *London*, 1836.
    pp. 32.   BM
    The BM copy bears a pencilled inscription,
    'By the discerning public's most discerning
    Servant, Dundonald'. [10th Earl of Dundonald,
    i.e. Thomas Cochrane.]
    A point by point criticism of George Walter's
    Evidence before a Committee of the House of
    Lords and a warning as to the danger of travel-
    ling on the London & Greenwich 'as at present
    constructed', i.e. on a continuous viaduct.

7234 LONDON & GREENWICH RLY. The Lon-
    don & Greenwich Railway Guide, con[t]ain-
LG ing an account of that bold and magnificent
    work, from its commencement at London
    Bridge. *London*, 1836. pp. 12, with frontis. G

7235 The RAILWAY Companion, in which the
    utility and advantages of the Canterbury &
    Whitstable Railway are clearly demonstrated
    . . . *Canterbury*, [1836.] pp. 27.   BM
    pp. 11–16, The Railway.

7236 SOUTH EASTERN RLY. London & Dover
    (South Eastern) Railway. Abstract of the
    Evidence given before the Committee of the
    House of Commons, with remarks thereon,
    1836. *London*, 1836. pp. 24.   BR

7237 SOUTH EASTERN RLY. South Eastern
    (London & Dover) Railway, incorporated 21
    June, 1836. Proceedings and General Meet-
    ing of Proprietors, held November 10th,
    1836. [*London*, 1836.] pp. 28, with fold. map.
                                                NLC
    First General Meeting.

7238 STEAD, J. From a morning paper. The
    Yorkshireman's Inn, Deptford. 'John Stead,
LG late the assisting Engineer of the London &
    Greenwich Railway, wishes to inform the
    inhabitants of Deptford . . . that he has re-
    ceived orders to provide a dinner . . . to
    consist of red herrings, lame ducks and
    farthing subjects, etc.' *Deptford*, October 17,
    1836. s.sh.   BM(MAPS)

7239 WALTER, G. The Evidence of George
    Walter, Esq., resident director of the London
LG & Greenwich Railway, on oath before a
    Committee of the House of Lords, July 1836,
    on the Direct Brighton Railway Bill, in
    which the capabilities and importance of the
    Greenwich Railway are made apparent.
    London, 1836. pp. 8.   BM

7240 WALTER, G. The London & Greenwich
    Railway and the Direct Brighton Railway:
LG extracts from the Evidence of George Walter.
    [*London*, 1836.] pp. 8.   BM(MAPS)

7241 MANSELL, G., *publisher*. The London &
    Greenwich Railway Guide, containing an
LG account of that bold and magnificent work,
    from its commencement at London Bridge,
    accompanied with [*sic*] a splendid engraving
    taken expressly for this work from a drawing
    on the spot, by an eminent artist. *London*,
    1837. pp. 12, with timetable & map.   PO

7242 WALKER, J. Report of James Walker . . .
    on the works of the London & Greenwich
LG Railway, made the 25th of August, 1837.
    London, 1837. pp. 8, with frontis. BM(Maps)

7243 SOUTH EASTERN RLY. Statement of the
    traffic, October 1838. *London*, [1838.] pp.
    23, with la. fold. map.   PC

*7244 WALTER, G. Explanatory notes on the Report of the Committee of Shareholders of the
LG London & Greenwich Railway. *London*, 1838. pp. 30.   BM(MAPS)
—— Addenda to 'Explanatory Notes . . .' *London*, 1838. pp. 8.   BM(MAPS)
G. Walter's defence of accusations against him. Dated 6 July, 1838.

7245 AUSTIN, C. Committee on the Greenwich Railway Bill and Station Bill and on the Croydon Railway and Station Bill. Speech of Mr. Austin. (House of Commons, 7 April, 1840.) *London*, [1840.] pp. 46.
BERMONDSEY PL
On behalf of the London & Croydon Rly.

7246 AUSTIN, C. In Parliament. Committee on the London & Greenwich Railway Enlarge-
LG ment and Station Bills. Speech . . . on the toll clause, May 19, 1840. [*London*,] 1840. pp. 11.

7247 EARNEST appeal of a Greenwich shareholder to the justice and consideration of
LG Parliament. *London*, 1840. pp. 16.   PO
The cost of widening the L. & G.'s viaduct should be borne by the four companies using it. The L. & G.'s share of the toll received by the London & Croydon from the South Eastern and the London & Brighton (one-fifth) is insufficient.

7248 GILBERT, L. The beauties and wonders of nature and science: a collection of curious,
LG interesting and valuable information for the instruction and improvement of the enquiring mind; with numerous illustrative engravings. *London*, [1840.] pp. 280.   BM
Contains short general accounts of contemporary railways, including the Liverpool & Manchester and the London & Birmingham. The London & Greenwich is illustrated by the frontispiece and two plates.

7249 MONEY, G. Greenwich Railway share-
LG holders. [*London*, 1840.] pp. 8.   G
On the directors' ruinous scheme for raising money for widening the line. Dated 3 Sept.,1840.

7250 WALTER, G. A letter from Mr. Walter to Mr. Wales, barrister . . . chairman of the
LG committee appointed to investigate his claim on the company; 13 February, 1840. *London*, 1840. pp. 15.   BM(MAPS)
The BM copy has a note in ink (unsigned) which states that G. Walter was in fact *in debt* to the L. & G. Rly.

7251 WOOD, W. P. Speech of W. P. Wood . . . counsel for the London & Greenwich Rail-
LG way Bill, in Committee of the House of Commons, Thursday April 2, 1840. pp. 62.
G

7252 WILKINSON, W. A. The toll question on railways exemplified in the case of the Croy-
LG don and Greenwich companies. *London*, 1841. pp. 16.   BM
This pamphlet is discussed in *Railway travelling and the toll question* (anon.), 1843.

7253 'JUSTUS.' A serio-comic, but very important little book to M–MB–RS OF P–RL–M–T
LG and others greatly interested, but not so immediately and paramountly, on high and public grounds. Important to be read, previously to the approaching meeting, by all proprietors of the London & Greenwich Railway unprivileged shares. By an author (and occasionally a speaker) on this subject only. [Cover title.]
London & Greenwich Railway. All is discovered! Who's the traitor? Query, plural? Ask Mr. Deep G–RN–Y. [*London*, Nov. 1842.] pp. 68.   G
A satire on the relationship between the L. & G. and the London & Brighton Rly., in which the former's virtue is upheld, although the management of this railway's affairs is criticised.

7254 POPE, J. Description of the permanent way of the South Eastern Railway. *London: Institution of Civil Engineers*, 1842. pp. 8, with diagrams.   PO
Excerpt, *Min. Proc. I.C.E.*

7255 MOGG, E. Mogg's South Eastern, or London & Dover Railway, and Tunbridge Wells, Hythe, Folkestone & Dover Guide; accompanied by a large official map of the line . . . *London*, July 1st, 1843. pp. iv, 4, 33.
IT

7256 RAILLERY on a very peculiar species of railway legislation. [*London*, 1843?] pp. 7.
LG   HRL
The L. & G. Rly.

7257 RAILWAY travelling and the toll question.
LG *London*, 1843. pp. 15.   BM
From no. 77 of the *Westminster Review*, May 1843.
Particularly with regard to the toll exacted from London & Croydon Railway passengers by the L. & G. The substance of two pamphlets is re-stated: 1, *Letter to H. Goulburn on the unequal pressure of the Railway Passenger Tax* by H. G. Lang (1842); and 2, *The toll question on railways exemplified in the case of the Croydon and Greenwich companies* by W. A. Wilkinson (1841).

7258 LONDON & CROYDON RLY. Statement of the directors of the Croydon Railway Company and their correspondence with the directors of the South-Eastern Railway Company, on the projected lines to North Kent, and on the leasing to them of the locomotive portion of the Croydon Railway. For circulation among the proprietors of the Croydon Railway. *London*, 1844. pp. 43.   NLC

7259 LONDON & GREENWICH RAILWAY.
LG [Documents: a collection of prospectuses, reports, maps & pamphlets, etc., issued between 1833 & 1844. 35 items.]   BM(MAPS)

7260 MEAD, J., *publisher*. The Illustrated Guide to the London & Dover Railway. *London*, [1844.] pp. 72, lxxii, with illus.   BM
Includes information on the railway and descriptions of its stations.

7261 PHIPPEN, J. Colbran's New Guide for Tunbridge Wells. 2nd edn. *Tunbridge Wells & London*, 1844. pp. x, 353, 4, with plate.   BM
    pp. 327–53, 'Descriptive particulars of the South Eastern Rly.'

7262 TIFFEN, W. The South-Eastern Railway Itinerary from Dover and London . . . times of arrival and departure of trains at the several stations; regulations adopted for the comfort and convenience of travellers . . . with engravings, map of the line . . . *Hythe*, 1842. pp. 23.   BM
—— *London*, [1844.] pp. [30.]   BM

7263 WHY should there be a railway from Greenwich to Gravesend? [*c.* 1844.] pp. 2. Signed 'A Man of Kent'.   BM
    Reasons in favour of railway communication for the Medway towns (North Kent line).

7264 BARLOW, P. W. Comparative advantages of the atmospheric railway system; with an Appendix containing experiments on the Tyler Hill inclined plane of the Canterbury & Whitstable Railway . . . *London*, 1845. pp. 40.   ICE

7265 The LONDON, Chatham & North Kent (Independent) and the South-Eastern (Dover) LCD railways. *London*, 1845. pp. 39.   BM
    Advantages of the L.C. & N.K. line over that approved by the Board of Trade (the South-Eastern).

7266 SCRIMGEOUR, R. S. Railways. Cause of property. Letters, etcetera, of R. S. Scrim-LG geour . . . on the property of the London & Greenwich Railway Company. *London*, 1845. pp. 58.   LSE
    Relations between the L. & G. and the S.E. Rly.

7267 AUSTIN, C. Speech of Mr. Austin on behalf of the South Eastern North Kent lines, before the Select Committee of the House of Commons. *London*, 1846. pp. 138.   H

7268 NORTH KENT RLY. House of Commons Select Committee on Group 14: North Kent and South Eastern railways. [*London*, 1846.] pp. 147.   PO
    Reports of proceedings.

7269 SOUTH EASTERN RLY. General statement of the position and projects of the company, 1845–6. *London*, [1846.] pp. 45, with la. fold. map.   BM
    Dated 27 December 1845.
    Includes a history of the S.E. Rly. (pp. 1–15) and proposals for a line into North Kent.

7270 NORTH KENT RLY. Reply to the statement put forth by the directors of the South Eastern Railway Company. *London*, 1846. pp. 46, with a fold. map of the proposed North Kent Rly.   BM

7271 AUSTIN, C. Speech of Mr. Austin on behalf of the South-Eastern lines, before the Select Committee of the House of Commons, April 26th & 27th, 1847. *London: C. Roworth & Sons*, [1847.] pp. 86.   IT

7272 SOUTH EASTERN RLY. Statement of the projects of the South Eastern Railway Company before Parliament, Session 1847. *London*, [1847.] pp. 21, with fold. map.   BM

7273 [SMITH, A.] Railways as they really are; or, Facts for the serious consideration of railway proprietors: no. 2, The Dover, or South Eastern Company. *London*, 1848. pp. 44.   BM
    'The source of the Panic traced by facts'; the writer explains that his only object is to stop the ruin of families and the havoc which is daily made by the bitterness of disappointment and poverty.

7274 BARLOW, P. W. Report to the directors of the South Eastern Railway Company, on permanent way. *London*, [1850.] pp. 16, with 2 fold. plates.   BM

7275 BARLOW, P. W. To the Chairman and directors of the South Eastern Railway, on the supply of water to be obtained from the North Kent district. [*London, c.* 1850.] pp. 7.   ICE
    'The district through which the North Kent line passes will yield a quantity of spring water sufficient for the supply of all London.' P. W. Barlow was Engineer to the S.E. Rly., 1844 to 1851.
—— another edn. '. . . to which is added the report of D. T. Ansted, F.R.S. . . .' *London*, 1850. pp. 21.   PC

7276 BROWNE, R. Observations on the South Eastern Railway goods traffic. *London*, November 1850. pp. iv, 107, with many tables.   BR
    A report to the Chairman, S.E. Rly., including comparisons with other railways. An entirely new basis required for the classification of goods traffic.

7277 WHITEHEAD, J. The key to railway investments. Part 5, South Eastern Railway; illustrated by a map of the district. *London*, 1850. pp. 17.   BM

7278 MEASOM, G. The Official Illustrated Guide to the South-Eastern Railway and all its branches. *London*, 1853. pp. viii, 104.   BM

7279 FISHER, J. Assessment of railways: some observations on the judgement delivered to the Court of Queen's Bench on Saturday the 18th of February in the case of The Queen *v.* The South-Eastern Railway Company. *London*, 1854. pp. 33.   BM

7280 'LANCASTRIENSIS.' The South Eastern Railway crisis. *London*, 1854. pp. 16.   BM
    Signed 'Lancastriensis'.
    Addressed to the proprietors of the S.E. Rly.

7281 REMARKS on the proposed Bromley Branch. By a South-Eastern Proprietor. *London*, 1854. pp. 10. BM
Warning that the line would not be profitable.

7282 STATEMENT of the proceedings in Parliament with reference to the construction of a
LCD direct and protected line of railway to Dover Harbour. *London*, 1855. pp. 24. BM
Proposed extension of the East Kent Rly. from Canterbury to Dover.

7283 WRIGHT, T. Guide to the Caterham Railway near Croydon. *London*, 1856. pp. 48, with fold. map. BM
Mainly topographical.

*7284 MEASOM, G. The Official Illustrated Guide to the South-Eastern Railway and its branches, including the North Kent and Greenwich lines. *London*, [1858.] pp. [xii,]324. UL(GL)

7285 SMILES, S. Statement in support of the proposed London Bridge & Charing Cross Railway submitted for the consideration of the directors of the South Eastern Railway by Samuel Smiles, John Charles Rees & Edward Ryde. *London*, 1858. pp. 29. LSE
'Private & confidential.'

7286 CONTRACTOR's jobs: no. 1, The East Kent Railway—London, Chatham & Dover: will
LCD it pay? *London*, 1860. pp. 40. BM
Reprinted from the *Railway Times*.
'Let the South Eastern Co. have nothing to do with them' [the East Kent Railway promoters].

7287 RELATIONS of the Brighton and South Eastern companies: a compilation of agreements and correspondence. *London*, 1860. pp. 95, 7. BM
Correspondence includes exchanges concerning the Caterham Rly. (22 letters); Portsmouth Rly. (4 letters); proposed Uckfield & Tunbridge Wells Rly. (11 letters and 10 more in an addenda made up of 'further correspondence'); Eastbourne & South-Eastern Rly. (3 letters).

7288 SOUTH EASTERN RLY. Report of the General Manager and Secretary on the relations of the South Eastern and Brighton companies. *London*, 1863. pp. 31. LSE
Signed 'C. W. Eborall & S. Smiles'.

7289 TIMBS, J. Walks and talks about London.
LCD *London*, 1865. pp. xii, 310. BM
pp. 258–80, 'Railway London'. London Bridge Station, the building of the Charing Cross and Cannon St. extensions (S.E. Rly.) and the Blackfriars & Farringdon extension (L.C. & D. Rly.). Contains much information relating to demolition of property and the objections and difficulties which accompanied these works.

7290 LONDON, Chatham and Dover Railway. Complication made clear; or, The exact
LCD condition of each interest defined. For the use of the debenture-holders, shareholders, and the public. *London*, 1866. pp. 27. BM

7291 LONDON, CHATHAM & DOVER RAILWAY COMMITTEE OF MAIN LINE SHARE-
LCD HOLDERS. Report of the Committee of Investigation appointed at a meeting of shareholders on the 31st day of August, 1866 . . . *London*, 1866. pp. 62. BM
Current L.C. & D. affairs in general, with financial statements.

7292 PETO, S, M. London, Chatham & Dover Railway: report of the proceedings at a
LCD meeting of the constituents of Sir S. M. Peto . . . held at Bristol . . . *London*, 1866. pp. 34. ICE
Peto explaining his relationship with the L.C. & D.: texts of letters.

7293 LONDON, CHATHAM & DOVER RLY. Gardner and others *v*. the London, Chatham
LCD & Dover Railway. Judgement of Lord Justice Turner and Lord Justice Cairns in reference to debenture holders. *London*, 1867. pp. 29. NLC

7294 LONDON, CHATHAM & DOVER RAILWAY COMMITTEE OF MAIN LINE SHARE-
LCD HOLDERS. Report of the Committee of the Main Line Shareholders appointed 3 December 1866. *London*, 1867. pp. 30. BM
'We have endeavoured to trace the progress of the company to its present position, which if not remedied, threatens the utter ruin of the shareholders' interest.'

7295 DIXON, J. London, Chatham & Dover Railway: considerations on the position and
LCD prospects of the company, addressed to its debenture-holding & other creditors. *London*, 1869. pp. 24. BM

7296 LONDON, Chatham & Dover Railway Co.: a few remarks on reconstruction and con-
LCD solidation. By a Holder of Mortgages. *London*, 1869. pp. 18. BM
Discusses Salt's scheme for economic reconstruction of the company, and suggests improvements and modifications to enable fusion of component undertakings.

7297 [SOUTH EASTERN RLY.] All London and Europe; or, The South Eastern Railway, its position, prospects and reversionary value, now that its capital account is closed. Second edition. *London*, 1869. pp. 54. BR
Hopes of a prosperous future for the S.E. Rly. resulting from the completion of the extensions to Charing Cross and Cannon Street, the completion of the new main line via Sevenoaks and the end of large-scale expenditure.

7298 CECIL, R. A. T. G. [Marquis of Salisbury] *and* CAIRNS, H. McC. [Baron Cairns].
LCD London, Chatham & Dover Arbitration Award: first (second & final) award. *London*, 1870,71. 2 parts, pp. 56, 23. LSE
The Marquis of Salisbury and Baron Cairns were arbitrators appointed by the Court of Chancery under the Arrangements Act (1869)

to settle the affairs of the L.C. & D. Rly., in financial difficulties over its Metropolitan and City Extensions. The report contains full schedules, with lists of all awards made.

7299 ABBOTT, W. The London, Chatham & Dover Railway: its position analysed and its
LCD prospects reviewed. *London*, 1874. pp. 15.
                                        LSE
A financial review followed by a survey of existing and future plans, extensions, etc., and relations with the South Eastern Rly.

7300 PHILP, R. K. South Eastern Railway Panoramic Guide. *London*, 1874. pp. 48, with map. ·   BM
A route book.

7301 WHETHAM, C. Letter from Alderman Sir Charles Whetham, late auditor, to the shareholders of the South-Eastern Railway Company. *London*, [1876.] pp. 19.   NLC
Dated 9 February, 1876.

7302 PHILP, R. K. The London, Chatham & Dover Railway Panoramic Guide. *London*,
LCD [188-.] pp. 32.   SL
A route book.

7303 VINE, J. R. S. The Iron Roads Dictionary ... The London, Chatham & Dover Rail-
LCD way. *London*, 1880. pp. xxiv, 92.   BM
A route book, with maps and a short historical sketch.

7304 VINE, J. R. S. The Iron Roads Dictionary ... The South Eastern Railway and its through routes to the Continent. *London*, 1881. pp. xxv, 160.   BM
Contains a tabulated companion to all lines, including branches.

7305 SIR EDWARD WATKIN'S services to the shareholders in the Manchester, Sheffield & Lincolnshire, South Eastern, Metropolitan, and East London companies. *Manchester*, 16 July, 1885. pp. 4, with financial tables. BR
Signed 'An Unfortunate Shareholder'. Privately printed.
Alleged autocracy of E. W. Watkin.

7306 INSTITUTION OF MECHANICAL ENGINEERS. The I.M.E. Summer Meeting. De-
LCD scription of places to be visited. *Manchester*, 1886. pp. 32.   BR
Reprinted from the *Mechanical World*, August 13th & 20th, 1886.
pp. 29–32, 'Longhedge Locomotive Works, L.C. & D. Rly'.

7307 ABBOTT, W. The South Eastern Railway: a few facts on its management under Sir Edward Watkin ... during the years from 1866 to 1888, and its prospects for the future from a continuance of a system of 'supreme authority'. *London*, [1888.] pp. 19.   ICE

7308 DAWKINS, W. B. The discovery of coal near Dover ... *London*, 1890. pp. 11, with 2 diagrams.   BR
Reprinted from the *Contemporary Review*, April 1890.
Borings were made on the orders of E. W. Watkin, Chairman of the S.E. Rly. and of the Channel Tunnel Co.

7309 CORRESPONDENCE, etc. between the South Eastern and London & South Western railway companies as to the Charing Cross Railway, from 1861 to 1868. *London*, 1892. pp. 64.   BR

7310 [PATTINSON, J. P.] The South Eastern Railway, its passenger services, rolling stock, locomotives, gradients, and express speeds. By the author of 'British railways' ... *London*, 1895. pp. x, 32, with 3 plates. BM
Description of the line and travelling facilities. Tables of 151 runs.

7311 [PATTINSON, J. P.] The London, Chatham & Dover Railway, its passenger services,
LCD rolling stock, locomotives, gradients, and express speeds. By the author of 'British railways' ... *London*, 1897. pp. x, 38, with plate & many tables.   BM
About 200 trips are recorded.

7312 'DAILY MAIL.' Monopoly's last phase: proposed amalgamation of the London,
LCD Chatham & Dover and South-Eastern railways ... *London*, 1898. pp. 48, with illus. [*Daily Mail Red Book*, no. 1.]   BM
Articles and letters reprinted from the *Daily Mail*, and press comments from other sources.

7313 LONDON COUNTY COUNCIL. South Eastern & Chatham Railway service: preliminary report ... *London*, 1900. pp. 8, with tables.   BM
'The chaotic and disastrous condition of the passenger and goods traffic on the S.E. & C. Unpunctuality, irregularity, inadequacy of staff and unsuitable rolling stock.'

7314 LONDON, CHATHAM & DOVER RAILWAY SERVANTS SICK & BENEFIT SOCIETY.
LCD Rules (Revised rules). *London*, 1908. pp. 19.
                                        PO

South Eastern, Brighton, Lewes & Newhaven Railway Company
[not incorporated]

7315 ALEXANDER, W. J. Speech ... for the South Eastern, Brighton, Lewes & Newhaven Railway ... *London*, [1837.] pp. 45.
                                        BM
Speech in House of Commons in support of a proposed branch from the S.E. Rly. at Oxted.

7316 SOUTH EASTERN, BRIGHTON, LEWES & NEWHAVEN RLY. Abstract of the Evidence on the South-Eastern, Brighton, Lewes & Newhaven Railway. *London: C. Roworth & Sons*, 1837. pp. 14, with favourable comments added.   LSE

7317 SOUTH EASTERN, BRIGHTON, LEWES & NEWHAVEN RLY. Evidence given before the Committee of the House of Commons on the London & Brighton railways, on the subject of tunnels. Session 1837. *London: C. Roworth*, 1837. pp. 24.   NLC

Southern Railway

Historical

7318 SOUTHERN RLY. Ten years of progress: the Southern Railway, 1923 to 1932. [*London*, 1932.] pp. 32.   LSE

7319 SOUTHERN RLY. Southern Railway Company, 1923–1933. *Waterloo Station (London)*, August 1933. pp. 49.   BR
c   'For private circulation only.'
A chronological record, with twenty-seven financial and other tables.

**7320 DENDY MARSHALL, C. F. A history of the Southern Railway, compiled from various sources. *London: Southern Rly.*, 1936. pp. xi, 708, with many illus. incl. portraits, maps & company seals; 2 fold. plans, 4 col. plates, 7 tables & a bibliography.   BM
Includes histories of constituent companies.
Although sufficient as a general source of reference, the work is acknowledged to be unreliable and incomplete in its detail. Three errata lists have appeared—one printed, another reproduced from typescript and a third in MS. These are the work of H. V. Borley, C. E. Lee and others.

—— 2nd, enl. edn., revised by R. W. Kidner. *London: Ian Allan*, 1963. 2 vols., pp. 563.   BM
The history is extended from 1935 to 1948, and contains many additional illustrations, although the colour plates of the first edition are omitted. There are extensive tables of openings, electrifications, closures, and station re-namings, and an augmented bibliography. Some, but by no means all, of the corrections supplied by H. V. Borley, C. E. Lee, and others (see note to first edition, above) are incorporated.

7321 CENTENARY of Southampton Docks. *London: Railway Gazette*, 1938. pp. 643–50, with illus. & maps. [*Railway Gazette Supplement*, 14 October, 1938.]   pc

7322 SOUTHERN RLY. Exhibition of prints, original poster sketches, photographs, plans and models in connection with Southampton Docks Centenary . . . *London*, 1938. pp. 18.   IT
131 items.

7323 SOUTHERN RLY. One hundred years of Southampton Docks, 1838–1938. [*London*,] 1938. pp. 32, with illus. & maps.   IT
Cover title, 'Southampton Docks Centenary, 1938.'

7324 WEBB, B. Locomotive engineers of the Southern Railway and its constituent companies. *London: Ian Allan*, 1946. pp. 87, with illus., incl. portraits.   BM

L. & S.W.R.: J. V. Gooch, J. Beattie, W. G. Beattie, W. Adams, D. Drummond, R. Urie.
L.B. & S.C.R.: J. C. Craven, W. Stroudley, R. J. Billinton, D. E. Marsh, L. B. Billinton.
S.E.R.: J. Cudworth, J. Stirling.
L.C. & D.R.: R. T. Crampton, W. Martley, W. Kirtley.
S.E. & C.R.: H. S. Wainwright.
S.E. & C. & Southern Rly.: R. E. L. Maunsell.
Southern Rly.: O. V. Bullied.

7325 SOUTHERN RLY. Ashford Works Centenary, 1847–1947. [*London*,] 1947. pp. 47, with many illus. & fold. plan.   BM

7326 DAVIS, H. G. Waterloo: one hundred years in the life of a great railway station. *London: British Railways (Southern Region)*, [1948.] pp. 31, with 20 illus. (2 col.) and a plan. BM

7327 SAVILL, R. A. The Southern Railway, 1923 to 1947: a chronicle and record. *South Godstone: Oakwood Press*, 1950. pp. 30, with 18 c illus. on 8 plates & detailed chronological & alphabetical lists. [*Locomotion Papers*, no. 6.]   BM

7328 NOCK, O. S. The locomotives of R. E. L. Maunsell, 1911–1937. *Bristol: Edward Everard*, 1954. pp. x, 192, with 63 illus. on 37 plates; diagrams & tables in text.   BM

7329 VEALE, E. W. P. Gateway to the Continent: a history of cross-Channel travel. *London: Ian Allan*, 1955. pp. 96, with 41 illus. on 16 plates.   BM
Rail and steamer services of the L.C. & D., S.E., S.E. & C. and Southern railways.

7330 HARVEY, J. *pseud.* [Ralph H. Clark.] Early railway historical news: a short anthology of extracts from early books and journals relating to railways; period 1832–1853. (Southern Group.) *Merstham: the author*, [1956.] pp. 19. *Reproduced typescript.*   BM

7331 BUCKNALL, R. Boat trains and Channel packets: the English short sea routes. *London: Vincent Stuart*, 1957. pp. xi, 218, with col. frontis., 108 illus. on 46 plates, maps & diagrams in text & a bibliography of 29 items.   BM
The history of the boat and boat-train services of the South Eastern, the London, Chatham & Dover, the South Eastern & Chatham, the Southern Railway and British Railways (Southern Region).

7332 COURSE, E. A. The evolution of the railway network of South-East England. Thesis, Ph.D., University of London. 1958. 2 vols. (pp. 926), with many photographs & maps mounted in text. *Typescript.*   UL

7333 KIDNER, R. W. The Southern Railway. *South Godstone: Oakwood Press*, 1958. pp. 52, with 33 illus. on 12 plates, loco. lists & a

map. [*Oakwood Library of Railway History*, no. 56.] BM
The Southern Rly., 1923–47.

7334 MACK, L. A. Southern Electric service stock. *Sidcup: Electric Railway Society*, March 1958. pp. [4.] *Reproduced typescript.* [*Booklet no. 5.*] BM
An account of vehicles withdrawn from normal service and adapted for various special duties.

7335 MACK, L. A. Southern Electric main line stock. *Sidcup: Electric Railway Society*, 1959. pp. 20, with 4 illus. inserted. *Reproduced typescript.* BM

7336 ELLIOT, J. Early days of the Southern Railway. In 'Journal of Transport History', vol. 4, no. 4, November 1960. pp. 197–213, with plate (portrait of Herbert Walker.) BM
Memoirs on management and leading personalities of the Southern, particularly of H. Walker.

7337 HOLCROFT, H. Locomotive adventure: fifty years with steam. *London: Ian Allan*, [1962.] pp. 216, with 77 illus. on 32 plates & detailed tables. BM
Memoirs, Great Western Rly., South Eastern & Chatham Rly. and Southern Rly.

7338 DAY-LEWIS, S. Bulleid, last Giant of Steam. *London: Allen & Unwin*, 1964. pp. 299, with frontis., & 70 illus. on 34 plates. BM

Contemporaneous

7339 BENNETT, E. P. L. Tales of the Trains: being some impressions by an onlooker of a railway from behind the scenes. *London: Southern Rly.*, 1925. pp. 39, with illus. RC

7340 CONFERENCE COMMERCIALE FRANCO-BRITANNIQUE DES USAGES DE LA LIGNE HONFLEUR–SOUTHAMPTON DE LA COMPAGNIE SOUTHERN RAILWAY. [Honfleur, 6 Avril 1925.] [Report on the proceedings.] *Honfleur*, 1925. pp. 93[95], with illus., incl. portraits. IT
A conference of British importers and French exporters to discuss means of extending their commercial interests via the Southern Railway.

7341 LOCKWOOD, H. F. Report on working of Southern group of railways in England. *Calcutta: Railway Board, India*, 1925. pp. 13. [*Technical Paper*, no. 241.] LSE
Impressions gained on a two-months' tour of the Southern Rly. to study management and working.

7342 MITTON, G. E. The Southern Railway. 2nd edn. *London*, 1925. pp. iv, 91, with illus. & map inside covers. BM
Brief histories of the constituent companies form an introduction to a topographical survey of the places served.

*7343 SOUTHERN RLY. Locomotives of the Southern Railway, 1925. *London*, 1925. pp. 55, with 20 illus. of locos. RC

7344 The 'LORD NELSON' four-cylinder 4–6–0 express locomotive, designed by Mr. R. E. L. Maunsell. [*London*, 1926.] pp. 8, with illus. & diagrams (2 fold.). PC

7345 BARING, E. The Port of Southampton: its past, present and future. [*London*, 1928.] pp. 14, with illus. & maps. BR

7346 TILLING, W. G. Locomotives of the Southern Railway (Eastern Section). *London*, 1928. pp. 39[41], with lists & illus. BM
—— 2nd edn. *London*, [1929.] pp. 39[41]. IT

7347 WALLER, A. G. The proposed bridge at Charing Cross. *London*, February 1930. pp. 20, with 4 fold. maps & diagrams. TUC
pp. 7–10, History of Charing Cross (Hungerford) Bridge.

7348 BENNETT, E. P. L. Southern Ways and Means: illustrated by 'Fougasse'. *London*, [1931.] pp. 88. BM
A light-hearted introduction to Southern Rly. services for passengers.

7349 The FIRST main line electrification in England: completion of stage 1 of the Southern Railway's electrification to Brighton. *London: Railway Gazette*, 1932. pp. 30. LSE
Supplement, *Railway Gazette*, 22 July, 1932.

7350 SOUTHERN Railway electrification extension, London, Brighton and Worthing. *London: Railway Gazette*, 1932. pp. 64, with many illus. & diagrams. PC
Supplement, *Railway Gazette*, 30 December, 1932.

7351 SOUTHERN RLY. Southampton Docks extension. [*London*,] Nov. 1932. pp. 11, with 6 illus. & a map. IT

7352 WESTINGHOUSE BRAKE & SAXBY SIGNAL Co. The Brighton Line signalling. *London*, June 1933. pp. 23, with illus. & 2 fold. diagrams. BR

7353 The EASTBOURNE and Hastings electrification, Southern Railway. *London: Railway Gazette*, 1935. pp. 1277–1300, with many illus., diagrams & maps. PC
Supplement, *Railway Gazette*, 28 June, 1935.

7354 ELECTRIC railway traction: the Sevenoaks electrification, Southern Railway. *London: Railway Gazette*, 1935. pp. 261–72, with illus. & diagrams. PC
Supplement, *Railway Gazette*, 8 February, 1935.

7355 SOUTHERN RLY. Eastleigh Locomotive Works. [*London*, 1935.] pp. 23, with illus. & a fold. plan. IME

7356 TILLING, W. G. Locomotives of the Southern Railway (Central Section). *London: the author*, 1935. pp. 34, with lists & illus. RC

7357 SOUTHERN RLY. To the Continent by train-ferry-boat. [*London*, 1936.] pp. [16.] RC
Illustrated brochure.

7358 WESTINGHOUSE BRAKE & SIGNAL COMPANY. Signalling Waterloo to Hampton Court Junction, Southern Railway. *London*, 1936. pp. 28, with illus., maps & diagrams. LSE
Reprint, *Railway Gazette*, 13 Nov., 1936.

7359 ELECTRIC railway traction: the London–Portsmouth electrification, Southern Railway. *London: Railway Gazette*, 1937. pp. 1225–48, with many illus., diagrams & maps. pc
Supplement, *Railway Gazette*, 25 June, 1937.

7360 COCHRANE, W. Charing Cross Road and Rail Bridge. [*London*, 1938?] pp. 7, with 2 diagrams. TUC
Paper to be read before the Southern Rly. Debating Society, March 24, 1938.

7361 ELECTRIC railway traction: Mid-Sussex and Sussex Coast electrification, Southern Railway. *London: Railway Gazette*, 1938. pp. 1221–40, with illus., diagrams & maps. pc
Supplement, *Railway Gazette*, 24 June, 1938.

7362 KIDNER, R. W. How to recognise Southern Railway locomotives. *Sidcup: Oakwood Press*, 1938. pp. 24, with 16 illus. on 4 plates, diagrams & tables. pc

7363 ELECTRIC railway traction: Southern electrification, 1923–1939. *London: Railway Gazette*, 1939. pp. 57–76, with many illus. & diagrams. pc
Supplement, *Railway Gazette*, 30 June, 1939.

7364 BOX, F. E. With the Nine Elms top link to Salisbury. pp. 11, with 12 illus. & logs of journeys. SLS
Reprinted from the *Southern Railway Magazine*, August 1941.

7365 The ABC of Southern electrics; fully illustrated: complete descriptions of stock with motor unit numbers and headcodes. *Staines: Ian Allan*, [1943.] pp. 24. BM

7366 TILLING, W. G. The locomotives of the Southern Railway, Western Section. *London*, 1930. pp. 47, with fold. table. BM
Descriptions, illustrations and lists.
—— 4th edn. *London*, 1943. pp. 50. BM

7367 MODERN locomotives and electric traction of the Southern Railway. *London: Locomotive Publishing Co.*, 1944. pp. 30[32], illus. BM

7368 BOX, F. E. Gradients, Barnstaple & Ilfracombe branch, Southern Railway. *London: Ian Allan*, [1946.] pp. 11, with tables. [*Trains Illustrated. Supplement* no. 3.] BM

7369 BURRIDGE, F. H. A. Nameplates of the Southern Railway locomotives. *Bournemouth: the author*, [1946.] pp. 48, with 49 illus. & diagrams. RC

7370 CRESWELL, A. J. Names and numbers: GWR & SR: over 5000 engines recorded and classified. *Huddersfield: Quadrant Publications*, 1946. pp. 20. BM

7371 DARWIN, B. R. M. War on the Line: the story of the Southern Railway in war-time. *London: Southern Rly.*, 1946. pp. iv, 215, with illus. (4 col.) on plates, tables & a map. BM

7372 DRURY, G. C. Golden Arrow Album: souvenir of the restoration of a famous continental link. *London: Ian Allan*, 1946. pp. [30.] BM
Photographs with brief descriptions.

7373 GRASEMANN, C. Round the Southern fleet: a brief review of the Southern Railway's fleet in 1946. *London: Ian Allan*, [1946.] pp. 54[55]. BM
Illustrations and descriptions of twenty-seven vessels.

7374 Titans of the Track: Southern Railway. *London: Ian Allan*, 1944. pp. 40, with illus. BM
Locomotives.
—— 2nd edn. *London*, 1946. pp. 23[32], with historical notes.

7375 COCK, C. M. Electric traction on the Southern Railway. [*London*, 1947.] pp. 16, with maps, tables, diagrams & a chronology of electrification. IT
c
Paper, Institution of Electrical Engineers, 23 July, 1947. C. M. Cock was Chief Electrical Engineer, Southern Railway.
Two of the diagrams are of the feeder system and show the locations of all sub-stations.

7376 PIKE, S. N. Travelling on the Southern Railway; Waterloo edition: the journey mile by mile. *Worthing*, 1947. pp. 36. BM
Published by the author.
A route chart in twenty-seven sections, with an account of features of interest to be seen from the train.

*7377 TOWNROE, S. C. The Book of the 'Schools' class. *London: Ian Allan*, 1947. pp. 32, with illus. BM

7378 The ABC of Southern locomotives: a complete list of all Southern Railway engines in service. *Staines: Ian Allan*, 1942-8. BM
Various editions.

7379 TOWNROE, S. C. The 'King Arthurs' and 'Lord Nelsons' of the Southern Railway. *London: Ian Allan*, [1949.] pp. 47, with illus. [*Famous Locomotive Types*, no. 4.] BM

7380 BRITISH RAILWAYS (SOUTHERN REGION)—LECTURE AND DEBATING SOCIETY. Coming of Age Celebrations, 1950. Souvenir Programme. *London*, 1950. pp. 20, with portraits. IT

Southwold Railway

7381 BECKER, M. J. Story of Southwold. Edited by M. J. Becker . . . *Southwold: F. Jenkins*, 1948. pp. 155, with 50 illus. BM
pp. 84–6, The Southwold Rly.; with plate (facing p. 112).

7382 TONKS, E. S. The Southwold Railway. *Birmingham: the author*, 1950. pp. 43, with 21 illus., map & 3 diagrams. BM

Stafford & Rugby Railway Company
[not incorporated]

7383 The STAFFORD and Rugby Railway considered with reference to its bearings upon existing railways and upon the public interests. (By One of the Public.) [1841.] pp. 24. NLC
Addressed to the President of the Board of Trade. Objections to the proposed railway refuted.

Stocksbridge Railway
[industrial railway]

7384 GIBBONS, V. The Stocksbridge Railway Company: a brief survey. Compiled by Victor Gibbons. *Stocksbridge: Samuel Fox & Co.*, April 1955. pp. [7,] with 2 fold. maps. SLS

Stratford-upon-Avon, Towcester & Midland Junction Railway

*7385 DUNN, J. M. The Stratford-upon-Avon & Midland Junction Railway. *South Godstone: Oakwood Press*, 1952. pp. 30, with 16 illus. & a map on 8 plates, lists & illus. [*Oakwood Library of Railway History*, no. 10.] BM

Surrey Iron Railway

7386 BULSTRODE. On iron rail-ways. *In* 'Recreations in Agriculture' by James Anderson. *London*, 1799–1802. vol. 5, pp. 290–3. BM
A letter by Bulstrode on the Surrey Iron Railway.

7387 SURREY IRON RAILWAY. Minutes of the proceedings for the extension of the Surrey Iron Railway, ordered to be printed 14th October, 1802. [*London*, 1802.] pp. 10. BM
Reports of four meetings, 3 June, 29 September, 7 October, and 14 October, 1802.

7388 BANKS, E. The report of Edward Banks on the practicability and expense of a navigable canal proposed to be made between the Grand Southern Canal near Copthorne Common and Merstham, to communicate with the River Thames at Wandsworth, by means of the Surr[e]y Iron Railways. *London*, 1810. pp. 8, with fold. frontis. (map.) LC

7389 SHOBERL, F. The beauties of England and Wales; or, Delineations topographical, historical and descriptive. *London*, 1810–15. 18 vols. BM
vol. 14, Suffolk, Surrey & Sussex. Surrey section, pp. 24, 116, 127 and 153, the Surrey Iron Railway, 1813.

7390 PHILLIPS, R. A morning's walk from London to Kew. *London*, 1817. BM
—— A new edn. *London*, 1820. BM
pp. 75–6, The Surrey Iron Railway, and speculations on the extension of railways generally.
This work was first published serially in the *Monthly Magazine*, the passage relating to the S.I. Rly. appearing in the issue of 1 September, 1814, on p. 119.

7391 BING, F. G. The Grand Surrey Iron Railway . . . *Croydon: Croydon Public Libraries*,
b 1931. pp. 20, with 9 illus. & 2 maps; bibliography of 41 items. BM

7392 LEE, C. E. The world's first public railway: an account of the Surrey Iron Railway and the associated Croydon, Merstham & Godstone Railway . . . *London*, 1931. pp. 34, with 9 illus. & a map. *Reproduced typescript*. BM

7393 LEE, C. E. Early railways in Surrey: the Surrey Iron Railway and its continuation, the Croydon, Merstham & Godstone Iron Railway . . . *London*, 1944. pp. 40, with 10 illus. on 4 plates, map & illus. in text & bibliogr. notes. BM
Paper, Newcomen Society, 11 December, 1940.

7394 TOWNSEND, C. E. Further notes on early railways in Surrey. pp. 12,[8,] with 12 maps and an addenda slip, 'Appendix no. 3', inserted. pc
Paper, Newcomen Society, 11 January, 1950. Supplementing *Early railways in Surrey* by Charles E. Lee (1944). Some notes by C. E. Lee are added in an Appendix.

7395 HALL & CO. A century and a quarter: the story of the growth of our business from 1824 to the present day. By C. G. Dobson. *Croydon: Hall & Co.*, 1951. pp. x, 228, with many plates. pc
pp. 24–8, The Grand Surrey Iron Railway; with col. plate, 6 illus. and a map.

7396 LEE, C. E. The Surrey Iron Railway.
In preparation, by David & Charles, Dawlish.

Swansea & Mumbles Railway

7397 SPENCE, E. I. Summer excursions. 2nd edn. *London*, 1809. 2 vols.   BM
vol. 2, p. 98, letter 14, mentions a ride from Swansea to Oystermouth in 'a carriage of singular construction . . . on an iron railway'. Dated 3 August, 1808.

7398 A DESCRIPTION of Swansea and its environs . . . *Swansea*, 1813. pp. 63,[16.]   BM
pp. 12 and elsewhere, Swansea & Mumbles Rly. described.

7399 SWANSEA & MUMBLES RLY. Swansea & Mumbles Railway, 1804–1904: centenary survey, June 29 & 30, 1904. *Swansea*, 1904. pp. 37, with illus.   LSE

7400 SOUTH WALES TRANSPORT CO. Electrification of the Mumbles Railway, 1928. (Souvenir.) *London*, [1928.] pp. 32[33], with 17 illus. & map.   RC

7401 LEE, C. E. The first passenger railway, the Oystermouth, or Swansea & Mumbles line. *London: Railway Publishing Co.*, 1942. pp. 91, with illus. & maps.   BM

* 7402 LEE, C. E. The Swansea & Mumbles Railway. *South Godstone: Oakwood Press*, 1954. pp. 50, with 20 illus. & time-tables on 12 plates; maps & plans in text.   BM

7403 SOUTH WALES TRANSPORT CO. The oldest passenger railway in the world. (Swansea & Mumbles Railway.) *Swansea*, 1954. pp. [12,] with 12 illus. & a chronology. pc
Commemorating the 150th anniversary of the S. & M. Rly.

7404 SOUTH WALES TRANSPORT COMPANY. Swansea & Mumbles Railway: the chain of progress. *Swansea*, 1960. pp. [24,] with many illus.   pc
Souvenir brochure issued to commemorate the closing of the line, 5 January, 1960.

Taff Vale Railway

7405 SMYTH, W. H. Nautical observations on the port and maritime vicinity of Cardiff, with occasional strictures on the ninth report of the Taff Vale Railway directors, and some general remarks on the commerce of Glamorganshire. *Cardiff*, 1840. pp. viii, 100, 12, with 2 maps.   BM

7406 The TAFF Vale Railway Company and the freighters: a letter to Lord James Stuart, M.P. *Cardiff*, 1858. pp. 11.   BM
Addressed to the Chairman of the T.V. Rly. Co. and signed 'Olive Branch'. Asks him to arbitrate in the dispute.

7407 The TAFF Vale Railway Company *v.* the Amalgamated Society of Railway Servants, Richard Bell, James Holmes, Philip Hewlett, George W. Alcock, and John Pilcher. Heard

before Mr. Justice Wills and a special jury on the 15th December 1902. Judgement of Mr. Justice Wills. pp. 18.   LSE
Unpublished galley proof.

7408 ALLCHIN, M. C. V. Locomotives of the Taff Vale Railway; illustrated: types, building dates, etc. *Fareham: the author*, [1944.] pp. 14.   BM

7409 BARRIE, D. S. The Taff Vale Railway. *Sidcup: Oakwood Press*, 1939. pp. 35, with 10 illus. on 4 plates & a map. [*Oakwood Library of Railway History*, no. 2.]   BM
—— 2nd edn. *South Godstone*, 1950. pp. 43, with 11 illus. on 5 plates & a map.   BM

Talyllyn Railway

7410 COZENS, L. The Talyllyn Railway. *Sutton. the author*, 1948. pp. 24, with 7 illus., maps, tables, & extracts from the Act of Incorporation.   BM

7411 ROLT, L. T. C. A railway revived. *Birmingham: Talyllyn Railway Preservation Society*, [1955.] pp. 5[6], with 6 illus.   BM
Reprinted from the March–April 1955 issue of *Out of Doors*.
The Talyllyn Rly.

* 7412 TALYLLYN RLY. Official Guide. [*Towyn*, 1952–]
Various editions of a 16- to 40-page booklet with illustrations, time-tables and map. In progress.

7413 TALYLLYN RLY. The Talyllyn Railway in pictures, no. 1. [*Towyn*, 1955.] pp. 32.   BM
Thirty-six photographs with captions.

—— no. 2. [*Towyn*, 1959.] pp. 32.   BM
Forty-nine photographs (6 col.) with captions.

7414 ROLT, L. T. C. A railway in miniature; with photographs by Edwin Smith. *In* 'The Saturday Book', 20th edition. *London*, 1960. pp. 221–[236.]   BM

* 7415 ROLT, L. T. C. Railway adventure. *London: Constable*, 1953. pp. xiii, 175, with 14 plates.   BM
The story of the Talyllyn Railway and its revival by the Talyllyn Railway Preservation Society.

—— another edn. . . . with a new introduction. Foreword by John Betjeman. *Dawlish: David & Charles*, 1961. pp. xv, 176, with 25 illus., diagrams, time-tables & map on 16 plates. (Text reprinted.)   BM

Tamworth & Rugby Railway Company
[not incorporated]

7416 TAMWORTH & RUGBY RLY. Adjourned debate in the House of Commons, Monday March 6, 1837, on the prayer for revising a decision of the Standing Orders Committee. *London*, 1837. pp. 6.   BR

Taunton Grand Western Railroad Company
[not incorporated]

7417 TAUNTON GRAND WESTERN RAIL-ROAD. Report of a meeting of landowners, Taunton, 3rd January, 1825. [*Taunton*, 1825.] pp. 4.   BM
Resolved—'That a company be formed' and that 'locomotive steam engines would be of public advantage'.

Vale of Rheidol Light Railway

7418 COZENS, L. The Vale of Rheidol Railway. *Sutton: the author*, 1950. pp. 40, with 20 illus., 4 maps & diagrams.   BM

7419 DAVIES, W. J. K. The Vale of Rheidol Light Railway; with plans and drawings by A. L.
c Thomas. *London: Ian Allan*, [1960.] pp. 64, with 39 illus., 4 diagrams, gradient profile, 2 maps, chronology & bibliography.   BM
—— rev. ed. *London*, 1964. pp. 56, with 44 illus.   BM

Van Railway

7420 COZENS, L. The Van and Kerry railways, with the Kerry Tramway. *Highgate: the author*, 1953. pp. 44, with 19 illus. & 2 maps.   BM

Wantage Tramway

7421 HIGGINS, S. H. P. The Wantage Tramway: a history of the first tramway to adopt mechanical traction. *Abingdon: the author*, 1958. pp. xvi, 158, with 39 plates; 7 maps & plans. (Appendix. pp. 109–55.)   BM
A very detailed study.

Welsh Highland Railway

*7422 LEE, C. E. The Welsh Highland Railway. *Weybridge: Welsh Highland Railway Society*, and *Dawlish: David & Charles*, 1962. pp. 48, with 32 illus. & map on 16 plates, and 5 illus. (1 fold.) & map in text.   BM
A revision of relevant portions of the author's *Narrow gauge railways in North Wales* (1945), with additional photographs.

Welshpool & Llanfair Light Railway

7423 COZENS, L. The Welshpool & Llanfair Light Railway. *Highgate: the author*, 1951. pp. 32, with 11 illus., 3 maps & plans.   BM

7424 STEPHENSON LOCOMOTIVE SOCIETY—MIDLAND AREA. Historical notes and itinerary in connection with the last train on the Welshpool & Llanfair Light Railway on 3rd November 1956, organised by the Stephenson Locomotive Society, Midland Area. [*Birmingham*, 1956.] pp. [8,] with 4 illus. & a map.   SLS

*7425 WELSHPOOL & LLANFAIR LIGHT RAILWAY PRESERVATION COMPANY. The Welshpool & Llanfair Light Railway: an illustrated guide, containing a history of the railway, a description of the route into Welshpool, with notes on locomotives, rolling stock and other information. Compiled by Michael Wakeman from information supplied by Derek A. Bayliss. *Llanfair: Welshpool & Llanfair Light Railway Preservation Company*, [1963.] pp. [28,] with 17 illus., 3 maps & a gradient profile.   BM

West Somerset Mineral Railway

7426 CLINKER, C. R. The West Somerset Mineral Railway. [1951.] pp. 14[16]. *Reproduced typescript*, with map & diagrams, statistics & tables.   BR

*7427 SELLICK, R. The West Somerset Mineral Railway and the story of the Brendon Hill iron mines. By Roger Sellick, with contributions by J. R. Hamilton and M. H. Jones. *Dawlish: David & Charles; London: Phoenix*, [1962.] pp. 126, with frontis., 12 plates, illus., 3 maps (inserted) & tables.   BM

Weston, Clevedon & Portishead Railway
(Incorporated as the Weston-super-Mare, Clevedon & Portishead Tramways.)

7428 WESTON, CLEVEDON & PORTISHEAD LIGHT RAILWAYS. Official Guide. *Clevedon*, [*c*. 1910.] pp. 44, with illus.   PC

7429 MAGGS, C. The Weston, Clevedon & Portishead Railway. [*Lingfield:*] *Oakwood Press*, 1964. pp. 48, with 21 illus. on 8 plates, map, diagrams & tables. [*Locomotion Papers*, no. 25.]   BM

Wirral Railway

7430 HIGHET, C. The Wirral Railway. *Lingfield: Oakwood Press*, 1961. pp. 39, with 20 illus. on 8 plates, 2 maps & a table of locomotives. [*Oakwood Library of Railway History*, no. 17.]   BM

Wolverton & Stony Stratford Tramway

7431 HYDE, F. E. *and* MARKHAM, S. F. A history of Stony Stratford and the immediate vicinity . . . *Wolverton & London: McCorquodale & Co.*, 1948, pp. xi, 191, with illus.   BM
pp. 166–79, 'The coming of the railway and its consequences'. Includes an account of the Stony Stratford & District Light Rly. Co., with 2 illus.

Wotton Tramway

7432 WOTTON TRAMWAY. Rules & regulations for the conduct of the traffic and for the guidance of the officers and men engaged on the Wotton Tramway. January 1873. *Aylesbury: 'Bucks Herald' Office*, [1873.] (*Facsimile reprint, Abbey Press, Abingdon, and S. H. P. Higgins*, 1961.) pp. 48, with fold. table of fines.   BM

M HERALDRY AND LIVERY

7433 GORDON, W. J. Our home railways: how they began and how they are worked; with 36 coloured plates . . . and 300 illustrations . . . *London*, 1910. 2 vols., pp. xvi, 268; x, 248.

Also issued separately in 12 parts. Includes reproductions of 12 coats of arms, in full colour.

—— reprinted. *London: Ian Allan*, 1962, 63. [*Classics of Railway Literature.*]

Plates (including the coats of arms) in monochrome.

*7434 ELLIS, C. H. The trains we loved. *London: Allen & Unwin*, 1947. pp. 196.   BM

pp. 179–89, Locomotive and rolling-stock liveries of the British main-line companies, 1914.

7435 LAKE, G. H. British Railways' standard liveries, July 1949. pp. [6,] with col. diagrams.   IT

Reprinted from vol. 2, no. 3, n.s., June–July, 1949, of *Railway Pictorial & Locomotive Review*, with the colours added.

7436 CARTER, E. F. Britain's railway liveries: colours, crests and linings, 1825–1948. *London: Burke*, 1952. pp. xvi, 360, with 8 col. plates, 37 monochrome illus. on 8 plates, 109 diagrams, 30 coats of arms, & a fold. chart of 50 colours.   BM

—— 2nd edn. *London: Harold Starke*, 1963. pp. xvi, 350.

Includes a list of historic locomotives and coaches preserved, and a classified list of pre-Grouping locomotive colour plates which have appeared in the *Railway Magazine* and the *Locomotive Magazine*.

Fine art—Posters—Ceramics—Medals and tokens

For humorous drawing see **P**

7437 TAYLOR, T. The Railway Station: painted by W. P. Frith; described by Tom Taylor. *London*, 1862. pp. 88.   BM
A description of Frith's painting of Paddington Station, and of the 100 people depicted in it.

—— another edn. *London*, 1865. pp. 35. BM

7438 FRITH, W. P. My autobiography and reminiscences . . . *London*, 1887. 2 vols.   BM
vol. 1, pp. 327–35, 'Success of "The Railway Station".' (Frith's famous picture of Paddington Station.)

—— 7th edn. *London*, 1889. (pp. 220–5.)
BM

7439 POTTER, G. W. J. Railway medals and tokens. *Brighton*, 1901. pp. 18, with 28 illus. on 4 plates. [*Railway Club Library*, vol. 1.]   BM

7440 MOYAUX, A. Les chemins de fer autrefois et aujourd'hui et leurs médailles commemoratives: notice historique suivie d'un catalogue descriptif des médailles de tous les pays. Ouvrage illustré hors texte et dans le texte accompagné de onze planches en phototypie. *Bruxelles*, 1905. pp. xii, 262, with 40 plates.   BM

—— Supplement.
BM (Dept. of Coins & Medals)
Includes railways of Gt. Britain.

7441 COLUMBIA UNIVERSITY [New York]. The William Barclay Parsons Railroad Prints: an appreciation and a check list. (Compiled by Laura S. Young.) *New York*, 1935. pp. 58, with plate.   BM
The list includes prints of British railway scenes.

7442 LONDON & NORTH EASTERN RLY. Sign standards: letters, totem, figures, arrow. Rev. edn. *London*, October 1946. pp. 12. PC
Gill Sans letters and figures. Standard drawings for the guidance of staff.

7443 KLINGENDER, F. D. Art and the Industrial Revolution. *London: Noel Carrington*, 1947. pp. xiii, 232, with plates.   BM
pp. 115–30, 'The Railway Age'; with illus. Reproductions of early railway scenes by contemporary artists; the social background of the Railway Age; the railway navvy.

7444 THOMAS, B. Railways by day. *London & Letchworth: Amex Co.*, [1947.] pp. [8.] BM
Seven coloured impressions with short descriptive remarks.

7445 THOMAS, B. Railways by night. *London & Letchworth: Amex Co.*, [1947.] pp. [8.] BM
Seven coloured impressions with short descriptive remarks.

7446 'X.' Power potential: studies of locomotives at rest: a series of pencil drawings by 'X'. *Bournemouth: E. R. Gray*, 1947.   BM
1000 copies only, numbered.
Twelve drawings, with descriptions by E. Rankine Gray.

7447 LONDON TRANSPORT EXECUTIVE. Art for all: London Transport posters, 1908–1949. *London: Art & Technics*, 1949. pp. 39, with 68 plates (18 col.).   BM

7448 MANN, P. B. How to draw locomotives. *London: The Studio*, [1948.] pp. 63.   BM

—— new edn. *London*, 1949. pp. 62[63].
BM

7449 MANN, P. B. How to draw rolling stock. *London: Studio Publications*, 1949. pp. 62 [64].   BM
Carriages, wagons, etc.

7450 ELLIS, C. H. Travel on railways: being twenty-four coloured drawings of locomotives, trains and steamers owned by railway companies between 1835 and 1920, drawn by C. Hamilton Ellis. *London: British Railways*, 1951.   BR

7451 SABIN, F. T. Our early railways: catalogue of an exhibition of old railway prints, drawings and books. [*London*,] 1951. pp. 47. PC
253 items.

7452 SABIN, F. T. Catalogue of old railway prints, drawings and books. *London*, 1952. pp. 44, with 23 plates.   BM
235 items.

7453 SABIN, F. T. Catalogue of an exhibition of early railways: prints, drawings, books, etc. *London*, 1954. pp. 53, with 30 plates. BM
281 items.

7454 SABIN, F. T. Catalogue of an exhibition of early railways: paintings, drawings, prints & books. III. *London*, 1956. pp. 40, with 14 plates.   BM
241 items.

7455 SABIN, F. T. Road and Rail Exhibition: old prints, drawings, books, etc. *London*, 1958. pp. 18.   BM
  160 items.

7456 SABIN, F. T. Our early railways: old prints, drawings, illustrated books, etc.

(Spring Exhibition, 1960.) *London*, 1960. pp. 10.   BM
  193 items.

*7457 LONDON TRANSPORT BOARD. London Transport posters: with an introduction and notes by Harold F. Hutchinson. *London*, 1963. pp. 23, 124,[4.]   BM
  Fifty years of pictorial poster art represented in 124 colour plates.

For writings in praise of railways see also **Q**
For humour, satire and allegory see also **P**

Marginal symbols: **b** bibliographies
com commentaries

Bibliographies and Anthologies

7458 DONOVAN, F. P. The railroad in literature: a brief survey of railroad fiction, poetry,
b songs, biography, essays, travel, and drama
in the English language. *Boston, Mass.:*
com *Railway & Locomotive Historical Society*,
1940. pp. ix, 138, with plates & maps.　pc
Includes many items relating to railways and
tramways in the British Isles.

7459 SIMMONS, J. Journeys in England: an
anthology edited by Jack Simmons. *London: Odhams Press*, 1951. pp. 288.　BM
Of ninety items, the following extracts from
prose, verse, diaries and letters relate to railways, travelling conditions and other social
aspects of railways—13, 21, 24, 56–63, 66, 67
and 73.

7460 LEGG, S. The Railway Book: an anthology.
Edited by Stuart Legg. *London: Rupert
Hart-Davis*, 1952. pp. 256.　BM
153 items in prose and verse on various aspects of railways, past and present, with notes
on sources.

—— Reprinted, *London*, 1958.　BM

7461 IRVING, C. Sixteen On. Edited and with
an introduction by Charles Irving; illustrated
by C. W. Bacon. *London: Macmillan & Co.*,
1957. pp. xxii, 239.　BM
Sixteen short stories and excerpts, and ten
smaller pieces by various writers.

Works by Individual Authors

7462 AITKEN, W. Echoes from the Iron Road,
and other poems. By Inspector Aitken,
Glasgow & South Western Railway, Greenock. *Glasgow & Edinburgh*, 1893. pp. 319.
BM
125 poems in which aspects of railway life
are used to illustrate the author's religious
sentiments, e.g. 'Is your Home Signal clear?'
Prefaced by two biographical sketches of the
author.

7463 AITKEN, W. Lays of the Line. *Edinburgh*,
1883.　BR

7464 AITKEN, W. Rhymes and Readings.
Glasgow, 1880. pp. 184.　BM
Miscellaneous verse, including a few on
railways and railway life.

7465 ALDEN, W. L. Johnston's Adventure. *In
his* 'The Mystery of Elias G. Roebuck, and
other stories.' *London*, 1896. pp. [71]–88. BM
An encounter on a train journey.

7466 ALEXANDER, R. The Wrecker . . . from
the famous play by Arnold Ridley and Ber-

nard Merivale. *London: Eldon Press*, 1951.
pp. 247.　BM

7467 ANDERSON, A. Ballads and Sonnets.
London, 1879. pp. x, 199.　BM
Includes some of his railway poems.

7468 ANDERSON, A. Songs of the Rail. *London*,
1878. pp. 163.　BM
Thirty-four poems on railway life.

—— 2nd edn. *London*, 1878. pp. 163.　pc
—— 3rd edn. *London*, 1881. pp. 163.　pc
Nine of the poems (some appearing as revised
versions) are taken from his first collected
volume of poems, *A Song of Labour, and other
poems.* Dumfries, 1873. The author was a
platelayer on the Glasgow & South Western,
and subsequently became Chief Assistant
Librarian at Edinburgh University.

7469 BROWN, A. Later poems of Alexander
Anderson, 'Surfaceman'. Edited, with a
com biographical sketch, by Alexander Brown.
Glasgow & Dalbeattie, 1912. pp. xxxii, 287.
BM
pp. xvii–xxxii, Biographical sketch with
portrait.

7470 ANDERSON, I. H. Kate Suter and the Old
Stationmaster. *Inverness*, 1910. pp. 54. BM
A tale.

7471 AUDEN, W. Night Mail. [Poem.]　BM
'This is the Night Mail crossing the border . . .'

7472 AYLMER, F. Dickens Incognito. *London:*
com *Hart-Davis*, 1959. pp. 95, with illus. & map.
BM
Charles Dickens' secret journeys to Ellen
Ternan at Slough. Evidence of his private
affairs deduced from a study of codes and
abbreviations used in his diary.
Appended to the UL copy is an excerpt from
The Sunday Times of 13 December, 1959.
This consists of a letter from Graham Storey
concerning Felix Aylmer's assumption that a
child was born to Ellen Ternan and Charles
Dickens at Slough on 13 April, 1867, and a
reply from the author.

7473 BAIR, P. Faster! faster! *London: Eyre &
Spottiswoode*, 1950. pp. 226[227].　BM

7474 BAKER, T. The Steam Engine; or, The
powers of flame: an original poem in ten
cantos. *London*, 1857. pp. iv, 260.　BM
Cantos VIII, IX and X, 'Locomotive power',
on locomotives and various other aspects of
railways, include the Liverpool & Manchester
Rly., the Rainhill Trials, and navvies.

7475 BARNES, W. The Railroad. [Two poems.]
    BM
    1, 'I took a flight awhile agoo . . .'
    2, 'An' while I went 'ithin a train . . .'

7476 BARTLETT, E. G. The Case of the Thirteenth Coach. *London: Staples Press*, 1958. pp. 208.   BM

7477 BAYLOR, F. C. An incident of English railway travel. *In her* 'A Shocking Example, and other sketches.' *Philadelphia*, 1889. BM

7478 BELL, N. The Handsome Langleys. *London: Eyre & Spottiswoode*, 1945. pp. 350 [351].   BM
    Period, 1838–*c*. 1900; setting, the L. & N.W. Rly. in which Tring station and cutting are featured. Several parts of the story concern other railways.

7479 BELLOC, H. On conversations in trains. *In his* 'On Nothing, and kindred subjects.' *London*, 1908. pp. 81–8.   BM

7480 BELLOC, H. On railways and things. *In his* 'On Nothing, and kindred subjects.' *London*, 1908. pp. 69–79.   BM

7481 BETJEMAN, J. First and Last Loves. *London: Murray*, 1952. pp. xi, 244.   BM
    pp. 75–89, London railway stations. Previously published in *Flower of Cities: a book of London. Studies and sketches by twenty-two authors* (1949). pp. 13–30.

7482 BETJEMAN, J. The Metropolitan Railway: Baker Street Station buffet. [Poem.]   BM
    'Early Electric! with what radiant hope . . .'

7483 BETJEMAN, J. Monody on the Death of Aldersgate Street Station. [Poem.]   BM
    'Snow falls in the buffet of Aldersgate Station . . .'

7484 BETJEMAN, J. Parliament Hill Fields. [Poem.]   BM
    'Rumbling under blackened girders, Midland, bound for Cricklewood . . .'

7485 BETJEMAN, J. Pershore Station. [Poem.]
    BM
    'The train at Pershore Station was waiting that Sunday night . . .'

7486 BETJEMAN, J. South London Sketch, 1944. [Poem.]   BM
    'From Bermondsey to Wandsworth so many churches are . . .'

7487 BETJEMAN, J. Summoned by Bells. *London: John Murray*, 1960.   BM
    In chapter 6: '. . . Great was my joy with London at my feet . . .' (Boyhood reminiscences of the Underground.)

7488 BLUNDEN, E. The Branch Line. [Poem.] BM
    'Professing loud energy, out of the junction departed . . ,'

7489 BLUNDEN, E. From the Branch Line. [Poem].   BM
    'Brightest of red roofs . . .'

7490 BLUNDEN, E. No Continuing City. [Poem.]
    BM
    'The train with its smoke and its rattle went on . . .'

7491 BLUNDEN, E. Railway Note. [Poem.] BM
    'The station roofs curve off and line is lost in white thick vapour . . .'

7492 BOAS, G. The Underground. [Poem.] BM
    'The Underground goes round and round . . .'

7493 BONHAM, M. Rolliver. *In her* 'The Casino, and other stories.' *London*, 1948. pp. 142–54.   BM
    West Country branch line journey.

7494 BONHAM, M. The Train and the Gun. *In her* 'The Casino, and other stories.' *London*, 1948. pp. 42–8.   BM
    A boy's reactions as witness and rescuer to an accident.

7495 BRINDLEY, H. H. Where was Mr. Carker
com killed ? . . . *Cambridge*, [1911.] pp. 7.   pc
    Reprinted from the *Cambridge Review*, 27 April, 1911.
    Mr. Carker of *Dombey & Son*, by Charles Dickens, was run over by a train.

7496 BROOKE, R. The Night Journey. [Poem.] BM
    'Hand and lit faces eddy to a line . . .'

7497 BROWN, H. F. A Railroad Medley. [Poem.]
    BM
    'Out from the roar and the smoke . . .'

7498 BROWN, H. F. To a Great Western Broad Gauge Engine and its Stoker. *In his* 'Drift: verses' (1900). pp. 3.   BM
    'So! I shall never see you more . . .'

7499 BROWNE, D. G. The Stolen Boat Train. *London: Methuen*, 1935. pp. x, 281.   BM
    The *Golden Arrow* train of the Southern Rly.

7500 BULLETT, G. W. The Last Days of Binnacle. *In his* 'Baker's Cart and other tales.' *London*, 1925. pp. 143–72.   BM
    A fantasy, Central London Rly.

7501 CALDECOTT, A. Branch Line to Benceston. *In his* 'Not exactly Ghosts.' *London: Edward Arnold*, 1947. pp. 35–54.   BM
    A mystery story.

7502 CAMPBELL, R. W. Snooker Tam of the Cathcart Railway. *Edinburgh*, 1919. pp. 241.   BM
    A tale of a boy porter on the Glasgow suburban section of the Caledonian during the Great War.

7503 CAPEK, K. Intimate Things. *London*, 1935.   BM
    pp. 99–102, Railway stations.

7504 CARROLL, L. For the Train. *London*, 1932.
pp. 76.   BM
    Limited edition of 100 copies.
    pp. 2–4, 'The Song of the Train': a poem.
    pp. 67–76, 'Some Carrollean episodes concerning trains'.

7505 CARROLL, L. Through the Looking Glass.
    BM
    chap. 3, '. . . "Tickets please," said the guard . . .'

7506 [CARSON, H.] Railway Line to Fortune;
or, The power of a good name. *London*,
1881. pp. 110.   BM

7507 [CHANDLER, M.] A Description of Bath: a
poem, in a letter to a friend. *London:* [1733.]
pp. 18 fol.   BM
    On p. 16 is a description of Ralph Allen's
wagonway, constructed in 1731 for the conveyance of stone from the top of Combe Down
through the Widcombe Valley to the River
Avon at Dolemead:
           '. . . hence is seen
The new-made Road, and wonderful Machine,
Self moving downward from the Mountain's
    Height,
A Rock it's Burden of a Mountain's Weight!'
    This is apparently the first mention of railways in English Literature.
    The first two editions, [1733] and 1734 were
published anonymously, but subsequent editions, 1736 to 1767, have title-pages bearing the
author's name.

7508 CHESTERTON, G. K. Tremendous Trifles.
London: Methuen, 1909.   BM
    pp. 9–15, The Secret of a Train. (A wayside
station and a journey by night on the G.W.R.)
    pp. 219–24, The Prehistoric Railway Station.
(Symbolism in the life and being of railway
stations; in opposition to the views of John
Ruskin.)

7509 CHRISTMAS Tale: a night in a railway
carriage. *London*, 1873. pp. 22.   BM

7510 CHURCH, R. The Golden Sovereign.
London: Heinemann, 1957.   BM
    An autobiography of Richard Church's
youth and a sequel to his *Over the Bridge* (1955).
    pp. 6–10, recollections of daily tram journeys
along the Walworth Road, London. This
unique account provides a welcome counterblast to the current tendency to eulogize the
trams out of their true place in social history
and is a vivid reminder of aspects which were in
danger of being forgotten.

7511 CLEWES, W. Peacocks on the Lawn.
London: Michael Joseph, 1952. pp. 222. BM
    The story of an Irish light railway, 1903–24.

7512 CONNINGTON, J. J., *pseud.* [A. W. Stewart.] The Two Tickets Puzzle. *London*,
1930. pp. 288.   BM

7513 COLLIER, R. First Class Romance.   BM
    Reprinted in *Sixteen On* (1957), pp. 216–22.
    A humorous study of the personality of a
railway enthusiast.

7514 CONAN DOYLE, A. The Adventure of the
Bruce Partington Plans. *In his* 'His Last
Bow: some reminiscences of Sherlock

Holmes.' *London*, 1924. pp. 67–91.   BM
    Sherlock Holmes' train journeys are usually
quite uneventful. The time of arrival or departure has sometimes a significance, but nothing happens en route apart from a review of the
situation in the mind of the detective. His rail
journeys (not always accurately conceived) are
merely incidental to the movement of the story.
    In *The Adventure of the Bruce Partington
Plans*, however, certain features of the Metropolitan Railway are important elements in the
story.

7515 CONAN DOYLE, A. The Lost Special. *In
his* 'Round the Fire Stories.' *London*, 1908.
pp. 177–201.   BM
—— Reprinted in 'Sixteen On', edited by
Charles Irving, *London*, 1957. pp. 32–52. BM

7516 CORBYN, E. All along the Line. *London:
Barrie*, 1958. pp. 208.   BM
    A light novel. The setting is a seaside railway
station, dominated by an eccentric stationmaster.

7517 COWARD, N. Brief Encounter. [A play.] BM
    Part of the action takes place at a railway
station, winter, 1938–9.

7518 COWARD, N. Still Life: a play in five
scenes. *In* 'Tonight at 8.30: plays by Noel
Coward.' *London*, 1936. vol. 3, pp. 47–92.
    BM
    Set in the refreshment room at 'Milford
Junction'. Time, the present.

*7519 CRISPIN, E. Beware of the Trains.   BM
    Reprinted in *Sixteen On*, edited by Charles
Irving, 1957. pp. 197–207.
    Crime.

*7520 CROFTS, F. W. Crime on the Footplate.
In his 'Many a Slip.'   BM
    Reprinted in *Sixteen On*, edited by Charles
Irving, 1957. pp. 186–95.

7521 CROFTS, F. W. Death of a Train. *London*,
1946. pp. 282.   BM
    An 'Inspector French detective story'.
    War-time transport of secret equipment on
the G.W.R. and the Southern.

7522 CROFTS, F. W. Death on the Way. *London*, [1932.] pp. 285.   BM
    A mystery story involving some train working, Southern Rly.

7523 CROFTS, F. W. The Level Crossing. *In*
'Short stories of detection, mystery and
horror.' 3rd series, edited by Dorothy
L. Sayers. *London*, 1934. pp. 118–34.   BM
    A crossing keeper who overslept.

7524 CROFTS, F. W. The Mystery of the Sleeping-Car Express. *In* 'Great short stories of
detection . . .' 2nd series, edited by Dorothy
L. Sayers, 1931. pp. 242–63.   BM
    Previously published in the *Premier Magazine*,
1921.
    On the London & North Western, between
Preston and Carlisle.

7525 CROFTS, F. W. Sir John Magill's Last
Journey: an Inspector French case. *London:
Collins*, 1930. pp. 288.   BM

7526 CRONIN, A. J. Hatter's Castle. *London*, 1931. (29th impression 1952.)   BM
In the story, Denis is a victim in the Tay Bridge disaster of 1879. (Book One, ch. 12, pp. 147–56.)

7527 CUTHBERTSON, D. The life-history of Alexander Anderson, 'Surfaceman' . . .
com *Inveresk*, [1929.] pp. 139, with 3 portraits. pc
'Privately printed.'
A. Anderson, a platelayer on the G. & S.W. who became a librarian, wrote, among other works, a collection of poems entitled *Songs of the Rail*, 1878 (7468) above.

7528 DARLINGTON, W. A. A Chain of Circumstance.   BM
Reprinted in *Sixteen On*, edited by Charles Irving, 1957. pp. 120–41.
Romance on a country branch line.

7529 DE LA MARE, W. A Froward Child. [A chapter in his *Wind blows over* (1936).]   BM
A dramatic encounter on a train journey.

7530 DICKENS, C. Dombey and Son.   BM
In chapters 6 and 15 are accounts of the London & Birmingham Railway at Camden Town and of a trip to Birmingham. Carker, one of the characters in the story, meets his death by being run down by a train at Paddock Wood, S.E. Rly. (*See* 7495.)

7531 DICKENS, C. A Flight. *In his* 'Reprinted Pieces'.   BM
A short story featuring a journey from London Bridge to Folkestone.

7532 DICKENS, C. Lazy Tour of Two Idle Apprentices.   BM
Contains references to the L. & N.W. Rly. in the Carlisle district.

7533 DICKENS, C., *and others*. Mugby Junction. *London*, 1898. pp. 216[217].   BM
Reprinted from the Extra Christmas Number of *All the Year Round*, 1866.
Of eight short stories, three are centred on Rugby Station and its refreshment room, and three are on other railway subjects.
Barbox Brothers. By C. Dickens.
Barbox Brothers & Co. By C. Dickens.
Main Line: the Boy at Mugby. By C. Dickens.
No. 1 Branch Line: the Signalman. By C. Dickens.
No. 2 Branch Line: the Engine Driver. By Andrew Halliday.
No. 4 Branch Line: the Travelling Post Office. By Hesba Stretton.
—— L'Embranchement de Mugby; précédé de son histoire, d'après John Forster, traduite par Th. Bentzon. [*pseud.* Thérèse Blanc.] *Paris*, [1879.] pp. 128, with illus. BM
—— Mugbyn risteys. Suomentanut Suonio. Toinen, korjattu painos. *Helsingissä*, 1904. pp. 198.   BM
A translation into Finnish of the Christmas 1866 number of *All the Year Round*.
—— Mugby Junction and other stories printed in the corresponding style of Pitman's Shorthand. Twentieth Century edition. *London: Sir Isaac Pitman*, [1909.] pp. 123.   BM

7534 DICKENS, C. The Mystery of Edwin Drood.   BM
Several implied references to the S.E. Rly. at London Bridge and 'Cloisterham' (Rochester); also to the L.C. & D. Rly.

7535 DICKENS, C. Our Mutual Friend.   BM
References to the London & Greenwich Rly., the G.W.R. and Paddington Station.
In the postscript to this work, Dickens writes of his experience in the Staplehurst accident on the S.E. Rly. in 1865.

7536 DICKENS, C. Out of Town.   BM
In his *Reprinted Pieces* 'Out of Town' has a brief reference to the S.E. Rly. at Folkestone.

7537 DICKENS, C. The Uncommercial Traveller.   BM
The 'Calais Night Mail' refers to the railway at Dover, and 'Dullborough Town' to the railway at Rochester or Chatham.

7538 DICKINSON, E. 'I like to see it lap the miles. . . .' [Poem. No title.]   BM

7539 DOBELL, S. A Young Man's Song. [Poem.]   BM
'At last the curse has run its date . . .'

7540 DOLPHIN, M. I. E. More Songs from the Moorland. *Oxford*, 1924. pp. 99.   BM
Includes three railway poems: The Song of the Train, Murton Junction, and Voices in a Train.

7541 DU MAURIER, D. The Infernal World of Branwell Brontë. *London: Victor Gollancz*,
com 1960. pp. 260.   BM
pp. 120–34, B. Brontë during his period as booking clerk at Sowerby Bridge, and stationmaster at Luddenden Foot, Manchester & Leeds Rly., 1840–2.

7542 DWARRIS, F. W. L. Railway Results; or, The gauge deliverence: a dramatic sketch. *London*, 1845. pp. 43.   BM
A play in five acts.

7543 DYMENT, C. The Railway Game. *London: Dent*, 1962. pp. ix, 218.   BM
On pp. 52–65, and subsequently as a recurring theme, the author recalls his boyhood acquaintance with an invalid ex-railwayman whose passion for railways—and for the L.N.W.R. in particular, as opposed to the G.W.R.—takes the form of imaginary footplate journeys.

7544 EDWARDS, A. B. The Four-fifteen Express. *In* 'Mixed Sweets from Routledge's Annual, 1867.' pp. 114–34.   BM
A mystery story (G.E. Rly.).

7545 ELIOT, T. S. Skimbleshanks, the Railway Cat. *In his* 'Old Possum's Book of Practical Cats.'   BM

7546 ELLIS, C. H. Dandy Hart. *London: Victor Gollancz*, 1947. pp. 466.   BM
A novel, interwoven with many facts, incidents and scenes from railway history in Southern England during the period 1830–60. The story is centred mainly upon the L.B. & S.C. Rly., but the G.W.R. and the L. & S.W.R. are also featured.

7547 ELLIS, C. H. The Grey Men. *Oxford: O.U.P.*, 1939. pp. 256   BM
A mystery story, West Highland Railway.

7548 ELLIS, C. H. T.P.O.   BM
Reprinted in *Sixteen On*, edited by Charles Irving, 1957. pp. 210–15.

7549 EVANS, E. J. Death on the Line: a ghost story in one act . . . based on a short story by Charles Dickens, 'The Signalman'. *London*, 1954. pp. 26.   BM

7550 FERGUSON, J., *railway guard*. Stories of the Rail. *Perth*, [1924.] pp. 133.   RC
Nine stories from the *Perthshire Advertiser*.

*7551 FREEMAN, R. A. The Blue Sequin. *In his* 'The Famous Cases of Dr. Thorndike: thirty-seven of his criminal investigations as set down by R. Austin Freeman.' *London*, 1929. pp. 318–38.   BM
Paddock Wood—Hawkhurst branch.

—— Reprinted in 'Sixteen On', edited by Charles Irving, 1957.   BM

*7552 FREEMAN, R. A. The Case of Oscar Brodski. *In his* 'The Famous Cases of Dr. Thorndike: thirty-seven of his criminal investigations as set down by R. Austin Freeman.' *London*, 1929. pp. 3–53.   BM

7553 FRITH, H. Biography of a Locomotive . . . *London*, 1891. pp. 254, with 8 illus.   BM
Memoirs and short stories on railway life.

7554 GARNETT, E. Hill of Sheep; illustrated by Joan Kiddell Munroe. *London: Hodder & Stoughton*, 1955. pp. 192.   BM
Set in the Blea Moor district during the construction of the Settle & Carlisle line.

7555 GARVE, A. The Cuckoo Line Affair. *London: Collins*, 1953. pp. 192.   BM
A story of detection involving a railway journey in Essex—*not* on the Eridge–Polegate branch of the Southern, familiarly known as 'The Cuckoo Line'.

7556 GOULD, A. The Viaduct. *London: Hodder & Stoughton*, 1939. pp. 320.   BM
Railway construction in Devon, 1870's.

7557 GRAHAM, R. B. C. Beattock for Moffatt. *In his* 'Success.' *London*, 1902. pp. 139–154.   BM
Reprinted 1912.

7558 GRAY, J. The Engine. 1852. pp. 2.   BM
Verses, 'printed for, and sold by, the Honourable Company of Stokers'.

7559 GREENIDGE, T. L. Girls and Stations. *London: Fortune Press*, [1952.] pp. 62.   BM
Verses.

7560 GRIFFITHS, M. Dempster and Son. *London: Rich & Cowan*, 1938. pp. 358.   BM
The story of a family business building locomotives in Wolverhampton from 1885 onwards.

7561 'GRIP', *pseud*. How John Bull lost London; or, The capture of the Channel Tunnel. 4th edn. *London*, 1882. pp. 127.   BM
A forecast of French invasion via the proposed Tunnel.

7562 GROGAN, W. E. The 10.20 Express: a novel. *London*, [1913.] pp. 326[327].   BM
A mystery story in a Great Northern Rly. setting.

7563 HADFIELD, J. Love on a Branch Line. *London: Hutchinson*, 1959. pp. 290[291].   BM

7564 HARDY, T. Faintheart in a Railway Train. [Poem.]   BM
'At nine in the morning there passed a church . . .'

7565 HARDY, T. Midnight on the Great Western. [Poem.]   BM
'In the third-class seat sat the journeying boy . . .'

7566 HENDERSON, R. W. W. John Goodchild. *London*, 1909. pp. 323.   BM
Autobiographical fiction: George Stephenson; the London & Birmingham; railway enterprise and investment in the 1840's.

7567 HOUSE, H. The Dickens World. *London: O.U.P.*, 1941. pp. 231.   BM
pp. 137–52 and elsewhere, railways in Dickens' time and in his writings.

—— 2nd edn. *London*, 1942. pp. 231.   BM
—— Reprinted, *London*, 1950. [*Oxford Paperbacks*, no. 9.]

7568 HURNARD, J. Coach to Railway. [Poem.]   BM
'The coachman was an English character . . .'

7569 HURNARD, J. The Setting Sun: a poem in seven books. *London*, 1870.   BM
Book I, pp. 41–4, 'These things of only yesterday have passed . . .'

7570 HURNARD, J. The Steam Engine. [Poem.]   BM
'This may be called the age of ingenuity . . .'

7571 INNES, M. Appleby's End. *London: Gollancz*, 1945. pp. 152.   BM
The story opens (chaps. 1 and 2) with a rural train journey.

7572 INNES, M. Journeying Boy. *London: Victor Gollancz*, 1949. pp. 325.   BM
The story involves a train journey from Euston to Heysham (pp. 33–90) and one on a light railway in Ireland (pp. 137–42).

—— *Harmondsworth: Penguin Books*, 1961. pp. 235.   BM

7573 JENNINGS, P. The Bin-bangers. *In his* 'Even Oddlier.' *London: Reinhardt*, 1952. pp. [16]–18.   BM
Night travel by railway.

7574 JENNINGS, P. British Railways. *In his*
'Oddly Enough.' *London: Reinhardt &
Evans*, 1950. pp. [90]–93.   BM
In praise of the L.M.S. Rly.

7575 JENNINGS, P. Euston Sleepers. *In his* 'Even
Oddlier.' *London: Reinhardt*, 1952. pp.
[13]–15.   BM

7576 JENNINGS, P. The Ghost Tram. *In his*
'Oddly Bodlikins.' *London: Reinhardt*, 1953.
pp. [151]–153.   BM
Note: In the index and running title this
essay is wrongly named 'The Ghost Train'.

7577 JENNINGS, P. Metroland. *In his* 'Next to
Oddliness.' *London: Reinhardt*, 1955. pp.
[76]–79.   BM

7578 JENNINGS, P. No atomic trams yet, he says.
In his 'Oddly Enough.' *London: Reinhardt
& Evans*, 1950. pp. [17]–20.   BM

7579 JENNINGS, P. Third Class Sleepers. *In
his* 'Even Oddlier.' *London: Reinhardt*,
1952. pp. [9]–12.   BM

7580 JENNINGS, P. Tramophilia. *In his* 'Oddly
Enough.' *London: Reinhardt & Evans*, 1950.
pp. [69]–73.   BM

7581 JEROME, J. K. Three Men in a Boat.   BM
An excerpt with the title 'Waterloo' is
reprinted in *Sixteen On*, edited by Charles
Irving, 1957. pp. 118–19.

7582 KEANE, E. Heroes of the Line: stories of
railway rescue. *London*, [1893.] pp. 128. BM

7583 KEANE, E. The Signalman's Boy. [*London*,
1893.] pp. 16. [*Shaw's Penny Series*, no.
21.]   BM
'Those little brown muscular hands seized
the lever with a desperate grip.'

7584 KENWARD, J. The Manewood Line. *London: S. Paul*, [1937.] pp. 350.   BM
A story about a small railway somewhere in
the South of England.

7585 KINGSLEY, C. Morte. [Part 3 of 'North
Devon', one of his 'Prose Idylls, new and
old'.]   BM
'Exquisite motion . . .'

7586 LAWRENCE, D. H. Tickets, please. *In his*
'Complete short stories.' *London*, 1955. BM
On a tramway in the Midlands (Notts &
Derby Traction Co.).

7587 The LEISURE hours of a railway labourer
. . . *Edinburgh*, 1855. pp. 96.   BM
Poems.

7588 LOWRIE, C. Level Crossing. *London:
Ward Lock*, 1950. pp. 224.   BM
Built around the finance, construction and
parliamentary background to the promotion of
various railways in East Anglia in the 1840's.
Robert Stephenson is brought into the story.

7589 LYND, R. In the Train. *In his* 'The Pleasures of Ignorance.' *London*, 1921. pp.
108–14.   BM
'Let the stations be made more amusing.'

7590 LYND, R. Railway stations I have loved.
In his 'In Defence of Pink.' *London: J. M.
Dent*, 1937. pp. 67–75.   BM

7591 LYND, R. Trains. *In his* 'The Orange
Tree.' *London*, 1926. pp. 79–85.   BM
An appreciation of railways.

7592 'LYULPH.' A Girl at a Railway Junction's
Reply. By Lyulph. A New Year's story.
London, [1867.] pp. 24.   BM
A sequel to Charles Dickens' *Mugby Junction*.

7593 McGONAGALL, W. An Address to the
new Tay Bridge. [Poem.]   BM
'Beautiful new railway bridge o' the silvery
Tay . . .'

7594 McGONAGALL, W. The Newport Railway. [Poem.]   BM
'Success to the Newport Railway . . .'

7595 McGONAGALL, W. The Railway Bridge
of the Silvery Tay. [Poem.]   BM
'Beautiful railway bridge of the silv'ry Tay,
With your numerous arches and pillars in so
grand array . . .'

7596 McGONAGALL, W. The Tay Bridge Disaster. [Poem.]   BM
'Beautiful railway bridge of the silv'ry Tay
Alas! I am very sorry to say . . .'

7597 MACKAIL, D. Another Part of the Wood.
London, 1929. pp. 310[311].   BM
pp. 16–28, a branch line journey.

7598 MACKAY, C. Railways, 1846. [Poem.] BM
'No poetry in railways! foolish thought . . .'
This poem includes the verse commencing
'Lay down your rails, ye nations, near and far'...

7599 McLAREN, M. Return to Scotland. *London*, 1930.   BM
pp. 69–80, Essay no. 6, in which is an account
of 'walking the sleepers' from Tyndrum to
Rannoch on the Highland Rly.

7600 MAJENDIE, M. A Railway Journey. *In*
'Tales from Blackwood', new series, vol. 6,
no. 11. [1879.] pp. 158–76.   BM
From *Blackwood's Magazine*, April 1877.
An encounter on a train journey from Euston.

7601 MAXWELL, W. B. The Long-Distance
Train. In 'Great English short stories',
edited by Lewis Melville and Reginald
Hargreaves. *London*, 1931. pp. 837–50. BM
A station-master's wife, bored with life in a
flat above a large suburban station, is tempted
away by a handsome traveller. Period, 1920's.

7602 MILNE, A. A. A Train of Thought. *In
his* 'If I may.' *London*, 1921. pp. 114–18. BM
'Nowhere can I think so happily as in a train.'

7603 MONKHOUSE, C. The Night Express.
[Poem.]   BM
'With three great snorts of strength . . .'

7604 MUNRO, H. H. The Mouse. *In his* 'Complete short stories of "Saki".' 1930. BM

7605 NEALE, J. M. The Engine Drivers. *In his* 'Songs and Ballads for Manufacturers'. 2nd edn. *London*, 1850. pp. 21–22.   BM
'Water and flame to agreement came . . .'

7606 NEALE, J. M. The Railway Accident: a tale. *London*, 1848.   BM

7607 NESBIT, E. The Railway Children; with drawings by C. E. Brock. *London*, 1906. pp. viii, 309.   BM
—— another edn. reset with new illus. & format. *Redhill*, 1944. pp. 192.

7608 NOYES, A. The Electric Tram. [Poem.] *In his* 'Collected Poems'. *New York: Frederick A. Stokes Co.*, 1913. vol. 3.   BM
This poem is not included in later collections. 'Bluff and burly and splendid . . .'

7609 NOYES, A. In a Railway Carriage. [Poem.]   BM
'Three long isles of sunset-cloud . . .'

7610 NOYES, A. On a Railway Platform. [Poem.]   BM
'A drizzle of drifting rain . . .'

7611 PRIESTLEY, J. B. Man underground. *In his* 'Self-selected essays.' *London*, 1932. pp. 75–80.   BM
Philosophical thoughts on travelling by underground railway in London.

7612 QUILLER-COUCH, A. T. Delectable Duchy. *London*, 1893.   BM
pp. 65–74, Cuckoo Valley Railway. (The Bodmin & Wadebridge.)
pp. [203]–221, In the Train. 1, Punch's Under-study; 2, A Corrected Contempt.
Encounters on train journeys in Devon and Cornwall.

7613 QUILLER-COUCH, A. T. The Destruction of Didcot. *In* 'Echoes from the Oxford Magazine . . .' *London*, 1908. pp. 127–9. BM
A satire on Didcot Station, G.W. Rly.

7614 QUILLER-COUCH, A. T. Pipes in Arcady. *In his* 'News from the Duchy.' Reprinted in 'Sixteen On', edited by Charles Irving, 1957. pp. 75–86.   BM
A Cornish branch line fantasy.

7615 RADCLIFFE, G. On the Irish Mail. *In* 'Great short stories of detection, mystery and horror.' Third series, edited by Dorothy L. Sayers. *London*, 1934. pp. 389–400. BM
A confidence trick, L.M.S. Rly., between Euston and Holyhead.

7615a The RAILWAY Guard: the mail train to the North. Music published by J. W. Trayhearne . . . Printer, W. S. Forley. *London*, [18– *after* 1846.] s.sh.   BM
A broadside ballad in four stanzas with a chorus. Begins:
'At the terminus at Euston of the North Western Rail'

7616 A RAILWAY Junction; or, The romance of Ladybank. *In* 'Tales from Blackwood.' n.s., no. 4. [1878.] pp. 59.   RC
Reprinted from *Blackwoods Magazine*, October 1873. The North British Rly.

7617 The RAILWAY Truck. *London: E. Hodge*, [*c.* 1845.] s.sh.   BM
Verses commencing, 'A railway guard as I've heard tell . . .'

7618 RANDELL, W. L. Quaker Robins. *London*, 1910. pp. 320.   BM
A tale of railway life. (The choice of the name 'Quaker' is capricious.)

7619 READY, S. Mr. Hunter: a thriller for women in one act. *London: Samuel French*, 1945. pp. 29.   BM
Set in a station waiting-room.

7620 RHODE, J. Dead on the Track. *London: Collins*, 1943. pp. 192.   BM

7621 RIDGE, W. P. On Company's Service. *London*, 1905. pp. viii, 251.   BM
Stories of railway life.

7622 RIDGE, W. P. Thanks to Sanderson. *London*, 1911. pp. 308.   BM
A story of the domestic life of an inspector on the South Eastern Rly.

7623 RIDLEY, A. The Ghost Train: a play in three acts. *London*, 1931. pp. 112[115], with 3 plates.   BM
—— The Ghost Train; adapted from the play. By Ruth Alexander. *London*, 1927. pp. 319.   BM

7624 RODGERS, W. R. Express. [Poem.]   BM
'As the through-train of words . . .'

7625 RODGERS, W. R. The Train. [Poem.]   BM
'There with a screech stuck in her hair like a feather . . .'

7626 ROLT, L. T. C. Winterstoke. *London: Constable*, 1954. pp. 247.   BM
The social and industrial history of an imaginary Midlands town in which salient features of the English 19th century railway scene (construction, finance, competition) are exemplified.

7627 RUSKIN, J. The works of John Ruskin. Edited by E. T. Cook and Alexander Wedcom derburn. *London*, 1912. 29 vols.   BM
vol. 29, General Index, contains about 140 references to railways in his writings.

7628 SASSOON, S. A Local Train of Thought. [Poem.]   BM
'Alone, in silence, at a certain time of night . . .'

7629 SASSOON, S. Morning Express. [Poem.] BM
'Along the wind-swept platform . . .'

7630 SHARP, L. 'N.B.' Strange happenings. *London*, 1883. pp. 128.   BM
pp. 108–16, Underneath the ground. A story of a journey on the Metropolitan Rly.

7631 SITWELL, O. Travelling: by train. *In his* 'Penny Foolish: a book of tirades and panegyrics.' *London*, 1935. pp. 231–5.   BM
'Trains sum up all the fogs and muddled misery of the nineteenth century . . . Slums on wheels.'

7632 SMYTH, E. M. Adventure in a Train. *In* 'Mercury Book', 1926. pp. 156–69.   BM
Waterloo to Woking, 1902. A character study narrative.

7633 SOMERVILLE, E. O. *and* ROSS, M. Poisson d'Avril. *In their* 'Further Experiences of an Irish R.M.'   BM
Reprinted in *Sixteen On*, edited by Charles Irving, 1957. pp. 87–99.
Irish cross-country train journey.

7634 SPENDER, S. The Express. [Poem.]   BM
'After the first powerful plain manifesto . . .'

7635 SPENDER, S. In Railway Halls. [Poem.] BM
'In railway halls, on pavements near the traffic . . .'

7636 STEEL, A. B. Jorrocks' England. *London*, com 1932. pp. ix, 303.   BM
pp. 88–108, 'Travel; The Railway Age'. Railways and Society as revealed in the novels of Robert Smith Surtees.

7637 STEPHEN, J. K. Poetic Lamentation on the Insufficiency of Steam Locomotion in the Lake District. [Poem.]   BM
'Bright Summer spreads his various hue . . .'
Addressed to William Wordsworth, and reprinted from the *Pall Mall Gazette*, November 1882. Reprinted in *The Railway Book*, edited by Stuart Legg. *London*, 1952. pp. 60–1.

7638 STEVENSON, R. L. From a Railway Carriage. [Poem.]   BM
'Faster than fairies, faster than witches . . .'

7639 STEVENSON, R. L. The Iron Steed. [Poem.]
  BM
'In our black stable by the sea . . .'

7640 STEVENSON, R. L. Virginibus Puerisque. BM
In the essay, 'Ordered South', he suggests some pleasures which may be derived from a train journey by persons travelling for convalescence.

7641 STEVENSON, R. L. *and* OSBOURNE, L. The Wrong Box.   BM
An excerpt with the title 'Accident' is reprinted in *Sixteen On*, edited by Charles Irving, 1957. pp. 208–9.

7642 STIRLING, E. The Railway King!: a laughable farce in one act . . . *London*, [*c*. 1845.] pp. 20. [*Duncombe's British Theatre*, no. 431.]   RC
Identification with George Hudson is avoided.

7643 STRONG, L. A. G. Departure. *In his* 'The English Captain and other stories.' *London*, 1929. pp. 123–33.   BM
Country station setting.

7644 STRONG, L. A. G. The Gates. *In his* 'The English Captain and other stories.' *London*, 1931. pp. 83–98.   BM
A crossing keeper forgets to set his alarm.

7645 SUMMERS, G. Railway Rhymes. *Egremont: Arcadian Agency*, [1960.] pp. 72.   BM

7646 SUTTON, G. Fleming of Honister. *London: Hodder & Stoughton*, 1953. pp. 288.   BM
The story surrounds the building of the Settle & Carlisle Line, Midland Rly. in the 1870's.

7647 TEY, J. The Singing Sands.   BM
Opening paragraphs reprinted under the title 'Journey's End' in *Sixteen On*, edited by Charles Irving, 1957, p. 100.
The arrival of an early morning mail train from Euston.

7648 THACKERAY, W. M. Jeames on the Gauge Question. *One of his* 'Letters of Jeames.'
  BM
A short story, in London dialect, relating a journey from Paddington to Cheltenham, with change of carriage at Swindon and at Gloucester and the confusion entailed by the transfer of ninety-three packages and a baby.

7649 THACKERAY, W. M. The Speculators. *One of his* 'Ballads of Policeman X.'   BM
'The night was stormy and dark . . .'
This ballad includes the verse commencing 'Bless railroads everywhere . . .'

7650 THOMAS, G. O. Calm Weather. *London*, 1928.   BM
pp. 36–42, Cross-country journeys.
pp. 67–74, A corner of Essex. (Kelvedon & Tollesbury branch, L. & N.E. Rly.)

7651 THOMAS, G. O. Selected poems, old and new. *London: Allen & Unwin*, 1951. pp. 111.
  BM
pp. 93–4, 'In the train'.

7652 THOMAS, G. O. Sparks from the Fire. *London*, 1923.   BM
pp. 77–83, 'The Motorman'. A reverie on tram-driving.
pp. 87–96, 'On railways and theology'. The mystery of an apparent link between a reverence for railways and experienced divine transcendence (rather than theology).

7653 THOMSON, J. In the Train.   BM
'As we rush, as we rush in the train . . .'

7654 'TILBURY TRAMP', *pseud. of* C. J. Lever. Tales of the Trains: being some chapters of railroad romance. *London*, 1845. pp. viii, 156.   BM
Five short stories centred upon train journeys, with some verse and some sketches by 'Phiz'.
1, The coupé of the North Midland.
2, The white lace bonnet. (London & Brighton Rly.)
3, Fast asleep and wide awake. (London & Brighton Rly.)
(Nos. 4 and 5 are about railways in France and Belgium.)

7655 [TOWNSEND, R. E. A.] Visions of the Western Railways. *London*, 1838. pp. 90, 36.   BM
> Printed for private circulation.
> A poem.

7656 VALE, E. Elfin Chaunts and Railway Rhythms. *London*, 1914. pp. 62.   BM
> pp. 53 to end, four poems: The Royal Mail; the Liverpool Express; Song of the Central London Rly.; the Cornish Express.

7657 VEITCH, S. F. F. Duncan Moray, farmer. *London*, 1890. 2 vols.   BM
> A novel which includes (vol. 2, pp. 63 et seq.) local reaction to a proposed railway in rural Scotland.

7658 VICKERS, R. The Eighth Lamp.   BM
> Reprinted in *Sixteen On*, edited by Charles Irving, 1957. pp. 101–17.
> Metropolitan Rly. When the last train has gone, the station lights have to be switched off . . .

7659 W., B. The Engine-Driver: a petite drama in one scene. *Manchester*, [1895.] pp. 16. [*John Heywood's Series of Plays, Recitations for School & Popular Entertainments, etc.*, no. 29.]   BM
> A domestic melodrama.

7660 WALLACE, E. The Branch Line. *In his* 'Bones in London.'   BM
> Reprinted in *Sixteen On*, edited by Charles Irving, 1957. pp. 163–78.

7661 WARNER, S. T. Level Crossing. *In her* 'Garland of Straw.' *London: Chatto & Windus*, 1943. pp. 206–20.   BM
> A country crossing-keeper (G.W.R.), his niece, and soldiers billeted with them.

7662 WELLS, H. G. The Food of the Gods.   BM
> An excerpt with the title 'Charing Cross' is reprinted in *Sixteen On*, edited by Charles Irving, 1957. pp. 53–4.

7663 WHITECHURCH, V. L. Sir Gilbert Murrell's Picture. *In* 'Great short stories of detection, mystery and horror', 1st series, edited by Dorothy L. Sayers. *London*, 1928. pp. 492–504.   BM
> Didcot & Newbury branch, G.W.R.

7664 WHITECHURCH, V. L. Thrilling stories of the railway. *London*, 1912. pp. 248.   BM
> Fifteen short stories of crime and detection

on the railway. An extract—'Old Joe Salter sat in his little box at Tedworth level-crossing, stirring the fire in his stove with his wooden leg . . .' (!)

7665 WHITEHALL, C. The Buckinghamshire Railway. *Buckingham*, 1849. pp. 36.   BM
> A poem.

7666 WILLIAMS, R. Border Country. *London: Chatto & Windus*, 1960. pp. 350[351].   BM
> The story contains useful 'factual-based' detail on the daily life and working routine of a signalman on the Great Western Railway in Wales, from the early 1920's on. The narrative includes a number of general instructions, notices and telegrams issued by the National Union of Railwaymen and the Great Western Railway during the General Strike, 1926.

7667 WOOD, A. Phantom Railway. *London: Frederick Muller*, 1954. pp. 199.   BM
> A light novel about a disused branch line.

7668 WOOD, E. Oswald Cray: a novel. By Mrs. Henry Wood [Ellen Wood]. *London*, 1896.   BM
> pp. 73–89, a railway accident.

7669 WORDSWORTH, W. At Furness Abbey. [No. 48 of his 'Miscellaneous Sonnets', 1845.]   BM
> 'Well have yon railway labourers to this ground
> Withdrawn for noontide rest . . .'

7670 WORDSWORTH, W. On the projected Kendal & Windermere Railway. [Nos. 45 & 46 of his 'Miscellaneous Sonnets', 1844.]   BM
> 'Is there no nook of English ground secure . . .'
> 'Proud were ye, Mountains, when, in times of old . . .'

7671 WORDSWORTH, W. Steamboats, viaducts and railways. [Itinerary Poems of 1833, no. 42.]   BM
> 'Motions and means, on sea, on land, at war . . .'
> In the last line of no. 41 of this series mention is made of the viaduct and railway at Corby.

7672 [YONGE, C. M.?] The Railroad Children. 1855.   BM

7673 YOUNG, F. The Barrier Line. *In his* 'Letters from Solitude.' *London*, 1912. pp. 219–26.   BM
> Suffolk is rarely visited because would-be travellers are discouraged by the unpleasantness of Liverpool Street Station (London).

Anecdotes—Allegory—Curiosa and Miscellanea

*For biographical anecdotes see under relevant heading for the
subject of the anecdote*

Collective Works

7674 PARTON, J. Humorous poetry of the English language, from Chaucer to Saxe . . . [Compiled] by J. Parton. 13th edn. *Boston,* 1881. BM

The railway items are from *Punch, c.* 1850.
pp. 333–4, 'The Railway Traveller's Farewell to his Family.
''t was business call'd a father to travel by the rail . . .'
p. 375, 'The Railway of Life': an epigram.
'Short was the passage through this earthly vale . . .'
pp. 475–8, 'The Railway Gilpin'.
'John Gilpin is a citizen . . .'
pp. 478–80, 'Elegy, written in a railway station'. A satire on George Hudson.
'The station clock proclaims the close of day . . .'
p. 633, 'Railroad nursery rhyme'.
p. 643, 'Epitaph on a Locomotive'.
'Collisions four of five she bore . . .'

7675 PIKE, R. Railway adventures and anecdotes, extending over more than fifty years. Edited by R. Pike. *London,* 1884. pp. 296. BM

Over 300 items. In most cases the source is given.

—— 2nd edn. *London,* 1887. pp. 296. LSE
—— 3rd, *London,* 1888. pp. 296. BM

7676 REYNOLDS, M. Real railway anecdotes, from all sources. *Manchester & London,* [1893.] pp. 128. HRL

7677 RAILWAY BENEVOLENT INSTITUTION —IRISH BRANCH. Tales of the Rail by Railwaymen. *Dublin,* 1904. pp. vii, 112. BM

A selection of anecdotes and short stories, mostly humorous.

7678 'PUNCH.' Mr. Punch's Railway Book . . . *London:* 'Punch', [1905.] pp. 192, with 160 illus. [*Punch Library of Humour.*] BM

Extracts from *Punch.*

—— another edn. *London,* [1910.] pp. 192. BM

7679 BEST railway stories. *London: Richards Press,* 1927. pp. 120. BM

A collection of humour.

7680 AYE, John, *pseud.* [John Atkinson.] Humour on the Rail. *London,* 1931. pp. 157. BM

An anthology of personal observations and anecdotes.

7681 COTTERELL, S. J. A. Curiosities of railway literature . . . *Birmingham,* 1931. pp. [8.] BM

Limited to 100 copies.
Small extracts from early railway books and guides.

7682 THOMAS, S. E. Laughs along the Lines. Compiled by S. Evelyn Thomas. *Northolt: P. J. Press,* January 1944. pp. 48. BTCHR

Stories, jokes and drawings.

7683 LEGG, S. The Railway Book: an anthology. Edited by Stuart Legg. *London: Rupert Hart-Davis,* 1952. pp. 256. BM

153 items in verse and prose relating to various aspects of railways at all periods.

—— Reprinted, with paper covers. *London,* 1958. BM

Single Works

7684 L., W. C. The Railway Passenger. *London: Religious Tract Society,* [1835?] BM

7685 BYRNE, O. How to measure the Earth with the assistance of railroads. *Newcastle,* 1838. pp. 12. BM

Calculations based upon the geometry of railway gradients.

7686 The GHOST of John Bull; or, The Devil's Railroad. A marvellously strange narrative, dedicated—without permission—to such Members of Parliament as may feel inclined to turn their coats, Poor Law Commissioners and railroad directors in particular. *London,* 1838. pp. 71. BM

An anti-railway satire.

7687 A FURTHER discovery on the Manchester & Leeds Rail-Road. *Manchester: Kiernan,* [1838.] pp. 8. BM

Skeletons, swords, helmets, etc., unearthed in the building of the M. & L. Rly.

7688 [B., H.] An address to the inhabitants of the Eastern Counties of England; being a slight historical sketch of ancient roads, with a few observations on the adaptations of the modern railway to the development of the resources of a country. [*London,*] 1839. pp. xvi, 44. BM

In verse. By Henry Barrett?

7689 [B., H.] Pooh! Pooh! a poem, by one of Job's Comforters. [*London,*] 1839. pp. 23. BM

By Henry Barrett? Verses on the coming of railways to East Anglia. Reprinted in his *Reminiscences of railway making* (1845).

7690 WALLIS, J., *publisher.* Wallis's New Railway Game; or, Tour through England and Wales. *London*, [c. 1840.] BM
A large folding map designed for use as a railway version of 'snakes and ladders'.

7691 [CLAUGHTON, T. L.] Viæ per Angliam ferro stratæ. *Oxonii*, 1841. pp. 15. BM
A prize poem, described in *The Railway Centenary: a retrospect*, by Randall Davies (1925), on p. 44.

7692 FANSHAWE, F. Viæ per Angliam ferro stratæ. Carmen Latinum in Theatro Sheldoniano recitatum, die Junii XV, MDCCCXLI. *Oxonii*, 1841. pp. [9.] BM
A prize poem.

7693 [B., H.] Reminiscences of railway making: rhymes ... *London*, 1845. pp. iv, 122. BM
The BM copy is inscribed 'R. Patterson, Esq., Ch. of the Northern & Eastern Railway Co., with H.B.'s best comps. Not published.' [By Henry Barrett?]
Verses, mostly on the coming of railways to East Anglia, 1839–41.
pp. [71]–122[123], 'An address to the inhabitants of the Eastern Counties of England ... with some observations on the adaptation of the modern railway to the development of the resources of a country' (1839).

7694 The RAILROAD considered in a moral and religious point of view. By a Spiritual Watchman of the Church of England. *London*, 1845. pp. 18. BM
'And they cover fields and take them by violence . . .' (Micah, ch. 2, v. 2). Railways identified with Sabbath desecration, violence, fraud, and injustice, and described as 'the masterpiece of Satan'.

7695 SALA, G. A. Rain, Hail, Steam and Speed: trifles for travellers dedicated to the world in general and unprotected females in particular. By An Old Stoker. *London: Ackermann & Co.*, [1845.] pp. [21.] LSE
'Practical exposition of Mr. J. M. W. Turner's picture. One shilling plain, 2s. 6d. coloured.' Comic drawings on the discomforts of rail travel in the 1840's.

7696 The SPIRITUAL Railway. *London: C. Paul*, [c. 1845.] s.sh. BM
Eighteen verses commencing 'The line to Heaven by Christ is made'.
A shorter version, of six verses, is reproduced on a post-card and published by Ely Cathedral. It is a replica of the inscription on a tombstone in the South Porch, erected to the memory of William Pickering and Richard Edger, who both died in 1845. (*See* 7710.)

7697 RAILROAD Eclogues. *London*, 1846. pp. 36.
Satirical verses. BM

7698 The RAILWAY to Heaven. This line runs from Calvary through this vain world and the valley of the shadow of death, until it lands in the Kingdom of Heaven. London, [c.1845.] s.sh. BM
A broadside ballad—'Oh! What a deal

we hear and read, about railways and railway speed! Of lines which are or may be made, and selling shares is quite a trade . . .'

7699 CURR, J. The Learned Donkeys of eighteen hundred and forty seven ... being a review of the reviewers of 'Railway locomotion and steam navigation; their principles and practice'. *London: John Williams & Co.*, 1847. pp. 185–98. BM
Letters by John Curr to the editors of the *Mechanics Magazine*, the *Artizan*, and the *Civil Engineer & Architects' Journal*, etc. 'Ten thousand copies of this satire will be printed, to exhibit the mal-practices of mechanical critics.'

7700 The NEW Railway Guide; or, Thoughts for thinkers on the road from this world to the next, suited to travellers in the British Dominions and to all in all countries, with details of the various lines, and critical estimates of their comparative value, together with historical, topographical and other notices of the chief points and places of interest on the road: accompanied by an accurate and well-executed map of the principal competing lines from Time to Eternity. *Hanley: Allbut & Son*, 1848. pp. 32. BM
The lines are divided into two groups— 'Lines that lead to Perdition', and 'Lines that lead to Glory'.

7701 REACH, A. B. The Comic Bradshaw; or, Bubbles from the Boiler. Illustrated by H. G. Hine. *London*, 1848. pp. 64, with 47 illus. BM
Humorous essays.

7702 CROWQUILL, A. How he reigned and how he mizzled: a railway raillery. *London*, 1849. pp. 8. BM
Satirical drawings on George Hudson.

7703 RAILWAY Guide. *London*, 1849. pp. 28.
A railway 'Pilgrim's Progress'. AU

7704 WRIGHT, J. Christianity and commerce: the natural results of the geographical progression of railways; or, A treatise on the advantage of the universal extension of railways in our colonies and other countries and the probability of increased national intercommunication leading to the early restoration of the Land of Promise to the Jews. *London*, [1851.] pp. 162, with 5 fold. maps. LC

7705 The LATTER Days: railways, steam and emigration, with its consequent rapid peopling of the deserts, also the present going to and fro, and increase of knowledge, foretold by Isaiah, Daniel and Joel, and indicating the rapid approach of the End of the Latter Days. *Dublin*, 1854. pp. 24. BM
'Every valley shall be exalted and every mountain shall be made low and the crooked shall be made straight and the rough places plain.'

7706 DE LA MOTTE. Cousin Chatterbox's Railway Alphabet. *London: Dean & Sons,* [1855.] pp. [12.] [*Dean & Sons' Shilling Panorama Alphabets,* no. 2.]   BM
Cover title, *Railway ABC.*
'A is the arch which you see when you start ...'
Each letter is superimposed on to a line drawing.

7707 The RAILWAY Meeting: a satire dedicated to the pillaged and plundered shareholders of Great Britain. By a Lancashire Victim. *London,* 1856. pp. vii, 137.   BM
Verses.

7708 [ANCELL, G. W.] Donkey Express Company. *London,* [c. 1857.] pp. 2.   LSE
A 'prospectus'. 'Steam having proved a total failure . . .' Chairman, Mangold Wurzel, Esq. [G. W. Ancell.]
This is related to a series of 'notices' which G. W. Ancell issued under the pseudonym of 'George Hoy', criticising the services of the Eastern Counties Rly. (*See* 5829.) It is reproduced on p. 21 of *The Jubilee of the Railway News* (1914).

7709 AYTOUN, W. E. How we got up the Glenmutchkin Railway, and how we got out of it. *In* 'Tales from Blackwood', vol. 1, 1858. pp. 1–44.   BM
This comic satire on railway speculation in 1845 appeared originally in *Blackwood's Magazine* and has since been published in various collections of stories, sometimes under the title of 'The Glenmutchkin Railway'.

7710 FISHER, W. J., *publisher.* The Railway Tract. *Torquay,* [1859.] pp. 4.   BM
Includes 'The Gospel Railroad' with an introductory verse beginning 'In days of old the line to Heaven was rough and stony and uneven . . .' This verse is not found in versions bearing the title 'The Spiritual Railway' and commencing 'The line to Heaven by Christ is (was) made . . .' (*See* 7696.)

7711 WARD & LOCK, *publishers.* The Little Engineer; or, How a child may make a cardboard railroad and station without using any adhesive material. *London,* [1860.] pp. [8.]   BM
Hand coloured cut-out book with 'explanatory introduction'.

7712 SCRIBBLE, W. Dublin destroyed; or, The witches' cauldron of railway horrors! a mysterious Shakespeareana, in one act. 3rd edn. *Dublin,* [1862.] pp. 30.   BM
'. . . to shew how Dublin might be soon destroyed
By railway bridges and by line for train,
Till of her boasted beauties none remain . . .'

7713 BOND, R. Murray & Co.'s Book of Information for Railway Travellers and Railway Officials, illustrated with anecdotes, etc. *London,* 1865. pp. vi, 203.   LSE
R. Bond was Superintendent, Newport Stn., G.W. Rly.

7714 W., M. My Railway Adventure; or, All's well that ends well: a fact. *Margate: C. D. Dixon,* 1869. pp. 30.   BM
Verses.

7715 ROSSENDALE, A. Mr. Julep Judkin's first journey by rail from 'Home, sweet home'. *Birmingham,* 1870. pp. 17.   BM
A humorous monologue.

7716 RICHARDSON, S. T. The world's first railway jubilee. *Darlington & London,* 1876. pp. [40.] obl. 4°.   RC
Twenty humorous essays, with drawings.

7717 'VERITA.' The Engine-Driver's Christmas: a tale of Portland Prison. *London,* [1880.] pp. 19.   BM

7718 'GRIP.' How John Bull lost London; or, The capture of the Channel Tunnel. 4th edn. *London,* 1882. pp. 127.   BM
A forecast of a French invasion via the proposed Tunnel.

7719 SUBMARINA; or, Green eyes and blue glasses: an amusing spectacle of short sight, as exhibited by the glorious year of light A.D. 1882, recalled and recorded one hundred years after. (Channel Tunnel; danger to England or no danger?) *London,* 1882. pp. 48.   LSE

7720 'VINDEX.' England crushed: the secret of the Channel Tunnel revealed; being the literal translation of a secret despatch recently revised and adopted by an Austrian Federal Cabinet. (Warning—It will be dangerous to be found with this in possession on the Continent.) *London,* 1882. pp. 16.   BM
An imaginary German plan to regain its 'old Saxon province of Kent' by capturing the Tunnel and using it for reinforcements and supplies for the conquest of Gt. Britain.

7721 BIRD, F. J. Shunted: a sermon to railway men, preached at the Baptist Chapel, Walsworth Road, Hitchin, by the pastor, F. J. Bird . . . *London,* [1884.] pp. 16.   BM
'You were running well; who was it hindered you . . .?' Gal. v. 7.

7722 KENNEDY, W. S. Wonders and curiosities of the railway; or, Stories of the locomotive in every land. *Chicago,* 1884. pp. xvi, 254.   LSE
pp. 6–30 and elsewhere, anecdotes on railways in the British Isles.

7723 SITWELL, S. M. A Railway Garden; illustrated . . . *London: Christian Knowledge Society,* [1887.] pp. 159. [*Jubilee Series.*]   BM

7724 P., H. The New International Railway. [*London:*] *W. Freeman*, [1888.] s.sh. BM
A religious tract. The Bible likened to a railway guide book.

7725 N., J. Tramway car sketches. *Glasgow*, 1889. pp. 48. BM
Cover title, *Glasgow tramway car sketches*. Seventy-two humorous drawings depicting travelling conditions and episodes in the working life of tramway-men on the Glasgow horse trams.

7726 NEWMAN, J. Queer scenes of railway life; being narratives of some comical and strange incidents. *London*, 1889. pp. 124. HRL

7727 RAILROAD Alphabet. *London: George Routledge & Sons*, [1889.] pp. [14,] with pictures (some col.). BM

7728 HASWELL, J. A. The locomotive engine; to which is appended 'A Quaint Story of Steam'. *London*, [*c.* 1890.] pp. 15. IME
Reprinted from the *Newcastle Daily Chronicle*. A popular account, followed by (pp. 14–15) an article from the *Penny Magazine* entitled 'Atmos the Giant'.

7729 The RAILWAY Book: tales, sketches and descriptions for young people; with ninety illustrations. *London*, 1891. pp. 96. BM

7730 BERRY, A. B. A Dirge over the Broad Gauge, which came to an end on Friday May 20th, 1892. *Penzance*, May 1892. s.sh. pc
A poem: 'Gone is the broad gauge of our youth . . .' Reproduced in part in *The trains we loved*, by C. H. Ellis (1947). pp. 49.

7731 STANLEY, C. Railway Incidents (Railway Tracts). *London: George Morrish*, [1859.] 12 pts. (I–IV, 'Railway Incidents'; 5–12, 'Railway Tracts'.) BM
A series of extremely dogmatic evangelical tracts, each of 16 pages, recording encounters on train journeys:
I, The Son of God.
II, The Handcuffs.
III, Smashed to Pieces.
IV, The Lost Ticket.
5, Just in Time.
6, Conversation.
7, What a Contrast.
8, Progress.
9, An Interesting Question.
10, The Explosion.
11, I have my Ticket.
12, Over-Luggage.

7732 WEATHERBURN, R. Ajax Loquitur; or, The autobiography of an old locomotive engine. *London*, 1899. pp. 151. BM

7733 O'MOORE, M. Tips for Travellers; or, Wrinkles for the road and rail . . . *London*, 1899. pp. 158. BM
pp. 41–66, for railway travellers. Includes anecdotes.
—— Cheap edn. *London*, 1900. pp. 158. BM

7734 FROUDE, J. A. A Siding at a Railway Station: an allegory. *London*, 1905. pp. 34. [*Simple Life series*, no. 19.] BM
A train-load of humanity on the Journey of Life. Also published in his *Short studies on great subjects*, 4th series.

7735 PLEDGE, D. The Great Valley Railway: the magnitude of the station, the departure of the trains, the fare and other useful information: an allegory. [By the Rev. D. Pledge.] 14th edn. *London & Ramsgate*, [*c.* 1905.] pp. 80. BM
A railway 'Pilgrim's Progress'.

7736 LEAROYD, J. I. Mr. Learoyd's record: travels 1000 miles on British railway in a day. [*Halifax*, 1910.] pp. 3. BM
Reprinted from the *Halifax Courier*, 23 July, 1910.
From St. Pancras to Leeds and back, then to Carlisle and back again to St. Pancras.

7737 LEAROYD, J. I. Unique trip by train: 1000 miles in twenty hours. Mr. J. I. Learoyd's experiences . . . [*Halifax*, 1910.] pp. [7.] BM
Reprinted from the *Halifax Guardian*, 23 July, 1910.

7738 GREAT WESTERN RLY. Prevention of accidents. The 'Is it Safe?' pocket token. [*London*,] 1922. BR
A folder describing the use of a pocket talisman issued in connection with the 'Safety First' campaign for employees. A reminder to promote personal safety. 'Carry it with you always.'

7739 MYTTON, H. A Village Drama. (An allegory, with figures from the rate book.) *London: Great Western Rly.*, 1927. pp. 8. LSE
Reprinted from the *G.W.R. Magazine*, April 1927.
A melodrama showing how the G.W.R. has to pay high rates to local councils on which it has no representation.

*7740 HEATH ROBINSON, W. Railway Ribaldry. *London: Great Western Rly.*, 1935. pp. 96. BM
Scenes from G.W.R. history, and revelations of its running and administration methods. W. Heath Robinson's G.W.R. works on the lever, string and pulley principle, and this book portrays the extent and variety of its adaptation in a series of ninety-six drawings.

7741 GOWER, F. C. The First Subject Catalogue of Cigarette Cards. *London*, 1941. pp. 47. *Typescript*. BM
Includes twenty-six series on railways, railway history, construction and working, locomotives, and railway posters, issued between 1903 and 1939.

7742 EMETT, M. *and* EMETT, R. Anthony and Antimacassar. *London: Faber & Faber*, 1943. pp. [30.] BM
A fantasy for children, with humorous drawings.

7743 EMETT, R. Engines, Aunties and Others: a book of curious happenings. *London: Faber & Faber*, 1943. pp. [60.]   BM

Humorous drawings mostly concerning railways under war-time conditions.

7744 EMETT, R. Sidings and such-like. *London: Faber & Faber*, 1946. pp. [60.]   BM

Humorous drawings on railways, etc.

7745 EMETT, R. Home Rails preferred. *London: Faber & Faber*, 1947. pp. [57.]   BM

Humorous drawings; and a poem on the Kent & East Sussex Rly. by C. H. Bevan, 'The Farmers' Train'.

7746 EMETT, R. Saturday Slow. *London: Faber & Faber*, 1948. pp. [59.]   BM

Includes some humorous drawings on railways.

7747 EMETT, R. Buffers End: arrived at by Emett. *London: Faber & Faber*, 1949. pp. [43.] BM

Humorous drawings.

7748 EMETT, R. Far Twittering; or, The annals of a branch line . . . *London: Faber & Faber*, 1949. pp. [25.]   BM

Humorous drawings.

7749 EMETT, R. High Tea. *London: Faber & Faber*, 1950. pp. [44.]   BM

Humorous drawings, including some of railways and tramways.

7750 EMETT, R. *and* KEELING, V. The Emett Festival Railway. *Harmondsworth*, 1951. pp. 30. [*Puffin Cut-Out Book*, no. 7.]   BM

Model, designed by V. Keeling, of the train which ran during the Festival of Britain, 1951 (The Far-Twittering & Oyster Creek Rly.).

7751 EMETT, R. The Forgotten Tramcar and other drawings. *London: Faber & Faber*, 1952. pp. 43.   BM

Humorous drawings on tramways and railways.

7752 EMETT, R. Nellie, come home! *London: Faber & Faber*, 1952. pp. 38.   BM

A story for children, written and illustrated by Rowland Emett.

7753 WILSON, E. Save Time Guide to the London Underground Railways. *London: the author*, 1955. pp. [8.]   BM

Tells which car of any train will stop nearest the exit of any given station. A novel attempt to provide a useful aid for passengers.

7754 ELLIS, C. H. Rapidly Round the Bend: a short review of railway transport from the time of Abraham; written and illustrated by C. Hamilton Ellis . . . *London: Parrish*, 1959. pp. 120.   BM

7755 CANTERBURY COLLEGE OF ART—DEPARTMENT OF PRINTING. An episode in the history of the Canterbury & Whitstable Railway, one of the earliest of the passenger-carrying railways in Great Britain. *Canterbury*, 1960. pp. [4,] with 3 wood engravings.   PC

The text is composed of extracts from newspaper reports on the opening of the line. It is not presented as a complete account but as an example of the kind of work produced by the College, and was printed specially for inclusion in the *Miniature Folio of Private Presses*.

Q APPRECIATION OF RAILWAYS

The appeal of railways and locomotives—Railway aesthetics

*Note: In Section O, 'Railways in Literature', are many items
extolling railways which are not repeated here*

7756 GRAY, T. Observations on a general iron rail-way, shewing its great superiority over all the present methods of conveyance . . . *London*, 1820. pp. 22.   ICE
—— 2nd edn. *London*, 1821. pp. 60.   BM
—— 3rd, revised & considerably enlarged. *London*, 1822. pp. xii, 131.   RC
—— 4th, considerably improved. *London*, 1823. pp. xii, 131.   BM
—— 5th, 'with maps and plates illustrative of the plan.' *London*, 1825. pp. xxiv, 233.   BM

7757 ARGUMENTS in support of the establishment of railroads, and to show the necessity of legislative sanction. *London*, 1825. pp. 32.   PO

7758 HAMMOND, T. A few cursory remarks on railways, showing their beneficial tendency . . . *London*, 1835. pp, 32.   LSE
A lively retort to the anti-railway campaign of the *Morning Herald*.

7759 P., E. An essay to shew the advantages that will follow the progressive formation of railways throughout the kingdom. *London*, 1836. pp. 44.   BM

7760 GODWIN, G. An appeal to the public on the subject of railways. *London*, 1837. pp. 45, with bibliogr. notes.   BM
General advantages of railways.

7761 MUDGE, R. Z. Observations on railways, with a reference to utility and profit and the obvious necessity for a national system. *London*, 1837. pp. 73.   BM

7762 DIMMICK, L. F. A discourse on the moral influence of rail-roads. *Newburyport*, 1841. pp. 125.   BM

7763 STEPHEN, J. K. Poetic lamentation on the insufficiency of steam locomotion in the Lake District.   BM
'Bright Summer spreads his various hue . . .' Addressed to William Wordsworth, and reprinted from the *Pall Mall Gazette*, November 1882. Reprinted in *The Railway Book* edited by Stuart Legg (1952).

7764 FOXWELL, E. English express trains: two papers. *London*, 1884. pp. 128.   BM
1st paper, pp. 1–58, 'Apologetic'. The various beneficial effects of speed upon individual and social well-being. 'Railways are incessantly

persuading men into a disposition of more kindliness.'
2nd paper, pp. 59–128, 'Statistical'. Tables and notes on long runs, gradients, etc.

7765 CHESTERTON, G. K. Tremendous Trifles. *London: Methuen*, 1909.   BM
pp. 9–15, 'The Secret of a Train'. A wayside station and a journey by night on the G.W.R.
pp. 219–24, 'The Prehistoric Railway Station'. Symbolism in the life and being of railway stations; in opposition to the views of John Ruskin.

7766 YOUNG, F. Praise of the Railway. *In his* 'Memory Harbour: essays chiefly in description.' *London*, 1909. pp. 231–41.   BM
The Cornish Express of the Great Western and the Irish Mail of the London & North Western.

7767 SCOTT, J. Railway Romance and other essays. *London*, [1913.] pp. viii, 291.   BM
pp. [3]–137, Railway Romance. Ten essays, eight of which are on the fascination of railways and of railway life.

7768 MILNE, A. A. A Train of Thought. *In his* 'If I may.' *London*, 1921. pp. 114–18.   BM
'Nowhere can I think so happily as in a train.'

7769 THOMAS, G. O. On a Certain Town. *In his* 'Things big and little.' *London*, 1922. pp. 58–64 (61–64).   BM
Reminiscences of boyhood in Leicester; the fascination of watching trains.

7770 THOMAS, G. O. Sparks from the Fire. *London*, 1923.   BM
pp. 77–83, 'The Motorman'. A reverie on tram-driving.
pp. 87–96, 'On railways and theology'. The mystery of an apparent link between a reverence for railways and experienced divine transcendence (rather than theology).

7771 SQUIRE, J. C. Railroadiana. *In* 'Selected modern English essays.' *London: O.U.P.*, 1925. [*The World's Classics*, no. 280.] pp. [399]–405.   BM
A forecast of the increasing value of railway literature as 'collectors' items'.

7772 LYND, R. Trains. *In his* 'The Orange Tree.' *London*, 1926. pp. 79–85.   BM
An appreciation of railways.

7773 THOMAS, G. O. Calm Weather. *London*, 1928.   BM
pp. 36–42, Cross-country journeys.
pp. 67–74. A Corner of Essex. (Kelvedon & Tollesbury branch, L. & N.E. Rly.)

7774 'TIMES' *newspaper.* Third Leaders reprinted from 'The Times'; with an introduction by George Gordon. *London*, 1928. BM
pp. 65–7, By Train. (Comfort and delight of railway travelling.)
pp. 67–9, Travelling Companions. (Principles of selection.)
pp. 69–71, Meals in the Train. (Enjoyment of the unusual.)

7775 MORTON, J. B. The Old Trams. *In* 'Essays of the Year (1930–31)', compiled by Frederick J. H. Darton. *London*, 1931. pp. 187–92. BM
Sentiments aroused by the replacement of trams by buses in Ireland.

7776 THOMAS, G. O. The Master-Light: letters to David. *London*, 1932. BM
pp. 72–93(75–78), The appeal of railways.

7777 LISSENDEN, G. B. The civilising influence of transport. *London: Stockwell*, [1937.] pp. 32, with 5 tables. BM
The relationship of transport to the growth and progress of civilisation.

7778 GREVILLE, M. D. The individuality of British railways. pp. 30. *Typescript.* RC
Paper, Railway Club, December 1938.
The distinguishing features of individual companies and of British compared with foreign railways.
A previous paper on the same subject was read to the Club by Mr. Greville on 3 Dec., 1918 (pp. 21) and to the MS. of this he added a postscript dated 10 July, 1954.

7779 BETJEMAN, J. Parliament Hill Fields. *In his* 'New Bats in Old Belfries: poems.' *London: John Murray*, 1945. pp. 3–4. BM
'Rumbling under blackened girders, Midland, bound for Cricklewood . . .'

7780 PEACOCK, T. B. Railway pride and prejudice. *Halstead: the author*, 1946. pp. 12, with 4 plates. IT
An appreciation of aesthetics in railway equipment and the importance of beauty in design. Examples of semaphore signals illustrated.
This essay also appears in his *Musing on railways* (1948).

7781 THOMAS, G. O. Autobiography, 1891–1941. *London: Chapman & Hall*, 1946. pp. 267. BM
pp. 39–42, 69–71, 242–3, and intermittently, the author's interest in railways, including boyhood reminiscences of railways in Leicester.

7782 THOMAS, G. O. Bradshaw—his Book. *In his* 'Times may change.' *London: Epworth Press*, 1946. pp. [94]–96. BM
The wonder of railway organisation revealed in Bradshaw's time-tables.

7783 THOMAS, G. O. Hobbies and other people. *In his* 'Times may change.' *London: Epworth Press*, 1946. pp. [132]–136. BM
The value to human relationships of a hobby,

evidenced by the author's well-known and well-visited model railway.

7784 RAILWAY 'Hows'. *London: Transportation Press*, [1946.] pp. 32, with diagrams. BM
Fifteen items of engineering and operational interest.

7785 RAILWAYS Quiz. *London: Transportation Press*, [1946.] pp. 30. BM
400 questions and answers.

*7786 ELLIS, C. H. The trains we loved. *London: Allen & Unwin*, 1947. pp. 196, with 69 illus. on 40 plates (8 col.). BM

7787 GILL, E. Letters of Eric Gill; edited by Walter Shewring. *London: Jonathan Cape*, 1947. BM
pp. 269–74, On the 'Flying Scotsman'. Kings Cross to Grantham on no. 2582.

7788 THOMAS, G. O. Paddington to Seagood: the story of a model railway; with photographs by W. J. Bassett-Lowke, and diagrams. *London: Chapman & Hall*, 1947. pp. 131. BM
'A tribute to a hobby.' The companionship of railways, real and model.

7789 ACTON, H. M. M. Memoirs of an aesthete. *London: Methuen*, 1948. pp. 415. BM
pp. 124–6, the Oxford Railway Club.

7790 PEACOCK, T. B. Musing on railways. *Halstead: the author*, 1948. pp. 20, 16, 23, 12, with 29 plates & maps. BM
A cumulative edition of his four essays: A trip by the Wye Valley train; Monmouth to Coleford by rail; The Mistley, Thorpe & Walton Railway; Railway pride and prejudice.

7791 GREENIDGE, T. A Branch-line Holiday. *In* 'Holidays and Happy Days', by Oswell Blakeston. *London*, 1949. pp. 69–84. BM
The appeal of railways, particularly of the Isle of Wight.

7792 LEE, C. E. Some notes on the history of the Railway Club. [1950.] pp. 7. *Reproduced typescript.* RC

7793 TREACY, E. Steam up! *London: Ian Allan*, [1950.] pp. 80, with illus. BM
Essays on the pleasures of railways.

7794 LLOYD, R. The fascination of railways. *London: Allen & Unwin*, 1951. pp. 160, with 22 illus. on 16 plates. BM
Observations on railway working; journeys undertaken; the locomotive; the footplate-men; and stations, in ten essays.

7795 BETJEMAN, J. First and Last Loves. *London: J. Murray*, 1952. pp. xi, 244. BM
pp. 75–89, London railway stations. Previously published in *Flower of Cities: a book of London. Studies and sketches by twenty-two authors* (1949). pp. 13–30.

7796 ELLIS, C. H. The beauty of old trains. *London: Allen & Unwin*, 1952. pp. 147, with 68 illus. on 32 plates (8 col.). BM

7797 LEGG, S. The Railway Book: an anthology. Edited by Stuart Legg. *London: Rupert Hart-Davis*, 1952. pp. 256. BM
153 items in prose and verse relating to various aspects of railways at all periods.

—— Reprinted, with paper covers. *London*, 1958. BM

7798 LLOYD, R. Railwaymen's Gallery. *London: Allen & Unwin*, 1953. pp. 166, with 9 plates.
Eight essays. BM

7799 THOMAS, G. O. Farewell to Seagood. *In his* 'Window in the West.' *London: Epworth Press*, 1954. pp. [124]–128. BM
Thoughts on the closing of the author's 'Paddington to Seagood' model railway.

7800 THOMAS, G. O. Temple Meads. *In his* 'Window in the West.' *London: Epworth Press*, 1954. pp. [19]–25. BM
Thoughts on the fascination of railways, locomotives, and the life of stations, with a personal tribute to Bristol (Temple Meads), G.W.R.

*7801 'DESIGN.' Railways: a special issue compiled and arranged by John E. Blake. *London*, September 1955. pp. 44, with many illus. [*Design*, no. 81.] IT
A symposium:
The shape of the train. By C. H. Ellis.
Inside the train. By C. H. Ellis.
Station architecture. By J. M. Richards.
Publicity. By Anthony Adams.

7802 LLOYD, R. Farewell to Steam. *London: Allen & Unwin*, 1956. pp. 128. BM
The appeal of steam locomotives, and observations on railway working and railway travelling.

7803 MARLOW, N. Footplate and signal cabin. *London: Allen & Unwin*, 1956. pp. 222, with 15 plates. BM
An appreciation of railways, containing an account of the author's experiences as a wartime temporary signalman during university vacations. Also (pp. 75–137) essays on practical and human aspects of locomotive driving, including extracts from the diaries of David Joy (1840's) and of the trips on broad-gauge G.W. engines by A. H. Malan in 1891, followed by narratives of journeys undertaken by N. Marlow himself.

7804 COLLIER, R. First Class Romance. *In Sixteen On*, edited by Charles Irving, 1957. pp. 216–22. BM
A humorous study of the personality of a railway enthusiast.

7805 LYND, R. Railway stations I have loved. *In his* 'In Defence of Pink.' *London: J. M. Dent*, 1937. pp. 67–75. BM
The drab unfriendliness of London termini, and the appeal of small country stations.

7806 ABC Railway Quiz. *London: Ian Allan*, 1960. pp. 32, with illus. BM
275 questions and answers.

7807 BLUEBELL RAILWAY PRESERVATION SOCIETY. The Handbook of the Bluebell Line. *Tunbridge Wells*, [1960.] pp. 19, with 10 illus. & a map. BM
Historical and descriptive notes.

—— another edn. *Tunbridge Wells*, [1962.] pp. 32, with 16 illus., tables & map. BM

7808 LOCOLOG Book. *Hampton Court: Ian Allan*, [1960.] pp. [32.] BM
Blank pages ruled for number, code, and remarks 'for your spottings and jottings'.

7809 RANSOME-WALLIS, P. On railways, at home and abroad. *London: Batchworth Press*, 1951. pp, 299, with plates. BM

—— 2nd edn. *London: Spring Books*, [1960.] pp. 300. BM
pp. 15–18, Railway enthusiasts.

7810 FRASER, I. N. The Arbroath Affair, being an account of the 1959 Steam Engine Inquiry in which a traction engine and a gas works locomotive met together, enjoyed an unusual legal affair and won a resounding victory. Foreword by W. Michael Salmon, President, The Road Locomotive Society. *Arbroath: T. Buncle*, 1961. pp. 41, with 23 illus. on 16 plates. BM
A record of the proceedings which eventually authorised the housing of a traction engine and a locomotive in an engine-shed adjoining the owner's residence.

7811 ERWOOD, P. M. E. The Railway Enthusiast's Guide. *London: George Ronald*, 1960. pp. 159, with 25 illus. on 14 plates. BM
A directory of British and foreign railway clubs, museums, relics, societies, model railways, periodicals, etc.

—— 2nd edn. *Sidcup: Lambarde Press*, 1962. pp. 202, with 51 illus. on 32 plates. BM

7812 MORGAN, B. The Railway Lover's Companion; edited by Bryan Morgan. *London: Eyre & Spottiswoode*, 1963. pp. 555, with 54 line illus. BM
119 excerpts and short pieces from railway literature, descriptive and imaginative, and 29 in verse. Collected from the works of 73 authors.
The faulty alignment of the double title-page is common to the whole of the first edition and the second impression.

7813 THOMAS, G. *and* THOMAS, D. ST. J. Double headed: two generations of railway enthusiasm. Drawings by Kenneth Lindley. *Dawlish: David & Charles*, 1963. pp. 200, with 59 illus. on 24 plates and 40 text illus. by K. Lindley. BM
Twenty-nine essays by father and son on railway aesthetics, from the 1890's to the present day.

7814 JEANS, J. S. Railway Jubilee at Darlington, September 27–28, 1875: reports of proceedings and opinions of the press. *Darlington,* 1875. pp. 52. pc

7815 STRETTON, C. E. The railway collection at the Leicester Museum . . . *Leicester,* 1903. pp. [8.] BM

7816 LONDON & NORTH EASTERN RLY. Catalogue of the collection of railway relics and modern stock at Faverdale, Darlington, in connection with the Railway Centenary Celebrations, July, 1925. 4th edn. *York,* [1925.] pp. 95. BM
Pictures, prints, models, documents, signalling apparatus, locomotives, rolling stock and permanent way, lent by the main-line companies.

7817 LONDON, MIDLAND & SCOTTISH RLY. LMS Control: the magic wand of transport: the brains behind railway traffic movement: the 'all-seeing eye': British Empire Exhibition, Wembley, 1925. *London,* 1925. pp. 35, with illus. & diagrams. BR
Guide to an exhibit designed to show how trains are controlled.

7818 SCIENCE MUSEUM [London]. Land Transport: Railway Centenary Exhibition Supplement. Compiled by E. A. Forward. *London,* 1925. pp. 39. [*Catalogue of the Collections in the Science Museum.*] BM
Description of the 189 items which made up this special exhibition. No illustrations.

7819 SCIENCE MUSEUM [London]. Land Transport: IV, Railway construction and working. Compiled by E. A. Forward. *London,* 1927. pp. 84, with 20 illus. on 10 plates. [*Catalogue of the Collections in the Science Museum.*] BM
Description of 227 exhibits in the permanent exhibition.

7820 LONDON & NORTH EASTERN RLY The Railway Museum, York. Reading to accompany a set of lantern slides prepared and issued by the L. & N.E. Rly. [1929.] pp. 21. BR
Eighty-four paragraphs.

*7821 SCIENCE MUSEUM [London]. Land Transport: III, Railway locomotives and rolling stock. Compiled by E. A. Forward. *London,* 1923. pp. 96, with 20 illus. on 10 plates. [*Catalogue of the Collections in the Science Museum.*] BM
198 exhibits in the permanent exhibition described.

—— another edn. *London,* 1931. 2 parts. BM

Part One: Historical Review. pp. 99, with 52 illus. on plates.
Part Two: Descriptive Catalogue. pp. 118 [119], with 24 illus. on plates.

7822 [HULL.] RAILWAY MUSEUM. Catalogue of the Railway Museum, Paragon Station, Hull. [Compiled by Thomas Sheppard.] *Hull,* 1938. pp. 32, with 13 illus. [*Hull Museum Publication,* no. 200.] BM
Description of 344 exhibits.

7823 SOTHEBY & CO. The Phillimore Railway Collection: catalogue of the well-known and extensive collection of books, autograph letters, prints and pictures, maps, pottery, porcelain and glass, works of art, etc., relating to railways and locomotive engines. The property of the late John Phillimore . . . which will be sold by auction by Messrs. Sotheby & Co. . . . 28 April 1942. *London,* 1942. pp. 52. BM

7824 SOTHEBY & CO. The Dendy Marshall Railway Collection: catalogue of . . . books, autograph letters, prints and pictures, maps, pottery, porcelain and glass, etc. relating to railways and locomotive engines. Date of sale, Tuesday the 13th of November, 1945. *London,* 1945. pp. 26. BM
352 lots.

*7825 BRITISH RAILWAYS. Model railway: a brief description. *London,* 1949. pp. [6.] BM
A model railway used at various exhibitions.

7826 BRITISH TRANSPORT COMMISSION. The preservation of relics and records: report to the B.T.C. (Chairman, S. B. Taylor.) *London,* 1951, pp. 40, with 2 illus. BM
pp. 38–40, Locomotives and vehicles displayed or stored elsewhere than in the York Museum.

7827 NATIONAL BOOK LEAGUE. Railroadiana: an exhibition of railway books, prints and relics, organised by R. Morton Shand and the late Harold Wyatt. Catalogue of the exhibition held . . . September to November 1952. [*London,* 1952.] pp. 52. pc

7828 BRITISH TRANSPORT COMMISSION. London on Wheels: an exhibition of London travel in the nineteenth century, in the Shareholders' Meeting Room, Euston Station. *London,* 1953. pp. 30, with illus. BM
—— 2nd edn. *London,* 1962. pp. 24. BM

7829 FOYLE, W. & G. Railways: an exhibition of rare and early books, prints and original drawings illustrating the development of railways in Great Britain in the nineteenth century. 24th November until 18th December, 1954. *London,* [1954,] pp. 9. BR
139 items.

7830 NEWCASTLE UPON TYNE—TOWN MOOR AND PARKS COMMITTEE. Museum of Science and Engineering Catalogue. *Newcastle*, 1954. pp. 146.   pc
pp. 50–64, Room 4: Railways and Transport.

7831 ROLT, L. T. C. Transport treasures: some historical relics of British transport. *London: British Transport Commission*, 1956. pp. 32, with illus.   BM
Issued in connection with the B.T.C.'s exhibition in the Shareholders' Room at Euston. Includes a list of relics preserved. Not a catalogue.

7832 [YORK.] RAILWAY MUSEUM, YORK. Catalogue. [*London*,] 1933. pp. 46.   IT
—— rev. edn. [*York*,] 1947. pp. 45.   SLS
—— another edn. [*York*,] 1956. pp. 48. BM
—— Catalogue, less Briggs' Collection. [*York*, 1933.] pp. 35.   RC

7833 BRITISH TRANSPORT COMMISSION. The Railway Museum, York. *London*, [1958.] pp. [8.]   BR
A descriptive folder, with illus.

7834 BRITISH TRANSPORT COMMISSION. The Railway Museum, York: the background story of the exhibits. By L. T. C. Rolt. *London*, 1958. pp. 23, with illus.   BM

7835 SCHOLES, J. H. Transport treasures. *In* 'Journal of Transport History', vol. 5, no. 1, May 1961. pp. 22–32, with 8 illus. on 4 plates.   BM
Describing the work of 'British Transport Commission Historical Relics'. The formation of the Museum of British Transport at Clapham.

7836 MORGAN, B. Transport preserved. *London: British Railways Board*, 1963. pp 39, with 40 illus.   BM
A survey of the aims and progress of the Office of the Curator of Historical Relics, B.T.C., with illustrations of some of the exhibits currently on display at the Museum of British Transport, Clapham.

Q 2   MODEL RAILWAY ENGINEERING

Indoor model railways are generally excluded, but a place is made here for garden railways and actual engineering in miniature, these being directly related, technically and mechanically, to railway engineering proper

For passenger-carrying railways run for pleasure on gauges of 2 ft. and less see **D 6**

7837 THOMSON. Life of Thomson, lecturer on steam machinery, written by himself during confinement from the accidental fracture of a leg . .. *Berwick*, 1831. pp. 48.   pc
Includes (pp. 6–9) an account of his model steam locomotive.

7838 DICKSON, W. E. How to make a steam engine: a treatise for the instruction and amusement of ingenious boys . . . *London*, [1867.] pp. 112, with illus.   BM
pp. 87–9, model railway locomotive.

7839 The MODEL steam engine: how to buy, how to use, and how to construct it. By 'A Steady Stoker'. *London*, 1868. pp. 80, with illus.   BM
pp. 46–68, 'The locomotive engine and its representative models'.

7840 POCOCK, J. Model engine making in theory and practice; with over one hundred illustrations drawn by the author. *London*, 1888. pp. vii, 178.   BM
pp. 122–40, 'Slide-valve locomotive engine'.

7841 ALEXANDER, J. H. Model engine construction, with practical instructions . . . containing 21 working drawings . . . *London*, 1894. pp. viii, 324.   BM
—— 2nd edn. *London*, 1904. pp. x, 326. BM

7842 GREENLY, H. The model locomotive: its design and construction: a practical manual on the building and management of miniature railway engines . . . *London*, 1904. pp. 276, with 9 fold. plates & 370 illus.   BM

7843 GREENLY, H. Model steam engines: how to understand them and how to run them . . . fully illustrated with diagrams and sketches. *London*, [1907.] pp. 87.   BM
pp. 69–84, Model locomotives.

7844 SHORES, J. Model steam engines: the story of a clergyman's hobby; illustrated. *Newcastle upon Tyne*, 1911. pp. vii, 56, with frontis. & 66 illus. on 56 plates.   BM
Includes locomotives.

7845 [MARSHALL.] PERCIVAL MARSHALL & Co. Wonderful models: the romance of the world in miniature, and a complete encyclopaedia of model-craft. *London*, 1928. 2 vols., with fold. plates & many illus.   ELTHAM PL
Reprinted articles from the *Model Engineer*, and *Model Railway News*.

*7846 'L.B.S.C.' [i.e. L. Lawrence.] Shops, Shed and Road: a handbook on the construction and fitting of details and accessories for small power steam locomotives; with a Foreword by Percival Marshall . . . *London*, [1930]. pp. 176, with frontis, 15 illus. & 130 diagrams.   BM

7847 BASSETT-LOWKE LTD. Fifty years of model making. (The story of Bassett-Lowke Ltd from the turn of the century.) Recorded by George Holland. [*Northampton,* 1949.] pp. 64, with many illus.   BM

*7848 HAMBLETON, F. C. Locomotives worth modelling. *London: Percival Marshall,* [1949.] pp. 170, with diagrams.   BM

7849 'L.B.S.C.' [i.e. L. Lawrence.] How to build 'Princess Marina': an L.M.S. Mogul Class in 3½ ins. gauge. *London:* '*Mechanics*', [1949.] pp. 52, with diagrams.   BM

7850 TUSTIN, R. E. Garden railways. *London: Percival Marshall,* 1949. pp. 110, with many illus. & diagrams.   BM
    Railway civil engineering in miniature: a manual for the planning, construction and maintenance of layouts, structures, permanent way and signalling, with chapters on motive power, gauge, and rolling stock.

7851 BASSETT-LOWKE, LTD. Model railways: a handbook on the choice of model locomotives and railway equipment, including designs for rail formations, and model railway signalling. *Northampton: W. J. Bassett-Lowke & Co.,* [1905]. pp. 72, with frontis., & 76 illus. & diagrams.   pc
    Includes garden railways and locomotives.
    —— 2nd edn., rev. & enl. *Northampton* [1907.] pp. 82.   pc
    —— [3rd.] 'Model Railway Handbook.' *Northampton,* [1910.] pp. 91.   pc
    —— 4th, rev. & enl. *London & Northampton,* [1912.] pp. 96.   pc
    —— 5th, rev. & enl. *London,* [1914.] pp. 142.   PO
    —— 6th, rev. & enl. *Northampton,* [1920.] pp. 120.   pc
    —— 7th, *London, Edinburgh & Northampton,* [1922.] pp. 132.   pc
    —— 8th, by W. J. Bassett-Lowke and C. J. Allen. *London,* [1928.] pp. 135.   pc
    —— 9th, completely revised & rewritten, by W. J. Bassett-Lowke. *Northampton,* 1940. pp. 148.   BM
    —— 10th, *Northampton,* 1943. pp. 149. pc
    —— 11th, *Northampton,* [1944.] pp. 149. BM
    —— 12th, *Northampton,* [1946.] pp. 149. pc
    —— 13th, *Northampton,* 1947. pp. 149. pc
    —— 14th, *Northampton,* 1948. pp. 157. pc
    —— 15th, *Northampton,* 1950. pp. 157. BM

7852 GREENLY, H. Model steam locomotives, their details and practical construction . . . with 376 photographs, diagrams and working drawings. *London,* [1922.] pp. 311. BM
    —— 7th edn., revised by Ernest A. Steel. *London,* [1951.] pp. xi, 320.   BM

7853 GREENLY, H. Model steam locomotive construction and design . . . with 91 illustrations, including 15 practical working designs. *London,* 1934. pp. 60[62]. [*Model Maker Series,* no. 3.]   BM
    —— another edn. 'Greenly's model steam locomotive designs and specifications, revised by Ernest A. Steel . . . with 36 illustrations, including 20 practical working designs.' *London,* 1952. pp. 62. [*New Model Maker Series,* no. 2.]   BM

7854 'L.B.S.C.' [i.e. L. Lawrence.] Maisie: words and music. *London: Percival Marshall,* 1952. pp. viii, 131, with illus. & diagrams. BM
    A manual for building a 3½-inch gauge Great Northern Rly. Ivatt 'Atlantic' locomotive.

*7855 'L.B.S.C.' [i.e. L. Lawrence.] The Live Steam Book. *London: Percival Marshall,* 1950. pp. xii, 199, with illus. & diagrams.   BM
    A handbook for model locomotive engineers.
    —— another edn. *London,* 1954. pp. xiv, 209.

7856 DEWHIRST, N. A steam locomotive for 'O' gauge. *London: Percival Marshall,* 1955. pp. 84, with 15 fold. sheets of working diagrams.   BM
    A construction manual.

7857 WHITE, H. E. The maintenance and management of small locomotives. *London: Percival Marshall,* 1955. pp. 204, with many illus. & diagrams.   BM
    A manual for garden railway locomotives.

*7858 EVANS, M. Manual of Model Steam Locomotive Construction. *London: Percival Marshall,* 1960. pp. x, 158, with 80 illus. on 32 plates & 122 diagrams in text.   BM

7859 ELLIS, C. H. Model railways, 1838–1939. *London: Allen & Unwin,* 1962. pp. 139, with 60 illus. on 32 plates.   BM

Q 3   RAILWAY PHOTOGRAPHY

7860 MY BEST RAILWAY photographs. *London: Ian Allan,* 1946–9.   BM
    A series of booklets of photographs, with details of exposures, etc., and notes on technique. Except for nos. 5, 9, 12, 13 and 15, each booklet is entitled *My best railway photographs.*
    1, [L.M.S.] By E. Treacy. 1946. pp. 32.
    2, [S.R.] By O. J. Morris. 1946. pp. 33.

    3, [G.W.R. & S.R.] By M. W. Earley. 1946. pp. 32.
    4, [L.N.E.R.] By C. C. B. Herbert. 1947. pp. 32.
    5, More of my best railway photographs. [L.M.S.] By E. Treacy. 1947. pp. 32.
    6, [S.R. and G.W.R.] By S. C. Townroe. 1948. pp. 32.

7, [Various railways.] By H. C. Casserley. 1948. pp. 32.

8, [L.N.E.R.] By F. R. Hebron. 1948. pp. 32.

9, My best railroad photographs. [American railways.] By R. H. Kindig. 1948. pp. 32.

10, [Various railways.] By C. R. L. Coles. [1948.] pp. 32.

11, [Various railways.] By P. Ransome-Wallis. 1948. pp. 32.

12, More of my best railway photographs. [Mostly L.N.E.R.] By C. C. B. Herbert. [1949.] pp. [32.]

13, Still more of my best railway photographs. [L.M. Region.] By E. Treacy. 1948. pp. [32].

14, [1906–1949.] By H. G. Tidey. [1949.] pp. [32.]

15, More of my best railway photographs. [Various railways.] By M. W. Earley. 1949. pp. 32.

7861 MORRIS, O. J. The ABC of railway photography. *London: Ian Allan*, [1952.] pp. 32, illustrated with examples. BM

7862 MILLS, J. D. How to photograph trains. *London: Fountain Press*, 1957. pp. 95, with 34 illus. on 32 plates & tables. BM

7863 RANSOME-WALLIS, P. All about locomotives and trains and your camera. *London: Focal Press*, [March 1957.] pp. 55, with illus. [*Photo Guides*, no. 75.] BM

Q 4   ILLUSTRATIONS
Works composed of illustrations or in which illustrations are noteworthy either for quality or quantity, or both

7864 ALLEN, C. J. The Children's Railway Book. By 'Uncle Allen' (C. J. Allen). *London*, [1931.] pp. [192,] with col. frontis. & 11 col. plates. BM

7865 ALLEN, G. F. Locovariety. *London: Ian Allan*, 1947. pp. [31.] BM
Twenty-five photographs, with text by G. F. Allen.

7866 BUCKNALL, R. *and* BUDDEN, T. F. Railway memories . . . Two hundred and four photographs by Doctor Budden. *London*, 1947. pp. 248. BM
Published by the authors.

7867 LOCOMOTION. *London: Ian Allan*, 1948. pp. [32.] BM
Photographs of trains with descriptions.

7868 BASSETT-LOWKE, W. J. *and* COURTNEY, F. E. A Book of Trains. *Harmondsworth*, 1941. pp. 31, with illus., some col. [*Puffin Picture Books*.] BM
Introductory.
—— rev. edn. *Harmondsworth*, 1949. pp. 31. [*Puffin Picture Books*, no. 10.] BM

7869 GOLDING, H. The Wonder Book of Railways for Boys and Girls. *London*, 1911–1950. BM
Twenty-one editions with plates (some col.) and many illustrations. For many years the most popular of railway books for children.

7870 KNOW your own railways: no. 1. *Nottingham: John Ford Publications*, 1950. pp. 32. BM
Thirty photographs of trains with short descriptions.

7871 NUNN, G. W. A. British sources of photographs and pictures. *London: Cassell*, 1952. pp. viii, 220. BM
Includes fifteen for railways (photographs, postcards, prints and exhibitions).

7872 TRAINS in Colour. *London: Ian Allan*, [1949.] pp. 16. BM
Includes nine colour photographs.
—— another edn. *London*, [1952.] pp. 20, with 7 col. illus. BM

7873 SEMAN, O. M. Spotlight on railways. 1953. BM
Published by O. M. Seman.
A booklet containing eight photographs of locomotives, mounted.

7874 TRAINS Photopix. *London: Ian Allan*, [1949.] pp. [16.] 41 illus. of contemporary trains, with descriptions. BM
—— 2nd series. *London*, [1950.] pp. [16.] 33 illus. BM
—— 3rd, *London*, [1953.] pp. [16.] 35 illus. BM
—— 4th, *London*, [1953.] pp. [16.] 38 illus. BM
—— 5th, *London*, [1955.] pp. [16.] 29 illus. BM
—— 6th, *London*, [1955.] pp. [16.] 32 illus. BM

7875 ELLIS, C. H. A Picture History of Railways. *London: Hulton Press*, 1956. pp. 18 (text) & 408 illus. BM
Each illustration is described.

7876 LOCOMOTIVE PUBLISHING COMPANY. Exclusive Railway Photographs. First Catalogue. *Hampton Court: Ian Allan*, [c. 1957.] pp. [46.] PC
5000 items.

7877 ELLIS, C. H. The beauty of railways; with an introductory essay by C. Hamilton Ellis. *London: Parrish*, [1960]. pp. 21, with 128 plates. BM
162 pictures by various photographers. Introductory essay, pp. 1–21.

7878 ELLIS, C. H. British trains of yester-year: a pictorial recollection of the pre-1923 railway scene. *London: Ian Allan*, [1960.] pp. 124. BM
288 photographs, with historical and descriptive annotations.

7879 'RAILWAY WORLD.' Colour Album. *Hampton Court: Railway World*, June 1961. pp. 48, with 39 illus. (incl. 31 col.). BM
Cover title, *Railway Colour Album*.

7880 ADAMS, J. *and* WHITEHOUSE, P. B. Railway Picture Gallery. *London: Ian Allan,* 1962. pp. 96. BM

Eighty-three photographs of steam locomotives, trains and railway scenes of the past ten years.

7881 SIMMONS, J. Transport. *London: Vista*

Books, 1962. pp. x, 69, 199–206, with 239 illus. on 128 plates, & 82 notes. [*Visual History of Modern Britain* Series.] BM

A pictorial survey, introduced by a concise account of main features in the development of all forms of transport from the 13th century to the present day, with 56 illustrations relating to railways and tramways.

R   RESEARCH AND STUDY OF RAILWAYS AND RAILWAY HISTORY

Sources and methods—Bibliography

*7882 MENZLER, F. A. A. Rail and road statistics. [*London,* 1950.] pp. 352–75, with a bibliography. BM

Reprint, *Journal of the Royal Statistical Society,* series A (general), vol. 113, part 3, 1950. A survey of available sources for statistics.

7883 BRITISH TRANSPORT COMMISSION. Preservation of relics and records: report to the British Transport Commission. *London,* 1951. pp. 40, with plate. BM

Recommendations of a committee. (Chairman, S. B. Taylor.)

7884 BRITISH MUSEUM. Catalogue of Additions to the Manuscripts. The Gladstone Papers: Additional Manuscripts 44086–44835. *London,* 1953. pp. vi, 400. BM

Letters, memoranda, and privately printed matter relating to railways are indexed under 'Railways', 'Thomas Brassey', 'John Bright', 'William Fairbairn', 'George Carr Glyn', George Hudson', 'London & North Western Rly.', 'Henry Pease', 'Robert Stephenson', and 'E. W. Watkin'.

7885 JOHNSON, L. C. Historical records of the British Transport Commission. *In* 'Journal of Transport History', vol. 1, no. 2, November 1953. pp. 82–96. BM

7886 SIMMONS, J. Railway history in English local records. *In* 'Journal of Transport History', vol. 1, no. 3, May 1954. pp. 155–69, with 67 bibliogr. notes. BM

7887 JOHNSON, L. C. Preserving the transport story. pp. 9. *Reproduced typescript.* BTCHR

Paper, L.S.E. Railway Students' Association, 16 November, 1955.

An account of the aims and achievements of B.T.C. Historical Records, by its Archivist.

7888 BRITISH RECORDS ASSOCIATION. List of record repositories in Great Britain. *London,* 1956. pp. 46. [*Reports from Committees,* no. 5.] BM

155 repositories.

7889 WARDLE, D. B. Sources for the history of railways at the Public Record Office. *In*

'Journal of Transport History', vol. 2, no. 4, November 1956. pp. 214–34. BM

Records of the Ministry of Transport, Treasury, Board of Trade, Home Office and other departmental, legal, and patent records and maps.

7890 ROBBINS, M. What kind of railway history do we want? *In* 'Journal of Transport History', vol. 3, no. 2, November 1957. pp. 65–75, with 16 bibliogr. notes. BM

7891 CAMPBELL, J. M. Index to the Railway Magazine, 1897–1957. [1958.] *c.* 500 pp. *Typescript.* BR

Compiled for the use of the staff of B.T.C. Historical Records (now British Railways Board Historical Records). Three copies only; at London, York and Edinburgh.

A very detailed and accurate analysis of articles and significant smaller items arranged alphabetically by subject. Since Mr. Campbell's retirement from the B.T.C. in 1960 a continuation has been maintained on cards.

The Railway Magazine issues an index at the completion of each volume, but no general index has been published.

7892 SIMMONS, J. The Scottish records of the British Transport Commission. *In* 'Journal of Transport History', vol. 3, no. 3, May 1958. pp. 158–67, with 22 bibliogr. notes. BM

7893 BOND, M. Materials for transport history amongst the records of Parliament. *In* 'Journal of Transport History', vol. 4, no. 1, May 1959. pp. 37–52, with 17 bibliogr. notes. BM

Includes railways, notes on procedure with Bills and on the citation of Acts.

*7894 CLINKER, C. R. A Handlist of the principal sources of original material for the history of railways in England & Wales; compiled by C. R. Clinker. *Rugby,* March 1959 pp. 4. *Reproduced typescript.* BM

A tentative guide to the location of various classes of primary material, printed books and newspapers.

7895 PALMER, J. E. C. Railway periodicals of the nineteenth century published in the British Isles: a bibliographical guide. Submitted in May 1959 in part fulfilment

of the requirements of the Academic Post-Graduate Diploma in Librarianship of the University of London, 1959. pp. [100,] with diagrams. *Typescript.*   SL
(A revised edition is to appear in the *Library Association Bibliographies* series.)
This bibliography is a biblio-technical description of serial publications. It is hoped that in the compilation of a subsequent volume to the present bibliography this work will become a basis for analysing the subject content of railway periodical literature. (See end of Compiler's Introduction.)

7896 DYOS, H. J. Transport history in university theses. *In* 'Journal of Transport History', vol. 4, no. 3, May 1960. pp. 161–73.   BM
159 items, including railways, with locations.

7897 SHERRINGTON, C. E. R. Development and work of the Railway Research Service. pp. 15. *Typescript.*   PC
Paper, Canadian Railway Club, Montreal, November 1960.

7898 JOHNSON, L. C. British Transport Commission Archives: work since 1953. *In*

'Journal of Transport History', vol. 5, no. 3, May 1962. pp. 159–65.   BM

7899 FOWKES, E. H. Railway history and the local historian. *York: East Yorkshire Local History Society*, 1963. pp. 40, with a map. [*East Yorkshire Local History Series*, no. 16.]   BM

The nature of railway archives available in the York Collection of British Railways Board Historical Records, with examples showing the direct relationship of this material to actual railway history in Yorkshire.
Tables in the Appendix describe the classes of material available for individual railway and canal undertakings in Yorkshire, and there is a select annotated bibliography.

*7900 OTTLEY, G. Railway company prospectuses in the British Museum Library: a hand-list. *In preparation.*

*7901 OTTLEY, G. Railway history resources in the libraries and archives of the British Isles. *In preparation.*

S   STATISTICAL METHOD

The science of compiling railway statistics

For actual statistics see under the relevant subject

7902 MURLAND, J. W. Observations on Irish railway statistics. *Dublin*, 1849. pp. 13. LSE
Paper, Dublin Statistical Society.
The interpretation of statistics.

7903 HARRISON, J. T. On railway statistics. *In* 'Railway management', edited by J. Forrest. *London*, 1875. pp. 36–83.   BR

7904 ACWORTH, W. M. English railway statistics. [1902.] pp. 52.   BR
Read before the Royal Statistical Society, 16 December, 1902, and reprinted from the *Journal of the R.S.S.*, vol. 65, pt. 4, 31 Dec., 1902.
Deficiencies of currently available statistics, with an analysis of actual tables provided by some British railway companies, with American comparisons.

7905 BOAG, G. L. Manual of Railway Statistics. *London*, 1912. pp. 185, with specimen

reports and schedules & a bibliography (32 items).   BM

7906 KIRKUS, A. E. Railway statistics: their compilation and use. *London*, 1927. pp. x, 134.   BM
Includes, pp. 9–21, an historical review.

7907 RAILWAY CLEARING HOUSE. Instructions for the compilation of statistics rendered to the Minister of Transport by the railway companies in Great Britain in accordance with the Railways Act 1921 . . . and the Railway Companies Road Transport Acts, 1928 . . . *London*, Dec. 1928. pp. 118.   LSE
'Private and not for publication.'

7908 HALL, J. A. Compilation and use of railway cartage statistics. 1954. pp. 8, with specimen forms. *Typescript.*   IT
Paper, Institute of Transport, York, 11 Jan., 1954.

Many directories and tables are issued repetitively at regular intervals. Such periodical publications are outside the range of this Bibliography, but three important sources are appended (7948–50). For the documentation of nineteenth-century railway periodicals see J. E. C. Palmer's work, described at 7895.

7909 FOWLER. Fowler's Railway Traveller's Guide, showing the time of the departure of the trains, a distance table, a skeleton map of all the railways in Great Britain. [1840?] pp. 104. H
—— 2nd edn. [1840?] H

7910 OWEN, W. New Book of Roads . . . describing the principal roads and railways . . . new edn. *London*, 1840. pp. xxxii, 198. LSE
pp. 191–8, Railroads, with starting times of trains on the principal railways from London.

7911 RICHARDSON, T., *printer*. Richardson's Railway Guide and time and fare tables, showing the departure and arrival of the trains of every railway in England . . . illustrated with several views, and a railway map of England engraved expressly for this work. *London*, 1841. pp. 64. PC

7912 ROBINSON'S Railway Directory, containing the names of the directors of all the principal railways in Great Britain; derived from original sources. *London*, 1841. pp. 36. LSE
Arranged under companies.

7913 TUCK, H. Every Traveller's Guide to the Railways of England, Scotland, Ireland, Belgium, France and Germany, containing correct time and fare tables of every railway, illustrated with maps of the country through which the railway lines traverse. Compiled from original sources. *London*, 1843. pp. 64[65]. BR

*7914 [COLE, H.] Railway Chronicle Travelling Charts; or, Iron Road Books, for perusal of the journey . . . with numerous illustrations. *London*, [1846.] BM
A series of folding route charts. Each is headed by an illustration, usually of the terminal station of the particular railway.
London to Wolverton (London & Birmingham Rly.).
London to Watford (London & Birmingham Rly.).
London to Cambridge on the Eastern Counties.
London to Hanwell and Southall (G.W.R.).
London to Slough, Eton, and Windsor (G.W.R.).
London and Croydon (L. & C. Rly.).
London and Brighton (L. & B. Rly.).
London to Reigate (South Eastern Rly. and London & Brighton Rly.).
London to Tunbridge Wells on the South Eastern.
London to Basingstoke, Winchester, Gosport, on the South Western.
London to Basingstoke, Winchester, and Southampton on the South Western.
London to Kingston and Hampton Court (South Western Rly.).
London to Richmond (South Western Rly.).
London to Woking and Guildford (South Western Rly.).

7915 GLYNN, H. Reference Book to the incorporated railway companies of England and Wales, alphabetically arranged, including a list of their directors, offices and officers, constitution and capital, shewing also the lines suspended in Session 1847, and applications for Bills in 1848 . . . *London*, 1847. pp. xii, 227. BM

7916 GLYNN, H. A Reference Book to the incorporated railway companies of Ireland, alphabetically arranged, including a list of their directors, offices and officers, constitution and capital. Gauge of way, 5 feet 3 inches. *London*, 1847. pp. xvi, 84. with fold. map. UL(GL)

7917 GLYNN, H. Reference Book to the incorporated railway companies of Scotland, alphabetically arranged, including a list of their directors, offices and officers, constitution and capital. Gauge of way, 4 feet 8½ inches. *London*, 1847. pp. xl, 60, with fold. map & a chronological table (4 pages). BM

7918 TOPHAM'S Railway Timetable and Guide, dedicated, by kind permission, to George Hudson. *Derby*, July 1848. pp. 82. LSE
Down trains in black, downwards; up trains in red, upwards. All railways.

*7919 CHURTON, E. The Railroad Book of England; historical, topographical and picturesque . . . with a brief sketch of the lines in Scotland and Wales. *London*, [1851.] pp. xxxiv, 590, with illus. & fold. map. BM
Routes from London described.

7920 MACAULAY, Z. List of all stations on the railways of Great Britain, alphabetically arranged. *London*, 1851. pp. 76. NLC
—— 2nd edn. 'List of stations on the railways of Great Britain and Ireland, alphabetically arranged.' *London*, 1855. pp. 95. UL(GL)

7921 SHARPE'S Road Book for the Rail: Eastern Division; including the lines north of the Mersey and comprising the Lancashire & Yorkshire, Midland, Great Northern, North Eastern, Caledonian, North British, Eastern Counties, and neighbouring lines, upon a scale of ten miles to an inch . . . *London*, 1855. pp. 108. BM

Bound and published as one book with *Sharpe's Road Book for the Rail: Western Division.*

7922 SHARPE'S Road Book for the Rail: Western Division; including the lines south of the Thames and comprising the South Western, South Eastern, Brighton & South Coast, Great Western, North and South Wales, London & North Western, and neighbouring lines, upon a scale of ten miles to an inch . . . *London*, 1855. pp. 108. BM

Bound and published as one book with *Sharpe's Road Book for the Rail: Eastern Division.*

7923 ASHTON, J. Plan of the Improved Special Railway and Steam Navigation Guide, for Great Britain and Ireland. *London*, 1860. pp. 18. BM

A simplified form of time-table.

7924 [RAILWAYS of England.] [1860?] pp. 108. LSE

The LSE copy has no title-page.

A route book for railways in England and Wales.

7925 RAILWAY CLEARING HOUSE. Distances between the stations and junctions of the railways on which the Clearing House is in operation. *London*, 1853. pp. 200. BM

—— another edn. *London*, 1862. pp. 671. BM

7926 RAILWAY CLEARING HOUSE. Hand Book of the Stations. *London*, 1867–1956. BM

A comprehensive and authoritative directory to railway services in operation at stations, sidings, collieries, etc.

7927 BRADSHAW'S Itinerary of Great Britain, for railway & telegraphic conveyance to and from every town, village, and parish containing a population of 500 and upwards in England, Wales, and Scotland . . . to which is added a general railway station list . . . and complete map . . . *London & Manchester: W. J. Adams & Sons*, [1879.] pp. 175. IT

7928 ROLYAT, C. H. Rolyat's Commercial and Professional Railway Distance Guide. *Birmingham*, [1887.] pp. 160. BM

7929 SCOTT, W. J. The best way there: a way-book for the rail-faring fool: being a summary of competitive services for the chief towns . . . corrected to date, January 1892; with notes on speeds, punctuality, fares, rolling stock, etc. of all the railways in Great Britain, with hints as to scenery on some routes. *London*, 1892. pp. v, 116. BM

7930 FITZGERALD, P. The story of 'Bradshaw's Guide' . . . *London*, 1896. pp. 76, with 2 illus. BM

7931 HILL, A. The Complete Time Table constructed upon a new and improved design. *Glasgow*, [1897.] pp. 7. BM

A plan for a simplified time-table, with examples.

7932 HARROD, J. G. & Co. Royal Despatch of Great Britain and Ireland. *London*, 1880–1901. BM

Various editions. A gazetteer giving distances of stations from the nearest centres of population. About 20,000 entries to each edition.

7933 BEMROSE, W. & SON. Bemrose's Railway Rate Book of the stations, sidings and collieries on the English railways (with principal Scotch and Irish stations) alphabetically arranged. 4th edn. *London*, [1893?] 2 vols. BM

—— 6th edn. *London*, 1905. pp. xvii, 513.

7934 FREDERICK, I. W. The authentic story of Bradshaw's Railway Guides. *In* 'Jubilee of the Railway News, 1864–1914.' *London: Railway News*, [1914.] pp. 202–5, with illus. BM

7935 LEGGATT, J. E. The Irish Commercial and Railway Gazetteer, shewing every town and railway station in Ireland, alphabetically arranged . . . *London*, 1879. pp. 52. BM

With the name of the railway for each station.

—— 2nd edn. *Dublin & London*, 1893. pp. 93. BR

—— Appendix, 1898. pp. [4.] BM

—— 3rd, *Dublin & London*, 1907. pp. 98. BM

—— 4th, *Dublin*, [1917.] pp. 80. BM

7936 ST. PAUL'S CATHEDRAL. Divine Service in memory of those railwaymen who laid down their lives for their country, in the Great War, 1914–1918. [*London*]: *Railway Companies Association*, [1919.] pp. 152. BM

pp. 13–152, 'Names of railwaymen . . . who have died' alphabetically arranged under companies.

7937 DRING, E. H. Early railway time tables. *In* 'The Library', 4th series, vol. 2, no. 3, 1 December, 1921. pp. [137]–173, with reproductions and collations of early Bradshaws. BM

Read before the Bibliographical Society, 17 October, 1921.

7938 HARROD, A. F. The Indispensable Reference Guide and Gazetteer, containing the names of every city, town and village in England, arranged alphabetically, with postal address, county and railway stations, the accommodation and crane power at the stations, lines of railway, telegraph offices and mileage

from railway stations and telegraph offices to each place; also a special list of carting agents. *Hingham* (Norfolk), [1899–1923.] BM
Various editions.

7939 BILBROUGH, G. F. Bilbrough's Railway Mileage Tables, Great Britain . . . *Birmingham*, 1924. pp. viii, 387.   BM
'14,000 stations and junctions and some thousands of private sidings.'
—— rev. edn. *Birmingham*, 1928. pp. xvi, 424.   BM

7940 FELLOWS, R. B. A Railway Library: a list of railway books. *Sidcup: Four O's Publishing Company*, 1935. pp. [12,] with 9 illus. of locomotives. *Reproduced typescript.*   BM
pp. 1–2, 'Early Railway Companions'.

7941 SMITH, G. R. The history of Bradshaw: a centenary review of the origin and growth of the most famous guide in the world. *London & Manchester*, 1939. pp. 76, with 4 plates & illus.   BM

7942 FELLOWS, R. B. One hundred years of Bradshaw. pp. 26, with tables of first issues. *Typescript.*   RC
Paper, Railway Club, 2 May, 1940.

7943 LEE, C. E. The centenary of 'Bradshaw'. *London*, 1940. pp. 48.   BM
A history of the Bradshaw time-tables, with illustrated examples.

7944 BRITISH RAILWAYS. Book of Routes: information regarding alternative routes by which passengers may travel without additional charge. [*London*,] May 1952. pp. 63.   BM

7945 HOUSE, J. The Romance of Murray: the story of 110 years of achievement. *Glasgow*, [1952.] pp. 27, with illus., incl. portraits. RC
Murray's Diary (railway time-tables for Scotland), 1842 to 1952.

7946 RAILWAY Map of England & Wales and Scotland; reproduced by permission of the Railway Clearing House. *London: Ian Allan*, 1948.   BM
Cover title: *Sectional Maps of the British Railways.*
The R.C.H. map, showing the railways in December 1947, in book form on a scale of 7¼ miles to 1 inch. 39 pages of coloured maps, plus 13-page index at end.
—— [2nd edn.] *London: Ian Allan*, [1952.]   BM
Cover title: *British Railways Sectional Maps.*
This limp cover edition has 37 pages of maps only. Pages 38–9 of the previous edition (covering the North of Scotland) are omitted.

*7947 [CONOLLY, W. P. *and* VINCENT, U. A.] British Railways Pre-Grouping Atlas and Gazetteer. *London: Railway Publications*, [1958.] pp. 84.   BM
—— reprinted 1960 & 1963 as 2nd & 3rd editions.   BM
Forty-five maps with lines of railway in five distinguishing colours, devised by W. P.

Conolly, followed by (pp. 47–84) a gazetteer arranged as a key to the maps, compiled by U. A. Vincent. The Gazetteer includes also separate indexes to tunnels, water troughs, summits and viaducts. Scale *c*. 9 miles to 1 inch, with enlargements of complicated areas.

To this bibliography of monographs must be added three serial publications of exceptional importance as works of reference:

7948 RAILWAY Year Book. *London*, 1898–1932. 35 vols.   BM
A compendium of miscellaneous information, including historical sketches of individual railways, a chronological list of, railway events, 1602 to date, and biographies and portraits of prominent railwaymen.
—— Subsequently amalgamated with 'The Universal Directory of Railway Officials' 1894(–1932) to form 'The Universal Directory of Railway Officials and Railway Year Book. *London*, 1933/34–1949/50.   BM
—— Continued as 'Directory of Railway Officials and Year Book'. *London*, 1950/51– . *In progress.*   BM

*7949 BRADSHAW'S Railway Manual, Shareholders' Guide and Official Directory for 1863, vol. 15—1923, vol. 75. *London*, 1863–1923.   BM
Issued annually in continuation of *Bradshaw's Railway Almanack, Directory, Shareholders' Guide, and Manual for 1848* (2 editions, both published 1847) and *1849* (1848), *Bradshaw's General Railway Directory . . . for 1850–1852*, and *Bradshaw's Shareholders' Guide . . . for 1853–1862* (numbered in error vol. 5–14). Details of individual issues are set out in item no. 7895.
A detailed annual record of the history and contemporary position of most railways in the British Isles, with a directory of railway officials and railway maps with lines shown in distinctive colours.

*7950 BRADSHAW'S . . . Guide . . . no. 1, Dec. 1841—no. 40, Mar. 1845; no. 141, Apr. 1845—no. 1521, June 1961. *Manchester & London*.   BM
Time-tables of passenger train and steamship services throughout the British Isles.
Issued monthly with slight variations of title, beginning as *Bradshaw's Railway Guide; containing a correct account of the hours of arrival and departure of the trains of every railway in Great Britain . . .*
The earlier issues were mainly printed from the same setting of type as *Bradshaw's Railway Companion*, a booklet in smaller format published from 1839 to 1848 at irregular intervals (the first few issues being entitled *Bradshaw's Railway Time Tables and Assistant to Railway Travelling*), and the broadsheet published each month from Apr. 1841 to Dec. 1854 under the title *Bradshaw's Railway Time Tables*.
The full history of these and other timetables published by George Bradshaw, and the locations of copies (all except some of the earliest issues being in the British Museum) will be found from item nos. 7930, 7934, 7937, 7941, 7942 and 7943.

APPENDIX I

THE RAILWAYS ACT, 1921

[11 & 12 GEO. 5, ch. 55]

FIRST SCHEDULE

1	2	3
Groups	Constituent Companies	Subsidiary Companies
1. The Southern Group	1. The London and South Western Railway Company; the London, Brighton and South Coast Railway Company; the South Eastern Railway Company; the London, Chatham and Dover Railway Company; the South Eastern and Chatham Railway Companies Managing Committee.	1. The Bridgwater Railway Company; the Brighton and Dyke Railway Company; the Freshwater, Yarmouth and Newport (Isle of Wight) Railway Company; the Hayling Railways Company; the Isle of Wight Railway Company; the Isle of Wight Central Railway Company; the Lee-on-the-Solent Railway Company; the London and Greenwich Railway Company; the Mid Kent Railway (Bromley to St Mary Cray) Company; the North Cornwall Railway Company; the Plymouth and Dartmoor Railway Company; the Plymouth, Devonport and South Western Junction Railway Company; the Sidmouth Railway Company; the Victoria Station and Pimlico Railway Company.
2. The Western Group	2. The Great Western Railway Company; the Barry Railway Company; the Cambrian Railway Company; the Cardiff Railway Company; the Rhymney Railway Company; the Taff Vale Railway Company; and the Alexandra (Newport and South Wales) Docks and Railway Company.	2. The Brecon and Merthyr Tydfil Junction Railway Company; the Burry Port and Gwendreath Valley Railway Company; the Cleobury Mortimer and Ditton Priors Light Railway Company; the Didcot, Newbury and Southampton Railway Company; the Exeter Railway Company; the Forest of Dean Central Railway Company; the Gwendreath Valleys Railway Company; the Lampeter, Aberayron and New Quay Light Railway Company; the Liskeard and Looe Railway Company; the Llanelly and Mynydd Mawr Railway Company; the Mawddy Railway Company; the Midland and South Western Junction Railway Company; the Neath and Brecon Railway Company; the Penarth Extension Railway Com-

1	2	3
Groups	Constituent Companies	Subsidiary Companies
2. The Western Group —*cont*.		pany; the Penarth Harbour, Dock and Railway Company; the Port Talbot Railway and Docks Company; the Princetown Railway Company; the Rhondda and Swansea Bay Railway Company; the Ross and Monmouth Railway Company; the South Wales Mineral Railway Company; the Teign Valley Railway Company; the Vale of Glamorgan Railway Company; the Van Railway Company; the Welshpool and Llanfair Light Railway Company; the West Somerset Railway Company; the Wrexham and Ellesmere Railway Company.
3. The North Western, Midland, and West Scottish Group.	3. The London and North Western Railway Company; the Midland Railway Company; the Lancashire and Yorkshire Railway Company; the North Staffordshire Railway Company; the Furness Railway Company; the Caledonian Railway Company; the Glasgow and South Western Railway Company; the Highland Railway Company.	3. The Arbroath and Forfar Railway Company; the Brechin and Edzell District Railway Company; the Callander and Oban Railway Company; the Cathcart District Railway Company; the Charnwood Forest Railway Company; the Cleator and Workington Junction Railway Company; the Cockermouth, Keswick and Penrith Railway Company; the Dearne Valley Railway Company; the Dornoch Light Railway Company; the Dundee and Newtyle Railway Company; the Harborne Railway Company; the Killin Railway Company; the Lanarkshire and Ayrshire Railway Company; the Knott End Railway Company; the Leek and Manifold Valley Light Railway Company; the Maryport and Carlisle Railway Company; the Mold and Denbigh Junction Railway Company; the North and South Western Junction Railway Company; the North London Railway Company; the Portpatrick and Wigtownshire Joint Committee; the Shropshire Union Railways and Canal Company; the Solway Junction Railway Company; the Stratford-upon-Avon and Midland Junction Railway Company; the Tottenham and Forest Gate Railway Company; the Wick and Lybster Light Railway Com-

1	2	3
Groups	Constituent Companies	Subsidiary Companies
3. The North Western, Midland, and West Scottish Group— *cont.*		pany; the Wirral Railway Company; the Yorkshire Dales Railway (Skipton to Grassington) Company.
4. The North Eastern, Eastern, and East Scottish Group.	4. The North Eastern Railway Company; the Great Central Railway Company; the Great Eastern Railway Company; the Great Northern Railway Company; the Hull and Barnsley Railway Company; the North British Railway Company; the Great North of Scotland Railway Company.	4. The Brackenhill Light Railway Company; the Colne Valley and Halstead Railway Company; the East and West Yorkshire Union Railways Company; the East Lincolnshire Railway Company; the Edinburgh and Bathgate Railway Company; the Forcett Railway Company; the Forth and Clyde Junction Railway Company; the Gifford and Garvald Railway Company; the Great North of England, Clarence and Hartlepool Junction Railway Company; the Horncastle Railway Company; the Humber Commercial Railway and Dock Company; the Kilsyth and Bonnybridge Railway Company; the Lauder Light Railway Company; the London and Blackwall Railway Company; the Mansfield Railway Company; the Mid-Suffolk Light Railway Company; the Newburgh and North Fife Railway Company; the North Lindsey Light Railways Company; the Nottingham and Grantham Railway and Canal Company; the Nottingham Joint Station Committee; the Nottingham Suburban Railway Company; the Seaforth and Sefton Junction Railway Company; the Sheffield District Railway Company; the South Yorkshire Junction Railway Company; the Stamford and Essendine Railway Company; the West Riding Railway Committee.

ALPHABETICAL ARRANGEMENT OF CONSTITUENT AND SUBSIDIARY COMPANIES AMALGAMATED UNDER THE RAILWAYS ACT (1921)

Alexandra (Newport and South Wales) Docks and Rly. Co.	G.W.R.
Arbroath & Forfar Rly. Co.	L.M.S.
Barry Rly. Co.	G.W.R.
Brackenhill Light Rly. Co.	L.N.E.R.
Brechin & Edzell District Rly. Co.	L.M.S.
Brecon & Merthyr Tydfil Junction Rly. Co.	G.W.R.
Bridgwater Rly. Co.	S.R.
Brighton & Dyke Rly. Co.	S.R.
Burry Port & Gwendreath Valley Rly. Co.	G.W.R.
Caledonian Rly. Co.	L.M.S.
Callander & Oban Rly. Co.	L.M.S.
Cambrian Rly. Co.	G.W.R.
Cardiff Rly. Co.	G.W.R.
Cathcart District Rly. Co.	L.M.S.
Charnwood Forest Rly. Co.	L.M.S.
Cleator & Workington Junction Rly. Co.	L.M.S.
Cleobury Mortimer & Ditton Priors Light Rly. Co.	G.W.R.
Cockermouth, Keswick & Penrith Rly. Co.	L.M.S.
Colne Valley & Halstead Rly. Co.	L.N.E.R.
Dearne Valley Rly. Co.	L.M.S.
Didcot, Newbury & Southampton Rly. Co.	G.W.R.
Dornoch Light Rly. Co.	L.M.S.
Dundee & Newtyle Rly. Co.	L.M.S.
East & West Yorkshire Union Rlys. Co.	L.N.E.R.
East Lincolnshire Rly. Co.	L.N.E.R.
Edinburgh & Bathgate Rly. Co.	L.N.E.R.
Exeter Rly. Co.	G.W.R.
Forcett Rly. Co.	L.N.E.R.
Forest of Dean Central Rly. Co.	G.W.R.
Forth & Clyde Junction Rly. Co.	L.N.E.R.
Freshwater, Yarmouth & Newport (Isle of Wight) Rly. Co.	S.R.
Furness Rly. Co.	L.M.S.
Gifford & Garvald Rly. Co.	L.N.E.R.
Glasgow & South Western Rly. Co.	L.M.S.
Great Central Rly. Co.	L.N.E.R.
Great Eastern Rly. Co.	L.N.E.R.
Great North of England, Clarence & Hartlepool Junction Rly. Co.	L.N.E.R.
Great North of Scotland Rly. Co.	L.N.E.R.
Great Northern Rly. Co.	L.N.E.R.
Great Western Rly. Co.	G.W.R.
Gwendreath Valleys Rly. Co.	G.W.R.
Harborne Rly. Co.	L.M.S.
Hayling Rlys. Co.	S.R.
Highland Rly. Co.	L.M.S.
Horncastle Rly. Co.	L.N.E.R.
Hull & Barnsley Rly. Co.	L.N.E.R.
Humber Commercial Rly. and Dock Co.	L.N.E.R.
Isle of Wight Central Rly. Co.	S.R.
Isle of Wight Rly. Co.	S.R.
Killin Rly. Co.	L.M.S.
Kilsyth & Bonnybridge Rly. Co.	L.N.E.R.
Knott End Rly. Co.	L.M.S.
Lampeter, Aberayron & New Quay Light Rly. Co.	G.W.R.
Lanarkshire & Ayrshire Rly. Co.	L.M.S.
Lancashire & Yorkshire Rly. Co.	L.M.S.
Lauder Light Rly. Co.	L.N.E.R.
Lee-on-the-Solent Rly. Co.	S.R.
Leek & Manifold Valley Light Rly. Co.	L.M.S.
Liskeard & Looe Rly. Co.	G.W.R.
Llanelly & Mynydd Mawr Rly. Co.	G.W.R.
London & Blackwall Rly. Co.	L.N.E.R.
London & Greenwich Rly. Co.	S.R.
London & North Western Rly. Co.	L.M.S.
London & South Western Rly. Co.	S.R.

London, Brighton & South Coast Rly. Co.	S.R.
London Chatham & Dover Rly. Co.	S.R.
Mansfield Rly. Co.	L.N.E.R.
Maryport & Carlisle Rly. Co.	L.M.S.
Mawddy Rly. Co.	G.W.R.
Mid Kent Rly. (Bromley to St Mary Cray) Co.	S.R.
Mid-Suffolk Light Rly. Co.	L.N.E.R.
Midland & South Western Junction Rly. Co.	G.W.R.
Midland Rly. Co.	L.M.S.
Mold & Denbigh Junction Rly. Co.	L.M.S.
Neath & Brecon Rly. Co.	G.W.R.
Newburgh & North Fife Rly. Co.	L.N.E.R.
North & South Western Junction Rly. Co.	L.M.S.
North British Rly. Co.	L.N.E.R.
North Cornwall Rly. Co.	S.R.
North Eastern Rly. Co.	L.N.E.R.
North Lindsay Light Rlys. Co.	L.N.E.R.
North London Rly. Co.	L.M.S.
North Staffordshire Rly. Co.	L.M.S.
Nottingham & Grantham Rly. and Canal Co.	L.N.E.R.
Nottingham Joint Station Committee	L.N.E.R.
Nottingham Suburban Rly. Co.	L.N.E.R.
Penarth Extension Rly. Co.	G.W.R.
Penarth Harbour, Dock and Rly. Co.	G.W.R.
Plymouth & Dartmoor Rly. Co.	S.R.
Plymouth, Devonport & South Western Junction Rly. Co.	S.R.
Port Talbot Rly. and Docks Co.	G.W.R.
Portpatrick & Wigtownshire Joint Committee	L.M.S.
Princetown Rly. Co.	G.W.R.
Rhondda & Swansea Bay Rly. Co.	G.W.R.
Rhymney Rly. Co.	G.W.R.
Ross & Monmouth Rly. Co.	G.W.R.
Seaforth & Sefton Junction Rly. Co.	L.N.E.R.
Sheffield District Rly. Co.	L.N.E.R.
Shropshire Union Rlys. and Canal Co.	L.M.S.
Sidmouth Rly. Co.	S.R.
Solway Junction Rly. Co.	L.M.S.
South Eastern & Chatham Rly. Cos. Managing Committee	S.R.
South Eastern Rly. Co.	S.R.
South Wales Mineral Rly. Co.	G.W.R.
South Yorkshire Junction Rly. Co.	L.N.E.R.
Stamford & Essendine Rly. Co.	L.N.E.R.
Stratford-upon-Avon & Midland Junction Rly. Co.	L.M.S.
Taff Vale Rly. Co.	G.W.R.
Teign Valley Rly. Co.	G.W.R.
Tottenham & Forest Gate Rly. Co.	L.M.S.
Vale of Glamorgan Rly. Co.	G.W.R.
Van Rly. Co.	G.W.R.
Victoria Station & Pimlico Rly. Co.	S.R.
Welshpool & Llanfair Light Rly. Co.	G.W.R.
West Riding Rly. Committee	L.N.E.R.
West Somerset Rly. Co.	G.W.R.
Wick & Lybster Light Rly. Co.	L.M.S.
Wirral Rly. Co.	L.M.S.
Wrexham & Ellesmere Rly. Co.	G.W.R.
Yorkshire Dales Rly. (Skipton to Grassington) Co.	L.M.S.

APPENDIX II

Axholme Joint Rly. Committee
Birkenhead Rly. Co.
Cheshire Lines Committee
Dumbarton & Balloch Joint Rly.
Dundee & Arbroath Joint Rly.
East Kent Light Rlys. Co.
East London Rly. Joint Committee
Easton & Church Hope Rly. Co.
Forth Bridge Rly. Co.
Grangemouth Branch Rly.
Great Central & Midland Joint Committee (Lessees)
Great Central & Midland Joint Committee (Lessors)
Great Central & North Staffordshire Rly. Committee
Great Central & North Western Rlys. Joint Committee
Great Central, Hull & Barnsley & Midland Committee
Great Northern & London & North Western Joint Committee
Great Western & Great Central Rlys. Joint Committee (Lessees)
Great Western & Great Central Rlys. Joint Committee (Lessors)
Great Western & Great Central (Banbury Junction Rly.) Joint Committee
Great Western Rly. Co.
Halifax & Ovenden Joint Committee
Halifax High Level Joint Committee
Hammersmith & City Rly. Co.
Hammersmith & City Rly. Joint Committee
Kent & East Sussex Light Rly. Co.
King's Lynn Docks & Rly. Co.
London & North Eastern Rly. Co.
London Midland & Scottish and Great Western Rlys. Joint Committee
London Midland & Scottish and Great Western Rlys. Joint Committee (Severn & Wye and
    Severn Bridge Rly.)
London Midland & Scottish Rly. Co.
London Passenger Transport Board
Manchester, South Junction & Altrincham Rly. Co.
Mersey Rly. Co.
Methley Rly. Joint Committee
Metropolitan & Great Central Joint Committee
Metropolitan and London & North Eastern Rly. Cos.—Watford Joint Rly. Committee
Mid-Nottinghamshire Joint Rlys. Committee
Midland & Great Northern Rlys. Joint Committee
Midland & North Eastern Rly. Cos. Committee
Norfolk & Suffolk Joint Rlys. Committee
North Devon & Cornwall Junction Light Rly. Co.
Oldham, Ashton-under-Lyne & Guide Bridge Junction Rly. Co.
Otley & Ilkley Joint Line Committee
Princes Dock Branch Joint Rly.
Shrewsbury & Hereford Rly. Co.
Shropshire & Montgomeryshire Light Rly. Co.
Shropshire Rlys. Co.
Somerset & Dorset Rly. Joint Committee
South Yorkshire Joint Line Committee
Southern Rly. Co.
Southport & Cheshire Lines Extension Rly. Co.
Tenbury Rly. Co.
Tottenham & Hampstead Joint Committee
West Cornwall Rly. Co.
West London Extension Rly. Co.
West London Rly. Co.
Weymouth & Portland Rly. Co.
Whitechapel & Bow Rly. Co.
Whitechapel & Bow Rly. Joint Committee

Also any other body whose members consist wholly of, or of representatives of, two or more of the above-mentioned bodies.

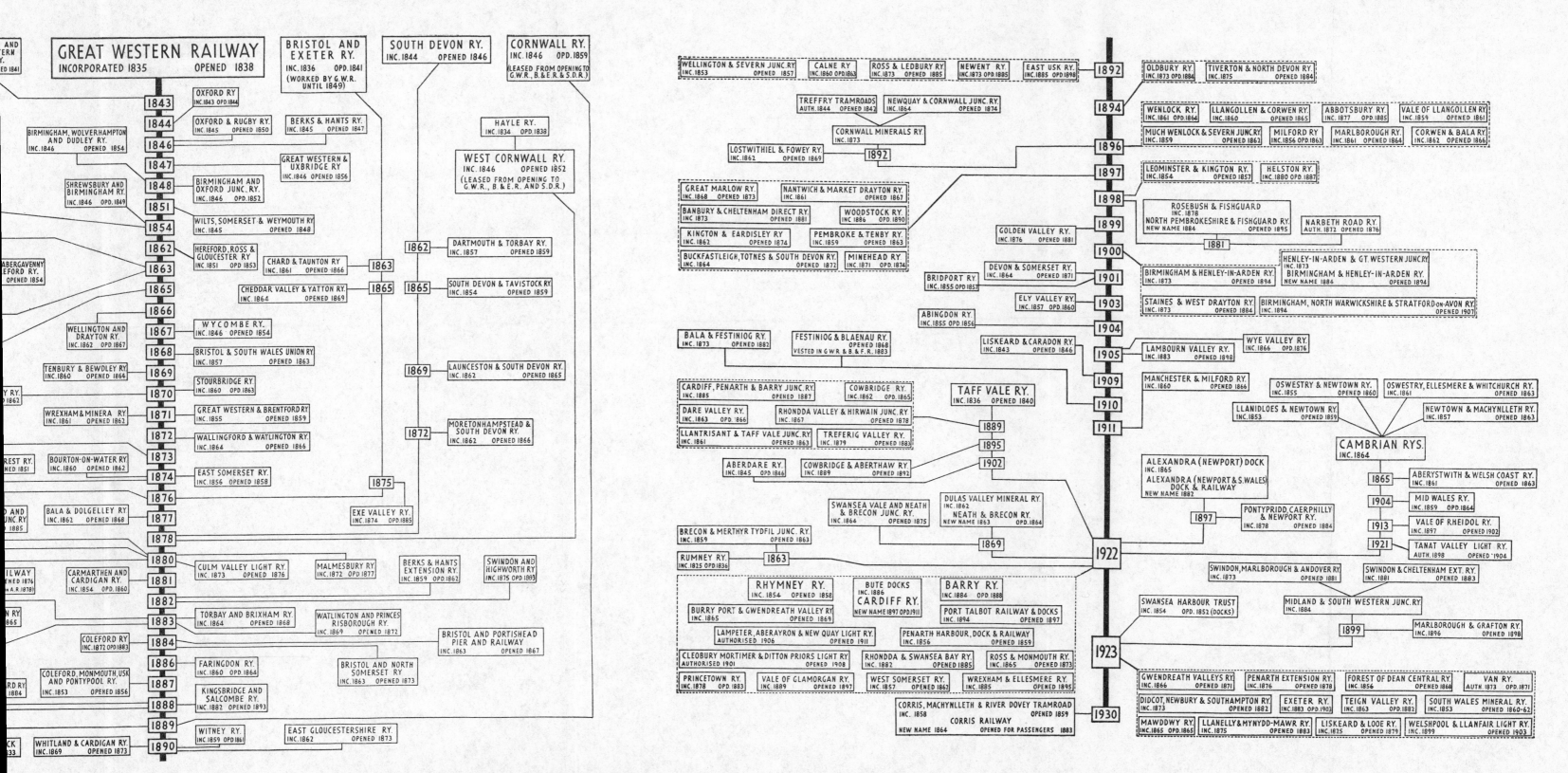

APPENDIX III

GENEALOGICAL TABLES of the Great Western Railway; London & North Western Railway; Midland Railway; and the London Passenger Transport Board. Devised by Charles E. Lee and reproduced from supplements to *The Railway Gazette*.

INDEX

AUTHORS IN CAPITALS, including corporate bodies as authors of their own publications.

Titles in italic, including differing cover titles.
No title entry is given when the author is an integral part (*Report by . . .*) (*Address to the proprietors by the Committee of the London & North Western Shareholders' Association*), or when the title has no identity without knowledge of its authorship (*Souvenir of the Corporation's Tramway Jubilee*).

Subjects and 'analyticals' in roman.

The Index is augmented by entries made from an analysis of subjects, subject relationships, persons, places, events, special aspects, and anything noteworthy within the wording of individual descriptions in the Bibliography (. . . with a chapter on the Channel Tunnel) (A letter to W. E. Gladstone . . .) (The tramways of Reading) (. . . with an account of the Rainhill Trial).
The notes appended to descriptions of items are included in this analysis. These attempt to provide, so far as this is practicable, a guide to knowledge in books which is not revealed, or not precisely defined, by the wording of title pages.
Thus the components of collective biographies and the hidden biographical emphases in historical works are brought to light (2896 *Twenty locomotive men* by C. Hamilton Ellis; 7336 *The early days of the Southern Railway* by Sir John Elliot in which Sir Herbert Walker is strongly featured, and 928 *The Underground Story* by Hugh Douglas with its detail on Charles Pearson and others).
Also included are the opening lines of poems ('Snow falls in the buffet of Aldersgate Station . . .').
Omission marks between references indicate that a subject is represented intermittently: thus, 4603 . . . 4622.
References are not repeated in subject entries which are immediately preceded by a similarly worded author entry, or immediately followed by a similarly worded title entry (Redruth & Chasewater Rly 1172: *Redruth & Chasewater Rly* 7183).

It is important to remember that although some works have duplicate and occasionally multiple placings within the Scheme it may sometimes still be necessary to refer to a heading in the Index other than the most obvious. In following up information on the Festiniog Railway, for example, it will be found that besides the main group of entries arranged under that heading in L 'Individual Railways' there will be in C3 'Railways in Wales' and in D2 'Narrow Gauge Railways' some works which have contributions to make.
It is hardly possible to index a bibliography so minutely as to include the complete range of subject matter contained within works of a very general nature. As a general rule, whenever a detailed study of a subject is required, it will be found profitable to examine the genus as well as the species (for Steam Locomotives, E7 as well as E8), not forgetting that the 156 items which make up the 'Generalia' section A provide 156 possible sources of information on any and every topic covered by the Bibliography. In cases like the Festiniog, which is an offspring of the marriage of two subject areas, 'Railways in Wales' and 'Narrow Gauge Railways', it will be found advisable to examine the genera from which the subject under survey proceeds.
Research will be facilitated by using the Bibliography in conjunction with a good general history. Among modern books *British Railway History* by C. Hamilton Ellis is unrivalled for subject coverage; *The Railways of Britain* by Jack Simmons, and for social aspects *The Railway Age* by Michael Robbins, both include authoritative annotated guides to the best reading on general and specific subjects.
A full account of the subject coverage of this Bibliography, material represented, and sources used, is given in the Compiler's Introduction (pages 13–20).

Baker, G. P. 1250

BAKER, George Sherston *A Handy Book on the Law of Railway Companies for the use of railway travellers* 5474

BAKER, John Clifford Yorke *The Metropolitan Rly* 910

BAKER, Joseph Allen *The London County Council and the tramways of London* 855
Tramway traction 2196

BAKER, T. *A Battling Life* 4938

BAKER, Thomas *Railway engineering; or, Field work preparatory to the construction of railways* 2547
The Steam Engine; or, The powers of flame 23 7474

BAKER, W. *Report ... with reference to the projected railways to the East and West India Docks and Blackwall* 761 5790

Baker Library, Harvard University Graduate School of Business Administration 391, 397

BAKER STREET & WATERLOO RLY *Baker Street and Waterloo Rly, March 1906. Description* 999

Baker Street Station alterations (1912) 1012

Baker Street Station Buffet [poem] 7482

Bakerloo Line (London underground railways) 999 1004 1118

Balance of transport components: air, rail, road, water 4764

BALD, William *Plan proposed by Sir James C. Anderson and J. W. Rogers, for establishing steam carriages for the conveyance of goods and passengers on the mail coach roads of Ireland* [with a letter at the end by Wm Bald] (1841) 326 1676
Report upon the proposed railways between Dublin, Navan, and Drogheda (1836) 1806

Baldock telpher (aerial cableway) 2390

BALDWIN, A. W. *Studies in Steam* 3071

BALDWIN, M. *Railway claims explained* 5155

Baldwin, Stanley 4588

BALFOUR, Arthur *Le Tunnel sous la Manche et les transports par ferry-boats* 2012

Balfour, Gerald William [2nd Earl of Balfour] 4689

Balfour's Light Railway Act (1889) 1775 2166

BALL, Alan W. *London underground railways (1863–1956). Bibliography* (1956) 914

Ballads and Sonnets (A. Anderson) 7467

BALLANTYNE, Robert Michael *The Iron Horse; or, Life on the line* 4017

BALLARD, Stephen *Cheap railways for rural districts* 2159 5089

BALLAST CORPORATION [Dublin] *Concise statement of the proceedings of the Ballast Corporation and the consequent state of the Harbour* (1833) 1751 1820

BALLEN, Dorothy *Bibliography of Road-making and Roads in the United Kingdom* (1914) 4499

Ballochney Rly 7000

Ballymena & Larne Rly 2155

Baltimore & Ohio Railroad: Centenary Exhibition and Pageant, 1927: Great Western Rly's brochure 6130

BANBURY F. G. *Railways Bill: memorandum by the Chairman of the Great Northern Rly Co.* (1921) 524 4537

Bandon & Crookhaven Rly & Transatlantic Packet Station 1691

Bangor (Caernarvonshire) 6332 7171

Bangor (Ireland) to Belfast: roadway or railway? (1933) 4626

BANISTER, Fred D. *Agreements between the L.B. & S.C.R. and the S.E.R. Co. relating to the use of the London and Redhill lines (1839–1898) ...* 6677 7202
Historical notes in reference to the lines of railway between Redhill and London 6676 7199

BANISTER, Thomas *Memoranda relating to the present crisis as regards our colonies, our trade, our circulating medium, and railways* (1848) 4331

Bankers' warning against speculation (1845) 5230

BANKES, Joyce H. M. *The first Lancashire locomotive* 403

BANKS, Edward *The report of Edward Banks on the practicability of a navigable canal proposed to be made between the Grand Southern Canal*

near Copthorne Common and Merstham, to communicate with the River Thames at Wandsworth by means of the Surrey Iron Railways (1810) 7388

BARANOWSKI, J. J. *Automatic railway signals* 3310
J. Baranowski's patent automaton distant signal 3289
J. Baranowski's patent automaton railway signals 3288

BARBER, L. H. *A family and a railway* 6672

BARBEY, Camille *Le Service actuel des trains rapides* 3875

BARBOUR, George F. *Letter to Edward Cardwell, President of the Board of Trade, on the occasion of his Bill for the prevention of railway accidents* (1854) 4007 4988

Barbox brothers 7533

Barbox Brothers & Co. 7533

BARCLAY, Andrew, Sons & Co. *Instructions for drivers of small locomotives* 2277

BARCLAY, Thomas *The Channel Tunnel* 1986

BARDSLEY, J. R. *The railways of Bolton, 1824–1959* 1331

BARING, Evelyn [1st Earl of Cromer] *The Port of Southampton: its past, present and future* 7345
Wages and Hours Arbitration. Award of the Earl of Cromer [Midland Rly] (1909) 4078

BARKER, Theodore Cardwell *A history of London transport: vol. 1* (1963) 754
A Merseyside town in the Industrial Revolution: St. Helens, 1750–1900 1321

Barking to Aldgate: tram services 822

BARLOW, Crawford *The New Tay Bridge* 2717

BARLOW, Henry Bernouille *A comparative account and delineation of railway engine and carriage wheels* 2758
Description of the outside-cylinder tank engine constructed by Sharp Brothers & Co., of Manchester (1848) 2947
Railway engine and carriage wheels, vol. 2 (1856) 2759

BARLOW, Peter *Experiments on the transverse strength and other properties of malleable iron with reference to its uses for railway bars* (1835) 2600 6436
Report on the weight of rails, the description of chairs and fastenings ... of the Liverpool & Manchester Rly (1837) 2606 6444
Report ... to the Earl of Ripon, President of the Board of Trade, on the atmospheric railway (1842) 329
Second report addressed to the directors and proprietors of the London & Birmingham Rly, founded on an inspection of, and experiments made on, the Liverpool & Manchester Rly (1835) 2606 6444
Treatise on the strength of timber, cast iron, malleable iron, and other materials 2410

Barlow, Peter 313 330 2601–4 2608 2615

BARLOW, Peter William *Comparative advantages of the atmospheric railway system, with an Appendix containing experiments on the Tyler Hill inclined plane of the Canterbury & Whitstable Rly* (1845) 339 7264
A description of the Southwark & City double line of subway, or tunnel (1873) 965
Investigation of the power consumed in overcoming the inertia of railway trains (1848) 354
On the relief of London street traffic, with a description of the Tower Subway (1867) 956 2303 2336
The relief of street traffic (1871) 963 2304
Report to the directors of the South Eastern Rly Co. on permanent way 7274
To the Chairman and directors of the South Eastern Rly on the supply of water to be obtained from the North Kent district (1850) 7275

BARLOW, William Henry *An analytical investigation of the Board of Trade Returns of the capital and revenue of railways in the United Kingdom* (1868) 3434
On the construction of permanent way of railways ... 2612

BARMAN, Christian *Early British railways* 392
An introduction to railway architecture 2687
Next Station 6152
Public transport 2426

BOARD OF TRADE—*continued*
Trade on the schemes for extending railway communication from Newcastle to Berwick (1845) 1375
Report of the Railway Department of the Board of Trade on the schemes for extending railway communication in Scotland (1845) 1555
Reports of the Railway Department of the Board of Trade on schemes for extending railway communications . . . 1845 426–7
Board of Trade (and Railway Department of the Board of Trade) **K 6**. *See also* Commissioners of Railways
accidents (1840–53) 4993
accidents (1874) 4965
accidents (1913–14) 5039–40
agricultural light railways (1894) 2173 5105
and railways **K 6**
and tramways 5437
Board of Trade Returns. *See below* railway returns (statistics)
brakes (1858–9) 3207 3209
brakes (1882) 3233
brakes (1893–1900) 3255
brakes (1894–8) 3251
carriage of explosives (1876) 5082
Departmental Committee on Railway Accounts and Statistical Returns (1910) 3584
Departmental Committee on Ventilation of London Underground Railways (1898) 981 2568
Eastern Union Rly: complaint against the Eastern Counties Rly (1860) 5835
Ebbw Vale case (1907) 4074 6111
gauge and the Gauge Commission (1846). *See* Gauge controversy between railways: Gauge Commission (1846)
goods clearing house for London (1919) 5144
horse railways (1860) 2334
Inspecting Officers: list 5353–4
interference in railway administration (allegations) (1845) 5373 5375
(1864) 5396
(1887) 5422
Irish railways (1845) 1679
light railways: rules (1896–7) 2180 2193
light railways for agriculture (1894) 2173 5105
London, Brighton & South Coast Rly (1883) 6748
opening of railways: requirements of Board of Trade (1892) 5428
private mineral railways and rates relief (1928) 5163
projected railways: (1845) 1268
in Scotland (1845) 1555
in Yorkshire (1845) 1439–40
railway and canal combination (1852) 359
Railway & Canal Traffic Act (1888) 5427
Railway & Canal Traffic Bill (1886–7) 5093 5422
Railway Board (proposal, 1845) 4318
Railway Department. *See* Board of Trade
railway extensions and amalgamations (1845) 427
railway legislation: deputation to the Board of Trade (1857) 4363–4
railway rates: (1886) 3551–2
(1887) 5422
(1889) 5099 5923
sugar (1893) 5103
railway rates control (1886) 4430 **4433**
railway reforms suggested: (1865) 4379
(1887) 4942
(1919) 5141
railway returns (statistics):
(1846–66) 3434
(1853–5) 3419 3421–2
(1858) 447
(1859–65) 452
(1867) 3530
(1870) 2625
(1870–1912) 63 3391
(1873): alleged inaccuracies 5009
(1875) 467
(1890–1906) 3466
(1904) 487
(1910) 492
(1912, 1913, 1916) 522 2074
(1913) 3703
(1913): alleged inaccuracies 519 5439
(1921) 529

features of returns outlined (1921) 4318
records preserved (documents relating to railways) 7889
tramways (1893) 5430
West Hartlepool Harbour & Rly Co. (1860) 7122
working conditions of railwaymen (1913) 4099
Board of Trade (H. L. Smith) 5348
Board of Trade and the Kentish railway schemes (1845) 1256 5373
Board of Trade inquiry into alleged victimisation of Midland Railway employees (National Union of Railwaymen, 1913) 4095
Board of Trade Returns. *See* Board of Trade: railway returns (statistics)
BOAS, Guy *The Underground* [poem] 7492
BOASE, Frederic *Modern English Biography* (1892–1921) 70 (Reprinted, *London: John Cass*, 1965)
Boat services. *See* Water services of railways: ships and boats owned and operated by railways
Boat trains **G 5** 724
Boat trains and Channel packets 724 3924 7331
Boats. *See* Water services of railways: ships and boats owned and operated by railways
Bobrinskoy, [Count] Alexis 5698
BODINGTON, Oliver E. *The Channel Ferry* 3901
The Channel Ferry in 'Jubilee of the Railway News' 3903
Bodleian Library, Oxford 229 231
BODMER, G. R. *The inspection of railway materials* 2418
Bodmin & Wadebridge Rly 1172
in literature 7612
Bodmin & Wadebridge Rly, 1834–1950 6617
BODY, Geoffrey *Light Railway Guide and Time-tables* (1963–) 2274
BOGLE, William R. *Cheap railway travelling* 4859
Nationalisation of railways 4448
Our railways and the zone system fully explained and practically illustrated, as applied to the Caledonian Rly Co. 3671 5664
Railway nationalisation 4453
Boiler explosions (1849) 2945
BOLAS, Thomas *An address to the members of the Railway Congress, London, 1895* 4443
The Chiswick level crossing fatality 5033
Confiscation of all railway property as a leading step in solving the labour problem 4444 5305
Equitable nationalisation of railway property on a constitutional basis 4447
Railway Reform Leaflets nos. 1 to 8 4443
BOLLAND, W. *Railways and the nation; problems and possibilities* 4475
State railways mean more employment 4879
Bolshevik Boards (1920) 4527
BOLTON, William F. *Railwaymen's Diesel Manual* 3139
Bolton: railways 1331 6426
tramways 1308 1312
Bolton & Leigh Rly 5592 (vol. 1) 6335 6376
BOLTON CORPORATION *Railway rates and charges: a general statement concerning rates and charges in operation upon British railways . . .* (1887) 5096
TRANSPORT DEPARTMENT *Abandonment of tramways, 29th March, 1947. Commemoration Dinner* 1308
BONAVIA, Michael R. *The economics of transport* 3507
Inland transport 4723
Lightweight diesel trains 3131
Some aspects of railway capital 3504
BOND, Maurice *Materials for transport history amongst the records of Parliament* 7893
BOND, R. Murray & Company's *Book of Information for railway travellers and railway officials* (1865) 4928 7713
BOND, R. C. *Some aspects of diesel traction* 3135
BOND, S. *A trader looks at transport* 5182
BONHAM, Margaret *Rolliver* 7493
The Train and the Gun 7494
BONNYN, William Wingfield *Seaton's patent safety rail* 2631
BONSER, Kenneth J. *Printed maps and plans of Leeds, 1711–1900* 1480
BONSOR, Noel Reginald Pixell *The Jersey Rly* 1915
Book about Travelling, past and present 32

Book and Programme of the Liverpool & Manchester Railway Centenary 6358
Book of Health 4935
Book of reference [railway surveying] 3405
Book of Routes (British Railways, 1952) 7944
Book of the Grand Junction Rly 6475
Book of the Locomotive 3016
Book of the Railway (J. R. Hind) 84
Book of the Railway (G. E. Mitton) 494 3732
Book of the 'Schools' class 7377
Book of Trains (W. J. Bassett-Lowke and F. E. Courtney) 7868
Book of Trains (A. Williams) 86
Booking office routine 3716 3765
Books, letters, prints and drawings (auction and exhibition catalogues) 7451–6 7823–4 7827 7829
Bookstalls **G 7**
literature 3943 4922
BOON, M. G. *How to construct free state railway and other national and municipal works of utility without loans* 4424
The ABC Railway Parcels Rate Guide versus rates by parcels post 3549
BOOTH, Charles *Life and labour of the people in London* 4060
Improved means of locomotion as a first step towards the cure of the housing difficulties of London 1082 4872
BOOTH, Henry *An account of the Liverpool & Manchester Rly* 313 2608 6402 6404 6449 6458 7094
The carrying question stated in reference to railways and canals; also, considerations on the mode of levying the passenger tax on railways 4300
Chemin de fer de Liverpool à Manchester: notice historique 6404
A letter to His Majesty's Commissioners on railways in Ireland (1836) 1659 6440
A Letter to Lord Campbell on 9 & 10 Victoria cap. 93, being an Act for compensating the families of persons killed by accidents (1854) 4989
Liverpool & Manchester Rly: extracted from 'An account of the Liverpool & Manchester Railway' by H. Booth 6450
Uniformity of time considered especially in reference to railway transit and the operations of the electric telegraph 4816
Booth, Henry 6315
Border Country 7666
BORGHT, Richard van der *Das Verkehrswesen* 47
BORLEY, Harold Vernon *London Transport railways: a list of opening closing and renaming dates of lines and stations* 755
Borley, Harold Vernon 7320
BOROUGH, C. M. *Calendar of the papers of the North Family from Wroxton Abbey* 231
'Borough' Guide to the Maryport & Carlisle Rly 6885
Borrow Bridge 5647–8
BOSCAWEN, Arthur Griffith *The Government and transport* 4701
BOSHART, August *Railway construction and operation* [technical dictionary] 2419
Railway rolling stock [technical dictionary] 3153
Boston, U.S.A.: tramways 2130
BOTT, William Eagle *A letter to Lord Campbell suggesting alterations in the law of rating railways* (1856) 4360
BOTZOW, Hermann S. D. *Monorails* 2391
Bouch, [Sir] Thomas 2738
BOUCHOT, J. C. *Invention de la locomotive par Cugnot* 2813
BOUGHEY, George Fletcher Ottley *Light railways and the effect of recent legislation thereon* (1899) 2199
BOULT, Wilfrid Swanwick *Boult's system of railway signalling* 3318
Signalling without contact 3320
BOULTON, Isaac Watt 2850
BOULTON, William Henry *The railways of Britain: their history, construction and working* 124
BOUND, Arthur F. *A review of the art of signalling* 3336
BOUND, John Arthur *Coastwise shipping and the small ports* 4737
BOURNE, John *A Catechism of the Steam Engine* 2969

Treatise on the steam engine (447) 2964
BOURNE, John C. *Drawings of the London & Birmingham Rly* 6465
The history and description of the Great Western Rly 5930
Bourne, John C. 5944
Bournemouth: tramways 1247
'Bournemouth Belle' train 2781
Bourneville transport 2278
BOUSSON, A. *Observations sur les chemins de fer d'Angleterre* 430
BOUTET, C. *Prevention of railway accidents* 4998
Bowaters' Sittingbourne railway 2302
BOWDLER, T. *An appeal to the public on the subject of Sunday trains on railroads* 4801
BOWEN, Frank Charles *Mail and passenger steamers of the 19th century* 3909
BOWES, Isaac *George Stephenson, the locomotive and the first public railway* 2460
Rails and waterways, George Stephenson . . . 2466
BOWKER, William R. *Management of electric tramways and light railways* 2217
Practical construction of electric tramways 2212
BOX, Charles Edmund *Liverpool Overhead Rly, 1893–1956* 6229
BOX, Frank E. *Gradients, Barnstaple & Ilfracombe branch, Southern Rly* 7368
With the Nine Elms top link to Salisbury 7364
Box Tunnel 2500
Boy at Mugby 7533
BOYD, James Ian Craig *The Festiniog Rly* 5708
The Isle of Man Rly 1910
Narrow-gauge rails in Mid-Wales 1620 2266
Narrow-gauge rails to Portmadoc 1616 2264 5704
BOYDELL, James *Explanatory remarks upon Boydell's patent for propelling locomotive engines* 2329
BOYLE, Edward *The law relating to traffic on railways and canals* 5488
BOYLE, Thomas *Hope for the canals!* 4332
BOYLET, Lionel J. *Eastbourne Tramways* 2407
BOYMAN *Eastern Counties Rly By Dimes & Boyman* (1834) 5789
Boys' Book of British Railways 653
Boy's Book of Locomotives 2988
Boys' Book of Railways 55
Boys' Book of World Railways 144
Boys' Power & Speed Library 647 3084
Brabourne, [Lord] 4433 5422
BRACE, George *1845 national delirium; or Hints on law and rail* 5227
BRACE, Harold W. *A Chronology of Gainsborough's railways* 1353
BRADBURY, Edward *The Dore & Chinley Rly: the Sheffield Independent's gossiping guide to the district* 6956
In the Derbyshire highlands 6574
Midland Rly sketches (By 'Strephon' [pseud. of E. Bradbury]) 6953
BRADFIELD, John Edwin *Mileage duties: case of the stage carriage proprietors* 4373 4927
The public carriages of Gt Britain 360
Street railways or street tramways will be mischievous and dangerous obstructions 847
Tramways or railways on Metropolitan streets will be mischievous and dangerous obstructions and nuisances 844
Bradfield, John Edwin 843 845
Bradford: railways 1144 1439 5592 (vol. 7)
tramways 1450 1456 1476
BRADFORD CORPORATION
The Bradford Picturesque Tram Guide (1903) 1456
Diamond Jubilee, 1898–1958 1476
Queries and replies re tramways 1450
Bradford Picturesque Tram Guide (1903) 1456
Bradford's first railway 5592 (vol. 7)
BRADLAUGH, Charles *The Channel Tunnel: ought the democracy to oppose or support it?* 1972
BRADLEY, Donald Laurence *The locomotives of the London, Chatham & Dover Rly* 7226
The locomotives of the South Eastern & Chatham Rly 7228
BRADLEY, Walter *The present aspect of finance in municipal passenger transport* (1946) 3505

Carter, Kenneth E. 2693

CARTER, S *Railway debentures and the Railway Commissioners* 5298 5411 (5412)
  Railway legislation: a letter to shareholders . . . (1874) 5296
  Railway legislation: letters on the subject of proposed transfer to Railway Commissioners of the power of fixing rates on railways (1874) 5403
  Railway legislation: the railway companies and the Railway Commissioners (1874) 3534 5404

CARTER, W. G. *Post Office (London) Rly* 5550

CARVALHO, Harold Nunes *The Channel Tunnel* 2026

CASE, Albert Haverlock *Port Talbot Rly & Docks. (General information as to facilities, together with a description of the Undertaking)* (1898) 6107

Case against nationalisation: what is best in the public interest? 4704

Case against railway nationalisation (E. A. Pratt) 4494

Case against the nationalisation of transport (British Railway Stockholders' Union) 4538

Case for a tube railway and electrification of the L. & N.E.R. (1947) 1231

Case for electrification of the railways (1935) 2669

Case for nationalization (A. E. Davies) 4530

Case for railway nationalisation (A. E. Davies, 1911, pp. 16) 4483

Case for railway nationalisation (A. E. Davies, 1913, pp. 262) 4492

Case for safeguarding railway employment 4170

Case law: railways **K** 7

Case of Oscar Brodski 7552

Case of Sir Humphrey Mackworth and of the Mine Adventurers . . . (1705) 163

Case of the Cheltenham petitions against the Bill [for the East Gloucestershire Rly] (1862) 6097

Case of the four Group railway companies for a reduction in railway labour costs (Railway Staff Conference, 1932) 4174

Case of the Grand Junction Rly Co. as opponents of the South Union Co. (Grand Junction Rly, 1837) 6447 (6448)

Case of the Leeds & Selby Rly Co., petitioners against the York & North Midland Railway Bill (1836) 7087

Case of the London Dock Company (1825) 759

Case of the Manchester South Union Rly Co. and the Cheshire Junction Rly Co. (Manchester South Union Rly, 1842) 5676 6883

Case of the railways considered (1852) 4984

Case of the Thames & Severn Canal Navigation Company opposing the Cheltenham & Great Western Union Railway Bill (1837) 6020

Case of the Thirteenth Coach 7476

Case of the village of East Acton (1836) 6016

Case of trade and industry against the Report of the Conference on Rail & Road Transport (1932) 4608

Case studies in national planning 605 2670

Cases relating to railways and canals 5462

CASSERLEY, Henry Cyril *British locomotive names of the 20th century* 2914
  Historic Locomotive Pocketbook 2904
  Locomotive Cavalcade 2885
  Locomotives of British Railways:
    Great Western Group 736
    London & North Eastern Group 686
    London, Midland & Scottish Group 699
    Southern Group 723
    Combined edition 2908
  The Midland & Great Northern Rly 1132 6972
  My best railway photographs 7860
  The Observer's Book of Railway Locomotives of Britain 2804
  Service suspended 650 3857
  Veterans of the track 2872

Cassier's Magazine. Electric Railway Number (1899) (Reprinted, 1960) 2200 2309

CASSON, Hugh *An introduction to Victorian architecture* 2685

Cast iron in railway architecture 2686

Cast iron sleepers 2619

CASTLE, Henry James *Contributive value a necessary element in the parochial principle of railway assessments* 4356

Engineering field notes on parish and railway surveying and levelling 2538

A few words to the shareholders of the Eastern Counties Rly Co. (1851) 1130 5818

Practical remarks on the principles of rating as applied to the proper and uniform assessment of railways, gasworks, waterworks . . . 4393

Practical remarks upon the Union Assessment Committee Act, 1862, showing how to apply the principles contained therein to the proper and uniform assessment of railway, gas, and water works . . . 4393

Railway curves 2530

'Castle' class, Great Western Rly 5949 6007 6154

'Castle' saga 6007

'Castles' of the Great Western Rly 6007

Catalogue of an exhibition of early railways: paintings, drawings, prints & books (F. T. Sabin, 1956) 7454

Catalogue of an exhibition of early railways: prints, drawings, books, etc. (F. T. Sabin, 1954) 7453

Catalogue of Books, reports, papers and articles relating to light railways (C. L. Thompson, 1895) 2087

Catalogue of old railway prints, drawings and books (F. T. Sabin, 1952) 7452

Catalogue of the collection of railway relics and modern stock at Faverdale, Darlington, in connection with the Railway Centenary Celebrations (1925) 79 7816

Catalogue of the Hopkins Railway Library 49

Catalogue of the William Barclay Parsons Collection (New York Public Library, 1941) 114

CATCHPOLE, Leslie Thomas *The Lynton & Barnstaple Rly, 1895–1935* 6873

Catechism of the Steam Engine 2969

Caterham Rly 6739 7283 7287

Caterham Rly (J. Spence, 1952) 7218

Caterham Rly [part of the souvenir programme, Caterham Railway Centenary] (J. Spence, 1956) 7223

CATERHAM RAILWAY CENTENARY COMMITTEE *Souvenir Programme of the commemoration of the first centenary of the opening of the Caterham Rly, 1856–1956* 7223

Catering services **G** 7

CATOR, G. H. *Twenty-five years at King's Cross.* (ex.) (p. 16)

Cattle traffic 3833
  entraining at Birkenhead 3842
  London & North Western Rly 6532

Cause and cure of railway labour disputes (1902) 4056

Causes of accidents in the coupling of railway vehicles and related operations, and measures for their prevention (International Labour Office, 1954) 4234

Causes of the explosion of steam engine boilers explained 2945

'CAUTUS' *A second letter to Sir Robert Peel on railway legislation* (1837) 308 5366
  Some words on railway legislation (1837) 5365

Cavan & Leitrim Rly 1801

Caxton Hall Conference (1919) 4117

CAYLEY, George *Essay on the means of promoting safety in railway carriages* 4977

CECIL, Robert Arthur Talbot Gascoyne [Marquis of Salisbury]
  London, Chatham and Dover Railway Arbitration Award (1870, 71) 7298

CEMENT AND CONCRETE ASSOCIATION *Concrete in railway construction* 2579

Centenaries Exhibition, 1852–1952; historical brochure (British Railways) 6248

Centenary celebrations, 9th–13th June, 1947. Brief guide to exhibition of Stephenson relics (Institution of Mechanical Engineers) 2478

Centenary history of the Liverpool & Manchester Rly 6361

Centenary of 'Bradshaw' 7943

Centenary of Crewe Locomotive Works 6781

Centenary of public railways (Stockton-on-Tees Railway Centenary Committee, 1925) 382 7034

Centenary of railway inspection 5353

Centenary of railways (L.M. & S. Rly, 1925) 6767

Centenary of Royal Albert Bridge, Saltash 2739 5997

Centenary of Shildon (L. & N.E. Rly) Institute 6238

DIGBY, W. P. *Statistics of British and American rolling stock* 2067 2763
Digest of English patents relating to propelling cars by traveling ropes or cables 2355
Digest of official statistics: earnings and hours of labour in the railway service, 1907 and later 4091
Digest of the law of carriers of goods and passengers by land and internal navigation 5499
Digest of the realities of the Gt Western Rly 6065
Digest on railway accounts 3468
DIGGES, J. G. *How the Cavan & Leitrim Rly Extension Bill was killed* 1801
Diglis branch, Oxford, Worcester & Wolverhampton Rly 6091
DILLON, James *On the railways of Ireland* 1714
DIMES and BOYMAN *Eastern Counties Rly* 5789
DIMMICK, Luther Fraseur *Discourse on the moral influence of rail-roads* 4806 7762
DIMOCK, Marshall E. *British public utilities and national development* 4623
Dining car services 3848 3856 3944 3951–2
Dining cars on British railways 3848
Diosy, Arthur 1990
DIRCKS, Henry *Account of a patent improved metallic wheel with wood-faced tyre* 2753
Direct Brighton Rly Bill (1836) 7239–40
Direct electric tramway traction with surface construction 2169
Direct London & Brighton Rly. Speech by D. Pollock 6702
Direct London & Brighton Rly. Speech by H. H. Joy 6698
Direct London & Exeter Rly 6232
Direct London & Manchester Rly 1267
Direct London & Manchester Rlys (proposed, 1845) 5229
DIRECT NORTHERN RLY *Comparative distances by Direct Northern, and London & York railways* 5900
Distances by Eastern Counties proposed Cambridge & Lincoln, and Lincoln, York & Leeds District & Independent 5902
Distances by Eastern Counties Extension from Cambridge 5901
The following is an accurate description of the route of this railway 5896
Memorial of the Provisional Committee (1845) 5903
Printed letter, addressed to 'My Lord Duke' concerning their necessity for crossing the Don Navigation by means of a fixed bridge (1845) 5904
Statement of the case and merits of the D N Rly 5897
Direct Northern Rly Co. from London to York 5907
Direct signalling (signalman in box to driver in cab) 3299 3305 3320 3323 3361
Directories **T**
Directors 3714 4365
 criticism of capitalist control (1931–2) 4163 4168
 lists (1841) 7912 (1847) 7915 (1894–1948) 7948 (1850–1948) 7949
Directory of Railway Officials and Year Book 7948
Dirge over the Broad Gauge 7730
Discipline, delays, licences . . . 880
Discomforts of early rail travel **K 2 tc**
Discomforts of excursion trips to Brighton (1863) 4842
Discourse on the moral influence of rail-roads 4806 7762
Discovery of coal near Dover 7308
Discussion Books 568 3502 4665
Discussion on Sabbath trains 4819 7112
Disease control and international travel 2086
DISNEY, Henry William *Law of carriage by railway* 5503
Displacement of the poor by railway construction **K 1 p** 1070–1 7289
Displays, exhibitions and pageants **Q 1**
Disraeli, Benjamin 4384 5840
Dissertation on the history of Traeth Mawr and the industrial results of the formation of the Embankment 5701
Dissolution of railways **F**
Dissolution of uneconomic lines (1846) 4325
Distance tables (general) **T**
Distance tables in miles and yards, Lancashire & Yorkshire Rly 6203

Distances between the stations and junctions of the railways on which the clearing system is in operation 7925
Distances by Eastern Counties extension from Cambridge 5901
Distances by Eastern Counties, proposed Cambridge & Lincoln, and Lincoln, York & Leeds District & Independent 5902
Distress caused by speculation **K 5** 7273
Distribution: a vital factor in sales (London, Midland & Scottish Rly) 6808
Distribution of population by facilities of rapid transit 4875
District Rly. *See* Metropolitan District Rly
District Rly and the London 'Circle' train service 974
'District' Signalman 1025
Diverse et artificiose machine 159
Dividends paid, and highest & lowest prices, 1875–90, of British railways 5303
Divine Service in memory of those railwaymen who laid down their lives for their country in the Great War, 1914–18 509 7936
DIXON, Frank Haigh *War administration of the railways in the United States and Gt Britain* 504 3702 5446
Dixon, John 379 7018
DIXON, Joshua *London, Chatham & Dover Rly: considerations on the position and prospects of the company* 7295
DIXON, Waynman *Intimate story of the origin of railways* 379 7032
DOBELL, Sidney *Young Man's Song* 7539
DOBLE, E. *History of the Eastern Counties Rly in relation to economic development* 5777
DOBSON, C. G. *A century and a quarter: the story of the growth of our business from 1824 to the present day* [Hall & Co.] 7395
Dobson, John H. 3972
Dock railways (owned and operated by port authorities) **D 3**
Docks (owned and operated by railways) **G 5** (1939–45) 597
Docks and inland waterways in Scotland owned by British Transport Commission 3918
Docks and Marine Department 3704 3902
Docks of the Gt Western Rly 6121
Documents of railways: collections in libraries and archives generally: a guide 7894 (7901)
 British Museum 1252 1497 1794 (7900) 5586 (5608) 5688 6311 7259 7884
 British Railways Board 7885 7892 7898–9
 London School of Economics 58 5599
 Parliament 7893
 Public Record Office 7889
Documents to be sent to the Railway Dept, Board of Trade previously to the second notice of the intention to open a railway being given 5415
DODD, A. H. *Industrial revolution in North Wales* 1608
Dodd, Barrodall Robert 7058
DODD, Cyril *Law relating to light railways* 2180
DODD, George *Railways, steamers and telegraphs* 29
Dodds, Isaac 2846
DODDS, J. K. *Gravity marshalling yards* 3844
DODDS, John *Railway reform a public necessity* 1705 4389
Dodds, Thomas Weatherburn 2846
DODGSON, G. *Illustrations of the scenery on the line of the Whitby & Pickering Rly* 7085
DODSHON, Edward *Memorandum on maximum railway rates for coal* 3568
DODSON, Gerald *Road and rail traffic law* 5508
DOHERTY, J. M. *Diesel railway traction* 2807
DOLLFUS, C. *Histoire de la locomotion terrestre: les chemins de fer* 97
DOLPHIN, Mary I. E. *More songs from the moorland* 7540
Dombey & Son (7495) 7530
DONCASTER CORPORATION *Story of Doncaster Corporation Transport, 1902–1952* 1467
Doncaster Gazette 5919
Doncaster Locomotive & Carriage Plant Works 6269
Doncaster Railway Works 2975 5589
Donegal: railways 1749–50

European Economic Community: transport policy 5204

European transport: the way to unity 2084

European War (1914–1918). *See* Great War (1914–18)

Euston and Crewe Companion 6790

Euston re-signalling (1952) 693

Euston Road: subsidence caused by the Metropolitan Rly (1885) 975

Euston Sleepers 7575

Euston (Euston Grove, Euston Square) Station 3265 6313 6367 6543
  bookstall 3945
  exhibition 7828 7831
  in literature 7647

Euston Station: a brief historical sketch 700

Euston to Heysham: a journey in fiction 7572

Euston to Watford electric train services 6391 6600

EVANS, Alfred Dudley *British railways and goods traffic: is the foreigner preferred?* 5108
  History and economics of transport 3397
  Transport: its history and economics 3397

EVANS, David Morier *The commercial crisis, 1847–48* 5261
  Facts, failures and frauds 5515

EVANS, Eric Jones *Death on the Line* 7549
  The Post Office (London) Rly: its equipment and operation 5546

EVANS, Frederick W. *Railway servants: an appeal to Parliament and the public* 4021

EVANS, George Heberton *British corporation finance, 1775–1850* 5212

EVANS, Gilmore *A treatise on the Railway & Canal Traffic Act, 1854* 5469

Evans, John *Lancashire authors and orators* 6426

EVANS, Martin *Atlantic Era: the British atlantic locomotive* 2909
  Manual of Model Steam Locomotive Construction 7858
  Pacific Steam: the British pacific locomotive 2910

EVANS, Walton W. *The Abt system of railway for steep inclines* 2358
  American v. English locomotives 2050 2968
  Extracts from English engineers' reports. [With] *A letter on the railway gauge question* 3669

'Evening Star' (last steam locomotive to be built by British Rlys) 3093

EVERARD, F. E. Welby *Light railways in Great Britain* 2225

EVERETT, J. *Panorama of Manchester and Railway Companion* 6434

EVERS, Henry *Steam and the steam engine: land, marine and locomotive* 2819

EVERSLEY, David Edward Charles *The Great Western Rly and the Swindon Works in the Great Depression* 5992
  The Great Western Rly Works, Swindon 5998

Every Traveller's Guide to the Railways of England, Scotland, Ireland, Belgium, France & Germany 7913

Everyday knowledge in pictures 2317

Everyday life on the railroad 4048

Evidence and opinions on the harbour of Valencia, Ireland, as to its fitness for a Western packet station 1889

Evidence concerning the High Level Bridge over the Tyne at Newcastle 1380 7115

Evidence given before the Committee of the House of Commons on the London & Brighton Railways on the subject of tunnels (1837) 4797 6709 7317

Evidence given before the Select Committee of the House of Commons on Observance of the Lord's Day (1832) 4793

Evil effects of Sabbath travelling proved by an appeal to facts, in a correspondence with the editor of the 'Scotsman' and a series of letters to the editor of the 'Daily Review' 4845

Evils of a diversity of gauge, and a remedy 4321

Evolution of L.N.E.R. locomotives 6233

Evolution of permanent way 216 390 2593

Evolution of railway vehicle suspension 2742

Evolution of railways (C. E. Lee) (162) 216 (232) 390 2593

Evolution of railways in the Wirral Peninsula 1198

Evolution of the locomotive engine (W. P. Marshall) 2833

Evolution of the locomotive engine (T. West) 2836

Evolution of the railway network of South East England 1156 7332

Evolution of the steam locomotive, 1803 to 1898 2834

Evolution of the Tube ticket office 915–16

EWALD, Kurt *20000 Schriftquellen zur Eisenbahnkunde* 113

EWEN, Herbert L'Estrange *History of railway letter stamps* 5521
  Priced Catalogue of the railway letter stamps of the U.K. 5522
  Railway newspaper and parcel stamps of the U.K. issued from 1855 to October 1906 5523
  Reference List of railway letter post stamps 5520

EWING, J. A. *Electric railways* 2306

Examen comparatif de la question des chemins de fer en 1839 en France et à l'etranger, et de l'intervention du gouvernement dans la direction et l'exécution des travaux 5368

Examination examined 7233

Examination into the respective merits of the proposed canal and iron railway from London to Portsmouth 1158

Examination of Prof. Barlow's reports on iron rails 2601

Examination of the 'Reply for the directors' of the Edinburgh, Leith & Newhaven Rly Co. 5697

Examples of preferential railway rates given on foreign sugar imported into this country (1893) 5103

Examples of station buildings and their cost 2709

Examples of the modes of setting out railway curves 2544

Excavating **E 2**

Exceptional freight: London & North Eastern Rly 6265

Exceptional rates: guide to traders (1927) 5160

Exchange Essays, no. 1 2128

Exchange Station, Manchester (London, Midland & Scottish Rly): re-signalling (1930) 3351

'Exchequer bill currency' for railway investments (proposal, 1846) 5245

Excluded publications pp. 15–16

Exclusive Railway Photographs. First Catalogue (Locomotive Publishing Co.) 7876

Excursion from Glasgow to Blair Atholl: engine, Highland Rly 4–6–0 no. 103 6170

Excursion traffic working **G 3**. *See also* Sunday trains (social and religious controversy)

Excursion train. The first excursion train (5 July, 1841) 4861

Excursion trains and services **G 3**

Excursion trips to Brighton, 1863: discomforts 4842

Excursions in Yorkshire by the North Eastern Rly 1443

Exemption of street railways, called tramways, from the railway passenger duty 5420

Exeter & Exmouth Rly 6644 6653

Exeter to Taunton (proposed Grand Western Railroad, 1825) 1392

Exeter, Yeovil & Dorchester Railway Bill 1171 6639 6643–4

Exhibited machinery of 1862: a cyclopaedia of the machinery represented at the International Exhibition 2761

Exhibition of freight rolling stock (1952) 3200

Exhibition of locomotive 'Southern Maid' 7188

Exhibition of locomotives, carriages, wagons and engineering plant at Willesden (1954) 2780

Exhibition of prints . . . in connection with Southampton Docks Centenary 7322

Exhibition of Railway Civil Engineering (1950) 2516

Exhibitions, displays, and pageants **Q 1**

Exide batteries for shunting locomotives 3104

Experience of British railways under war control 501 5444

Experiences of a railway guard 4094

Expériences sur la force transversale et les autres propriétés du fer malléable dans son application aux chemins de fer . . . 2600 6436

Experimental inquiry into the advantages attending the use of cylindrical wheels on railways 327

'Experimental' period in British railway history (1800–1830 . . . 1850) **B 2**

Experimental trip of the 'Great Western' new locomotive passenger engine (1846) 3648 6049

KNOWLES, G. *Observations on the expediency of making a line of railroad from York to Scarborough* 7100

KNOWLES, G. W. *Handbook on railways* 527

KNOWLES, James *The Channel Tunnel and public opinion* 1968

KNOWLES, L. C. A. *Industrial and commercial revolutions in Great Britain during the 19th century* 4261 5049

KNOWLMAN, B. *Report of an unofficial traffic survey: Southern Region, Western Section* 720

KNOX, C. *The Un-beaten Track* 584 6146

KOCHER, Ethel Madeleine *British railway catering* 3951

KOEHLER, G. *Lehrbuch der Bergbaukunde* 200

KOLLMANN, G. A. *Some observations on the imperfections of the present system of constructing railways* 2524 3166

KONSTAM, E. M. *Railway rating: law and procedure* 4625

Kress Library of Business and Economics, no. 3 391

KRUGER, J. A. *Design and operation of marshalling yards* 3835

KU, Chuan Hui *Railway station planning in Great Britain* 2689

L., J. F. *Train lighting by electricity* 3157

L., W.C. *The Railway Passenger* 7684

L. & N.W.R. 4-cylinder 4–4–0 compound passenger engines and the 2-cylinder 'Renown' class simples 6365

L. & N.W. Rly from 1830 to the present time: reproduced from the L. & N.W. series of pictorial postcards 6351

L. & S.W. Rly locomotives, 1872–1923 6616

L. B. & S.C.R. (O. J. Morris) 6688

L. B. & S.C.R. locomotives: an up-to-date survey from 1870 6685

'L.B.S.C.' [pseud. of L. Lawrence] *How to build 'Princess Marina'* 7849
  Live Steam Book 7855
  Maisie: words and music 7854
  Shops, Shed and Road 7846

L.C.C. Tramways (C. W. Matthews) 884

L.C.C. Tramways, and London electricity supply 878

L.M.A. Handbook 2791

L.M.R. Locomotive Reference Book 6861

L M S answers your questions 617

L M S at war 592 6845

L M S Book of the Train 6773 6829 6834

L M S centenary of opening of first main line railway 6777

L M S control: the magic wand of transport 6800 7817

L M S country lorry services 6814

L M S getting back to normal (1946) 6842

L.M.S.: its railways and its hotels 6803

L M S locomotives in colour 6849

L M S numbers, names and classes: L N E R second re-numberings: stock changes, L N E R, G W R, S R 3054

L.M.S.R. diesel-electric shunting locomotives 3124

L.M.S.R. locomotive casualty report system 3048 6838

L.M.S.R. Locomotive Reference Book 6861

L.M.S.R. modernised traffic control organisation 6847

L M S railhead storage and distribution, and other services 6806

L M S Research Laboratory, Derby: official opening ceremony (1935) 6823

L M S Route Books (*Who Runs may Read series*) 6834 6854–8

L.M.S. School of Transport, Osmaston Park, Derby. Official opening ceremony 6833

L.M.S. Works Training School 6850

L.N.E.R. and British Railways 6253

L.N.E.R. locomotives, 1938 6280

L.N.W.R. eight-coupled goods engines 6373

L.P.T.B. (London Passenger Transport Board) *See* London Transport

L.S.E. *See* London School of Economics

L.S.W.R. and Salisbury 6619

L.T.E. (London Transport Executive). *See* London Transport

LABELYE, Charles de. *See* De Labelye, Charles

Laboratory work by railways **G 8**

Labouchere, Henry 4302 4343 5391

Labour and capital on the railways 3392 3975

Labour and politics, 1900–1906 3992

Labour conditions. *See* Railwaymen: work and working conditions

Labour Discussion Series, no. 10 4716

Labour disputes. *See* Railwaymen: work and working conditions

Labour/management relations. *See* Railwaymen: work and working conditions

Labour organization on British railways 3704

LABOUR PARTY *British transport* 4750
  Fighting the Government for a guinea a week 4090
  National planning of transport 4610
  Notes on Tory transport policy 4741
  Post-war organisation of British transport (1943) 606 4683
  Transport for the nation 621 4718
  RESEARCH AND INFORMATION DEPARTMENT *Electricity interests and the L.C.C. Tramways* 886

Labour Party 1104–5 2011 (3992) 4268 4588 4656 4681 4684 4690 4716 4740–1
  policy: criticisms 658 1106
  See also Socialism and railways

Labour problems. *See* Railwaymen: work and working conditions

Labour relations in London Transport 1062

Labour relations on the railways, 1835–1875 3985

LABOUR REPRESENTATION COMMITTEE *Why our railways should be nationalised* 4452

Labour Representation Committee 3992

LABOUR RESEARCH DEPARTMENT *Fair play for railwaymen* 4228
  Justice for railwaymen: can the companies afford it? 4198
  Labour and capital on the railways 3392 3975
  London fares 3625
  The London Traffic Combine 1109 4611
  The National Wages Board and after 4177
  Railways for the nation 3396 4694
  Report to the N.U.R. on publicity work undertaken in connection with the recent strike, October 6, 1919 4115
  Transport robbery: exposure of Tory plan 639 4742
  Wages and profits on the railways 4169

Labour Research Department 3493 3495 4168 4181
  See also Fabian Research Department *and* New Fabian Research Bureau

Labour White Papers 4169 4177

Labouring classes: displacement by railway construction **K 1 p** 1070

Labour's right to combine 4046 6588

LABRYN, P. *Internal combustion locomotives and motor coaches* 3120

Lacey's Railway Companion and Liverpool & Manchester Guide (A. Freeling, 1836) 6441

Lady Charlotte Guest: extracts from her journal, 1833–1852 393

Lady clerks 4110

LAHORE Gabriel-Placide *Projet de construction d'une chaussée avec ou sans tunnel de Calais à Douvres* 1942

LAIGHT, J. C. *The economics of inland transport* 3509

LAING, Austen *The obligation to carry* 4758

LAING, John *The railway dilemma* 5291

LAING, Samuel *Audit of railway accounts: letter to the proprietors of the L.B. & S.C.Rly Co.* 3417 4348
  Letter to the working men in the employment of the L.B. & S.C.Rly Co. on the present contest between the Amalgamated Society of Engineers and the employers (1852) 6735
  Observations on Mr. Strutt's amended Railway Regulation Bill now before Parliament (1847) 5386
  Railway taxation 4339 6732

LAING ART GALLERY [Newcastle upon Tyne] *George Stephenson Centenary Exhibition* (1948) 2482

LAKE, Charles Sidney *Locomotive management: cleaning, driving, maintenance* 3086
  The locomotive simply explained 3034
  Locomotives of 1906 2989
  Locomotives of 1907 2992
  The world's locomotives 2984

Nine Elms Locomotive Depot workings 7364
Nine Elms wharfs and warehouses (1853) 5075 6651
Nine lives of Citizen Train 2097
1914–1918 (railways during the Great War). *See*
　Great War (1914–18)
1918–23 (period). *See* Post-war recovery (1918–23)
1919 railway strike and the settlement of January
　1920 4123
1920's and 1930's (period) **B 6**
1930's (period) **B 6**
1940's (period) **B 7, B 8, B 9, B 10**
1945–1947 (period). *See* Post-war recovery (1945-47)
1951 Design Congress (Council of Industrial Design)
　2736
Nineteen Hundreds, being the story of the
　Buckinghamshire towns of Wolverton and Stony
　Stratford during the years 1900–1911 1183
Nineteenth century (period) **B 2, B 3**
Nineteenth Century and after [a periodical] 507
　1103 3598 4519 4640
Nineteenth century railway carriages in the British
　Isles 3186
Nippers (ticket nippers) 3582
NIXON, Charles *Description of the tunnels situated*
　between Bristol and Bath on the Great Western
　Rly 6031
NIXON, Frank *Notes on the engineering history of*
　Derbyshire 1214
NNOKES, George Augustus. *See* Nokes, George
　Augustus
No atomic trams yet, he says 7578
No Continuing City [poem] 7490
No more interest to pay upon debenture debts . . .
　(By M. N., 1861) 5283
'No poetry in railways! foolish thought . . .' 7598
NOBLE, Celia Brunel *The Brunels, father and son*
　5970
[NOBLE]. JOHN NOBLE & CO. *City of Dublin*
　Tramway 1754
　Drawing and description of the Crescent Rail; also,
　　an article on street railways 2129
　Facts respecting street railways 2130
　Liverpool tramways: explanatory statement and
　　map (1866) 1277
　Metropolitan tramways and omnibus
　　misrepresentations: a reply to Mr. Bradfield's
　　pamphlet on tramways or railways on
　　Metropolitan streets (1867) 845
　Metropolitan tramways: explanatory statement and
　　map, proving the advantages of tramways . . .
　　(1867) 846
　Observations upon Mr. Bradfield's pamphlet on
　　tramways or railways on metropolitan streets
　　(1866) 843
　Street tramways as they will affect the ordinary
　　users of the roads and householders: a reprint of
　　a pamphlet recently issued by the London General
　　Omnibus Company, with observations thereon
　　(1868) 2134
　Tramways as a means of facilitating the street
　　traffic of the Metropolis 842
Noble science: a few general ideas on foxhunting 4803
NOCK, Oswald Stevens *Boy's Book of British*
　Railways 653
　Branch lines 2106
　British locomotives at work 3061
　British locomotives from the footplate 3076
　British railway construction and operation: no. 1,
　　semaphore signals 3362
　British railways in action 3887
　British steam railways 148
　British trains, past and present 2746
　The Caledonian Rly 5636
　Father of Railway: the story of George
　　Stephenson 2489
　Fifty years of railway signalling 3276
　Fifty years of Western express running 5988
　Four thousand miles on the footplate 3083
　The Great Northern Rly 5889
　The Great Western Rly: an appreciation 5982
　The Great Western Rly in the 19th century 6004
　The Great Western Rly in the 20th century 6008
　Historical steam locomotives 2902
　The 'Kings' and 'Castles' of the Great Western Rly
　　6154
　The locomotives of R. E. L. Maunsell, 1911–1937
　　7328

The locomotives of Sir Nigel Gresley 6241
Locomotives of the L.N.E.R.: standardisation and
　renumbering 6298
Locomotives of the North Eastern Rly 7042
Locomotives of the Premier Line in pictures 6374
The London & North Western Rly 6386
Main lines across the Border 1496
The Premier Line: the story of London & North
　Western locomotives 6374
The railway engineers 2441
The Railway Race to the North 1495
The Railways of Britain, past and present 122
Scottish railways 1518
Signalling from the driver's point of view 3366
The South Eastern & Chatham Rly 7230
Steam locomotive: a retrospect of the work of eight
　great locomotive engineers 2890
The steam locomotive in traffic 2807
Steam locomotive: the unfinished story of steam
　locomotives and steam locomotive men on the
　railways of Gt Britain 2895
William Stanier: an engineering biography 6796
NOKES, George Augustus *Railway control by*
　railway stockholders, not by railway directors
　(By G. A. Nnokes) 3705. *See also* Sekon,
　George Augustus [pseud. of G. A. Nokes]
Non-paying services: the public's view 4905
Non-stop runs by trains in Gt Britain, 1845–1928
　3859
NORDMANN, Hans *Die Frühgeschichte der*
　Eisenbahnen 220
Norfolk: tramways 1363
Norfolk Chronicle 5805
Norfolk Rly 5779 5805 5809 5814 5818
NORMAN, L. G. *The health of London's travelling*
　public 4964
NORMINGTON, Thomas *The Lancashire &*
　Yorkshire Rly 6184
NORRIE, Charles Matthew *Bridging the years: a*
　short history of British civil engineering 2518
NORRIS, J. E. *The railways of Worcester* 1435
NORRIS, J. T. *A Guide to the Eastern Counties Rly*
　containing an account of the rise and progress of
　the company . . . (1839) 5800
NORRIS, John *The Stratford & Moreton Tramway*
　1142
　Waterways to Stratford 1142
NORRIS, W. *Address to the Southampton Chamber*
　of Commerce upon a direct communication by
　railway and steam ferry between Southampton
　and South Wales 1162
NORRIS, W. S. *Railways: the object is to achieve*
　the largest number of the cleanest, most
　comfortable, fastest and cheapest trains
　throughout the country 4734
Norris locomotives in England, 1838–1842 2877
North [family] 177 229 231
North, Francis [Baron of Guilford] 177 229 1371
NORTH, Roger *The life of Francis North* 177 1371
North American Review 2068
North British and Glasgow & South Western
　amalgamation (Glasgow Chamber of Commerce,
　1890) 1577
NORTH BRITISH LOCOMOTIVE COMPANY
　History of the North British Locomotive Co.
　2888
　Locomotives for narrow gauge railways 2258
　North British Locomotive Company. An account of
　　the manufacture of locomotives and war material,
　　1914–1919 3011
NORTH BRITISH RLY *Epistles of Peggy written*
　from Scotland (1910) (ex.)
　Souvenir of the opening of the North British Station
　　Hotel, Edinburgh (1902) 7010
North British Rly **L** (historical 6982–6988:
　contemporaneous 6989–7010; and in collective
　works 5582 . . . 5608)

Constituent railways are indexed separately

accidents 4969 4974. *See also* Tay Bridge *and*
　Tay Bridge Disaster
and Newcastle (1861) 7006
and the Caledonian Rly (1858) 7004
and the Glasgow & South Western Rly (proposed
　transfer to the North British, 1889–90) 1577–8
　5663 5729
and the London & North Western Rly (1861) 7006

Publicity: railway facilities **G 6**
Publicity (essay, by A. Adams) 7801
Publicity Department 3929
'PUBLICOLA' *Letter to a Member of Parliament on the subject of the proposed Manchester & Birmingham Extension Rly* (1839) 6474
'PUBLICUS' *Stroud & Severn Rail Road* . . . 1236
PUDNEY, John *The Hartwarp Light Rly* (1963) (*ex.*)
   The Thomas Cook story 3858
Puffin Cut-Out Book 2401 7750
Puffin Picture Books 2432 3060 7868
'Puffing Billy' and the prize 'Rocket' (*ex.*)
Pullman and perfection 3855
PULLMAN CAR COMPANY *The story of the Pullman organisation* 3851
Pullman Car Company 3190 3952
Pullman Car Company (F. D. M. Harding) 3861
Pullman cars **E 12** 3181 3851 3855 3863
Pullman in Europe 3863
Pullman Review (L.C.C., 1932) 892
Pullman train services **G 3**
PULLON, J. T. *Description of the proposed elevated single rail railway to Roundhay Park* 1452 2361
PUNCH *Elegy written in railway station* 7674
  . *Epitaph on a Locomotive* 7674
   Mr. Punch's Railway Book 7678
   Railroad nursery rhyme 7674
   Railway Gilpin 7674
   Railway of Life 7674
   Railway Traveller's Farewell to his Family 7674
Punch Library of Humour 7678
'Punch's Railway' [the West London Rly] 319 964 2409 6363
Punch's Under-study 7612
Punctuality of trains. *See* Unpunctuality of trains
Purchase of railways by the state (E. H. S. Stanley) 4442
Purchase of the railways by the state (T. Lea) 4408
PURVIS, R. *Sir William Arrol: a memoir* 2731
PYM, Jethro *Iron Ways, bridges, rails and rolling stock: cheap transit combined with steam farming* 5074

Quaint Story of Steam 7728
Quaker Journal (W. Lucas) 1250
Quaker Robins 7618
Quakers and railways. *See* Friends (Quakers) and railways
Quakers in commerce 109
Quarry wagonways (early) **B 1**
Quarterly Journal of Science 4406
Quarterly Review 4518
Quartermaster-General's Office, Horse Guards 5558
Queen Mary of the Iron Road 589 6785
Queen of Scots (G. F. Allen) 2781
'Queen of Scots' new Pullman-de-luxe all steel trains (L. & N.E. Rly) 6261
Queen's Highway . . . 1712
Queer scenes of railway life 7726
Queries and replies re tramways (Bradford Borough Council) 1450
Quest for Crisis 1747 4773b
QUESTED, John *Treatise on railway surveying and levelling* 2536
Question du Tunnel sous la Manche 1922
Question of railway organisation 3729
Question of the Age: how to avert the horrors of a general war (1877) 4417
Question of the gages commercially considered 3654
Quick Spotter Book series 3070 3074
Quicker way to London Airport 4753
QUILLER-COUCH, Arthur T. *A Corrected Contempt* 7612
   The Cuckoo Valley Rly 7612
   Delectable Duchy 7612
   The Destruction of Didcot 7613
   In the Train 7612
   Pipes in Arcady 7614
   Punch's Under-study 7612
QUIN, Michael Joseph *Letter to the House of Commons on railways in Ireland* (1839) 1671

R., L. G. *Is home trade in home productions worth having?* 5101
R.C.A. and its path of progress 4154
R.C.H. (*Railway Clearing House*): *what it is and what it does* 3688
RADCLIFFE, Frederick Peter Delmé *Noble science* 4803
RADCLIFFE, Garnett *On the Irish Mail* 7615
Radcliffe, Joshua 6204
RADCLYFFE, E. *Six views on the Dublin & Drogheda Rly* 1809
RADFORD, George *State services* 4510
Radial system 2337
Radio communication in industrial railway operation 2287
Radio dramatisation of railways in wartime 585
RAE, W. Fraser *The business of travel* 3846
RAIDABURGH, G. P. *Origin and development of the railway rail* 2589
Rail: its origin and progress 13
Rail-air-plan (Railway Companies Association, 1944) 4689
Rail and highway competition in England 4676
Rail and platform plans of British stations 2580
Rail and road statistics (F. A. A. Menzler) 4733 7882
Rail and road transport: speech at L.M.S. Annual General Meeting, 1937 (J. C. Stamp) 4652
Rail and the electric telegraph 12
Rail and the Rod 4850
Rail and waterway competition: pleasing dividends 1694
Rail coaches. *See* Railcars
Rail formations 2650-1
Rail laying **E 3**
Rail modernisation (Financial Times, 1958) 673
Rail/road competition *See* Road/rail relationships
Rail Speed Pocket Chart 3885
Rail transport (H. M. Hallsworth) 5178
Rail transport at particular periods **B**
Rail transport in particular areas (general history and description of railways and tramways) **C**
Rail transport industry 559
Railcar, 1847–1939 2107
Railcar progress around the British Isles 3142
Railcar service, Birmingham to Cardiff, Great Western Rly (1934) 6141
Railcars (rail coaches) 357 2094–5 2221 2240 3020 3024 3027 3029 3031 3142
   Great North of Scotland Rly 5872
Railhead distribution, Great Western Rly (1929) 6135
Railhead distribution (Great Western Rly) 6138
Railings, gates and fences for railways 3375
Raillery on a very peculiar species of railway legislation (1843) 7256
Railplane system 2379 2383–5 2387
   London suburbs (proposed, 1935) 2387
   Ribble Bridge (proposed, 1928) 1300
Railplane system of transport 2387
Railroad [poem] (W. Barnes) 7475
Railroad accounting in America versus England 2068 3470
Railroad Alphabet (1889) 7727
Railroad Book of England 7919
Railroad Children (C. M. Yonge?) 7672
Railroad considered in a moral and religious point of view 7694
Railroad Eclogues 7697
Railroad Guide from London to Birmingham (J. Thomas, 1839) 6480
Rail-road impositions detected; or, Facts and arguments, being an exposé of the estimates for the Grand Northern Rly 5219 5739
Railroad impositions detected; or, Facts and arguments to prove that the Manchester & Liverpool Rly has not paid 1% nett profit . . . 5218 5582 6432
Railroad in literature 7458
Railroad Medley (poem, H. F. Brown) 7497
Railroad mismanagement, its evils and remedy 3423
Railroad Monthly Journal 1675
Railroad nursery rhyme (Punch, 1850) 7674
Railroad problem 5408
Railroad transportation: its history and its laws 5477
Railroadiana (An essay, by J. C. Squire) 7771
Railroadiana: a new history of England 4799 6459

RAISTRICK, Arthur *Dynasty of iron founders . . .* 227
RALPH, Henry *Railway days and railway ways* 5947
Rambles on railways 454
RAMELLIS, Augustini de *Diverse et artificiose machine* (1588, 1620) 159
RAMMELL, T. W. *New plan for street railways* 2330
Rammell, T. W. 2338
Ramp operated cab signal 3299
RAMSAY, James A. B. [Lord Dalhousie]. *See* Dalhousie, [Earl of]
Ramsbottom, John 2863 2890
RANDALL, F. Oliver *Hundred of Hoo Rly* 7224
RANDALL, J. *Handbook to the Severn Valley Rly* 6098
RANDELL, Wilfrid L. *Messengers for mankind* 5529
   Quaker Robins 7618
Randell, William 2491
Random hints on railways and railway legislation 1257 3411 5390
Rank bad planning of London Transport 1118
RANKINE, David *Popular exposition of the effect of forces applied to draught . . .* 271
RANKINE, William John Macquorn *Experimental inquiry into the advantages attending the use of cylindrical wheels on railways* 327
Ransome, James 109
RANSOME-WALLIS, Patrick *All about locomotives and trains and your camera* 7863
   Concise Encyclopaedia of World Railway Locomotives 2807
   Gas turbine in railway service 2807
   Horizon Book of Railways 151
   Locomotives through the lens 3068
   Men of the footplate 3988
   My best railway photographs 7860
   On engines in Britain and France 3091
   On railways, at home and abroad 146 1893 6863 7227 7809
   Organization of a steam motive power depot 2807
   Snowdon Mountain Rly 7198
   Unconventional forms of motive power 2807
   The world's smallest public railway: the R.H. & D. 7191
RANSOMES & RAPIER *The tramway nuisance and its true remedy* 2153
Rapid-acting Vacuum Brake and its successes 3254
Rapid transit in the future 784 2376
Rapidly Round the Bend 7754
RAPIER, Richard Christopher *On the fixed signals of railways* 3301
Rapport sur le chemin de fer établi suivant le système atmosphérique de Kingstown à Dalkey 1831
RASTRICK, J. M. *See* Rastrick, John Urpeth
RASTRICK, John Urpeth *Liverpool & Manchester Rly. Report on the comparative merits of locomotive and fixed engines as a moving power* 6402
   Rainhill Notebook 6361
   Report [to the Manchester & Cheshire Junction Rly] (1836) 6875
   West Cumberland, Furness & Morecambe Bay Railway. Report on the intended line of railway from Lancaster to Maryport, via Furness and Whitehaven (1839) 1152
   West Cumberland, Furness & Morecambe Bay Rly. Reports (1838) 1151
Rastrick, John Urpeth 1152 6409 6875
Rates **F 1**. *See also* Rating of railways (taxation)
   and agricultural marketing costs (1906) 5110 5112–13
   and the cost of living (and food) 3609
   aspect of railway administration **F 1**
   consignor aspects **K 4**
   government control 5403–4 5411 5455
   international comparisons 2058 3591 3619 5094–5
   revision (1925) 5156
Rates charged by British railway companies in respect of the carriage of foreign & colonial farm, dairy & market garden produce: the railway companies' case 3574
Rates, charges, fares and tolls **F 1**
Rates of carriage to and from Liverpool (1865) 1276 3528

Rates of pay and conditions of service: claims for modifications referred, January 1931 (National Wages Board) 4166
Rates of pay and conditions of service of British Railways salaried staffs (T.S.S.A., 1953, 1956) 4244
Rates of pay and conditions of service of conciliation grades (N.U.R., 1927) 4146
Rates of pay and conditions of service of locomotive and electric trainmen (A.S.L.E.F., 1953) 4227
Rates of pay and conditions of service of railway operating staff, 1907–1922 (G.W. Rly) 4135
Rates of pay and conditions of service of railway salaried and conciliation staff (N.U.R., 1950) 4213
Rates of pay and conditions of service of railway workshop staff (Confederation of Shipbuilding & Engineering Unions, 1945) 4202
Rates of pay and conditions of service of railway workshop staff and railway electrical staff (N.U.R., 1953) 4230
RATHBONE, Hannah Mary *Letters of Richard Reynolds, with a memoir of his life* 187
RATHBONE, S. G. *Tramways. Report of special committee appointed by the Council [Liverpool Borough Council]* (1874) 1281
Rating of railways (taxation) **K** 3704
   (1864 to 1914) 4256
   and poor relief **K 1** 4340–1
   Great Western Rly 4576 7739
   international comparisons 4418
   London & South Western Rly and Mitcheldever parish 6636
   relief for private mineral lines (1928–9) 5163 5165
Rating of railways (G.W. Rly) 4472
Rating of railways (C. Penfold) 4308
Rating of railways (E. Ryde) 4392
Rating of railways in England and Wales compared with the railways in Ireland and the effects of the parochial principle of rating 4418
Rating of railways: statement of the railway interest handed to Mr. Lewis 4341
Rating of railways: the G.W.R. and Tilehurst parish 4350
Rationale of railway administration 4322
Rationalisation of the railways (The Beeching Plan, 1963) 4773
Rationalization of British railways 567 3501 3769
'Ratty': a history of the Ravenglass & Eskdale Rly 7181
RAVEN, [Sir] Vincent Litchfield *Railway electrification and electric locomotives* 2664
   Report with reference to the working of compound engines compared with the working of other classes of engines on the N.E. Rly 7136
Raven, [Sir] Vincent Litchfield 3101 6243
Ravenglass & Eskdale Narrow Gauge Rly 7180
RAVENGLASS & ESKDALE RLY *Handbook* (1962) 7182
Ravenglass & Eskdale Rly 2270 7180–3
Ravensworth wagonway, Tanfield 217
Raw materials: freight handling, holding and storage by railways (1952) 5192
Rawlinson, Robert 4000
RAWSON, William *Address to the shareholders of the Lancashire & Yorkshire Rly Co. on the present crisis in their affairs* (1848) 6200
   Diary of a director 6556
Rawtenstall: tramways 1329 1336
RAWTENSTALL BOROUGH COUNCIL *Golden Jubilee of the Rawtenstall Corporation Transport Department, 1908–1958* 1329
RAYMOND, S. E. *Selling transport* 3941
RAYNES, J. R. *Engines and men* 3973
Re Driver Gourlay, concerned in the Arbroath disaster . . . Report of proceedings taken by the A.S.R.S. for his defence 4071
REA, Samuel *Railways terminating in London* 777
REACH, Angus Bethune *The Comic Bradshaw; or, Bubbles from the Boiler* 7701
READER, E. R. *The British coasting trade* 4648
Readers' Guide to Books on Transport (Library Association—County Libraries Section, 1950) 125
Reading (Berkshire): station bookstall 3945
   tramways 1179
   Western Region facilities 737

Royal Commission on Transport: memorandum to the
   Minister of Transport (Railway Companies'
   Association, 1932) 4617
Royal Commission on Unemployment (1931) 4167
Royal Commission. See Parliament (heading note)
Royal Despatch of Gt Britain and Ireland 7932
ROYAL ECONOMIC SOCIETY The state in
   relation to railways 5438
Royal Economic Society 553 3487 4471
ROYAL ENGINEERS. See Army—Royal
   Engineers
Royal Engineers, Professional Papers 5574
Royal Geographical Society 2008
Royal Hotel, Lowestoft 5832
ROYAL INSTITUTE OF BRITISH ARCHITECTS
   —Library Railway stations, 1949–1956: a select
   list of references to material in the R.I.B.A.
   Library 2737
Royal Institute of International Affairs 2082
Royal Institute of Public Administration 646
   3711 3782
Royal Institution of Great Britain 112 2657
Royal Irish Academy (p. 14)
Royal Journey 2749
Royal journeys 139 6348
Royal Mail 5534
The Royal Mail [poem] 7656
Royal Naval Reserve: train services for
   mobilisation scheme (1897) 5562
Royal Philosophical Society of Glasgow 3633
Royal railways with uniform rates 3588 4498 5545
Royal Road; being the history of the L. & S.W. Rly
   6608
Royal Scot (G. F. Allen) 2781
Royal Scot (A. Anderson) 692 710
Royal Scot and her forty-nine sister engines 6768
'Royal Scot' locomotive 6785 6815 6835
'Royal Scot' train 692 2781 4196 6815 6834–5
   6858
Royal Scottish Society of Arts 3228 4267
Royal Society 3287
ROYAL SOCIETY FOR THE PREVENTION OF
   ACCIDENTS I.C.I. Engineering Codes and
   Regulations, Group A, vol. 1 (4). Railways and
   haulages: design: safety precautions (1950) 2288
   I.C.I. Engineering Codes and Regulations, Group A,
   vol. 1 (5). Railways and haulages: operation and
   maintenance: safety precautions (1951) 2290
Royal Society of Health 4963
Royal Statistical Society 558 781 3569 4733 6587
   7904
Royal trains E 6
Royal United Service Institution 669 1990 2345
   2980 5557 5561 5568
Royal Victualling Yard, Deptford: suspension
   railway (1823) 250
Royal Wessex, and the Bournemouth Belle 2781
ROYLE, Robert W. Railways Act, 1921 532
Royston & Hitchin Rly 5893
Ruabon Coal Company 6086
Ruabon coal traffic 6092
Rubber and railways 2770
Rubber and railways in the 19th century 2750
Rubber buffers 2750
RUDGARD, Harold L.M.S.R. locomotive casualty
   report system 3048 6838
Rudimentary treatise on locomotive engines 2965
Rudimentary treatise on railways (E. D. Chattaway,
   1855–6) 445 3420
Rudimentary treatise on railways (R. M. Stephenson,
   1850) 14
Rudimentary treatise on the locomotive engine 2965
Rudimentary treatise: tubular and other girder
   bridges 2707
Rudiments of civil engineering for the use of
   beginners 2560
RUEGG, Louis Henry The history of a railway
   [The Salisbury & Yeovil] 6607
   Salisbury & Yeovil Rly: a centenary reprint of
   'The History of a Railway' 6607
RUELL, David Evidence given before the Select
   Committee of the House of Commons on
   Observance of the Lord's Day (1832) 4793
Rugby 6933
Rugby Locomotive Testing Station 3065
Rugby Locomotive Testing Station 3085
Rugby Station: in literature 7533 7592

Ruhmesblätter der Technik von den Urerfindungen bis
   zur Gegenwart 205
Rule Book (Railway Clearing House, 1945) 3776
Rule books (p. 16)
   tramways 858 1339
Rules and data for the steam engine, both stationary
   and locomotive, and for railways, canals, and
   turnpike roads 315
Rules and regulations for railway operation 3753
Rules for observance by employees (Rule Book)
   (Railway Clearing House, 1933) 3776
Rules for ranging railway curves with the theodolite
   and without tables 2537
'Rumbling under blackened girders, Midland,
   bound for Cricklewood . . .' 7484 7779
Ruminations on railways: no. 1, Railway speculation
   5232
Ruminations on railways: no. 2, The Railway Board
   of Trade 5376
Run through South Wales via the L. & N.W. Rly 6570
Runaway wagons 1399 2504
Running of railway trains on the Sabbath (Edinburgh,
   1846) 4814
Running powers. See Co-operation between railways
Rural transport 1224 1383
RUSH, Robert W. The Garstang & Knott End Rly
   5719
   The Lancashire & Yorkshire Rly and its
   locomotives, 1846–1923 6186
   The tramways of Accrington, 1886–1932 1336
RUSKIN, John [Somervell, R.] Protest against the
   extension of railways in the Lake District, with a
   preface by John Ruskin 4854
   The works of John Ruskin: edited by E. T. Cook
   and A. Wedderburn 4777 7627
Ruskin, John 4778 (7508) (7765)
Russell, Charles 4330 6058
RUSSELL, H. V. The financial position of British
   railways for the second half-year of 1883 471
   The financial position of British railways on 4th
   May, 1884 473
RUSSELL, Harold H. Railway rates and charges
   orders 3579
RUSSELL, John Engineering notes as to light
   railways 2176
Russell, Lord John 942 1688–9 4330 4338 4795
   4832 4921
RUSSELL, John Scott On the nature, properties and
   applications of steam and on steam navigation
   2934
RUTHERFORD, William Tables for estimating the
   contents in cubic yards of the earthwork of
   railways and other public works 2546
RUTHVEN, John [Essay] in Essays on rail-roads
   (1824) 251
RUTTER, John New Guide to Weston-Super-Mare
   (1843) 6033
RYDE, Edward Rating of railways 4392
Ryde, Edward 7285
Ryde Pier tramway 2091
Ryton 7068
RYVES, Frances Workman's Train: a tale of
   Greater London (1910) (ex)
RYVES, Reginald Arthur The. Channel Tunnel
   project 2024

S., G. W. Brief history of the rise of Cardington
   Street factory during 100 years 3949
S., H. U. Handbook to the Newcastle & Carlisle Rly
   (1851) 7117
S.E. & C.R. locomotives, 1874–1923 7216
S.S. 'Arnhem' 6297
Sabbath and railway trains: letter addressed to the
   Marquis of Bradalbane, Chairman of the Scottish
   Central Rly Co. 4815
Sabbath and the railway (1847) 4821
Sabbath made for man: a sermon 4846
Sabbath passenger trains: report of the great public
   meeting . . . Edinburgh & Glasgow Rly (1847)
   4817 6998
Sabbath railway system practically discussed 4824
Sabbath trains. See Sunday trains
SABIN, Frank T. Catalogue of an exhibition of early
   railways: paintings, drawings, prints and books
   (1956) 7454

Practical tunnelling as exemplified by Bletchingley and Saltwood Tunnels 2566

The public works of Great Britain (1846) 2409

Report upon the project of the Calcutta & Diamond Harbour Rly & Dock Co. 3410

Secto-planography 2522

SIMNETT, W. E. *Progress and possibilities of electrification* 395 2662

Railway amalgamation in Gt Britain 3636

SIMON, H. *Hilf's system of wrought-iron permanent way for railways* 2628

SIMON, Henry Andrews *The law relating to railway accidents* 4996

SIMON, Herbert *About railways* 2432

SIMONS, William *Our railway system: a scheme for converting it into national property* 4427

SIMPSON, Charles Reginald Hanbury *Locomotives and their working* 2797

The reciprocating steam locomotive 2807

SIMPSON, E. J. *See* John, Evan, [pseud. of E. J. Simpson]

SIMPSON, F. D. *The story of the Colne Valley* 5683

SIMS, E. A. *Note on the methods by which the provisions regarding rates and fares embodied in the English Railways Act of 1921 were framed* 3616

SINCLAIR, [Sir] John *Statistical Account of Scotland* (1791–99) 1523

Sinclair, R. 2896

SINGER, Charles *History of technology* 2434

Singing Sands 7647

Single line working during repairs or obstruction by means of pilotman 3358

Single lines: operation 3796

'Single-phase' electrification: first installation in Gt Britain 6962

SINGLETON, Frederick Bernard *History of Yorkshire* 1486

Sir Edward Watkin: a Canadian view 7225

Sir Edward Watkin's services to the shareholders in the Manchester, Sheffield & Lincolnshire, South Eastern, Metropolitan, and East London companies (By 'An Unfortunate Shareholder') 7305

Sir Eric Geddes correspondence with Mr. A. W. Gattie on transport reform 4522

Sir Gilbert Murrell's Picture 7663

Sir John Magill's Last Journey 7525

Sir John Rennie's line (H. H. Joy) 6699

Sir Waterloo: fragments of the biography of a Sussex lad 6680

Sir William Arrol: a memoir 2731

Sirhowy Valley and its railways 1357

SITES, James N. *Quest for Crisis* 1747 4773b

Sittingbourne: Bowaters' railway 2302

SITWELL, Osbert *Travelling by train* 7631

SITWELL, S. M. *A Railway Garden* 7723

Six coloured views on the Liverpool & Manchester Rly 6420

Six great railwaymen 130

Six months tour through the north of England (A. Young, 1770–1) 166

Six views on the Dublin & Drogheda Rly 1809

Sixpenny Guide to the Skye Rly 6163

Sixteen-mile fare stages 4394

Sixteen On 7461

16th century wagonways **B 1**

Sixth decade, 1946–1956 (British Electric Traction Co.) 2104

Sixty years in the wilderness (H. W. Lucy) 7194

Sixty years of engineering scientific and social work (F. Fox) 2443

Sixty years of progress (Aberdeen Corporation Transport Dept.) 1514

SKEAT, W. O. *Decapod locomotive of the Great Eastern Rly* 5782

SKEGG, J. E. *Transport staff welfare* 4207

Skeletons, swords and helmets unearthed, Manchester & Leeds Rly (1837) 7687

SKELLORN, S. B. *Railway business and accounts* 3438

Sketch of the history of old St Pancras Church and its grave-yard, with an account of the recent desecration of the burial ground attached thereto 4849

Sketch of the principal and most interesting objects

observed in a tour along the railway from Birmingham to Derby . . . 6939

Sketch of the railroad from Carlisle to Greenhead 7084

Sketches of our information as to railroads 264 313 7059 7094

Sketches of the coal mines in Northumberland and Durham 5061

Sketches of the Forth Bridge; or, The Giant's Anatomy from various points of view 2720

SKEY, Robert S. *Report to the Committee of the Birmingham & Liverpool Junction Canal, on the present state of the competition between the canal carriers using that line and the Grand Junction Rly Co.* (1841) 6488

SKILLERN, William J. *The Caerleon tramroad* 1361

Monmouthshire rail tour, 7 May, 1960: itinerary 1358a

Train and track: a booklist 121

Skillern, William J. p. 21

Skimbleshanks the Railway Cat 7545

Skipton & Colne extension 1268 1439

Skye Rly 6163

SLADEN, M. *Somerset & Dorset Rly* 6673

Slamannan Rly 7000

Slate industry: Great Western Rly 6112

SLATER, Humphrey *The Channel Tunnel* 1925

SLAUGHTER, Mihill *Railway traffic tables: 1849, 1850, 1851, 1852* 5271

Slavery on Scottish railways 4033

SLEEMAN, John Frederick *British public utilities* 3713

Sleepers: cast iron 2619

Sleigh, W. W. 4982

SLICK, Sam *Letter-bag of the Great Western* (1839) (*ex.*)

Sligo, Leitrim & Northern Counties Rly 1879–80

Sligo Leitrim & Northern Counties Railway Auction [Sale catalogue] (1959) 1880

Slip coach services 3852

Slip coach working. *See* Passenger train services

SLOANE, John S. *A few words on tramways and light railways applicable to the requirements of Ireland at the present time* (1883) 1773 2158

Slough: signalling installation (1914) 6115

Slough and Charles Dickens 7472

Slough to Windsor branch, G.W. Rly 4825 5218 5582 6066 6432 6648

SLOUS, Frederick L. *Stray leaves from the scrape book of an awkward man* 5933 6675

SLUGG, J. T. *Reminiscences of Manchester fifty years ago* (1881) 6321

Small talk at Wreyland 5959

SMART, Harry Cuff *The R.C.H. (Railway Clearing House) what it is and what it does* 3688

The Railway Clearing House 3689

Smart, Harry Cuff 3686

SMART, William *Railways and the nation* 4586

Smashed to pieces [tract] 7731

SMEATON, John *Narrative of the building and a description of the construction of the Eddystone Lighthouse with stone* 170

Reports of the late John Smeaton 180

SMILES, Robert *Brief Memoir of the late William Muir* 3376

Memoir of the late Henry Booth of the Liverpool & Manchester and afterwards of the L. & N.W. Rly 6315

Metropolitan District Rly: opening of the line from Blackfriars Bridge to the Mansion House Station (1871) 964

Metropolitan locomotion 1

SMILES, Samuel *Autobiography of Samuel Smiles* 7203

Industrial biography: iron workers and tool makers 189

Life of George Stephenson, railway engineer (24) (363) 2471 (2812)

Lives of the engineers (George & Robert Stephenson) (2451) 2472 (6310)

Railway property: its condition and prospects 5272

Statement in support of the proposed London Bridge & Charing Cross Rly submitted for the consideration of the directors of the South Eastern Rly by Samuel Smiles, John Charles Rees, and Edward Ryde 7285

Story of the life of George Stephenson 2471

WILLIAMSON, John Wolfenden *A British railway
behind the scenes* 3763 6817
Railways today 623 655
WILLIS, R. Carrington *My fifty-one years at
Euston* 6780
Willoughby, [family]: records 232
WILLOX, John *Guide to the Edinburgh & Glasgow
Rly* (1842) 6995
Wills, [Mr Justice] 4058 7407
WILLSON, Hugh Bowlby *Reports and
correspondence on the 'patent compound rail'*
2614
WILMOT, Graham Francis Albion *The evolution
of railways in the Wirral Peninsula* 1198
The Railway in Finchley 817
WILSON, A. *Memorandum as to suggested railway
connections in the east end of Glasgow from
Bridgeton Cross* 1573
WILSON, Brian Geoffrey *ABC, miniature railways*
2404
The Central London Rly 909
Unusual railways 399 2389 2393
WILSON, Edward *Save Time Guide to the London
Underground Railways* 7753
WILSON, Francis Raynar *Railway signalling:
automatic* 3342
Railway signalling: mechanical 3344
WILSON, Frank Edward *The British tram* 2114
WILSON, Geoffrey *Britain's transport crisis: a
Conservative's view* (1960) 4771
WILSON, George *On colour blindness in relation
to the danger attending the present system of
railway and marine coloured signals* 4992
*Researches on colour-blindness with a supplement
on the danger attending the present system of
railway and marine coloured signals* 3286
WILSON, George Lloyd *An appraisal of nationalised
transport in Great Britain* 635
Nationalization of transport in Great Britain 636
WILSON, George Robert Stewart *The Railway
Inspectorate* 5357
WILSON, Harold *The financial problem of British
transport* (1951) 638 656 5333
WILSON, Henry *Hints to rail-road speculators . . .*
5065 5236
WILSON, Henry Raynar *Mechanical railway
signalling* 3328
Power railway signalling 3331
*Railway accidents: legislation and statistics 1825
to 1924* 4969
Railway signalling 3327–8
The Safety of British railways 4968
WILSON, Hugh Bowlby. *See* Willson, Hugh
Bowlby
WILSON, Hugh Geoffrey Birch. *See* Wilson,
Geoffrey
WILSON, John *Description of the continuous brake
invented in 1848* 3228
*Railways. The prevention of accidents arising in
connection with the doors of the carriages* 5040
WILSON, Philip Whitwell *The Greville Diary* 6356
WILSON, Reginald *Economics of transport, with
special reference to road-rail questions in the
United Kingdom* 3513 4767
*Finance in public administration with particular
reference to passenger transport* 3508
For and against monopolies in transport 4756
Space and transport 4891
*Technical modernization and new freight charges
on British Railways* 5205
Wilson, Robert A. (p. 22)
WILSON, Thomas *The railway system and its
author, Thomas Gray* 364 4369
Wilts, Somerset & Weymouth Rly 6046 6641
Wiltshire: railways 1431–3
Winch system 2347
WINCHESTER, Clarence *Railway wonders of the
world* 100
Wind blows over 7529
Windsor branch, Great Western Rly 4825 5218
5582 6066 6432 6648
Windsor railway schemes (1847) 6645
Windsor, Slough & Staines Atmospheric Railway
Bill 6048
WINDSOR, STAINES & SOUTH-WESTERN RLY
*Statement of the directors respecting their
arrangements with the Commissioners of Her*

*Majesty's Woods as to the W.S. & S.W. Rly
and the contemplated Windsor improvements*
(1848) 6648
Windsor Station, Great Western Rly: station-
master's memoirs 4024
Winkworth, Derek W. 719
WINN, Rowland George Allanson *The goods
clearing house system and machinery explained*
2576
WINSLOW, I. Everson *Electric tramways: overhead
construction* 2219
Electric tramways: surface contact systems 2219
Tramway feeders 2219
WINSTONE, Reece *Bristol as it was, 1914–1900*
1402
Bristol as it was, 1939–1914 1403
Bristol in the 1890's 1404
WINTER, J. B. *The principal head boards and
lights of the L.B. & S.C. Rly* 6754
Winterstoke 7626
Wire Tramway Company 2339 2350
Wire tramways: description of the various systems . . .
2350
Wire tramways: Hodgson's patents 2339
Wireways (aerial wireways, cableways or 'telphers')
161 205 2350 2360 2367 2378 2390
mediaeval 205
Wirral: railways 1198
Wirral lines, London, Midland & Scottish Rly:
electrification 6837
Wirral Rly 7430
*Wirtschaftsführung und Finanzwesen bei den
englischen Eisenbahnen* 3485
With men, horses or otherwise 389
With the British Expeditionary Force, 1917–1919
5575
With the Nine Elms top link to Salisbury 7364
'With three great snorts of strength . . .' 7603
*Withdrawal of Sabbath passenger trains neither a
violation of contract with the Government nor an
infringement of rights of conscience* 6999
Wodson. Richardson versus Wodson 4346
WOHL, Paul *Road and rail in forty countries* 4641
Woking: London & South Western Rly Servants
Orphanage 6662
Woking to Guildford (London & South Western
Rly) 6614
WOLFE, A. G. *The nationalisation of the railway
system* 4446
Wollaton Hall 206
Wolverhampton: in railway fiction 7560
tramways 1406
Wolverhampton Chamber of Commerce 4421 5090
Wolverhampton to Porthdynllaen (proposed railway,
1839) 6479
Wolverton & Stony Stratford Tramway L
Wolverton Carriage & Wagon Works 3188
Wonder Book of Railways (1911 . . . 1950) 7869
*Wonderful effects of the Peterborough &
Northampton Railway* 6496
Wonderful inventions 37
Wonderful models 7845
Wonders and curiosities of the railway 7722
Wontner, John 4793
WOOD, Andrew. *See* Wood, Samuel Andrew
WOOD, Ellen [Mrs. Henry Wood] *Oswald Cray*
7668
WOOD, F. T. *Transportation facilities of London
and Paris as of October 1913* 786
WOOD, Mrs. Henry. *See* Wood, Ellen
WOOD, Nicholas *Introductory letter of Nicholas
Wood to the directors of the Great Western Rly*
(1838) 6021 6024
On the conveyance of goods along rail-raods 248
*A practical treatise on rail-roads and interior
communication in general* 294
Report on a central line of railway in Scotland 7104
Report to the directors of the Great Western Rly
(1838) 6021
Wood, Nicholas 287 2615 6429
WOOD, Owen T. *The design and construction of
earthworks* 2570
WOOD, Samuel Andrew *Introducing the
engine-driver and the signalman* 4249
Phantom Railway 7667
WOOD, T. McKinnon *The so-called 'commercial
audit' of the L.C.C. Tramways* 877